encyclopedia of
fundamentalism

ROUTLEDGE ENCYCLOPEDIAS OF RELIGION AND SOCIETY

David Levinson, *Series Editor*

The Encyclopedia of Millennialism and Millennial Movements

Richard A. Landes, *Editor*

The Encyclopedia of African and African-American Religions

Stephen D. Glazier, *Editor*

The Encyclopedia of Fundamentalism

Brenda E. Brasher, *Editor*

encyclopedia of
fundamentalism

Brenda E. Brasher, Editor

Religion & Society
A Berkshire Reference Work

ROUTLEDGE
New York   London

Published in 2001 by

Routledge
29 West 35th Street
New York, NY 10001

A Berkshire Reference Work
Copyright © 2001 by Berkshire

Printed in the United States of America on acid-free paper.

10 9 8 7 6 5 4 3 2 1

Library of Congress Cataloging-in-Publication Data
Encyclopedia of fundamentalism / edited by Brenda E. Brasher.
      p. cm. — (Religion and society)
   "A Berkshire Reference work."
   Includes bibliographical references and index.
   ISBN 0-415-92244-5 (alk. paper)
   1. Fundamentalism—Encyclopedias.   I. Brasher, Brenda E.
1952–   II. Routledge encyclopedias of religion and society.

BL238.E63 2001
200'.9'403—dc21
                        2001019951

Contents

Editorial Advisory Board

List of Entries

List of Abbreviations

KJV   King James Version

NAB   New American Bible

NASB New American Standard Bible

NIV   New International Version

NJB   New Jerusalem Bible

NRSV New Revised Standard Version

OEB   Oxford English Bible

RSV   Revised Standard Version

Introduction

The *Encyclopedia of Fundamentalism* introduces the root components of a widespread, populist, socio-religious movement that emerged in twentieth-century Christian Protestantism, known as Fundamentalism. For Fundamentalists, the only viable faith was one organized around a literal interpretation of the Bible. They identified it as the sole, supreme inerrant conveyor of divine truth, and adhered to the hermeneutical principle that its religious truth must not pass through a filter of human interpretation but was unambiguously communicated by a transcendent power, and must be understood as such, and claimed. While some Fundamentalist-like assumptions can be found in most, if not all, religious traditions, Fundamentalists advanced an absolutist claim to religious truth, and displayed an emphatic intolerance of others that starkly demarcated them from other religiously inspired actors of their era. Fervent, exclusive, religious clarity achieved via an erasure of doubt (justified by the claim that the Bible was the inerrant Word of God) was the hallmark trait of religious Fundamentalism. Those who adopted this conviction gradually became referred to within Christian circles as Fundamentalists, due in part to the movement's close association with a twelve-volume series of essays entitled *The Fundamentals* (1900–1915). These essays were the initial salvo in a struggle between conservative and liberal Protestant Christians to define the essence of Christianity that endured throughout the twentieth century and into the twenty-first century.

Historically, Fundamentalism was closely correlated with the rise of modernism and the accompanying rationalization of public life. In the realm of religion, the Fundamentalist movement was a popular means of revolt against modernism by traditional Christians at serious odds with the dominant values of a rapidly developing modern, technological, capitalistic society, and often squeezed out of meaningful participation in it as well. In the twentieth century, modern communication and transportation technologies united substantial segments of the world into what Marshal McLuhan famously opined was a "global village." Religious practitioners comfortable with this development welcomed it and responded to it in kind. Ecumenical and inter-religious cooperation within and among religions flourished. Religious Fundamentalists, however, resisted and vociferously denigrated the tolerance of religious pluralism intrinsic to the civil society that modernity brought. They maintained that the compromises of religious truth necessary for the modern state to exist were blasphemous, and must be rejected.

Christian Fundamentalism in the United States

In the United States, Christian Fundamentalism appeared in two waves. The first wave surfaced at the beginning of the twentieth century, in the form of an accelerated conflict between conservative, predominantly Calvinist Protestants and moderate-to-liberal Protestants. The former accused the latter of being corrupted by the intellectual and social developments of modernity. Conservative Protestants fought the modern theologies liberals embraced, particularly the Christian socialism advocated by social gospelers such as Walter Rauschenbush that valued acting on behalf of the poor and oppressed over orthodox belief. Fundamentalists viewed such liberal efforts to define the essence of Christianity as political action as overstepping the province of God.

The rejection of a theology centered on social ethics by Christian conservatives was only one component of Fundamentalists broad rejection of modernism, which they believed was undermining the cultural and moral power of Christian faith. Fundamentalists insisted that the essential, stable, eternal truths of sacred text were the only fundamentals one could or needed to know. Denying that traditional higher education was necessary to understand biblical texts, they insisted that biblical truths were easily intelligible to any and all. Thus, anti-intellectualism (though not antirationalism) permeated the movement. Higher biblical criticism, Darwin's theory of evolution, liberalization of gender roles, the suffrage movement, and countless other developments of modernity were targeted by Christian Fundamentalists for assault.

As the twentieth century progressed, two world wars tragically forged and occupied a world stage. The end of each was decisive for Fundamentalism, albeit in contrary ways. The end of World War I unleashed a paroxysm of nostalgia that drew people to Fundamentalism's symbolic goods of "rock hard certainty." However, that attraction was short lived, as an act that thrust Fundamentalists into the public eye around the world also gave it a major public defeat: the Scopes "Monkey Trial."

It was during the spring of 1925 that Fundamentalists publicly denounced the teaching of evolution by a Dayton, Tennessee high-school teacher, John T. Scopes. The trial, which ran from 10–25 July drew agnostic Clarence Darrow to the trial as defense attorney, while Evangelical, populist preacher and politician William Jennings Bryant led the defense. As the trial progressed, journalists from around the world depicted the Fundamentalist-appealing, creationist arguments advanced by Bryant as ludicrous. By the trial's close, many non-Fundamentalist Christians had joined the nonreligious in using the term "Fundamentalist" as a pejorative. From this point on, a persistent segment of the population would equate Fundamentalism with a narrow-minded religious bigotry that only those unacceptably out of touch with the modern world could adopt. In the end, Scopes lost his case; however, the guilty verdict was undermined when Scopes was fined $100, the minimum amount the law allowed.

Soon after the trial, Fundamentalists lost a second battle, the one they had been waging for doctrinal control of historic Christian institutions. Some opted to stay within traditional Christian denominations, and would gradually become known as Christian Evangelicals. Those who carried on under the banner of Fundamentalism were the ones who left, and formed their own churches, schools, and eventually universities. During the next several decades, while Fundamentalists engaged in institution building, their internal orientation made it appear to the wider populace as if Fundamentalism had vanished. But this was not the case.

When World War II ended, a series of events began that resulted in a reemergence of Fundamentalists into the public eye. It started when idealistic political figures such as Eleanor Roosevelt attempted to capitalize on the global attention being paid to international issues by inaugurating universal human rights deliberations. To Fundamentalists, the concrete movement toward a world ethics, world law, and what former U.S. President George Bush—many decades later—referred to as a New World Order, were a terrifying betrayal of trust in divine sovereignty. To Fundamentalists, local leaders might be necessary for practical reasons; but only one authority rightfully governed the world. It was not reason or human consensus. It was the authority of the divine.

It took several decades for their rejection of this development to come to the fore, but by the 1970s, Fundamentalists refused to remain on the sidelines any longer. They once more captured attention when they reentered the public stage to combat what they perceived to be the misguided direction of public life. This was Fundamentalism's second wave. With significant institutional strength now at their command, these second-wave Fundamentalists produced a number of reactionary, theocratic political movements with religious leaders at their head. Though not a direct descendent of the original Fundamentalist movement, second-wave Fundamentalists were both like and unlike their predecessors. Where first-wave Fundamentalists stood in stark contrast to the culture of their time and were eventually dismissed as outdated and irrelevant, second-wave Fundamentalists were sophisticated players in contemporary media culture. They advanced leaders such as Pat Robertson and Jerry Falwell, adept at promoting a culturally current public image, who exploited radio, television, and eventually, the Internet to the full.

Where first-wave Fundamentalists were among the least politicized groups in the country, second-wave Fundamentalists had leaders who were politically active and savvy. Still, although they strove to be less rigid ideologically than their predecessors, second-wave Fundamentalists like the Fundamentalists before them, espoused absolute confidence in a literal, inerrant Bible.

As it was for the first-wavers, gender was a prominent issue. They decried the feminist movement, condemned liberal churches' ordination of women, and lauded an energized masculinity. Bill McCartney's The Promise Keepers, headquartered in Boulder, Colorado, was an outgrowth of the redirected masculinity these movements encouraged. Similar to the first movement, creationism came to the fore for the second wave of Fundamentalism. Conservative Christians organized special purpose groups that promoted the teaching of creationism in public schools.

Fundamentalist, Evangelical, and Pentecostal: Similarities and Differences

Fundamentalists share a significant overlap of ideas with Christian Evangelicals, who outnumbered them substantially. The easiest way to distinguish the two is by the adage that Evangelicals cooperate with other Christian groups, while Fundamentalists do not. Yet a noticeable difference exists with regard to intra-religious cooperation between first- and second-wavers. While first-wavers were absolute purists over this issue, second-wave Fundamentalists have engaged in some intra-religious cooperative ventures such as participation in local magisteriums.

Pentecostals advocate Fundamentalist beliefs, but center their religious practice on what they understand to be 'gifts of the spirit" such as glossolalia and faith healing. Fundamentalists exclude Pentecostals from their fold, for they believe that such activities belonged to a past age and are not valid in the present. Consequently, while Pentecostals may claim to be Fundamentalist, Fundamentalists insistently reject the classification of Pentecostals as one of their own.

Beyond the United States and Christianity

As a religious movement, Fundamentalism swept through religious traditions around the globe. Grasping the international dimensions of Fundamentalism is vital to understanding how its ideas spread in the contemporary world, as well as how, why, and when they vary. American Christian Fundamentalists, for example, espouse beliefs that differ significantly from British Christian Fundamentalists, even though some of the American ideas such as dispensational premillennialism were British imports.

Variations of Fundamentalism appeared among the adherents of Islam, Hinduism, Buddhism, Judaism, and other religious traditions, as conflicts arose among them over what valid interpretations of those traditions were, and what, if any, tolerance of other religious traditions was possible. Fractious debates between Fundamentalists and non-Fundamentalists within religious traditions became a dominant feature of twentieth-century religion, and contributed much to its defining spirit; however, the notoriety Fundamentalists achieved by the close of the twentieth century belied their actual numbers. For example, at the cusp of the third millennium, sociologists estimated that no more than ten percent of Protestant Christians were Fundamentalists.

The volatile Fundamentalist combination of absolutist beliefs and small numbers have yielded Fundamentalist streams within a variety of religions whose adherents despair of humankind, and perceive the God or the gods they worshipped as despairing of humankind as well. Because of this, Fundamentalists throughout the world exhibit a magnetic attraction to any End-Times narratives associated with their tradition.

Certain feminist scholars argue that Fundamentalism—rather than being an intrinsic development of particular religious traditions—is actually a response against the liberalization of women's roles that occurred in the twentieth century. Fundamentalism, they contend, developed is a patriarchal backlash against the women's movement, whose objective is to countermine the overarching goal of the women's movement of encouraging women to understand their own experiences as an authoritative ground for speech and political action.

Among academics specializing in religious studies, a contentious argument roils on over whether the term "Fundamentalism" can be appropriately applied to religions other than Christianity. The editors of this Encyclopedia of Fundamentalism have concluded that it can. Throughout the Encyclopedia, entries use the term "Fundamentalism" in relationship to movements within a variety of religious traditions (albeit often with significant qualifications). By so doing, the editors hope to provide a platform that encourages comparative work among certain religious movements in Hinduism, Islam, Judaism, and others that developed roughly during the same period as Christian Fundamentalism. Like Christian Fundamentalism, these movements attempted to blockade religious authority from most, if not all, outside critique, and fence off adherents from the influence of contemporary culture beyond their religion. Taken together, they constitute the global phenomenon that is religious Fundamentalism.

Acknowledgments

At some level, all texts are collaborative efforts, but encyclopedias are explicitly and quite thoroughly so. The *Encyclopedia of Fundamentalism* intentionally includes contributions from scholars with diverse academic backgrounds in the fields of religious studies, sociology, biblical studies, psychology, history, and others. The goal of this cross-field approach was to provide readers with the richest possible overview of scholarly approaches to and understandings of Fundamentalism, one of the dominant religious movements of our age. The quality of contributions scholars produced for this volume surpassed even my high hopes for the work in this regard. While it is scant reward for the effort they made, I encourage readers to attend to the names of contributors who produced the various entries. My warmest thanks go to sub-field editors Jeffrey Kaplan and Richard Flory for insightful contributions to the complex organizational work necessary for this project, to Berkshire Publishing Group for the outstanding work they did shepherding the project through to completion, and to Routledge for their support of such a serious academic endeavor.

Brenda E. Brasher

Bibliography

Ammerman, Nancy. (1987) *Bible Believers: Fundamentalists in the Modern World.* New Brunswick, NJ: Rutgers University Press.

Bartholomeusz, Tessa, and Chandra Richard De Silva, eds. (1998) *Buddhist Fundamentalism and Minority Identities in Sri Lanka.* Berkeley: University of California Press.

Belcove-Shalin, Janet, ed. (1995) *New World Hasidim: Ethnographic Studies of Hasidic Jews in America.* Albany, NY: SUNY Press.

Bendroth, Margaret. (1993) *Fundamentalism & Gender, 1875 to the Present* New Haven, CT: Yale University Press.

Boone, Kathleen. (1989) *The Bible Tells Them So: The Discourse of Protestant Fundamentalism.* Albany, NY: SUNY Press.

Brasher, Brenda E. (1998) *Godly Women: Fundamentalism & Female Power* New Brunswick, NJ: Rutgers University Press.

Carpenter, Joel. (1997) *Revive Us Again: The Reawakening of American Fundamentalism.* New York: Oxford University Press.

DeBerg, Betty. (1990) *Ungodly Women: Gender and the First Wave of American Fundamentalism.* Minneapolis, MN: Fortress Press.

Dekmejian, R. Hrair. (1985) *Islam in Revolution: Fundamentalism in the Arab World.* Syracuse, NY: Syracuse University Press.

Diamond, Sara. (1995) *Roads to Dominion: Right-Wing Movements and Political Power in the United States.* New York: The Guilford Press.

Gorenberg, Gershom. (2000) *The End of Days: Fundamentalism and the Struggle for the Temple Mount.* New York: Free Press.

Harris, Harriet. (1998) *Fundamentalism and Evangelicals.* New York: Oxford University Press.

Hiro, Dilip. (1989) *Holy Wars: The Rise of Islamic Fundamentalism.* New York: Routledge.

Lawrence, Bruce. (1989) *Defenders of God: The Fundamentalist Revolt against the Modern Age.* San Francisco: Harper & Row.

———. (1998) *Shattering the Myth: Islam beyond Violence.* Princeton, NJ: Princeton University Press.

Marsden, George M. (1980) *Fundamentalism and American Culture* New York: Oxford University Press.

Marty, Martin, and R. Scott Appleby, eds. (1991, 1993–1995) *The Fundamentalism Project,* vols. 1–5. Chicago: University of Chicago Press.

Saha, Santosh, and Thomas Carr. (2001) *Religious Fundamentalism in Developing Countries.* Westport, CT: Greenwood Press.

Strozier, Charles. (1994) *Apocalypse: On the Psychology of Fundamentalism in America.* Boston: Beacon Press.

Tibi, Gassam. (1998) *The Challenge of Fundamentalism: Political Islam and the New World Disorder.* Comparative Studies in Religion and Society, No. 9. Berkeley: University of California Press.

Abortion

Abortion, the deliberate expulsion of a human fetus, became a religiously charged political issue during the last quarter of the twentieth century and was vigorously opposed by Evangelical American Protestants. No issue so bitterly pitted these Christians against the nation's prevailing legal and political culture. Abortion became a rallying cry for the so-called religious right and was, in large part, responsible for the organized mustering of a constituency hitherto politically somewhat inchoate.

Abortion was generally legal throughout the United States, subject to certain restrictions, until the nineteenth century. Reliance on herbs, potions, and "old wives'" remedies, however, produced haphazard results. Eventually, surgical abortion was made routinely possible by anesthesia and advances in obstetrics. Its increased incidence prompted a reconsideration of violently terminated pregnancies. The medical profession was a persuasive lobby against the practice and by the last decades of the nineteenth century, abortion was illegal virtually everywhere. The social consensus against abortion remained in place well into the twentieth century but began to weaken toward century's end. In 1969, for instance, New York State largely legalized the practice. It was regarded as a local issue, however, and remained largely invisible at the national political level.

This state of affairs changed drastically with a Supreme Court decision, *Roe v. Wade* (1973), which removed virtually all restraints on abortion at all jurisdictional levels. The court's decision was so broad and so unexpected that it shocked much of the public. Within the Evangelical community there was a sense of bewilderment—a belief that an assault had been launched on basic Christian values. The resented decision seemed just one more of so many "bolts from the blue" issued by the judiciary without broad societal comment. The *Engle v. Vitale* case (1962), which effectively eliminated school prayer, was another such instance. More liberal observers, however, might argue that these decisions merely codified ongoing popular change in American social behavior.

The theological grounds for the Evangelicals' hostile reaction toward abortion requires careful examination. The Bible, on which Evangelicals rely, is silent on the subject. Furthermore, unlike the Roman Catholic Church, Protestants possess no *magisterium* to provide a uniform and authoritative teaching. In fact, much Protestant tradition militates against a common moral stance, vesting, as it so often does, authority in local congregations and assemblies. There would seem to be no compelling theological stricture that would prompt such uniform Evangelical hostility. Nevertheless, Evangelical denominations, at least since *Roe v. Wade*, have largely opposed "abortion on demand." (The so-called mainline denominations have been more ambiguous.)

This antiabortion stance seems linked, in part, to Evangelical endorsement of traditional mores, often stereotyped as "family values." The nuclear family, wedded parents and their children, is regarded as the irreplaceable building block of personal and social morality. The ideal family is often portrayed in slightly patriarchal terms, with the wife honored

SELECTION FROM: ROE V WADE, 41 US 113 (1973)

To summarize and to repeat:

1. A state criminal abortion statute of the current Texas type, that excepts from criminality only a life-saving procedure on behalf of the mother, without regard to pregnancy stage and without recognition of the other interests involved, is violative of the Due Process Clause of the Fourteenth Amendment.

    (a) For the stage prior to approximately the end of the first trimester, the abortion decision and its effectuation must be left to the medical judgment of the pregnant woman's attending physician.

    (b) For the stage subsequent to approximately the end of the first trimester, the State, in promoting its interest in the health of the mother, may, if it chooses, regulate the abortion procedure in ways that are reasonably related to maternal health.

    (c) For the stage subsequent to viability, the State in promoting its interest in the potentiality of human life [p165] may, if it chooses, regulate, and even proscribe, abortion except where it is necessary, in appropriate medical judgment, for the preservation of the life or health of the mother.

2. The State may define the term "physician," as it has been employed in the preceding paragraphs of this Part XI of this opinion, to mean only a physician currently licensed by the State, and may proscribe any abortion by a person who is not a physician as so defined.

    In Doe v. Bolton, post, p. 179, procedural requirements contained in one of the modern abortion statutes are considered. That opinion and this one, of course, are to be read together.(67)

    This holding, we feel, is consistent with the relative weights of the respective interests involved, with the lessons and examples of medical and legal history, with the lenity of the common law, and with the demands of the profound problems of the present day. The decision leaves the State free to place increasing restrictions on abortion as the period of pregnancy lengthens, so long as those restrictions are tailored to the recognized state interests. The decision vindicates the right of the physician to administer medical treatment according to his professional judgment up to the points where important [p166] state interests provide compelling justifications for intervention. Up to those points, the abortion decision in all its aspects is inherently, and primarily, a medical decision, and basic responsibility for it must rest with the physician. If an individual practitioner abuses the privilege of exercising proper medical judgment, the usual remedies, judicial and intra-professional, are available.

primarily as mother, and the husband, as head of family, for his role as father. There is much in the Judeo-Christian tradition that supports such a familial portrayal. God is uniformly regarded throughout the Bible as father to humankind—portrayed, in turn, as His children. The sanctity of the family in Evangelical thought thus expresses a profound Christian sociology and anthropology. For a parent to "slaughter" its own unborn children flies in the face of this biblical model, at least to Evangelicals.

Abortion was but one of a number of issues that prompted first unease and, then, outrage among Evangelicals. Other issues included liberalized por-nography laws, militant feminism, and the so-called sexual revolution that attended chemical birth control. The abortion issue doubtless generated the most intense sense of moral indignation, but it gained urgency by being grouped with other issues that seemed, when taken together, little better than systematic aggression against the Christian family. In this sense, Evangelical Christians did not look for a fight but had one forced upon them by a belligerent and crusading liberal culture. They reacted with organized political activity unprecedented since the antislavery, Sabbatarian, and temperance campaigns of the nineteenth century.

Lobbying organizations, most prominently the Moral Majority and the Christian Coalition, made restricting, or even eliminating, abortion a top priority. At times, the spokesmen for these lobbies were strident and controversial, the most prominent being the Rev. Jerry Falwell of the Moral Majority. These lobbies, in turn, provoked vehement opposition from proabortion lobbies such as the National Organization of Women. Despite a nearly identical position on the issue between Evangelicals and the Roman Catholic Church, there was relatively little concerted action between them. It is possible that the inveterate conservative Protestant suspicion of the Church of Rome made such cooperation problematic.

Organized Evangelical lobbying doubtless played a role in securing legislative restrictions on abortion at the state level. Federal courts, however, always overturned these. In 1999, one Evangelical publicist noted sadly: "In perhaps the biggest and costliest battle waged by conservative Christians, twenty years of fighting has won nothing" (Thomas and Dobson 1999: 24). The Evangelical lobby also attacked late-term abortions, which it denominated "partial birth abortions." The abortion issue doubtless caused many Evangelical voters to drift toward conservative Republican candidates, frequently seen as more hostile than Democrats toward abortion. At the time of the 2000 national election, Evangelical opposition to abortion remained a potent political issue.

There is no question that many Evangelicals are deeply offended at the violent end to life, however the fetus is regarded, which is the essence of abortion. Evangelical thought, as the twentieth century gave way to the twenty-first, was, however, divided on the overall issue of the sanctity of life. Once again, a contrast may be drawn with a Roman Catholic Church that, as a unified body, can enunciate a systematic position. It teaches a "consistent ethic of life," and in recent years has extended this to oppose not just abortion but also capital punishment and the use of violence in international affairs. Evangelicals were far more likely to support capital punishment—even urge it upon the state. This seeming logical contradiction regarding human life undercut the authority of Evangelicals on the abortion issue. There was evidence at century's end to suggest that opposition to abortion was leading some Evangelicals to reconsider their stance on capital punishment.

Robert K. Whalen

Bibliography

Graber, Mark A. (1996) *Rethinking Abortion: Equal Choice, the Constitution and Reproductive Politics*. Princeton, NJ: Princeton University Press.

Green, John C., James L. Gath, Corwin E. Smidt, and Lyman A. Kellstedt. (1996) *Religion and the Culture Wars: Dispatches from the Front*. New York: Rowman & Littlefield Publishers, Inc.

Luker, Kenneth. (1984) *Abortion and the Politics of Motherhood*. Berkeley: University of California Press.

Reed, Ralph. (1996) *Active Faith: How Christians Are Changing the Soul of American Politics*. New York: Free Press.

Smidt, Corwin E., and James M. Penning. (1997) *Sojourners in the Wilderness: The Christian Right in Comparative Perspective*. New York: Rowman & Littlefield Publishers, Inc.

Thomas, Cal, and Ed Dobson. (1999) *Blinded by Might: Can the Religious Right Save America?* Grand Rapids, MI: Zondervan Publishing.

Adventism. *See* Seventh-Day Adventists

African-American Holiness-Pentecostal Movement

Specific African-American sects refer to themselves as either "Holiness" or "Pentecostal," but the distinction between the two forms is not clear-cut. Indeed, within the black community, there is a strong tendency to group these two categories together by referring to them as "Sanctified–churches" (Hurston 1981). Sanders (1996: 19–20) delineates five types of organizations within the African-American Holiness-Pentecostal movement: (1) bodies that retained their unique black Holiness identity following the Pentecostal revival (e.g., the Church of Christ (Holiness), USA; (2) the black Holiness sects that became predominantly black Pentecostal sects (e.g., the Church of God in Christ); (3) the interracial Holiness sects that evolved into predominantly black Pentecostal sects (e.g., the Fire-Baptized Holiness Church of God in the Americas); and (4) the interracial Pentecostal sects that evolved into predominantly black Pentecostal sects (e.g., the Pentecostal Assemblies of the World).

The Development of the Black Holiness-Pentecostal Movement

The Holiness movement emerged largely as an effort to restore John Wesley's doctrine of "entire sanctification" within white Methodism following the Civil War. Initially, the Holiness movement, according to Synan (1971: 40), "began as an urban force among the better educated circles" and included "leading figures in the Methodist church," but its most radical wing attracted primarily Methodists and some Baptists in the rural South and Midwest. Most of the major white Holiness sects developed during the Jim Crow era and, like populism, often exhibited racist elements. Occasionally poor whites and blacks broke with prevailing segregationist patterns and joined together for interracial Holiness fellowships.

The first African-American Holiness sects emerged in the rural areas of the South. The United Holy Church (established in 1886 in Method, North Carolina), perhaps the earliest black Holiness sect, merged with several other small bodies in 1902 with the assistance of W. H. Fulford, a black elder in the predominantly white Fire-Baptized Holiness Church, and later became a full-fledged Pentecostal sect. In 1889, William Christian established a Holiness sect called the Church of the Living God, in Wrightsville, Arkansas, and asserted that the "saints" of the Bible were black (Simpson 1978: 259), a messianic-nationalist belief not uncommon among African-American Holiness-Pentecostal sects. While several black Holiness bodies arose out of the African Methodist Episcopal and African Methodist Episcopal Zion churches, most emerged as schisms from Baptist associations and conventions (Shopshire 1975: 51).

C. H. Mason and C. P. Jones started another African-American Holiness sect in the Mississippi Valley. Mason, who began his ministry in the Mt. Gale Missionary Baptist Church in Preston, Arkansas, underwent sanctification in 1893 and joined C. P. Jones, J. A. Jeter, and W. S. Pleasant in conducting a Holiness-style revival in Jackson, Mississippi, in 1895. After being expelled from the Baptist Church, Mason and Jones established a congregation in Lexington, Mississippi, which they eventually named the Church of God, but renamed shortly thereafter

the Church of God in Christ to distinguish it from the white-controlled Church of God (Jones 1975: 147).

The origin of the Pentecostal movement per se, as opposed to its historical predecessor, has been the subject of much debate. Various scholars point to Charles Fox Parham's House Bible School in Topeka, Kansas, in 1901, as the genesis of modern Pentecostalism. While indeed Parham's teaching that glossolalia constitutes overt evidence of a convert's reception of the Holy Spirit played a significant role in the beginnings of Pentecostalism, the interracial Azusa Street Revival of 1906 to 1909 in Los Angeles under the leadership of William J. Seymour, a black Holiness preacher and former student at Parham's House Bible School, "acted as the catalytic agent that congealed tongue-speaking into a fully defined doctrine" (Synan 1971: 121). In early 1907, Charles H. Mason, J. A. Jeter, and D. J. Young spoke in tongues during their five-week stay at the Azusa Street Mission. After he returned to his headquarters in Memphis, Mason asked an assembly of the Church of God in Christ (COGIC) that the sect become a Pentecostal group—a move that compelled C. P. Jones to establish the Church of Christ (Holiness), USA (Cobbins 1966).

The initial interracial character of the Pentecostal movement began to break down in the years following the Azusa Street Revival. C. H. Mason ordained many white ministers of independent congregations because the COGIC was one of the few legally incorporated Holiness-Pentecostal bodies in the mid-South. In 1914, COGIC-ordained white ministers formed the Assemblies of God in Hot Springs, Arkansas, at a gathering that reportedly was addressed by Bishop Mason. In 1924, the division along racial lines of the Pentecostal Assemblies of the World, which initially had "roughly equal numbers of Negroes and whites as both officials and members," formally ended the interracial period in American Pentecostalism (Synan 1971: 221).

While the roots of the African-American Holiness-Pentecostal movement in the rural South still await detailed examination, Goldsmith's (1985) analysis of the emergence of the movement on the Georgia coast provides some clues. As elsewhere, the black Baptist and Methodist missionaries who arrived on the Georgia coast following the Civil War were appalled by the ecstatic rituals practiced by the ex-slaves. By the end of the nineteenth century, "the energetic 'shout' had disappeared from the [St. Simons] island's religious worship, and the stately hymns sung by the Baptist nationally were adopted in its place" (Goldsmith 1985: 90). In their evolution from conversionist sects into mainstream denominations, many black churches emulated the somber worship style of the white middle-class churches, even though the members of the former continued to occupy an inferior social status. The initial converts to "holiness" did not renounce membership in the Baptist churches, but their ministers and fellow congregants objected to their ecstatic outbursts and ultimately forced them out. According to Goldsmith, "The appearance of Pentecostal 'sanctification' on the Georgia coast offered a means of disregarding the dominant socio-economic criteria for measuring success in life. Material measures were jettisoned in favor of a binary distinction between 'sinner' and 'saint'" (1985: 94).

Flourishing beyond its roots in the rural South, the black Holiness-Pentecostal movement has functioned for some time as an urban phenomenon as well. After his split with Jones, Mason located the headquarters of the COGIC in Memphis, one of the largest cities in the South. As Sernett (1997: 95) observes: "As a result of the Great Migration the Pentecostal and Holiness movements, which spawned scores of groups other than COGIC and the Church of Christ (Holiness), USA, became important alternatives to the near hegemony of the Baptist and Methodist denominations." Elsewhere, Sanders (1996: 123) has characterized the "Sanctified church tradition" as an "African-American Christian reform movement that seeks to brings its standards of worship, personal morality, and sociocultural concern into conformity with principles of holiness and spiritual empowerment." In her recent compendium of black Holiness-Pentecostal bodies, Dupree (1996) lists 73 "Trinitarian Pentecostal groups," 137 "Apostolic Pentecostal groups," and 106 "evangelical charismatic or neo-Pentecostal groups." African-American Holiness-Pentecostal sects include the Church of All Nations established by Elder Lucy Smith in Chicago in 1916; the Church of Our Lord Jesus Christ of the Apostolic Faith established by Bishop R. C. Lawson in Harlem in 1918; the Church of God established by Solomon Michaux in 1921 in tidewater Virginia; the United House of Prayer for All People on the Rock of the Apostolic Church established by "Sweet Daddy" Grace in 1921 in Wareham, Massachusetts; and the Crenshaw Christian Center established by K. C. Price in 1973 in Los Angeles.

The Politico-Religious Organization of the African-American Holiness-Pentecostal Movement

The Sanctified movement consists of numerous religious associations as well as independent congregations. At the ideological level, Holiness-Pentecostal sects vary from those that are Trinitarian to those that are Unitarian in terms of their view of the Godhead. Even more so than the Baptist and Methodist traditions, fission and fusion have characterized the movement. The COGIC spawned the First Unity of God in 1927; the Church of God in Christ, Congregational, in 1932; and the Church of God in Christ, International, in 1969. Despite the loss of some of its membership to various schismatic groups, the COGIC has grown into the largest black Pentecostal body in the world, claiming to have some 6,5,000,000 members in 12,816 churches (Mead and Hill 1995: 114).

While in theory most Sanctified associations exhibit an episcopal polity in that they are overseen by a bishop or board of bishops, in reality their politico-religious organization tends to combine aspects of the Episcopal, Presbyterian, and Congregational forms. The larger associations have created boards, assemblies, committees, and councils at the national,

Fundamentalist minister and congregants at a church in Tidewater, Virginia in 1975. The church membership is unusual in that it includes whites and African-Americans. PHOTO COURTESY OF KAREN CHRISTENSEN.

regional, and even local levels to administer affairs such as evangelism, Sunday schools, publications, and pensions. For example, the COGIC is governed by the General Board of Twelve Bishops and the General Assembly, which elects the former. The General Assembly meets during the Annual Convocation in November and April.

Historically, Sanctified congregations have held their greatest appeal for lower- and working-class African Americans. In contrast to the relatively modest socioeconomic composition of most Sanctified congregations, Lincoln and Mamiya (1990: 163) maintain that "more than half of COGIC members are within the coping middle-income strata (largely working-class and some middle-class)." As a consequence, black Holiness-Pentecostal congregations are housed in facilities that range from storefronts, house churches, and apartments in cities and simple frame structures in small towns and rural areas to substantial edifices in urban areas.

While the COGIC and various other Sanctified churches maintain a relatively patriarchal politico-religious structure, many Sanctified sects have provided women with opportunities to achieve religious leadership. Sociologist Cheryl Townsend Gilkes states:

> The Sanctified Church dignified the role of black working women, providing the positive moral support for their role within their families and communities. Some churches ... actually ordained women to the ministry. In the context of the South, their ecclesiastical titles were respected in spite of their race. In other regards, churches such as the Church of God in Christ proffered social roles that carried titles of respect, dress, codes, and institutional authority to travel throughout the South. (1986: 29)

The Mt. Sinai Holy Church of America is an example of the heights many women have attained in the African-American Holiness-Pentecostal movement. Bishop Ida Robins formed the sect in Philadelphia in 1923, later appointing Elmira Jeffries to serve as "vice-bishop" (Fauset 1971: 13–21). Although Mt. Sinai Holy Church also has many male officers, women make up a notable portion of its elders and ministers. While the COGIC does not ordain women ministers, it does permit women to oversee congregations that do not have a male pastor.

The Role of the African-American Holiness-Pentecostal Movement

Various social scientists have interpreted the African-American Holiness-Pentecostal movement as an adjustment to the social disorganization that many black migrants faced upon arrival in the cities of the North and the South. They view testimonies and various ecstatic rituals as providing members with a cathartic release from the frustrations and anxieties that social dislocation created in their everyday lives. Sanctified congregations often substitute high religious status as "saints," bishops, elders, missionaries, and mothers for a relatively humble social status in a racist and class society.

Anderson (1979: 224) maintains that Pentecostalism in general emerged as a response to the transition from competitive to monopoly capitalism during the period from 1890 to 1925. While in theory the Holiness-Pentecostal movement rejected "the world," in reality it encouraged its followers to adjust to the processes of industrialization and urbanization. In a similar vein, Paris (1982: 147) asserts that black Pentecostalism emphasizes "the mediation of an economy of salvation and not the secular political economy." While the African-American Holiness-Pentecostal movement historically has a strong accommodative orientation in its eschewal of social protest, in recent decades some Sanctified ministers and congregations have become involved in protest activities that challenge racist and even classist features of the American political economy. The COGIC provided the headquarters for the sanitation workers' strike, which was punctuated by the assassination of Dr. Martin Luther King, Jr., in Memphis in 1968. An increasing number of Sanctified people have won political offices in city councils and state legislatures and have obtained minor political appointments in the executive branch of the federal government.

Theologically speaking, Sanders (1996: 140) asserts that Sanctified people can be best characterized as "liberal literalists" "because the exilic experience of being black in a racist society forbids them to follow uncritically conservative, fundamentalist readings fostered by descendants who used the Bible to justify slavery." While the Holiness-Pentecostal movement is generally viewed as anti-intellectual, the mainstreaming process occurring within its ranks as various members have become educated has resulted in the formation of a Sanctified intelligentsia. These have included or include individuals such as James S. Tinny, a professor at Howard University and the organizer of the Pentecostal Coalition for Human Rights in 1980; James Leonard Lovett, a COGIC pastor and the first dean of the C. H. Mason Theological Seminary at the Interdenominational Theological Seminary in Atlanta; and Pearl Williams-Jones, a music professor at the University of the District of Columbia and a musician at the Bible Way Temple in Washington, D.C. (Sanders 1996: 121).

At any rate, black Sanctified sects exhibit the complex and vacillating juxtaposition of protest and accommodation characteristic of African-American religion in general (Baer and Singer 1992). Most black Holiness-Pentecostal sects struggle to make a bad situation better without daring to risk small gain by openly challenging the oppressive structures of the larger society. A few, however, include politically liberal and even radical ministers who lead their congregations in social protest activities and/or become part and parcel of larger social movements for social justice.

Hans A. Baer

See also Azusa Street Revival; Black Church, The; Pentecostalism

Bibliography

Anderson, Robert Mapes. (1979) *Vision of the Disinherited: The Making of American Pentecostalism.* New York: Oxford University Press.

Baer, Hans A., and Merrill Singer. (1992) *African-American Religion in the Twentieth-Century: Varieties of Protest and Accommodation.* Knoxville: University of Tennessee Press.

Cobbins, Ortho B. (1966) *History of the Church of Christ (Holiness) U.S.A., 1885–1965.* New York: Vantage Press.

Dupree, Sherry Sherrod. (1996) *African-American Holiness-Pentecostal Movement: An Annotated Bibliography.* New York: Garland Publishing Company.

Fauset, Arthur H. (1971) *Black Gods of the Metropolis.* Philadelphia: University of Pennsylvania Press.

Gilkes, Cheryl Townsend. (1986) "The Role of Women in the Sanctified Church." *Journal of Religious Thought* 43, 1: 24–41.

Goldsmith, Peter D. (1985) *When I Rise Cryin' Holy: African-American-Denominationalism on the Georgia Coast.* New York: AMS Press.

Hurston, Zora Neale. (1981) *The Sanctified Church.* Berkeley, CA: Turtle Island.

Jones, Lawrence. (1975) "The Black Pentecostals." In *The Charismatic Movement*, edited by Michael P. Hamilton. Grand Rapids, MI: Wm. B. Eerdmans.

Lincoln, C. Eric, and Lawrence H. Mamiya. (1990) *The Black Church in African-American Experience.* Durham, NC: Duke University Press.

Mead, Frank S., and Samuel S. Hill. (1995) *Handbook of Denominations in the United States*, 10th ed. Nashville, TN: Abingdon Press.

Paris, Arthur E. (1982) *Black Pentecostalism: Southern Religion in an Urban World.* Amherst: University of Massachusetts Press.

Sanders, Cheryl Jeanne. (1996) *Saints in Exile: The Holiness-Pentecostal Experience in African American Religion and Culture.* New York: Oxford University Press.

Sernett, Milton C. (1997) *Bound for the Promised Land: African American Religion and The Great Migration.* Durham, NC: Duke University Press.

Shopshire, James Maynard. (1975) "A Socio-Historical Characterization of the Black Pentecostal Movement in America. PhD dissertation, Northwestern University.

Simpson, George Eaton. (1978) *Black Religions in the New World.* New York: Columbia University Press.

Synan, Vinson. (1971) *The Holiness-Pentecostal Movement in the United States.* Grand Rapids, MI: Wm. B. Eerdmans.

America, as a Christian nation

Religious belief became a definitive force in American politics and culture in the closing decades of the twentieth century. While religion has always been an important part of life in the United States, and has played a significant role in the nation's history, only recently has the meaning of America's religious past become a point of concentrated contestation.

Since the public resurgence of American Fundamentalism and the regeneration of the political right in the latter part of the last century, politicians, educators, and the media have been forced to take seriously the cries of the religiously devout who crave a restoration of "Christian America." Organizations such as the Christian Coalition and James Dobson's

THE MAYFLOWER COMPACT (1620)

In the name of God, Amen. We, whose names are underwritten, the Loyal Subjects of our dread Sovereign Lord, King James, by the Grace of God, of England, France and Ireland, King, Defender of the Faith, e&.

Having undertaken for the Glory of God, and Advancement of the Christian Faith, and the Honour of our King and Country, a voyage to plant the first colony in the northern parts of Virginia; do by these presents, solemnly and mutually in the Presence of God and one of another, covenant and combine ourselves together into a civil Body Politick, for our better Ordering and

Preservation, and Furtherance of the Ends aforesaid; And by Virtue hereof to enact, constitute, and frame, such just and equal Laws, Ordinances, Acts, Constitutions and Offices, from time to time, as shall be thought most meet and convenient for the General good of the Colony; unto which we promise all due submission and obedience.

In Witness whereof we have hereunto subscribed our names at Cape Cod the eleventh of November, in the Reign of our Sovereign Lord, King James of England, France and Ireland, the eighteenth, and of Scotland the fifty-fourth. Anno Domini, 1620.

Source: The University of Oklahoma College of Law.
A Chronology of Historic Documents. www.law.ou.edu

Focus on the Family are among the most powerful interest groups who propose a return to a bygone era in which they believe Christians, as they define the term, ruled the nation. According to these conservative interest groups the values that characterized the "Christian" country of previous generations have eroded in this era of abortion, open homosexuality, declining respect for authority, violence, and "secular humanism." Complementing the agendas of these political organizations are the thousands of lesser-known Fundamentalist teachers, preachers, theologians, and a handful of historians. From a wide representation of America's Protestant denominations, such men and women articulate varying interpretations of God's relationship with American churches that privilege the United States as having a distinct Christian heritage.

Other Christian groups, such as the Sojournors, are less interested in revisiting a past that they view as saturated with racial discrimination, patriarchy, weapons of mass destruction, and unrelenting capitalist exploitation. It is against the beliefs of such left-leaning Evangelicals, and non-religious American citizens, that Fundamentalists attempt to carve out a distinct vision of the historical past. Imbedded in their

reading of American history is an undeniable "godly heritage." Appeals to this Judeo-Christian ethic, supposedly revealed in the origins and founding of America, have had a tremendous rhetorical influence in recent years; however, the development and history of such a position has been more complicated. What is at stake in the telling of history is power—power to determine the future of the country, and power to determine the telling of the past, complete with its winners and losers, heroes and villains. Within colonial and Revolutionary America are histories defined by conflicting interpretations that illustrate the heart of the debate over America as a Christian nation.

Christian America(?): Religion in the Founding and Independence of a Nation

Most Fundamentalists argue that any "objective" student will see within America's historical origins, from the first colonists to the War of Independence, a clear foundation for their claims of a Christian past. They often skip, however, to the Puritans' mission in America, dismissing their North American predecessors. The first Americans were of course Native Americans. By the end of the fifteenth century,

American Indians had created hundreds of different societies with distinct languages, cultures, and religions. Diversity defined the pre-Columbian experiences of these peoples, but among the similarities that anthropologists have discovered is cohesion within their experiences of the ordinary and extraordinary. Religion and culture, however differently expressed, were unassailably entwined in the Native American world.

The initial Europeans to visit North America were Roman Catholics. Florida's St. Augustine, established in 1565, became the first permanent colony founded in what is now the United States. Spanish Catholics had, by the end of the sixteenth century, sent out missionaries to many of the local Indian tribes. Catholics were the first non-native settlers on the West Coast as well. In the mid-1700s, Father Junipero Serra established an impressive line of mission stations up and down the California coast. Adding to the influence of Catholicism in early America was Lord Baltimore, who in the 1630s was granted a charter for Maryland, which he established as a refuge for persecuted Catholics.

In 1607, English colonists settled their first permanent colony in North America. Under the leadership of John Smith, the English named their new home Jamestown, which was located on the mouth of the Chesapeake Bay in Virginia. Having witnessed Spain's tremendous financial prosperity that had resulted from her New World endeavors, the English decided to try to profit in North America. Quick rewards, not establishing a Christian colony, were the motivating force behind almost all of the first Virginian settlers. Fostering peaceful relations with the natives was among the many difficulties that the new colonists faced. The famous marriage of Pocahontas to John Rolfe, and her conversion to Christianity, has become a celebrated myth in American history, and one that epitomizes the conflict over the telling of history between those who envision a Christian past and those who do not.

The religious Right views the Pocahontas story as evidence of the Christian mission of Virginia, and the work of courageous men and women who carried the gospel into virgin territories. Historians of Native America interpret the story differently. This union was little more than the result of political maneuvering by the English and the local Indian leader Powhatan, who oversaw a large confederacy of tribes, according to the latter. Both the Indians and the English hoped to bring the other group under their political authority. Powhatan's plan was to unite his daughter, Pocahontas, to the English. It had been Powhatan's practice to marry his children to the leaders of other powerful Indian tribes in order to foster friendly relations, which he believed would succeed with the English too. With the Pocahontas–Rolfe marriage, Powhatan had achieved his goal of an alliance and the British, in return, could celebrate Pocahontas as their first native Christian convert, which made their exploitation of Indian lands seem more justifiable, at least according to many historians. Such interpretations of colonial history, which dominate university classrooms, have impassioned the leaders of the new Right. Frustrated with what they refer to as "revisionist" history, they long for a return to the visions of the past that celebrated the missionary aspects of colonization, rather than those that focus on the colonists' material self-interests.

A few short years later, in 1620, the first Pilgrims arrived in Plymouth, Massachusetts. In the struggles and ideals of the first New Englanders, modern Christians find their greatest inspiration for envisioning American as a Christian nation. Frustrated with the state of the Church of England, the Pilgrims abandoned their homes in search of a place where they could protect their lifestyle from England's corruption as well as raise children in their faith. The Pilgrims believed that they secured an unbreakable covenant with God in the New World, which was chronicled by Plymouth's governor William Bradford. A few groups of Fundamentalists believe that the Mayflower Compact actually represents a shift from Israel to the United States as God's chosen nation, although the major political groups do not often make such hubris claims explicit.

Another powerful myth in the debate over America as a Christian nation is the Puritan notion of the "city on the hill," which was coined by a second group of Christian dissenters who arrived in Massachusetts ten years after the Pilgrims. Although this group also believed that the Church of England had been corrupted, they did not intend to separate from it. Instead, as their governor John Winthrop articulated, they sought to establish a godly, utopian society in the New World, one that would demonstrate the legitimacy of the Puritan faith to the English. The Puritans would then be welcomed back to England where they could lead a religious and political reformation. But this was not to be. Despite the best efforts of the Massachusetts leadership to maintain a unified religious colony, dissenting voices arose almost immediately. Among the earliest and most prominent was Roger Williams, a friend of Winthrop and a young pastor who had arrived with the original settlers. Williams believed that the Puritan experiment was inherently flawed. A colony that compelled people to go to church and participate in Christian worship actually brought nonbelievers into sacred space, thereby contaminating it. Therefore, Williams believed, the church should be completely separate from state and social institutions. Williams is widely credited by historians on all sides of the Christian American debate for articulating the notion of a separation of church and state, which has become a definitive aspect of American life. For his views, Williams was banned to Rhode Island, where he founded a colony for Puritan dissenters. Some Evangelical historians, who do not subscribe to the views of the Right, find in Williams a powerful criticism of modern attempts to Christianize America. They argue, as Williams did, that mixing politics with religion results in the bastardization of the Christian faith, not the betterment of the polity.

Anne Hutchinson added to the troubles of the Puritan leadership by claiming to receive revelation directly from God. Quakers too, who first arrived in Massachusetts in 1656, regularly challenged the authority of Puritan leaders and were persecuted as a result. Although the Massachusetts Bay Colony had the strongest "Christian" heritage (as modern Fundamentalists would define Christian), they never maintained a consensus on the relationship between government and church authority. By the second generation, the Puritan leadership was forced to compromise its requirements, with the famous halfway covenant, in order to adapt to a generation that lacked the religious radicalism of their parents. By the end of the seventeenth century, Plymouth was absorbed by the Massachusetts Bay Colony, which was well on its way to losing its countercultural critique of Europe and instead, developing a complex and thriving merchant economy.

Protestants and Catholics were not the only religionists in early America. Jews added yet another voice in the development of the colonies. Originally settled in Brazil, pockets of Jews moved to New Amsterdam—the Dutch colony that would become New York—during the 1650s when Portugal conquered Brazil. Within ten years Jews were buying property, serving in the militia, and engaged in colonial commerce in North America. The first synagogue was established in 1692. Toward the end of the seventeenth century another religious people found homes in large numbers on the soil of North America. Victims of a forced migration, African slaves from many geographical regions arrived with a diverse set of religious systems.

Telling the story of slavery in America has become one of the seminal political issues implicit in debates over Christian America. Historians of slavery have persuasively shown how the religions of Africa, including Islam, had a tremendous effect on the American colonies. The religious Right, on the other hand, dismisses such evidence of African influences on Evangelicalism as the product of a biased, anti-Christian multiculturalism. They emphasize instead the many slaves who converted to the Christian faith and the truly undeniable ways in which the "invisible institution" of the Christian Church provided a refuge and a sense of liberation for many African Americans.

The middle colonies of Pennsylvania, New York, New Jersey, and Delaware were settled in the late 1600s and early 1700s. Distinguished by their tremendous ethnic diversity, immigrants from Germany, Scotland, and Ireland made the middle colonies the least "English" of British North America. Many colonists came to America hoping to improve their economic condition, while religious liberty also attracted groups like the Anabaptists. Among the most famous religious leaders was William Penn, who established a refuge for Quakers in Pennsylvania. Penn promoted toleration of other religious groups in his colony, including many Protestant groups and Catholics. The influence of Quaker beliefs in cities like Philadelphia cannot be overstated. There is a consensus among historians that religion did in fact dramatically shape life in Philadelphia, but whether or not the Christianity of Quakerism matches the faith espoused by the contemporary Right is an open question.

Many Christian schools, and virtually all Christian-home school curriculums, ignore the radical religious diversity found in America's origins. Narratives of the Puritans are privileged, while Catholics, Jews, Anabaptists, Muslims, and Native American and African religions are minimized. Even within the New England colonies, about which children are extensively taught, the religious Right often ignores the multiplicity of religious views. The Puritan leadership was so adept at masking the voices of dissent in their colonies that it has become convenient for those seeking to reestablish a Christian nation to parade New Englanders as the founders of a vision parallel to their own. However, a closer look at the evidence of such people as Quakers, Roger Williams, and Anne Hutchinson in the colony complicates such political appeals.

The second epoch in American history in which Fundamentalists ground their claims for a "godly American heritage" is within the American Revolution, which they connect to the Great Awakening and the ideology of the "Founding Fathers." Although its magnitude may have been somewhat overstated in the past, few historians discount the importance of the Great Awakening in American religious history. The revivals of the mid-eighteenth century came at a time when there were important new innovations in communication, most obvious in the distribution of newspapers. Historians have persuasively argued that the Awakening did have an important effect on the Revolution in that it provided the first unifying experience for the colonies. Colonists no longer thought of themselves so much as "Virginian" or "Pennsylvanian" but as American, with a culture that was distinct from Britain. Most important, however, Awakening revivalists infused in their audiences a belief that the common person could trust his or her own instincts. No longer did established authorities have to be deferred to, but the religious impulses of the regular man and woman were valued. This populist faith reemerged in the early 1800s and again with the Pentecostal revivals of the early 1900s, which may be Evangelicalism's greatest legacy in America. Most historians agree that a new national identity, a communications revolution, and the fracturing of traditional authorities, all spawned by the Awakening, contributed to colonists' abilities to unite against England during the Revolution.

However, the religion of most of the Revolutionary leaders was not the faith of Jonathan Edwards, George Whitefield or John Wesley. According to historian Catherine L. Albanese (1999), the religion of the war was "Civil Religion." It did, as many modern Fundamentalists argue, appropriate ideas from Puritanism. The belief in a dualistic world with good battling evil, an unrelenting sense of the providence of God, and melodramatic interpretations of world events did have unquestionable Puritan roots. However, Puritanism was not the only tradition to be

drawn from. Integrated with Puritan rhetoric and ideas was the European Enlightenment. Emphasizing humans' abilities to work for a better world, the Enlightenment defined God as removed from events of this world. Replacing an active deity was the God of reason, natural law, and natural rights. While the Bible provided much of the rhetoric of the patriots' bloody war, it was a deistic God, who had set the universe in motion with specific laws, which they honored. The most obvious convergence of the Puritan ideology and Enlightenment philosophy appeared in Freemasonry, with its elaborate rituals and emphasis on an architect Deity. Fifty-two of the fifty-six signers of the Declaration of Independence were Masons.

Although there were Founding Fathers and Mothers who could be classified as "Christian" by modern Evangelical standards, such as Patrick Henry and John Jay, they were the exception. Evangelical historians Noll, Marsden, and Hatch argue that leaders such as George Washington, Thomas Jefferson, and Benjamin Franklin, although adhering to belief in a deity, were not orthodox Christians in the sense that modern Fundamentalists or Evangelicals would define the faith. They denied the atonement, the nature of biblical revelation, and the legitimacy of Jesus' miracles. One only has to look at Thomas Jefferson's Bible, devoid of Christ's Resurrection, for this to be obvious.

Fundamentalist historians, on the other hand, are quick to point out the professions of Christian belief that saturated public life during this era. Most people of the Revolutionary generation did want to instruct their children in the virtues of the Christian faith and did see organized Christianity as a purifying influence in society. State constitutions are superb examples of the influence of the Christian faith in this period. Many of them expressed an obvious religious devotion to some form of Christianity. Constitutions supported enforcement of Christian rituals like the Sabbath; they prohibited blasphemy; and some used tax revenues to support state churches. However, the omission of such statements of belief in the United States Constitution complicates historians' interpretations of the success of Christianity in defining America.

Evangelical religion again surged after the war during a series of revivals. This was so apparent that a French visitor to America, Alexis de Tocqueville, expressed amazement on its influence on the society he encountered. At the same time, however, many immigrants came to the United States carrying with them religions from their homelands. By the Civil War, Catholicism had become the largest single religious group in the country. New denominations were formed, and new religious movements emerged, such as the Church of Jesus Christ of Latter-day Saints and the Disciples of Christ. The diversity that had defined American religion when the first colonists anchored their ships off the North American coast has only increased exponentially since.

The Legacy of America's Religiously Diverse Origins

The political battles between the Right and the Left in America will continue. What is yet to be determined is the ways in which the religiously faithful understand and reshape the terms of the debate. Many will continue to look to the past in which they see a better epoch while others will focus on the future where they believe that justice and liberty for all may yet be found. It is undeniable that religion has saturated America's past, and more research will only help us sort out the complex issues that have been raised by Fundamentalists. However, as more voices continue to be heard, it will become increasingly difficult for any Americans to find a religious consensus in a country that prides itself on individual rights and democratic freedom.

Matthew A. Sutton

See also Campus Crusade; Campus Crusade for Christ; Ku Klux Klan; Megachurches; Moral Majority; Nativism; Promise Keepers; Radio; Televangelism

Bibliography

Albanese, Catherine L. (1999) *America, Religions and Religion*, 3rd ed. New York: Wadsworth Publishing Company.

Noll, Mark, Nathan Hatch, and George Marsden. (1989) *The Search for Christian America*. Colorado Springs: Helmers and Howard.

Noll, Mark, ed. (1990) *Religion and American Politics, From the Colonial Period to the 1980s*. New York: Oxford University Press.

Roark, James, Michael Johnson, Patricia Cline Cohen, Sarah Stage, Alan Lawson, and Susan Hartmann. (1998) *The American Promise: A History of the United States*. Boston: Bedford Books.

Angels

During the last quarter of the twentieth century, angels became a prominent feature of popular Evangelical literature. As one scholar noted, "to ignore the subject of angels is to miss one of the comeback stories of the century" (Noll 1998: 11). This interest was part of a general revival of curiosity about spiritual beings, demonic as well, which pervaded American culture. There was some serious theological discussion of angels, but the general tone was one of treacly sentimentalism.

Angels are frequently mentioned in the Bible and have provided a subject for such artistic and theological giants as St. Augustine, St. Thomas Aquinas, Dante, Milton, and, more recently, Karl Barth. Modern Evangelical fascination with angels, however, owes little to such precursors and much to the late-twentieth-century American fascination with the occult. Demonic possession (demons being the satanic counterpart to angels) was a staple of many popular movies, such as *The Exorcist* and *The Omen*. There was, likewise, a broad fascination with superior creatures from beyond the earth, manifested in the 1950s as the "flying saucer" craze and by the UFO mania of the 1980s and 1990s, with its tales of alien abduction. Meanwhile, benign extraterrestrial creatures were featured in such vastly popular films as *Close Encounters of the Third Kind* and *E.T.* While not angels per se, this menagerie of unearthly beings—some malign, some friendly, all powerful—possessed many of the traits traditionally assigned them.

The presence of angels in the Evangelical imagination owes some of its currency, paradoxically, to a treatment of demons. C. S. Lewis's *The Screwtape Letters* (1949), a humorous account of a clutch of inept devils frustrated in their continued attempts to lead human souls into damnation, became immensely popular among Evangelicals after World War II. The existence of spiritual beings active in the daily life of humankind was thus normalized.

In the midst of this renewed interest in occult creatures, the Rev. Billy Graham, the century's most renowned evangelist, published *Angels: God's Secret Agents* (1975). Graham's book, which sold in the hundreds of thousands and remains in print, was a folksy, anecdotal, even saccharine account of angelic presence. No work of theology, it nevertheless had unrivalled mass appeal. Graham's almost iconic status among Evangelicals made angels an accepted presence in their devotional life. The theme was picked up in popular Evangelical fiction, especially Frank Peretti's 1985 novel *This Present Darkness*.

Hollywood was quick to sense the commercial potential of the angel craze. There is a long tradition of sentimental American films that portray angels lending the down-and-out a helping hand: *The Bishop's Wife*, for instance, or the classic *It's a Wonderful Life*, both from the 1940s. This theme was repeated during the 1990s with such films as *Angels in the Outfield* and *The Preacher's Wife*. On television, a long-running dramatic series, *Touched by an Angel*, provided weekly episodes centered on a gang of meddlesome angels who turn up wherever needed. Biblical angels, especially in the Old Testament, are awe-inspiring, even menacing. In American Evangelical culture, however, popular religiosity converted such alarming creatures into benevolent, if somewhat insipid, celestial busybodies. Whether such an amalgam of occultism, sentimentalism, and commercial opportunism has theological staying power in Evangelical life was open to question as the twenty-first century began.

Robert K. Whalen

Bibliography

Adler, Mortimer J. (1982) *The Angels and Us*. New York: Macmillan.

Boros, Ladislaus. (1977) *Angels and Men*. New York: The Seabury Press.

Graham, Billy. (1975) *Angels: God's Secret Agents*. Garden City, NY: Doubleday.

Keck, David. (1998) *Angels and Archeology in the Middle Ages*. New York: Oxford University Press.

Noll, Stephen F. (1998) *Angels of Light, Powers of Darkness: Thinking Biblically about Angels, Satan & Principalities*. Downers Grove, IL: Intervarsity Press.

Angelus Temple

Located in Echo Park, near downtown Los Angeles, the striking white-domed structure called Angelus Temple is now an historic landmark. At one time, it was the centerpiece of the flourishing evangelistic ministry of Aimee Semple McPherson (1890–1944). The cornerstone was dedicated on 1 January 1923, and from its opening day, the 5,300–seat auditorium was filled to capacity at every meeting for almost twenty years. The Temple also served as the mother church of the International Church of the Foursquare Gospel, also founded by McPherson.

The controversial evangelist was "Sister Aimee" to her multitude of followers across the nation and in several foreign countries. Ultimately, Aimee Semple McPherson crossed the United States many times, attracting large crowds at her evangelistic crusades. Not only did she preach the gospel, but she also had a remarkable healing ministry that produced thousands of testimonies of miraculous healings.

It was her supporters who urged her to locate in one place and build a headquarters church. A site overlooking Echo Park Lake was selected and work began on the sanctuary building as well as an accompanying residence for McPherson and a nearby structure to house L.I.F.E. (Lighthouse of International Foursquare Evangelism) Bible College, also founded by McPherson. The inside of the Temple contained two balconies; above the platform was a huge mural depicting a scene based upon a vision that the evangelist had had. The domed sanctuary served not only to accentuate McPherson's preaching but also the music of the majestic pipe organ, considered to be one of America's finest at the time. The Temple also included a prayer tower in which volunteers prayed around the clock for needs that arrived by mail and by telephone. Lines of people waited outside for the doors to open for Sister Aimee's famed "illustrated sermons" on Sunday evenings. Ambulances brought the sick from hospitals to join the many others who flocked to the healing services. In addition, the Temple carried out a remarkable program of food and clothing distribution to the homeless and hungry of Los Angeles, particularly during the Depression years.

Following Aimee Semple McPherson's death in 1944 at age 54, Angelus Temple continued to serve as the mother church of the Foursquare denomination, now a worldwide movement. Attendees of services at the Temple were increasingly multiethnic, reflecting the changing area in and around Echo Park. L.I.F.E Bible College was relocated to San Dimas, California. Angelus Temple still attracts many visitors who can still get a sense of its remarkable past.

Mary Ann Lind

See also Evangelicalism; Healing, Faith; Preaching

Antichrist

The term "Antichrist" barely appears in Scripture. Only two minor epistles, 1 John and 2 John, actually use the term and its meaning even there is fairly obscure. Yet, from the earliest times, the concept of the Antichrist has captured the popular imagination. The Antichrist represents the ultimate enemy of Christ who will appear in the final chapter of history to lead the forces of Satan in one last desperate battle against the forces of God. This concept factors significantly in modern Fundamentalist thought because his appearance is believed to begin the sequence of events that will eventuate in the return of Christ and God's final victory over evil. Thus, even though Fundamentalism teaches that the Antichrist's tyranny and deceit are to be feared, his appearance is nonetheless eagerly anticipated as it will signal the first stages of the establishment of God's kingdom here on earth.

Early History of the Idea

The word "Antichrist" appears in both 1 John and 2 John, two of the shortest and least-read books in the Bible. These books were written at a pivotal time in early Christian history. There was as yet no clear-cut set of doctrines that all Christians believed. 1 and 2 John are actually letters that identify a specific group of persons who, while claiming to be Christians, understood Christianity in ways that the author disagreed with. This group claimed to have been anointed by the Spirit and that they therefore participated directly in God's divine spirit. Because they believed that they had direct and unmediated access to God, they rejected the emerging Christian doctrine that only Jesus could mediate between humans and God. The author of 1 and 2 John makes it clear that this group's reliance upon personal experience rather than the historical Jesus made it impossible to still consider them Christian. The author then warns against these persons. They are nonconformists. He calls them deceivers and antichrists (2 John 1:7). The Bible, then, uses the word "antichrist" to identify specific persons who lived in the early Christian world but who did not conform to the doctrines that were beginning to emerge as orthodox Christian belief. The term "antichrist" is thus used in the Bible to identify those who hold diverging beliefs about Jesus: "This is the antichrist, he who denies the Father and the Son" (1 John 2:22, RSV).

The Bible contains other passages that identify an enemy of God who will appear in the final days before the Second Coming and final judgment. Both the books of Daniel and Revelation contain rich apocalyptic imagery describing a beast who will appear in the End Times to lead the forces of evil in one last battle against the forces of God. It seems that most Christians intuitively associated the term "Antichrist" with this beastlike enemy of God, despite the fact that the Bible itself never makes this connection. Modern Fundamentalists continue to make this connection and read the books of Daniel and Revelation in hope of finding information about the nature and identity of the feared beast who will emerge in the final days to be Satan's ally in a last, desperate assault on Christ and His church. They believe that Revelation explains how the Antichrist will take control of the world economy "so that no one can buy or sell unless he has the mark, that is, the name of the beast or the number of its name" (13:17). The "number of its name," 666, supplies modern Fundamentalists with an all-important clue about the beast's identity. While academic scholars believe that the number 666 was a code term for the Roman emperor, Nero Caesar, Fundamentalists continue to devise intricate methods for connecting various people, events, or cultural movements with this curious number.

During the Middle Ages, Christian writers developed elaborate theories about the expected Antichrist. Most concluded that his life would be a perverse opposite of the life of Christ. Medieval theories suggested that the Antichrist would be born of a whore, be of Jewish parentage, and would be possessed by the devil, who will instruct him in the powers of deception and tyranny. It was further thought that the Antichrist would enter Jerusalem, rebuild the temple, and convert the Jews, who will initially embrace him as their ally. He will then gain political and religious power, send out false prophets, destroy belief in Jesus as the Son of God, and demand to be worshiped as God. Then, at the height of the Antichrist's false rule, Christ will return in the clouds and slay him in the Battle of Armageddon that will inaugurate Christ's millennial rule as described in Revelation.

By the Protestant Reformation, the idea of the Antichrist had become politicized. Protestant leaders beginning with John Wycliff (d. 1384) began charging that the pope was the Antichrist, trying to deceive the world with a false church structure. Martin Luther (1483–1546) considered the belief that the pope is the Antichrist to be a life and death matter for all true Christians. The pope returned the favor, branding all Protestants as agents of the Antichrist. While few Catholics would still subscribe to that view, many conservative Protestants still identify the pope as the Antichrist.

Development of the Idea in American Protestant Fundamentalism

The majority of colonial Americans were associated with Protestant churches that linked the pope and all of Catholicism with the deceitful work of the Antichrist. This made it easy at the dawn of the French and Indian War to equate Catholic France with the Antichrist, as well. A few decades later, many American colonists decided that King George III had not sufficiently separated the Church of England from Catholicism and that he, too, was associated with the Antichrist. From that time on, American Protestants have had a tendency to "demonize" the nation's political adversaries by labeling them the Antichrist or at least agents of the Antichrist. This continued well into the twentieth century when each successive leader of the Soviet Union was identified by Protestant Fundamentalists as the Antichrist poised to conquer the world and persecute faithful Christians.

Various Chinese and Arab leaders have also been nominated as possible embodiments of the Antichrist. Other kinds of "outsiders" have also been the targets of apocalyptic speculation. Jews, labor leaders, socialists, feminists, and spokespersons for New Age religious philosophies have all been identified by modern Fundamentalists as in league with the beast of Revelation. However, no group of persons has been more vilified in fundamentalist theories concerning the coming Battle of Armageddon as secular humanists. All humanist causes such as evolutionary biology, world peace, and ecology are suspect in the minds of Fundamentalists who view them as deceitful means whereby the Antichrist hopes to lure unsuspecting Christians from single-minded devotion to Christ and the Bible.

Because Fundamentalism's apocalyptic beliefs assert that the Antichrist will appear in the period just before the Second Coming, it is difficult for Fundamentalist writers to resist the temptation to speculate about the precise person or cultural movement that most closely strikes them as the ultimate enemy of Christ. Recent attempts to identify the Antichrist in American society have even included rap music, computer technology, the European Economic Union, and ecumenical religious movements. All of these identifications remind us that Fundamentalism is not only a theological position; it is also a social and cultural movement. Fundamentalism emerged as a deliberate stance "over and against" many of the secularizing trends that define contemporary American culture. It is by its very nature polemical, thriving in opposition to its perceived enemies. The concept of the Antichrist allows Fundamentalists to name, dramatize, and mythologize their enemies in ways that foster a crisis mentality. By labeling an enemy as the Antichrist, even the most extreme efforts to eradicate this enemy become justified as pious actions undertaken in the name of God. To this extent, apocalyptic identifications of the Antichrist often reveal a hateful or mean-spirited side of Fundamentalist opposition to the surrounding culture.

Significance of the Idea

Christian Fundamentalists view the Antichrist as the Satan-inspired person (or cultural force) who will emerge in the final days to wage one last battle for dominion over this world. The appearance of the Antichrist will trigger the entire sequence of events enumerated in Fundamentalists' apocalyptic beliefs about the Second Coming. For this reason, contemporary Fundamentalists devote a great deal of energy deciphering the "signs of the times" in an effort to determine whether the Antichrist is yet among us and, if so, to determine his exact identity. Fear of the Antichrist's imminent arrival has value for converting persons to the Fundamentalist cause. Proselytizing activities frequently warn persons about the Antichrist's treachery in hope of motivating them to make a more determined commitment to conservative, Bible-based teachings. Outsiders interpret such apocalyptic thought as symbolic of deep-seated psychological and sociological fear among Fundamentalists. Indeed, efforts to "name the Antichrist" appear most frequently when Fundamentalists feel threatened by external enemies or by their own subjective impulses to believe in ideas that will lead them outside the narrow world of fundamentalist thought. By labeling such threats as the work of the Antichrist, they can alleviate their fear and be reassured by the fact that the Bible prophesies their ultimate triumph over all worldly enemies.

Robert C. Fuller

See also Armageddon; Christ; Devil and Satan, The; End Times; Evil; Jesus; Messiah

Bibliography

Boyer, Paul. (1992) *When Time Shall Be No More: Prophecy Belief in Modern American Culture.* Cambridge, MA: The Belknap Press of Harvard University Press.

Fuller, Robert. (1995) *Naming the Antichrist: The History of an American Obsession.* New York: Oxford University Press.

Lindsey, Hal. (1970) *The Late Great Planet Earth.* Grand Rapids, MI: Zondervan Publishing.

McGinn, Bernard. (1994) *Antichrist: Two Thousand Years of the Human Fascination with Evil.* San Francisco: HarperSanFrancisco.

Antifeminism

The antifeminist aspects of Fundamentalist discourse and practice vary across religious movements, and are subject to specific historical and cultural contexts. Common to all of them, however, is an attempt to uphold patriarchal social constructions of gender and "traditional" sex roles. This reinforcement of patriarchy is the trait that Christian Fundamentalism most clearly shares with the other forms of religious belief that have also been called "Fundamentalist." This characteristic is most evident across the Abrahamic tradition of the three monotheistic religions: among Fundamentalist Israeli Jews, within both Sunni and Shi'ite Muslim communities in various countries, and within the current revival of evangelical Protestantism emanating from the United States—but it is also evident in Fundamentalist Hindu and Buddhist movements. Fundamentalists argue that men and women are by divine design, *essentially* different, and they aim to preserve the separation between public and private, male and female, spheres of action and influence. All seek to control women and the expression of sexuality, and to keep women subordinated to men both in the home and in the public world (including business and government).

Fundamentalists define themselves by identifying their enemies: modernism, secularism, communism, homosexuality, and especially, *feminism.* They actively work against feminist concerns and legislation involving gender equality, pay equity and comparable worth, reproductive choice, sexuality education,

and domestic violence. In their resistance to work that articulates women's rights *as* human rights, they stand opposed to the Convention on the Elimination of All Forms of Discrimination Against Women (CEDAW; see Howland 1999; Rose 1999). Majid Tehranian takes the antifeminist animus of Fundamentalism as an example of the attempt to control the interpretation of "human rights and liberation" (Marty and Appleby 1993: 12), arguing that: "The reassertion of patriarchal values in reaction to modern feminist values is reflected in the fundamentalist discourses against abortion, coeducation, unveiling, and more generally, women's full and equal participation in social, economic, and political life" (Tehranian 1993: 314).

In Islam, Judaism, and Christianity, "fundamentalism is primarily a radical patriarchalism" that represents a protest movement against the increasing egalitarianism between the sexes (Riesebrodt 1993). In the twentieth century, "a weakening of the insistence on absolute distinctions between female and male roles, a growing pressure on married women to enter the paid, work force, and a diminution of male monopoly on cash income contrived to challenge the legitimacy of patriarchal authority" (Hardacre 1993: 135). The struggle for women's and children's rights as human rights poses a fundamental threat to "traditional" cultural orders and social structures, and especially to secondary male elites. John Hawley's description of the Fundamentalist Hindu movement, where the traditional status of middle-class men is threatened on many fronts, correlates nicely with the assessment of Protestant Fundamentalism both at the turn and end of the twentieth century in the United States, and Shi'ite Fundamentalism in Iran. Bruce Lawrence's reference to Fundamentalism as the realm of "second-tier male elites" relates to men's insistence on controlling the means of social reproduction in order to maintain male dominance of the middling areas of society where jobs are increasingly contested by women. When trying to regain control of something around them, the people of working and middle-class ranks note that the family, school, and church are the social institutions most accessible to them (see Lawrence 1988; Brouwer 1996; Gifford 1996; Rose 1996; Hawley 1994; and Marty and Appleby 1993). Certainly the "second tier" of male authority can reassert itself on this level more successfully than in the macroeconomic or world political level. The first tier male elite—those who control the major financial institutions and/or manage the corporate structures—are not so preoccupied with this kind of patriarchal restoration.

Changes in the status of women that challenge these "traditional" patriarchal cultural orders and organizations provoke various responses from Fundamentalist groups, ranging from the Taliban's restricting women's access to basic education and medical care to conservative Christian groups in the United States lobbying against reproductive choice and for "abstinence only" sex education. The pro-family, pro-life platform of the New Religious Right (NRR) in the United States unabashedly supports patriarchy, and privileges men's rights over women's rights, and parents' rights over children's rights. Spokespersons for the NRR made this clear in their opposition to the Fourth World Conference on Women. James Dobson, who heads up the largest Christian Right organization in the United States, Focus on the Family, warned that the United Nations Conference on Women represented: "the most radical, atheistic, anti-family crusade in the history of the world.... The extremists who are ... promoting this conference are a million miles outside the American mainstream.... It is a mystery to me how such enormous threats to our spiritual and cultural heritage have slithered into out midst without due notice or alarm" (Dobson 1995: 1). The Family Research Council argued that the conference reflected "a radical feminist agenda that denigrate[d] motherhood and the traditional family" by addressing the "unequal power relations" in the family and the desire of women "to achieve greater equality between women and men in economic and political spheres" (Dobson 1995: 1). [These feminists], writes Gary Bauer, "wanted to enshrine the 'rights'of adolescents to information and medical services where sex and AIDS were concerned and without 'interference from parents'"; although, "parents rights were not completely overruled, they were subordinated to 'the best interests of the child'"(Family Research Council 1995: 1).

When the world seems incomprehensible or spinning out of control, people will seize upon the oldest and simplest traditions of order to reassert control—and patriarchy is one of those. As Karen McCarthy Brown argues, "women become the magnets for the fear raised by everything else that seems out of control. The degree to which control is exercised over women is therefore a key to the profundity of stresses felt by most persons and groups. Fundamentalism is a product of extreme social stress"(1994: 197). An antifeminist stance characterizes Fundamentalist movements across religious traditions because patriarchy lies at the core of Fundamentalist belief.

Susan D. Rose

See also Abortion; Christian Home, Ideal; Male Headship; Pastor's Wife

Bibliography

Bendroth, Margaret L. (1993) *Fundamentalism and Gender, 1875 to the Present*. New Haven, CT: Yale University Press.

Brouwer, Stephen, Paul Gifford, and Susan Rose. (1996) *Exporting the American Gospel: Global Christian Fundamentalism*. New York: Routledge.

Brown, Karen McCarthy. (1994) "Fundamentalism and the Control of Women." In *Fundamentalism and Gender*, edited by John Hawley. Oxford: Oxford University Press.

Dobson, James. (1995) "The Family Under Fire by the UN." *Focus on the Family Newsletter* (August).

Family Research Council. (1995) "UN: Bound for Beijing." *Washington Watch: Special Report* (24 August) 6: 1.

Goodwin, Jan. (1994) *Price of Honor: Muslim Women Lift the Veil of Silence on the Islamic World*. New York: Little, Brown, and Co.

Hardacre, Helen. (1993) "The Impact of Fundamentalisms on Women, the Family, and Interpersonal Relations." In *Fundamentalisms Observed: Reclaiming the Sciences, the Family, and Education*, vol. 2, edited by Marty Martin and Scott Appleby. Chicago: University of Chicago Press, 129–150.

Hawley, John S. (1994) *Fundamentalism and Gender*. New York: Oxford University Press.

Howland, Courtney W. (1997) "The Challenge of Religious Fundamentalism to the Liberty and Equality of Rights of Women: An Analysis under the United Nations Charter." *Columbia Journal of Transnational Law* 271, 35: 283–285.

Howland, Courtney W., ed. (1999) *Religious Fundamentalisms and the Human Rights of Women*. New York: St. Martin's Press.

Lawrence, Bruce. (1989) *God's Defenders: The Fundamentalist Revolt Against the Modern Age*. New York: Harper and Row.

Marty, Martin, and Scott Appleby, eds. (1993) *Fundamentalisms Observed: Reclaiming the Sciences, the Family, and Education*, vol. 2. Chicago: University of Chicago Press.

Rieesebrodt, Martin. (1993) *Pious Passion.* Berkeley: University of California Press.

Rose, Susan D. (1988) *Keeping Them Out of the Hands of Satan: Evangelical Schooling in America.* New York: Routledge.

———. (1999) "Christian Fundamentalism: Patriarchy, Sexuality, and Human Rights." In *Religious Fundamentalisms and the Human Rights of Women*, edited by Courtney Howland. New York: St. Martin's Press, 9–20.

Stacey, Judith. (1990) *Brave New Families.* New York: Basic Books.

Tehranian, Majid. (1993) "Fundamentalist Impact on Education and the Media: An Overview." In *Fundamentalisms Observed: Reclaiming the Sciences, the Family, and Education*, vol. 2, edited by Marty Martin and Scott Appleby. Chicago: University of Chicago Press, 313–340.

Antimodernism

Antimodernism is a global-wide reaction to modernity and to its chief signifiers: high-tech industrialism, bureaucratic depersonalization, radical individualism, and above all, secularism, a decrease in religion's importance as a guidepost for conduct. It arises from concern about urban sprawl, democratic leveling, environmental catastrophe, gross inequality, and pandemics, along with the A-bomb, the gulag, and the death camp, all of which are alleged to be consequences of modernization.

Locating the Subject

Antimodernism typically assumes a harsh right-wing "back-to-basics" form; however, it can also be leftist and environmentally "green, " as with Earth First! and the so-called Unabomber, Ted Kaczynski. Either way, it should be distinguished from *post*modernism. Both anti- and postmodernisms rebuke modernity; however, they do so from entirely different standpoints. Antimodernists respond to the specter of a "brave new (modernist) world" by nostalgically fantasizing of God-centered local communities rooted in faith and piety. Postmodernists, in contrast, announce the "death of god" and then embrace relativism, ambiguity, and artificiality. Antimodernists consider postmodernism not as an alternative to

modernism but as its nihilistic culmination in a "culture of death."

The antimodernist impulse is evident in all contemporary major world religions. There is the nationalistic, kosher-insistent Orthodox Jew as well as the violently misogynist Islam of the Iranian mullahs and the Taliban rulers. There has even been an attempt to resurrect the ancient Hindu custom of holy war by the Bharatiya Janata Party in India. The particular flavor of each of these antimodernisms is seasoned by the cultural context out of which it emerges. In all cases, however, its chief carriers are literate but jobless, unmarried male youth marginalized and disenfranchised by the juggernaut of modernity. The situation is analogous in America. Traditionally, the most enthusiastic audience for antimodernist polemics in the United States has been the rural South, a region seemingly left behind by the march of American progress. At the outset of the twenty-first century, antimodernists find that the agrarian populations of the resource-rich, job-poor Rocky Mountains are fertile soil for the implantation of their reactionary seed.

American Antimodernism

The term "antimodernism" in American religious discourse refers to the non-progressive participant in two overlapping debates within Evangelical Protestantism. The first debate concerns how the Bible should be read; the second concerns what the proper mission of the church should be. Both debates ultimately revolve around a deeper question: specifically, the role that the driving force of modernization, science, should have in everyday life.

How to Read the Bible

Modern science has always constituted a formidable challenge to biblically based worldviews. As early as the fifteenth century the Polish astronomer, Copernicus, dared to argue that the earth was only one of a number of planets, not the center of the universe. For this he was condemned by the Catholic Church as a threat to orthodoxy. Two and a half centuries later, geologist William "Strata" Smith (1769–1839) would explode Archbishop Ussher's claim that the world was created in 4000 BCE. This, by identifying fossil types millions of years old. A more severe blow was struck by the English naturalist, Charles Darwin, in 1859, when in his "preliminary sketch" *On the Origin of Species*, he shattered the Genesis account of Creation by explaining biological variation through a blind process of natural selection. When human artifacts were uncovered in proximity to skeletons of long-extinct beasts at the beginning of the twentieth century, together with proto-human skulls datable before the biblical Flood, many modernists drew a seemingly obvious conclusion: Man was not specially created by God; he has evolved from apes.

As discomfiting as these findings and theories have been to Bible students, they are properly seen as harassing forays in the modernist attack on tradition. The vanguard, so to say, also inspired by science, comes from a different direction. It is known today by the phrase "the Higher Criticism."

During the mid-1800s, German scholars, having translated, dated, and authenticated legal documents, mythologies, and philosophies from around the world, came to a shocking conclusion: The Scriptures are neither unique, nor are they historically accurate. Not only are many Bible accounts—including those in Genesis and the story of the Ten Commandments—anticipated in earlier repositories such as the Babylonian Genesis and the Laws of Hammurabi, comparable themes are also found in Hesiod's Cosmogony, the German sagas, the Hindu Puranas, the Laws of Manu, and even in the non-European Aztec codices. One implication drawn from this by modernists was that read correctly or "esoterically," the Bible is a symbolic rendering of affairs. It is not a literal picture of the past. While proponents of the Higher Criticism argued over the Bible's symbolic meaning—some insisting that the tale of the god–man Jesus' death and Resurrection be interpreted as an allegory of personal psychological growth, while others argued that the same tale is a hyperbolic propaganda intended for political purposes—all concurred that the *wrong* way to understand the Bible is "exoterically" or literally. The first chapters in the Book of Genesis, therefore, like the accounts of Jesus' life, may be good poetry, but they are not good historiographies.

The Church's Mission

As the prestige of science grew during the nineteenth century, modernists began contemplating the possibility of using its theories to engineer solutions to the social problems of an emerging American civilization, such as unemployment, overcrowding, ignorance, vice, and disease. Academically, the product of this modernist project was the establishment of the social sciences, most notably the disciplines of sociology and social work. In the religious realm, the same impetus led to the Social Gospel, that is, to the idea that Christianity should be coupled to science so that its charitable intentions can be implemented more cost effectively.

Social Gospel clergy organized themselves into the Federal (now National) Council of Churches in 1908. They believed that the mission of the modern church should be to scientifically address public issues. Among other things this meant advocating the "Christian" acquisition and use of private property. Support for labor unions and shorter work weeks, lobbying for child labor laws and safer working conditions, and working to pass public health measures, unemployment benefits, and government pensions were seen as important to the Christian vocation as frequent attendance at church.

This progressivist rendition of the Protestant mission made little sense to rural preachers who were already skeptical of "German" ideas such as those recounted earlier. Furthermore, they were unsympathetic to urban social problems, many of which were associated in their minds with "un-American," "Romanish" immigrants. Instead, they urged a return to "old-fashioned revivalism." Included in the revival message were the following themes: First, do not waste time futilely trying to interfere with the divine order of things, for the poor and downtrodden shall always be with us; prepare instead for the imminent Second Coming of Christ when justice shall be achieved. Second, the way to prepare for the Last Days is not to modernize society through Social Gospel activism, which is simply socialism parading behind a facade of religiosity; it is instead to sanctify one's private moral life by renouncing gambling, sports, drink, and dance. Notable among the names associated with this last sentiment are the renowned preacher, Dwight L. Moody (1837–1899), baseball player turned evangelist, Billy Sunday (1863–1935), and Baptist minister, William Bell Riley, (1861–1947) founder of the World's Christian Fundamentals Association (WCFA).

Struggles between Modernists and Antimodernists

The "war against modernism" was formally announced by the WCFA in 1919. Following as it did on the heels of the Prohibition Amendment to the Constitution, the declaration was greeted with both joy and confidence by its proponents. To say that the ensuing struggle was bitter is an understatement. Modernist clergy defamed the opposition as "backward thinking," "unrespectably emotional," "sectarian," "non-civic," "bigoted," and even "neurotic." Antimodernists gleefully returned the insults. Modernists, they alleged, were "spiritually dead secular humanists," "pagan-worshiping sodomites," "comsymps (communist sympathizers)," and "Jew lovers" (Roy 1953). The struggle eventually found political expression. In the 1920s, tens of thousands of antimodernist Protestants affiliated themselves with nativist groups like the Ku Klux Klan, which as a consequence enjoyed political success in a number of states in the Old Confederacy, as well as in Indiana and Oregon. During the 1950s and 1960s, antimodernists played pivotal roles in the right-wing Christian Anti-Communist Crusade and the John Birch Society. Two and three decades later, their racist, anti-Semitic rhetoric largely tempered, antimodernists became avid supporters of the Moral Majority and the Christian Coalition, two powerful lobbies. For their part, promodernists associated themselves with the liberal wing of the Democratic Party, eventually helping to implement the New Deal, Fair Deal, Civil Rights, and Great Society programs. By 1950 all major American Protestant denominations had fractured on modern/antimodernist lines: Methodism, Presbyterianism, Baptism, Lutheranism, and Campbellism (the latter into the modernist Disciples of Christ and the antimodernist Church of Christ).

Three of the most newsworthy battles between the two forces were fought during the 1920s. First was the failed attempt in 1922 to oust liberal Baptist minister Harry Emerson Fosdick (1878–1969) from his pulpit at the First Presbyterian Church in New York after he angrily challenged the congregation with this question, "Shall the Fundamentalists Win?" The second battle involved the passage of thirty-seven bills in twenty state legislatures from 1921 to 1929 outlawing the teaching of evolution. This culminated in 1925 in Tennessee with the Scopes "Monkey Trial," successfully prosecuted by three-time presidential candidate and biblical literalist William Jennings Bryan (1860–1925). The third battle was Fundamentalist minister J. Gresham Machen's unsuccessful attempt to seize control of the Presbyterian Seminary at Princeton University, New Jersey, in 1929 and put an end to the Higher Criticism.

Victory in Defeat

Because promodernists lost only the second of these battles, they claim to have won the war. In retrospect, however, it is now clear that their pronouncements of victory were premature. For the irony is that for all their prating against modernity, antimodernist clergy were far more amenable than their opponents in utilizing modern technology. They were the first to pay local syndicates for airtime to broadcast taped sermons. Later, they jumped at the opportunity to access public cable television, to establish their own television networks, and to adopt the use of short-wave radio as a religious medium. All of this instead of transmitting their messages live (and free) through the mainline radio and television networks, from which they had been strategically excluded by modernist clergy. To circumvent their exclusion from the major (modernist) publishing houses and booksellers, antimodernists set up their own independent printers; they were also among the original users of desktop publishing technology to issue multicolored, slick-page magazines, broadsheets, and commercial-quality books. Led by the model of Charles Fuller's *Old Fashioned Revival Hour*, antimodernists were also the first to borrow modern theatrical logistics for Evangelical purposes: multistaging professional spectacles, using the talk-show format, and lately, implementing in-house big screen projection. They also used computerized mailing systems, direct-dial counseling, and research-based, targeted marketing. With this arsenal of devices antimodernists rapidly began increasing their share of the American religious market in 1940, while promodernists began to lag behind. The (modernist) United Methodist, Presbyterian USA, Episcopal, Disciples of Christ, and United Church of Christ lost an average of fifty percent of the religious market in the four and half decades after 1940. The (antimodernist) Southern Baptist, Assemblies of God, Church of the Nazarene, and Church of God, in contrast, averaged a more than 170 percent growth in their shares during the same period. The deeper irony, of course, is that because the advocates of antimodernism were compelled to defeat the devil of modernity with the devil's own tools, the real victor in the war between modernism and antimodernism may have been the devil himself.

James Aho

See also Biblical Inerrancy; Christian Research Institute; Creationism; Entertainment Industry; Evolution and Antievolution; Hinduism, Fundamental; Islamic Fundamentalism; Judaism, Fundamental; Liberalism; Literalism; Rock Music; Secularism; World Council of Churches

Bibliography

Ammerman, Nancy. (1987) *Bible Believers: Fundamentalists in the Modern World*. New Brunswick, NJ: Rutgers University Press.

Finke, Roger, and Rodney Stark. (1992) *The Churching of America, 1776–1990*. New Brunswick, NJ: Rutgers University Press.

Roy, Ralph. (1953). *Apostles of Discord*. Boston: Beacon Press.

Sandeen, Ernest. (1970). *The Roots of Fundamentalism: British and American Millenarianism 1800–1930*. Chicago: University of Chicago Press.

Anti-Semitism

The term "anti-Semitism" specifically refers to anti-Jewish attitudes and practices. Jews throughout history have had to contend with damaging prejudicial beliefs about themselves as a religious or cultural group as well as discriminatory actions that limit their social, political, and economic choices and opportunities. Although the conditions this term describes are ancient, the word "anti-Semitism" is relatively recent, having been coined only in the latter part of the nineteenth century to describe a racialized, secular conception of the Jewish people as being biologically different from and inferior to Christian Europeans. However, the earliest manifestations of anti-Jewish beliefs begin with the origins of Christianity and are supported by New Testament texts. Both Catholics and Protestants, including Fundamentalists who rely on the Bible as literal truth, have used biblical texts to justify anti-Jewish animosity. It is thus necessary to distinguish the two interrelated but distinct aspects of anti-Jewish sentiment—one originating in the ancient world, the other in the nineteenth century, although both manifestations are often collectively termed "anti-Semitism."

The Origins of Anti-Semitism

Anti-Jewish sentiment dates from the very beginnings of Christianity and is woven through the fabric of Christian–Jewish relations. Whether supported by Christian theological authority, including the Catholic Church, various Protestant denominations, or New Testament texts, anti-Jewish belief is rooted in the Jewish rejection of Jesus as the Messiah. Although recognizing Jesus as a wise teacher and even a prophet, Jews nevertheless considered Him a mortal. Their historic rejection of the essential Christian belief in the divinity of Christ provoked Christian hostility and condemnation. The Book of Matthew, for example, portrays the Roman governor, Pontius Pilate, reluctantly giving in to the demands of Jewish priests and the populace to crucify Jesus. They condemned Jesus for seditiously representing Himself as king of the Jews. Pilate symbolically washed his hands, proclaiming in Matthew 27:24 (AV), "I am innocent of the blood of this just person." The crowd responded, according to the Gospel (Matthew 27:25), by saying, "His blood be on us, and on our children." Here, then, the New Testament lays on Jews an impossible and unending burden of shared responsibility for the killing of Christ, also known as deicide (literally, the killing of God). The text claims that Jews acknowledged their culpability and defiantly accepted a corporate responsibility extending to unborn generations. There are additional examples of specifically anti-Jewish texts in the Christian canon, such as John or the Book of Acts.

Separately or taken together as literal truth, these texts as well as other sources of Christian theological authority justified centuries of discrimination and violence against Jews, including mass expulsions. The First Crusade, for example, exhorted by Pope Urban II in 1095, ignited Christian religious fervor, unleashing a wave of attacks against Jews, especially in the Rhineland. Faced with the threat of conversion to Christianity or death, many Jews chose martyrdom over baptism. Christian zealots terrorized Jews, slaughtering nearly the entire Jewish population of Worms and Mainz. The Jews of Spain, having lived there for over a thousand years, suffered banishment following the church-sponsored Inquisition of 1492. Expulsions, massacres, and lesser forms of violence perpetrated against Jewish communities have punctuated European history from the Middle Ages through the first half of the twentieth century.

However, Christian anti-Jewish beliefs and actions legitimated by the New Testament or church authority depended on distortions of the historical record. The crime of deicide proclaimed in Matthew, for example, is inconsistent with what historians know about the social and political conditions in Roman Palestine. The dominant role of Roman political authority is pivotal in understanding the death of Jesus. Yet the Christian Bible consistently minimizes the role of that authority, expressing the culpability of the Jewish religious leadership hostile to the messianic claims of Jesus.

Anti-Semitism in the Middle Ages

In the twelfth century, medieval folk beliefs disseminated through peasant oral tradition and promoted by some segments of the church also played an important role in nurturing anti-Jewish hostility and violence. Peasant folklore represented Jews as demonic enemies of Christendom, allies of Satan bent on attacking the sacred symbols of Christianity or even killing Christians themselves. A widely held popular medieval belief claimed, for example, that the alleged Jewish hatred of Jesus extended to the theft of communion wafers, the literal embodiment of Christ, in order to desecrate and torture His body. Even in the twentieth century, while Christians celebrated Easter, Jewish communities feared attacks from peasants determined to punish Jews for killing Jesus. Jews were also charged with sacrificing Christian children at Passover to obtain their blood, believed to be an essential ingredient in the preparation of the unleavened bread of Passover. Known as "the blood libel," this medieval defamation showed remarkable staying power as it too continued into the twentieth century, particularly in eastern Europe, where it emboldened and justified peasant assaults on Jewish life and property. Implicit in the "blood libel" was the belief that Jews and Judaism were demonic and parasitic elements in Christian Europe. Other folk legends, such as charging Jews with poisoning wells, continued into the recent past.

The complicity of the Catholic Church in anti-Jewish peasant violence is reflected in beliefs and prayers that encouraged anti-Jewish feeling. Until 1959 when Pope John XXIII rescinded it in an effort to diminish anti-Jewish feeling in the church, the phrase "perfidious Jews" figured in the Catholic liturgy on Good Friday. The pope's action recognized the role of Christian liturgy in engendering hostility against Jews.

Anti-Jewish Sentiment during the Reformation

Although the Protestant Reformation brought a more positive attitude toward the Hebrew Bible, the continuing refusal of Jews to convert to Christianity led to Protestant fulmination as vituperative as the anti-Jewish denunciations emanating from Catholic authority. Protestant theologians also cultivated anti-Jewish malice. In the sixteenth century, for example, Martin Luther condemned Jews for blasphemy and urged the destruction of synagogues, the confiscation of Jewish holy texts, and the expulsion of Jews from German territory.

Defamatory Christian beliefs effectively limited the capacity of Jews to control their lives. Theologically based animosity toward Judaism had important social, economic, and political consequences for the Jewish communities of Europe. From the twelfth through the eighteenth centuries, imposed restrictions channeled Jews into stigmatized occupations, such as money-lending. Jews, moreover, had to live in residentially segregated locales, or ghettoes and had to observe curfews and other serious constraints on their freedom of action. These social and economic measures in turn reinforced the belief among the Christian majority that the Jews were different, a people apart and worthy only of suspicion and contempt.

Ironically, as Jews suffered the consequences of demonization and political domination by the Christian majority, they also had to endure medieval legends that depicted them as bent on world domination. The notorious fraudulent document, *Protocols of the Learned Elders of Zion* (widely distributed in the early 1900s), played on old beliefs about nefarious Jewish elders plotting to control the world. Purporting to reveal the secrets of a Jewish conspiracy to seize power, the *Protocols* are nothing more than a modern version of medieval peasant delusions about a conspiratorial alliance between Jews and Satan, the archenemy of Christ and Christendom. Although exposed as a lie on many occasions, the *Protocols* served as a pretext in the twentieth century to legitimate genocide by the Nazis. In the United States, they inspired the vicious series, "The International Jew," in Henry Ford's anti-Semitic newspaper, the *Dearborn Independent*. Others, including ministers such as Gerald L. K. Smith, disseminated Ford's series and the *Protocols* and added their own scurrilous and hateful messages against Jews and other minorities.

Anti-Semitism in Post-Reformation Europe

Beginning in the eighteenth century the effects of the Enlightenment and the French Revolution permitted fundamental changes in the centuries-old status of

Jewish life in areas of western Europe. Granted civil rights and religious freedom, first in France and then in certain states in Germany and other parts of Europe, Jewish communities made a historic break with a social past that excluded them from participation in the mainstream of a Christian-dominated world. Once they were granted citizenship and civil rights, Jews gained greater access to secular education, the professions, and other social positions from which they had been barred since the Middle Ages. Many Jews were thereby able to ascend economically and socially over the course of the nineteenth and early twentieth centuries. They adopted a way of life consistent with a modern secular world as differences between themselves and non-Jews diminished along many lines, including dress, language, cultural outlook, and shared national allegiances.

Still, Jewish social and economic success affronted many non-Jews who were envious of Jewish achievements. At those times when ethnic nationalism and economic insecurity intensified, old anti-Jewish attitudes resurfaced and Jews were made scapegoats once again for the existing social and economic crises and cultural dislocations.

A new form of secular rather than strictly religious anti-Jewish sentiment emerged based on allegations of racial difference. "Scientific racism" contended that the Jews were biologically distinct, representing an inferior race that threatened the alleged purity of the dominant and superior Aryan "race" of Europe. Pseudoscientific authority purported to identify Jewish physical distinctiveness and related behaviors deemed disagreeable. Europe's Jews appeared once again to be an alien, polluting element within ethnic nation-states such as Germany. Nazism was the culmination of these claims and ultimately responsible for the extermination of two-thirds of Europe's Jewish population in World War II.

Fundamentalist Anti-Semitism in the United States

Over the past fifty years some Christian thinkers have tried to come to terms with the historic role of Christianity in the persecution of European Jewry. Christian self-scrutiny and acknowledgment of complicity in anti-Jewish beliefs and practices are all the more critical in the wake of the destruction of European Jewry in World War II.

Still, theologically grounded anti-Semitism continues in the United States and elsewhere. For example,

in 1980, Bailey Smith, the president of the Southern Baptist Convention, said that "God Almighty does not hear the prayer of a Jew." Smith was speaking to a group of Fundamentalist Christians. Proclaiming his friendship with Jews and denying that his remarks were anti-Semitic, Smith said, "I am pro-Jew. I believe they are God's special people, but without Jesus Christ they are lost. No prayer gets through that is not prayed through Jesus Christ. Jews have an argument with me because they have an argument with the New Testament" (*New York Times* 1980: A-18). Significantly, protests against Smith's remarks emanated not only from rabbis and Jewish community spokesmen but also from enlightened Baptist leaders who criticized Smith both on sociopolitical and theological grounds. One critic contended that Baptists have always defended religious liberty and that position required respect for the religious beliefs of other people. Moreover, he argued that Smith's view of God was limiting and restrictive.

Smith's position was not unique. Religious pluralism implicitly challenges the certainty of Evangelical Fundamentalist forms of Christianity that emphasize literal interpretations of the Bible. Other modes of religious thought simply represent repudiations of the one true word of God. Since Jews reject the Christian message, many Fundamentalists believe they have a special, divinely ordained mission to proselytize Jews and other unbelievers. Assuming, moreover, that the United States is a Christian country, some Fundamentalists have historically promoted efforts to insinuate their version of Christianity into public policy. In the nineteenth century, for example, they urged a constitutional amendment declaring Christ's authority in the United States. At the same time, the evangelist Dwight L. Moody on a missionary tour in the 1870s told his audiences that the Jews had killed Jesus and exhorted his listeners to convert them. More recently, Evangelical Christians including Jerry Falwell and Pat Robertson have been equally energetic in trying to promote the incorporation of Christian views into public policy.

Much of today's Fundamentalist Christianity embodies the same contradictions expressed by Reverend Smith. For Fundamentalists, Jews are worthy of admiration because their relationship to God precedes Christianity. But Smith condemned Jews as "lost" without Jesus. Consequently, Jews regard his position as anti-Semitic and intolerant, for it recapitulates the same ancient Christian failure to recognize the legitimacy of Judaism on its own terms. In other words, it encounters Judaism as a continuing repudiation of the most essential element of Christianity—Jesus as Messiah.

The well-known support of many Fundamentalist groups for Israel is also symptomatic of a determined incapacity to see Judaism as a distinct religion worthy of respect in its own right rather than as a living negation of Christian doctrine. That is, many Fundamentalists believe that supporting the in-gathering of Jews to biblical Israel is but a necessary prelude to the return of Jesus, when Jews will finally accept the truth of His divinity. Theological anti-Semitism within Christianity has a very long history indeed. Its future is assured as long as the Bible is read as history and the values of religious pluralism and mutual tolerance are rejected.

Jack Glazier

Bibliography

"Baptist Leader Criticized for Statement about Jews." (1980) *New York Times* A-18.

Dinnerstein, Leonard. (1994) *Antisemitism in America.* New York: Oxford University Press.

Hall, Stanley G., III. (1993) *Christian Anti-Semitism and Paul's Theology.* Minneapolis, MN: Fortress Press.

Ruether, Rosemary Radford. (1974) *Faith and Fratricide: The Theological Roots of Anti-Semitism.* New York: Seabury Press.

Selzer, Robert M. (1980) *Jewish People, Jewish Thought: The Jewish Experience in History.* New York: Macmillan.

Singer, David G. (1986) "From St. Paul's Abrogation of the Old Covenant to Hitler's War Against the Jews: The Responses of American Catholic Thinkers to the Holocaust 1945–76." In *Anti-Semitism in American History*, edited by David A. Gerber. Urbana: University of Illinois Press, 386–406

Apocalypse

An apocalypse is an imminent confrontation, cataclysmic event, or transformation of epochal proportion. Apocalypticism often manifests itself as a rhetorical style or mobilization strategy used by people who believe in an impending battle between good and evil about which they and a select few have forewarning. The apocalyptic tradition can be traced through Zoroastrianism, Judaism, Christianity, Islam, and other religions, as well as secular belief systems. Apocalyptic themes permeate literature, art, and music in the United States, from Moby Dick to Dick Tracy to Tracy Chapman.

The word "apocalypse" evolves from the Greek, *apokalypsis,* which means unveiling hidden information or revealing secret knowledge concerning unfolding human events. The word "revelation" is another way to translate the idea of *apokalypsis.* Thus, the words "apocalypse," "revelation," and "prophecy" are closely related. Prophets, by definition, are apocalyptic.

The Christian Apocalypse

In Christianity, the Apocalypse refers to a cataclysmic struggle with the evil forces of the Antichrist in the End Times. Periods of Catholic apocalyptic fervor spanned many centuries, often spawning periods of intense repression and violence, but periodically generating peaceful and reflective movements as well. In recent decades, the Catholic Church has deemphasized apocalyptic interpretations of biblical verses, although it still flourishes in small subcultures such as the Marianists.

Within Protestant Fundamentalism, the interpretation of biblical prophecy to set the exact timing and order of events in the apocalyptic End Times is the subject of hundreds of books and tracts. Christian premillennialists often generate apocalypticism through their expectation that the End Times will bring the return of Christ, who will then reign for one thousand years—the millennium. While some premillennialists believe they are "raptured" up into God's embrace prior to the End Times apocalyptic battles—encouraging passivity—others believe they must struggle within secular society as long as possible—encouraging activity. Christian postmillennialists are apocalyptic activists in their quest to take over secular society and hold it for the thousand years they believe is required to bring the return of Christ. Preterists and amillennialists argue against apocalyptic interpretations of the Bible that see current relevance or timetables. All millennial movements are apocalyptic in some sense, even when positive and hopeful; but not all apocalyptic movements are millennial.

Christian apocalypticism is based on many sources in the Bible, including the Old Testament books of Daniel and Ezekiel, and the New Testament Gospel of Matthew. The primary biblical source,

Daniel 12:2

2. **And many of them that sleep in the dust of the earth shall awake, some to everlasting life, and some to shame and everlasting contempt.**

Joel 2:30–31

30. **And I will shew wonders in the heavens and in the earth, blood, and fire, and pillars of smoke.**
31. **The sun shall be turned into darkness, and the moon into blood, before the great and the terrible day of the LORD come.**
32. **And it shall come to pass, that whosoever shall call on the name of the LORD shall be delivered: for in mount Zion and in Jerusalem shall be deliverance, as the LORD hath said, and in the remnant whom the LORD shall call.**

however, is the Book of Revelation, the last book of the Christian New Testament. Revelation, the chronicle of an apocalyptic vision, was written about 95 CE, but parts derive from prophetic elements of the Book of Daniel and other Old Testament books. The identity of John of Patmos, the author of Revelation, is disputed, but most experts suggest it was not the same John, the disciple of Jesus, who authored the fourth Gospel.

A primary theme of Protestant apocalypticism is that as the End Times battles approach to cleanse, through fiery destruction, a world polluted by sin and materialism—there is hope. As evangelist Billy Graham explains, "There can be no new world under present conditions. Something dramatic has to happen to alter man and his world. That leaves us with only one absolute certainty about the future: Christ as the Prince of Peace, with the government upon His shoulders" (1983: 228).

Apocalyptic Themes in U.S. History

In the United States the witch-hunts in Salem and throughout New England in the colonial period are an example of apocalypticism. The Civil War was seen by many in apocalyptic terms of good versus evil, with the words to the "Battle Hymn of the Republic" clearly qualifying it as an apocalyptic anthem. Prior to the early 1900s, references to apocalyptic prophecy were commonplace in popular culture. For example, in a speech against slavery in 1857, abolitionist orator Frederick Douglass complained about materialism trumping prophetic morality. Quoting from Revelation 14:6, Douglass admonishes:

... if such a people as ours had heard the beloved disciple of the Lord, exclaiming in the rapture of the apocalyptic vision, "And I saw another angel fly in the midst of heaven, having the everlasting gospel to preach to them that dwell on the earth, and to every nation, kindred, tongue, and people;" they, instead of answering, Amen Glory to God in the Highest, would have responded,—but brother John, *will it pay?* Can money be made out of it? Will it make the rich richer, and the strong stronger? How will it effect property? In the eyes of such people, there is no God but wealth; no right and wrong but profit and loss. ... [Our] national morality and religion have reached a depth of baseness than which there is no lower deep. (1985: 197)

Consider the range of biblical knowledge Douglass assumes in his audience. In addition to using apocalyptic images from biblical prophecy, Douglass himself uses apocalyptic rhetoric in casting the struggle in terms of battles between good and evil, with slavery and materialism on one side, and abolition and spirituality on the other. The contempt shown by Douglass for political and religious leaders who refuse to stand up against slavery is typical of the apocalyptic rhetorical style, and is reprised fifty years later by the Fundamentalist movement who held mainstream Protestant leaders in contempt for succumbing to the allures of modernity.

Fundamentalism and Apocalyptic Politics

Fundamentalism emerged in opposition to mainstream Protestant denominations seen as betraying Christianity in an attempt to accommodate liberalism and modernity. Almost immediately this was grafted onto an apocalyptic fear of internal subversion that gained strength after the Bolshevik Revolution in Russia. Frank Donner, in *The Age of Surveillance* (1981: 47–48), describes the process:

> Bolshevism came to be identified over wide areas of the country by God-fearing Americans as the Antichrist come to do eschatological battle with the children of light. A slightly secularized version, widely shared in rural and small-town America, postulated a doomsday conflict between decent upright folk and radicalism—alien, satanic, immorality incarnate

Liberals, secular or religious, were seen as greasing the slide down the slope toward communism and the one-world government ruled by the Antichrist. Thompson points out that the right-wing political and social movements representing what historian Richard Hofstadter called the paranoid style are more accurately seen as having an apocalyptic style. A variety of Christian Right movements since World War II mobilized grass-roots activism through the use of antiliberal apocalyptic rhetoric, especially in the areas of anticommunist, antifeminist, antigay, and antiglobalist campaigns. More secular conservative groups did likewise, especially in campaigns against the ecology movement.

The mainstreaming of apocalypticism received a major boost when, in 1983, Ronald Reagan cited scriptural authority to demonize the Soviet Union as an "evil empire." Halsell (1986) noted that some evangelists, including Jerry Falwell, Hal Lindsey, and Pat Robertson, hinted that use of atomic weapons might be part of the inevitable final battle of Armageddon. As FitzGerald explains:

> ... elements of premillennialist thinking seem to exist in vague and diffuse form quite generally in the United States. Fundamentalist theology, for example, dictates that God and the Devil are everywhere immanent; thus, politics is not simply the collision of differing self-interests but the expression of a transcendent power struggle between the forces of good and the forces of evil.... If the United States is the "Christian nation," then the Soviet Union must be the "evil empire." (1985: 106)

Ironically, Kovel notes that "Whatever its claims to be a scientific understanding of society, Marxist Communism showed unmistakable influences of Revelation in its central texts, indeed, in its whole sense of mission, in the rising of the underclass to overthrow the 'beast' of capital (corrupt as the Whore of Babylon) and redeem history" (1994: 77). When Communists sing the "Internationale," they salute the apocalyptic "final conflict."

There are hundreds of books with apocalyptic themes aimed at Christian Evangelicals and Fundamentalists, see, for example, Lindsey and Carlson (1970), Lindsey (1997), and Graham (1983). By the time the 1974 prophecy book, *Armageddon, Oil, and the Middle East Crisis* was revised and republished during the Gulf War, it had sold over one million copies.

Year 2000 and the Apocalypse

The approach of the calendar year 2000 excited millennial expectation and apocalyptic rhetoric among Fundamentalists and the broader Evangelical community. The Promise Keepers men's movement brought tens of thousands to stadium events, and many attending the massive October 1997 Stand in the Gap rally in Washington, D.C., expressed their belief that they would witness the apocalypse in their lifetime.

Most Evangelical leaders sought to dampen overt apocalyptic expectation, as did some Fundamentalist leaders. One sector of Fundamentalism, however, pulled out all the stops in their house organs of apocalyptic awareness. A typical example was David Webber, who warned that "Because of exploding population (Gen. 6:1); increase of knowledge and travel (Dan. 12:4); and the ability to wage war in the heavens (Joel 2:30, 32), global war and cyberwar may break out before the end of this century!" (1996: 201). Webber writes that Joel 2:2–4 "could indicate ... a demonic army unleashed from the pit of hell, as described in Revelation 9. Or verses 5–10 might denote an alien invasion from outer space by fallen angels who give their allegiance to Satan, the fallen angelic prince (Luke 10:18)" (1996: 204).

Theoretical Frameworks

There have been numerous theories put forward for explaining apocalyptic beliefs. Strozier (1994) takes the psychological approach, claiming apocalyptic thinking reflects a broken self-identity within a person, leading to an inability to deal with the present on a personal, societal, and metaphysical level. Lamy

(1996) and Thompson (1996) argue that while apocalyptic millennialism has many sources, it generally can be tied to some type of societal conflict or resistance to change. Fuller says apocalyptic fervor is complex, and part of a "literary and theological tradition," that is "transmitted through a variety of cultural institutions that are relatively immune" to certain "social or economic forces" (1995: 9–10, 191–200). Other theories examine natural disasters or other hardships, relative deprivation, and loss of status.

O'Leary has constructed a theory of how millennial rhetoric is used to manage concepts of time, authority, and evil. Apocalyptic beliefs that demonize, says O'Leary, come from a literal interpretation of prophecy that sees a physical battle between good and evil that functions on a societal level, along with a specific timetable and geography for how God intervenes in earthly affairs with a final judgment. Not all interpretations of the images and metaphors in Revelation fit this category, but any attempt to reduce the Bible verses "to literal and factual content inevitably distorts the deliberately metaphorical language of prophecy" (1994: 42). This is not a new view. St. Augustine argued that the signs of the End Times were present throughout history, and thus should not be interpreted as signals. O'Leary divides apocalypticism into the tragic and comedic modes:

> In the tragic periodization of history, calamities appear as part of a predetermined sequence that will culminate in the reign of Antichrist, whose final defeat will be followed by the millennial kingdom. In Augustine's provisionally comic view of history ... calamities become episodes, recurrent events that all human communities must face without recourse to an apocalyptic understanding, while the millennial kingdom becomes an obscure allegory of the church in the present age. Augustine explicitly invokes the comic perspective when he cautions readers to be skeptical in evaluating apocalyptic claims ... [the] comic interpretation of the Apocalypse thus neutralizes its predictive function. What remains is the exhortation of the saintly life and the aesthetic functioning of the text experienced as allegory. (1994: 75)

Other analysts take a more skeptical approach. "What makes apocalypse so compelling," argues Quinby, "is its promise of future perfection, eternal happiness, and godlike understanding of life." She adds, however, that "it is that very will to abso-

lute power and knowledge that produces its compulsions of violence, hatred, and oppression." Apocalyptic demonization "fuels discord, breeds anxiety or apathy, and sometimes causes panic." Quinby claims that this process can happen at the individual, community, national, or international level (1994: 162).

Fenn (1997) sees apocalyptic rituals both as a way to mediate social change and transfer power between generations; and to challenge, at least metaphorically, death itself. He also sees fascist movements using apocalyptic rhetoric to defend imperiled traditional communities based on race or kinship against the bewildering and intrusive forces of modernity. Wistrich (1985) traces the apocalyptic paradigm of Nazism and writes of the millennial roots of their plans for a thousand-year Reich.

While agreeing that human nature has a nasty side, Reston looks for a way out of the dilemma by noting that God may have a different way to read the clock. "If counting time might be different, could the very nature of apocalypse, as we generally understand it, be different as well? We understand apocalypse to be sudden, but what, to a deity, is suddenness? We understand it to be total and all-encompassing, but who says it can't be limited? It must be dramatic, but in the modern attention span, a four-hour drama is boring by its nature" (1998: 275).

Apocalypse promises transformation, and the resulting changes—emerging from the fission of metaphysical expectation—produce physical social or political struggle. This can move a society toward greater liberty and equality or toward authoritarianism and genocide. Berrigan (1997) is one of many who give voice to apocalyptic aspirations that seek to build community and compassion. These visionaries carry forward an apocalyptic tradition of liberation that locates evil in the will to oppress, rather than embodied by specific demonized individuals or groups.

Chip Berlet

See also Apocalyptic Literature; End Times; Eschatology

Bibliography

Abanes, Richard. (1998) *End-Time Visions: The Road to Armageddon?* New York: Four Walls Eight Windows.

Berrigan, Daniel. (1997) *Ezekiel: Vision in the Dust.* Maryknoll, NY: Orbis Books.

Boyer, Paul. (1992) *When Time Shall Be No More: Prophecy Belief in Modern American Culture.* Cambridge, MA: The Belknap Press of Harvard University Press.

Camp, Gregory S. (1997) *Selling Fear: Conspiracy Theories and End-Times Paranoia.* Grand Rapids, MI: Baker Books.

Cohn, Norman. (1993) *Cosmos, Chaos and the World to Come: The Ancient Roots of Apocalyptic Faith.* New Haven, CT: Yale University Press.

Donner, Frank J. (1981). *The Age of Surveillance: The Aims and Methods of America's Political Intelligence System.* New York: Knopf.

Douglass, Frederick. ([1857] (1985) "The Significance of Emancipation in the West Indies." Speech, Canandaigua, New York, 3 August, 1857; collected in pamphlet by author. In *The Frederick Douglass Papers. Series One: Speeches, Debates, and Interviews.* Vol. 3: *1855–63,* edited by John W. Blassingame. New Haven, CT: Yale University Press, 183–208.

Fenn, Richard K. (1997) *The End of Time: Religion, Ritual, and the Forging of the Soul.* Cleveland: Pilgrim Press.

FitzGerald, Frances. (1985) "Reflections: The American Millennium," *The New Yorker* (11 November), 88–113.

Fuller, Robert C. (1995) *Naming the Antichrist: The History of an American Obsession.* New York: Oxford University Press.

Graham, Billy. (1983) *Approaching Hoofbeats: The Four Horsemen of the Apocalypse.* Minneapolis, MN: Grason.

Halsell, Grace. (1986) *Prophecy and Politics: Militant Evangelists on the Road to Nuclear War.* Westport, CT: Lawrence Hill.

Herman, Didi. (1997) *The Antigay Agenda: Orthodox Vision and the Christian Right.* Chicago: University of Chicago Press.

Johnson, George. (1995) *Fire in the Mind: Science, Faith, and the Search for Order.* New York: Knopf.

Kaplan, Jeffrey. (1997) *Radical Religion in America: Millenarian Movements from the Far Right to the Children of Noah.* Syracuse, NY: Syracuse University Press.

Kovel, Joel. (1997) *Red Hunting in the Promised Land: Anticommunism and the Making of America.* London: Cassell.

LaHaye, Tim. (1975) *Revelation: Illustrated and Made Plain,* rev. ed. Grand Rapids, MI: Zondervan Publishing.

Lamy, Philip. (1996) *Millennium Rage: Survivalists, White Supremacists, and the Doomsday Prophecy.* New York: Plenum.

Landes, Richard. (1995) *Relics, Apocalypse, and the Deceits of History: Ademar of Chabannes, 989–1034.* Harvard Historical Studies, 117. Cambridge, MA: Harvard University Press.

———. (1996) "On Owls, Roosters, and Apocalyptic Time: A Historical Method for Reading a Refractory Documentation." *Union Seminary Quarterly Review* 49:1–2,165–185.

Lindsey, Hal, with C. C. Carlson. (1970) *The Late Great Planet Earth.* Grand Rapids, MI: Zondervan Publishing.

Lindsey, Hal. (1997) *Apocalypse Code.* Palos Verdes, CA: Western Front.

O'Leary, Stephen D. (1994) *Arguing the Apocalypse: A Theory of Millennial Rhetoric.* New York: Oxford University Press.

Quinby, Lee. (1994) *Anti-Apocalypse: Exercises in Genealogical Criticism.* Minneapolis: University of Minnesota Press.

Reston, James, Jr. (1998) *The Last Apocalypse: Europe at the Year 1000 A.D.* New York: Anchor Books.

Robbins, Thomas, and Susan J. Palmer, eds. (1997) *Millennium, Messiahs, and Mayhem: Contemporary Apocalyptic Movements.* New York: Routledge.

Rosenfeld, Jean E. (2000) "A Brief History of Millennialism and Suggestions for a New Paradigm for Use in Critical Incidents." In *Millennialism, Persecution, and Violence: Historical Cases* [Religion and Politics series], edited by Catherine L. Wessinger. Syracuse, NY: Syracuse University Press.

Smith, Christian, ed. (1996) *Disruptive Religion: The Force of Faith in Social-Movement Activism.* New York: Routledge.

Strozier, Charles B. (1994) *Apocalypse: On the Psychology of Fundamentalism in America.* Boston: Beacon Press.

Thompson, Damian. (1998) *The End of Time: Faith and Fear in the Shadow of the Millennium.* Hanover, NH: University Press of New England.

Walvoord, John F. (1990) *Armageddon, Oil and the Middle East Crisis,* rev. ed. Grand Rapids, MI: Zondervan Publishing.

Webber, David. (1996) "Cyberspace Storm Troopers Rampage." In *Raging into Apocalypse: Essays in Apocalypse IV,* edited by William T. James. Green Forest, AK: New Leaf Press, 201–213.

Wistrich, Robert. (1985) *Hitler's Apocalypse: Jews and the Nazi Legacy.* New York: St. Martin's Press.

Apocalyptic Literature

The word "apocalyptic" derives from the Greek word *apokalypsis,* which literally means "uncovering." The primary characteristic of apocalyptic literature is not necessarily a final cataclysm; rather it is the revelation of divine knowledge to a human being. This knowledge, however, is often about the end of the world. The word "apocalyptic" developed its meaning as a term associated with a body of Jewish literature produced in the first few centuries before Christ. To understand apocalyptic literature one must understand these texts. The main features of apocalyptic literature will be summarized here and some of the most important apocalyptic compositions—*1 Enoch*, Daniel, and Revelation—will be reviewed. (For other apocalyptic works, see Collins 1998; Charlesworth 1985.) This will provide a historical context with which to understand the production of modern apocalyptic literature by Fundamentalists.

Common Features of Apocalyptic Literature

Apocalyptic literature is a product of Second Temple Judaism. The Second Temple period is demarcated by the rebuilding of the Jerusalem Temple in the fifth century BCE and its destruction by the Romans in 70 CE. The late Second Temple period is characterized by popular dissatisfaction with a succession of oppressive rulers (Hellenistic, Hasmonean, and Roman). (For a review of this history, see Shanks 1999: 231–298.) The religious and cultural crises of this period had a lasting influence on Judaism. Jews tried to reconcile their belief that they were the people chosen by God with the oppression facing them. God's deliverance was not manifested in the present, and was seen as deferred to the eschatological future. This delay of vindication is expressed in apocalyptic literature.

The visions depicted in apocalyptic literature are often intentionally cryptic. Interpretation requires revelation from a higher source. Quite often an angel interprets the scene for the visionary (see, e.g., Daniel 7:17–27). In apocalyptic literature the appeal to revelation is paramount. It underscores the perception that the world does not make sense on its own, but rather needs information from the divine realm in order to be fully understood. This literature discloses heavenly secrets. The content of these visions can be knowledge about the scope of human history, the nature of the angelic world, or information about the cosmos generally not permitted to humans. It can also contain information about events associated with the end of the world and the Final Judgment. In this sense it is eschatological literature. The Final Judgment represents an expected intervention by

God in the End Times to correct wrongs caused by the reign of evil in the human world.

The recipient of apocalyptic visions is often pseudonymous, which means that they are attributed to a figure other than the author of the composition. The visionary is often a revered figure from the past, which gives his revelations additional force and legitimacy. The Book of Daniel, for example, was written in the second century BCE but is set in the sixth century BCE.

Apocalyptic literature is also dualistic in that its eschatological scenarios depict the world as dominated by two rival powers, one good, one evil. Apocalyptic texts also frequently demarcate history into a sequence of periods, such as in Daniel 9, to show that history is unfolding according to God's predetermined plan. The author often places his own day at the end of this historical sequence to give his description of the coming judgment more immediacy (see Daniel 9:27). This literature is thus deterministic. It is written in light of a conviction that all the events are known and ordained by God. It is produced to show that God is in control when that does not appear to be the case.

One complication is the difference between "apocalypse" and "apocalyptic." "Apocalypse" is a genre—a type of literature with specific features and intents that help one categorize it. It is a "genre of revelatory literature" that typically features a pseudonymous recipient of visions that disclose secrets about the cosmos and/or human history, often given and/or interpreted by an angel (Collins 1998: 5). It may also include tours of the heavenly world given by angels to the visionary. Nevertheless, a text can be apocalyptic but not an apocalypse if it has some apocalyptic motifs but does not fully fit the definition of that genre. It is analogous to the fact that a literary work can be poetic without necessarily being a poem. For our purposes, the distinction between "apocalypse" and "apocalyptic" is less important than clarifying the dominant characteristics of apocalyptic literature. (For more information on the genre apocalypse, see Collins 1998.)

Apocalyptic literature developed in the Second Temple period but has antecedents that are much older. Many scholars consider these antecedents to include Mesopotamian mythology (see *1 Enoch* later), the ancient Persian religion of Zoroastrianism, which is highly dualistic, and the biblical prophets (VanderKam 1984; Cohn 1993; Collins 1998: 23–37). The visions interpreted by an angel in Zechariah and

1 Enoch 102:1–4

In those days, when he hurls out against you terror of fire, where shall you flee, and where shall you find safety? When he flings his word against you, will you not faint and fear? All the luminaries shall faint with great fear; the whole earth shall faint and tremble and panic. . . . The children of the earth will seek to hide themselves from the presence of the Great Glory, trembling and confounded. You, sinners, you are accursed forever; there is no peace for you! But you, souls of righteousness, fear not; and be hopeful, you souls that died in righteousness

the war of Gog and Magog in Ezekiel 38–39, for example, are features commonly found in apocalyptic literature (see also Isaiah 24–27, 56–66; and Zechariah 9–14). Apocalypticists responded to the oppression and instability of the late Second Temple period in part by appropriating and reinterpreting older traditions. A more precise understanding of the features of apocalyptic literature, however, demands an examination of some of the most important apocalyptic works.

1 Enoch

1 Enoch is a large work in which revelations that disclose secret knowledge on such topics as the final judgment and the angelic world are given to Enoch. It is comprised of five compositions: the Book of the Watchers (chaps. 1–36), the Similitudes of Enoch (chaps. 37–71), the Astronomical Book (chaps. 72–82), the Book of Dreams (chaps. 83–90), and the Epistle of Enoch (chaps. 91–107). The Epistle of Enoch contains the Apocalypse of Weeks, which is a distinct unit (chaps. 93:1–10; 91:11–17). The Book of Dreams also contains a distinct work, the Animal Apocalypse (chaps. 85–90). Most of these works were written in the second century BCE; the exceptions are the Astronomical Book, which is probably from the third century BCE, and the Similitudes, which is probably from the first century CE. (This corpus cannot be fully examined here, but for more information, see Charlesworth 1985: 5–89; Collins 1998: 43–84.)

This corpus of disparate texts is bound by the figure of Enoch. He is known from the Bible (Genesis 5:24), and is the seventh descendent after Adam. Enoch corresponds to a figure from Mesopotamian mythology called Enmeduranki. He was the seventh king according to an ancient Sumerian chronology, and was legendary as a recipient of revelations. This suggests that the inspiration for the Jewish Enoch came from Mesopotamian sources (VanderKam 1984).

The texts of *1 Enoch* recount revelations given to Enoch. He is an intermediary figure between the human and divine realms. In the Book of Watchers, angels lift Enoch into the skies and give him a "heavenly tour." He is shown how the universe functions: "I saw the winds which turn the heaven and cause the start to set—the sun as well as all the stars. I saw the souls carried by the clouds. I saw the path of the angels . . . and the firmament of the heaven above" (18:4–5). Throughout *1 Enoch* cosmological and eschatological secrets are disclosed to him: "my eyes saw there [in the west] all the secret things of heaven and the future things" (52:1); "my eyes saw the secrets of lightning and thunder, and the mysteries of the winds" (41:3; cf. 59:1; 69:16–25; 71:3). In the Apocalypse of Weeks, Enoch recounts information given to him about human history, such as the number of periods it is divided into, and what happens when that sequence of periods is complete. The revelation of divine secrets is a chief characteristic of *1 Enoch*.

Some Enochic works are political. The Animal Apocalypse is an allegory in which figures of biblical history are represented as animals. The Jews are portrayed as sheep. One sheep sprouts "a great horn," who leads the rams to attack the eagles, vultures, and other animals that have been ravishing the sheep (90:10–11). God eventually gives a sword to the sheep, who kill the other animals (90:19). The sheep with the horn is widely thought to be Judas Maccabee, who led a Jewish revolt against the Hellenistic rulers of Israel in the 160s BCE. This military action was caused in part by oppressive policies and disdain for Jewish tradition by these foreign rulers. Jews were forced to sacrifice swine upon the altar of the temple, copies of the Torah were burned (1 Maccabees 1:56), and Jewish religious festivals were suppressed (cf. 1 Maccabees 1:10–15; 2 Maccabees 4:7–38; Shanks 1999: 231–264). This apocalypse provided a divine revelation that alluded directly to the current political crisis in a way that portrayed it as a period of oppression to be followed by one of victory and deliverance.

The description of deliverance frequently includes a description of the judgment of God, in which the wicked are vanquished and the righteous are rewarded. In the Apocalypse of Weeks, after the tenth and final period of human history, the angels will execute God's judgment (91:15). Descriptions of the Final Judgment occur throughout *1 Enoch* (cf. 38:1–6; 54:7–10; 61:9; 90:26; 106:17–19). In the Epistle of Enoch, the promise of judgment provides hope for Jews suffering from oppression. A time is foretold when wrongs shall be reversed: "Be hopeful, you righteous ones, for the sinners shall soon perish from before your presence. You shall be given authority upon them. . . . In the day of the tribulation of the sinners, your children shall be raised up" (96:1–2).

After the elimination of the wicked, the righteous will be rewarded in the End Times. They will be transformed and given life in heaven. In the Apocalypse of Weeks, after the judgment, "the first heaven shall depart and pass away; a new heaven shall appear; and all the powers of heaven shall shine forever sevenfold" (91:16). In the Animal Apocalypse, after the judgment, the sheep are invited to live in the house of the Lord where they are transformed into white bulls (90:31–39). Apocalyptic literature describes the End Times not only to predict the downfall of the wicked but also to give the righteous hope that God will give them a form of existence that is far better than the one they currently have.

The Book of Daniel

This Old Testament text is a collection of tales and visions ascribed to Daniel, a legendary sage who has the ability to interpret dreams (2:25–49). Ostensibly its stories take place in Babylonia, where a Jewish community was living in exile in the sixth century BCE. It has twelve chapters, the first six of which are tales from the Babylonian royal court. (For more information, see Collins 1993: 127–273.) Chapters 7 to 12 contain apocalyptic visions.

In Daniel 7, Daniel has a dream of four beasts: a lion with eagle's wings, a bear with three ribs in its mouth, a leopard with four bird's wings and four heads, and a beast with iron teeth and ten horns. An additional horn sprouts from the fourth beast. Three horns fall off because of this little horn, which has human eyes and a mouth full of boasting (7:8). Then "the Ancient of Days" (God) judges him. A messianic figure called the Son of Man appears before God, who gives him everlasting dominion (7:14; Collins 1993: 304–310). Christians have traditionally understood the Son of Man to represent Jesus Christ (cf. e.g., Matthew 24:30; Mark 2:10; Collins 1993: 90–112). An angel then interprets the dream for Daniel. He is told that each beast represents a kingdom, and discloses that the little horn stands for a wicked ruler who will have a reign of terror for "a time, two times and half a time," a cryptic reference to three and a half years, after which the people of God will be given dominion (7:25–27, NRSV). Daniel 9 is a historical apocalypse, like the Apocalypse of Weeks. It contains a vision based on Jeremiah 25 that outlines a period of seventy "weeks of years" (that is, 490 years). The author's own day was placed at the end of that period. At the end of the sequence suffering will be widespread until it comes to its ordained end (9:24–27).

Daniel 10–12 recounts the history of Israel from the fourth to the second centuries BCE, beginning with the conquests of Alexander the Great. It is concerned with the Hellenistic Seleucid and Ptolemaic Empires that formed as a result of the breakup of Alexander the Great's empire in 332 BCE. It culminates in the reign of Antiochus Epiphanes, who ruled the Seleucid Empire from 175 to 164 BCE. He attacked Jewish religious customs and desecrated the temple (1 Maccabee 1:37; Daniel 11:31). These events led to the Maccabean Revolt. The temple was desecrated for roughly three and a half years (7:25). The rededication of the temple in 164 BCE is celebrated today as Hanukkah.

Daniel 10–12 provide the spiritual backdrop to these political events, portraying them as a result of angels warring with one another (10:20–21). This account of these historical episodes culminates in a period of anguish "such as has never occurred since nations first came into existence" (12:1). After this the dead shall be raised, and all will be judged. Those deemed righteous will be given a celestial existence, raised up to the heavens where they will shine like stars (12:3–4).

The visions of Daniel 7–12 are responses to the oppression and instability that characterized the

Revelation 14:14–20

14. And I looked, and behold a white cloud, and upon the cloud one sat like unto the Son of man, having on his head a golden crown, and in his hand a sharp sickle.

15. And another angel came out of the temple, crying with a loud voice to him that sat on the cloud, Thrust in thy sickle, and reap: for the time is come for thee to reap; for the harvest of the earth is ripe.

16. And he that sat on the cloud thrust in his sickle on the earth; and the earth was reaped.

17. And another angel came out of the temple which is in heaven, he also having a sharp sickle.

18. And another angel came out from the altar, which had power over fire; and cried with a loud cry to him that had the sharp sickle, saying, Thrust in thy sharp sickle, and gather the clusters of the vine of the earth; for her grapes are fully ripe.

19. And the angel thrust in his sickle into the earth, and gathered the vine of the earth, and cast it into the great winepress of the wrath of God.

20. And the winepress was trodden without the city, and blood came out of the winepress, even unto the horse bridles, by the space of a thousand and six hundred furlongs.

period of the Maccabean Revolt. They recount in cryptic and mythic language current events. They are not a call for military action, as is the Animal Apocalypse, but, instead, sought to provide an eschatological framework in which current events should be understood. Like the Epistle of Enoch, their visions, in part, were designed to provide solace. Daniel's visions indicated that the current suffering and upheaval is all part of God's plan, and that they will be followed by a period in which the righteous shall be immeasurably rewarded. One of the accomplishments of apocalyptic literature is that it can make a moment of suffering cause to be optimistic about the future.

The Book of Revelation

Revelation was probably written close to the end of the first century CE. Like the Jewish apocalypses, it contains visions of heavenly secrets not normally given to humanity. The book is centered around the death and Resurrection of Jesus, which signals the unfolding of an ordained eschatological scenario. Its visions depict the systematic implementation of the destruction of the world. In Revelation 6–8, for example, seven seals on a scroll are opened, with each one accompanied by an act of destruction. The opening of the seventh seal is followed by seven angels blowing trumpets, with each trumpet blast causing an act of destruction.

Revelation depicts a world filled with wickedness. Chapter 13, for example, has a vision of a beast with ten horns and seven heads (based on Daniel 7). He persecutes the faithful and leads people to worship the dragon, who represents Satan (13:4–8; Yarbro Collins 1979: 89–93). There is also a vision of a harlot riding on the dragon. The woman is referred to as "Babylon the Great" who is "drunk with the blood of saints" (17:5–6). This name illustrates that the harlot represents the dominant political empire at the time: Rome. Babylon is a cryptic reference to Rome, since Rome destroyed the Jerusalem Temple in 70 CE, as Babylon had done in the sixth century BCE. John is given a vision of her downfall, which is accompanied by the angels rejoicing in heaven (18–19). The beast is eventually captured by armies led by Christ and is thrown alive into a lake of burning sulfur (19:11–21). Then the dragon is thrown into the Abyss, after which begins the thousand-year reign of Christ on earth (the origin of the term "millennialism") (20:3). After this period, there is a final war in which the nations of the world, led by Gog and Magog (see Ezekiel 38–39), attack Israel. The armies are destroyed by fire from heaven (20:11), after which God judges the world. Those who are deemed righteous are rewarded with a transformed existence. The earth passes away as God creates a "new heaven and a new earth" (21:1). He also creates a new Jerusalem, made of gold and precious stones, where there is no darkness, but only the light of God

HAL LINDSEY, *THE LATE GREAT PLANET EARTH* (1970)

The nature of the forces which the Lord will unleash on that day against the armies gathered in the Middle East is described in Zechariah 14:12 (KJV):

'And this shall be the plague wherewith the LORD will smite all the people that have fought against Jerusalem; Their flesh shall consume away while they stand upon their feet, and their eyes shall consume away in their holes, and their tongue shall consume away in their mouth.'

A frightening picture, isn't it? Has it occurred to you that this is exactly what happens to those who are in thermonuclear blast? It appears that this will be the case at the return of Christ.

p. 175.

(21:10–21; 22:5; cf. 7:15–17). This is where the faithful will dwell eternally.

Revelation shows a pattern similar to other apocalyptic compositions—revelations of the heavenly world and the future are given to provide an eschatological framework for understanding the current situation. Although it is not clear that there was widespread persecution of Christians when Revelation was written, the book is adamantly opposed to the dominion of Rome (Collins 1998: 273). It depicts Christians as suffering under her rule. The Book of Revelation is an apocalypse that describes the end of the world in a way that alluded to the contemporary situation of its audience. It promised Christians that the current moment of hardship and suffering would be eventually followed by one of eternal bliss.

Modern Apocalyptic Literature

The production of apocalyptic literature is not confined to the Second Temple period. Apocalypticists have continued to write in Judaism, Christianity, and Islam. (For more information about this rich amount of literature, see Schneemelcher 1991: 542–752; McGinn 1998 and 2000.) This article concentrates on apocalyptic literature written by modern Christian Fundamentalists.

Since apocalyptic literature provides revelations about the eschatological future, the production of apocalyptic compositions by Fundamentalists is enormous. Among the most well known are Hal Lindsey's *The Late Great Planet Earth* (1970), the tracts of Chick Publications, and the *Left Behind* novels (1995–) by Jerry Jenkins and Tim LaHaye, which depict the unfolding of the End Times. Books, pamphlets, tracts, web pages, and cassette tapes by Fundamentalists about the nature of the end of the world and the return of Christ can all be considered apocalyptic.

Modern apocalyptic literature typically includes traditional elements of Christian eschatology. Among the most important are the Antichrist, an evil figure who will have worldly power in the End Times (cf. 2 Thessalonians 2; 1 John 2; 4:3; 2 John 7; Revelation 13, 17) and the Rapture. This doctrine is based on 1 Thessalonians 4:13–17 and claims that all pious Christians will be physically ascended to heaven in a single moment. The *Left Behind* novels describe the End Times from the perspective of those who were not taken up.

Basic elements of apocalyptic literature as developed in Second Temple Judaism are core elements of apocalyptic writing by modern Fundamentalists. Chief among them is the concept of revelation; however, unlike Second Temple apocalyptic literature, the claim of revelation is not based on angelic visions. It is based on the Bible itself, which is understood as the source of revelation, being the inerrant Word of God. Descriptions of the End Times by Fundamentalists routinely appeal to biblical authority. For example, Hal Lindsey, in his *The Late Great Planet Earth*, explains his predictions for world upheaval and Christ's return by writing "In this book I am attempting to step aside and let the prophets speak" (1970: 6). In this view, the Bible is seen as a road map that explains, if properly interpreted, how the End Times will unfold.

Modern apocalyptic literature, like that of Second Temple Judaism, frequently is intended to provide an eschatological framework for current events. The establishment of the state of Israel and instability in the Middle East, for instance, are often the basis of eschatological speculation. Hal Lindsey offers an elaborate prediction: World War III will begin with a joint Russian and pan-Arabic assault upon Israel while the Jews are under the dominion of the Antichrist (1970: 146–168). Revelation 16:12 suggests to him that Red China will also invade the Middle East (Ibid: 162). Ezekiel 39:6 is taken as a proof text for a full-scale nuclear war, as is Zechariah 14:12 (Ibid: 161, 175). This war is construed as the tribulation that precedes the violent return and judgment of Christ. All who remain will eventually be rewarded with eternal life in heaven (Ibid: 178).

Though farfetched, Lindsey's eschatological scenario has common characteristics of apocalyptic literature. Like Second Temple apocalyptic writings, political tensions are understood in light of a larger eschatological perspective. The conviction that one is living in a time of violence and wickedness is taken as an indication that an eschatological scenario is currently unfolding. David Wilkerson, in *The Vision* (1974), writes "Let the fabric of society disintegrate. Let mankind go to the drunken brink of disaster. . . . The future is . . . under His control so we need not fear. God has it all preprogrammed. He knows the exact moment Christ will return" (Boyer 1992: 297). Both Second Temple and modern apocalypticists frequently construe current events as preceding a time when wickedness will be purged and the pious will be immeasurably rewarded. For Fundamentalists, this is inextricably linked to the return of Christ.

Conclusion

Apocalyptic literature has been written and read for more than two thousand years. It has consistently had a broad appeal due to its claim to impart knowledge directly transmitted from the divine realm. Apocalyptic literature is popular in part because it provides an eschatological framework with which current events should be understood. Apocalypticists have an ability to provide solace and hope to people living in difficult times. By describing wickedness and tribulations in rich detail, it makes its ordained defeat all the more triumphant. It provides comfort by construing suffering and instability as signs that the faithful will soon receive their eschatological rewards.

Matthew Goff

See also Apocalypse; End Times

Bibliography

Armstrong, Karen. (2000) *The Battle for God*. New York: Alfred A. Knopf.

Boyer, Paul. (1992) *When Time Shall Be No More: Prophecy Belief in Modern American Culture*. Cambridge, MA: The Belknap Press of the Harvard University Press.

Charlesworth, James H., ed. (1985) *The Old Testament Pseudepigrapha*. New York: Doubleday.

Cohn, Norman F. (1993) *Cosmos, Chaos, and the World to Come: The Ancient Roots of Apocalyptic Faith*. New Haven, CT and London: Yale University Press.

Collins, John J. (1993) *Daniel*. Minneapolis: Fortress Press.

———. (1998) *The Apocalyptic Imagination*, 2nd ed. Grand Rapids, MI: Wm. B. Eerdmans.

Lindsey, Hal, with C. C. Carlson (1970) *The Late Great Planet Earth*. Grand Rapids, MI: Zondervan Publishing.

McGinn, Bernard. (1998) *Visions of the End. Apocalyptic Traditions in the Middle Ages,* 2nd ed. New York: Columbia University Press.

———. (2000) *Antichrist: Two Thousand Years of the Human Fascination with Evil,* 2nd ed. New York: Columbia University Press.

Schneemelcher, Wilhelm. (1991) *New Testament Apocrypha,* 2nd ed. Cambridge, UK and Louisville, KY: James Clark and Co. and Westminster John Knox.

Shanks, Herschel, ed. (1999) *Ancient Israel: From Abraham to the Roman Destruction of the Temple.* 2nd ed. Washington, DC: Biblical Archaeological Society.

VanderKam, James C. (1984) *Enoch and the Growth of an Apocalyptic Tradition.* Washington, DC: Catholic Biblical Association.

Yarbro Collins, Adela. (1979) *The Apocalypse.* Collegeville, MN: The Liturgical Press.

Armageddon

Armageddon is mentioned in the Bible as the place in Israel where the "kings of the whole world" will gather their demon-inspired armies "for the battle on the great day of God Almighty" (Revelation 16:14–16, NIV). In popular usage, however, the term "Armageddon" has been used to refer to a wide range of apocalyptic and catastrophic events leading to the end of the world. The Bible refers to Armageddon only once: "the place that in Hebrew is called Armageddon" (Revelation 16:16). While its precise meaning and location still confound biblical scholars, many devotees of Bible prophecy connect *har magedon* with the mountain of Megiddo that rises above the Plain of Jezreel, some thirty-five miles southeast of modern Haifa. Megiddo was a military stronghold and the scene of many battles in ancient Israel (Joshua 12:21; Judges 1:27; 5:19; 2 Kings 8:27; 23:29). Some biblical texts and prophecies imply that Megiddo will be the site of a climactic battle between the forces of God and Satan (e.g., Ezekiel 38–39).

Various religious movements have made much of Armageddon imagery in their prophetic systems, including Jehovah's Witnesses and Mormons. Dispensationalist premillennialists, popular in the United States since the late nineteenth century, make the Battle of Armageddon the capstone of a series of events leading up to the Second Coming of Jesus Christ. Using various biblical texts, they construct an elaborate scenario of the End Times. At the end of the "Great Tribulation," a number of clearly identified national coalitions will gather their armies in Israel for a final apocalyptic battle, which ends in the annihilation of the Antichrist's armies and total victory for the armies of King Jesus. The victorious Messiah will then assume David's throne in Jerusalem, from which he will reign for a thousand years. Speculation about the approach of Armageddon thus became a mainstay of Fundamentalism in the twentieth century, as well as the conviction that real believers will be "raptured" long before the battle occurs.

Such imagery has moved far beyond convinced dispensationalist believers, due to the breakout impact of Hal Lindsey's *The Late Great Planet Earth* (1970) and the enormously popular series of *Left Behind* novels by Tim LaHaye and Jerry Jenkins (1995–). Apart from such prophetic speculation, the term "Armageddon" has been widely adapted to refer to any apocalyptic or catastrophic event with "world-ending" potential. Patriots during the American Revolution often drew on such biblical imagery in describing their struggle for independence against Great Britain and the Antichrist King George. Both sides during the Civil War termed the conflict "Armageddon," as *The Battle Hymn of the Republic* illustrates. Many identified the horrors of the two World Wars as Armageddon. Finally, at the end of the twentieth century, many have referred to impending ecological or environmental disasters or the possibility of nuclear annihilation in the same apocalyptic terms.

Timothy P. Weber

See also Apocalypse; Apocalyptic Literature; End Times

Bibliography

Boyer, Paul. (1992) *When Time Shall Be No More: Prophecy Belief in Modern American Culture.* Cambridge, MA: The Belknap Press of the Harvard University Press.

Clouse, Robert G., Robert N. Hosack, and Richard V. Pierard. (1999) *The New Millennium Manual: A Once and Future Guide.* Grand Rapids, MI: Baker Book House.

LaHaye, Timothy F., and Jerry B. Jenkins. (1995–) *Left Behind.* Wheaton, IL: Tyndale House Publishers.

Arminianism

The theological stance of Arminianism originated in the seventeenth century as a reaction against the Calvinist doctrine of predestination, with an assertion that God's sovereignty and man's free will were incompatible. Jacobus Arminius (1560–1609), a Dutch Reformed theologian of the University of Leiden, entered into a highly publicized debate with his colleague Francis Gomarus concerning the Calvinist interpretation of the divine decrees concerning election and reprobation. Arminius affirmed that these decrees were based on God's divine foreknowledge of either a freely willed acceptance or rejection of God's extended love. Arminius argued that the divine omniscience knows that the divine will effects sovereignty through a love that is so omnipotent as to suffer the contradictions of human rejection. Arminius saw the divine will in terms of the power of love rather than of unmitigated force. God's will as unceasing love is seen as the determinative initiator and arbiter of human destiny.

The next understanding of Arminianism was put forth in the Remonstrance (1610), a theological statement written by J. Uytembogaert and submitted to the States General of the Netherlands. The States General called on the Synod of Dort (1618–1619) to condemn the Remonstrance. The defenders of the document, called the Remonstrants, had never

Selection From: *ORATIONS OF ARMINIUS, ORATION I: THE OBJECT OF THEOLOGY*

But God is himself the Object of Theology. The very term indicates as much: for Theology signifies a discourse or reasoning concerning God. This is likewise indicated by the definition which the Apostle gives of this science, when he describes it as "the truth which is after godliness." (Tit. i, 1.) The Greek word here used for godliness, is eusebeia signifying a worship due to God alone, which the Apostle shews in a manner of greater clearness, when he calls this piety by the more exact term qeosebeia All other sciences have their objects, noble indeed, and worthy to engage the notice of the human mind, and in the contemplation of which much time, leisure and diligence may be profitably occupied. In General Metaphysics, the object of study is, "BEING in reference to its being;" Particular Metaphysics have for their objects "intelligence and minds separated and removed from mortal contagion." Physics are applied to "bodies, as having the principle of motion in themselves." The Mathematics have "relation to quantities." Medicine exercises itself with the human body, in relation to its capacity of health and soundness." Jurisprudence has a reference to "justice, in relation to human society." Ethics, to "the virtues." Economics, to "the government of a family;" and Politics, to "state affairs." But all these sciences are appointed in subordination to God; from him also they derive their origin. They are dependent on him alone; and, in return, they move back again, and unto him is their natural re-action. This science is the only one which occupies itself about the BEING of beings and the CAUSE of causes, the principle of nature, and that of grace existing in nature, and by which nature is assisted and surrounded. This object, therefore, is the most worthy and dignified of all, and full of adorable majesty, It far excels all the rest; because it is not lawful for any one, however well and accurately he may be instructed in the knowledge of all the sciences, to glory in the least on this account; and because every one that has obtained a knowledge of this science only, may on solid grounds and in reality glory in it. For God himself has forbidden the former species of boasting, while he commands the latter. His words by the prophet Jeremiah, are "Let not the wise man glory in his wisdom; but let him. that glorieth glory in this, that he understandeth and knoweth me." (ix, 23, 24)

Source: Arminius, Jacobus. *The Works of James Arminius*. Christian Classics Ethereal Library. www.ccel.org.

come under the teaching of Arminius. The heart of this Remonstrant Arminianism lay in the assertion that human dignity requires an unimpaired "freedom of the will." To these thinkers, it was reason rather than alienable love that was determinative of human choice.

In England in the seventeenth century, the term "Arminianism" was used by opponents to label the high church theories of episcopacy and church discipline put forth by Archbishop Laud. The latitudinarians of Oxford and Cambridge also became labeled as Arminians by the Calvinist Puritans of their day. Then, in the eighteenth century, the Wesleyan movement developed the label "Methodist-Arminianism"

to distinguish itself from the revivalism of George Whitefield. John Wesley accepted the term and used it in the title of his magazine (*The Arminian Magazine*) with the phrase "that God willeth all men to be saved." Wesley went to Amsterdam in the Netherlands to secure data on the life of Arminius, which he then published in the first issue of the magazine. Wesley's reappraisal of the theology of Arminius was based on Arminius's works and sharply distinguished it from the Arminianism of the rationalist Remonstrants of Holland as well as the Arminianism of England in the preceding century.

In the United States, Methodist theology as put forth by systematic theologians in the theological schools reverted to the views of the Remonstrants, leading to theological disparities between British Methodist theology and that of nineteenth-century American Methodism. The renaissance of Calvinism under the influence of Karl Barth and modern studies of John Calvin also revived interest in Arminius as well as a reevaluation of Arminianism. This doctrine was integrated into the American Holiness movement of the latter part of the nineteenth century and later into the Pentecostalism that arose out of this movement. It did not, however, directly influence Protestant Fundamentalism, which arose in the early part of the twentieth century. This form of Protestantism was more influenced by the Calvinism that dominated nineteenth-century Evangelicalism and the Calvinism of a group of conservative theologians at Princeton Seminary. Arminianism does not seem to be an issue in the post-denominationalism that is currently exploding in postmodern America.

Leland Edward Wilshire

See also Calvinism; Great Awakening; Holiness, Wesleyan

Bibliography

Geisler, Norman L. (1999) *Chosen but Free*. Minneapolis, MN: Bethany Publishers.

Harrison, Archibald W. (1937) *Arminianism*. London: Duckworth.

Rugh, Gilbert W. (1991) *Calvinism and Arminianism*. Lincoln, NE: Sound Words.

Tyacke, Nicholas. (1997) *Puritanism, Arminianism and Counter Revolution*. London: Arnold.

Aryan Nations

The Aryan Nations is both a national Christian Identity movement and a communal settlement centered in Hayden Lake, Idaho. It came into being with pastor Richard Butler's 1973 move from multiracial southern California to the primarily white enclave of northern Idaho near Coeur d'Alene.

The Aryan Nations would attract a disparate group of disaffected young white men, particularly recently released prison inmates, as a result of its prison outreach ministry spearheaded by the Aryan Nations's prison journal *The Way*. Other Aryan Nations publications include the periodicals *Calling Our Nation* and *Aryan Nations*. The Aryan Nations outreach features the effective use of pastor Richard Butler's sermons on cassette tape as well.

The most complete program of the Aryan Nations is found in the eponymous premier edition of the organization's newsletter. This foundational creed provides a remarkable insight into the mind-set of the separatist aspirations of the movement in the 1980s. Opening with a detailed explanation of the symbolism of the swastika-like Aryan Nations emblem, the document then segues into a detailed political manifesto that begins, fittingly enough, with the question of "population and race." Here, the Christian Identity's emphasis on the descent of Caucasian man from Adam is blended with the "science" of eugenics. In particular, miscegenation is expressly forbidden.

Next, the Aryan Nations turns to the problem of private property. Here, what is demanded is a utopian socialism in which the nation's productive capacity in the forms of agriculture and industry will be placed under communal control to be administered "in the national and racial interest." This is followed by a brief section on industry and finance in which the "financial system of International Jewish Capitalism" is to be abolished, all adults are expected to be productive contributors to society, and loaning money at interest is to be abandoned.

The subject of Aryan youth follows and is given more attention. Here the model is Platonic by way of National Socialist Germany. Youth movements for both boys and girls are mandated:

> In young men the Aryan ideal is of physical and athletic fitness, reliability and determination of character, proficiency in chosen livelihood-occupation, and general usefulness to the community.

> In young women the accent is primarily on fitness for motherhood and homemaking, but also on athletics and arts. For the rest, the Aryan warrior ideal is touted, as is a call for discipline, race consciousness, and obedience to the laws of God.

The role of women is of particular concern to the Aryan Nations. Here, an Aryan woman's primary duty is clear:

> Every child that an Aryan mother brings into the world is a battle waged for the existence of her people.

The program of the National Aryan Women's Movement has a truly single point—the child.

Then, among idealized calls for feminine purity and paeans to the complimentary nature of the separate roles for the Aryan male and female, the manifesto cannot resist the passing observation that it is far better to be "the mother of healthy Aryan children than to be a clever woman lawyer."

When the document turns to more global questions, much of the specificity found in discussions of social relations vanishes. For example, Aryan law is described as something that is to be followed more in spirit than in the letter, and judges are given wide latitude to apply the law in the racial and national interest. Much the same applies to the formation of the Aryan armed forces. The underlying concept is that the battle is for race and not territory! The Aryan army is to defend "Aryan freedom" and the "whole of the Aryan state."

But what constitutes the Aryan state? The following section "Constitution and World Outlook," the longest in the document, seeks to elaborate. First, the primacy of the leadership principle is affirmed. The putative Aryan state will be explicitly National Socialist in structure. Thus, the constitution will reflect the divinely ordained interests of the Aryan people, and will brook no dissent, because: "Intolerance of opposing ideas is necessary to strength." In 1979, however, the movement's vision had yet to disengage from the central paradigm of the nation-state. World leadership in the cold war world was vested in the United States, and thus leadership of the world to come would rest with the Aryan United States. Yet, the seeds of something greater are nonetheless present:

> The Aryan views not only his State and nation, but his race throughout the earth; and he works for "understanding and union between the different language groups of the one ordained ruling race." Against the international organization of Jewry, he sets his World Aryan Christian Union.

The sections which follow, on culture and education, respectively, are both of a piece. On the one hand, they contemptuously reject "intellectualism" in favor of spirit. On the other hand, culture is seen as the genetic possession of the Aryan people. No other racial group is capable of possessing this priceless gift from God to the Aryan folk. Surprisingly, the only section dealing explicitly with religion is one of the document's briefest. The entire exposition is neatly summed up in the opening sentences: "Christianity [is] for the Aryan is Race; and Race is Christianity. Race is Soul seen from without; and Christianity is Soul seen from within." With this genetic vision of religion, all that need be added is the rather contradictory assertion that to be truly Aryan, Christianity "must be purged of all remnants of Jewish thought."

The penultimate section reprises economics, stating again that agriculture is to be the foundation of the Aryan state, while the document closes with the standard assertion that communism is Jewish and thus a contemporary mask of Satan.

What is perhaps most important in the Aryan Nations foundational document is its generic nature. There is little in it that is so specifically Christian Identity that other sectors of the race movement would be put off from becoming associated with the organization. If anything, National Socialism rather than Christian Identity provides the document's primary thrust.

This appeal thus attracted many of the disaffected. Most were content to attend the annual Aryan Nations Congress, although a few of the most committed donned pastor Butler's snappy imitation Nazi uniforms and became full-time residents of the compound. It was here that men like Robert Mathews, Gary Yarbrough, and Frank Silva talked late into the night of their hopes and dreams, and thus gave birth to the Order (Silent Brotherhood). However, the Order's emergence and brief but violent revolutionary career owed much to the frustration of the Aryan Nations residents with the steady diet of dreamy promises of impending apocalypse and white renaissance, which contrasted so sharply from Richard Butler's cautious disinclination to go beyond words to the propaganda of the deed.

Other contradictions ate away at the Aryan Nations' base of support among its resident faithful. There has, for example, been in recent years a fruitless search for a successor to Butler, which has not coincidentally coincided with the defection of several senior followers. The most interesting of these defections is arguably that of Floyd Cochrane, to whom the implications of the Aryan Nations's fixation with race eugenics was graphically driven home in bunkhouse conversation when a fellow race warrior casually noted that Cochrane's own son, born with a cleft palate, would probably have to be eliminated under the New Order. This seems to have brought home the practical implications of the ideology for the first time and Cochrane not only left the movement but he renounced his racialist beliefs as well. Carl Franklin, a man who was widely expected to succeed Butler, departed as well, forming the New Church of Jesus Christ Christian of Montana.

Throughout the 1980s, not only did the Aryan Nations's residential population decline, but the attendance at the Annual Congress dropped precipitously as well. Part of the problem was that in the wake of the successful efforts of the Anti-Defamation League (ADL) to outlaw paramilitary training at such gatherings, it simply was not as much fun anymore. Moreover, acutely aware of the presence of federal agents and private spies working for groups like the ADL, the ever-cautious Butler had allowed little of the kind of fiery rhetoric that had once typified the Congress.

As the movement declined, relations with the citizens of Coeur d'Alene appeared to reach their nadir in 1986 to 1987, with a series of bombings of the homes of local human rights activists. Following the bombings, an unspoken truce of sorts emerged for a time. The truce was broken, however, with an attack by drunken and panicky Aryan Nations guards on a woman and her son who were driving by the compound. The resulting civil suit taken on by the Southern Poverty Law Center headed by Morris Dees provided the citizens of Coeur d'Alene with a long-sought opportunity to rid themselves once and for all of their controversial neighbors. Thus, in 1999, a jury verdict against pastor Butler and his organization all but guaranteed that the Aryan Nations's property would have to be sold to meet the group's multimillion-dollar debt.

In a last ditch attempt to save the doomed organization, Richard Butler briefly added the name Aryan National Alliance to that of the Aryan Nations and the Church of Jesus Christ Christian, both of which became part of the liquidation sale of the Aryan Nations's compound. The Aryan National Alliance was short-lived, however, as the website—the only public face of the organization—defected to another Identity ministry, the Church of True Israel.

Jeffrey Kaplan

See also Ku Klux Klan

Bibliography

Aho, James A. (1990) *The Politics of Righteousness: Idaho Christian Patriotism.* Seattle: University of Washington Press.

Barkun, Michael. (1994) *Religion and the Racist Right: The Origins of the Christian Identity Movement.* Chapel Hill: University of North Carolina Press.

Ezekial, Raphael. (1995) *The Racist Mind.* New York: Viking Press.

Flynn, Kevin, and Gary Gerhardt. (1990) *The Silent Brotherhood.* New York: Signet.

Kaplan, Jeffrey (1997) *Radical Religion in America: Millenarian Movements rrom the Far Right to the Children of Noah.* Syracuse, NY: Syracuse University Press.

Ridgeway, James. (1990) *Blood in the Face.* New York: Thunder's Mouth Press.

Ascension

The Ascension of Jesus Christ celebrates the change of His presence in the world. He is no longer circumscribed by time and place, but is universally present in His glorified humanity. According to Mark 16:19, Luke 24:51, and Acts 1:9, the apostles or some of the apostles witnessed Jesus being "lifted up, and a cloud took him out of their sight" (Acts 1:9, RSV). While Luke 24:50–53 can be read to imply that the Ascension took place on the evening of the day of the Resurrection, Acts 1:3 states clearly that it occurred forty days after the Resurrection: "appearing to them during forty days."

In the Pilgrimage of Etheria, a description of a journey by a woman in the late fourth century, there is a reference to a worship service at the Church of the Nativity at Bethlehem on the fortieth day after Easter. At the same time, it must be noted that Etheria does not mention that this is a celebration of the Ascension.

In the early church, the entire fifty days between the Resurrection and Pentecost were understood as a commemoration of the mighty acts of redemption revealed in the Resurrection, the Ascension, and the giving of the Holy Spirit (Pentecost). These "Great Fifty Days" make up a single festival, of which the Ascension is one part. The Ascension is a bridge between the Resurrection and Pentecost. Without the Resurrection there could be no Ascension, and the Ascension makes possible the coming of the Holy Spirit.

The Ascension is confessed in the Apostles' and Nicene Creeds ("He ascended into heaven, and is seated at the right hand of the Father"). His being

Mark 16:19

19. So then after the Lord had spoken unto them, he was received up into heaven, and sat on the right hand of God.

Luke 24:51

51. And it came to pass, while he blessed them, he was parted from them, and carried up into heaven.

Acts 1:9

9. And when he had spoken these things, while they beheld, he was taken up; and a cloud received him out of their sight.

seated at the right hand of the Father has been interpreted differently by Martin Luther and John Calvin. Luther insisted that "at the right hand of the Father" meant everywhere because the Father does not have a right hand. Calvin insisted that the right hand of the Father is a place and that the humanity of the ascended Christ is localized at that place. These different interpretations have influenced the understanding of the presence of Jesus Christ in the Lord's Supper. Those who agree with Luther stress the Real Presence—that is, Jesus Christ is present in His humanity and divinity—and those who agree with Calvin stress a spiritual presence—that is, Jesus Christ is present only in His divinity.

The theological importance of the Ascension is that it marks a definite ending of the earthly ministry of Jesus Christ, and demonstrates that His Resurrection was not a return to the conditions of this life, but a completion and transformation of this life through the removal of earthly limitations. The paradox of the Ascension is that it does not take Christ out of the world, removing Him from history and the life of humanity, but that it enables Him to be right in the midst of history and our human affairs. The Ascension inaugurates a new era in the redemptive activity of God, and it sets the stage for the coming of the Holy Spirit at Pentecost.

Donald S. Armentrout

See also Resurrection (Christ)

Bibliography

Davies, John Gordon. (1958) *He Ascended into Heaven: A Study in the History of Doctrine.* London: Lutterworth Press.

Milligan, William. (1892) *The Ascension and Heavenly Priesthood of Our Lord.* London: Macmillan Press.

Assumption

The Assumption of the Blessed Virgin Mary, celebrated on 15 August, is one of fifteen Marian feasts on the current Roman Catholic liturgical calendar. It celebrates the dogma that at the end of her life Mary was taken (assumed) body and soul into heaven. The dogma was promulgated by Pope Pius XII on 1 November 1950, in the papal bull *Munificentissimus Deus* (the most munificent God). The dogma asserts that:

"The universal Church, in which the Spirit of Truth dwells, and which he infallibly guides to perfect knowledge of revealed truths, has shown its faith many times in the course of the centuries. Bishops from all over the world with almost perfect unanimity have petitioned that the truth of the corporeal Assumption of the Blessed Virgin Mary into heaven be defined as a dogma of the divine, Catholic faith. The truth of this dogma is based on Sacred Scripture and is deeply rooted in the hearts of the faithful. It is sanctioned by the worship of the Church from the most ancient times. It is completely consonant with all other revealed truths. It has been explained and proclaimed by the study, the knowledge, and the wisdom of theologians. In consideration of these reasons, We judge that in God's providence the time has come to proclaim solemnly this wonderful privilege of the Virgin Mary.... We, therefore, do pronounce, declare, and define as a divinely revealed dogma: The Immaculate Mother of God, Mary ever Virgin, after her life on earth, was assumed, body and soul, to the glory of heaven." (Clarkson 1955: 213).

In Eastern Orthodoxy the Assumption is known as *Koimesis*, "falling asleep," or the Dormition of the Blessed Virgin Mary.

This belief was unknown in the early church and there is no reference to it in Scripture. Early on, however, there began to develop a Marian devotion and great respect for Mary as the One who gave Jesus His human flesh. Irenaeus of Lyons (ca. 130–200) referred to Mary as the Second Eve, whose obedience to God's call reversed the effects of the First Eve's sin. A popular term for Mary, used by Athanasius (d. 373) and Apollinaris (ca. 310–390) was *theotokos*, the "One who gave birth to God," which is also translated "Mother of God," or "Bearer of God." Cyril of Alexandria (d. 444) insisted on using the term *theotokos*, and the Council of Ephesus (431) and the Council of Chalcedon (451) affirmed the use of the term. The dogma does not say whether Mary died, and it is supported by the fact that no relics of Mary's body have been found.

Most Protestants object to the doctrine of the Assumption and the doctrine of the Immaculate Conception, that is, that Mary was free from original sin. The Assumption raises difficulties in ecumenical dialogues in that there is no biblical evidence for it. The Assumption of the Blessed Virgin, body and soul, into heaven is one of the great privileges granted to her by God for consenting to be the mother of Jesus Christ. It is also the only dogma proclaimed since the 1870 decree on papal infallibility.

Donald S. Armentrout

See also Cult of Mary

Bibliography

Brown, Raymond, Karl P. Donfried, Joseph A. Fitzmyer, and John Reumann., eds. (1978) *Mary in the New Testament: A Collaborative Assessment by Protestant and Roman Catholic Scholars.* Philadelphia: Fortress Press.

Clarkson, John F., ed. (1955) *The Church Teaches: Documents of the Church in English Translation.* St. Louis: B. Herder Book Co.

Healy, Killian. (1982) *The Assumption of Mary.* Wilmington, DE: Michael Glazier, Inc.

Atonement

The atonement, the means by which a righteous God can redeem and accept sinful human beings, has been a central question in Christian biblical and historical theology. Principally using materials from the Bible, Christian theologians have proposed answers to this question, comprising theories of atonement. Most center on the meaning of the death of Jesus Christ.

American Protestant Fundamentalism inherited a high view of God's righteousness and human sin from the Calvinist tradition tracing back to New England Puritanism. Many seventeenth- and eighteenth-century American Calvinists thus advocated a substitutionary (also called "vicarious") view of the atonement, whereby Christ's death worked primarily to appease God's wrath against sin. This view had origins in the *Cur Deus homo* of Anselm of Canterbury (c. 1033–1109). The nineteenth century was generally inhospitable to strict Calvinist views, and other Christian theories of atonement came to dominate the theological landscape. The governmental view, held by early-nineteenth-century Calvinists like Edwards Amasa Park (1808–1900), proposed that Christ's death took place to display the seriousness of sin and hence to deter people from sinful behavior. Other, less Calvinistic views were proposed as well. Park's contemporary, Horace Bushnell (1802–1876), advocated a moral influence theory of atonement (with roots at least as early as Peter Abelard [1079–1142]), in which Christ's life and death work supernaturally to show the depth of divine love and to prompt sinners to turn in love to God. Nineteenth-century Unitarians held a view in which Christ's death was an example of a sacrificial life: humans do not need regeneration for God's approval, but they do need the model of self-sacrificial love.

These nonsubstitutionary views became widely accepted among liberal Protestants of the late nineteenth and early twentieth centuries, precipitating a theological outcry among conservatives. Presbyterian theologians at Princeton University, such as Charles Hodge (1797–1878), B. B. Warfield (1851–1921), and J. Gresham Machen (1881–1937), led the conservative response. They saw human sin as an offense against a holy God, the consequence of which was eternal separation from God. Yet when Jesus Christ—God incarnate—died for human sin, He paid sin's penalty and His death was substituted for human death. *The Fundamentals* (1910–1915), a twelve-volume statement of Evangelical orthodoxy, contained essays advocating this substitutionary view of the atonement. While never as divisive an issue as biblical inerrancy or biological evolution, conservatives in the major denominations often made this view of the atonement a litmus test for theological orthodoxy. The 1910 Presbyterian General Assembly, for example, ruled Christ's substitutionary atonement one of five "essential" doctrines, a ruling reaffirmed in 1916 and 1923. When the World's Christian Fundamentals Association was formed in 1919, its doctrinal statement, drafted by Wheaton College president Charles Blanchard, included the "substitutionary sacrifice" of Christ as one of its nine articles.

This view of the atonement thus became part of a theological package embraced widely by Fundamentalists. Joel Carpenter (1997) argues that Fundamentalists relied on substitutionary atonement to buttress their firm adherence to religious conversion, thereby emphasizing the supernatural character of redemption. They considered the doctrine of substitutionary atonement foundational to saving faith. When Edward J. Carnell (1919–1967) began to distance himself from Fundamentalism in the 1950s, his Fundamentalist opponent John R. Rice (1895–1980) accused him of extending the right hand of fellowship to those who "spit on the blood of Jesus, [and] deny the inspiration of the Bible and the blood atonement" (Harris 1998: 41]). For Fundamentalists, beliefs about the atonement separated true from false Christians. Fundamentalists, however, are not the only Christians who have upheld the doctrine of substitutionary atonement. Many British and American conservative Evangelicals, such as John Stott, have tried to make the atonement a central theme in Evangelical preaching and doctrine, while avoiding the Fundamentalist tendency to make it a point of separation.

R. Bryan Bademan

See also Sin and Sinners

Bibliography

Aulen, Gustaf. ([1931] 1969) *Christus Victor: An Historical Study of the Three Main Types of the Idea of the Atonement,* translated by A. G. Herbert. New York: Macmilllan.

Bushnell, Horace. (1866) *The Vicarious Sacrifice, Grounded in Principles of Universal Obligation.* New York: C. Scribner's Sons.

Carpenter, Joel A. (1997) *Revive Us Again: The Reawakening of American Fundamentalism.* New York: Oxford University Press.

Grensted, Laurence William. (1920) *A Short History of the Doctrine of the Atonement.* Manchester: University Press.

Harris, Harriet A. (1998) *Fundamentalism and Evangelicals.* Oxford: Clarendon Press.

Machen, J. Gresham. (1923) *Christianity and Liberalism.* Grand Rapids, MI: Wm. B. Eerdmans.

Marsden, George M. (1980) *Fundamentalism and American Culture: The Shaping of Twentieth-Century Evangelicalism: 1870–1925.* New York: Oxford University Press.

Stott, John R. W. (1986) *The Cross of Christ.* Downers Grove, IL: InterVarsity Press.

Azusa Street Revival

Regarded by many religious historians as one of the founding events in the modern Pentecostal movement, the Azusa Street Revival resulted from the efforts of William Joseph Seymour, an African-American preacher who had briefly attended Charles F. Parham's Bible school in Houston, Texas. Parham, who had founded the Apostolic Faith movement in Baxter Springs, Kansas, stressed the idea that speaking in tongues, or glossolalia, was the necessary outward expression of the baptism of the Holy Spirit. The third stage following conversion (or regeneration) and sanctification in the process of Christian maturation, the baptism of the Holy Spirit had already been recognized by many in the Holiness movement. Parham's innovation involved his insistence on glossolalic evidence of the believer's having received this divine gift.

Seymour accepted a call to pastor a Nazarene church in Los Angeles and took Parham's theory with him to the West Coast. His belief that those who had not spoken in tongues had not actually received the baptism of the Holy Spirit offended many church members, some of whom had claimed that experience for most of their lives. Following Parham, Seymour argued that they had only experienced sanctification and that another spiritual "experience" awaited them. When the church expelled Seymour, he began to hold meetings in the homes of sympathetic individuals, and on 9 April 1906, an eight-year-old boy was apparently the first among his congregation to experience the baptism of the Holy Spirit evidenced by glossolalia. Seymour, who was joined by two other students from Parham's school, Lucy Farrow and J. A. Warren, then rented an abandoned Methodist church at 312 Azusa Street in Los Angeles and began a three-year series of meetings characterized by a variety of ecstatic, charismatic expressions, including both speaking and singing in tongues as well as prophecy.

The success of Seymour's revival in terms of numbers was phenomenal. Crowds of people began to flock to the Azusa Street Mission, attracted, in part, by sensationalistic newspaper accounts. By late summer an estimated twelve hundred people could be found attending a prayer meeting at the site. The San Francisco earthquake, which occurred in late April 1906, also contributed to the revival's success. Frank Bartleman, a local Holiness evangelist who had participated in Seymour's prayer meetings even before he moved to Azusa Street, publicized the idea that the devastating quake signaled the imminence of the apocalypse and encouraged readers of his tracts to join the revival while there was still time.

By the end of the revival's first year (1906), some nine Pentecostal congregations, including one led by Bartleman, were established in Los Angeles. Though the movement had begun under the instigation of an African-American preacher whose original West Coast congregation had been an African-American Holiness church, the Pentecostal movement in southern California was interracial from its inception. Seymour's colleagues from Texas, Farrow and Warren, were black, but Bartleman was white, as were many of those who attended meetings at the Azusa Street church during the spring and summer of 1906.

Though Seymour was officially affiliated with Parham's Apostolic Faith movement, his mentor did not immediately capitalize upon the successes in Los Angeles, preferring apparently to focus his attentions on spreading his message in the Midwest. He finally made a trip to the West Coast in October 1906 and found two features of the Azusa Revival disturbing.

Though he had shown some sensitivity to African-American spiritual needs during his career, Parham could not accept the racial intermixing and equality that characterized the Azusa Street activities. His advocacy of the British Israel theory (that the ten tribes of Israel that disappeared from the Old Testament historical record during the Assyrian captivity were the forebears of the Anglo-Saxons) contributed to a strong belief in white superiority. Moreover, Parham did not believe that some of the glossolalia among participants in the Los Angeles revival was legitimate. He held that after the initial speaking in tongues that evidenced the baptism of the Holy Spirit, Pentecostal believers would be spreading their message through xenoglossia (using earthly languages, which they spoke through divine intervention). He dismissed much of the Azusa Street glossolalia as mere babbling. When he unsuccessfully tried to assert his influence in the Azusa movement, Parham opened the door to the development of Pentecostal groups to rival his Apostolic Faith organization. These groups eventually included the Church of God in Christ, the Apostolic Overcoming Holy Church of God, and Triumph the Church, and Kingdom of God in Christ—all African-American denominations. However, the influence of the revival on Azusa Street in Los Angeles also contributed to the emergence of many white-oriented Pentecostal groups such as the Assemblies of God and the United Pentecostal Church.

William M. Clements

See also Black Church, The; Evangelicalism; Pentecostalism; Speaking in Tongues

Bibliography

Goff, James R., Jr. (1988) *Fields White Unto Harvest: Charles F. Parham and the Missionary Origins of Pentecostalism.* Fayetteville: University of Arkansas Press.

Hollenweger, W. J. (1972) *The Pentecostals: The Charismatic Movement in the Churches.* Minneapolis, MN: Augsburg.

Baconian Science

Baconian science is loosely derived from the work of Sir Francis Bacon (1561–1626), an English Enlightenment empiricist and philosopher who advocated scientific study through induction, or the belief that general laws could be inferred from observable facts. Bacon's philosophy relied heavily on common sense, and it became popular in the United States during the nineteenth century, especially among Evangelical Christians attempting to challenge Charles Darwin's theory of evolution. Most Evangelicals considered evolution irreconcilable with the account of divine creation recorded in the Bible and they attempted to scientifically prove the existence of God in order to counter the claims of scientists who increasingly favored the Darwinian hypothesis.

During the nineteenth century, most Evangelicals within the United States held science in high esteem, often incorporating scientific concepts into their teachings. Evangelicals firmly believed that an objective science would substantiate biblical explanations. After the theory of evolution began to gain wider acceptance, however, Evangelicals maintained that mainstream science had become too subjective, and they sought to return it to greater objectivity through adherence to the Baconian method. This phenomenon became most pronounced following the emergence of Fundamentalism during the 1920s.

Despite Fundamentalists' admiration of Baconian science, they twisted it to their own ends. While they denounced evolution as theoretical nonsense when contrasted with the supposed rationality of Baconian science, they rarely applied the Baconian method to the natural world for which it was intended. Instead, they used it as a method for biblical interpretation, insisting that the Bible should be understood literally. Fundamentalists could, with common sense, deduce the uncomplicated meaning of the biblical text through the Baconian process of induction. Reading the biblical text in this way is not as simple as it first appears, however, for the reader brings preconceived ideas to the interpretation that distort any ideal of an unbiased reading.

But Fundamentalists went further. They attempted to use the Baconian method to devise a science of creation that could counter evolutionary claims. This "creation science," as it came to be known, rested on the presumption that the Bible is itself a scientific text, containing the blueprint for divine creative action. Rather than develop a coherent, comprehensive theory, contemporary creation scientists seek to undermine what they view as weak links in evolutionary thought. By focusing on the perceived flaws in evolution, they fail to offer a compelling critique for secular explanations. Moreover, Fundamentalists accept as fact a pseudo-Baconian model for analyzing the Bible and for positing a biblically based view of natural history that is itself as interpretative as the evolutionary explanation proposed by secular science.

Following World War II and the rise of the "neo-Evangelical" movement, creation science became more widespread and it emerged as an issue of contentious debate within the United States. At its heart lay a model for scientific inquiry that Fundamentalists partially co-opted in an attempt to credibly critique evolutionary science. In the process, they not only distorted Bacon's intentions, but they furthered the seemingly irreconcilable differences between modern science and Fundamentalism.

Scott Lupo

See also Creationism; Evolution and Antievolution

Bibliography

Marsden, George M. (1980) *Fundamentalism and American Culture: The Shaping of Twentieth-Century Evangelicalism: 1870–1925.* New York: Oxford University Press.
———. (1991) *Understanding Fundamentalism and Evangelicalism.* Grand Rapids, MI: Wm. B. Eerdmans.
Noll, Mark. (1994) *The Scandal of the Evangelical Mind.* Grand Rapids, MI: Wm. B. Eerdmans.

Baptism

Baptism is, in its many forms, an initiatory rite involving the ritualistic application of water to a professing novitiate. As it is known to the West, baptism dates to the very earliest years of the Common Era, though whether John the Baptist (6? BCE–27? CE) or his second cousin, Jesus (5? BCE–29? CE), initiated Christian baptism is a matter of some theological discussion. Jewish proselyte baptism, Hindu washings, and the baptism of various mystery cults are among the non-Christian instances of the rite. These other examples, however, differ from Christian baptism in that they are simply ceremonial washings, whereas Christian baptism is a public demonstration of the covenantal relationship between the "baptisand" (the individual being baptized) and God. This relationship is especially poignant to the believing Christian, because the immersion in or application of water symbolizes the spiritual death that should have been the believer's but was instead suffered physically by Christ.

Christian Baptism

Christian baptism is linked symbolically to three Old Testament (OT) phenomena, all of which were signs of God's covenant with His chosen people. First, in his letter to the Christians scattered throughout the ancient world, Peter refers to the Noachian flood as an analog to baptismal salvation in Christ (1 Peter 3:18–22). Second, Paul regards the Israelites' crossing of the Red Sea (the final trial in their escape from captivity in Egypt) as a baptism (1 Corinthians 10:1–4). Third, and perhaps less obviously, Paul calls baptism a "circumcision made without hands" (Colossians 2:8–15, KJV). By virtue of the cleansing deluge, Noah and his family (thus, humankind) were saved and brought into communion with Yahweh. The passing through the water of the Red Sea further sealed the covenant God made with Abraham. Finally, just as Jesus came to fulfill the law, baptism fulfills circumcision in its spiritual, rather than physical, signification of a bestowing of the Holy Spirit upon the baptisand.

John the Baptist, who was prophesied as "one crying in the wilderness" in the OT (Isaiah 40:3) was descriptively named for the baptism by water in which his followers participated. Christian baptism is generally considered not to have begun with John, though no New Testament (NT) author requires John's baptisands to be rebaptized after the Resurrection of Jesus or after Pentecost. The main difference between Christian baptism and John's baptism is in the attitude toward the risen Christ. John baptized in anticipation of the Messiah, while baptism after the Resurrection is performed with a definite knowledge of who the Messiah is and precisely what baptism means to the believer and the church at large. The baptism of the Spirit to which John refers in Matthew 3:11 is known as Pentecost, or the bestowing of the Holy Spirit (and His gifts) upon the believers, which occurred shortly after Jesus' ascension into heaven (Acts 1,2).

Though only once does Jesus explicitly command believers to baptize (the Great Commission, Matthew 28:19; the parallel passage found in Mark 16:15–16 is generally considered an inauthentic and late addition to Mark), the practice quickly assumed a very important place in the early church. As early as 60 to 100 CE, *The Didache*, a handbook for new converts to the faith, provided techniques for administering the rite, including a prescription of immersion in running water and fasting before the event for the baptizer, the baptisand, and any others in the community who are able (7:1–4). These early, formal rules are a sign of the church's earnest adoption of baptism probably no later than the end of the first century. Furthermore, such church fathers as Irenaeus (125?–202? CE), Tertullian (155?–225? CE), and Origen (185?–254? CE) write of baptism and its practice in the early church.

1 Peter 3:18–22

18. For Christ also hath once suffered for sins, the just for the unjust, that he might bring us to God, being put to death in the flesh, but quickened by the Spirit:

19. By which also he went and preached unto the spirits in prison;

20. Which sometime were disobedient, when once the longsuffering of God waited in the days of Noah, while the ark was a preparing, wherein few, that is, eight souls were saved by water.

21. he like figure whereunto even baptism doth also now save us (not the putting away of the filth of the flesh, but the answer of a good conscience toward God,) by the resurrection of Jesus Christ:

22. Who is gone into heaven, and is on the right hand of God; angels and authorities and powers being made subject unto him.

1 Corinthians 10:1–4

1. Moreover, brethren, I would not that ye should be ignorant, how that all our fathers were under the cloud, and all passed through the sea;

2. And were all baptized unto Moses in the cloud and in the sea;

3. And did all eat the same spiritual meat;

4. And did all drink the same spiritual drink: for they drank of that spiritual Rock that followed them: and that Rock was Christ.

Colossians 2:8–15

8. Beware lest any man spoil you through philosophy and vain deceit, after the tradition of men, after the rudiments of the world, and not after Christ.

9. For in him dwelleth all the fullness of the Godhead bodily.

10. And ye are complete in him, which is the head of all principality and power:

11. In whom also ye are circumcised with the circumcision made without hands, in putting off the body of the sins of the flesh by the circumcision of Christ:

12. Buried with him in baptism, wherein also ye are risen with him through the faith of the operation of God, who hath raised him from the dead.

13. And you, being dead in your sins and the uncircumcision of your flesh, hath he quickened together with him, having forgiven you all trespasses;

14. Blotting out the handwriting of ordinances that was against us, which was contrary to us, and took it out of the way, nailing it to his cross;

15. And having spoiled principalities and powers, he made a shew of them openly, triumphing over them in it.

Classifications of Baptism

John C. Lambert (1857–1917) appropriately distinguishes among the subject, mode, administrator, and formula of baptism, each of which has been the subject of debate at some point in the history of the Christian Church. The debate surrounding baptism generally takes the form of infant versus believer. Infant baptism is performed by the Catholic Church, the Eastern Orthodox Church, and many Protestant denominations, including the Methodists, Presbyterians, Lutherans, and Anglicans. In this practice, infant children of believing parents or parent are baptized. The baptism of whole households in the NT and Jesus' attitude toward children in general are cited as biblical foundations for this practice. Contrarily, proponents of believers' baptism insist that baptism is a rite in which only those believers who can enunciate its meaning may participate.

Proponents cite the lack of any mention of infant baptism in the NT and significance of the rite itself as grounds for their view.

Three modes of baptism—immersion, affusion (pouring), and aspersion (sprinkling)—are practiced today by various sects. Though no mention is made in the Bible of the mode of John's or subsequent baptisms, immersion and affusion are probably the only two that were practiced in the early church; aspersion is almost certainly a late development.

In most Protestant denominations, the administrator of baptism is an official or representative of the church, because baptism is not only a public acknowledgment of the subject's covenant with God, but also the church's recognition of the baptisand's membership (both spiritually and organizationally). The Catholic Church, viewing baptism as necessary for the salvation of one's soul, allows laity to baptize in emergencies (when death is imminent) if no priest is present.

The predominant formula for baptism, "I baptize you in the name of the Father, of the Son, and of the Holy Spirit," is derived from Jesus' Great Commission (Matthew 28:19). Though early apostolic baptism was generally in "the name of Jesus Christ," nearly all modern sects of Christianity baptize using Jesus' formula.

The modern Fundamentalist Christian, with regard to Lambert's classifications, is baptized as a believing child or adult, through immersion, by a church official, in "the name of the Father, of the Son, and of the Holy Spirit." Currently, the major debates surrounding baptism involve the subject and the mode. Fundamentalists do not baptize infants, because infants are unable to understand the significance of the rite, and there is no conclusive evidence of infant baptism occurring in the NT. Furthermore, Fundamentalists practice immersion because of their interpretation of the Greek verb frequently used in the NT, *baptizo*. Though scholars cannot agree, Fundamentalists insist that "to dip" is the primary meaning of the word. Even if it were proven that "to dip" is not the meaning of *baptizo* as it was used in the NT, today's Fundamentalists would probably continue in their practice of immersion, a vivid physical representation of the death Christ suffered (going under the water) and his victorious Resurrection (emerging therefrom).

W. Zachary P. Holt

See also African-American Holiness-Pentecostal Movement; Speaking in Tongues (Glossalalia)

Bibliography

Arbesmann, Rudolph, tr. (1950) *Tertullian: Apologetical Works*, vol. 10. New York: Fathers of the Church, Inc.

Armour, Rollin Stely. (1966) *Anabaptist Baptism*. Scottdale, PA: Herald Press.

Beasley-Murray, George Raymond. (1973) *Baptism*. Grand Rapids, MI: Wm. B. Eerdmans.

Berkhof, Louis. (1941) *Systematic Theology*. Grand Rapids, MI: Wm. B. Eerdmans.

Bromiley, Geoffrey W. (1979) "Baptism." In *The International Standard Bible Encyclopedia*, vol. 1, edited by Geoffrey W. Bromily. Grand Rapids, MI: Wm. B. Eerdmans.

———. (1984) *Evangelical Dictionary of Theology*. Grand Rapids, MI: Baker Book House.

Dockery, David S. (1992) *Dictionary of Jesus and the Gospels*. Downers Grove, IL: InterVarsity Press.

Dods, Marcus. (1906) *Dictionary of Christ and the Gospels*, vol. 1. New York: Charles Scribner's Sons.

Dunn, J. D. G. (1962) *New Bible Dictionary*. Leicester, UK: InterVarsity Press.

Gavin, Frank Stanton Burns. (1928) *The Jewish Antecedents of the Christian Sacraments*. London: Society for Promoting Christian Knowledge.

Kleist, James A., tr. (1948) *The Didache*. London: Longmans, Green & Co.

Lambert, John Chisholm. (1903) *The Sacraments in the New Testament*. Edinburgh: T. & T. Clark.

Lindsay, Thomas M. (1979) "Baptism (Non-Immersionist View)." In *The International Standard Bible Encyclopedia*, vol. 1, edited by Geoffrey W. Bromily. Grand Rapids, MI: Wm. B. Eerdmans.

Robertson, A. T. (1979) "Baptism (The Baptist Interpretation)." In *The International Standard Bible Encyclopedia*, vol. 1, edited by Geoffrey W. Bromily. Grand Rapids, MI: Wm. B. Eerdmans.

Baptists

The Baptists form a Protestant denominational family that originated in the sixteenth and seventeenth centuries, which combined beliefs from both continental Anabaptism and English Congregationalism. They affirm that baptism is only appropriate for those old enough to confess their personal faith in Jesus Christ and that immersion is the only true form of baptism.

John Smyth, an English nonconformist clergyman, rebaptized himself in early 1609 and thus is designated as the first Baptist. Thomas Helwys subsequently established the first Baptist church in England in 1612. Baptist churches now make up the largest Protestant denominational community in North America.

Baptist Beliefs

Throughout their history down to today Baptists generally have held to six basic convictions. First, they believe in a "gathered church," that is, a regenerate church membership. This is an understanding of the church as a community of Christian believers gathered together by the witness of the Holy Spirit. According to Baptist belief, the local church is composed of those who have been born again by the Holy Spirit and who have been brought to personal and saving faith in the Lord Jesus Christ. In their worship services they stress preaching and conversion.

The second belief is the acceptance of the radical notion of the priesthood of all believers. The church is not governed by a distinctive class of priests; instead, all members share in the ministry and mission of the local church. In a Baptist worship service, the pastor "leads in prayer," he does not pray by himself. Most of the prayers are unwritten and voiced extemporaneously. Each church works out its own order. In church government, each member is given an opportunity to share in the decision-making. The church calls pastors and deacons to functional leadership roles. Ordination as a pastor is simply the church's recognition of a divine call to a particular ministry in the church and of the gifts needed for the fulfillment of that call. Deacons form an advisory council to work with the pastor or pastors in providing leadership for the church's total ministry.

Third, Baptists share a conviction that the congregation stands under the Word of God. They uphold the principle of "the supreme authority of Scripture in matters of faith and practice." Conflicts over the interpretation of the Bible have divided the ranks of Baptists, but there is still no higher court of appeal in matters of faith and practice.

Baptists' fourth conviction is that they are participants in the gospel ordinances. They avoid the term "sacrament" and prefer the word "ordinance," stressing that baptism and the Lord's Supper were the only orders ordained by Jesus. The Baptist position on baptism is that only true believers, thus excluding infants, are proper candidates for baptism because the ceremony is a visible sermon about Christ's death and Resurrection and the faith of the candidate is part of that message. Baptism is considered the truth of the spiritual union of the believer with the Lord Jesus Christ in His death, burial, and Resurrection and is a symbolic expression of the gospel and moral cleansing. Full immersion is seen as the only proper mode of baptism. The ordinance of the Last Supper is viewed as a symbolic expression of the once-for-all event of Christ's crucifixion and is usually observed monthly or quarterly.

Fifth, Baptists acknowledge "the autonomy of the local church," that is, the local church exercises its own authority and regulates its own affairs. Membership in the local church is based solely on salvation in Christ and baptism by immersion on the authority of New Testament example and command. Before joining the church, a convert usually makes a confession of faith in baptism before the church congregation. Members are received by a membership transfer letter from other Baptist churches, or if a transfer letter cannot be secured, by a statement of personal experience of the believer's baptism. The decision of whether to accept the candidate rests with the church members who vote on each candidacy in a congregational meeting. Regular "business meetings" or "church meetings" give church members the opportunity to openly discuss or debate church matters and vote their decision. Baptists are generally encouraged to participate in the life of the church at large, by assisting in associations of churches, missionary societies, or denominational conventions.

Finally, Baptists have celebrated the concept of a "free church in a free state." To the sixteenth-century Anabaptists on the European continent and the early Baptists in England religious liberty was of utmost importance. The conviction emerged that this religious liberty was based on the New Testament and thus humans are of infinite worth and have rights of unique personal existence conferred upon them by God. They insist that the church and state have two different responsibilities and two separate and distinct kinds of authority. Government should exercise its authority only in civil affairs not in religious affairs. Baptists are not committed to any single theory of government or political philosophy but hold strongly to the concept of separation of church and state.

Baptist Divisions

Differences among Baptists have caused many divisions within the Baptist community. Even as the Baptists began as free congregations in England, there emerged two distinct theological groups. The Regular Baptists held Calvin's predestination as their basic theology and the General Baptists were Arminian in theology and thus believed in free will. When Baptists came to America, there were continued splits. One controversy involved evangelism and missionary activity. One group began forming associations to do missionary work while the other, known as the Primitive (or antimissionary) group, believed that only God could evangelize and humans should not presume to do God's work.

Baptists in the United States

Political and cultural cleavages in American history have also divided the Baptists. Until the Civil War, there were Baptists in the South who supported slavery while there were some ardent Baptists in the North who supported the abolitionist movement. In the nineteenth century a Southern church movement called the "Landmarkers" argued that there was a valid and unbroken succession of Baptist churches since the time of the New Testament. They refused to join in cooperative ventures with other Baptist churches and would not accept transfer letters of church membership. They practiced "closed communion," which was only open to baptized members of the local church and believed any baptismal immersion not performed by a Baptist church was an "alien immersion." The beliefs of the Landmarkers can still be found in local churches in the South. An alliance of Fundamentalist Baptists was formed during the years 1923 to 1932 and took the title of the Baptist Bible Union. In 1932, members of the Baptist Bible Union left the Northern Baptist Convention to form the General Association of Regular Baptist Churches. Members from a modern moderate Fundamentalist fellowship stayed in the convention until 1947 when they left to form the Conservative Baptist Association. In the South, a controversial Baptist preacher started the World Baptist Fellowship in the 1930s and saw it split into the Baptist Bible Fellow-

ship of the late 1940s. At present, the Southern Baptist Convention is the largest Baptist denomination with 1.8 million members in 2001; it is also the largest of all Protestant denominations. The Southern Baptist Convention is conservative in its theology but does not accept such tenants of the American Fundamentalist movement as the pre-Tribulation rapture and dispensational eschatology. In the twentieth century, other Baptists have also divided over issues of centralized denominational structures and theological inclusiveness.

Black churches are a dominant segment of the Baptist community in America. African Americans have been historically drawn to the Baptist family of churches because of their lack of formality, the absence of ritual, and the democratic spirit of the Baptist congregations. The first African-American Baptist church was organized around 1773 at Silver Bluff in Georgia. After the Civil War, nearly one million African-American Baptists worshiped in their own churches.

Some Baptists were involved in the American Fundamentalist movement in the early twentieth century. The term "Fundamentalist" was first coined in 1920 by the Baptist clergyman Curtis Lee Laws in his weekly newspaper the *Watchman-Examiner*. In his words, Fundamentalists were those "who still cling to the great fundamentals and who mean to do battle royal for the faith." Interestingly, Laws originated this title because he rejected such contemporary descriptive terms as "conservative," "premillennialist," or "Landmarker." Most Baptists today span the theological spectrum from moderate to conservative. The Baptists in America have produced such well-known figures as Walter Rauschenbush, a theologian of the Social Gospel; Martin Luther King, Jr., the nonviolent civil rights leader; and Billy Graham, the world-famous evangelist. Jerry Falwell, founder of the Moral Majority, was active in conservative politics for a time but has since returned to the pastoral ministry of his Thomas Road Baptist Church.

Leland Edward Wilshire

See also Baptism; Black Church, The; Moral Majority; Televangelism

Bibliography

Freeman, Curtis W., et al. (1999) *Baptist Roots: A Reader in the Theology of a Christian People.* Valley Forge, PA: Judson Press.

Selection From:
THE BAPTIST FAITH AND MESSAGE.
A STATEMENT ADOPTED BY THE SOUTHERN BAPTIST CONVENTION ON JUNE 14, 2000

XV. The Christian and the Social Order

All Christians are under obligation to seek to make the will of Christ supreme in our own lives and in human society. Means and methods used for the improvement of society and the establishment of righteousness among men can be truly and permanently helpful only when they are rooted in the regeneration of the individual by the saving grace of God in Jesus Christ. In the spirit of Christ, Christians should oppose racism, every form of greed, selfishness, and vice, and all forms of sexual immorality, including adultery, homosexuality, and pornography. We should work to provide for the orphaned, the needy, the abused, the aged, the helpless, and the sick. We should speak on behalf of the unborn and contend for the sanctity of all human life from conception to natural death. Every Christian should seek to bring industry, government, and society as a whole under the sway of the principles of righteousness, truth, and brotherly love. In order to promote these ends Christians should be ready to work with all men of good will in any good cause, always being careful to act in the spirit of love without compromising their loyalty to Christ and His truth.

Exodus 20:3–17; Leviticus 6:2–5; Deuteronomy 10:12; 27:17; Psalm 101:5; Micah 6:8; Zechariah 8:16; Matthew 5:13–16,43–48; 22:36–40; 25:35; Mark 1:29–34; 2:3ff.; 10:21; Luke 4:18–21; 10:27–37; 20:25; John 15:12; 17:15; Romans 12–14; 1 Corinthians 5:9–10; 6:1–7; 7:20–24; 10:23–11:1; Galatians 3:26–28; Ephesians 6:5–9; Colossians 3:12–17; 1 Thessalonians 3:12; Philemon; James 1:27; 2:8.

Source: The Hall of the Southern Baptist Convention Reformation. www.members.nbci.com

Grenz, Stanley. (1985) *The Baptist Congregation: A Guide to Baptist Belief and Practice.* Valley Forge, PA: Judson Press.

McNutt, William Roy. (1959) *Polity and Practice in Baptist Churches.* Chicago: Judson Press.

Shelley, Bruce L. (1973) *What Baptists Believe.* Wheaton, IL: C. B. Press.

Stewart, Howard R. (1974) *Baptists and Local Autonomy. The Development, Distortions, Decline and New Directions of Local Autonomy in Baptist Churches.* Hicksville, NY: Exposition Press.

Bavarian, Illuminati *See* Illuminati, The

Beast, The

The beast is an apocalyptic image derived from the biblical Book of Revelation. While the exact interpretation of the beast varies among Fundamentalists, it is depicted as a monotonous entity that will terrorize the world in the last days when its infamous mark will be forced on the inhabitants of the earth. In Revelation 13:1–2, the author, presumably John, paints a vivid portrait of a hideous creature rising from the sea. The beast possessed "ten horns and seven heads." Furthermore, it was "like a leopard, its feet were like a bear's, and its mouth was like a lion's mouth" (NRSV). This unsightly beast is a composite of apocalyptic imagery presented in the Book of Daniel. In Daniel 7, four beasts are depicted that represent progressive political empires prior to the establishment of the divine kingdom. In interpreting

Revelation 13:1–4

1. And I stood upon the sand of the sea, and saw a beast rise up out of the sea, having seven heads and ten horns, and upon his horns ten crowns, and upon his heads the name of blasphemy.
2. And the beast which I saw was like unto a leopard, and his feet were as the feet of a bear, and his mouth as the mouth of a lion: and the dragon gave him his power, and his seat, and great authority.
3. And I saw one of his heads as it were wounded to death; and his deadly wound was healed: and all the world wondered after the beast.
4. And they worshipped the dragon which gave power unto the beast: and they worshipped the beast, saying, Who is like unto the beast? who is able to make war with him?

the vision in Daniel 7, Fundamentalists often follow the explanation of the *Scofield Reference Bible* (1909), which identifies the lion with wings as the Babylonian Empire, the bear as the Medo-Persian Empire, the leopard as the Greek Empire, and the horrible fourth beast as the Roman Empire. The Beast of Revelation 13:1–2, by incorporating the creatures described in Daniel 7, assumes their strength, making it at once powerful and frightful. Yet the symbolism of the beast appears to have a dual meaning: representing both the final world empire and its chief human agent, a person capable of incalculable evil. A second "beast from the earth" in Revelation 13:11–12, enforces obeisance to the first beast and is more commonly referred to as the "false prophet" of Revelation 19:20.

While some scholars argue that the Beast of Revelation 13:1–2 described conditions within the Roman Empire of the first century CE, the mysterious symbolism of the vision made it the subject of fascination in subsequent centuries. During the French Revolution many ascribed prophetic significance to dramatic events unfolding on the European continent, believing they fulfilled both Daniel 7 and Revelation 13. More recently, Fundamentalists in the United States largely accept the apocalyptic descriptions popularized by Hal Lindsey in *The Late Great Planet Earth* (1970), which identifies the final world dictator as the leader of a revived Roman Empire, a political superstate of ten kingdoms that will arise out of the European Union. Some Fundamentalists integrate the persona of the beast, a political despot, with popular conceptions of the Antichrist, a wicked pseudo-religious figure, although the word "antichrist" appears only in the Epistles of John and it is

unclear in Revelation if such an identification is viable. Nonetheless, the beast wields tremendous power and speculation abounds regarding his telltale mark, the feared "666." While some identify 666 with the name of the Roman emperor Nero Caesar, other contemporary designations include credit cards and computers. Fascination with the beast remains as evidenced by the recent best-selling series, *Left Behind* (1995–2000), by Tim LaHaye and Jerry Jenkins, including a volume entitled *The Mark: The Beast Rules the World*. It is likely that the ancient image of the beast will continue to evoke fear and wonder for generations to come.

Scott Lupo

See also Antichrist; Mark of the Beast

Bibliography

Boyer, Paul. (1992) *When Time Shall Be No More: Prophecy Belief in Modern American Culture*. Cambridge, MA: The Belknap Press of Harvard University Press.

LaHaye, Tim, and Jerry Jenkins. (2000) *The Mark: The Beast Rules the World*. Carol Stream, IL: Tyndale House.

Lindsey, Hal. ([1970] 1973) *The Late Great Planet Earth*. New York: Bantam Books.

McGinn, Bernard. (1994) *Antichrist: Two Thousand Years of the Human Fascination with Evil*. San Francisco: HarperSanFrancisco.

Scofield, Cyrus Ingerson, ed. ([1909] 1998) *The Scofield Reference Bible*. New York: Oxford University Press.

Bible

The Christian Bible consists of two parts, the Old Testament (OT) and the New Testament (NT). The original OT was written in Hebrew (with some minor portions in Aramaic) and the NT in Greek. All present-day Bibles in English and other modern languages are translations and paraphrases of those two languages. Each of the two testaments presents a covenant (that is, an agreement established by God with His people): the OT presents the covenant made through Moses (Exodus 24:8; 2 Kings 23:2), and the later NT presents the new covenant made through Jesus Christ (Matthew 26:28).

The OT contains thirty-nine books written over a thousand-year period beginning in approximately 1450 BCE. The NT contains twenty-seven books written over about sixty years, with the earliest (some of the letters by the apostle Paul) now thought by scholars to have been written only a few years after the death and Resurrection of Christ.

The Bible is both a collection of books and a single book. It is a collection of books in view of its having been written by many different human beings, each with a different personality and writing style. However, conservative Christians—and Fundamentalists among them—see the Bible as one book in view of its writing having been superintended in detail by God. Fundamentalist Christians accept the Bible—in its "autograph" copy—as inerrant; that is, the writing of the original copy of each book of the Bible was so minutely superintended by the Holy Spirit that it contains no errors, factual or verbal. The Bible is a book written by some forty authors living in different times and places, most of whom did not know of one another's writings or even existence. Therefore, the Bible is a composition with only slight human means of achieving self-consistency, but which nevertheless has one overall message and one aim: the glorification of God through the salvation of His people. It is seen as the Word of God in written form.

Contents and Canon of the Bible

While the NT is roughly one-third the length of the OT, this part of the Bible is accepted by virtually all Christians as vitally important to the people of God. This acceptance rests upon two beliefs: (1) that its writers were inspired by God, and (2) that God Himself, in the person of Jesus Christ, formed the basis for its entire message through His words and actions while on earth.

The Roman Catholic and Eastern Orthodox churches accept twelve additional books as valid components of the OT, books that are not accepted by the Protestant Christian denominations, including Fundamentalists. These twelve books, often called the Apocrypha, were assessed by the leaders of the Protestant Reformation as "useful" but not divinely inspired. This lower level of perceived authority was based on the late dates perceived for the composition of these books, along with no copies having been found of them in Hebrew.

Some of the apocryphal books are Tobit, certain additions to Daniel and to Esther, Judith, the Epistle of Jeremiah, the Book of Baruch, Ecclesiasticus (not Ecclesiastes), the Wisdom of Solomon, and 1 and 2 Maccabees.

The OT in English translation is organized into four groups of books: the Law, History, Poetry, and the Prophets. The Law contains the first five books of the OT: Genesis, Exodus, Leviticus, Numbers, and Deuteronomy. The second group, History, contains Joshua, Judges, Ruth, 1 and 2 Samuel, 1 and 2 Kings, 1 and 2 Chronicles, Ezra, Nehemiah, and Esther. The third group, Poetry, consists of Job, Psalms, Proverbs, Ecclesiastes, and Song of Solomon. The remaining seventeen books of the OT, Isaiah through Malachi, make up the Prophets.

The NT also falls into four groups, the Gospels (from an Old English word meaning "good news"), History, Letters, and Revelation. There are four gospels—Matthew, Mark, Luke, and John—each named for its writer. There is only one book of History, the Book of Acts. The third group, Letters (often called the Epistles), consists of all the remaining NT books except the last, from Romans through Jude. And the last category, like the second, is comprised of a single book, Revelation.

The known history of canonicity (decisions as to whether individual books are authentically inspired or not) in both testaments is long and largely uncertain. What is known with considerable certainty is that the OT collection (canon) was effectively chosen and closed in about 90 CE in the teaching house of Jamnia. The NT canon was developed from books known and used by different Christian congregations. From these, the presently accepted twenty-seven book canon was chosen and closed in the fourth century CE.

Historical Accuracy of the Bible

While some skeptics have accused the writers of the Bible of myth-making, more recently the Fundamentalist view that the Bible's accounts are accurate records has been supported to some extent by archeology. To cite only three such cases regarding the OT, in Judges 1:27–35 and in Joshua 13:2–6, we are given lists of unconquered territories in Canaan. At several of the sites mentioned (Beth-Shean, Megiddo, and Gezer are among them), archeological evidence supporting the biblical accounts has been found. Again, in 1 Kings 7:9–10, the Bible describes Solomon's palace as having been built of sawn stones (ashlar) of eight and ten cubits in size. And in verse 11 the corresponding courtyard is described as having "three courses of hewn stone" and "a course of cedar beams." These methods of construction are the same as those found in Israelite masonry dating from Solomonic times. And once more, Joshua 6 describes the falling of Jericho's defensive walls. This account has been debated by archeologists since the 1930s, with recent analysis (in the 1980s) affirming the biblical account.

In the NT, Luke wrote both the gospel bearing his name and the Book of Acts, the two books together constituting one-fourth of the NT. Luke's accuracy as a historian has been verified by archeologists, one in particular having examined evidence for Luke's descriptions of nine islands, fifty-four cities, and thirty-two countries, finding no errors at all.

But while archeology often agrees with the biblical account, making Scripture plausible even to the skeptic, this branch of history alone cannot persuade even the willing inquirer of the Bible's theological message. The Fundamentalist conviction is that only the Holy Spirit, working within the inquirer who reads the Bible, can make it possible for one to accept the Bible's message as having its origin in God.

In contrast to the Roman Catholic Church, which views doctrine as properly emanating from its hierarchy and from its interpretation of the Bible, Fundamentalists—as heirs of the Protestant Reformation—see the Bible as the sole unimpeachable authority on earth for the formation of spiritual doctrine. Both views are in strong contrast to secular culture's adherence to intellectual fashions, with their inherent instability and self-contradictions. Fundamentalists, apparently in an attempt to solidify this biblical basis for a worldview, interpret the Bible more literally than do other Protestant Christians.

Text and Translations of the OT

Until 1947, the oldest known manuscript of the OT was approximately one thousand years old. The fact that this text was itself the result of many scribal copies of copies, long since lost or decayed, gave rise to the common belief that the original reading had suffered greatly through the accumulation of scribal errors.

In 1947, however, the Dead Sea Scrolls were discovered, among which were the remains of a text one thousand years older than the oldest previously known text. This pre-Christian copy allowed scholars to determine how much of the text had been distorted through repeated copying. The result was that there had been no significant distortion of the text, only minor scribal errors.

Other evidence of the reliability of the Hebrew Bible comes from the Samaritan text of the first five books of the OT. Because the Samaritan community broke off all official and religious contact with the Jews at Jerusalem, their text was transmitted in a line of copies independent of those leading from the Dead Sea Scrolls to our modern text. This independent Samaritan line of descent, dating from approximately the fifth century BCE, again affirms the trustworthy transmission of the Hebrew text over a surprisingly great expanse of time.

Beginning in the third century BCE, the OT was translated into Greek for the benefit of Jews who understood Greek but not Hebrew. Because the first five books were translated by approximately seventy scholars, this translation is called the Septuagint, the Latin word meaning "seventy."

Text and Translations of the NT

NT manuscripts in the original Greek exist in a vast array, seventy-six of them written on papyrus and dating from the second and third centuries CE, together with another group of almost three thousand on parchment, the earliest of which date from the fourth century CE. And finally there exist nearly two thousand lectionary manuscripts, portions of NT books to be read aloud in early Christian worship services, with various datings up to the tenth century CE.

Translation of the NT into Latin began in the third century CE, and was revised by Jerome in the late fourth century. The Latin version is frequently called the Vulgate, indicating its intended use for the bene-

THE BIBLE ON THE BIBLE

Matthew 26:28
For this is my blood of the new testament, which is shed for many for the remission of sins.

Proverbs 15:1
A soft answer turneth away wrath, but grievous words stir up anger.

John 1:46
Authorized version: And Nathanael said unto him, Can there any good thing come out of Nazareth? Philip saith unto him, Come and see.
New International version: Nazareth! Can any good come from there? Nathanael asked. Come and see, said Philip.

fit of those common people of the time who did not understand Greek.

Text and Translations in English

While it is possible that the Bible as a whole was translated into Old English, only fragments and individual books survive today in this early and very Germanic form of English (sometimes called Anglo-Saxon). These date from the seventh century CE to the beginning of the ninth century. Translations into Middle English were similarly fragmentary, except for the important work by John Wycliffe and his associates in the late fourteenth century. All of these translations were made from the Vulgate. The first translation of the NT into English from the original Greek was by William Tyndale, who used the newly printed NT in Greek published by Erasmus in the early sixteenth century.

The first translation of the complete Bible into Modern English was published in 1535 by Miles Coverdale. The "Matthew" Bible followed in 1537. In 1539 the Great Bible was published, so called because of its large size. This revision of the Matthew Bible has had a strong influence on subsequent translations of the Bible into English. Henry VIII allowed this Bible to "go abroad among our people," with the result that a copy was made available to be seen and read in every church under Henry's rule.

In 1557 the Geneva NT was published. This translation was the first in English to use verse divisions (which were originally used in a Greek-language edition published in 1551). The year 1568 saw publication of the Bishops' Bible, so called because a great deal of the work was done by various English bishops. In 1582 Roman Catholic Englishmen in France brought out the Rheims-Douay translation of the NT in an attempt to counteract effects of the various Protestant translations. The corresponding translation of the OT was produced in 1609 to 1610.

In 1604 King James I agreed to the formation of a team of fifty-four scholars from both Oxford and Cambridge universities to translate the entire Bible. In 1611 the Authorized Version (also called the King James Version) was published, replacing the Great Bible in English churches. The Authorized Version, in one form or another, is still in use by many Fundamentalist churches as of this writing, though numerous other Christian churches have moved to newer translations using a style of English that is more accessible to the contemporary reader.

In the four centuries since publication of the Authorized Version, there have been a great number of revisions, translations, and paraphrases of the Bible. Chief among these are the Revised Version (1885), the Revised Standard Version (1952), the New English Bible (1961), the Jerusalem Bible (1966 [a Catholic translation]), the New American Standard Version (1971), and the New International Version (1978).

Conclusion

Though the Bible as embraced by Judaism, Catholicism, and Protestant Christianity differs in its content, when seen as a whole, the uniformity of accepted content is remarkable. All three groups accept at least the thirty-nine books contained in the Protestant OT, and both Catholic and Protestant Bibles contain the same twenty-seven books of the NT.

While certain passages are understood to be parabolic and/or poetic, and therefore not meant to be understood literally, the text as we have it seems to have been copied with surprising accuracy through the ages, and the historical portions of the Bible show significant signs of being plausible as records of actual events. These assurances from textual and archeological studies testify to a certain amount of reliability in the Bible, but they cannot form the deciding factor for the inquirer who is considering the adoption of the Bible's theological message.

No autograph copy of any book of the Bible exists, but this is true of many documents, including the autograph copies of works by Shakespeare. The text in the original languages has been translated into English many times, most notably into the Authorized Version, a favorite of most Fundamentalists.

John J. Brugaletta

See also Bible Conferences; Bible Schools; Bible Study; Biblical Criticism; Biblical Inerrancy; New Testament; Old Testament; Preaching

Bibliography

Geisler, Norman, and Thomas Howe. (1992) *When Critics Ask.* Wheaton, IL: Victor.

Hoerth, Alfred J. (1998) *Archeology and the Old Testament.* Grand Rapids, MI: Baker House Books.

Hoffmeier, James K. (1996) *Israel in Egypt: The Evidence for the Authenticity of the Exodus Tradition.* New York: Oxford University Press.

Mazar, Amihai. (1990) *Archeology of the Land of the Bible: 10,000–586 B.C.E.* New York: Doubleday.

Strobel, Lee. (1998) *The Case for Christ: A Journalist's Investigation of the Evidence for Jesus.* Grand Rapids, MI: Zondervan Publishing.

Bible Conferences

One of the key institutions in forming and promoting Protestant Fundamentalism in the United States was the Bible conference. Large interdenominational conferences, often held in vacation settings, served both as centers for spreading Fundamentalist teaching and as rallying points for assembling the elements of the Fundamentalist coalition that emerged in the early twentieth century.

Laying the groundwork for the development of Bible conferences was Pietism, an eighteenth-century movement within the Protestant state churches of Europe that stressed holy living. Pietists often formed "little churches within the church," small groups of believers, often led by laypersons, who met together apart from an official church setting for Bible study, prayer, and mutual encouragement. These informal meetings provided a pattern for Evangelical Protestantism in Britain and North America in which Christians who shared a common heartfelt piety cooperated across denominational lines in evangelistic and devotional efforts.

This Pietist influence is evident in several British conferences that contributed to the rise of American Bible conferences. At the Albury (1826–1828) and Powerscourt (1831–1836) conferences, John Nelson Darby and others outlined the dispensationalist version of premillennialism that became predominant in American Fundamentalism. The '59 Revival in Northern Ireland saw the practice of what were known as "believers' meetings," small gatherings for Bible study along the lines of Pietist "little churches within the church." Later in the nineteenth century, the Keswick conventions (begun in 1875) became popular centers for Bible teaching with a stress on Christian holiness expressed in surrender of one's will to God and achieving victory over conscious sin. Also a factor was the Mildmay Conference founded by Anglican clergyman William Pennefather in 1864.

The "believers' meetings" in Ireland gave rise to the most important American Bible conference, the Niagara Bible Conference. A private Bible study group begun in imitation of the believers' meetings gradually changed into a public conference. The conference held annual meetings in Niagara-on-the-Lake, Ontario, from 1883 to 1897. Under the leadership of Presbyterian clergyman James H. Brookes of St. Louis, Missouri, Niagara became a major center of premillennial teaching. Some historians regard the fourteen-point Niagara creed as the first creed of the Fundamentalist movement. The Niagara conference eventually ended amid disputes over the timing of Christ's return for the church: whether it would come before or after God's judgment of the world through a Great Tribulation period.

Arising about the same time as Niagara and perhaps as influential was the Northfield Bible Conference begun by American evangelist D. L. Moody in Massachusetts. Moody followed the pattern of the Mildmay Conference of Pennefather, whom he had met in Britain. Holding his first meetings in 1880 and 1881 and then continuously from 1885, Moody established his Northfield Conference as a center for conservative Bible teaching. In addition to a prophetic emphasis, Moody brought in speakers who added a strong element of Keswick teaching, leading C. I. Scofield to call Northfield "the American Keswick." Along with these annual summer conferences, the Fundamentalist movement also owes its origin to American Bible and Prophetic Conferences held in New York (1878), Chicago (1886 and 1914), Allegheny, Pennsylvania (1895), and Boston (1901). These centralized meetings attracted more attention to the prophetic movement, and the volumes of published addresses from these sessions served to publicize and explain premillennial teaching. In all of these conferences, speakers generally held to what may broadly be called a "Bible conference theology." It rested on three pillars: an unswerving commitment to biblical inerrancy (as influenced by Princeton Theological Seminary), premillennialism (normally of the dispensationalist variety), and Keswick holiness piety. Not coincidentally, all three emphases became prominent features of Fundamentalist theology.

The first half of the twentieth century saw a remarkable growth in Bible conferences. After the demise of Niagara, A. C. Gaebelein founded the Sea Cliff Bible Conference in New York, one of the fruits of which was C. I. Scofield's influential reference Bible. Often, leading evangelists or ministers founded these conferences, such as R. A. Torrey's Montrose Bible Conference in Pennsylvania. The importance of such conferences to the Fundamentalist movement can be seen in the fact that the World's Christian Fundamentals Association (the first major interdenominational Fundamentalist organization) set up a committee to oversee and coordinate Bible conferences in the 1920s. Typical of these conferences,

and perhaps the most influential, was the Winona Lake Bible Conference in northern Indiana. Founded by Presbyterian minister Solomon C. Dickey in 1895 and patterned on Northfield, Winona also stressed cultural elements, including the establishment of a successful chautauqua program. Winona attracted some of the leading lights of Fundamentalism, such as evangelist J. Wilbur Chapman (the first director of its Bible conference), antievolution crusader William Jennings Bryan (who served as its president), and evangelist Billy Sunday (who made his summer home in Winona Lake).

After the Fundamentalist–modernist controversy of the 1920s, Fundamentalists began to assemble their own network of schools, mission boards, and publishing houses to replace those they viewed as lost to theological liberalism. The Bible conferences became major focal points in this network, creating centers for interdenominational fellowship and the exchange of ideas. The conferences helped spread Fundamentalism as they had earlier spread premillennial prophetic teaching. After the middle of the twentieth century, however, Bible conferences declined in popularity. Aging facilities, theological dissension, and changing tastes in both leisure and worship among Evangelicals combined to end the heyday of the conference movement. The patterns of the Bible conferences, however, remain evident in the youth camps, seminars, and retreats still popular among Fundamentalist and Evangelical audiences.

Mark Sidwell

See also Keswick Movement

Bibliography

Beale, David O. (1986) *In Pursuit of Purity: American Fundamentalism since 1850.* Greenville, SC: Unusual Publications.

Sandeen, Ernest. (1970) *The Roots of Fundamentalism: British and American Millenarianism, 1800–1930.* Chicago: University of Chicago Press.

Bible Schools

The Bible school movement emerged in the late nineteenth and early twentieth centuries as a result of the influence of mass evangelists such as Dwight Moody

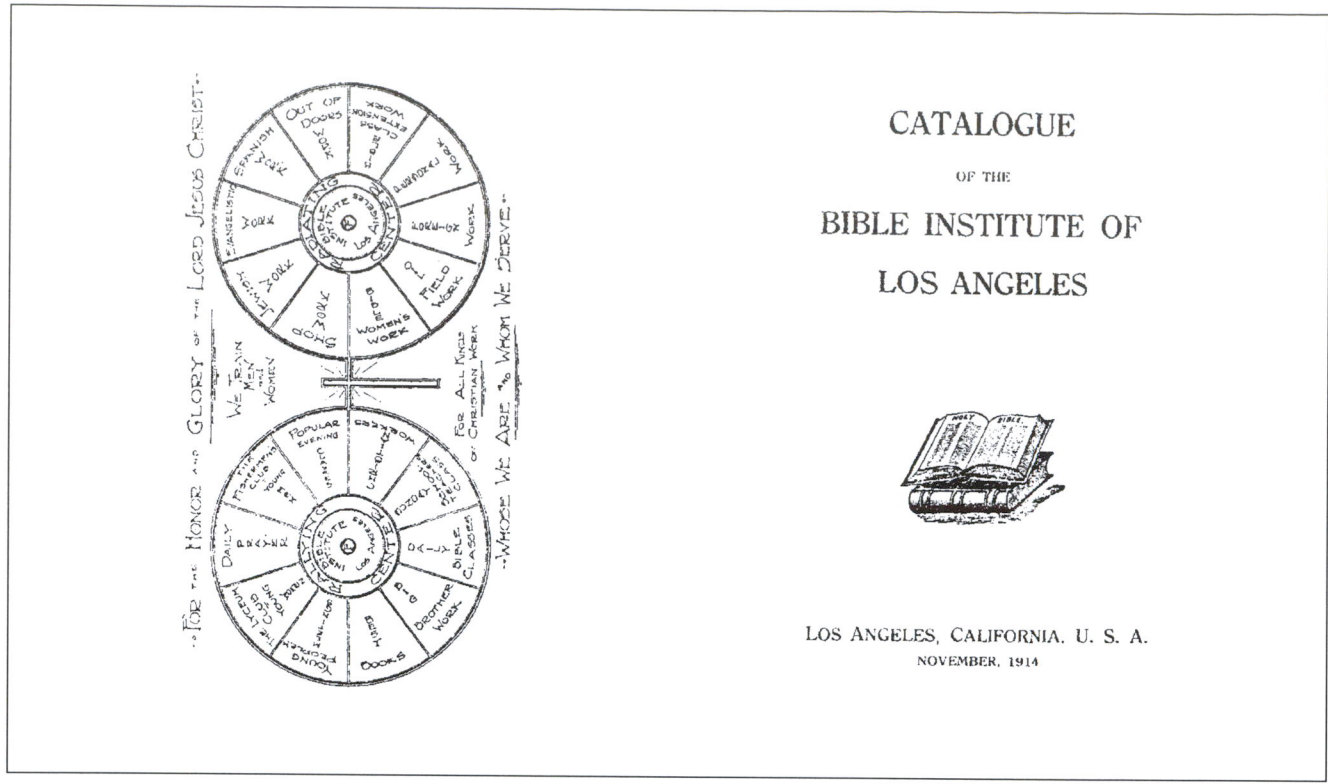

CATALOGUE

OF THE

BIBLE INSTITUTE OF

LOS ANGELES

LOS ANGELES, CALIFORNIA. U. S. A.
NOVEMBER, 1914

Front piece and title page of the *Catalog of the Bible School of Los Angeles.* Courtesy of Richard Flory.

(1837–1889), the belief in the power of education to promote individual and social change, and as a reaction toward liberalization within American Protestantism in general, and its colleges and seminaries in particular. Moody had famously issued a call to train "Christian workers" as "gap men" to stand in the gap between the seminary trained ministers, many of whom he believed had lost touch with their parishioners, and the common person. This call was heeded by many church leaders who established their own Bible schools, the majority of which were in urban areas. By 1900, fourteen Bible schools had been established; by 1920, there were twenty-six more; and although not all survived, by 1945, 108 had been established. Currently, there are eighty-six schools listed as being member institutions of the American Association of Bible Colleges, and although not strictly Bible schools, one hundred additional schools are listed as members of the Coalition for Christian Colleges and Universities.

The first two Bible schools were Nyack, founded in 1882 as the "New York [City] Missionary Training College for Home and Foreign Missionaries," and Moody Bible Institute, founded in 1886 as the "Chicago Evangelization Society." They were estab-lished to train Christian lay persons in the "English Bible" and practical methods of evangelization for use both in the United States and in foreign missions. As the differences between Fundamentalists and modernists increased in the early years of the twentieth century, Bible schools took on added importance for the Fundamentalist movement, acting as institutional centers within Fundamentalism. The schools operated as organizing and networking centers for Fundamentalist leaders, and the theological and ideological teachings of Fundamentalist Christianity were disseminated largely through these schools and their various activities, which included not only classroom instruction and evangelistic outreach but also radio programs, magazines and newsletters, extension courses, and Bible conferences.

The Student Body

The Bible schools educated and trained their students in Bible study and in evangelistic methods, often with the purpose of preparing them to become "full-time Christian workers." The students tended to be somewhat older and had already held jobs and whether their goal was for full-time Christian work or simply to improve their biblical literacy, all had a desire to engage in some form of Christian work. The entrance requirements emphasized Christian experience and a desire to serve in Christian work, with academic requirements, where indeed they had such requirements, limited to a "common school" education.

The schools were open to both men and women, with female students often outnumbering male students. Although these were fairly Victorian institutions in terms of expectations for men and women, both sexes were equally active in various urban ministries. As well, many Bible schools advertised the ethnic diversity of their student body by including pictures of students of "different nationalities" in their catalogs. One photograph from Moody Bible Institute (ca. 1920), shows a group of young men with identities listed such as Japanese, "Porto Rican," "Assyrian," "Russian Jew," "American Negro," and several other American and European nationalities.

Programs and Courses

The Bible school curriculum consisted of both classroom training and practical application of the classroom study. In the early years of the Bible schools, classroom study consisted of one or two years of coursework in subject areas such as Bible study, missions, music, and teacher training. Over time, however, the curriculum expanded to three and sometimes four years, and different specializations for the students were offered. These specializations were rooted in a core of Bible study classes, but were intended to provide more extensive training in specific areas of ministry, with a diploma awarded upon completion of the chosen course of study. In its 1920–1921 catalog, Moody Bible Institute listed five separate "courses" of study—Bible, Bible-Music, Music, Missionary, and Sunday School—in which there were seventeen different subject areas included in different combinations depending on the course of study chosen. The different subject areas included English Bible, biblical psychology, evangelism, public speaking, missions, and music (15–44).

"Practical work," in parallel to the classroom study, was also required. The students were asked to venture out into the city for various evangelistic activities. This classroom–work study relation is clearly demonstrated in the Bible Institute of Los Angeles' representation of the relationship between these two activities. The various classroom activities, such as the

Bible classes, prayer groups, and men's and women's groups, were referred to as the "Rallying Center," while the students' evangelistic activities, such as "Spanish Work," "Out of Doors Work," "Foreign Work," "Oil-field Work," "Shop Work," and "Jewish Work," were referred to as the "Radiating Center." For the Bible Institute of Los Angeles, these two types of activities were intimately linked.

The Development of Bible Schools

As Bible schools developed over time, and particularly after 1940, they patterned themselves along the lines of a college model, both in terms of curriculum, academic degrees, and the upgrading and professionalization of their faculty. As a response to demand from the Fundamentalist constituency for college-level programs, as well as to external developments such as the GI Bill—which made it possible for the returning servicemen and women to enroll in college programs—Bible schools expanded their programs to accommodate the greater numbers of students. As a result, two basic forms of schools developed: one, the Bible college, and the other, the Fundamentalist-oriented liberal arts college.

Guatemalan children at a summer Bible school run by U.S. missionaries in a remote mountain village, 1976. PHOTO COURTESY OF KAREN CHRISTENSEN.

DWIGHT L. MOODY'S VISION OF A BIBLE TRAINING SCHOOL

I believe that we have got to have gap-men—men to stand between the laity and the ministers; men who are trained to do city mission work. . . . We need the men that have the most character to go into the shops and meet these hardhearted infidels and skeptics. They have got to know the people and what we want is men who know that, and go right into the shop and talk to men.

Never mind the Greek and Hebrew, give them plain English and good Scripture. It is the sword of the Lord that cuts deep. If you have men trained for that kind of work, there is no trouble about reaching the men who do not go into the churches.

My idea is to have the people study mornings and have some ministers of different denominations give them a good Bible lecture and visit every family in their district and every night preach the simple Gospel.

I do not want you to misunderstand me, but the ministers are educated away from these classes of people. Not that it is too much education, but it is their training that has been away from them. For instance a boy grows up to school, he is kept at school until he is ready to go to college, and then to college, and from college to the theological seminary, and the result is he comes out of a theological seminary knowing nothing about human nature, doesn't know how to rub up to these men and adapt himself to them, and then gets up a sermon on metaphysical subjects miles above these people. We don't get down to them at all; they move in another world. What we want is men trained for this class of people.

Source: Getz, Gene A. [revised and updated by James M. Vincent] (1986[1969]).
MBI: The Story of Moody Bible Institute. Chicago: Moody Press, p. 22.

The Bible college model consisted of the same, or similar, core biblical studies requirements as in the Bible school, but also offered academic majors in what were previously simply courses of study. In addition, new general education requirements were added, which although similar to those at any other college or university, were appropriately integrated with Fundamentalist Christian teachings. The liberal arts college model was in part patterned after other long-established schools like Wheaton College (Illinois), in which along with general education requirements, several liberal arts majors were established, while maintaining the religion course requirements in some modified form, from the Bible school days. In some cases this meant keeping the same number of religion courses, whereas in others, it meant reducing the number of those courses. Since the 1980s, many of the former Bible schools have moved to a university model, offering professional graduate programs usually in religious studies oriented toward professional ministry, psychology, and missions.

Conclusion

Throughout their development, Bible schools have played an important role in the Fundamentalist movement by providing an institutional center that has produced many of the Fundamentalist leaders throughout the last century, as well as an ideological center where future generations of Fundamentalist youth continue to be trained.

Richard W. Flory

See also Missions; Preaching; Sunday Schools

Bibliography

Bible Institute of Los Angeles. (1914) *Catalogue*. Los Angeles, CA: Bible Institute of Los Angeles.

Brereton, Virginia Lieson. (1990) *Training God's Army: The American Bible School, 1880–1940*. Bloomington and Indianapolis: Indiana University Press.

Carpenter, Joel A. (1997) *Revive Us Again: The Reawakening of American Fundamentalism*. New York: Oxford University Press.

Getz, Gene A. (1986 [1969]) *MBI: The Story of Moody Bible Institute*, revised and updated by James M. Vincent. Chicago: Moody Press.

Moody Bible Institute. (1920–1921) *Catalogue*. Chicago: Moody Bible Institute.

Ringenberg, William C. (1984) *The Christian College: A History of Protestant Higher Education in America*. Grand Rapids, MI: Wm. B. Eerdmans.

Bible Study

Bible study usually refers to personal or group study of biblical passages, entire books of the Bible, or topics from selected biblical passages. Participants learn how to interpret the meaning of the text and how it relates to their own life situations, all for the purpose of personal spiritual growth in their relationship with God. Christians study the Bible because Jesus regularly referred to the Scriptures (at that time the Hebrew Bible) as a clear and trustworthy source of revelation from God (Matthew 5:17–19; Luke 24:27). Many statements in the Old and New Testaments attest to the character of Scripture and the importance of knowing and studying it diligently. The people of Israel, for example, were to know the Scriptures well enough to teach them to their children in formal and informal settings (Deuteronomy 6:6–7). The Psalms claim that the truth of the Word of God gives wisdom to live life, revive the soul, bring joy to the heart, and provide warning and great reward in one's life (Psalms 19:7–11; 119:130). In 2 Timothy 3:16–17, the Scriptures are described as "God-breathed" and a valuable spiritual guide for life.

Personal Bible Study: A Historical Survey of Its Use

When one considers the claims Scripture makes about its dynamic nature, it is rather surprising that personal Bible study is a relatively modern practice in Christendom. Historically this appears to be related to two factors: (1) the availability of the Scriptures in printed form (or lack of it) for individual Christians, and (2) the encouragement (or lack of it) to study the Bible by church leaders. Modern Fundamentalism, taking its core values from the Protestant Reformers, has promoted Bible study groups within the modern church more than at any other time in history. George M. Marsden, noted historian of the Fundamentalism movement, writes, "Fundamentalism did not develop in seminaries, but in Bible conferences, Bible schools, and perhaps most importantly, on the personal level of small Bible-study groups where the prophetic truths could be made plain" (1982: 61–62).

The Protestant Reformation

Reacting against the authority of the Roman Catholic Church, many of the Protestant Reformers (from the fourteenth to sixteenth centuries) contended for the right of every Christian to examine the Scriptures for him or herself. This led to the translation of the Scriptures from Greek, Hebrew, and Latin into the languages of the common people. John Wyclif (1328–1384), who produced the first English translation, wrote, "The New Testament is of full authority, and open to the understanding of simple men. . . . " In addition, the invention of the printing press greatly assisted in the dissemination of copies of Scripture. Martin Luther (1483–1546) encouraged people to study the Bible for themselves, based on his conviction "*Sola Scriptura*" ("Scripture alone") as the only authority in the life of a Christian. Later, European groups like the Anabaptists and the Puritans in England established small-group Bible studies as a source of spiritual and emotional strength within their ranks.

Modern Fundamentalism

The practice of personal and group Bible study, presently practiced in many denominational groups, was strongly encouraged by conservative, Evangelical leaders in the nineteenth and twentieth centuries. D. L. Moody (1837–1899), C. I. Scofield (1843–1921), R. A. Torrey (1856–1928), and others promoted the personal study of the printed word through their expositional teaching of the Bible. The publishing of the *Scofield Reference Bible* (1909) was later followed by a series of others (*Ryrie Study Bible, NIV Study Bible, NASB Study Bible*), all intended to encourage personal Bible study through the inclusion of background and explanatory footnotes with the

Matthew 5:17–19

17. Think not that I am come to destroy the law, or the prophets: I am not come to destroy, but to fulfill.
18. For verily I say unto you, Till heaven and earth pass, one jot or one tittle shall in no wise pass from the law, till all be fulfilled.
19. Whosoever therefore shall break one of these least commandments, and shall teach men so, he shall be called the least in the kingdom of heaven: but whosoever shall do and teach them, the same shall be called great in the kingdom of heaven.

text. Within these circles, personal devotion has come to mean Bible study and prayer.

Bible Study Methodology

Observe the Text

Look carefully at the passage and its place in the Bible in order to identify features that may have a bearing on its meaning. These factors include genre (type of literature in which the passage is written), historical background, or cultural and metaphorical expressions that come from the writer's background.

Read and Meditate upon the Text

Determine the main theme represented in the passage and try to understand how each part of the passage contributes to the overall "big idea." This is both an intellectual and a spiritual exercise.

Interpret the Text

Make observations about the meaning of the text, initially taking into consideration what the terms would have meant to its original author and readers. Bible study resources can be helpful in identifying and clarifying important background issues.

Apply the Text

Building on the application to the original recipients of the passage, determine the present application to life today. This process involves the convicting work of the Holy Spirit, taking universal spiritual principles that were true "then and there" and applying them "here and now."

John C. Hutchison

See also Bible Schools; Biblical Inerrancy; Missions; Preaching; Sunday Schools

Bibliography

Dixon, Rev. A. C. (1990) "The Scriptures." In *The Fundamentals: The Famous Sourcebook of Foundational Biblical Truths*, edited by Charles Feinberg. Grand Rapids, MI: Kregel Publications, 661–668.

Fee, Gordon, and Douglas Stuart. (1993) *How to Read the Bible for All Its Worth*, 2nd ed. Grand Rapids, MI: Zondervan Publishing.

Lindsell, Harold. (1977) *The Battle for the Bible*. Grand Rapids, MI: Zondervan Publishing.

Marsden, George M. (1982) *Fundamentalism and American Culture: The Shaping of Twentieth-Century Evangelicalism: 1870–1925*. Oxford, UK: Oxford University Press.

Russell, Walt. (2000) *Playing With Fire: How the Bible Ignites Change in Your Soul*. Colorado Springs, CO: Navpress.

Shelley, Bruce. (1982) *Church History in Plain Language*. Waco, TX: Word Books.

Biblical Criticism

Until the eighteenth century most of Christianity accepted the biblical writings as historically accurate, but with the period of the European Enlightenment, a very different interpretation began to emerge. The Enlightenment was a historic shift away from the knowing of truth from divine revelation and toward the discovery of truth through rational and empirical methods in which human reason became the only valid epistemological process. Reason, among those influenced by the shift, displaced revelation and the Bible became a central focus for this form of rational analysis.

Emergence and Purpose of Biblical Criticism

The process of secularization had begun with the abandonment of supernatural entities and explanations of life and existence for those based upon reason, science, and logic. The Bible, as the literary and religious foundation of much of Western civilization, was soon made the focus of intense critical study, using methods of scholarship that could be applied for the analysis of any form of historical literature. Thus, modern biblical criticism was born.

The word "criticism" means the use of discursive analysis leading to a rational evaluation. "Biblical criticism" refers to an examination of biblical texts using the methods that were developed primarily by German scholars in the nineteenth century, which came to be called "Higher Criticism." This criticism, which dealt with how and why the texts of the Bible were written, would eventually include source, form, literary, historical, narrative, and redaction criticism. Source criticism examines the written sources used in the writing and compilation of the biblical texts. Form criticism studies the ways the stories were transmitted from the time of Jesus to the time of the writing of the Gospels, especially as they were passed on and modified while in the oral form of transmission. Literary criticism identifies the specific kind of writing a text is, its literary genre, such as poetry, narrative, history, or fiction. Redaction criticism focuses upon the work of the final compiler of each text and how that compiler may have edited, composed, and changed the oral and written materials that were available at the time in order to make the stories or text address the redactor's own historical, religious context.

"Lower Criticism" would refer to the work of textual scholars who sought to understand, as best as possible, what was the actual wording of the original biblical texts since no original manuscripts of the biblical writings exist, only copies of copies, with many of the New Testament texts dating from the fourth to fifth centuries CE. Initially, the promoters of biblical criticism sought to show the Bible to be incorrect, contradictory, and historically unreliable. In time, some liberal theologians and scholars began to adapt the various forms of criticism to portray that, although the Bible was not without inaccuracies, myths, legends, fictions, symbolization, and while diminishing the emphasis upon supernatural events (miracles), the Bible could still be maintained to be significant for faith and living. Such scholars thought the Bible conveyed spiritual truths through fallible, humanly created stories using human language and ideas.

Biblical criticism asked such questions as: who were the authors of the texts; when and where were they written; who was the intended audience; what was the historical, religious, political, and social contexts for the writing; what form, or genre, of literature was it; were there oral and written sources used to compose the writing; what process of composition and editing did the text undergo; what was the role and input of the final writer/editor/compiler; how was symbolism used; and were myths from other cultures and religions adapted for use in the text? Basically, biblical criticism sought to interpret the biblical texts within their historical, literary contexts, searching for how and why the texts were written. Through the principles of hermeneutics (interpretation) and the methods of exegesis (analysis of a text in its context), biblical criticism was a departure from how the Bible had often been read and understand.

The Response of Fundamentalism to Biblical Criticism

In 1895 at the Niagara Bible Conference, a list of five basic, or fundamental, beliefs was written. The first belief was the inerrancy of the Bible. Taking the name from a series of pamphlets called "The Fundamentals: A Testimony to the Truth, " (1910–1915), what soon thereafter came to be called Fundamentalism was a response to what were perceived to be direct challenges and attacks against the validity of the Bible and of Christianity itself. With this reaction, Fundamentalism would see itself in a battle for the soul of the Christian faith in which biblical Fundamentalists were the true believers under attack from a vast variety of the degenerative ideas of the modern age.

The nineteenth century had ended with theories of an enormously long process of evolutionary development (Darwinism). These therories were based on a mechanical, natural selection that seemed to many to eliminate the role and need for a Creator (God), on geological evidence for enormous aeons of time instead of the accepted age of the earth at only a few thousand years, and on the gradual secularization of societies with a diminished role of the church. For the first time in human history, there were significant numbers of agnostics and theoretical atheists. That the Bible itself was coming under intense scholarly scrutiny using the same methods as those for analyzing any historical texts, was the epitome of all that was wrong with "modernism" and when reason, not revelation, became central. Revivalism, which would become of great importance in Fundamentalism, had declined. The periods of early, great awakenings or times of revivalism were historically distant. With what was thought to be an all-out attack upon the Bible and Christian faith, belief in the Bible came to be the basis for a call for a new age of revivalism to overcome the evil ideas and forces at work in the modern world.

One of the "fundaments" upon which Fundamentalism was based, and which to this day unites Christian Fundamentalists more than anything else, is the belief in the inerrancy of the Bible because it comes from God and God does not deceive or dilute truth. The biblical texts were to be read in a strictly literalist way because the Bible was not like any other ancient or modern book. It was believed to have supernatural origins that led it to serve as the source of individual and societal significance. To apply the methods of biblical criticism to the Bible was seen as desacralizing it and rejecting the communication and content of God's truths and teachings to humanity.

Fundamentalism, in its reaction against a scientific method in which "truth" was equated with "facts" and historical accuracy, came to embrace the same criteria for truth as was held by the science it rejected. Fundamentalism believes that truth, including in the Bible, signifies factually, historically correctness. Thus, because the Bible is held to be true, everything in the Bible is historically and factually correct. Other forms of Christianity disagree with this view of what constitutes biblical truth, but it is the hallmark of Fundamentalism.

Therefore, Fundamentalism rejects the work of biblical criticism and very actively opposes it with its own position. To Fundamentalism, biblical criticism is one of the destructive products of the Enlightenment and threatens to sever Western civilization from its religious foundations. Furthermore, based upon the Fundamentalist view of the dualism of the natural versus the saved-by-grace person, only those who are "saved" by God can really understand the purposes and teachings of the Bible.

In today's age of "postmodernism," Fundamentalists continue to regard biblical criticism as a threat to true Christianity. They see postmodernism's rejection of the very possibility of universal truths and values as a logical consequence of what began when reason was exalted over the ancient revelation of the Bible. They believe that if the Bible is rejected and its truths disparaged by critical analysis, then nihilism and relativism are not long in coming.

Fundamentalism's View of the Bible

The Fundamentalist belief is that the Bible and the "Word of God" are identical. Although God used humans and human writings for the purpose of revealing divine truth, He did not allow those human writers to make any mistakes or errors; therefore, in their original languages (Hebrew, Aramaic, Greek) the autographs, or original texts, contained no errors whatsoever, neither of fact, geography, chronology, and so forth. This literal inerrancy is so central to Fundamentalism that it is its defining belief and source of identity, giving Fundamentalists a sense of belonging to a community that possesses the light in the midst of the prevailing darkness. Even though the original biblical manuscripts are not available, Fundamentalism maintains this view. Any errors that did appear in the Bible are because of human errors in copying and transmission over the centuries. For this reason, Fundamentalism does accept "Lower Criticism" and its work to decipher the actual wording of the original text as much as is scholarly possible. For many English-speaking Fundamentalists, the King James Version (1611 CE) of the Bible is the closest to an inerrant translation. Of course, biblical criticism counters by saying that this version of the Bible has many inaccuracies that more modern translations have eliminated by means of archeological, philological, and textual work.

Fundamentalists usually understand themselves to be the biblical "faithful remnant" who remain faithful to God's truth while all about them there is dilution, distortion, deception, heresy, and disbelief. Fundamentalism sees itself as the only fully correct manifestation of Christianity precisely because it is "Bible-believing." The only source of divine revelation is the Bible and that Bible demands to be read literally as the infallible, verbally inerrant word of God. To Fundamentalism the admission that the Bible may contain errors of any sort would be a slippery slope toward placing any and all biblical passages and writings under suspicion, thereby destroying the very foundation of Christianity.

Inerrancy puts Fundamentalism in conflict with many theories of modern science. Whereas most scientists claim that the universe is many billions of years old and began with a singular, primordial explosion ("Big Bang") and the earth itself is several billion years old, Fundamentalism's reading of the first creation story in the Book of Genesis places the beginning of the universe and earth only some six to ten thousand years ago in a creative act of God with no huge sweeps of time and no gradual evolution of humans from lesser beings. Another example of this conflict is the famous Scopes "Monkey Trial" in Tennessee in 1925. At that trial a public school teacher, John Scopes, was the defendant accused of teaching Darwinian evolution. Scopes was defended by Clarence Darrow and the opposing counsel was the famous orator, William Jennings Bryan. Scopes lost the trial, but when Bryan turned the trial away from the question of responsibility to decide what is taught in the public schools and into a fierce debate about the inerrancy of the Bible taking precedence over the empirical findings of science, Fundamentalists seemed to many people to be dismissed as an enclave of uneducated, anachronistic religious fanatics.

The Revival of Fundamentalism

Although debate continues over creation and evolution, Fundamentalism ended the twentieth century as one of the most significant religious movements of the age. It skillfully used the technology of the age to call for a return to a biblically based worldview that rejects the very science that produced that technology. Fundamentalists recognized the need for education and the negative perception of Fundamentalism from the Scopes trial gradually faded, as the movement's image improved socially and economically. While not abandoning its millennarian view that the state of the world would soon come to a destructive end and that Christ would soon return, more attention seems to have been given to aiding the poor around the world as well as focusing primarily upon converting individuals to Fundamentalist beliefs before it was too late.

While many people in the twentieth century were greatly distressed over either the loss of the traditional meaning of life, or its growing ambiguity—as is evidenced in art, literature, music, philosophy, and more—Fundamentalism was unwavering in its insistence on the Bible's validity and it being the only pure source of scientific, historical, and religious truths. It became one of the more rapidly growing religious movements in the last third of the century most likely because of its claims of certainty of truth, clarity of morals, and assurance of salvation.

Fundamentalism has rallied around its continued opposition to theories of evolution and has advocated that if evolution must be taught in public schools, then the creation stories in Genesis should be taught as well. This is especially important with the development of the Fundamentalist-inspired "creation science" or "scientific creationism," which says that the Bible's version of the beginnings ("genesis") of the world and human life is scientifically accurate and should be presented at the very least as an alternative scientific explanation. While the courts have usually not sided with the position of Fundamentalism, it remains undeterred in proclaiming the Bible to be the only sure and true source of knowledge about God, humanity, and the world.

Alan Altany

See also Antimodernism; Biblical Inerrancy; Creationism; Secularism

Bibliography

Adam, A. K. M. (1995) *What Is Postmodern Biblical Criticism?* Minneapolis, MN: Fortress Press.

Armstrong, Karen. (2000) *The Battle for God.* New York: Alfred A. Knopf.

"Bible Studies." http://www.biblebelievers.com/BibleStudies.html

"Biblical Criticism." http://www.religioustolerance.org/chr_hcri.htm

"Biblical Fundamentalism." http://www.biblebelievers.net/Fundmentalism/kjcfunda.htm

Bray, Gerald. (2000) *Biblical Interpretation: Past & Present.* Downers Grove, IL: Intervarsity.

Carpenter, Joel. (1997) *Revive Us Again: The Reawakening of American Fundamentalism.* Oxford: Oxford University Press.

Elwell, Walter, and J. D. Weaver (1999) *Bible Interpreters of the Twentieth Century.* Grand Rapids, MI: Baker Book House.

Friedman, R. E. (1987) *Who Wrote the Bible?* New York: HarperSanFrancisco.

Grant, Robert McQueen. (1984) *A Short History of the Interpretation of the Bible.* Minneapolis, MN: Fortress Press.

"How Various Christians Interpret the Bible." http://www.religioustolerance.org/chr_inte.htm

"Inerrancy." http://www.religioustolerance.org/inerrant.htm

Lawrence, Bruce. (1989) *Defenders of God: The Fundamentalist Revolt Against the Modern* Age. San Francisco: Harper & Row.

Marsden, George. (1991) *Understanding Fundamentalism & Evangelicalism.* Grand Rapids, MI: Wm. B. Eerdmans.

McKim, Donald. (1998) *Historical Handbook of Major Biblical Interpreters.* Downers Grove, IL: Intervarsity.

Montague, George T. (1997) *Understanding the Bible: A Basic Introduction to Biblical Interpretation.* Mahwah, NJ: Paulist Press.

Society of Biblical Literature: Electronic Journals. http://www.sbl-site2.org/e-journals.php3.

Thiselton, Anthony. (1997) *New Horizons in Hermeneutics.* Grand Rapids, MI: Zondervan Publishing.

Biblical Inerrancy

Inerrancy is a theory about the authority of the Christian Bible. It holds that the original writings—the "autographs"—are free of error in all about which they speak, matters scientific and historical as well as theological and moral. Their errorless status is based on the work of the Holy Spirit, the third Person of the Trinity, who superintended the biblical words used to describe the events that took place and to express the teachings given.

The language of "inerrancy" regarding scriptural authority emerged in the late eighteenth and early nineteenth centuries, given prominence by orthodox Protestant theologians. Its concern for exactitude, and the treatment of the Bible as a reliable source of information about all aspects of the world, reflected the growing influence of science. Inerrantists sought to counter the incursions of the Enlightenment with their own form of empirical and rational argument.

The Views of Modern Inerrantists

The concept of inerrancy today is regularly confused with the view of oracularity. The latter asserts that the words of the original Scripture were dictated by the Holy Spirit, becoming the literal oracles of God. The former, inerrancy, takes account of the human factor in the process of inspiration, adducing the varying vocabulary pools, styles of authorship, and literary conventions found in the different books of the Bible, with God protecting the authors from the erroneous use of their words. While allowing for authorial creativity in the writing process, therefore, inerrantists assert that such takes place under a divine supervision that precludes mistakes of any kind on any and every topic considered. While sharing the common conviction of Scripture's plenary inspiration, inerrantists divide into conservative, moderate, and liberal parties. Conservative inerrantists trust the transmissive power of the Holy Spirit to assure that certain received versions and translations carry the authority of the inaccessible autographs. This perspective is noted for its practice of harmonizing apparently conflicting reports of events or teachings, arguing for the historical veracity of accounts of the world's beginnings and endings, and attacking critical scholarship as the tool of "secular humanism."

Moderate inerrantists allow for a more influential role of the human factor in the creation of the originals, in particular the impact of culture and the conditioning of the text by historical context. Historical and literary criticism that discloses oriental hyperbole in reportage of events, the function of other genre such as narrative in biblical writing, and the limitations in ancient cosmology is not rejected, although a sharp eye is kept out for the intrusion of an antisupernaturalist bias in biblical scholarship. Textual criticism that seeks for the closest approximation to the yet inaccessible originals is actively pursued. While the autographs are sacrosanct in all respects, subsequent editions and translations bear the marks of the human hand, which make possible small errors in historical and scientific details. The salvific heart of Scripture in matters of faith and morals, however, is secured, because the trajectory of the Spirit's power that produced the originals assures the absolute trustworthiness of today's approved texts.

Liberal inerrantists acknowledge a greater role for the human factor in the creation of the errorless autographs, as well as in the transmission process, granting a larger place for the legitimacy of historical, literary, and textual criticism. The most notable feature of this view is the insistence on the recognition of varying genre in biblical writings. It looks for authorial intention, reading, for example, accounts of the world's creation and consummation as theological in genre and housed in primitive cosmology, and therefore not to be treated as "informational," that is, accurate history in the modern sense.

THE CHICAGO STATEMENT ON BIBLICAL INERRANCY

Articles of Affirmation and Denial

Article I

We affirm that the Holy Scriptures are to be received as the authoritative Word of God.

We deny that the Scriptures receive their authority from the Church, tradition, or any other human source.

Article II

We affirm that the Scriptures are the supreme written norm by which God binds the conscience, and that the authority of the Church is subordinate to that of Scripture.

We deny that Church creeds, councils, or declarations have authority greater than or equal to the authority of the Bible.

Article III

We affirm that the written Word in its entirety is revelation given by God.

We deny that the Bible is merely a witness to revelation, or only becomes revelation in encounter, or depends on the responses of men for its validity.

Article IV

We affirm that God who made mankind in His image has used language as a means of revelation.

We deny that human language is so limited by our creatureliness that it is rendered inadequate as a vehicle for divine revelation. We further deny that the corruption of human culture and language through sin has thwarted God's work of inspiration.

Article V

We affirm that God's revelation in the Holy Scriptures was progressive.

We deny that later revelation, which may fulfill earlier revelation, ever corrects or contradicts it. We further deny that any normative revelation has been given since the completion of the New Testament writings.

Article VI

We affirm that the whole of Scripture and all its parts, down to the very words of the original, were given by divine inspiration.

We deny that the inspiration of Scripture can rightly be affirmed of the whole without the parts, or of some parts but not the whole.

(cont.)

Evangelical Interpretations of Inerrancy

Inerrancy is sometimes deployed as the criterion of faithfulness in Evangelical circles. It may function as a loyalty oath for faculty in some Evangelical seminaries or a litmus test for membership in Evangelical societies, and may be written into the charters of Evangelical para-church movements.

The heated controversies surrounding inerrancy, and the misunderstandings over its meaning, have prompted many Evangelicals to look for other ways to assert and interpret biblical authority. One avenue pursued is to espouse an "infallibilist" rather than an "inerrantist" view of Scripture. The former holds that Scripture is written for "salvific" purposes, to convert people to Christ and to nurture them in the Christian life. Hence it is viewed as an instrument of salvation utterly trustworthy in faith and morals, not an encyclopedia of knowledge on all human concerns. Infallibilists acknowledge Scripture's cultural conditioning in matters of science and history and accept historical-critical and literary-critical

THE CHICAGO STATEMENT ON BIBLICAL INERRANCY (cont.)

Article VII

We affirm that inspiration was the work in which God by His Spirit, through human writers, gave us His Word. The origin of Scripture is divine. The mode of divine inspiration remains largely a mystery to us.

We deny that inspiration can be reduced to human insight, or to heightened states of consciousness of any kind.

Article VIII

We affirm that God in His Work of inspiration utilized the distinctive personalities and literary styles of the writers whom He had chosen and prepared.

We deny that God, in causing these writers to use the very words that He chose, overrode their personalities.

Article IX

We affirm that inspiration, though not conferring omniscience, guaranteed true and trustworthy utterance on all matters of which the Biblical authors were moved to speak and write.

We deny that the finitude or fallenness of these writers, by necessity or otherwise, introduced distortion or falsehood into God's Word.

Article X

We affirm that inspiration, strictly speaking, applies only to the autographic text of Scripture, which in the providence of God can be ascertained from available manuscripts with great accuracy. We further affirm that copies and translations of Scripture are the Word of God to the extent that they faithfully represent the original.

We deny that any essential element of the Christian faith is affected by the absence of the autographs. We further deny that this absence renders the assertion of Biblical inerrancy invalid or irrelevant.

Article XI

We affirm that Scripture, having been given by divine inspiration, is infallible, so that, far from misleading us, it is true and reliable in all the matters it addresses.

We deny that it is possible for the Bible to be at the same time infallible and errant in its assertions. Infallibility and inerrancy may be distinguished, but not separated.

Article XII

We affirm that Scripture in its entirety is inerrant, being free from all falsehood, fraud, or deceit.

We deny that Biblical infallibility and inerrancy are limited to spiritual, religious, or redemptive themes, exclusive of assertions in the fields of history and science. We further deny that scientific hypotheses about earth history may properly be used to overturn the teaching of Scripture on creation and the flood.

Article XIII

We affirm the propriety of using inerrancy as a theological term with reference to the complete truthfulness of Scripture.

We deny that it is proper to evaluate Scripture according to standards of truth and error that are alien to its usage or purpose. We further deny that inerrancy is negated by Biblical phenomena such as a lack of modern technical precision, irregularities of grammar or spelling, observational descriptions of nature, the reporting of falsehoods, the use of hyperbole and round numbers, the topical arrangement of material, variant selections of material in parallel accounts, or the use of free citations.

Article XIV

We affirm the unity and internal consistency of Scripture.

We deny that alleged errors and discrepancies that have not yet been resolved vitiate the truth claims of the Bible.

Article XV

We affirm that the doctrine of inerrancy is grounded in the teaching of the Bible about inspiration.

We deny that Jesus' teaching about Scripture may be dismissed by appeals to accommodation or to any natural limitation of His humanity.

Article XVI

We affirm that the doctrine of inerrancy has been integral to the Church's faith throughout its history.

We deny that inerrancy is a doctrine invented by Scholastic Protestantism, or is a reactionary position postulated in response to negative higher criticism.

Article XVII

We affirm that the Holy Spirit bears witness to the Scriptures, assuring believers of the truthfulness of God's written Word.

We deny that this witness of the Holy Spirit operates in isolation from or against Scripture.

Article XVIII

We affirm that the text of Scripture is to be interpreted by grammatico-historical exegesis, taking account of its literary forms and devices, and that Scripture is to interpret Scripture.

We deny the legitimacy of any treatment of the text or quest for sources lying behind it that leads to relativizing, dehistoricizing, or discounting its teaching, or rejecting its claims to authorship.

Article XIX

We affirm that a confession of the full authority, infallibility, and inerrancy of Scripture is vital to a sound understanding of the whole of the Christian faith. We further affirm that such confession should lead to increasing conformity to the image of Christ.

We deny that such confession is necessary for salvation. However, we further deny that inerrancy can be rejected without grave consequences both to the individual and to the Church.

Source: International Council on Biblical Inerrancy. *Historic Church Documents.* www.reformed.org.

scholarship, albeit alert to the appearance of an antisupernaturalist bias in its methods and conclusions. Infallibilists have their own internal differences, some holding to a uniform pattern of faith and morals throughout Scripture, others seeing a progression of teaching within the Bible, and still others judging all theological and moral assertions in Scripture by their conformity to the norm of Christ.

Biblical Inerrancy and Fundamentalism

The relation of the claims for biblical inerrancy to Protestant Fundamentalism is a complex one. Many inerrantists, especially moderate and liberal ones, are not self-identified Fundamentalists. In fact, they share with infallibilists the current attempt to distinguish themselves as *Evangelicals* from those who are *Fundamentalists*. Fundamentalism, so understood, is a mind-set that sharply divides up the world between "us" and "them," and wages a religious war in kind, the armies of light against the armies of night. Evidence of such is the struggle in some American denominations for the control of its seminaries, agencies, and congregations. While all its members or leaders might profess inerrancy in some form, the true test of faithfulness becomes the espousal of conservative inerrancy as the *Kampfbegriff*, the "fighting word," in the warfare against the heresy everywhere thought to be found. Thus, Fundamentalism, as it functions in American church life in particular, is the focus on one of a longer list of "fundamentals" of the earlier movement, inerrancy, becoming the defining characteristic of a faithful church and believing Christian.

Gabriel Fackre

See also Bible; Bible Study; Literalism; New Testament; Old Testament

Bibliography

Fackre, Gabriel. (1987) *The Christian Story*. Vol. 2 of *Authority: Scripture in the Church for the World*. Grand Rapids, MI: Wm. B. Eerdmans.

Geisler, Norman L., ed. (1979) *Inerrancy*. Grand Rapids, MI: Zondervan Publishing.

Henry, Carl F. H. (1979) *God, Revelation and Authority*. In *God Who Speaks and Shows, vol. IV*. Waco, TX: Word.

Youngblood, Ronald, ed. (1984) *Evangelicals and Inerrancy*. Nashville, TN: Nelson.

Biblical Inspiration

Why is Scripture authoritative? The Protestant Reformers answered that "this Word of God was not sent nor delivered by the will of man, but that *holy men of God spake as they were moved by the Holy Ghost . . .* to commit his revealed will to writing (Cochrane 1966: 190). The Second Vatican Council stated the Roman Catholic view in similar terms: "Divine revelation, which is contained and presented in Holy Scripture, was committed to writing under the Holy Spirit's influx" (Flannery 1979: 11). Classical Christianity, therefore, holds that the authority of the Bible rests on its "inspiration," the unique knowledge-giving work of the Holy Spirit, the third Person of the Trinity.

Warrants are sought within Scripture itself for its singularly inspired status. 2 Timothy 3:16 (NRSV) is the text most frequently cited: "All scripture is inspired by God [*theopneustos*, God-breathed] and is useful for teaching, for reproof, for correction, for training in righteousness." Also referenced are more general texts such as John 20:31 ("But these are written so you may come to believe."); 2 Peter 1:19–21 ("we have the prophetic message . . . a lamp shining in a dark place"); and 2 Peter 3:15–16 ("our brother Paul wrote to you according to the wisdom given to him"). This limited textual evidence prompts the judgment that the doctrine of inspiration, like the doctrine of the Trinity, rests, finally, on inference from the total witness of Scripture. Giving further reason is the belief that the Spirit speaks from within its pages ever and again to the church that chose by the process of canonization to make itself accountable to "the Word written."

Perspectives on Biblical Inspiration

That Scripture is inspired is generally held to be the case in all branches of the church, but opinion is divided on *how* inspiration takes place. Some have spoken of the work of the Holy Spirit as the "dictation" of its very words, the vowel points in ancient Hebrew included. Most Christian traditions have taken another tack because of the variety of writing styles and language pools discernible in the different books of the Bible. Those who have wanted to press the case for the biblical words being errorless without espousing the dictation theory speak of the *superintendence* of the original writings by the Holy Spirit. Such protects the human and culturally shaped language of the Bible from mistakes in anything about which it speaks, with "plenary verbal inspiration" becoming a key formulation.

Another perspective on the *how* of biblical inspiration stresses the work of the Holy Spirit in bringing to light the theological and moral content of Scripture. Here the words of the Bible are treated as human testimony to, or vehicles of, the "Word" that is contained in Scripture. Allowance is thereby made for the cultural conditioning of its writers, with critical scholarship given a role in separating the time-bound aspects of the Bible from its perennial truth. This content view of inspiration takes various forms, from Evangelical "infallibilists" seeking the salvific essentials in Scripture, to the Roman Catholic focus on its "plan of salvation"(Vatican II), the traditional Protestant quest for the "gospel" substance of Scripture, the scholar's interest in the "ideas" of the Bible to a more "existential" understanding of Scripture as the occasion for an enlightening and convincing Word to be spoken to the heart of believers or to the mind of the Christian community.

Along with the differences between those who associate inspiration with words or content is the debate between the exponents of individual or social inspiration. The former assert the individual authors to be inspired, either in mantic fashion in seizures of the Spirit, or through a more cognitive infusion entailing words or insights, or in intuitive experiences with revelatory import. The latter interpret inspiration communally. This can mean placing the locus of the Spirit's work initially in the traditions of Israel and subsequently in the earliest Christian communities, moving from oral to written stages, with special status given to the Bible's final form. Social inspiration can also be understood as a work begun in biblical times but continuing now in varied ways—in church, academy, and social experience—that bring out the *sensus plenior*, the fuller meaning of Scripture, or in a more restricted fashion in which a magisterium (viz., the teaching office of the Roman Catholic Church) or a community of hermeneutical privilege (viz., the oppressed) is the medium of a continuing inspiration.

Implicit in the foregoing is yet another dispute on the *how* of inspiration, its locus in the past or present. Those who find inspiration taking place in Scripture as such, in any form—words, ideas, authors, ancient communities—give pride of place to the past. Those who speak about continuing inspiration—in persons or interpreting communities—accent the importance of the present. The latter also applies to the more general understanding of the subject at hand, Scripture as "inspiring," that is, able to evoke new ideas or commitments quite apart from any reference to a special work of the third Person of the Trinity.

Catholic and Protestant Views of Inspiration

While both Scripture and the subsequent tradition of the church are considered by historic Christian faith to be authoritative and interrelated, priorities are also honored. Roman Catholic teaching describes Scripture as the *norma normans et non normata* (the norm that governs but is not governed—the Council of Trent). A comparable Protestant view is found in the Lutheran Book of Concord, which teaches that Scripture is the *norma normans* (the norm that

governs) and tradition is the *norma normata* (the norm that is governed). The work of the Holy Spirit in establishing priority in authority is sometimes described in terms of the *inspiration* of Scripture as primary and the *illumination* of the church as secondary.

Biblical inspiration can be viewed in the context of the wider concept, revelation, and is so understood in many Christian traditions, either explicitly or implicitly. Revelation is the disclosure of who God is and what God does. Scripture gives us a narrative of the divine disclosure. It begins with an "original revelation" in Creation, but one soon distorted by the fall of the world into sin. Enough knowledge of the purposes of God to keep the Story going forward is preserved through the covenant with Noah, a "general revelation" in conscience and history. "Special revelation" occurs in the actions of God among a chosen people—Israel. Its fullness appears as the Word of God becomes flesh in Jesus Christ. The trustworthy record and interpretation of the acts of God in Israel and Christ is given by the Holy Spirit through the inspiration of the Old and New Testaments. The reception of the knowledge so communicated is made possible by the work of the same Spirit in the illumination of the church—granting it a right interpretation and growing understanding of its truth, of individuals within it as their hearts and minds are enlightened, and finally, of the world in its entirety at the eschatological close of the Story, when we no longer "see in a mirror, dimly, but . . . see face to face" (1 Corinthians 13:12).

Gabriel Fackre

See also Bible Study; Biblical Inerrancy; Common Sense Philosophy; Holy Spirit

Bibliography

Achtemeier, Paul J. (1980) *The Inspiration of Scripture: Problems and Proposals.* Philadelphia: The Westminster Press.

Cochrane, Arthur C., ed. (1966) "Reformed Confessions of the 16th Century." In *The Belgic Confession of Faith, 1561.* Philadelphia: The Westminster Press, 185–219.

Fackre, Gabriel. (1997) *The Doctrine of Revelation: A Narrative Interpretation.* Edinburgh Studies in Constructive Theology. Edinburgh: Edinburgh University Press and Grand Rapids, MI: Wm. B. Eerdmans.

Flannery, Austin. O. P., ed. (1975) "Vatican Council II: The Conciliar and Post-Conciliar Documents." In

The Dogmatic Constitution on Divine Revelation. Collegeville, MN: The Liturgical Press, 750–765.

Gnuse, Robert. (1985) *The Authority of the Bible: Theories of Inspiration, Revelation and the Canon of Scripture.* New York: Paulist Press.

Black Church, The

Numerous scholars refer to the "Negro church" or "black church" in their discussion of African-American religion in the United States (DuBois 1903; Mays and Nicholson 1933; Woodson 1945; Frazier 1974; Wilmore 1983; Lincoln and Mamiya 1990). Implicitly, this term generally refers to African-American Baptist and Methodist churches of various types, but it also has been applied to many other religious bodies within the African-American experience. While the concept of the black church has a certain analytical value, it also tends to essentialize the African-American religious experience that has not been uniform or monolithic. The black church, especially during the twentieth century, took a multiplicity of interrelated trajectories. Early on, various African-American social scientists made it possible to appreciate religious pluralism among black people (Jones 1939; Fauset 1971; Drake and Cayton 1945). The same holds true for "fundamentalism" in African-American religion, as there is both diversity across the spectrum of black churches and also variation from Fundamentalism in white American churches.

In addition to exemplifying the variety and richness of African-American social life, the black church tells us much about the position and condition of black people in the United States. Through religion, African Americans found a voice, indeed multiple and variegated voices, to express not only their spiritual quest but also their earthly trials and social yearnings. In this interplay of worldly and otherworldly images, African Americans constructed their cultural identity. Consequently, African-American politics has always had and continues to have a decidedly religious slant, while African-American religion is deeply political. African-American religions derive from many sources, but three are of central significance: (1) influences from various parts of Africa; (2) borrowings from the patterns of European and American cultures; and (3) religious responses of African Americans to their subordinate status within the racist and classist structure of a capitalist political economy.

The "Invisible Institution" under Slavery

As opposed to the organized congregations that developed among free blacks, particularly in the North during the antebellum (pre–Civil War) period, Frazier (1974) referred to the religion of the slaves as the "invisible institution." Slaves worshipped in a variety of settings: with whites, with free blacks, exclusively with fellow slaves, and in private. Since they often did not find services in white-controlled churches to be especially meaningful, many resented the requirement to attend and, consequently, met for services apart from whites whenever the opportunity arose. Such meetings were conducted in the slave quarters, "praise houses" (small buildings for worship), "hush arbors" (secret meeting places), or, if greater seclusion was required, deep in the woods, swamps, and caverns.

The Black Church Independence Movement

Scholars referring to "independent" black churches during the antebellum period often fail to emphasize that independence is a matter of degree. Black churches included unaffiliated black congregations; black congregations pastored by a white minister and others by a black minister, which were affiliated with a white-controlled association or denomination; congregations affiliated with a separate black church regional association; and congregations affiliated with a black national denomination, such as the African Methodist Episcopal (AME) Church. Despite limits on their freedom, independent black churches constituted the one institution where African Americans were able to come together as a community, especially in the South.

The appearance of separate black Baptist churches was an outgrowth of the First and Second Great Awakenings during the eighteenth century. More black people were attracted to the Baptists than to the Quakers, Anglicans, Congregationalists, Presbyterians, and even the Methodists. While most early black Baptist churches were pastored by free people or ex-slaves, several of them were established by slaves. During the first decade of the eighteenth century, the African Baptist faith took root among Northern blacks, many of whom were fugitive slaves and free blacks from the South. Black Methodists, although slower to found independent churches, were able to move toward denominational structures well before their Baptist brethren. The growth of both the AME Church and the African Methodist Episcopal (AME) Zion Church occurred primarily in the North during the antebellum period. The aftermath of the Civil War had an unparalleled impact on the growth of black church membership, transforming the South into a vast missionary territory. While both the AME and AME Zion churches entered the South as bitter rivals, they also faced fierce competition from the Methodist Episcopal Church, a white-controlled institution based in the North and, after 1870, the Colored (later Christian) Methodist Episcopal Church.

The Black Rural Church

In 1900, more than ninety percent of African Americans still resided below the Mason–Dixon line. The outmigration of African Americans from the rural South to both the cities of the North and the South had a significant impact on the black rural church during the first half of the twentieth century. As a consequence, most black churches in the countryside have not had regular or full-time ministers. The common responses to the shortage of ministers have been intermittent scheduling of Sunday services and greater lay control over church affairs. Many of the black Baptist churches in small Southern communities are not affiliated with any of the national Baptist denominations, the first of which—namely, the National Baptist Convention, USA—was formed in 1895.

Johnson (1941: 169) contends that the black rural church is a "conservative institution" whose "greatest value appears to be that of providing emotional relief for the fixed problems of a hard life." In his assertion that the "black church functioned as the institutional center of the modern civil rights movement," Morris (1984: 4) is by and large referring to the complex of black urban churches in the South rather than its rural counterparts. Nevertheless, an unknown number of black rural churches did play a supportive role in the civil rights movement, and some were among the many Southern black churches burned or bombed during the 1960s.

The Diversification of African-American Religion during the Twentieth Century

The rural church was the "sentimental" model that the migrants hoped to participate in when they attended the large mainstream Baptist and Methodist congregations of the North and the South. Since they often felt marginal in the class-stratified mainstream churches, many migrants attempted to recreate the ethos of the rural church in storefronts and house churches. The migrants frequently established independent Baptist congregations that often sooner or later became affiliated with one of the national Baptist conventions. Often, however, the migrants were attracted to the "gods of the black metropolis" (Fauset 1971), that is, the charismatic prophets and messiahs who established a wide array of Judaic, Islamic, Holiness-Pentecostal (Sanctified), and Spiritual sects as well as groups such as the African Orthodox Church and Father Divine's Peace Mission movement. The Depression accelerated the process of religious diversification. As Wilmore (1983: 163) asserts, "the black community, by the end of the 1930s, was literally glutted with churches of every variety."

Most African-American religious groups fit into one of several types: mainstream denominations, messianic-nationalist sects, conversionist sects, and thaumaturgical sects (Baer and Singer 1992). The mainstream churches are committed, at least in theory, to a reformist strategy of social action that will enable blacks to become better integrated into American society. Although many of their congregations conduct expressive religious services, churches affiliated with mainstream denominations often display a strong commitment to political protest, social uplift, and church-related colleges. Members of these churches frequently view institutional racism as a barrier to the attainment of the American Dream. Most mainstream congregations are affiliated with the three National Baptist conventions—the AME Church, the AME Zion Church, and the Christian Methodist Episcopal Church—but some are affiliated with various white-controlled denominations, particularly the Catholic, United Methodist, Presbyterian, and Congregational churches.

Messianic-nationalist sects generally are established by charismatic messianic figures who promise to deliver black people from white oppression. In their initial stages, these sects reject "Negro identity" and define blacks as the original human beings. Messianic-nationalist sects express strong criticism of white racism and create alternative communities, businesses, and schools. African-American messianic nationalism has exhibited Judaic, Islamic, and Christian forms. Black Judaic or Hebraic sects include the Church of the Living God, the Pillar Ground of Truth for All Nations, the Church of God and Saints of Christ, and the Original Hebrew Israelite Nation.

Islamic sects include the Moorish Science Temple founded by Noble Drew Ali in Newark around 1913, the Nation of Islam established by Wallace D. Fard in Detroit in 1930, the Ahmadiya Moslem movement based in Chicago, and the Hanafis of Washington, DC. Following the mysterious death of Fard in the early 1930s, Elijah Muhammed moved the main contingent of the Nation of Islam to Chicago from where it gradually spread to other cities. The Nation underwent rapid growth in the 1960s due to the charismatic and militant style manifested by Malcolm X, who had converted to Islam while in prison. Following the assassination of this leader in 1965 and the death of Elijah Muhammed in 1975, Wallace D. Muhammed led the transformation of the Nation of Islam into the American Muslim Mission. To counter the Mission's shift to orthodox Islam, Louis Farrakhan established a reconstituted Nation of Islam. Farrakhan served as the key organizer of the One Million Man March in March 1995—the "greatest black manifestation thus far in US history" (Gardell 1996: 5).

The smallest wing of messianic nationalism remained within the Christian fold. It has included the African Orthodox Church established by George McGuire as the religious arm of Marcus Garvey's Universal Negro Improvement Association, and the Black Christian National Church established by Albert Cleage, a former United Church of Christ minister who began to assert in the 1960s that Jesus was a revolutionary who came to free peoples of color from white oppression.

Conversionist sects characteristically adopt expressive forms of religious behavior, such as shouting, ecstatic dancing, and glossolalia (speaking in tongues) as outward manifestations of "sanctification." They stress a puritanical morality and are often otherworldly and apolitical, although some congregations engage in social activism. Conversionist sects encompass a wide array of Holiness-Pentecostal (or Sanctified) sects and smaller Baptist sects. The Church of God in Christ (COGIC) is the largest African-American conversionist sect. Although it still exhibits many conversionist elements, this body has been undergoing a process of mainstreaming. Other conversionist bodies include the Church of Christ (Holiness), USA; the Pentecostal Assemblies of the World; and the National Primitive Baptist Convention. Although the more established conversionist bodies, such as the COGIC, prohibit women from serving as bishops and pastors, many others were established by women and have female pastors and overseers of associations.

Thaumaturgical sects maintain that the most direct means of achieving socially desired objectives, such as financial prosperity, prestige, love, and health, or to obtain esoteric knowledge and develop a positive attitude, is to engage in various magico-religious rituals. These groups generally accept the cultural patterns, values, and beliefs of the larger society but tend to eschew social activism. Spiritual churches constitute the foremost example of the thaumaturgical sect (Baer 1984). These groups blend together elements from American spiritualism, Roman Catholicism, African-American Protestantism, and voodoo or Haitian *vodun* as well as, depending upon the association or congregation, other religious traditions, such as New Thought, Judaism, Islam, and astrology. Most Spiritual churches are small and cater primarily to the lower class, but others are large and cater to the affluent working and middle classes. The Metropolitan Spiritual Churches of Christ with some eighty congregations is the largest of the many Spiritual associations. Even more so than Sanctified churches, Spiritual churches provide women with a vehicle for attaining religious leadership. Although not a part of the Spiritual movement per se, the United Church and Science Living Institute, founded by the Reverend Frederik Eikenrenkoetter (better known as Rev. Ike), is the best known of the African-American thaumaturgical sects.

Fundamentalism in African-American Religion

Relatively little has been written about Fundamentalism among African-American religious groups, in contrast to that written about this topic in white religious groups in the United States. Like their counterparts, most black Baptists and Holiness-Pentecostals accept a literal interpretation of the Bible. Undoubtedly, many middle-class members of the National Baptist conventions and the African Methodist churches, as well as members of black congregations in various white-controlled mainstream denominations, subscribe to a figurative or an allegorical interpretation of the Bible. Indeed, a growing number of young black men and women have obtained training from predominantly white liberal seminaries, such as Union Theological Seminary in New York City, and the generally liberal Interdenominational Theological Center affiliated with Atlanta University, a prominent black institution. From a theological perspective,

Sanders (1996: 140) asserts that Sanctified people (and presumably many black Baptists and some black Methodists) constitute "liberal literalists" because they are not a part of white Fundamentalism, which has a long history of supporting conservative political stances, harkening back to a defense of slavery in the nineteenth century to the contemporary agenda of the religious Right. While Spiritual people often believe in a literal interpretation of the Bible, their acceptance of various unorthodox beliefs clearly distinguish them from the great majority of Christian Fundamentalists. Finally, the original African-American Islamic sects adopted theological beliefs that clearly differentiate them from Islamic Fundamentalism as it exists in the Middle East. Conversely, the reconstituted Nation of Islam perhaps may be defined as an Islamic neo-Fundamentalist Islamic sect of sorts in that it asserts that it accepts the "fundamentals" of the original Nation of Islam as taught by W. D. Fard and Elijah Muhammed.

Hans A. Baer

See also African-American Holiness-Pentecostal Movement; Azusa Street Revival

Bibliography

Baer, Hans A. (1984) *The Black Spiritual Movement: A Religious Response to Racism.* Knoxville: University of Tennessee Press.

Baer, Hans A., and Merrill Singer. (1992) *African-American Religion in the Twentieth-Century: Varieties of Protest and Accommodation.* Knoxville: University of Tennessee Press.

Drake, St. Clair, and Horace R. Cayton. (1945) *Black Metropolis.* New York: Harcourt, Brace.

DuBois, W. E. B. (1903) *The Negro Church in America.* Atlanta: Atlanta University Press.

Fauset, Arthur H. (1971) *Black Gods of the Metropolis.* Philadelphia: University of Pennsylvania Press.

Frazier, E. Franklin. (1974) *The Negro Church in America.* New York: Schocken.

Gardell, Mattias. (1996) *In the Name of Elijah Muhammed: Louis Farrakhan and the Nation of Islam.* Durham, NC: Duke University Press.

Johnson, Charles. (1941) *Growing Up in the Black Belt: Negro Youth in the Rural South.* Washington, DC: American Council on Education.

Jones, Raymond. (1939) "A Comparative Study of Religious Cult Behavior among Negroes with Special Reference to Emotional Conditioning Factors." *Howard University Studies in the Social Sciences* 2, 2.

Lincoln, C. Eric, and Lawrence H. Mamiya. (1990) *The Black Church in the African-American Experience.* Durham, NC: Duke University Press.

Mays, Benjamin E., and Joseph R. Nicholson. (1933) *The Negro Church.* New York: Institute of Social and Religious Research.

Morris, Aldon D. (1984) *The Origins of the Civil Rights Movement: Black Communities Organizing for Change.* New York: Free Press.

Sanders, Cheryl Jeanne. (1996) *Saints in Exile: The Holiness-Pentecostal Experience in African American Religion and Culture.* New York: Oxford University Press.

Wilmore, Gayraud S. (1983) *Black Religion and Black Radicalism.* Maryknoll, NY: Orbis Books.

Woodson, Carter Goodwin. (1945) *The History of the Negro Church,* 2nd ed. Washington, DC: Associated Publishers.

Blasphemy

Blasphemy, as it is generally understood today, is irreverence toward the holy name of God. Whether ascribing to God qualities that are not His or denying qualities that are His, blasphemy is regarded as a grave moral sin in Judaism, Christianity, and Islam. More generally, blasphemy can be defined as calling unholy that which the blasphemer knows to be holy, or vice versa. Blasphemy is, then, an active and intentional neglect, whether in word or deed, of the distinction between the divine and the mundane.

Blasphemy is related to both apostasy and heresy, but is unique in its causes and effects. By rejecting his own religion, the apostate claims there is a better way to the Truth or salvation. Misguided or not, the heretic tries to better his religion for all its adherents by proposing a view that dissents from orthodoxy. The blasphemer, however, attempts to alter the very nature of God.

God gave to Moses, who in turn gave to the Israelite nation, the primary Old Testament (OT) injunction against blasphemy in the form of the Third Commandment: "Thou shalt not take the name of the Lord thy God in vain" (Exodus 20:7; Deuteronomy 5:11, KJV). Notably, the name of Yahweh was generally the only thing that could be blasphemed in the ancient Jewish world. So important is this commandment that Jews are forbidden by custom to say the name of God, lest it be mispronounced (see Tetragrammaton). This custom is prudent, as the OT penalty for blasphemy is death by stoning,

2 Timothy:1–5

1. This know also, that in the last days perilous times shall come.
2. For men shall be lovers of their own selves, covetous, boasters, proud, blasphemers, disobedient to parents, unthankful, unholy,
3. Without natural affection, trucebreakers, false accusers, incontinent, fierce, despisers of those that are good,
4. Traitors, heady, highminded, lovers of pleasures more than lovers of God;
5. Having a form of godliness, but denying the power thereof: from such turn away.

though modern-day penalties for blasphemy in the Jewish world do not include capital punishment (Leviticus 24:16).

In the New Testament (NT), the Greek verb *blasphemeo* is used with either God or man as its object. It is made clear several times in the NT that blasphemy is among the most repugnant of sins (Matthew 15:19; Colossians 3:8; 2 Timothy 3:1–5). Jesus Himself was accused by some of His Jewish contemporaries of blasphemy, including claiming the ability to forgive sin (Matthew 26:65; Mark 14:64; Luke 5:21; John 10:33). Because only God can forgive sin, they reasoned, Jesus had called Himself God by making such a claim. Jesus said that all blasphemies are forgivable, except blasphemy against the Holy Spirit, which is an "eternal sin" (Mark 3:28–29; Luke 12:10). Modern critics debate the meaning of this statement, but the Fundamentalist Christian generally takes it literally, meaning that blasphemy against the Holy Spirit is an unpardonable sin, resulting in eternal, fiery torment.

Islamic law is clear on the matter of blasphemy. In many Islamic countries, the death penalty is still on the books as the appropriate punishment for blasphemy, though its use today is much rarer than it was up until the twentieth century. Apostasy, as well, is punishable by death. The notion of blasphemy takes on a new dimension in Islam, because in addition to its Judeo-Christian meanings, to the Muslim it connotes treason. This reasoning is easily understood considering the inextricable relationship between religion and the state in the Islamic world.

W. Zachary P. Holt

Bibliography

Ali, Maulana Muhammad, tr. (1995) *The Holy Qur'an.* Columbus, OH: Ahmadiyyah Anjuman Isha'at Islam Lahore, Inc. USA

Archer, Gleason L. (1973) *Baker's Dictionary of Christian Ethics.* Grand Rapids, MI: Baker Book House.
Davids, Peter H. (1988) *Encyclopedia of the Bible*, vol. 1. Grand Rapids, MI: Baker Book House.
Green, William S. (1999) *The Encyclopedia of Judaism*, vol. 1. New York: Continuum Publishing Company.
Hughes, Thomas Patrick. (1885) *A Dictionary of Islam.* London: W. H. Allen & Company.
Levy, Leonard W. (1981) *Treason Against God: A History of the Offense of Blasphemy.* New York: Schocken Books.
Martin, R. P. (1962) *New Bible Dictionary.* Leicester, UK: InterVarsity Press.
Stein, Gordon. (1985) *The Encyclopedia of Unbelief.* Buffalo, NY: Prometheus Books.
Werblowsky, R. J. Zwi, and Geoffrey Wigoder, eds. (1997) *The Oxford Dictionary of the Jewish Religion.* New York: Oxford University Press.

Body of Christ, The

"The body of Christ" is a biblical metaphor for the church of Jesus Christ, which is found exclusively in the letters of the apostle Paul to the Corinthians (1 Corinthians 10:16, 17; 12:4–27), Romans (12:4–8), Ephesians (1:22–23; 2:14–16; 3:4–7; 4:11–16; 5:22–33), and Colossians (1:24; 2:18–19; 3:15). While the term "church" is sometimes used in Scripture for a local assembly of believers ("The church of God which is at Corinth," 1 Corinthians 1:2), it is also used in reference to the "universal church," the whole spiritual body of Christian believers, regardless of location, circumstances, or time, from Pentecost until the return of Christ. The church is a living organism, composed of a number of essential and mutually dependent parts, all of which partake of a common life. "The body of Christ" appears to be used exclusively as a metaphor for the universal church (Ephesians 1:22–23). Membership in this body belongs to those who are true believers in Christ (1 Corinthians 1:20) and who by virtue of that fact have been baptized into His body by the Holy Spirit (1 Corinthians 12:13). Several important concepts are drawn from the parallel between the members of the natural body and the members of the body of Christ.

Unity

There is but one true church, and as the physical body is one and yet has many members, so it is with the body of Christ (1 Corinthians 12:12; Romans 12:4–5). Paul reminds his readers of the time when Jew and Gentile were separate from Christ and from each other, but now have been brought together by the death of Christ and made into one new man, Christ having reconciled both in one body to God by putting to death the enmity between them (Ephesians 2:12–16; 4:4–5). The concept of unity is expressed in the specific work of the Spirit in which all true believers are baptized into the one body of Christ, and in the reality of the headship of Christ. Christ exercises sovereignty and direction as head of the church, bringing about the proper working of each part of the body and causing its growth, which results in the building up of itself in love (Ephesians 4:15–16). He, as the head of the church, is the savior of the body, it is subject to Him, it is loved, cleansed, nourished, cherished by Him, and the consummation will be reached when Christ presents it to Himself as a glorious church without fault or wrinkle, which is holy and blameless (Ephesians 5:22–29; Colossians 1:18; 2:18–19).

Diversity

As the physical body is one yet has many members, and all the members, though many, are one body, so, writes Paul, is Christ's body (1 Corinthians 12:12–14). He notes that there are varieties of gifts, of ministries, and of effects, yet it is the same God who works all things in all persons with the ultimate goal that these manifestations of the Spirit would be for the common good or mutual profit of the body (1 Corinthians 12:4–7). The varieties of gifts and ministries are listed in 1 Corinthians 12:8–10 and 28–30, in Romans 12:6–8, and a third, shorter list is located in Ephesians 4:11. This may simply be a shortened list, or it may present gifted individuals who are given to the body as a whole. Paul notes that Christ gave these gifted individuals to the church "for the equipping of the saints for the work of service" whose goal is to build up the body of Christ in spiritual maturity, "to the measure of the stature which belongs to the fulness of Christ" (Ephesians 4:12–13, NASB).

Mutual Dependence

As each member of the physical body is important in fulfilling its purpose, so the various members of the body of Christ are necessary to make His body complete and to fulfill its purpose. The Spirit distributes gifts to each one individually just as He wills, and God places each one of the members in the body just as He desires (1 Corinthians 12:7–24) so that "there should be no division in the body," so that members "should have the same care for one another" (1 Corinthians 12:25), and so that the church may be edified or built up by the use of the spiritual gifts distributed to the individual members of the body (1 Corinthians 14:4, 5, 12, 26). Thus, it is clear that members of the body are dependent on one another so that each may profit spiritually by the full ministry of the body members, even as each contributes his or her ministry to the whole.

Spirituality

The "born again" life of the individuals who make up the church finds its origin in the Person and work of the Holy Spirit, for Jesus said, "Unless one is born of water and the Spirit, he cannot enter into the kingdom of God. . . . [T]hat which is born of the Spirit is spirit" (John 3:5–6). The apostle Paul enlarges this concept with his statement that those who believe are baptized into the body of Christ by the Spirit, and "we were all made to drink of one Spirit" (1 Corinthians 12:13 To drink of the Spirit implies identification with Him and dependence upon Him in spiritual life, enlightenment, sustenance, and power. The result of the Holy Spirit's work in the member of Christ's body is perhaps best seen under the heading of the "fruit of the Spirit" (Galatians 5:22–23), which is nothing less than the growth of the character of Christ in the believer.

The Purpose of the Gifted Men of Ephesians 4:11

The gifted men of Ephesians 4:11 are given by Christ to His body in order to accomplish certain purposes:

1 Corinthians 10:16–17

16. The cup of blessing which we bless, is it not the communion of the blood of Christ? The bread which we break, is it not the communion of the body of Christ?

17. For we being many are one bread, and one body: for we are all partakers of that one bread.

1 Corinthians 12:4–27

4. Now there are diversities of gifts, but the same Spirit.

5. And there are differences of administrations, but the same Lord.

6. And there are diversities of operations, but it is the same God which worketh all in all.

7. But the manifestation of the Spirit is given to every man to profit withal.

8. For to one is given by the Spirit the word of wisdom; to another the word of knowledge by the same Spirit;

9. To another faith by the same Spirit; to another the gifts of healing by the same Spirit;

10. To another the working of miracles; to another prophecy; to another discerning of spirits; to another divers kinds of tongues; to another the interpretation of tongues:

11. But all these worketh that one and the selfsame Spirit, dividing to every man severally as he will.

12. For as the body is one, and hath many members, and all the members of that one body, being many, are one body: so also is Christ.

13. For by one Spirit are we all baptized into one body, whether we be Jews or Gentiles, whether we be bond or free; and have been all made to drink into one Spirit.

14. For the body is not one member, but many.

15. If the foot shall say, Because I am not the hand, I am not of the body; is it therefore not of the body?

16. And if the ear shall say, Because I am not the eye, I am not of the body; is it therefore not of the body?

17. If the whole body were an eye, where were the hearing? If the whole were hearing, where were the smelling?

18. But now hath God set the members every one of them in the body, as it hath pleased him.

19. And if they were all one member, where were the body?

20. But now are they many members, yet but one body.

21. And the eye cannot say unto the hand, I have no need of thee: nor again the head to the feet, I have no need of you.

22. Nay, much more those members of the body, which seem to be more feeble, are necessary:

23. And those members of the body, which we think to be less honourable, upon these we bestow more abundant honour; and our uncomely parts have more abundant comeliness.

24. For our comely parts have no need: but God hath tempered the body together, having given more abundant honour to that part which lacked:

25. That there should be no schism in the body; but that the members should have the same care one for another.

26. And whether one member suffer, all the members suffer with it; or one member be honoured, all the members rejoice with it.

27. Now ye are the body of Christ, and members in particular.

(1) to build up the body through the ministry of its "equipped" membership (4:12); (2) to promote the unity of the faith and the full knowledge of the Son of God (4:13); and (3) to foster the spiritual growth of the members of the body (4:14–15).

Wayne S. Flory

See also Christ

Bibliography

Chafer, Lewis Sperry. (1948) *Systematic Theology*, vol. 1. Dallas: Dallas Seminary Press.

McGrath, Alister E. (1994) *Christian Theology*. Cambridge, MA: Basil Blackwell Inc.

Ryle, John C. (c.1890) "The True Church." In *The Fundamentals*, edited by R. A. Torrey and updated by Charles L. Feinberg. (1958) Grand Rapids, MI: Kregel Publications, 552–556.

Saucy, Robert L. (1972) *The Church in God's Program*. Chicago: Moody Press.

Born Again

The term "born again" is a translation of a Greek phrase γεννηθῇ ἄνωθεν (*genneethee anoothen*), which can also be interpreted as "born anew" or "begotten from above." The term within its biblical setting is traceable to John 3:3–7 where Jesus told an enquirer, a Pharisee named Nicodemus, that he must be born anew or born again before entering the kingdom of God. Being born again is essentially a spiritual experience, denoting a change of heart or inner disposition, which comes when a person is converted to the Christian faith. The term is the same as that for regeneration or new birth, which Christians generally believe is achievable by the operation of the Holy Spirit to cleanse a person from every filth and thus become a new spiritual person. Being born again emphasizes the communication of a spiritual life in contrast to antecedent spiritual death, while regeneration stresses the beginning of a new spiritual state. This is one of the drastic teachings of Jesus to His audience, and it has never been stated so impressively before or since. Roman Catholics, Protestants, and other Christians all agree on the necessity of being born again, but differ in the manner it is accomplished in the individual.

The Biblical Background

In the Old Testament, the idea of being born again or of a regeneration is mainly applied to the work of God in bringing the nation of Israel back from idolatry and syncretism, and causing the nation to turn to Jehovah God as its Creator and Sustainer. Some of the prophets, particularly Jeremiah and Isaiah, declared that such a national rebirth will signal the beginning of the messianic rule over the people.

In the New Testament, being born again is applied significantly to the person who experiences purification brought about by God's Spirit. The Pauline and Johannine writings affirm that being born again is a once-for-all divine work whereby the sinner, who before was previously spiritually dead, is brought to life when he or she responds to the saving revelation of God in Christ. Though there is a unique factor to the Christian teaching of new birth, a similar phenomenon was also found in the pagan cults and in the mystery religions in the Greco-Roman world.

"Born Again" and Its Contemporary Application

"Born again" is an old term within the vocabulary of Evangelical Christianity, but it received much attention from the mid-1970s in connection with the Charismatic Renewal in North America and abroad. By the late 1970s, it was not uncommon to find the term "born again movement" used for some Pentecostal and charismatic churches that consider being born again as the primary Christian experience. In distancing themselves from Evangelicals, charismatic Christians make a distinction between being born again and baptism of the Holy Spirit. The former is assumed to be the first conversion experience while the latter is an experience after being born again when the Holy Spirit fully indwells in the life of the believer.

Revival services, Evangelical meetings, and personal witnessing often create the appropriate setting in which to experience the new birth. Sermons and exposition from the Scriptures on these occasions can induce a sense of guilt, and then launch the sinner into a conscious consideration of his or her life, and, finally, an attempt to seek God's forgiveness—hence, being born again. Yet, there are those who claim to be nominal Christians and become born again when they experience crises in their lives, and then join Fundamentalist groups as a last resort.

Fundamentalists insist strongly on this teaching by repudiating all the previous notions of who a Christian is. A person's previous background, which may include baptism, confirmation, Christian parentage, prayer and fasting, activities in the church, among many other activities, does not make him or

John 3:3–7

3. Jesus answered and said unto him, Verily, verily, I say unto thee, Except a man be born again, he cannot see the kingdom of God.

4. Nicodemus saith unto him, How can a man be born when he is old? can he enter the second time into his mother's womb, and be born?

5. Jesus answered, Verily, verily, I say unto thee, Except a man be born of water and of the Spirit, he cannot enter into the kingdom of God.

6. That which is born of the flesh is flesh; and that which is born of the Spirit is spirit.

7. Marvel not that I said unto thee, Ye must be born again.

her a Christian, nor can these be substituted for the new birth, which is essentially a spiritual experience. Therefore, all sins and deceitful pleasures must be renounced in order to be born again. In addition to spiritual blessings such as joy, satisfaction, and peace, which come after the new birth, it is only after the conversion experience that the privileges meant for Christians can be enjoyed.

The nature of the change in a born-again Christian can be dramatic and possibly traumatic; it can take place within a short time or over a long period. The change consists of the renunciation of the sinful lifestyle of the past, followed by purification from the defilement of sin, and the implanting of a new spiritual life, and finally the cultivation of a new moral attitude. Consequent upon being born again, a Christian is qualified to be baptised in water and partake in the Lord's Supper. In fact, a person who has been baptised in water before being born again is made to repeat the process. Fundamentalists believe that there is no regeneration that does not produce spiritual activities.

A born-again Christian lives righteously and portrays a new moral disposition that is clearly visible to all. In the Fundamentalist's religious thought, a born-again Christian must live a life that is in conformity with the biblical teachings. He or she must be distinguished from ordinary churchgoers and the rest of the world, work hard in any secular job, and have an impeccable character. The born-again Christian does not live a life of moral degeneracy, especially in the world where moral bankruptcy pervades all known cultural settings. For Fundamentalists, it is inconceivable to claim to be born again and still live a life full of worldly sensuality and pleasures. An immoral Christian is a contradiction in terms to a life that has been "begotten from above."

Conclusion

"Born again" has become an important religious vocabulary, a distinguishing identity, and a prerequisite for adherence to the religious culture of Fundamentalists. "Are you born again?" is a common question of most Fundamentalists. The expected answer is "Yes." Thereafter, further questions such as "when" and "how" often follow. Against the perceived ungodliness in society, Fundamentalists believe that a Christian must clearly stand out in his or her lifestyle, and this is only possible after being born again.

Matthews A. Ojo

See also African-American Holiness-Pentecostal Movement; Evangelicalism

Bibliography

Brown, Raymond E. (1966) *The Gospel According to John (I-XII)*. Garden City, NY: Doubleday.

Bruce, F. F. (1985) *The Real Jesus*. London: Hodder & Stoughton.

Bultmann, Rudolf. (1952) *Theology of the New Testament*, vol. 1. London: SCM Press, Ltd.

Dugan, Richard. (1978) *How To Know You Are Born Again*. Van Nuys, CA: Bible Voice, Inc.

Hefner W. Robert, ed. (1993) *Conversion to Christianity: Historical and Anthropological Perspectives on a Great Transformation*. Berkeley and Los Angeles: University of California Press.

Metzger, Bruce Manning. (1983) *The New Testament: Its Background, Growth and Content*, 2nd ed. Nashville, TN: Abingdon Press.

Calling

The early Christian community portrayed in Acts 13 suggests a divine coordination between the internal call of God to individuals and the external ordination and sending out by the church: " . . . the Holy Spirit said, 'Set apart for me Barnabas and Saul for the work to which I have called them.' Then after fasting and praying they laid their hands on them and sent them off" (Acts 13:2–3, NRSV). In the history of the church the relationship between a perceived internal call and a public selection by church authorities or the congregation is rarely so clear or harmonious. Compounding this tension is the ever-changing association between church and state. From the Puritans to the emergence of American Fundamentalism in the 1920s and beyond, the notion of calling has varied widely in the United States, depending on the perceived intensity of mission, congregational or denominational support, and political circumstances.

The Puritans who arrived in New England were heirs of the Reformed "middle way" between the Anabaptist vision of the church as a free association of regenerate lay priests and the sacramentalism of a Roman Catholicism that views the priest as God's special agent in dispensing grace through the Eucharist. A dynamic tension between these poles was experienced by Puritan ministers who moved from a situation of intermittent persecution in England to one of relative establishment in the New World.

The first half of the eighteenth century witnessed a wave of new immigrants who were more concerned with economic prosperity than religious freedom or purity. Some revivalist ministers like Gilbert Tennent (1703–1764) worried about "the danger of an unconverted ministry" among nonrevivalist clergy and called for new recruitment efforts so that the masses could hear the gospel: "The most likely Method to stock the Church with a faithful Ministry, . . . the publick Academies being so much corrupted and abused generally, is, To encourage private Schools, or Seminaries of Learning, which are under the Care of skilful and experienced Christians; in which those only should be admitted, who upon strict Examination, have in the Judgment of a reasonable Charity, the plain Evidences of experimental Religion" (1983: 80). But as the nineteenth century drew near, challenges were mounted against the legal, medical, political, and ministerial professions as well as the institutions that educated them. A strong anticlerical sentiment ensued. Democratizing influences such as these paved the way for many uneducated people to sense God's calling. Story-telling and humor with personal rapport became the trademark of good preaching rather than well-scripted, learned sermons. These sweeping changes were most evident in the Methodist campgrounds, but transcended denominational boundaries and doctrinal distinctions. Churches that bucked the trend and insisted on highly educated clergy were bypassed. Many new denominations were created.

At the end of the nineteenth century and the beginning of the twentieth, even before the Fundamentalist–modernist debate broke out in the 1920s, a "crises of missions" generated a new sense of calling to many. This crisis derived from the belief that they were living in the last days before Christ's return. Time was short. For those who adopted the

Acts 13:1–3

1. Now there were in the church that was at Antioch certain prophets and teachers; as Barnabas, and Simeon that was called Niger, and Lucius of Cyrene, and Manaen, which had been brought up with Herod the tetrarch, and Saul.
2. As they ministered to the Lord, and fasted, the Holy Ghost said, Separate me Barnabas and Saul for the work whereunto I have called them.
3. And when they had fasted and prayed, and laid their hands on them, they sent them away.

premillennial dispensational End Times scenario, evangelization of the world could not wait. Two key figures in this development were Arthur Tappan Pierson (1837–1911) and George Muller (1805–1898).

Pierson was a conservative Presbyterian minister who successfully served in several urban American churches. In the 1870s, while a pastor in Detroit, he began to doubt his own conversion and belief in the progressive march toward the realization of God's Kingdom. In 1879, George Muller convinced him of a premillennial interpretation of Scripture that anticipated the world's deterioration until Christ's return. Muller also directed many orphanages in Bristol, England, on a "faith" basis—not asking for financial support, but expecting God to provide for their needs. Both Pierson and Muller participated in the Niagara Bible conferences that were formative in the emerging Fundamentalism. The combination of premillennial dispensational theology and the call to go to the mission field by "faith" in student mission conferences—most notably the Northfield, Mt. Hermon conferences convened by Dwight L. Moody (1837–1899)—was critical in an explosion of interest in missionary outreach. These students returned to their own campuses, repeating Pierson's assertion that "all should go, and go to all." The Student Volunteer Movement for Foreign Missions was born out of this context and within fifteen years, thousands of students responded to the call. Pierson and others started independent mission-sending agencies to supplement the denominational mission boards and to handle the large cadre of recruited students who could not possibly be funded through the traditional denominational donation structures. Later, these new agencies became caught up in the Fundamentalist–modernist struggle and over time recruited and sent far more missionaries to foreign fields. The "faith" method of fund-raising was adopted and employed by both domestic and foreign mission agencies. To this day, the "call" to many students to serve in campus parachurch ministries or abroad in Evangelical and Fundamentalist mission agencies is often confirmed by their ability to raise monthly financial support from both churches and individuals.

Douglas Milford

See also Bible Schools; Campus Crusade for Christ; Missions; Preaching; Rescue Missions

Bibliography

Hall, David, D. (1972) *The Faithful Shepherd: A History of the New England Ministry in the Seventeenth Century.* Chapel Hill: University of North Carolina Press.

Hatch, Nathan O. (1989) *The Democratization of American Christianity.* New Haven and London: Yale University Press.

Robert, Dana L. (1990) "'The Crisis of Missions': Premillennial Mission Theory and the Origins of Independent Evangelical Missions." In *Earthen Vessels: American Evangelicals and Foreign Missions, 1880–1980,* edited by Joel A. Carpenter and Wilbert R. Shenk. Grand Rapids, MI: Wm. B. Eerdmans, 29–46.

Tennent, Gilbert. (1983) "The Danger of An Unconverted Ministry." In *Issues in American Protestantism: A Documentary History From Puritans to the Present,* edited by Robert Ferm. Gloucester, MA: Peter Smith, 73–83.

Calvinism

Calvinism, a tradition of Christian dogma originating with the reformer John Calvin (1509–1564), has become the foundational theology for many reformed denominations throughout history. It has received the label "reformed theology" to distinguish it from Lutheran theology, which also emerged in the sixteenth century. The term "Calvinism" has been used in several different senses over the past three centuries. Neither John Calvin nor his followers chose this term. It was first used by Roman Catholics in the sixteenth century as a pejorative term for the followers of Calvin. In the seventeenth century the term was used by the opposition in response to the teachings of Jacob Arminius. John Calvin himself would not have accepted it as a good description of his own doctrine and often made comments to that affect in his writings. He believed that the doctrine he put forth was nothing more or less than the teaching of the Scriptures found in the Old and New Testaments. Yet Calvinism is largely derived from Calvin's own interpretation and exposition of Scripture. Using the most up-to-date techniques of biblical exegesis developed by the humanists of his day, he wrote commentaries on most of the books of the Bible, summing up his findings in various editions of the *Institutes of the Christian Religion* (first edition in 1536, final edition in 1551).

The Essence of Calvinism

The essence of Calvinism is generally determined on the basis of each individual's own particular theological or philosophical presuppositions. Some view it on the basis of two principles. The first principle is the commitment to the Bible as the final authority. Calvin believed that the Bible was the Word of God, bringing God's revelation to man in documents written under the inspiration of the Holy Spirit. He insisted that the Bible is the only source of man's knowledge of God and of His will and works. He believed that although creation and providence reveal God's power and divinity, both nature and man have been so corrupted by sin that they cannot be an adequate means of God's self-manifestation. Creation and providence do not reveal anything concerning God's redeeming activity.

The second principle of Calvinism is the doctrine of the omnipotent sovereignty of God. God is completely and fully sovereign, thus everything exists only by the creative decision and providential action of God. The continued existence and operation of the universe, including the free actions of man, are sustained and determined from moment to moment by the mysterious and all-powerful providence of God.

Out of His ultimate will God allowed man to sin although man dies according to his own will and desire, alienating himself from God. At the same time, God in His grace purposed to redeem man from his sins and bring him to glory. Later reformed creeds have differed in interpreting Calvin in regard to the scope of God's predestination. The Scots Confession of 1560 and the Westminster Confession of Faith of 1647 declare a "double predestination," which states that God has determined both to whom He wills salvation (the elect) and those to whom He wills judgment (the nonelect), both to the glory of God. The Heidelberg Catechism of 1563 and the Second Helvetic Confession of 1566 state a "single predestination," that God is responsible for the salvation of the elect but those who are damned have chosen this path themselves.

Calvinism after Calvin

The term "Calvinism" is also used to specify the development and advancement of Calvin's doctrines by his followers or those who claim to be his followers. His successor in Geneva, Theodore Beza, modified certain lines of development in Calvinism. He placed the doctrine of predestination under the heading of God and Providence, whereas Calvin had discussed it in the Person and Work of Christ. Beza thus injected a powerful element of speculative determinism into the doctrine. Beza also emphasized literalism in the doctrine of the inspiration of the Bible, which introduced a biblical interpretation that differed from that of Calvin's.

The five articles of the Synod of Dort took upon itself this post-Calvin "Calvinism." It included the assertion that Christ died only for the elect, a belief statement that Calvin himself did not formally propose. While this formulation of thought was made explicit by Calvin in his writings, it was further elaborated in the late sixteenth century and partially summarized in the Canons of the Council of Dort (1618). These canons are commonly known as the Five Points of Calvinism: (1) the total depravity of man; (2) unconditional election, (3) limited or particular atonement, (4) irresistible grace, and (5) perseverance of the saints.

Theodore Beza's determinist elements were modified by the introduction of the theology of "the covenants," which sought to draw attention away from the doctrine of absolute predestination to the successive covenants made by God with man. This

Selection from: *INSTITUTES OF THE CHRISTIAN RELIGION* BY JOHN CALVIN, BOOK 1, CHAPTER 8: "THE CREDIBILITY OF SCRIPTURE SUFFICIENTLY PROVED IN SO FAR AS NATURAL REASON ADMITS, SECTION 1.

1. IN vain were the authority of Scripture fortified by argument, or supported by the consent of the Church, or confirmed by any other helps, if unaccompanied by an assurance higher and stronger than human Judgment can give. Till this better foundation has been laid, the authority of Scripture remains in suspense. On the other hand, when recognising its exemption from the common rule, we receive it reverently, and according to its dignity, those proofs which were not so strong as to produce and rivet a full conviction in our minds, become most appropriate helps. For it is wonderful how much we are confirmed in our belief, when we more attentively consider how admirably the system of divine wisdom contained in it is arranged—how perfectly free the doctrine is from every thing that savours of earth—how beautifully it harmonises in all its parts—and how rich it is in all the other qualities which give an air of majesty to composition. Our hearts are still more firmly assured when we reflect that our admiration is elicited more by the dignity of the matter than by the graces of style. For it was not without an admirable arrangement of Providence, that the sublime mysteries of the kingdom of heaven have for the greater part been delivered with a contemptible meanness of words. Had they been adorned with a more splendid eloquence, the wicked might have cavilled, and alleged that this constituted all their force. But now, when an unpolished simplicity, almost bordering on rudeness, makes a deeper impression than the loftiest flights of oratory, what does it indicate if not that the Holy Scriptures are too mighty in the power of truth to need the rhetorician's art?

Hence there was good ground for the Apostle's declaration, that the faith of the Corinthians was founded not on "the wisdom of men," but on "the power of God," (1 Cor. 2:5), this speech and preaching among them having been "not with enticing words of man's wisdom, but in demonstration of the Spirit and of power," (1 Cor. 2:5). For the truth is vindicated in opposition to every doubt, when, unsupported by foreign aid, it has its sole sufficiency in itself. How peculiarly this property belongs to Scripture appears from this, that no human writings, however skilfully composed, are at all capable of affecting us in a similar way. Read Demosthenes or Cicero, read Plato, Aristotle, or any other of that class: you will, I admit, feel wonderfully allured, pleased, moved, enchanted; but turn from them to the reading of the Sacred Volume, and whether you will or not, it will so affect you, so pierce your heart, so work its way into your very marrow, that, in comparison of the impression so produced, that of orators and philosophers will almost disappear; making it manifest that in the Sacred Volume there is a truth divine, a something which makes it immeasurably superior to all the gifts and graces attainable by man.

Source: Christian Classics Ethereal Library. www.ccel.org.
Calvin, John (1845–1846) *Institutes of the Christian Religion.*
A new translation by Henry Beveridge, Esq. Edinburgh: Calvin Translation Society.

was first expounded by the theologian Johannes Cocceius. The Westminster Confession of Faith (1647), written by English Puritans, was influenced by covenant theology. The English Puritans, especially the theologian William Perkins, also developed the concern for personal sanctification, which was separate from Calvin's insistence upon the objective reality of church and sacraments. In the eighteenth century, such English-speaking Evangelicals as Jonathan Edwards and George Whitefield combined the doctrine of irresistible grace with a personal experience of salvation.

"Calvinism" also refers to the theological emphasis on forms of church organization, worship, and discipline that became widespread in the sixteenth century in France, Holland, the Palatinate in Germany, Scotland, and elsewhere. This emphasis was adopted by the Reformed and Presbyterian churches. In France, there was a minority of Calvinists who were known by the name "Huguenots." In the eight-year Wars of Religion, these Huguenots faced off against the Roman Catholic faction led by the royal court and the Catholic nobles. Out of this continued conflict the Huguenots had to develop a theory of resistance and rebellion beyond that elucidated by Calvin.

Calvinism was brought over to America with the Pilgrims and the Puritans. Later, Jonathan Edwards allowed for greater freedom of the will in responding to conversionist preaching. His critics became known as the "old Calvinists," whereas his followers became known as the "New Divinity Men." This modification in doctrine provided a theological basis for many American Calvinists to participate in the first and second Great Awakenings.

Contemporary Calvinism

Many different theological interpretations can be found in contemporary Calvinism—from liberalism to neo-orthodoxy and conservative beliefs. The Presbyterian Church (USA) and other Presbyterian denominations along with various Reformed denominations mostly hold to a broad church or "confessional" belief. The Presbyterian Church (USA) holds to *The Book of Confessions* and the current *Book of Order*. There is a debate among modern historians over whether nineteenth- and twentieth-century Calvinism has influenced the American Fundamentalist movement or whether a similar belief in inerrancy emerged on

its own within American Fundamentalism, possibly from previous nineteenth-century conservative theological trends. There is the "Old Princeton" theology held by certain professors at Princeton Theological Seminary from its founding in 1812 to its reorganization in 1921. As critics attacked Calvinist orthodoxy, a series of Princeton professors defended the Calvinist stand with the doctrine of an inerrant Scripture in the original autographs. Some of these same Princeton professors were critical of many aspects of the emergent Fundamentalist movement.

Leland Edward Wilshire

Bibliography

Bratt, John H. (1973) *The Heritage of John Calvin*. Grand Rapids, MI: Wm. B. Eerdmans.

McNeill, John Thomas. (1954) *The History and Character of Calvinism*. New York: Oxford University Press.

Meeter, H. Henry. (1990) *The Basis Ideas of Calvinism*, 6th ed. Grand Rapids, MI: Baker Book House.

Schnucker, Robert V., ed. (1988) *Calviniana: Ideas and Influence of Jean Calvin*. Kirksville, MO: Sixteenth Century Journal Publishers.

Campus Crusade for Christ

Campus Crusade for Christ is a nondenominational conservative parachurch organization focusing on evangelism and discipleship. It was created on the campus of the University of California, Los Angeles (UCLA), in 1951 by William R. "Bill" Bright (1921–), a former entrepreneur and recent graduate of the new Fuller Evangelical Seminary. A revival among UCLA's student leaders and athletes gave Bright's fledgling organization immediate publicity and paved the way for steady growth during the 1950s. Central to Campus Crusade's success was Bright's avoidance of internal Fundamentalist squabbles and utilization of a simple, nondenominational "spiritual sales pitch" eventually standardized in his famous, and widely adopted, tract, "The Four Spiritual Laws."

The acquisition of a new headquarters and training center at Arrowhead Springs Resort near San Bernardino, California, in 1962 marked the beginning of an Institute of Biblical Studies, which trained Crusade workers for an increasingly diverse set of programs. Among the new initiatives were evangelism among American military personnel, evangelism training for laypersons and business professionals, and Athletes in Action, a program seeking to evangelize athletes and sports fans through exhibitions with college and professional teams (mostly basketball).

These new programs set the stage for a period of meteoric growth and visibility in the 1970s that saw Campus Crusade's staff grow to nearly ten thousand—five times the number it employed in 1969. Among its successful efforts was "EXPLO '72," a June 1972 youth congress that utilized publicity surrounding the Jesus People Movement to attract more than eighty thousand high school and college age youth to Dallas for a week of evangelism and discipleship training. An international missions-themed follow-up, EXPLO '74, drew an estimated crowd of 1.3 million to Seoul, South Korea. But it was the intensive evangelistic campaign "Here's Life America" that truly put Campus Crusade into the national spotlight in the United States. Using the slogan "I Found It!" the strategy revolved around a savvy combination of interchurch cooperation and the use of billboards, bumper stickers, television specials, and telephone counseling. Between the years 1973 and 1978, "Here's Life America" campaigns were carried out in over 250 metropolitan areas in the United States.

While Bill Bright personally identified with the so-called religious Right on any number of issues and campaigns during the 1980s and 1990s, Campus Crusade's resources concentrated on expanding its traditional emphases on evangelism and discipleship. In recognition of the United States' growing ethnic diversity, it began new campus programs aimed specifically at Hispanic, Asian, and African-American students. Additionally, Campus Crusade was a major player in cooperative efforts among American Evangelicals to promote evangelism and Christian education in Russian schools after the unraveling of the Soviet Union in the 1990s. Perhaps the organization's biggest success, however, was the "Jesus" film, an adaptation of the Gospel of St. Luke originally distributed to American theaters in 1979. Subsequently translated into more than five hundred languages for use as a low-key tool for foreign evangelism, Campus Crusade claimed by the late 1990s that more than one billion people had viewed the "Jesus" film.

Campus Crusade for Christ is second only to the Billy Graham Evangelistic Association in size, influence, and historical importance among the Evangelical parachurch organizations that emerged from

Fundamentalism in the wake of World War II. From a sprawling new headquarters (1991) in Orlando, Florida, it continues to expand its operations worldwide. Its annual operating budget for the year 2000 was estimated at almost three hundred million dollars per year, supporting a full-time global staff of nearly fourteen thousand workers.

Larry Eskridge

Bibliography

Bright, Bill. (1970) *Come Help Change the World*. Old Tappan, NJ: Fleming H. Revell.

———. (1977) *A Movement of Miracles*. San Bernardino, CA: Campus Crusade for Christ.

Quebedeaux, Richard. (1979) *I Found It! The Story of Bill Bright and Campus Crusade for Christ*. San Francisco: Harper and Row.

Richardson, Michael. (2000) *Amazing Faith: The Authorized Biography of Bill Bright*. Oxnard, CA: Waterbrook Press.

Zoba, Wendy Murray. (1997) "Bill Bright's Wonderful Plan for the World." *Christianity Today* (14 July): 14–20, 22, 24, 26–27.

Catholic Fundamentalism

Gabriel Daly's identification of integralism as "the Catholic form of fundamentalism" (1985: 776) has been adopted by John Coleman (1989) and others (Hebblethwaite 1988; *America* 1986) as a label for a variety of right-wing Catholic groups in the second half of the twentieth century. The very term, "Catholic Fundamentalism" distinguishes it from Protestant varieties that tend to be interested in prophecies about the end of the world, or in a literal interpretation of the Bible. Catholics are not distinguished by either of these religious preoccupations. Indeed, the American Catholic bishops issued a pastoral statement (*Origins* 1987) on biblical Fundamentalism that encourages the critical study of the Bible rather than a literal reading of it. Yet, if Fundamentalism is militant opposition to modernity rooted in an experience of isolation or a social, political, and intellectual phenomenon whose adherents care passionately about "old time religion" in a number of forms, then there is family resemblance between Catholic and Protestant Fundamentalism (Marsden 1980). Although the Catholic version is not a coherent movement, those groups and individuals who might be identified as Fundamentalists believe they have the power to shape a particular kind of Catholicism by their criticisms of the post–Vatican II church.

The Vatican II Council (1962–1965) and the dissent surrounding the birth control encyclical, *Humanae Vitae* (1968), quickly became rallying points for Catholics in the second half of the twentieth century. These two events along with major changes in liturgical understanding and practice are more important in defining Catholic Fundamentalism than political, economic, or social issues. Right-wing Catholics also share a posture of resistance to modernity that allows them to assume a common cultural context: they believe they have held steady while the world around them has changed. Their experience suggests that the Catholic ability to shape a religious identity formed in faith and measured in obedience to the teaching of the church has been lost in the last thirty years. While most of them do not wish to return to the nineteenth century or the 1950s, they are, nevertheless, heartbroken and angry at what has happened since the council and sometimes conflicted about what to do about it. Many of them who consider themselves loyal and faithful Catholics felt betrayed by the post-conciliar church. The markers they had always counted on to describe their faith—dogmatism, Latin, a lack of ambiguity in moral teaching, set forms of worship, unchanging moral codes, and papal power clearly invoked and cheerfully obeyed—seemed to have been eroded by the council. Although right-wing (or traditional, conservative, or Fundamentalist) Catholics are a minority of the American Catholic population, they have created hundreds of groups clustered around a wide variety of themes. Nearly all of them have websites and links, and although it is impossible to name all of these groups, some general connecting themes can be identified.

Marian Piety

Devotees of the Virgin Mary who believe that she has made appearances in the twentieth century are generally advocates of a strong papacy and opponents of the modern world. In their experience, Mary comes to bring warnings from heaven about dangerous ideas. For example, in the 1950s, "Our Lady of Necedah" (Wisconsin) spoke against communism at the very time that philosophy was under congressional investigation. In the last two decades of

the twentieth century, Mary is reported to have appeared in a variety of places in the United States—most notably in Georgia and Arizona—to exhort people to prayer. Mary also upholds traditional family values, including the idea that women should not work outside the home (Zimbdars-Swartz 1995; cf. Perry and Echeverria 1988). The Blue Army of Mary, founded to promote devotion to "Our Lady of Fatima" (a Marian apparition in Portugal in the early twentieth century) is the largest organization of the Cult of Mary and a source of information about Marian devotion.

Conservative Catholics

Those Catholics who long for a return to a time when sacred identity was clearly transcendent, moral norms rigorously upheld, papal authority respected, and personal piety rooted in a vertical relationship with the deity are sometimes called Fundamentalists (Cuneo 1987, 1997). Many believe that Vatican II has not been properly interpreted and that the *aggiornamento* policies of Pope John XXIII (1958–1963) have gone too far. Those in this group who teach at Catholic colleges and universities, but who feel marginalized or isolated in those settings, belong to the Fellowship of Catholic Scholars, founded in the mid-1970s to oppose what they saw as dangerous trends in Catholic intellectual life (J. Hitchcock 1997). Conservative Catholics who want to show their collective loyalty to the pope, especially in the light of Vatican teaching about birth control, may belong to Catholics United for the Faith. Catholics who find a special calling as antiabortion activists may join the Pro-Life Action League or Catholics United for Life. Conservative Catholics have generally been encouraged by the restorationist policies of Pope John Paul II (1978–) and are intensely loyal to him.

Conservative Catholic Nuns

Although most American nuns are represented by the Leadership Conference of Religious Women, traditionalist sisters have formed a separate organization, the Council of Major Superiors of Women Religious. These women subscribe to four tenets: freely given obedience to the pope and the church; the wearing of a distinctive religious habit as a sign of poverty and consecration to God; the importance of community life as essential to common prayer and spiritual growth; and active participation in community-based ministries that bring Christ to the young, the sick, the poor, and those who seek a deeper relationship with God. Traditional nuns are supported by the Institute for Religious Life, a national organization of bishops, priests, and laypersons who support traditional vocations and expressions of religious life.

Lefebvrist Traditionalists

Far from being grounded on an essential respect for the present leadership of the church, traditionalists who follow the teaching of the late French archbishop Marcel Lefebvre (d.1991) and his clerical Society of St. Pius X, reject the Vatican II Council and directly challenge the authority of the pope. Lefebvre was an astute ecclesiastical politician who understood that a pope acting with a council holds an unassailable position and that the only way to counteract Vatican II was to refuse to accept it. Unlike conservatives who believe that the council has not been properly interpreted, these traditionalists reject the council altogether and identify themselves primarily by way of the Council of Trent (sixteenth century) and Vatican I (1870). Where they might be called Fundamentalists is in their claim to define real or true Catholicism against any attempt to find religious identity in collegiality, pluralism, or ecumenism, values they believe simply reflect "liberty, equality, and fraternity," the odious values of the French Revolution (Dinges 1997; Komonchak 1997).

Catholic Separatists

The Lefebvrist movement is usually linked to the desire to preserve the Tridentine Mass (the Latin Mass as specified at the Council of Trent in distinction from the "Novus Ordo," the new vernacular Mass translated into Latin and rooted in the new liturgical piety of the Vatican II Council). The desire to provide the opportunity for Catholics to hear a Tridentine Mass was the impetus behind the Traditionalist movement founded by Gommar DePauw, a Belgian-born priest teaching in America who took issue with the new liturgy decreed by Vatican II. The Catholic Traditionalist movement later found a hero in and martyr in archbishop Lefebvre, and spawned hundreds of separatist centers throughout the United States. Many of those who support this initiative inhabit a mental universe that is alert to conspiracy theories (e.g., they may believe that there have been

papal plots with Moscow, or that the church has been invaded and is now controlled by Freemasons). The two most active sectors of the Tridentine Mass movement are the Society of St. Pius X, and a splinter group, the Society of St. Pius V.

Opus Dei

Catholic Fundamentalists sometimes belong to European movements with a presence in the United States. Communio e Liberazione, for example, was founded in Italy in 1926 as a populist movement with a political agenda. It appeals to those who hope to restore "true" or "authentic" values to the Catholic Church. The most famous European movement, however, is Opus Dei, founded in Spain in 1928 by the priest José Maria Escrivá Balaguer, whose controversial beatification in 1992 attracted nearly a quarter of a million people to St. Peter's Square. With nearly seventy-five thousand members and twelve thousand priests in more than fifty countries, Opus Dei aims to promote piety among the laity by appealing to well-educated, highly disciplined Catholics who, in their ordinary jobs, can penetrate society in ways not open to priests. Members of this strictly hierarchical and authoritarian structure are taught that Opus Dei is God's perfect instrument, sinless and virtually incapable of error. Unlike most organized groups who must report and work through a local bishop, Opus Dei is a personal prelature of the pope: it can operate anywhere in the world with or without the support of local ecclesiastical authorities. Opus Dei has a reputation for secrecy, rigorous practices of mortification, and political intrigue. It tends to have passionate defenders and detractors, so it is not altogether well served in the books written about it, and it is surrounded by controversy, partly because of its supposed influence at the Vatican. (Opus Dei is notoriously difficult to describe because of the secrecy of its documents and the general controversy that surrounds it. For a general introduction, see Casanova 1982. See also *America* 1995, Walsh 1989, and Estruch 1995.)

Antifeminist Laywomen

When the American bishops decided to write a pastoral letter on women in the early 1980s, they opened a series of national listening sessions to hear women describe their experiences in the church. The initial sessions were attended mostly by nuns and lay-

Selections from: *ENCYCLICAL LETTER OF HIS HOLINESS POPE PAUL VI. HUMANAE VITAE (ON THE REGULATION OF BIRTH)*

Illicit Ways of Regulating Birth

14. In conformity with these landmarks in the human and Christian vision of marriage, we must once again declare that the direct interruption of the generative process already begun, and, above all, directly willed and procured abortion, even if for therapeutic reasons, are to be absolutely excluded as licit means of regulating birth [14].

Equally to be excluded, as the teaching authority of the Church has frequently declared, is direct sterilization, whether perpetual or temporary, whether of the man or of the woman [15]. Similarly excluded is every action which, either in anticipation of the conjugal act, or in its accomplishment, or in the development of its natural consequences, propose, whether as an end or as a means, to render procreation impossible [16]. . . .

The Church Guarantor of True Human Values

18. It can be foreseen that this teaching will perhaps not be easily received by all: Too numerous are those voices—amplified by the modern means of propaganda—which are contrary to the voice of the Church. To tell the truth, the Church is not surprised to be made, like her divine Founder, a "sign of contradiction" [22], yet she does not because of this cease to proclaim with humble firmness the entire moral law, both natural and evangelical. Of such laws the Church was not the author, nor consequently can she be their arbiter; she is only their depositary and their interpreter, without ever being able to declare to be licit that which is not so by reason of its intimate and unchangeable opposition to the true good of man.

In defending conjugal morals in their integral wholeness, the Church knows that she contributes toward the establishment of a truly human civilization; she engages man not to abdicate from his own responsibility in order to rely on technical means; by that very fact she defends the dignity of man and wife. Faithful to both the teaching and the example of the Saviour, she shows herself to be the sincere and disinterested friend of men, whom she wishes to help, even during their earthly sojourn, "to share as sons in the life of the living of God, the Father of all men" [23].

women with feminist views who raised questions of equality, due process in regulation of religious life, inclusive language, and women's ordination. When the first draft of the letter reflected these concerns, conservative Catholic women who had felt marginalized since the council were galvanized into action. They blamed what they called "radical feminists" for the demise of the family and the destruction of the church. A small group of conservative women, led by Helen Hull Hitchcock, a recent convert to Catholicism, met in St. Louis in 1984 to protest the process of the pastoral letter, claiming that it privileged a small minority of Catholic women in sessions that were designed to elicit complaints. They founded Women for Faith and Family as an ad hoc response to the controversy surrounding the proposed pastoral letter. As the group grew, it created a place to amplify the voices of Catholic women who affirm papal teaching, particularly about women. Their first project was the "Affirmation for Catholic Women," an eight-point statement and petition that affirmed the distinctiveness of women's nature (as meant for childbearing), legitimate subordination of women in service of the family and the sanctity of life. The petition condemned sex education in schools and any attempt to secure ordination for women (H. H. Hitchcock 1997).

Educational Initiatives

Catholics have protested against the direction of the Catholic school system at nearly all levels. In the closing decades of the twentieth century, American Catholics have joined the home-schooling movement partly as a protest against sex education in the schools and partly to preserve the kinds of religious instruction that children received in Catholic schools in the 1940s and 1950s. The two most prominent home-schooling corporations serving children in grade school and high school are Our Lady of the Rosary in Bardstown, Kentucky, and Seton Home School in Front Royal, Virginia. Parents can rent copies of the *Baltimore Catechism* (used by Catholic school children until the 1970s), find the textbooks that were used in Catholic schools before the council, and receive instructional help from staff members. Books, statues, and prayer cards of the preconciliar era are, for home-schoolers, treasures of a Catholic culture to be passed on to the next generation. At the college level, four new colleges have been founded since the council to protest the directions taken by Catholic higher education since the early 1960s. Thomas Aquinas College (Santa Paula, California), Magdalen (Warner, New Hampshire), Thomas More (Merrimack, New Hampshire), and Christendom (Front Royal, Virginia) are lay-founded, lay-led experiments in high education linked by a shared belief in objective truth and the means to attain it. They define their college curriculum in Catholic terms by way of a Great Books approach and by providing a campus atmosphere that is saturated with Catholicism (Weaver 1997).

Following Marsden's (1980) understanding of Fundamentalism as a flexible alliance that resists efforts to conform to a universal description, it is fair to say that the concept of Catholic Fundamentalism has to admit some ambiguity of definition. Gabriel Daly (1985) connects modern Catholic Fundamentalists with those people who opposed modernism either as a movement or as any impulse to threaten the integrity of a Catholicism built upon a strategic alliance of scholastic methodology, Canon Law, and magisterial control over ecclesiastical structures. With the dismantling of scholasticism by the council and the reform of Canon Law, Catholic Fundamentalists have become strangers in their own land, threatened, Daly says, with "cognitive misery" and constrained to take a stand on the battlefront of moral and administrative authority. Parallels between Roman Catholic and Protestant Fundamentalists can be found in a profound sense of disinheritance: Catholic Fundamentalists are most at home in a triumphalist, exclusive, world-transcending church and often homeless in the modern, pluralistic context.

Because Catholics in general are not eschatologically minded, it is not surprising that millennialism is not a major aspect of Catholic Fundamentalism as opposed to its Protestant cousin. At the same time, the fears of the sample groups mentioned here have some resonance in the apocalyptic plot as outlined in the Bible. There is a sense that the church is at war with the powers of darkness, that the faithful are being tested by way of terrible suffering, and that Catholicism, real Catholicism, demands conscious resistance and heroic action. The anticipated reward changes somewhat from group to group, but takes the general form of a return to the past where transcendence, mystery, supernaturalism, and moral absolutes characterize a society with real power to persuade and to unify religious people. The mythic picture of a church constituted by a grateful and obedient people under the direction of a wise and benevolent pope, sometimes presented to Catholics as the reality of medieval Catholicism, is a hope for the future for many Catholic Fundamentalists.

Mary Jo Weaver

See also Catholics United for the Faith; Cult of Mary; Opus Dei; Wanderer, The

Bibliography

America. (1986) Issue on Catholic Fundamentalism, 115 (12 September).

America. (1995) Issue on Opus Dei, 172 (25 February).

Casanova, Jose V. (1982) "The First Secular Institute: The Opus Dei As a Religious Movement-Organization." *Annual Review of the Social Sciences of Religion* 6: 243–285.

Coleman, John. (1989) "Who Are the Catholic Fundamentalists." *Commonweal* 16 (27 January): 42–47.

Cuneo, Michael. (1987) "Conservative Catholicism in North America." *Pro Mundi Vita Dossiers*—Europe/North America 36 (January): 1–30.

———. (1997) *The Smoke of Satan: Conservative and Traditionalist Dissent in Contemporary American Catholicism.* New York: Oxford University Press.

Daly, Gabriel. (1985) "Catholicism and Modernity." *Journal of the American Academy of Religion* 53: 773–796.

Dinges, William D. (1995) "We Are What You Were: Roman Catholic Traditionalism in America." In *Being Right: Conservative Catholics in America*, edited by Mary Jo Weaver and R. Scott Appleby. Bloomington: Indiana University Press, 241–270.

Estruch, Joan. (1995) *Saints and Schemers: Opus Dei and Its Paradoxes*. Translated by Elizabeth Ladd Blick. New York: Oxford University Press.

Hebblethwaite, Peter. (1988) "A Roman Catholic Fundamentalism." *Times Literary Supplement* (5–11 August): 866.

Hitchcock, Helen Hull. (1995) "Women for Faith and Family: Catholic Women Affirming Catholic Teaching." In *Being Right: Conservative Catholics in America*, edited by Mary Jo Weaver and R. Scott Appleby. Bloomington: Indiana University Press, 163–185.

Hitchcock, James. (1995) "The Fellowship of Catholic Scholars: Bowing Out of the New Class." In *Being Right: Conservative Catholics in America*, edited by Mary Jo Weaver and R. Scott Appleby. Bloomington: Indiana University Press, 186–210.

Komonchak, Joseph A. (1995) "Interpreting the Council: Catholic Attitudes toward Vatican II." In *Being Right: Conservative Catholics in America*, edited by Mary Jo Weaver and R. Scott Appleby. Bloomington: Indiana University Press, 17–37.

Marsden, George M. (1980) *Fundamentalism and American Culture: The Shaping of Twentieth-Century Evangelicalism 1870–1925*. New York: Oxford University Press.

"Pastoral Statement for Catholics on Biblical Fundamentalism." (1987) *Origins* 17 (5 November): 376–377.

Perry, Nicholas, and Loreta Echeverria. (1988) *Under the Heel of Mary*. London: Routledge.

Walsh, Michael. (1989) *The Secret World of Opus Dei: An Investigation into the Secret Society Struggling for Power within the Roman Catholic Church*. San Francisco: HarperSanFrancisco.

Weaver, Mary Jo. (1995) "Self-Consciously Countercultural: Alternative Catholic Colleges." In *Being Right: Conservative Catholics in America*, edited by Mary Jo Weaver and R. Scott Appleby. Bloomington: Indiana University Press, 33–324.

Zimdars-Swartz, Sandra L. (1995) "The Marian Revival in American Catholicism: Focal Points and Features of the New Marian Enthusiasm." In *Being Right: Conservative Catholics in America*, edited by Mary Jo Weaver and R. Scott Appleby. Bloomington: Indiana University Press, 213–240.

Catholics United for the Faith

A 15,000–member international organization of lay Catholics, Catholics United for the Faith (CUF) supports papal teaching and condemns dissent. Catholicism has always been informed by a tension between progressives and traditionalists, what Meriol Trevor called "the prophets and the guardians." Before Vatican II (1962–1965), that dialectic was generally a clerical phenomenon (occurring at the institutional level or in theological circles). Since the council, however, dedicated laity have been an integral part of it. CUF is a case in point.

Founded by the late H. Lyman Stebbins in 1968 to rally around the pope in the wave of dissent following the publication of *Humanae Vitae* (the encyclical condemning all forms of artificial birth control), CUF was inspired by Vatican II, which called for lay activism, and is defined by an uncompromising loyalty to the pope. As such, it is on the side of "the guardians." When Stebbins founded the group, he said, "in this period when there is so much contumacious defiance of God-given authority, the church needs, and we owe, our unswerving support of her teaching and ruling authority" (Sullivan 1995: 112f).

The international headquarters is located near Franciscan University in Steubenville, Ohio, and currently serves a number of local chapters both in the United States and in other nations. CUF is alert to "unorthodox" activity and assiduous in reporting dissenters to the Vatican. Its constructive mission supports doctrinal and intellectual formation in the orthodox Catholic faith. The organization publishes a monthly newsletter, *Lay Witness*, has a website (www.cuf.org) and a toll-free telephone number (800–MY FAITH).

Mary Jo Weaver

See also Catholic Fundamentalism; Opus Dei; Wanderer, The

Bibliography

Sullivan, James A. (1995) "Catholics United for the Faith: Dissent and Loyalty." In *Being Right: Conservative Catholics in America*, edited by Mary Jo Weaver and R. Scott Appleby. Bloomington: Indiana University Press, 107–137.

Trevor, Meriol. (1969) *Prophets and Guardians: Renewal and Tradition in the Church.* Garden City, NY: Doubleday.

Chiliasm

A formal term of Christian theology, *chiliasm* derives from the Greek term meaning "a thousand," and is a synonym for millennialism—the expectation that at some point in the future the physical world will transform into a just and peaceful society, known to Christians as the "reign of the Saints," or of Christ.

Millennialism and the Fundamentalist Movement

Millennialism and Fundamentalism overlap in many areas. On a purely historical level, theologians' early efforts to define the "fundamentals" of faith grew out of a period of intense apocalyptic expectations of the imminent millennium. Close ties drew together the English theologian John Nelson Darby (1800–1882), the first to articulate the premillennial dispensationalist vision; James Brookes (1837–1897), who founded the first premillennial journal in the United States (*The Truth for Christ*) and played a prominent role in virtually every one of the Niagara Conferences (1875–) as long as he lived; Cyrus I. Scofield (1843–1921), who produced the *Scofield Reference Bible* (1901–1909); and the group of theologians who wrote *The Fundamentals* around 1910 to 1915 (Sandeen 1970). Thus, Fundamentalism was born out of a succession of apocalyptic and postapocalyptic crises in Protestant millennialism during the nineteenth and early twentieth centuries.

Apocalyptic Expectations

In the broader context of millennial thinking, Darby's rereading of the sacred history as seven dispensations allowed apocalyptic hope to survive the disastrous failure of more specific calculations (e.g., William Miller's timetable for Christ's return between 1843 and 1844) and the postmillennial abolitionism of the Civil War period (1840–1865). A curious parallel can be found among early twelfth-century historians of sacred history, such as Rupert of Deutz, Anselm of Havelberg, and Gerhoh of Reichersberg, who developed "dispensationalist schemata," in several cases of the "Seven Church Ages." Their efforts to restructure the Christian past were an attempt to revive apocalyptic expectation in the aftermath of the "First" Crusades' failure to inaugurate the millennium (1096–1100) (Morrison 1992). In this sense, Fundamentalism can be seen as an enclave movement that coalesced after millennial disappointment.

The millennial dimension pervasive to Fundamentalism is fueled by Fundamentalists' tendency to read the social forces of modernity as manifestations of the Antichrist's growing power, leading directly and imminently to the apocalyptic Tribulation. This view of the modern West on the verge of catastrophic collapse was widely held at the end of the nineteenth century among both religious and secular thinkers (e.g., Oswald Spengler and Thomas Carlyle). Premillennialism especially targeted the secularizing morality of liberal, activist ("post")millennialism, with its lofty moral goals and this-worldly (utopian) reform programs (1878 Niagara Creed, V). Indeed, any effort to deemphasize a Christ-centered millennialism was almost, ipso facto, defined as modernism. The antimodern elements of both premillennialism and Fundamentalism account for the frequent role that global conspiracy theories played in later apocalyptic episodes of Fundamentalism (e.g., Pat Robertson's *New World Order* [1992]). A central antimodern thread links the Masonic conspiracy texts of the nineteenth century to the Jewish conspiracy of the *Protocols of the Elders of Zion* (1904) and to the later twentieth-century view that the Antichrist will first arise as a benign, liberal, world leader who will come to power via the United Nations.

Millennial beliefs added another element to Fundamentalists' hostility to Darwin. Of course, Darwin's account cast doubt on the Genesis narrative of Creation, and undermined Christian moral notions by placing a rapacious ethic of "survival of the fittest" at the core of the evolutionary process. In addition, its chronological framework destroyed the dominant structure of Western Christian millennialism, the schema of the 6,000 years from Creation to the sabbatical millennium (O'Leary, 1994). The defense of Genesis against Darwin, and the inerrant truth of the entire biblical text, gave birth to a major theological activity among the emerging Fundamentalist community—the search for the "signs" and calculations of coming apocalyptic events. Indeed, "modern sensibilities" attacked with particular vigor and contempt the apocalyptic exegeses with which people "read" the signs of Christ's coming in the Scriptures and in world events. The first and most vital battle of Fundamentalist literalism, then, was to preserve the biblical record as a source of apocalyptic millennial expectation. And, of course, the more passive the anticipation (as in premillennialism in which Jesus returned does most of the work creating the new heavens and new earth), the more important that the exegesis work with an inerrant text.

A Sign of the End Times and Zionist Premillennialism

Perhaps the most striking and consequential of the Christian Fundamentalists' millennial beliefs concern the idea that before or at the premillennial appearance of Jesus, "Israel shall be restored to their own land" (1878 Niagara Creed, XIV). This premillennial commitment combined with Zionism (a secular form of "post-" or activist millennialism) and forged a long and consequential alliance between Protestant Christian Evangelicals and Fundamentalists and Zionists. Christian desire to see the Jews return to Zion connects the Blackstone Proclamation of 1891 to the Balfour Declaration of 1917 to the modern-day alliance between the Fundamentalists and the Israeli Likud Party. In the aftermath of dated expectations of the Rapture in 1981 and 1988, much of this "Zionist" premillennialism shifted its attention from awaiting apocalyptic dates to promoting the rebuilding of the third temple by messianic Jews.

At the core of this cooperation and mutual appreciation, however, lies an underlying instability. Fundamentalists favor the Jews and wish—contrary to almost all earlier Christian positions on the matter—to see them flourish, primarily in expectation that the final days will witness the return of the Jews to Israel and their conversion to Christianity. The hope for Jewish restoration has found a great response among Jews, climaxing in the creation and success of the Zionist nation-state (thus intensifying millennial expectations among Christians in 1948, 1967, and 1981). The conversion of the Jews, however, has never found a strong resonance among Jews, and past efforts have often led to antagonism and the Christian use of force to coerce it. In that sense, the current close association between Fundamentalists and Jews resembles the first part of a common cycle of Jewish–Christian relations in the West. The cycle begins with a period of close cooperation, followed by violent outbreaks of anti-Judaism, in many cases

fueled initially by millennial hopes for voluntary conversion and subsequently, after the bitter disappointment, by a sense of betrayal and (post) apocalyptic scapegoating—such as among the monastic reformers in eleventh-century France (Landes 1996) or the British Israelites in the twentieth-century United States (Katz and Popkin 1998).

More broadly, a comparative psychological analysis, which permits one to speak of Jewish, Christian, Muslim, even Hindu Fundamentalism, also marks the underlying millennial dynamics. The anxiety provoked by a modernizing world that changes rapidly and systematically disadvantages older authorities produces powerful abreactions, among them the rejection of modernity as the force leading to apocalyptic destruction, and the retreat to older forms of religious certainty. Some of these abreactions destabilize and revitalize (apocalyptic episodes) and others stabilize and reform (Fundamentalist enclaves). The alternating current between them creates a continuous feedback of mutually enforcing commitments and revivals. While the (antimodern) apocalyptic tradition is never too far from the surface of most Fundamentalist ideologies (e.g., Islam and Judaism), no other religion approaches the depth and intimacy of the Christian tradition's association between formal millennialism (premillennial dispensationalism) and Fundamentalism.

Richard Landes

See also Antimodernism; Dispensationalism; Israel; Jews; Premillennialism

Bibliography

Brasher, Brenda. (1998) *Godly Women: Fundamentalism and Female Power*. New Brunswick, NJ: Rutgers University Press.

Gorenberg, Gershom. (2000) *The End of Days: Fundamentalism and the Struggle for the Temple Mount*. New York: Free Press.

Katz, David, and Jeremy Popkin. (1998) *Messianic Revolution: Radical Religious Politics to the End of the Second Millennium*. New York: Hill and Wang.

Landes, Richard. (1996) "The Massacres of 1010: On the Origins of Popular Anti-Jewish Violence in Western Europe." In *From Witness to Witchcraft: Jews and Judaism in Medieval Christian Thought*, edited by Jeremy Cohen. Wolfenbüttel, Germany: Wolfenbüttler Karl Mittelalterlichen-Studien, 79–112.

Mendel, Arthur. ([1992] 2000) *Vision and Violence*. Ann Arbor: University of Michigan Press.

Morrison, Karl. (1992) "The Exercise of Thoughtful Minds: The Apocalypse in Some German Historical Writings." In *Apocalypse in the Middle Ages*, edited by Richard K. Emmerson and Bernard McGinn. Ithaca, NY: Cornell University Press, 352–373.

O'Leary, Stephen. (1994) *Arguing the Apocalypse: A Theory of Millennial Rhetoric*. Cambridge MA: Harvard University Press.

Sandeen, Ernest R. (1970) *The Roots of Fundamentalism: British and American Millenarianism, 1800–1930*. Chicago: University of Chicago Press.

Strozier, Charles B. (1994) *Apocalypse: On the Psychology of Fundamentalism in America*. Boston: Beacon Press.

Christ, The

The words "The Christ" occur frequently in the New Testament as a title applied to the Lord primarily by others. On three occasions it is expressly accepted by Him (John 4:26; Matthew 16:17; Mark 14:61–62), but only once does He use it of Himself (John 17:3). This oft-used name carries with it the Old Testament promises of salvation and the fulfillment of messianic prediction that are brought to fulfillment in the New Testament.

Linguistic Background

The word "Christ" is derived from the Greek verb *christos*, which means "to anoint."

This term is the translation of the Hebrew word uniformly used in the Septuagint version of the Old Testament. It signifies the symbolic anointing with holy oil, whereby men ordained of God to special service in His economy—such as priests, prophets, and kings—were not only set apart and consecrated, but gifted and endowed for that holy service that demanded powers above and beyond those naturally belonging to man. The oldest and most sacred usage of unction or anointing was that carried out at the coronation of a king. The oil was poured out upon his head, a ceremony regarded as sacred from earliest times and observed faithfully in Israel. Such anointing was reserved exclusively for the king, which accounts for the fact that "His anointed" (1 Samuel 12:3, 5; NASB) became a synonym for the king.

Although the ceremonial anointing of the priests may have come after that of the king in history, there is ample evidence that the rite was a part of the preparation of the Old Testament priest to fulfill his office. This is mentioned almost matter of factly in Leviticus 4:3, 5: "the anointed high priest." The only recorded instance of the anointing of a prophet is in 1 Kings 19:16 (NASB), where it stands in context with the command to anoint a king: "Elisha ... you shall anoint as prophet in your place."

In the prophetic portions of the Old Testament, this designation is given to a particular personage who is spoken of as the one who is coming to free Israel from her yoke and to set her upon God's pathway. In all the passages where this "Deliverer" is mentioned by David, the royal prophet, he is plainly viewed as being a coming king. David, in Psalm 2, pictures the heathen raging and the people imagining a vain thing "against the Lord and against His anointed."

Isaiah also uses the term "the anointed" with reference to the promised Deliverer (Isaiah 61:1–2), but sees him primarily as a prophet or great teacher. He quotes him as saying, "The Spirit of the Lord Jehovah is upon me; because Jehovah has anointed me to preach good tidings unto the meek.... " (Revised Version of 1901.)

Daniel is the other prophet who uses the title "the anointed one" of the great coming personage foretold by the prophets, and he clearly designates him as not only a prince, but also as a high priest, an expiator of guilt ("Seventy weeks are decreed upon thy people ... to anoint the most holy," Daniel 9:24, Revised Version of 1901). Westcott (1884) summarizes the meaning of the title "Christ" and its Old Testament equivalent "Messiah" as marking generally one who had been given a divine gift for the fulfillment of a divine office. All limited offices, all partial endowments of earlier anointed ones, or "christs," were preparatory foreshadowings of "The Christ," in whom every work of prophet, priest, and king found its perfect consummation. Chafer (1948) concurs in the opinion that the word "Messiah" contemplates Christ as the final or greatest Prophet, the final Priest, and the final King.

Development of the Messianic Idea

Having considered the Old Testament usage of the term "Messiah," it is important to consider briefly the development of the messianic idea in the Old

Testament Scriptures, together with its perfect fulfillment in Jesus Christ. The first intimation that God would provide redemption for the fallen race came with God's confrontation of Adam and Eve in the garden where they fell. The first promise of a redeemer, a person through whom redemption would come, was made on this occasion when God promised victory over the tempter through the "seed of the woman" (Genesis 3:15, NASB). Thus, very early in history, both the divine and human sides of the hope for redemption were revealed and called for the incarnation of God in human flesh.

Prior to Abraham's time, the coming redemption was not narrowed to any segment of the whole race, but the bearing of the hope and the production of the redeemer was then restricted to his descendants (Genesis 12:3 [NASB], "In you all the families of the earth shall be blessed."). In Jacob's day, the line of the redeemer's ancestry was restricted to Judah, and for the first time it was intimated that the redeemer might be a Messiah—an anointed king (Genesis 49:10 [NASB], "The scepter shall not depart from Judah.... ").

With the accession of David to the throne, the fact of the redeemer's humanity became prominent. David and his descendants upon the throne became the mediatorial representatives of God. The hope of redemption had become at last truly a "Messianic hope" (2 Samuel 7:12–13 [NASB], "I will raise up your descendant after you.... I will establish the throne of his kingdom forever."). As the representative of Jehovah, the anointed Davidic king was for the salvation of Israel from her enemies. And, although Israel did not understand it, he was for the salvation of all men as well.

The history of the Davidic dynasty with the failure of Solomon and Jeroboam, and the consequent separation of ten of the twelve tribes, dimmed the hope of redemption through a man; hence, in the years after Jeroboam the divine character of the Messiah became more prominent in messianic prediction (Isaiah 40:10 [NASB], "Behold, the Lord God will come.").

In addition, the prophecies specify more clearly how that Messiah should not be merely the dynasty, or any group of the kings, but a certain definite person (Isaiah 11:1 [NASB], "Then a shoot will spring from the stem of Jesse"; Isaiah 9:6, "For a child will be born to us."). Further, in the prophecies regarding this one, two distinct lines of prediction developed:

(1) that of the suffering servant who would be the savior of the whole world, and (2) that of reigning king who would destroy the wicked at his coming and fulfill all Jewish hopes for their nation. While Isaiah 52:13 to 53:12 speaks of the suffering servant, and Zechariah 9:9–10 displays the reigning king, both lines of prophecy unite in one passage in Zechariah 12:1–11. This two-sidedness of Old Testament prediction of the coming salvation—the human as opposed to the divine, the suffering as opposed to the glory—is described and interpreted beautifully by Delitzsch (1952) in his commentary on Psalm 72. Using the metaphor of two stars of promise arising from opposite directions in the night of the Old Testament prophecies, he notes that one describes its path from above downward, and the other its path from below upward. The former is the promise of Jehovah who is about to come, and the latter is the prophecy of the Son of David. These two stars ultimately meet, blend together into one star, and the night vanishes and it is day. "This one Star is Jesus Christ, Jahve and the Son of David in one person, the King of Israel and at the same time the Redeemer of the world, in one word, the God-man" (Delitzsch 1952: 300).

It is not the divine sonship of the Lord that constitutes Him The Christ, and it is not the Davidic sonship that constitutes Him the Messiah, but it is the two inseparably united that make Him "The Christ."

New Testament Significance

The name "Christ" is a title applied to Jesus by others and accepted by Him as a correct description of His person and work. It is important to note that the title as used in the New Testament carries with it all that is implicit in the Old Testament title "Messiah." In addition, it retains in the New Testament its Old Testament covenant flavor signifying that Christ is the anointed King who will rule over the theocracy of Old Testament and New Testament prophecy, in keeping with the covenant God made with David. It was founded on divine revelation and both Jesus and the apostles make use of it (Matthew 20:20–21; Luke 24:21; Acts 1:6) without any attempt to explain its meaning. It was this background of meaning that made Herod uneasy at His birth, resulting in the slaughter of the babies (Matthew 2:4); and it was this recognized meaning that resulted in His death (Matthew 26:63).

Matthew 20:21–31

21. And he said unto her, What wilt thou? She saith unto him, Grant that these my two sons may sit, the one on thy right hand, and the other on the left, in thy kingdom.

22. But Jesus answered and said, Ye know not what ye ask. Are ye able to drink of the cup that I shall drink of, and to be baptized with the baptism that I am baptized with? They say unto him, We are able.

23. And he saith unto them, Ye shall drink indeed of my cup, and be baptized with the baptism that I am baptized with: but to sit on my right hand, and on my left, is not mine to give, but it shall be given to them for whom it is prepared of my Father.

24. And when the ten heard it, they were moved with indignation against the two brethren.

25. But Jesus called them unto him, and said, Ye know that the princes of the Gentiles exercise dominion over them, and they that are great exercise authority upon them.

26. But it shall not be so among you: but whosoever will be great among you, let him be your minister;

27. And whosoever will be chief among you, let him be your servant:

28. Even as the Son of man came not to be ministered unto, but to minister, and to give his life a ransom for many.

29. And as they departed from Jericho, a great multitude followed him.

30. And, behold, two blind men sitting by the way side, when they heard that Jesus passed by, cried out, saying, Have mercy on us, O Lord, thou Son of David.

31. And the multitude rebuked them, because they should hold their peace: but they cried the more, saying, Have mercy on us, O Lord, thou Son of David.

Luke 24:21

21. But we trusted that it had been he which should have redeemed Israel: and beside all this, to day is the third day since these things were done.

Acts 1:6

6. When they therefore were come together, they asked of him, saying, Lord, wilt thou at this time restore again the kingdom to Israel?

While the disciples understood that He was The Christ (Matthew 16:16) in the strict Old Testament sense, it is of value to observe how often they were charged not to make Him known by this title. The prohibition was undoubtedly based on the fact that the offer of the kingdom to the nation was conditioned on repentance; the nation refused to repent, and the representatives of the nation, the Sanhedrin, conspired to put Jesus to death. In God's plan, this earthly kingdom was already postponed to a second coming, and the prohibition was in accord with discretion and wisdom, since to proclaim it publicly would have been tantamount to treason under the Roman government. The prohibition lasted only until Christ's death; afterward, it became a favorite title because: (1) it was necessary to show He was still "The Christ"; (2) in spite of His death, faith in "The Christ" indicated hope in the final fulfillment of covenant prophecy; and (3) His death would enable the proclamation of "The Christ" throughout the Roman Empire without fear of the charge of treason. There was no recorded instance where the Jewish meaning for "Christ" was changed after His death, and thus covenant and prophecy demanded the retention of the theocratic idea in the title of Christ. Any such change would have involved rejection of the Davidic covenant and the declaration that the Jews had been mistaken in their conceptions of the Messiah and must receive Jesus as "The Christ" on some other grounds.

The fact of the retention of the full messianic idea in the title is seen in that the apostles constantly pointed believers to the Second Coming for a glorious realization of the promises intimately connected with the Christhood of the Lord. It is clear from the Scripture that when He comes again, He comes as "The Christ," the anointed King who is to reign as David's son and Lord just as covenant and prophecy required. The judgment seat will be established, the saints when He comes to reign will reign with Christ (Revelation 20:4), and the saints at Christ's appearing will appear with Him in glory (Colossians 3:4; see also Philippians 3:20; Revelation 11:15; 1 Thessalonians 5:9, 23; 1 Corinthians 15:21–23; Acts 17:30–31).

Furthermore, Scripture indicates that the last opposition of the kings of the earth will be against "The Christ," who has aroused their anger by coming to assert His claim to kingship over the whole earth (Revelation 11:15, 18). Instead of being wise, acknowledging the Son and giving willing obedience, they resist "The Christ" and perish under His wrath (Psalms 2). It is The Christ, coming to manifest Himself as such, who is opposed, and all opposition is effectively dealt with by Him as the mighty theocratic king.

If the title "The Christ" is filled with theocratic meaning, and it is, the question arises, What value does the term have for believers living in the present age? It is as the Messiah that He comes to be the savior of the world (cf. Isaiah 53), and therefore a proper conception of Him as The Christ is a vital one to a proper understanding of a completed redemption. The saints who are destined to be kings are specially declared to be "Christ's body" (1 Corinthians 12:27), and will be associated in rulership with Him (Revelation 20:6). Christ is the head of the body, and the honor and exaltation of the head are communicated to the body.

The preaching of the first preachers of the new age was centered in "The Christ": Peter preached Christ (Acts 2:30–36); Philip preached Christ (Acts 8:5, 12); and Paul preached Christ (Acts 9:20, 22). It was necessary to declare prominently the name of Christ in order to reach the Jewish heart and to satisfy the longing of the Gentiles for deliverance from the bondage of sin.

Conclusion

The New Testament title "The Christ" has special reference to the theocratic order and rule as centered in the person of the Old Testament Redeemer who is identified as the Lord Jesus in a host of New Testament passages. In the use of the name, the Lord and the apostolic writers never divorce it from either of the lines of Old Testament messianic prediction: the Suffering Servant and all that the suffering entailed together with the salvation it purchased, and the glorious reigning King whose return will inaugurate the earthly kingdom of biblical prophecy.

Wayne S. Flory

See also Messiah; Second Coming

Bibliography

Chafer, Lewis Sperry. (1948) *Systematic Theology*. Dallas: Dallas Seminary Press.

Cremer, Hermann. (1895) *Biblico-Theological Lexicon of New Testament Greek*. Edinburgh, UK: T. & T. Clark.

Delitzsch, Franz. (1952) *Biblical Commentary on the Psalms*. Grand Rapids, MI: Wm. B. Eerdmans.

Eager, George B. (1949) "Anointing." In *International Standard Bible Encyclopedia*, vol. 1. Grand Rapids, MI: Wm. B. Eerdmans, 138.

McClintock, John, and James Strong, eds. (1902) "Christ." In *Encyclopedia of Biblical, Theological, and Ecclesiastical Literature*, vol. 2. New York: Charles Scribner's Sons, 260.

Peters, George N. H. (1952) *The Theocratic Kingdom of Our Lord Jesus the Christ*. Grand Rapids, MI: Kregel Publications.

Westcott, Brooke Foss. (1884) *The Revelation of the Father*. London: Macmillan and Company.

Christian Coalition

The Christian Coalition is an outgrowth of religious broadcaster Pat Robertson's failed campaign for the Republican presidential nomination in 1988. Formed in October 1989, the well-marketed organization is demonstrative of the political and media expertise of conservative Evangelical and Fundamentalist Christians who seek to play a prominent role in American political life. Supporters of the Christian Coalition form an active grass-roots organization that backs conservative Christian candidates for public office. The Coalition's clout has grown considerably since its formation, and Republican nominees for president, most recently George W. Bush, openly court the

Coalition's backing. The Christian Coalition's political activism stems from its belief that the United States has traditionally been a Christian nation and that concerted efforts are necessary to stop the spread of secularism that its supporters maintain threatens America's survival.

The Christian Coalition is only the latest prominent organization to surface in the emergence of the "Religious Right" since the 1970s. In 1976, conservative Southern Democrat Jimmy Carter, a self-proclaimed "born-again" Christian captured the presidency. But Carter's troubled term in office, coupled with his moderately left-wing commitment to social equity, led many Fundamentalists to support more conservative candidates. Fundamentalist Jerry Falwell, chancellor of Liberty University and broadcaster of the *Old Time Gospel Hour*, founded his politically active Moral Majority in 1979. Falwell's organization helped Republican Ronald Reagan defeat Carter in the 1980 presidential election, and Falwell became influential during the first Reagan term. He gradually distanced himself from direct political involvement, however, a role soon enthusiastically filled by Pat Robertson, founder of the Christian Broadcasting Network (CBN) and the main presenter on the popular *700 Club*. The son of a former United States senator, Robertson often seemed more interested in politics than religion and regularly filled his program with political commentary. Robertson's disappointing showing in the early Republican primaries led him to exit the 1988 presidential election, but not politics. Ironically, Robertson came to have greater political influence through the Christian Coalition than he had as a presidential candidate.

During the early and mid-1990s, the Christian Coalition, under the day-to-day leadership of its executive director, Ralph Reed, became a viable force in conservative politics. Reed, a talented political strategist with a Ph.D. in American history, became a high-profile spokesman for the Coalition and found many admirers within Republican ranks during the first years of Bill Clinton's presidency when Republicans often vociferously sought to counter Clinton's policy initiatives. Although Reed stepped down as executive director of the Coalition in 1997, the organization continues to thrive under Robertson's overall direction.

The Christian Coalition takes a number of controversial positions. It opposes abortion and among its goals is the eventual reversal of *Roe v. Wade*, the 1973 United States Supreme Court decision that legalized abortion. The organization is also against homosexuality, which Robertson has publically denounced, as well as federal hegemony in national affairs. Such conservative positions are likely to make the Christian Coalition a major presence in American politics during the administration of George W. Bush.

Scott Lupo

See also Media, Mass; Moral Majority; Promise Keepers; Televangelism

Bibliography

Capps, Walter H. (1990) *The New Religious Right: Piety, Patriotism, and Politics.* Columbia: University of South Carolina Press.

Foege, Alec. (1996) *The Empire God Built: Inside Pat Robertson's Media Machine.* New York: John Wiley and Sons.

Rozell, Mark J., and Clyde Wilcox. (1995) *God at the Grass Roots: The Christian Right in the 1994 Elections.* Lanham, MD: Rowman and Littlefield.

Watson, Justin. (1997) *The Christian Coalition: Dreams of Restoration, Demands for Recognition.* New York: St. Martin's Press.

Christian Home, Ideal

The church and the home are two institutions that are central to Christian Fundamentalists' religious ideals. While the church is considered a safe haven for troubled souls, the home is regarded as a challenge to believers because it is constantly buffeted by the permissive society. In fact, most Fundamentalist groups believe that the continuing spiritual vigor of their members is intricately linked to their marriages and family lives. Hence, regulations of sexual behavior, marriage, and the home constitute an important concern for such groups.

Marriage and the Home Life among Fundamentalists

Most Fundamentalist groups strive to have their marriages and homes structured according to strict Christian principles. Although there are some differing views as to what constitutes these principles, for

PATRIA CHRISTIAN SCHOOL

Patria represents a unique thrust in elementary school education. The concepts on which Patria is founded introduce a new dimension into the Christian School curriculum and could well spearhead a new movement across this nation.

Patria's special features include:

- **a program in which the child's learning process is a total family experience**
- **a Christ-centered curriculum that includes grading on selected subjects taught by the parents**
- **classes where parents learn the practical application of scriptural principles to successful family living**
- **a link which ties together home, school and church in a meaningful way**

Patria is a Greek word meaning family. It is also a derivative of the Greek word for father. Webster defines the family as parents and children and therefore, the Patria Christian School is, in essence, the Family Christian School. As an arm of the home Patria seeks to enhance the biblical concept of the family, with the father as the head and its members in submission to him. Children are taught in an environment where scriptural principles are predominant. History is taught as His Story. Science is presented as the revelation of His Creation. Math depicts God as unchanging. (Two plus two is always four.)

The staff of Patria is pledged to academic and spiritual excellence in a Christ-centered atmosphere!

From brochure, Patria Christian School, Portsmouth, VA

the majority of Christian Fundamentalists the understanding is that the ideal Christian home is expected to be radically different from the societal standards. Moreover, it is also believed that the Christian family is becoming the target of satanic attacks with the aim of causing disunity in the church. Therefore, Christians must resist the corrupting influences of worldliness. Some even go to the extent of discouraging the reading of books on marriage written by non-Christians, or visiting counselors or family planning clinics that are not sanctioned by the leaders of the groups.

The foundation of the religious group and the composition of its membership influence to what extent and in what manner these groups will attend to marriage and family life. For groups in which the majority of the members are young singles, this issue is of particular concern when these members begin to settle into marriage, especially if such a demographic change diminishes their active involvement. In other cases, the introduction of administrative and organizational procedures among the first-generation members often brings about the establishment of rules that govern marriage and the home as part of the changing organizational structure of the group. The

Christian home is second only in sanctity to the church; therefore, Fundamentalists believe strongly in its foundations, such as the choice of a mate and the nature of the courtship and marriage.

The Principal Priorities

Christian Fundamentalists share definite ideas about marriage and the family. The most important is that marriage and the home should be Christ-centered and guided by the Scriptures. Marriage is a God-ordained institution, and the scriptural regulations define its operation. Companionship, procreation, and the prevention of fornication are often stated to be the reasons for marriage.

The choice of one's mate partly determines the future of the home; therefore, believers must pray for God's guidance in selecting their mates. Moreover, believers should not allow the ridicule of friends, the anxiety of parents, and other outside influences to rush them into making a hasty choice. Once that choice is made, the courtship must be free from sexual intimacy. Fundamentalists have attempted to sustain moral purity by stressing the doctrine of holiness and applying such to the lifestyles among their

MOTHERHOOD

What, then, does make a Mommie in the truest sense of the word? There must be some answer and it is probably a combination one! Mommie thought back to the bathnight and Daddy helping with the children. "That's it—or part of it," she decided. "It's the sense of doing the work together, the sharing of the burden and responsibility, the mutual dependence one upon the other. Something . . . not everything, but something is missing when being a Mommie is an all-alone job. God recognized that, for He said, 'I will be a father to the fatherless.'"

But is just having children and bringing them up to the best physical beauty and moral perfection enough? Isn't there a higher conception of motherhood, a God-given understanding?

Mommie thought of the things that had been whispered to her heart when each time she first knew there was another baby on the way. "Another, Lord? My hands are now so full."

"I know it, child, . . . I filled them, and I'll supply the grace and strength. . . . Will you take another one to raise for Me? And I'll be there."

What could one do but gladly receive the trust, rejoicing that one had been so blessed? And looking forward to the future years, if the Lord tarry, one sees eight grown sons and daughters in His service, and one senses a fulfillment. The heavy burdened years seem but a dream, and one begins to perceive what it means to be a mother."

Source: Aldrich, Doris Coffin. (1949) *Musings of a Mother.* Chicago: Moody Press, p. 88.

young members. Christians who strive to have an ideal home should not marry unbelievers. This is considered a scriptural commandment, and defying it constitutes a sin. Some groups even encourage marriages within their folds. Members can freely marry outsiders and bring them into the church but not vice versa.

The husband and wife have separate but specific roles in the ideal Christian home. Marriage is strictly monogamous and the family is headed by the husband. He is responsible for the spiritual, financial, and social needs of the household. Among his responsibilities are to love his wife with a constant and selfless love, lead the family in daily devotion, provide guidance to the children, and drive the family to church activities. The wife has a subsidiary role as the husband's helpmate. In time past, many wives were full-time mothers who stayed at home; however, contemporary economic reality has forced some to join the labor force. Nonetheless, child-rearing and cooking are still the prerogatives of the wife. The wife is expected to be obedient and submit completely to the husband. Even if the husband is an unbeliever, the wife's submissive role is not lessened, but she is expected to pray constantly for the spouse's conversion. This male prescription for the dominance of women may be shocking to feminists, but this idea is prevalent among Fundamentalists.

In the ideal Christian home, the expectation is that the parents, rather than society, will exert the greatest spiritual and moral influence on the children. The parents share the responsibility of raising and caring for the children under God's guidance. In fact, the parents must ensure their children's spiritual growth by relating closely to the Bible, and telling Bible stories in order to impart the Christian ideal to them. Generally, the picture of an ideal home is that of the parents and children sitting together to pray or read the Bible, or attending church with Bible in hand. Children are also taught how to recognize sinful situations and overcome temptation. When they become teenagers, the church is always at hand to enroll them into the youth or teenagers clubs.

Love must radiate among members and disagreements should be amicably settled. Divorce is discouraged, and believers who have divorced their partners are judged to be less committed to the Christian ideals, and may be excluded from the group. Concerning sexual relations, Fundamentalists differ on whether to use artificial family planning methods. However, most are pro-life and view any legislation allowing abortion as abhorrent. Cultural and societal expectations greatly influence how a Fundamentalist copes with childlessness. Other than praying for miraculous intervention, modern medical treatments such as fertility drugs and in vitro fertilization are often encouraged. Adoption is considered the last resort.

The methods used to enforce compliance of regulations on marriage and the home life include regular teaching sessions, sermons, Bible studies, and the reading of selected devotional books written by the leaders. The emphases on marriage and the home are also taught as aspects of the doctrine of holiness or as one's responsibility to God. The expected standard of holy life is generally measured against biblical standards and the permissiveness in the society. Moreover, counseling sessions are arranged, and seminars on marriage and the home are included in programs of conferences and camp meetings.

Conclusion

Marriage and the home are the bedrock of the Christian society envisaged by Fundamentalists. Therefore, the importance placed on the doctrine of the ideal Christian home is meant to subordinate members to the leaders, to test fidelity to church doctrines, to show the distance of the religious organizations to the wider society, and to eventually transform the individual and ultimately the society. Revivalist movements are only long-lasting if they develop institutional forms, mostly puritanical in conception. Fundamentalist groups often attempt to encompass the whole life of their members, and as such regulations about the home are institutional means of achieving dominance over the lives of their members.

Matthews A. Ojo

See also Abortion; Antifeminism; Bible Study; Male Headship; Pastor's Wife

Bibliography

Ammerman, Nancy Taton. (1987) *Bible Believers: Fundamentalists in the Modern World*. New Brunswick, NJ: Rutgers University Press.

Forster, Lawrence. (1984) *Religion and Sexuality*. Urbana and Chicago: University of Illinois Press.

Hastings, Adrian. (1973) *Christian Marriage in Africa*. London: Society for Promoting Christian Knowledge.

Lamanna, Mary Ann, and Agnes Riedmann. (1985) *Marriages and Families: Making Choices Throughout the Life Cycle*. Belmont, CA: Wadsworth Publishing.

Ojo, Matthews A. (1997) "Sexuality, Marriage and Piety among Nigerian Charismatic Movements." In *Rites of Passage in Contemporary Africa*, edited by James L. Cox. Cardiff: Cardiff Academic Press, 180–197.

Rassieur, Charles L. (1988) *Pastor, Our Marriage Is in Trouble: A Guide to Short-term Counselling*. Philadelphia: The Westminster Press.

Christian Research Institute

The Christian Research Institute (CRI), located in Rancho Santa Margarita, California, was founded by Walter Martin (1928–1989) in 1960 as an apologetic ministry (defenders of Christianity) against alternative faiths and beliefs, both within and outside of the church. Its mission for the last sixty years has been "to provide Christians worldwide with carefully researched information and well-reasoned answers that encourage them in their faith and equip them to intelligently represent it to people influenced by ideas and teachings that assault or undermine orthodox, biblical Christianity" (http://www.equip.org). CRI attempts to achieve its mission through five specific goals, spelled out by the acronym EQUIP: "E" stands for essentials, or the basic tenets of biblical Christianity, so that believers may differentiate the true faith from heretical ones. "Q" represents the word "questions." CRI promotes itself as a resource center to answer people's questions regarding Christian beliefs. "U" stands for user-friendly. CRI presents accurate information in its simplest form, so to be easily understood. The Institute also prides itself on integrity, "I." The organization is fiscally accountable, belonging to various regulators including the Better Business Bureau, the Internal Revenue Service, and the Evangelical Counsel for Financial Accountability (ECFA). (During the late 1990s, however, CRI found itself embroiled in many scandals including a dispute over current president and CEO Hank Hanegraaff's book royalties for *Christianity in Crisis*, and temporary membership withdrawal from ECFA.) Finally, "P" represents parachurch. CRI is committed to the use of local churches as the medium for evangelism and education.

CRI maintains an extensive website and online bookstore, publishes the quarterly magazine

Christian Research Journal, offers degree and nondegree courses in conjunction with Christian colleges, and broadcasts a daily radio show, *Bible Answer Man*, hosted by Hanegraaff. In 1995, it had an annual revenue in excess of three million dollars.

Beth Marie Forrest

Bibliography

"Apology Follows Hanegraaff Attack." (1997) *Christianity Today* 41 (11 August): 54.

"Apologetics Ministry Resolves Wrongful Termination Suit: Other Ex-Employees Still Question Book Royalties." (1995) *Christianity Today* 39 (11 September): 88.

Christian Research Institute. http://www.equip.org.

Church

The word "church" comes from the Anglo-Saxon word *cirice*, which is derived from the Greek word *to kyriakon*, meaning the "Lord's house" or the "Lord's body." The English word translates the New Testament word "ekklesia," used in the early Greek city-states to signify the assembly of citizens summoned by a herald to vote on an issue. In the Septuagint, a pre-Christian Greek translation of the Hebrew Old Testament, the word "ekklesia" referred to Israel as assembled for religious and cultic purposes (Deuteronomy 31:30; 1 Kings 8:55). With the essential connection with Israel of the new people of God (Galatians 6:16), the New Testament writers followed the usage of the Septuagint and spoke of those who were united by a common confession of Jesus as Lord.

The Nature of the Church

In Christianity, the church ("ecclesia") or "called out ones," is a community founded on the teachings of Jesus Christ and striving to bear witness to Christ's gospel. The church in the New Testament goes back to the disciples associated with Jesus during His earthly ministry. As they were gathered on the day of Pentecost they received His Spirit poured out upon them, empowering them to witness unto Him as the risen Christ (Acts 1:8). In the imagery of the apostle Paul, the church is the body of Christ and Christ is the head of His body. The church is thus a spiritual communion of the whole people of God. Within church history there emerged a distinction between the "invisible church" and the "visible church." In the invisible church its members enjoyed the invisible grace of the Spirit (1 Corinthians 12:4) that enlivened them into one body and united them to Christ the head (Ephesians 4:15–16). This is sometimes called the "communion of saints."

Christian history reflects different interpretations of what the church is and how it should be organized. Roman Catholics traditionally united around apostolic authority based on Scripture and church tradition mediated through the bishops. With Vatican II, the identification of the church with the papacy and the institution was rejected in favor of an understanding of the church as a mystery and sacrament subsisting in the Catholic Church. Orthodox and Anglican traditions stressed the role of the episcopacy in the definition of the church. Churches of the Reformation reasserted the Scripture as the true measure of apostolicity. The true church was to be distinguished by the faithful preaching of the Word, the proper celebration of the sacraments, and the exercise of church discipline. The Calvinist churches promoted church discipline along with the integrity of the Word and affirmation of the sacrament. This is the mark of the visible church. To the Reformer John Calvin, the invisible church included "all the elect from the beginning of the world." Yet Calvin saw no possibility of achieving a pure church or the equation of the invisible church and visible church. Only God was capable of separating the "wheat" from the "tares." Calvin posited, however, "presumptive tests" composed of a confession of faith, the example of one's life, and partaking of the sacraments that one could use here on earth. Congregationalists and Baptists emphasized the authority of Christ as expressed through the congregation. The local congregation consists of men and women who acknowledge the Lordship of Jesus Christ and seek His will and govern themselves through congregational vote, covenant, and participation. The "gathered church" of the continental Anabaptists argued that all the members of the church have had a conversion experience and that they are free of state control.

The Organized Church

The concept of an organized church has been rejected by certain groups. John Nelson Darby, leader of the Plymouth Brethren, argued for the rejection of denominations. This has not been true, however, in the United States where dispensational theology has

1 Corinthians 12:4–6

4. Now there are diversities of gifts, but the same Spirit.

5. And there are differences of administrations, but the same Lord.

6. And there are diversities of operations, but it is the same God which worketh all in all.

Ephesians 4:15–16

15. But speaking the truth in love, may grow up into him in all things, which is the head, even Christ:

16. From whom the whole body fitly joined together and compacted by that which every joint supplieth, according to the effectual working in the measure of every part, maketh increase of the body unto the edifying of itself in love.

been the mainstay of the American Fundamentalist movement, but the assembling of churches into some sort of fellowship has been accepted. One group has even called themselves the "Independent Fundamentalist Churches of America." There are some conservative denominations in the United States that would find themselves in agreement with the tenants of American Fundamentalism but have kept their denominational name. In addition, there are certain individual churches in various denominations that would informally classify themselves as holding to the beliefs of the Fundamentalist movement in America. There are also individuals in local churches who would hold beliefs similar to American Fundamentalism. In the contemporary United States, there are local churches who proclaim that they are "nondenominational," that is, they are not affiliated with the "mainline" Protestant denominations. Some of these nondenominational churches, however, have banded together into fellowships that are called by the same name, have their own hierarchy, confessional statements, and schools or training institutes. They thus operate as denominations whether or not they wish to be called a denomination.

Conclusion

The word "church" has come to have a wide variety of subsidiary or popular meanings. It has been used to signify a denomination, such as the "Methodist Church" or "the Lutheran Church." In the popular mind, the word "church" is often associated with a church building. It may also refer to the programs and services provided to a specific constituency by a local church in a particular geographical location.

Leland Edward Wilshire

Bibliography

Alston, Wallace M. (1984) *The Church*. Atlanta, GA: John Knox Press.

Berkouwer, Gerrit Cornelius. (1976) *The Church*. Grand Rapids, MI: Wm. B. Eerdmans.

Halton, Thomas P. (1985) *The Church*. Wilmington, DE: M. Glazier.

Küng, Hans. (1976) *The Church*. Garden City, NY: Image Books.

Pannenburg, Wolfhart. (1963) *The Church*. Philadelphia: Westminster Press.

Church of God

The Church of God is a Christian fellowship that began in 1881 with the acceptance by the minister Daniel S. Warner (1842–1895) of the idea of Holiness, which Methodists saw as a baptism or second act of the Holy Spirit that came to Christians and made them perfect in love. Warner called together a group of like-minded people, many formerly members of the General Eldership of the Churches of God in America, and together they declared themselves free from creeds and denominational labels. Their only allegiance would be to the apostolic church, though their interpretation of the Bible closely resembled that of the Methodists. The Church of God promoted a relationship to God established by repentance of sins and faith in Christ and the need of church members to seek perfection. The church uniquely came to understand God's Church as a divine institution, the one true church, composed of all true Christian believers and certainly not limited to the fellowship created by Warner. The realization of the nature of the church leads toward its unity. Membership in the church was obtained through the salvation of Christ and no worldly acts of joining were necessary. The Church of God members were also amillennialists, believing that the imminent event culminating human history would be Christ's return and that God would not establish any earthly millennial reign. Many Fundamentalists, being staunch premillennialists, did not accept the Church of God's stance.

The Church of God movement is currently composed of a spectrum of conservative Evangelical Christian denominations. The name "Church of God" is believed to be the only appropriate and biblical one by which the true church established by Jesus called itself. Many of the older denominations such as the Church of God (Anderson, Indiana) participated in the nineteenth-century Holiness movement, while others, such as the Church of God International (Cleveland, Tennessee), grew out of the Pentecostal revival that swept through the Holiness movement at the beginning of the twentieth century. Although Holiness churches are divided doctrinally from most Fundamentalists (who came from a Calvinist theological tradition), they share the same allegiance to a literalist interpretation of the Bible, the affirmation of what are considered essential Christian beliefs, and an emphasis on evangelism.

Most of the denominations that selected the name also saw themselves taking a step away from sectarian labels (Methodist, Baptist, Lutheran, etc.). However, as the number of new denominations with the same name appeared, some means of distinguishing among them was developed, usually by adding the city and state in which they were headquartered to their name.

The Church of God movement spread internationally through the early nineteenth century, and congregations can now be found across the Caribbean, Africa, Europe, and the South Pacific. The church generally sided with the Fundamentalist cause in the 1920s and 1930s but did not take part in the major battles. In the last half of the twentieth century, it identified with the Evangelical movement though it is not a member of the National Association of Evangelicals. The Church of God headquarters remain in Anderson, Indiana, where Warner Press, its publishing house, and a college and theological seminary have been established.

J. Gordon Melton

See also Holiness, Wesleyan

Bibliography

Callen, Barry L., ed. (1979) *The First Century*, 2 vols. Anderson, IN: Warner Press.

Sterner, R. Eugene. (1960) *We Reach Our Hands in Fellowship*. Anderson, IN: Warner Press.

Church of the Nazarene

The Church of the Nazarene is a Protestant denomination that is one of the more prominent representatives of the nineteenth-century Holiness movement that spread through the several Methodist churches in North America. Its founder, Phineas Bresee (1838–1915) began his career as a minister in the Methodist Episcopal Church in Iowa and California. In 1894, at the end of his career, he requested the bishop to grant him a special appointment to the Penial Mission, a small independent Holiness mission in Los Angeles, California. When the bishop refused, he left the church and accepted the tasks of leading the mission. The following year, he began a new career as the pastor of the first Church of the Nazarene. His work was so successful that a second congregation was started in Berkeley, California, in 1897. Other congregations soon emerged and in 1905 Bresee became the general superintendent.

The Church of the Nazarene grew through a series of mergers with other small independent Holiness associations. Its 1907 merger with the Pentecostal Church on the East Coast led to a new name, the Pentecostal Church of the Nazarene; however, with the spread of the competing Pentecostal sects that emphasized speaking in tongues, the original name of the church was resumed in 1919. The church began to develop outside of the United States in 1915 when it merged with the Pentecostal Church of Scotland. The various mergers throughout the twentieth century did not dampen evangelistic zeal, and missionaries supported by the church spread its message to more than fifty countries worldwide.

The Church of the Nazarene follows a traditional Holiness perspective. Members are expected to have had a saving experience of faith in Jesus Christ and to be either actively seeking sanctification or to have reached that state. Like other Holiness groups, the Nazarenes hold that believers can seek and receive the baptism of the Holy Spirit, which both empowers them and makes them perfect in love. All members are required to adhere to a code of strict behavior, which includes refraining from alcohol, tobacco, and other recreational drugs, illicit sex, and secret societies. Members are expected to tithe.

While generally favoring the Fundamentalist cause during the 1920s and 1930s, the Church of the Nazarene remained separate from the movement due in large part to the Calvinist theological perspective adopted by most Fundamentalist leaders. However, the Nazarenes generally agreed with the literalist interpretation of the Bible, the necessity of faith in Christ, and the need to affirm traditional Christian beliefs. In the decades since World War II, it identified with the worldwide Evangelical movement and in 1984 joined the National Association of Evangelicals.

The Church of the Nazarene has its headquarters in Kansas City, Missouri, where its publishing house, Beacon Hill Press, and the Nazarene Theological Seminary are located. At the beginning of the new century, the church reported a membership in excess of 1,300,000, with slightly more than half the membership produced by its worldwide missionary endeavor. The church is especially strong in the Caribbean and Africa. In the 1950s, a Church of the Nazarene minister, Glenn Griffith, became disenchanted with the church, complaining that it and other prominent Holiness churches were becoming too worldly. Griffith led a movement calling for the formation of the Bible Missionary Church to accommodate those who accepted his charges.

J. Gordon Melton

See also Holiness, Weslyan; Pentacostalism

Bibliography

Purkiser, W. T. (1983) *Called unto Holiness II*. Kansas City, MO: Nazarene Publishing House.

Redford, M. E. (1948) *The Rise of the Church of the Nazarene*. Kansas City, MO: Beacon Hill Press.

Smith, Timothy. (1962) *Called unto Holiness*. Kansas City, MO: Nazarene Publishing House.

Churches of Christ

The Church of Christ is an international association of conservative Evangelical Christian congregations that emerged out of the efforts in the revivals and camp meetings held on the American frontier in the early nineteenth century. Barton Stone (1772–1844), a Presbyterian minister in Kentucky, observed the famous revival at Cane Ridge. Motivated by his experience with the revival and his previous doubts about several points of Presbyterian doctrine, he and several colleagues organized the independent Springfield presbytery in 1804. However, within months they also concluded that presbyteries were invalid and after penning their conclusions in "The Last Will and Testament of the Springfield Presbytery," resolved to be known as "Christians only."

Meanwhile, Thomas Campbell (1763–1854), a minister in an independent branch of Scotch Presbyterianism, migrated to America. He had worked for the reunion of the several Scottish churches with little to show for his efforts. Then in 1809, he founded the Christian Association of Washington, Pennsylvania, to promote Christian unity. A basic principle (that became the group's motto) defined the new approach, "Where the Scriptures speak, we speak; where the Scriptures are silent, we are silent." Joined by his son Alexander Campbell, who had come to share many of his father's opinions, Campbell continued his study of the Scriptures. He ordained Alexander in 1811.

Principles and Practices of the Movement

Though working separately in different states, Stine and the Campbells were reaching many of the same conclusions. For example, they accepted baptism by immersion as the proper scriptural mode. They rejected the making of creeds, the Bible being sufficient, and rejected denominational labels. The Campbells operated through the Redstone Baptist Association for several years, but began to gather congregations that described themselves as simply "Disciples of Christ." In 1832, the followers of Stone and the Campbells met together and over the next few years united as a single fellowship known variously as the Churches of Christ or the Christian church (Disciples of Christ). They were joined by similar groups in Virginia that had been raised up by former Methodist James O'Kelly and in New England by Abner Jones and Elias Smith, both former Baptists.

The movement as it emerged by the middle of the nineteenth century saw itself as restoring first century Christianity. Campbell, writing in 1850 in his periodical, the *Millennial Harbinger*, suggested that it was held together by several points of agreement including the Scripture as the sole authority, Christ as Messiah and Savior, the ancient church order; the authority of the Messiah and the apostles (i.e., the New Testament), above that of the Old Testament; and cooperation among churches. Members were organized into autonomous congregations that believed in baptism by immersion and observed the Lord's Supper weekly. Baptism and the Lord's Supper were seen as ordinances commanded by Scripture, not sacraments. Theological constructs (including Calvinism, Arminianism, Trinitarianism, and Unitarianism) were rejected as unbiblical. Such constructs and the creeds they generated served primarily to create disunity in the Church.

As the restoration movement grew, it manifested an extreme form of Congregationalism. There were no associations or conventions above the congregations, and churches were tied together merely by a sense of fellowship and agreement with the position articulated by the Campbells. The movement was served by a variety of periodicals that represented the different emphases. Schools were founded and sponsored by local congregations and supported by the freewill offerings.

Conflicts in the Movement

In the decades following the American Civil War, tensions entered the movement with the more conservative congregations finding spokespersons in David Lipscomb and Tobert Fanning in Nashville, Tennessee, and Austin McGary of Austin, Texas. Lipscomb became editor of the *Gospel Advocate* and McGary of *Firm Foundation*, the two most popular periodicals advocating the conservative cause. They championed the rejection of instrumental music in the churches (a practice being adopted in some of the northern urban congregations) and opposed the organization of missionary societies (though not the support of missionaries by local churches). They also opposed the new modernist theology that came to be advocated by some leading northern Restoration ministers and the participation of Christian ministers in the emerging ecumenical movement.

By the early twentieth century, tensions within the Restoration movement led to its split with most of the northern churches evolving into the denomination now known as the Christian Church (Disciples of Christ). The largely southern congregations, especially in Tennessee and Texas, became known as the Churches of Christ, with 1906 generally taken as the date of separation. Eventually a third division of the Restoration movement would distinguish itself as the Christian churches and Churches of Christ.

The nature of their organization, lacking a formal denominational structure, their manifest anticreedal approach, and the fact that most people with "modernist" sympathies had associated with the Disciples of Christ, kept the Churches of Christ from being ravaged by the Fundamentalist-modernist controversy. Their sympathies plainly lay with the Fundamentalist cause and its emphasis on biblical authority. Also, their questioning of the doctrine of the Trinity and attachment to various specific biblical admonitions found little sympathy with Presbyterian and Baptist Fundamentalist leaders.

The Fundamentalist issues were, of course, discussed in the periodicals serving Churches of Christ congregations. In the early nineteenth century, a controversy developed over the issue of premillennialism and the dispensational theology that underlay it. Premillennialism, the idea that Christ would return to earth and establish a thousand-year reign, was advocated by a new periodical, *Word and Work*, published in Louisville, Kentucky. Though the idea was rejected by the larger body of the church, there was no mechanism by which the idea and its supporters could be banished. Gradually, through mid-century, the premillennialist Churches of Christ became an identifiable subgroup within the larger movement.

Through the support of missionaries and schools by individual churches, the Churches of Christ have become a large international denomination in the twenty-first century. There have retained their emphasis in local church autonomy and eschew any form of denominational structures. They have also refrained from association with any ecumenical structures including the National Association of Evangelicals and the World Evangelical Fellowship, seeing these as the wrong approach to church unity. The Churches of Christ have an estimated 1.2 million members in the United States and another 750,000 members scattered in congregations worldwide.

J. Gordon Melton

Bibliography

Churches of Christ Around the World. (1990) Nashville, TN: Gospel Advocate Company.
Harrell, David Edwin. (1973) *The Social Sources of Division in the Disciples of Christ.* Athens, GA: Publishing Systems.

Hatch, Nathan O. (1989) *The Democratization of American Christianity*. New Haven, CT: Yale University Press.

West, Earl. *Search for the Ancient Order*, 4 vols. (1950–1987) Nashville, TN; Indianapolis, IN; and Germantown, TN: The Gospel Advocate Company and Religious Book Service.

Common Sense Philosophy

Originating as a reaction against the skepticism of Scottish philosopher David Hume (1711–1776) and the idealism of Irish philosopher George Berkeley (1685–1753), Common Sense Philosophy, or Scottish Realism, has profoundly influenced American Protestant thought. Taking the empirical ideas of John Locke (1632–1704) to their philosophical extremes, Hume and Berkeley asserted that the material universe cannot be assumed to exist outside of the individual's sensory impressions. Even an individual's very existence, Hume suggested, is a product of sensory impressions and can only be recognized as an unverifiable inference. Furthermore, Hume questioned the validity of revealed religion by declaring that the evidence for God's existence is beyond the realm of empirical proof or disproof.

Thomas Reid (1710–1796), a Scottish minister and professor at Glasgow University, rejected the metaphysical speculations of Hume and Berkeley in his *Inquiry into the Human Mind on the Principles of Common Sense* (1764). Claiming that man could confidently understand the world as perceived through the medium of his five senses, Reid advocated a "common sense" approach to philosophical discernment. All knowledge, he explained, is built upon certain self-evident principles that are obvious to every person possessing common sense. Among the self-evident principles affirmed by the Common Sense philosophers were existence outside of perception, the natural functioning of the universe, an intuitive sense of morality, and a belief that the world and all other things that exist must have a cause of origination.

John Witherspoon (1723–1794), a Presbyterian minister and educator from Scotland, carried the ideas of Common Sense Realism to America when he accepted the presidency of the College of New Jersey (which later became Princeton University) in 1768. Witherspoon instructed his students in the principles of the Scottish philosophy, thus establishing it as an integral component in the development of the highly influential Princeton Theology. With the graduation and dissemination of Witherspoon's students, Common Sense Philosophy also made its way into the theological instruction of Harvard, Yale, and numerous other institutions of higher learning. The rapid growth of nineteenth-century Scottish Realism ultimately shaped the theological beliefs of the Calvinists, Unitarians, Primitivists, and nearly every Evangelical movement in antebellum America. Furthermore, it has continued to hold a position of considerable sway among conservative American Christians.

The effects of Scottish Realism on modern Fundamentalist Christian thought are most profoundly observed in their views of Scripture and apologetics. From Scottish philosophy Fundamentalists have gained a "common sense" view of Scripture for the ordinary man. Convinced that the Bible contains the complete and all-sufficient revelation of God, both logically and scientifically sustainable, Fundamentalists maintain that Scripture was made for the purpose of popular comprehension. Therefore, they contend, the only thing necessary for a proper understanding of God's Word is the implementation of common sense while reading it. This same common sense, they further explain, is all that is necessary to recognize the existence of God. Noting the elements of intelligent design in the universe and the need for all things to have an initial cause, Fundamentalists point to God as the obvious designer and first cause of the universe.

Richard J. Cherok

See also Bible Study; Biblical Inerrancy

Bibliography

Ahlstrom, Sydney E. (1955) "The Scottish Philosophy and American Religion." *Church History* 24: 257–272.

Broadie, Alexander. (1990) *The Tradition of Scottish Philosophy: A New Perspective on the Enlightenment*. Savage, MD: Barnes and Noble.

Grave, S. A. (1960) *The Scottish Philosophy of Common Sense*. Oxford, UK: Clarendon Press.

Robinson, Daniel S., ed. (1961) *The Story of Scottish Philosophy: A Compendium of Selections from the Writings of Nine Pre-eminent Scottish Philosophers, with Bibliographical Essays*. New York: Exposition Press.

Communism

Fundamentalist Protestant Christians during the second half of the twentieth century correctly regarded communism as a potentially fatal threat to a Christian America. The intensity of their fear, however, led many to conflate the United States with Christianity, until patriotism became an article of faith. No religious group was so overtly patriotic or as vehemently opposed to "socialism." Evangelicals, though, paid a price for this vehemence as they became stereotyped as mindless reactionaries wrapped in the American flag.

The 1917 Russian Revolution was militantly antireligious. For a time, early in the 1920s, all things "red" were suspect in America. The prominent evangelist, the Rev. Billy Sunday, routinely lambasted "bolshevism," which he blamed for widespread American labor disturbances. This helped set a recurrent pattern among Fundamentalists of ascribing social unrest to communist infiltration, rather than injustice, and prompted others to regard them as uncaring. For the most part, however, Evangelicals had other things to worry about during the interwar years as the Great Depression created a domestic crisis of such staggering proportion that foreign affairs seemed a distant concern.

Some historians, who take their inspiration from the Cold War Era, have typed Evangelicals as reflexive political reactionaries. This was not necessarily the case, although during the 1930s Gerald L. K. Smith did preach an anticommunism jumbled with other supposed social evils. However, it was the American South, drenched as it was in Fundamentalism and Pentecostalism, which most consistently supported the liberal New Deal. The Tennessee Valley Authority and the Rural Electrification Administration together constituted a quasi-socialization of the power industry—and were vastly popular in the South. Whatever a local pastor might think, the general southern populace, which included a huge reservoir of Fundamentalists, supported such measures—or at least Franklin Roosevelt.

It is significant that during the interwar years some religious liberals were attracted to socialism at a time when theological tension between them and conservative Evangelicals was especially intense. Naïveté about communism on the part of some leftist clergy seemed almost deliberate, as with the one-time Yale Divinity School professor who insisted: "It would be a error to consider the Soviet leader [Stalin] a willful man who believes in forcing his ideas upon others" (Roy 1960: 177). Most were not so fatuous, of course, but religious liberalism and political radicalism did keep a certain company during the 1930s. This was noted by Fundamentalists, already besieged, as they thought, by a contemptuous religious modernism. Eventually, it proved easy to add the charge of lack of patriotism to apostasy in their contest with the religious Left. Toward the end of the interwar period, certain Fundamentalists compounded their anticommunism with anti-Semitism, racism, and anti-Catholicism. Such an amalgam of villains was somewhat illogical. Communism and the Catholic Church, for instance, were antithetical. This promiscuous casting about for adversaries gave certain Fundamentalists more than just a tinge of fanaticism.

In 1941, the American Council of Christian Churches (ACCC) was founded, in part, to crusade against perceived communist infiltration of American life—one of many threats seen lurking in the social landscape. The ACCC appealed especially to those who regarded America as an historical Protestant bastion, now under assault from foreign influence of all kinds. By no means did it speak for all Fundamentalists. More politically centrist Evangelicals founded the National Association of Evangelicals to distinguish themselves from this strain of Christianity.

Anticommunism became a defining characteristic of Evangelical and Fundamentalist thought only after World War II, when patriotic triumphalism combined with legitimate fear of Soviet aggression. If Soviet communism was, for perfectly valid reasons, regarded as irretrievably hostile to Christianity, it followed that America, Russia's great rival, must be God's chosen nation. As one historian noted: "The fundamentalism of the cross was now supplanted by a fundamentalism of the flag" (Hofstader 1963: 131). The investigation of communism in the United States made early in the 1950s by Senator Joseph McCarthy, much criticized for his excesses, provided an ideal rallying point for Evangelicals who conflated America and Christianity. Carl McIntire, a long-time luminary of the political and theological right, formed the International Council of Christian Churches (ICCC) in opposition to the far larger World Council of Churches, which he perceived as leftist. Other Fundamentalists crusaded against communism: for instance, the Rev. Billy James Hargis. Both he and McIntire used radio to preach their ultrapatriotic brand of Christianity to a wide audience.

BEHIND COMMUNISM

There is vastly more to communism than is often suspected by the most shrewd observers of the communist conspiracy. It is doubtful that even the brilliant, warped personalities who formed and shaped the rise of communism could have foreseen the aggressive and irresistible way in which it would sweep all before it, threatening all of mankind with the very real possibility that the Red flag would some day fly over the whole earth . . . .

The real cause of communism is *spiritual* sickness, a lack or loss of faith in God, the social order, morality, and law . . . . The Christian explanation for the successful advances of communism and socialism, and the partial impotence of conservatism is—SATAN! . . . No communist, not even Lenin, unaided by a Satanic force, could possibly have planned for all the successes communism has enjoyed . . . .

It shall be our purpose to set before the reader the frightening way in which the Evil One has been preparing to bring communism its present stunning victories. This is the answer from the Bible, and, in the writer's opinion, there is no other rational explanation.

There seems to be little doubt that communism is the embodiment of "antichrist," the dread being spoken of in Holy Scripture whose task is to try to place the world under a single, God-defying, totalitarian state, where no person may even buy or sell except he who will "worship" the "antichrist." Communism alone fits this prediction.

Source: McBirnie, William Stewart. (c. 1968) *The Real Power behind COMMUNISM*. Glendale, CA: Center for American Research and Education, pp. 3, 5–6, 13–14.

This ultrapatriotism of the Evangelical Right should be seen within historical context. Hostility toward communism was a staple of American life throughout the Cold War era. Their 1930s flirtation with Marxist doctrine left a few liberal theologians vulnerable to charges of being communist-sympathizers. Attacks on such individuals, as well as others, for allegedly traitorous views were intemperate, to say the least, but not strikingly out of place in the charged ideological atmosphere of the 1950s. Even a relatively irenic evangelist such as Billy Graham warned against the communist menace and, at least initially, supported Senator McCarthy. For many years, it was fashionable in liberal circles to mock Evangelicals for their obsession with the redundantly described "godless, atheistic communists." The ultra-patriotism of many Evangelicals doubtless furthered their image as rubes in the minds of the American intelligentsia.

The winding down of the Cold War during the 1980s gradually lessened the urgency of anticommunism in the Evangelical worldview. The immensely influential Rev. Billy Graham had, as early as the 1960s, taken his Evangelical message behind the Iron Curtain. While most Fundamentalists doubtless agreed with the anticommunism of the Evangelical Right, the very stridency of such voices seemed more than ever an embarrassment to the larger religious community. Then, too, Evangelicals were increasingly sympathetic toward those who suffered from social injustice and less inclined to dismiss them as communist dupes.

The passing of the Soviet Union finally removed the urgency that many Evangelicals had felt toward Marxism. Patriotism, of course, continued to be a staple of Fundamentalist thought. For instance, in the 1990s, the Rev. Jerry Falwell, an especially prominent preacher, proclaimed that the "free-enterprise system" was endorsed in the Old Testament Book of Proverbs, thus sanctifying not just America but its capitalist system in the bargain. But, although America remained "God's country," Evangelical anticommunism largely faded with the old century.

Robert K. Whalen

See also America, as a Christian nation; Nationalism; Nativism; World War I; World War II

Bibliography

Craig, Robert H. (1992) *Religion and Radical Politics: An Alternative Christian Tradition in the United States.* Philadelphia: Temple University Press.

Hofstader, Richard. (1963) *Anti-intellectualism in American Life.* New York: Vintage Books.

Kater, John L., Jr. (1982) *Christians on the Right: the Moral Majority in Perspective.* New York: Seabury Press.

Roy, Ralph Lord. (1960) *Communism and the Churches.* New York: Harcourt, Brace and Co.

Speer, James A. (1984) "The New Christian Right and Its Parent Company: A Study in Political Contrasts." In *New Christian Politics*, edited by David G. Bromley and Anson Shupe. Macon, GA: Mercer University Press.

Conversion

Conversion is a term that has several connotations, including the popular one of a sudden change of attitude and values, if not basic personality, involved in a decision to join or commit to a religious group or set of beliefs. This definitional approach, which influenced much earlier social science research on conversion, is rather cognitive in orientation, and assumes that the essence of a conversion experience is about an individual changing his or her basic views about life and how to achieve "salvation." The prototype for this view of conversion, widely accepted within Fundamentalist circles, is Saul of Tarsus who, reputedly after being struck down quite literally on the road to Damascus, became an instant believer in Jesus Christ, and went on to become Paul, and to act out his new-found beliefs as perhaps the most famous of the founders of the early Christian Church (Acts 9).

Conversion is also a term used in more recent social scientific literature dealing with recruitment to social movements, which refers specifically to joining or deciding to participate in a religious group. Thus, the term can have both a traditional theological and cognitive interpretation as in the conversion of Paul, as well as a straightforward and even mundane sociological and social psychological meaning that refers to the social processes involved with recruitment to religious groups. This latter perspective, which first developed in more general studies of recruitment to nonreligious social movements, focuses on behav-

ioral and affective elements in the process, assigning them primacy over strictly cognitive and theological considerations. Indeed, there is an assumption in most social science–oriented literature on recruitment and conversion that attitudes and beliefs follow behavior, and derive from the experience of the participant within a given social context. The modern social science approach to conversion will undergird this brief analysis, which examines a few key interrelated issues concerning conversion. These major issues will illustrate a basic paradigm change that has occurred in how social scientists view conversion and recruitment in general.

"Old Wineskins" in Conversion Research

The "old paradigm" that governed research and scholarship about conversion for decades could be thought of as containing several perspectives.

Conversion As Psychopathology

For many years the social science literature on conversion and recruitment often involved an implicit assumption that those who converted to or joined deviant movements were suffering from some sort of mental problem or deficiency. "Religion as a crutch" was the metaphor, with those writing about religious conversion assuming that something was wrong with people who would convert. This approach to conversion was often fueled by either Marxian or Freudian perspectives that defined religion as a projected illusion (Freud) or an opium for those suffering from false consciousness about the causes of their lot in life (Marx). This psychopathological view of conversion was often applied to those joining Fundamentalist groups.

Conversion As Deterministic

Earlier views of conversion and recruitment also seemed to assume that such phenomena occurred as a result of the action of social, psychological, or even religious forces or personages over which the individual had little control. Freudian perspectives on conversion focused on alleged problems caused by suppressed sexual desires, implying that religious interest derived from sublimated efforts at controlling the libido. More sociological approaches stressed social conditions that would drive people to despair, causing them to turn to religion as a last resort to deal with their problems. Theological perspectives would focus on an intervention by deity or an agent of deity who would effect the conversion, as with Saul of Tarsus.

Conversion As a Psychological Phenomenon

Earlier efforts by social scientists to explain conversion and recruitment often were quite psychological and individualistic in their orientation. The conversion research focused on finding the individual problem or condition that had led a person to adopt a religious solution to a felt problem. This perspective often was demonstrated by the administration of personality assessment instruments to or clinical assessment (sometimes quite crude and anecdotal in nature) of converts to see how they differed from "normals," and how the conversion experience had changed their lives. Case studies were used in efforts to explain conversion even within the sociological literature.

Conversion As a Total and Rapid Change of Life

Conversion to a religious group, including Fundamentalist ones, was viewed, following the Pauline metaphor described earlier, as something that happened suddenly and that involved a complete change of the personality. While the literature did allow for the occasional gradual conversion and the fact that some so-called conversions were not true ones because they did not involve total transformation, the assumption of much scholarly social science writing was that conversion was quick and thorough, and anything else was of little interest and not worthy of study.

The New Paradigm

A different approach to conversion developed out of studies of social movements in the 1960s and 1970s. Those studying participation in the political movements of the 1960s were often from similar demographic categories to the participants they were studying, and sometimes found themselves in agreement with the views and values of the participants. It was difficult for these researchers to assume that what the participants were experiencing was pathological and deterministic in nature. It was also problematic to conceptualize participation only in strictly psychological terms, since the movements where large and ongoing multisegmented collective actions. Close observation revealed serious problems with any assumption that a rapid and thorough personality change took place with participation, as well.

This new view of participation in these secular social movements, perhaps best exemplified by Jerome Skolnik's *The Politics of Protest* (1969), was also evolving within the ranks of the researchers who had studied new religious social movements of the 1960s and 1970s. For some of the same reasons, sociologists and psychologists of religion studying participation in religious groups found it difficult to accept the traditional psychopathological, deterministic, psychological, and total/rapid view of conversion to the new religions, including new variants of Fundamentalist-oriented groups such as the Jesus Movement.

Instead, a more humanistic perspective was developed that stressed *volition* on the part of participants, who were not assumed to be suffering from some mental disorder as they made their choice to participate. This new paradigm also was more cognizant of the social nature of conversion and recruitment to religious movements, and that the process of involvement in such groups was often lengthy, with considerable negotiation taking place between the individual potential converts and the group. In addition, the negotiations were not nearly as one-sided as some would assume. Researchers also became aware that so-called conversion seldom involved a total transformation, but was often partial, with people keeping their options open to better offers as they played the role of convert.

In the "new paradigm," participants were not viewed as passive objects being taken advantage of by anyone and everyone, but instead were defined as "seekers," looking for ways to improve themselves and even to act out their ideals using religious groups. This new perspective found superfluous any assumption of total personality change, and instead focused on the kinds of behavioral changes that might accompany participation in a religious group, noting that many of the behavioral changes were obviously positive ones. Individuals were studied as they became involved in conversion careers, moving from group to group and experience to experience, seeking a better life.

Researchers also began to focus on the act of leaving or disaffiliation from religious groups, because there were nearly as many such acts as there were acts of conversion. This was made obvious as researchers finally began to attend to the very high attrition rates of most newer religions, as well as their relatively small size. This broader view, encompassing joining as well as leaving, led to a fuller understanding of conversion to religious groups in contemporary society. This perspective focused attention on the problem of commitment (or lack thereof) of many in today's society, and led some scholars to redefine the meaning of conversion in modern times. This more sophisticated approach to conversion and recruitment also drew attention to some religious groups, many of them more or less Fundamentalist Christian in orientation, that managed to counter the trend of smallness, and develop into megachurches not only by attracting many people but managing to maintain their participation. Calvary Chapel is an example of such large nondenominational churches that have grown very rapidly and are now found virtually worldwide.

Denominational Switching

Denominational switching is a well-known phenomenon that involves people changing their religious affiliation, but within the broad religious tradition of which they are a part. Usually there are not significant behavioral changes accompanying such a change. Switching is particularly prevalent in a pluralistic society such as the United States, which has many different religious groups available to citizens. Switching sometimes occurs with marriage between people of different faiths, with one spouse agreeing to join the religious group of the other. Switching is also related to movement on the class ladder in societies that have different religious groups available, with certain groups associated with specific social classes.

Denominational switching is not defined by most scholars as true conversion because the consequences of switching are not usually thought to be very pervasive or dramatic. However, the modern social science perspective outlined in the "new paradigm" may suggest that switching is not as dissimilar as some have assumed. The phenomenon of individuals who are involved in religious groups joining more Fundamentalist versions of their faith, or choosing another more "Fundamentalist" religious group, can be defined as simple switching or, depending on the pervasiveness of life changes undergone by the converts, it could be thought of as conversion. But if so defined, the social science perspective would seem more applicable to understanding the phenomenon.

Brainwashing As Conversion

A modern variant of the old, deterministic paradigm of conversion is the idea of "brainwashing," which has become a widely accepted, even hegemonic, way of defining conversion to controversial religious groups, including some Fundamentalistic ones. This concept was developed in writings that purported to explain Communist takeovers in China and the experience of U.S. prisoners of war during the Korea War, situations supposedly fraught with physical coercion. The application of such terms as "brainwashing" or "mind control" to any experience of people voluntarily joining and participating in religious groups in contemporary society is questionable. While the modern social science view is antithetical to concepts such as brainwashing, the concept has achieved considerable popular acceptance, even if contradicted by considerable evidence that terms like "brainwashing" are ideological weapons for use against unpopular groups, organizations, or lifestyles.

Conversion to Fundamentalist groups is not inexplicable, therefore requiring ambiguous and loaded terms such as "brainwashing" for a full explanation. Most scholars now believe that conversion to Fundamentalist groups (and most other religious groups) involves ordinary people making choices to change their lives in ways that they define as better. An understanding of such choices is not enhanced by assuming that converts are turned into "robots" by powerful preachers practicing some mysterious techniques. A more mundane view that recognizes the social and volitional nature of most conversion or switching events is much more valuable as an explanatory approach.

James T. Richardson

See also Missions

Bibliography

Barker, Eileen. (1984) *The Making of a Moonie: Brainwashing or Choice?* Oxford: Basil Blackwell.

Bromley, David. (1998) *The Politics of Religious Apostasy.* Westport, CT: Praeger Press.

———, and James Richardson. (1983) *The Brainwashing/Deprogramming Controversy.* New York: Edwin Mellen.

Lofland, John, and Norman Skonovd. (1981) "Conversion Motifs." *Journal for the Scientific Study of Religion* 20: 373–385.

Malony, Newton, and Samuel Southard. (1992) *Handbook of Religious Conversion*. Birmingham, AL: Religious Education Press.

Marty, Martin, and Frederick Greenspahn. (1988) *Pushing the Faith: Proselytism and Civility in a Pluralistic World*. New York: Crossroad Publishing.

Muffler, John, John Langrod, James Richardson, and Pedro Ruiz. (1997) "Religion." In *Substance Abuse: A Comprehensive Test Book*, 3rd ed. Baltimore: Williams and Wilkins, 492–499.

Paloutzian, Raymond, James Richardson, and Lewis Rambo. (1999) "Religious Conversion and Personality Change." *Journal of Personality* 67: 1047–1080.

Rambo, Lewis. (1993) *Understanding Religious Conversion*. New Haven, CT: Yale University Press.

Richardson, James T. (1985) "Active Versus Passive Converts: Paradigm Conflict in Conversion/Recruitment Research." *Journal for the Scientific Study of Religion* 24: 163–179.

———. (1993) "Mergers, Marriages, Coalitions, and Denominationalization: The Growth of Calvary Chapel." *SYZYGY: Journal of Alternative Religion and Culture* 2: 205–224.

———. (1993) "A Social Psychological Critique of Brainwashing Claims about Recruitment to New Religions." In *Handbook of Cults and Sects in America*, edited by Jeffrey Hadden and David Bromley. Greenwich, CT: JAI Press, 75–94.

———, Mary Stewart, and Robert Simmonds. (1978) "Conversion to Fundamentalism." *Society* 15 (4): 46–52.

Robbins, Thomas, and Dick Anthony. (1990) *In Gods We Trust*, 2nd ed. New Brunswick, NJ: Transaction Books.

Stark, Rodney. (1965) "Psychopathology and Religious Commitment." *Review of Religious Research* 12: 165–176.

Straus, Roger. (1979) "Religious Conversion and a Personal and Collective Accomplishment." *Sociological Analysis* 40: 158–165.

Covenant

"Covenant" has been a central theme in the Judeo-Christian tradition for the past two millennia. The concept has been defined in a variety of ways at different times in a number of different religio-cultural traditions. It is a subject that has been exhaustively examined and debated by scholars operating from divergent disciplinary perspectives. The focus here is on the complex history of covenant as an organizing principle for contemporary Fundamentalism. From this perspective it should be emphasized that the concept covenant has served as a cultural resource that has been continuously redefined to meet the needs of a variety of times and traditions. It is particularly important to juxtapose covenant to contract in understanding the significance of covenant for contemporary Fundamentalism.

"Contract" also has roots that can be traced more than two millennia. Elements of contractual thought can be found in ancient Greek philosophy as well as in Roman law, but it only emerges as a recognizable tradition in the seventeenth century with the work of Thomas Hobbes and John Locke. The concept of covenant, of course, has biblical roots from which distinct Christian and Jewish traditions developed as well as separate streams of thought within branches of the Christian tradition. The two concepts are closely interrelated as various religious traditions contributed to the development of contractual forms; for example, twelfth-century canon law stipulated for the first time that consensual agreements were legally, and not simply morally, binding in ecclesiastical courts. Seventeenth-century Puritanism drew liberally on contractual logic in interpreting the relationship between God and humankind, and in so doing elevated the importance of autonomy, voluntarism, and rational interest that are foundational to contractual logic.

Development of Covenant Theology

The term "covenant" appeared in the Protestant tradition in late-sixteenth-century Calvinism but was expanded and reconceptualized in seventeenth-century Puritan theology. John Witte (1987) identifies three notable developments. First, the covenant of works was defined as tracing back to the creation of the world rather than as having been established with the chosen people of Israel and thus was universalized to all humankind. The Fall of humankind constituted a violation of that covenant, and it was through Christ's intercession that a second covenant of grace was established, based on faith rather than adherence to law, through which salvation could be attained. Second, the covenant of grace was understood as a mutually accepted contract binding on both God and humankind. Third, a variety of covenant forms were identified through human history. The result was that Puritans regarded themselves as bound by a series of covenants: a national covenant between God and his elect; a political covenant involving God, the civil ruler, and the people; a church covenant requiring the establishment of community churches with specific worldly responsibilities; and a marital covenant involving mutual promises of spousal fidelity. Puritan doctrine emphasized both the free choice and the absolute obligation of these covenants. Their obligatory nature stemmed not only from the Christian requirements of avoidance of sin, love for neighbors, and unfaithfulness but also from the convictions that social order required compliance and that each small covenant found its roots in the original Creation covenant. Among the most important implications were the expanded importance of human autonomy and voluntarism, heightened individual responsibility as well as obligation to the community, and affirmation of an absolute responsibility to honor obligations.

Robert Bellah (1992) describes how the Puritan tradition transferred to America in a unique form that created a mythic mandate for America long before a nation-state was established. America was conceived by its first European inhabitants both as an undefiled, Edenic state of nature and as a barbaric, inhospitable wilderness. Early settlers came to regard themselves as a chosen people on a divine mission to create a garden in the midst of this wilderness. The notion of a chosen people produced a strong sense of covenant with God and with one another. The centrality of conversion as a liberating, salvationist experience also produced covenantal obligations that reinforced an ethically grounded community. Alongside this biblical tradition stood the contractual tradition, deriving from Hobbes and Locke, which understood social order to rest on maximization of individual self-interest. In this view the social, common good would inevitably emerge from individuals' pursuit of their own self-interest. During the nineteenth century a movement developed to sever contract law from its connection to religious principles and found contracts in rationalistic principles of individual autonomy and free will. Contractual organization gained clear ascendancy in the public sphere institutions, most notably the state and economy; covenantal forms of social relations oriented church, family, racial/ethnic, and informal personal relationships in the private sphere.

The Concept of Covenant in Fundamentalist America

Fundamentalism as a movement in America began in the late nineteenth century with the emergence of urban centers, an industrial economy, ethnic and religious diversity, a secular scientific knowledge base, and liberalization of religious theology in mainline denominations. As Nancy Ammerman (1991) has observed, at its inception Fundamentalism constituted an organized movement to resist growing institutional differentiation and cultural pluralism. Indeed, Fundamentalism is most likely to be located socially and geographically where contractual and covenantal forms encounter one another. While Fundamentalism exhibits considerable internal disagreement and conflict, its major defining characteristics involve a reassertion of covenantal forms characteristic of the era in which the movement began. Thus, Fundamentalists reaffirm the covenant individually through life-transforming decisions for Christ; separating themselves collectively in churches, thereby preserving a faithful remnant that continues to honor its covenantal obligations; creating marriages and families centered on pledges to spiritual commitments; actively evangelizing to bring others within the covenant, thereby assuring the spiritual destinies of their fellows; seeking to bring a fallen nation back to its sacred covenantal purpose; asserting the absolute truth of covenantal provisions by defending biblical inerrancy; and reaffirming independent divine agency in the form of premillennialist expectations.

Conclusion

Both the concepts of covenant and contract have long, intersecting histories. The emergence of Puritanism and its subsequent development in America created a unique sense of spiritual purpose. Covenantal forms of social relations became increasingly marginalized as contractual forms came to dominate the public sphere. Fundamentalism constitutes one historic reaction to dominant contractualism through which religious communities seek to reassert the primacy of the covenant and integrate their lives individually and collectively through covenantally organized churches, families, and communities. Fundamentalism's unique characteristics constitute a collective commitment to spiritually based lives that honor the obligations of their covenant with God.

David G. Bromley

See also America, As a Christian Nation; Old Testament

Bibliography

Ammerman, Nancy. (1987) *Bible Believers: Fundamentalists in the Modern World.* New Brunswick, NJ: Rutgers University Press.

———. (1991) "North American Protestant Fundamentalism." In *Fundamentalisms Observed,* edited by Martin Marty and R. Scott Appleby. Chicago: University of Chicago Press, 1–65.

Bellah, Robert. (1992) *The Broken Covenant.* Chicago: University of Chicago Press.

———, Richard Madsen, William Sullivan, Ann Swidler, and Steven Tipton. (1985) *Habits of the Heart: Individualism and Commitment in American Life.* Berkeley: University of California Press.

Bromley, David, and Bruce Busching. (1988) "Understanding the Structure of Contractual and Covenantal Social Relations: Implications for the Sociology of Religion." *Sociological Analysis* 49: 15–32.

Elazar, Daniel. (1996) *Covenant and Commonwealth: From Christian Separation through the Protestant Reformation.* New Brunswick, NJ: Transaction.

Hartman, David. (1985) *A Living Covenant: The Innovative Spirit in Traditional Judaism.* New York: Free Press.

Witte, John. (1987) "Blest Be the Ties That Bind: Covenant and Community in Puritan Thought." *Emory Law Journal* 36: 579–601.

Creation

Creation is the view that everything but God was brought into existence by God, Who alone has always existed. This is in contrast with various alternative views: (1) that the cosmos has always been and there are no Gods at all (atheism); (2) that the cosmos is itself God (pantheism); (3) that the cosmos is God's "body" while God is its "spirit" (panentheism); and (4) that the cosmos is merely something shaped by God or the gods, but that its matter has always existed (dualism; various forms of polytheism). Creation is the teaching of the Bible and of traditional Judaism, Christianity, and Islam. Here we sketch the teaching given in the Old and New Testaments as understood by Evangelical and Fundamental Christians. Their views on how to relate the idea of creation to scientific data range over a spectrum, which may be subdivided into young-earth (or recent) creation, old-earth (or progressive) creation, and theistic evolution (or fully gifted creation).

At its most basic level, the act of creation is the bringing into existence of that which did not previously exist. In this sense creation is spoken of as *ex nihilo* (Latin, "from nothing"). The Creation account in Genesis seems to apply this idea to the universe as a whole (heaven and earth), and perhaps to life and to the human spirit, but not, for example, to the human body. The creation of other spirit beings (angels, etc.) is mentioned in the Bible but not narrated in Genesis; perhaps these belong to another, earlier created order. God's other creative actions in Genesis may alternatively have been *ex nihilo* creation, or his miraculous working with existing materials, or his nonmiraculous (providential) guidance of natural processes. Whether time and space were also created with the cosmos has been debated.

God's creation of the cosmos was a free, personal action. He was not constrained by any logical necessity nor by need for companionship. Christians would see God as having always enjoyed such companionship because of the three-person nature of his being (the Trinity). Genesis tells us that God created all things by means of His Word, that is, His spoken command. Christians understand this Word (from the opening verses of John's Gospel) to be Jesus before He became a human. We learn from Genesis that God's Spirit hovers over the waters at Creation. Apparently the Holy Spirit works within the created order to carry out God's purposes. God is thus both within and beyond his creation (immanent and transcendent). God's purpose in creating was to "declare His glory," that is, to demonstrate His character—wisdom, goodness, power, justice, compassion, and more—to the personal beings He would create, and to share these and other good things with them. The Creation is initially good—in fact "very good." But God also created free, moral beings who could choose either to trust and obey Him, or to doubt and reject Him. The Bible's main story line tells what happened as a result of the disobedience of the first humans, and how God subsequently reached out to rescue people from the consequences of their own and others' rebellion against Him. The great dilemma of how God can be both a just judge and yet merciful to those who deserve punishment is solved when God Himself suffers their punishment and provides their righteousness by becoming a created human in Jesus

Genesis 1:1

1. In the beginning God created the heavens and the earth.

Genesis 1:26–27

26. And God said, Let us make man in our image, after our likeness: and let them have dominion over the fish of the sea, and over the fowl of the air, over the cattle, and over all the earth, and over every creeping thing that creepeth upon the earth.
27. So God created man in his own image, in the image of God created he him; male and female created he them.

Hebrews 11:3

3. Through faith we understand that the worlds were framed by the word of God, so that things that which are seen were not made of things which do appear.

Psalm 19:1

1. The heavens declare the glory of God; and the firmament sheweth his handywork.

Psalm 102:25–27

25. Of old hast thou laid the foundation of the earth, and the heavens are the work of they hands.
26. They shall perish, but thou shalt endure; yea, all of them shall wax old like a garment; as a vesture shall thou change them, and they shall be changed.
27. But thou art the same, and thy years shall have no end.

---

of Nazareth, living a life of perfect obedience, and dying a criminal's death nailed to a wooden cross.

Humans were created "in God's image." Though this concept is not explained anywhere in the Bible, it seems to be intended to contrast with the animals being made "according to their kinds." The point seems to be that humans share some features with God that the animals do not. As animals are called "irrational" in the New Testament, rationality is apparently part of this. Many passages indicate that humans are spirits (who can survive death), so that this is included in our resemblance to God. Other such features are presumably moral and artistic capabilities, probably a part of our spirituality. Humans were created to have responsibility and rule over at least the earthbound part of Creation. This means that we as humans are responsible under God for how we treat the plants, animals, and nonliving environment around us, as well as for how we treat one another. Our ability to do this successfully has been badly disrupted by our rebellion against God, as has our behavior in all of the other authority relation-

ships we inhabit: God/human, government, employment, marriage, and family.

The idea that we and the cosmos are created has profound effects on how we are to view reality, and (if true) on the meaning and value of our lives. Unlike the other worldviews mentioned in the first paragraph, Creation explains both the existence of real, objective standards of ethics, logic, and beauty, along with the fact that people regularly violate these standards—thus, the simultaneous existence of both good and evil, and why the one is different from and preferable to the other. It explains why humans are more valuable than animals and why we view cannibalism with horror but need not (and cannot) extend this to eating meat and vegetables. It explains why we have longings for a life beyond this one, and how God can be just even though justice is not always done in this life. According to the Bible, our cosmos has not always existed, and one day it will come to an end. It is "wearing out." One day it will be replaced with a new heaven and a new earth, in which all will be well.

Robert C. Newman

See also Creationism; Evolution and Antievolution

Bibliography

Bromiley, Geoffrey W. (1979) "Creator." In *International Standard Bible Encyclopedia,* 1: 802–804.

Buswell, J. Oliver. (1962–1965) *Systematic Theology of the Christian Religion.* Grand Rapids, MI: Baker House Books.

Carter, Charles W. (1983) *A Contemporary Wesleyan Theology,* 2 vols. Grand Rapids, MI: Zondervan Publishing.

Chafer, Lewis Sperry. (1947–1948) *Systematic Theology.* Dallas: Dallas Seminary Press.

Dabney, Robert L. ([1878] 1972) *Lectures in Systematic Theology.* Grand Rapids, MI: Zondervan Publishing.

Demarest, Bruce, and Gordon Lewis. (1987) *Integrative Theology.* Grand Rapids, MI: Zondervan Publishing.

Erickson, Millard J. (1983) *Christian Theology,* 3 vols. Grand Rapids, MI: Baker House Books.

Grenz, Stanley J. (2000) *Theology for the Community of God.* Grand Rapids, MI: Wm. B. Eerdmans.

Grudem, Wayne A. (1994) *Systematic Theology.* Grand Rapids, MI: Zondervan Publishing.

Harrison, Roland K. (1975) "Creation." In *Zondervan Pictorial Encyclopedia of the Bible,* 1: 1020–1025.

Hodge, Charles. ([1873] 1973) *Systematic Theology,* 3 vols. Grand Rapids, MI: Wm. B. Eerdmans.

Lindsay, James. (1979) "Creation." In *International Standard Bible Encyclopedia,* 1: 800–802.

Oden, Thomas C. (1987) *The Living God: Systematic Theology: Volume One.* San Francisco: Harper and Row.

Pieper, Francis. (1917–1924) *Christian Dogmatics,* 3 vols. St. Louis: Concordia.

Strong, Augustus Hopkins. (1907) *Systematic Theology,* 8th ed. Valley Forge, PA: Judson.

Williams, J. Rodman. (1988–1992) *Renewal Theology: Systematic Theology from a Charismatic Perspective,* 3 vols. Grand Rapids, MI: Zondervan Publishing.

Creationism

Creationism, broadly understood, includes the whole range of (usually conservative) Christian attempts to reconcile nature and the Bible on origins. In a narrower sense, it means a specific subset—the view that God created the world just a few thousand years ago. As the broader use includes the narrower, both are discussed here.

Historical Background

Traditional Christian interpretation of the biblical account in Genesis by such theologians as Ambrose (339–397), Thomas Aquinas (1225–1274), Martin Luther (1483–1546), and John Calvin (1509–1564), saw the cosmos as created in a literal week only a few thousand years ago. Though a few had speculated with Augustine (354–430) that the Creation may have been instantaneous and the week just God's way of explaining this to humans, no one had seen any need for a more ancient Creation nor a longer time-span for this to occur.

In the late 1700s, however, systematic study of the geologic record by geologists Abraham Gottlob Werner (1749–1817), William Smith (1769–1839), and James Hutton (1726–1797) began raising problems for this traditional view. By the 1840s most geologists had concluded the earth was far older than a few thousand years, and a number of Christian thinkers had proposed models for interpreting the Genesis account along these lines. Churchmen Thomas Chalmers (1780–1847) and William Buckland (1784–1856) proposed what came to be called the Gap or Restitution theory. This theory stated that the earth and universe are very old (as evidenced by geology), but the biblical Creation account narrates a recent restoration of the earth and the re-creation of life following a great catastrophe that had desolated the planet. As modified by George H. Pember (1837–1910), this view came to be widely disseminated in the older editions of the *Scofield Reference Bible.* It was probably the dominant view among Evangelicals until the 1960s. Another old-earth model was the Day-Age theory. Here the biblical account and the geologic record refer to the same events, but the days of Genesis are long periods rather than twenty-four hours. A number of geologists, including James Dwight Dana (1813–1895), J. William Dawson (1820–1899), and Hugh Miller (1802–1856) came to advocate this view, along with numerous theologians such as Franz Delitzsch (1813–1890), John Peter Lange (1802–1884), Charles Hodge (1797–1878), and Alexander Maclaren (1826–1910). Others, however, resisted these moves as unnecessary accommodations to scientific speculation and abandonment of the plain teaching of the Bible. Theologians Robert L. Dabney (1820–1898), a Presbyterian, and Francis Pieper (1852–1931), a Lutheran, are representative of this response.

Meanwhile, by the early 1800s, philosopher David Hume (1711–1776) had convinced many that miracles were incredible, that enlightened people should seek to understand nature and history without them. In his *Origin of Species* (1859), the English naturalist Charles Darwin (1809–1882) presented a theory to eliminate miracles from biological origins. His proposal produced a storm of controversy that has continued to this day. Nevertheless, by the end of the nineteenth century, most biologists accepted some form of evolution, though many had reservations about Darwin's particular mechanism. Darwin thus added another factor to the origins debate: what parts did God, miracle, and evolution have to play in all this? A number of Evangelical Christians sought to harmonize evolution with the Genesis account, producing models invoking both evolution and God. Early proponents of such theistic evolution included botanist Asa Gray (1810–1888), geologist James Dwight Dana (1813–1895), theologian-geologist George Frederick Wright (1838–1921), and theologian Augustus Hopkins Strong (1836–1921).

The Fundamentalist–Modernist Controversy

The impact of Hume and Darwin widened the rift between conservatives and liberals in Christendom, leading to the Fundamentalist–modernist controversy of the twentieth century. This struggle pitted modernists, who sought to reshape Christianity along nonmiraculous lines, against Fundamentalists, who believed that God really had performed such miracles as narrated in the Bible. In response to liberal teachings, conservatives issued a series of pamphlets entitled *The Fundamentals* (1910–1915), which were sent to every pastor in the United States. Darwinism was one of the teachings to which the series reacted. Yet, the main threat was clearly atheistic forms of evolution, as two of the four authors responding to Darwinism were the theistic evolutionists James Orr (1844–1913) and G. Frederick Wright. From about 1890 to 1940 the mainline denominations in the United States were the battleground between the two camps. However, by the outbreak of World War II, most of these denominations had come under the control of the modernists.

The famous Scopes "Monkey Trial" of 1925 was one battle in this war, but it was fought in the public square rather than in the churches, for the fight concerned how biology should be taught in the public schools. Though the trial resulted in a technical victory for the conservatives, its long-term effect was to establish a Darwinian monopoly on teaching biology in public education. The Fundamentalists retired to lick their wounds, but proceeded to found a number of organizations concerned with science and Scripture on origins. Several groups lasted for a few years, but the two that have survived to the present are the American Scientific Affiliation (ASA), founded in 1941, and the Creation Research Society (CRS), founded in 1963. The ASA had a broadly Evangelical statement of faith and included proponents of all the basic models to reconcile nature with Scripture. But by the early 1960s, its leadership had come to be dominated by theistic evolutionists, so a number of young-earth creationists withdrew to form the CRS. Other current organizations that promote one of the basic models include the Institute for Creation Research, the Bible-Science Association (both young-earth), the Interdisciplinary Biblical Research Institute, and Reasons to Believe (both old-earth).

Basic Models to Reconcile Nature with Scripture

The major views by which Evangelicals and Fundamentalists have sought to relate the biblical data to that of modern science can be classified in various ways, but a threefold division (with considerable variety within each) is the most common: (1) young-earth creation, (2) old-earth creation, and (3) theistic evolution.

Young-Earth Creation

Sometimes called recent creation, creation science, or scientific creationism, this view proposes that the universe and all its contents were created a few thousand years ago (suggestions range from six to twenty thousand years). Everything was created in the span of six consecutive twenty–four hour days, the simplest reading of the Genesis account. The geologic strata and the fossils found in them are not a history of millions of years, but the result of a worldwide flood at the time of Noah that destroyed all animal life not on the Ark. Proponents of this view differ on what part of the current diversity among animals was originally created versus what has developed since the flood. Creationist George McCready Price (1870–1963) was an important early proponent of the idea that the flood could explain the geological strata. Henry M. Morris (1918–) and John C. Whitcomb (1924–) popularized this approach in *The*

THOUGHTS ON CREATIONISM

" . . . a superintellect has monkeyed with physics, as well as with chemistry and biology"

Fred Hoyle, "The Universe: Past and Present Reflection," p. 16

"The information content of a simple cell has been estimated as around 1012 bits, comparable to about a hundred million pages of the *Encyclopaedia Britannica*."

Carl Sagan, "Life" in *Encyclopaedia Britannica* (1970), 13:1083B

"The chance that higher life forms might have emerged [by chance] is comparable with the chance that a tornado sweeping through a junk-yard might assemble a Boeing 747 from the materials therein."

Fred Hoyle, "Hoyle on Evolution," Nature (12 Nov 1981), p. 105

"The extreme rarity of transitional forms in the fossil record persists as the trade secret of paleontology."

Stephen Jay Gould, *Natural History* 86, #5 (1977), p. 14

"Well, we are now about 120 years after Darwin . . . ironically, we have *even fewer* examples of evolutionary transitions than we had in Darwin's time. By this I mean that some of the classic cases . . . have had to be discarded or modified . . . "

David Raup, *Field Museum Bulletin* 30 #1 (1979), p. 25

" . . . despite the detailed study of the Pleistocene mammals of Europe, not a single valid example is known of phyletic (gradual) transition from one genus to another."

Steven M. Stanley, *Macroevolution: Pattern & Process* (1979), p. 82

Genesis Flood (1961), and within a decade it had nearly replaced Chalmers and Buckland's Gap theory as the preferred Evangelical view on origins. Other recent proponents of this view include scientists Stephen A. Austin, Thomas Barnes, Leonard Brand, Wayne Frair, Robert Gentry, Duane Gish, Ken Ham, Russell Humphreys, Paul Nelson, and Barry Setterfield.

Old-Earth Creation

Sometimes called progressive creation, this view accepts the standard dating provided by geology for the earth and its strata, and by astronomy for the universe, so that the cosmos is seen as some 15 billion years old, the earth perhaps 4.5 billion, with the earliest living things appearing as soon as the earth had cooled enough to support life, perhaps 3.8 billion years ago. Proponents disagree on how to understand the days of Genesis (whether ages, days separated by long gaps, days on which the account was revealed to Moses, or a literary device with no chronological significance). Old-earth creationists differ from theistic evolutionists (discussed later) in denying that the scientific evidence favors macroevolution—the gradual development of all life's diversity from a single primordial creature—feeling instead that God has intervened in some way or other at various times in history to provide new life forms that would otherwise never have arisen. Small-scale evolution (microevolution) of varieties within the created kinds is typically affirmed. Old-earth creationists agree that Adam and Eve are special creations of God rather than natural developments from the apes, but disagree considerably on how far back in the past humans were created. Recent proponents of this view include Gleason L. Archer, James Montgomery Boice, Norman L. Geisler, Alan Hayward, Russell W. Maatman, Robert C. Newman, Pattle P. T. Pun, Hugh Ross, John L. Wiester, and Daniel E. Wonderly.

Theistic Evolution

One proponent calls this view "fully gifted creation." Like old-earth creation, this view accepts the standard scientific dating for the universe, the earth, the various geologic strata, and the fossils within them. Unlike old-earth creation, however, theistic evolutionists believe that macroevolution has actually occurred, but that this was not a random, mindless, unguided process as many secular evolutionists (such as Stephen Jay Gould, Richard Dawkins and Daniel Dennett) believe. Instead, God guided the process by means of his providential oversight of all that happens. Theistic evolutionists disagree whether Creation involved any miraculous intervention besides the origin of the universe, but a number put such intervention at the creation of life and of humans, while others see the origin of life and the development of humans from the apes as divinely guided natural processes. Proponents of this view include Henri Blocher, Richard H. Bube, Michael Denton, Keith B. Miller, George L. Murphy, John Polkinghorne, Howard J. Van Till, and David L. Wilcox.

The Intelligent Design Movement

A recent development in the controversy over origins has come to be labeled the "intelligent design movement." Following a resurgence of conservative Christianity beginning in the 1960s, a culture war has been heating up between materialists and theists. Materialists believe that reality is basically matter-energy and impersonal forces, with minds being only a late development in the history of the universe. Theists believe that behind physical reality is a Mind that has designed and produced all that we see.

In 1982 and 1985, a pair of court decisions in Arkansas and Louisiana struck down new laws in those states that permitted teaching of Creation alongside evolution in public schools. The U.S. Supreme Court concurred in 1987. Yet, a number of observers felt that these decisions were flawed because (1) a narrow definition of Creation was used in the decisions that made Creation a religious view while evolution was not; and (2) a narrow definition of science was used that ruled out in advance any evidence that might point to agency from beyond nature.

Meanwhile, evidence had been accumulating that our universe and the life within it seems to be strangely designed. As early as 1913 Lawrence J. Henderson's book *The Fitness of the Environment* noted many unusual features of chemistry that were just right for life to exist. By the 1950s, physicists had noticed a number of unusual relationships between the basic constants of nature. This picture has sharpened considerably since then as many striking examples of "fine-tuning" have been discovered in cosmology, physics, chemistry, and biology, summarized in such books as Paul Davies's *Accidental Universe* (1982), John Barrow and Frank Tipler's *The Anthropic Cosmological Principle* (1986), Hugh Ross's *The Creator and the Cosmos* (1993), and Michael Denton's *Nature's Destiny* (1998). To many, these features point to a Mind behind the universe. To others, they merely indicate that intelligent life will only exist in those universes where everything is just right; therefore, there must be many more universes where everything is not all right and consequently there is no life. In biology, Darwin's theory has long been thought to have explained away apparent design. It is merely the result of natural selection rather than the work of a Designer. Yet, Michael Denton's *Evolution: A Theory in Crisis* (1986) and Michael Behe's *Darwin's Black Box* (1996) drew attention to numerous features in living things that suggest they could not have arisen by chance. Materialists have responded that perhaps nature itself has (impersonal) forces that produce the kind of order needed. Berkeley law professor Phillip E. Johnson has been a prime mover in the intelligent design movement, beginning with his book *Darwin on Trial* (1991), followed up with additional books and extensive speaking and writing. Mathematician-philosopher William A. Dembski has provided a rigorous account of how to distinguish design from randomness or law-bound behavior in his book *The Design Inference* (1998) (see Dembski 1998 and 1999 for a sketch of this approach).

Conclusion

How everything came to be is one of the most basic and debated questions we can ask. Evangelicals and Fundamentalists contend that both the Bible and nature indicate the universe is created and God is its

Creator. When and how this occurred are disputed. That the universe has not always been, and that the universe and life are strikingly designed, continues to appear more certain as scientists probe to the edges of the universe and to the depths of cells, molecules, and elementary particles.

Robert C. Newman

See also Creation; Evolution and Antievolution

Bibliography

Ackerman, Paul D. (1986) *It's a Young World After All: Exciting Evidences for Recent Creation*. Grand Rapids, MI: Baker Book House.

Behe, Michael. (1996) *Darwin's Black Box: The Biochemical Challenge to Evolution*. New York: Free Press.

Brand, Leonard. (1997) *Faith, Reason, and Earth History: A Paradigm of Earth and Biological Origins by Intelligent Design*. Berrien Springs, MI: Andrews University Press.

Dembski, William A. (1999) *Intelligent Design: The Bridge Between Science & Theology*. Downers Grove, IL: InterVarsity Press.

———, ed. (1998) *Mere Creation: Science, Faith & Intelligent Design*. Downers Grove, IL: InterVarsity Press.

Denton, Michael. (1998) *Nature's Destiny: How the Laws of Biology Reveal Purpose in the Universe*. New York: Free Press.

Gillespie, Charles Coulston. (1951) *Genesis and Geology: The Impact of Scientific Discoveries upon Religious Beliefs in the Decades before Darwin*. Cambridge, MA: Harvard University Press; reprinted 1959, New York: Harper and Row.

Hagopian, David, ed. (2001) *The Genesis Debate: Three Views on the Days of Creation*. Mission Viejo, CA: Crux Press.

Livingstone, David N. (1987) *Darwin's Forgotten Defenders: The Encounter between Evangelical Theology and Evolutionary Thought*. Grand Rapids, MI: Wm. B. Eerdmans and Edinburgh, UK: Scottish Academic Press.

McIver, Tom. (1988) *Anti-Evolution: A Reader's Guide to Writings before and after Darwin*. Jefferson, NC: McFarland and Co.; reprinted 1992, Baltimore and London: Johns Hopkins University Press.

Moreland, J. P., and John Mark Reynolds, eds. (1999) *Three Views on Creation and Evolution*. Grand Rapids, MI: Zondervan Publishing.

Newman, Robert C., and Herman J. Eckelmann, Jr. (1977) *Genesis One and the Origin of the Earth*. Downers Grove, IL: InterVarsity Press; reprinted 2000, Hatfield, PA: Interdisciplinary Biblical Research Institute (IBRI).

Newman, Robert C., and John L. Wiester, with Janet and Jonathan Moneymaker. (2000) *What's Darwin Got to Do with It? A Friendly Conversation about Evolution*. Downers Grove, IL: InterVarsity Press.

Numbers, Ronald L. (1992) *The Creationists*. New York: Alfred A. Knopf.

———, gen. ed. (1995) *Creationism in Twentieth-Century America*, 10 vols. New York: Garland Press.

Price, David, John L. Wiester, and Walter R. Hearn. (1986) *Teaching Science in a Climate of Controversy: A View from the American Scientific Affiliation*. Ipswich, MA: American Scientific Affiliation.

Ross, Hugh. (1995) *The Creator and the Cosmos: How the Greatest Scientific Discoveries of the Century Reveal God*. Colorado Springs, CO: NavPress.

Wells, Jonathan. (2000) *Icons of Evolution: Science or Myth? Why Much of What We Teach about Evolution Is Wrong*. Washington, DC: Regnery.

Whitcomb, John C., Jr., and Henry M. Morris. (1961) *The Genesis Flood*. Philadelphia: Presbyterian and Reformed.

Wiester, John L. (1983) *The Genesis Connection*. Nashville: Thomas Nelson; reprinted 1992, Hatfield, PA: Interdisciplinary Biblical Research Institute (IBRI).

Wonderly, Daniel E. (1987) *Neglect of Geologic Data: Sedimentary Strata Compared with Young-Earth Creationist Writings*. Hatfield, PA: Interdisciplinary Biblical Research Institute (IBRI).

Van Till, Howard. (1986) *The Fourth Day: What the Bible and the Heavens Are Telling Us about the Creation*. Grand Rapids, MI: Wm. B. Eerdmans.

———, Robert E. Snow, John H. Stek, and Davis A. Young. (1990) *Portraits of Creation: Biblical and Scientific Perspectives on the World's Formation*. Grand Rapids, MI: Wm. B. Eerdmans.

Young, Davis A. (1982) *Christianity and the Age of the Earth*. Grand Rapids, MI: Zondervan Publishing.

Youngblood, Ronald F., ed. (1986) *The Genesis Debate: Persistent Questions about Creation and the Flood*. Nashville, TN: Thomas Nelson; reprinted 1990, Grand Rapids, MI: Baker Book House.

Cult of Mary

Catholic Fundamentalism has traditionally been identified with cults and sects devoted to the Virgin

Pilgrims gather at the Conyers apparition site. PHOTO COURTESY OF VICTOR BALABAN.

Mary. There are currently hundreds of Marian visionaries around the world, from Canada to Syria, Japan to Rwanda, Russia to Venezuela. Those in Medjugorje, in the former Yugoslavia, have been particularly influential in recent years. The messages at all these sites are believed by pilgrims to provide a single extended warning, given in different times and different places, of how the Apocalypse, the price of mankind's drifting away from true Catholic devotion, will occur.

The Cult of Mary must be viewed as part of a larger spectrum of contemporary Catholic Fundamentalism, consisting of widely scattered groups of Catholic traditionalists, separatists, and visionaries. They are linked by the underlying assumption that the Catholic Church is, at best, misguided, and at worst, the victim of sinister conspiracies. Virtually all these groups are characterized by a longing for the moral certainties of pre-Vatican II Catholicism and a profound reaction against liberal and reforming trends within the church—birth control, abortion, homosexuality, women priests, and more. Unlike Protestant Fundamentalism, Catholic Fundamentalism takes place within the context of a centralized church that is the ultimate arbiter of faith. Therefore, individuals and groups who are in disagreement with church doctrine, and yet who still wish to remain Roman Catholics, find themselves in a dilemma. Because Vatican II and all the attendant changes were instituted by the church itself, and to question the authority of a pope is to question Catholicism itself, an alternate source of authority must be found.

Schisms in the Catholic Church

Traditionalist organizations such as Catholics United for the Faith and the Orthodox Roman Catholic Movement, and Catholic antiabortion groups such as Catholics United for Life, or the Pro-Life Action League, still look to the Vatican for authority and hope to reform the church from within. Other, more schismatic, groups have found alternate sources of authority by concluding that the present pope, or the last several popes, have all been impostors, Jews, Freemasons, or communists, bent on destroying the church. Espousing a doctrine called "sedevacantism" (from the Latin "empty chair"), they hold that the papacy has been vacated, because the changes instituted since the Vatican II could not have been put in place by a true pope. Therefore, Catholic separatist organizations, such as the Tridentine Latin Rite Church, reject all popes since Vatican II as false antipopes, and at the extreme, The Apostles of Infinite Love in Quebec, Canada, have taken this sedevacantist doctrine to its logical conclusion and its leader, the former Gaston Tremblay, has proclaimed himself the true pope, Gregory XVII.

The Cult of Mary occupies a special middle ground between these traditionalist and separatist paths, seeking to use the supernatural authority of the messages of Marian visionaries as a way to mediate the cognitive dissonance between believers' Catholic convictions and their misgivings about contemporary Catholicism. Marian apparitions exist at the intersection of two contrary cultures: the formal theology of the church and a more magical, forbidden world of folk Catholicism. As a result, Marian cults are always at risk of moving from traditionalism to separatism, from within the church to outright schism.

Some Marian apparitions, such as those at Rue de Bac, La Salette, and Lourdes, have been approved by the church. This potential for approval holds out the possibility that believers may be able to simultaneously believe in the authority of traditionalist messages from a visionary and still be good Catholics. If the church does ultimately disapprove, then the contradictions inherent in apparitions are brought to the surface and devotees are faced with a dilemma. Do they renounce the site and the visionary? Or do they shift their allegiance to the visionary and disobey the bishop? In one direction lies obedience to a church they feel is misguided, and in the other lies heresy.

Only the potential for official approval by the church holds out the possibility of resolving these tensions.

A shrine that has made the leap into heresy is in Necedah, Wisconsin. In the early 1950s, Necedah was probably one of the most famous apparition sites in the world, so large that in August 1950, one hundred thousand pilgrims came to hear the visionary, Mary Anne Van Hoof, relate a message from the Virgin similar to the ones from Conyers. But, as has been the case in nearly all American sites, the cult of Necedah was officially condemned, once in 1955 and again in 1970. As a result, devotees of Necedah formed their own schismatic sect, For My God and My Country Incorporated, and to this day, a community of several hundred "shrine people" continue to live at the site.

History of Marian Apparitions

Although devotion to Mary has a long history in the Catholic Church, the Fundamentalist Cult of Mary as it is known today is a nineteenth- and twentieth-century phenomenon, particularly shaped by the two major apparitions, La Salette and Fatima. In 1846, François-Mélanie Mathieu (known also as Melanie Calvat) and Pierre-Maximin Giraud, two peasant children in the village of La Salette, France, saw the figure of a weeping woman bathed in light. She told the children of crop failures and famine if people did not return to the church and observe the Sacraments. She warned that walnuts would go bad and grapes would rot. A few days later, Mélanie and Maximin returned to the site and claimed that a natural spring now flowed at the spot where the Virgin had appeared. The spring soon became known for healings, and La Salette was transformed into a pilgrimage site. Although less well known today, La Salette was a world famous site throughout the nineteenth century. Melanie's apocalyptic, populist, and fairly anticlerical post-La Salette writings helped give rise to apocalyptic Marian popular literature. This genre of millennial apocalyptic writing was common in the Middle Ages and derives ultimately from the Bible, particularly the Book of Revelation and the Book of Daniel. Melanie's writings brought this tradition into the milieu of lower-middle-class Catholics in southern Europe, and later, to America. The Marian movement that developed was populist and most closely identified with the lower middle and working classes.

The most important apparitions in the development of twentieth-century Marian Fundamentalism were those at Fatima, Portugal, in 1917. A great deal of the popular fascination with Fatima focuses on the so-called Third Secret of Fatima. On 13 June and 17 July 1917, Lucia dos Santos and her two cousins reported that part of the message they had received from the Virgin that day was a secret. The children were questioned about the secrets, not only by friends and family but also by local officials such as the mayor, who threatened to have them boiled alive in oil if they did not tell. In her later writings, Lucia described a three-part secret received on 13 July. The first part was a vivid and frightening vision of hell. The second part was the revelation of the devotion to the Immaculate Heart of Mary, from Lucia of Fatima, and a message stressing the need for the consecration of Russia as a way to obtain grace and mercy for the entire world. Lucia also alluded to a third part of the secret, one that she could only reveal to the pope. In 1943, Lucia did write down the third part of the secret. It was placed in a sealed envelope, which the bishop of Leiria kept in his safe until 1957. In 1957, the secret was sent to the Vatican, but there is no record as to what was done with it.

The contents of the Third Secret of Fatima became a subject of intense speculation in Marian circles, and have remained so ever since. During World War II, it was assumed that the secret referred to the outcome of the war. In the postwar years, the third secret was taken to refer to the ongoing struggle between the church and communism. As with all apparitions since the Middle Ages, it was presumed that Mary was interceding to save a beleaguered community, in this case the entire world. The key to defeating the forces of godless communism was for all sinners to renew their devotion to the Immaculate Heart of Mary. This interpretation was particularly encouraged by church authorities in Europe, who considered it their mission to bring young communist sympathizers back to the church.

In the 1950s the belief arose that the Third Secret was going to be made public in 1960. When this did not happen, a variety of scenarios were proposed as to why Pope Paul VI was unable to make the secret known. Some versions simply reasoned that it could not be made public while Lucia was still alive, but more elaborate scenarios were discussed where the secret was considered to be too dangerous to be disseminated. Some reports had the pope weeping or falling unconscious upon reading the secret. On 26 June 2000, the Vatican made the Third Secret public.

The message was not one of world destruction nor one of overwhelming horror. Instead, it described an "angel with a flaming sword" who pointed to earth and shouted "penance, penance, penance," and a "bishop clothed in white" who was killed by bullets and arrows, which the Vatican identified as the 1981 assassination attempt on John Paul II.

Predictably, some Fundamentalist Catholic groups immediately attacked the text of the Third Secret released by the Vatican as a hoax, maintaining that the "real" Third Secret is still being kept from the public. The secret had not answered all their questions, nor had it solved their problems. The underlying needs and tensions that feed Fundamentalism everywhere, and the difficulty of maintaining faith in a rapidly changing world, are still present and cannot ultimately be resolved.

Victor Balaban

Bibliography

Carroll, Michael P. (1986) *The Cult of the Virgin Mary: Psychological Origins*. Princeton, NJ: Princeton University Press.

Cuneo, Michael. (1997) *The Smoke of Satan: Conservative and Traditionalist Dissent in Contemporary American Catholicism*. New York: Oxford University Press.

Kselman, Thomas A. (1983) *Miracles and Prophesies in 19th Century France*. New Brunswick, NJ: Rutgers University Press.

Pelikan, Jarosalv. (1996) *Mary Through the Centuries: Her Place in the History of Culture*. New Haven, CT: Yale University Press.

Turner, Victor, and Edith Turner. (1978) *Image and Pilgrimage in Christian Culture: Anthropological Perspectives*. New York: Columbia University Press.

Zimdars-Swartz, Sandra L. (1991) *Encountering Mary: Visions of Mary from LaSalette to Medjugorje*. Princeton, NJ: Princeton University Press.

Decalogue

The Decalogue, or Ten Commandments, is found in the Book of Exodus of the Bible. Exodus 20:1–17 and Deuteronomy 5:6–21 relate that God (Yahweh) revealed these commandments to Moses on Mt. Sinai. Moses was a former murderer who had repented of his sins. Yahweh gave him another chance and Moses became a great leader of his people. Among his many accomplishments as prophet, leader, and deliverer was his passing on of the Decalogue or Ten Commandments to Israel on two stone tablets.

The first three commandments (four in some religious traditions) relate to the Hebrew's duties to God and the remainder to their obligations to each other. Thus, worshipping of false gods and idols is prohibited as is taking the Lord's name in vain, or violating the Sabbath by working. Another commandment enjoins parental respect on the Hebrews. Those who honor their parents are promised that their "days may be long in the land which the Lord your God gives you" (Exodus 20:12, KJV). The list of prohibitions includes murder, adultery, theft, bearing false witness, and coveting a "neighbor's wife, or his manservant, or his maidservant, or his ox, or his ass, or anything that is your neighbor's" (Exodus 10:1–17, NJB).

Different religious traditions (Judaism, Roman Catholicism, Orthodoxy, and various Protestant denominations) organize and number the Ten Commandments in different ways. Judaism, for example, counts the prologue ("I am the Lord your God, who brought you out of the land of Egypt, out of the house of bondage" [Deuteronomy 5:6–22, NJB]) as constituting the First Commandment. Medieval Christianity, however, joined the prologue to the prohibition against idolatry and false gods to form the First Commandment and arrived at the number ten by separating the coveting of a neighbor's wife and property into two commandments. Greek Orthodox and Protestant Reformed traditions, however, join the prologue and the prohibition against false gods into one commandment, and then view the prohibition against idols as the Second Commandment.

Biblical scholars also differ in their dating of the Ten Commandments. Dates vary from between the sixteenth and thirteenth centuries BCE to after 750 BCE or later. In any case, the commandments are of a piece with general moral traditions in the Middle East. They sum up a general code of relationships between Hebrews and Yahweh and between Hebrews and one another. The commandments grew in importance for Christians in the thirteenth century CE by becoming part of a manual for those preparing to confess their sins. In time and with the rise of Protestantism, the Ten Commandments found their way into catechisms as a basic part of instruction in the faith.

The Ten Commandments helped to forge a new community of believers who kept peace among themselves by following a common moral code. It replaced the need for a large bureaucracy and military organization to protect life and property and it helped establish the Kingdom of Yahweh, extending divine sanction to the well-being of the community. Responsibility for one's actions was an essential part of the general contract that Israel had made with God. Society itself was a sacred thing, created by agreement with God. Therefore, any violation

Exodus 20:1–17

1. And God spake all these words, saying,
2. I am the LORD thy God, which have brought thee out of the land of Egypt, out of the house of bondage.
3. Thou shalt have no other gods before me.
4. Thou shalt not make unto thee any graven image, or any likeness of any thing that is in heaven above, or that is in the earth beneath, or that is in the water under the earth:
5. Thou shalt not bow down thyself to them, nor serve them: for I the LORD thy God am a jealous God, visiting the iniquity of the fathers upon the children unto the third and fourth generation of them that hate me;
6. And shewing mercy unto thousands of them that love me, and keep my commandments.
7. Thou shalt not take the name of the LORD thy God in vain; for the LORD will not hold him guiltless that taketh his name in vain.
8. Remember the sabbath day, to keep it holy.
9. Six days shalt thou labour, and do all thy work:
10. But the seventh day is the sabbath of the LORD thy God: in it thou shalt not do any work, thou, nor thy son, nor thy daughter, thy manservant, nor thy maidservant, nor thy cattle, nor thy stranger that is within thy gates:
11. For in six days the LORD made heaven and earth, the sea, and all that in them is, and rested the seventh day: wherefore the LORD blessed the sabbath day, and hallowed it.
12. Honour thy father and thy mother: that thy days may be long upon the land which the LORD thy God giveth thee.
13. Thou shalt not kill.
14. Thou shalt not commit adultery.
15. Thou shalt not steal.
16. Thou shalt not bear false witness against thy neighbour.
17. Thou shalt not covet thy neighbour's house, thou shalt not covet thy neighbour's wife, nor his manservant, nor his maidservant, nor his ox, nor his ass, nor any thing that is thy neighbour's.

---

threatened or challenged the Divine Order of things. Religious morality thus became the basis for political and communal identity and stability.

Frank A. Salamone

See also Justice; Law, Old Testament

Bibliography

Barcellos, Richard. (2001) *In Defense of the Decalogue: A Critique of New Covenant Theology*. Enumclaw, WA: Wine Press Publishing.

Fox, Emmet. (1993) *The Ten Commandments: The Master Key to Life*. San Francisco: Harper.

Freedman, David M., Jeffrey C. Geoghegan, and Michael M. Homan. (2000) *The Nine Commandments: Uncovering the Hidden Pattern of Crime and Punishment in the Hebrew Bible*. New York: Doubleday.

Spong, John Selby, and Denise G. Haines. (2001) *Beyond Moralism: A Contemporary View of the Ten Commandments*. New York: Saint Johann Press.

Depravity

As a result of the Fall described in Genesis 3, Western Christian theologians taught that human nature was corrupted by sin. As a result of their disobedience, Adam and Eve, originally created without sin, became sinful in their very nature. In Romans 5:12 (NRSV), Paul taught that sin entered the world through the disobedience of Adam, "and so death spread to all because all have sinned." Saint Augustine, following a Latin translation of the Bible, interpreted the last phrase of this verse as "in whom all have sinned." Because all people were "in Adam," he taught that all people inherited an innate depravity, or original sin, passed on through the propagation of the human race. The sin of an individual does not create a state of depravity; rather, specific acts of sin rise out of a sinful, or depraved, nature.

Although other understandings of original sin developed in Christian theology, the Augustinian doctrine of inherited depravity prevailed in the West, and especially in Protestant theology. For Fundamentalism, one of the most significant developments in Christian understandings of depravity was the Synod of Dort (1618–1619), which created a doctrinal statement used by many Reformed denominations (and the basis for what would later be called, somewhat inaccurately, the "five points of Calvinism"). In the Canons of the Synod of Dort, the state of humanity was described as one of "total depravity" (total in the sense of affecting the totality of human abilities and faculties, not total in the sense of depraved as one could possibly be). Prior to the Fall, human beings were created pure, holy, and innocent. After the Fall, however, the heart, mind, and will were all corrupted by sin. Not only was the will inclined toward sin rather than goodness, but the mind was blinded by the ravages of sin, affecting the human capacity of reason. Although the Fall did not obliterate the image of God in every person—and some realization of the existence of God, the difference between right and wrong, and so on, still remained—human beings after the Fall were powerless to come to salvation by their own power. Fallen humanity is "dead in sin." This depraved nature is passed on from parent to child, so that from birth children are not only guilty of sin, but powerless to resist sin. Since those with a fallen nature cannot choose good, salvation comes entirely through divine choice (election), and involves bringing the fallen nature, which is dead in sin, to life (regeneration).

Variants on this perspective tend to dominate later Fundamentalist theology, including Fundamentalist Presbyterians, many Baptists, and some branches of the Plymouth Brethren. Lewis Sperry Chafer, (1871–1952) professor of theology, one of the founders of the Dallas Theological Seminary, and author of one of the most influential Fundamentalist systematic theology texts, advocates a Calvinistic doctrine of depravity. He goes even further than Dort, however, in two ways. First, Chafer teaches that the entire cosmos after the fall is "wholly evil," and entirely under the authority and power of Satan. Because of the depth of depravity of the entire cosmos, it is destined for destruction, rather than redemption. This doctrine has significant repercussions on the Fundamentalist view of cultural and political involvement. Second, in salvation a new, "spiritual" nature is added to the sinful, or "carnal" nature. Both natures remain, but the spiritual Christian lives according to the new nature, not the old. It is possible, however, for a believer to be a "carnal Christian," dominated by the carnal nature despite the presence of a spiritual nature.

Not all Protestant Fundamentalists, however, draw from the Calvinistic theological tradition. The Independent Christian Church and Churches of Christ, originating in nineteenth-century America, reject the doctrine of an inherited depraved nature. Many Fundamentalist groups have been heavily influenced by the revivalism of Charles Finney (1792–1875) and his teaching on "moral depravity." Finney rejected what he called "constitutional sinfulness," and taught that sin is always a matter of voluntary choice by free moral agents. Baptist minister John Rice (1895–1980), founder of the widely read Fundamentalist magazine *The Sword of the Lord*, strongly condemned what he called "hyper-Calvinism," by which he meant the Canons of Dort and Calvinist doctrines of depravity. His basic reasoning is much like that of Finney: if God calls sinners to repent, they must be able to respond, since it would be unreasonable for God to command sinners to do what is not within their power. (This view has similarities with a fourth century CE heresy called Pelagianism, which denies original sin and holds that man has perfect freedom to do right or wrong). While both Islam and Judaism give sin a central place in its belief system, neither has a doctrine of depraved human nature.

Depravity of the fallen world is a frequent theme in much Fundamentalist Christian "last days" literature, which examines biblical prophecies of the return of Christ and the end of the world. An

Selection from:

THE CANONS OF DORDT,
FORMALLY TITLED THE DECISION OF THE SYNOD OF DORDT ON THE FIVE MAIN POINTS OF DOCTRINE IN DISPUTE IN THE NETHERLANDS

The First Main Point of Doctrine
Divine Election and Reprobation
The Judgment Concerning Divine Predestination
Which the Synod Declares to Be in Agreement with the Word of God
and Accepted Till Now in the Reformed Churches,
Set Forth in Several Articles

Article 1: God's Right to Condemn All People

Since all people have sinned in Adam and have come under the sentence of the curse and eternal death, God would have done no one an injustice if it had been his will to leave the entire human race in sin and under the curse, and to condemn them on account of their sin. As the apostle says: The whole world is liable to the condemnation of God (Rom. 3:19), All have sinned and are deprived of the glory of God (Rom. 3:23), and The wages of sin is death (Rom. 6:23).

Article 2: The Manifestation of God's Love

But this is how God showed his love: he sent his only begotten Son into the world, so that whoever believes in him should not perish but have eternal life.

Article 3: The Preaching of the Gospel

In order that people may be brought to faith, God mercifully sends proclaimers of this very joyful message to the people he wishes and at the time he wishes. By this ministry people are called to repentance and faith in Christ crucified. For how shall they believe in him of whom they have not heard? And how shall they hear without someone preaching? And how shall they preach unless they have been sent? (Rom. 10:14–15).

Article 4: A Twofold Response to the Gospel

God's anger remains on those who do not believe this gospel. But those who do accept it and embrace Jesus the Savior with a true and living faith are delivered through him from God's anger and from destruction, and receive the gift of eternal life.

Article 5: The Sources of Unbelief and of Faith

The cause or blame for this unbelief, as well as for all other sins, is not at all in God, but in man. Faith in Jesus Christ, however, and salvation through him is a free gift of God. As Scripture says, It is by grace you have been saved, through faith, and this not from yourselves; it is a gift of God (Eph. 2:8). Likewise: It has been freely given to you to believe in Christ (Phil. 1:29).

Source: *Historic Church Documents.* www.reformed.org

increase in sin and depravity is described as one of the signs of the last days in passages such as Matthew 24:12. In 2 Timothy 3:1–8, certain sins are listed that describe people in the last days, such as "lovers of money . . . without love . . . lovers of pleasure rather than God." The King James version lists "without natural affection" as one of these sins, which is usually interpreted in Fundamentalist theology as a reference to homosexuality. Sexual sins are frequently emphasized as the prime examples of moral depravity, and homosexuality is sometimes even called "the lowest level of human depravity." In sermons and devotional literature, an emphasis on depravity can serve both to heighten hope in the nearness of the return of Christ, as well as intensify the believer's sense of separation from the world. In this latter sense, "depravity" can serve as a marker that sharply differentiates the fallen world from the Christian, creating a sharp contrast from the purity of pre-fallen humanity and redeemed humanity.

Russ P. Reeves

See also Apocalyptic Literature; Fall of Humankind; Sin and Sinners

Bibliography

Canons of the Synod of Dort. (1619) *Third and Fourth Heads of Doctrine.*

Chafer, Lewis Sperry. (1947) *Systematic Theology*, vol. 2. Dallas: Dallas Seminary Press.

Pelikan, Jaroslav. (1971) *The Emergence of the Catholic Tradition*. Chicago: University of Chicago Press.

Sexton, Clarence. (1997) "What God Says about Gay Rights." *The Baptist Vision*, September 1, 1–7.

Devil and Satan, The

Through the centuries of recorded history the embodiment of evil has been called many names: Satan, devil, serpent, Antichrist, Mephistopheles, Lucifer, witch, demon, Mara, Beelzebub, Belial, black cat, Beast. These are the tangible forms of evil, not mere metaphysical sinister forces with no meat to their bones. But who is the master and who the servant? Even if we agree that in Western thought the devil or Satan are the principal choreographers from hell, they are not seen as identical figures over time.

While the metaphysical idea of evil appears across time and place, Peter Stanford observes that the figure of the devil has ancestry in "the ancient civilizations of the Near East and in Judaism and Islam" (1996: 2). The roots may trace to Set, the Egyptian god, or Ahriman, the Zoroastrian force of evil. The word "devil" originally derives from the word for "slanderer," while Satan comes from "accuser," but these figures appear variously throughout history as a tester, a tempter, or a trickster. It seems the devil is in the details.

In Genesis the evil serpent tempts Eve and Adam with fruit from the Tree of Knowledge about good and evil. According to Elaine Pagels, "Adam's sin was not sexual indulgence but disobedience. . . . The real theme of the story of Adam and Eve is moral freedom and moral responsibility. Its point is to show that we are responsible for the choices we freely make—good or evil—just as Adam was" (1989: xxiii). Yet, for centuries Christianity followed the view of Augustine that the Fall from Grace in Eden involved sex, leaving little doubt that if idle hands were the devil's playthings, then the cards were dealt with carnal knowledge.

By undermining God's command the serpent of Genesis is cursed, and reptilian forms are often used to represent evil in the Bible. Revelation describes a war in heaven where "The great dragon was hurled down—that ancient serpent called the devil, or Satan, who leads the whole world astray" (Revelation 12:7–9, NIV). Revelation also describes evil beasts, and an Antichrist who serves Satan by attempting to fool Christians into renouncing Jesus. These are examples of Satan as trickster or tempter. In other biblical roles, Satan, in the book of Job, is an angel of God, serving as the tester of faith. Satan causes the destruction of Job's entire household: family, servants, livestock, and house. Although in agony over his loss, Job "fell to the ground in worship," saying "Naked I came from my mother's womb, and naked I will depart. The Lord gave and the Lord has taken away; may the name of the Lord be praised" (Job 1:20–21). Still not satisfied, Satan causes Job to be covered in painful sores. Again, Job refused to curse God (Job 1–2). Therefore, a person "with the patience of Job" is someone who can withstand even the test of Satan. These passages are often invoked by faithful Christians at times of great misfortune or death; and are cited as part of a larger theological discussion over the relationship between an all-powerful

God and the devil, and why bad (evil) things happen to good (Godly) people.

The Devil's Disciples

According to Carus, the "saddest side of the Devil's history appears in the persecution of those who were supposed to be adherents of the Devil; namely, sectarians, heretics, and witches" (1996: 306). Indeed, devil worshipping is a charge that has been leveled against dissidents of all stripes. Pagels finds in early Christianity, "the use of Satan to represent one's enemies [which] lends to conflict a specific kind of moral and religious interpretation, in which 'we' are God's people and 'they' are God's enemies, and ours as well" (1996: xix). Pagels quips, "Satan has, after all, made a kind of profession out of being the 'other'" (1996: xviii).

What Christians conceive as evil and the embodiment of evil has varied over time. This has even led to serious schisms and battles within Christianity—including campaigns against the Gnostics, the Paulicians, and the Cathars—and disputes among missionaries sent across the Atlantic to "New Spain." According to Robert Fuller, "During the first three centuries of Christian thought, the identities of Satan and the Antichrist were frequently intertwined," but after that, "The Antichrist has generally been understood to be Satan's chief disciple or agent for deceiving humanity in the final days" (1995: 5, 31). The idea of the devil as an incarnate powerful evil demon leading a battle against God gains prominence in the eight and ninth centuries in Christianity.

From the 1100s through the 1500s, Christianity experienced a period of militant millennialism, and the faithful paid special attention to identifying the Antichrist and his evil followers, who were seen as in league with the devil. In the thirteenth century, according to Carus, "the Devil reached the acme of his influence" (1996: 282). During this century, the original papal inquisition was largely directed against dissenters linked to Satanic influence. The charge frequently served an opportunistic purpose. The Christian order of the Knights Templar was accused of "bestial idolatry" by "an avaricious king of France ... anxious to deprive them of their wealth" (1996: 306–307).

When some Freemasons constructed a history linking their order to the Knights Templar, they inherited the charges of Satanic conspiracy. The later Spanish Inquisition, in the fifteenth century, often targeted converted Jews and Muslims who were suspected of aiding the devil or engaging in forbidden practices. By taking a hard line in opposition to the practice of magic and witchcraft, Christian authorities taught followers that some persons in league with the devil possessed special powers and skills. Alliance with the devil might be through demonic possession or soul-selling; it might also manifest itself as spreading the false religion of the Antichrist, or recalcitrant sinfulness; or even be traced to alleged bloodlines from the biblical Cain. No matter the conceptualization of demonic allegiance, the response was often brutal, ranging from exorcism, to torture, to execution. With this reading of the relationship between the devil and certain demonized individuals, the seeds of future witch-hunts were sown. Even when church officials tried to downplay the idea of the devil or Satan and the process of demonization, it often flourished at a popular level.

Jews have long been a special target of Christian demonization. The Christian Church linked Jews to the Antichrist as early as the second century. By the twelfth century, Jews were being charged with the ritual murder of children, poisoning of wells, desecration of communion bread and wine, and other calumnies. The demonization of Jews as magical agents of the powerful devil gained strength during the sixteenth-century Renaissance and the Reformation. During this period, the earlier false allegations about Jews secretly engaging in murder and desecration again became widely believed among Christians. Martin Luther believed Jews were Satanic agents of the Antichrist in what he thought were the approaching End Times, although he also included orthodox Catholics loyal to the papacy, the Turkish invaders of Europe, and, eventually, just about everyone who disagreed with him. In the early 1900s, Christian anti-Semites in Russia popularized the hoax document *The Protocols of the Elders of Zion*, again suggesting Jews were Satanic agents of the Antichrist in a period of apocalyptic millennialism.

Legacies of Demonization

Robert Fuller ties demonization and scapegoating to apocalyptic and millennialist fervor, but argues that it is universal and "rooted in the psychological need to project one's 'unacceptable' tendencies onto a demonic enemy" (1995: 168). Fundamentalist movements in the United States often have reflected this type of an apocalyptic Manichaean framework of absolute good versus absolute evil—a tendency that encourages demonization of opponents. Jeffrey Kaplan notes this: "framework requires the adherent to see the world as the devil's domain, in which the tiny, helpless 'righteous remnant' perseveres through the protection of God in the hope that, soon, God will see fit to intervene once and for all in the life of this world" (1997: 171). Ironically, this dualism reflects the ideas of the early Gnostics and other groups considered heretics by Christian ideologues. The colonial settlers brought the idea of devout Christians battling the devil to New England where in the 1600s a series of witch-hunts frequently singled out nontraditional women, and established a paradigm for demonization that later targeted Freemasons, Catholics, immigrants, anarchists, socialists, and labor organizers.

Frank Donner and Joel Kovel argue that from about 1915 until 1990, the main Fundamentalist outlet for demonization took the form of right-wing anticommunism. This expanded into a general linkage of any form of collectivism or globalism to Satan's plan—outlined in the Book of Revelation—for a one-world government. The biblical basis for this political viewpoint was sometimes obscured. For instance, the book *Trilaterals Over Washington* (1979) appears to be a secular antiglobalist critique, but it takes on a new dimension when the illustration on the cover is identified as the many-headed beast mentioned in Revelation, which in turn gives added meaning to the inside graphic with the headline: "The Trilateral Commission: the Devil's Triangle of your future" (Sutton and Wood 1979).

Some politically active conservative Christians believe they are engaged in "Spiritual Warfare" against Satanic forces. Discussion of this is unremarkable within the Christian Right, even among savvy policy analysts and lobbyists. A 1984 booklet from the Free Congress Research and Education Foundation titled *The Morality of Political Action: Biblical Foundations* includes a defense of Christian political activists misleading or tricking opponents, claiming it is justified by the higher purpose of the Christian struggle against evil. The publication advises that while opponents may be doing the work of the devil, it would be wrong to publicly accuse them of being "a card-carrying member of Satan's band," not because it might be untrue, but because it falls under "the scope of the Lord's command: 'Judge not lest ye be judged'" (Marshner and Rueda 1984:47.)

Since the 1960s many Fundamentalist Protestants and apocalyptic Catholics have seen the hands of the devil behind what they characterize as godless political liberalism, especially the feminist movement and gay rights. They argue that "secular humanism" is displacing biblical mandates in society. George Marsden says this idea "revitalized fundamentalist conspiracy theory." According to Marsden, "Fundamentalists always had been alarmed at moral decline within America but often had been vague as to whom, other than the Devil, to blame. The 'secular humanist' thesis gave this central concern a clearer focus that was more plausible and of wider appeal than the old mono-causal communist-conspiracy accounts. Communism and socialism could, of course, be fit right into the humanist picture; but so could all the moral and legal changes at home without implausible scenarios of Russian agents infiltrating American schools, government, reform movements, and mainline churches" (1991: 109). After the collapse of communism in Europe, this preexisting theoretical framework helped transfer concern for Satan's agenda among Fundamentalists from the Red Menace to other demonized targets in a relatively seamless manner.

Fear of Satanism

For certain Fundamentalists, Satan is not just the tempter but a palpable presence luring children away from God and toward sin. At Christian bookstores, parents can purchase numerous books on the topic with titles such as *The Satan Seller*, *Teens and Devil Worship*, and *The Devil's Web: Who Is Stalking Your Children For Satan?* In the 1980s this belief system helped spur concerns about Satanic ritual abuse that some critics labeled an hysteria. According to Gerry O'Sullivan:

> The satanic panic combines the worst of several scares peculiar to the eighties—terrorism, secular humanism, drugs and child-kidnapping—to frame a largely Christian, populist critique of mass cultural forms. But its analyses remain mired in conspiracy thinking, racism, eschatological anticipation, and the displacement of what are primarily familial ills (child abuse and incest) onto highly secretive and hooded outsiders....
>
> The satanism scare is "about" several things, among them: the demonization of adolescent behavior through folkloric and often lurid accounts of bloodletting, cannibalism and sex; a struggle over the constitution of knowledge elites ... and the

ideological reinstitution of the family as racially pure, intact, and continually threatened from without by dark and hooded people emerging from the shadows to steal "our" tow-headed children. (1991, para. 14–15

O'Sullivan argued the fears of Satanism echo and "reiterate the medieval blood libel" (1991, para. 14) against Jews (as did *The Protocols of the Elders of Zion*), but in an adapted and sanitized form to fit contemporary society in the 1980s.

As the millennial year 2000 approached, Sara Diamond reported that even some Christians who were dubious of explicit End Times claims were reenergized by the idea of the 2000th anniversary of Christianity as a time not only for aggressive evangelism but also "spiritual warfare" against demonic forces (1997: 206–210). One Fundamentalist production company, Jeremiah Films, issued a thirteen-part video series "Pagan Invasion," which included a program claiming Halloween was a pretense for Satanic abduction. Apocalyptic rhetoric about Satan can be vivid. The militant antiabortion website "Nuremberg Files" launched a project with the argument that "Satan hates [the] project because it actually has the power to interfere with the delivery of his daily diet of slaughtered babies. Satan gets very angry when his favorite food (sacrificed human babies) fails to be delivered.... Interrupting Satan's food source is a great reason to help us with this project! How's this for a bumper sticker? Starve Satan: Stop Abortion.

Conclusion

Discussing the devil and Satan may seem obscure in an increasingly secularized age with the Internet and cell phones, but Pagels points out that today, "Many religious people who no longer believe in Satan, along with countless others who do not identify with any religious tradition, nevertheless are influenced by this cultural legacy whenever they perceive social and political conflict in terms of the forces of good contending against the forces of evil in the world" (1996: 182). Satan's literary legacy alone embraces not only the Bible but Dante's *Inferno*, Goethe's *Faust*, the quintessentially American *The Devil and Daniel Webster*, and the very postmodern television series *Buffy the Vampire Slayer*.

There is a vast range of beliefs about the devil and Satan within Christianity in general and Fundamen-

talism in particular, and even these ideas have changed over time. While some variations promote demonization, even some politically conservative Fundamentalist Christians warn against this tendency. One such group, the Institute for the Study of Religion in Politics (ISRP) argues that: "if the price of reestablishing a 'public Christian culture' in this country means that the church must ostracize its opponents, ghettoize the adherents of other religions and cultures, make enemies of women who choose abortion, demonize homosexuals, etc., as it seeks to gather political power into its hands—maybe, just maybe, the price isn't worth paying" (ISRP website). Christian authors ranging from the mainstream John Bevere to the avant-garde René Girard also warn against demonization. They stand in opposition to those for whom the devil and Satan are not just the embodiment of evil, but sinister leaders whose followers must be tracked down and exposed—perhaps even eliminated.

Chip Berlet

See also Antichrist; Evil; Fall of Humankind; Sin and Sinners

Bibliography

Bevere, John. (1997) *The Bait Of Satan: Your Response Determines Your Future.* Lake Mary, FL: Creation House.

Boyer, Paul, and Stephen Nissenbaum. (1974) *Salem Possessed: The Social Origins of Witchcraft.* Cambridge, MA: Harvard University Press.

Carus, Paul. ([1900] 1996) *The History of the Devil and the Idea of Evil.* New York: Gramercy/Random House.

Cervantes, Fernando. (1994) *The Devil in the New World: The Impact of Diabolism in New Spain.* New Haven: Yale University Press.

Cohn, Norman. ([1957] 1970) *The Pursuit of the Millennium,* rev. and expanded ed. New York: Oxford University Press.

———. (1993) *Cosmos, Chaos and the World to Come: The Ancient Roots of Apocalyptic Faith.* New Haven: Yale University Press.

———. ([1967] 1996) *Warrant for Genocide: The Myth of the Jewish World Conspiracy and the Protocols of the Elders of Zion.* London: Serif.

Cuneo, Michael W. (1997) *The Smoke of Satan, Conservative and Traditionalist Dissent in Contemporary American Catholicism.* Oxford: Oxford University Press.

TEENS AND DEVIL-WORSHIP

Over the years Hollywood has led many to believe that the devil is a hideously ugly creature with red skin, black eyes, cloven hooves, dagger-like fangs, and horns. He has been portrayed by artists as a half human/half animal mutation resembling that which only our most terrifying nightmares could design. But no where in the Bible do we find such descriptions of Satan. In fact, quite the opposite is true. The Old Testament describes him before he fell from heaven and clearly states that he was full of wisdom and perfect in beauty (Ezek. 28:12) . . . .

This is tremendously important. Simple logic tells us that the average person is not tempted by anything that tastes dreadful, smells terrible, or appears unattractive. Instead, we are tempted by those things that are delicious, smell heavenly, and are pleasing to the eyes . . . .

Naturally, if Satan presented the real facts to those he tempts, the vast majority would want nothing to do with him. After all, who really wants to end up on death row because they followed the devil's instructions to murder their family members? Who really wants to beat a friend to death with a baseball bat in a satanically inspired frenzy? Who really wants to end up as an unwilling human sacrifice to Satan? But again, he makes it look so good.

Keeping the above in mind, the next logical question is *Why*. Why does anyone decide to worship the devil?

Source: Evans, Charles G.B. (1991) *Teens and Devil-Worship: What Everyone Should Know*.
Lafayette, LA: Huntington House, pp. 23–24.

Diamond, Sara. (1989) *Spiritual Warfare: The Politics of the Christian Right*. Boston: South End Press.

———. (1997) "Political Millennialism within the Evangelical Subculture." In *The Year 2000: Essays on the End*, edited by Charles B. Strozier and Michael Flynn. New York: New York University Press, 206–216.

Evans, Charles G. B. (1991) *Teens and Devil-Worship: What Everyone Should Know*. Lafayette, LA: Huntington House.

Frazier, James George. ([1890] 1959) *The New Golden Bough: A Study in Magic and Religion*, abridged, edited by Theodor H. Gaster. New York: Criterion Books.

Fuller, Robert. (1995) *Naming the Antichrist: The History of an American Obsession*. New York: Oxford University Press.

Girard, René. (1979) *Violence and the Sacred*. Baltimore: Johns Hopkins University Press.

Gow, Andrew Colin. (1995) *The Red Jews: Antisemitism in an Apocalyptic Age 1200–1600*. Leiden, Netherlands: E.J. Brill.

Hsia, R. Po-chia. (1988) *The Myth of Ritual Murder: Jews and Magic in Reformation Germany*. New Haven, CT: Yale University Press.

Institute for the Study of Religion in Politics (ISRP). http://www.isrp.org/welcome.html.

Kaplan, Jeffrey. (1997) *Radical Religion in America: Millenarian Movements from the Far Right to the Children of Noah*. Syracuse, NY: Syracuse University Press.

Karlsen, Carol F. (1998) *The Devil in the Shape of a Woman: Witchcraft in Colonial New England*. New York: W. W. Norton.

Kovel, Joel. (1994) *Red Hunting in the Promised Land: Anticommunism and the Making of America*. New York: Basic Books.

Lea, Henry Charles. ([1887–1888] 1961) *The Inquisition of the Middle Ages*, abridged by Margaret Nicholson. New York: Macmillan.

Lurker, Manfred. (1987) *A Dictionary of Gods and Goddesses, Devils and Demons*. London: Routledge and K. Paul.

Marsden, George M. (1991) *Understanding Fundamentalism and Evangelicalism*. Grand Rapids, MI: Wm. B. Eerdmans.

Marshner, William H. and Enrique T. Rueda. (1984) *The Morality of Political Action: Biblical Foundations*, booklet. Washington, DC: Free Congress Research and Education Foundation.

Munk, Linda. (1997) *The Devil's Mousetrap: Redemption and Colonial American Literature*. New York: Oxford University Press.

Nathan, Debbie, and Michael Snedeker. (1995) *Satan's Silence: Ritual Abuse and the Making of a Modern American Witch Hunt*. New York: Basic Books.

Oberman, Heiko A. (1984) *The Roots of Anti-Semitism: In the Age of Renaissance and Reformation*, translated by James I. Porter. Philadelphia: Fortress Press.

O'Shea, Stephen. (2000) *The Perfect Heresy: The Revolutionary Life and Death of the Medieval Cathars*. New York: Walker & Company.

O'Sullivan, Gerry. (1991) "The Satanism Scare." *Postmodern Culture* 1, 2 (January), electronic journal.

Pagels, Elaine. (1989) *Adam, Eve, and the Serpent*. New York: Vintage.

———. ([1979] 1989) *The Gnostic Gospels*. New York: Vintage

———. (1996) *The Origin of Satan*. New York: Vintage.

Pulling, Pat, with Kathy Cawthon. (1989) *The Devil's Web: Who Is Stalking Your Children for Satan?* Lafayette, LA: Huntington House.

Richardson, James T., Joel Best, and David G. Bromley, eds. (1991) *The Satanism Scare*. New York: Aldine De Gruyter.

Rose, Susan D. (1990) *Keeping Them Out of the Hands of Satan: Evangelical Schooling in America*. New York: Routledge.

Stanford, Peter. (1996) *The Devil: A Biography*. New York: Henry Holt.

Starkey, Marion L. ([1949] 1969) *The Devil in Massachusetts: A Modern Inquiry into the Salem Witch Trials*. Garden City, NY: Anchor Books/Doubleday.

Sutton, Antony C., and Patrick M. Wood. (1979) *Trilaterals Over Washington*. Scottsdale, AZ: The August Corporation.

Warnke, Mike, with David Balsiger and Les Jones. (1972) *The Satan Seller*. South Plainfield, NJ: Bridge Publishing.

Woods, William Howard. (1974) *A History of the Devil*. New York: Putnam.

Dispensationalism

Dispensationalism is an interpretation of salvation history popular with American Evangelical Protestants, including Fundamentalists. The chief characteristic of this system of theology is the division of God's dealings with humankind into discrete eras. In each such era, God offers salvation under somewhat different circumstances, only to see it inevitably refused. The number of such eras, or dispensations, varies by school, but seven is the number most often cited. The current dispensation will end with the Rapture, a divine act that removes the saved from earth just before the Tribulation, a period of unspeakable woe. The Tribulation is to end with Christ's Second Advent and what follows will be the new millennial dispensation.

Fundamentalist dispensationalism is traceable, in part, to John Nelson Darby (1800–1882), a nineteenth-century Irish cleric. Darby was a premillennialist; that is, he believed that the Second Advent precedes the thousand-year period of earthly bliss that many Evangelicals understand as the meaning of Revelation 20:1–3. Premillennialism was a salient feature of nineteenth-century Evangelical Protestantism in England and, especially, the United States. Dispensationalism is thus inseparable from premillennialism. Darby systematized premillennial dispensationalism, furthered Evangelical philo-Semitism, and originated the Rapture as a stock part of Evangelical theology. Nevertheless, dispensationalism remains alien for much the larger part of the Christian world, including Catholicism, Orthodoxy, and the mainline Protestant faiths down to the present.

Christianity, along with the other Abrahamic faiths, Islam and Judaism, is rooted in a salvation history that largely corresponds to chronological time on earth. Significant events in these faiths can be located in historic time, often to a precise year, date, and even time of day. For instance, the Crucifixion is thought to have occurred at a specific site in Jerusalem on the morning after Passover about the year 33 CE. Likewise, the prophet Muhammad is known to have died on 8 June 632 CE.

This specific historicity of the Abrahamic faiths contrasts with that of most other religions, ancient and modern. For instance, it was a common article of classical religion that Venus sprang full-grown from the forehead of Zeus. However, it occurred to no one in ancient Greece to assign a specific date to an event that occurred in mythic time and so does not correlate with human history on this planet.

Christianity, like the other Abrahamic faiths, is thus perforce a philosophy of history. God reveals Himself in time as calculated by ordinary human chronology, and history is invested with direction and purpose. Once the early chapters of Genesis are past, the Bible deals largely with actual historical events and identifies their spiritual significance. In Christian thought, the most crucial such event is the ministry of Jesus. While the Resurrection is not an accepted fact for all, the Gospel account of it is minutely specific as to time and place. It is understood as an epochal event that in the most dramatic way imaginable changes the relationship between God and His creation.

However, there are earlier instances in the biblical account in which the Deity ratifies a new constitution between Himself and humankind. The Exile from the Garden, the covenant given Noah after the Flood, the calling of Abraham, and the Ten Commandments are such instances. Even though some of these events occur in mythic time, there is a degree of historicity about most of them. The point is that history is not a bland continuum but is episodic. Time—real time— passes, and as it does God regularly amends His covenant with humankind.

Dispensationalism codifies such amendments in the divine–human relationship in an explicitly schematic manner. All Christians, whether Fundamentalist or not, agree that the death and Resurrection of Jesus alters for all time the relationship between God and humanity. The very fact that the Bible is divided into Old and New Testaments indicates the epochal nature of the alteration. In this regard, Fundamentalist thought differs not at all from Roman Catholic, Orthodox, or other Protestant belief. It does, however, differ elsewhere in its interpretation of sacred history and this is due, in large part, to its premillennial eschatology.

Premillennialism and Dispensationalism

Fundamentalism and premillennialism evolved together throughout the nineteenth century. The belief that Jesus might soon return to inaugurate a millennial reign on earth quickly spread from Great Britain to America during the years just after the American Revolution. For many, the millennium formed an era as distinct in salvation history as those recognized by the two biblical testaments. As early as 1797, the Boston cleric Abraham Cummings in his *A Dissertation on the Introduction and Glory of the Millennium* explicitly identified three dispensations: the Old Testament, the New Testament, and the millennium. The concept of distinct dispensations additional to the two traditionally recognized by

Christians in their division of the Bible into Old and New Testaments was thus introduced early in American religious thought.

Nineteenth-century American premillennialists dissected sacred history ever more minutely. Their outlook was essentially legalistic, in that they treated the Bible as a contract between God and humanity, best understood as a series of sequential governing clauses—the dispensations. This mind-set, in turn, reveals the chasm that steadily opened during the first half of that century between certain Evangelicals and more liberal Protestant thought.

The rise to prominence of the historico-critical method during the nineteenth century constituted a revolution in biblical scholarship. The new analysis approached Scripture as an historical document that, like any other, must be understood within the context of the time during which it was written. Prophecy, along with much else, was reevaluated in light of increased knowledge of its historical setting, along with a rigid critique of internal evidence. Scholars argued, for example, that the Book of Daniel was not even prophecy but was, instead, a retrospective interpretation of the recent past cast in the guise of prediction in order to legitimize a known outcome. The Book of Revelation, they also argued, was likewise not a prophecy of distant events but a denunciation of the contemporary Roman world in which it was written and its supposed predictions really just inspirational poetry crafted to sustain persecuted Christians.

The premillennial movement that flourished during these same years considered this new scholarship as anathema. Premillennialism is grounded absolutely and entirely in prophetic scripture. If that scripture were treated merely as inspirational poetry written to offer succor during a transient and long-ago period of persecution or, worse, not prophecy at all but, like Daniel, just a political tract in religious guise, then the foundation for premillennialism simply ceased to exist. There was thus a clear incentive for premillennialists to refute the historico-critical method and insist that the Bible is inerrant.

This is the background against which dispensationalism emerged. Premillennialists realized that their treasured eschatology was lost if they failed to insist on an inerrant (or "literal") interpretation of the Bible. It is no surprise, then, that as the nineteenth century wore on, premillennialists, in the United States especially, were the ones who most uncompromisingly insisted on just such a "literal"

JOHN NELSON DARBY ON DISPENSATIONALISM

The detail of the history connected with these dispensations brings out many most interesting displays . . . But the dispensations themselves all declare some leading principle or interference of God, some condition in which He has placed man, principles which in themselves are everlastingly sanctioned of God, but in the course of these dispensations placed responsibly in the hands of man for the display and discovery of what he was, and the bringing in their infallible establishment in Him to whom the glory of them all rightly belonged . . . In every instance, there was a total and immediate failure as regarded man, however the patience of God might tolerate and carry on by grace the dispensation in which man has thus failed in the outset; and further, that there is no instance of the restoration of a dispensation afforded us, though there might be partial revivals of it through faith.

The paradisaical state cannot properly perhaps be called a dispensation in this sense of the word; but as regards the universal failure of man; it is a most important instance . . . Corruption, disorder, violence were the consequences of this, until the Lord destroyed the first world created . . .

Here dispensations, properly speaking, begin. On the first, Noah I shall be very brief . . . The first account after his call we have of faithful Abraham which as a minuter circumstance I also pass briefly over . . .

But to take up the point of the dispensation-obedience under the law by which life was to be: this obedience they undertook; and Moses returned to receive the various orderings of divine appointment as under it, and the two tables of testimony. But this dispensation which met the failure of the world . . .

The ordinance or dispensation of priesthood failed in like manner. Before Aaron and his sons had gone out of the door of the tabernacle of the congregation, because the anointing oil of the Lord was upon them, Nahab and Abihu had already offered stranger fire and been consumed before the Lord . . .

The kingly dispensation failed in the same way as did the nation under the previous ordering which made way for the king (see Judges 2) . . . till the provocations of Manasseh set aside all hope of recovery or way of mercy in that dispensation. The same is true of universal rule transferred to the Gentiles: Nebuchadnezzar, the golden head, sets up the golden image, persecutes the faithful, and is turned into the image of a beast for his pride.

understanding of Scripture. And, as exemplified by the just-quoted Rev. Cummings, premillennialists had early on joined a third dispensation—the millennium—to the two recognized by traditional Christianity. Such a categorizing mentality when combined with an unyielding defense of an inerrant Bible clearly had the potential to subdivide sacred history into ever-finer gradations. Moreover, it will be remembered, the Abrahamic religions all implicitly tend in this direction by their insistence on the significance of "real," that is, chronological, time. The elements were present for someone to systematize sacred history in a manner that, at once, remained rooted in the biblical narrative, understood that narrative in the light of premillennial eschatology, and

rested on a literal reading of the Word. Such an interpreter would, at the same time, clearly go against the current of modern biblical scholarship. During the last half of the nineteenth century, this interpreter emerged in the person of the Irish cleric John Nelson Darby.

John Nelson Darby's Influence

Dispensationalism, it must be stressed, did not originate wholly with Darby. Christians had always divided salvation history into the two epochs of Old and New Testaments. Likewise, a dispensational triad that added the millennium to the two Testaments was a commonplace of premillennial literature

The rejection of our blessed Lord proved that no present mercy or grace, no present interference of God in goodness here would meet the wilful and persevering enmity of the human heart, but only showed it in its true light. But this never being set up as a dispensation but only the manifestation of His Person (by faith), I pass by. The last we have to notice, in a humbled sense of sin in us, is the present, where we are apt to take our ease in the world . . . the dispensation of the Spirit. Much has been said, with strong objection to it, as to the apostasy or failure of this dispensation. The results are but too plain . . .

But the point which is proved is that this is not merely that it is in a bad state now, but that like all others it broke down in the commencement-no sooner fully established than it proved a failure . . . The remnant have been preserved . . . but the dispensation was gone. We belong to a better glory . . .

And as he cannot desire, so neither does Scripture present the restoration of a dispensation; it never justifies its actual condition; and though grace and faith may, as I have said, effect revivals during the long-suffering of God, the dispensation, as such, is actually gone, that the glory of the principle contained in it may shine forth in the hands of Messiah. The attempt to set this dispensation on another footing, as to its continuance, than those dispensations which have failed already, not only shows ignorance of the principles of God's dealings . . .

And the close of all dispensation, and the end of all question and title of authority shall come, and all be finished, God shall be all in all without question and without failure . . .

Reference to the second chapter of Galatians will confirm and establish the point historically as to the present dispensation . . . In fact the Gentile dispensation, as a distinct thing, took its rise at the death of Stephen, the witness that the Jews resisted the Holy Ghost: as their fathers did, so did they.

Source: Darby, John Nelson. "The Apostasy of the Successive Dispensations."
Quoted in *John Nelson Darby (1800–1882): The Father of Premillennial Dispensationalism*.
www.virginiawater.co.uk.

for at least two generations beforehand. Darby, however, elaborated a systematic dispensational scheme and endowed it with at least one truly novel element—the Rapture. The resultant explication of sacred history today flourishes on countless prophetic charts in innumerable Evangelical Sunday school rooms. It also separates much of Fundamentalism from the biblical scholarship of the last two centuries.

John Nelson Darby was an Irish cleric who abandoned an earlier practice of law in favor of the Gospel. Despite his reputation as a caring pastor, he gradually withdrew from the parish ministry, convinced that the Anglican Church was "in ruins." Eventually, he left that church and was instrumental in founding the Plymouth Brethren, a small denomination that was soon established in the United States as well. The Brethren was founded on the premillennial eschatology Darby embraced and that, in turn, rested on the biblical literalism just described. Darby divided sacred history into seven dispensations, beginning with the "Adamaic," in each of which humankind willfully rejects God's proffered salvation. That number became more or less the norm in dispensational thought, although commentators occasionally separate the biblical narrative into slightly different categories. Each of these dispensations has the nature of a contract, with salvation the consideration, but the terms of agreement vary by dispensation. For example, the tender to Abraham differs significantly from the arrangement offered earlier to Adam.

Had Darby stopped there, his compartmentalization of sacred history might have made an interesting, if somewhat abstruse, theology, but not much more. However, to this he added the doctrines of the Rapture and the Great Parenthesis (as it came to be called). In effect, Darby taught that there are two Second Advents, and the Rapture is concerned with the first. Those called to be saved will be mysteriously spirited out of the world "to meet the Lord in the air." (1 Thessalonians 4:17, RSV) The Tribulation then follows, a time of Satanic triumph, from which the elect are safely insulated with Christ. The Tribulation ends when Christ returns a second time, now visible to all, and initiates the millennium.

The Rapture offers the exciting psychological prospect of being one of the select few to be dramatically plucked out of humdrum life while the rest of humanity wallows in unimaginable woe. Airplanes in mid-air will be left suddenly without their pilots while cars, their drivers, whisked away by Jesus, will careen crazily down the nations' freeways. A popular late twentieth-century Evangelical film shows a distraught wife rushing into the family bathroom, only to find her husband mysteriously gone and his electric razor humming mindlessly in the washbasin.

The Jews fascinated Darby, as they did all premillennialists. It was a staple that the "Children of Abraham" would be "restored" to Israel. Insofar as he subscribed to this belief, Darby was not exceptional. What was unusual, however, was his insistence that promises made by God at the calling of Abraham remain valid. Although Christianity may seem to supersede Judaism, it is, in reality, just a temporary detour. Darby called the Christian era a "parenthesis" in sacred history, necessitated by the Jews' faithlessness to the Covenant. He discerned a difference between "Israel" and the "church." "Israel" is the eventual fulfillment of God's covenant with the Jews. The "church" is what God has done in the meantime. If all this made perfect sense to Darby and his followers, it outraged countless other Christians who alleged that it reduces Christianity to a sort of historical warm-up act before the main attraction.

Darby traveled extensively in the United States during the latter decades of the nineteenth century and received a respectful hearing for his dispensational theology among Evangelicals. His philo-Semitism was also well received. In the early twentieth century, an American disciple, the attorney

Cyrus I. Scofield, produced his hugely influential *Scofield Reference Bible*, a dispensational gloss that made Darby's ideas easily accessible. It soon became a fixture in countless Evangelical pulpits and Sunday school classrooms.

By the early decades of the twentieth century, and certainly by the 1920s, Fundamentalism was recognized as a prominent, if controversial, strain of American Protestant Christianity. Most Fundamentalists embraced premillennialism, attracted in part by its "literal" interpretation of Scripture. It was not, however, axiomatic that Fundamentalists must therefore embrace Darby's dispensationalism, since premillennialism had flourished without it for generations. Dispensationalism proved enticing, however, to the quasi-legalistic theological outlook of most premillennialists. Its neat compartmentalization of sacred history had an affinity with a mind-set already given to categorization through long years of cataloging prophetic epochs, apocalyptic beasts, and bewildering symbols. As for Darby's philo-Semitism, this was a perfect fit with the long-standing premillennial belief that the Jews remained God's chosen people.

Today, and for several generations past, dispensationalism and premillennialism are nearly synonymous in Evangelical theology, or at least that portion of it popularly labeled Fundamentalist. In its own way, dispensationalism contributed to the divergent paths taken by Evangelical and liberal Protestantism throughout the late nineteenth century and into the twentieth century. Convinced that they understood the Word of God through its plain semantic meaning, Evangelicals occupied themselves refining their theology through categorizing and schema. Meanwhile, liberal Protestant theologians moved steadily toward an understanding of the Bible that increasingly understood it in terms of past historical situations and present ethical dilemmas. Dispensationalism both exacerbated and exemplified this divide.

Robert K. Whalen

See also Noahide Covenant; Premillennialism; Rapture; Resurrection (Christ)

Bibliography

Bass, Clarence B. (1960) *Backgrounds to Dispensationalism*. Grand Rapids, MI: Wm. B. Eerdmans.

Boyer, Paul. (1992) *When Time Shall Be No More: Prophecy Belief in Modern American Culture*. Cambridge, MA: The Belknap Press of Harvard University Press.

Erfid, James M. (1986) *End-Times: Rapture, Antichrist, Millennium*. Nashville, TN: Abingdon Press.

Sandeen, Ernest R. (1970) *The Roots of Fundamentalism: British and American Millenarianism 1800–1930*. Chicago: University of Chicago Press.

Dominion Theology

Dominion theology is the Christian Reconstructionist blending of historic Calvinism (with its notions about "calling" and work) and postmillennialism (with its view that Christians are to "usher in the Kingdom of God"). Reconstructionists developed these ideas and disseminated them widely within the Fundamentalist Christian subculture. By the 1980s aspects of postmillennialism and especially dominion theology had taken hold in many churches, but it was especially well received in Pentecostal circles.

Reconstructionists teach that Satan was defeated in Christ's Resurrection and that we are currently living in the thousand-year reign of the Kingdom of God promised in the Bible. They draw parallels between the restoration of the Creation and a three-step understanding of individual salvation. Christians are saved instantaneously at the point they accept Christianity, they increasingly experience the fruits of that salvation as they work through it in their daily lives, and they are finally and completely sanctified at the culmination of history. Postmillennialist Reconstructionists see a similar process at work in Creation that was redeemed with the Resurrection, in which the Kingdom of God is increasingly apparent as history progresses (and as Christians labor to build it), and which will be perfectly established at Christ's Second Coming (thus, his coming is "postmillennial").

This eschatology was laid out in a technical way in Marcellus Kik's *An Eschatology of Victory* (1971), developed in R. J. Rushdoony's *Thy Kingdom Come* (1971), and made accessible to people in the pews by virtue of the work of David Chilton. Chilton's *Paradise Restored* (1985) was widely read and highly influential. The book argues that the "great tribulation" predicted in the Book of Revelation actually referred to the destruction of Jerusalem in 70 CE, and that all the other incidents that twentieth-century American Christians read as future predictions were also events that had already occurred—including the beginning of the Kingdom of God. Chilton's later work *Days of Vengeance* (1987), a commentary on the Book of Revelation written at a more technical level, was also well received in the subculture.

While many Christians place the Crucifixion and Resurrection at the center of their theology, Reconstructionists begin and end with the Creation account. In the Book of Genesis, God creates Adam and Eve to "keep the garden" and tells them to have dominion over all the earth. In Reconstructionism (and therefore dominion theology) the fall from grace inhibited human ability to fulfill the mandate for which they had been created: dominion. The purpose of the Resurrection is to restore humanity to grace and renew the purpose for which humans were created: work. The central importance of work to human life and human purpose is drawn from John Calvin's teaching about work as "calling."

During the 1980s conservative Christians (Fundamentalists, Evangelicals, Pentecostals, and others) adopted Reconstructionist postmillennialism in a piecemeal way. While most did not explicitly jettison their premillennial dispensationalism (the idea that things on earth would get increasingly worse until Christians were "raptured" away and the apocalyptic battle would usher in Christ's "premillennial" return), they adopted, instead, what became known as "dominion theology." They chose to stop focusing on what would happen eschatologically and instead, focused on Christ's command that, until He returned, Christians were to disciple the nations and take dominion over the earth.

Those Christians began to organize because of their concern that America was drifting from its "holy calling as a Christian nation" and specifically because the changing values of America were impinging on their own family and church lives. As Moen (1989) has argued, it was often issues about taxation (Internal Revenue Service "tyranny") and the regulation of Christian schools that propelled Fundamentalists into local politics. Dominion theology provided much of the theological foundation for the New Christian Right (NCR) in that Fundamentalists who had believed that things were to get worse until Christ returned were unlikely to become involved in attempts to bring about political change. Dominion theology, on the other hand, called them to efforts to "return America to its place as a Christian nation" and to take dominion, "in the name of Jesus," over the power structures that they believed were leading the nation toward destruction.

In addition to the political implications of this theology, the economic implications became increasingly central, especially among Pentecostals. While groups such as Maranatha Ministries flirted with dominion theology and postmillennialism, other Pentecostals (e.g., the Reverend Fred Price, Bishop Earl Paulk, Jim and Tammy Bakker) developed a variation on dominion theology that came to be known as the "name it and claim it Gospel." These teachers rejected traditional Christian teachings about suffering and poverty and argued that God wanted to bless His people but His blessing required their unquestioning faith. They argued that authentic faith would lead to material blessing; and they lived lives that demonstrated their closeness to God in material terms. Despite its abuses, rather than being merely a theology of justification for the wealthy, the "name it and claim it Gospel" ironically functioned as a liberation theology of sorts. It was targeted primarily to social groups struggling with poverty, dislocation, and disenfranchisement: Price's Crenshaw Christian center is an African-American church in urban Los Angeles, whereas the Bakkers (and similar television preachers) draw primarily rural poor white Christians.

Dominion theology, postmillennialism, and Christian reconstruction may be inseparably intertwined among Reconstructionists but it must be emphasized that most Christians drew on bits and pieces of the worldview to create a theological mosaic that fits their circumstances.

Julie J. Ingersoll

See also Calling; Creation; Premillennialism; Postmillennialism

Bibliography

Barron, Bruce. (1992) *Heaven on Earth?* Grand Rapids, MI: Zondervan Publishing.

Chilton, David. (1985) *Paradise Restored.* Tyler, TX: Reconstruction Press.

———. (1987) *Days of Vengeance.* Fort Worth, TX: Dominion Press.

DeMar, Gary. (1989) *God and Government*, 2nd ed. Brentwood, TN: Wolgemuth and Hyatt.

Kik, Marcelus. (1971) *An Eschatology of Victory*. Phillipsburg, NJ: Presbyterian and Reformed Publishing.

Moen, Matthew C. (1989) *The Christian Right and Congress.* Tuscaloosa: University of Alabama Press.

North, Gary. (1973) *Introduction to Christian Economics.* Vallecito, CA: Craig Press.

———. (1981) *The Dominion Covenant.* Tyler, TX: Institute for. Christian Economics.

Rushdoony, Rousas John. (1971) *Thy Kingdom Come.* Phillipsburg, NJ: Presbyterian and Reformed Publishing.

———. (1972) *Institutes of Biblical Law.* Nutley, NJ: The Craig Press.

———. (1982) *Law and Society: Institutes of Biblical Law*, vol. 2. Vallecito, CA: Ross House Books.

Thoburn, Robert L. (1984) *The Christian and Politics.* Tyler TX: Thoburn Press.

Whitehead, John W. (1977) *The Separation Illusion.* Milford, MI: Mott Media.

Doubt

Philosophically, doubt is considered to be a state of mind or intentionality that a subject can hold about some proposition. As such it is normally defined by reference to two other states of mind: ignorance, where the subject is unaware of the proposition; and certitude, where the subject either unequivocally affirms or unequivocally denies the proposition.

Philosophers identify between doubt and certitude a mediate intentionality that is given status as a mental state in its own right—opinion. One holds an opinion when one either affirms or denies a proposition but remains open to the possibility that the affirmation or denial may be incorrect. It follows, therefore, that when one is in doubt about a proposition one suspends one's judgment of either the truth or falsity of that proposition despite being fully aware of the proposition and all that it entails.

Generally speaking, theologians do not question this philosophical placement of doubt within the range of possibilities of human knowledge. Where differences emerge is in the area of practical application. Philosophers generally want to understand the conditions under which any form of doubt is reasonable. Theologians want to understand the conditions under which doubt in matters of religious faith is reasonable. To a lesser extent, the latter group, quite opposed to philosophers, may also strive to understand the emotions that can accompany doubt in matters of religious faith—emotions such as anxiety,

The scientist has a lot of experience with ignorance and doubt and uncertainty, and this experience is of very great importance, I think. When a scientist doesn't know the answer to a problem, he is ignorant. When he has a hunch as to what the result is, he is uncertain. And when he is pretty darned sure of what the result is going to be, he is in some doubt. We have found it of paramount importance that in order to progress we must recognize the ignorance and leave room for doubt. Scientific knowledge is a body of statements of varying degrees of certainty—some most unsure, some nearly sure, none *absolutely* certain.

Richard P. Feynman, "*What Do You Care What Other People Think?: Further Adventures of a Curious Character*"

guilt, and despair. Although popularly assumed to be antithetical to religious belief, as a preliminary state of mind that necessarily precedes the discovery of truth, doubt can be considered a required ingredient of the process by which religious faith becomes religious conviction.

The Meaning of Doubt

The word "doubt," as commonly used, signifies a suspension of judgment or lack of conviction on the part of a subject about some claim. However, a closer examination of the word's origins reveals further meaning. The word "doubt" has been a part of the English language since the thirteenth century. It is an assimilated form of the Old French word *doutere*, which itself is a form of the Latin verb *dubitare*. Modern English has intentionally retained the silent "b"—as it has for another Latinate word, "debt"—to mark the word's Latin origin. Grammatically, *dubitare* is the verbal form of the Old Latin *dubo*, which is derived from *duo* ("two"). The notion of duality in the word "doubt" is seen more clearly in German than in English, where the German word for doubt, *Zweifel*, is dominated by the prefix *zwei*, meaning "two."

Christian homiletics has made much of this etymology, insisting that doubt connotes a state of vacillation between "two minds": certain belief and unbelief. Though it sometimes insists that doubt warrants the same moral consequences as unbelief, both the etymology and philosophical definition cited above clearly show that doubt is substantially different. Doubt indicates that both sides of a claim—its affirmation and its denial—are fully recognized. This distinction is often overlooked in conservative or Fundamentalist theologies that tend to define faith as belief in a specified set of propositions or "fundamentals" and doubt as tantamount to their denial. Nor must doubt always lead to skepticism, as conservatives sometimes fear. Skepticism implies that there is no hope of ever affirming or denying a claim under consideration, whereas doubt insists that this is true only of the present and need not hold for future considerations.

Doubt As Methodology

Doubt has long been considered a necessary component of the search for knowledge. In Eastern traditions, doubt in the ability of the bodily senses to perceive the full nature of reality—a doctrine summarized in the Indian teaching of *maya* ("illusion")—is considered a major step on the path toward enlightenment. In Western traditions, doubt is thought to play an essential role in the progress toward knowledge of the truth. In Western philosophy, for example, it is commonly understood that putting a claim "in doubt" is an essential prerequisite to verifying, and then being able to act upon, that claim. This methodological use of doubt had its origins in the teachings of the Greek philosopher Socrates as they were expounded upon by Plato. These early Greek thinkers conceived of philosophy as an attitude of mind that used doubt and questioning to bring fundamental opinions to greater clarity and coherence. Critics of Socrates feared this method harbored a moral unwillingness to arrive at any sort of certainty. Plato's work was in part an answer to this criticism. In upholding certitude on positions that have successfully passed through the screen of doubt, Plato demonstrated the essential link between the attainment of certitude and the questioning posture demanded by doubt. Another thinker in this tradition is the seventeenth-century French philosopher, Descartes, who made of doubt a systematic methodology. His purpose was to use even the slightest possibility of doubt to reveal those "clear and distinct" ideas that cannot logically be doubted, and upon which the foundations of true knowledge can be built. Finally, doubt was used expressly in the modern existentialist tradition to emphasize the distinction between authentic and inauthentic human existence. Inauthentic existence, or what the French philosopher Jean-Paul Sartre called "bad faith," is an existence that doubts nothing and assents to everything conventional without question. By contrast, authentic existence is one that doubts and questions accepted conventions, treating each as an opportunity for moral decision. This latter stance, added the Danish philosopher Kierkegaard, requires a "leap of faith," a state of mind that transcends the ordinary dichotomy between unbelief and certainty, doubt and belief. Theologian Paul Tillich, whose work was strongly influenced by the existentialists, lists doubt as a potentially redemptive element in faith. He claimed that when doubt becomes the basis of a willingness to "leap" into a deeper level of faith commitment, then it can be redemptive. To live out an authentic faith in the modern world on Tillich's terms means necessarily to embrace doubt.

Conclusion

Doubt can be defined as a position of mind intermediate between unbelief and certainty. It obtains not where ignorance of a proposition interferes with its valid appraisal, nor where confidence in a proposition's truth or falsity inhibits further inquiry, but only where there is true openness and warrant for debate regarding the proposition. As a methodology, doubt interjects a certain sense of humility into the process of cultivating knowledge. Doubt counsels hesitation before all the evidence has been carefully and impartially weighed. Again, doubt does not always lead to a nihilistic skepticism. Rather, it is best thought of as a necessary prerequisite for the sort of moral certitude that lends conviction to one's knowledge of the truth. This may be especially so in the case of religious belief.

Thomas Kinsell Carr

Bibliography

Barth, Karl. (1999) *The Christian Life*. Edinburgh: T&T Clark.

Descartes, René. (1994) *A Discourse on Method*. London: Everyman Library.

Kierkegaard, Søren. (1978) *Søren Kierkegaard's Journals and Papers*. Indianapolis: Indiana University Press.

Sayre, Kenneth M. (1997) *Belief and Knowledge: Mapping the Cognitive Landscape*. New York: Rowman & Littlefield.

Tillich, Paul. (1986) *The Dynamics of Faith*. San Francisco: HarperCollins.

Ecumenical Movement

The word "ecumenism" is from classical Greek and refers to the "whole world," but in the early centuries of Christianity "ecumenical" was used to designate special gatherings of church bishops and leaders of the worldwide, or universal, church. These were the ecumenical councils such as the Council of Nicaea and the Council of Chalcedon. Since the late nineteenth century, the term has been used to refer to a movement to begin a process of promoting greater Christian unity after centuries of schism and splitting.

As such, the ecumenical movement began in the late nineteenth century within Protestant Christianity, where the number of different denominations had grown into the hundreds. National movements of Christian students were formed in Great Britain, Germany, the United States, and elsewhere to generate the idea of Christian unity. Later, the World Council of Churches and the Roman Catholic Church began to participate as well, with the impetus for Catholicism coming from the Second Vatican Council (1962–1965). Therefore, by the end of the twentieth century, much of Christianity was participating in ecumenical (intrareligious) dialogue, often between two specific churches or denominations.

Ecumenical Practice

The ecumenical movement sought to restore a unity among Christians in a vision of the universality of the Christian message and resulted at times in actually reversing denominational splits that had previously occurred. However, with actual mergers and reunification being such a slow and complex process, the movement sought to bring Christians of different denominations and from the main branches of Christianity (Protestantism, Eastern Orthodoxy, Roman Catholicism) together for such activities as prayer, humanitarian aid, Bible study, worship services, theological discussions, formal dialogue, and more, all based upon a vision of Christianity needing to be a united witness for Christ in society and the world.

Thus, ecumenism has been an effort within Christianity to overcome the polemics and divisions that have historically taken place among the diverse forms of Christianity, such as the schism between the eastern (Eastern Orthodox) and western (Roman Catholic) churches in the eleventh century and the fracturing of the western church beginning in the sixteenth century with the Protestant Reformation and the response of Roman Catholicism.

Ecumenism and Fundamentalism

Christian Fundamentalist churches have generally not participated in the ecumenical movement and do not see a theological purpose in doing so. As Fundamentalism is a religious perspective based upon the propositional expression of what is considered true, it can be identified as a form of theological and ecclesiastical exclusivism in which truth is understood to have been verbally conveyed by God to humanity through what came to be the texts of the Bible, Old Testament and New Testament. As such, Fundamentalist's belief in the verbal inerrancy of the Bible, their historical objection to evolution, biblical criticism, and modernism in the late nineteenth century, as well as their view that only individuals who are Christians and who accept the inerrancy of the Bible have a clear knowledge of God and God's revelation, have led them to defer from active participation in the ecumenical movement.

While there exists a pluralism of branches, denominations, and sects within Christianity, Fundamentalists tend to reject other forms of Christian theologies and biblical criticism as either wrong or, minimally, less correct than their views. Therefore, Fundamentalists seek more to convert others to their positions than to engage in dialogues with those who have other positions. Moreover, there is the idea that they do not have much to gain from the others since they believe Fundamentalism to be the truest form of Christianity, the form most in harmony with the earliest Christian Church. Thus, since dialogue requires each position to take seriously the views of the others, even to the point of possibly changing or even adopting some of those views, Fundamentalists' religious exclusivism really precludes them from both wanting to engage in ecumenical discussions and activities and from being invited by ecumenical Christian groups from participating.

For ecumenism the difficulty is that Fundamentalism has become a very significant presence in contemporary Christianity (as well in other major religions), representing a very large number of Christians. Thus, it is a way of being religious in the modern (and postmodern) world for a large segment of Christians and its very existence calls for a historical understanding as to the roots and continued appeal of Fundamentalism. As long as non-Fundamentalists think of Fundamentalism as a religious aberration and as long as Fundamentalists think of other Christians as in need of conversion to the only true path, ecumenical dialogue seems implausible.

The Future

Since what is meant by ecumenical within Christianity is the sense of a universal, worldwide religious tradition, the ecumenical movement remains incomplete as long as Fundamentalism is not a participant. For any change in this situation to occur would seem to require some major changes in attitude by both Fundamentalists and by Christian non-Fundamentalists. At this time, there do not seem to

be strong indications that such foundational changes in attitude have taken place.

Alan Altany

See also World Council of Churches

Bibliography

"AD2000 Ecumenical Evangelism: A Warning!" (2000) Fundamental Evangelistic Association. http://www. FundamentalBibleChurch.net/fbcad200.htm

Appleby, R. Scott, and Martin E. Marty. (1995) *Fundamentalisms Comprehended (The Fundamentalism Project*, Vol. 5). Chicago: University of Chicago Press.

Armstrong, Karen. (2000) *The Battle for God*. New York: Knopf.

Braaten, Carl. (1998) *Mother Church: Ecclesiology and Ecumenism*. Minneapolis, MN: Fortress Press.

Carpenter, Joel. (1997) *Revive Us Again: The Reawakening of American Fundamentalism*. Oxford: Oxford University Press.

Cope, Brian, and Michael Kinnamon, eds. (1997) *The Ecumenical Movement: An Anthology of Keys Texts and Voices*. Grand Rapids, MI: Wm. B. Eerdmans.

Cunningham, Lawrence. (1999) *Ecumenism: Present Reality and Future Prospects*. Notre Dame, IN: University of Notre Dame Press.

Gros, Jeffrey, Eamon McManus, and Ann Riggs. (1998) *Introduction to Ecumenism*. Mahwah, NJ: Paulist Press.

Marsden, George. (1991) *Understanding Fundamentalism and Evangelicalism*. Grand Rapids, MI: Wm. B. Eerdmans.

"Update on the Ecumenical Movement." (2000) Brethren Revival Fellowship. http://www.brfwitness.org/Articles/2000v35n3.htm

Wacker, Grant. (2000) "The Rise of Fundamentalism." National Humanities Center. http://www.nhc.rtp. nc.us:8080/tserve/twenty/tkeyinfo/fundam.htm

Elohim

The reverence given to God is exhibited in Jewish life by the recognition that God's being transcends all forms of human constructs in both thought and expression. It is this belief that led the ancient Israelites to avoid uttering God's sacred name, Yahweh. This reticence to evoke the inexpressible name, Yahweh, is united paradoxically with the persistent quest to invoke God by the right name. One attempt to negotiate this form of pietistic expression is witnessed in the Pentateuch, the first five books of Jewish and Christian Scriptures, in which other designates are employed to name God. "Elohim," or its singular, "eloha," is a lengthened form of the ancient Semitic word "El," and one such name that appears for God. The singular form, eloha, is most frequently seen in the writings of Job, but rarely appears outside this book. By contrast, its plural, elohim, is one of the most common names given to God among the ancient texts and conveys the idea of the Jewish covenant (e.g., the "true" God, or the God of Israel).

With the introduction of "Higher Criticism" in biblical studies, the etymology of this term has proven to be problematic for some Fundamentalist circles. The use of the plural form, for example, has led some Christian Fundamentalists to espouse an interpretation of the text that is shaped by an underlying historicism. In contrast to understanding the use of the plural as an expression of the majesty or greatness of God—an interpretation first espoused in the Reformation era by the likes of Thomas De Vio Cajetan and John Calvin—Fundamentalists have suggested that the use of the plural must be understood in light of the Trinity. Following this line of Trinitarian thinking, it is asserted that the ancient text forecasts the coming of Jesus and the Holy Spirit.

Such lines of interpretation are further complicated by the use of "elohim" to refer to deities such as Dagon (1 Samuel 5:7) and Marduck (Daniel 1:2). The reference to these gods potentially complicates the issue for Fundamentalist interpreters. Not only were these gods of a single, as opposed to a triune, nature, but they also stand outside the purview of monotheism. Further still, the reference to a female goddess using the term "elohim" raises questions of interpretative consistency in the designation of God's nature.

Debates over the origin and meaning of this term are not reserved to Christianity alone, however. The name given to God also conjures up complications for Judaism and its relationship to the modern Jewish state. Jewish Fundamentalists are engaged in a debate with moderates over the implications of key terms taken from the tradition (Silberstein 1993: 13). The intensity of the debate is no less true for interpretations surrounding "elohim," or "the God of Israel." Jewish Fundamentalists reject the modern state of Israel, arguing its secular agenda is a "deviant" expression of Zionism, which subverts tradition. Elohim, the God of Israel, they argue, will restore the true

nation of Israel according to God's plan, not humanity's efforts.

Kent A. McConnell

See also Israel; Jews; Judaism, Fundamental

Bibliography

Cohon, Samuel S. (1987). *Essays in Jewish Theology.* Cincinnati, OH: Hebrew Union College Press.

Girdlestone, Robert Baker. (1981 reprint) *Synonyms of the Old Testament; Their Bearing on Christian Doctrine.* Grand Rapids, MI: Wm. B. Eerdmans.

Katz, Steven T. (1977) *Jewish Ideas and Concepts.* N.p.: Keter Publishing House Jerusalem, Ltd.

Ravitzky, Aviezer. (1996) *Messianism, Zionism, and Jewish Religious Radicalism.* Chicago: University of Chicago Press.

Silberstein, Laurence J., ed. (1993) *Jewish Fundamentalism in Comparative Perspective: Religion, Ideology, and the Crisis of Modernity.* New York: New York University Press.

Thuesen, Peter J. (1999) *In Discordance with the Scriptures: American Protestant Battles over Translating the Bible.* New York: Oxford University Press.

End Times

Protestant Fundamentalism devotes substantial attention to what is variously called, along with other names, the End Times, End of the World, Last Judgment, and Second Advent. It supposes that history, and probably the earth itself, are finite and will perish in accordance with divine will. This cataclysm will correspond with the return of Jesus Christ, who will judge the living and the dead. What follows is the "new heaven and a new earth" (Revelation 20:1, RSV). The details of these events are matters for speculation. What is essential is that the current state of affairs will utterly and forever cease.

The theological study of the End Times is called eschatology and has been part of Christianity from its inception. Jesus warned, "there will be such tribulation as has not been from the beginning of the creation which God created until now, and never will be." (Mark 13:19, RSV) This apocalyptic theme is repeated throughout the Pauline letters and elsewhere in the New Testament, especially the Book of Revelation. There is, as well, an apocalyptic strain in both the Old Testament and other Jewish sacred literature. To this day, the Second Advent remains dogma in Catholic, Orthodox, and Protestant theology.

After the immediate post-Apostolic period, and certainly by the time of the Roman emperor Constantine, the Christian church began to dampen apocalyptic speculation. Jesus had not yet returned and the church had to find its way in the world. Eschatology was not discarded, but for many centuries thereafter it was deemphasized. From time to time during the medieval era there were brief apocalyptic disturbances but these were quickly suppressed.

It was largely due to the English Civil War, and then the French Revolution, that End Times speculation eventually became crucial to Fundamentalism. The political turmoil of the seventeenth century reignited apocalypticism among English Protestants, while the French Revolution of the next century gave eschatology an enormous impetus. Soon after the American Revolution, English apocalypticism traveled to the new United States.

During the first half of the nineteenth century, many American evangelicals, following the lead of British writers, concluded that Jesus Christ must soon return in judgment and initiate the millennium. They were known as premillennialists because they located the Second Advent before the millennium. These American premillennialists were largely Calvinist in theology, social conservatives, and given to a literal reading of the Bible. This literalism was inevitable if prophecy was to be taken seriously and not dismissed as so much poetry. The gloomy apocalyptic outlook accorded with the Augustinian theology of these Calvinists, while it also justified their suspicion of social reform: only Christ's return would bring meaningful social relief. Thus, by the mid-century, several of the essential elements of Fundamentalism were in place, derived from End Times speculation.

In the latter decades of the nineteenth century, this nascent Fundamentalist eschatology was amplified by the dispensationalism of John Nelson Darby (1800–1882). He also added his unique doctrine of the Rapture. These various doctrines were popularized in a series of influential prophetic conferences and by century's end were well established in some Protestant thought.

During the twentieth century, Fundamentalism split off from the general body of American Protestantism. By the 1920s, at the latest, it was recognized as a distinct—and highly controversial—aspect of American Christianity. The End Times theology that helped prompt Fundamentalism flourished along with it. Since then, eschatology has remained integral to Fundamentalist thought. Its characteristics of biblical literalism, social conservatism, and Augustinian theology denote modern Fundamentalism.

It is possible to sketch a basic End Times theology as believed today by most conservative evangelicals, whether Fundamentalist or Pentecostal. Both camps are notably quarrelsome about details, but a general outline is easily seen. To begin with, the End Times is believed to be laid out in biblical prophecy, especially the Book of Revelation. This prophecy must be read "literally," but this does not mean a slavishly grammatical reading. It signifies, rather, that its puzzling imagery must be understood to have real significance and to foretell actual events in shaded language. It emphatically is not merely figurative or of transient historical interest.

Prophecy is interpreted in anticipation of the Second Advent. There has always been a debate between futurists and historicists over this interpretation. The futurists, associated with Darby, are probably in the majority and hold that Christ can return at any time. The historicists, more prevalent in the nineteenth century, believe that prophecy foretells events that must first occur and that these are locatable in history.

As prophecy is fulfilled, the earth will become, morally, an ever-darker place. Evil will triumph, the saints will undergo persecution, and a demonic figure, the Antichrist, will rise to power. At the moment of their greatest peril, Christ, during the Rapture, will pluck the elect out of the world. There follows the Tribulation, a period of unimaginable earthly woe, that ends only when Christ returns with His elect. Evil will be vanquished and Jesus will initiate the millennium, during which He may personally reign on earth from Jerusalem. What follows next is controverted, but it may be a final apostasy that leads to the physical end of the world and its replacement by the New Jerusalem.

The Jews occupy a central place in all of this. Fundamentalists long predicted that Israel would be "reestablished" in Palestine, which, in fact, happened in 1948. The Jews must eventually regain their favored place as a priestly people. As a result, Fundamentalists usually support the present Israeli state.

The cosmic drama of the End Times offers great psychological fascination. Every story has its ending and this is earth's. Eschatology promises the punishment of evil and the triumph of good, while it thrills believers with the prospect of the Rapture. Insofar as Fundamentalist End Times theology anticipates Christ's return in glory it is entirely within the Christian tradition. Nevertheless, the mainline Protestant churches, as well as the Roman Catholic and Orthodox churches, regard the rest of Fundamentalist eschatology as flawed. Although not necessarily heretical, it seems to them a fanciful embroidering of a sound Christian tenet.

Robert K. Whalen

See also Apocalypse; Apocalyptic Literature; Eschatology; Premillennialism; Rapture; Second Coming

Bibliography

Boyer, Paul. (1992) *When Time Shall Be No More: Prophecy Belief in Modern American Culture.* Cambridge, MA: The Belknap Press of Harvard University Press.

Cohn, Norman F. (1961) *The Pursuit of the Millennium.* New York: Harper Torchbooks.

Garrett, Clark. (1975) *Respectable Folly: Millenarians and the French Revolution in France and England.* Baltimore: Johns Hopkins University Press.

Weber, Timothy P. (1992) *Living in the Shadow of the Second Coming: American Premillennialism: 1875–1925.* New York: Oxford University Press.

Entertainment Industry

Fundamentalists have always believed in the power of entertainment. On the one hand, they have been wary of entertainment, believing that it can rouse inappropriate passions and distract people from the leading of a moral, God-centered life. On the other hand, throughout their history, Fundamentalists have sought to harness the power of entertainment in their efforts to introduce the gospel to nonbelievers. Although emotional and energetic preaching has been the centerpiece of Fundamentalist conversion, the twentieth-century development of the dramatic television and film industries in the United States provided new avenues for proselytization efforts.

These two seemingly contradictory approaches to entertainment reflect Fundamentalism's uneasy relationship with storytelling. Stories of the Bible, Torah, Qur'an, or other holy scriptures have long been viewed as authoritative sources offering guidance for the living of a faithful life. Stories reflecting what they take to be the fundamental messages of holy scriptures may serve to introduce people to salvation. Stories that are not believed to rest upon the same authority are considered questionable at best, requiring critical interpretation or, in some cases, censorship.

Censorship Efforts

In 1937, eighty million people attended the cinema on a weekly basis in the United States—more than three times the estimated weekly attendance at Protestant, Catholic, and Jewish houses of worship combined. Religious leaders sought various avenues to limit or mitigate the influence of films on their flock. From its beginnings, however, the film industry has successfully promoted self-regulating policies. One of the earliest forms of self-regulation was the Motion Picture Producers and Distributors Association (MPPDA), formed in 1922 by several prominent studio heads. Will Hays, a Presbyterian, was named MPPDA's director. While he was ostensibly charged with policing the morality of the film industry, his dubious achievement may have been that during his tenure virtually no coordinated effort was mounted toward regulation of the film industry. Roman Catholics, along with other religious groups, were concerned about film's deleterious effects on young people. With the formation of the Legion of Decency in 1934, the Catholic hierarchy launched a campaign aimed at convincing American Catholics to boycott films they deemed objectionable. In an effort to staunch the flow of Catholic business from the industry, the Production Code Administration (PCA) was formed in 1934 and was charged with reviewing scripts and films for morally offensive material. This appeased Fundamentalists and others concerned with film's morality. For two decades, films were scrutinized by the PCA, a reign that ended with the Supreme Court's 1950 ruling that broke up the monopoly of the studio system and granted the right to free speech to filmmakers.

The Legion of Decency's power was waning just as the Fundamentalist and Evangelical presence on the American landscape was ascending. Fundamentalist leaders, who increasingly saw themselves as the guardians of American morality, had learned an important lesson from the Legion of Decency's earliest days: the power of the boycott. Throughout the following decades, Fundamentalists put teeth into the censorship movement by taking aim at particular films and television programs. Rather than addressing grievances to the industry directly, they sought to influence the faithful in their consumptive habits. In 1977, Donald Wildmon, then a Methodist minister in Mississippi, initiated a "Turn the TV Off" week among his constituents. The timing was right and the idea quickly spread. Upward of a million people reportedly participated in the boycott, and the National Federation for Decency (NFD) organization (now known as the American Family Association) was born.

This organization, like many Fundamentalist and Evangelical organizations, has focused on representations of sexuality. One of their earliest efforts targeted the American Broadcasting Company (ABC) sitcom *Soap*, which was protested by a coalition that included the Southern Baptist Christian Life Commission and the U.S. Catholic Conference, among others. In 1980, the NFD united more than 150 conservative organizations into the National Coalition for Better Television (NCBT). The NCBT sought to identify sponsors of television programming that featured "gratuitous sex and violence," urging constituents to boycott the sponsor's goods. The NCBT was lent legitimacy when Procter & Gamble's chairman withdrew support from some fifty television programs deemed objectionable by the NCBT.

In 1985, Wildmon's organization united with the National Association of Evangelicals to form Christian Leaders for Responsible Television (CLeaR-TV). This coalition produced a Statement of Concern, highlighting four problem areas in the entertainment industry: violence, sex, profanity, and negative stereotyping of Christians. While the document called on networks to address these concerns, it followed the pattern of earlier efforts and relied primarily on a monitoring of television programs for objectionable content and a subsequent boycott of television program sponsors. This time, however, the coalition was met with a different strategy. Network executives defused the protests by meeting with CLeaR-TV leaders, preempting criticisms of CLeaR-TV's supporters. No changes in policy resulted.

Though its record for industry change has been spotty, the NFD and associated efforts have been successful in the realm of educating the faithful about objectionable content. In recent years, the organization has called on Christians to boycott all Disney-related theme parks and programs in response to Disney's purported support of homosexuality, this time forming a coalition with the Southern Baptist Convention and the radio and video ministry Focus on the Family, among others. Highlighted among Disney's offenses were the ABC television sitcom *Ellen*, the first prime-time program to feature a self-identified lesbian playing a character who struggles with and eventually claims her identity as a lesbian. Other boycotts have been mounted against the Fox reality television program *Temptation Island* and films such as *Chasing Amy*, as well as video games that feature sexually dominant females.

Today, the entertainment industries rarely request that Fundamentalists and other religious leaders provide feedback on films or television programs prior to their release. In fact, past events have taught Fundamentalists to be wary of such solicitations of critique by the industry. When Fundamentalists heartily condemned the controversial film *The Last Temptation of Christ* after an invited prerelease screening, their objections became an important part of the film's publicity. Thus, while boycotting and condemning objectionable films has been a favored approach, such strategies present Fundamentalists with a dilemma in the era of round-the-clock news coverage ignited by controversy. Campaigns mounted against a certain film or television program might generate awareness of objectionable material, but the increased awareness that results can also trigger an increase, rather than a limit to, interest in the material on the screen.

Using Entertainment for Proselytizing

As the United States was coming out of the Depression, Fundamentalists were increasingly experimenting with film and television, most commonly adapting the format of radio into televangelism. Dramatic proselytizing films modeled after Hollywood features, however, had their beginnings with the Baptista film mission, founded by Charles O. Baptista in 1942. Baptista produced films for churches along with projector equipment (including "The Miracle" projector). The company was unable to remain financially viable, however, and they closed their doors in 1965. Baptista may have been an inspiration for Great Commission Films, a production company begun in 1949 and incorporated into the Billy Graham Evangelistic Association as World Wide Pictures (WWP) in 1952. Their films, referred to by the organization as "modern-day parables," employed dramatic stories designed to introduce nonbelievers to the gospel. With the support of a growing establishment headed by Billy Graham (1918–), an evangelist well respected by Fundamentalists and more moderate Christians, WWP achieved remarkable success in the sophisticated marketing and distribution of their films.

Mr. Texas, borrowing from the popular Western genre and released in 1951, was the organization's first feature-length film. While this and subsequent films of the decade were seen primarily at church events, WWP's film *The Restless Ones* (1965) was the first-ever Christian film to be shown in commercial theaters. More recent Christian films that received wide viewership through distribution in commercial theaters or on television included *Joni* (1979), *The Hiding Place* (1975, 1980, and *Cry from the Mountain* (1985). International distribution of WWP's films began in 1968, with translations available in many languages. Graham's organization claims that in 1995, more than eighty-three thousand people received salvation after watching a WWP film.

Billy Graham's organization largely targeted the adult film audience, whereas Campus Crusade for Christ has produced films aimed at the college student and, more recently, teen audiences. The organization claims that their film *Jesus* (1979), which has been translated into 355 languages, has been seen by an estimated 750 million people. While there have been some theater showings, the film is distributed for small-group use in homes as well as in churches.

Some films with overtly Christian themes and purposes have achieved commendable success at the box office in recent years. *The Omega Code* (1999), funded by the Trinity Broadcasting Network, is one noteworthy example. The film, based on the best-selling book *The Bible Code*, took in a remarkable $2.4 million on its opening weekend, placing in the top ten films for the week. Although most film critics dismissed it as a poorly written B movie, a widespread church-based campaign among Fundamentalists and conservative Christians buoyed the film to its success. The film *Left Behind* (2000), based on the best-selling pre-Tribulation novel series by popular Evangelical writers Tim LaHaye and Jerry Jenkins, received equally dismal reviews. However, its box office success may have been understated due to the fact that its small distribution company chose to release the film after the videotape version had been available for several months through Christian retailers.

Fundamentalists have increasingly supported efforts to reform the entertainment industry from within. Beginning with the writings of popular Evangelical author Francis Schaeffer in the 1970s, conservative Christians have moved away from their separatist approach to the film industry and instead have believed that they could view and participate in Hollywood film productions while keeping their own worldviews intact. Universities such as Regent and Liberty each offer courses in film production and criticism, and Fuller Theological Seminary, along with numerous conservative churches located in southern California, offer support for conservative Christians seeking to work within the Hollywood system. Believing in the importance of infiltrating and therefore offering alternatives within large-scale entertainment productions, the Los Angeles Film Studies Center, sponsored by the Council for Christian Colleges and Universities, offers a Hollywood internship program that regularly trains and places young Christians within the film industry.

Fundamentalists and the Alternative Entertainment Industry

Most of the Billy Graham and Campus Crusade for Christ films, as well as the newer Christian films in theatrical release, were explicitly created in an effort to introduce nonbelievers to the gospel. Indeed, they were promoted with the admonition that believers should bring their nonbelieving friends to the showings at the local theater or church. These films served a secondary purpose as well, of course: they provided entertainment and inspiration for the growing number of persons affiliated with Christian churches and parachurch organizations in the United States and around the world. Believers may not have been the intended audience, but with the rise of the Christian retailing industry in the 1970s and 1980s, they made up an important and lucrative market.

Dramatic films and videos (both those produced explicitly for Christian audiences and older Hollywood releases now deemed appropriate family fare) take their place on the shelves of Christian bookstores alongside books of fiction and self-help, Christian video games, and recorded Christian music. All of these items are now part of a Christian market that functions as a kind of alternative entertainment industry. The development of this industry is due in part to the growth of in-home technologies such as videocassette recorders and portable audio systems that make it possible for Fundamentalist families to exercise greater choice about what their family will consume. With commercial theater, radio, and network television no longer acting as bottlenecks that limit distribution of Christian materials, this industry has flourished.

In addition to the burgeoning Christian music industry, one prominent development within this alternative entertainment industry is the growth of family-oriented dramatic fare. The eminently successful *Veggie Tales* video series must be considered the centerpiece of this development. Produced by Big Idea Productions for the child audience, the series uses humor and animation to teach lessons such as honesty, truthfulness, forgiveness, and kindness that are, as the producers claim, "rooted in the Bible." In addition to Christian retail stores and Christian websites, the videotapes have achieved such widespread success in the United States that they are available at numerous grocery and discount chain stores nationwide, in addition to such large online retailers as Amazon.com and eToys. Enjoyed by Fundamentalists as well as less conservative Christians, the *Veggie Tale* series is a marker in the successful crossover of such explicitly religious products to the commercial marketplace. While the *Veggie Tales* series arose as an entrepreneurial project, the older, more established production companies associated with televangelistic efforts have entered the fray, as well. Focus on the Family, long a purveyor of Christian advice on the radio with a significant distribution network for self-help books as well as audio and videocassettes, now produces and distributes the *Adventures in Odyssey* series on video and audiotapes for children as a competitor to *Veggie Tales*.

Fundamentalists and the Entertainment Industry outside the United States

It is difficult to compare the censorship and entertainment efforts of U.S. Protestant Fundamentalists to similar efforts in other parts of the world, primarily because of the scope, size, and profitability of the American entertainment industry and the nascent yet quickly growing Christian entertainment industry also based in the United States. Most other conservative religious groups, such as those in the Muslim-dominated Middle Eastern countries, operate under vastly different relations among the state, religious organizations, and media industries.

An interesting parallel to the American entertainment industry is found in India's successful dramatic film and television programs. There, the ancient myth of the Mahabharata, believed to enshrine the philosophical basis of Hindu religious beliefs, is the basis for an enormously successful "sacred soap" that is broadcast weekly on the state-owned television channel Doordarshan. The fact that this broadcast appears on the government's monopoly channel exacerbates rising concerns about Fundamentalist beliefs in contemporary India. In India, as in other parts of the world, including the United States, religion, culture, and entertainment remain intertwined with politics in ways that make it difficult to conceive of clear distinctions among them. Hinduism in India, Islam in several Middle Eastern countries, Judaism in Israel— the religious leaders in these places increasingly enter and produce materials as alternatives to the fare available through commercial channels. As televangelism's popularity continues to wane around the world, the growth of dramatically inspired entertainment options for the family are bound to increase within the Fundamentalist audience, both in the United States and abroad.

Lynn Schofield Clark

See also Antimodernism; Campus Crusade for Christ; Preaching; Radio; Secularism; Televangelism

Bibliography

Archives of the Billy Graham Center Evangelism Library. http://www.wheaton.edu/bgc/library.

Ferre, John, ed. (1990) *Channels of Belief: Religion and American Commercial Television.* Ames: Iowa State University Press.

Gillespie, Marie. (1995) *Television, Ethnicity, and Social Change.* London and New York: Routledge.

Moore, Lawrence (1994) *Selling God: American Religion in the Marketplace of Culture.* Oxford, UK: Oxford University Press.

Schultze, Quentin J. (1991) *Televangelism and American Culture: The Business of Popular Religion.* Grand Rapids, MI: Baker Book House.

Eschatology

Eschatology is from the Greek word *eschatos* meaning "last things," or the "end of the world." Eschatological belief has been important throughout Judeo-Christian history because both the Hebrew scriptures and the sacred texts of Christianity—especially the

1 Thessalonians 4:16–17

16. For the Lord himself shall descend from heaven with a shout, with the voice of the archangel, and with the trump of God: and the dead in Christ shall rise first:

17. Then we which are alive and remain shall be caught up together with them in the clouds to meet the Lord in the air: and so shall we ever be with the Lord.

Book of Revelation—describe events that will unfold in the last days. Eschatology looms large in the history of Fundamentalism, because Fundamentalists have historically embraced biblical inerrancy and a literal reading of the scriptures, including the eschatological portions.

In the late nineteenth century and throughout the twentieth century, the most widespread eschatological belief system among American Fundamentalists (as well as among the larger community of Evangelical and charismatic Protestants), was premillennial dispensationalism. "Premillennia" means that Christ will return to earth *before* the millennium, the thousand-year era of universal righteousness foretold in Revelation 20:6–7, while "dispensationalism" refers to the belief that God has dealt with his chosen people, the Jews, and with the Gentiles, in a series of distinct epochs—or dispensations—in each of which the means of grace has differed.

Premillennial dispensationalism was elaborated in the mid-nineteenth century by the Irish clergyman John Nelson Darby (1800–1882), a leader of the Plymouth Brethren sect. It spread rapidly to the United States, where Darby made several preaching tours, and was integral to the emerging Fundamentalist movement. Darby taught that the signs of the end foretold by Christ to the disciples (Mark 13, Matthew 24–25, Luke 21), and in other texts, meant that the present dispensation, the Church Age, was rapidly nearing its close. (Darby carefully avoided setting a date, however.) These End Time signs included wars, wickedness, and disruptions in nature. Later, dispensationalists also saw the rise of Zionism, the 1917 Balfour Declaration, and the Jews' return to Palestine as important signs of the approaching end.

In Darby's scheme, woven from passages found in Isaiah, Daniel, Ezekiel, the Gospels, 1 Thessalonians, 1 and 2 John, Revelation, and elsewhere, the present dispensation will end with the Rapture (1 Thessalonians 4:16–17), when all true believers will "meet the Lord in the air" (1 Thessalonians 4:17, RSV). Then will come the Great Tribulation, a brief but dreadful interval during which the Antichrist (the "Beast" of Revelation) will arise to rule a revived Roman Empire and then the whole world. After seven years, Christ will return, in company with His saints, to vanquish the Antichrist's armies at Armageddon (an ancient battlefield near Haifa). Christ will establish His kingdom in a rebuilt Temple in Jerusalem and reign on earth for a thousand years as prophesied in Revelation. After one final battle with the Antichrist, the Last Judgment will be made, the New Heaven and New Earth, and the end of the long cycle of human history that began in the Garden of Eden.

This belief system attracted many American followers in the years 1880 to 1920, the same period that saw the emergence of Fundamentalism as a distinct movement within Evangelical Protestantism. The Niagara Bible Conference of 1895, a landmark in the rise of Fundamentalism, included Christ's literal and bodily return among the five fundamentals of the faith. The publication of *The Fundamentals* (1910–1915) and the formation of the World's Christian Fundamentals Association in 1919, with their affirmation of biblical literalism, the divine inspiration, and inerrancy of Scripture, and the premillennial Second Coming, deepened the link between Fundamentalism and dispensationalist eschatology. Indeed, historian Ernest Sandeen argued in *The Roots of Fundamentalism* (1970) that premillennial dispensationalism, more than any other single factor, precipitated the rise of Fundamentalism in Great Britain and America.

With some variations of detail, Darby's system was spread by prophecy conferences, thousands of pastors and touring evangelists, as well as fundamentalist Bible schools such as Moody Bible Institute, Bob Jones University, and Dallas Theological Seminary. Cyrus R. Scofield (1843–1921) was particularly important. He was an advocate of Darby's system whose annotated *Reference Bible* (1909), a key dispensationalist text, sold millions of copies and remained in print (in revised form) a century after its publication. Meanwhile, *post*millennialism, a quite different system of eschatological interpretation, won favor in liberal Protestant and social-gospel circles. According to this view, the millennium can be achieved in the present age, through Christian effort, missionary activity, and social-justice campaigns to uplift the poor and oppressed.

It was premillennialism that flourished in Fundamentalist circles and beyond, however. After World War II, dispensationalists found prophetic significance in the rise of the United Nations and the European Common Market, the nuclear arms race, the Cold War conflict with Russia, the ever-rising tide of wickedness and secularism, the establishment of Israel in 1948, and Israel's capture of Jerusalem's Old City in 1967. Dispensationalism was now increasingly spread by magazines like *Eternity*, *Moody Monthly*, and *Midnight Call*; mass-market paperbacks; television evangelists like Jerry Falwell and Jack Van Impe; films; videocassettes; and even the Internet and World Wide Web. Fundamentalist and Pentecostalist missionaries, their efforts supplemented by global religious broadcasting via communications satellites, spread these beliefs more widely still, especially in Africa and Latin America.

America's best-selling nonfiction book of the 1970s was *The Late Great Planet Earth* (1970), a popularization of dispensationalism by Hal Lindsey, a campus evangelist and graduate of Dallas Theological Seminary. Eschatalogical interest soared in the late twentieth century, not only among Fundamentalists, but across American society. Opinion polls of the 1980s and 1990s suggested that some forty percent of Americans embraced the dispensationalist End Times scenario—the Rapture, the Great Tribulation, the Battle of Armageddon, and so forth.

These beliefs helped shape many Americans' view of world events in the Cold War era and beyond. With the collapse of the Soviet Union, many prophecy believers saw the rise of international organizations, multinational corporations, and media empires, and a computer-based global economy as preparing the way for the Antichrist. The "Left Behind" series of novels, a fictionalized version of premillennial dispensationalism by Tim LaHaye, a leader of the religious Right, and Jerry B. Jenkins of *Moody Monthly*, sold many millions of copies in the later 1990s. As a new century dawned, eschatological interest among Fundamentalist and charismatic

Christians—as well as many others—showed no signs of abating in America and other countries where these beliefs had taken root.

Paul S. Boyer

See also Apocalypse; Apocalyptic Literature; Dispensationalism; End Times; Last Things; Premillennialism; Prophecy; Rapture; Second Coming

Bibliography

Bass, Clarence B. (1960) *Backgrounds to Dispensationalism*. Grand Rapids, MI: Wm. B. Eerdmans.

Boyer, Paul. (1992) *When Time Shall Be No More: Prophecy Belief in Modern American Culture*. Cambridge, MA: The Belknap Press of Harvard University Press.

Sandeen, Ernest R. (1970) *The Roots of Fundamentalism: British and American Millenarianism, 1800–1930*. Chicago: University of Chicago Press.

Weber, Timothy P. (1987) *Living in the Shadow of the Second Coming: American Premillennialism, 1875–1982*, rev. ed. Chicago: University of Chicago Press.

Eternal Life

Eternal life normally refers to that form of human existence that is believed to follow death. More narrowly, it refers to the continued postmortem existence of the human self in a realm outside of the ordinary space–time dimension of earthly existence. In Greek philosophy, eternal life was attributed only to the rational part of the soul, a part devoid of the accidents of personality. Moreover, this rational part—the "mind" or "reason"—was understood by the Greeks to be innately divine, with an existence not only succeeding the death of the body but preceding it as well. Traditional Christian theology rejected the Greek conception of eternal life for two reasons: because the biblical doctrine of creation "from nothing" (*ex nihilo*) assumes for all things apart from God a temporal existence; and because the Christian notion of bodily resurrection implies the indissoluble unity of the human person—body and soul—both before and beyond death. More positively, Christian theology states that (1) each individual soul is created from nothing along with the creation of the body; and (2) after death the whole person, body and soul, are

John 17:3

3. And this is life eternal, that they might know thee the only true God, and Jesus Christ, whom thou hast sent.

resurrected to a form of eternal life determined by God at the Last Judgment."

The notion of "eternity" as it is used to define the experience of time after death warrants clarification. There is a long-standing disagreement in Christian tradition between those who hold eternity to mean an endless sequence of passing moments and those who hold it to mean an infinite, changeless present. At stake in this debate are consequent notions of what the human experience of eternal life is like. By those who favor an eternity of infinite duration, eternal life is described in terms analogous to earthly existence. Certain biblical references seem to favor this reading, speaking metaphorically of eternal life as a "wedding" and a "great banquet." The alternate view, eternal life as a timeless infinite "now," was strongly influenced by Greek thought, which held time and change to be inseparable correlates. God's perfection demanded the quality of changelessness, hence also timelessness. In this view, eternal life is rendered as a perpetual "vision of God" (*visio Dei*) in which the resurrected believer participates in God's own timeless self-love. Biblical support for this notion comes from the Gospel of John where Jesus is understood to have equated eternal life with "knowing God" (John 17:3). The Western notion of eternal life is to be distinguished from notions of the afterlife in Eastern traditions. The norm for the latter is reincarnation, the transmigration of the human soul after death into another earthly life. Reincarnation is thought of as an endless cycle of birth, death, and rebirth until, after sufficient spiritual growth is accumulated in that cycle for enlightenment to occur, the soul leaves the earthly plane to become one with the infinite realm of true reality, the universe's ground and source. Not only do Western notions of eternal life reject the possibility of more than one earthly life, they also deny the possibility of union of the human self with God.

In conservative Christian theology, eternal life is normally understood to be manifested in two very different ways, depending on how one fares in the Last Judgment: either one is condemned for reasons of punishment to an eternity in hell, or one is elevated for reasons of reward to an eternity in heaven. Roman Catholic theology adds an intermediate realm to its account of heaven: a place of "purgation" where unconfessed sins too grievous to allow entrance into heaven, but not so grievous as to deserve hell, are repented for. In the last century, the notion of hell has come under attack from various fronts. It has been said that the idea of hell is alien to God's universal and unconditional love for humankind. More recent criticism has come from accounts of the "near-death experience," which have been nearly universally positive and heaven-like. The doctrine of hell is defended by conservative theologians

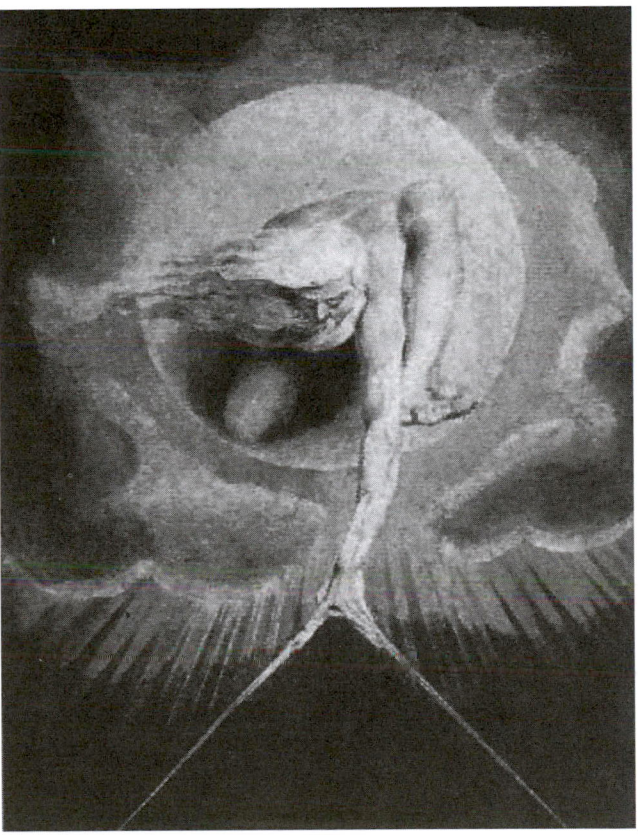

William Blake, *Ancient of Days.*

as logically consequent to the notion of free will, which is itself thought to be essential to the ethical integrity of the doctrines related to salvation and redemption.

Thomas Kinsell Carr

See also Hell, Heaven, and Purgatory

Evangelicalism

The term "Evangelical" generally refers to the New Testament and, less generally, to Martin Luther's "rediscovery of the gospel" in the sixteenth century. However, the evolution of Evangelicalism in America, where it became the most influential religious and social movement in American history, has produced some rather specialized characteristics that set it apart from the mainstream of American Protestantism.

The Great Awakening

The visits of George Whitefield, an Anglican itinerant preacher, to the American colonies in the 1730s and 1740s triggered a widespread Evangelical revival known as the Great Awakening. Whitefield built upon and knit together disparate revivals in the colonies: the pietistic awakenings among the Dutch in the Raritan Valley of New Jersey, the revival in Jonathan Edwards's congregation in Northampton, Massachusetts, and the sacramental seasons among the Scots-Irish Presbyterians in the middle colonies. One way to understand the peculiarities of Evangelicalism in North America, then, would be to see it as the eighteenth-century combustion of Pietism, Presbyterianism, and the remnants of Puritanism in the revival fires of the Great Awakening.

Despite the persistence of some ethnic and theological differences, all manifestations of the Great Awakening emphasized the necessity of some kind of conversion followed by a piety that was warmhearted and experiential—or, in the argot of the day, experimental"—against the coldly rationalistic religion characteristic of the upper classes and the ecclesiastical establishment. Although it is perilous to generalize about such a broad and internally diverse movement, Evangelicalism in America has largely retained those characteristics of a centrality of con-

version, the quest for an affective piety (perhaps best exemplified by John Wesley's Aldersgate experience in 1738, when he found his heart "strangely warmed"), and a suspicion of wealth, worldliness, and ecclesiastical pretension.

Eighteenth-century Evangelicals, known as New Lights, helped to shape American culture in the Revolutionary era and beyond. Evangelicals generally lined up with the Patriots during the Revolution, and Evangelical leaders such as Isaac Backus joined Enlightenment deists like Thomas Jefferson in an unlikely alliance to press for religious disestablishment, which was codified in the First Amendment to the U.S. Constitution.

Second Great Awakening

The Second Great Awakening stoked the revival fires once again in three different theaters of the new nation: New England, western New York, and the Cumberland Valley. Each theater made its own distinctive contribution to antebellum Evangelicalism. The revival fervor in New England gave rise to benevolent and reform societies such as the temperance movement, the female seminary movement, prison reform, and abolitionism. Lyman Beecher, for example, invested considerable energy into his campaign to outlaw dueling.

The contribution of the western New York phase of the Second Awakening was theological and tactical. Whereas Jonathan Edwards had insisted that revivals were a "surprising work of God," Charles Grandison Finney in western New York believed that his "new measures" would precipitate revival. Finney also emphasized the role of human volition in the salvation process. Ever since, American Evangelicalism has eschewed Calvinist notions about predestination in favor of Finney's Arminian doctrines that exalt the individual's ability to "choose God" and thereby take control of his or her spiritual destiny; such notions doubtless had a certain resonance in the new nation among a people who had, only recently, taken control of its political destiny.

The contribution of the Second Great Awakening in the South is rather more complex. The revival certainly functioned as a civilizing force in a frontier society of widely scattered settlements, prodigious alcohol consumption, and notoriously rowdy behavior. Circuit riders, a product of the great organizing genius of American Methodism, brought religion to

Selection from: THE KNOWLEDGE OF JESUS CHRIST THE BEST KNOWLEDGE DELIVERED BY GEORGE WHITEFIELD

I determined not to know any thing among you, save Jesus Christ,
and him crucified. 1 Corinthians 2: 2.

The persons to whom these words were written, were the members of the church of Corinth; who, as appears by the foregoing chapter, were not only divided into different sects, by one saying, "I am of Paul, and another, I am of Apollos;" but also had man amongst them, who were so full of the wisdom of this world, and so wise in their own eyes, that they set at nought the simplicity of the gospel, and accounted the Apostle's preaching foolishness.

Never had the Apostle more need of the wisdom of the serpent, mingled with the innocency of the dove, than now. What is the sum of all his wisdom? He tells them, in the words of the text, "I determined not to know any thing amongst you, save Jesus Christ, and him crucified."

A resolution this, worthy of the great St. Paul; and no less worthy, no less necessary for every minister, and every disciple of Christ, to make always, even unto the 3end of the world.

In the following discourse, I shall,

FIRST, Explain what is meant by "not knowing any thing, save Jesus Christ, and him crucified."

SECONDLY, Give some reasons why every Christian should determine not to know any thing else. And

THIRDLY, Conclude with a general exhortation to put this determination into practice.

FIRST, I am to explain what is meant by "not knowing any thing, save Jesus Christ, and him crucified."

By Jesus Christ, we are to understand the eternal Son of God. He is called Jesus, a Savior, because he was to save us from the guilt and power of our sins; and, like Joshua, by whom he was remarkably typified, to lead God's spiritual Israel through the wilderness of this world, to the heavenly Canaan, the promised inheritance of the children of God.

He is called CHRIST, which signifies anointed, because he was anointed by the Holy Ghost at his baptism, to be a prophet to instruct, a priest to make an atonement for, and a king to govern and protect his church. And he was crucified, or hung (O stupendous love!) till he was dead upon the cross, that he might become a curse for us: for it is written, "Cursed is every man that hangeth upon a tree."

Source: *Historic Church Documents*. www.reformed.org

A handbill from Nigeria announcing a gospel celebration. COURTESY OF MATTHEWS A. OJO.

the people; Baptists, the other major religion of the South, ordained their own ministers without regard for clerical education. Camp meetings, still a fixture of religion in the South, lured thousands for socializing, preaching, conversion, and, very often, spectacular displays of religious enthusiasm. Evangelicalism has surely left its mark on Southern culture, witness the persistence of backwoods camp meetings and baptisms, Evangelical revivals, and public prayers at high school football games.

The social reforming impulse emanating from Protestantism in the North, however, soon clashed with Southern mores. Evangelicalism in the antebellum South came to be identified with the social order, especially after Nat Turner's rebellion in 1831, which obliterated any public qualms that Southerners harbored about the morality of slaveholding. Southern Evangelicals saw themselves at odds with Northern abolitionists over the issue of slavery. Each side marshaled its own theological position, either in defense or in opposition to slavery, confident of divine sanction. Southern Evangelicalism turned inward and became increasingly insular in the face of attacks from the North. The sectional conflict divided denominations before it sundered the Union, thereby creating institutional schisms that, in some instances, still fester. (Although the Presbyterians and the Methodists mended their sectional differences, for instance, the Southern Baptist Convention never reunited with its Northern counterparts.)

Protestant Fragmentation

The Emancipation Proclamation removed the one adhesive, abolitionism, that had united Northern Evangelicals, so that after the Civil War Evangelicalism in the North began to dissipate in a flurry of theological controversies and denominational disputes. The publication of Charles Darwin's *The Origin of Species* in 1859 had gone virtually unnoticed amid the building sectional tensions, but in the waning decades of the nineteenth century, Evangelicals began to recognize its implications for literalistic interpretations of the Bible. The discipline of higher criticism emanating from Germany, moreover, cast further doubt on the infallibility of the Scriptures. American Protestants, especially in the North, waged fierce battles over biblical inspiration. Conservatives, notably A. A. Hodge, B. B. Warfield, and the theologians at Princeton Theological Seminary, reasserted the divine inspiration of the Bible, even insisting

upon its inerrancy in the original autographs. In contrast, liberal theologians such as Charles A. Briggs at Union Theological Seminary took a less rigid, more progressive view.

Social and economic factors, particularly the industrialization and urbanization of American culture in the decades following the Civil War, exaggerated the divide within American Protestantism. Whereas earlier in the century Evangelical optimism about the perfectibility of both the individual and society had unleashed various reform efforts directed toward establishing the biblical millennium in America, by the close of the century teeming, squalid tenements populated by immigrants, most of them non-Protestant, hardly looked like the precincts of Zion. In the face of such squalor and the frustrated ambitions for a Protestant empire, disappointed Evangelicals adjusted their eschatology. No longer did they believe that their efforts could bring about the millennium; instead, they adopted an interpretive scheme of the Bible called "dispensational premillennialism." Dispensational premillennialists insisted Christ would come at any moment to "rapture" the true Christians from the earth and unleash His judgment against a sinful world. While Evangelicals retreated to dispensationalism and despaired of social reform, their liberal counterparts embraced the Social Gospel, which held that God redeems not only individuals but sinful social institutions as well.

Pentecostalism and Fundamentalism

Another strain of Evangelicalism, Pentecostalism, emerged at the turn of the twentieth century. On the first day of the new century, 1 January 1901, Agnes Ozman, a student at Bethel Bible College in Topeka, Kansas, began speaking in tongues, a spiritual language akin to babbling. This practice, first mentioned in the second chapter of the Acts of the Apostles, when the early Christians spoke in tongues on the day of Pentecost, soon spread throughout the lower Midwest, to Texas, and then, through the agency of an African-American hotel waiter, William J. Seymour, to Los Angeles in 1906. Seymour's preaching triggered the famous Azusa Street Revival, an event that drew thousands for spectacular demonstrations of the Pentecostal gifts, especially divine healing and speaking in tongues. Converts from the Azusa Revival then fanned out across North America and the world, spreading their Pentecostal message.

While Pentecostals emphasized the affective dimensions of the faith and cared little for theological niceties, Evangelical and liberal Protestants clashed again in the 1910s and 1920s. Responding to various assaults on Evangelical orthodoxy, two oil tycoons, Lyman and Milton Stewart of Union Oil in California, financed the publication of a series of pamphlets called *The Fundamentals*, which outlined what the writers regarded as the essentials of orthodoxy: biblical inerrancy, the Virgin Birth, Christ's Atonement and Resurrection, the authenticity of miracles, and the system of dispensational premillennialist biblical interpretation. These "five points of Fundamentalism" became the focus of doctrinal struggles in the 1920s, with the "Fundamentalists" (hence the name) defending the doctrines against the "modernists" or liberals.

With rare exceptions, the Fundamentalists lost those struggles for power within Protestant denominations. Although some resolved to stay within mainline churches in hopes of checking the drift toward liberalism, most left to form independent churches or denominations, such as J. Gresham Machen's Orthodox Presbyterian Church. An even larger defeat for the Fundamentalists came in Dayton, Tennessee, in 1925, at the infamous Scopes "Monkey Trial." Although Fundamentalists, represented in the courtroom by William Jennings Bryan, actually won the case against John T. Scopes (his conviction was later overturned on a technicality), they lost badly in the courtroom of public opinion. The merciless lampoons of H. L. Mencken and other journalists covering the trial succeeded in portraying Fundamentalists—and, by extension, Evangelicals—as uneducated country bumpkins, a stereotype that, unfairly, persisted through the end of the twentieth century.

The Evangelical Subculture and the Religious Right

After the 1920s, Evangelicals, perceiving that American culture had turned against them, retreated from public life, but they did not disappear. Instead, they set about building a huge and intricate subculture of churches, denominations, Bible institutes, colleges, seminaries, Bible camps, mission societies, and publishing houses that provided the foundation for their resurgence in the 1970s. A central figure in the renewal of Evangelicalism was a charismatic young preacher named Billy Graham (1918–). Reared in

North Carolina and converted to Evangelical Christianity as a teenager, Graham attended Bob Jones College and then transferred to Wheaton College, an Evangelical school located west of Chicago. Graham not only had a knack for preaching, he also had a knack for self-promotion. He rose to prominence at a unique moment in history, when various new media technologies were emerging, and he seized on them with a vengeance and made himself into something of a cultural icon at the middle of the twentieth century. Graham rejected much of the narrowness and censoriousness of the Fundamentalist strain of Evangelicalism in favor of a more tolerant "New Evangelicalism," which sought to communicate effectively with the masses. His very public friendships with a succession of U.S. presidents, moreover, from Dwight Eisenhower to Bill Clinton, served to legitimize Evangelicalism once again in the eyes of the public.

Exactly half a century after the humiliation of the Scopes Trial and coincident with the presidential campaign of Jimmy Carter, a Southern Baptist Sunday school teacher, Evangelicals, especially Southerners, began to reassert themselves in the political arena. Although they deserted Carter for Ronald Reagan in 1980, Evangelicals, led by preacher-activists like Jerry Falwell and Pat Robertson (who himself would mount a credible campaign for the Republican presidential nomination in 1988), made their presence felt in American politics, in part through the advocacy of a loose network of politically conservative organizations known collectively as the religious Right. Not all Evangelicals, however, are politically conservative. During the 1980 campaign, for instance, all three of the major candidates for president—Carter, Reagan, and John B. Anderson, a liberal Republican who ran as an independent—claimed to be Evangelicals.

The "Americanness" of Evangelicalism

Despite the surprise registered by pundits and the media over Evangelical political activism, Evangelicals in recent years have merely reclaimed their historic place in American public discourse. Evangelicals in the nineteenth century, more than any other group, shaped the nation's political and social agenda, just as they had provided important support for the patriot cause in the eighteenth century. The return of Evangelicalism to public life has also served to gradually erode popular perceptions of

Evangelicals as backward and somehow opposed to technology and innovation. Evangelicals, in fact, have consistently been pioneers in mass communications—the open-air preaching in the eighteenth century that prefigured the patriot rhetoric during the Revolution; the Methodist circuits on the frontier that anticipated grass-roots political organizations; the adroit use of broadcast media in the twentieth century, from the radio preachers of the 1920s to the televangelists of the 1970s, which provided a model for such acknowledged masters of political communication as Franklin Roosevelt and Ronald Reagan.

Evangelicalism—from the revival tradition of the eighteenth and nineteenth centuries to the militant Fundamentalism of the 1920s to Pentecostalism with its emphasis on speaking in tongues and other gifts of the Holy Spirit—is deeply imbedded in American life, in part because of its promise of salvation available to all, intimacy with God, and a community of fellow believers.

Randall Balmer

See also America, as a Christian nation; Dispensationalism; Great Awakening; Pentecostalism; Premillennialism; Speaking in Tongues

Bibliography

Balmer, Randall. (1999) *Blessed Assurance: A History of Evangelicalism in America.* Boston: Beacon Press.

———. (2000) *Mine Eyes Have Seen the Glory: A Journey into the Evangelical Subculture in America,* 3rd ed. New York: Oxford University Press.

Carpenter, Joel A. (1997) *Revive Us Again: The Reawakening of American Fundamentalism.* New York: Oxford University Press.

Heyrman, Christine Leigh. (1997) *Southern Cross: The Beginnings of the Bible Belt.* New York: Alfred A. Knopf.

Marsden, George M. (1980) *Fundamentalism and American Culture: The Shaping of Twentieth-Century Evangelicalism: 1870–1925.* New York: Oxford University Press.

Smith, Christian, and Michael Emerson. (1998) *American Evangelicalism: Embattled and Thriving.* Chicago: University of Chicago Press.

Stout, Harry S. (1991) *The Divine Dramatist: George Whitefield and the Rise of Modern Evangelicalism.* Grand Rapids, MI.: Wm. B. Eerdmans.

Evil

In traditional Christian theology, evil was brought into the cosmos via sin. From birth, each human is tainted and thus inclined toward sin. Sin is both an individual and collective phenomenon and serves to separate us from God. It manifests through such unfavorable human emotions as fear, pride, and selfishness, emotions that lead to the corruption of the world around us. The story of Adam, Eve, and the snake is read as the introduction of sin, but this reading has little effect on the Fundamentalist understanding of evil.

For Christians, the essential theological problem of evil has been that of how one can reconcile a just and good God with a substantially evil world. To this dilemma, centuries of Christian philosophers have offered theories, defending the position of Monism or considering the role of free will, to name just two. John Hick's *Evil and the God of Love* (1966) and Stephen T. Davis's *Encountering Evil: Live Options in Theodicy* (1981) both consider approaches to the problem of evil in Christian thought.

Yet because Fundamentalist Christians have a pretheoretical worldview, the mythic and philosophical approaches have not heavily influenced their understanding of evil. Their approach is decidedly eclectic, as individual Fundamentalists draw their own conclusions about the meaning and purpose of a particular evil. In *Bible Believers,* sociologist Nancy Ammerman observed how one group of Fundamentalists struggled to make sense of a freak tornado that struck a nearby town. "Everyone was sure that so unusual an occurrence must bear a divine message, but not everyone agreed on what that message might be" (1987: 70–71). Some suggested the storm was a sign of the End Times. Others believed the town was being punished for its sins. Another possibility was the event would cause some to turn to God.

Each possibility, and others, were well within reason and what's more, group members rethought their ideas as the conversation developed. This example reinforces the point that Fundamentalists commonly advance personal theories for evil events. As Ammerman noted, "The only intolerable possibility was that the whole thing was 'merely natural.' Explanations do not have to form a logical whole, but there must be an explanation, one that includes divine activity" (1987: 71).

For conservative Christians, it is far more important to maintain faith in God's supreme control than to advance complex theories of the nature of evil in the world. At the same time, Fundamentalists look around them and see a world drenched with evil. Where the New Testament considers Satan the "prince of this world" (John 12:31, NIV), Fundamentalists wholeheartedly agree. They read the decrease in family stability and increase in immorality and sin as signs of evil's influence. In their supernatural worldview, every event can be allied with the efforts of God or Satan and thus bears the mark of good or evil.

Fundamentalists perceive God's direct influence on their lives in every way. Therefore, a setbacks and personal tragedies can often be viewed as "tests" from God. Orthodox Christians may feel that personal tragedies are obstacles to be overcome and these events lead to an increase in one's faith. Tragic events are often seen as tests of faith that can only be probably understood in retrospect, when the believer recognizes the good that resulted. For example, looking back at a misfortune, Fundamentalists often note that a particular event which appeared to be evil in fact strengthened their or someone else's relationship with the Lord. Though one may not be able to recognize the good in a car accident or a life-threatening storm, for Fundamentalists, believing that God turns the tragic to the good is a necessary part of faith. It is God's will that everyone be saved; therefore, even an apparent tragedy can be part of God's plan if it leads one down the right path. As Ammerman wrote, "Because the trials may result in good, the trials themselves are often attributed to God" (1987: 65).

The New Testament is a model for this thinking. The foremost example is the crucifixion of Jesus, symbolic of the evil of nonbelievers and also an event that God turned into the greatest triumph. Moreover, Fundamentalists take comfort in recalling the incarnation; Jesus' suffering is further evidence that God appreciates the depth of human suffering and acts to mitigate our pain. They have faith that the all-good and all-powerful God can easily turn evils in their lives into victories and can point to multiple examples in their own lives where God intervened and transformed a tragedy into a blessing.

Fundamentalists consider Satan the second potent influence is their lives and a figure that is the basis for much evil. Whereas mainstream Christian denominations have largely jettisoned serious consideration of Satan, Fundamentalists consider the devil an actual being who has the power to nega-

tively alter their lives. The devil may attempt to persuade the believer to sin or cause painful events that undermine the believer's assuredness.

Differing Views among Fundamentalists

In the early part of the twentieth century, famed Fundamentalist preacher Billy Sunday (1862–1935) often spoke of the threat of the devil. His simple message and enthralling presentation proved highly effective for thousands of Evangelical Christians. He preached that the devil induced Christians to drink alcohol, to abuse their families, and to confuse right from wrong. Today, hints of Sunday's stories in which he battled the devil can be found in the literature of "spiritual warfare." These numerous books catalogue stories of possession, demonic attacks, and the tools that Christians can use to defend against Satan's attacks. C. Peter Wagner has been an influential voice in this contemporary battle against evil. Another is Frank Peretti who, in the 1980s, sold millions of copies of his novels such as *This Present Darkness* (1986) and *Piercing the Darkness* (1989), which described dramatic battles between demons, angels, and the humans caught in the middle.

Other Fundamentalists who take a less aggressive approach toward defeating evil may consider Satan's attacks as opportunities to grow in faith. Though the devil's threat is no less real and dangerous, Fundamentalists are confident that Satan can only succeed by sabotaging the believer's faith. With God's support, Satan's threat is seriously diminished. The devil creates obstacles in the life of the believer but once again, God often intervenes to turn Satan's attack toward the good. Having overcome another hurdle, the believer's faith is further substantiated.

Premillennialism

A third consideration of the Fundamentalist understanding of evil involves their eschatological worldview. The prior consideration of God and Satan's influence helps shed light on the orthodox Christian's own world. Yet global evils such as nuclear war and tragic earthquakes are often more closely connected with premillennialism, the Fundamentalist interest in the end of the world. To be sure, many elements of premillennialism have no association with evil. The creation of the Jewish state, for one, is a key event for premillennial forecasters but in and of itself the event has no evil import. Yet Fundamentalists take other occurrences such as environmental devastation and the increased possibility of nuclear destruction as signs of the impending end of the world.

Like most other beliefs considered here, premillennialism does not have the same appeal for every Fundamentalist nor is there a uniform approach to understanding the last days. Yet in the 1970s the best selling title of the entire decade was Hal Lindsey's *The Late Great Planet Earth*, a fact that speaks to the popularity of the subject matter. For many conservative Christians, the end of the world is closely connected with a variety of evils, both natural and moral.

Psychotherapist Charles Strozier interviewed several Fundamentalists in his *Apocalypse: On the Psychology of Fundamentalism in America* and noted the list of global evils that are closely associated with the end of the world. The Gulf War, nuclear proliferation, and the spread of AIDS were just a few of the nearly endless examples of apocalyptic evidence to which Fundamentalists refer. Strozier noted that many Fundamentalists "draw strength from the approaching Apocalypse"; one church he studied committed to greater social activism knowing that the End Times were near (1994: 13). This is because the Apocalypse, while connected to contemporary global evils, is not in itself an unfavorable event. The availability of Apocalypse paraphernalia such as rapture watches ("one hour nearer the Lord's return") and the success of the *Left Behind* series of novels by Tim LaHaye and Jerry Jenkins, a collection of books that make an action-adventure story out of the final battle between good and evil, speak to the comfort and even enthusiasm of apocalyptic contemplation.

The Fundamentalist belief in God, Satan, and premillennialism plays heavily in the Fundamentalist views of evil. As noted earlier, Fundamentalists often reinterpret the meaning of events in retrospect so that moral and natural evils become altogether different. To a Fundamentalist, war is not evil if it is part of God's plan. This is not to say that Fundamentalists have no category of evil in their worldview. On the contrary, for them, the world is organized into radical polarities of good and evil. Fundamentalists find evil throughout the dominant culture around them. What's more, the sheer quantity of evil far outstrips that of the good, although good will unquestionably win out in the end. For conservative Christians, the appropriate path is the narrow one that leads closer to God; evil is any experience, decision, or event that takes a different path. The pretheoretical nature of Fundamentalism allows for great flexibility in recognizing and describing experiences of evil. Evil is not found in a given event, but in the interpretation of that event. Stated simply, Fundamentalist evil can be anything that counters the conservative Christian message.

Shanny Luft

See also Devil and Satan; Original Sin; Sin and Sinners

Bibliography

Ammerman, Nancy. (1987) *Bible Believers: Fundamentalists in the Modern World.* New Brunswick, NJ: Rutgers University Press.

Barr, James. (1978) *Fundamentalism.* Philadelphia: The Westminster Press.

Boyer, Paul. (1992) *When Time Shall Be No More: Prophecy Belief in Modern American Culture.* Cambridge, MA: The Belknap Press of Harvard University Press.

Lindsey, Hal. (1972) *The Late Great Planet Earth.* New York: Bantam Books.

Strozier, Charles B. (1994) *Apocalypse: On the Psychology of Fundamentalism in America.* Boston: Beacon Press.

Wagner, C. Peter. (1990) *Wrestling with Dark Angels.* Ventura, CA: Regal Books.

Weber, Timothy. (1983) *Living in the Shadow of the Second Coming: American Premillennialism 1875–1982.* Grand Rapids, MI: Zondervan Publishing House.

Evil Empire

As part of the prophetic scenario for the end of the world accepted by many Fundamentalists, the Evil Empire—Gog in Old Testament terms—will join forces with Satan in the final rebellion against God at the end of the millennium. Introduced most clearly by the prophet Ezekial and picked up in Revelations, Gog in alliance with Magog is supposed to come from a location to the north of Israel for the Battle of Armageddon.

Christian exegetes have attempted to identify Gog since at least the fourth century, with an early favorite being the Scythians, which was the identification favored by Jewish interpreters of prophecy. Muslims, especially the Ottoman Turks, dominated interpretation from the thirteenth through eighteenth centuries. By the early nineteenth century, Russia began to be cast as the empire from the north, and the emergence of the Soviet Union in the early twentieth century confirmed that identification and dominated the thought especially of American Fundamentalists even after the Soviet dissolution in 1990.

The early case for equating Russia with the evil empire rested in large part on the translation of Ezekiel 38:3 (KJV), which equates Gog with "the chief prince of Meshech and Tubal." The *King James* translation rendered the Hebrew *nesi rosh* as "chief prince," but later biblical scholars argued that *rosh* was a proper name and that the phrase should read "prince of Rosh." Moreover, "Rosh" came to be viewed as an early form of "Russia" with "Meshech" and "Tubal" as Moscow and Tobolsk. By the time that Cyrus Scofield (1843–1921) published his influential *Reference Bible* in 1909, he could unequivocally claim that Gog referred to a coalition of northern powers headed by Russia.

The triumph of the Bolsheviks and the emergence of the Soviet Union reinforced the equation. American Fundamentalists did not need to reinterpret Hebrew texts to support their belief that the godless communists who spread their hegemony over eastern Europe after World War II and were attempting to do so in other parts of the world constituted the evil empire. The idea pervades the writings of prophecy interpreters during the last half of the twentieth century and emerged into the mainstream of foreign relations when President Ronald Reagan explicitly identified the Soviet Union as the "evil empire" during an address delivered to the National Association of Evangelicals in 1983. More than a decade previously when speaking to a group of California legislators, the future president had argued forcefully for an identification of Russia with Gog.

The thaw in the Cold War during the 1980s and the collapse of the Soviet empire did not perceptibly affect the identification of Gog with Russia. Some commentators on prophecy held that the apparent softening of the Soviet regime was merely a ruse, while others suggested that the relative peace that occurred after *glasnost* was itself a sign that the End Times were imminent and that the Soviet Union would reemerge clearly as the evil empire and fulfill Ezekiel's prophecy by assuming the principal adversarial role in the final conflict. Russia remained the prophesied nation whose invasion of Israel would precipitate the ultimate global confrontation that would leave all but the righteous in ruins.

William M. Clements

See also Apocalypse; Communism; End Times

Bibliography

Boyer, Paul. (1992) *When Time Shall Be No More: Prophecy Belief in Modern American Culture.* Cambridge, MA: The Belknap Press Harvard University.

Cohn, Norman. (1993) *Cosmos, Chaos and the World to Come: The Ancient Roots of Apocalyptic Faith.* New Haven, CT: Yale University Press.

Wojcik, Daniel. (1997) *The End of the World As We Know It: Faith, Fatalism, and Apocalypse in America.* New York: New York University Press.

Evolution and Antievolution

Surveys suggest that the majority of religious Americans find the biological theory of evolution controversial and that their views on the topic vary considerably (Scott 1997). Some of these views are linked to religious beliefs—but not all. In no industrialized nation have antievolutionists been so active and so successful as in the United States. Antievolutionist sentiments are growing abroad, however, but usually—as among Turkish Muslims—as a result of a strong religious bias. As a group, Protestant Fundamentalists in the United States are more likely than members of most other religious groups to find the evolutionary theory to be inconsistent with religious beliefs, but not every opponent of evolution is a Fundamentalist. In the last decades of the twentieth century Fundamentalists campaigned against the theory of evolution by promoting creationism as an alternative and prohibiting or limiting the teaching of evolution in the public schools.

Evolution

Evolution in its most basic sense can be summarized in the concept that "Change through time has occurred and the present is different from the past" (Scott 1997: 265). Evolution is now most commonly used to refer specifically to biological evolution, that is: "Living things descend with modification from ancestors through the process of natural selection" (Scott 1997: 265). The theory of evolution by natural selection was proposed by Charles Darwin (1809–1882) and Alfred Russell Wallace (1823–1913). Both sought to account for the rise and extinction of all species on the basis of variation, which, they argued, can be found within all species. The environment (nature) selects from preexisting variation and over time causes species to change and become better adapted to their respective environments. Darwin and Wallace contended that as species modify to changing environments, they eventually diverge so much from the original species that they themselves become separate, new species. Thus, "natural selection" accounts for both the origin and extinction of species and operates to make each species as well adapted to its particular environment as possible. According to Darwin and Wallace, evolutionary change has no particular direction because adaptive traits do not always arise when they are needed and most, if not all, species eventually face extinction. Antievolutionists, to the contrary, assert that the universe and all life forms came into existence by the direct acts of a creator believed to be external and independent of the natural universe.

While evolutionary theory is predicated on a random view of the universe, and, by implication, is atheistic, Charles Darwin—its most famous exponent—was not personally antagonistic toward religion and religious ideas. While at Cambridge, he studied to be a clergyman. With but few exceptions, Darwin's 1859 book *Origin of Species* was well received among clergy, and James R. Moore (1979: 92) concludes that by the end of the nineteenth century most leading Christian thinkers in both Great Britain and the United States had come to terms with Darwin's theory of natural selection. Though the major intellectuals of his day either ignored or welcomed Darwin's theory, it enjoyed widespread acceptance among scientists and educators. By the end of the nineteenth century the educational establishment in the United States had incorporated Darwin's ideas. In 1895, for example, the National Education Association advocated including the theory of evolution in high school textbooks.

Antievolution

Organized opposition to the theory of evolution in the United States was relatively late in coming and roughly corresponds to the emergence of Fundamentalism as a religious and political movement (ca. 1909–1912). Some historians have portrayed Fundamentalists as open enemies of science whose assertions that the Genesis account is a literal statement put them at odds with major findings in biology, geology, astronomy, chemistry, physics, anthropology, archaeology, and paleontology. But this is a distortion.

Evolutionary theory was only a secondary target of Fundamentalists. Their primary objective was to force out what they saw as "modernism" and "liberalism" from mainline Protestant denominations. It has been argued that Fundamentalists were opposed to evolution and evolutionary theory largely because the liberal denominations seemed to support it. Whatever their reasons for opposing evolution, Fundamentalist groups lacked the necessary funding to bring the issue to a focus, and they did not have a strong media presence until after World War II.

The Scopes "Monkey Trial"

The most famous battle between evolutionists and antievolutionists took place in Dayton, Tennessee. In January 1925 the Tennessee House of Representatives passed a bill making it unlawful for state-supported schools to teach any theory denying the divine Creation as taught by the Bible. The bill, proposed by representative John Washington Butler of Lafayette, made violation of this law a misdemeanor that carried a fine of $100 to $500. In May, John Thomas Scopes, a high school science teacher in Dayton, at the instigation of the American Civil Liberties Union (ACLU), agreed to test the constitutionality of the law. The ACLU provided Scopes with legal counsel, including the eminent Chicago attorney Clarence Darrow. Three-time presidential candidate William Jennings Bryan joined the prosecution team. The trial lasted eight days, from 10 to 18 July. On the seventh day of the trial, Bryan submitted to a lengthy examination by Clarence Darrow in which Bryan affirmed his belief in Old Testament miracles (e.g., that Joshua commanded the earth to stand still) and his acceptance of the Genesis account of Creation. The outcome of the trial was never in doubt because Scopes's defense attorneys had already admitted that Scopes has taught the forbidden theory. He was convicted after less than ten minutes of jury deliberation, and fined $100. William Jennings Bryan died just five days later.

The Scopes trial was one of the most highly publicized legal battles in American history, and in many respects rivals the coverage given to the O. J. Simpson murder trial in 1995 (Numbers 1998: 77). Scholars continue to debate the trial's significance. Some (e.g., Eve and Harrold, 1991) see the Scopes trial as the climax of the antievolution movement in America, while others (e.g., Webb 1994) view it as the beginning of a new stage in the battle between evolutionists and antievolutionists.

CLARENCE DARROW QUESTIONS WILLIAM JENNINGS BRYAN AT THE SCOPES TRIAL, 20 JULY 1925

DARROW: You have given considerable study to the Bible, haven't you, Mr. Bryan?

BRYAN: Yes, sir, I have tried to.

DARROW: Well, we all know you have; we are not going to dispute that at all. But you have written and published articles almost weekly, and sometimes have made interpretations of various things.

BRYAN: I would not say interpretations, Mr. Darrow, but comments on the lesson.

DARROW: If you comment to any extent, those comments have been interpretations?

BRYAN: I presume that my discussion might be to some extent interpretations, but they have not been primarily intended as interpretations.

DARROW: But you have studied that question, of course?

BRYAN: Of what?

DARROW: Interpretation of the Bible.

BRYAN: On this particular question?

DARROW: Yes, sir.

BRYAN: Yes, sir.

DARROW: Then you have made a general study of it?

BRYAN: Yes, I have. I have studied the Bible for about fifty years, or some time more than that. But, of course, I have studied it more as I have become older than when I was but a boy.

DARROW: Do you claim that everything in the Bible should be literally interpreted?

BRYAN: I believe everything in the Bible should be accepted as it is given there. Some of the Bible is given illustratively; for instance, "Ye are the salt of the earth." I would not insist that man was actually salt, or that he had flesh of salt, but it is used in the sense of salt as saving God's people.

DARROW: But when you read that Jonah swallowed the whale—or that the whale swallowed Jonah, excuse me, please—how do you literally interpret that?

BRYAN: When I read that a big fish swallowed Jonah—it does not say whale.

DARROW: Doesn't it? Are you sure?

BRYAN: That is my recollection of it, a big fish. And I believe it, and I believe in a God who can make a whale and can make a man, and can make both do what He pleases.

Much has been written concerning Bryan's testimony at the trial. It is apparent from the court transcript that Bryan interpreted the days of Genesis as vast stretches of time. But was he consistent with the views held by Fundamentalists of his day? Numbers (1998: 80–81) makes a strong case that few Fundamentalists in 1925 insisted on a young earth. Fundamentalists did not speak out against Bryan, and there is little evidence that they felt betrayed. A majority of Fundamentalists, Numbers contends, followed the *Scofield Reference Bible*'s interpretation, in which the first book of Genesis described two separate beginnings, one "in the beginning," and the other, eons later when God placed Adam and Eve in the Garden of Eden. Between these two beginnings, the earth underwent a series of great catastrophes as may be discerned from the fossil record. Few Fundamentalists of the time, Numbers argues, were committed to a strict, literal interpretation of the Bible and most allowed for leeway in the interpretation of Scripture.

The Battle in the Schools

Public schools have always been the major battleground. Between 1922 and 1929, forty-six state legislatures considered bills that would have made it illegal to teach evolution. Only three states actual-

DARROW: Mr. Bryan, doesn't the New Testament say whale [Matthew 12:40]?

BRYAN: I am not sure. My impression is that it says fish, but it does not make so much difference. I merely called your attention to where it says fish, it does not say whale.

DARROW: But in the New Testament it says whale, doesn't it?

BRYAN: That may be true. I cannot remember in my own mind what I read about it.

DARROW: Now, you say the big fish swallowed Jonah, and he remained how long—three days—and then he spewed him up on the land. You believe that the big fish was made to swallow Jonah?

BRYAN: I am not prepared to say that; the Bible merely says it was done.

DARROW: You don't know whether it was the ordinary run of fish or made for that purpose?

BRYAN: You may guess; you evolutionists guess.

DARROW: But when we do guess, we have the sense to guess right.

BRYAN: But you do not do it often.

DARROW: You are not prepared to say whether that fish was made especially to swallow a man or not?

BRYAN: The Bible doesn't say; so I am not prepared to say.

DARROW: You don't know whether that was fixed up specially for the purpose.

BRYAN: No, the Bible doesn't say.

DARROW: But do you believe He made them—that He made such a fish, and that it was big enough to swallow Jonah?

BRYAN: Yes, sir. And let me add, one miracle is just as easy to believe as another.

DARROW: It is for me.

BRYAN: It is for me, too.

DARROW: Just as hard?

BRYAN: It is hard to believe for you, but easy for me. A miracle is a thing performed beyond what man can perform. When you get beyond what man can do, you get within the realms of miracles; and it is just as easy to believe the miracle of Jonah as any other miracle in the Bible.

DARROW: Perfectly easy to believe that Jonah swallowed the whale?

BRYAN: The Bible says so. The Bible doesn't make as extreme statements as evolutionists do.

---

ly passed such bills—Tennessee, Mississippi, and Arkansas—although Oklahoma prohibited the use of textbooks that promoted evolution, and Florida condemned the teaching of evolution as "improper and subversive"; however, the teaching of evolution science was never illegal in Florida.

After the Soviet Union launched Sputnik in 1957, Americans embarked on unprecedented efforts to improve science education in the public schools. Proevolution texts were widely distributed, and evolution was promoted as the "centerpiece" of modern biology (Numbers 1988). Antievolutionists were still active during this period, but they did not receive as much media attention as previously.

During the 1970s, antievolutionists attempted to ban the teaching of evolution or argued that it should be presented on an equal footing with creation science. Although antievolutionists have given lip service to the so-called scientific problems of evolution, Scott (1997: 263) contends that they are motivated primarily by their apprehensions over the implications of evolution for religion. Literalists (whether Christians, Jews, or Muslims) fear that if their children learn evolution, they will cease to believe in God and, therefore, will not experience salvation.

During the 1980s, bills promoting equal time for the teaching of evolution and creation science were introduced in twenty-six state legislatures, but only the bills introduced in Arkansas and Louisiana became law. The Arkansas bill became the focus of much media attention. It was challenged by proponents and opponents of both creationism and evolution. Many opponents of the bill—including leaders of the Methodist Church, the Roman Catholic Church, the Episcopal Church, the African Methodist Episcopal Church, the Presbyterian Church, and Reform Jews—were not Fundamentalists. However, a number of Southern Baptist ministers and Rev. Bill McLean, the lead plaintiff, clearly would have placed themselves in the Fundamentalist camp. In 1982, Arkansas' equal time law was declared unconstitutional in Federal District Court, but the failure of the Arkansas bill did little to halt efforts to pass equal time legislation elsewhere. Unlike the Arkansas bill, the Louisiana law was never challenged in the state courts. It remained on the books until 1987, when the U.S. Supreme Court decided that equal time laws like Louisiana's violated the clause establishing separation of church and state because such laws serve a religious, not a scientific, purpose (Larson 1985; Numbers 1998).

Such battles are far from over. In 1969, the California Board of Education issued guidelines for its public school biology courses. The board recommended equal time for the Genesis account of Creation. Proposals for equal time gained renewed attention following an influential 1978 article by Wendell Bird published in the *Yale Law Review*. Bird's article posed a legal justification for the teaching of creation science whenever evolution science was taught in the public schools and gave additional credence to the doctrine of equal time. In 1999, the Kansas School Board voted 6 to 4 to downplay the importance of evolution in its statewide curriculum standards. The most hotly contested local election in 2000 was the Republican primary for a seat on the Kansas State Board of Education in which conservative Linda Holloway, who had voted for the new standards, raised more than $90,000 in campaign contributions. Moderate Republican Sue Gamble, who said she wanted to reverse the new standards, raised over $36,000. By comparison, a typical candidate for a seat on the Kansas School Board spends less than $2,000. Gamble—the moderate—won the election.

Antievolutionism, Creationism, and Fundamentalism

Despite continued judicial opposition to the teaching of creationism in public schools, the battle continues as increasingly more American parents choose to educate their children at home or in private schools that teach creationism. Creationists have developed variations of creation theory that accounts for evidence of evolution in the geological record and might also be more acceptable to the courts and to public officials. They believe these theories should be taught alongside the evolutionary theory. For example, a Dallas-based creationist organization, The Foundation for Thought and Ethics, has sponsored an antievolutionist supplemental biology textbook entitled *Of Pandas and People*. The text does not explicitly mention God or Creation, but tacitly argues for an "intelligent design" of life forms and the abrupt appearance of new species.

Many of these activities do not reflect the interests and concerns of Fundamentalists. In fact, much recent literature on the antievolution movement has been devoted not to Fundamentalists but to scientific creationists. It should be kept in mind that not all creationists are Fundamentalists and comparatively few Fundamentalists would call themselves creationists. Many creationist organizations—like the American Scientific Affiliation, the Creation Research Society, and the Institute for Creation Research—were founded by well-established scientists and scholars, and most of the leadership within these organizations have earned Ph.D.s in the biological sciences, physics, and/or engineering. Fundamentalists have little influence in these organizations. Creationist groups, it could be argued, mainly address one another (see Toumey 1994).

According to Eve and Harrold (1991: 3), the debate between creationists and evolutionists centers on five basic issues: 1) Is the universe divinely created or did it come into existence without the intervention of any supernatural forces? 2) Is the earth thousands of years old or is it billions of years old? 3) Does life begin out of nothing or is it a result of chemical processes? 4) Can one species become another or is there only modification within a species? 5) Did humans evolve from other life forms or do humans represent a unique and separate creation? Some creationists reject evolution outright along with any scientific conclusion that is contrary to their faith. This stance dominated the antievolution movement in the 1920s. Toumey (1994: 6) calls these creationists "apocalyptic separatists." A majority of Fundamentalists would fit within this category. Other creationists, known as "scientific creationists," accept the value and authority of science. For scientific creationists, the conflict between science and creationism is illusory. They claim that the scientific evidence is consistent with a literal reading of Genesis and attempt to show where scientists favoring evolution have made mistakes. Gould (1983: 18) maintains that creationism is any conviction that a higher power had a hand in the origin of the universe, the earth, and, most important, in living beings. He further argues that many evolutionary scientists must therefore consider themselves creationists. In recent years, scientific creationists of varying stripes have upstaged Fundamentalists in battles over the teaching of evolution in the public schools. It is mainly creationists who have captured the bulk of American media and scholarly attention. As Toumey (1992: 6) observes, "The argument that the authority of modern science rests with creationism, not evolution, has convinced numerous Americans, including many who are not Fundamentalist Christians."

Stephen D. Glazier

See also Antimodernism; Creation; Creationism; Liberalism

Bibliography

Eve, Raymond A., and Francis B. Harrold. (1991) *The Creationist Movement in Modern America.* Boston: Twayne Publishers.

———. (1994) "Who Are the Creationists?" *Population Review* 38: 65–76.

Gould, Stephen Jay. (1983) *Hen's Teeth and Horses' Toes: Further Reflection in Natural History.* New York: W. W. Norton.

Harrold, Francis B., and Raymond A. Eve, eds. (1995) *Cult Archaeology and Creationism: Understanding Pseudo-Scientific Beliefs about the Past.* Iowa City: University of Iowa Press.

Hayward, James L. (1998) *The Creation/Evolution Controversy: An Annotated Bibliography.* Lanham, MD: Scarecrow Press.

Larson, Edward J. (1997) *Summer for the Gods: The Scopes Trial and America's Continuing Debate over Science and Religion.* New York: Basic Books.

Moore, James R. (1979) *The Post-Darwinian Controversies: A Study of the Protestant Struggle to Come to Terms with Darwin in Great Britain and America.* New York: Cambridge University Press.

Numbers, Ronald L. (1992) *The Creationists: The Evolution of Scientific Creationism.* New York: Alfred A. Knopf.

———. (1998) *Darwin Comes to America.* Cambridge, MA: Harvard University Press.

Scott, Eugenie C. (1997) "Anti-Evolution and Creationism in the United States." *Annual Review of Anthropology* 26: 263–289.

Toumey, Christopher. (1994) *God's Own Scientists: Creationists in a Secular World.* New Brunswick, NJ: Rutgers University Press.

Webb, George K. (1994) *The Evolution Controversy in America.* Lexington: University of Kentucky Press.

Fall of Humankind

The Fall was the result of the first act of disobedience of Adam and Eve, as described in Genesis 3. Eve, the first woman, was tempted by the serpent, who promised that if she ate the fruit of the "Tree of Knowledge of Good and Evil" at the center of the Garden of Eden, she would become like God. She ate, and encouraged Adam to eat as well. As a result of their disobedience, the first couple was expelled from the Garden, Eve was sentenced to suffer pain during childbirth, and Adam was sentenced to work the earth for food. In addition, the serpent was cursed, and God placed enmity between the serpent and the woman, as well as their "seed" (offspring). God declared that the "seed of the woman" would "crush the serpent's head," while the serpent would "bruise his heel." Even before the development of the New Testament, some saw the Fall as the loss of an original state of immortality, and the serpent identified with Satan. Paul (Romans 5:12–21; 1 Corinthians 15:22) identified the Fall as the source of both death and sin in the world, which Christ, the "second Adam," reversed. Early Christian theologians continued this tradition, also interpreting the "seed of the woman" as Christ, who defeated the power of Satan (death) at the cross. Later Christian theologians, notably Augustine in the fourth century, taught that one of the results of the Fall was sinful nature and depravity, passed on to the descendants of Adam. In addition to eventual physical death, the Fall was seen as bringing spiritual death, or separation from God and eternal punishment. Concepts of inherited sin are not found in Jewish or Islamic interpretations of Genesis.

One vital element of Fundamentalist Christian interpretation of Genesis 3 is historicity of Adam and Eve and the details of the Fall. Interpretations of the early chapters of Genesis that do not emphasize the literal, factual nature of the narrative are seen as in effect denying the reality of original sin and humanity's fallen nature, in addition to rejecting the divine inspiration of the Bible. A small minority of Pentecostal sects, primarily those associated with healing evangelist William Branham (1909–1965), have advocated what they call the "serpent–seed" doctrine, teaching that the seduction of the serpent was a sexual seduction. After sexual intercourse between Eve and Satan, on the same day Adam impregnated Eve, creating twins in her womb from separate fathers, Cain from Satan, and Abel from Adam. Branham taught that he had been sent to preach to the children of Abel, while the children of Cain were predestined for hell. Other groups that could be classified as Fundamentalist advocate distinctive variants of the serpent–seed doctrine. For those affiliated with the white supremacist Christian Identity movement, the descendants of Cain are the Jewish people, while for the African-American sect Nation of Yahweh, the children of Cain are whites. For the Unification Church, the children of Cain are those infected with selfishness, including atheists and communists.

Russ P. Reeves

See also Anti-Semitism; Depravity; Sin and Sinners

Genesis 3:11–24

11. And he said, Who told thee that thou wast naked? Hast thou eaten of the tree, whereof I commanded thee that thou shouldest not eat?

12. And the man said, The woman whom thou gavest to be with me, she gave me of the tree, and I did eat.

13. And the LORD God said unto the woman, What is this that thou hast done? And the woman said, The serpent beguiled me, and I did eat.

14. And the LORD God said unto the serpent, Because thou hast done this, thou art cursed above all cattle, and above every beast of the field; upon thy belly shalt thou go, and dust shalt thou eat all the days of thy life:

15. And I will put enmity between thee and the woman, and between thy seed and her seed; it shall bruise thy head, and thou shalt bruise his heel.

16. Unto the woman he said, I will greatly multiply thy sorrow and thy conception; in sorrow thou shalt bring forth children; and thy desire shall be to thy husband, and he shall rule over thee.

17. And unto Adam he said, Because thou hast hearkened unto the voice of thy wife, and hast eaten of the tree, of which I commanded thee, saying, Thou shalt not eat of it: cursed is the ground for thy sake; in sorrow shalt thou eat of it all the days of thy life;

18. Thorns also and thistles shall it bring forth to thee; and thou shalt eat the herb of the field;

19. In the sweat of thy face shalt thou eat bread, till thou return unto the ground; for out of it wast thou taken: for dust thou art, and unto dust shalt thou return.

20. And Adam called his wife's name Eve; because she was the mother of all living.

21. Unto Adam also and to his wife did the LORD God make coats of skins, and clothed them.

22. And the LORD God said, Behold, the man is become as one of us, to know good and evil: and now, lest he put forth his hand, and take also of the tree of life, and eat, and live for ever:

23. Therefore the LORD God sent him forth from the garden of Eden, to till the ground from whence he was taken.

24. So he drove out the man; and he placed at the east of the garden of Eden Cherubims, and a flaming sword which turned every way, to keep the way of the tree of life.

Bibliography

Chafer, Lewis Sperry. (1947) *Systematic Theology*, vol. 2. Dallas: Dallas Seminary Press.

Williams, Norman Powell. (1927) *The Ideas of the Fall and of Original Sin*. London: Longman, Green, and Co.

False Prophets

In the Hebrew Scriptures, the issue of false prophecy is related to the overarching concern with false gods and idolatry. The main polemic is found in Deuteronomy, which cautions the Israelites not to pay heed to prophets and diviners who entice them to serve other gods, even if the portents they predict come true. This situation is to test God's people; the false prophets will be put to death (Deuteronomy 13:1–5). Deuteronomy 18:20 underscores this issue; yet, in this passage, one may tell a true prophet from a false one when the former's divinations prove correct. Hence, a true prophet both speaks in the true God's name and is validated by subsequent events. Deuteronomy's scenarios for true and false prophethood are fully realized in the contest between the prophet Elijah and the prophets of Baal (1 Kings 18:17–40) and the confrontation between King Ahab and the dissident, but true, prophet Micaiah ben Imlah (1 Kings 22:1–38; see also 1 Kings 13; Jeremiah 14:13–16).

False prophets in the New Testament are associated with both the acceptance of the gospel message

Deuteronomy 13:1–5

1. If there arise among you a prophet, or a dreamer of dreams, and giveth thee a sign or a wonder,

2. And the sign or the wonder come to pass, whereof he spake unto thee, saying, Let us go after other gods, which thou hast not known, and let us serve them;

3. Thou shalt not hearken unto the words of that prophet, or that dreamer of dreams: for the LORD your God proveth you, to know whether ye love the LORD your God with all your heart and with all your soul.

4. Ye shall walk after the LORD your God, and fear him, and keep his commandments, and obey his voice, and ye shall serve him, and cleave unto him.

5. And that prophet, or that dreamer of dreams, shall be put to death; because he hath spoken to turn you away from the LORD your God, which brought you out of the land of Egypt, and redeemed you out of the house of bondage, to thrust thee out of the way which the LORD thy God commanded thee to walk in. So shalt thou put the evil away from the midst of thee.

and the messianic prophecies of the Last Days. Jesus cautions His followers that "false messiahs and false prophets will appear" in His name at the End Times, producing "signs and omens, to lead astray, if possible, the elect" (Mark 13:22, NRSV; cf. Matthew 24:4, 23–26; Luke 21:8). Even those who act in His name may have a deficient personality or intent. "Beware of false prophets, who come to you in sheep's clothing but inwardly are ravenous wolves. You will know them by their fruits," warns Jesus in the Sermon on the Mount (Matthew 7:15–16). These sentiments intensify in the Epistles, where in 1 John false prophets are linked to the spirit of the Antichrist, though here the test of truth is the acceptance or denial of Jesus as the Christ (2:18–27; 4:1–6; cf. 2 Peter 1:16–2:22; Galatians 1:6–12).

Arguably the most famous false prophet in the Bible is the second Beast of Revelation. This beast is a deceiver who "performs great signs" and exercises authority on behalf of the first beast, who makes war against the saints and blasphemes God. This false prophet animates an image of the first beast so that it can "even speak and cause those who would not worship the image of the beast to be killed"; then it marks all participants in the economy with the name or number of the beast (Revelation 13:5–18). These beasts become, in Christian tradition, the archetypal Antichrist and his prophet, both in league with Satan. False spirits come forth from these three to gather the forces of the world against God in the battle of Armageddon (16:13–16). Ultimately, the first beast and the false prophet are thrown into the lake of fire and tormented for eternity, joined by Satan after Christ's thousand-year reign (19:20–20:10). Apocalyptically minded Christians have compared subsequent prophets throughout history against this End-Times scenario in anticipation of the Tribulation and Christ's Second Coming.

Dereck Daschke

See also Beast, The; End Times; Eschatology; Messiah; Second Coming; Tribulation

Bibliography

Aukerman, Dale. (1993) *Reckoning with Apocalypse: Terminal Politics and Christian Hope*. New York: Crossroad.

Lindsey, Hal. (1972) *Satan Is Alive and Well on Planet Earth*. Grand Rapids, MI: Zondervan Publishing.

Strecker, Georg. (1996) *The Johannine Letters*. Minneapolis, MN: Augsburg Fortress.

Wilson, Robert R. (1980) *Prophecy and Society in Ancient Israel*. Philadelphia: Fortress.

Fascism

The term "fascism" refers to a form of secular politics born of the convulsions of modernity whose belief in the nation or race rather than God's Word as the foundation of reality makes it, in theory, the antithesis of Fundamentalism. Yet, in practice a number of fascism's manifestations have exhibited a striking, if ultimately spurious, resemblance to movements and regimes based on Fundamentalist forms of religion. Moreover, some political phenomena in Israel, India, and the contemporary United States demonstrate how the two can become inextricably bound together to a point where a genuine hybrid seems to occur, defying neat categorization. The potential for a superficial affinity and even substantive kinship existing between the two phenomena resides in their shared need to put an end to the radical pluralism of values and lack of faith characteristic of "modern" life in secular, "Westernized" societies and in their conviction that the (perceived) decadence of the contemporary world is destined to give way to a comprehensive rebirth or palingenesis. This is a biblical term (see John 3:7) that derives from the Greek *palin* (again) and *genesis* (birth). Palingenesis has been used to describe religious, biological, and sociopolitical transformations. In times of acute social crises palingenetic myths—which present the contemporary period of (perceived) decay and disintegration as about to give way to a new era, a new order, and a new man—naturally can come to exert considerable appeal once modernization is felt to be eroding the (imagined) homogeneity of many "traditional" religious and national communities. Paradoxically, the origins of both fascism and Fundamentalism in intransigent resistance to the decay of "traditional" communities bound together by unquestioned beliefs and certainties makes them both manifestations of the modernity against which they rebel.

Parallels and Distinctions between Fascism and Fundamentalism

The relationship of fascism to Fundamentalism is likely to remain a highly contentious subject because of the inability of experts in the social sciences to arrive at a consensus about the precise meaning of either term. Certainly protagonists of movements would nowadays tend to dissociate themselves from both terms because they have both acquired deeply pejorative connotations of fanaticism, hatred, and violence in common usage. While some scholars see fascism driven by a barbarian or pathological will to power, which denies it any substantive ideology or coherent worldview, others see it as primarily a revolt against socialism, the Enlightenment, or modernity itself. Others still have treated fascism, alongside communism, as a modern, secularized form of millennialism and hence a "political religion" in the full sense of the word—an approach that

makes it impossible to draw neat distinctions between religion and any sort of overtly utopian form of revolutionary extremism.

Any writings such as this therefore have recourse to artificially discrete and tidy definitions of the key words (known as "ideal types") to delimit their meaning. The premise of the following analysis is that, in line with the findings of much recent scholarship, fascism is best seen (for analytical or heuristic purposes) as a revolutionary variant of modern nationalism at the heart of whose ideology, policies, tactics, and actions lies a vision of national rebirth in a postliberal new order. This is a process in which, guided by a visionary elite, the historical nation-state or the core ethnic group (*ethnie*) that forms it finally overcomes the forces of decadence and disintegration that have threatened to extinguish it and becomes a rejuvenated, harmonious "community of destiny." True to the spirit of "modern" nationalism, which demonstrated its mobilizing power so spectacularly in the French Revolution and World War I, fascists imagine their "nation" to be forged by unique historical and cultural factors, and to exist in its own right within its own historical and physical space, that is, its homeland.

In contrast to liberal nationalism, however, the "people" is for fascists an organic entity that has fallen into a state of spiritual decadence and collective amnesia. Their task is to "awaken" it so that it becomes aware once more of the greatness of its pioneering mission within human history. This means purging it spiritually (and in the case of Nazism even eugenically) of degeneracy so as to forge it into a new type of society and create a "new man" (*homo fascistus*), using the inspiration of a glorious past to create an alternative form of modern state based on the regenerated national community. The fascist ideological basis for the "new order" is not sacred texts or even a single theoretical source, but a highly eclectic and overtly man-made synthesis of ideas that may be both modern and traditional, secular and religious, adapted to the unique historical situation in which each nation finds itself.

Fundamentalism also takes the form of a crusade against decadence. It too wants to awaken the people, to remind them of the true destiny from which they have strayed, to show them where they belong. However, at least in orthodox religious contexts, Fundamentalists conceive the "people" as a community of believers created by a divine force for a metaphysical mission that is not necessarily bound up with exclusive claims to a particular territory. Its historicity is thus inseparable from a suprahistorical reality, and its role within the divine cosmos is invisible to nonbelievers. This means that fascists and Fundamentalists approach issues concerning their "chosen" people with a radically different perspective on time. Though the fascist invests the life of the nation with a mythic significance that transcends personal, profane time and hence bestows onto national heroes a form of eternity, the suprapersonal realm that it occupies is bound by the life span of the nation within historical time. It is what one expert on fascism has called "an indeterminate secular otherworld, 'immortal' yet of this world" (Schnapp 1992: 30). For the Fundamentalist the nation cannot be the supreme or ultimate reality, since historical time itself is transcended by an infinite reality inhabited by a supreme being or "timeless" absolute whose will is being actualized or whose "eternal" cosmic laws are being lived out in and through the nation, no matter how oblivious it has become of its true, sacred identity and mission within secular time. A lucid glimpse into the abyss which yawns between the fascist and religious concept of a suprapersonal reality and the redemption it promises once prompted Adolf Hitler to declare: "To the Christian doctrine of the infinite significance of the individual soul . . . I oppose with icy clarity the saving doctrine of the nothingness and insignificance of the individual human being, and of his continued existence in the visible immortality of the nation." (Rauschning1940: 225.)

The extreme resentment (and sometimes violence) with which Fundamentalism resists and combats the modern world is thus not revolutionary, but reactionary and conservative. It attempts to reestablish what it conceives to be the religion's true traditional or orthodox religious values based on divine revelation, whether in the form of sacred texts or the pronouncements of a visionary religious leader on whom God has bestowed charisma in the original Greek sense of "divine grace." This contrasts glaringly with fascism, which, no matter how much its ideologues use and abuse religious discourse, rejects Scripture and holy men as a primary source of understanding and legitimation. It thus chooses its leaders not from the clergy but from secular individuals endowed with charismatic authority of a strictly secular kind who seek to foment passions that well up not from pious fervor, but from a heightened sense of cultural and national identity. Unlike Islamic militants such as the Lebanese and Iranian Hizbollah or the Taleban in Afghanistan, fascism seeks to inaugurate, not a theocracy in which power over the secular plane of reality is wrested from "man" and returned to God, but an ethnocracy in which the "people" is returned to itself. The salvation it achieves is thus of a terrestrial, human kind. Its martyrs are great military leaders and anonymous war heroes, not prophets and saints.

Interwar Conflations of Fascism and Established Christianity

The distinctions being drawn here between fascism and Fundamentalism hopefully become clearer when applied to a synoptic view of interwar fascism. In the wake of World War I, which demonstrated the awesome destructive power of nationalism as a mobilizing myth, fascism naturally tended to take the form of ritual, charismatic politics wherever it gained critical mass as a populist force. Hence, the two fascist movements that conquered power, Fascism in Italy and Nazism in Germany, made a systematic attempt to use this type of politics to sacralize the state and turn nationalism into a "civic religion" based on a revival of Roman and Aryan virtues, respectively.

Those who assume that Christians should be immunized by their faith against being duped by the secular travesties of religion manifested in leader cults and the worship of the race might see in the refusal of Jehovah Witnesses to bow to the authority of Nazism and their terrible persecution under the Third Reich a manifestation of the ideal relationship that should exist between Christianity and fascism. In practice, however, the courageous stands taken by the Protestant theologian Dietrich Bonhoeffer or the Catholic Archbishop von Galen against the Third Reich were very much the exception and there was no mass resistance to fascism on theological grounds in interwar Europe. This fact raises extremely complex issues both in the history of Christianity and the secularization of the West, as well as in the nature of religion and human psychology. Perhaps one factor in explaining the failure of a purportedly Christian Europe to "stop fascism" was the human propensity for what George Orwell's *1984* (originally published in 1949) termed "double-think," namely, "the power of holding two contradictory beliefs in one's mind simultaneously, and accepting both of them." Another was the Christian Churches' long tradition of legitimizing the ambitions of the secular state and the nationalist or imperialist ambitions of its leaders, thereby giving its blessing to innumerable human atrocities committed in the name of Christ down the centuries.

However, any neat (ideal-typical) distinctions between fascism and orthodox Christianity—and hence by extension with Fundamentalism as a form of ultraorthodox or heterodox religion—that exist on paper are blurred even further by the fact that fascism is a chameleonic ideology that survives by tailoring its ideology of national rebirth to the culture and history of the "nation" it seeks to regenerate. It thus has no scruples about combining incongruous elements, the modern with the antimodern, the secular with the religious—a process known as "syncretism. Such syncretism is anathema to orthodox forms of established religion, and especially to Fundamentalism, which is driven by the urge to keep faith pristine and uncontaminated by extraneous elements. As a result, the relationship of fascism with established Christianity between the two world wars varied enormously from country to country. As a rule, wherever society was extensively secularized fascism reflected this, just as its degree of anti-Semitism or the extent of its imperialistic ambitions were conditioned by how deeply these sentiments were already entrenched in popular culture. Thus, the British Union of Fascists, apart from some maverick English clergymen, generally ignored Christianity altogether, while Nazism "at the top" was religious only in a deeply pagan and anti-Christian sense, even if for pragmatic reasons it postponed suppressing the Churches. This was so as not to alienate the many millions of "ordinary" Germans who managed with varying degrees of torment or complacency to reconcile their Christian beliefs with a fervent commitment to the racial revolution instituted by the Nazis. There was even an energetic faction of deeply anti-Semitic nationalists within the Evangelical Church called "German Christians." After Hitler's election as chancellor, these nationalists sought to Nazify the Lutheran Church from within, but by the end of 1934 had been neutralized by a counterattack from more resolutely orthodox Lutherans who formed a Confessional Church (which nevertheless colluded extensively with the Third Reich).

In Italy, Fascism started out as anticlerical and republican, but the Lateran Pacts of 1929 reconciling the Vatican with the Italian Kingdom and the Fascist State was a landmark in the insidious process by which Mussolini's regime legitimated and normalized itself. In practice this meant that millions of con-

ventionally devout Italians mastered this ability so well that the glaring theological contradictions between Christian and Fascist faith were fudged. When members of the Catholic clergy became enthusiastic devotees of Mussolini, it produced what historians have called "'clerical Fascism," which anticipated the modern hybridization of Fundamentalism and racist politics.

If ideal-typical boundaries between fascism and established religion become fuzzy in the case of German Christians and "clerical Fascists," there are several cases where the conflation of fascism with politics is even greater. In contrast to Britain, Germany, and even Italy, much of Spain had only traveled a short distance down the road of modernization, and a myth of pagan ancestry equivalent to that provided by an Aryan or Roman past was thus precluded to the Falange. It thus had recourse to the vision of a "'new Catholicity," which, though a phrase evocative of religious Fundamentalism, proves on closer inspection to be quite the opposite. Catholicism was for Falangists to be gutted of its devotional, transcendental, Christ-centered core and used purely instrumentally for its mythic power as a signifier of Spain's glorious imperial past in the "golden" sixteenth century. Moreover, it betokened a spiritual "faith" that, being antirational, anti-individualist, and antimaterialist, made it the archenemy of liberalism, Marxism, and democracy. The same is true of other interwar forms of fascism where ingredients of the nation's established religion were blended into a syncretic myth of national palingenesis, such as the Belgian Rex (Catholicism), the South African Ossewabrandwag (Dutch Reformed Christianity), and the Finnish Lapua Movement (Lutheranism).

The incorporation of established religion into fascism in the interwar period perhaps reached it ultimate conclusion in the ideology of the Iron Guard. The importance of the Orthodox Church to Romanian history and identity led its leader Corneliu Codreanu (who cut his ideological teeth in ultranationalist rather than Christian milieux) to assert that the whole Romanian people, past, present, and future was destined to be resurrected collectively on Judgment Day. This prophesy forms no part of orthodox Christian thinking and is not sanctioned by any heterodox biblical tradition indigenous to Romania. Rather, Codreanu was perverting a long-standing Christian apocalyptic tradition concerned with the fate of the elect in the "Last Days" to give mythic power and legitimation to his secular nationalist vision of rebirth and the destruction of its alleged enemies, principally Jews and communists. Hence, even though the elite of his movement called themselves the "Legionaries of the Archangel Michael," they fought not to restore the purity of the Christian faith, but of the Romanian people.

The Iron Guard can be seen as the precursors of a number of postwar ultranationalists for whom religion is reduced to a signifier of nationhood and a myth disseminated in order to mobilize racial hatreds. Some of them perpetuate the fascist call for national palingenesis, such as Pamyat in Russia (which uses the Russian Orthodox Church as a discriminator of "Russianness"), or the Afrikaner Werstandsbeweging (AWB) in South Africa which, having given up attempts to sabotage the dismantling of the apartheid system in the 1990s, is now seeking to create a separatist white homeland in the new South Africa. The AWB's symbol consists of three sevens representing the biblical cypher for the divine Truth, which is destined to overcome the forces of the Antichrist, whose apocalyptic number is 666. Yet they are set out in such a way as to deliberately evoke the Nazi swastika, thus epitomizing fascism's capacity to appropriate religion when it suits its cause. Meanwhile, ultranationalists in Northern Ireland and the Balkans routinely assert their religious identity in order to pursue their separatist or irredentist claims, just as the Croatian and "Catholic" Ustasha did in interwar Yugoslavia. They thereby perpetuate a millennial Christian tradition of riding slipshod over Christ's supranational message of love and forgiveness in order to legitimate territorial conquest and the destruction of enemies.

The Postwar Hybridization of Fascism and Fundamentalism

Though most candidates for genuinely fundamentalist forms of fascism fail the test when purist (ideal-typical) definitional criteria are applied, the modern era has produced several forms of politics in which a fundamentalist form of religion has apparently undergone such an intense process of secularization in upholding nationalist or racist claims within historical time, and the suprahistorical realm of eternity has receded so far from the concerns of the believers, that a genuine hybrid seems to have resulted. According to some experts, Fundamentalism cannot by definition accommodate alien "secular" elements to form hybrids. However, it is characteristic of the

modern age, which can be seen as a vast experimental laboratory for the modification, transformation, and creation of ideologies, that the hybridization of ideologies that are theoretically irreconcilably opposed to each other has become a relatively common phenomenon. Like living entities ideologies are constantly mutating and adapting to the prevailing cultural habitat and sociopolitical space in which they operate. In the late nineteenth century, revolutionary Marxism developed reformist varieties, and more recently even fascism has produced a successful democratic version of itself in Italy's National Alliance. In the same way, monarchy, once a divine institution, has become secular and constitutional, while commercialized, "commodified" variants of Eastern mysticism and religious sects have become commonplace.

One ideal habitat for the hybridization of fascism and Fundamentalism is Israel, a secular state with both biblical and historical claims to be the legitimate homeland of the Jews. In this country, communities of highly orthodox Hasidic Jews coexist with secularized "liberal" ones in an intrinsically fragile political situation saturated with ultranationalist energies. Such energies are a natural consequence of the Nazi attempt to commit genocide against all Jews under the cover of World War II, the violent birth pangs of the State's creation in 1948, and the continued hostility of surrounding Arab nations, especially the millions of displaced Palestinians, to Israel's very existence. In such a cauldron of supercharged mythic forces it is inevitable that some (highly marginalized) variants of ideology have arisen at the heart of the ultraorthodox "religious Right" (notably Kahanism) in which religious and political energies are synthesized in the demand for a rebirth that is simultaneously of Judaism as the religion of the Jewish people and of Israel as its homeland, rescued from the decadence of liberalism, socialism, and materialism.

In contemporary India a fascistized form of Fundamentalism for a time has exerted considerable impact on mainstream politics. The Bharatiya Janata Party (BJP) was formed in 1980 as the political expression of Hindutva, a form of Hindu Fundamentalism. Rejecting the principle of religious pluralism within a secular state that was the cornerstone of postcolonial India under Nehru, the BJP sees Hinduism as the spiritual essence of an organic national community and the inspiration of its rebirth in a new just order based on the precepts of the God Rama. As one of the party ideologues puts it, "Hindutva awakened the Hindus to the new world order where nations represented the aspirations of people united in history, culture, philosophy, and heroes" (Meghani 2000: 1). At the time of sectarian violence over the rebuilding of the Ayodhya temple in the early 1990s, BJP activists called for a national "awakening" (Jagriti). Some of its militants denounced Muslims as enemies of "true" Indians in terms deeply reminiscent of Nazi propaganda campaigns against Jews. Meanwhile, its more radical leaders promised its followers rebirth from India's political, economic, social, and moral decadence. This rebirth would come after a purging storm of violence against the Muslims who were undermining the cohesion of Indian society. Since the BJP formed a government in 1997 its policies for India's Hinduization have been extensively moderated. India's democratic parliamentary system has been retained and the ruthless cultural and ethnic cleansing called for by its radicals when out of power has not taken place. However, the program to turn India into a nuclear power capable of annihilating (Islamic) Pakistan is consistent with a form of religious politics in which Fundamentalism at one point acquired a fascist complexion.

Yet it is the United States, whose birth as a nation was deeply bound up for many Americans with millennial Christian hopes of a New Jerusalem, and where Fundamentalist and revivalist variants of Christianity—some highly heterodox—continue to play such a crucial role both sociologically and mythically in some of its political subcultures. This provides the most propitious conditions for a symbiosis of Fundamentalist values with fascist forms of nationalism. Not only does the United States host countless varieties of nonconformist creeds, cults, sects, and new religions that it has already brought forth, but the formation of the Ku Klux Klan (KKK) in the aftermath of the American Civil War opened up a permanent political space for modern fusions of religion and politics. Yet as long as the bulk of the United States' population continued to believe that they were living in the dominant nation of the "New World" and that its rise to ever greater power and hegemony over the rapidly declining "Old World" would continue indefinitely, the structural basis for a mass movement of palingenetic ultranationalism promising to rescue America from decline did not exist. Even the Depression of the 1930s did not destroy this myth, marginalizing all attempts to emulate Fascist Italy or Nazi Germany.

However, in the postwar era the American Dream started to give way to the (equally mythic) nightmare scenario that the nation's strength as an economic, political, and military superpower was ebbing away, that the "melting pot" principle of ethnic assimilation and equality of civil rights was generating conditions of racial civil war, and that the "Caucasian" whites were rapidly becoming politically impotent outcasts in "their own" country. At this point a political and social climate formed which encouraged the appearance of movements based not on restoring Christianity or America to its former purity, but on the need for a cleansing hurricane of violence from which a new America would emerge— a vision that admitted both Fundamentalist and fascist interpretations.

This peculiar conjuncture of historical factors has led to the proliferation in the contemporary United States of scattered religious sects, many of them with minuscule memberships, in whose creed white supremacy rather than Christian worship plays a central role. As a result, however far removed from secular brands of nationalism in principle, they now operate de facto as indigenous sources of organized racial hatred and violence on a par with fascist groups and "groupuscules" (numerically minute groupings whose strength derives from the extensive network of kindred spirits that they help form). Indeed, the boundaries between the religious Right and neo-fascism have become increasingly fuzzy over the last two decades. This merging is due to their shared belief in the need for a national and international insurrection against the evils of racial and cultural mixing, the Zionist Occupation Government (ZOG), and the New World Order embodied in the United Nations, combined with the extensive linkages between many racist groups fostered by the Internet. A notable example of this symbiosis is provided by the KKK. Though originally a reactionary mass movement of white Protestant resistance to the emancipation of the blacks and (in the 1920s) to mass immigration from Europe, by the 1970s it had undergone a steep decline in membership and fragmented into scores of small and often competing regional cells. Since then it has forged links with racist skinheads and pagan neo-Nazi groups, a development that led to the joint staging of elaborate Aryan "Fests" in which cross-burnings take place amidst swastikas, and to Klan websites merchandising Nazi insignia.

It is against this background that a remarkable process of hybridization has taken place between fascism and a cluster of highly heterodox and deeply divided permutations of Christianity known collectively as Christian Identity (CI), all ultimately derived from a wayward nineteenth-century form of biblical exegesis known as British Israelism. This identified the ten tribes of Israel who did not return to the Holy Land in the eighth century BCE with European peoples, and hence was originally far from anti-Semitic. However, during the period of mass immigration to North America after World War I it was transformed into an outlandish rationalization of belief in the innate superiority of the "Aryans." Its distinctive feature is the "two seeds" doctrine which maintains that, while whites are descended from Abel, Jews are the offspring of Satan's intercourse with Eve. Whether CI can legitimately be called "Fundamentalist" depends entirely on the definition applied. The term can be restricted to movements that base themselves on a return to the "fundamental doctrine" from which a religion has grown, and which are therefore "ultraorthodox" in a way sanctioned by the interpretations of Scripture of a religious caste, clergy, or priesthood. This could be taken to exclude CI, which is in Protestant terms anything but orthodox in its highly selective readings and racist exegesis of biblical texts (see Barkun 2000: 80–83). However, it is extremely difficult in practice to define "orthodoxy" in any of the world's major religious traditions, especially in the case of post-Reformation Christianity, and particularly in the nonconformist United States. If definitions instead emphasize Fundamentalism's emphasis on the translation of a religion into a militant, fanatical form of political and social program based on a literal interpretation of key texts that are sacred to it, then CI sects fit the description more closely.

In the last decades of the twentieth century the ideology of CI groups such as The Covenant, Sword, and Arm of the Lord, The Church of Israel, Aryan Nations, Children of Yahweh, the Christian Defense League, and Kingdom Identity Ministries, blended into their distinctive amalgams of biblical, apocalyptic, historical, anti-Semitic, racist, and conspiratorial theories. The ingredients of these theories were taken from New Age cults, survivalism, and the Patriots' movement, as well as from neo-Nazi variants of white supremacism. As a result, the CI's calls for a crusade against America's contemporary ethnic mixing and moral decadence, whatever their roots in millennialism, now represent de facto highly syncretic permutations of palingenetic ultranationalism, that is, fascism (which could be dubbed "millenary-anism"!) perfectly adapted to the peculiarities of the United States's thriving racist and nonconformist subcultures. This explains why CI ideas have percolated into the ideologies of American neo-Nazis and skinheads who in Europe would identify with exclusively secular or pagan forms of racism. It is no coincidence, therefore, that one of the United States's most notorious right-wing terrorist groups of the postwar era, the Order (otherwise known as the Silent Brotherhood, or Holy Order of Aryan Warriors), brought together militant racists from CI, Odinist (neopagan), and conventional neo-Nazi backgrounds. Though traditional fascist studies have tended to ignore the ease with which nonconformist religion can combine with fascism in the racist subcultures in which CI groups have taken root, this has enabled the United States, which played a negligible role in interwar fascism, to make a major contribution to the revision of contemporary fascism away from slavish imitation of its interwar role models, Fascism and Nazism.

Nor should the hybridization of heterodox religious Fundamentalism with elements of fascist racism in the United States be thought of as exclusive to white supremacism. The America of the 1930s saw the emergence of an (in orthodox terms) equally aberrant form of Islam based on belief in a Lost Nation of Asia of African descent, practically a mirror image of the British Israel "Christian" foundation myth. The resulting movement, The Nation of Islam, went on to gain a high public profile in the 1950s and 1960s when Malcom X (assassinated in 1965) was its national spokesman. Under the subsequent leadership of Louis Farrakhan, The Nation proved its ability to stage a mass demonstration of ethnic solidarity on a scale of which white supremacists can only dream when hundreds of thousands participated in the Million Man March of 1995.

The BJP also illustrates the latent capacity of most organized religions to fundamentalize, politicize, and fascistize themselves when the forces of secularization create the right historical conditions in a traditional non-Western culture. For the time being, however, it is the peculiar sociological, cultural, and mythic habitat created within both black and white enclaves of socially marginalized North Americans that looks likely to produce the most vigorous and viable hybrids of the religious and political energies discussed here. Nor are the new hybrids once engendered, white or black, confined to America. Thanks to the web, Nazified Christian Fundamentalism is now effectively a dialect of "cyberfascism" readily downloadable to inspire the formation and activities of groupuscules wherever religiously inclined whites succumb to the temptation of diagnosing the state of the world in terms of decadence and palingenesis. This has created the basis for the emergence of a Euro-American radical Right, which was unthinkable in the days when Fascism and Nazism were at the peak of their power. Meanwhile, the Nation of Islam's peculiar blend of religion and politics, especially its use of Islam as a signifier of a nonwhite identity, has found receptive ears in black communities in the Caribbean, Asia, and sub-Saharan Africa.

In an age dominated by increasing globalization, materialism, multiculturalism, economic dysfunctions, and ecological crises, the attraction exerted on small, highly marginalized groups within the spiritually homeless and materially dispossessed in Westernized countries by combinations of fascism and racism with occultism, paganism, apocalyptic Christianity, or radical Islam is liable to grow rather than wane. Nor should the dangers of collaboration between groups that on paper remain deeply divided ideologically be underestimated. White and black supremacists certainly have more respect for each other than for "race traitors," as a letter from the Grand Dragon of the Knights of the KKK to Minister Louis Farrakhan, leader of the Nation of Islam, graphically illustrates (Kaplan 2000: 555–556). Indeed, racists are increasingly prone to bury the many differences that their convictions should logically create for the sake of their common crusade against multiculturalism, miscegenation, and mindless materialism. In this context, the plea for a racial ecumenicalism made in an open letter written by imprisoned Order member Gary Lee Yarbrough in 1983 acquires a special resonance: "Whether you are National Socialist, Klan, Odinist, Christian Identity, Skinhead, Creator, or any other cult, creed, faith, or persuasion of our cause does not matter.... Our faith is our Race, and our Race is our faith!!!" (Kaplan 2000: 531)

Roger Griffin

See also Communism; Hinduism, Fundamental; Ku Klux Klan; Nationalism; World War II

Bibliography

Akenson, Donald Harman. (1992) *God's Peoples: Covenant and Land in South Africa, Israel, and Ulster.* Ithaca, NY and London: Cornell University Press.

Barkun, Michael. (1997) *Religion and the Racist Right: The Origins of Christian Identity Movement.* Chapel Hill and London: University of North Carolina Press.

———. (2000) "Christian Identity." In *The Encyclopedia of Millennialism and Millennial Movements*, edited by Richard Landes. New York: Routledge.

Bharatiya Janata Party. http://www.bjp.org.

Christian Research Institute. http://www.hearnow.org/id.htm.

Conkin, Paul. (1997) *American Originals: Homemade varieties of Christianity.* Chapel Hill: University of North Carolina Press.

Gentile, Emilio. (1996) *The Sacralization of Politics in Fascist Italy.* Cambridge, MA: Harvard University Press.

Griffin, Roger. (1995) *Fascism.* Oxford: Oxford University Press.

———. (March 1998) "'I am no longer human. I am a Titan. A god!' The Fascist Quest to Regenerate Time." Electronic Seminars in History. http://www.ihr.sas.ac.ua/ihr/esh/quest.html.

Kaplan, Jeffrey. (1997) *Radical Religion in America. Millenarian Movements from the Far Right to the Children of Noah.* Syracuse, NY: Syracuse University Press.

———, and Leonard Weinberg. (1998) *The Emergence of a Euro-American Radical Right.* New Brunswick, NJ: Rutgers University Press.

———. (2000) *Encyclopedia of White Power.* New York and Oxford: AltaMira.

Laqueur, Walter. (1996) *Fascism. Past, Present, Future.* Oxford: Oxford University Press.

Meghani, Megir. (2000) "Hindutva: The Great Nationalist Ideology." http://www.bjp.org/philo.htm

Nation of Islam. http://www.finalcall.com.

Ontario Consultants on Religious Tolerance. http://www.religioustolerance.org/cr_ident.htm.

Orwell, George. ([1949] 1987) *1984.* London: Penguin Books.

Rauschning, Hermann. (1945) *The Voice of Destruction.* New York, G.P. Putnam's Sons.

Schnapp, Jeffrey. (1992) "Epic Demonstrations." In *Fascism, Aesthetics, and Culture*, edited by R. J. Golsan. Hanover, NH: University Press of New England.

Turner, Richard Brent. (1997) *Islam in the African-American Experience.* Bloomington: Indiana University Press.

Final Judgment

In Fundamentalist religions, "Final Judgment" refers to a moment, typically after or on the cusp of the end of time, in which a divine being judges the sinfulness of humanity. Most closely associated with Christianity and Islam, the Final Judgment is not unknown in Asia and Native American religions. In an ancient Indian text, the late Vedic *Taittirîya Âranyaka*, it is said that a king named Yama will divide those who have spoken truthfully and those who have lied at some appointed time in the future. This same king seems to appear in later Chinese texts as Yen-lo or Yen-lo Wang. With nine other Chinese kings, he will be the administrator of the punishments in hell. At a fixed time, their impartial judgment will be final. In Japanese Buddhism, King Yama or Yen-lo is known as Enma-ô. In a similar fashion, the oral traditions of the Native-American Hopi people tell of a "Day of Purification." On this day, great divine helpers will attempt to save the world from a coming period of terrible evils. If enough people remain true of heart, the helpers will succeed, the world will be preserved, and a new age of peace and prosperity will come. However, if they do not, the majority of the world and its peoples will be destroyed. Although these and a few other examples of non-Judaic beliefs about a final judgment do exist, it is in Islam and Christianity where the influence of a somewhat obscure ancient Judaic concept of Final Judgment flowers into a powerful force of belief.

Judaism

A few ancient Judaic texts refer to a Final Judgment of God. The seventh chapter of the Book of Daniel describes a scene in which a divine force judges the human kingdoms. In the fiftieth chapter of the *Apocalypse of Enoch*, there is an explicit description of a righteous god standing in judgment of humans. The sinners will be punished. Chapter 51 goes on to relate that the dead shall be resurrected and judged by the chosen one of God. In chapter 7 of *Esdras*, God sitting in this moment of judgment is also mentioned. Although this tradition was most likely very influential in the later development of the idea of Final Judgment in Islam and Christianity, it does not figure prominently in Jewish traditions except in very specific messianic Jewish sects that are themselves heavily influenced by Islam and Christianity.

Islam

In Islamic traditions, the relationship between individual human acts and a final judgment is most clear. In the Qur'an, "just balances" will be set up and every wrong an individual has committed will be brought out to be weighed (21:49). This will occur after the Day of Resurrection, which is associated with the Final Judgment of all mankind at the end of time, called *yawm al-dîn*. This day will be one of great catastrophes throughout the world and "no soul will be able to help another, for the decision belongs to God" (82:19). Before the end of time, all individual human actions are being irrefutably documented in divine books. Those books will then be produced during the Final Judgment. Each person must then review their lives as recorded in the books and each will be commanded: "Read your book! Today you are yourself a reckoner against yourself!" (17:13) In the case of Islam, those who are judged worthy will be allowed into an afterlife of paradise beginning after the end of time on the Day of Resurrection. Those who are judged unworthy will be thrown into hell.

Christianity

Although less clearly defined than in Islam, the concept of a Final Judgment is equally important in Christian traditions. In chapter 25 of the Gospel of Matthew, Jesus tells the parable of the Last Judgment: the "Son of Man" is to sit on His earthly throne at the end of time. "And before him shall be gathered all nations: and he shall separate them one from another, as a shepherd divideth *his* sheep from the goats"(Matthew 25:32, KJV). Those who have acted out of love for their neighbors will receive eternal life, and those who have not will be sent into eternal punishment. Although this description is only found in the Gospel of Matthew, it does appear to be referred to in other biblical texts. Acts 17:31 states, "Because he hath appointed a day, on which he will judge the world...." In Acts 10:42, Christ "is he which was ordained of God *to be* the Judge of quick and dead." In 2 Corinthians 5:10 and Romans 14:10, it states that we must all appear before God's judgment. In this way, though less directly than in Islam, the Final Judgment is associated with the *parousia* or the Second Coming of Christ. There is, however, in the Christian tradition, some confusion about whether the judgment of individuals occurs

Matthew 25:31–46

31. When the Son of man shall come in his glory, and all the holy angels with him, then shall he sit upon the throne of his glory:

32. And before him shall be gathered all nations: and he shall separate them one from another, as a shepherd divideth his sheep from the goats:

33. And he shall set the sheep on his right hand, but the goats on the left.

34. Then shall the King say unto them on his right hand, Come, ye blessed of my Father, inherit the kingdom prepared for you from the foundation of the world:

35. For I was an hungred, and ye gave me meat: I was thirsty, and ye gave me drink: I was a stranger, and ye took me in:

36. Naked, and ye clothed me: I was sick, and ye visited me: I was in prison, and ye came unto me.

37. Then shall the righteous answer him, saying, Lord, when saw we thee an hungred, and fed thee? or thirsty, and gave thee drink?

38. When saw we thee a stranger, and took thee in? or naked, and clothed thee?

39. Or when saw we thee sick, or in prison, and came unto thee?

40. And the King shall answer and say unto them, Verily I say unto you, Inasmuch as ye have done it unto one of the least of these my brethren, ye have done it unto me.

41. Then shall he say also unto them on the left hand, Depart from me, ye cursed, into everlasting fire, prepared for the devil and his angels:

42. For I was an hungred, and ye gave me no meat: I was thirsty, and ye gave me no drink:

43. I was a stranger, and ye took me not in: naked, and ye clothed me not: sick, and in prison, and ye visited me not.

44. Then shall they also answer him, saying, Lord, when saw we thee an hungred, or athirst, or a stranger, or naked, or sick, or in prison, and did not minister unto thee?

45. Then shall he answer them, saying, Verily I say unto you, Inasmuch as ye did it not to one of the least of these, ye did it not to me.

46. And these shall go away into everlasting punishment: but the righteous into life eternal.

simultaneous to the Final Judgment or if it occurs at the time of each individual's death.

In Fundamentalist Christianity, typically a distinction is made between the Final Judgment of God on the world in general and the particular judgment of each individual that would occur at the time of death when the soul separates from the body. Especially associated with Catholicism, the idea of a particular judgment holds that, at the time of death, the soul either enters a beatific vision, if the soul is judged good, purgatory if the soul is judged to be redeemable, or hell if the soul is judged to be beyond redemption. Then, during the Final Judgment, the souls in purgatory are moved either to the final position of eternal life with God or condemned to forever be separated from God.

This confusion between the particular judgments and the Final Judgment derives from very different descriptions of judgment in the Gospel of Matthew versus that in the Gospel of John. The description of the Final Judgment and Resurrection in the Gospel of Matthew is very similar to that in Islam and is thought to be based in Judaic thought. In the Gospel of John, however, we find something much more like a particular individual judgment. Though God the Father "has committed all judgment unto the Son" (5:22), one who believes and follows the Son "has everlasting life, and shall not come into condemnation; but is passed from death unto life" (5:24). From this Gospel, it would seem that one's belief or disbelief in the teachings of Jesus during life result in an immediate decision by Christ about one's worthiness to pass on into eternal life or be condemned to hell. Although unclear, various sects of Christianity have dealt with these difficult passages in different ways.

Conclusion

While the idea of a great Final Judgment is most closely associated with Islam and Christianity, it does appear in some completely distinct religious traditions. The basis for both the Islamic and Christian visions of a Final Judgment is most likely rooted in an older Judaic tradition, which is closely intertwined with conceptions of systems of law in relation to sin, guilt, and individual responsibility. In Islam, this is most clear with its very distinct vision of a Final Judgment of individuals at the end of time in which irrefutable evidence from each person's life is read from a divine book. However, in the Christian traditions some blurring occurs between a Final Judgment at the end of time that is much like that of Islam and particular judgments of each individual at the end of his or her life. In Catholic thought, the particular judgment is emphasized over the Final Judgment. In most cases of Fundamentalism, however, the powerful image of a Final Judgment of the world combined with the end of time and the judgment of both the living and dead individuals has become a primary focus of belief.

Robert Glenn Howard

See also Apocalypse; Armageddon; End Times; Hell, Heaven, and Purgatory; Sin and Sinners

Bibliography

Brandon, Ernest Alfred Wallis. (1967) *The Judgement of the Dead: The Idea of Life after Death in the Major Religions.* New York: C. Scribner's and Sons.

Cavallin, Hans Clemens Caesarius. (1974) *Life after Death: Paul's Argument for the Resurrection of the Dead in I Cor.* Lund, Sweden: Gleerup.

Charles, Robert Henry ([1912] 1964) *The Book of Enoch.* Mokelumne Hill, CA: Health Research.

Churn, Law. (1998) *Heaven and Hell in Buddhist Perspective.* Delhi: Pilgrims Book.

Keith, Arthur Berriedale. (1990) *Indian Mythology.* New Delhi: Mittal.

Nagel, Tilman. (2000) *The History of Islamic Theology from Muhammad to the Present,* translated from the German by Thomas Thornton. Princeton, NJ: Markus Wiener Publishers.

Newport, Kenneth G. C. (2000) *Apocalypse and Millennium: Studies in Biblical Exegesis.* Cambridge: Cambridge University Press.

Robinson, John A. T. (1957) *Jesus and His Coming: The Emergence of a Doctrine.* New York: Abington Press.

Waters, Frank. (1963) *Book of the Hopi,* drawings and source material recorded by Oswald White Bear Fredericks. New York, NY: Viking Press.

Free Methodist Church

The Free Methodist Church is the result of the convergence of three forces upon the Methodist Episcopal Church (now a constituent part of the United Methodist Church) in the mid-twentieth century. First, a new Holiness movement began to emerge in the church, emphasizing the need for believers to seek sanctification—a second experience of the believer with God analogous to the experience of repentance and faith that brought them into the faith. It was claimed that the experience of sanctification would empower the believer, remove the taint of original sin, and make the person perfect in love. Second, the church had already been divided by the slavery controversy that had originally led many proslavery people into the Methodist Episcopal Church, South. During the 1850s, however, strong debates over slavery continued in the Methodist Episcopal Church between the majority group who were opposed to slavery but favored a gradual ending to the practice and the abolitionists who demanded an immediate end to human bondage. Third, the Methodist Episcopal Church was in the process of change. It began to tolerate membership in secret societies, the selling/renting of church pews, and the use of choirs. Within the Genesee Conference (western New York State), a group emerged who championed the cause of entire sanctification, abolition, and less tolerance toward such practices as the selling of church pews to privileged members. In 1858, the leader of this movement, Rev. Benjamin Titus Roberts (1823–1893) was expelled from the Genesee Conference (thus losing his ministerial appointment). Other ministers and laypersons who shared his opinions were also asked to leave.

Roberts appealed his situation to the 1860 General Conference, but when it failed to accept his appeal, he and his followers organized the Free Methodist Church. The "free" in the name implied an assertion of freedom from bought or rented pews, ecclesiastical domination, and sin. The church adopted the doctrinal statement of the Methodist Episcopal Church, the Twenty-five Articles of Religion, though it modified them and added a paragraph on entire sanctification. In 1974, it adopted a new statement of faith written without reference to the Twenty-five Articles, though it did not substantively modify the church's position.

The Free Methodist Church was for many years headquartered at Winona Lake, Indiana, the sight of a Christian campground and the Billy Sunday Tabernacle. Fundamentalist evangelist Billy Sunday had retired to Winona Lake. Recently, the church moved its headquarters, including the publishing house, Life and Light Press, into a new World Ministries Center in Indianapolis, Indiana. The church adopted a modified Episcopal church polity from its parent organization, although bishops have less power than in United Methodism. The burden of running the church is shared by clergy and laypersons. A general conference is the highest legislative body, which not only sets the general rules but also elects the bishops. Very soon after its formation, the church took up the missionary enterprise that has taken it around the world. The church experienced spectacular growth in the later twentieth century. It now reports more than 350,000 members residing outside North America compared to 80,000 in the United States and Canada. Related churches, products of the missionary enterprise, can now be found in Mexico, Paraguay, Brazil, Taiwan, Hong Kong, the Philippines, India, several African nations, and the Dominican Republic.

Like most Holiness bodies, the Free Methodist Church did not play a central role in the Fundamentalist–modernist controversy, although generally it sided with the more conservative Fundamentalists. Its Wesleyan background and acceptance of the Holiness perspective generally alienated it from the overwhelmingly Calvinist (Baptist, Presbyterian) leadership of the Fundamentalist movement; however, it was aligned with the movement's assertion of traditional Christian doctrines and its focus on the authority of the Bible.

During the early decades of the twentieth century, Free Methodists reacted to the Universalist understanding of the gospel, that eventually all would be saved. In 1921 it added an article of religion on heaven as the reward of the righteous and hell the destiny of unbelievers. The church has from its beginning advocated its members' living the holy life. It accepted the General Rules written by Methodism's founder, John Wesley, to which it added its own four special rules: adherence to Christian standards of attire (modest, nonostentatious), abstention from alcohol, tobacco, and recreational drugs, cessation of memberships in secret oath-bound organizations, and recognition of only biblical grounds for divorce (desertion or adultery). Members eschew any hint of racism and decry the social and political discrimination directed against ethnic minorities. Members are expected to tithe and traditionally Free Methodists have been among the highest and most faithful contributors to their church.

Through the last half of the twentieth century, the church has become aligned with the larger Evangelical movement (which has in turn become more open to the Holiness and Pentecostal perspective) and, in 1944, it joined the National Association of Evangelicals. The church's alignment with the Evangelical position was manifest in the new statement of faith that affirmed the authority of the Holy Scriptures, which are believed to have been given without error and which were faithfully recorded and transmitted without corruption of any essential doctrine.

J. Gordon Melton

See also Holiness, Wesleyan

Bibliography

Hogue, William T. *History of the Free Methodist Church*, 2 vols. (1915) Chicago: Free Methodist Publishing House.

Marston, Leslie R. (1960) *From Age to Age a Living Witness*. Winona Lake, IN: Life and Light Press.

Taylor, J. Paul. (1963) *Holiness, the Finished Foundation*. Winona Lake, IN: Life and Light Press.

Free Will

The term "free will" has a long history of controversy and interpretation in the history of Christian thought, complicated by related discussions of God's absolute power (omnipotence) and foreknowledge (omniscience), and by questions arising from the application of God's grace to human beings, such as whether human beings are able to accept or reject the divine offer of grace. In general, it may be said that free will denotes the power or ability of the individual to make real choices that are not coerced or determined by any cause outside of the will itself. In the Christian tradition, it is generally agreed that God created human beings with an original freedom or ability to choose between good and evil, although there remain considerable differences as to the origin and nature of this freedom. Likewise, most Christians have agreed that after the sin of Adam this original freedom was compromised by the power of sin, although here too there remain considerable differences as to the extent and effects of sin on human freedom, as well as the power of grace to restore human freedom. Finally, all Christians agree that the final state of glory in heaven will be characterized by the perfection of human freedom, in which sin will not be possible.

Early Christian Thought on Free Will and Predestination

Discussion about free will has assumed greater importance in the Western Christian tradition due principally to the influence of St. Augustine (354–430). In the Augustinian view, human beings after the Fall inherited a sin nature, which renders the human will incapable of choosing good or avoiding evil. Although the will remains free to make real choices, all such choices are inevitably tainted with sinful self-interest. One question that arises from this Augustinian perspective on sin and free will, which has been of some importance to Protestant Fundamentalists, is whether human beings are free to accept or reject the grace of Christ. Augustine argued that human beings cannot freely choose God by their own natural ability without a prior gift of grace, and that God has eternally chosen those to whom He will give this grace and ultimately salvation. This idea, called "predestination," has led to many controversies over whether predestination is taught in the Bible, and if it violates human freedom and moral responsibility. It is important to note, however, that in the Augustinian paradigm true freedom of the will is conceived as the power to love God and to do His will. A choice to sin, therefore, while made freely in the sense that a person is not compelled to sin, nevertheless leads to a loss of freedom because it strengthens the power of sin over the will and alienates the soul from its true destiny.

During the Protestant Reformation of the sixteenth century, the question of free will surfaced again within the framework of new controversies about predestination, the nature of God's grace, and the power of sin over the human will and intellect. Martin Luther (1483–1546) opposed a late medieval tendency to assert the natural power of human beings to do good and to love God freely apart from supernatural grace. But it is also true that Luther's conception of God's sovereign will, and his conception of grace as divine favor had ample precedents in late medieval theologians like William of Ockham (1285–1347) and Gabriel Biel (1420–1495). In a famous dispute over free will with the Catholic humanist, Erasmus (1466–1536), Luther affirmed that the corruption of human nature has left the will powerless to choose good and avoid evil. He therefore reasserted the doctrine of predestination. These views were expressed in his principal work on the topic, usually translated into English as *Bondage of the Will* (1525), although properly speaking, only the choices of the will are bound by sin. An analogy may be helpful: the will is like a piano out of tune: one is free to play any song, but any song played on this piano will always be out of tune.

In these essential points, John Calvin (1509–1564) did not differ greatly from Luther. However, it was the Arminian controversy in the early seventeenth century that most decisively influenced future attitudes of Protestant Fundamentalists about free will. Jacobus Arminius (1560–1609), a Dutch Reformed pastor and theologian, asserted that God predestined some to eternal life based only on His foreknowledge of those who would freely repent and trust in Christ. For Arminius, the will was free to resist or to accept the offer of divine grace. He affirmed this position against other Reformed theologians, who asserted that the intellect is blind and the will completely powerless to respond to the divine call apart from a special work of prevenient grace. Theologically, Arminianism brought the issue of predestination into sharper focus as the antithesis of free will, or expressed differently, as God's sovereignty versus human freedom. Historically, Arminianism influenced later Protestant Fundamentalists through eighteenth-century Methodism and various Baptist groups that made antipredestination a standard of religious identity.

Protestant Fundamentalist Views on Free Will

The British and American Evangelical revivals of the eighteenth and nineteenth centuries form the immediate historical antecedents of Protestant Fundamentalist views on free will. In the English revivals, George Whitefield (1714–1770) and John Wesley (1703–1791) split in part over the issue of predestination and free will. Whitefield was a Calvinist. Wesley, who was the founder of the Methodist Church, continued to hold a Calvinist view of corrupt human nature, but he also affirmed that there is a universal prevenient grace common to all human beings that enables a person to freely accept or reject the offer of salvation. In the British colonies of North America, most of the early-eighteenth-century revival leaders followed the Reformed tradition of George Whitefield and English Puritanism. Jonathan Edwards (1703–1758), the most prominent theologian of the revivalist party in America, wrote a complex defense of a Calvinist view entitled *Freedom of the Will* (1754). In this work, Edwards argued that the will possesses a natural ability to love God, but lacks the inclination to do so until the grace of God transforms its inclinations, or desires.

The strict Calvinism of Edwards, however, was not to succeed in the self-reliant democratic atmosphere of American life. With the exception of a few pockets of Reformed intellectual influence, American Protestantism in the nineteenth century was characterized by the triumph of Arminianism and Methodism. This trend is seen most notably among revival leaders of the Second Great Awakening, such as Timothy Dwight (1752–1817), Lyman Beecher (1775–1817), and Charles Finney (1792–1875). While claiming to be the successors of Edwards, these men gradually modified their Reformed views, giving more emphasis to the methods of achieving revival than to the independent and sovereign work of God apart from human instrumentality. Finney did not in theory abandon the doctrine of election (predestination), but suggested that election of some to eternal life was simply the result of God's final goal for the moral governance of the universe; hence, a rational means to an end and not an arbitrary act of divine will. Expanding on Edwards's idea of natural ability, Finney argued in his *Systematic Theology* (1846) that human beings are free in the sense of possessing a natural ability to repent and obey God. A person's choices, therefore, are not bound inevitably by sin arising from a prior sin nature; rather, sin consists only in the act of sinning itself, and the possession of free will is necessary for any act to be regarded as sinful or righteous.

Finney's modifications of traditional Reformed ideas on sin and free will became the common and unexamined assumptions of Protestant Evangelicalism toward the end of the nineteenth century. The most important revivalist of this period, Dwight L. Moody (1837–1899), shared most of Finney's assumptions about human nature. He emphasized a simple gospel that could be understood by the common person and freely accepted with a little common sense and emotional persuasion. Also important (but somewhat opposite to the tendency of Fundamentalists in the twentieth century), Moody subordinated doctrine to practical Christian living and soul saving, making earlier denominational divisions over predestination and free will of secondary importance. Most twentieth-century Fundamentalists have continued to follow Moody's commonsense approach, which emphasizes the role of human decision making more than God's sovereign initiative in human salvation. This can be seen, for example, in the popular practice of coming forward at the end of an evangelistic crusade to repent and make a decision to follow Christ. Known as an "altar call," this practice is usually accompanied by emotive music and special pleadings that are designed to overcome resistance to conversion.

Many of the Fundamentalist denominational groups in the twentieth century have their roots in nineteenth-century sectarian movements that were Wesleyan in character. For example, both the Cumberland Presbyterian Church and the Christian Church (Disciples of Christ) distanced themselves from a Calvinistic heritage by embracing an Arminian doctrine of free will. The Methodist Church experienced a repeated process of schism from the mid-nineteenth to early twentieth century, creating a large number of Fundamentalist Holiness sects that emphasized a Wesleyan doctrinal identity. Most of these groups resisted the growing influence of theological liberalism and emphasized free will and the power of the individual to live a perfected life with the assistance of sanctifying grace. Although Fundamentalist, these sects were often isolated from Presbyterian and Baptist Fundamentalists due to their distinctive views on free will and perfectionism. Among these were the Free Methodists, Wesleyan

Methodists, and after the Civil War, the Church of the Nazarene, the Church of God (Anderson), the Christian and Missionary Alliance, and many other groups bearing the name "Holiness." Twentieth-century Pentecostal denominations, having their roots in the Fundamentalist Wesleyan-Holiness tradition, also affirm free will.

Among Baptist Fundamentalists there is more diversity on the issue of free will. Although a majority of Baptists in America have theological roots in Puritan Calvinism, there was in the early American revivals an alternative tradition of Arminian Baptists, some even identifying themselves explicitly as "Free Will Baptists." Finney revivalism, on the one hand, and the growth of theological liberalism on the other, contributed to an erosion of Calvinism among Northern Baptists in the nineteenth century. Southern Baptists preserved more of a Calvinistic heritage than did their northern counterparts. In general, the Fundamentalist crusade against theological modernism required a subordination of traditional reformed doctrinal issues such as predestination and free will, for the sake of defending other doctrines (such as biblical authority) that seemed more important to Baptist Fundamentalist identity.

In spite of the widespread antipathy in America for strict subscription to predestination and total depravity, such views did influence American Fundamentalists through the Old School Presbyterian tradition of Princeton Seminary. While all historians agree that the Princeton doctrine of biblical inerrancy was crucial to Fundamentalism, there is less agreement about the importance of Princeton's Reformed doctrines of sin and grace. Some, following the lead of George Marsden, tend to emphasize the role of Reformed orthodoxy as the matrix in which the Fundamentalist movement grew and developed. An alternative view, advocated by Donald Dayton, emphasizes that Fundamentalists were more influenced by Methodist revivalism and Wesleyan theological distinctives. This discussion has led one historian to quip that "fundamentalists were Calvinists while sitting down, but Arminians on their feet." The controversy is probably best resolved by recognizing that Fundamentalist views on free will and total depravity are a variegated and complex mosaic of Reformed and Wesleyan influences.

Among independent or nondenominational Fundamentalists, members of "Bible churches," the influence of Bible schools and independent seminaries was important. A significant source of Calvinist influence came from the Fundamentalist theologian Lewis Sperry Chafer (1871–1952), president of Dallas Theological Seminary. Chafer defended an explicit Calvinism in his *Systematic Theology* (1948): total depravity, predestination, and the need for grace to move the human will to accept the gospel. Yet in spite of these affirmations, independent dispensational Fundamentalists like Chafer maintained a remote relationship to the Reformed tradition of Princeton Seminary, because they felt that it did not share their emphasis on revivalism, personal evangelism, Bible-centered teaching, and personal piety.

During the 1920s, Fundamentalist opposition to liberalism and evolution sometimes contributed to new theological concerns about free will and predestination. For the more Reformed-minded Fundamentalists, the doctrine of free will led inevitably to theological liberalism, just as it apparently had in New England Congregationalism with the emergence of Unitarianism in the early nineteenth century. For Wesleyan Fundamentalists, Calvinistic doctrines of predestination and total depravity made evangelism and Holiness teachings seem superfluous. Finally, in the context of the antievolution crusade, Fundamentalists often pointed out that evolution implied a form of social and biological determinism that destroyed human freedom and reduced human beings to a level of brutish existence.

Daniel W. Draney

See also Arminianism; Grace; Sin and Sinners

Bibliography

Basinger, David, et al. (1986) *Predestination and Free Will: Four Views of Divine Sovereignty and Human Freedom.* Downers Grove, IL: InterVarsity Press.

Chafer, Lewis Sperry. (1948) *Systematic Theology.* Dallas TX: Dallas Theological Seminary.

Dayton, Donald. (1993) "The Search for the Historical Evangelicalism: George Marsden's History of Fuller Seminary As a Case Study." *Christian Scholar's Review* 23: 12–33

Guelzo, Allen. (1989) *Edwards on the Will: A Century of American Theological Debate.* Middletown, CT: Wesleyan University Press.

Lindstrom, Harald. (1946) *Wesley and Sanctification: A Study in the Doctrine of Salvation.* Stockholm: Nya Bokforlage Aktiebolaget.

Marsden, George M. (1980) *Fundamentalism and American Culture: The Shaping of Twentieth-Century Evangelicalism: 1870–1925*. New York: Oxford University Press.

Muller, Richard A. (1986) *Christ and the Decree: Christology and Predestination in Reformed Theology from Calvin to Perkins*. Durham, NC: Labyrinth Press.

Wallace, Dewey. (1982) *Puritans and Predestination: Grace in English Protestant Theology, 1525–1695*. Chapel Hill: University of North Carolina Press.

Weisberger, Bernard. (1948) *They Gathered at the River: The Story of the Great Revivalists and Their Impact Upon Religion in America*. Boston: Little, Brown and Co.

Fundamentals, The

The Fundamentals, a twelve-volume series of articles dedicated to a restatement of conservative Christian theological teachings, were conceived and funded by the California oil millionaire Lyman Stewart (1840–1923). Stewart was a Presbyterian lay leader in Los Angeles who had dedicated much of his activity and economic resources toward combating the influence of modernist theology within Christianity. In addition to his funding publication of *The Fundamentals*—at a cost of $200,000—Stewart's activities included purchasing and distributing Christian magazines to his oil-field workers, and funding a faculty position in Bible studies at Occidental College (Los Angeles) on the condition that the teaching was "thoroughly Scriptural" and that the school "be established as an out and out Christian school" (Stewart 1896).

The twelve volumes of *The Fundamentals* were originally published from 1910 to 1915, and distributed free of charge to "every pastor, evangelist, missionary, theological professor, theological student, Sunday school superintendent, Y.M.C.A. and Y.W.C.A secretary in the English speaking world" (*The Fundamentals*, vol. 1). The distribution of all twelve volumes totaled three million copies worldwide. In all, ninety articles were written by sixty-four authors. The authors were either American, British, or Canadian men who were representative of a broad range of conservative and millenarian scholars, ministers, and laypersons. Following the original publication, *The Fundamentals* were republished as a four-volume set in 1917 and in one volume in 1958 and again in 1990. Each of the subsequent editions were slightly different from the original: in the 1917 edition, ten additional articles were included; in the 1958 and 1990 editions, only sixty-five articles were included, and those that were included had been "edited and revised" by various Fundamentalist scholars.

Three separate themes are addressed in *The Fundamentals*: a core of articles are devoted to the defense of the inerrancy of Scripture; a second set focuses on traditional theological issues such as apologetics, the nature and work of the trinity, the doctrines of sin and salvation; and, finally, the remaining articles cover such diverse categories as personal testimonies, attacks on competing forms of belief (such as Mormonism, Christian Science, and Roman Catholicism), the relationship between science and religion, and appeals for missions and evangelism.

The articles concerning biblical inspiration uniformly mounted a strong defense of complete inerrancy of Scripture and tended to approximate a "dictation theory" approach. James M. Gray, then the dean (1904–1934) of Moody Bible Institute, stated that by "miraculous control" the Bible was an "absolute

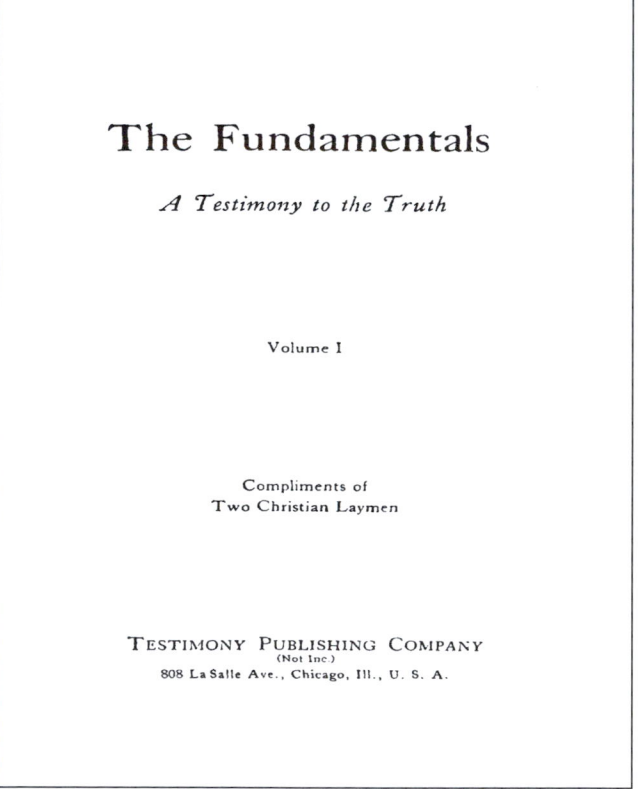

Title page of *The Fundamentals*. COURTESY OF RICHARD FLORY.

LYMAN STEWART'S REFLECTION

Now that we are closing up the final details of The Fundamentals, my thoughts have reverted to you very frequently, and especially to that Sunday afternoon, when in our [Baptist] Temple Auditorium [in Los Angeles], you were replying to something that one of those infidel professors in Chicago University had published, and during which lecture I was very definitely impressed to ask for an interview with you. As I have thought about that since, it seems as though the Lord must have given me courage to ask for the interview as I naturally have a great shrinking from meeting strangers, and this matter which I had to present to you I had never mentioned to a single soul, not even my own wife. So you were the first that heard it and when you remarked, "It is of the Lord; let us pray," I was deeply impressed.

Source: Lyman Stewart to A.C. Dixon. July 29, 1915. Dixon Papers, XI-6, Southern Baptist Historical Commission Library (Quoted in Sandeen p. 188).

Regarding ministers in the churches and the important role that Lyman Stewart saw *The Fundamentals* playing in the churches

Of course there are a great many 'wolves in sheep's clothing' among such a multitude, but there are also among them the 'salt of the earth.' These are the men from whom the present generation of the Anglo-Saxon people, as well as the large portion of the heathen world, are, in a large measure, to receive their spiritual instruction, and hence the great importance of getting them, as far as possible into line for true service. The spiritual welfare of the present generation requires it; the safety of foreign missionary work demands it. It is a work that will count for both time and eternity. . . . The best and most loyal Bible teachers in the world are supposed to be enlisted in the preparation of this 'Testimony,' and . . . these articles will doubtless be the masterpieces of the writers.

Source: Lyman Stewart to Milton Stewart. October 26, 1909. Stewart Papers, Biola University (Quoted in Sandeen p. 195).

---

transcript" of God's mind. The Reverend George S. Bishop (author and pastor of the First Reformed Church in Orange, New Jersey) spoke of the "'dictated inspiration' of the entire Bible and even referred to it as 'a Book dropped out of heaven'" (Marsden 1980: 122). In contrast, the few articles that dealt with the question of the relationship between religion and science show that at this point within the emerging Fundamentalist movement, there was an allowance for a position that argued for the compatibility of certain forms of evolutionary theory and the biblical record. George Frederick Wright, a geologist from Oberlin College, Ohio, argued that evolution need not exclude God's creative work: "If anything is to be *evolved* in an orderly manner from the resident forces of primordial matter it must first have been *involved* through the creative act of the Divine Being" (Marsden 1980: 122). Similarly, James Orr, a professor of theology at the United Free Church College in Glasgow, argued that "'Evolution,' in short, is coming to be recognized as but a new name for 'creation,' only that the creative power now works from *within*, instead of, as in the old conception, in an *external*, plastic fashion. It is, however, creation none the less" (*The Fundamentals*, vol. 4: 103). These views were edited out of the Orr and Wright articles in the 1958 and 1990 editions of *The Fundamentals*, making their articles more in line with the complete rejection of any form of evolutionary teaching that came to characterize Fundamentalism after the Scopes "Monkey Trial" in 1925.

Richard W. Flory

Bibliography

The Fundamentals: A Testimony to the Truth, 12 vols. (1910–1925) Chicago: Testimony Publishing Company.

The Fundamentals: A Testimony to the Truth, 4 vols. (1917) Chicago: Testimony Publishing Company.

The Fundamentals for Today, 1 vol. (1958) Grand Rapids, MI: Kregel Publications.

The Fundamentals: The Famous Sourcebook of Foundational Biblical Truths, 1 vol. (1990) Grand Rapids, MI: Kregel Publications.

Marsden, George M. (1980) *Fundamentalism and American Culture: The Shaping of Twentieth-Century Evangelicalism, 1870–1925*. New York: Oxford University Press.

Sandeen, Ernest R. (1970) *The Roots of Fundamentalism: British and American Millenarianism, 1800–1930*. Chicago: University of Chicago Press.

Stewart, Lyman to Rev. W. S. Young, D. D. 26 July 1896. *Stewart Papers*, Biola University, La Mirada, California.

Gifts of the Spirit

Fundamentalists, as a group, have shown a great deal of interest in the Gifts of the Spirit. This has been noted particularly in the last quarter of the twentieth century. It is important to make a distinction between the "gift" of the Spirit and the "gifts" of the Spirit. The gift of the Spirit is given to a person at the moment of salvation. A spiritual gift, however, is a special endowment given by the Holy Spirit for the purpose of enhancing the ministry of the church as a whole (1 Corinthians 12:7).

In the Old Testament, the Spirit of God gave gifts in a much more limited way and such gifts were normally associated with the design and building of the dwelling place of God. For example, Bezalel and Oholiab were given special gifts for the task of building the Tabernacle in the wilderness (Exodus 31:1–11). Saul, the first king of Israel, was given a special "filling of the Spirit," which probably related to his being given prophetic and administrative gifts (1 Samuel 10:6).

The Major Scriptures

There are primarily four New Testament references to "gifts." In order of their probable dates of writing, the first is 1 Corinthians 12–14, followed by Romans 12:3–8, Ephesians 4:7–16, and 1 Peter 4:10–11. Common to all of these passages is the concept that the "gifts" are not natural abilities, but rather are God-given ministries for the benefit of a group of Christians. The Corinthian writings are the most extensive and are somewhat apologetic in tone.

In the Corinthian passages, it appears that the apostle is principally interested in explaining the nature and use of two gifts: prophecy and tongues. These gifts are provided by the risen Christ as a means of carrying out His commission to the church. There is a correlation between Christ ascending to the right hand of the Father and the descent of the Holy Spirit (Ephesians 4:7–8) in Christ giving gifts (Ephesians 4:8).

None of the New Testament passages presents a comprehensive list of all of the gifts. Even in the Pauline writings, there is no single list that would provide a key to all the others. In 1 Corinthians 12:8–11 and 12:28, the longest lists occur. Taken together, the four principal passages cited in the first paragraph do make the gifts of oral communication preeminent—that is, those through the apostles and prophets. The other gifts are then to enhance the ministry of the Word of God.

The Terms Used

The passages in 1 Corinthians follow Paul's purpose to answer one of the questions that the Corinthians had asked (Note 7:1, and the formula, "Now concerning...."). In this case, it is "concerning spiritual gifts." The word "gifts" is not in the original language. Literally, the term *pneumatikon* is translated as "spiritualities" and could be interpreted as a reference to spiritual gifts (or things) or to spiritual persons.

A second term, *charismaton*, appears in 1 Corinthians 12:4. This term means that these are "gracious gifts," that is, they are not earned but are sovereignly bestowed by God. Two other terms follow that seem

Ephesians 4:7–16

7. But unto every one of us is given grace according to the measure of the gift of Christ.

8. Wherefore he saith, When he ascended up on high, he led captivity captive, and gave gifts unto men.

9. (Now that he ascended, what is it but that he also descended first into the lower parts of the earth?

10. He that descended is the same also that ascended up far above all heavens, that he might fill all things.)

11. And he gave some, apostles; and some, prophets; and some, evangelists; and some, pastors and teachers;

12. For the perfecting of the saints, for the work of the ministry, for the edifying of the body of Christ:

13. Till we all come in the unity of the faith, and of the knowledge of the Son of God, unto a perfect man, unto the measure of the stature of the fullness of Christ:

14. That we henceforth be no more children, tossed to and fro, and carried about with every wind of doctrine, by the sleight of men, and cunning craftiness, whereby they lie in wait to deceive;

15. But speaking the truth in love, may grow up into him in all things, which is the head, even Christ:

16. From whom the whole body fitly joined together and compacted by that which every joint supplieth, according to the effectual working in the measure of every part, maketh increase of the body unto the edifying of itself in love.

to explain the nature of these "gifts.": *diakonion*, or "ministries" and *energematon*, or "energies,"; that is, active spiritual energy. These may be the three dimensions of the spiritual gifts.

Pertinent Questions about the Gifts

The first question relates to the lists as being *comprehensive*. There is no means by which this can be answered, but the fact that there are variances within the four texts would seem to preclude that idea. Many in the contemporary church believe that there are spiritual gifts bestowed upon people in congregations today—gifts necessary to the congregation but which were not even dreamed about in the apostolic period.

A second question that has vexed interpreters has to do with the *permanence* of the gifts, that is, have any of these gifts ceased to be provided for by the church or are they all expected to be the legacy of the church from the time in which they were bestowed until the time that Christ shall return? There are arguments on both sides. The argument that they are not permanent is at least twofold: (1) The precise meanings of such gifts as "the word of wisdom" or "the word of knowledge" is not clear. (2) The reference in 1 Corinthians 13:8 seems to indicate that at least "tongues," "prophecy," and "knowl-

edge" are not permanent. And those who hold to the permanence of the gifts would find it difficult to authenticate "Apostles" in the present, particularly considering the qualifications of such in Acts 1:21–22.

A third question has to do with the knotty problem of "tongues." Is this some kind of "Holy Spirit" language, or is this expression to be interpreted as a miraculous ability to speak a language unknown to the one who is given the gift of speaking? Those who hold to the first idea refer to the King James translation of *"unknown* tongues," although the term "unknown" is not in the original as is demonstrated by its being italicized. Those who favor the second view take their point from the experience of Pentecost when the believers were miraculously speaking in the languages, even in the dialects, of those who were hearing them. (Acts 2:5–11)

The Purpose of the Gifts and the Place of Love

It is obvious that the gifts are not for one's personal benefit. Rather, they are given for the benefit of others. This is what Paul meant when he wrote that they were given "for the common good" (1 Corinthians 12:7). The gifts are the means by which God's people will mature. This is the emphasis in the passage in Ephesians 4.

Paul centers his discussion in 1 Corinthians on the mediating principle of love. In Chapter 13, love is not a gift but rather an attitude in the exercising of one's gifts. Those who are specially gifted are not to become proud but rather to display the *agape* love that is always concerned with the welfare of the other person.

Richard I. McNeely

See also Salvation; Speaking in Tongues

Bibliography

Brown, Steve. (1999) *Follow the Wind*. Grand Rapids, MI: Baker House Books.

Bruner, F. Dale. (1970) *A Theology of the Holy Spirit*. Grand Rapids, MI: Wm. B. Eerdmans.

Fee, Gordon D. (1994) *God's Empowering Presence*. Peabody, MA: Hendrickson.

Ferguson, Sinclair B. (1996) *The Holy Spirit*. Downers Grove, IL: InterVarsity Press.

Packer, J. I. (1984) *Keep In Step With the Spirit*. Downers Grove, IL: InterVarsity Press.

Ruthven, Jon. (1993) *On the Cessation of the Charismata*. Sheffield, UK: Sheffield Academic Press.

Walvoord, John F. (1954) *The Doctrine of the Holy Spirit*. Wheaton, IL: Van Kampen Press.

God and God's Will

Determining the will of God has been and continues to be a difficult undertaking for many Christians. In addition, the subject has often been misunderstood by dealing with peripheral matters such as the *geographical place* where one should minister, the *person* one should marry, or whether to marry at all, as well as a host of other options such as ascertaining the particular profession one should enter or the skills that one should acquire. All of these are questions relating to finding God's will. Should Christians, as Gideon of old, put out fleeces to determine what is or is not the will of God?

Three Aspects of the Will of God

God's Decretive Will

The concept of God's control over all things is basically confessed by all those within the Fundamentalist camp. First, there is the fact that God does order His universe. He does so as the Sovereign Lord and exercises His will through His omniscience and His omnipotence. This concept of God's will may be defined as God's *decretive will*. It is that which God decrees. Whatever the Lord desires in heaven and earth He does (Psalms 135:6). For example, it is by the will of the Father that people come to Christ (John 6:37–39), and Jesus promises that those who come will never be driven away. This is more than a mere desire on the part of God and certainly is not dependent upon human will; it is an assurance that God will bring this about. Further, in the New Testament, there are statements of what God desires. The Greek word for this is *thelo*. Such desires often pertain to His redemptive work in Jesus Christ. In John 1:13 (NIV), John notes that it is God's will in giving the "right to become children of God." But there is the recognition that a person may not know just what God has ordained or what God's disposition toward a given goal may be. For example, Paul's desire to visit the Christians in Rome is conditioned by his declaration, "I pray that now at last by God's *will* the way may be opened for me to come to you" (Rom 1:10, NIV [italic not in original]). In such cases, the concept of God's will rests upon God's initiative entirely.

God's Dispositive Will

Second, there is an aspect to God's will that is not always determined. Peter, in a conditional clause, notes that "it is better, if it is God's will, to suffer for doing good rather than for doing bad things"(1 Peter 3:17, Tr. Richard I. McNeely). All Christians will not suffer, hence the use of the word "if." Too, in 1 Thessalonians 4:3, the apostle notes that it is God's will that His people be sanctified, particularly as it relates to their morality, but it is clear that this is not automatic as coming from the sovereign hand of God. Some of God's people will fail in their moral lives. In fact, the New Testament recognizes the human responsibility in obedience.

God is also pleased with expressions of gratefulness even in situations that are unfavorable (1 Thessalonians 5:16–18). This same thought is echoed in Peter's exhortation to his readers to submit to the authority of pagan rulers, "for it is God's will that by doing good, you should silence the ignorance of foolish men" (1 Peter 2:15, AV). It is also clear that in some of these cases this is not a *predetermined* thing but rather something that brings pleasure to the Creator. Sproul calls this *the will of disposition* (Sproul 1992: 69).

God's Preceptive Will

The third portrayal of God's will relates to those clear commands that God gives (such as the Law) and in the New Testament, the commandments, and exhortations. Some have referred to these as the *preceptive will of God* (Sproul 1992: 69). Though these declarations are clearly revealed, there is the possibility of not carrying them out.

The Old Testament

Though most of the questions regarding God's will come from Christians, it is important to note that even in the Old Testament, the concept of God's will was clearly stated. In the account of Adam and Eve in the Garden of Eden, there was a clear statement of God's will. Generous as it was, it placed a taboo only on partaking of the fruit of the tree of the knowledge of good and evil (Genesis 2:16–17).

The Law given at Sinai is an expression of the will of God, and the acclaim of the people of Israel. "We will do everything the Lord has said," demonstrates a clear understanding of the required obedience to God. God expected His covenant people to do His will. David wrote, "I desire to do Your will, O my God; Your law is within my heart" (Psalms 40:8, NIV). The angels of God also do His will (Psalms 103:20–21). That "obedience is better than sacrifice" is a clear Old Testament teaching (Psalms 40:6; see also 1 Samuel 15:22 and Micah 6:6–8, NIV).

The New Testament

There are a number of terms relating to the concept of God's will. Only two are of particular pertinence to the scope of this article. The first has to do with the Greek word *thelo* and its noun, *thelema*. These are the principal terms translated as "to will" or "will" in the New Testament. The second concept is found in the verb *boulomai* and its two nouns, *boule* and *boulema*. Most commentators believe that both *thelo* and *boulomai* are used synonymously, while others believe that there are still some distinctions. For the latter, *thelo* expresses more of a desire and is not as determinative as *boulomai*, which would be used in a more narrow sense of that which God intends and consequently carries out. Thus, *boulomai* would mean "I purpose or intend," while *thelo* would express the idea of "I desire."

For those with Calvinist leanings, *boulomai* would have reference to God's sovereignty in all things, and

the word would have particular relevance to God's decree. For those of Arminian leanings, such distinctions would not be made. God's intention (*thelema*) would only be realized by the human decision to receive Christ.

The Teaching

In the prayer that Jesus set forth as a model prayer, one of the major petitions is "Your will be done on earth as it is in heaven" (Matthew 6:10; Luke 11:2, NIV). This also was the petition of the Lord as He prayed in Gethsemane (Matthew 26:42; Luke 22:42). Compared to the Synoptics, the Gospel of John has more references to the Lord's recognition that He was on earth to do the will of the One who sent Him (4:34, 5:30, 6:38–39), but John also presents instruction on discerning the will of God. "If anyone chooses to do God's will, he will find out whether my teaching comes from God or whether I speak on My own," Jesus declared in John 7:17 (NIV). Here human volition is involved, but in chapter 6, the will (*thelema*) of God seems squarely to rest with God's initiative as Jesus avows that anyone who comes to Him will come because of the Father's drawing him (6:37, 39, 44).

Although Luke in the Acts frequently uses the word *thelo*, he shows a particular preference to the words associated with *boulomai*. Peter's sermon at Pentecost asserts of Christ, "This man was handed over to you by God's set purpose (*boule*) and foreknowledge; and you, with the help of wicked men, put Him to death by nailing Him to the cross" (Acts 2:23, NIV). The same thought is echoed in Acts 4:28 as the believers, while in prayer, recognized that behind the death of Christ was God's determinate will. Luke's use of the *boulomai* words in Acts seems to set them apart from *thelo*. This is demonstrated by the translations found in the New International Version. Often, *boulomai* is translated as someone "wanting" to do something. However, in each instance, this is more than just a wish; it is an intention. An example of this is in Acts 25:20. Festus, the governor, is reiterating Paul's case to Herod and Agrippa. He notes, "I was at a loss how to investigate such matters; so I asked if he (Paul) would be willing (*bouloito*) to go to Jerusalem and stand trial there on these charges." Obviously, Paul was not about to do that. Festus was not asking if it would please (*thelo*) Paul to go, but would he make a resolution to go. Wisely, Paul said "No!"

Determining the Will of God

The New Testament's teaching on "knowing God's will" obviously has nothing to do with knowing God's *decretive will*. Such a search will only end in frustration. There are many facets of God's will that are secret to God alone. However, there is not a mystery to God's *preceptive will*. The commandments are quite clear: generally, when one seems uncertain about God's will, it has to do with His *dispositional will*. Central to one's quest to determine God's *dispositional will* is the interaction with Paul's exhortation in Romans 12:1–2 (NIV): "Therefore I urge you, brothers, in view of God's mercy, to offer your bodies as living sacrifices, holy and pleasing to God—this is your spiritual act of worship. Do not conform any longer to the pattern of this world, but be transformed by the renewing of your mind. Then you will be able to test and approve what God's will is—His good, pleasing, and perfect will."

There are certain conditions, then, for ascertaining God's *dispositional will*. It begins with a commitment of oneself to God, body and spirit (or body and mind). In the same manner as any sacrifice in the Old Testament, so the believer's presentation is to be a holy one and one that is acceptable or pleasing to God. Conformation to the culture is to be superseded by a transformation, and this is a deliberate mental exercise. It is significant that the instruction of the apostle is not to spend long periods in prayer (though that may be necessary and automatic), but that there is to be a deliberate and intentional presentation of oneself to God. Another test comes from Philippians 4:7–8. A peaceful heart and an examination of the moral value of the thing sought is imperative. The reward is the acquisition of an understanding of God's will.

An Association between God's *Dispositional Will* and God's *Decretive Will*

The instruction in Romans 8 is that the Spirit of God prays for God's people "according to God" (literal statement of verse 27). The translators have correctly interpreted this to mean "in accordance with the will of God." Then, in the verses that follow, those things that God has decreed for His people are listed. One of them is that believers should be "conformed to the likeness of his Son" (verse 29). This is where the purpose of God and God's pleasure come together. The litmus test of whether or not one is doing the will of God is to subject it to the test of whether or not one can apply the character and behavior of Jesus Christ to the given situation. Conformity to Christ is the key. As Apostle Paul exhorted the believers in Corinth, "Follow my example, as I follow the example of Christ" (1 Corinthians 11:1, NIV). The Greek word translated "follow" is the term from which derives our word "mimic." How then can this be applied to knowing God's will? A student, for example, should be the kind of student Jesus would have been. The attitude toward the acquisition of knowledge should be that which one could imagine of Jesus Christ. A businessman could apply the same test. How would Jesus run this business? This is not some kind of faddish What Would Jesus Do, but demands careful study of Scripture to understand the completeness of Christ's obedience to the Father. One's motives as well as one's actual behavior are to be tested by their conformity to the likeness of God's Son.

Richard I. McNeely

Bibliography

Boice, James. (1979) *Awakening to God.* Vol. 3 of *Foundations of the Christian Faith.* Downers Grove, IL: InterVarsity Press.

Michaels, J. Ramsey. (1988) "The Will of God." In *The International Bible Encyclopedia.* Grand Rapids, MI: Wm. B. Eerdmans, 4: 1064–1067.

Sittser, Gerald L. (2000) *The Will of God As a Way of Life.* Grand Rapids, MI: Zondervan.

Sproul, R. C. (1977) "Discerning the Will of God." In *Our Sovereign God,* edited by James M. Boice. Grand Rapids, MI: Baker House Books, 106–107.

———. (1992) *Essential Truths of the Christian Faith.* Wheaton, IL: Tyndale.

Gospel

Taken from the Greek word *evangelion* meaning "good news," the gospel is the central message of Christian revelation, claiming the good news of human redemption in the life of Jesus Christ. The term was used as early as 9 BCE, but its association with the preaching of Jesus in Mark 1:1—"The beginning of the good news of Jesus Christ, the Son of God" (Metzger and Murphy 1991: NT 48)—and other canonical writings concerning Jesus' teachings soon eclipsed all vernacularisms. The apostle Paul's frequent reference to the term in his writings demonstrates his audience readily understood the focus and breadth of the "Christian gospel" message. While Paul occasionally employed terms such as "the gospel of God," "my gospel," and "our gospel" (Romans and 2 Corinthians), the single source of the gospel was clearly understood among early Christian audiences. Nevertheless, for first-century Christians whose communal authority was defined by the Septuagint and a recently developed oral tradition concerning the teachings and acts of Jesus, determining and incorporating the "authentic" gospel message in the fledgling church was a process replete with ambiguities and compromise. Not until the middle or end of the second century was the authority of the gospel writers established and even then, varying expressions of the good news were articulated and adhered to by the scattered communities of Christian believers (Chadwick 1967: 32–45). Furthermore, just as early confessors of Christianity grappled with the meaning and application of the good news found in the life of Jesus Christ, so too have subsequent generations of the faithful appropriated and proclaimed different aspects of the gospel message.

Shifting Allegiances to the Gospel Message in Twentieth-Century America

For centuries the gospel message was viewed as both a historically accurate description of the life of Jesus and as a prescriptive claim upon the lives of the faithful. Prior to the American Civil War, these elements of interpreting the Scriptures were regarded as equally valid, and shaped religious life accordingly. Between the close of America's great internal conflict and the nation's entry into World War I, however, many of the nation's Protestant denominations encountered profound, yet often subtle challenges in the area of hermeneutics. The growing acceptance of higher critical methods on biblical scholarship soon shook the very epistemological foundation upon which Protestantism had rested for centuries. Some of the deepest fractures to eventually surface concerned the meaning and message of the gospel.

By the close of the nineteenth century vastly different expressions about the role of the Scriptures in one's faith life were forming throughout the United States. Given the profound shift in cultural currents that accompanied modernity, liberal Protestants set out on a new tact of religious profession and practice

in order to keep the faith socially viable. At the center of this effort was a new interpretation of Jesus and His message. It is estimated that among one-third of the nation's religious practitioners, the balance once struck between religious profession and accepting the gospel as historically accurate was lost. For a significant number of Americans, the advancement of Christ's Kingdom was no longer associated with the coming of supernatural events and the salvation of souls, but instead was identified with the progress of human morality and history. God's purposes, it was assumed, were immanent in the unfolding of human history. Earlier faith claims about Jesus' physical Resurrection, Virgin Birth, and the cosmic ushering in of a new age of human morality were considered pure folly among liberal Protestants.

The Good News Revealed

Protestant Fundamentalists balked at this new interpretation of the gospel message. Reasserting what they understood to be the Truth found in Scripture, Fundamentalist interpreters constructed an apologetic rooted in the Baconian method that sought to reassert the "facts" of the gospel message. This literalist hermeneutic tended to catalog the gospel message into a series of factual propositions to which the listener only need to assent in order to find redeeming faith. The gospel account, in particular, gave Protestant Fundamentalist theology its greatest expression and consequently its greatest differences with liberals and moderates. Its influence was evident in the "five points" of Fundamentalism.

Whether the student of Fundamentalism places the publication of *The Fundamentals*, a series of articles appearing between 1910 and 1915, and its so-called accompanying five points at the center or periphery of their understanding, the dissemination and subsequent importance of this work cannot be overlooked. As George M. Marsden maintains, *The Fundamentals* proved to be "a symbolic point of reference for identifying a 'fundamentalist' movement" (1980: 119). Of the five points identified by Fundamentalists as being "fundamental" to Christian profession, several are largely shaped by the Fundamentalists' interpretation of the gospel accounts. Perhaps the most significant assertion made by these articles following the claim of inerrancy is the belief in the physical Resurrection of Jesus Christ. As an attempt to combat the seemingly growing cleavage between God and modern society, conservative Protestant Evangelicals—later to be identified as Fundamentalists—redoubled their efforts and aggressively asserted claims about Christian orthodoxy based on a theology grounded in supernaturalism. By asserting the divinity of Jesus and His physical Resurrection after the Crucifixion, Fundamentalists sought to shed Christian theology of its recent liberal trappings of higher criticism. By the end of the 1920s, the Fundamentalist reaction to liberal Protestant hermeneutics was full-blown, creating a rift among American Protestants that realigned the cultural landscape of the nation.

The Fulfillment of Truth: Fundamentalist Hermeneutics and the Gospel Message

To the Christian Fundamentalist the prescriptive quality of the gospel message, which is held as the inerrant word of God, is intricately related to what the gospel describes as historical fact. The significance of the gospel account rests squarely on the hard historical certainty of the Incarnation and Jesus' fulfillment of what was ordained by God. For Fundamentalists, the authority and significance of the gospel message is not conditioned upon interpretations of Jesus as the extraordinary moral teacher of His day who revealed great truths about the human condition, but is grounded upon the a priori assertion of Jesus as the anointed Christ, the miraculous Redeemer whose Virgin Birth and divinity was foreknown by God and foretold by the Hebrew prophet Isaiah to coming generations (Isaiah 7:14). The assumed prescriptive nature of the Scriptures as it relates to truth is readily visible in many aspects of Fundamentalist life. One revealing example of this popular epistemology was evident in an 8 January 1979 letter to the editor of the *Christian News*. This letter read in part: "The Jesus Christ Whom I know from Holy Scriptures, who was God, and IS God, never usurped the AUTHORITY OF THE HOLY SCRIPTURES to transfer that AUTHORITY TO HIMSELF. The JESUS CHRIST Whom I know ... always subjected Himself to the AUTHORITY of 'IT IS WRITTEN.' ... JESUS CHRIST did not get up on the stage of this world and 'AD LIB IT.' ... the HOLY SCRIPTURES were 'SCRIPT' for Jesus' whole Life, Action and Words" (Hamann 1980: 11). Such examples of reducing the gospel message to legally and historically deterministic terms are not uncommon. Rather than proclaiming the good news of Jesus the Christ, all of Scripture is understood as a historical narrative recording doctrinal truths in which even the most ancillary text must consistently articulate the truth.

Against the swelling sea of scientific inquiry that no longer viewed knowledge as fixed truths or special revelation, Fundamentalists reasserted the message of Jesus' redemptive action on the cross as the only source of objective truth. As a series or collection of truth propositions, Fundamentalists argue the inquirer only need to submit their reason to the claims of Scripture and assent to the literal demands of the text to have truth revealed. While Fundamentalists were not the first to make this epistemological move, their demand for the complete and total allegiance to an inerrant word as the only means of discerning truth was a tactical move to salvage the battered vessel of Christian faith from the shoals of modernity. This crude reductionism of reasoned inquiry coupled with the claim of scriptural inerrancy, however, put Fundamentalists at odds with the Christian tradition itself. As Peter J. Thuesen observed in his study on the development of biblical hermeneutics, by the late nineteenth and early twentieth centuries the "truth-value" of the gospel rested solely upon notions of "a desire for textual and historical veracity." Unlike previous generations of Christians for whom the authenticity of the gospel message was wedded to their corporate ecclesiastical setting, for the modern Christian such apparatus was largely ignored as interpreters probed the text for evidence of its historical accuracy, which it was assumed, conditioned its veracity (Thuesen 1999: 4–15). Without such ecclesiastical guidelines at hand, Fundamentalist reading of the Scriptures tended to deemphasize historical causation and bolster claims about a supernaturally determined course of human history. The Scriptures chronicled the supernatural events of the past and predicted God's interaction with world history in the future. Such episodic action on the part of the Divine, Fundamentalists believed, culminated in the life of Jesus. Thus, the gospel message contains a power, force, and truth beyond human recognition. In fact, for Fundamentalists, the gospel and truth are synonymous terms. In their opposition to the trends of the modern world, Fundamentalists' defense of the gospel message has been a defense of truth. It is this conceptualization of the truth intricately woven in their perceived defense of it that has given Christian Fundamentalism its vitality and a type of "gospel identity."

195

"Gospel Identity"

The gospel message is not only descriptive of Jesus' life, but also has a prescriptive quality for Fundamentalists that delimit the community's identity, its associations, and course of action. The Pauline conception of being "made anew" by the gospel message is not only a powerful metaphor for Christian Fundamentalists but also one that reorients their entire lives. Fundamentalists' identity with the gospel is reinforced among members of the community through ritual enactments, formulaic expression, and the orientation of space. Their willingness to express this gospel identity has clearly defined the Fundamentalists' relationship to the wider society. Joel A. Carpenter, an astute observer of Fundamentalism, suggested that Fundamentalists shared with their Evangelical brethren the "language of postconversion" spiritual formation and understanding. This was the language of a sanctified life, which welcomed the repentant into full fellowship, but also bestowed upon them the assurance to proclaim the truth boldly in whatever they did and wherever they went. Adherents of this new identity subsequently reordered and adapted nearly every aspect of their lives in accordance with this newfound assurance of the gospel message. "As people of the Book," Carpenter reflects, "fundamentalists made it the identifying totem of their movement" (Carpenter 1997: 74). The gospel as the "totem" of Fundamentalist life and identity has materialized in two notable areas of religious life: the ritual association of the gospel to Fundamentalist identity and the reorientation of physical space.

"Gospel Ritual"

Marsden persuasively argued that Protestant Fundamentalism is a movement shaped by paradox (1980: 43–48). Perhaps nowhere is this characteristic more evident than in the Fundamentalist's eschewing of modern society while at the same time fervently embracing its technological advances in communication. Fundamentalists have retooled the revivalist tradition of their Evangelical ancestors by adopting the latest technologies to spread the gospel message. Through this means of adaptation, Fundamentalists have been innovative in the development of new and meaningful rituals for their communities. One such example is the use of the radio broadcast, which can spread the gospel by reaching large numbers of potential converts. In addition, by going to the airwaves Fundamentalist leaders were no longer ensnarled by traditional denominational barriers. Disparate communities of Fundamentalists could be united at a certain level and able to form their own gospel identity by listening to the message on the radio broadcasts.

Coinciding with the use of mass media was the development of the Gospel Tabernacle movement among Evangelicals and Fundamentalists during the 1920s and 1930s. Somewhat eclectic in their makeup (some of the earliest gathering involved Pentecostals, Evangelicals, and Fundamentalists), the Tabernacle movement brought together charismatic leaders and laity to worship as a collected body celebrating in the gospel. In their selection of music, "Tab" services mirrored the eclecticism of the faith traditions of those gathered. However, because of the growing popularity of radio at these religious gatherings, the music began to evolve with the radio audience in mind. Gospel songs were particularly suited for this medium because of their simple lyrics, stirring themes, and upbeat tempos. The gospel message set to music and conveyed over the airwaves enabled distant listeners to sing along with their spiritual brethren. Whether going to "Tab" on Sunday afternoons in person or listening to it on the radio, Fundamentalists of different generations and locales participated in religious activity closely aligned and readily identifiable with the gospel. At these and similar types of gatherings, practitioners listened to popular orators, were led in a close reading of the Scriptures, and sang gospel songs that posed questions such as "Are you washed in the blood of the Lamb?" These events became the defining rituals for Fundamentalists and dramatically oriented their lives as the gatekeepers of gospel truth (Carpenter 1997: 124–140).

"Gospel Space"

An allegiance to the gospel and work toward its dissemination has also redefined physical space among Fundamentalists. Spreading the gospel was a Fundamentalist ritual that not only could potentially transform the state of an individual's soul, but could transform ordinary or secular space into a sacramental one. Though this practice is not unique to Fundamentalism, it has shaped the lives of numerous followers. The urban gospel tabernacle, perhaps the best-known and most influential manifestation of the

Fundamentalists' evangelicalism, is but one example of this kind of self-styled reorganization. "Gospel tabernacles" adapted old theater buildings and dilapidated auditoriums used by Evangelicals and Fundamentalists as a forum for urban revival campaigns. These evangelistic gatherings attracted a broad array of Evangelicals and Fundamentalists and focused on such themes as "the Gospel of full salvation and present and complete sanctification" and "the provision Christ has made in the Gospel for our physical redemption through divine healing." Sensational preaching styles punctuated the gospel message of salvation while gospel singers entertained the audience, who often participated in the singing of familiar tunes. Evangelical Paul Rader, one of the most popular preachers of this parachurch forum, drew significant crowds of Chicagoans from 1915 to 1921. So convinced was Rader of this method and approach to evangelizing, he decided to formally found the Chicago Gospel Tabernacle in 1922 and urged the Christian and Missionary Alliance to reorganize to promote gospel tabernacles throughout the country (Reid 1990: 970).

The adaptation of secular space for spiritual means is also demonstrated by the establishment of new Fundamentalist churches. For example, Jerry Falwell of the Thomas Road Baptist Church—who has fallen in and out of grace with Fundamentalist leaders—started his church in Lynchburg, Virginia, in 1956 with thirty-five members who met for worship in the vacated Donald Duck Bottling Company building. In 1968, the church began recording its services for the ever-expanding medium of television and called these services *The Old-Time Gospel Hour*. By the mid-1980s, the congregation had more than 18,000 members (Reid 1990: 427).

Kent A. McConnell

See also Fundamentals, The; Gospel Music; New Testament; Orthodoxy; Televangelism

Bibliography

Carpenter, Joel A. (1997) *Revive Us Again: The Reawakening of American Fundamentalism*. New York: Oxford University Press.

Chadwick, Henry. (1967) *The Early Church*. New York: Penguin Books.

Cross, Frank L., and Elizabeth A. Livingstone, eds. *The Oxford Dictionary of the Christian Church*. New York: Oxford University Press.

Hamann, Henry P. (1980) *The Bible Between Fundamentalism and Philosophy*. Minneapolis, MN: Augsburg Publishing House.

Hutchison, William R. (1992) *The Modernist Impulse in American Protestantism*. Durham, NC: Duke University Press.

Lawrence, Bruce B. (1989) *Defenders of God: The Fundamentalist Revolt Against the Modern Age*. New York: Harper and Row.

Marsden, George M. (1980) *Fundamentalism and American Culture: The Shaping of Twentieth-Century Evangelicalism, 1870–1925*. New York: Oxford University Press.

Metzger, Bruce M., and Roland E. Murphy, eds. (1991) *The New Oxford Annotated Bible*. New York: Oxford University Press.

Reid, Daniel G., Robert D. Linder, Bruce L. Shelley, and Harry S. Stout, eds. (1990) *Dictionary of Christianity in America*. Downers Grove, IL: InterVarsity Press.

Thuesen, Peter J. (1999) *In Discordance with the Scriptures: American Protestant Battles over Translating the Bible*. New York: Oxford University Press.

Gospel Music

The Christian Church has a long musical history, as do many religions. The apostle Paul, in his letters to the churches in Ephesus and Colossi, wrote of singing psalms, hymns, and spiritual songs. He told them to sing and make music to God (Ephesians 5:19; Colossians 3:16). The Anglican and Reformed churches have had a tradition of singing the Psalter, and the church universal has sung hymns for nearly two millennia. Gospel songs, or spiritual songs, have emerged with more centrality since the Great Awakenings in North America and England. The great hymn writer Charles Wesley (1707–1788) composed much of the music that was sung during the First Great Awakening (1725–1769); however, by the Second Great Awakening (1800–1830) a shift had begun in American religious patterns. Coupled with influences from the Enlightenment, English-speaking Protestant Christianity increasingly began to focus on the individual and its music reflected this trend. After the Enlightenment the church shifted from hymnody to gospel music.

What is the difference between hymns and gospel music? Hymns focus on one's attitude toward God, His character and actions, or His purpose in human life. Gospel songs more often focus on the human condition and one's relation to God. Sacred songs moved from articulate theological statements to simple messages that were easily understood and the tunes changed from complex to simple melodies. This trend mirrored the growing number of popular songs with simple lyrics and melodies that pervaded the general culture, such as "The One Horse Open Sleigh" (Jingle Bells) and "The Man on the Flying Trapeze." Gospel music, therefore, is another form of popular religious music in the vein of Luther's adaptations of the spiritual songs using popular tunes sung in the taverns of the time.

Gospel Music and the Great Awakenings

Gospel music is a truly American music form and continues as a popular form of religious music. Gospel music of a Fundamentalist variety, as opposed to the variety that emerged from the African-American community, came out of the camp meeting and revivalist tradition of the mid- and the late nineteenth century after the Second Great Awakening. Another major transformation in American Protestantism from the First Great Awakening to the Second was the mitigation of the Calvinistic traditions of evangelists Jonathan Edwards (1703–1758) and George Whitefield (1714–1770) by the Arminianism of John Wesley (1703–1791). This transformation echoed the theological shift from God's sovereignty to man's, especially as American Protestantism urged a personal religious experience and conversion. The songs also encouraged those in the fold to reach out to others through missionary and evangelistic efforts.

Throughout its revivalist history, American gospel music and mass evangelism have gone hand-in-hand (Ellsworth 1979: 92). The preachers' message of sin and salvation has continually resonated with the populace, and the message has always been better conveyed when the preacher was aided by a gospel song leader. Evangelist Dwight L. Moody (1837–1899) had Ira Sankey (1840–1908); Daniel Webster Whittle (1840–1901) had Philip Bliss (1838–1876); Billy Sunday (1862–1935) had Homer Rodeheaver (1880–1955); and Billy Graham (1918–) had George Beverley Shea (1909–).

Another key period in the development of gospel music came during the Sunday school movement, which arose amidst the growth of the public school movement advocated by Horace Mann (1796–1859). Sunday schools filled many individuals' need for

social interaction, instruction in reading and writing, and other learning opportunities. Music was also central to the Sunday school movement because songbooks were created for these schools.

Some scholars have articulated a Third Great Awakening that encompassed the years 1870 to 1925. The so-called Gilded Age and Progressive Era saw an urban crisis as many rural Americans moved into the large cities and the forces that created Fundamentalism emerged as a definable movement. It was during this period that gospel music evolved, composed by key figures like Bliss, Sankey, and Rodeheaver. Their songs spoke to the growing urban masses and were compiled into songbooks that echoed the themes of the revivalist tradition: triumph, awakening, service, good news, salvation, praise, and victory.

Prominent Music Evangelists

Philip Paul Bliss is believed to be the first individual to use the phrase "gospel music" in a consistent fashion to denote that form of music that strongly emerged after the Civil War. It first appeared in his *Gospel Songs* (1874), which was compiled with Whittle for use in their revival meetings (Reynolds 1978: 94). Showing great promise, it is unknown what Bliss could have written if his life had not been cut short by a train wreck when he was 38 years old. Bliss is most known for his hymns "Hold the Fort" (1870), "Jesus Loves Even Me" (1871), "Hallelujah, What a Saviour" (1875), and "Wonderful Words of Life" (1874).

Despite being blind from poor treatment by a doctor as an infant, American hymn writer Fanny Crosby wrote more than 8,000 hymns, though she did not start writing until she was nearly 45 years old. Undisputedly, Crosby was one of the most (if not the most) prolific hymn writers of all time, authoring hymns under no fewer than seventy-five pseudonyms. For many years, Fanny was under a contract to submit three hymns per week to her publisher, Biglow and Main Company, a major gospel music publishing house (Foote 1968: 267). At times she was able to complete six to seven hymns a day. Some of her best-loved and well-sung hymns are "Blessed Assurance" (1873), "He Hideth My Soul" (1890), "Near the Cross" (1869), and "Rescue the Perishing" (1869).

In the latter half of the nineteenth century, Dwight L. Moody rose to prominence in America and abroad. Though Moody originally sought to unite with Philip Bliss, one cannot think of Moody without also thinking of Ira Sankey. It was their union, after meeting at a YMCA meeting, that established the model of mixing preaching and singing, both solo and corporate, still in use today by many evangelists. As well as being a soloist, Sankey wrote roughly 1,200 songs during his career and was best-known for his tunes to the hymns "The Ninety and Nine" (1868) and "Trusting Jesus" (1876). For the last thirteen years of his life Sankey served as the president of Biglow and Main Company.

Following the lead of Moody and Sankey, the next major evangelist–soloist pair was Billy Sunday and Homer Rodeheaver. After serving in the Spanish–American War, Rodeheaver attended Ohio Wesleyan University. He intended to study law, but felt called into ministry. After some years on his own as a musical evangelist, in 1909 he joined fiery evangelist Billy Sunday. He worked with Sunday for the next twenty years. Rodeheaver eventually established his own gospel publishing house, the Rodeheaver-Ackley Company (it later became the Rodeheaver Hall-Mack Company). In 1920, he founded a gospel music recording company, Rainbow Records. Rodeheaver is considered to be the most prolific recorder of sacred songs in the pre-microphone era of acoustical recording, with some of his offerings being sold via the Sears and Roebuck catalog.

The legacy of Bliss, Crosby, Sankey, and Rodeheaver has been carried on in more recent times by Alfred B. Smith (1916–). Smith, a graduate of Billy Graham's alma mater Wheaton College, was the founder of Singspiration Music and served as a songwriter for Moody Bible Institute. Starting in the 1930s Smith began producing gospel songbooks, which were later published under the Singspiration label. The first issue of that label was printed at Wheaton College in 1941. Smith also continued the practice of gospel composers establishing their own publishing organizations. His gospel-laden and most well-known work is probably "For God So Loved The World" (1938)

Conclusion

American religious movements, particularly Fundamentalism, have succeeded in creating populist forms of religion; and this has also been true of gospel music and its wide range of forms. Gospel music is characterized by simple and repetitive lyrics, uncomplicated, easily learned melodies, and its emphasis on personal religious experience. The shift in sacred music away from complex hymns to gospel music, both musically and theologically, mimics the shift in American religion from traditional services to camp meetings and revivals. The music of yesterday was no longer suited to the times and had to make way for more accessible forms.

David B. Malone

See also African-American Holiness-Pentecostal Movement; Great Awakening; Preaching; Radio; Televangelism

Bibliography

Blackwell, Lois S. (1978) *The Wings of the Dove: The Story of Gospel Music in America*. Norfolk, VA: Donning.

Crafts, Wilbur F. (1877) *Song Victories of "the Bliss and Sankey Hymns," being a Collection of One Hundred Incidents in Regards to the Origin and Power of the Hymns Contained in "Gospel Hymns and Sacred Songs."* Boston: D. Lothrop.

Ellsworth, Donald Paul. (1979) *Christian Music in Contemporary Witness: Historical Antecedents and Contemporary Practices*. Grand Rapids, MI: Baker Book House.

Foote, Henry Wilder. (1968) *Three Centuries of American Hymnody*. Hamden, CT: Archon Books.

Lorenz, Ellen Jane. (1980) *Glory, Hallelujah!: The Story of the Camp Meeting Spiritual*. Nashville, TN: Abingdon Press.

Olson, Bob. (n.d.) "Homer Rodeheaver, Pioneer of Sacred Records." http://www.garlic.com/~tgracyk/rodeheaver.htm.

Patrick, Millar. (1962) *The Story of the Church's Song*. Richmond: John Knox Press.

Porter, Thomas Henry. (1981) "Homer Alvan Rodeheaver (1880–1955): Evangelistic Musician and Publisher." Ed.D. thesis, New Orleans Baptist Theological Seminary.

Reynolds, William Jensen. (1978) *A Joyful Sound*. New York: Holt, Rinehart and Winston.

Routley, Erik. (1952) *Hymns and Human Life*. Grand Rapids, MI: Wm. B. Eerdmans.

Sadie, Stanley, and John Tyrrell, eds. (2001) *The New Grove Dictionary of Music and Musicians*. New York: Grove's Dictionaries.

Sallee, James. (1978) *A History of Evangelistic Hymnody*. Grand Rapids, MI: Baker Book House.

Sankey, Ira David. (1907) *My Life and the Story of the Gospel Hymns and of Sacred Songs and Solos*. New York: Harper.

Whittle, Daniel W., ed. (1877) *Memoirs of Philip P. Bliss.* New York: A.S. Barnes and Co.

Wilhoit, Melvin Ross. (1982) "A Guide to the Principal Authors and Composers of Gospel Song of the Nineteenth Century." D.M.A. thesis, Southern Baptist Theological Seminary.

Grace

While the term "grace" in its broadest sense contains the concepts of joy, pleasure, delight, sweetness, charm, and loveliness, its general biblical usage is centered in the concept of favor, whether merited (deserved) or not. In this sense, Luke speaks of Jesus' development as a child, growing "in favor (grace) with God and men" (Luke 2:40, 52; NASB). However, in its more specific New Testament reference to Christian salvation, the term is used for the kindness or favor God bestows upon those who deserve nothing, granting to sinners pardon for their offenses and opening the doorway to eternal salvation through Jesus Christ. The apostle Paul, in Romans 5:6–10, characterizes the undeserving nature of mankind as "helpless," "ungodly," "sinners," and as "enemies." Nevertheless, through the operation of divine grace (Romans 3:24), Christ died for us, we have been justified by His blood, and shall be saved from the wrath of God through Him—thus, the well-known and often used simple definition of grace as "the unmerited (undeserved) favor of God."

Usage

In this specific sense of "unmerited favor," grace is used in the New Testament to include practically every aspect of God's work in our behalf. Grace is an attitude of God toward man (Ephesians 2:7), it is a work of God on behalf of man (Titus 2:11), a gift of God given to man (Ephesians 4:7), and a power of God working in man (1 Corinthians 15:10). Faith in Christ has provided believers with a standing in grace in which we abide and experience all the blessings of salvation (Romans 5:2; Acts 13:43). In fact, in the New Testament "grace" practically becomes a synonym for Christianity itself. Worthy of note in this connection is Paul's custom of closing his letters with a benediction which mentions "grace" alone, as

if nothing else were needed (1 Corinthians 16:23; Galatians 6:18; Philippians 4:23; Colossians 4:18; 1 Thessalonians 5:28; 2 Thessalonians 3:18).

Source

The New Testament text demonstrates that grace finds its source in the triune God: the Father is "the God of all grace" (1 Peter 5:10), Paul writes of "the grace of our Lord Jesus Christ" (2 Corinthians 8:9), and the Holy Spirit is characterized as "the Spirit of grace" (Hebrews 10:29). However, grace is most clearly seen in the person of the Son and best understood in His life and work. John the Apostle wrote that "we saw His glory," which was "full of grace and truth," that we have received of His fullness which is characterized as "grace upon grace," and that while the law was given by Moses, grace and truth were realized through Jesus Christ" (John 1:14–17). Paul, in Titus 2:11–13, practically uses "Grace" as a title for Christ, writing that "the Grace of God has appeared." He explains that this grace has brought salvation, that it provides instruction for godly living, and the expectation or blessed hope of Christ's return.

Grace and Law

While John has said that grace was "realized through Jesus Christ" (John 1:17), that is not to say that grace was unknown in Old Testament revelation, for it has never been absent from God's dealings with man. While found again and again in the sacrifices of Abraham, Isaac, and Jacob, it is institutionalized in the sacrificial system of the nation of Israel. Having declared the commandments to Moses (Exodus 20, esp. vv. 24–25), God commanded the building of an altar for burnt offerings and peace offerings and promised that in every place where He caused His name to be remembered, He would come and bless His people. Thus, in the midst of law-giving, grace was pictured in the sacrifices of the Old Testament, as God in this way provided the means whereby man might live in relationship with Him.

It is a glorious New Testament truth that with the life, death, and Resurrection of Jesus Christ, the requirements of the Law have been fulfilled and the righteousness of Christ has been imputed to the believer (placed to the believer's account). Thus, one's relationship with God is based solely upon

Romans 5:6–10

6. For when we were yet without strength, in due time Christ died for the ungodly.

7. For scarcely for a righteous man will one die: yet peradventure for a good man some would even dare to die.

8. But God commendeth his love toward us, in that, while we were yet sinners, Christ died for us.

9. Much more then, being now justified by his blood, we shall be saved from wrath through him.

10. For if, when we were enemies, we were reconciled to God by the death of his Son, much more, being reconciled, we shall be saved by his life.

Romans 3:23–26

23. For all have sinned, and come short of the glory of God;

24. Being justified freely by his grace through the redemption that is in Christ Jesus:

25. Whom God hath set forth to be a propitiation through faith in his blood, to declare his righteousness for the remission of sins that are past, through the forbearance of God;

26. To declare, I say, at this time his righteousness: that he might be just, and the justifier of him which believeth in Jesus.

God's grace, rather than upon Law works or upon a mixture of grace and works. In fact, Paul declares that grace and works are mutually exclusive: "But if it is by grace, it is no longer on the basis of works, otherwise grace is no longer grace" (Romans 11:6). This is not to say that righteous living is unimportant under the sovereignty of grace. Paul wrote, "The Law came in so that the transgression would increase; but where sin increased, grace abounded all the more ... even so grace would reign through righteousness to eternal life through Jesus Christ our Lord" (Romans 5:21).

The Breadth of the Work of Grace

The grace of God in Christ does not merely recover what was lost in Adam, but provides "much more" besides (Romans 5:15, 17, 20). In fact, grace brings every blessing of salvation to the believer: election (Romans 11:5), forgiveness (Ephesians 1:7), calling (Galatians 1:15), comfort and hope (" ... God ... has given us eternal comfort and good hope by grace...." 2 Thessalonians 2:16), salvation in its totality (Ephesians 2:8; "For by grace you have been saved through faith; and that [i.e., salvation by grace through faith] not of yourselves, it is the gift of God"), spiritual strength (2 Timothy 2:1), justification (Titus 3:7), standing in grace (Romans 5:2), ministry

by grace ("To me ... this grace was given to preach to the Gentiles.... " Ephesians 3:8), eternal life (Romans 5:21), the complete area of spiritual growth ("But grow in grace"; 2 Peter 3:18), all that we are and do in Christ ("But by the grace of God I am what I am, and His grace toward me did not prove vain; but I labored even more than all of them, yet not I, but the grace of God with me"; 1 Corinthians 15:10). Thus, grace is responsible for the totality of salvation: past, present, and future.

Wayne S. Flory

See also Salvation

Bibliography

Chafer, Lewis Sperry. (1943) *Grace*. Chicago: Moody Press.

Erickson, Millard. (1992) *Introducing Christian Doctrine*. Grand Rapids, MI: Baker Book House.

McGrath, Alister E. (1994) *Christian Theology*. Cambridge, MA: Basil Blackwell Inc.

Scofield, Cyrus Ingerson. (n.d.) "The Grace of God." In *The Fundamentals*, edited by R. A. Torrey and updated by Charles L. Feinberg (1958). Grand Rapids, MI: Kregel, 398–407.

Thiessen, Henry C. (1979) *Lectures in Systematic Theology*. Grand Rapids, MI: Wm. B. Eerdmans.

Great Awakening

The Great Awakening commonly describes a series of revivals that swept through the American colonies between 1739 and 1743. These revivals involved Evangelical preaching, often in open-air services and before large groups of people. Calvinist in theological emphasis, the Great Awakening was characterized by strong religious emotionalism: sermons typically placed great stress upon the depravity of unredeemed humanity, the wrath of God, the necessity of conversion—or, as it was termed, the "New Birth"— and the unconditional election of the saints. Listeners were forcefully and repeatedly exhorted to forge a personal relationship with Christ, and, during services, often experienced profound emotional reactions such as bursting into tears, fainting, convulsions, visions, and trances.

Historically, the Great Awakening movement is associated with the Evangelical Revival, occurring at the same time in the Church of England, and with the emergence of eighteenth-century pietism throughout Western Europe. It is also part of a series of revivals, or periods of spiritual "wetness," that occurred in America at regular intervals throughout the late seventeenth and early eighteenth centuries. The last of these, taking place in the Connecticut River valley between 1734 and 1735, and described by Jonathan Edwards in his *A Faithful Narrative of the Surprising Work of God* (1737), in many respects served as a precursor to and blueprint for the Great Awakening itself. However, the Great Awakening stands out in this context as a culminant and transformational event for a number of reasons. Because of the geographical range over which it extended, the number of clergymen actively participating, and the sizes of the audiences attending services and testifying to converting experiences, it established revivalism as a major cultural force in American culture. Moreover, the depths of controversy it raised created crucial ruptures within the participating churches, permanently dividing liberal and Evangelical Christians, and effectively destroying America's parochial system. Finally, the methods of preaching evolved during the Awakening and the doctrinal struggles following its conclusion did much to define American Evangelicalism.

The Revivalists

The preaching of George Whitefield (1714–1770) was the immediate catalyst for the Great Awakening. As a Calvinist Anglican preacher he had already achieved a reputation in England for his ability to move audiences to profound emotional responses. Whitefield was reportedly of singularly remarkable oratorical ability: he had a powerful, sonorous voice, capable of being heard at great distances, and would always speak extemporaneously, using dramatic gestures and illustrations to vividly depict the horrors of damnation and the wonders of conversion. Encouraged partially by accounts of the 1734–1735 revival, Whitefield undertook an extended preaching tour of the American colonies, beginning in Philadelphia in 1739, traveling through the middle colonies and the South, and ending in New England in 1741. Throughout, he maintained a vigorous schedule, often preaching twice a day, to crowds of up to 30,000 people. Many clergymen, impressed by Whitefield's results, joined in his efforts and also began itinerant preaching. Of these, the most prominent was Gilbert Tennent, a Presbyterian from Philadelphia who was encouraged by Whitefield to travel to New England, and who continued to tour this region after Whitefield's departure. Other important supporters included Benjamin Colman, the senior pastor in Boston; Jonathan Dickinson; Jonathan Edwards, the most able defender of revivalist theology; and Thomas Prince, Jr., the editor of *The Christian History*, the journal of the revivalist movement.

Consequences of the Great Awakening

Although the majority of Congregationalist and Presbyterian clergymen initially supported the Awakening, as its influence began to wane, its spiritual validity fell into question. The ensuing debate served to exacerbate tensions already existing within the participating churches. Objections to the Great Awakening on the part of non-revivalist clergy were focused on a number of issues: the practices of itinerant preaching and lay exhorting, which disrupted ecclesiastic order and bred resentment and jealousy among the clergy; the disparaging attitude many of the Evangelical preachers such as Whitefield or, more extravagantly, James Davenport, assumed toward those not actively involved with the revivals; and what the non-revivalists viewed as the promulgation of doctrinal errors. These issues led to fissures that divided both the Presbyterian and Congregational Churches into pro-revival and anti-revival factions.

In the Presbyterian Church, the "New Side" supporters of the Great Awakening, led by Tennent and

Selection from: "SINNERS IN THE HANDS OF AN ANGRY GOD" A SERMON DELIVERED BY JONATHAN EDWARDS IN ENFIELD, CONNECTICUT ON JULY 8, 1741

Their foot shall slide in due time. Deuteronomy 32:35
In this verse is threatened the vengeance of God on the wicked unbelieving Israelites, who were God's visible people, and who lived under the means of grace; but who, notwithstanding all God's wonderful works towards them, remained (as vers 28.) void of counsel, having no understanding in them. Under all the cultivations of heaven, they brought forth bitter and poisonous fruit; as in the two verses next preceding the text.—The expression I have chosen for my text, their foot shall slide in due time, seems to imply the following things, relating to the punishment and destruction to which these wicked Israelites were exposed.

1. That they were always exposed to destruction; as one that stands or walks in slippery places is always exposed to fall. This is implied in the manner of their destruction coming upon them, being represented by their foot sliding. The same is expressed, Psalm 72:18. "Surely thou didst set them in slippery places; thou castedst them down into destruction."

2. It implies, that they were always exposed to sudden unexpected destruction. As he that walks in slippery places is every moment liable to fall, he cannot foresee one moment whether he shall stand or fall the next; and when he does fall, he falls at once without warning: Which is also expressed in Psalm 73:18,19. "Surely thou didst set them in slippery places; thou castedst them down into destruction: How are they brought into desolation as in a moment!"

3. Another thing implied is, that they are liable to fall of themselves, without being thrown down by the hand of another; as he that stands or walks on slippery ground needs nothing but his own weight to throw him down.

4. That the reason why they are not fallen already and do not fall now is only that God's appointed time is not come. For it is said, that when that due time, or appointed time comes, their foot shall slide. Then they shall be left to fall, as they are inclined by their own weight. God will not hold them up in these slippery places any longer, but will let them go; and then, at that very instant, they shall fall into destruction; as he that stands on such slippery declining ground, on the edge of a pit, he cannot stand alone, when he is let go he immediately falls and is lost.

Source: *Historic Church Documents*. www.reformed.org.

Dickinson, broke from the "Old Side" Synod of Philadelphia and formed the Synod of New York. These factions, however, engaged in little dialogue. The defining struggle between pro-revivalists and anti-revivalists occurred within the Congregational Church of New England. For the anti-revivalists ("Old Lights"), the Great Awakening was pernicious because it seemed to them to consist largely of dangerous religious enthusiasm that verged on antinomianism. The pro-revivalist ("New Light") apologists insisted that, despite its flaws, the Awakening was a legitimate work of God and an instrument for the diffusion of the Holy Spirit. To them, the Great Awakening constituted a return to the pietistic and "experimental" (experiential) approach to religion evident in the first generation of New England Puritans, which had been in remission for much of the eighteenth century. Moreover, they saw the non-revivalists' opposition as betraying a tendency to Arminianism—that is, to the belief that grace is not irresistible, but conditional on human cooperation.

Charles Chauncy and Jonathan Edwards were the leading disputants in this controversy, and they engaged in a protracted debate about the nature of divine grace, the value the affections should be afforded in the conversion experience, and, ultimately, the nature of religious psychology itself. As a result of this exchange—Edwards wrote *The Distinguishing Marks* (1741), *Some Thoughts Concerning the Revival* (1742), and *The Religious Affections* (1746), and Chauncy responded with *Enthusiasm Described and Caution'd Against* (1742) and *Seasonal Thoughts* (1743)—the distinct theological assumptions guiding the pro-revivalists and the anti-revivalists were refined, and the sects that came to dominate nineteenth-century theological thought gradually took shape. The "Old Lights" moved to a liberal Christianity that, for many, eventually found expression in Unitarianism. The Evangelically inclined "New Lights" produced the New Divinity movement, as well as other forms of Calvinism and revivalism prominent in the nineteenth century.

Significance

Although of great consequence for the evolution of American religious history, the larger significance of the Great Awakening has been subject to much dispute. Some scholars have argued that it inaugurated a fundamental change in consciousness that contributed to the American Revolution. Others have asserted that it constituted a retrograde expression of a Calvinist theology that had become untenable, and in fact only delayed the spread of the Enlightenment in America. Recently, much critical attention has been paid to the way in which writers, both contemporary with and subsequent to the Great Awakening, have attempted to construct it so as to make it validate particular readings of history.

James Hewitson

See also Calvinism; Evangelicalism; Holiness, Wesleyan; Pentecostalism; Preaching

Bibliography

Bushman, Richard L., ed. (1970) *The Great Awakening: Documents on the Revival of Religion, 1740–1745.* New York: Atheneum.

Butler, Jon. (1982) "Enthusiasm Described and Decried: The Great Awakening As Interpretive Fiction." *Journal of American History* 69.2:. 305–325.

Gaustad, Edwin Scott. (1957) *The Great Awakening in New England.* New York: Harper.

Goen, C.G., ed. (1972) *Works of Jonathan Edwards: The Great Awakening.* New Haven, CT: Yale University Press.

Heimert, Alan. (1966) *Religion and the American Mind, From the Great Awakening to the Revolution.* Cambridge, MA: Harvard University Press.

Heimert, Alan, and Perry Miller, eds. (1967) *The Great Awakening: Documents Illustrating the Crisis and Its Consequences.* Indianapolis: The Bobbs-Merrill Company, Inc.

Lambert, Frank. (1994) *"Pedlar in Divinity": George Whitefield and the Transatlantic Revivals, 1737–1770.* Princeton: Princeton University Press.

———. (1999) *Inventing the "Great Awakening."* Princeton: Princeton University Press.

Stout, Harry S. (1986) *The New England Soul: Preaching and Religious Culture in Colonial New England.* New York: Oxford University Press.

———. (1991) *The Divine Dramatist: George Whitefield and the Rise of Modern Evangelism.* Grand Rapids, MI: Wm. B. Eerdmans.

Gush Emunim

In the mid-1970s the religio-political movement of Gush Emunim (Bloc of the Faithful; henceforth GE) gained widespread public attention in Israel for its militant political actions carried out in the name of the Jewish religion. Followers of GE started settling hilltops in the occupied territories in the West Bank that were regarded internationally as Palestinian lands. To better understand the characterization of GE as a religious Fundamentalist movement, it is first necessary to delineate the convergence of historical events after World War II and the particular interpretation of a certain spectrum of the Israeli society based on the Jewish tradition.

The creation of the nation-state of Israel in Palestine by the secular Zionists constituted a huge theological dilemma for the religious sector. According to Jewish doctrine, the final redemption occurs when the Messiah returns to the Promised Land and reestablishes a divine kingdom in Palestine. For the Haredim (commonly known as ultra-Orthodox Jews), the secular nation-state by the secular Zionists was interpreted as a revolt against the divine will and thus seen as a blasphemic act. In contrast, the first Chief Rabbi of Israel, Abraham

Isaac Kook (1865–1935), and subsequently his son, Zvi Yehuda Kook (1891–1982), both of whom became the ideological heads of GE, interpreted the newly established nation-state as a sign of the beginning of the return of the Messiah. In their view, the secular Zionists were mere assistants in a divinely inspired plan.

The Six-Day War in 1967 provided another momentum for fostering the Kooks' interpretation. Because of the unexpected dimension of Israel's victory by capturing East Jerusalem with its Jewish holy sites and biblical Judea and Samaria, it was interpreted as the proof of the ongoing process of messianic redemption. However, the catalyst for the formation of GE was the Yom Kippur War in 1973 when Israel was on the brink of losing the war. Followers of the ideology of GE, previously a loose circle of students in the Merkaz Harav Yeshiva in Jerusalem led by the charismatic personality of Rabbi

Moshe Levinger, officially founded GE. For them the near war debacle was seen as Godly punishment for reducing the efforts to redeem (settle) the Holy Land. Therefore, they believed that the return of the Messiah could be hastened by Jews settling "the Whole Land of Israel," as it is written in the Bible.

For the followers of GE the settlement of the occupied territories in the West Bank became tantamount to all other religious commandments. They believed that the settlement was a divine precept to hasten the messianic process. Because their intent was opposed by local Palestinians as well as fellow Jews, they employed militant acts to realize their goal. In 1984 members of GE attempted to blow up the Arab mosques at the Temple Mount in Jerusalem. They tried to justify their militant actions religiously. Aran (1991: 291) stated that, for them, "an IDF rifle and tank have the same values as the prayer shawl and phylacteries; soldiers are as important as

Confrontation between national-religious Jews and ultra-Orthodox Jews near the wailing wall in Jerusalem. PHOTO COURTESY OF HERMANN MAIBA.

Talmudic scholars, and settlers are a particularly saintly group."

Even though GE never constituted more than a few thousand activist-believers, its actions had profound impacts. After the Likud Party took power in 1977 it adopted a policy to successively settle parts of the occupied territories and therefore took the agenda out of GE hands. The signing of the peace agreement between leaders Yitzhak Rabin and Yasir Arafat in 1993 and the concurrent hand over of occupied territories of biblical homeland to the Palestinians created an ideological void for the GE activists. Even though GE has since disappeared from the public stage, its interpretation of messianic redemption lies dormant, awaiting new historical circumstances to be taken up once again.

Hermann Maiba

See also Judaism, Fundamental

Bibliography

Aran, Gideon. (1991) "Jewish Zionist Fundamentalism: The Bloc of the Faithful in Israel (Gush Emunim)." In *The Fundamentalism Project*. Vol. 1, *Fundamentalism Observed: Reclaiming the Sciences, the Family, and Education*, edited by Marty Martin and Scott Appleby. Chicago: University of Chicago Press, 265–344.

Caplan, L., ed. (1987) *Studies in Religious Fundamentalism*. Albany: SUNY Press.

Demant, Peter. (1994) *Jewish Fundamentalism in Israel: Implications for the Mideast Conflict*. Jerusalem: IPCRI.

Don-Yehiya, Eliezer. (1991) "The Book and the Sword: The Nationalist Yeshivot and Political Radicalism in Israel." In *The Fundamentalism Project*. Vol. 4, *Accounting for Fundamentalism*. Chicago: University of Chicago Press, 264–302.

Landau, David. (1993) *Piety and Power: The World of Jewish Fundamentalism*. New York: Hill and Wang.

Lustick, Ian S. (1988) *For the Land and the Lord: Jewish Fundamentalism in Israel*. New York: Council for Foreign Relations.

Sivan, Emmanuel, and Menachem Friedman. (1990) *Religious Radicalism and Politics in the Middle East*. Albany: SUNY Press.

Sprinzak, Ehuh. (1986) *Fundamentalism, Terrorism, and Democracy*. Washington, DC: Wilson Center.

———. (1991) *The Ascendance of Israel's Radical Right*. New York: Oxford University Press.

Haredim

The term "Haredim" refers to a variety of groups making up the ultra-Orthodox wing of Judaism. It derives from the ancient Hebrew, meaning those who "tremble" before the word of God (Isaiah 66:5), often rendered "God-fearers." The Haredi movement originated as a negative reaction to the eighteenth-century Haskalah (Jewish Enlightenment). Its roots reach back to both classical rabbinic Judaism and Hasidism, the pietist movement founded by Israel ben Eliezer, the Baal Shem Tov (c. 1700–1760). While some Jews attempted to reconcile faith and practice with modern values, the Haredim opposed assimilation and compromise with secularity. The principal feature of the Haredi movement is strict observance of *halachah* (Jewish law). In contrast to modern forms of Orthodoxy, the Haredim are committed to unyielding separatism and a set of distinctive folkways inherited from premodern Eastern European Jewish culture. Since the Holocaust the Haredim have existed in insular, countercultural communities in Israel, North America, and parts of Western Europe. The most famous community is the Mea Shearim district of Jerusalem. In the 1990s worldwide membership was estimated at 540,000. Long known for political quietism, Haredim in Israel have been active in partisan politics. Unlike the Gush Emunim (Bloc of the Faithful), whose members espouse a radical religious nationalism, many Israeli Haredim—especially the Neturei Karta (Guardians of the City)—reject secular and religious Zionisms. They question the Jewish identity of Reform and Con-

Haredim in the streets of Mea Shearim, Jerusalem. PHOTO COURTESY OF HERMANN MAIBA.

servative Jews and converts. The description of the Haredim as Jewish Fundamentalists is a matter of scholarly debate. Some scholars dismiss the category of Jewish Fundamentalism altogether.

Peter A. Huff

See also Judaism, Fundamental

A FEW TEACHINGS OF THE BA'AL SHEM TOV

The Growing Tree
Rabbi Uri taught:

"Man is like a tree. If you stand in front of a tree and watch it incessantly to see how it grows and to see how much it has grown, you will see nothing at all. But tend to it at all times, prune the runners, and keep the vermin from it, and all in good time - it will come into its growth. It is the same with man: all that is necessary is for him to overcome his obstacles, and he will thrive and grow. But it is not right to examine him every hour to see how much has been added to his growth."

Breaking Impulses
A young man gave a note of request to the rabbi of Rizhyn. He had written to ask God's help in breaking his evil impulse. The rabbi's eyes laughed as he looked at him: "You want to break impulses? You will break your back, and your hip, yet you will not break an impulse. But if you pray and learn and work in all seriousness, the evil in your impulses will vanish of itself."

A Prayer
The rabbi of Koznitz said to God:

"Lord of the world, I beg of you to redeem Israel. And if you do not want to do that, then redeem the goyim [non-Jews]."

Books
Once the rabbi of Kobryn said:

"If it were within my power, I should hide everything written by the zaddikim. For when a man has too much knowledge, his wisdom is apt to be greater than his deeds."

Depending on God
Rabbi Moshe Leib said:

"How easy it is for a poor man to depend on God! What else has he to depend on? And how hard it is for a rich man to depend on God! All his possessions call out to him: "Depend on us!"

Source: *Stories of Ba'al Shem Tov.* www.totalb.com

Bibliography

Heilman, Samuel. (2000) *Defenders of the Faith: Inside Ultra-orthodox Jewry.* Berkeley: University of California Press.

———, and Menachem Friedman. (1991) "Religious Fundamentalism and Religious Jews: The Case of the Haredim." In *Fundamentalisms Observed*, edited by Martin E. Marty and R. Scott Appleby. Chicago: University of Chicago Press, 197–264.

Levy, Amnon. (1989) *The Haredim.* Jerusalem: Keter Publishing House.

Healing, Faith

Faith healing is the belief that mental or physical ailments are cured through a supernatural act of God in response to an act of faith. Claims of miraculous healings, while present throughout Christian tradition, took on particular importance with the precursors to the Fundamentalist movement. Since its systemization in the mid-nineteenth century, the practice of faith healing has served both as a major source of contention within Fundamentalism and, somewhat ironically, as a means of reintegrating aspects of the movement back into mainstream society. The doctrine remains prominent today, particularly within Pentecostal and charismatic circles, and has been a main vehicle in spreading Christian Fundamentalism among indigenous cultures in Africa, Latin America, and parts of Asia.

Nineteenth-Century Beginnings

During the late nineteenth century, the acceptance of faith healing was motivated by a number of cultural and theological factors. The era was marked by an increased interest in health and hygiene, yet professional medicine at this time remained more adept at diagnosing disease than treating it. In this vacuum, a number of alternate theories of health flourished, from pseudoscientific theories of animal magnetism to those of a more overtly religious nature such as Christian Science. In fact, much of the conservative Christian development of faith healing was in response to what was seen as theological errors in these alternate approaches. Religious trends within Christianity also contributed to an increased emphasis on faith healing. Many prominent church leaders were discarding the long-held Protestant conviction that miracles had ceased with the death of the apostles. In addition, biblical interpretation shifted away from its dependence on educated clergy toward increasing literal homespun interpretations. Many of these new interpreters had grown discontented with a perceived coldness in the church and looked for solutions in early Christian practices, such as the baptism of the Holy Spirit, which was recorded in the Book of Acts—a book that also spoke of miraculous healings. Finally, those who continued to hold to traditional Christian belief felt themselves under attack from an increasingly scientific world. Higher Criticism challenged notions of biblical inerrancy and many of its miraculous stories. Modern miracles, it was believed, could end these objections.

A number of individuals with apparent healing gifts first brought public attention to faith healing in the late nineteenth century. Episcopalian layman Charles Cullis (1833–1892) is considered the American father of faith healing. His long-standing care for the sick (Cullis studied homeopathic medicine and started a hospice for terminally ill patients) came to include faith healing in 1873 after hearing reports from Europe. By 1880 he was actively promoting the practice in New England. Adoniram Judson Gordon

(1836–1895), a Baptist minister from Boston, was another early proponent of faith healing. Although Gordon had only a limited faith-healing ministry, he influenced many with his book *Ministry of Healing* (1892), one of the clearest defenses of the movement. Albert Benjamin Simpson (1843–1919), a Presbyterian minister, went further in incorporating faith healing as an integral part of his ministry. After learning of faith healing from Cullis and then reportedly experiencing it himself, Simpson founded a number of faith homes (residences set aside for those seeking faith healing) and conducted numerous meetings devoted to its teaching and practice. Together, Cullis, Gordon, and Simpson codified the belief and practice of faith healing in the nineteenth century.

The central tenants of faith healing during the nineteenth century rested on the literal interpretation of several biblical passages. Isaiah 53:4–5 was interpreted to promise freedom from sickness and disease through the death of Christ just as it promised freedom from sin (a belief often referred to as "healing being found in the atonement"). The miraculous cures of Jesus further reinforced that this health would be realized miraculously through faith. Finally, two key passages in the Book of James were interpreted in a way that linked sickness to sin and unanswered prayer to impure motives or a lack of faith. The sick were thus encouraged to spend time in prayer and self-reflection, and to confront any spiritual barriers to health that might emerge. Only when a person's spiritual life was in order could he or she claim God's promise of healing. Most early faith healers believed the promise of health was unconditional, and thus taught that the use of doctors, medicine, and other medical means was not acting on faith and would impede recovery. However, as an increasing number of people were not healed despite their faith, and as medical technology continued to improve, such prohibitions against medicine were softened or eliminated altogether. It was reasoned that God could work though medical means as well as prayer.

Unlike most early practitioners who viewed faith healing as simply a spiritual means to health available to all believers, a second group used it to authenticate a unique message or special authority. Most prominent and controversial was John Alexander Dowie (1847–1907), a Scottish-born Australian evangelist and faith healer. After immigrating to the United States and, in 1894, basing his healing ministries in Chicago, his prominence grew exponentially.

But unlike other faith-healing advocates, Dowie believed his apparent ability to heal was his own unique gift, signifying a special prophetic status. He also never moderated his views on why some were not healed, steadfastly claiming that all such people continued in sin (which could include both using medical means and disagreeing with Dowie). Ultimately, the deaths of several of his followers resulted in his arrest and unsuccessful prosecution for practicing medicine without a license. By 1896 he founded his own denomination (the Christian Catholic Church), and later his own utopian community, Zion, Illinois. Though Dowie's followers ultimately rejected his prophetic claims in 1906, his extreme views of faith healing reverberated long after his demise. Far less confrontational, but equally influential was Maria Woodworth-Etter (1844–1924), the matriarch of the faith-healing revival meeting. Though Woodworth-Etter saw her meetings as primarily evangelistic, she was best known for her faith healing, prophecies, trances, and visions. Such practices, which would later emerge in Pentecostalism, drew large crowds, but kept her on the periphery of most religious circles.

The Pentecostal Movement

When the Pentecostal movement emerged at the turn of the twentieth century, its message of the restoration of miraculous signs and wonders (including speaking in tongues) almost immediately divided the Fundamentalist movement as it coursed through the networks created by Simpson, Dowie, Woodworth-Etter, and others. Most early Pentecostals adopted Dowie's controversial views on faith healing, simplistically linking sin and sickness and using miraculous healing as evidence that they were set apart. Most Fundamentalists, who either rejected faith healing or held to the moderate views of Simpson and Gordon, believed Pentacostalism reflected poorly on conservative theology in general and became among the movement's fiercest opponents. Such opposition to faith healing was not new, however. Conservative Presbyterian theologians from Princeton Seminary believed it was irresponsible not to use the medical establishment and theologically incorrect to place the promise of healing in the atonement. With the emergence of Pentecostalism, many Fundamentalists who had been at odds with the Princetonians on other issues adopted their critique of faith healing. Sickness, they claimed, was a part of human exis-

tence that God allowed believers to experience; human ingenuity—doctors and medication—was the main vehicle for healing. Many Fundamentalists returned to believing that God no longer performed miracles, using dispensational theology to defend their perspective; others held that while God might occasionally choose to miraculously heal, such occurrences were the exception.

The isolation of faith healing to the Pentecostal movement did not last long, however, due in large part to healing revivalist Aimee Semple McPherson (1890–1944). Unlike many Pentecostals of the time, McPherson avoided exclusivism and theological disputes, and held Simpson's more moderate views on faith healing. McPherson viewed her prayers for healing as only one side of her message, though it was the reports of the apparent effectiveness of those prayers that first drew people to her meetings. Combined with her physical attractiveness and excellent communication skills, McPherson became a national celebrity by the early 1920s. While McPherson was not without her own controversies, the net effect of her ministry was to reintroduce a new generation of Americans to the practice of faith healing in a way that was largely acceptable to the average citizen.

Healing Revivals and the Charismatic Movement

As Pentecostal denominations such as the Assemblies of God matured in the 1940s, many of the movements' more ebullient practices, including faith healing, were minimized. In response to this trend, a new wave of unaffiliated healing revivalism emerged in an attempt to revive these practices. The healing revivals of the late 1940s were started by William Branham (1909–1965) and were perpetuated by his able organizer Gordon Lindsay (1906–1973). Despite early successes, Branham briefly retired from public ministry in 1948. Left without anyone to promote, Lindsay focused his considerable organizational acumen on promoting several lesser-known revivalists and ultimately transforming a handful of isolated regional movements into a nationwide phenomenon. By 1949 Lindsay had a magazine with a circulation of thirty thousand, and his convention of healing revivalists had more than one thousand attendees a year later. Though most participants saw themselves as simply returning to earlier Pentecostal beliefs, they significantly altered the classic Pentecostal view by

Isaiah 53:4–5

4. Surely he hath borne our griefs, and carried our sorrows: yet we did esteem him stricken, smitten of God, and afflicted.

5. But he was wounded for our transgressions, he was bruised for our iniquities: the chastisement of our peace was upon him; and with his stripes we are healed.

Acts 3:1–16

1. Now Peter and John went up together into the temple at the hour of prayer, being the ninth hour.

2. And a certain man lame from his mother's womb was carried, whom they laid daily at the gate of the temple which is called Beautiful, to ask alms of them that entered into the temple;

3. Who seeing Peter and John about to go into the temple asked an alms.

4. And Peter, fastening his eyes upon him with John, said, Look on us.

5. And he gave heed unto them, expecting to receive something of them.

6. Then Peter said, Silver and gold have I none; but such as I have give I thee: In the name of Jesus Christ of Nazareth rise up and walk.

7. And he took him by the right hand, and lifted him up: and immediately his feet and ankle bones received strength.

8. And he leaping up stood, and walked, and entered with them into the temple, walking, and leaping, and praising God.

9. And all the people saw him walking and praising God:

10. And they knew that it was he which sat for alms at the Beautiful gate of the temple: and they were filled with wonder and amazement at that which had happened unto him.

11. And as the lame man which was healed held Peter and John, all the people ran together unto them in the porch that is called Solomon's, greatly wondering.

12. And when Peter saw it, he answered unto the people, Ye men of Israel, why marvel ye at this? or why look ye so earnestly on us, as though by our own power or holiness we had made this man to walk?

13. The God of Abraham, and of Isaac, and of Jacob, the God of our fathers, hath glorified his Son Jesus; whom ye delivered up, and denied him in the presence of Pilate, when he was determined to let him go.

14. But ye denied the Holy One and the Just, and desired a murderer to be granted unto you;

15. And killed the Prince of life, whom God hath raised from the dead; whereof we are witnesses.

16. And his name through faith in his name hath made this man strong, whom ye see and know: yea, the faith which is by him hath given him this perfect soundness in the presence of you all.

---

reinforcing Dowie's belief that faith healing depended on a particularly gifted person. Moreover, the new wave of faith healers believed the cause of mental or physical ailments was not a person's sin, but rather outside causes (often supernatural). The faith healer became the go-between of the physical and spiritual worlds; an individual's illness was part of a cosmic battle between good and evil.

Faith healer and evangelist Oral Roberts (1918–), while starting with many of these stark supernatural beliefs, ultimately took the middle ground between the more extreme healing revivalists and those who ignored faith healing. As such, Roberts facilitated interaction between numerous religious traditions. Born in poverty to a Pentecostal minister in Oklahoma, Roberts began an independent ministry in 1947 focusing almost exclusively on healing and demon possession. Roberts quickly gained considerable prominence through his wildly successful revival meetings and the unparalleled efficiency of his organization. Not content with the smaller Pentecostal circles, however, Roberts shifted his attention outward toward wider cooperation and cultural integration in the mid-1960s. To aid this accommodation, Roberts softened the harder edges of faith healing practice and rhetoric. He moved away from the supernatural language of faith healing by linking health to a positive mental attitude. In 1965 he founded Oral Roberts University, which eventually boasted a fully accredited medical school. In 1968 the lifelong Pentecostal took the unheard-of step of becoming a member of the Methodist Church. Simultaneously, Roberts's accommodation spread ideas of faith healing into mainstream denominations. Roberts was a founding member of the Full Gospel Business Men's Fellowship International, a nondenominational organization that spawned the charismatic movement in mainline Protestant and Roman Catholic circles. Roberts was also integral in bridging the divide between Pentecostals and the more moderate Fundamentalists (self-titled "neo-Evangelicals"), the successors of those who had spurned faith healing a generation before.

In the 1970s the theme of faith healing would reemerge in diverse and often contradictory settings. Some evangelists, like Kenneth Hagin, Kenneth Copeland, and Jim and Tammy Bakker, followed Roberts's lead by wedding classic promises of physical health to material success, forming the "Faith Movement." Logically tying wealth to long-held beliefs in healing not only won new followers, but also salved the consciences of upwardly mobile second- and third-generation Pentecostals who had been raised to believe that poverty was a necessary component of piety. On the opposite end of the spectrum, faith-healing themes could be found in the counter-cultural "Jesus Movement," which explicitly shunned wealth and traditional power structures in lieu of simple, often communal lifestyles.

Conclusion

The belief in faith healing shows no signs of abatement. Pentecostal and related independent churches throughout the world have experienced exponential growth, due in part to the practice of faith healing, which is easily adaptable to local customs and non-Western conceptions of health. Such churches in Latin America, the Caribbean, Africa, and East Asia have been among the most vibrant in the world.

{The Yoido Full Gospel Church in Seoul, South Korea, for example, had more than 600,000 members in 1990). Similar trends are evident in the West. Most conservative Evangelicals and Fundamentalists accept at least some form of faith healing (usually aligned with the more muted later beliefs of Simpson and Gordon). The charismatic movement continues to thrive in Protestant and Roman Catholic congregations throughout the United States and Europe. Moreover, recent medical studies linking mental and physical health have made aspects of faith healing attractive to those without any beliefs in the supernatural.

From its beginnings in the 1870s the faith-healing movement has been both compelling and controversial. Though the doctrine has revolved around several central themes, including the relation of sin to disease, God's relation to the physical world, and issues of unanswered prayer, the answers to these questions are often as numerous as faith healing practitioners. Although at times the belief caused sharp divisions, it also brought together unexpected allies. Both the changing conceptions of health on the one side and the continued flourishing of Fundamentalism on the other suggest that the practice of faith healing in its many forms will continue well into the future.

Timothy E. Gloege

See also African-American Holiness-Pentecostal Movement; Angelus Temple

Bibliography

Anderson, Robert Mapes. (1979) *Vision of the Disinherited: The Making of American Pentecostalism.* New York: Oxford University Press.

Blumhofer, Edith L. (1993a) *Aimee Semple McPherson: Everybody's Sister.* Grand Rapids, MI: Wm. B. Eerdmans.

———. (1993b) *Restoring the Faith: the Assemblies of God, Pentecostalism, and American Culture.* Urbana: University of Illinois Press.

Cox, Harvey. (1995) *Fire From Heaven: The Rise of Pentecostal Spirituality and the Reshaping of Religion in the Twenty-first Century.* Reading, MA: Addison-Wesley Publishing.

Cunningham, Raymond J. (1974) "From Holiness to Healing: The Faith Cure in America 1872–1892." *Church History* 43, 499–513.

Dayton, Donald W. (1987) *Theological Roots of Pentecostalism.* Peabody, MA: Hendrickson Publishers.

Harrell, David E., Jr. (1975) *All Things Are Possible: The Healing and Charismatic Revivals in Modern America.* Bloomington: Indiana University Press.

Hollenweger, Walter. (1988) *The Pentecostals.* Peabody, MA: Hendrickson Publishers.

Martin, David. (1990). *Tongues of Fire: The Explosion of Protestantism in Latin America.* Cambridge, MA: Blackwell Publishers.

Poewe, Karla, ed. (1994) *Charismatic Christianity As a Global Culture.* Columbia: University of South Carolina Press.

Wacker, Grant. (1985) "Travail of a Broken Family: Evangelical Responses to Pentecostalism in America." *Journal of Ecclesiastical History* 47: 3, 505–528.

Hell, Heaven, and Purgatory

Heaven is ordinarily understood by Fundamentalist or conservative Christians as the dwelling place of God or the gods, and/or spiritual beings who have been found worthy, or who have been made worthy, to dwell within a realm of perfection and bliss. The term, which has etymological relations to words meaning "sky" or "celestial sphere," is to be distinguished from both the earthly plane of space/time dimensionality, and the underworld abode of the damned. The latter, hell, is the reserve of spiritual beings whose earthly lives were judged to be lacking of the qualities associated with sanctity. According to traditional Catholicism, there lies in between these two spiritual realms the domain of purgatory, a place for the temporary sojourn of souls who are destined for heaven but are not yet ready to receive its blessings in full. All three concepts received much and varied interpretation in all religious traditions as they developed over the centuries. In general, heaven is understood to be the highest good attainable by humans, hell the most punitive demerit, and purgatory the intermediate realm between the two. In more recent decades, and in keeping with recent developments in biblical hermeneutics and psychological theories, heaven, hell, and purgatory have all been subject to a more symbolic reading. Conservative Christians, for the most part, reject these theories.

Heaven in the Western Religions

The Hebrew Bible annotates a development in the religious notion of heaven. The earliest strands of Jewish biblical tradition regard the heavenly sphere, that realm beyond the visible sky, as the dwelling place of Yahweh, from which Yahweh rules the earth, establishes its laws of behavior and religious devotion, and judges the day-to-day activities of humans. While a few select prophets were allowed to transcend life to that realm after death, it was not understood as the future dwelling place of ordinary believers. Rather, it was thought that all people, both the good and the transgressors of God's laws, would "sleep" eternally without reward or punishment in an

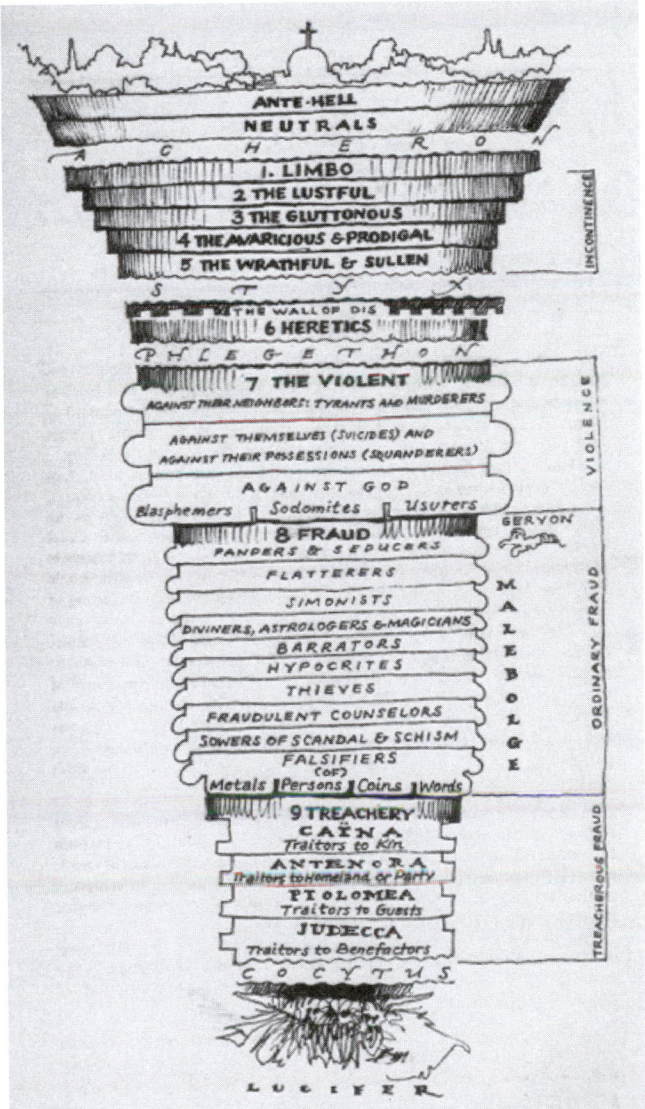

Dante's Map of Hell. HTTP://MARTIN.CARTHAGE.EDU.

underground region called "Sheol." In later strands of tradition, this view altered to include the idea of heaven as the postmortem resting place of those found to be righteous at the Day of Judgment, who would be miraculously "resurrected" or revivified in spiritual form to live eternally in the presence of God.

Christianity, born within the nexus of beliefs of later Judaism, along with the beliefs of certain post-Jewish apocalyptic sects, viewed heaven and its reward of the intellectually fulfilling *visio Dei* ("vision of God") as the hope of all true followers of Jesus Christ. "Heaven is the greatest good," writes Christian apologist and Boston College professor of philosophy, Peter Kreeft. "It is the reason God banged out the Big Bang 18 billion years ago. Next to the idea of God, the idea of heaven is the greatest idea that has ever entered into the heart of man, woman or child" (1990: 3). Christian rhetoric portrays heaven as humanity's "true home," a relief from earthly trials, the righting of all injustices, the end of all pain and suffering, and the everlasting experience of perfect beauty, bliss, fellowship with others, and connection to God. Roman Catholic doctrine adds the teaching that all souls destined for heaven, but who are not yet pure enough to enter it, must pass time in "purgatory" where they will be cleansed through obedience and devotion.

Islam, founded six centuries after the birth of Jesus, and influenced strongly by the same Jewish matrix that gave Christianity its start, views heaven as the unalterable reign of Allah's (God's) will, to which all faithful Muslims must go after death. Perhaps taking a cue from early Christian tradition, the Qur'an, Islam's bible, teaches that after death souls must pass certain tests, which for some may include a sojourn in hell, before entering into the blissful state of heaven. These tests are designed to evaluate the individual's understanding of the all-encompassing will of Allah as well as his or her devotion to the teachings of Muhammed, Islam's founding prophet.

Heaven in the East

Concepts of heaven vary considerably in the dominant Eastern religions of Hinduism and Buddhism. Hinduism's teachings of heaven are especially pluriform, relying as it does on a variety of deity-centered devotional practices and beliefs. Some gods are thought to reward their devotees with postmortem existences of bliss in a spiritual realm, while others

are thought to mediate a more disintegrated existence after death where the individual soul becomes one with the ultimate ground of all existence. Buddhism's beliefs can generally be divided into two primary types: that heaven is a space-time dimension similar to our present one, reserved for the faithful, wherein all suffering ceases and a life of continual bliss and enlightenment is preserved; and that heaven is the ultimate fulfillment of the teaching of *anatta*, or "non-self," by means of which the boundaries circumscribing the individual ego are shattered and a state of perfect nothingness obtains. Both traditions are in agreement, however, that the heavenly afterlife is one in which all forms of *dukha*, or "suffering," cease eternally.

Both Hinduism and Buddhism agree that the final moments of life prior to bodily death are all important to determining one's postmortem state. To be in a condition of enlightenment at the point of death, a mental state in which all earthly desires have ceased and perfect inner peace reigns, is the hope of every faithful Hindu and Buddhist. It is this state which is the key that unlocks the gateway to eternal paradise. All those who die without benefit of such enlightenment are fated to be born again, or reincarnated, in another earthly life. The law of karma is thought to be operative here. Karma is like the spiritual baggage that is carried from one life to the next. Evil deeds accrue bad karma, which both hinders one's attempts at reaching enlightenment, and also dictates that the next life lived will be worse than the prior one. Good deeds, however, merit good karma, and so both facilitate enlightenment and the enjoyment of earthly delights in the next life.

Concepts of Hell, East and West

Hell is traditionally defined in all religious traditions as the abode or state of being of souls that are damned to postmortem punishment. In the earliest forms of religion, hell is thought to be a gloomy subterranean realm where the souls of unenlightened heathen reside eternally (the Greek Hades); a dark region in the lower world in which both good and evil souls exist as shadowy figures (the ancient Israelite Sheol); or a nebulous existence in which the soul might eventually fade into nonexistence (as in certain North American Indian tribes). The view that hell is the punitive dwelling place of the damned after a Last Judgment, a place of suffering and torment, is a later development held commonly by the religions of Zoroastrianism, later Judaism, Christianity, and Islam.

The Christian view of hell, based on Jewish concepts, generally regards hell as the fiery domain of the devil and his evil angels, and a place of eternal damnation for those who have lived a life of sin and denial of God. This view was reinforced by the pre-scientific philosophizing of St. Augustine's *City of God*, and by the poetic presentations of Dante's *Inferno* and Milton's *Paradise Lost*. Some early Christian thinkers, such as Origen of Alexandria and Gregory of Nyssa, questioned the eternity of hell, insisting that God will extend mercy to all in time. The majority Christian view, however, teaches that hell is a state of punishment for those who reject God's offer of salvation. In more recent times, Christian theologians have come to question this view, forwarding the logic that eternal torment inflicted by divine decree is incompatible with the idea of God as infinite love, and that divine justice could never demand for finite human sin the infinite penalty of unending pain (cf. Hick 1994: 200–201). In 1995, the Anglican Church of England took the historic step of removing from the Book of Common Prayer all references to hell as a fiery realm of eternal torment, replacing them with the phrases "separation from God" and "annihilation" as indicative of the fate of the damned.

In Hinduism, it is believed that all actions have consequences and that evil actions have evil consequences. Such evil consequences may include time spent between incarnations in one or more of the twenty-one hells beneath the netherworld. However, Hinduism teaches that this consignment in hell is not of ultimate significance. It is, rather, a preparatory exercise intended to correct bad habits in the hope that they will not be carried on into the next life. It is also believed that eventually all souls will reach a state of everlasting nirvana, or blissful union with the Ultimate, even though it may take many life periods to attain this.

By contrast, Buddhism denies the existence of both the individual soul and an Ultimate. Nevertheless, there exist in popular Buddhist mythologies multiple hells as realms of punishment and expiation after death. In certain ancient Buddhist traditions, there is described a judgment that takes place immediately after death: the virtuous are allowed to enter immediately into one of the Buddhist paradises while sinners go to one of the many hells where they undergo a period of fixed punishment prior to their next rebirth. This time in hell can be shortened by the intercessions made on behalf of the departed by family and friends.

Purgatory

The concept of purgatory is that of an intermediate state between our present existence and the eternal heavenly life. This idea has been developed within Roman Catholic theology as the next stage of life for those who die in a state of unconfessed sin. It is generally understood that most people fall into this category: they are destined by God's grace to enter heaven, but there remain too many imperfections for their immediate admittance. As the name implies, purgatory (Latin, *purgare,* "to make pure") exists to purify the soul from all that would hinder it from receiving the beatific vision of God in heaven. While purgatory is not understood to be a place of torment, it is a place of rigorous self-examination and discipline. It is also believed that friends and family should pray for their departed loved ones in purgatory, and that those prayers are efficacious in ensuring that the time in purgatory is spent wisely.

In the fifteenth and sixteenth centuries, the saying of masses for souls in purgatory became a major ecclesiastical industry. Indulgences, or promises of the remittance of specific periods of purgatorial sentences, were sold for a price by less scrupulous priests. It was largely this that provoked the violent condemnation of Martin Luther, and therefore precipitated the Reformation. Consequently, the notion of purgatory has been in disrepute among most Protestant Christian denominations. In recent decades, however, certain Protestant theologians have spoken about the possibility of "progressive sanctification after death" (Hick 1994: 202), invoking thereby a kind of purgatorial state for those who die in an imperfect state.

Thomas Kinsell Carr

See also Catholic Fundamentalism; Eternal Life; Hinduism, Fundamental; Islamic Fundamentalism; Judaism, Fundamental; Sheol

Bibliography

Hick, John. (1994) *Death and Eternal Life*. Louisville, KY: Westminster Press.

Kreeft, Peter. (1990) *Everything You Ever Wanted to Know about Heaven, but Never Dreamed of Asking*. New York: Ignatius Press.

Heresy

Heresy is an identification referring to false religious teaching or erroneous doctrine. Heresy often represents to many religious Fundamentalists dangerous compromises with modernity and secular culture. Fundamentalists, whatever their sort, have universally fought to preserve traditional essentials of ancient faith and orthodoxy defined by religious leaders, historical consensus, or sacred writings.

The English word "heresy" originates from the Greek word *hairesis*, which in ancient Greek culture meant either a "choice," as in a "course of action," or a group or party with distinctive teachings, customs, or common purposes. In the early centuries of Christianity, *hairesis* came to designate teachings associated with religious groups that dissented from Catholic tradition. *Hairesis* especially became identified with erroneous teachings and inferior doctrine and resulted in condemnation by ecclesiastical authorities. Heresy, however, was not simply doctrinal error. Church leaders believed it threatened the purity of the church and led Christians away from the path of salvation. Throughout the history of the church, various heresies have emerged that have prompted harsh punishment from zealous defenders of tradition. Debates over doctrinal truth and error and the condemnation of heretics continued within Christianity into later centuries, quickly emerged within Protestantism, and in some respects, are common to every religious tradition.

The identification of heretical ideas and the perception of the heretic are largely dependent on perspective. From the position of religious authorities who have either defined correct doctrine or are committed to upholding tradition, the heretic is seen as an infidel and corrupter of the true faith. Often, however, those protesting official dogma or dissenting from religious institutions regard themselves as possessing a higher form of faith—a faith that was lost amid the institutional machinery of the official church. Similarly, while the orthodox, or those holding to codified dogma, have used the brand of heresy pejoratively, others have argued that heretics are often progressive harbingers of positive innovation and persons of deep faith, genuine sincerity, and unusual piety.

Heresy As Doctrinal Accommodation

While heresy and orthodoxy as identifications are somewhat problematic in nature, within the various fundamentalisms of the globe, heresy has almost universally referred to some form of doctrinal accommodation to modernity—a departure or dilution of ancient faith. Fundamentalism, in all its manifestations, is concerned with recapturing an adherence to older conceptions of faith and practice. Twentieth-century Islamic Fundamentalist sects such as the Muslim Brotherhood, Soldiers of God, and Holy Flight have all made efforts to reclaim the "classical experience" of Islamic faith and the "original meaning" of its message (Hunter 1990: 61). The National Pure Service Society, a Fundamentalist sect within Hinduism, has emphasized similar attitudes in their efforts to recover a more unadulterated observance of Dharma, the Hindu standard of conduct and social behavior. Within ultra-Orthodox Judaism, some have maintained their commitment to reclaiming ancient boundaries and traditional understandings of divine providence. Perhaps the most illustrative example of Fundamentalist notions of heresy and reaction against doctrinal compromise, however, can be found within American Protestant Fundamentalism, especially during the first decades of the twentieth century. Believing they were responsible for maintaining the purity of the church and for preserving traditional understandings of God, Jesus, and the Bible, Protestant Fundamentalists fought to purge America's denominations and Christian institutions of theological infidelity. The identification of heresy and the subsequent efforts to eradicate it lay at the heart of the Fundamentalist debates with theological liberalism, so-called modernism, and the New Theology.

Modernism, Liberalism, and the New Theology

In the eighteenth and nineteenth centuries, Americans were confronted with many social and religious changes. Many of these seemed to challenge traditional views of God and the natural world. The ideas of the German philosopher Immanuel Kant (1724–1804), for example, called into question the objective nature of reality and placed the individual, instead of God, at the center of human experience. The Enlightenment, with its confidence in human reason and belief in human autonomy, took America by storm and produced a thirst for liberty and democratic ideals. After 1859, Darwinism, along with the theory of evolution, gained momentum within educational circles and scientific inquiry led many to question traditional understandings of human origins. With the influx of immigrants during the nineteenth century came a new level of ethnic diversity, religious pluralism, and ideological competition. The Industrial Revolution created new social structures within American culture and the religious ideas of European theologians and biblical scholars also challenged American Evangelical notions about God and Scripture.

From this turmoil emerged a movement of Christian theology that sought to adjust the Christian faith and its doctrines to accommodate the "modern" scientific and intellectual advances of the nineteenth century. Liberalism, the New Theology, or modernism, as it was also called, recognized that traditional Christian theology might not withstand the challenges of shifting intellectual and cultural trends and sought to save it by "reformulating doctrines in the light of new biblical and scientific knowledge" (Conkin 1998: 54). Liberalism incorporated the thought of German theologians such as Frederick Schleiermacher (1768–1834) and Albrecht Ritschl (1822–1889) and found points of agreement with Unitarian notions of God and the experiential emphasis in transcendentalism. Liberalism also shied away from narrow theological boundaries and creeds and practiced openness in membership. Liberals possessed a progressive understanding of Revelation that emphasized the immanence of God, or His action within temporal processes. Modernists believed that traditional dogma was tied to older social structures and was thus provisional. Contemporary understandings of religion were more relevant to the changing world and were by nature more sophisticated, useful, and reliable. Many were optimistic about human progress and found social action to be the most appropriate form of Christian service.

Liberals were also quick to adopt innovative methods of biblical study and progressive conclusions about biblical authorship through the science of literary criticism. Many of these methods flourished in the universities of Germany and were popularized in the nineteenth century by scholars such as K. H. Graf and Julius Wellhausen. Liberals tended to be more imaginative in their reading of Scripture and were willing to look beyond literal interpretations. Given the biblical difficulties uncovered by modern scholarship, liberals could not affirm the doctrine of biblical inerrancy. Neither could they affirm the deity of Christ as defined by Fundamentalists nor justify belief in supernatural events such as Christ's miracles, His Virgin Birth, or Resurrection. Liberal theologians and modernists admitted there were essential differences between themselves and Fundamentalists. Many agreed their understandings were unorthodox and some were proud to admit a radical departure from traditional Christianity. Others, however, saw the New Theology as a reclamation of the true essence of Christianity—the essence that was lost to the institutional faith of orthodox Christianity. At times, modernists claimed that orthodox doctrines were human inventions and turned the tables by declaring Fundamentalists as the true heretics. In his famous debates with conservative Baptist John Roach Straton, New York Unitarian Charles Francis Potter declared the doctrine of the deity of Christ to be the "supreme heresy of Christian theology" (Potter 1924: 13).

American Fundamentalists on the Defensive

Many Evangelicals became alarmed at the spread of liberal theology and believed that modernists were sacrificing too much in their efforts to save Christianity. For many, in fact, any accommodation to secular or humanistic influences meant a departure from the ancient and unchanging truth of Christian orthodoxy: "adaptation constituted nothing less than heresy" (Ammerman 1991: 14). Convinced that the forces of truth waged a perennial, cosmic battle with the forces of falsehood, Fundamentalists believed that they, like many throughout the history of the church, faced the challenge of refuting error and protecting Christian truth in its original form. Theological modernism represented an evil of gigantic proportions that promised not to save the Christian faith, but to destroy it. Fundamentalists believed the church was suffering from internal corruption, or "apostasy," and were convinced that America's denominations were turning away from the great doctrines of the faith.

A common reaction among religious conservatives, American Fundamentalists rallied around certain essential doctrines or "fundamentals" deemed to represent the heart of Christian orthodoxy and that seemed to be especially under attack by liberal heretics. Although there existed no universally endorsed list of these essentials, the Presbyterian Church USA set forth in 1910 five points of doctrine that are representative of the Fundamentalist position: the inerrancy of Scripture, the Virgin Birth of Christ, the substitutionary Atonement, the bodily Resurrection of Christ, and Christ's miracle working power. In 1931, historian Stewart Grant Cole listed in

Selection From: *CHRISTIANITY AND LIBERALISM* BY J. GRESHAM MACHEN

Two lines of criticism, then, are possible with respect to the liberal attempt at reconciling science and Christianity. Modern liberalism may be criticized (1) on the ground that it is un-Christian and (2) on the ground that it is unscientific. We shall concern ourselves here chiefly with the former line of criticism; we shall be interested in showing that despite the liberal use of traditional phraseology modern liberalism not only is a different religion from Christianity but belongs in a totally different class of religions. But in showing that the liberal attempt at rescuing Christianity is false we are not showing that there is no way of rescuing Christianity at all; on the contrary, it may appear incidentally, even in the present little book, that it is not the Christianity of the New Testament which is in conflict with science, but the supposed Christianity of the modern liberal Church, and that the real city of God, and that city alone, has defenses which are capable of warding off the assaults of modern unbelief. However, our immediate concern is with the other side of the problem; our principal concern just now is to show that the liberal attempt at reconciling Christianity with modern science has really relinquished everything distinctive of Christianity, so that what remains is in essentials only that same indefinite type of religious aspiration which was in the world before Christianity came upon the scene. In trying to remove from Christianity everything that could possibly be objected to in the name of science, in trying to bribe off the enemy by those concessions which the enemy most desires, the apologist has really abandoned what he started out to defend. Here as in many other departments of life it appears that the things that are sometimes thought to be hardest to defend are also the things that are most worth defending.

In maintaining that liberalism in the modern Church represents a return to an un-Christian and sub-Christian form of the religious life, we are particularly anxious not to be misunderstood.

"Un-Christian" in such a connection is sometimes taken as a term of opprobrium. We do not mean it at all as such. Socrates was not a Christian, neither was Goethe; yet we share to the full the respect with which their names are regarded. They tower immeasurably above the common run of men; if he that is least in the Kingdom of Heaven is greater than they, he is certainly greater not by any inherent superiority, but by virtue of an undeserved privilege which ought to make him humble rather than contemptuous.

Such considerations, however, should not be allowed to obscure the vital importance of the question at issue. If a condition could be conceived in which all the preaching of the Church should be controlled by the liberalism which in many quarters has already become preponderant, then, we believe, Christianity would at last have perished from the earth and the gospel would have sounded forth for the last time. If so, it follows that the inquiry with which we are now concerned is immeasurably the most important of all those with which the Church has to deal. Vastly more important than all questions with regard to methods of preaching is the root question as to what it is that shall be preached.

Source: Machen, J. Gresham. (1923) *Christianity & Liberalism*. New York: Macmillan, pp. 7–8.

addition the deity of Christ and His future bodily return. Although these doctrines were not the only points of orthodox belief, they were those that represented the Fundamentalist agenda.

Like many global fundamentalisms, American Fundamentalism sought to demonstrate and reclaim a sense of ancient faith. Perhaps the most important "fundamental" doctrine for American Fundamentalists was the inerrancy of Scripture. For American Fundamentalists, orthodoxy was built on the ancient teachings of Scripture and thus provided a firm sense of authority. Fundamentalists were convinced that the Bible was divinely inspired and without error in its original manuscripts and although the doctrine of inerrancy may not have been officially declared before the nineteenth century, American Fundamentalists believed it had always been assumed by orthodox Christians. Since the Bible represented divine authority, to discredit it, as liberal scholars were doing, constituted the ultimate heresy.

American Fundamentalists also found support for their doctrines from the pages of Christian history. In an effort to lay claim to ancient origins, they pointed to the creeds and council declarations of the early church despite the fact that they felt little, if any, affinity with Roman Catholicism. Doctrines such as the deity of Christ, His Virgin Birth, and Resurrection were affirmed in the Nicene (325 CE) and Chalcedonian (451 CE) Creeds.

American Fundamentalists on the Offensive

American Fundamentalists responded quickly and militantly to the perceived heresies within liberal theology. They took to heart the admonition in Jude 3 (NAS) to "contend earnestly for the faith which was once for all delivered to the saints" and lifted their attacks from pulpits, podiums, publishing houses, and radio broadcasts. Fundamentalist criticisms of liberal theology were designed to demonstrate the irreconcilable nature of the two camps, bolster the ranks of the faithful, and demonize the heretical opposition. In 1910, conservatives began publishing a set of volumes called simply, *The Fundamentals*. Throughout the twelve volumes, various prominent Fundamentalists identified, described, and argued against liberal heresies and especially sought to defend the supernatural character of Christianity and the inerrant nature of Scripture. Fundamentalist periodicals arose with names like *The Watchman Examiner*, *The Truth*, and *The King's Business*. Fundamentalist Bible colleges also published periodicals such as Moody Bible Institute's *The Moody Monthly*. Prominent Fundamentalist leaders penned polemic treatises as well. Mennonite Fundamentalist John Horsch, for example, wrote *Modern Religious Liberalism: The Destructiveness and Irrationality of Modernist Theology* in 1920 and well-known Princeton University professor J. Gresham Machen (1881–1937) published his scholarly assault, *Christianity and Liberalism* in 1923. (Machen, so completely appalled by liberalism, argued that the movement did not even constitute Christian heresy, but another religion altogether.)

Also in the 1920s, Northern Baptists and Presbyterians experienced fervid debate within their denominational structures. Presbyterian Fundamentalists found leadership not only in J. Gresham Machen but also in popular Presbyterian activist, William Jennings Bryan (1860–1925). Harry Emerson Fosdick (1878–1969) became the focus of Fundamentalist attacks during his tenure as minister of New York's First Presbyterian Church. In his famous sermon, "Shall the Fundamentalists Win?" Fosdick denied the importance of the Virgin Birth of Christ, rejected biblical inerrancy and the Second Coming.

William Bell Riley (1861–1947) and John Roach Straton (1875–1929) were two of the more prominent Fundamentalist leaders for conservative American Baptists. The University of Chicago Divinity School, a Baptist institution, provoked repeated and strong condemnation from Fundamentalists. A number of Chicago faculty members were outspoken modernists, including George Burman Foster (1857–1918), Gerald Burney Smith (1868–1929), and Shailer Matthews (1863–1941). Matthews's important defense of liberal theology emerged in 1910 entitled *The Gospel and the Modern Man*.

Increasingly after 1925, American Fundamentalists responded to the proliferation of liberalism by severing ties with "apostate" denominations, congregations, and institutions that harbored heretics and assigned them to positions of leadership. More radical Fundamentalists advocated separation as the "duty of God's people" whenever a church or denomination became irreparably heretical or "passed the point of reform." Carl McIntire (1906–), who founded the International Council of Christian Churches in protest to the modernist leanings of the Federal Council of Churches, likened the Fundamentalist movement of separation to the Protestant Reformation of the sixteenth century: "The doctrine of separation is the doctrine of the purity of the church—nothing more and nothing less" (McIntire 1952: 3–5). Throughout the 1930s and 1940s, the tendency toward separation resulted in thousands of independent Bible churches and "tabernacle" fellowships, a new network of independent mission agencies, and a host of parachurch organizations.

Due in part to the fact that the world's fundamentalisms owe their existence to orthodoxy's "confrontation with modernity," heresy is a concept common to virtually every movement of religious Fundamentalism (Hunter 1990: 57). Like many militant religious conservatives, American Fundamentalists narrowed their definition of orthodoxy, opposed the spread of perceived infidelity with fervid conviction, and frequently advocated formal separation from the influences of theological modernism.

Jared S. Burkholder

See also Antifeminism; Antimodernism; Biblical Inerrancy; Liberalism; Secularism

Bibliography

Ammerman, Nancy T. (1991) "North American Protestant Fundamentalism." In *Fundamentalisms Observed*, edited by Martin E. Marty and R. Scott Appleby. Chicago: University of Chicago Press, 1–65.

Brown, Harold O. J. (1984) *Heresies: Heresy and Orthodoxy in the History of the Church*. Peabody, MA: Hendrickson Publishers.

Conkin, Paul K. (1998) *When All the Gods Trembled: Darwinism, Scopes, and American Intellectuals*. New York: Rowman and Littlefield Publishers, Inc.

Henderson, John B. (1998) *The Construction of Orthodoxy and Heresy: Neo-Confucian, Islamic, Jewish, and Early Christian Patterns*. Albany, NY: SUNY Press.

Hunter, James Davison. (1990) "Fundamentalism in Its Global Contours." In *The Fundamentalist Phenomenon: A View from Within; A Response from Without*, edited by Norman J. Cohen. Grand Rapids, MI: Wm. B. Eerdmans, 56–71.

McIntire, Carl. (1952) *The Testimony of Separation*. Collingswood, NJ: Christian Beacon Press.

Pelikan, Jaroslav. (1990) "Fundamentalism and/or Orthodoxy? Toward an Understanding of the Fundamentalist Phenomenon." In *The Fundamentalist Phenomenon: A View from Within; A Response from Without*, edited by Norman J. Cohen. Grand Rapids, MI: Wm. B. Eerdmans, 3–21.

Potter, Charles Francis. (1924) "Was Christ Both God and Man?" In *Fundamentalist Verses Modernist: The Debates between John Roach Straton and Charles Francis Potter*, edited by Joel A. Carpenter. New York: Garland Publishing, 11–101.

Higher Criticism

"Higher criticism" is the name given to a type of biblical criticism distinguished from textual or "lower criticism." Whereas lower criticism deals with textual minutiae, higher criticism addresses the larger aspects of Bible study, such as authorship, date, cultural context, and authority of biblical books. With roots in the Enlightenment, higher criticism reached its zenith in the nineteenth century with scholars questioning the historical reliability of the Bible and challenging the supernatural underpinnings of traditional Christian faith. Although North American scholars and pastors were familiar with the higher critical method as early as the 1870s, it was not widely accepted until after World War I. Higher criticism, along with Darwinian evolution and philosophical modernism (the belief that historic Christian beliefs had to be modified so that they would fit squarely with modern science), was the expressed enemy of North American Protestant Fundamentalists who affirmed the inerrancy of Scripture and defended the Bible as historically factual.

History of Biblical Criticism

Modern biblical criticism began in the period of the Enlightenment. During the Age of Reason, thinkers applied new methods of empirical science to the study of all disciplines, including the Bible. Because of their commitment to rationalism and natural theology, British Deists were opposed to the supernatural. They argued that prophecies should not be taken literally and that miracles that violated the natural order were falsely fabricated by biblical authors. Continental Pietists pushed for a subjective and spiritual reading of the text which valued not only the Bible's literal meaning but its practical effect on the reader who was asked not only to understand but to live out scriptural counsel. Other European scholars applied new linguistic methods to the Bible, seeking to discover the literal historical meaning within its original historical context. Using this new rigid scientific method, writers began to question the authorship and canonicity of several biblical books. By 1800 many continental biblical scholars were reading the Bible like any other work of literature, arguing it was not intended to be read as history, but as poetic, aesthetic, literary expression. The historical reliability of the biblical text had been called into question. Needless to say, North American Fundamentalists held suspect this entire tradition of biblical criticism because it challenged the clear, simple truths that they took to be at the center of the Christian faith.

Biblical criticism is generally divided between lower criticism and higher criticism. The purpose of lower criticism (or "text criticism") is to restore the original text. This is difficult because no autographs of biblical works exist; so the task of text critics is to examine the more than five thousand manuscripts and fragments in existence and reconstruct, to the best of their ability, the original. Desiderius Erasmus (probably 1469–1536) was the father of modern textual criticism, but it did not come into its own until the nineteenth century.

In the nineteenth century, higher criticism took center stage in European and North American study of the Bible. Higher criticism (or "historical criticism") sought to achieve an accurate historical understanding of the Bible by viewing documents within their historical and cultural contexts. The discoveries of never-before-seen documents dating from the biblical era, along with advances in philology, archeology, and the study of non-Christian religions led some to conclude that ancient Judaism and early Christianity were not unique but had much in common with religions in surrounding cultures.

The Emergence of a New Criticism

Adherents to the "History of Religions" school began to place biblical belief and practice in the context of ancient cultures. To these scholars, the Bible was not a timeless theological text delivered from the hand of God, but a reflection of a strange and far-off culture wholly different from the modern world in language, worldview, images, and symbols. Form critics argued that oral traditions lay behind biblical texts; as a result, biblical authors were not writing down the words of God, but instead were simply collectors and arrangers of various stories and traditions. As higher criticism blossomed, tradition critics, sociological interpreters, and literary critics called into question almost every traditional Christian affirmation.

Julius Wellhausen (1844–1918) argued that the Pentateuch was not written by Moses but was the product of several authors long after the events within it took place. Other scholars questioned the dates of prophetic books and argued that they were written much later than originally thought—after the events prophesied in them had actually taken place. William Wrede (1859–1906) argued that the Gospel of Mark contained not true stories about Jesus but the theological reflections of the author. Many thinkers questioned the authorship and canonicity of several New Testament books. Broadly speaking, this newer scholarship relied on evolutionary notions—histories, stories, and writings all evolve over time, as does religious consciousness itself. In the end the supernatural was dismissed—miracles were unverifiable, Jesus was a historical figure and not divine, and Judaism as well as Christianity were culturally conditioned like all other world religions.

Very few Americans accepted these new radical ideas without reservation before World War I; however, pastors and scholars became acquainted with the higher critical method beginning in the 1870s. The entrance of these views into North American circles corresponded with a surge in professionalization in major universities. At this time, universities began offering graduate study on the European model where science was held up as the only way to truth and higher critical methods were valued as the best way to study the Bible. In addition, the Society of Biblical Literature formed in the 1880s, coordinating the efforts of biblical scholars nationally along higher critical lines.

Although new critical approaches to the Bible would eventually become the intellectual norm in North America, they received mixed reviews throughout the late nineteenth century. Presbyterian David Swing (1830–1894) was tried for heresy in 1874, largely because he insisted that all religious expressions were dependent upon the culture within which they were formulated and could not be understood apart from that culture. In the early 1880s, Presbyterian Charles A. Briggs (1841–1913) of Union Theological Seminary argued for cautious acceptance of new criticism. His heresy trial in the early 1890s has been called "a landmark in the popularization of Higher Criticism" (Hutchison 1976: 116). In the 1880s, leading liberals like Washington Gladden (1836–1918), Newman Smyth (1843–1925), Phillips Brooks (1835–1893), Henry Ward Beecher (1813–1887), Alexander V. G. Allen (1841–1908), Theodore Munger (1830–1910), and various professors at Andover Seminary championed higher critical scholarship. The liberal theology that grew out of those new critical methods was systematized by scholars like William Newton Clarke (1841–1912) and William Adams Brown (1865–1943), and popularized by clergy like Harry Emerson Fosdick (1878–1969). After 1900 most of the recognized universities in North America had swung over to the new views. In general, theological liberals affirmed divine immanentism within human culture, the essential goodness of humanity, and the social ramifications of Christianity; and they denied the deity of Christ, the uniqueness of Christianity among world religions, and New Testament miracles. Adhering to the principle of modernism, they consciously adapted religious ideas to modern culture and scientific inquiry.

The Fundamentalist Response

Noting this swing to liberalism, conservative biblical critics developed a coherent theology expressed in *The Fundamentals* (1910–1915), a series of articles written as an all-out theological and cultural attack against modernism, theological liberalism, evolution, and higher criticism of the Bible. Fundamentalists eventually settled on five "fundamentals" of the faith: infallibility of the Bible; the Virgin Birth; substitutionary Atonement; bodily Resurrection of Jesus, and the imminent premillennial return of Christ. The battle lines were drawn. Fundamentalists and liberals grew increasingly divided over issues of biblical criticism. In general, conservative biblical critics argued that the antisupernatural bias and evolutionary speculations of the new critics disqualified them as scholars altogether. Those who upheld the new criticism thought that when conservatives stubbornly failed to recognize recent gains in scholarship by clinging to outmoded conceptions of the supernatural, they forfeited their right to existence in the modern academy. Eventually, North American universities became the domain of liberal scholarship committed to higher critical method, and Fundamentalists nurtured their own educational and ecclesiastical institutions.

Kurt W. Peterson

See also Biblical Criticism

Bibliography

Elliott, John H. (1993) *What Is Social-Scientific Criticism?* Minneapolis, MN: Fortress Press.

Hutchison, William R. (1976) *The Modernist Impulse in American Protestantism.* New York: Oxford University Press.

Marsden, George M. (1980) *Fundamentalism and American Culture: The Shaping of Twentieth-Century Evangelicalism, 1870–1925.* New York: Oxford University Press.

Marty, Martin E. (1986)*The Irony of It All, 1893–1919.* Vol. 1 of *Modern American Religion.* Chicago: University of Chicago Press.

Noll, Mark. (1992) *A History of Christianity in the United States and Canada.* Grand Rapids, MI: Wm. B. Eerdmans.

Smith, H. Shelton, Robert T. Handy, and Lefferts A. Loetscher. (1963) *1820–1960.* Vol. II of *American Christianity.* New York: Charles Scribner's Sons.

Torrey, Reuben A. (1911) *The Higher Criticism and the New Theology.* New York: Gospel Publishing House.

Hinduism, Fundamental

Some contemporary Hindu scholars question whether or not Hinduism can have a "fundamentalist" nature, because unlike Islam or Christianity, some difficulty exists in identifying the "fundamentals" of Hinduism upon which all of its some 800 million adherents can agree. Not only are the origins of Hinduism somewhat clouded in ancient history, but the major tenets are difficult to define. Nevertheless, before a consideration of what may constitute Hindu Fundamentalism, it is helpful to explore the origins and gradual development of Hinduism into one of the world's great religions.

History and Literature

As nearly as can be ascertained, the civilizations of Harappa and Mohenjo-Daro, located along the Indus River in present-day Pakistan, were the sites where certain religious activity first appeared as early as the third millennium BCE. Archeological evidence of these Indus sites indicates worship of the god Shiva, later to become the Destroyer in the vast pantheon of Hindu gods and goddesses. It was during the Indo-Aryan invasion of c. 1500 to 1000 BCE, however, that the major principles of what would eventually be called "Hinduism" became evident. The Aryans recorded sacred literature in the ancient language of Sanskrit. The collection of hymns to the gods, poetry, chants, epic tales, and legends were collectively known as the Vedas. The best known of the Vedic literature was the Rig Veda, which explained the four original classes (varna) that became the basis for the caste system, now an inextricable part of Hinduism. The castes were believed to have been placed in the order in which they had emerged from the body of the original cosmic man. The Brahmins emerged from the head and thus became the priests, the highest caste. The Kshatriyas were from the arms and thus comprised the warriors. The Vaishyas, from the thighs, constituted the artisans and farmers. Finally, the Sudras came from the feet and comprised the day

HINDU DEFENDERS ARMY

"You are allowed to perform last rites of my body you may perform them in any manner. But I am to express herewith a specific wish. The river Indus (Sindhu), on the banks of which our Pre- historic Rishis composed the Vedas is the Boundary of our Bharatvdrsha i.e. Hindusthan. My ashes may be sunk in the Holy Sindhu river when she will again flow freely under the aegis of the flag of Hindusthan. That will be the sacred day for US. It hardly matters even if it took a couple of generations for realising my wish. Preserve the ashes till then, and if that day would not dawn in your life time, pass on the remains to posterity for translating my desire into reality."

~Sri Nathuram Godse

This is a network of proud Hindu fundamentalists working to defend Sanatana Dharma and promote the Hindutva philosophy. Down with the Christians, Muslas and Pseudo-Seculars who have tried to take over and ruin our Bharat for so long! Hindu Rashtra ki Jaya! Har Har Mahadev!!!

The only requirement for joining is that you be a website owner who believes in the cause of Hindutva. Sites in the ring may deal with any Hindu topics such as Soldiers of Hindutva, Bharatiya politics, Hindu philosophy, etc. NO anti-Hindutva material is tolerated!!!

Source: *Hindu Defenders Army.* www.hinduweb.org.

---

laborers and those with menial tasks. Eventually, those outside of these categories were thought of as pariahs or "outcasts," also known as "Untouchables." Strong evidence also exists to conclude that the early caste system was not only identified with occupation, but was also based upon skin color, with Sudras being the darkest.

Many of the Hindu pantheon of some 330 million gods and goddesses made their appearance during the Vedic period and seemed to center around the worship of various aspects of nature such as fire, darkness, thunder, and the like. The religious rituals that developed around the worship of these many deities were to maintain a balance of the universe or rita, "the true order." Thus the Aryan period, also referred to as the Vedic period, was characterized by an assimilative process from the preexistent Indus civilization.

The unification of northern India, which began around 1000 BCE, further consolidated the principles of Hinduism. One of the greatly revered pieces of Hindu literature, the Mahabharata, was written around 1000 BCE and reflects Indian life during this period. At its core, this epic tale tells of a king who marries the goddess Ganga, representative of the Gangetic Plain of India. Another of the sacred Hindu texts of this era introduced several other principles identified with the religion in general. The Upanishads contain discussions regarding the soul of man (Atman) and the ultimate destination of release (Moksha) or oneness with the universe. Most contemporary Hindus subscribe to both of these principles.

The Vedic texts as well as subsequent literature perpetuate two other principles that are virtually inseparable from Hinduism: karma and reincarnation. Karma is the universal law of cause and effect; one's actions in this life will predetermine situations in the next life. Thus, karma is a concomitant of reincarnation (samsara). As the centuries progressed, the three principles of karma, reincarnation, and caste became interdependent. One's actions in the present life will determine what caste one is reincarnated into with the ultimate goal being to reach a state of Moksha, or release, in which one's Atman, or soul, is united with the spirit of the universe (Brahman). In order to attain good karma, one must pursue the paths of Yoga such as Karma Yoga, Bhakti Yoga, or Jnana Yoga, each of which is a system of behavior.

The last of the sacred books of Hinduism is the Bhagavad Gita, often referred to simply as the "Gita." In this "Song of the Blessed One," the reader may find a number of epic tales of heroism and acts of the gods and goddesses. The most famous and appealing character of the Gita is Krishna, the charioteer of Arjuna, the great warrior. In a dialogue with Arjuna, Krishna explains the true nature of reality and the path to salvation through indifference and detachment. Thus, the Gita has traditionally been appealing to the masses who believe that Krishna's explanation is relevant to them. Krishna, depicted with light blue skin and as playing his flute, often appears in popular Hindu art.

The Hindu Gods

Although Krishna remains a popular figure in Hinduism, there are three prominent gods in the vast pantheon of Hindu gods and goddesses. Most Hindus believe that there are three forces at work in the universe: creation, preservation, and destruction. Brahma, the Creator, may be seen in a newborn baby or in the sunrise of a new day. Vishnu, the Preserver, may be seen in early middle age or at noontime. Shiva, the Destroyer, may be seen in old age or the setting of the sun. But, because of reincarnation, all things become new and the cycle is perpetuated.

Principles of Faith

With all of these aforementioned principles in mind, one might conclude that if Hinduism has "fundamentals," they are as follows: (1) the belief in an impersonal universe dominated by a universal cosmic energy force into which all souls will eventually merge; (2) the belief in a complex and extensive myriad of gods and goddesses, all of whom are a manifestation of a single entity; (3) the belief in karma, caste, and reincarnation; and (4) a belief in certain actions and behaviors in order to establish good karma and, thus, ultimately be released into a state of Moksha, a return to oneness with the universe. While Hinduism may be the most esoteric of the world's great religions, most Hindus would probably agree on these four principles of faith. At the same time, one most remember that Hinduism is complex, highly individualistic, and pluralistic.

Fundamentalism in India

If there are Hindu fundamentals, what, then, is Hindu "Fundamentalism"? In few nations around the world is a religion and a national identity so fully integrated. The root of the word "India," the language "Hindi," and the religion Hinduism is the same. Thus, the land, language, and religion are intertwined. Few persons outside of India are Hindu, except those who have emigrated, and Hinduism has had little appeal through conversion. Herein lies one of the reasons for the existence of modern-day Hindu Fundamentalism. There is great pride among many Indians, not only in their nation and the very land itself, but also in being Hindu. To many, to be Indian is to be Hindu and to be Hindu is to be Indian. In fact, in the 1800s, when India was colonized by the British, there was a Hindu Renaissance in which Indians, with the encouragement of some British scholars, attempted to rekindle pride in Indian culture. The literature, poetry, and other publications of the Hindu Renaissance planted the seeds of Indian nationalism, which eventually bore fruit under the leadership of Mohandas Gandhi in the twentieth century; however, Gandhi did not use Hinduism as a tool to motivate the masses to force the British out.

In the last few decades of the twentieth century, a new aspect of Hinduism emerged, primarily in response to what is perceived as a threat to Hindus and to India from Islam and Christianity within India. Islam, as a religious and cultural force, entered India during the Mughal invasions, which began gradually in the tenth century CE. Hindu Fundamentalists today look back to an event that took place in 1025 CE in what is the present-day state of Gujarat. Muslims under the leadership of Sultan Mahmud of Ghazni destroyed the Somanth Temple, a Hindu holy site located at Prabhasa Patan. A thousand Brahmins a day had worshipped at this temple and its destruction has become a historical motif and example of Muslim aggression in contemporary Hindu Fundamentalist ideology.

In 1923, *Hindutva: Who Is a Hindu?* was written by Vinayak Savarkar, a Brahmin. He postulated that "Hinduness" is rooted to the soil of India and had its origins in the Vedic period. Thus, Muslims and Christians are foreigners whose allegiance is to a holy land located outside India. This appeal to ethnic Hindu nationalism may be considered the beginning of the modern Hindu Fundamentalist movement known as Hindutva. Most recently, the Hindutva movement has gained momentum both politically and culturally. The goal has been nothing short of the establishment of a Hindu *rashtra*, a Hindu state.

Accompanying the rise of the Hindutva movement was the remarkable national response to a television production of the Hindu epic, *The Ramayana*.

Telecast on Sunday mornings from 25 January 1987 to 31 July 1988, the impact was unexpected. From obscure villages that collected money to rent a television, to the high-rise apartments of Mumbai (Bombay), the nation ceased activity as Indians watched the ancient epic come alive. Ram iconography followed as this ancient Hindu god became something of a cult figure. Chariot processions that reenacted Ram's glory often stirred up a determination to liberate Ram's birthplace at Ayodhya, which was occupied by Muslims. This campaign to free temple sites taken over by Muslims was also a policy of the Vishwa Hindu Parishad (VHP), or Hindu World Congress, founded in 1964. The VHP especially singled out the Babri Masjid in Ayodhya, which was subsequently destroyed on 6 December 1992. The destruction of the Ayodhya mosque was hailed as a great victory for the Hindutva movement as well as a statement of Hindu nationalism.

In the temple wars that followed, more than two thousand persons were killed in Mumbai and Calcutta as temple burnings and personal attacks took place. The VHP called upon Hindus to make holy bricks for the rebuilding of the Ayodhya temple; the bricks poured in from Hindus all over the world. Interestingly, those who feel strongest about the Ayodhya mosque come from the large population of urban, educated, but unemployed young persons. Their unfulfilled expectations fuel their frustrations, which have contributed to Hindu Fundamentalism.

In recent years, Hindu Fundamentalism has taken on definite political overtones with the rise to power of the Bharatiya Janata Party (BJP), which appeals to the strong nationalistic desire of Hindu Fundamentalists. In 1996, the BJP briefly held an electoral majority and thus the prime ministerial position under Atal Behari Vajpayee. Since then, it has been an important component in coalition governments in India, although its support is by no means equally dispersed throughout the country. The BJP has campaigned on a platform that accuses the other major parties of being "secular." In 1998, under the strong endorsement of the BJP and the leadership of Vajpayee, India tested a nuclear device. This event shocked the international community and initiated fears of a high-stakes nuclear arms race in South Asia between India and Pakistan. But, for Hindu Fundamentalists and nationalists, the successful testing of a nuclear device was a great accomplishment for India. The tests were dubbed "Operation Shakti" in a reference to the Hindu god of fire and power. For many,

Indian nuclear power was looked upon as a long-awaited rite of passage into the world community of leading nations, which would at last garner India the international respect it deserves. The tests became a tangible symbol that unlocked emotions of primal will to power and assertion of Hindu supremacy. Hindutva rhetoric intensified, especially against Muslim Pakistanis. Other Hindu nationalists saw India's rising nuclear power as a way to redress the perceived weakness of India brought on by the long period of British colonialism.

Finally, it would appear that Hindu Fundamentalism is associated with a backlash against the rising tide of globalization that increasingly influences India. Whereas some in the BJP see aggressive participation in world markets as a way to increase India's voice in the world, others, especially in the Hindutva movement, see globalization as a corrosive influence on India. The latter group sees consumerism as evidence of Westernization and moral pollution that erodes the more esoteric aspects of Hinduism, which emphasize detachment and nonpossessiveness. Thus, Hindu Fundamentalism can best be summarized as nationalistic in its major identifications. Rooted in a religious identity that lays claim to geography, it has in recent years been most evident in the BJP political activities and in the rise of the Hindutva movement. Increased modernization and globalization in India may serve to strengthen Hindu Fundamentalism or may actually weaken its appeal as more Indians seek a more modern way of life.

Mary Ann Lind

Bibliography

Keay, John. (2000) *India: A History*. New York: Grove Press.

Talbot, Ian. (2000) *India and Pakistan*. London: Hodder Headline Group.

Tharoor, Shashi. (1997) *India: From Midnight to the Millennium*. New York: Harper.

Wolpert, Stanley. (1999) *A New History of India*. New York: Oxford University Press.

Holiness, Wesleyan

The Wesleyan Holiness movement, also known simply as the Holiness movement, has roots in the perfectionist agitation that swept North American society in the 1830s. Its distinctive teaching, which held that all Christians needed a second religious experience to cleanse and empower believers for lives of service, drew its inspiration from John Wesley's controversial teaching that all Christians might become perfect in love. The movement's founders were Methodist preacher and abolitionist Timothy Merritt and a pair of Methodist sisters from New York City, Sarah Worrall Lankford and Phoebe Worrall Palmer. These Methodists insisted that they were merely resurrecting the neglected Methodist teaching that all Christians might experience "Christian perfection" in this life. The common term for the experience became "entire sanctification"—although it was known by numerous other titles such as "the second blessing," "the higher Christian life," "the rest of faith," "full salvation," and "perfect love." As defined by the Worrall sisters, the experience of entire sanctification (which drew its inspiration from the thought and experience of such Methodist luminaries as John Fletcher and William Carvosso) taught that by a simple act of faith one could claim the experience of full salvation apart from any personal evidence. By the late 1840s, testimonies to the experience of full salvation were commonplace. A decade later, prominent Presbyterians, Baptists, Episcopalians, Dutch Reformed, and Congregationalists had entered into the higher Christian life, even as North American–style perfectionism had spread to Great Britain through the ministries of James Caughey and Phoebe Palmer. In the decades following the Civil War, Holiness agitation found a ready audience among smaller bodies, such as the Methodist-related United Brethren and Evangelical Association, and among Friends and Mennonites.

Emergent Holiness Groups

In spite of this, by the 1880s, independent Holiness churches began to appear in New England, the Midwest, and California. Such developments incited an extended debate on the nature of the church, which led to the formation of the Church of God reformation movement and the establishment of such groups as the Church of God (Anderson, Indiana) in 1881 and the Church of God (Holiness) USA in 1883.

Perhaps the most familiar public manifestation of the Holiness movement has been urban Holiness missions. Most often associated with The Salvation Army, these "rescue missions" played a significant role in the life of the Holiness movement, at least since 1850 when Phoebe Palmer founded the Five Points Mission in New York City. By the 1890s, even as Holiness teaching in Methodism became more controversial, Phoebe Palmer's "shorter way to holiness" was being challenged on the right by thoughtful Methodists and National Holiness Association (NHA) leaders and on the left by a growing body of radicals who believed that entire sanctification was only gained after a protracted period of repentance and spiritual struggle (known as "death route" salvation). Frequently embracing such controversial new teachings as the premillennial return of Jesus, critics of the NHA, including Cincinnati publisher Martin Wells Knapp, founded the International Apostolic Holiness Union in 1897. By 1901, when Knapp left the Methodist Episcopal Church, the premillennial teaching had become the norm, even for NHA loyalists.

The Growth of the Holiness Movement

Beginning in the 1890s, the "come-outer" sentiment intensified and additional independent churches and regional Holiness denominations were founded. Increasingly radicalized by the depression of the 1890s, these churches, often convinced that the return of Jesus was imminent, embraced such increasingly radical proposals as the redistribution of wealth and the communal ownership of property. In this climate, more moderate voices, such as California pastor Phineas Bresee, began laying the foundation for transcontinental Holiness churches. In spite of the loss of many potential Holiness adherents to Pentecostalism in the wake of the 1906 Azusa Street Revival, by the 1920s the followers of Bresee and Knapp had organized two national Holiness churches, the Church of Nazarene and the Pilgrim Holiness Church.

Among Methodists, Holiness camp meetings, distinctly Holiness schools, such as Asbury College, Taylor University, and Chicago Evangelistic Institute, and periodicals, such as Henry Clay Morrison's *Pentecostal Herald*, continued to thrive. During the 1920s, Asbury College emerged as perhaps the key institutional expression of Wesleyan Holiness Fundamentalism. Led by Morrison and his key associates Andrew Johnson, John Paul, Harold Paul Sloan, and George Ridout, Asbury vigorously opposed the emerging liberalism in North American Methodism. In 1923, Asbury Theological Seminary was established on the campus of Asbury College to provide an alternative to the perceived liberalism of Methodism's official seminaries. However, most Wesleyan denominations were never deeply involved in the Christian Fundamentalist movement of the 1920s. This was especially true of the largest bodies, such as the Church of the Nazarene, Salvation Army, Church of God (Anderson, Indiana), and the Pilgrim Holiness Church. Although deeply conservative, such bodies continued to emphasize the traditional subjective theology of the Holiness movement, which remained suspicious of Christian Fundamentalism's tendency to reduce Christianity to "right" belief.

In the years following World War II, the Holiness movement continued to experience steady growth. Reflecting the greater demand for an educated clergy, theological seminaries emerged in North America, India, the Philippines, Africa, and Korea. In 1965, the Wesleyan Theological Society was founded while a number of young Wesleyan scholars such as Timothy L. Smith, Donald W. Dayton, and Mildred Bangs Wynkoop emerged as international scholars of note.

The Inter-Church Holiness Convention

While deeply concerned with personal behavior, the Holiness movement struggled with changing cultural mores. In 1951, conservatives within the Holiness denominations, especially the Church of the Nazarene and the Wesleyan Methodist Church, organized the Inter-denominational Holiness Convention, which later became the Inter-Church Holiness Convention (IHC). These conventions challenged the established NHA, now known as the Christian Holiness Partnership, for the position as the primary ecumenical Holiness body. Although a minority within the Holiness movement, the IHC grew into a significant international constituency consisting of a number of small denominations and independent congregations. This body of Wesleyans readily identified themselves as Fundamentalists. In the 1990s—ironically amid discussions of the presumed death of the Holiness movement—membership in Holiness-related bodies, not including Holiness Pentecostals or Keswick-related Evangelicals, passed the ten million mark. In fact, this suggests that while for most North American Christians,

the Holiness movement is in the midst of a serious identity crisis, it is perhaps a sign of the movement's continued vitality that Holiness adherents from Africa, Asia, the Caribbean, and South America are increasingly setting the agenda for the movement.

William C. Kostlevy

See also African-American Holiness-Pentecostal Movement; Free Methodists

Bibliography

Jones, Charles Edwin. (1974) *Perfectionist Persuasion: The Holiness Movement and American Methodism, 1867–1936.* Metuchen, NJ: Scarecrow Press.

Kostlevy, William C., with Gari-Anne Patzwald. (2001) *Historical Dictionary of the Holiness Movement.* Lanham, MD: Scarecrow Press.

Holy *See* African-American Holiness-Pentecostal Movement; Holiness, Weslyan; Holy Spirit

Holy Spirit

Sometimes referred to as "the Cinderella of the Godhead," the person of the Holy Spirit is often confused as an extension of God the Father and/or God the Son. Though mentioned in the Old Testament, the fullest development of the teaching about the Holy Spirit is found in the New Testament. There are several issues involved in a study of the doctrine of the Holy Spirit, but the most important is the confusion involving the personality of the Holy Spirit. Part of the confusion comes as one discovers that the Hebrew word, *ruach*, and the Greek word, *pneuma*, are both neuter in gender. So the natural assumption is that the Spirit is an "it," that is, a force or influence, rather than a person. A second area of confusion has to do with the "Godhood" or deity of the Holy Spirit. The personality and deity of the Spirit are both intrinsic to the nature of the person of the Holy Spirit and are often considered together. Other teachings about the Holy Spirit have to do with the Spirit's work.

The Person of the Holy Spirit

Historic Christianity from the Council of Nicaea (325 CE) confessed that whereas God is one in essence (nature), there are three distinct persons called the Father, the Son, and the Holy Spirit whose distinctions are real, not merely nominal (that is, in name only), and who share the same numerical essence of Oneness.

It should be noted that the word "trinity" does not appear in the biblical text, but the concept is certainly there, and as a result, the church has held to a triunity in God. It is not a teaching that can be logically explained. As A.W. Tozer (1961) once observed, this teaching is apprehended by the heart, not with the mind. The nature of God is incomprehensible, so such an idea of God as three in persons but one in essence should not be used as a basis for unbelief.

The Spirit is a person as demonstrated in three basic ways: first, the Spirit is presented in Scripture as a person; second, by the attributes and works ascribed to the Spirit, He is both personal and is God; third, the pronouns used in reference to the Spirit demonstrate both His personality and Godhood.

What is the biblical evidence for the personality of the Holy Spirit? The Holy Spirit can be *grieved* (Ephesians 4:30). The argument that a force or influence cannot be grieved is a valid one. The Holy Spirit can also be *quenched* (1 Thessalonians 5:19, AV). One of the clearest statements regarding the personality of the Holy Spirit is the teaching of our Lord as recorded in John 14–17, appropriately called "the Upper Room Discourse." The context is that our Lord is about to go to the cross; His relationship with His apostles is about to change. He then presents a comprehensive teaching about what will happen in the days ahead.

In John 14:16, Jesus announces that He will send "another" Paraclete (Comforter, Counselor, Helper) to be with His people forever. The term "another" means "another of the same kind as he (Jesus) was." Further, He is identified as "the Spirit of truth." Then Jesus notes that the Spirit is known to His apostles in that "he lives with you," but, there will be a new relationship, "he will be *in* you." Every reference to the Holy Spirit in these three chapters presents the Spirit as personal, not merely a power or an influence.

The second line of evidence for the personality and deity of the Spirit has to do with the attributes and works ascribed to the Holy Spirit. The terms "holy" (Ephesians 4:30), "truth" (John 14:17), and "Lord" (2 Corinthians 3:18) give credence to both the Spirit's personality and deity. He is called "God" in Acts 5:3–4. And Matthew's record of the Great Commission iterated by the Lord, "baptizing them in the name of the Father and of the Son and of the Holy Spirit" further demonstrates the Spirit's equality with the other two members of the Godhead. That the Holy Spirit can be sinned against (Matthew 12:31–32) indicates not only His personality but His deity as well.

The works of the Holy Spirit are the works of God. The Holy Spirit was present at Creation (Genesis 1:2; Job 33:4), He is the "inspirer" of Scripture (2 Peter 1:21), and He is the agent of the new birth (John 3:6), and the power behind resurrection (Romans 8:11).

The third line of evidence for the personality and deity of the Holy Spirit is found in the pronouns that are used. As has been noted, both the Old Testament and New Testament words for "spirit" are neuter. The rule of grammar is that a pronoun must agree with its nearest antecedent in number and gender. By this rule, all pronouns used for the Spirit should be singular (as they are) and neuter in gender. There are situations in which this gender rule is put aside, however. Such a clear reference is found in John 15:26: "When the Paraclete, the Spirit of truth, shall come, *whom* I will send to you from the Father . . . *that one* shall witness concerning me" (Tr. Richard I. McNeely). The italicized words are masculine pronouns.

Together, these point to the Spirit as a person and as a member of the triune Godhead. The Bible presents the Spirit as more than a Sustainer, but active in all the works of God as are the Father and the Son.

The Works of the Holy Spirit

The presence of the Holy Spirit in the Old Testament is not as clearly developed as is His role in the New Testament period. However, the Spirit was present at Creation (Genesis 1:2; Job 33:4). The Spirit fills various people for great exploits. For example, it is implied that the Spirit filled Bezalel and Oholiab for the task of constructing the Tabernacle in the wilderness and all its furnishings (Exodus 31:3). It is noted that some of the judges of Israel were endowed by the Spirit with special wisdom and strength. The phrase, "the Spirit of the LORD came upon . . ." occurs eight times in the Book of Judges (3:10; 6:34; 11:29; 13:25;

14:6; 14:19; 15:14; 15:19). Samuel prophesies that the Spirit of God will come upon Saul, Israel's first king (1 Samuel 10:6, cf. v. 9). David was endowed by the Spirit (1 Samuel 16:13).

In the New Testament, there are many functions of the Spirit of God that are carried over from the Old Testament, but these functions seem to be more specific in the New Testament. For example, it is clear that the Holy Spirit did indwell some in the Old Testament, but there was no universal indwelling of the Spirit with God's people. The indwelling was for a special purpose, and it was not permanent. David's request in confessing his sin was "Take not your Holy Spirit from me" (Psalms 51:11, Tr. Richard McNeeley). Jesus spoke of the Spirit's work as having been "with you but He shall be in you" (John 14:17). The revelation that Jesus gave concerning the Spirit in John 14–16 assures the believers of a permanent indwelling by the Spirit. This is echoed particularly by Paul in such passages as Romans 8:9. Most important, the Holy Spirit is the agent of regeneration or the cause of one becoming "born again" (John 3:6).

A third work of the Spirit and one unique to the New Testament period is the *baptism of the Spirit*. Introduced by John the Baptist, he said, "I baptize you with water for repentance. But after me will come one who is more powerful than I, whose sandals I am not fit to carry. He will baptize you with the Holy Spirit and with fire" (Matthew 3:11; Mark 1:8, NIV). There seems to be a partial fulfillment of this when on the evening of His Resurrection, He said to them, "Receive the Holy Spirit." But at the time of His Ascension, He noted that there would yet be a time before the Holy Spirit would come upon them in power (Acts 1:5). This took place on the Day of Pentecost (Acts 2), and Peter's comment of that event in Acts 11 demonstrated that they had indeed been baptized with the Holy Spirit (Acts 11:15–17). Peter's words seem to indicate that speaking in tongues, which sometimes accompanied such events, was not the norm. In fact, it may not have happened at all between Pentecost and Peter's encounter with Cornelius in Acts 10 and 11, a time lapse of ten or eleven years from Pentecost. According to 1 Corinthians 12:13, the baptism of the Holy Spirit is given to every Christian. The New Testament does not teach a distinction between a baptism *with* the Holy Spirit and a baptism *by* the Holy Spirit. Both the prepositions, "with" and "by," are translations of the same Greek word, *en*.

However, another work of the Spirit that is not true of all believers is the "filling of the Spirit." Such filling was not a new event. Zacharias, the father of John the Baptist, and his wife Elizabeth, were both "filled with the Holy Spirit," and the results of the filling were the words of praise to God for His grace in sending the Messiah (Luke 1:41, 67). In the apostolic age, Paul commands his Ephesian readers, "Be filled with the Spirit" (5:18). Throughout the Book of Acts, there are many instances in which one of God's messengers was "filled with the Spirit" (2:4; 4:8; 4:31; 13:9).

In a disputed passage, there are some within Fundamentalism who believe that the Holy Spirit is one of whom it is said, "the one who now holds it [secret power of lawlessness] back will continue to do so until He is taken out of the way" (2 Thessalonians 2:7, Tr. Richard McNeeley). In other words, even though things are bad, they will get worse when this One is removed. Those who hold to this position believe that such a removal of the Spirit will take place at the Rapture (1 Thessalonians 4:16–17) when the Spirit is removed with the people He indwells.

The Holy Spirit is active in the hearts of those who are unbelievers. Christ's words in John 16:8–11 indicate that the Spirit "will convict the world of guilt in regard to sin, and righteousness and judgment." The sin spoken of in this passage is the sin of not believing in Jesus as the Christ, the Son of God (see John 20:30–31). The righteousness is explained as the fact that Jesus will be leaving and that God's demonstration of human righteousness in Jesus will no longer be seen. The judgment has to do with the verdict that the "prince of this world," Satan, the Tempter, the Serpent, has been condemned.

The Spirit and the Word of God

Jesus was filled with the Holy Spirit from His mother's womb (Luke 1:15). Just as the Spirit of God filled the Living Word, so the Spirit is the agent behind the Written Word of God. Paul declares, "All Scripture is inspired by God" (2 Timothy 3:16), and Peter explains how this came about as "men spoke from God as they were carried along by the Holy Spirit" (2 Peter 1:21).

The principal work of the Spirit is to glorify the Son (John 16:14). That is the work of the Spirit in the life of a believer. The result of the Spirit's work will be the production of a genuinely spiritual person. The evidence of that spirituality will not be boasting about being Spirit-filled, but will evidence itself in one's love and commitment to Christ in speech and behavior (Ephesians 5:18–21; Colossians 3:16–17). Indeed, the Spirit of God works behind the scenes to glorify the Son, for in giving glory to the Son, the Father is also glorified (John 16:14–15).

Richard I. McNeely

See also Baptism; God and God's Will

Bibliography

Boice, James. (1979) *Awakening to God.* Downers Grove, IL: Intervarsity Press.

Brown, Steve. (1999) *Follow the Wind.* Grand Rapids, MI: Baker Book House.

Bruner, F. Dale. (1970) *A Theology of the Holy Spirit.* Grand Rapids, MI: Wm. B. Eerdmans.

Chafer, Lewis Sperry. (1948) *Systematic Theology,* vol. 6. Dallas: Dallas Theological Seminary Press.

Morey, Robert. (1996) *The Trinity.* Iowa Falls, IA: World Bible Publishers.

Tozer, A. W. (1961) *The Knowledge of the Holy.* San Francisco: HarperCollins.

Walvoord, John F. (1954) *Theology of the Holy Spirit.* Wheaton, IL: Van Kampen Press.

Illuminati, The

Among some groups with millennialist or apocalyptic world views, there is a particular conspiracy theory claiming that within Masonic lodges is a secret group called the Illuminati that controls the world. Real Freemasons—members of several branches of a fraternal society that meets in Masonic lodges–are not particularly millennialist or apocalyptic, but they have become entwined in this longstanding conspiracy theory about plots for world control.

Freemasons were first accused of being the devil's disciples in the late 1700s, an idea that flourished in the United States in the 1800s. Those who embrace this theory often point to symbols associated with Freemasonry, such as the pyramid and eye on the back of the one-dollar bill, as evidence of the conspiracy. The original allegation of a conspiracy within Freemasonry to control the world can be traced back to British author John Robison who wrote a 1798 book in which the full title explains the basic premise: *Proofs of a Conspiracy Against All the Religions and Governments of Europe, carried on in the secret meetings of Free Masons, Illuminati, and Reading Societies, collected from good authorities*. Robison influenced French author Abbé Augustin de Barruel, whose first two volumes of his eventual four-volume study, *Memoirs Illustrating the History of Jacobinism* (1797–1798), beat Robison's book to the printer.

Both Robison and Barruel discuss the attempt by Bavarian intellectual Adam Weishaupt to spread the ideas of the Enlightenment through his secretive society, the Order of the Illuminati, founded in 1776. Weishaupt, a professor of Canon Law at the University of Ingolstadt in Germany, was banished in 1786 by the government, and the Order of the Illuminati was suppressed.

Weishaupt, his Illuminati society, the Freemasons, and other secret societies are portrayed by Robison and Barruel as bent on a conspiracy using front groups to spread their influence and eventually establish world domination. Barruel claimed the conspirators wanted to destroy both Christianity and the monarchies of Europe. He described the Illuminati as prophets of "revolutionary Equality and Liberty" responsible for causing the French Revolution. Robison, a professor of natural philosophy at the University of Edinburgh in Scotland, argued that the Illuminati evolved out of Freemasonry, and called the Illuminati philosophy "cosmopolitism." The books of both men promote three conspiracist contentions still circulating today: (1) the Enlightenment themes of equality and liberty undermine respect for private property and the natural social hierarchy; (2) there is a secret conspiracy to destroy Christianity; and (3) people who encourage free-thinking and international cooperation are disloyal cosmopolitans and subversive traitors, out to destroy national sovereignty, promote moral anarchy, and establish political tyranny. These conspiracist themes soon merged with the idea that individual Masons influenced by the Order of the Illuminati were in league with the devil (as agents of the Antichrist)—a claim that quickly became entwined with allegations that Jews were behind the plot. These claims of conspiracy made their way to the United States in the 1800s, generating Protestant suspicion about Freemasons and Catholics. Later they were modified to demonize

ADAM WEISHAUPT, FOUNDER OF THE ILLUMINATI, QUOTED IN JOHN ROBISON'S *PROOFS OF A CONSPIRACY* (1798)

The great strength of our Order lies in its concealment; let it never appear in any place in its own name, but always covered by another name, and another occupation. None is fitter than the three lower degrees of Free Masonry; the public is accustomed to it, expects little from it, and therefore takes little notice of it. Next to this, the form of a learned or literary society is best suited to our purpose, and had Free Masonry not existed, this cover would have been employed; and it may be much more than a cover, it may be a powerful engine in our hands. By establishing reading societies, and subscription libraries, and taking these under our direction, and supplying them through our labours, we may turn the public mind which way we will . . . . A Literary Society is the most proper form for the introduction of our Order into any state where we are yet strangers.

Source: Robison, John (1967/1798) *Proofs of a Conspiracy*. Boston: Western Islands, p. 112.

Catholics, and in the early 1900s, served as a template for the anti-Semitic hoax document, the *Protocols of the Elders of Zion*.

Chip Berlet

See also Anti-Semitism

Bibliography

Barruel Abbé Augustin. ([1797–1798] 1995) *Memoirs Illustrating the History of Jacobinism*, 2nd ed. revised and corrected, translated by Robert Clifford, reprinted in 1 vol. Fraser, MI: Real-View-Books.

Berlet, Chip, and Matthew N. Lyons. (2000) *Right-Wing Populism in America: Too Close for Comfort*. New York: Guilford Press.

Cohn, Norman. ([1967] 1996) *Warrant for Genocide: The Myth of the Jewish World Conspiracy and the Protocols of the Elders of Zion*. London: Serif.

Hofstadter, Richard. (1965) *The Paranoid Style in American Politics and Other Essays*. New York: Knopf.

Johnson, George. (1983) *Architects of Fear: Conspiracy Theories and Paranoia in American Politics*. Los Angeles: Tarcher/Houghton Mifflin.

Robison, John. ([1798] (1967) *Proofs of a Conspiracy Against All the Religions and Governments of Europe, carried on in the secret meetings of Free Masons, Illuminati, and Reading Societies, collected from good authorities*, 4th ed. with postscript. Boston: Western Islands.

Imam, The Last

The Last Imam is a central figure in Shi`ite Islam eschatology. From a historical point of view, his name was Muhammad al-Mahdi, a descendant of the Prophet Muhammad, who disappeared under mysterious circumstances in 873 CE. While the probability is that he was murdered by the ruling `Abbasid dynasty (which had kept his family imprisoned for some thirty years previously), Shi`ites believed that he went into a period of occultation (*ghayba*). This occultation is divided by Shi`ite scholars into two parts: the Lesser Occultation (874–941 CE), which was characterized by communication from the missing Imam in the form of letters, and the Greater Occultation, which persists until the present day.

Shi`ite apocalyptic beliefs focus around the activities of Muhammad al-Mahdi, who is the Twelfth and final Imam (hence the name Twelver Shi`ites for the majority of Shi`ites who believe in his return). He will appear in Mecca, at the Ka`ba, and gather a band of 313 followers to himself. Quickly he will fight the enemies of the Shi`a, mainly Sunnis, and defeat them, after which he will usher in a messianic kingdom of righteousness that will last for hundreds of years.

Although the figure of Muhammad al-Mahdi has always been central to Twelver Shi`ites, for the most part during the last four hundred years expectation of his appearance has been minimal (most Shi`i rulers have not encouraged such beliefs). But with the advent of Ayatollah Ruhollah al-Khumayni (d. 1989) and his preaching first against the Shah of Iran, Muhammad Reza Pahlavi, and then with the success of the Islamic Revolution in Iran (1978–1979), this expectation became more pronounced. The change in emphasis was largely brought about by the symbiosis of Khumayni's writings and those of `Ali Shariati, a prominent Iranian sociologist. Shariati "sought to do away with the traditional notion that until the Second Coming of the Hidden Imam, one must accept secular, unjust government" (Rinehart 1997: 159). This attitude dovetailed with Khumayni's ideas about changing society, and especially the necessity to defend and preserve Islam without waiting for the Twelfth Imam to appear.

In essence, Khumayni called for a state in which the powers of the Twelfth Imam would be delegated (to a large extent) to the *fuqaha'* (religious jurisprudents) who would defend the Islamic nature of the society and create a messianic state previous to the revelation of the Imam (Khumayni 1981: 76, 84–85, 145–146). Thus, according to this activist interpretation of Twelver Shi`ism, the Muslim believer can and must participate in the building of a just messianic society.

David Cook

See also Mahdi; Shi'a Islam

Bibliography

Amir-Moezzi, Mohammed. (1994) *The Divine Guide in Early Shi`ism: The Sources of Esotericism in Islam*, translated by David Streight. Albany, NY: SUNY Press.

Arjomand, Sa`id. (1984) *The Shadow of God and the Hidden Imam: Religion, Political Order and Societal Change in Shi`ite Iran from the Beginnings to 1890*. Chicago: University of Chicago Press.

Khumayni, Ayatollah Ruhollah. (1981) *Islam and Revolution: Writings and Declarations of Imam Khomeini*, translated by Hamid Algar. Berkeley: Mizan Press.

———. (n.d.) *Selected Messages and Speeches of Imam Khomeini*. Tehran: Ministry of National Guidance.

al-Majlisi, Muhammad al-Baqir. ([1700] 1983) *Bihar al-anwar*. Beirut: Mu'assasat al-Wafa', vols. 51–53.

Rinehart, James. (1997) *Revolution and the Millenium*. Westport, CT: Praeger Press.

Immaculate Conception

The Immaculate Conception affirms that Mary, the mother of Jesus, was conceived without the stain of original sin. This Roman Catholic doctrine was formally defined by Pope Pius IX on 8 December 1854—but only after asking the bishops of the church what their people believed. In spite of the important role that devotion to Mary plays in Catholic faith and culture, the church has only four "official" Marian doctrines: the perpetual virginity of Mary and the title "Mother of God" (*Theotokos*, literally "God-bearer") (both dating from the fourth century), the Immaculate Conception, and the Assumption of the body of Mary into heaven (defined in 1950).

The Immaculate Conception is the most misunderstood of the four doctrines. In fact, the doctrine is not found explicitly in Scripture, but two texts have been cited in its support. In Genesis 3:15, God says to Eve, "I will put enmity between you and the woman, and between your offspring and hers; He will strike at your head, while you strike at his heel" (NAB). Though referring literally to the abhorrence the children of Eve have for snakes, the Christian tradition has seen here a promise of Christ's victory over the serpent or devil. Thus, Mary, called the "new Eve" from the second century, has frequently been represented in Christian art as crushing the head of the serpent. Luke 1:28 has Gabriel greeting the young Jewish girl, Mary, as "hail, full of grace [Vulgate translation], the Lord is with you."

The doctrine of Mary's conception has been a matter of dispute. Though the concept of original sin had not yet been formulated by Augustine, Ephraem of Syria (306–373) and Ambrose (339–397) taught that Mary was free of all stain of sin. Many of the Eastern fathers followed this opinion and a feast commemorating Mary's conception began in the East in the late seventh century and eventually spread throughout the church. Augustine (354–430) taught that Mary was free from personal sin through God's special grace, but he insisted that as one born of conjugal intercourse she inherited original sin. Bernard of Clairvaux (1090–1153), though greatly devoted to Mary, followed Augustine's opinion. He in turn influenced the thirteenth-century scholastic theologians, Bonaventure, Albert the Great, and Thomas Aquinas, all of whom rejected the Immaculate Conception. John Duns Scotus (1266–1308), by introducing the concept of "preservative redemption," reconciled Mary's freedom from original sin with Christ's universal redemptive work. In 1854, however, in *Ineffabilis Deus*, Pope Pius IX declared, "the Most Blessed Virgin Mary from the first moment of her conception was, by the singular grace and privilege of Almighty God, in view of the merits of Christ Jesus the Savior of the human race, preserved immune from all stain of original sin" (Denzinger and Schönmetzer 1965: 3900). Two things should be observed about this definition. First, it does not deny that Mary herself has been redeemed by Christ; indeed it affirms it. Mary cannot be thought equal to the Redeemer. Second, it asserts that in the divine plan of salvation, Mary has been chosen to benefit from Christ's salvation from the moment of her conception. The doctrine of the Immaculate Conception affirms God's providential care for the mother from whom the divine son would be born, and thus, for the environment in which He would be nurtured. In Christ, grace triumphs over sin and its effects.

Thomas P. Rausch, S.J.

See also Cult of Mary

Bibliography

Denzinger, Henricus, ed., reedited by Adolfus Schönmetzer. (1965) *Enchiridion Symbolorum: Definitionum et Declarationum de Rebus Fidei et Morum* (Handbook of symbols: Of definitions and declarations concerning faith and morals). New York: Herder.

Jelly, Frederick M. (1986) *Madonna: Mary in the Catholic Tradition.* Huntington, IN: Our Sunday Visitor.

O'Connor, Edward Dennis. (1958) *The Dogma of the Immaculate Conception: History and Significance.* Notre Dame, IN: University of Notre Dame Press.

Incarnation

Incarnation is fundamentally based on the idea that the divine can appear in human form. The concept of incarnation can be found in various religions, but its most enduring expression is its use in Christian theology with reference to Jesus Christ. Incarnation is indeed the most central and complex of all Christian doctrines. It affirms that Jesus Christ, the divine Logos or the second person of the Trinity, assumed human form, that He was and is truly and fully God, and that this veritable hypostatic union is perpetual. The Christian doctrine of the incarnation states that God in one of the forms of God's triune being, while continuing to be God, has revealed the Godself to humankind for their redemption by appearing among them as a man. This man called Jesus is held to be the incarnate Word or Son of God. The incarnate one remains the paradigmatic example of the God–human encounter. Jesus as God incarnate mediates God to humanity and also in His consummate humanity, represents humanity to God.

The Incarnation in Scripture

The dogma of incarnation took some time to come to full fruition. The disciples of Jesus initially thought of Jesus as no more than a charismatic prophet. As time went on they began to believe Him to be the promised prophet, someone analogous to a new Moses (Deuteronomy 18:15) and later the Messiah (Mark 8:29). The earliest incarnation language had an adoptionist tone. Examples include the description of Jesus as "designated Son of God in power according to the Spirit" (Romans 1:4, RSV) or "God has made him both Lord and Christ" (Acts 2:36). A more refined language can be found in the writings of Paul. According to him, "God was in Christ" (2 Corinthians 5:19) and in the Epistle to the Hebrews he said "God spoke of old to our fathers by the prophets; but in these last days he has spoken to us by a Son" (1:1–2). The strongest affirmation of incarnation is in the famous words in the prologue to John's Gospel: "The Word became flesh and dwelt among us" (1:14) and also in John's statement that "The Word was with God, and the Word was God" (1:1).

Historical Background of Incarnational Christianity

The doctrine of the incarnation was hotly debated over the first five centuries of the Christian era. The need to provide a clear understanding of the hypostatic union between God and Jesus Christ was the basis of the ecumenical councils of Nicea (325 CE), Constantinople (381), Ephesus (431), and Chalcedon (451). These councils vehemently opposed Arianism (the denial of the Son's eternal divinity), Nestorianism (the denial that the divine–human Christ could be conceived as one), Monotheletism (the denial of two wills, divine and human, in Christ), Apollinarianism (the denial of Christ's human spirit), and

Eutychianism (the denial of Christ's two natures). The final and conclusive incarnational position reached at the Council of Chalcedon states that in Jesus Christ there are two natures, the human and divine, each complete and entire; they are unmixed, yet they are not separated but united together in one person. The Chalcedonian formula has become the essential definition of the doctrine of incarnation and the basis of Christological orthodoxy. With various corrections, it endured through the Middle Ages and was utilized by several Protestant churches at the time of Reformation. In fact, the basis of traditional Christology and incarnation is the two-nature doctrine of the Chalcedonian definition, which speaks of "one and the same Christ, Son, Lord, Only-begotten, recognized in two natures, without confusion, without change, without division, without separation; the distinction of natures being in no way annulled by the union, but rather the characteristics of each nature being preserved and coming together to form one person, not as parted or separated into two persons, but one and the Same Son and Only-begotten God the Word, Lord Jesus Christ."

Modern Criticisms

Several scholars have criticized the Chalcedonian definition. Frederick Schleiermacher in *The Christian Faith* (1821) vigorously opposed the Chalcedonian formula on logical grounds. He maintained that its principal terms, "person" and "nature," were shrouded in mystery and had been used in a confusing manner. He proposed a new approach that would be based on the humanity of Jesus. He consistently maintained that in Jesus alone do we encounter a perfect or mature humanity, and that this embraces a complete God-consciousness, which he also refers to as an essential indwelling of God in that person. Although Schleiermacher rejected the traditional Chalcedonian formula, he believed that he was reformulating an important doctrine of incarnation. Later in the nineteenth century, theologian Albrecht Ritschl criticized Chalcedon because of its intellectual or scholastic dimension. Theologian Adolf Harnack has also labeled incarnational Christology as a Hellenizing of the Gospel, which had resulted in putting the person of Christ at the core of the proclamation, rather than the kingdom of God. In the contemporary period, John Hick in *The Myth of God Incarnate* (1977) suggests that the incarnation is a mythological or poetic way of expressing Jesus' sig-

nificance for humanity. He further states that the symbolic statement that Jesus was God and the Son incarnate is not literally true, because it has no literal meaning. Hick also elaborates on what is intended by the mythical language of the creed of incarnation as agreed upon at Chalcedon. Hick's summation regarding the language of Chalcedon is based on his opinion that myth and symbol are not indicative but expressive and that their real significance is to express a valuation and evoke an attitude.

Conclusion

Be it as it may, there is no doubt that the doctrine of the incarnation represents an important cornerstone in Christian theology. This doctrine is particularly important in our contemporary world because it provides the lens to look at God's work and action in the material world as well as a way to understand the action of the Word in different cultures and traditions. The Fourth Gospel and the Epistle to the Ephesians affirm that the Word is at work in all things. There is no part of human life and experience that is foreign to Him. According to Maximus the Confessor, "The Word of God, who is God wills at all times and in all places to work the mystery of his embodiment."

Akintunde E. Akinade

See also Jesus; Trinity

Bibliography

Hebblethwaite, Brian. (1987) *The Incarnation*. Cambridge, UK: Cambridge University Press.

Hick, John, ed. (1977) *The Myth of God Incarnate*. Philadelphia: The Westminster Press.

Islamic Fundamentalism

In the modern world, the term "Fundamentalism" appears most often in reference to two major religious traditions: American Evangelical Protestantism and Islam. Its application in other realms, such as Judaism and Hinduism, is much less axiomatic, according to those who usually employ the term, such as Western journalists, commentators, and analysts. But whereas American Protestant "Fundamentalists"—sometimes described as "angry Evangelicals"—are seen by some

The Dome of the Rock in Jerusalem. PHOTO COURTESY OF HERMANN MAIBA.

as out-of-touch, narrow-minded, and threatening only at the ballot box (insofar as they usually vote Republican), Islamic "Fundamentalists" are viewed by many in the West not only as a global ideological threat but also as a military menace. Thus, of all the world's "Fundamentalisms," the Islamic brand is the best-known, most discussed (a recent Internet search yielded 47,100 entries under the topic), most-feared and yet least understood version.

Definition

There is an ongoing, heated debate among scholars of Islam and the Middle East concerning the usage of the term "Fundamentalism." (This struggle has long since been lost in the media and popular discourse, but specialists obstinately refuse to abandon the field of battle.) The term "Fundamentalism" arose in the American Protestant circles of the late nineteenth and early twentieth centuries as a religious-oriented ideology aimed not only at fending off the attacks of Darwinism and Marxism on the Christian world-

view but also at countering the developing field of biblical criticism. "Fundamentalism" was finally named as such, and codified, in the twelve-volume work *The Fundamentals: A Testimony of the Truth*, published from 1910 to 1915 by a group of Protestant laymen. The focus of the books was doctrinal, specifically rearticulating five essential points: biblical inerrancy; Jesus' divinity, the Virgin Birth, and Jesus' substitutionary Atonement, physical Resurrection, and eventual return. Today, Protestant Fundamentalism has moved into the realm of criticizing social praxis (e.g., homosexuality, abortion) but is at root belief-oriented along the same lines as delineated a century ago.

Beliefs

Scholars who object to the term "Fundamentalism" in an Islamic context do so primarily on the grounds of its Christian origin and furthermore argue that the interjection of this term continues Western semantic and ideological imperialism, even when arabicized as *usuliyah* and employed by Arabs themselves. However, insofar as for both Christians and Muslims, "fundamentalism is orthodoxy in confrontation with modernity" (Hunter 1990: 57), the term is applicable to the Islamic world. The key concept of modernity, or Western (and now de facto global) thought since the eighteenth-century Enlightenment, is the divorce of revelation and reason and the ramifications thereof: the separation of religion and state, the relegation of religion to an increasingly smaller section of the public square, and unbridled faith in science and technology to solve all of humanity's problems. Both American Protestant and Muslim Fundamentalists reject all or part of this modernist credo. Both, likewise, believe in the transformability of society through politics (though disagreeing on the degree of militancy required). And today, both agree that a return to the proper praxis of their respective faiths will cure societal ills. Therefore, while some scholars prefer the terms "Islamic revivalism," "Islamic reformism," "Islamic radicalism," or "Islamism," "Fundamentalism" is acceptable in an Islamic context.

Muslim Fundamentalists add several other key points to their rejection of modernity that differentiate their brand of the ideology from that of Protestant Christians. First, they believe that after the time of the Prophet Muhammad (d. 632 CE) and his first four caliphs ("successors")—Abu Bakr (d. 634), Umar (d. 644), Uthman (d. 656), and Ali (d. 661)—history took a wrong turn as illegitimate leaders usurped power. This grave situation was exacerbated by Western imperialism, beginning with the Spanish Reconquista and the Crusades, continuing with Napoleon's occupation of Egypt in 1798 and the British and French Mandate system after World War I. American military (the Gulf War) and cultural imperialism is seen as part of this long tradition of Western oppression. The current phase of tyrannical rule is one in which Arab, Turkish or, until 1979, Iranian leaders foolishly adopted Western ideas in order to maintain their power. Second, Muslim Fundamentalists believe that only the return of legitimate Islamic rule will cure the *ummah*, or "Islamic community," of its socioeconomic, political, and cultural malaise. Most Fundamentalists look to human efforts to bring this about, although some look to the major Islamic eschatological figure—known as al-Mahdi, the "rightly guided one," to Sunnis and the "Hidden Imam" to Shi'ites — to usher in utopia. Finally, Muslim Fundamentalists believe in *tawhid*, literally "profession of faith in monotheism," but also short-hand for a Pan-Islamic state based on *Sharia*, or "Islamic law," that supersedes the artificial nationalistic boundaries created by Western colonialists.

Influential Islamic Fundamentalists

There are six major figures whose influence has been crucial to modern Islamic Fundamentalism. Taqi al-Din Ahmad Ibn Taymiyah (d. 1328), who lived in Damascus, is revered for his calls to jihad ("holy war" or "religious struggle") against non-Muslims (in his time the Mongols) and for his criticism of the pantheistic/polytheistic practices of the Sufis, or Islamic mystics. Ibn Taymiyah's teachings were adopted by Muhammad Ibn Abd al-Wahhab (d. 1792) in Arabia. His views included calls for a literal interpretation of the Qur'an, *tawhid*, and criticism of the Sufis and of the Ottoman rulers of Arabia for their allegedly lax Islamic practices. Abd al-Wahhab's interpretation of Islam was adopted by the founders of the state of Saudi Arabia and made its official ideology.

The other four fathers of Islamic Fundamentalism all lived in the twentieth century. Hasan al-Banna (d. 1949) and Sayyid Qutb (d. 1966) were both Egyptian. The former was an "inclusive Fundamentalist" who wanted to rehabilitate society from within by making it more Islamic and accepted the theoretical possibility of reconciling Islamic and Western political theory. al-Banna founded al-Ikhwan al-Muslimun, the "Muslim Brotherhood," now operative in most Arab countries. His ideological offspring was Qutb, an "exclusive Fundamentalist," who wished to overthrow society and create an Islamic state; he rejected the coexistence of Islam with Western ideas like multiparty democracy. al-Banna was assassinated and Qutb was executed by the Egyptian government for his unremitting criticisms of President Gamal Abdel Nasser.

Sayyid Abu `A'la Mawdudi (d. 1979) is, as a Pakistani, the only non-Arab or non-Iranian regarded as an influential Fundamentalist. He advocated a "theodemocracy" in which all Muslims, not just the elite, would interpret and practice Islamic law. Illegitimate Western-created nation-states would thus be supplanted by an Islamic state.

The final major influential modern Islamic Fundamentalist is the only Iranian one: Ayatollah Khomeini (d. 1989). Khomeini played a major role in overthrowing the secular Iranian government of

Shah Mohammad Reza Pahlavi in 1979 and establishing the Islamic Republic of Iran. The Ayatollah's major ideological presupposition—now political reality in Iran—was *vilayet-i faqah*, the "guardianship of the interpreters of Islamic law." This was a new development in Islamic thought, for despite the always close relationship between mosque and state since the time of the Prophet Muhammad, religious leaders had not actually directed politics. Thus, Western commentators are mistaken when they label Iran a "Fundamentalist" state that turns the clock back centuries; actually, Iranian Islam is quite radical (albeit antimodernist, at least ideologically).

Conflicting Islamic Fundamentalist Views

Post-revolutionary Iranian Shi'ite religio-political thought shares several characteristics with Sunni Fundamentalism: primarily the need to overthrow regimes and reshape society and Pan-Islamic aspirations. However, until very recently the two brands of "Fundamentalism" were separated by the uniquely Shi'ite eschatological view about the Hidden Imam, which differs from the Sunni view of the Mahdi. For the Sunnis the Mahdi is one of two good eschatological figures—the prophet Jesus being the other—who returns before the end of time to battle the forces of evil and establish global social justice and Islam. The Sunnis see the Mahdi and Jesus as restoring the halcyon days of Prophetic rule. Shi'ites who make up about fifteen percent of the world's one billion Muslims, believe that after the fourth caliph, Ali, was assassinated, the legitimate leadership of the community passed to their imams (like Ali, descendants of the Prophet) rather than to the usurper Sunni Umayyads from Damascus. The particular brand of Shi'ism now predominating in Iran holds that the eleventh imam after Ali—the Twelfth Imam—went into a state of occultation, whence he will return one day as the Mahdi. Since the Arab defeat in the Six-Day War of 1967, increased eschatological yearnings among the Sunnis for the Mahdi have converged with the Shi'ite example of how to create an Islamic state without the actual presence of the Hidden Imam and produce a new kind of eschatological Fundamentalism. The Islamic Revolution in Iran, however, has proved enormously influential to Sunni Muslim Fundamentalists just by virtue of its existence, which proves that an Islamic revolutionary state is a real possibility.

Of these six major thinkers who influenced twentieth-century Islamic Fundamentalism, only two—Abd al-Wahhab and Khomeini—were able to put their ideas into practice directly. Nevertheless, Islamic Fundamentalism, both Sunni and Shi'ite, has taken concrete form over the last fifty years in particular, drawing upon all the ideas of these thinkers (as well as others).

Islamic Fundamentalist Groups

The Wahhabis, who formed a synergistic relationship with the ruling al-Saud family of Arabia, are viewed by many in the West as Fundamentalist Muslims, considering their limitations on the rights of women, strict "eye for an eye" judicial punishments, and prohibition of any but Islamic worship in the kingdom of Saudi Arabia. Many other Muslims, however, consider the Saudi state an illegitimate one, given its alliance with the United States and the alleged immoral practices (e.g., gambling, sexual excesses) of many members of the ruling house, as well as their failure to more equitably distribute the kingdom's vast economic wealth.

The Muslim Brotherhood, since its founding by al-Banna, has spread to most Arab countries. While not enjoying state sponsorship, the Brotherhood has nonetheless (or perhaps for that very reason) moved from the fringes into the political mainstream by virtue of its social welfare and educational ventures (e.g., running schools, providing loans for the needy) and in fact in countries like Jordan has had members elected to the national assembly. As such, this organization epitomizes the concept of "inclusive Fundamentalism."

Hamas is a Palestinian offshoot of the Muslim Brotherhood, founded during the *intifadah*, or "uprising," against Israeli occupation that began in 1987. The word is a double entendre in Arabic: its intrinsic meaning is "enthusiasm," or "fighting spirit" and it is also an acronym for *harakat al-muqawimah al-islamiyah*, "the Islamic resistance movement." Headed by Shaykh Ahmad Yasin and supported by Iran, it constitutes the popular religious alternative to the officially secular Palestine National Authority, Yasir Arafat's de facto government that grew out of the Palestine Liberation Organzation (PLO). Hamas advocates the Islamization of Palestinian (and Israeli) society in order to achieve an Islamic state. The Islamic Jihad is another, more radical offshoot of the

Muslim Brotherhood that differs from Hamas primarily in its open advocacy of an armed struggle against the Israelis, preceding the society's total Islamization. This group lionizes Sayyid Qutb and the Ayatollah Khomeini.

The Taliban rule most of Afghanistan today. This is truly a Sunni Fundamentalist group, founded, with the assistance of Pakistan, in the wake of the 1980s Soviet occupation. (*Talib* is an Arabic word meaning "claimant" or "scholar," although often rendered in the Western press as "student.") The Taliban ordered women to veil upon leaving their homes, men to grow beards, all books but the Qur'an destroyed and, most recently, two huge statues of Buddha—symbols of the country's "pagan" past—razed. The Taliban has also been accused of harboring, and assisting, the terrorist leader Usama bin Laden.

Hizb Allah, or "Hizbullah," means "party of God" and is a Shi'ite group. Headquartered in Lebanon, where the Shi'a outnumber both Sunnis and Christians, Hizb Allah originated during the 1970s civil war as an offshoot of the Amal militia. This group has close ties with Iran and fought against the Israelis in both southern Lebanon and northern Israel. They are Pan-Islamic and view themselves as a bridge between Arab and Iranian Fundamentalists.

Conclusion

The term "Fundamentalism," despite its Christian provenance, is applicable—mutatis mutandis—to an Islamic context. Rejection of modernism and creation of an Islamic state to cure societal ills are the two major characteristics of Islamic Fundamentalism, whether it manifests as a state-sponsored (the Wahhabis, Taliban) or state-tolerated (Muslim Brotherhood) ideology, an alternative power bloc (Hamas) or an extra-governmental radicalism (Islamic Jihad, Hizb Allah). Some Fundamentalist groups, such as al-Qa'idah (the "base" or "control"), headed by the renegade Saudi Usama bin Laden, operate more as peripatetic, militant cells. His group, for example, is not permanently sited in any one country in order to effect change there but rather moves from place to place (e.g., Sudan, Afghanistan), striking targets of opportunity. Its major goal is to encourage Pan-Islamic struggle against the West (bin Laden styles himself a modern Salah al-Din, who retook Jerusalem from the Crusaders). Such groups as this differ from the major sedentary Islamic Fundamentalist movements not in their ideological bent but rather in the degree of violence they are willing to utilize against Western (primarily American) interests. Islamic Fundamentalism, of both the Sunni and Shi'ite varieties, will exist until the Muslim world comes to terms with modernity and with its own colonial past. Until then, Islam will remain for many—now that communism has lost its allure—the only viable ideological rival to post-Enlightenment democratic capitalism.

Timothy R. Furnish

See also Imam, The Last; Mahdi; Shi'a Islam; Taliban

Bibliography

Abu-Amr, Ziad. (1994) *Islamic Fundamentalism in the West Bank and Gaza: Muslim Brotherhood and Islamic Jihad.* Bloomington: Indiana University Press.

Ahmad, Rif`at Sayyid. (1998) *al-Harakah al-islâmîyah al-râdîkâlîyah fî Misr* [The radical Islamic movement in Egypt]. Beirut: Markaz al-Dirâsât al-Istrâtîjîyah wa-al-Buhûth wal-al-Tawthîq.

`Ammârah, Muhammad. (1998) *al-Usûlîyah bayna al-gharb wa-al-islâm* [Fundamentalism between the West and Islam]. Cairo: Dâr al-Shurûq.

Arjomand, Sa'id Amir. (1995) "Unity and Diversity in Islamic Fundamentalism." In *Fundamentalisms Comprehended*, edited by Martin E. Marty and R. Scott Appleby. Vol. 5 of *The Fundamentalism Project*. Chicago: University of Chicago Press, 179–198.

al-Azmeh, Aziz. (1993) *Islams and Modernities.* London: Verso.

Azzam, Maha. (1993) "Islamist Attitudes to the Current World Order." *Islam and Christian–Muslim Relations* 4, 2: 247–256.

"A Biography of Osama [sic] bin Laden." (1999) Frontline. http://www.pbs.org/wgbh/pages/frontline/shows/binladen/who/bio.html.

Carré, Olivier. (1995) "From Banna to Qutb and 'Qutbism': The Radicalization of Fundamentalist Thought under Three Regimes." In *Egypt from Monarchy to Republic: A Reassessment of Revolution and Change*, edited by Shimon Shamir. Boulder, CO: Westview Press, 181–194.

Choueiri, Youssef M. (1993) "Theoretical Paradigms of Islamic Movements." *Political Studies* XLI: 108–116.

———. (1997) *Islamic Fundamentalism.* London: Pinter.

Israel

Eisenstadt, S. N. (1996) "The Jacobin Component of Fundamentalist Movements." *Contention* V, 3: 155–170.

Esposito, John L. (1992) *The Islamic Threat: Myth or Reality?* New York: Oxford University Press.

Fukuyama, Francis. (1992) *The End of History and the Last Man.* New York: Free Press.

Fuller, Graham E., and Rend Rahim Francke. (1999) *The Arab Shi`a: The Forgotten Muslims.* London: Mac-Millan Press, Ltd.

Furnish, Timothy R. (2001) "Eschatology As Politics, Eschatology As Theory: Modern Sunni Arab Mahdism in Historical Perspective." Ph.D. diss., Ohio State University, Columbus, Ohio.

Hassan, Riffat. (1990) "The Burgeoning of Islamic Fundamentalism: Toward an Understanding of the Phenomenon." In *The Fundamentalist Phenomenon: A View from Within, a Response from Without*, edited by Norman J. Cohen. Grand Rapids, MI: Wm. B. Eerdmans, 151–171.

Hunter, James Davison. (1990) "Fundamentalism in Its Global Contours." In *The Fundamentalist Phenomenon: A View from Within, a Response from Without*, edited by Norman J. Cohen. Grand Rapids, MI: Wm. B. Eerdmans, 56–72.

Huntington, Samuel P. (1996) *The Clash of Civilizations and the Remaking of World Order.* New York: Simon and Schuster.

Jansen, Johannes J. G. (1997) *The Dual Nature of Islamic Fundamentalism.* Ithaca, NY: Cornell University Press.

Kramer, Martin. (1993) "Hizbullah: The Calculus of Jihad." In *Fundamentalisms and the State: Remaking Polities, Economies and Militance*, edited by Martin E. Marty and R. Scott Appleby. Vol. 3 of *The Fundamentalism Project.* Chicago: University of Chicago Press, 539–556.

Lewis, Bernard. (1993) *Islam and the West.* New York: Oxford University Press.

Moussalli, Ahmad S. (1993) "Two Tendencies in Modern Islamic Political Thought: Modernism and Fundamentalism." *Hamdard Islamicus* XVI: 51–78.

———. (1999) *Moderate and Radical Islamic Fundamentalism: The Quest for Modernity.* Gainesville: University Press of Florida.

Pelikan, Jaroslav. (1990) "Fundamentalism and/or Orthodoxy? Toward an Understanding of the Fundamentalist Phenomenon." In *The Fundamentalist Phenomenon: A View from Within, a Response from Without*, edited by Norman J. Cohen. Grand Rapids, MI: Wm. B. Eerdmans, 3–21.

Ryan, Patrick J. (1984) "Islamic Fundamentalism: A Questionable Category." *America* 151: 437–440.

Schmidtke, Sabine. (1987) "Modern Modifications in the Shi`i Doctrine of the Expectation of the Mahdi (Intizar al-Mahdi): The Case of Khumaini." *Orient* 28: 389–406.

Sivan, Emmanuel. (1985) *Radical Islam: Medieval Theology and Modern Politics.* New Haven, CT: Yale University Press.

Tibi, Bassam. (1988) *The Crisis of Modern Islam: A Preindustrial Culture in a Scientific-Technical Age*, translated by Judith van Sievers. Salt Lake City: University of Utah Press.

Watt, William Montgomery. (1988) *Islamic Fundamentalism and Modernity.* New York: Routledge.

Weaver, Mary Anne. (2000) "The Real Bin Laden." *The New Yorker* (24 January): 32–38.

Zonis, Marvin, and Daniel Brumberg. (1987) *Khomeini, the Islamic Republic of Iran, and the Arab World.* Harvard Middle East Papers Modern Series, V. Cambridge, MA: Center for Middle Eastern Studies.

Israel

When speaking of Israel one must exert extreme caution, especially in light of the twentieth-century Holocaust, for Israel is neither a doctrine nor an abstract concept, but a real people (*laos*) and a nation (*ethnos*) in space and time. Israel as a community has a special place with God that no other nation enjoys, for God called Israel into being to be both a witness to His divine revelation and reconciling mediation to the world.

Israel in the Old Testament

The call of Israel can be placed in the Creation narrative where God blesses Adam with the charge to "be fruitful and multiple" (Genesis 1:22), but God's covenant with Abraham is understood to be the comprehensive event where God formalizes this relationship. The call of Abraham was to leave his country and his kin and to go to the Land that God would apportion for him because God was going to make him a great nation, make his name great, and bless him (Genesis 12:1–2). The covenant is reiterated in Genesis 15 and finally formalized in Genesis 17. Here God pronounces the covenant (in Hebrew *brit*) to be an everlasting or perpetual (*olam*) covenant to be with not only Abraham but also his descendants for generations to come (2–10). Circumcision was the sign of covenant (10) and the promise of the Land was to be an "everlasting possession" (8). More important, the covenant is met by only God for Abraham mysteriously falls asleep during which time God moved between the divided pieces of sacrifice (Genesis 15:17). In this way, the covenant with Abraham, as representative of Israel, is to be regarded as *unilateral* or *one-sided*, that is, it is not dependant on Abraham. Because God's covenant was both everlasting and unilateral with Israel, the conclusion must be drawn that the covenant continues to this day.

The purpose of the covenant was so that "all nations on earth will be blessed" (Genesis 18:18; 22:18; NIV) because Abraham was the "father of many nations" (Genesis 17:4–7). The name "Israel" is attributed to Abraham's grandson Jacob by God (Genesis 32:28; 35:10). Born of Jacob are twelve sons who each become the seedbed for the Twelve Tribes of Israel. It is through the lineage of Judah, Jacob's son by Leah, that Christ was born (cf. Matthew 1:1–16; Luke 3:33; Hebrews 7:14).

From the time of Moses to Saul (c. 1500–1000 BCE), Israel matures from a people into a great nation. The tribe of Levi is set apart as a priesthood to mediate between God and the people. The Tabernacle and Ark of the Covenant are constructed to be the dwelling place of God. Israel moves into the land of Canaan and fulfills one of the covenant promises. This marks the period of the judges. These men and women were appointed by God to deliver the people from an oppressor (cf. Jude 2:16–18). The judges quickly lose sight of their divine calling and Israel, desiring to be like other nations, rejects God as king and petitions Samuel to anoint a monarch over them (1 Samuel 8:5). Saul is appointed as king, marking the beginning of Israel's monarchy. The unified monarchy is short-lived and the kingdom is divided under the reign of Rehoboam, son of Solomon (1 Kings 12). Eventually, Israel is exiled from the Land and an established remnant of God's people perpetuates the covenant.

Israel in the New Testament

Jesus comes as a Jew, a descendant of David, Judah, and Abraham, not to the nations but to the "lost sheep of the house of Israel" (Matthew 15:24). It is not surprising, therefore, that Jesus proclaims to the Samaritan women "salvation is from the Jews" (John 4:22). Israel brings forth Jesus the Messiah as a Jew and, as a Jew, Jesus brings forth the kingdom of God (Romans 9:5). This is illustrated in Jesus' charge to the disciples to begin their mission efforts first to Jerusalem, then Judea, Samaria, and beyond (Acts 1:8).

The apostle Paul understands that Jesus was the "seed" (descendant) of Abraham and through him all nations of the earth would be blessed (Galatians 3:16). Apart from Christ, Gentiles remain alienated from God and outside the commonwealth of Israel (Ephesians 2:11). Only through Christ are the Gentiles grafted into the trunk of Israel and established as heirs to the promise of Abraham (Galatians 3:29). Therefore, the barrier between Jew and Gentile has been removed and the two groups enjoy communion with God through the Holy Spirit (Ephesians 2:19, 22). Romans 9–11 is the longest treatise in Paul's writings on the place of Israel in history and in the consummation of all things. Twice in chapter 11 Paul states that God did not reject Israel (1, 2), but he points out that despite the people's continual stubbornness and rebellion they were elected by God for the reconciliation of the world (11, 15). Israel, according to Paul, will continue to experience a hardening of the heart and mind until the full measure of Gentiles have been saved and then all Israel will be saved (26). If in their obstinacy those outside of Israel find an inheritance through God's covenant with Abraham, then how much more will the world be blessed in Israel's obedience during the final days.

Israel Today

Today we see God continually working in and through Israel as a continuation of His covenant with Abraham. In 1948, Israel was reestablished as a nation-state and once again the people (*laos*) are restored as a nation (*ethnos*) to their promised land (*topos*). Theologically, there has been a post-Holocaust movement in which supersessionism (the belief that the church in the New Testament superseded or replaced Israel as the people of God) has been rejected. For dispensational Fundamentalists, Israel plays a central role in interpreting and predicting the final days. They too see the church superseding Israel for the church inherits the spiritual blessings of God and ascends to the heavens to be in eternal communion with God. Israel, on the other hand, inherits only the earthly eternal blessing of the land and remains on New Earth (Chafer 1948: 23). Some Reformed theologians understand the covenant promises of God to be fulfilled in Jesus Christ. Therefore, Israel's unbelief of Jesus as the Messiah results in a cutting off from the blessings of God. At the center of the debate over a future for Israel is interpretative methodology. Premillennial dispensationalists tend to interpret literally and specifically Old Testament prophecies concerning Israel. Reformed scholars tend (again, generally speaking) to interpret allegorically and spiritually passages about Israel.

Robert T. Leach

Bibliography

Barth, Karl. (1936–1969) *Church Dogmatics*. Edinburgh: T and T Clark.

Chafer, Lewis Sperry. (1948) *Systematic Theology*, vol.4. Dallas, TX: Dallas Theological Press.

Holwerda, David E. (1995) *Jesus & Israel: One Covenant or Two?* Grand Rapids, MI: Wm. B. Eerdmans.

House, H. Wayne. (1998) *Israel: The Land and the People.* Grand Rapids, MI: Kregel.

Kaiser, Walter C. (1998) *A History of Israel.* Nashville, TN: Broadman and Holman.

Sonderegger, Katherine. (1992) *That Jesus Christ Was Born a Jew: Karl Barth's Doctrine of Israel.* University Park, PA: Penn State Press.

Soulen, R. Kendall. (1996) *The God of Israel and Christian Theology.* Minneapolis, MN: Fortress Press.

Torrance, David W., ed. (1982) *The Witness of the Jews to God.* Edinburgh: Handsel Press.

Torrance, Thomas F. (1983) *The Mediation of Christ.* Exeter, UK: Paternoster Press.

Jehovah's Witnesses

The Jehovah's Witnesses emerged in the 1870s as a loosely organized Adventist movement led by Charles Taze Russell (1852–1916). From Jehovah's Witnesses' inception, Witnesses were fundamentalists with strong millennial tendencies. Initially known as "Bible Students," "Millennial Dawnists," or "Russellites," the Watchtower Bible and Tract Society was legally incorporated in the United States in 1884; the group officially adopted the name Jehovah's Witnesses in 1931. Although American in origin, fewer than one-fourth of Jehovah's Witnesses lived in the United States by the end of the twentieth century, at which time the Society in the 1990s claimed a worldwide membership of over 5.5 million with U.S. membership at approximately one million. As such, it is one of the largest individual fundamentalist organizations in the world.

Witness life is based on a regimen of active proselytizing and regular participation in five weekly meetings at their Kingdom Halls where members study Society literature and learn effective recruiting skills and techniques. Individuals are encouraged to log one to ten hours a week in "field ministry" (proselytizing) as "Publishers"; "Regular Pioneers" average 70 hours per month; "Auxiliary Pioneers," 50 hours per month; and "Special Pioneers," 140 hours per month.

The Society's biweekly magazines, *The Watchtower* and *Awake!* are important sources of information about Witness beliefs and practices. *The Watchtower* magazine is the most authoritative source of ideological guidance from the organization; the periodical *Awake!* is a popular magazine that brings a "theocratic" perspective to bear on common issues and problems of everyday life. The Society publishes its own Bible translation, the *New World Translation* (rev. ed. 1984). Although Witnesses regularly use other established Bible translations, they prefer to use the NWT for study and proselytizing. The translation is an important source of Witness doctrine, and the Witnesses' distinctive communal dialectic (sometimes referred to as "theocratic English") is based in part on the NWT's unique English style. The WTS published a substantial official history, *Jehovah's Witnesses: Proclaimers of God's Kingdom* (1993).

Organization

The Watchtower's model for its international, interracial society is the *theocracy*. According to the Society, Jehovah's theocratic kingdom currently appears on earth in the global network of congregations composed of individuals of almost every race and culture. Through its circuit and district overseers, each congregation answers to its branch office, and that office operates under the direct oversight and authority of the Governing Body located in the movement's world headquarters in Brooklyn, New York.

The Society's Governing Body, representatives of the 144,000 "anointed" ones destined to reign with Christ in heaven over his millennial kingdom, provides exclusive and comprehensive guidance to Jehovah's contemporary organization. Authority and leadership within the Watchtower Society is a type of anonymous, institutionalized charisma. Only the privileged "anointed class" of the 144,000 has access to this charismatic power. In practice, only a handful of elderly men at the Society's headquarters in Brooklyn serve as God's "channel of communication." That group, called the Governing Body, represents the "Faithful and Discreet Slave" prophesied in Matthew 24:45–47, and only they can discern the "true meaning" of the biblical text. Interestingly, the "new light" that they believe Jehovah makes available to his faithful "anointed" in these "evil last days" is based in the Bible itself. That is, while the Bible itself is necessarily perfect, its meaning is not always clear without this privileged organizational guidance. Therefore, what the Bible really "means" is available only to this special class, and even then Jehovah is only gradually enlightening his faithful as the End draws closer.

It is this distinction that clearly sets off Jehovah's Witnesses from other fundamentalist groups.

The WTS's ultimate objective is a kind of *frictionless theocracy* that eliminates all slippage within its theocratic economy, filtering out disruptive *noise*, exorcising local particularities and idiosyncrasies potentially in conflict with the homogenizing designs of Jehovah's theocratic monologue. The vertical distribution of theocratic power emanating from the theocratic center in Brooklyn permeates Witness culture, facilitating the WTS's production of global uniformity. This dynamic can be observed, for example, in the WTS's creation and translation of its literature. Almost all the major writing occurs in Brooklyn, at the center of Jehovah's visible theocracy, where it is first composed in the Society's (apparent) Truth language, i.e., English, before it is then translated into other world languages. It appears that any local material that finds its way into print must always receive the theocratic imprimatur from Brooklyn headquarters.

Distinctive Beliefs and Practices

A posture of world rejection entails the rhetorical exorcism of Witness discourse in which words and doctrines are purged of their "Babylonish" associations. This purge of all vestiges of corrupt Babylon demands more than simple lexical correctness. Jehovah's people must be *theocratically correct* in every way. This desire for theocratic correctness involves not only the eradication of the corrupt language of Babylon; it also requires the theological exorcism of ideological remnants of corrupt Babylon. Watchtower literature proclaims that:

> A religion may *claim* to advocate worship of the true God of the Bible and it may use the name of his Son, Jesus Christ, but of what value is this if it is contaminated with Babylonish doctrines and practices? . . . [W]e need to make a clean break from any and all organizations of Babylon the Great. We need to quit sharing in their activities.

Thus Witnesses reject the traditional Christian doctrine of the Trinity because they consider it neither rational nor scriptural, and they claim that the very notion of triune gods evidences pagan corruption.

The traditional doctrines of the immortality of the soul and eternal torment in Hell are rejected by Witnesses because they too originated in pagan antiquity, not in the Bible. What appears as a particularly idiosyncratic claim is the Witness' insistence that Jesus was crucified on a single-beamed "torture stake," not on a tau-shaped cross. Witnesses argue that the tau-shaped cross has ancient pagan fertility associations, although the phallic imagery of a single-beamed stake gives them no pause. In one issue, *The Watchtower* declared that:

> there are common threads going through the confused tapestry of the world's religions. Many religions have their roots in mythology. Nearly all are tied together by some form of belief in a supposed immortal human soul that survives death and goes to a hereafter or transmigrates to another creature. Many have the common denominator of belief in a dreadful place of torment and torture called hell. Others are connected by ancient pagan beliefs in triads, trinities, and mother goddesses. Therefore, it is only appropriate that they should all be grouped together under the one composite symbol of the harlot "Babylon the Great."

Witnesses likewise reject the traditional celebration of festivals and holidays (including Christmas, New Year's Day, Easter, and personal birthdays) on the grounds that they actually originated in Babylon the Great. Witnesses believe that:

> Those that make up the Christian organization of Jehovah's witnesses are persons who have separated themselves from the many religions of both pagandom and Christendom. By attending meetings at one of their Kingdom Halls, you can see for yourself the difference this has made.

God's people must treat his name as holy and make it known throughout the earth. . . . There is only one people that is really following Jesus' example in this regard. Their main purpose in life is to serve God and bear witness to his name, just as Jesus did. So they have taken the scriptural name "Jehovah's Witnesses."

Millennialism

Despite numerous delays and recalculations of the endtime, Witnesses continue in their tenacious struggle to proclaim Jehovah's imminent kingdom on earth. Witness scholar M. James Penton argues that in fact the Witnesses have "preached millenarianism longer and more consistently than any major sectarian movement in the world" (1985: 7). The year 1914 is a pivotal date for Witnesses, as it signifies the time when Watchtower prophetic interpretation indicates that "Jesus Christ began to rule as king of God's heavenly government." One Watchtower publication, *Reasoning from the Scriptures* (p. 87), summarizes that:

> Christ as King did not immediately proceed to destroy all who refused to acknowledge Jehovah's sovereignty and himself as Messiah. Instead, as he had foretold, a global preaching work was to be done. . . . As King he would direct a dividing of peoples of all nations, those proving to be righteous being granted the prospect of everlasting life, and the wicked being consigned to everlasting cutting off in death. . . . In the meantime, the very difficult conditions foretold for "the last days" would prevail. . . . Before the last members of the generation that was alive in 1914 will have passed off the scene, all the things foretold will occur, including the "great tribulation" in which the present wicked world will end.

Jehovah's Witnesses manifest a sort of catastrophic millennialism, as they confidently expected the entire globe to be purged and cleansed at Armageddon in preparation for the imminent millennial paradise. But some beliefs and practices suggest that catastrophic and progressive millennialisms are not necessarily exclusive categories. Witnesses believe that in some important sense, the power of the millennium is *already present*, albeit in a qualified or attenuated form.

They see their international, interracial organization as a foretaste of the millennial paradise.

Watchtower literature defends the Society's aggressive construction projects by explaining that these buildings will likely endure the ravages of Armageddon and prove useful in the global educational work required in the millennium. In effect that means that Witnesses are laying the *material* as well as the spiritual infrastructure of the millennial kingdom. Witness iconography is characterized by the visual motif of life in the paradise earth, where the earth is restored to its Edenic purity, and people of every conceivable color and ethnic/racial group are joined together in eschatological bliss.

The End of the End?

Currently the Watchtower Society appears to be undergoing a historic transition in which their millennial urgency is weakening and their characteristic sectarian resoluteness is increasingly succumbing to dynamics of moderation and accommodation.

After decades of disappointment, deferral, and ex post facto reinterpretation of prophecy, the WTS slowly divested in date-setting and grounded their millennial expectations in arguments based on the "signs" of the Last Days that indicated the End must occur within a literal "generation" of 1914. According to the 1 November 1995, issue of *The Watchtower* magazine, the Watchtower Society finally relinquished its long-standing claim that the "End" (i.e., Armageddon and Paradise) would take place within a literal generation of 1914. The Witnesses are now operating—for the first time in their 125-year history—without a specific temporal horizon to frame their millennial expectations. The implications of this revision of the Watchtower Society's prophetic timetable are not certain.

Jehovah's Witnesses rely on the same *terminus a quo*—1914—as the temporal anchor for their millennial expectations. They still insist that Jesus returned *invisibly* in 1914 and is now enthroned over his theocratic kingdom. In other words, 1914 marks the *beginning* of the End; according to Witness doctrine, these last days will soon culminate in the cathartic destruction of Armageddon and the miraculous transformation of planet Earth in the millennial paradise. After the 1995 redefinition of the meaning of "this generation" in Matthew 24:34, Witnesses are now forced to rely exclusively on their adaptation of the apocalyptic "sign argument" to support their claim that the (visible/

literal/physical) End is near. Based on the prediction of eschatological woes found in the Synoptic Gospels "little apocalypse" (Matthew 24 and parallels), Witnesses insist that the global catastrophes of the twentieth century (e.g., war, famine, disease, natural disasters, etc.) cumulatively provide undeniable evidence that this "evil world system" is nearing its end.

In Witness discourse this practice is always qualified by the insistence on the "spiritual" and unstable nature of Jehovah's theocratic presence in this "evil world system." The period between 1914 and the End is something of a liminal space where Jesus is legally but "invisibly" enthroned over his millennial kingdom, but in which Satan is more powerful than ever in his rage against Jehovah's people. Satan knows his time is up, but he makes every effort to win over individuals from the faithful remnant of Jehovah's people. Witnesses explain that the present time is analogous to the spinning blade of an electric fan after it has been unplugged, or that the disastrous "signs" of the end are comparable to the death throes and involuntary jerks of a beheaded snake.

Joel Elliott

See also Seventh-Day Adventists

Bibliography

Festinger, Leon et al. (1956) *When Prophecy Fails: A Social and Psychological Study of a Modern Group That Predicted the Destruction of the World.* New York: Harper and Row.

Mankind's Search for God. (1990) Brooklyn, NY: WBTS.

Moorhead, James H. (1993) "The Millennium and the Media." In *Communication and Change in American Religious History,* edited by Leonard I. Sweet. Grand Rapids, MI: Wm. B. Eerdmans, 216–238.

O'Leary, Stephen D. (1994) *Arguing the Apocalypse: A Theory of Millennial Rhetoric.* New York: Oxford University Press.

Penton, M. James. (1985) *Apocalypse Delayed: The Story of Jehovah's Witnesses.* Toronto: University of Toronto Press.

Reasoning from the Scriptures. (1985, 1989) WBTS of Pennsylvania, Inc.

The Truth That Leads to Eternal Life. (1968) Brooklyn, NY: WBTS.

Wilson, Bryan R. (1978) "When Prophecy Failed." *New Society* (26 January): 183–184.

You Can Live Forever on Paradise on Earth. (1982, 1990) Brooklyn, NY: WBTS.

Zygmunt, Joseph F. (1970) "Prophetic Failure and Chiliastic Identity: The Case of the Jehovah's Witnesses." *American Journal of Sociology* 75: 926–948.

Jesus Christ

One of several defining doctrines of Christian Fundamentalism has been its view of Jesus Christ—both His identity and the significance of His life and death. Similar to the Fundamentalist view of the Bible (the written Word of God), believed to be both human and divine in its origin, so the Living Word of God, Jesus Christ, is both human and divine in nature (John 1:1, 14). Questions about His humanity, His deity, and their relationship have historically been at the heart of many heresies about Him. Fundamentalist Christianity has not only defended a Christ who was both human and divine but also claims that His life demonstrates a supernatural involvement of God in human history. Belief in the Virgin Birth, Jesus' power to do miracles, His Resurrection from the dead, and His substitutionary payment for the sins of others on the cross are foundational doctrines of conservative Christianity and its view of Jesus.

A second characteristic that distinguishes historic Christian Fundamentalism has been its confidence in the Bible (especially the Gospels) as a trustworthy record of Jesus' life and the response of people to Him. Very little is known about Jesus outside of the New Testament, and Fundamentalist claims are therefore based almost entirely on Scripture. While the modernist viewpoint has disputed traditional views of Jesus' identity, the skepticism is really grounded in presuppositions that deny the truthfulness of the Gospel accounts and the possibility of supernatural elements in the earthly ministry of Jesus. The debate, therefore, is not ultimately about sources, but one's assumptions about the Bible. Christian Fundamentalism, following the historic orthodox view of Christ, believes faith in the biblical record is the most consistent way to understand Jesus' life, His teachings, and the historic commitment of His followers.

His Name

The name "Jesus Christ" reflects both Jesus' human identity and His Messianic mission. It is derived from his given name "Jesus" (the Hebrew root meaning is similar to ""Joshua": "one who saves or delivers") and the title "the Christ," a Greek expression for Messiah or "anointed one." First known as "Jesus of Nazareth," the expression "Jesus, the Christ" was probably used by his earliest converts (Matthew 16:16; Acts 5:42) and later the title became a part of his name (Romans 1:7; James 1:1; 1 Peter 1:1).

Source Information

There is little historical information about Christ outside of Christian writings, though there are a few references. He is mentioned in the writings of Jewish historian Josephus (*Antiquities*) and pagan writers Pliny, Tacitus, and Suetonius, but little information is provided beyond the fact that He had some followers, He performed healings, He was condemned to death by Pontius Pilate, and His later followers sang hymns referring to Him as God. While some pseudoepigraphical writings appeared between 150 and 350 CE (e.g., Infancy Gospel of Thomas), their historical accuracy was denied by the early church and they were therefore not included with the canonical Gospels.

The conservative Christian's view of Christ is therefore dependent on the presentation of the Gospels Matthew, Mark, Luke, and John. The first three, often designated the synoptic ("seeing together") Gospels, were probably written within a brief time period (c. 50–70 CE) and earlier than John's Gospel (c. 90–100 CE). The synoptic Gospels have many similarities and were likely drawn from similar written and oral sources about Jesus, including eyewitness accounts from many (Luke 1:1–4) and information from the apostles Matthew, Peter, and Paul as well as Mary the mother of Jesus. Though the historical information overlaps in the synoptic Gospels, each provides unique information and perspectives about Jesus' earthly life, demonstrating they were intended for different audiences with unique writing purposes. The Gospel of John serves a distinctive and supplementary role. Writing at the end of the first century, he adds material not included in the earlier Gospels and recounts Jesus' life more in the form of a theological treatise to combat false teaching about Christ at that time.

The Biblical Teaching about Jesus Christ

Just as announced by the angel Gabriel, Jesus was born in Bethlehem (most likely in 5 BCE, rather than in 1 CE) to a Jewish virgin named Mary, who was betrothed to a carpenter, Joseph, both being from Nazareth and descendants of David (Mark 1:9, Luke 1:26–2:7). Little information is known about Jesus' childhood and young adult years, with the exception of a story about His celebration of the Passover at twelve years of age with His family (Luke 2:41–50). There are also summarized statements about Jesus' physical, intellectual, and spiritual growth to manhood (Luke 2:51–52).

His Ministry

John, the baptizer, was much like an Old Testament prophet and prepared the Jews for a Messiah's ministry, calling them to repentance and preparation for a new religious movement of sorts. Jesus' baptism by John in the Jordan River introduced His Messianic ministry (Matthew 3:1–17; Mark 1:1–13; Luke 3:1–22; John 1:29–35). He was quickly tempted (tested) by Satan, the god of this world, and remained perfectly obedient to the will of God the Father (Matthew 4:1–11; Mark 1:12–13; Luke 4:1–13). He selected twelve disciples and began preaching a message of repentance and preparation for the kingdom of God (Mark 3:13–19; John 1:35–51). While offering Himself as Messiah to the Jews (John 1:11), He also offered salvation to the Gentiles and outcasts of society (Mark 2:15–17; Luke 15:1–32; 19:10). Jesus taught as one who had authority in contrast to the rigid legalists who represented the Judaism of that time (Matthew 7:28–29). The authority of His words was confirmed by His miraculous works, both authenticating His claims to be Messiah (John 2:1–11; Matthew 8–9; Mark 1:21–2:12; Luke 5:12–26).

There are two noteworthy turning points in Jesus' earthly ministry. The first followed the clear, public rejection of His claims to be Messiah by the religious leadership of Israel (Matthew 12:22–37). After repeated Messianic proofs through His words and works (Matthew 4–11), the "unpardonable sin" passage indicates a willful rejection of these claims in favor of accusing Jesus of demon possession. Following this, Jesus instituted a change of direction in His ministry. He focused less upon public demonstration and more intently on developing His disciples; in conjunction with this He began to teach more extensively through parables about a new understanding of the Old Testament concept kingdom of God (Matthew 13:1–52). Later, a second turning point was represented by Peter's confession, "You are the Christ, the Son of the Living God." Christ indicated this conviction in Peter's heart could only come by super-natural revelation in response to faith, and began to predict more clearly the events surrounding His coming death (Matthew 16:13–21; Mark 8:27–31). He moved steadfastly toward Jerusalem and the cross.

His Death and Resurrection

The Gospel writers devote a remarkable amount of attention to the events of the week just preceding Jesus' death and Resurrection. Twenty of the sixty-eight chapters (almost thirty percent) of the synoptic Gospels are allocated to the events following Palm Sunday, and John, who likely had copies of the other three Gospels, chose to devote ten of twenty-one chapters from his Gospel (John 12–21). The reason for this emphasis is implicit in Jesus' teaching, and explicitly stated in later preaching from Acts and the rest of the New Testament. Christ's death and Resurrection were historical events that would culminate the theological meaning of His life.

The Biblical Teaching about Jesus Christ: His Identity As Messiah and God

John Stock writes an important chapter called "The God Man" in *The Fundamentals*, a series of twelve paperback volumes published between 1910 and 1915. These treatises, which are identified as the source of the modern term "fundamentalist" (used after 1920), became the theological reference for conservative Christian views. It is clear from history, and from Scripture, that the question of Jesus' deity and His Messiahship has always been a "watershed" issue for Christians. But, what did He claim about Himself? (1) He claimed to be the Son of God (Matthew 11:25–27; Mark 12:1–9; John 3:18); (2) He claimed equality with God the Father (John 5:18; 10:38; 14:9); (3) He claimed to have authority that can only be attributed to God, such as power to forgive sins (Mark 2:5–7; Luke 7:48–49), power to raise His own body from the grave (John 2:19–21), authority to determine people's eternal destiny (Matthew 10:32–33; Mark 8:34–38); and (4) He claimed to be the Messiah or Christ (Mark 8:27–30; 14:61–62). The name "Son of Man," Jesus' favorite self-designation, is quoted in more than eighty passages with unmistakable Messianic significance (Daniel 7:13–14). When examining many of these stories it is clear that Jesus' opponents knew exactly what He was claiming and called it blasphemy (Matthew 26:63–64; Luke 22:70–71).

The committed followers of Christ who became the early church believed Jesus of Nazareth was the Christ, God come in the flesh. The Epistles make this explicitly clear (Philippians 2:9–11; Colossians 1:16–17; Hebrews 1:1–3). Jesus Christ is referred to as "Lord"(Romans 10:9), "Creator" (Colossians 1:16), and "God" (Romans 9:5; 2 Thessalonians 1:12; Titus 2:13; 1 John 5:20).

Fundamentalist Beliefs Expressed through Early Christian Symbols

Although "Fundamentalist" is a modern term, certain fundamental beliefs about Jesus Christ have been defended throughout church history. Early Christian inscriptions reveal the most significant beliefs about Christ, and probably those that were challenged by others. The symbol of the fish (see Figure 1) symbolized a simple confession of faith about Christ.

The Greek word for "fish," *ichthus* served as an acronym (I-CH-TH-U-S) for

> Iesus (Jesus)
> Christos (Christ)
> Theos (God)
> Uios (Son)
> Soter (Savior)

All five of these Greek letters were also superimposed in the early Christian symbol of a circle traversed by four diagonals (see Figure 2).

Also included in early Christian icons was the familiar symbolism of "the alpha and the omega" (Revelation 1:8; first and last letters of the Greek alphabet); this was a reference to the eternality of Jesus Christ, the Son of God as "the beginning and the end" (see Figure 3).

These symbols reflected a creedal belief among early followers of Christ that He was both human and divine. Early challenges to these claims came from groups like the Ebionites and the Gnostics. The Ebionites, a Jewish group committed to monotheism, denied Christ's deity and believed Jesus, the son of Mary and Joseph, became Messiah after obedience to the Mosaic Law and reception of the Holy Spirit at His baptism. The Gnostics came to a similar conclusion based on the Greek philosophical presuppositions. Their dualistic system denied the possibility of the spiritual realm mixing with the evil physical realm. The apostles Paul and John addressed early forms of these views in the New Testament writings, claiming that in the Incarnation of Jesus Christ the

Figure 1. Christian inscription including symbol of the fish (early Roman period).

Figure 2. Christian symbolism for Christ (Roman period).

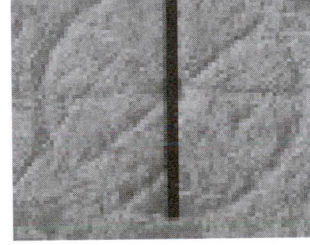

Iesus

Christos

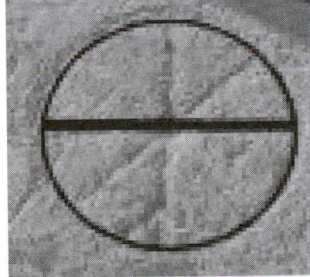

Theos (God)

Uios (Son)

Soter (Savior)

Inscription using symbols for Jesus Christ (superimposed I-X) and the alpha and omega (Roman period).

fullness of God came to dwell in human form (Colossians 2:9; John 1:1, 14; 1 John 1:1–4).

The Early Christological Debates: 350–450 CE

After Christianity became the official religion of the Roman Empire, several prominent cities and the bishops of the church within them (called "archbishops") competed to extend their spiritual and political influence. Schools of religious thought from Alexandria and Rome competed with the influence of Antioch and Constantinople. In this competitive climate debates arose to address a number of heresies about the person of Christ. Arianism (fourth century), for example, believed that Jesus Christ was not the true God nor equal with God because He (the Logos) was created by God before the creation of the world. Apollinarius (fourth century) reasoned from a psychological point of view that at the Incarnation the divine (the Logos) displaced Jesus' human nature, thus denying the completeness of His humanity. Another heresy, Nestorianism (fifth century), described Christ essentially as two persons rather than one person with two natures. Eutychianism (fifth century) combined the two natures so completely that the human nature was completely absorbed in the divine. Eutyches reasoned that as a drop of honey which falls into the sea dissolves in it, so the human nature of Christ is lost in the divine.

The Council of Chalcedon in 451 CE addressed all of these issues in a decision that has been the view of Christian orthodoxy to the present. Nearly four hundred bishops and theologians gathered to confirm the following truths: that Jesus Christ is one person who has two natures, the human and the divine. He is truly God and truly man. The differences of the two natures is not diminished by their union, but the attributes and essence of both human and divine natures are united in one person. Jesus is not a

249

Luke 1:1–4

1. Forasmuch as many have taken in hand to set forth in order a declaration of those things which are most surely believed among us,
2. Even as they delivered them unto us, which from the beginning were eyewitnesses, and ministers of the word;
3. It seemed good to me also, having had perfect understanding of all things from the very first, to write unto thee in order, most excellent Theophilus,
4. That thou mightest know the certainty of those things, wherein thou hast been instructed.

divided person, but one being who is both human and the Son of God.

The Modern Search for the Real Jesus

While the earliest historical debates about Christ centered on the relationship of His humanity and deity, the modern discussion has questioned accuracy of the biblical information about him. Prior to the eighteenth century no one expressed a need to search for "the historical Jesus" because the Christ of the Gospels was believed to be an accurate record. Enlightenment thinking, however, treated the Bible as any other book and questioned its claims about the supernatural. Thus, the "historical Jesus" was assumed to be different from the "Christ of faith" depicted in the New Testament. This search for the real Jesus in the nineteenth century, later called "the old quest," gave way to the skepticism of Barth and Bultmann who taught that a search for a historically accurate Jesus was impossible and theologically meaningless. Their followers moderated their views in the 1950s in what is now called "the new quest." The "third quest," beginning in the 1970s, renewed the attempt to rediscover the historical Jesus and took more seriously His Jewish background, but held strongly to the skepticism and literary criticism of the earlier quests. In short, all modern attempts to "discover" Christ that deny the accuracy of the canonical Gospel accounts have produced skeptical or widely divergent conclusions. Modern perspectives, such as those of the "Jesus Seminar" (a New Testament study group), have popularized this skepticism and denounced the naiveté of traditional views of Jesus. In contrast, conservative Christianity has held firm to the fundamental beliefs of orthodox, historical Christianity. Trust in the historical accuracy of the Gospels, including the super-natural elements of Christ's life, has proven to be one of the most significant elements of Christian Fundamentalism.

Conclusion

One's view of Christ is related to one's view of Scripture; therefore, it is not surprising that the most vigorous modern attacks on traditional Christology have denied the trustworthiness of the biblical accounts concerning Him. One of the tenets of Christian Fundamentalism is its commitment to the record of the Gospels as the most consistent way to explain Jesus Christ and the historical responses to Him. Walter Elwell, a professor at Wheaton College, Illinois, offers some helpful insight into this subject:

> Given Christian presuppositions, the story makes perfect sense; given non-Christian presuppositions, the rejection of the sources as unreliable is understandable. It is not really a question of the sources, but a question of the interpreter of the sources. Second, the Gospel writers and their subject matter argue in favor of truthfulness. They were attempting to present a true account of Christ (Luke 1:1–4) and were willing to die for the results; Third, the church from the beginning believed that God had a hand in the writing of the material and that guaranteed its trustworthiness. Fourth, the Gospels are all we have. If they are allowed to speak for themselves, they present a consistent picture that gave rise to the Christian faith, which has been confirmed in the lives of believers throughout the centuries. The simple fact is there is no other Jesus available than the one presented in the Gospels. Either that is accepted or one creates his or her own Jesus on the basis of what is thought to be possible or likely. (1996: 396)

C. S. LEWIS REFLECTS ON JESUS

"You must make your choice. Either this man was, and is, the Son of God: or else a madman or something worse. You can shut Him up for a fool, you can spit at Him and kill Him as a demon; or you can fall at His feet and call Him Lord and God. But let us not come with any patronising nonsense about His being a great human teacher. He has not left that open to us. He did not intend to."

Selection from: C. S. Lewis. ([1943] 1974) *Mere Christianity*,
New York: Macmillan, 56

The term "Fundamentalist" has its greatest historical meaning during the twentieth century in the aftermath of the modernist–Fundamentalist controversy of the 1920s. The belief in "fundamental" truths about Christ, however, has spanned the centuries since He walked on this earth. Jesus claimed to be the promised Messiah and He claimed to be God. He taught that personal faith in His life, death, and Resurrection gave eternal life to anyone who followed Him (John 3:16–18; 5:24). Though these truths were discussed, defined, and sometimes debated in the early centuries of Christianity, they have consistently remained the foundation of Christian orthodoxy. Fundamentalist Christianity remains committed to the belief that the Christ of faith is the Jesus of history as presented in Scripture; to deny the Jesus of the Gospels is to invent another Christ.

John C. Hutchison

See also Biblical Inerrancy; Messiah; Resurrection (Christ); Second Coming; Sermon on the Mount

Bibliography

Bruce, Frederick Fyvie(1974) *Jesus and Christian Origins Outside the New Testament.* Grand Rapids, MI: Wm. B. Eerdmans.

Elwell, Walter. (1996) "Jesus Christ." In *Evangelical Dictionary of Biblical Theology.* Grand Rapids, MI: Baker House Books, 396–406.

Green, Joel, Scot McKnight, and I. Howard Marshall, eds. (1992) *Dictionary of Jesus and the Gospels.* Downers Grove, IL: InterVarsity Press.

Marsden, George M. (1982) *Fundamentalism and American Culture: The Shaping of Twentieth-Century Evangelicalism: 1870–1925.* Oxford, UK: Oxford University Press.

Shelley, Bruce. (1982) *Church History in Plain Language.* Waco, TX: Word Books.

Stock, John. (1990) "The God Man." In *The Fundamentals: The Famous Sourcebook of Foundational Biblical Truths,* edited by Charles Feinberg. Grand Rapids, MI: Kregal Publications, 279–292.

Wilkins, Michael, and J. P. Moreland, eds. (1995) *Jesus Under Fire: Modern Scholarship Reinvents the Historical Jesus.* Grand Rapids, MI: Zondervan Publishing.

Jews

Since the rise of the Fundamentalist movement in the latter decades of the nineteenth century, Fundamentalist Christians have had an abiding interest in the Jewish people. Strongly influenced by a dispensationalist-premillenialist messianic faith, Fundamentalists have viewed the Jews as the heirs and continuers of the Sons of Israel, and the objects of the biblical prophecies about a restored kingdom of David during the messianic age. The Jews, they believed, were destined to play a central role in the events that would lead to the arrival of the Messiah, as well as during the messianic age itself. Since the later decades of the nineteenth century, Fundamentalist Christians have shown a continuing interest in the Jewish people, their fate, the prospect of their return to Zion, and their conversion to Christianity.

A Sign of the End Times and Reconstruction of the Temple

Fundamentalists were engaged in attempts to restore the Jews to Palestine even before the rise of political

Zionism. When the Zionist movement came about in 1897, Fundamentalist Christians welcomed it wholeheartedly, seeing in it a "sign of the time" that indicated that this era was ending and the events of the End Times were about to begin. Fundamentalists were delighted by developments such as the new Jewish settlements in Palestine, the rejuvenation of the Hebrew language, and the Balfour Declaration of 1917, in which Britain promised to help build a national home for the Jews in Palestine. Following the Scopes "Monkey Trial" in 1925, Fundamentalist interest in the fate of the Jews, while remaining strong, became more passive. This reality changed in the 1970s with the resurgence of Fundamentalism in American public life. Fundamentalists were particularly impressed by the results of the Six-Day War in 1967 and the Israeli conquest of biblical territories, including the historical parts of Jerusalem. For many Christian Fundamentalists, the war proved that the State of Israel was created for a purpose, and the messianic age was soon to begin. Their interest in Israel and their support for that country intensified.

Following the Six-Day War, many Fundamentalist Christians were convinced that the Jews should build the temple in Jerusalem in preparation for the arrival of the Messiah. On 19 August 1969, Dennis Michael Rohan, a twenty-eight-year-old Australian influenced by the premillenialist faith, set fire to the El Aksa mosque on the Temple Mount in an attempt to clear the ground for the rebuilding of the biblical temple. The mosque burned, local Arabs rioted, and Rohan was arrested, put on trial, found insane, and placed in an institution for the mentally ill. While Rohan's actions were extreme, other Fundamentalists have also promoted the idea that the Jews start building the temple. Christian Fundamentalists tried to research the Temple Mount in an attempt to discover the exact location of the temple and have lent their support to groups of Jewish Fundamentalists who have advocated, and at times prepared for the building of the temple. In 1999, the Israeli government became particularly concerned that Christian Fundamentalists in cooperation with Jewish extremists would plot to bomb the Temple Mount mosques in an attempt to bring about the Apocalypse and hasten the arrival of the Messiah. Israel extradited a number of Fundamentalist Christians and refused entry into the country to many others.

Pro-Israeli Fundamentalism

Fundamentalist Christian involvement with Israel did not remain confined to efforts to promote the building of the temple. Fundamentalists have organized tours to the country and come as volunteers to work in kibbutzim or in archaeological digs. Since the late 1960s, they became ardent supporters of Israel in the American public arena, advocating American political and financial support for the Jewish state. A warm relationship developed between Christian Fundamentalists and the more right-wing Likud Israeli government when the Likud Party was in power. In the 1980s, Israel's prime minister, Menachem Begin, bestowed the Jabutinsky Medal on two leading Fundamentalists, Jerry Falwell, leader of the Moral Majority, and Pat Robertson, founder of the Christian Broadcasting Network, in recognition of their support for Israel. Dozens of pro-Israeli Fundamentalist organizations were founded from the 1970s to the 1990s, with the largest and most visible of such groups being the International Christian Embassy in Jerusalem (ICEJ). The ICEJ advocates right-wing Israeli politics, musters support for Israel among conservative Protestants around the world, and is known for its yearly festivals in Jerusalem during the Feast of Sukkot (Tabernacles), to which thousands of conservative Protestant supporters come from dozens of countries.

Evangelizing the Jews

In addition to their support for Zionism and Israel, Fundamentalists have also been engaged in extensive missionary work among the Jews. Coming into being during the same years that gave rise to the Fundamentalist movement, the missions, like Fundamentalist pro-Zionist activity, have represented the interest of Fundamentalists in the Jews and their fate. Evangelizing the Jews received high priority in the Fundamentalist camp, which generously supported missions to the Jews. Since the late nineteenth century, dozens of missions sponsored by conservative Christians, employing hundreds of missionaries, have been busy propagating Christianity among the Jews. Missions to the Jews, such as the American Board of Missions to the Jews (currently the Chosen People Ministries) or Jews for Jesus, have been among the largest and better budgeted missionary agencies of conservative Protestant Christianity in the twentieth century. Since the 1970s, Jews for Jesus, a missionary group that broke away from the American Board of Missions to the Jews, has become the largest missionary group to labor among the Jews. With a yearly budget of about $20 million and more than one hundred field evangelists operating all over the world, Jews for Jesus has been one of the more dynamic and visible conservative Protestant missions. In addition to evangelizing Jews, missions to the Jews also work to promote among conservative Christians the idea of the centrality of the Jews in God's plans for humanity. They also organize tours to Israel and distribute material about the country. Jews for Jesus named its musical band "The Liberated Wailing Wall," indicating its warm support of Israel and its belief in the country's special destiny.

The missionary ideology changed significantly during the 1970s to 1990s. Missionaries began to promote the idea that Jews could retain their ethnic and cultural heritage at the same time that they accept Christianity. The new ideology has been enhanced by the rise of Messianic Judaism, a movement of Jewish converts to Evangelical Christianity who view themselves as Jews and Christians at the same time. Within the conservative Protestant community, Messianic Jews have worked to promote even further the notion of the centrality of Israel in God's plans for humanity.

While Jewish leaders have responded enthusiastically to the pro-Zionist and pro-Israeli activity of Fundamentalist Christians, their reaction to the missionary activity has been very different. They see the missions as a threat to Jewish survival, as well as a continuation of the age-old Christian wish to do away with Judaism and with Jewish existence outside of the Christian Church. The Jewish reaction has been far from unified, however: Jews have often shown curiosity and come to hear the missionary message. Missions have offered material aid to needy Jewish immigrants in urban areas as a means to attract them to the missions, and many Jews are more than willing to receive such help. At the same time, Jewish leaders and organizations have protested against the activity of the missions and called on Christians to stop missionizing Jews. From the 1950s to the 1970s, liberal and mainline Christian churches closed missionary agencies that focused on Jews, and the only missions that are currently operating have a conservative Fundamentalist character and sponsorship.

Fundamentalist Christian Attitude toward Jews

Missions are not the only realm in which Jews and Fundamentalist Christians have not seen eye to eye. While Fundamentalist Christians continued to view the Jews as the chosen people, destined to become once again God's covenant nation, they have not necessarily admired Jewish culture and values, and often have a deep-seated ambivalence toward Jews. In the Fundamentalist view, Jews have not yet accepted Jesus as their Savior, and are thus spiritually and morally lacking. Fundamentalists have taken particular exception to Jewish secular culture and values, which they see as shallow and decadent. They are disappointed and resentful that Jews have turned away from the religion of their ancestors but have chosen secular lives and ideologies, or have joined religious groups other than conservative Protestantism. During the late nineteenth century to the middle decades of the twentieth century, many Fundamentalists held the stereotypical image of Jews as political radicals involved in revolutionary activities. Some Fundamentalist leaders, such as William Riley or Arno Gaebelein, viewed the forged *Protocols of the Elders of Zion*, which spoke about a Jewish conspiracy to overtake the world, as authentic. A sociological survey, taken in the early 1960s in America, which examined the opinions on Jews held by members of different religious groups, found that conservative Protestants were more likely to be prejudiced against Jews on a day-to-day basis than liberal Protestants or Roman Catholics. However, a similar survey taken in the mid-1980s found a large decline in anti-Jewish prejudices among conservative Protestants and a more appreciative outlook on Jews. This change in attitude was due in large degree to the increasing exposure to Jews among conservative Christians since 1967 and the growing acquaintance of this segment of Christianity with Israel and the realities of Jewish life. At the turning of the twenty-first century, the complex and ambivalent attitude of Fundamentalist Christians toward Jews has remained strong. They have supported Israel vis-à-vis the Palestinian *Intifada* (the uprising against Israel) at the same time that they have continued to promote an extensive network of missionary activity among the Jews.

Yaakov S. Ariel

See also Anti-Semitism; Elohim; Gush Emunim; Haredim; Israel; Jews for Jesus; Judaism, Fundamental; Temple

Bibliography

Ariel, Yaakov. (1991) *On Behalf of Israel: Fundamentalist Attitudes towards Jews, Judaism and Zionism.* New York: Carlson.

———. (2000) *Evangelizing the Chosen People: Missions to the Jews in America 1880–2000.* Chapel Hill: Univesity of North Carolina Press.

Greenberg, Gershom. (2000) *The End of Days: Fundamentalism and the Struggle for the Temple Mount.* New York: Free Press.

Lindsey, Hal. (1970) *The Late Great Planet Earth.* Grand Rapids, MI: Zondervan Publishing.

Rausch, David A. (1979) *Zionism within Early American Fundamentalism.* New York: Edwin Mellen Press.

Simon, Merrill. (1984) *Jerry Falwell and the Jews.* Middle Village, NY: Jonathan David.

Walvoord, John F. (1966) *Israel in Prophecy.* Grand Rapids, MI: Zondervan Publishing.

Jews for Jesus

The term "Jews for Jesus" began as a slogan in the early 1970s and came to designate Jewish believers in Jesus, that is, Jews who have embraced the Christian faith yet retained their identity as Jews. The group that formally carried the name "Jews for Jesus" originated in 1970 in San Francisco. Moishe Rosen, a missionary of the American Board of Mission to the Jews, decided to turn his evangelistic energy to Jewish members of the counterculture. The new organization adapted its evangelization messages and manners to the style of the baby boom generation. Members of the group wore jeans and T-shirts, grew their hair, and embraced the musical trends of the day. Jews for Jesus also gave expression to the new emphasis in American culture on searching for roots and taking pride in one's ethnicity. It advocated the idea that Jews did not have to give up their identity as Jews, but rather could retain it at the same time as they embraced Jesus as their Savior. The missionary organization used Jewish names, symbols, and expressions in its missionary literature. It also emphasized its support for the State of Israel, called its musical band "The Liberated Wailing Wall," and incorporated Israeli and Hasidic music in its musical repertoire. Starting out as a local group in the San Francisco Bay area, Jews for Jesus has grown to become the largest mission to the Jews, with branches all over the world.

Jews for Jesus has become part of a larger movement of Jewish Christians that came about in the 1970s and 1980s. Often calling themselves messianic Jews, such communities have promoted the idea that Jews who embrace Christianity should not assimilate into the Christian culture and do not have to join Christian denominations, but instead should retain their Jewish heritage and create their own communities. Jewish–Christian congregations differ as to the amount of Jewish tradition they choose to retain. The more "traditionalist" communities have introduced Arks and Torah scrolls into their assemblies; their members wear yarmulkes during services; and they celebrate Jewish holidays such as Chanukah and Purim. All Jewish–Christian congregations celebrate Passover, and most have chosen to conduct their prayer meetings on Friday nights or Saturday mornings. There are also many Jewish believers in Jesus who have joined regular Christian congregations but see themselves as Jewish.

Jewish believers in Jesus consider themselves to have transcended the historical boundaries between Judaism and Christianity, overcoming old, seemingly irreconcilable differences and injuries to amalgamate the Christian faith with Jewish ethnicity. This notion has served as a source of energy and a sense of mission. By the beginning of the twenty-first century, there have been more than three hundred congregations of Jewish Christians in America, as well as dozens more in Israel and throughout the Jewish world—and the movement is growing. Jews for Jesus and the movement of Jewish believers in Jesus in general have stirred strong reaction among Jews and Christians. Jews, on the whole, have reacted negatively to Jewish believers in Jesus and have refused to recognize Jewish–Christian congregations as legitimate synagogues. Jewish organizations and leaders of different affiliations (whether Orthodox, Conservative, Reform, or Reconstructionist) are in agreement that one cannot be Jewish and Christian at the same time. Evangelical Christians, on the other hand, have accepted Jewish believers in Jesus, as the latter share the faith and values of the conservative Evangelical segment of Christianity. This shows great adaptability and openness on the part of Evangelical Christianity in relation to ethnic plurality and new, innovative modes of Evangelical expressions. It also reflects the growing appreciation by this segment of

Christianity for Jews as the object of biblical prophecies and as a nation destined to regain its old status as the Chosen People.

Yaakov S. Ariel

Bibliography

Ariel, Yaakov. (2000) *Evangelizing the Chosen People: Missions to the Jews in America 1880–2000.* Chapel Hill: University of North Carolina Press.

Feher, Shoshonah. (1998) *Passing Over Easter.* Walnut Creek, CA: Altamira Press.

Lipson, Juliene G. (1990) *Jews for Jesus: An Anthropological Study.* New York: AMS Press.

Pruter, Karl. (1987) *Jewish Christians in the United States: A Bibliography.* New York: Garland Publishing.

Rausch, David A (1982), *Messianic Judaism: Its History, Theology and Polity.* New York: Edwin Mellen Press.

Rosen, Moishe, and William Proctor. (1974) *Jews for Jesus.* Old Tappen, NJ: Fleming H. Revell.

Judaism, Fundamental

What distinguishes Jewish forms of religious Fundamentalism from Protestant counterparts is not the belief in the absolute truth of their religious doctrine but the fundamental importance of adhering to religious practice as set forth in Jewish religious law. In other words, what is most important to Jewish Fundamentalists is not the right belief as such but the realization of the written religious tradition in their daily life. The German word *Kulturreligion* expresses exactly this point that biblical injunctions have to be realized in everyday life. It would be more accurate to speak in the Jewish case of ortho-praxis since the Latin word *doxa* means "belief." Jewish Fundamentalism is therefore an attempt to practice their religion today in an unbroken tradition that began with Moses at Mount Sinai. Different strands within the Jewish Fundamentalist spectrum vary in their interpretation of what their religious tradition means today and how present-day occurrences must be interpreted in light of this tradition. Jews believe that they are the chosen people of God, who appeared before Moses at Mount Sinai to bestow upon him God's commandments for His people. These commandments were later termed the five books of Moses, Pentateuch, or the old Bible. God also gave

them the Holy Land in Palestine—where Jewish tribes lived until 70 CE. The Romans drove the Jews out of their Promised Land and Jews lived from 70 CE until the late nineteenth century scattered around the world. Their exile was religiously interpreted as godly punishment for not living in accord with the religious commandments. According to the religious interpretation, their return to their homeland in Palestine was envisioned for when all Jews would live according to the tradition. Then, the Messiah would return and reerect the Jewish kingdom in Palestine. Exile and redemption (seen in the return to the Holy Land) are key concepts in Judaism as is Messianism. Jewish Fundamentalist movements differ in their interpretation of the present State according to these concepts.

Jewish Ultra-Orthodoxy

The ultra-Orthodox Jews are known by different names. People outside their community call them Hasidic Jews or Haredim (singular Haredi). The term "haredi" is taken from Isaiah 66:5—"Hear the word of the Lord, you who tremble [haredim] at His word" (Weinfeld 1991). Therefore, this word describes Jews who are God-fearing and punctilious concerning the religious commandments. They attempt to observe all 613 commandments (*mitzvot*) and believe that ritual slippage lessens the spiritual worth of the Jewish community. Worse yet, it delays the coming of the Messiah and the day of redemption. Even though Israeli Haredim live in the Promised Land, they interpret their existence in Israel as still living in exile.

They can be easily identified because they wear distinctive garb as fulfillment of the biblical injunctions. Men wear long, black caftans, long stockings, beards, side curls, and hats (sometimes made of fur). Women wear modest outfits, always long-sleeved dresses or blouses and skirts (never pants) and hats, wigs, or scarfs on their heads. The largest Hasidic communities are in Jerusalem, Bnei Brak, near Tel Aviv, and in certain neighborhoods in the New York City boroughs of Brooklyn and Manhattan. It is estimated that the ultra-Orthodox population in Israel comprise about four to ten percent of the total population of just over six million.

Ultra-Orthodoxy emerged in the last third of the nineteenth century in Europe, particularly in central and Western Europe, as a reaction to and in opposition to the changes and reforms sweeping through

Selection from: WHAT IS BITACHON (TRUST?) IN G-D?

The common perception of this concept is that we trust in G-d that whatever happens to us will be good. That is, we believe G-d is good, and that whatever endeavor we undertake and any situation we find ourselves in, then because G-d is good, things will be good.

Of course, there are two possible outcomes. Either the event will turn out good, or it won't. So what happened? The usual explanation is that it depends on whether we are worthy or not. That is, if we merit it, then it will be for the good, if not, then it won't be for the good.

Now, even those who explain Bitachon this way, will qualify things slightly. That is, if a bad occurrence happens, then true, it is a bad occurrence to us. That is, on the revealed plane to us this appears bad. However, on the hidden level it is good. That is, everything that occurs to us G-d intends for our good. At a particular time an event might appear to us to be bad, however, the inner intent is for our good.

Sometimes, after the passage of time this inner goodness in the event will become apparent to us, and sometimes it might never become revealed. Still, our Trust in G-d is that G-d is good and that we believe even the revealed bad contains within it a deeper inner good (just not perceivable by human-kind).

This is where things usually end. But the Rebbe asks a further question. What is the simple meaning of Trust? Does not trust mean that we trust that G-d will give us a revealed good? What would the point be in trusting that G-d is going to deliver us a revealed bad, but a concealed good? Something is really not very good until we can really see in a revealed way that the thing is good. Until then, for all practical purposes it is bad. Besides, what would the use of our trust be?

Sure we trusted, but we got bad. Our trust had nothing to do with what we got. It was our merits. The same thing would have occurred if we did not trust.

The Rebbe brings a quote from Chovos Levavos. That we trust in G-d, the One who grants good to those who deserve and those who do not deserve.

From this he goes on to point out that Bitachon is not a philosophical principle. It is an avodah (service) in itself. By actively trusting in G-d, we make a change in our situation.

Tefillah (Prayer) & Teshuva (Repentance [or better Return]) have the ability to change our situation. Through teshuva we become meritorious. Though before we were not deserving of a certain thing, through teshuva we transform ourselves.

The same is through Bitachon. By trusting in G-d, that G-d is good and that all we receive from G-d is good, we transform ourselves.

Source: Gutfreund, Yechezkal-Shimon. (2001) In *A Guide to Chabad Literature*. www.kesser.org.

Jewish communities as the result of the Enlightenment. Jews responded to this encroaching modernization either by assimilating to these changes, by acculturating to the changes while still upholding certain traditional values, or by resisting change. Hasidic Jews chose to resist by attempting to separate themselves from the outside culture and people. Their approach is described in Heilman's (1992) metaphor of the gatekeeper who attempts to keep the outsiders out and the insiders in.

People and groups classified as ultra-Orthodox are not a unified group. In fact, three major streams within the ultra-Orthodoxy can be distinguished: the Hasidim, the Misnagdim, and the Sephardic ultra-Orthodox Jews. The founder of the Hasidic movement was Israel ben Eliezer, also known under the

Entrance to Mea Shearim ultra-Orthodox neighborhood in Jerusalem. PHOTO COURTESY OF HERMANN MAIBA.

acronym Ba'al Shem Tov. The distinguishing characteristic of the Hasidic movement is that they introduced spiritualistic and charismatic elements into keeping the Jewish religious tradition. The rebbe, or rabbi, became all-important and it was crucial for all fellow Hasidim to be close to him. The rebbe of a Hasidic community ("court" in their terminology) became the unifying agent for binding his adherents together into a single, close-knit society. In contrast, the Misnagdim (opponents) stress the attachment to the written text and therefore focus their religious practice on the study of the Talmud and Torah. The Misnagdic rabbi, rav, bases his authority on his scholarship of the biblical texts and not on doing miracle and spiritual work. Whereas the Hasidic and the Misnagdic movement emerged at the end of the nineteenth century, the Sephardic ultra-Orthodoxy appeared on the politico-religious scene much later. Mass immigration of Sephardic Jews (of Spanish or North African descent) to Israel and their discrimina-

tion by the Ashkenazi establishment (Jews from Central and East European background), propelled this group to form its own religious movement. They established Misnagdic-style *yeshivot* (Jewish seminaries for religious studies) and emphasized the study of the biblical texts. What distinguishes them from the Misnagdic movement is that the rank and file of the Sephardic stream cannot be described as full-blood ultra-Orthodox. While the Sephardic leadership study in the *yeshiva* and live a virtuous life according to the *mitzvots* (religious commandments), this cannot be said for the majority of the followers. What holds this movement together is their common interest based on their ethnicity vis-à-vis the Ashkenazi hegemony. However, all three streams share their counter-acculturative position toward the secular culture of the Israeli society. Counter-acculturative Orthodoxy is thus best described by their attachment to traditional Judaism (and in particular the version of it practiced in Eastern Europe) and a rejection of the emphasis on the freedom of the individual as the quintessential feature of the modern world.

Furthermore, ultra-Orthodox groups are distinguished by the manner in which they attempt to achieve their goals, be it in an active and conflictual manner or in a passive manner. Passive traditionalists, also termed "quietists," cut themselves off from outside influences, whereas active traditionalists fight for their way of life by trying to change the outside world. Both approaches are found within the ultra-Orthodox camp. The largest organization of Hasidic Jews, Agudat Israel, represents, thus far, the moderate and passive position among the ultra-Orthodox. They participate in parliamentary politics and it can be said that they gave up their radical position at the political bargaining table in exchange for governmental subsidies for their institutions. In contrast, Neturei Karta (Guardians of the City) and Edah Haredit (The Pious Community) are the more activist and extremist groups in the ultra-Orthodox community. For both, the establishment of the state of Israel by the secular Zionist was an act of rebellion against God. In their view, the Zionist interfered in the godly realm by hastening His return. They believe that to force the Messiah by human deed will bring God's wrath over them. For this reason, the Satmar Hasidim fight fiercely against every aspect of Zionist politics and culture since the founding of the nation-state. The Satmar community also maintains its isolation from the outside world, including Jews who are not Satmar. By contrast, the Lubavitch Hasidim actively proselytize fellow Jews to convert to ultra-Orthodoxy (*Ba'al teshuvah*).

For the most part, the American Hasidic communities pursue the passive counter-acculturative approach toward the American society and body politic. But, in Israel in recent years, even the more passive Haredim have adopted a more confrontational approach. Cultural, political, demographic, and socioeconomic factors within the Israeli society have been contributing to rising tensions between the ultra-Orthodox sector and the secular Israeli society. In short, this heightening tension was the result of the high birthrate of the ultra-Orthodox (on average, seven children per family), the increasing economic dependency on government subsidies, and a growing unwillingness of the secular majority to finance a lifestyle of people who attempt to tell them how they should live. According to Heilman and Friedman, "the true haredim tremble and cannot be content to be simply passive in their traditionalism; they must

be active in their Kulturkampf, ever demonstrating the religious 'truth' to the majority who are enticed by the hedonistic pleasures of contemporary culture and who thus submit to desire" (1991: 216).

Hermann Maiba

Bibliography

Caplan, L., ed. (1987) *Studies in Religious Fundamentalism*. Albany, NY: SUNY Press.

Friedman, Menachem, and Heilman C. Samuel. (1991) "Religious Fundamentalism and Religious Jews: The Case of the Haredim." In *Fundamentalism Observed*, edited by Martin Marty and R. Scott Appleby. Vol. 1 of *The Fundamentalism Project*. Chicago: University of Chicago Press, 197–264.

Hadden, Jeffrey K. (1992) "Religious Fundamentalism." In *Encyclopedia of Sociology*, vol. 3, edited by Edgar Borgatta and Marie Borgatta. New York: Macmillan 1637–1642.

Heilman, Samuel. (1983) *People of the Book*. Chicago: University of Chicago Press.

———. (1992) *Defender of the Faith: Inside Ultra-orthodox Jewry*. New York: Pantheon Books

Ultra-Orthodox Jews at the Wailing Wall in Jerusalem. PHOTO COURTESY OF HERMANN MAIBA.

Landau, David. (1993) *Piety and Power: The World of Jewish Fundamentalism.* New York: Hill and Wang.

Lawrence, Bruce B. (1989) *Defender of God: The Fundamentalist Revolt against the Modern Age.* San Francisco: Harper and Row.

Lustick, Ian S. (1988) *For the Land and the Lord: Jewish Fundamentalism in Israel.* New York: Council of Foreign Relations.

Silberstein, L. J., ed. (1993) *Jewish Fundamentalism in Comparative Perspective: Religion, Ideology, and the Crises of Modernity.* New York: New York University Press.

Weinfeld, Moshe. (1991) *Deuteronomy 1–11: A New Translation with Introduction and Commentary,* 1st ed. New York: Doubleday.

Justice

Justice is a central teaching in the Judeo-Christian tradition, which is modeled in the relationship of the chosen people with God, symbolized in the covenant. That relationship of justice extended to every other person in the community, who, because of his or her relationship with God, had to be treated with justice. God's justice required justice of His followers to each other, including the "least" in the community. Out of these relationships arose responsibilities and demands. The just person was faithful to these responsibilities and demands.

The Old Testament

The Old Testament or Hebrew Scriptures makes clear human responsibility to care for the hungry. In the Scriptures, God enjoins people to ensure that others have sufficient food. Taking care of the earth is part of the responsibility to feed the hungry. At the onset of human life, God commands Adam and Eve to care for the earth. God promises to provide for people through His providence but, in turn, there is human responsibility to be accountable for those less fortunate. This message of accountability for those most prone to poverty, including hunger, recurs throughout the Hebrew Scriptures. The Israelites must remember the foreigner, the orphan, and the widow, all of whom are the must liable to suffer the pangs of poverty. Deuteronomy 24:19–22 (NJB) ties God's providence to human responsibility for others:

When you gather your crops and fail to bring in some of the grain that you have cut, do not go back for it; it is to be left for the foreigners, orphans, and widows.... When you have gathered your grapes once, do not go back over the vines a second time; the grapes that are left are for the foreigners, orphans and widows. Never forget that you were slaves in Egypt; that is why I have given you this command.

Additionally, Deuteronomy enjoins the setting aside one-tenth of the harvest for "immigrants, orphans, and widows" (14:28–29). Moreover, there is to be no usury, defined as lending at interest to those in need (Exodus 22:25). Furthermore, the Israelites are to cancel all debts every seventh year (Deuteronomy 15:1–2, 7–11). Finally, every fiftieth year was set aside to be a Year of Jubilee. At that time, people returned property to the family of the original owner. The law sought to prevent the concentration of wealth and ensure that every family could have the means to feed itself.

The Prophets

The theme of justice runs through the writings of the prophets. Everyone is entitled to justice. A typical example is that of Amos. Amos denounced those people who sought wealth at the cost of riding over the rights of the poor and needy. Moreover, those people who wallowed in luxury and ignored the plight of the poor came in for special reproach. Amos connected his message of justice to the worship of the true God. Idolaters seek fertility and prosperity and shirk any social responsibility. Followers of the true God must be personally responsible for social justice and live the pursuit of luxury and the easy life (Amos 1:6–15, 2:10–12, 9:13–15).

Human justice must pattern itself on the justice of God. The Psalms have many passages that reiterate the message. For example, "[God] always keeps his promises; He judges in favor of the oppressed and gives food to the hungry" (Psalms 146:6–7). In another passage, it is written: "Happy are those who are concerned for the poor; the Lord will help them when they are in trouble" (Psalms 41:1).

The various books of wisdom and the wisdom literature repeat the same theme of justice. The Book of Proverbs, for example, offers the following: "If you refuse to listen to the cry of the poor, your own cry will not be heard" (21:13). Another verse states:

"Speak out for those who cannot speak, for the rights of all the destitute. [D]efend the rights of the poor and needy" (31:8–9).

In sum, the Hebrew Scriptures evidence great concern for justice and its application to all. To be just is to imitate God. God's justice is connected with his loving providence, and all His followers are to go and do likewise.

The New Testament

The New Testament teaching on justice is a continuation and expansion of the teachings of the Hebrew Scriptures. Additionally, the New Testament sees Jesus Christ as the Son of God, who lived, died, and rose from the dead. Jesus, Christians believe, sets the example for doing good and dispensing justice. The nature of that justice is clear from the actions of Jesus; namely, it is to aid the poor and oppressed people. Jesus in Luke 4:18–19 refers to the prophecy of Isaiah to mark out His mission and sense of justice:

> The Spirit of the Lord is upon me,
> because he has anointed me to bring good news to
> the poor.
> He has sent me to proclaim release to the captives
> and recovery of sight to the blind,
> to let the oppressed go free,
> to proclaim the year of the Lord's favor.

The justice that Jesus preached extended to those who were often despised by the elite of society—that is, those who were at the lowest end of the social structure, such as poor people, women, Samaritans, lepers, children, prostitutes, and tax collectors. Jesus accepted the rich but made His acceptance dependent upon repentance as evidenced by acts of social justice—giving all one had to the poor, for example.

This message of justice is carried into Jesus' depiction of the Day of Judgment. At that time He calls the elect to Him, saying "Come you blessed of my Father, for I was hungry and you fed me." To their question about when they fed Him, He replies "When you did it to the lowliest of my brothers (and sisters)." He condemns those who are damned by saying that they refused to provide works of charity to Him when He was hungry, thirsty, and sick. Refusing to help the least of His people is refusing to help Jesus (Matthew 25:31–46).

True justice for Jesus often led Him to ignore the letter of the law to get to its spirit. He praised the spirit of the Hebrew Scriptures while violating those laws that tried to keep Him from working His cures on the Sabbath. In so doing, the message that unjust laws need not be obeyed was conveyed to many of His followers. The need to take care of all humans—that we are our brother's keepers—is a message that runs through the Hebrew Scriptures and the New Testament.

Justice As an Attribute of God

In both the Hebrew Scriptures and the New Testament, justice is considered as a sign of the power of God as well as of His grace. Abraham, for example, has no fear in standing up to God on a matter of justice, telling Him that He cannot judge the just in the same manner as He does the wicked. God, for Abraham, must act justly, for it is in His nature to do so (Genesis 18:25). In Deuteronomy the theme of justice as an attribute of God is found in this passage:

> I charged your judges at that time: "Give the members of your community a fair hearing, and judge rightly between one person and another, whether citizen or resident alien. You must not be partial in judging: hear out the small and the great alike; you shall not be intimidated by anyone, for the judgment is God's. Any case that is too hard for you, bring to me, and I will hear it." (1:16–17)

Additionally, God is a rock, perfect and just (Deuteronomy 32:4). That justice is an attribute of God should be part of any ruler. So Samuel notes that David administered justice to all the people equally (2 Samuel 8:15). David's son, Solomon, was even more renowned than David for his wisdom and justice: "All Israel heard of the judgment that King Solomon had rendered; and they stood in awe of the king, because they perceived that the wisdom of God was in him, to execute justice" (1 Kings 3:28).

The Book of Job provides an interesting test of God's justice. However, Job refuses to charge God with injustice even in the midst of his trials. He speaks quite forcefully to God but never lays the charge of injustice against Him even as he states that he does not deserve the treatment he is receiving: "The Almighty . . . we cannot find him; he is great in power and justice, and abundant righteousness he will not violate" (Job 37:23).

This attribute of God, justice, is carried over to the New Testament. God is not only just; He is Justice Personified. Those who do just things are allowing Him to act through them. Matthew 12:18 states that God the Father notes that Jesus is His chosen and beloved servant. So pleased is the Father that He puts the Spirit on Jesus so that He can proclaim justice to the rest of the world. There are many passages in the Gospel that repeat the message of justice coming from God through Jesus to His followers. In turn, it is their responsibility to do justice to others.

The message of justice runs through the entire New Testament, continuing from the Old Testament, to the Book of Revelations. For example, "And they sing the song of Moses, the servant of God, and the song of the Lamb: 'Great and amazing are your deeds, Lord God the Almighty! Just and true are your ways, King of the nations!'" (Revelation 15:3).

For the authors of the Hebrew Scriptures and the New Testament, believers must pursue justice, but may not get justice. In fact, only in dispensing justice will the believer be rewarded. For the believer, the pursuit of justice is a prerequisite for salvation and earning God's reward: "Justice, and only justice, you shall pursue, so that you may live and occupy the land that the LORD your God is giving you. (Deuteronomy 16:20)" In another instance, "Thus says the LORD: Maintain justice, and do what is right, for soon my salvation will come, and my deliverance be revealed" (Isaiah 56:1).

Justice consists in giving every person his or her due. However, in light of the Scriptures, that due is seen from a different perspective. God, the Scriptures say, is no respecter of persons. The due that is owed is seen to be that which is owed to God. James sums up this view of justice in the following passage:

My brothers and sisters, do you with your acts of favoritism really believe in our glorious Lord Jesus Christ? For if a person with gold rings and in fine clothes comes into your assembly, and if a poor person in dirty clothes also comes in, and if you take notice of the one wearing the fine clothes and say, "Have a seat here, please," while to the one who is poor you say, "Stand there," or, "Sit at my feet," have you not made distinctions among yourselves, and become judges with evil thoughts? Listen, my beloved brothers and sisters. Has not God chosen

the poor in the world to be rich in faith and to be heirs of the kingdom that he has promised to those who love him? (James 2:1–5)

Conclusion

In both the Old and New Testaments, justice entails responsibilities to others, including stewardship of the world and care for all in that world. The New Testament explicitly extends that care to those who are not simply our neighbors in the physical sense but to all people in the world. Concern for the oppressed is a basic theme of the Scriptures. Stewardship is not for the purpose of self-enrichment. It is for the care of all that God has created. There is special concern for all the oppressed throughout the Scriptures. Justice also entails repentance. The New Testament expands on this theme of justice. John the Baptist, for example, preaches repentance, which includes the sharing of one's possessions with those less favored. Jesus characterized His own earthly ministry by service to the poor, the outcasts, and the downtrodden. Justice is required of the believer as part of the contract God made with His chosen people and which Jesus extended to all people. The believer holds that God shows this justice, tempered with mercy, to us and to all other humans.

Frank A. Salamone

Bibliography

Adamiak, Richard. (1985) *Justice and History in the Old Testament.* 2nd ed. Cleveland: John Zubal.

Barrett, Lois. (1999) *Doing What Is Right: What the Bible Says about Covenant and Justice* (Peace and Justice Series, vol. 7). Scotsdale, PA: Herald Press.

Dershowitz Alan M. (2001) *The Genesis of Justice: 10 Stories of Biblical Injustice That Led to the 10 Commandments.* New York: Warner Books.

Herzog, William R. (1999) *Jesus, Justice, and the Reign of God: A Ministry of Liberation.* Louisville, KY: Westminster John Knox Press.

Hollyday, Joyce. (1994) *Clothed with the Sun: Biblical Women, Social Justice, and Us.* Louisville, KY: Westminster John Knox Press.

Schussler Francis, and Elisabeth Schussler Fiorenza. (1999) *Book of Revelation: Justice & Thought.* Minneapolis: Fortress Press.

Justification

Justification by faith, biblical language that achieved a high priority in the sixteenth-century Reformation, has not been one of the principal doctrines of American Fundamentalism. Rather, it has been assumed as part of a larger bulwark of Christian doctrine supported by teachings considered of prior importance in defending the faith against alien forces in public life, whether earlier in the twentieth century or contemporaneously.

Despite the emphasis given by Paul in his letters to the Romans and the Galatians, justification by faith has been of only minor importance in the development of the early church. Taking over Greco-Roman assumptions in which the Law of God holds together a hierarchical structure ordering all of being, formative theologians assumed that the Law was the original way of salvation, rendered ineffective by the power of sin. Christ's work, replacing the old Law with the new covenant, is to both clarify what is required and to provide the grace necessary to turn the believer from the flesh to the spirit. Justification, restoration to the righteousness called for by the Law, occurs in this transition, as the morally unregenerate are rehabilitated by God's grace.

Historical Development of the Doctrine

There were two serious challenges to these assumptions in the early church. Pelagius and his heirs argued in the early fifth and again in the early sixth centuries that the Law and the human will are so sufficient to moral conversion that little grace is necessary. Julian of Eclanum was the most capable of such critics, engaging St. Augustine in running controversy. Augustine countered by suffusing the traditional scheme with grace, emphasizing the corruptibility of reason, the unreliability of the will, and finally the absolute power of God's predestination in, for example, *On Grace and Free Will*. Pelagianism and later semi-Pelagianism were officially condemned by the Synod of Carthage in 418 and the Synod of Orange in 529.

Justification by faith assumed far greater importance in the Reformation, as theologians translated the concept of grace through faith of Romance language–speaking Europe into the culture of the Germanic language–speaking north. Significantly, both Luther and Calvin (a Francophone who eventually gained significant influence in Germany) began their work with the later Augustine, but eventually they developed diverging ideas.

Oriented by Paul's apocalyptic as well as his conviction of Christ's death and Resurrection, Luther challenged the assumption that the Law was originally salvific. From the beginning, it was always God's intention to redeem both Creation and creature in Christ Jesus. Consequently, the Law is provisional, having its limits as well as its end. Just as Christ comes before the Law theologically, faith takes priority over works of the Law. To be justified is to be defined in relation to Christ, in Luther's own phrase, "to be what Adam and Eve were meant to be," creatures living by faith in the Creator while caring for other creatures and the Creation. In such faith, the believer confesses both the continuing force of sin and the power of the Holy Spirit, simultaneously saint and sinner. Righteousness is a relational rather than a legal quality. Moral improvement is not a goal to be sought but a by-product of faith. Significantly, as Luther broke the preserve that the medieval church had maintained through the enforced use of Latin, his linguistic and theological translation found its most appreciative audience in Germany and other Germanic-speaking areas, such as Scandinavia and Finland. They became legally and later culturally Lutheran.

When the sixteenth-century Reformation spread to southwestern Germany and Switzerland, Luther's understanding of justification encountered opposition. Working scripturally, relying on the later Augustine and the earlier Luther, Jean Calvin also translated, setting out a doctrine of justification much more significant historically for American evangelicalism and its Fundamentalist expression. Calvin smoothed out and gave cohesion to Luther's eschatologically driven, relationally oriented dialectics. He began with the doctrine of God's predestining to establish the priority of Christ's justifying work; filled out the doctrine of inspiration to clarify the authority of the biblical word; worked out the arguments for the bondage of the will with language of total depravity; argued the priority of the Law in shaping Christian life; and sought to present the city of Geneva to the larger world as a beacon on the hill showing the way to a transformed society. Grace-driven, Christ-centered justification was once more a process of rehabilitation in which morally unregenerate sinners are restrained and restored by legal standards.

While the Lutherans went north, the reformed of southwest Germany, Strasbourg, and then Geneva went west and northwest, to France, the Netherlands, and the British Isles. From there, they provided the original European immigrants to North America. The doctrine of justification that they brought with them was Calvinistic, recently purged of Arminian or free will tendencies by the Synod of Dort in 1624.

In the meantime, Catholicism had undergone its own reformation, most importantly in the Council of Trent. Instead of using the later Augustine view, so important to both Luther and Calvin, the bishops at Trent looked to his earlier work. Holding with the rejection of both a full and a semi-Pelagianism, they nevertheless insisted on the synthesis of God's grace and the human will in applying the self to achieving a legally measurable righteousness.

The most important step in the transition from European Calvinism to American evangelicalism occurred during the Great Awakening, particularly in the 1740s. The church in Europe had been able to rely on the coercive power of the state to maintain itself. The American frontier provided initially what the American constitution later guaranteed: open spaces beyond the claim of the established church. Freedom of choice was a de facto political reality, whatever might have previously been said about it psychologically or theologically by the great theologians of the western European church. No matter how valiantly theologians like Jonathan Edwards fought against it, freedom of the will became a defining feature of the Evangelical doctrine of justification.

Fundamentalism has taken various forms: the early-twentieth-century fight against modernism, the later Christian militancy against the perceived liberal dilution of historic Christianity, and the more recent Baptist dispensationalism. At its center, however, the understanding of justification that emerged with American evangelicalism has remained virtually unchanged. The emphasis on Christ's substitutionary Atonement begins with the assumption that God's original intention in the Law was salvific. The Lord Jesus took upon Himself the consequences of human disobedience, propitiating God's wrath so that He can offer grace. The believer, accepting the proffered grace in a free decision of the will, is then justified, applying the self to the standard of the Law for personal and subsequently public moral transformation.

James A. Nestingen

See also Calvinism; Free Will; New Testament

Bibliography

Bloesch, Donald G. (1978) *Essentials of Evangelical Theology.* San Francisco: Harper and Row.

Calvin, John. (1960) *Institutes of the Christian Religion.* Philadelphia: The Westminster Press.

Luther, Martin. (1957) "The Freedom of the Christian." In *Luther's Works.* Philadelphia: Muhlenberg Press.

Marsden, George M. (1991) *Understanding Fundamentalism and Evangelicalism.* Grand Rapids, MI: Wm. B. Eerdsmans.

K

Keswick Movement

Geographically, Keswick is a small resort town located in the beautiful Lake Country of northwestern England and the location of a religious conference held there annually since 1875. Yet, Keswick is much more than a place or a successful conference that was transplanted to other locations around the globe. For adherents it was all about living a "higher life" with victory over sin and helping others to do the same. An examination of the Evangelical spiritual terrain in the late nineteenth and early twentieth centuries reveals Keswick theology and its brand of spirituality at the intersection of many religious movements, including Pentecostalism, the Wesleyan-Holiness movement, and early North American Fundamentalism. Mapping this territory is necessary, not only to understand the Keswick movement but also the religious and social impulses that gave birth to it and which it, in turn, helped to set in motion.

Indigenous Precursors

While some view the origin of the Keswick movement in England as primarily an American Wesleyan-Holiness import (without the perfectionist doctrine that was troublesome to the Reformed clergy), this ignores the many religious developments in Britain and on the European continent that helped to pave the way for later transatlantic influence. The Mildmay conferences, for instance, were of major importance.

Mildmay began with the Anglican priest William Pennefather (1816–1873), whose multifaceted min-istries focused on personal holiness, missionary outreach, social ministry, women's organizations, Christian unity, and the impending return of Christ. These latter two emphases, unity and Christ's return, respectively, reflect the influence of the ecumenically minded Evangelical Alliance upon Pennefather and the fact that he was a nephew of John Nelson Darby (1800–1882), who did much to define and promote dispensational premillennialism in both Britain and North America. Denominational distinctions were downplayed. The motto that was later given to the Keswick Convention, "All one in Christ," just as easily would have fit Mildmay. Low-church Anglicans, many Brethren and Quakers, were drawn to Mildmay and its message. Its format was equally important. Mildmay broke new ground in raising the expectation of an annual conference among the Evangelical faithful to routine status. Through Pennefather's encouragement of lay teaching and ministry by women (something quite rare in England at the time), Mildmay also prepared the way for the American Holiness evangelists who followed. Reactions to these evangelists shaped the birth and the development of Keswick teachings at critical junctures.

The American Perfectionists

Ironically, the American Holiness movement that played an important role in the genesis of Keswick in England would never have come into being if it were not for the English-born founder of Methodism, John Wesley (1703–1791), and his emphasis on a second work of sanctifying grace beyond conversion to do away with sin and live a holy life. His message and

Postcard of the Keswick Convention tent with sign "All One in Christ Jesus." COPYRIGHT G. P. ABRAHAM, LTD., N.D. C 1962.

method were transplanted to America's expanding frontier and became the root from which the later Holiness movement sprouted, bursting the denominational structure of Methodism.

Wesley's perfectionist strand was later appropriated and magnified by two prominent educators and revivalists from Oberlin College, Asa Mahan (1799–1889) and Charles Grandison Finney (1792–1875). Calvinist opponents branded this form of perfectionism the "Oberlin heresy," yet their very opposition did much to publicize the cause. However, it was the publication of William Edwin Boardman's (1810–1886) book, *The Higher Christian Life* (published in 1858 and republished a short time later in London), that did even more to lay the groundwork for the spread of perfectionist doctrine and piety to the non-Methodist world in England. Having prepared the way in print, Boardman and other evangelists, male and female, departed for Britain to reinforce their message of living a higher Christian life without sin.

The Birth, Growth, and Spread of Keswick

Having benefited from the kind of annual conferences that Mildmay inspired, the Anglican Vicar of St. John's at Keswick decided, along with his Quaker friend, to call a new meeting, the "Keswick Union Meetings for the Promotion of Practical Holiness" in 1875. The Quaker-born, American Holiness evangelist couple, Hannah Whitall Smith (1832–1911) and Robert Pearsall Smith (1827–1899), were invited along with other leading speakers in the English convention network. The Smiths' approach resembled the American Holiness camp meetings and carried a perfectionist message. Shortly before the big tent meeting, however, Robert Smith withdrew to America under rumors of sexual impropriety. Already hypersensitive to the criticism of staunch Calvinist ministers about the perfectionist tradition and their ready charge of antinomianism, Keswick organizers began to downplay perfectionist language inherent in holiness circles and embraced a view of sin more in line with low-church Anglicans, Brethren, Quakers, and Baptists. Sin could not be eradicated instantaneously or completely. Nevertheless, "victory" over sin remained the Keswick trademark. Sin, though still present, could be kept in check by faith, through the power of the Holy Spirit. The annual conference was well received and grew quickly.

Whether due to shrewd salesman instincts honed earlier in life, or other reasons, the visiting American evangelist Dwight L. Moody (1837–1899) managed to walk the fine line between the American Holiness evangelists and their Reformed critics in England. Both, at times, claimed him for their own. But when the Wesleyan clergy in Sunderland complained that he was overly Calvinist, Reformed ministers came to his defense. This perception of Moody was critical because he returned to America and introduced Keswick spirituality to the millenarian movement. The millenarians were deeply suspicious of Holiness theology and it is probable that Moody would have been rejected had he identified himself too closely to them. Instead, through the Keswick-type Northfield conferences he convened in New England and through his invitation to a steady stream of British Keswick speakers to the American religious conference network, Moody did much to infuse the Fundamentalist movement with an emphasis on holiness and living a life of victory over sin. An official American Keswick movement was subsequently established in 1913 with conferences in Princeton, New Jersey, and Stony Brook, New York, and then at Keswick, New Jersey, in 1923 where the theme of personal holiness and the premillenial return of Christ coexisted. Often the two themes were linked, Christ's imminent return serving as an impetus for holy living and missionary outreach.

The Holy Spirit and the Spirit of the Age

Scholars of religion have recently begun to uncover ways in which Keswick on both sides of the Atlantic reflected large cultural shifts at work. In the religious milieu of New England, for example, transcendentalism, New Thought, and the Keswick/Higher Life teachings can all be seen as responses to some of the same intellectual and cultural trends that gave rise to English romanticism and German idealism. Advocates of these diverse movements shared intuitionist approaches to knowledge, spiritualized interpretations of Scripture or literature, and a thirst for a more direct experience with the Holy (however defined). The Higher Life spirituality and theology of Keswick shared many notions of personal peace, power, and wealth in common with New Thought in the American Gilded Age. This had an enormous impact on the emerging Pentecostal movement and the later independent charismatic "Word of Faith" churches and their gospel of prosperity through the influence

of Essek William Kenyon (1867–1948). Given the worldwide growth of Pentecostalism, this understudied aspect of Keswick deserves further attention.

Douglas Milford

See also Evangelicalism; Holiness, Wesleyan

Bibliography

Bebbington, David. (1992) *Evangelicalism in Modern Britain: A History from the 1730s to the 1980s*. Grand Rapids, MI: Baker Book House.

Bundy, David. (1993) "Keswick and the Experience of Evangelical Piety." In *Modern Christian Revivals*, edited by Edith L. Blumhofer and Randall Balmer. Urbana and Chicago: University of Illinois Press.

Sandeen, Ernest. (1970) *The Roots of Fundamentalism: British and American Millenarianism 1800–1930*. Chicago: University of Chicago Press.

Simmons, Dale H. (1997) *E. W. Kenyon and the Postbellum Pursuit of Peace, Power, and Plenty*. Lanham, MD, and London: Scarecrow Press.

Wacker, Grant. (1985) "The Holy Spirit and the Spirit of the Age in American Protestantism, 1880–1910." *Journal of American History* 72, 1: 45–62.

Kingdom of God

The meaning of the New Testament term "Kingdom of God" has been the subject of extensive discussion in twentieth-century biblical studies. It is generally agreed that the term is best understood in an active sense as the reign of God. A central issue has been whether this reign is a reality that began with the life and ministry of Jesus, or if Jesus expected a future coming of God's reign as a final and cataclysmic victory over the forces of evil. Some liberal and mainline Protestant interpretations of the Kingdom of God have tended to emphasize, on one extreme, a gradualist perspective, in which the Kingdom of God is gradually realized in history through the spread of the Christian religion. On the other extreme, many Protestants believe that the Kingdom of God will only be established after Christ returns to earth, defeats the power of Satan, and establishes His reign on earth for a thousand years of peace—the millennium. This interpretation, known as premillennialism, has been the majority opinion among Fundamentalists, although it should be noted that some Fundamentalists in the Reformed and Wesleyan traditions do not accept this view.

The term "Kingdom of God" also took on a new theological significance for Fundamentalists who followed the system of biblical interpretation known as dispensationalism. In this form of premillenialism, Jesus' teachings about the kingdom referred more specifically to a restoration of an earthly kingdom to Israel. Because the Jews rejected Christ, however, the establishment of this kingdom has been postponed until Christ's Second Coming, at which time the promises of a new Davidic kingdom will finally be fulfilled. This view led dispensational Fundamentalists to distinguish between the Gospel of the Kingdom, which was intended for the Jews, and the Pauline Gospel of Grace, which was directed to the church.

Fundamentalists often asserted that premillenialism was an essential doctrine of the Christian faith that if denied would inevitably lead to error and even apostasy. They severely criticized the traditional Catholic interpretation that the Kingdom of God could in some sense be identified with the institutional church. They also criticized the Reformed view that the Kingdom of God was a present spiritual reality of God's rule in the life of every believer. These interpretations seemed to deny the idea of the Kingdom as a future perfect reign of God. Moreover, dispensational Fundamentalists insisted that promises of a restored kingdom to Israel must be understood literally, not as having been set aside or spiritually fulfilled in the church. In 1957, George Ladd led an effort to reestablish what he called historical premillenialism in his book, *The Gospel of the Kingdom* (1957), against the dispensational ideas represented by Dallas Theological Seminary. For Pentecostal Fundamentalists, the return of Christ and the establishment of His millennial reign would be preceded by visible signs and wonders. Therefore, Pentecostals emphasized speaking in tongues, healing, and miracles as preparation for the victory of Christ over the devil and the inauguration of the Kingdom of God on earth.

Daniel W. Draney

See also Dispensationalism; Premillennialism

Bibliography

Ladd, George Eldon. (1957) *The Gospel of the Kingdom*. Grand Rapids, MI: Wm. B. Eerdmans.

Ryrie, Charles Caldwell. (1965) *Dispensationalism Today*. Chicago: Moody Press.

Weber, Timothy P. (1979) *Living in the Shadow of the Second Coming: American Premillenialism 1875–1982*. Chicago: University of Chicago Press.

Willis, Wendell, ed. (1987) *The Kingdom of God in 20th-Century Interpretation*. Peabody, MA: Hendrickson Publishers.

Ku Klux Klan

The Ku Klux Klan (KKK) is the longest-lasting extremist right-wing movement in U.S. history. Founded in the late 1860s, the Klan has collapsed and reappeared many times. At the beginning of this century, it continues to have a presence on the American political landscape. Throughout history, all Klan groups trace their ideological heritage to the post–Civil War era Klan, but in other ways they differ considerably. Some are highly organized with a military model of hierarchy, leadership, and membership, while others are much more fluid, with unclear and shifting leadership and memberships. Some Klan groups claim to renounce violence and promote themselves as white interest groups, whereas others more explicitly advocate racial violence and revolutionary terrorism. They also differ in their membership and political message, yet all support a pernicious agenda of racial and religious bigotry, along with social and cultural conservatism.

History and Development

Many competing groups have taken the name of "Ku Klux Klan" in various historical periods. The first were gangs of Southern rural white men who violently opposed racial and political realignment in the U.S. South at the end of the Civil War. This Klan fomented a bloody sweep of lynchings, assaults, arson, and destruction and expropriation of property across the former states of the Confederacy. Their hatred was directed at African-American former slaves, Northern representatives of the Reconstruction government, and whites thought to be sympathetic to the new racial order. These Klan groups collapsed in the mid-1870s because of federal government pressure and as a new structure of white supremacist laws, agricultural sharecropping, and a

Klan billboard along rural road near Fayetteville, North Carolina, in 1968. PHOTO COURTESY OF DAVID LEVINSON.

racially exclusive political system shored up the privilege of white supremacism earlier enforced by the system of slavery.

A second Klan wave emerged in the mid-1910s and gained strength through the mid-1920s. It was extensive in the North as well as the South, in large urban areas that were absorbing new immigrants as well as more racially and religiously homogenous small towns and rural areas. This Klan drew between two and three million members, including about a half-million women, from a range of social classes, from small business owners and professionals to those from the working and lower classes. In many communities in which it took root, the 1920s Klan enlisted a substantial proportion, even a majority, of the white, native-born, Protestant population. It collapsed precipitously in the late 1920s, as the result of financial and sexual scandals and as passage of severe immigration quotas undercut one of the Klan's most visible political issues.

The next Klan groups appeared in the late 1960s and early 1970s during the turbulent period of social and school racial desegregation in the South. This Klan recruited largely from populations of poorly educated and economically marginal white men in the rural South and unleashed a wave of violence and terror against African Americans.

Today's Klan emerged in the late 1980s, as part of a broader upsurge in racist activity. This wave of organized racism was fueled by economic restructuring and decline in certain sectors of the economy, notably small-scale agriculture and industrial work, as well as by the increased use of xenophobic, racist, and homophobic rhetoric by politicians from the conservative political mainstream. The Klan also grew because of internal factors, especially alliances with previously antagonistic racist and neo-Nazi leaders, made possible in part by decisions by several Klan leaders to de-emphasize anti-Catholicism and even to welcome Catholic members along with their traditional base among Protestant Fundamentalists. Also influential were international efforts to forge a transnational "pan-Aryan" movement that proclaimed the interests of all non-Jewish whites (Aryans) to be in opposition to those of Jews and all nonwhites, making anti-Semitism as central as race to the international racist agenda. Most of the several dozen or so Klan groups remained small during the 1980s and 1990s, many declining even further in the face of federal investigations of the extreme right after the bombing of the Oklahoma City federal building in 1995.

The Klan's ideological flexibility is one reason for its longevity. Every Klan proclaims virulent racism

WHY WE LIGHT THE CROSS

Mortal man wonders in awe, at the sight of a huge cross set upon a hill, encircled by those who placed it there. Adorned in White robes and hoods, they perform the age old rituals, then in somber silence approach the cross, and set ablaze the symbol of Christianity. To most men this act of igniting a symbol of the Christian faith may seem barbaric or even next to anti-Christian, but nothing could be farther from the truth.

The Truth Is; Klansmen hold the Cross in most high reverence. We of the American Knights of the Ku Klux Klan, Honor the Holy Cross, as a symbol of Christian Faith, and recognize the Sacrifice of Holy Blood, which was shed, that all men might receive forgiveness of sin, and have life everlasting. We light the Cross in recognition that,

JESUS CHRIST IS THE LIGHT OF THE WORLD

As light drives out darkness, so knowledge and truth dispel ignorance and superstition. The lighting of the Cross was originally taken from the lighting of signal fires upon the mountain tops of Scotland as a warning of danger from an invading enemy. So we of the American Knights of the Ku Klux Klan light the cross as a warning signal to all men of the impending disaster that is facing our Nation if it continues on it's present course without God.

We also light the Cross, as a tribute to Jesus Christ in recognition of his sacrifice, and willingness to die for our sins. We endeavor to warn of the dangers of interracial mixing, and teach those who will listen and learn, the ways of the Klan. We feel it is our duty to prepare ourselves, and those of our race, for the hard road ahead, while the Government over this Nation turns like a rabid dog upon the very people who support it.

We of the American Knights of the Ku Klux Klan want you to understand that there is a difference between Lighting a cross and a Cross burning.

The lighting of a cross is a religious ceremony, performed in reverence to the Lord Jesus Christ, in recognition of his sacrifice.

The burning of a cross is an illegal act of violence against a person or a person's home, while invading their privacy with the intent to harass, intimidate, or do bodily harm. This act of burning a cross is usually performed by irate citizens who do not understand the rules of the Klan, but wish to use the influence of the Klan to scare their victims, by burning a cross usually less than ten feet tall in the persons yard or against the home.

We of the American knights of the Ku Klux Klan, wish to take this opportunity to invite you to join us and learn the meaning of true Klan craft, and help us build a better Nation for our children to grow up in and call home.

Source: American Knights of the Ku Klux Klan. www.americanknights.com

against African Americans and other racial minority groups. Most are also deeply anti-Semitic, proclaiming that a Jewish conspiracy rules the world to the detriment of all Aryans. But other aspects of the Klan's message have changed over time, tailored to the different groups of people it seeks to recruit. In the 1920s, a period of high immigration to the United States, the Klan promoted an "America-first" and anti-Catholicism agenda, along with hatred of African Americans and Jews. By the late 1980s, however, few Klan groups were actively promoting anti-Catholicism. Instead, many targeted Hispanics and

Chicano/as, Asians and Asian Americans, and gay men and lesbians as their main enemy groups and some have moderated their xenophobic appeals to support an international "pan-Aryan" movement.

A second reason that the Klan has been fairly durable over time is its compatibility with some aspects of Protestant Fundamentalism. Indeed, many Klan groups have regarded adherents to Protestant Fundamentalist beliefs and congregations as their most likely recruits. This was particularly true for the 1920s Klan, which relied on Protestant ministers for some of its spokespersons and absorbed entire local Protestant congregations in some areas of the United States. Today, the Klan's connection to Protestantism is much more attenuated, as many have been influenced by the ideology of "Christian Identity." Christian Identity, based loosely on an eighteenth- and nineteenth-century British theology known as "British Israelism," denounces traditional Protestant teachings, preaching instead a vicious theology that views Jews, African Americans, and other persons of color as the literal offspring of Satan and white Anglo-Saxon Christians as the true lost tribe of Israel, that is, the chosen people of God.

Kathleen M. Blee

See also Anti-Semitism; Aryan Nation; Nativism

Bibliography

Barkun, Michael. (1994) *Religion and the Racist Right: The Origins of the Christian Identity Movement.* Chapel Hill: University of North Carolina Press.

Bennett, David. (1988) *The Party of Fear: From Nativist Movements to the New Right in American History.* Chapel Hill: University of North Carolina Press.

Blee, Kathleen M. (1991) *Women of the Klan: Racism and Gender in the 1920s.* Berkeley: University of California Press.

———. (2001) *Inside Organized Racism: Women and Men in the Hate Movement.* Berkeley: University of California Press.

Chalmers, David M. (1981) *Hooded Americanism: The History of the Ku Klux Klan.* Durham, NC: Duke University Press.

McLean, Nancy. (1994) *Behind the Mask of Chivalry: The Making of the Second Ku Klux Klan.* New York: Oxford University Press.

Last Things

The contents of eschatology or the Christian doctrine of the last things include human death, judgment, heaven and hell, and the afterlife. Christians hold that the most important of the last things is the various events that will herald the end of this world. Christians generally believe that human history will not continue in endless cycles, but that there will be a finality to it in the future. The end of the world will come not by any natural disaster, nor nuclear explosion, nor any revolutionary process, but by God's direct action, which eventually will usher in a permanent order of righteousness and heavenly bliss in the new spiritual world.

Apocalypticism and millennialism are forms of eschatology. Apocalypticism is the belief that the events heralding the end of the world are imminent, and involve a catastrophic and a harshly retributive end. Apocalyptists believe in the dissolution of this present world that is evil, and its replacement by the triumph of good. Millennialism is an expectation of the last things based on the interpretation of Revelation 20:1–10 in which Satan is bound and thrown into a bottomless pit for a thousand years. With the removal of Satanic influence from world affairs, a new world order will ensue, characterized by peace, freedom, material prosperity, and the reign of righteousness under Christ's rule. Essentially, millennialism concerns earthly salvation executed according to divine plan. There are conflicting opinions about the details of the millennialist doctrine: some scholars have argued that the references to the last things in the Scriptures and Jesus' teachings on the subject are figurative and, hence, subject to various interpretations, while others hold that the scriptural passages referring to the last things should be taken literally.

Eschatology in the Bible

There is much reflection on the idea of the last things in the Old Testament. It has always been an important Jewish belief that God will surely bring about some changes in the course of human history. Prophets like Isaiah, Jeremiah, Amos, Joel, Daniel, and Ezekiel prophesied about the last things. Jewish apocalyptic thought and literature flourished considerably during the inter-testamental period when powerful overlords frequently frustrated the struggle for national independence. Thereafter, Jews began to await a divine intervention through the Messiah, who would end all human sufferings.

Jesus' teachings also contain reference to the last things. In Matthew 24:1–44, Jesus predicted certain apocalyptic events that will precede the end of the world. The disciples based their eschatological belief on Jesus' teachings, but did not understand the meaning of some of the expressions He used. For example, before Jesus' Ascension, the disciples asked Him, "Lord, will you at this time restore the kingdom to Israel?"(Acts 1:6, RSV). The disciples had hoped that the end of the world would have a political reality for the nation of Israel. However, Jesus had a contrary idea. The Book of Revelation, written at the close of the first century, contains much imagery of the last things. The book, in figurative expressions, presented a future in which Satan would be defeated and the saints rescued. In addition, a detailed description is given of life on earth in the new world. This description has inspired countless interpretations of the end of the world.

The Understanding of Eschatology in Contemporary Times

Since the first century, Christians have anticipated the end of the world because certain of Jesus' predictions have come to pass. For example, Paul wrote to correct the Christians in Thessalonica, who attached immediacy to Christ's Second Coming, and in anticipation had stopped working and had abandoned all ordinary pursuits. Such an overwhelming reliance on the end of the world encouraged some Christian sects to predict a particular date for the end of the world. The first of such was the Montanist movement in the second and third centuries. Later, the revolt in Münster in 1534, which was supported by Anabaptists, was inspired by an apocalyptic vision of the end of the world. There have been countless apocalyptic predictions throughout history.

Christians of all eras have been preoccupied by the imagery used in the Scriptures about the last things, and have sought to understand them in relation to the events occurring around them. For example, premillennialists believe that Christ's Second Coming will be preceded by signs including wars, famines, earthquakes, the preaching of the gospel to all nations, a great apostasy, the appearance of the Antichrist, and the Great Tribulation. Thereafter, there will be a period of peace and righteousness in the world under Christ's control. Christ will destroy the power of Satan during the millennium, the dead will be resurrected, and the last judgment will be conducted. The wicked will be eternally condemned while the righteous will be rewarded. Premillennialism has dominated the theology of Protestant Fundamentalism in North America. In contrast, postmillennialists accept that human agency, particularly the evangelization of the world, will usher in Christ's Second Coming.

More important, there is no general agreement on the precise timing of the events of the last things. The New Testament understands the last days to have begun with the ministry of Jesus, particularly with reference to some of Jesus' parables on the Kingdom of God. Yet, some Christians believe that the last days were ushered in in 33 CE when the Christian Church was inaugurated at Pentecost. Thus, the signs of the Messianic age, namely, healing, exorcism, miracles, and the proclamation of the Good News, are regarded as stages of the last things. Others date the last days from 1914, when the world wars began; these events were seen as manifestations of the Antichrist. Still others believe that the End Times began in 1948 with the restoration of Israel as a nation. Despite these various opinions, there is general agreement on the judicial role of Jesus in the End-Times order of things.

The doctrine of the last things is central to the way Protestant Fundamentalists understand the Bible as literalists; hence, they often look with distrust at others holding contrary views. The belief that Christ's Second Coming is imminent has energized them to preach the gospel near and far. Consequently, the evangelization of the world becomes a necessary preparation to usher in the End Time. Fundamentalists are always prepared by continually scrutinizing contemporary events to find the fulfillment of prophecies ushering in the end of the present age.

Conclusion

The doctrine of the last things has continued to fascinate and shape the minds of Christians and, in certain cases, has determined political and social response to world issues. The millennial message of God's direct intervention to reverse history and to overcome evil with good has given hope to Christians throughout history, especially in times of persecution. More recently, sociologists have tried to detach eschatology from its traditional biblical mooring and analyze it as a social phenomenon or extreme prophetism. The approach of the year 2000 initially fuelled expectation about the end of the world, but with the beginning of the new millennium attention is turning to other world issues that are closely related to the biblical predictions. Certainly, the focus on the end of the world is intricately linked to the expectation of a better life in the future.

Matthews A. Ojo

See also Apocalypse; End Times; Eschatology

Bibliography

Eddleman, H. Leo, ed. (1969) *Last Things*. Grand Rapids, MI: Zondervan Publishing.

Gloer, W. Hullit, ed. (1988) *Eschatology and the New Testament*. Peabody, MA: Hendrickson Publishers.

Pentecost, J. Dwight. (1958) *Things to Come: A Study in Biblical Eschatology*. Grand Rapids, MI: Zondervan Publishing.

Robbins, Thomas, and Susan J. Palmer, eds. (1997) *Millennium, Messiah, and Mayhem: Contemporary Apocalyptic Movements*. New York: Routledge.

Strozier, Charles B. (1994) *Apocalypse: On the Psychology of Fundamentalism in America*. Boston: Beacon Press.

Law, Old Testament

God gave the Mosaic Law to the nation of Israel. It is an essential part of the Mosaic Covenant, which stands as a binding covenant between the nation of Israel and Yahweh their God. Yahweh chose Israel to be His people (Deuteronomy 7:6–8) and Israel accepted this relationship (Exodus 24:1–11, especially 3–8). As a result, it was necessary to define the particulars of this covenant between Israel and Yahweh.

The Nature of the Law

The legal material of the Mosaic Covenant is introduced by the narrative of Genesis 1 through Exodus 19, which provides the background to Yahweh's redemption of Israel from bondage in Egypt. The content of this legal material is found in the remainder of the Pentateuch, Exodus 20 through Deuteronomy 33, interspersed with further narrative on the story of Israel. There are more than 600 laws in this section of the Old Testament.

It is common to divide the Law into various collections of laws: the Ten Commandments (Exodus 20; Deuteronomy 5); the Book of the Covenant or Covenant Code (Exodus 21–23); the Priestly Code (Leviticus 1–16); the Holiness Code (Leviticus 17–26); and the Deuteronomic Law (Deuteronomy 12–26). The Law is expressed in various formulas depending on the situation for which a particular law has been given (e.g., hypothetical situations, secret sins, establishing boundaries for behavior), grouped into subcategories. Casuistic or case law, one major subcategory, is evidenced by the "if . . , then" formula: "if" some event happens, "then" this action is to be the consequence (cf. Deuteronomy 22:22). It makes reference to specific cases in the life of people based on hypothetical situations. Apodictic law, another major subcategory, is a direct command (both affirmative and negative) that clearly establishes general boundaries of behavior. These include the highly recognizable "thou shall not" formula of the Ten Commandments (cf. Exodus 20:3, 12). There are three other subcategories related to those noted above. The first is prohibitions or negative commands, which refer to hypothetical offenses that do not carry a fixed penalty. They simply define an action that is not to occur in Israel (cf. Leviticus 19:14). It is similar to the apodictic law (negative). Second, the death law refers to hypothetical offenses just like the prohibitions or negative commands, but it carries a fixed penalty of death. Not only is one not to engage in such activity in Israel, the person who does will surely be put to death (cf. Exodus 21:15). Third, the curse refers to regulations that are a further development of prohibitions or negative commands and death law. The laws are designed to maintain purity in the nation, and focus on those violations of the law that are performed in secret (e.g., moving a neighbor's boundary mark while he is not present, cf. Deuteronomy 27:17). The judgment is of a divine nature. The person who commits such a violation is cursed (cf. Deuteronomy 27:17, 24).

The Function of the Law

The Law had three basic functions for the nation of Israel. First, it was a constant reminder that Yahweh had led them out of Egypt, redeeming them with His outstretched arm from slavery (cf. Deuteronomy 6:20–25). It was out of gratitude for this redemption that they in turn lived a life that was pleasing to him. Obedience to the Mosaic Law, then, was not to be a heavy burden on a people bound by slavery. It was to be a gracious response of a people who had been freed from bondage and who now wanted to demonstrate their love to the One who granted the redemption and who alone is worthy of such obedience.

Second, the Law defined the nature of the relationship with Yahweh and with one another in the covenant community. Because of Yahweh's holy character, a relationship with Him required certain qualities that were to be expressed to Him as well as to one another. The essence of the Mosaic Law, as clearly revealed by Christ in Matthew 22:34–40, is love for Yahweh and for fellow humans (cf. Matthew 23:23). The Mosaic Law is not simply a list of rules on how to live, which must be obeyed. It is a manner of living that shows Israel how to properly express love for Yahweh and their fellow Israelite. It sets forth certain principles that show how this love will be manifested in everyday life.

Third, the Law offered the nation of Israel the opportunity to receive atonement when they failed to abide by the Law. Inevitably, the Israelites would disobey the Law, but forgiveness was available. Yahweh, in His grace, created the opportunity for His people to maintain a proper relationship with Him if they would only humble themselves and do what was necessary to atone for the wrongs they committed. It is actually one of the most amazing realities of the Law. As Yahweh gave the law and required the nation of Israel to be obedient, He also extended grace for when they were not obedient. Thus, the Law, which requires holy obedience, also makes provision for disobedience.

The Purpose of the Law

The Law is given in the context of a covenant between the nation of Israel and Yahweh. As with all covenants, the Mosaic Covenant included both promises and obligations (Exodus 19–24; 25:1–Leviticus 26:46; Deuteronomy 1–31). The promises of the Mosaic Covenant are that Yahweh would offer the blessings of peace, rest, and provision (Exodus 19:5b–6; Leviticus 26:40–45; Deuteronomy 30:1–10). For the people to experience the blessings of the covenant, they had to obey the stipulations of the law code (Exodus 19:5a, 8; Exodus 24:3, 7; Leviticus 26:46; 27:34; Deuteronomy 28:1, 15; 29:10ff; 30:15–20). This is found primarily in Exodus 19:5–6, but it is reiterated throughout Israel's history (cf. Deuteronomy 7:6–8). Fidelity to this covenant (i.e., obedience) would result in blessings; infidelity (i.e., disobedience) would result in, not only the removal of blessings, but in specific penalties (cf. Leviticus 26; Deuteronomy 28). This basic principle of blessing and penalty in relation to obedience and disobedience is at the heart of Israel's relationship with Yahweh.

The Law defined the relationship between Yahweh and the nation of Israel. It provided a standard of how the nation of Israel was to live. They were no longer to live as other nations or however they pleased (cf. Leviticus 18:24–28); instead, they were to live in a faithful manner to the Yahweh with whom they were in a covenant relationship. The ultimate goal of the Law was to provide instruction to the nation of Israel concerning how to maintain covenant fidelity in their relationship with Yahweh. He is a holy God and as such requires holiness on the part of His people (Deuteronomy 7:6; Leviticus 11:44–45). The Law defines this holiness that Israel was to evidence. The message of the Old Testament is clear concerning Israel's inability to live a holy life, but the Law included provision for the breaking of its laws. It spells out clearly how people were to pay their debt if they failed in any detail of the Law. Therefore, a relationship with Yahweh could be maintained, even though the Law had been broken, as long as the stipulations regarding restoration provided in the Law were followed.

Various Misunderstandings Concerning Yahweh and the Law

Three questions must be answered to better understand the basic premise of the Law for the nation of Israel: Were sins just "covered" or were they "forgiven" for the nation of Israel? Was Yahweh's only concern in the Old Testament outward obedience? Why is Yahweh so legalistic in the Old Testament and full of grace in the New Testament?

The first question can be answered initially by stating that although the Israelites offered only animal sacrifices, they received forgiveness of sins (cf. Leviticus 4:20, 26, 31). The apparently contradictory teaching in Hebrews 10:4, which states "for [it is] impossible [for] the blood of bulls and goats to take away sins" (Tr. David Lee Talley) concerns the permanency of the problem of sin. For this problem the blood of Jesus Christ was absolutely essential. The blood of bulls and goats would be ineffective. However, the blood of bulls and goats could bring forgiveness for an offense committed against the Mosaic Law. The "forgiveness" that was granted was on the level of the Mosaic Covenant, that is, it took care of sin on that level. It is not a salvific forgiveness, but rather forgiveness for an offense committed against the stipulations of the Mosaic Law.

The second question is whether Yahweh's only concern in the Old Testament was outward obedience. The Mosaic Law assumed Abrahamic faith as it was founded on the Abrahamic Covenant (Exodus 2:24; 6:4–5; Leviticus 26:42). Sincere obedience to the Law was, then, an outward expression (i.e., obedience) of an inward reality (i.e., faith or love for Yahweh). Out of a deep love for Yahweh, the Israelites were to obey His commands. Jesus summarized the Law in the word "love," that is, love for Yahweh and love for fellow human beings (Matthew 22:34–40). This does not imply simply obedience, but

Matthew 22:34–40

34. But when the Pharisees had heard that he had put the Sadducees to silence, they were gathered together.

35. Then one of them, which was a lawyer, asked him a question, tempting him, and saying,

36. Master, which is the great commandment in the law?

37. Jesus said unto him, Thou shalt love the Lord thy God with all thy heart, and with all thy soul, and with all thy mind.

38. This is the first and great commandment.

39. And the second is like unto it, Thou shalt love thy neighbour as thyself.

40. On these two commandments hang all the law and the prophets.

---

rather the attitude of the heart toward Yahweh and fellow humans. In fact, Jesus condemned the hypocrites—those who were more interested in their own obedience than in expressing their hearts in such a way that the other, whether Yahweh or neighbor, received a taste of goodness (cf. Matthew 23:23). The "weightier provisions" of the Law concerned how the effective work of God (through the Law in a person's life) was experienced by others through relationship, not the degree to which legalistic self-righteous obedience occurred. Yahweh asked for sincere obedience of the heart, not perfunctory religious observance (cf. 1 Samuel 15:22; Joel 2:13, and other prophetic pleas). He did not simply want circumcision of the flesh (this was the outward sign of the covenant), which was outward conformity, but rather circumcision of the heart (cf. Leviticus 26:41; Deuteronomy 10:15–17; 30:6; Jeremiah 4:4; Romans 2:28–29), inward transformation. Throughout the Bible, God calls for genuine heart devotion.

The last question is why is Yahweh so legalistic in the Old Testament and full of grace in the New Testament? Many claim that the Law is a system of works with no grace. Thus, the Old Testament is often referred to as the age of Law and the New Testament as the age of Grace. However, from the very beginning of Yahweh's relationship with Israel, His love and grace are evident (cf. Exodus 2:23–25; 19:3–6; Joel 2:13). In fact, it is His love and grace that provide the basis for the covenant (cf. Deuteronomy 7:6–8; 9:4–6). Israel was the chosen "lover" of Yahweh, but if they wanted to enjoy the blessings of the relationship, they had to demonstrate faithfulness (i.e., treat Yahweh as their "lover"). The Law defined how they could be faithful and express their love. It was not enough for Israel to simply obey the stipulations of the Law, they were to gladly obey in gratitude for all that Yahweh had done on their behalf. Grace is also evidenced in the forgiveness that was available within the Law (cf. Leviticus 4:20, 26, 31).

The Application of the Law to the Contemporary Christian

Is the Law binding on Christians today? This is basically an interpretational issue, and the primary confusion in this area is that Christians will apply some laws but reject others. For example, a Christian might say that homosexuality is wrong and cite Leviticus 18:22, which states, "Do not lie with a man as one lies with a woman; that is detestable." However, that same person might not have any problem wearing a cotton-blend shirt even though Leviticus 19:19 states, "Do not wear clothing woven of two kinds of material." This is obviously inconsistent. All of the laws must be equally binding. However, they are binding for the Christian today in a different manner than they were for the Israelite. The Law was specifically given to the nation of Israel to define how they were to live in relationship with Yahweh as defined by the Mosaic Covenant. The coming of Christ did not nullify the Law, rather Christ fulfilled it. Further, in 2 Timothy 3:16 it states that "all Scripture" is "profitable for doctrine, reproof, correction, and instruction in righteousness." Therefore, the Law continues to play a role in the lives of contemporary Christians.

Although the Law is binding on Christians today, it finds different expression. The Law is now written on the heart (Jeremiah 31:33) and is to be lived as such. Consider the following implications of this. First, many laws are clearly applied to a Christian's life, such as "thou shall not murder" (Exodus 20:13).

Other laws find different expression for Christians. The law, "thou shall not muzzle the ox while he is threshing" (Deuteronomy 25:4; cf. 1 Timothy 5:18 and 1 Corinthians 9:9), is applied metaphorically to Christians as "Let the elders who rule well be considered worthy of double honor, especially those who work hard at preaching and teaching" (1 Timothy 5:17). Sacrifice takes a new expression as Christians are called to present their own bodies as a "living sacrifice, holy and acceptable unto God" (Romans 12:1–2). Finally, still other laws are full of principles that Christians must discern so that they can apply them to their lives. In these cases, Christians have to study the laws, glean the laws' principles, and then apply them to their lives. This is obviously easier for a law such as "Remember the Sabbath day to keep it holy" (Exodus 20:8) than it is for one such as "Do not cook a young goat in its mother's milk" (Exodus 23:19). The central principle for Christians is to have the Law written on their hearts so that it transforms the way they live.

Conclusion

The Mosaic Law, properly understood, does not present as many barriers as students of the Old Testament assume when they first encounter it. It is also not so easily applied in certain instances as might initially be assumed. However, once the basics of the topic are understood, Mosaic Law is fascinating to explore.

David Lee Talley

See also Decalogue; Old Testament

Bibliography

Dillard, Raymond B., and Tremper Longman, III. (1994) *An Introduction to the Old Testament.* Grand Rapids, MI: Zondervan Publishing.

Walton, John. (2000) *A Survey of the Old Testament,* 2nd ed. Grand Rapids, MI: Zondervan Publishing.

Liberalism

Like its Fundamentalist counterpart, liberalism in the United States cannot be conceptualized as a unified historical movement. Lacking a codified set of doctrines and possessing few systematic organizational structures, it has drawn supporters from many denominations. Therefore, liberal theology and its manifestations within American culture are best treated as the aggregate of disparate individuals and groups in support of a number of essential precepts. While contributions to this mind-set have been offered by numerous Catholics and Jews, American Protestantism has led the liberal effort during the past two centuries, with Protestant thinkers often situated as formidable adversaries to conservative Evangelicals and Fundamentalists.

Beginning with early-nineteenth-century Unitarians and Congregationalists, Protestants emphasized the core principle of liberalism—the immanent rather than transcendent nature of the sacred. Later liberal commentators functioning under the influence of newly burgeoned biblical criticism, would augment this theme by suggesting a more historicized approach to Scripture and doctrine that stressed contextual malleability, rather than fixedness. Related issues such as the harmonious relationship between religion and science, the God-ordained progress of the nation, and the necessary involvement of the church within the realm of culture furthered an ideological divide between religious liberals and conservatives.

Early-Nineteenth-Century Roots of the Liberal Tradition

While many early liberal Protestants resisted the embrace of modern culture that was characteristic of later thinkers, their general revolt against Calvinist doctrines of human depravity and the unbreachable separation of this and otherworldly spheres prefaced the birth in America of a more dynamic liberalism to emerge at century's end. At institutions such as Harvard University, theologians frequently took exception to orthodox beliefs of the first Great Awakening, calling for an end to depictions of God as alienated from His Creation and accentuating the notion of universal divine love. The transcendent deity of Calvinism, it was claimed, had created a dissociation between religion and society, relegating religious behavior to a domain of scholasticism that failed to comment upon the valuable role of pious feelings within the realm of the social.

Noting this false divide between sacred and profane, William Ellery Channing (1780–1842), minister of Federal Street (Unitarian) Church in Boston, praised religion's advancement "from the cell of the monk, and the school of verbal disputant, into life and society" (1843: 138). Other early liberals like Horace Bushnell (1802–1876) would echo Channing's call for religion's active engagement with culture, suggesting that entities such as the church and the scientific community should not be at odds. Ultimately, these predecessors to a more fervent liberalism reflected a growing confidence in, rather than denial of, the ability for religious individuals to find redemption and effect change within a worldly realm much maligned by their Calvinist forefathers.

The Birth of Modern Liberalism

Despite these early stirrings, it was not until the 1870s that liberalism became firmly entrenched in American religious life. In a post–Civil War climate that witnessed the emergence of Darwinism and the advent of biblical scholarship utilizing historical and literary methods, threats to accepted understandings of Christian faith abounded. Conservative doctrines intent upon promoting the Genesis account of Creation or the derivation of Scripture from divine inspiration met with significant challenges within this milieu. In addition, late-nineteenth-century American culture faced a gamut of modern changes spawned from industrialization and urbanization. These transformations led many liberals to further emphasize the imperative role of the church in confronting problems of immigration, labor strife, and urban poverty—an emphasis much different from that of traditional Evangelicals who focused the majority of their attention on saving individual souls.

Liberals of the late nineteenth century willingly espoused Christocentric philosophies premised on the conviction that Jesus' role as moral exemplar should overshadow His redemptive sacrifice and atonement for sins. However, these individuals were also crafting apologetics that were meant to ground Christianity within a more secure foundation through the discerning of new religious truths. Henry Ward Beecher (1813–1887), pastor of Plymouth Congregational Church in Brooklyn, was one of the first to disparage a reliance upon ancient doctrines, advocating a "Life School" of pastoral care focused on understanding individuals rather than creeds. Advancing evolutionary theory and sentiments of destined human progress, he proposed that Evangelicals must understand new intellectual premises if they are to effectively speak to their congregations. He wrote in the early 1870s, "If ministers do not make their theological systems conform to the facts as they are; if they do not recognize what men are studying, the time will not be far distant when the pulpit will be like a voice crying in the wilderness" (1889, vol. 1: 88–89). Though not a theologian, Beecher nevertheless echoed the sentiments of New Theology by emphasizing the progress of the kingdom of God made manifest in American civilization and conjoining the natural and supernatural into a unified whole.

By the 1880s, American liberals were growing acquainted with European scholarship through theological training abroad. Of the two preeminent challenges to orthodox theology, Darwinism and the historical critique of the Bible, the latter caused the greatest debate among late-nineteenth-century religious thinkers. The Higher Criticism of theologians such as Friedrich Schleiermacher (1768–1834) buttressed a flourishing trend among liberals to note the conditional rather than timeless nature of Scripture. William Newton Clarke (1840–1912), Baptist theologian at Hamilton (later Colgate) Theological Seminary in New York, published the first systematic treatment of liberal theology. Claiming that the authority of Scripture was not monolithic, Clarke suggested that its prestige did not reside in "minute accuracy of statement," but in "the living and effective conveyance of truth concerning God and Man" (1898: 18, 36). Thus, liberal scholars utilized the techniques of "scientific history" to situate the Bible as a varied anthology compiled over thousands of years. Despite their perceived radical nature, these efforts ultimately sought to preserve Scripture as the chief source of theology by reinterpreting it within modern contexts. Nevertheless, this approach was seen as a substantial challenge for conservative Evangelicals intent on upholding the miraculous content of the Bible, inducing much consternation from those opposed to "hypothesis-weaving and speculation."

Liberalism and the Social Gospel

Darwinism, much maligned by orthodox Christians who viewed it as a call for godless naturalism, met with a variety of interpretations within liberal camps. While resonating with liberalism's embrace of empirical methods, natural selection undermined a teleology premised upon the inherent progress of nature. Therefore, evolutionary theory was often interpreted through a Spencerian lens, with emphasis placed on a developmental model of historical

Selection From: ON THE ELEVATION OF THE LABORING CLASSES, A LECTURE BY WILLIAM ELLERY CHANNING DELIVERED IN BOSTON, MASSACHUSETTS, FEBRUARY 1840

Such are some of the circumstances which inspire hopes of the elevation of the laboring classes. To these might be added other strong grounds of encouragement, to be found in the principles of human nature, in the perfections and providence of God, and in the prophetic intimations of his word. But these I pass over. From all I derive strong hopes for the mass of men. I do not, cannot see, why manual toil and self-improvement may not go on in friendly union. I do not see why the laborer may not attain to refined habits and manners as truly as other men. I do not see why conversation under his humble roof may not be cheered by wit and exalted by intelligence. I do not see why, amidst his toils, he may not cast his eye around him on God's glorious creation, and be strengthened and refreshed by the sight. I do not see why the great ideas which exalt humanity—those of the Infinite Father, of perfection, of our nearness to God, and of the purpose of our being—may not grow bright and strong in the laborer's mind. Society, I trust, is tending towards a condition in which it will look back with astonishment at the present neglect or perversion of human powers. In the development of a more enlarged philanthropy, in the diffusion of the Christian spirit of brotherhood, in the recognition of the equal rights of every human being, we have the dawn and promise of a better age, when no man will be deprived of the means of elevation but by his own fault; when the evil doctrine, worthy of the archfiend, that social order demands the depression of the mass of men, will be rejected with horror and scorn; when the great object of the community will be to accumulate means and influences for awakening and expanding the best powers of all classes; when far less will be expended on the body and far more on the mind; when men of uncommon gifts for the instruction of their race will be sent forth to carry light and strength into every sphere of human life; when spacious libraries, collections of the fine arts, cabinets of natural history, and all the institutions by which the people may be refined and ennobled, will be formed and thrown open to all; and when the toils of life, by a wise intermixture of these higher influences, will be made the instruments of human elevation.

Source: *Harvard Classics Series* (1909).

---

design. Essential for such development was the involvement of the church within society, a call for divine immanence achieved in part from 1870 to 1920 by the Social Gospel movement. A remaking of the social order, motivated by dramatic changes accompanying the rise of the city and the growth of industry, was viewed by many liberals as the only way to ensure the ceaseless advancement of the kingdom of God on earth.

Theodore Munger (1830–1910), within the liberal manifesto *The Freedom of Faith* (1883), defined the New Theology as different from the old based on a number of crucial points. Among a list that included a call for less antagonism between faith and the material world, Munger prescribed a replacement of "excessive individuality" by "a truer view of the solidarity of the race" (1883: 11–44). The substitution of community for individuality was further espoused by Washington Gladden (1836–1918), a Congregationalist minister who published nearly three dozen books calling for cooperation to replace capitalistic competition and advocating the causes of American labor. Baptist minister and theologian Walter Rauschenbusch (1861–1918) became immersed in similar concerns in 1885 as pastor of the Second German Baptist Church in New York City's Hell's Kitchen. Witnessing firsthand the problems of the working class, Rauschenbusch later wrote the most significant document of the movement, *Christianity and Social Crisis* (1907), while teaching at Rochester Theological Seminary in New York. To supplement these scholarly offerings, most major denominations created commissions to confront pressing social issues, and in 1908, the Federal Council of Churches (to become the National Council of Churches in 1950) was formed by liberal Protestant denominations. Perhaps the most familiar response to crisis was the founding of social agencies and settlement houses, best exemplified by Jane Addam's Hull House in Chicago. While sometimes criticized as an effort by middle-class Americans to inculcate Victorian values into a new urban population, the Social Gospel nevertheless demonstrates both the theoretical and practical ways in which liberals sought to actualize a belief in the immanent nature of God.

The Liberal–Fundamentalist Conflict

In the 1910s, with America witnessing the dawn of a distinct theology of Fundamentalism, vociferous critics emerged to challenge liberal theology's hold on mission boards and educational institutions. Works such as William Bell Riley's *The Menace of Modernism* (1917) and J. Gresham Machen's *Christianity and Liberalism* (1923) attacked disbelief in miracles and revelation, the denial of the unique authority of Scripture, and a view of Christ as moral exemplar rather than supernatural Savior. Adding to this rising tide of controversy was a dispensational premillennialist viewpoint held by some Fundamentalists. This belief in the coming of Christ prior to the millennium stood in dire opposition to a progressive view of American social change. Instead of promoting social programs, premillennialists sought to restrain evil as much as possible while waiting for Christ's return. This growing divide between liberalism and orthodoxy led Machen to place the former camp entirely outside the fold of Christianity. As he wrote, "What the liberal theologian has retained after abandoning to the enemy one Christian doctrine after another is not Christianity at all, but a religion which is so entirely different from Christianity as to belong in a distinct category" (1923: 8).

Responses to these Fundamentalist critiques came from a number of prominent liberals. Harry Emerson Fosdick (1878–1969), a Baptist preacher occupying the pulpit of the First Presbyterian Church in New York City, protested the growing intolerance among conservative Christians in his sermon, "Shall the Fundamentalists Win?" (1922). Chiding the dichotomous views of Fundamentalism within a tumultuous historical context that necessitated unity, Fosdick called for an embrace of liberalism's modern and ecumenical perspective. Shailer Matthews (1863–1941), a theologian and educator at the University of Chicago Divinity School, perhaps best represents Protestant modernism during this era. Working out of a university that was considered the liberal headquarters of the country and colluding with like-minded colleagues such as Edward Scribner Ames (1870–1955), Matthews advocated a focus on individual religious experience rather than metaphysical systems. Reiterating the liberal belief that Christian orthodoxy was failing to address the concerns of the age, he wrote in *The Faith of Modernism* (1924), "The world needs new control of nature and society and is told that the Bible is verbally inerrant. It needs a means of composing class strife, and is told to believe in substitutionary atonement. It needs a spirit of love and justice and is told that love without orthodoxy will not save from hell" (1924: 10). The offering of such outmoded doctrines, claimed Matthews, could only result in a tragic dissociation of religion from the world. Despite a liberal push for religious inclusiveness, modernist precepts lead many Fundamentalists to break away from their denominations and form separatist groups intent on preserving conservative theology.

The Waning of Liberalism and Its Continuing Influence

While the Scopes "Monkey Trial" of 1925 marked a victory for liberals over Fundamentalists in the United States, by this date theological liberalism was on the wane. The atrocities of World War I had drastically shaken a faith in the inherent progress of the world. In addition, a liberal reliance upon German biblical scholarship had been taken to task by conservatives who allied it with the moral collapse of that nation, implicating modernist scholars along with the Kaiser. Amplifying this loss of coherence and credibility within liberalism was the rise of neoorthodoxy, a crisis theology that called for a return to Scripture and an acknowledgement of the Bible's authority over individual or social experience. Spawned from the works of Karl Barth (1886–1968) and perpetuated by "realist" thinkers such as Reinhold Niebuhr (1892–1970), neoorthodoxy attempted to reinstate the divide between supernatural and natural, returning to notions of human sinfulness rejected by liberalism. While liberals criticized this new challenge by questioning its abandonment of social justice, the once impassioned reliance upon a progressive "spirit of the age" drew to a close with the dawn of the Great Depression and World War II.

While many scholars view the 1930s as the terminus of religious liberalism in the United States, the ideology's influence continues to be present in a variety of forms. For instance, the methods of Higher Criticism are used at most institutions of higher education. In addition, many denominations have reworked their overarching theology to prioritize hopes for salvation over notions of depravity. Perhaps most important, liberalism's receptiveness to the problems of everyday life crafted a new ministerial mode within mainline Protestantism. From the civil rights movement of the 1950s and 1960s and its fusing of racial justice and piety, to the organization of the Universal Fellowship of Metropolitan Community Churches in 1968 to address ministry to homosexuals, to the multifarious religious dimensions of the women's movement in America, liberals have demonstrated the capacity to retain a belief in divine immanence within a context of rapid social change.

Aaron K. Ketchell

See also Antimodernism; Evolution and Antievolution; Secularism

Bibliography

Beecher, Henry Ward. (1889) *Yale Lectures on Preaching*, 3 vols. New York: Fords, Howard and Hulbert.

Buckham, John W. (1919) *Progressive Religious Thought in America: A Survey of the Enlarging Pilgrim Faith.* Boston: Houghton, Mifflin and Co.

Carpenter, Joel A., ed. (1988) *The Fundamentalist-Modernist Conflict: Opposing Views on Three Major Issues.* New York: Garland Publishing.

———. (1997) *Revive Us Again: The Reawakening of American Fundamentalism.* New York: Oxford University Press.

Cauthen, Kenneth. (1962) *The Impact of American Religious Liberalism.* New York: Harper and Row.

Channing, William E. (1843) *The Works of William E. Channing, D. D.*, 6 vols. Boston: James Munroe and Co.

Clarke, William Newton. (1898) *An Outline of Christian Theology.* New York: C. Scribner's and Sons.

Handy, Robert T., ed. (1966) *The Social Gospel in America, 1870–1920.* New York: Oxford University Press.

Hudson, Winthrop S. (1992) *Religion in America: An Historical Account of the Development of American Religious Life.* New York: Macmillan.

Hutchison, William R., ed. (1968) *American Protestant Thought: The Liberal Era.* New York: Harper and Row.

———. (1976) *The Modernist Impulse in American Protestantism.* Cambridge, MA: Harvard University Press.

King, William McGuire. (1996) "Liberalism." In *The Encyclopedia of American Religious History*, vol. 1, edited by Edward L. Queen II, Stephen R. Prothero, and Gardiner H. Shattuck, Jr. New York: Facts on File, 1129–1145.

Lippy, Charles H. (1996) "Social Christianity." In *The Encyclopedia of American Religious History*, vol. 2, edited by Edward L. Queen II, Stephen R. Prothero, and Gardiner H. Shattuck, Jr. New York: Facts on File, 917–931.

Machen, J. Gresham. (1923) *Christianity and Liberalism.* New York: Macmillan.

Marsden, George M. (1980) *Fundamentalism and American Culture: The Shaping of Twentieth-Century Evangelicalism, 1870–1925.* New York: Oxford University Press.

Matthews, Shailer. (1924) *The Faith of Modernism.* New York: Macmillan.

Munger, Theodore T. (1883) *The Freedom of Faith.* Boston: Houghton, Mifflin and Co.

Rauschenbusch, Walter. ([1907] 1964) *Christianity and the Social Crisis.* New York: Harper and Row.

Riley, William Bell. (1917) *The Menace of Modernism.* New York: Christian Alliance.

Literalism

Literalism is the method of biblical interpretation most often associated with Fundamentalism. It is popularly taken to signify that Scripture must be believed according to the plain meaning of its language as used in ordinary speech. In the event that its meaning contradicts known facts or flies in the face of logic, then the facts are to be disregarded and the logic ignored. An example of this approach would be the often-heard line that while the Bible states a whale swallowed Jonah, it must still be believed if it said that Jonah swallowed the whale. Because literalism is likely to produce such patent absurdities, it is often derided outside of Evangelical circles as credulous, even simpleminded.

This popular conception of literalism is, however, somewhat flawed in that it does not allow for the subtlety that biblical Evangelicals do, in fact, often bring to Scripture. Fundamentalists are as aware as anyone else that certain biblical passages, if taken in their exact grammatical meaning, become risible. Likewise, they are fully aware that much of the Bible, prophecy especially, uses figurative language. While the term *literalism* is commonly used, a more accurate description of Fundamentalist exegesis would be inerrancy. The Bible, it is alleged, never falls into error; but this is different from believing that one must adhere slavishly to its exact grammatical meaning. The distinction between literalism and inerrancy is thus crucial.

The authority of the Bible, heretofore virtually unquestioned in Christendom, was impugned by the Western scientific revolution. Then, in the nineteenth century, the new historico-critical scholarship, pioneered in Germany, demoted the Bible to merely an historical document to be believed or not depending on both external and internal evidence. Thus, even for pious Christians, the veracity of Scripture was under skeptical assault by the nineteenth century. In America, these changes in the intellectual climate prompted many to develop new approaches to biblical exegesis.

Numerous Protestants, such as Horace Bushnell, used linguistic theory and the historico-critical method to abstract spiritual significance from the Bible in lieu of its strict contextual meaning. Where biblical cosmology, that is, the Creation story in Genesis, conflicted with modern science, they concentrated on the imputed moral significance of the biblical narrative and discounted its literal meaning. This approach eventually became the norm in liberal or mainline Protestantism.

During the nineteenth century, however, significant numbers of Protestants rejected any challenge to biblical authenticity, whether based in science or literary criticism. In a high-stakes gamble, they charged the Bible to be utterly true or entirely unreliable. More liberal theologians were aghast at this "all or nothing" approach, which seemed to make the validity of Jesus' ministry hang on the accuracy of Bronze Age cosmology.

The debate over biblical authority was especially crucial to premillennial Evangelicals. Their treasured eschatology depended on a close reading of biblical prophecy. Of all Protestants, they could least afford an exegesis that demoted those texts to inspirational poetry or passé historical documents. Prompted to defend their "literal" interpretation of these essential prophecies, else lose their whole theology, they were backed into a position of likewise insisting on the complete validity of all Scripture.

There were, as well, countless local pastors and laity uninterested in modern science and biblical criticism and exceedingly uncomfortable with any criticism of biblical veracity. There was relatively little debate among such people, for whom a simple reaffirmation along the lines of "the Bible tells me so" sufficed. However, there were also knowledgeable biblical scholars who insisted that modern reservations about the Bible were as meaningless as, one theologian put it, flecks of sandstone in the marble of the Parthenon. The intellectual center of such scholarship, down to the end of the nineteenth century, was Princeton University.

Despite popular stereotypes, biblical literalists never asserted that the Bible must be read in a mindlessly grammatical fashion. They made ample allowance for the nonliteral meaning of its language and frequently quarreled vehemently over its proper interpretation. They parted company with their liberal counterparts in their belief that the Bible was free of error. It might, indeed, be confusing or ambiguous and reasonable men might differ on its meaning; however, confusion in the mind of the reader did not impugn the text.

Throughout the nineteenth century, conservative Protestants, especially among the premillennialists, steadily developed their own theories of biblical inerrancy. Easily regarded as a pigheaded refusal to acknowledge contemporary science, it was at least as much a serious academic endeavor to exposit an alternative approach to sacred literature. By the end of the century, a considerable scholarship had evolved that supported an inerrant Bible and if it was unconvincing to many it was far from intellectually negligible.

In the early twentieth century, differences between those wedded to biblical inerrancy, now called Fundamentalists, and liberal Protestants exploded into open warfare. The resultant conflict edified no one. Liberal savants, such as the Rev. Ralph Emerson Fosdick, were scathing toward biblical literalism, such as in his essay "Shall the Fundamentalists Win?" Hurt and bewildered by this attack on their religion, Fundamentalists were at least as intemperate in their response. The 1925 Scopes "Monkey Trial" so exposed conservative Evangelicals to such withering ridicule that the chasm between mainline and Fundamentalist faiths over biblical authority became unbridgeable. It remains so to this day.

By the early twenty-first century, an inerrant Bible was at the core of much Evangelical belief. It was the approach taken by such popular media-savvy pastors as the Rev. Billy Graham and was taught in Evangelical seminaries. A considerable ally was recruited to the Fundamentalist cause with the rise of Pentecostalism, which relied heavily on strict adherence to the Acts of the Apostles. These Evangelicals posited unique interpretations of scientific evidence, such as "Creation Science," in lieu of most contemporary cosmology and biology. In nearly all scholarly circles, these interpretations were ridiculed or ignored. Although more subtle than its critics allow, Fundamentalist biblical inerrancy lacks respect in secular academic circles.

Robert K. Whalen

See also Biblical Criticism; Biblical Inerrancy; Prophecy

Bibliography

Boone, Kathleen C. (1989) *The Bible Tells Them So: The Discourse of Protestant Fundamentalism.* Albany: SUNY Press.

Bushnell, Horace. (1965) *Horace Bushnell*, edited by H. Shelton Smith. New York: Oxford University Press.

Hatch, Nathan O., and Mark A. Noll. (1982) *The Bible In America: Essays in Cultural History.* New York: Oxford University Press.

Marsden, George. (1982) *Fundamentalism and American Culture.* New York: Oxford University Press.

Lord's Supper

The Lord's Supper refers to the New Testament event (Matthew 26:26; Mark 14:22–26; Luke 22:14–20)

where Jesus Christ convened His disciples on the night He was betrayed to partake and participate both in His body and His blood. Symbolically and sacramentally, His body was represented with bread and His blood with wine. The Lord's Supper is also referred to as the Eucharist (from the Greek word *eucharisteo* meaning "to give thanks") in more traditional Christian churches and Communion or Mass in Catholic and Angelical traditions.

It is clear from other New Testament passages that the apostles perpetuated the Lord's Supper and it became an ordinance (cf. sacrament) in the early church. The apostle Paul writes in 1 Corinthians that he understands the command "to do this in remembrance" of Christ (11:24–25) because by the partaking of the Lord's Supper the community was "proclaiming the Lord's death" until His Second Coming (11:26). Paul continues to add prohibitions and admonitions concerning the reverence of this ordinance (11:27–32).

In Genesis 14:18, the high priest Melchizedek brings forth bread and wine to Abraham as a blessing from God. In acknowledgment of this blessing Abraham offers to God a tenth of all he owns. The author of the Books of Hebrews testifies that Jesus Christ is our eternal High Priest in the order of Melchizedek (Hebrews 6:20ff). Certainly, this Old Testament typology of both the elements and of Jesus' priesthood is not coincidental. Rather, it must be seen as a significant signpost of the future offering of Christ's body and blood.

The Gospel of John gives one of the clearest and most theological interpretations of the Lord's Supper, yet strangely it is overlooked by most theologians. There, Jesus identifies Himself as "The bread of Life" (6:48) and says "Whoever eats my flesh and drinks my blood remains in him, and I in him" (6:56, NIV). As Christ offers Himself to communicants as body and blood, bread and wine, believers mutually participate with Christ.

Major Views on Significance and Meaning

There is much debate over the significance of the Lord's Supper. One of the perennial debates is whether the elements (bread and wine) are simply symbolic of Christ's body and blood or if there is a mystical transformation of the elements into the real presence of Christ. The point of controversy is over how literal Christ's words, "This is my body," are to be interpreted. The four historical views follow.

John 6:48–56

48. I am that bread of life.

49. Your fathers did eat manna in the wilderness, and are dead.

50. This is the bread which cometh down from heaven, that a man may eat thereof, and not die.

51. I am the living bread which came down from heaven: if any man eat of this bread, he shall live for ever: and the bread that I will give is my flesh, which I will give for the life of the world.

52. The Jews therefore strove among themselves, saying, How can this man give us his flesh to eat?

53. Then Jesus said unto them, Verily, verily, I say unto you, Except ye eat the flesh of the Son of man, and drink his blood, ye have no life in you.

54. Whoso eateth my flesh, and drinketh my blood, hath eternal life; and I will raise him up at the last day.

55. For my flesh is meat indeed, and my blood is drink indeed.

56. He that eateth my flesh, and drinketh my blood, dwelleth in me, and I in him.

Catholicism tends to see the elements as transfiguring into the real presence of Christ. In this view, called transubstantiation, the bread and wine are changed into the *actual* body and blood of Christ. This event of transfiguration occurs, and only occurs, as an ordained priest consecrates the elements (sacerdotalism). All participants in the Lord's Supper literally partake of the real body and blood of Christ although the appearance of the bread and wine remain unchanged. The Council of Trent (1545–1563) affirmed this position as official Roman Catholic dogma. Like Romanism, Greek Orthodoxy sees the Lord's Supper as the focal point of Christian worship, but where the former understands the event as centered on Christ's death and Resurrection, the latter sees the Second Coming of Christ as the theological center.

The Lutheran view is similar to the Catholic view in that Martin Luther (1483–1546) took seriously Jesus' words. His view, called consubstantiation, differs from Rome's in that the bread and wine *interpenetrate* the body and blood of Christ. In this manner, the elements contain or coexist with (*con-*) Christ. Luther rejected sacerdotalism because it put the primacy of the transformation in the spoken words of the priest. For Luther, Christ alone is efficient to consecrate the bread and wine, although the administration of the Lord's Supper should be by an ordained minister.

Ulrich Zwingli (1484–1531) and John Calvin (1509–1564) are thought to be the proponents of the Reformed view, although arguably their views differed (Hodge 1995: 626ff). Nonetheless, the Reformed view understands the bread and wine as *spiritually* contained in the body and blood of Christ. The participant communes with Christ through the partaking of the bread and wine by means of the power and presence of the Holy Spirit. It is in and through the Holy Spirit that Christ's real presence is exhibited in the communicant as a means of grace. This position is found in the Westminster Confession of Faith.

Calvin's view was quite similar to Zwingli's in that he understood Christ not to be present in the elements. Rather, the bread and wine are *representative* of Christ and function as a reminder of His death and Resurrection. It is by faith that the individual receives the benefits of Christ. The presence of Christ, either literally or spiritually, is not to be found in the bread and wine.

Lord's Supper and Fundamentalism

It is difficult to identify Fundamentalism's interpretation of the Lord's Supper because it is a complex movement over many decades and this doctrine is not considered one of the Fundamentals. Generally, in the early part of the movement the reformed traditions would have adhered to the Westminster Confession of Faith when interpreting the Lord's Supper. The sacrament is understood as the mystical communion of Christ with His body, the church, whereby He departs His grace and spiritual gifts by means of His Holy Spirit.

The fourth view—the bread and wine being *representative* of Christ—is the most common in Evangelicalism and Fundamentalism. Rejecting the language of sacrament, this ordinance or institution of Christ is understood as having a commemorative and proclamative effect as it evokes the death and Resurrection of Christ. There is no real presence of Christ in the bread and wine, they merely serve as symbols or signs to remind and proclaim to the believer Christ's death and Resurrection. This is evident in the frequency in which the local church institutes the Lord's Supper, which can be quarterly or yearly. Congregations aligning themselves more with the Calvinistic or Lutheran interpretations typically offer the Lord's Supper monthly or even weekly. Given Fundamentalism's avoidance of alcohol, grape juice is typically used in place of wine in the feast of the Lord's Supper, in contrast with liturgical churches (e.g., Roman Catholic, Anglican, and Episcopalian), which use wine.

Robert T. Leach

See also Jesus; Resurrection (Christ); Westminster Confession

Bibliography

Beveridge, Henry, tr. (1989) "Calvin, John." In *Institutes of the Christian Religion*, reprint ed. Grand Rapids, MI: Wm. B. Eerdmans, 555–621.

Chafer, Lewis Sperry. (1948) *Systematic Theology*. Dallas: Dallas Theological Press.

Erikson, Millard. (1985) *Christian Theology*. Grand Rapids, MI: Baker House Books.

Hodge, Charles. (1995) *Systematic Theology*, Vol. III. Grand Rapids, MI: Wm. B. Eerdmans.

Torrance, Thomas F. (1962) "Doctrinal Consensus on Holy Communion." *Scottish Journal of Theology* 15: 1–35.

Westminster Confession of Faith. (1646) Electronic version © 1991 by BibleWorks, L.L.C.

Zizioulas, John. (1994) "The Eucharist and the Kingdom of God (Part 1)." *Sourozh* 58: 1–12.

Love

The theme of love pervades the Bible—the love of God, God's love for those who believe in Him, and the love people are expected to have for one another. The covenant that exists between God and His people is a central concept in both the Old Testament and the New Testament. This covenant is at the core of Fundamentalism's strict view of what constitutes love.

Love in the Hebrew Scriptures

The Psalms sum up the notion of love in the Old Testament or Hebrew Scriptures. In the words of the psalmist, "He determines the number of the stars and calls them each by name. Great is our Lord and mighty in power; his understanding has no limit ... the Lord delights in those who fear him, who put their hope in his unfailing love" (Psalms 147:4, 5, 11, NJB).

The notion of the unfailing love of God for those who follow His ways and respect His laws is found throughout the Hebrew Scriptures. It is repeated in numerous passages and variations. Deuteronomy 11:27–28, for example, promises "a blessing, if you obey the commandments of the Lord your God ... and a curse, if you will not obey." The case of Jacob, who depends upon himself rather than God, provides an example of the manner in which "poetic justice" illustrates the way that rewards, or punishments, flow from a person's actions. "Jacob" translates as "supplanter," or more generally as "deceiver," from the manner in which he took his twin's place. In fact, Jacob became renowned for his scheming. He met up with his own uncle, who surpassed him in being a master of deception (Genesis 29:4–30). Similarly, when the Israelites are reported to have desired idolatry, they found themselves in Babylon (Exodus 20:3–4; Deuteronomy 11:28–30). Therefore, when people fail to follow the love of God, they are given something according to their nature: "I judged them according to their conduct and their actions" (Deuteronomy 36:19). The Hebrew Scriptures expect that the person who believes in God will be generous because God is seen as being generous toward His people (Malachi 3:10). This generosity shows itself in sharing with those who are in need. Goods are given to people who are generous because they know how to use those goods to help the community. The contractual relationship of love is in keeping with the notion of the covenant.

The Hebrew word for "covenant" is *briyth*, which refers to a compact between two people. It depends on each party living up to the terms of the compact: "But God said, 'No, but Sarah, your wife shall bear you a son, and you shall call his name Isaac; and I will establish My covenant with him for an everlasting covenant for his descendants after him'" (Genesis 17:19). A covenant, moreover, is conditional. Thus, to receive the love of God, one must give love to others: "Now then, if you will indeed obey My voice and keep My covenant, then you shall be My own possession among all the peoples . . . "(Exodus 19:5). Love, then, was part of the agreement the Hebrew people made with God: "Know therefore that the Lord your God, He is God, the faithful God, who keeps His covenant and His loving kindness to a thousandth generation with those who love Him and keep His commandments but repays those who hate Him, to their faces, to destroy them; He will not delay with him who hates Him, He will repay him to his face" (Deuteronomy 7:9–10). Love is part of the strict justice that figures so prominently in the Hebrew Scriptures.

New Testament and Love

The New Testament builds upon the Old Testament notion of love, as it does with so many other ideas. Jesus, for example, sums up the entire law in stating that people must love God and their neighbor. Everything else flows from that command. When Jesus was asked what is the greatest commandment, He replied, "Thou shalt love the Lord thy God with all thy heart, and with all thy soul, and with all thy mind. This is the first and great commandment. And the second is like unto it, Thou shalt love thy neighbor as thyself. On these two commandments hang all the law and the prophets" (Matthew 22:37–40). St. Augustine paraphrases these words in stating that people should love God and do what they will—because a person who loves God will only do what is right.

What has come to be known as The Sermon on the Mount—most likely a collection from a number of Jesus' sermons—summarizes Jesus' message of love. The basic theme is love of God and neighbor. The fact that the Sermon is set on a mountain, or hill, signifies a contact with God. Jesus began the Sermon by saying that God will provide what people need. It is the task of humans to seek the Kingdom of God and God's justice. Thus, the Sermon on the Mount, as presented in the Gospels, stresses that those people are blessed who are meek, pure in heart, and otherwise as trusting as children. And, as trusting children, they will perform the good works that their father enjoins on them. Thus, love of God leads to love of neighbor and is expressed through deeds.

Commentators note that love reflects the love that God has for His people (Matthew 6:12, 14, 15). The love that a Christian gives others is an expression of the love that God has for His people. The Sermon on the Mount especially emphasizes this point. The Lord's Prayer (Our Father), for example, states, "Forgive us our debts as we forgive our debtors" (Matthew 6:12). Proof that a person is forgiven, in other words, is demonstrated in that person's willingness to forgive others. In the Sermon on the Mount, Jesus notes that the spirit of the Law of Moses is love. All the regulations that had grown around it tended to obscure the spirit of the law.

There are many types of love. *Agape*, meaning "love feast," is the Greek word for relational love; that is, love that is returned. It is nonerotic love, founded on moral loyalties, on benevolence, and wishing another well. The "love feast" so prominent in Fundamentalist beliefs is based on agape. For the Fundamentalist, this love is grounded in the very nature of God. One John (4:9) says, "By this the love (agape) of God was manifested in us, that God has sent His only begotten Son into the world so that we might live through Him." The Beatitudes begin with the relationship of humans with God and the rest concern relationships with one another. In sum, the basic idea of love of God and love of neighbor as one's self is repeated. Paul expands on the theme of love in this way: "Love is patient, love is kind. It does not envy, it does not boast, it is not proud. It is not rude, it is not self-seeking, it is not easily angered, it keeps no record of wrongs. Love does not delight in evil but rejoices with the truth. (1 Corinthians 13:4–6)

Peter presents a version that is in harmony with Paul's, but returns to the basic idea of a covenant, one of the basic themes of Fundamentalists: "All of you, live in harmony with one another; be sympathetic, love as brothers, be compassionate and humble. Do not repay evil with evil or insult with insult, but with blessing, because to this you were called so that you may inherit a blessing" (1 Peter 3:8–9).

Fundamentalism and Love

The Fundamentalist view of love is in conformity with their general organizational principles. They believe that there is a membership chosen by God and that these members are sharply distinguished from people in other groups. The leaders of the group are authoritarian, in imitation of God, and provide clear-cut boundaries on behavior. Only those who follow all these principles are worthy of God's love. That love is conditional, based on the principle of the covenant from the Hebrew Scriptures. Love is often expressed through condemnation of false teachers, fallen-away Christians, and the world. For the Fundamentalist, the world is inherently evil, and those who love God must hate the world.

Fundamentalists view unconditional love as weak, as a violation of the covenant. For them, true love is relational and conditional. It can only exist in justice in which both parties are faithful to their basic commitments. To love someone who has defaulted smacks of liberalism and weakness, and liberalism is a key enemy of the Fundamentalist. It is considered a weak movement that would do greater harm than good through its compromises. For the Fundamentalist, love must be tough, for it is not love to allow a sinner to continue in error and risk the loss of his or her immortal soul. Fellowship is not possible with those who fail to live up to their obligations. Instead, love is found in the process of correcting the sinner's errors and praying for that sinner to repent.

The Fundamentalist believes that people who really do "speak the truth in love" are those whom liberals and modernists accuse of being deficient in love. They quote Paul's statement," Am I become your enemy because I tell you the truth? (Galatians 4:16). Fundamentalism teaches that speaking the truth to correct those in error is, in fact, a means to show love to them. Compromise with error—moral, secular, or in teaching—is the antithesis of love. For the Fundamentalist, truth is found in a literal interpretation of Scripture. Therefore, there is a great deal of error in the teaching and behavior of other Christians. There is a kind of Manichaean tendency to their thought, dividing reality into good and evil. The world is evil while the Kingdom of God is good. Creation appears to be evil in itself and therefore people cannot take joy in the things of this world, much less love them.

Broader social concerns are not of importance to the Fundamentalist. Rather, personal salvation and private morality are of overriding importance. Free-market ideas and even authoritarian regimes may be to the Fundamentalist's liking because he or she can compel people to be "good," or at least to act in a manner that is deemed good by the Fundamentalist. To act in accord with God's precepts is to earn His love; hence, harsh measures are really loving ones.

This perspective is one that theologians term a "Church of Law," contrasting it with a "Church of Love." In the first, sharp distinctions are drawn between the "saved" and the "unsaved." A God of judgment and wrath is prominent in the worship of this church. In the Church of Love all people are children of a loving God. This God issues a call to people to aid those who are in need and suffering. He also desires an end to hatred and prejudice.

Critics of Fundamentalism state that it views love as weak. To be strong, love and truth need to be united; otherwise, love degenerates into a weak liberalism that is blind to sin and evil. These critics state that the Fundamentalists desire a God who can smite His enemies and punish them for their evil ways. Yet, most Fundamentalists reject a truth without love approach. Arguing that if the first approach is weak, the second is too legalistic, they stress the need for love to temper justice. Fundamentalists who embrace the love and truth approach quote the following passages of the Bible: "Beloved, let us love one another; for love is of God, and he who loves is born of God and knows God. He who does not love does not know God; for God is love" (1 John 4:7–8)."Beloved, if God so loved us, we also ought to love one another. No man has ever seen God; if we love one another, God abides in us . . . "(1 John 4:11–12).

True love to the Fundamentalist is an interest in and a concern for another person as a person. That love is not unconditional; it has responsibilities, including the obligation to help that person save his or her soul. Judgment and even condemnation is inherent in God's love. To save someone it is sometimes necessary to hate that which threatens the loved one's life.

Frank A. Salamone

Bibliography

Almond, Gabriel, Emmanuel Sivan, and R. Scott Appleby. (1995) "Fundamentalism: Genus and Species." In *Fundamentalisms Comprehended*, edited by Martin E. Marty and R. Scott Appleby. Chicago: University of Chicago Press, 399–424.

Armstong, Karen. (2000) *The Battle for God*. New York: Alfred A. Knopf.

Beale, David O. (1986) *In Pursuit of Purity: American Fundamentalism since 1850*. Greenville, SC: Unusual Publications.

Carpenter, Joel A. (1997) *Revive Us Again*. New York: Oxford University Press.

Dalhouse, Mark Taylor. (1996) *An Island in the Lake of Fire: Bob Jones University, Fundamentalism, and the Separatism Movement*. Athens: University of Georgia Press.

Hadden, Jeffrey K. (1992) "Religious Fundamentalism." In *Encyclopedia of Sociology*, edited by Edgar F. Borgatta and Marie Borgatta. New York: Macmillan, 3: 1637–1642.

Lawrence, Bruce. (1989) *Defenders of God: The Fundamentalist Revolt Against the Modern Age*. San Francisco: Harper and Row.

Marty, Martin, and R. Scott Appleby. (1991) *Fundamentalisms Observed. The Fundamentalism Project*, vol. 1, edited by Martin R. Marty and R. Scott Appleby. Chicago: University of Chicago Press.

Marty, Martin, and R. Scott Appleby. (1993) *Fundamentalisms and Society. The Fundamentalism Project*, vol. 2, edited by Martin R. Marty and R. Scott Appleby. Chicago: University of Chicago Press.

Nielsen, Niels S. (1993) *Fundamentalism, Mythos, and World Religions*. Albany, NY: SUNY Press.

Woodberry, Robert D., and Christian S. Smith. (1998) "Fundamentalism et al.: Conservative Protestants in America." *Annual Review of Sociology* 24: 25–56.

Mahdi

At once an apocalyptic dream, an eschatological process, a centennial event, and a fervent hope, the term "Mahdi" has come to encompass a number of meanings in Islamic belief. The Mahdi, an Arabic term that translates as "the guided one," is a relatively late development in Islamic belief. The term is not mentioned in the Qur'an, and appears first in the Hadiths (noninspired traditions of the Prophet), where it is attributed most reliably to Muhammad ibn al-Hanafiyyah, a traditionalist who resisted the imposition of kingship on the Islamic community under the Ummayads (661 CE). This context is important because it is believed that the Mahdi, like eschatological figures in Christianity and Judaism, will give refuge to the weak and the oppressed, assure divine justice in this world, and establish peace, power, and prosperity in the posthistorical world to come. In the Hadiths, the promise of the Mahdinate was to restore Islam to its original purity under the Prophet.

As a refuge for the oppressed, the complex of beliefs surrounding the Mahdi were the most developed in Twelver Shi'ism, where the Mahdi was identified with the Twelfth Imam, who was named Muhammad but who is known in Shi'ite belief as "the Awaited Mahdi" (al-Mahdi-l-Muntazar). The Twelfth Imam went into occultation in 873 CE, and the eschatological scenario that surrounded him fell into a pattern that would be immediately familiar to both Christianity and Judaism. At some future time, when the earth becomes full to bursting with sin and corruption, the Twelfth Imam as Mahdi will return, for a time, to defeat evil and establish a reign of jus-

tice on the earth. However, this reign will be interrupted by the appearance of al-Dajjal, the cyclops-like Islamic antichrist figure. The evil of the Dajjal will bring about a final battle of good versus evil whereby the Dajjal will be defeated by the heavenly host led by a returned Jesus (Isa), bringing to an end historical time.

The Mahdi is an important concept in Sunni Islam as well. In one belief, the Mahdi is a figure who, in accord with the promise of the Prophet, will reappear every one hundred years to purify and redeem the Islamic community (Ummah). This belief has inspired pretenders to the title to spectacular acts of resistance. The most successful Mahdi figure of the modern era was the Sudanese religious teacher and revolutionary leader, Muhammad Ahmad ibn as Sayyid Abd Allah, who in 1880 proclaimed himself Mahdi. In 1882 he declared a jihad (religious struggle) against the Anglo-Egyptian colonial government of the time. Deeming his followers to be *Ansar* (companions) and assuring them of God's promise of victory, the forces of the Mahdi swept to power in 1884, most famously defeating and beheading the British commander Charles George Gordon. Once in power, the Mahdi established Islamic law (Sharia) and undertook a strict Islamization of Sudanese society while promising to spread the jihad to all parts of the Islamic world. However, he became rather too addicted to the pleasures of the harem, and the jihad remained yet another of the broken redemptive promises that litter the history of the Islamic world. Today, the descendants of Muhammad Ahmad, taking the family name of al-Mahdi, remain one of the most important political clans in the nation.

Nearly one hundred years later, the latest claimant of the title of Mahdi was revealed during the dramatic and bloody seizure of the Grand Mosque in Mecca in 1979. On 20 November 1979, a group of armed revolutionaries led by Mohammad ibn Saif al-Otaybi killed the Saudi guards and proclaimed over the Mosque's loudspeaker system the appearance of a new Mahdi in the person of his brother. Little is known of this Mahdi, who was killed when Saudi Royal Guards stormed the Mosque. Juhayma, however, was the leader of the revolt, which was ultimately crushed only after French troops were airlifted into the Mosque, in violation of Islamic law, which forbids non-Muslims from setting foot in the Sacred Precincts. In the end, the mission of this Mahdi had no more impact on the course of the Islamic world than had that of the Sudanese Mahdi, and the Islamic Ummah, Sunni, and Shi'i alike, must wait still longer for a surcease of the oppression of this world.

Jeffrey Kaplan

See also Shi'a Islam

Bibliography

Jafri, S. H. M. (1979) *The Origins and Early Development of Shi'a Islam.* Beirut:Libraieri du Liban.

Kechichian, Joseph A. (1990) "Islamic Revivalism and Change in Saudi Arabia: Juhayman al-'Utaybi's 'Letters' to the Saudi People." *Muslim World* 80, 1 (Jan.).

Lacey, Robert. (1981) *The Kingdom: Arabia and the House of Sa'ud.* New York: Avon Books.

Lapidus, Ira M. (1988) *A History of Islamic Societies.* Cambridge, UK: Cambridge University Press.

Momen, Moojan. (1985) *An Introduction To Shi'i Islam.* New Haven, CT: Yale University Press.

Sachedina, Abdulaziz Abdulhussein. (1981) *Islamic Messianism.* Albany: SUNY Press.

Male Headship

Proper relations between men and women are a central concern for Fundamentalists. There are several doctrines that govern gender relations but none is more crucial than the doctrine of "headship." This teaching is based on several biblical passages, such as, "wives be subject to your husband as you are to the Lord. For the husband is the head of the wife just as Christ is the head of the church, the body of which he is the Savior. Just as the church is subject to Christ, so also wives ought to be, in everything, to their husbands" (Ephesians 5:22–24, RSV). Also, "wives be subject to your husbands as is fitting in the Lord" (Colossians 3:18).

Most Fundamentalists teach that husbands are to provide leadership for their families, that is, they are to exercise headship. Most often this has meant that spiritual direction for the family is the responsibility of husbands and fathers and that final decision-making power resides with husbands. The corollary teaching is the doctrine of women's submission, drawn from the same texts.

In practice, headship and submission take a variety of forms. Some Fundamentalists take these doctrines very seriously and attempt to apply them in detail to daily reality. Every family decision of any significance is made by the husband/father. Certain Fundamentalist families divide tasks according to those that are seen as leadership and those that are seen as support functions, such as the handling of family finances. These families believe that it is the man's role as head to handle the family finances, whereas in other families such tasks are considered clerical work and therefore assigned to the wife. Headship is interpreted in primarily spiritual terms and it becomes the central responsibility of the husband/father to give the family spiritual direction, such as leading family devotions, and other duties.

In still other contexts, Judith Stacey (1990) has found what she calls "patriarchy in the last resort." The husband may be the head of the home with final decision-making authority in Fundamentalist families but, in light of the fact that he is obligated to consider his wife's opinions, desires, and needs (as a loving leader would), he is never permitted to "lord it over her." The result is assent to the idea that "if it comes to it" he must make the final decisions. However, that assent is tempered by the reality that it doesn't "come to it," because if it did that would be evidence that he was not "lovingly leading his family."

While the headship–submission relationship is most often understood to apply to husbands and wives, some, more extreme Fundamentalists argue that there are implications of this doctrine, based on the created natures of men and women, that are applicable to society in general. In an important work laying out "biblical" gender relations, Piper and Grudem (1991) argue that because, in their view,

Ephesians 5:22–25

22. Wives, submit yourselves unto your own husbands, as unto the Lord.
23. For the husband is the head of the wife, even as Christ is the head of the church: and he is the saviour of the body.
24. Therefore as the church is subject unto Christ, so let the wives be to their own husbands in every thing.
25. Husbands, love your wives, even as Christ also loved the church, and gave himself for it;

Colossians 3:18–19

18. Wives, submit yourselves unto your own husbands, as it is fit in the Lord.
19. Husbands, love your wives, and be not bitter against them.

---

men are created to lead and women are created to submit, any time women are placed in authority over men it not only violates the doctrine of headship but also the essential natures of both the man and the woman. Fundamentalists of this sort believe that there ought to be specific roles in society designated for men and women, respectively.

This so-called traditionalist perspective, however, is not the only one found within Fundamentalist circles. Since the 1970s there has been an active feminist movement that has argued that, correctly interpreted, the Bible requires equality and "mutual submission" in marriage. Such feminists point out that the Bible places husbands as the "heads" of their wives in a way that parallels Christ's headship over the church. Since Christ's "headship" led to the ultimate act of submission (the giving up of his own life) the "real" meaning of this text, in their view, is that all Christians are to submit to one another—especially so for husbands and wives. While only a minority viewpoint in popular circles, this perspective holds much sway in elite circles (authors, publishers, schools, etc.) and has impacted the ways in which even traditionalist Fundamentalists understand headship.

This issue has become one of the most contentious for Fundamentalists and it has broad symbolic significance. In many circles assent to this doctrine (as repugnant as it is in the secular world) has become a badge of allegiance to Fundamentalism. For example, as Fundamentalists solidified their hold on the Southern Baptist Convention, they used gender issues to draw boundary lines: specifically, among several gender-related resolutions adopted, one admonished wives to submit to their husbands'

headship. Even in the case of "patriarch in the last resort," Fundamentalist men and women who embrace headship and submission at a theological level mark themselves as loyal insiders against the outside world of the unsaved.

For traditionalists meaning comes for women via their gendered roles of wife and mother and for men via their gendered roles of leader and provider. Everyday activities become significant when they are seen as part of a cosmic plan. The hierarchical structure of gender relations replicates a hierarchically ordered universe in which God is sovereign and each aspect of creation is assigned a place in the chain of authority. By fulfilling appropriate roles in a gendered dualism, men and women mirror the cosmic reality of the relationship between Christ and the church, God and creation. Chaos is kept at bay.

Julie J. Ingersoll

See also Antifeminism

Bibliography

Bushnell, Katherine C. (n.d.) *God's Word to Women*. North Collins, NY: Ray B. Munson.

Gilder, George. (1986) *Men and Marriage*. Gretna, LA: Pelican Publishing.

Harding, Susan. (2000) *The Book of Jerry Falwell*. Princeton, NJ: Princeton University Press.

Piper, John, and Wayne Grudem. (1991) *Recovering Biblical Manhood and Womanhood*. Wheaton, IL: Crossway Books.

Rice, John R. (1941) *Bobbed Hair, Bossy Wives, and Women Preachers*. Murfreesboro, TN: Sword of the Lord Publishers.

Stacey, Judith. (1990) *Brave New Families: Stories of Domestic Upheaval in Late Twentieth Century America.* San Francisco: BasicBooks.

———, and Susan Elizabeth Gerard. (1990) "'We are Not Doormats': The Influence of Feminism on Contemporary Evangelicals in the United States." In *Uncertain Terms: Negotiating Gender in American Culture*, edited by Faye Ginsberg and Anna Lowenhaupt Tsing. Boston: Beacon Press.

Mark of the Beast

One of the more enigmatic verses of the Bible, Revelations 13:18 (NIV) presents an age-old riddle that apocalypticists, propagandists, and in recent years, popular entertainers have tried without success to fathom. The verse warns: "This calls for wisdom. If anyone has insight, let him calculate the number of the beast, for it is man's number. His number is 666."

The Antichrist figure marked by 666 is associated most commonly with the Roman emperor Nero Caesar, persecutor of the early Christian community, whose name in Hebrew letters translates to 666, the numerical value equivalent of the Beast of Revelations. When Nero died, however, historical time did not end, Jesus did not return in glory, and the hunt for the "real" Antichrist of Revelations began in earnest. No subsequent generation would be without villains thought to carry the Mark of the Beast and who would thus, in due time, assume the appointed eschatological role of the Antichrist.

The utility of the epithet "Antichrist" needs little explication here. Where once the term was attached to pagan persecutors, it was seamlessly transformed into the common coin of medieval Christian polemic. Heretical sects held the pope of the day to be the dread Beast of Revelations, and the papacy was not loath to respond in kind. With the Reformation, the Mark of the Beast was held by many Lutherans to be carried by Pope Leo X, while for many of his Catholic opponents, Luther himself seemed to be the living embodiment of the Antichrist's timeless evil.

Although the Mark of the Beast is a belief system most associated with Christianity, it should be noted that in Islam, the figure of al-Dajjal has marked similarities to the Beast of Revelations. Based on the Hadith literature, al-Dajjal is conceived as an eschatological figure similarly marked by deformity, most commonly, a cyclopsian eye in the center of his forehead. The Dajjal was once much feared in Islam, and more recently serves as a figure of fear for naughty children. Islam, however, did not use the belief in the same polemical sense as did Christianity.

Today, the Mark of the Beast 666 continues to fascinate, although it is taken most seriously only in the more religious realms of American conspiracy theory. Even the most cursory Internet search on the number 666 will produce a proliferation of pages dedicated to the proposition that the Mark of the Beast may be found in Social Security numbers, scanner bar codes, and most recently, tattoos favored by twenty-something wannabe rebels without a particular cause. More seriously, some high-profile Fundamentalist and Evangelical ministers—Pat Robertson comes most to mind—have revived the practice of utilizing the Mark of the Beast as polemic, speculating that this or that world leader, or more grandly, processes such as globalization under the rubric of the "New World Order," are the fulfillment of the dread prophesy of Revelations 13:18.

Jeffrey Kaplan

See also Antichrist; Beast, The

Bibliography

Bousset, William. (1896) *The Antichrist Legend.* London: Hutchison and Co.

Halperin, David J. (1976) "The Ibn Sayyad Traditions and the Legend of Al-Dajjal." *JAOS* 96, 2 (April–June): 213–225.

McGinn, Bernard. (1994) *Antichrist: Two Thousand Years of the Human Fascination with Evil.* New York: HarperSanFrancisco.

Media, Mass

The relationship between Fundamentalism and the mass media is a curious one. While many Christian Fundamentalists in the United States routinely criticize mass media industries, citing their perceived role as secularizing agents in American society, Fundamentalist groups are generally adept at exploiting the mass media for evangelistic purposes. In fact, Christian Fundamentalists are often among the most professional, talented, and technologically savvy of media producers, carefully crafting publications, radio and television programs, and Internet websites to appeal to nationwide audiences. Capable use of mass media has ironically made many Fundamentalist media organizations and the messages they distribute more a reflection of the consumerism that pervades American culture than most Fundamentalists would either recognize or admit.

American Evangelicalism and Mass Media

Christian Fundamentalists' utilization of the mass media is not a recent phenomenon. Since the settlement of the American colonies, Evangelical leaders have relied on advertised public gatherings to rally the faithful and spread the message to the unconverted. During the First Great Awakening in the eighteenth century, skillful preachers such as George Whitefield helped forge a more open environment for evangelical Christianity, eroding the strength of the established churches by arguing that individuals could directly petition God for forgiveness and blessings. Whitefield accomplished this through a forceful, charismatic personality that appealed to mass sentiment. The succeeding Second Great Awakening of the early nineteenth century escalated this trend. Influential on the frontier, this second great Evangelical revival fostered the growth of numerous sects and denominations within American Protestantism. Moreover, by emphasizing the emotional experience of salvation rather than doctrinal details, the movement attracted a broader audience. Whereas early Protestant reformers such as Martin Luther lauded education as an integral part of faith, American Evangelicalism reflected the burgeoning democratic and anti-intellectual impulses evident in the frontier experience. In a land that prized ingenuity and practicality, making a decision for Christ could be accomplished free from the fetters of state-sanctioned religion or educational background.

This marketplace of potential converts invited religious entrepreneurs who capitalized on Americans' attraction to innovation. Evangelicals took advantage of social and cultural changes that enhanced their efforts to spread the gospel. Improved transportation networks, which facilitated more efficient mail delivery as well as the increased shipment of raw materials to factories for the production of paper, contributed to a boon in the publishing industry after 1820. As a result of more cost-effective publishing, an increasingly literate number of Americans gained access to widely circulated printed materials.

Evangelicals enthusiastically embraced this new market, distributing countless tracts, books, and advertisements. Even among conservative premillennialists who anticipated the imminent return of Christ, most notably William Miller and his followers, print media provided a useful venue for spreading their message.

The Rise of Radio Evangelism

Technological advances during the early twentieth century afforded greater opportunities for advancing the Evangelical cause. The widespread use of radio after 1920 promised to make worldwide evangelism possible. In 1921, Pittsburgh's Calvary Episcopal Church began broadcasting its weekly services, inaugurating what is regarded as the first religious program over station KDKA in Pittsburgh. The following year, Paul Rader, the conservative pastor of the Chicago Gospel Tabernacle, began broadcasting over Chicago station WHT, earning the distinction as the first "radio evangelist" in the United States. Although radio broadcasting remained rudimentary throughout the 1920s, a number of other religious leaders recognized the potential of the medium and individuals such as the flamboyant Aimee Semple McPherson, founder of the famed Angelus Temple in Los Angeles, established private broadcast stations devoted exclusively to religious programming.

Fundamentalism and Mass Media

The religious debates of the 1920s that coalesced around the Scopes "Monkey Trial" in 1925 galvanized the emerging Fundamentalist wing of American Evangelicalism. Despite the obvious antimodernism permeating Fundamentalist thought, Fundamentalists maintained the Evangelical tradition of using the mass media to spread their message. Fundamentalist publications, such as the popular *Moody Bible Institute Monthly*, evidenced considerable circulation gains during the 1930s and 1940s. Perhaps more noticeable was the Fundamentalists' use of radio. Although some Fundamentalists remained suspicious of the medium, considering it a corrupting form of "entertainment," the majority saw it as essential to warning a dying world of the wages of sin.

Fundamentalist broadcasters faced early challenges from the major radio networks, such as the National Broadcasting Company (NBC) and the Columbia Broadcasting System (CBS), which, in conjunction with mainline religious bodies, refused to sell time to independent preachers. The Federal Communications Commission required that the major networks provide broadcast space for public affairs programming or risk federal intervention. This government-mandated allocation, which came to be known as "sustaining time," became dominated by such organizations as the Federal Council of Churches, which effectively monopolized the airwaves. Fundamentalists turned to local radio-station owners who generally welcomed the paid programming. Eventually, newly formed networks such as the Mutual Broadcasting System agreed to sell time to nonmainline conservative groups. The threat to Fundamentalist broadcasters remained, however. The Institute of Education by Radio, which studied religious broadcasting, pressured the networks to limit programs sponsored by independent churches and even the Mutual Broadcasting System complied in 1944. Opposition from the religious establishment to conservative broadcasters contributed to the formation of the National Association of Evangelicals in 1942, which two years later authorized the establishment of the National Religious Broadcasters, a conservative group dedicated to improving the quality and protecting the rights of independent broadcast ministries.

Fundamentalist radio ministries thrived despite the organized opposition. In 1937, Charles Fuller began broadcasting his *Old Fashioned Revival Hour* over the Mutual Broadcasting System. A master in the use of simple, understandable language, Fuller's program was a success with national audiences and by 1942 it was aired on 456 stations. Following Mutual's bow to pressure from the Institute for Education by Radio, Fuller was forced to buy time for the *Revival Hour* on independent stations, but his popularity remained. In 1949, Fuller's program was picked up by the recently formed American Broadcasting Company (ABC) network. Other radio evangelists faced more pronounced obstacles. Controversial Fundamentalist J. Harold Smith, who angered the Federal Council of Churches with his denouncement of their supposed liberal theological and political positions, was forced to leave the air by the Federal Communications Commission in 1953. The ingenious Smith then moved his operation south of the Texas border where he bought time on a 100,000–watt station that broadcast to most of the United States—an act that maintained his audience.

Ironically, Fundamentalist broadcasters forced to navigate the treacherous waters of commercial radio became more adept at utilizing the medium than did speakers from the established churches accustomed to receiving allocated airtime. This competitive atmosphere—because a paid broadcast required an interested audience capable of sustaining it—led to considerable diversity among radio preachers. Former baseball player turned evangelist Billy Sunday understood the value of engaging his audience and he became a captivating performer, both in his public appearances and over his popular radio program. Sunday's messages, which often included shouting and other comic theatrics, aided him in attracting attention as he denounced the spiritual malaise he believed characterized society. Others, such as Herbert W. Armstrong, came from backgrounds in professional advertising, which well-prepared them for mass media. Armstrong began broadcasting his Fundamentalist *Radio Church of God*, later renamed the *World Tomorrow*, over a local station in Eugene, Oregon, in 1934. Undoubtedly aided by his previous professional training, Armstrong built his ministry, which also included the *Plain Truth* magazine, into one of the most recognized in the United States. Many in Armstrong's radio audience eventually coalesced into a denomination, itself initially called the Radio Church of God, with congregations located around or near the media centers that carried his broadcast.

Televangelism

Diverse, generally charismatic radio personalities who thrived on sensationalism (such as the perceived impending end of human civilization and rampant moral decay) fueled public fascination with Fundamentalism and helped make it the most recognized form of Evangelical belief from the 1920s through the 1940s. The fascination carried over to television. Fundamentalist Percy Crawford, host of *Youth on the March*, became the first independent televangelist to broadcast over network television in 1950. A decade later, Crawford bought station WPCA in Philadelphia, making him the first independent televangelist to own a television station. Numerous other conservative Evangelicals, each displaying considerable flair for the stage, such as Rex Humbard and Oral Roberts, launched television ministries. Billy Graham began broadcasting his revivals over television in 1957. Three years later, the Federal Communications Commission ruled that commercial networks could use paid broadcasting to fulfill their obligations for "sustaining time," effectively removing the barriers to independent broadcasters. A critical move, the Federal Communications Commission decision enabled Fundamentalists, previously forced into the "wilderness" of commercial broadcasting, to emerge as leaders in the field of religious media as a result of their experience and media savvy. Beginning in 1964, independent televangelists were also able to acquire inexpensive time over newly created ultrahigh frequency (UHF) television.

Some early entries to the field of religious television become enduring successes. In 1961, Pat Robertson formed the Christian Broadcasting Network (CBN), which five years later began airing its flagship program, the *700 Club*. By 1977, Robertson's network began operating over satellite, pioneering international television broadcasting for independent broadcasters. Robertson was not alone. In 1973, Paul Crouch founded the Trinity Broadcasting Network. Four years later, it was the first Christian network to launch twenty-four hour broadcasting. Under Crouch's direction, the network also bought television stations throughout the United States and around the world. Concurrently, other television ministries cultivated solid audiences during the 1970s, creating a host of charismatic stars, among them Jimmy Swaggart, Jim and Tammy Bakker, and Jerry Falwell.

Mass Media and the Religious Right

Mass media also proved influential in the formation of the religious Right during the late 1970s and the 1980s. While some Fundamentalists eschewed politics altogether, viewing it as a worldly endeavor, many constituted the more conservative wing of the political movement that formed around Jerry Falwell's Moral Majority in 1979 and was reinvigorated with the establishment of Pat Robertson's Christian Coalition ten years later. The Christian Coalition makes skillful use of direct advertisements, radio and television appeals, such as those featured on the *700 Club*, and Internet websites to rally support for political positions and candidates. Fundamentalists' attraction to such political efforts is not surprising. They have a history of using the mass media to highlight political causes. Notable examples include Carl McIntire and

Billy James Hargis, both rabid anticommunists who openly advocated right-wing political positions. In the days before the evolvement of the religious Right, McIntire and Hargis offered politically interested Fundamentalists boisterous commentary on contemporary political events.

The Exportation of Fundamentalism

Christian Fundamentalists also used the mass media to extend their religious message beyond the North American continent. In 1931, independent Evangelicals began broadcasting from Ecuador; following World War II, broadcasters gradually extended their programs into Europe and Asia. Government oversight of European stations made broadcasting on the continent and in Britain difficult, although not impenetrable. Beginning in 1953, Herbert W. Armstrong obtained time on the powerful Radio Luxembourg, covering much of Europe with his message. By the time of Armstrong's death in 1986, his freely distributed, staunchly Fundamentalist *Plain Truth* magazine was published in seven European languages. More recently, the widespread use of satellite television and the crumbling of the former Soviet Union have created more opportunities for media expansion in Eastern Europe and Russia, and Evangelicals readily entered this market during the 1990s. Meanwhile, Evangelicals continued to use the media in an attempt to further the Protestant revival currently underway throughout much of Latin America.

Fundamentalism and Mass Media Today

At the beginning of the twenty-first century, Christian Fundamentalists remain adroit exploiters of the mass media. There is a proliferation of Fundamentalist radio, television, and Internet sites, and Fundamentalists continue to show their skill in the field of publishing. Hal Lindsey's *Late Great Planet Earth*, first published in 1970, and the more recent *Left Behind* (1995–2000) series by Tim LaHaye and Jerry Jenkins have been runaway best-sellers, demonstrating that such Fundamentalist ideas as premillennial dispensationialism are widely circulated in American national life. Conservative Evangelicals have also made a thriving business of gospel music, skillfully creating recordings that appeal to mass audiences. Surprisingly, however, few Christian Fundamentalists credit mass media evangelism with their conversion to Christ, often citing the influence of other Christians instead. Mass media appears to confirm Fundamentalists in their religious convictions, ending the sense of isolation that many feel within secular culture, while simultaneously raising the profile of Christian Fundamentalism in American society.

Fundamentalists' utilization of the mass media is itself characteristic of American culture. In a consumer-based, media-driven society that relies on sophisticated imagery, Fundamentalists and the wider Evangelical movement in general, have subscribed to the promise of American commercialism. Unlike Islamic Fundamentalists' use of the mass media in Iran, for example, which is closely linked to the state, American Fundamentalists are forced to compete in the marketplace, often relying on stylish advertising to sell their well-packaged products. Christian Fundamentalists ardently contend that their message is undiluted by the mass media they so effectively manipulate, but by courting popular appeal, Fundamentalists' critique of American society is diminished and they appear to be but another extension of American culture rather than a manifestation of divine work. Yet the Fundamentalists' approach to the media is unlikely to change, for it is this adaptability to the surrounding mass culture, through two centuries of skillful media exploitation, that has made Evangelical Christianity an enduring feature of American life.

Scott Lupo

See also Evangelicalism; Radio; Televangelism

Bibliography

Bendroth, Margaret Lamberts. (1996) "Fundamentalism and the Media, 1930–1990." In *Religion and Mass Media: Audiences and Adaptations*, edited by Daniel A. Stout and Judith M. Buddenbaum. Thousand Oaks, CA: Sage Publications, 74–84.

Boyer, Paul. (2001) "The Chameleon with Nine Lives: American Religion in the Twentieth Century." In *Perspectives on Modern America: Making Sense of the Twentieth Century*, edited by Harvard Sitkoff. New York: Oxford University Press, 247–274.

Carpenter, Joel A. (1997) *Revive Us Again: The Reawakening of American Fundamentalism*. New York: Oxford University Press.

Erickson, Hal. (1992) *Religious Radio and Television in the United States, 1921–1991: The Programs and Personalities*. Jefferson, NC: McFarland and Co.

Fishwick, Marshall W. (1995) *Great Awakenings: Popular Religion and Popular Culture*. Binghamton, NY: Haworth Press.

Hoover, Stewart M. (1988) *Mass Media Religion: The Social Sources of the Electronic Church*. Newbury Park, CA: Sage Publications.

Jorstad, Erling. (1993) *Popular Religion in America: The Evangelical Voice*. Westport, CT: Greenwood Press.

Kintz, Linda, and Julia Lesage, eds. (1998) *Media, Culture, and the Religious Right*. Minneapolis: University of Minnesota Press.

Melton, J. Gordon, Phillip Charles Lucas, and Jon R. Stone. (1997) *Prime-Time Religion: An Encyclopedia of Religious Broadcasting*. Phoenix, AZ: Oryx Press.

Morgan, David. (1999) *Protestants & Pictures: Religion, Visual Culture, and the Age of American Mass Production*. New York: Oxford University Press.

Schultze, Quentin J. (1991) *Televangelism and American Culture: The Business of Popular Religion*. Grand Rapids, MI: Baker Book House.

———. (1996) "Evangelicals' Uneasy Alliance with the Media." In *Religion and Mass Media: Audiences and Adaptations*, edited by Daniel A. Stout and Judith M. Buddenbaum. Thousand Oaks, CA: Sage Publications, 61–73.

Megachurches

The term "megachurch" generally refers to any congregation with a sustained average weekly attendance of two thousand persons or more. Most discussions of megachurches focus solely on very large Protestant Christian congregations in the United States—of which there are roughly six hundred. If Roman Catholic churches were included, the total number of U.S. megachurches would be closer to 2,200. Likewise, there are significant numbers of megachurches throughout the world, especially in Korea, Brazil, and several African countries, although no exact counts exist for this worldwide phenomenon. The largest megachurches in America average near 20,000 in attendance; however, several churches in Korea claim over 250,000 attenders.

Although large congregations have existed throughout Christian history, there has been a rapid proliferation of churches with massive attendance since the 1970s. As such, some researchers suggest that this church form is a unique collective response to distinctive cultural shifts and changes in societal patterns throughout the industrialized, urban, and suburban areas of the world.

While size is the most immediately apparent characteristic of these congregations, the Protestant megachurches in the United States generally share many other traits. Virtually all these megachurches have a conservative theology, even those within mainline denominations. Not surprisingly, the majority of Protestant megachurches are affiliated with either the Southern Baptist Convention or the Assemblies of God or are nondenominational.

The vast majority of megachurches (over eighty percent) are located in the southern Sunbelt of the United States—with California, Texas, Georgia, and Florida having the highest concentrations. Most megachurches are located in suburban areas of rapidly growing sprawl cities such as Los Angeles, Dallas, Atlanta, Houston, Orlando, Phoenix, and Seattle. These large churches often occupy prominent land tracts of fifty to one hundred acres near major traffic thoroughfares. They generally have significant parking lots and sanctuaries that are able to accommodate the vast numbers of worshipers they attract.

Megachurches tend to grow to their great size within a very short period of time, usually in less than ten years, and under the tenure of a single senior pastor. Nearly all megachurch pastors are male, and are viewed as having considerable personal charisma. The senior minister often has an authoritative style of preaching and administration and is nearly always the singular dominant leader of the church. Supporting these senior pastors are teams of five to twenty-five associate ministers, and often hundreds of full-time staff. The church hosts a multitude of social, recreational, and aid ministries. Likewise, a majority of megachurches employ intentional efforts at enhancing congregational community, such as home fellowships and interest-based small group meetings. Contrary to expectations, these congregations promote intense personal commitment in a majority of their members but also have a large percentage of anonymous spectators in their ranks.

Few megachurches have been exceptionally large for longer than the tenure of their current minister. Evidence suggests, however, that these churches can remain vital following a shift in leadership from the founder to his successor. Although some researchers argue the era of megachurch proliferation is drawing to a close, the total number has increased by ten percent between 1995 and 2000. It seems clear that reports of the demise of the megachurch are greatly exaggerated.

Scott Thumma

See also Sunday Schools

Messiah

The term "messiah" originates from the Hebrew word *mashiahk*, meaning "one who is anointed." A messiah heralds the arrival of a utopian epoch. For Christians the messianic figure is Jesus Christ. Messianic speculation focuses on a dramatic moment of transition represented by the advent of an eschatological (End Times) king. The emergence of this figure is understood as a decisive turning point in history that demarcates the present age from one that is (for the believer) much better. In many accounts of the End Times, the utopian epoch comes after one fraught with tribulation and upheavals of a vast magnitude. Times of great suffering and catastrophe can thus be interpreted as a sign that the end is near. But to appreciate messianic thought more thoroughly its biblical and Jewish origins must first be understood.

The Hebrew Bible Context

In the Hebrew Bible the word "anointed one" (*mashiahk*) often refers to kingship. In ancient Israel, the king in his coronation ritual was anointed with oil (1 Samuel 10:1; 16:13; 1 Kings 1:39; 1 Chronicles 29:22, NRSV). Priests were also anointed with oil (Leviticus 4:5; 6:15), and, at times, prophets were as well (Isaiah 61:1). According to the royal ideology of ancient Israel, the act of anointing with oil signified that the king was selected by God to rule. In this period "messiah" did not have an eschatological meaning, but rather helped legitimize the king's political authority in the present. Saul, the first king of Israel, is called the Lord's "anointed" (*mashiahk*) in 1 Samuel 12:3, 5; 24:4:6; and 26:9. The most important king of Israel was David. God, in 2 Samuel 7, promises to him and his descendants the right to rule over Israel forever. The term *mashiahk* often refers to David or his dynasty. In Israel the title often represented David's exalted status, and that God has bestowed special favor upon him and his dynasty:

for example, Psalm 18:50 reads: "He [God] saves his king time after time, displays his faithful love for his anointed (*meshihko*), for David and his heirs forever" (cf. Psalm 2:2; 20:6; 28:8; 45:6–7; 89:20–38; 132:10; 2 Samuel 19:22; 22:51; 23:1).

The Davidic monarchy fell in 586 BCE, when Judah was conquered by Nebuchadnezzar II, king of Babylon. The Jerusalem Temple, which was the central religious site of Judaism, was destroyed and many Jews were deported to Babylon (see 2 Kings 24–25). Many considered the last legitimate king to be Jehoiachin, of the Davidic line, who was deported in 597 BCE (2 Kings 24:15). Prophets proclaimed that an idealized Davidic king would come to restore the monarchy. This Davidic king would return to Israel at some future point to inaugurate an idealized period of prosperity (Jeremiah 23; 33; Ezekiel 34). Representative of this tradition is Isaiah 11:1–9, which reads in part: "a shoot shall grow out of the stump of Jesse [David's father], a twig shall sprout from his stock. . . . He will strike the country with the rod of his mouth and with the breath of his lips bring death to the wicked." The reign of this "shoot" will begin a utopian period of peace and stability in Israel: "The wolf shall dwell with the lamb, the leopard lie down with the kid. . . . The lion will eat hay like the ox. The infant will play over the den of the adder." This future Davidic king is sometimes called "the Branch," a botanical metaphor that signifies that his kingship will grow and prosper (Jeremiah 23:5–6; Zechariah 3:8; 6:12; Collins 1995: 25).

Cyrus, the Persian emperor who conquered the Babylonians, is also called the Lord's "anointed" (*mashiahk*) (Isaiah 45:1). He allowed the Jews who were exiled in Babylon to return to Israel in 538 BCE. As a Gentile (non-Jew), he is not the Davidic king who will deliver Israel. Rather, the title "messiah" signifies that he was chosen by God to free the Jews.

Some in Judah seem to have placed messianic hopes upon a man named Zerubbabel around 520 BCE. Zerubbabel has the distinction of arguably being the first Jewish messiah. He was of the Davidic line, since he was the grandson of King Jehoiachin (1 Chronicles 3:16). He helped rebuild the Temple, which was destroyed in 586 BCE, amid speculation that this would usher in God's return to Jerusalem, restore the monarchy, and deliver Israel from its enemies: "Tell Zerubbabel, governor of Judah: I [God] shall shake the heavens and the earth; I shall overthrow the thrones of kings, break the power of heathen realms. . . . On that day, says the Lord of Hosts, I shall take you, Zerubbabel son of Shealtiel, my servant, and I shall wear you as a signet ring, for it is you I have chosen" (Haggai 2:21–23; cf. Zechariah 3:8–10; 4:6–10; 6:12–14). In this oracle the might of God and the restoration of Israel is represented by the act of God's choosing a descendent of David to rule Judah.

Messianism in the Late Second Temple Period

The Second Temple period is demarcated by the rebuilding of the Jerusalem Temple in the fifth century BCE and its destruction by the Romans in 70 CE. The late Second Temple period is characterized by popular dissatisfaction with a succession of oppressive rulers (Hellenistic, Hasmonean, and Roman). (For an overview of this history, see Shanks 1999: 231–298.) It was a time of religious and cultural crises that had a profound impact on Judaism. Jews tried to reconcile their belief that they were the chosen people of God with the oppression facing them. Since God's deliverance was clearly not visible in the present, it was seen as deferred to the eschatological future. Belief in the future reign of an idealized Davidic king was similarly transferred to an eschatological period. There are many depictions of the End Times from this period. Some allocate a role for a figure who will provide deliverance in the eschatological future; others do not. There is also variety of opinion about the identity of this figure. In some cases it is the Archangel Michael (Daniel 12:1; Revelation 12:7), with others it is Elijah (Malachi 4:5; Mark 9:12), and still others an enigmatic figure named Melchizedek (Collins 1995: 162). There were also different opinions as to what kind of a role a messianic figure was thought to have in the End Times. Often his duties included heralding not only redemption from sin and deliverance from oppression but also the resurrection of the dead and the day of final judgment.

The Dead Sea Scrolls illustrate the various forms of messianic speculation in this period. Many of these texts were written in the first century BCE and are associated with a sect of Jews that lived at Qumran; for example, the Isaiah Pesher (a text referred to by scholars as 4Q161; "pesher" is a kind of biblical interpretation) interprets Isaiah 11 (quoted in the Hebrew Bible section). It claims this biblical passage refers to "the Branch of David which will sprout in the final days. . . ." In one manuscript of the War Scroll (4Q285), which describes a final eschatological war between the angels and the Gentiles, the

Matthew 24:6–9, 27–30

6. And ye shall hear of wars and rumours of wars: see that ye be not troubled: for all things must come to pass, but the end is not yet.

7. For nation shall rise against nation, and kingdom against kingdom: and there shall be famines and pestilences, and earthquakes in diverse places.

8. All these are the beginning of sorrows.

9. Then they shall deliver you up to be afflicted, and shall kill you: and ye shall be hated of all nations for my name's sake.

27. For the lightning cometh out of the east and shineth even unto the west; so shall also the coming of the Son of Man be.

28. For wheresoever the carcase is, there will the eagles be gathered together.

29. Immediately after the tribulation of those days shall the sun be darkened, and the moon shall not give her light, and the stars shall fall from heaven, and the powers of heaven shall be shaken:

30. And then shall appear the sign of the Son of man in heaven: and then shall all the tribes of the earth mourn, and they shall see the Son of man coming in the clouds of heaven with power and great glory.

Revelation 11:15

And the seventh angel sounded; and there were great voices in heaven, saying, the kingdoms of this world are become the kingdoms of our Lord, and of his Christ; and he shall reign forever and ever.

"Branch of David" helps lead the angels in battle. In the longer version of the War Scroll, the Archangel Michael leads them (cf. Daniel 12; Revelation 12). Some texts conceive of more than one messianic figure. They assert the coming of the "messiahs of Aaron and Israel" (Community Rule 9:11; Damascus Covenant 20:1). Such messianism distinguishes Davidic and priestly aspects of messianic speculation. One emphasizes the coming divine deliverance as a vanquishing of political enemies; the other understands it as the purification of Israel from sin. These dual messiah texts consider those roles to be distinct yet conjoined (Collins 1995: 74).

Acute messianic hopes are found in the *Psalms of Solomon* (c. 40 CE; Charlesworth 1985, 2: 639–670). The seventeenth psalm beseeches the Lord to send his messiah to deliver Jerusalem from the Romans: "See, Lord, and raise up for them [the Jews] their king, the Son of David, to rule over your servant Israel" (v. 21). This king will "judge peoples and nations in the wisdom of his righteousness" and "will have gentile nations serving him under his yoke" (vvs. 29–30). The psalm ends by proclaiming "their king shall be the Lord Messiah" (v. 32). This is one of the most explicit pre-Christian testimonies of messianic expectation. (For more on Second Temple Jewish messianism, see Collins 1995.)

Messianic Traditions in the New Testament

This swirl of Jewish messianic traditions coalesced around the person of Jesus Christ. "Christ" derives from the Greek *christos*, which is a translation of the Hebrew *mashiahk* (cf. John 1:41; 4:25–26). "Christ" is a messianic title. The Israelite tradition of an idealized Davidic king anointed by God to rule is stressed in the New Testament. Jesus is frequently called the Son of David (Matthew 1:1; Mark 10:47). He is also frequently called the "Son of Man" (Matthew 24:44). The "Son of Man" is an eschatological king described in Daniel 7 who, many Christians believe, prefigured Christ (cf. 1 Enoch 48). Many Christians also believe that the "Servant Songs" of Isaiah, which describe the persecution and restitution of a "servant" (the most important song is in Chapters 52:13–53:12), foretold the suffering of Jesus and His ordained role as atoning for the sins of the world (Isaiah 53:7–12; Matthew 8:17; Luke 22:37; Ehrman 1999: 236). The Gospels proclaim that Christ will return amidst great tribulation: "Immediately after the suffering of those days the sun will be darkened, and the moon will not give its light; the stars will fall from heaven, and the powers of heaven will be shaken. Then the sign of the Son of Man will appear in heaven, and then all the tribes of the earth will mourn, and they will see 'the Son of

Man coming on the clouds of heaven' with power and great glory" (Matthew 24:29–30; cf. Mark 13:24–26; Luke 21:25–28; Daniel 7:13; Allison 1998: 145). The Book of Revelation 13:3–10 claims that the period of Christ's reign will be preceded by an age of wickedness where demonic figures hold sway. Revelation also asserts that the overthrow of the dominion of Satan and the Antichrist will begin a reign of Christ on earth that will last one thousand years (Revelation 20:1–6).

The eschatological scenario that is associated with Jesus includes the Final Judgment: "Be alert at all times, praying that you may have the strength to escape all these things that will take place, and to stand before the Son of Man" (Luke 21:36; Allison 1998: 144–145). At the moment of judgment the wicked who prosper in this life will be punished, and the righteous who are downtrodden shall be vindicated: "For all who exalt themselves will be humbled, and those who humble themselves will be exalted" (Luke 14:11; see also 13:29–30; Mark 10:31). Some early Christians traditions hold that the dead will be raised so that they too can be judged: "the hour is coming when all who are in their graves will hear his voice and will come out—those who have done good, to the resurrection of life, and those who have done evil, to the resurrection of condemnation" (John 5:28–29; cf. Revelation 20:12; Allison 1998: 136–141).

The Gospels stress that these eschatological events are imminent: "The time is fulfilled, and the kingdom of God has come near; repent, and believe in the good news" (Mark 1:15). The early followers of Jesus did not claim to know when these events would unfold (Matthew 25:13), but that they would take place in the near future: "You also must be ready, for the Son of Man is coming at an unexpected hour" (Luke 12:40; see also 1 Thessalonians 5:2; Mark 13:33–37; Ehrman 1998: 160–161). The imminence of Jesus' return gave His teachings an urgency that helps explain their centrality in the Christian tradition.

Messianic Traditions in Rabbinic Judaism

While Christianity appropriated Jewish messianic traditions, they also continued their development within Judaism itself. Rabbinic Judaism abounds in messianic speculation. It is beyond the scope of this article to explore these traditions, however (see Klausner 1955; Lenowitz 1998). Many rabbis taught that there was a figure known as Messiah ben David ("Son of David"). He was to arrive in glory to vanquish the enemies of Israel, lead the return of the exiles to Israel, begin the resurrection of the dead, foster the redemption of their sins before God, and inaugurate a period of bliss. This is often called the "World to Come." It is described idyllically. At that time the "righteous sit with crowns on their heads" and in this period there will be "no business transactions, no envy, no hatred, no rivalry" (Babylonian Talmud, *Berakoth* 17a). In recent times, a group of orthodox Jews believed that Rabbi Menachem Schneerson (1902–1994), who lived in Brooklyn, was the messiah.

The Messiah in Modern Fundamentalism

Fundamentalists assert the inerrancy of the Bible, and that it should be read literally. Biblical descriptions of the End Times are interpreted as prophecies about events that will actually occur. One hallmark of messianic thought in Fundamentalism is that current events correlate with biblical prophecies that proclaim Jesus' return. The idealized future is generally portrayed as in stark contrast to the modern world. War, poverty, environmental abuse, and secular humanism are frequently taken as signs of the rise of wickedness and chaos that will precede the reign of Christ. The Reconstructionist movement, for example, founded by Gary North and Rousas John Rushdoony, asserts that the coming reign of Jesus will abolish democracy, the separation of church and state, abortion, federal welfare programs, and many other features of modern society (Armstrong 2000: 361).

Jesus' messianic role in Fundamentalist thought is often a counterpoint to negative assessments of contemporary society. Doug Clark, in his *Shockwaves of Armageddon* (1982), writes that "It is such a marvelous comfort to Christians to know that Jesus Christ is coming and that He will snatch us up and out of this mundane sphere of living" (Boyer 1992: 299). The descriptions of Jesus in the New Testament are used to support the conviction that the modern world is corrupt and wicked, and that Jesus will return to punish the sinners and reward the righteous. Jesus' messianic duty is to be the eschatological hero who will implement this ordained punishment and vindication.

Christ's return is often construed as a time of extreme violence. An early-twentieth-century Fundamentalist, Isaac M. Haldeman, wrote that Christ's "garments are dipped in blood, the blood of others. He descends that he may shed the blood of men" (Armstrong 2000: 172). The judgment and battles that will accompany Christ's return will only cause suffering, it is commonly thought, to the unbeliever. Those who profess Jesus Christ to be their personal savior (Romans 10:13) will be spared. During the Gulf War, one Fundamentalist told a reporter: "[The end] is definitely coming. It's freaky but it doesn't scare me, because I'm a Christian. It will be other people who suffer" (Boyer 1992: 329).

Many Fundamentalists believe in the Rapture, which is based on a literal interpretation of 1 Thessalonians 4. It claims that believers will be physically taken up to heaven to spare them from the wrath of God that will descend upon the earth. The raptured ones are thought to participate in Christ's millennial reign. In *Jesus Is Coming* (1982), Paul Lee Tan writes: "Have you ever been a king? If not, do not despair. Someday you will be a king. You will reign with Christ over the millennial earth" (Boyer 1992: 323; cf. Revelation 5:10; 20:1–6). In some Fundamentalist circles, messianic traditions of an End-Times king are expanded to be an eschatological reward for all who follow Jesus.

Conclusion

Messianism is rooted in traditions from ancient Israel about the reign of an idealized Davidic king who will deliver Israel from its enemies. The first followers of Christ interpreted those traditions as being embodied by Jesus who would return to deliver the faithful in the eschatological future. Modern Fundamentalists also subscribe to this view.

In Fundamentalism, Jesus is often understood as a hostile force ordained to destroy the world. To legitimate this view, they assert that the Bible presents a unified, unambiguous portrayal of this understanding of Jesus. This view cannot accommodate the diversity of traditions about Jesus preserved in the New Testament. He is both the warrior with the sword at the End Times (Revelation 19) and the sage who admonishes one to turn the other cheek (Matthew 5). The hostility with which they often view the world polarizes the perception of Jesus into a figure of judgment and war. He is thus hailed as the eschatological king who will deliver the faithful from a wicked world doomed to perish.

Matthew Goff

See also Christ; End Times; Final Judgment

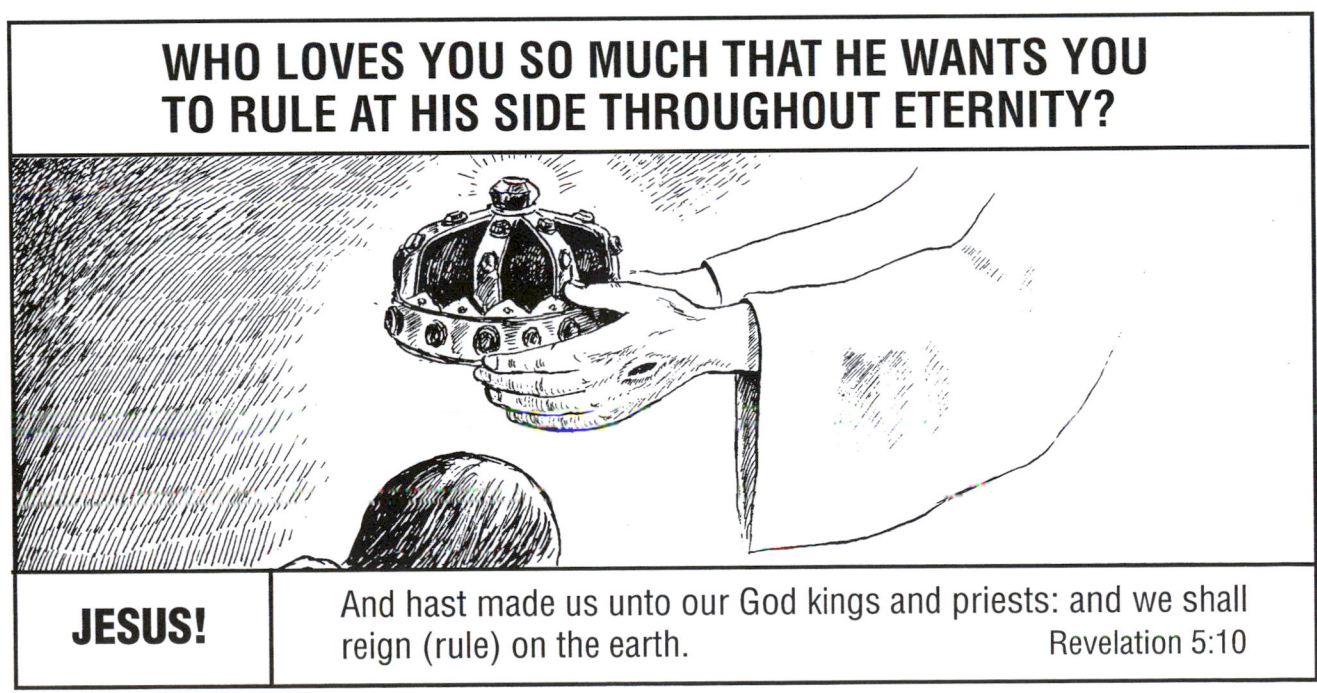

WHO LOVES YOU SO MUCH THAT HE WANTS YOU TO RULE AT HIS SIDE THROUGHOUT ETERNITY?

JESUS! And hast made us unto our God kings and priests: and we shall reign (rule) on the earth. Revelation 5:10

Illustration from "The Love Story," p. 19. CHICK PUBLICATIONS, ONTARIO, CA, 1977. USED BY PERMISSION.

Bibliography

Allison, Dale C. (1998) *Jesus of Nazareth: Millenarian Prophet*. Minneapolis, MN: Fortress Press.

Armstrong, Karen. (2000) *The Battle for God*. New York: Alfred A. Knopf.

Boyer, Paul. (1992) *When Time Shall Be No More: Prophecy Belief in Modern American Culture*. Cambridge, MA: Harvard University Press.

Charlesworth, James H., ed. (1985) *The Old Testament Pseudepigrapha*. New York: Doubleday.

Collins, John J. (1995) *The Scepter and the Star: The Messiahs of the Dead Sea Scrolls and Other Ancient Literature*. New York: Doubleday.

Ehrman, Bart D. (1999) *Jesus: Apocalyptic Prophet of the New Millennium*. New York: Oxford University Press.

Hendrick, Charles W. (1999) *When History and Faith Collide: Studying Jesus*. Peabody, MA: Hendrickson Publishers.

Klausner, Joseph. (1955) *The Messianic Idea in Israel: From Its Beginning to the Completion of the Mishnah*. New York: The Macmillan Company.

Lenowitz, Harris. (1998) *The Jewish Messiahs: From the Galilee to Crown Heights*. New York: Oxford University Press.

McGinn, Bernard. (1994) *Antichrist: Two Thousand Years of the Human Fascination with Evil*. San Francisco: HarperSanFrancisco.

Shanks, Herschel, ed. (1999) *Ancient Israel: From Abraham to the Roman Destruction of the Temple,* 2nd ed. Washington, DC: Biblical Archaeological Society.

Mid-Tribulationism

A minority of premillennialists hold to the mid-Tribulational view, which teaches that the Rapture of the church will occur midway through the "Seventy Weeks of Daniel" (Daniel 9:20–27). While all premillennialists expect the Rapture (Latin, *rapio*) or the spiriting away of the church around the time of the Second Coming, they have sometimes vehemently disagreed on the timing of the coming Tribulation.

In comparison to the pre- and post-Tribulational positions, the mid-Tribulational view of the Rapture was the most recent to emerge within premillennialism. Though its origin is not completely clear, this perspective seems to have been first articulated in 1941 by Norman B. Harrison in his book *The End: Rethinking the Revelation*. Unlike most other premillennialists who called the entire "Seventy Weeks of Daniel" the Tribulation, Harrison insisted that the Great Tribulation occupied only the last three-and-a-half years of the Tribulation's seven years. Consequently, Harrison preferred to call himself a pre-Tribulationist. However, dispensationalists who already used that term to describe their belief that Jesus will rapture the church before the "Seventy Weeks of Daniel" insisted on calling this view mid-Tribulationism.

Harrison based his view on a variety of biblical arguments. He noted the frequent mention of forty-two months in key prophetic texts in Scripture (Daniel 7:25; 9:27; 12:7; Revelation 11:2–3; 12:1) that described the pouring out of divine judgment on the world. Thus, he claimed, the Great Tribulation will not begin until the seventh trumpet in Revelation 11, which he placed midway through the last seven years before Christ's return. During the first half of the "Seventy Weeks of Daniel," the church will witness the rise of the Antichrist, his increasing control over the world scene, and the persecution of those who refuse to pledge him allegiance by receiving his mark.

Mid-Tribulationists contend that their view corrects pre-Tribulationism's unsupported claim that the Rapture will be secret and without any preceding prophesied events, as well as its inability to locate the Rapture in the Olivet Discourse of Matthew 24. Despite such critiques, mid- and pre-Tribulationists still divide the Second Coming of Christ into two phases: when Christ comes *for* His saints (the Rapture) and *with* His saints (the Second Coming proper). Few Fundamentalists have followed this view. It is usually seen as a mediating position (both exegetically and chronologically) between the other two more popular alternatives of pre- and post-Tribulationism.

Timothy P. Weber

See also Premillennialism; Pre-Tribulationism; Post-Tribulationism; Rapture; Tribulation

Bibliography

Archer, Gleason L., et. al. (1984) *The Rapture: Pre-, Mid-, or Post-tribulational?* Grand Rapids, MI: Zondervan Publishing.

Harrison, Norman B. (1941) *The End: Rethinking the Revelation*. Privately printed.

Pentecost, J. Dwight. (1958) *Things to Come*. Grand Rapids, MI: Dunham Press.

Militia

The 19 April 1995 bombing of the Alfred P. Murrah Federal building in Oklahoma City, Oklahoma, in which 167 people, including 19 children, died, is considered one the worst acts of domestic terrorism the United States has ever experienced. Timothy McVeigh and Terry Nichols, arrested and later convicted of the crime, had been associated with a militia group in Kingman, Arizona, and the larger murky world of right-wing Patriots and survivalists. The militias, Americans soon learned, were armed and angry at the U.S. government for eroding the rights of American citizens. Many professed a "patriotic" stance, while others were separatists. They practiced and preached survivalism, preparing for the collapse of civilization, or fearing that a conspiracy to create a socialist one-world government and a "new world order" was unfolding in America and the world.

The Oklahoma City bombing also brought into relief the ideas of the Patriot movement, from which the militias had emerged. Organized in the same loose fashion as the militias, but older and more broadly based, Patriot leaders have reached out in recent years to the emerging militia and survivalist movements. The Patriot movement endorses a strong nationalist philosophy, expressing the views of "super" patriotic Americans, who see America as a Christian land and Americans as a chosen people. Some militia and Patriot leaders fancy themselves as "constitutionalists," employing legal and constitutional analysis of the nation's founding documents, including the Constitution and its Amendments, which they believe to have been inspired by God. The spring 1996 standoff between the Federal Bureau of Investigation (FBI) and the Montana Freemen, resulted from the Freemen's "constitutional" analysis and "common law" procedures and courts to sanction their flouting of local, state, and federal laws, in their attempt to create a separatist and autonomous "township."

The conspiracy theory weaved by militias and Patriots argues that the new world order will be controlled by a cadre of powerful economic, political, and cultural elites. Based in international organizations such as the World Bank and the United Nations, in global think tanks, multinational corporations, and cultural or humanitarian organizations, the goal of the conspiracists is to build a global socialism that will require Americans to share their prosperity with the rest of the world, ultimately leading to impoverishment and oppression of the population. The laws and rules that govern the new global order and instituted by the new world government will take precedence over the federal government of the United States.

Farther down the road of the militia and survivalist right are racist and neo-Nazi paramilitary groups, who see Jews behind the conspiracy to create a one-world government and the new global order. With the racist and anti-Semitic theology of Christian Identity as their justification, they blame the Jewish Antichrist, or the Zionist Occupation Government (ZOG), which rules in Washington, taking its orders from internationalist Jews in Israel, the United Nations, and the Fortune 500. Attracting old-line hate groups like the Ku Klux Klan and inspiring newer ones like the Aryan Nation Alliance (formerly the Aryan Nations), the militias and Patriot movement have helped to legitimate racist and anti-Semitic hate groups by providing a populist antigovernment umbrella for them to share.

Prior to the Oklahoma City bombing the militia and antigovernment chorus had been rising. There had been the 1992 shoot-out at Ruby Ridge, Idaho, between U.S. marshals and Randy Weaver, an adherent to Christian Identity, who had resisted arrest on illegal weapons charges. Weaver's wife and fourteen-year-old son and a U.S. marshal were killed during the shoot-out. The next year Americans and the world witnessed the horror of Waco, Texas, where, in an attempt to serve a warrant on illegal weapons charges, would-be messiah David Koresh and the Branch Davidians came into fatal contact with the FBI and the Bureau of Alcohol, Tobacco and Firearms (ATF). "Ruby Ridge" and "Waco" became rallying cries for a growing movement of Americans angry at their government and fearful of what many predicted would be the imminent collapse of American society and the oppression of its people. Two years to the day, and apparently in revenge for the Waco "attack," the Oklahoma bombing occurred. While Patriot and militia leaders were quick to condemn the action, especially where so many innocent civilians were killed, they also argued that they were not surprised by the event, given recent government attacks on its citizens. Oklahoma City, many predicted, might be just the beginning.

The militia and paramilitary groups particularly despise federal law enforcement agencies such as the FBI and the ATF, because they enforce the laws that Patriot and militia members find so repulsive, including the Brady Bill requirement for a seven-day waiting period before purchasing a gun and the ban on assault rifles. Among militias federal law enforcement has been demonized as part of a larger conspiracy to take away American's most basic rights. Through networks created on the Internet; via an extensive literature that includes all manner of desktop published books, pamphlets, and newsletters; videos and cassette tapes; as well as talk radio programs and grass-roots organizations, Patriots, militia members, survivalists, and white supremacists are finding common ground in their fear and loathing of government, law enforcement, and the emerging "new world order." By the mid-1990s there were militias in every state in the United States with numbers estimated between 20,000 and 60,000.

Since its peak in the mid-1990s, the militia movement and the numerous related antigovernment- or survivalist-oriented groups have come under heavy surveillance from law enforcement. The militias seem to have backed off and lost energy and support. Still, the ranks of militias, survivalists, Patriots, and white supremacists remain a part of the American countercultural landscape.

Philip Lamy

See also Anti-Semitism; Aryan Nation; Ku Klux Klan

Bibliography

Abanes, Richard. (1996) *American Militias: Rebellion, Racism, and Religion.* Downers Grove, IL: InterVarsity Press.

Berlet, Chip, and Matthew N. Lyons. (2000) *Right-wing Populism in America: Too Close for Comfort.* New York: Guilford Press.

Junas, Daniel. (1995) "Rise of the Citizen Militias: Angry White Guys with Guns." *Covert Action Quarterly* (Spring): 20–25

Lamy, Philip. (1996) *Millennium Rage: Survivalists, White Supremacists, and the Doomsday Prophecy.* New York: Plenum.

Millerites

Millerites are so named because they were followers of William Miller (1782–1849), a well-respected New York farmer who became convinced that the Second Coming of Jesus Christ would occur in 1843. Origi-nally a deist, Miller aligned himself with the Baptist Church and became a staunch supporter of premil-lennial Christianity following his service in the War of 1812. Miller developed an attraction to the apoca-lyptic books of the Bible, focusing on an obscure passage in Daniel 8:14 that refers to a period of 2,300 days that must elapse before the sanctuary is restored. Like many premillennialists, Miller inter-preted "a day for a year" and elongated the span of time to 2,300 years. He then added the 2,300-year fig-ure to the date of the Jewish scribe Ezra's commis-sion to rebuild the temple at Jerusalem, an event that occurred in 485 BCE, and arrived at the year 1843 CE.

Miller gradually publicized his calculations and his message attracted considerable attention, much to the chagrin of some other revivalists in Jacksonian America who found their audiences dwindling and who had asked the sensationalist Miller to reinvigo-rate their crowds. In 1839, Miller met a Boston minis-ter, Joshua V. Himes, and the two began to work together to exploit the mass media to spread the mes-sage of the approaching advent. They circulated a number of periodicals, including *Signs of the Times* and *The Midnight Cry*. The Millerites proved adroit at using the mass media, creating publications that incorporated visual effects such as drawings of prophetic symbols and the use of detailed charts out-lining the timetable of prophetic events. Publication efforts were enhanced by numerous public ap-pearances during the 1830s and early 1840s and the convening of a number of conferences to discuss prophecy. Attendance at Miller's public lectures often numbered in the thousands, and his fame quickly spread throughout the eastern United States and even in Great Britain as people from different walks of life gathered in support of his prophetic message.

As the date drew near, however, trepidation arose among some of the leading Millerites over narrowing the prediction of the advent to a specific day. In January 1843, Miller himself noted that his prophetic timetable was not based on the Gregorian calendar and that the return of Christ could occur at any time between 21 March 1843 and 22 March 1844. When the year passed without event, public criticism of the movement grew and the Millerites attempted to dis-cover the reason for their disappointing failure. By August 1844, the date was reconfigured by Millerite Samuel Snow to 22 October 1844, a date that received a belated endorsement from Miller. When the Second Coming failed to occur according to the revised sce-nario it became known as the "Great Disappointment." Most Millerites suffered a profound sense of psychological disorientation and loss, and many deserted the cause they had once committed their lives to advancing. Nonetheless, some saw divine guidance in Miller's work and a remnant of the movement coalesced into the Seventh-Day Adventist Church.

Scott Lupo

See also Apocalypse; Eschatology

Bibliography

Boyer, Paul. (1992) *When Time Shall Be No More: Prophecy Belief in Modern American Culture*. Cambridge, MA: The Belknap Press of Harvard University Press.

Conkin, Paul K. (1997) *American Originals: Homemade Varieties of Christianity*. Chapel Hill, NC: University of North Carolina Press.

Morgan, David. (1999) *Protestants & Pictures: Religion, Visual Culture, and the Age of American Mass Production*. New York: Oxford University Press.

O'Leary, Stephen D. (1994) *Arguing the Apocalypse: A Theory of Millennial Rhetoric*. New York: Oxford University Press.

Miracles

In common usage, a miracle is a pleasing extraordinary act or event in the physical world that does not follow the known laws of nature, and is therefore attributed to the presence and intervention of a supernatural or divine power. In a more restricted sense, Christian miracles are wonderful phenomena that reflect God's revelation to humankind. Miracles are as old as the world itself, and they continue to gain ascendancy. They are a distinguishable mark of the divine, hence, belief in miraculous events pervades all known cultures and is a feature of practically all religions. Some cultic practices of traditional religions often seen as "magical arts" can be regarded as miracles, but not in the manner that Christians understand the term. The reasons why miracles occur frequently within certain religious traditions and not others are best explained by the religious adherents.

Miracles do not follow scientific principles, hence some people such as agnostics and skeptics deny all or most miracles or explain them as natural phenomena. This rejection, however, does not obliterate the fact of miraculous assertion by all religious cultures of the world, particularly Christianity. Those who reject miracles assert that the laws of nature are self-evident and uncaused by any other power. On the contrary, Christians believe that God, who is the creator of the universe, has the power to intervene in nature. Hence, whenever miracles occur, God introduces a new agent into the laws of nature. Miracles are inexplicable but very often explanations are adduced as to why and what miracles stand for in various cultures of the world.

Miracles in the Bible

The Bible records numerous miracles, which occurred in various contexts, at different times, in different localities, and affected diverse people. Although there are many events in the Old Testament that are considered miraculous, greater attention has always been paid to the New Testament miracles recorded in the Gospels, particularly those performed by Jesus Christ because they strengthened the divine origin of Christianity. The Bible records that miracles were performed by the divine including God Himself, Jesus Christ, the Holy Spirit, servants of God such as prophets, and in some cases by agents of Satan such as the Egyptian magicians, the witch of Endor, Simon the magician, and more. Miracles by satanic agents, however, were regarded as counterfeits and of low quality, and in some cases they did not stand the test of time.

The Old Testament recounts numerous miraculous events. The Israelites believe that it is only God who does wondrous things in human history. Accounts of some miracles performed by God with significant impact on human history are given in Psalms 136:1–26. The Creation was the first miraculous event in human history, and thereafter God performed miracles directly or through human agents. For example, the miracles performed by Moses were many, and include the ten plagues brought upon the Egyptians, the parting of the waters of the Red Sea, and the provision of food for the Israelites in the wilderness on their journey to Canaan. These miracles were seen as revelation of the saving presence of God; hence, to serve God became an obligation for the Israelites.

Certain prophets in the Old Testament such as Elijah and Elisha performed various miracles in-

John 2:1–11

1. And the third day there was a marriage in Cana of Galilee; and the mother of Jesus was there:
2. And both Jesus was called, and his disciples, to the marriage.
3. And when they wanted wine, the mother of Jesus saith unto him, They have no wine.
4. Jesus saith unto her, Woman, what have I to do with thee? mine hour is not yet come.
5. His mother saith unto the servants, Whatsoever he saith unto you, do it.
6. And there were set there six waterpots of stone, after the manner of the purifying of the Jews, containing two or three firkins apiece.
7. Jesus saith unto them, Fill the waterpots with water. And they filled them up to the brim.
8. And he saith unto them, Draw out now, and bear unto the governor of the feast. And they bare it.
9. When the ruler of the feast had tasted the water that was made wine, and knew not whence it was: (but the servants which drew the water knew;) the governor of the feast called the bridegroom,
10. And saith unto him, Every man at the beginning doth set forth good wine; and when men have well drunk, then that which is worse: but thou hast kept the good wine until now.
11. This beginning of miracles did Jesus in Cana of Galilee, and manifested forth his glory; and his disciples believed on him.

cluding raising the dead to life, ceasing the rain for three and a half years, and enabling an axe's head to float on water. All these miracles were performed through the intervention of the spirit of God who was working with these men. These miracles authenticate God's omnipotence and authority over His creation.

The New Testament records various miracles performed by Jesus Christ in the course of His earthly ministry. His birth was miraculous because Mary, His mother, conceived without any sexual relationship with a man. Jesus' first miracle is recorded as the turning of water into wine at a marriage feast in Cana (John 2:1–11). This miracle occurred on obedience to Jesus' instruction to fill pots of water, and the water was transformed instantly into wine of excellent quality. Jesus performed His miracles on a variety of objects: on nature, vegetation, humans, and more. The miracles of Jesus have precisely the same message as His words and actions. While the parables and preaching of Jesus were verbal proclamation of the kingdom of God, His miracles were physical demonstrations of the nature of the kingdom. Miracles were carried beyond Jesus' life and ministry into the era of the apostles. In fact, Christians of the first century believed that the miracles of Jesus formed an essential part of the presentation of the gospel. In this regard, many miracles performed by the apostles after Pentecost are recorded in the Acts of the Apostles.

Miracles in Contemporary Times

There are countless examples of miraculous performances by saintly individuals throughout Christian history. For example, between the second and fifth centuries, the fathers of the Greek and Latin churches such as Justin Martyr, Irenaeus, Tertullian, and Origen attested that miracles were real, and further, that Christians have performed many miracles, mostly miraculous healings, in the name of Jesus Christ. E. Cobham Brewer (1966) attempted to present data of hundreds of miracles performed by some church fathers, saints, and the pious in Christian history from the New Testament era until the nineteenth century. All the recorded miracles are ascribed to the intervention of God in human history.

Strewn within the fabric of African Church history are notable faith healers and prophets whose ministries witnessed significant miraculous phenomena. Among them were Joseph Ayo Babalola (1904–1959), William Wade Harris of Liberia (1865–1929), Simon Kimbangu of the Congo (1889–1951), and Benson Idahosa of Nigeria (1939–1998). Parallel events took place in the Western world where revivalists, televangelists, and faith healers such as Kathryn Kuhlman, T. L. Osborn, Charles G. Finney, Oral Roberts, Kenneth E. Hagin, Benny Hinn, and Reinhard Bonnke recorded many astonishing miracles, and thus wielded great religious influence in their society. The patterns of ministry and healing methods may have varied depending on the faith healer, the location, and the period, but the miracles were very similar. These faith healers used prayers, prophecy, icons, and material objects such as candles, olive oil, water, scarves, or handkerchiefs. Testimonies of miraculous events performed by these preachers and healers have enlarged their status, and indirectly contributed to the expansion of their religious organizations.

Today, revival services, retreats, camp meetings, conventions, and evangelistic crusades have become the prominent settings associated with miracles. Many Christian preachers believe that evangelistic activities ought to go hand in hand with miraculous events. Sermons and readings from the Scriptures often proclaim that God is interested in giving miracles to His people. In the Pentecostal and charismatic churches, the proclamation of "power evangelism" has become a common feature and a major method of enlistment.

Of all miracles, miraculous acts of healing have received much attention in human history, particularly in Christianity. In fact, there are more records and testimonies of physical healing than any other type of miracle. For example, many such physical healings were recorded in connection with Kathryn Kuhlman, who made Pittsburgh, Pennsylvania, the center of her healing ministry from the 1940s to the 1960s. Medical treatment had often proved to be unhelpful, and when healed most of the people had their healing verified by independent experts. Twenty-one of Kuhlman's miracles were recorded in her best-selling book *I Believe in Miracles* (1962). Pentecostal and charismatic groups portray their acts of healing as more efficacious than what modern medical treatment can offer. There are many reasons why people look to miraculous healings. First, the mystery of certain illnesses and the quest for cures continue to make people rely on the supernatural. Second, there is an ongoing recognition of the connection between religion and healing. The definitions of diseases and illnesses are particularly influenced by religious cultures. Third, modern medicine reaches only a small portion of the population in underdeveloped countries. Finally, physical healing provides the incontrovertible evidence of the reality of miracles to a doubting world.

Christian Fundamentalism and Miracles

Fundamentalists accept the reality of miracles, but the attention given to the miraculous by many churches and preachers is a source of contention for many. Fundamentalists believe that the first miracle a person can experience is that of a spiritual healing of the new birth. Miraculous transition from a sinful life to a saintly one is due to the intervention of the Spirit of God; therefore, the experiences of salvation and sanctification take precedence over all other miracles.

Miracles are regarded as signs of the presence of God among His people, especially when Christians invoke the Spirit of God in prayer and fasting. Because the cure for bodily ills is believed to be linked to spiritual healing, Fundamentalists cannot accept a bodily miracle without a concomitant spiritual healing. Therefore, teachings of holiness, righteousness, faith, and love are a means by which to achieve miracles. Lasting miracles, according to Fundamentalists, can only occur with devotion and piety rather than the contrary.

Fundamentalists believe that only gifted holy persons can perform genuine miracles. Those who sin habitually and still perform miracles are suspect. Yet, the performance of miracles is not the yardstick or evidence of holy living; God can work through anyone or anything to bring about His saving grace to humankind. The decision of who will have power to perform miracles resides with God. Since demonic people also perform miracles, Fundamentalists do not attach importance to miraculous events except when they are performed within the realm of faith in Christ alone. Furthermore, they regard miracles as only a temporary relief to sufferers before they are finally ushered in to a place of eternal bliss and rest. Miracles are designed to turn people toward God and awaken a sense of dedication and commitment. Miracles are viewed as part of God's redemptive act, hence Fundamentalists teach that churches should incorporate the teaching and practice of miracles into their evangelistic activities. They are one of the products of revivals that strengthens Fundamentalists' belief that God has the ultimate power.

Significance of Miracles

Miracles are a revelation of the divine power. A miraculous event convinces people that the numinous is present. In addition, miracles are credentials for claimants to religious authority in the form of leadership. But more important, miracles are proof of the sanctity of a holy person. In fact, faith healers in every culture are seen as divine agents and their activities have always had much social impact in their societies. Moreover, when miracles occur within religious praxis they are accepted as the superiority of one religion over the others. For instance, the God of Elijah in 1 Kings 18 was seen as superior over Baal in the contest on Mount Carmel because a miracle accompanied Elijah's offering. The miracles performed by Jesus confirmed that He was the Messiah. Following this, miracles also confirm the divine nature of the Christian faith. Furthermore, since most miracles are acts of mercy, they could be viewed as spiritual blessings to the recipients of miracles. Finally, miracles are part of the ongoing ministry of the church; they project the image of God, promote the church ministry, and make it more visible in the society.

Conclusion

Miracles do take place, particularly in Christian tradition. Miracles are sought after by many because they strengthen the faith of adherents. However, a question that needs further consideration is "Are miracles an end in themselves or a means to an end?" Miracles are reflective of particular patterns of religious thought and a perspective of the universe. The constant preoccupation with miraculous healings signals a paradigm shift from the scientific worldview to a religious one. Although, the more illiterate societies tend to rely on the miraculous, the acceptance of the miraculous by any people indicates a recognition of the supernatural. That the natural and the supernatural worlds are organically linked is a belief that has often been confirmed by miraculous events.

Matthews A. Ojo

See also Angels; Healing, Faith; Virgin Birth

Bibliography

Brewer, E. Cobham. (1966) *A Dictionary of Miracles: Imitative, Realistic and Dogmatic.* Philadelphia: J. N. Lippincott Company.

Brown, Colin. (1984) *Miracles and the Critical Mind.* Grand Rapids, MI: Wm. B. Eerdmans.

Isichei, Elizabeth. (1995) *A History of Christianity in Africa: From Antiquity to the Present.* Grand Rapids, MI: Wm. B. Eerdmans.

Kuhlman, Kathryn. (1962) *I Believe in Miracles.* New York: Pyramid Books.

Lockyer, Herbert. (1961) *All the Miracles of the Bible.* Grand Rapids, MI: Zondervan Publishing.

Lucas, Ernest, ed. (1997) *Christian Healing: What Can We Believe.* London: Lynx Communications.

Smedes, Lewis B., and David Allan Hubbard, eds. (1987) *Ministry and the Miraculous: A Case Study at Fuller Theological Seminary.* Pasadena, CA: Fuller Theological Seminary.

Westberg, Granger E., ed. (1979) *Theological Roots of Wholistic Health Care.* Hinsdale, IL: Wholistic Health Centers, Inc.

Williams Don. (1989) *Signs, Wonders, and the Kingdom of God: A Biblical Guide for the Reluctant Skeptic.* Ann Arbor, MI: Vine Books.

Wimber, John. (1986) *Power Evangelism.* San Francisco: Harper and Row Publishers.

Missions

Evangelism and missions have always been at the very heart and soul of the Fundamentalist movement. As a militant reform movement for traditional Orthodox Christianity, Protestant Fundamentalists seek to not only correct what they perceive to be the drift away from orthodoxy, but they are committed to the propagation of their faith through evangelism and missions. In the words of Nancy Ammerman (1994: 149), "They are an evangelistic people, anxious to share what they have found, anxious for others to experience the grace they claim."

To fully appreciate the impact of Fundamentalism on missionary activity it is necessary to examine (1) the theological imperatives that fuel the missionary enterprise, (2) the social milieu and ethos of missions in Fundamentalist circles, (3) the growth and spread of Fundamentalist mission activity, and (4) the impact on international Christianity of the Fundamentalist missions.

Fundamentalist Theology and Missions

The peculiar nature of Fundamentalist theology has a direct impact on the message, motive, and methodology of missions. In respect to their message, Fundamentalist missionaries give priority to proclaiming a message that is focused upon the life and ministry of Jesus Christ, particularly His Virgin Birth, miraculous ministry, death on the cross for the sins of humanity, physical Resurrection from the dead, and promise to return. For Fundamentalists, those who hear this message need to then respond with per-

American missionary family based in Peru (with adopted Peruvian son) in publicity photograph used by the Wycliffe Bible Translators to raise money for translating the New Testament into Huaylas Quichua, c. 1993. PHOTO COURTESY OF KAREN CHRISTENSEN.

sonal acts of repentance from sin and commit to godly living. This means not only rejecting all forms of sin but separation from compromise with it, including disassociation from any organizations, activities, or individuals that might also compromise the pure teachings of the Scriptures.

In respect to their motivation for missions, Fundamentalist missionaries find urgency in their beliefs about the "End Times." They have sought to hasten the coming of their Lord by proclaiming the Gospel to every tribe and people in fulfillment of the prophecy that the Second Coming of Christ would follow the accomplishment of this task. Furthermore, in their reading of the "signs" of the End Times they are convinced that the end of the present age is near and that the church must increase its efforts, for Jesus has already declared in John 9:4 (KJV), "I must work the works of Him who sent Me, as long as it is day; night is coming, when no man can work." With no hope of realizing reform of the world, Fundamentalists seek to save as many individuals as possible while there is still time.

Fundamentalists are also motivated by the belief that salvation and eternal life can only be obtained by faith in Jesus Christ and that no redeeming merit can be found in any other religion. Likewise, they hold to the conviction that they alone represent the true Gospel of Jesus Christ and that as the sole remnant of believers they bear the weight of responsibility for carrying out God's mission to the world. In tandem with the colonial mentality that the underdeveloped world constituted "the white man's burden," Fundamentalists embraced the concept that the salvation of the lost is their burden.

Fundamentalist theology also impacts their missionary methodology by holding missionaries to a standard of strict biblicism. All missionary activities are to be carried out according to models and standards as outlined in the Bible. Important books that spell out these standards include the *Bible Basis of Mission* (1964), by Robert Glover; *Missionary Methods: St. Paul's or Ours* ([1912] 1962), by Roland Allen; and *Biblical Theology of Missions*, by George Peters (1972). Their theology of missions also gives primacy to the tasks of evangelism, conversion, and church planting, causing Fundamentalists to prioritize ministries that proclaim their brand of truth, produce new converts, and start new (doctrinally correct) churches.

Social Milieu and Ethos of Fundamentalism

Because Fundamentalism is as much a product of its social and historical context as its theology, it is not surprising to discover that Fundamentalist

GOD'S WORD IN EVERY LANGUAGE?

Wycliffe Bible Translators and its sister organization, the Summer Institute of Linguistics, aim to translate the Word (primarily the New Testament) into every language of the world. This mission springs from what is considered a condition for the millennial return of Jesus to earth in Revelation 14.6: *And I saw another angel fly in the midst of heaven, having the everlasting gospel preach unto them that dwell on the earth, and to every nation, and kindred, and tongue, and people.*

The organizations were founded in 1942 and were the offspring of Camp Wycliffe, a linguistics training school founded in 1934 by William Cameron Townsend, a missionary to the Cakchiquel Indians of Guatemala. Camp Wycliffe was named for John Wycliffe (1330?–1384), an English church reformer. Wycliffe has over 5,000 career and short-term members working in more than 70 nations. They are supported by individual and church donations.

Wycliffe was known throughout the Cold War for its pioneering linguistics and missionary work in remote places. It was, however, also criticized for its involvement with repressive government regimes in Latin America, and what some described as encouragement of exploitive U.S. aid, including CIA covert actions.

Wycliffe describes its mission as educational and social: "holistic people-centered development." The publicity materials of SIL explain that its focus is on the study of unwritten languages and it has a faculty of anthropologists and linguists, many of whom are active in the scholarly community.

Further Reading

Colby, Gerard with Dennett, Charlotte. (1995) *Thy Will Be Done—The Conquest of the Amazon: Nelson Rockefeller and Evangelism in the Age of Oil.* New York: HarperCollins.

Stoll, David (1991). *Is Latin America Turning Protestant?: The Politics of Evangelical Growth.* Berkeley and Los Angeles: University of California Press.

Karen Christensen

---

missionary activity bears the imprint of that social milieu. In order to propagate their brand of Christianity, free from the corrupting influence of modernism, Fundamentalists have established scores of new mission societies and have started a host of new (separatistic) national churches, schools, and ministries that are mirror images of their American founders. This has virtually internationalized the theological distinctives and denominational issues of American Christianity.

Fundamentalists are also convinced of the pervasive nature of sin and its influence on the degeneration of contemporary culture, resulting in a hostile stance toward the world and its cultural institutions. This has a wide-ranging consequence on their mission activities. They seek to avoid ministries that focus on improving the quality of human life (com-munity development, social welfare, education other than Bible training, and more) and emphasize instead evangelistic tasks. In tension with this anti-culture perspective is a naive captivity to a belief in the possibility of founding a Christian republic and a hyperpatriotism to American values because these are embodied in their perception that America's founding fathers were motivated by Christian principles. Their failure to separate the essence of the gospel message from its cultural context indicates that Fundamentalist missionaries are prone to advocating an (idealized middle-class Victorian) American form of Christianity in the countries where they serve. Their hostile attitude toward culture also inspires them to seek to reform individuals by attacking what they perceive to be sinful practices without consideration of the social consequences of the changes they are advocating. New converts who embrace this message are inevitably caught in the conflict between the demands of their traditional culture and the requirements of their new faith. This results in what has become known as an "extractionist" approach to conversion. New converts are pressured to deny their traditional cultures, reject all aspects of their traditional religions, and remove themselves from their former associations.

The Fundamentalist missionaries are generally the product of Fundamentalist Bible schools. Starting in the late nineteenth century these Bible schools grew in number until there were well over 160 with annual enrollments of more than 25,000 students. The curriculum at these institutions was confined almost exclusively to Bible study, missions, pastoral ministries, and evangelism. By 1956 at the height of the Fundamentalist movement, Moody Bible Institute, which was the largest of the Bible schools, had an enrollment of over 1,000 students and some 3,600 graduates had already entered into some type of foreign missionary service.

Fundamentalist Mission Agencies: Their Growth and Activities

Measuring the growth and accomplishments of the Fundamentalist mission agencies is not an easy task because there is little agreement among Fundamentalists as to who actually represents them. The Fundamentalist historian George Dollar (1973) sought to identify mission agencies that were representative of Fundamentalism in 1973 by grouping forty-five agencies into three categories: militant Fundamentalist agencies (seventeen mission boards), moderate Fundamentalist agencies (eleven mission boards), and modified Fundamentalist or "new Evangelical" agencies (seventeen mission boards). Together, these missions constituted approximately ten percent of the total North American Protestant mission force in 1979. This list, even at the time of its writing, does not provide a reliable guide for Fundamentalist missions inasmuch as it has noticeable gaps, including the very Fundamentalist New Tribes Mission, which had some 1,500 members during that period. Furthermore, it does not accommodate the porous nature and dynamic growth of Fundamentalism that has since added or dropped mission agencies from this list.

If we broaden the definition of what constitutes a Fundamentalist by including those mission agencies that are conservative in doctrine and practices but not as separatistic in their affiliations, then another way to look at the strength and growth of Fundamentalism in missions can be found in the reports of two associations of missions—the Interdenominational Foreign Missions Association (IFMA) and the Evangelical Foreign Missions Association (EFMA). The IFMA was formed in 1917 by several well-known missions with strong Fundamentalist ties. By 1967 the IFMA represented almost one-third of the North American Protestant mission force and, today, continues to grow in numbers. The EFMA was formed in 1945. Its goal was to develop a wider fellowship and cooperation among conservative Christians who were not members of the IFMA, including conservative or Fundamentalist denominational missions, Pentecostals, and charismatic organizations. Their choice of the term "Evangelical" also represents a growing movement among conservative and Fundamentalist churches who agree with the principal doctrines of Fundamentalist groups but who are divided about method. (They advocate greater cooperation with Christians from other [non-Fundamentalist] traditions including Pentecostals and charismatic Christians, and a more reformist stance toward culture and society.) In 1967 missionaries serving with the EFMA represented one-quarter of the total North American Protestant missionary force and their numbers also continue to grow. Since 1960 missionaries serving under the oversight of the IFMA–EFMA represent well over one-half of North American Protestant missions.

These numbers still do not represent the total influence of Fundamentalism in missions inasmuch as many Fundamentalist agencies refuse to be associated with either the IFMA or the EFMA. Statistics from the *Mission Handbook 1998–2000* (1997) reveal that the number of missionaries serving with the ten largest unaffiliated missions who identify themselves as either Fundamentalists or as conservative Evangelicals totals over eight thousand, representing still another twenty-one percent of the missionary force. Clearly, at the beginning of the twenty-first century, Fundamentalists and Evangelicals represent well over three-quarters of the total North American Protestant missionary force serving more than one year. Their numbers have grown from some four thousand missionaries in 1900 to more than forty-two thousand by the year 2000. They are deployed in more than 192 different nations with approximately thirty-three percent serving in Latin America, thirty percent in Asia, twenty-two percent in Africa, ten percent in Europe, and four percent in Oceania.

The Impact on International Christianity by Fundamentalist Missions

How effective have Fundamentalist missions been during their almost one hundred years of missionary activity? Again, this is a difficult question to answer because the greatest strength of Fundamentalism has been in the manner in which it has focused its ministries on the transformation of individual lives, and it is not possible to measure character, discipleship, and holiness. Furthermore, the failure of Fundamentalists to address the social implications of personal conversion and transformation has sometimes led to confusion, conflict, and contradiction in the larger ebb and flow of international politics, national loyalties, or social issues. Indeed, Fundamentalist attempts to form public policy have sometimes proven to be disastrous. (One example is that of the clumsy attempt by Fundamentalist believers in Guatemala under the leadership of Rios Montt to reform their government.) Such failures in the public arena have sometimes given the impression that Fundamentalism itself has been a failure and yet its missionary work continues to grow and new churches filled with fresh converts are added annually. Statistics have never been published to measure the growth of Fundamentalism overseas and can only be presumed to be a fraction of the total number of individuals who are now classified as Evangelicals worldwide. How big a fraction one wishes to make them will depend upon how tightly one defines the term "Fundamentalist." Nevertheless, the total number of Evangelicals in the world has grown dramatically as evidenced by the following figures:

Evangelicals by Region in 1990.

Region	Population (in millions)	Evangelicals (in millions)	Christian Percentages (%)		
			Total	Prot.	Evang
Africa	480.8	63	48.1	20.2	13.2
Asia	2,940.3	90	7.3	3.9	3.1
Europe	507.9	14	77.2	18.3	2.8
Latin America	412.7	44	90.9	12.1	11.1
Oceania	26.5	4	66.8	37.0	15.8

Fundamentalist Missions and the Future

By 1980 the total number of North American mission societies increased to 649, with the greatest number of these representing conservative churches and Fundamentalist believers. This is an increase from only 45 mission agencies in 1880, one hundred years earlier. The number of missionaries serving with Fundamentalist and Evangelical mission boards continues to show a steady increase, but once again it is difficult to quantify their influence because of the fluid boundaries between Fundamentalism and Evangelicalism within conservative Christianity.

In a recent trend, Fundamentalist and Evangelical missionaries have also begun to enhance their ministries through the extensive use of short-term missionaries, who serve for anywhere from a period of a few weeks to twelve months. In 1996 there were more than 66,000 short-term missionaries serving under North American mission agencies, representing a more than 150 percent increase in the number of long-term missionaries.

The Evangelical, or reform, branch of Fundamentalism has also become much more sophisticated in respect to its missionary methodology, and continues to have an influence on the more conservative branches of Fundamentalism. In one instance, contemporary missionary statesmen and scholars have begun to engage in more serious academic reflection on their missionary activities through the new emerging discipline of missiology. As an academic discipline missiology has sought to incorporate the theoretical insights and academic strengths of studies in anthropology, theology, and mission history to create an integrated field of study that will realize immediate benefits for the future work of missions. Two new societies, The American Society of Missiology and The Evangelical Missiological Society (which is the more conservative and Fundamentalist agency), now hold annual meetings to discuss current mission issues and to promote missionary scholarship. This new reflective approach to missions is a wholesome harbinger for the future of missions as the years of hard work by Fundamentalist and Evangelical missionaries begins to show a growing number of followers and the formation of international communities of believers whose presence will increasingly influence national development.

Douglas Hayward

See also Bible; Bible Schools; Bible Study; Conversion; End Times; Gospel; Salvation; Sin and Sinners; Southeast Asia

Bibliography

Ammerman, Nancy. (1994) "Accounting for Christian Fundamentalisms: Social Dynamics and Rhetorical Strategies." In *Accounting for Fundamentalisms*, edited by Martin Marty and Scott Appleby. Chicago: University of Chicago Press, 149–172.

Dollar, George. (1973) *A History of Fundamentalism in America*. Greenville, SC: Bob Jones University Press.

Gasper, Louis. (1963) *The Fundamentalist Movement*. The Hague: Mouton and Co.

Johnstone, Patrick. (1993) *Operation World*. Grand Rapids, MI: Zondervan Publishing.

Siewert, John, and Edna Valdez. (1997) *Mission Handbook 1998–2000*. Monrovia, CA: Mission Advanced Research and Communications Center (MARC).

Stoll, David. (1994) "Jesus Is Lord of Guatemala: Evangelical Reform in a Death-Squad State." In *Accounting for Fundamentalisms*, edited by Martin Marty and Scott Appleby. Chicago: University of Chicago Press, 99–123.

Wilson, Samuel. (1980) *Mission Handbook: North America Protestant Ministries Overseas*, 12th ed. Monrovia, CA: Missions Advanced Research and Communications Center (MARC).

Moral Majority

The Moral Majority was a controversial, politically conservative lobby with a largely Evangelical Protestant membership that flourished briefly during the closing years of the twentieth century.

Historical Background

The Moral Majority came into being during a period of intense social change in the United States. This change stemmed, in part, from the radical politics of the Vietnam protests of the 1960s. In addition to this were the deeper historical and technological innovations in American life. For example, women participated increasingly in commercial and political life throughout the twentieth century, a movement accelerated by World War II. Innovations in birth control, especially "the pill," likewise wrought a transformation of sexual mores. Traditional familial roles were questioned and former taboos, such as out-of-wedlock births, ceased to apply. Welcomed by some, these changes offended and alarmed others.

A series of judicial decisions also exacerbated conservative social sensibility. In 1962, the *Engle v. Vitale* Supreme Court decision seemed to sever any connection between the public schools and religion. Then, in 1973, in *Roe v. Wade*, that same court effectively legalized abortion "on demand" throughout the United States and overturned long-standing legislative prescription in the several states. Quite apart from the substance of these decisions, which was immensely controversial, political conservatives were deeply offended that such sweeping social renovation was made by a nonelected and largely secretive body, from which there was no appeal.

A New Constituency

The Rev. Jerry Falwell, pastor of the Thomas Road Baptist Church in Lynchburg, Virginia, was a highly successful "televangelist" whose *Old Time Gospel Hour* was seen nationally. His own congregation was large and thriving. He was a talented and ingratiating speaker. In 1979, Falwell founded the Moral Majority to mobilize what he saw as Americans offended by the changing social milieu but bereft of an effective means of protest. The core tenets of the organization were based on the sanctity of the traditional nuclear family. Homosexuality was seen to threaten the family—although precisely how was left somewhat unclear. Abortion was especially detested and the Moral Majority advocated grass-roots political work through state legislatures to overturn or modify *Roe v. Wade*. (The courts largely frustrated such efforts, despite frequent legislative success.) The organization also lobbied to restore prayer and religious observance in the public schools. It also excoriated pornography.

The Moral Majority's main constituent was politically conservative Evangelical Protestants, a group that enjoyed steady and impressive growth in membership throughout the twentieth century. Several denominations fit this category, but the various Baptist conventions came to epitomize it in the popular mind. As a rule, this group was not notably political and certainly not a monolithic voting bloc.

However, segments of it were briefly galvanized by the rhetoric of the Moral Majority.

Officially, the Moral Majority welcomed members from all religious persuasions and counted non-Evangelical Protestants, Roman Catholics, and Jews among its members. This slight ecumenicism, however, did not convince the general public that the organization was other than a vehicle for Evangelical Protestantism and the public was largely correct. It was often derided as "Fundamentalist," but that term is much too amorphous and, fairly or not, laden with pejorative connotation to accurately describe its Evangelical makeup.

It is likely that the influence of the Moral Majority on national politics was grossly exaggerated. At its height, it claimed a membership of seven million, but even a neutral scholarly estimate of 800,000 members at its peak may be too high. Most of its "state chapters" existed on paper. It served as a useful whipping boy for political and social liberals, who uniformly denounced it, and, ironically, it thus may have been more useful to its foes than friends. Regardless, in 1986 Falwell announced a new organization, the Liberty Foundation, that effectively superseded the Moral Majority and thereafter little was heard of the former lobby.

The General Reaction toward the Moral Majority

The general reaction toward the Moral Majority among commentators and the non-Evangelical public was instructive and not altogether consistent. Much was made of the presence of the clergy in its councils and there were dark warnings regarding the Jeffersonian tradition in America of separation of church and state. However, no such strictures were applied to left-leaning clergy active in politics, of which there was a host: Rev. Martin Luther King, Rev. Jesse Jackson, and the Rev. William Sloan Coffin, to name but a few. There was, as well, a well-established tradition of clerical involvement in American social issues, especially the Social Gospel of the post–Civil War era, consistently endorsed by liberal scholars. One must conclude that it was the content of the Moral Majority's message that alarmed critics, while the church and state issue was something of a red herring.

Falwell's crusading rhetoric annoyed many. Often, it was needlessly apocalyptic and self-righteous. Further, it tended, in the opinion of more than a few,

to scapegoat entire populations, especially homosexuals. More detached scholars might have noted, although few did, that the condemnatory language of the Moral Majority fit exactly into a long tradition of Protestant jeremiads that included the "Demon Rum" crusade of the nineteenth century. Society had largely survived such perceived evils and was likely to endure present ones with equal aplomb.

On the other side, the anti-Falwell rhetoric and alarms about the Moral Majority reached a pitch that can best be described as fatuous. In 1980, a cabinet secretary espied the emergence of an "Ayatollah Khomeini in this country." The doctrine of separation of church and state was wheeled out and interpreted to mean that Evangelical Christians, precisely because they were Evangelical Christians, were somehow forbidden to engage in political activity. The anti-Falwell hysteria ultimately discredited itself by so excoriating the legitimate exercise of common civil rights of speech and assembly. In 1989, the Moral Majority was officially disbanded by Falwell, and in the end, the group seems historically something of a tempest in a teapot.

Robert K. Whalen

See also New Christian Right

Bibliography

Fackre, Gabriel. (1982) *The Religious Right and Christian Faith*. Grand Rapids, MI: Wm. B. Eerdmans.

Georgiana, Sharon Linzey. (1989) *The Moral Majority and Fundamentalism: Plausibility and Dissonance*. New York: E. Mellen Press.

Kater, John. (1982) *The Moral Majority in Perspective*. New York: Seabury Press.

Snowball, David. (1991) *Continuity and Change in the Rhetoric of the Moral Majority*. New York: Praeger Publishers.

Mormons, Fundamentalist (Polygamous)

In American society, the term "Fundamentalist" generally refers to Protestant Christians, usually associated with various Evangelical-conservative religious bodies (e.g., the Southern Baptist Convention, the Assemblies of God, the Churches of God, the Seventh-Day Adventists, etc.), which accept a literal interpretation of the Bible. These groups are contrasted with the more mainstream denominations (e.g., Episcopalians, Presbyterians, Methodists, Roman Catholics, etc.) that take a more figurative or allegorical view of the Bible. But, in the Intermountain West—the nation's Mormon stronghold—"Fundamentalist" generally refers to various individuals or groups who continue to believe in the practice of "plural marriage" or polygyny—often referred to as "The Principle." According to Bennion, mainstream Mormons and Mormon Fundamentalists adhere to different conceptions of God:

> Mainstream Mormons are torn between two poles: a belief that Jesus is the God and the "Father" of this world and a belief that he is the "Brother" who is to help his brothers and sisters find their way back to the Father. Fundamentalists believe that Christ is the Son who will take over the Father's place in the hierarchical schema and that Adam is the Father, the God of this world. (Bennion 1998: 21)

Mormon Fundamentalists also reject the Mormon Church's lifting of the ban that excluded black males from the priesthood and disapprove of the church's willingness to shorten the original temple garments in order to accommodate for more contemporary dress styles.

The Emergence and Development of the Mormon Fundamentalist Movement

Although the Proclamation Manifesto of 1890 presented by Wilford Woodruff, the president of the Church of Jesus Christ of Latter-day Saints at the time, theoretically prohibited "plural marriage" or polygyny among Mormons residing in the United States, this practice continued unofficially among members of the church hierarchy as well as for Mormons in Mexico and Canada into the early twentieth century. At a time when the total membership of the Mormon Church was between 200,000 and 250,000, O'Dea (1957: 246) estimates that the number of Mormons living in polygynous households during the years 1890 to 1904 was approximately 21,000 to 28,000. In 1904, after being forced to testify at a U.S. Senate committee hearing that he lived with his plural wives, President Joseph F. Smith (1838–1918), founder of the Mormon Church, issued the "Second Manifesto," which reiterated that plural marriage was forbidden and adding that those entering such an arrangement would be excommunicated from the church. Two active polygynists among his apostles—John W. Taylor and Matthias Cowley—were dismissed from their positions shortly afterward. Beginning in the 1920s, the Mormon Church began to assist law enforcement agencies in the prosecution of polygynists. Despite repeated church warnings, various individuals and groups continued to practice polygyny, an activity that still flourishes in the Intermountain West. The continuation of plural marriage served as one of the several rationales for many of the Mormon sects that appeared over the course of the twentieth century.

John Tanner Clark served as a central figure in the emergence of the Fundamentalist movement. He was excommunicated from the church in 1905 for having circulated letters condemning the Manifesto and the General Authorities. Most Fundamentalist sects point to a statement by Lorin Woolley on September 29, 1929, as the rationale for their practice of plural marriage. Woolley claimed that John Taylor, a polygynist president of the church, called seven men together in September 1886 shortly before his death and told them that plural marriage was not to disappear from the face of the earth. Taylor allegedly ordained Samuel Bateman, George Q. Cannon, John W. Woolley, Lorin Woolley, and Charles Wilkins (not all of whom were present at the "secret meeting") as apostles and patriarchs to continue the practice of plural marriage. Claiming direct authority from Taylor, Lorin Woolley ordained Leslie Broadbent, John Y. Barlow, Joseph W. Musser, and Charles Zittig to be high-priest apostles of the "Council of Friends" (van Wagoner 1986: 209).

On April 4, 1931, President Heber J. Grant announced that the Mormon Church would offer legal assistance in the prosecution of individuals engaged in plural marriage. Following the church's "Final Manifesto" in 1933, the Utah legislature passed a bill on March 14, 1935, declaring "unlawful cohabitation" a felony. Apparently in response to the stringent position, a month later the Fundamentalists came "out of the closet" and began a monthly magazine, *Truth*, which continued to be published for the next 15 years and was devoted to the defense of The Principle. The decision by its editor, Joseph W. Musser, to publish the speeches and writings of the nineteenth-century Mormon leaders contributed to the church's concerted effort to suppress *Truth*. As Bradley (1993: 37–38) observes, *Truth* functioned as a "means of reconciliation among the different factions

THE PROCLAMATION MANIFESTO OF 1890

To Whom it may concern:

Press dispatches having been sent for political purposes, from Salt Lake City, which have been widely published, to the effect that the Utah Commission, in their recent report to the Secretary of the Interior, allege that plural marriages are still being solemnized and that forty or more such marriages have been contracted in Utah since last June or during the past year, also that in public discourses the leaders of the Church have taught, encouraged and urged the continuance of the practice of polygamy—

I, therefore, as President of the Church of Jesus Christ of Latter-day Saints, do hereby, in the most solemn manner, declare that these charges are false. We are not teaching polygamy or plural marriage, nor permitting person to enter into its practice, and I deny that either forty or any other number of plural marriages have during that period been solemnized in our Temples or in any other place in the Territory.

One case has been reported, in which the parties allege that the marriage was performed in the Endowment House, in Salt Lake City, in the Spring of 1889, but I have not been able to learn who performed the ceremony; whatever was done in this matter was without my knowledge. In consequence of this alleged occurrence the Endowment House was, by my instructions, taken down without delay.

Inasmuch as laws have been enacted by Congress forbidding plural marriages, which laws have been pronounced constitutional by the court of last resort, I hereby declare my intentions to submit to those laws, and to use my influence with the members of the Church over which I preside to have them do likewise.

There is nothing in my teachings to the Church or in those of my associates, during the time specified, which can be reasonably construed to inculcate or encourage polygamy; and when any Elder of the Church has used language which appeared to convey any such teaching, he has been promptly reproved. And I now publicly declare that my advice to the Latter-day Saints is to refrain from contracting any marriage forbidden by the law of the land.

Wilford Woodruff
President of the Church of Jesus Christ of Latter-day Saints.

Source: *Mormon Manifesto one-1890.* www.polygamyinfo.com

---

of fundamentalist Mormons." In 1936, fifteen Fundamentalist leaders were arrested and convicted for practicing polygyny. After eleven of these men agreed to refrain from advocating plural marriage, they were paroled.

Around 1929 a group of polygynists living at Lee's Ferry in southwestern Utah decided that it would be safer to move to Short Creek in the remote Arizona Strip in the extreme northwest corner of the state. When in 1935 the Arizona authorities prosecuted two residents for practicing polygyny, Joseph Musser and John Barlow came to assist them and viewed Short Creek as a place where a large number of Fundamentalists could await the millennium. When Musser lost interest, the aging Barlow remained its spiritual leader and ordained one of its residents to be his successor. The community operated on a quasi-communal basis called "United

Effort," and since there were few local jobs and the land was harsh, many of the men worked elsewhere and contributed their wages to a common fund.

Given its status as a showcase for polygyny, it is not surprising that over the years the community experienced harassment and periodic raids. The last of these occurred in July 1953, upon the order of the Arizona governor, when more than one hundred police officers raided Short Creek and arrested thirty-six men and women. National outrage forced the authorities to release the women and 263 children who had been taken into custody. As van Wagoner (1986: 204) observes, "The $600,000 'Operation Short Creek' failed to eradicate polygamy.... Men returned from their jail sentences to their wives and children with increased resolve to 'live the principle' of polygamy." Since then, law enforcement agencies have looked the other way. The community grew and spilled over into Utah. Bradley (1993: 182) reports that "[b]y 1992, more than 4,500 fundamentalists lived in the town known after 1962 as Colorado City/ Hildale." The community operates Barlow University, which offers two-year degrees and certificates. Its catalog states that the curriculum "is directed primarily to provide education for members of the Fundamentalist Church of Jesus Christ of Latter-day Saints" (quoted in Altman and Ginat 1996: 51).

Diversity within the Mormon Fundamentalist Movement

As is characteristic of religious sects, the Mormon Fundamentalist movement has had more than its share of schismatic tendencies (Shields 1982). Much of the contention within the movement has revolved around the issue of who holds the "keys" or the authority of the priesthoods and the rights of succession to the council leadership. Fundamentalists often refer to various factions by names of their leaders (e.g., Johnsonites, Allredites, etc.). Most Fundamentalists regard themselves to be members of the Mormon Church, even if they have been excommunicated by it.

The Short Creek and Salt Lake communities of the Fundamentalists grew throughout the 1940s but splintered in the early 1950s. When Barlow died in 1949, Musser took over the reins of leadership, but his ailing health prompted some members to question his decisions. His appointment of his personal naturopath, Rulon Allred, to the council in the 1950s prompted the Short Creek community to rebel. LeRoy Johnson emerged as its leader, and their

church came to be known as the Fundamentalist Church of Jesus Christ of Latter-day Saints. He led the group until his death at age 98 in 1986 (Altman and Ginat 1996: 47).

Although not as well known as the Short Creek or Colorado City groups, the Apostolic United Brethren or the Allredites probably constitutes the largest of the Mormon Fundamentalist sects. Its some ten thousand members are scattered about in branches in Arizona, New Mexico, Utah, Wyoming, Idaho, Montana, Canada, and Mexico (Bennion 1998: 17–26) The sect has its administrative base in Bluffton, a suburb of Salt Lake City. Many of the branches, including the well-known Pinesdale community at the base of the Bitterroot Mountains in Montana, practice "United Order"—a form of communalism that seeks to rejuvenate nineteenth-century utopian ideals. Owen Allred has led the group since his brother's assassination in 1977.

The most turbulent faction within the Fundamentalist movement is connected with the LeBaron family of Mexico. The sect, called the Church of the Firstborn of the Fulness of Time [sic], claimed that its politicoreligious hierarchy was of a higher status than either those of the other Fundamentalist groups or the Mormon Church. In addition to internal violence within the LeBaron sect, Ervil LeBaron was convicted of masterminding the assassination of Rulon Allred in 1977, and for conspiring the unsuccessful murder of his own brother, Verlan (van Wagoner 1986: 217).

Probably the most colorful of the various Fundamentalist sects is the Church of Christ of Solemn Assembly started by pistol-packing Alex Joseph as a schism from the Allderites in 1975. After he and his fifteen or so wives and their children were evicted from Bureau of Land Management land in southern Utah, Joseph and members of his sect incorporated the town of Big Water.

Several other Fundamentalist sects also exist, such as the Latter-day Church of Christ or the Davis County Cooperative. Furthermore, enclaves of independent Fundamentalists are scattered about the Intermountain West and California. Law enforcement agencies have estimated that as many as fifty thousand individuals are members of Fundamentalist households. A fair number of Fundamentalists may continue to be members of the Mormon Church, patiently awaiting the day when the higher form of marriage will be reinstated by its leaders. At any rate, as Driggs observes,

Fundamentalist Mormons are very traditional. Families and children are extremely important, indeed are the primary focus of community life. Divorce or, in the case of plural families, a "cancellation of sealings," is frowned upon, though it does occur. Community sexual mores are very restrictive, beginning with extreme modesty in dress and appearance. (Driggs 1991: 51)

The Mormon Fundamentalist Movement as an Effort to Revitalize Modern Mormonism

Whereas Mormonism emerged as a nineteenth-century revitalization movement that tended to cater to people on the fringes of the larger society, over time it evolved from a religious utopia in the Midwest to a virtual theocratic nation-state in the Intermountain West to a global theocratic corporation in which religious and business leadership became synonymous. Twentieth-century Mormonism increasingly came to replicate patterns of class stratification existing in the larger American capitalist society. While the precursors of the Mormon Fundamentalist movement predate the Great Depression, its greatest appeal was to numerous working-class Mormons at a time when they began to perceive significant socioeconomic differences between themselves and the leaders of their church. Even today, the Mormon Fundamentalist movement appears to be, by and large, a working-class movement. Although little research has been done on the socioeconomic composition of the Mormon Fundamentalist movement, anthropologist Janet Bennion provides the following profile of a sample of 1,024 converts to the Allred group.

[O]nly 69% (706) had graduated from high school. Of that number, 12% (143) had earned a college degree, and 23% (236) had attended college. Overall, blue-collar labor was the most common profession (35% or 358 individuals), with a smaller percentage in the occupations of manufacturer (12% or 82 individuals), teacher (21% or 215 individuals), administrator (6% or 61 individuals), and salesperson (26% or 266 individuals). (Bennion 1998: 65)

Elsewhere, Altman and Ginat (1996: 84), based upon their study of an urban Fundamentalist group and a rural Fundamentalist group, note that "[f]amilies in our sample are from middle and lower socioeconomic levels."

Historically, the Mormon Fundamentalist movement has attempted to revitalize the doctrines and practices that have been either discarded or held in abeyance by mainstream Mormonism during the twentieth century. The movement, along with various other Mormon sects such as the Levites or the Aaronic Order (Baer 1988), has sought to resurrect cooperative and egalitarian ideals that its members have associated with nineteenth-century Mormonism. In many ways, the Fundamentalists regard plural marriage, their practice of United Order or Effort, and their adherence to the Adam–God concept as symbols of an earlier Golden Age that the Mormon Church abandoned as it evolved into a respectable institution that has become part and parcel of mainstream American life. In contrast to its stance between the 1920s and 1950s when it actively cooperated with law enforcement agencies in the prosecution of Fundamentalists, the Mormon Church in recent decades has adopted a laissez-faire stance toward the Fundamentalist movement and also tends to either downplay or ignore the centrality of plural marriage at an earlier time in its history. Nevertheless, the Mormon Church still does "seal" plural wives to men in its temple marriages. In essence, the church has relegated the issue of plural marriage to the "celestial" kingdom or the highest level of the Mormon afterlife where a man may eventually evolve into a God accompanied by his Goddess-wives. Ironically, closer to this earth, a Canadian court ruled in 1992, in a case involving the Colorado City group, that a law-banning polygyny violated constitutional guarantees of religious freedom. A leader of the sect viewed this decision as an indication that plural marriage would eventually be legalized in the United States (Altman and Ginat 1996: 58). At any rate, U.S. legal authorities have not prosecuted Mormon Fundamentalist polygynists for years.

Hans A. Baer

Bibliography

Altman, Irwin, and Joseph Ginat. (1996) *Polygamous Families in Contemporary Society.* Cambridge: Cambridge University Press.

Baer, Hans A. (1988) *Recreating Utopia in the Desert: A Sectarian Response to Modern Mormonism.* Albany: SUNY Press.

Bennion, Janet. (1998) *Women of Principle: Female Networking in Contemporary Mormon Polygyny.* New York: Oxford University Press.

Bradley, Martha Sonntag. (1993) *Kidnapped from That Land: The Government Raids on the Polygamists of Short Creek.* Salt Lake City: University of Utah Press.

Driggs, Ken. (1991) "Twentieth-Century Polygamy and Fundamentalist Mormons in Southern Utah." *Dialogue* 24: 44–58.

O'Dea, Thomas F. (1957) *The Mormons.* Chicago: University of Chicago Press.

Shields, Steven L. (1992) *Divergent Paths of the Restoration: A History of the Latter Day Saint Movement.* Bountiful, UT: Restoration Research.

Van Wagoner, Richard S. (1986) *Mormon Polygamy: A History.* Salt Lake City: Signature Press.

Mormons, Mainstream and Protestant

Since its emergence in upstate New York in 1830, Mormonism has manifested fundamentalist or literalist tendencies in several ways: (1) its emphasis on the *Book of Mormon* as a literal record of Israelites who populated the New World; (2) the insistence of certain Mormon sects, whose adherents are often referred to in the Intermountain West as "Fundamentalists," to continue the practices of polygyny or "plural marriage" and communal living characteristic of nineteenth-century Mormonism; and (3) a pattern of accepting certain literal interpretations of the Bible characteristic of Protestant Fundamentalism. This article focuses on the last of these tendencies. In contrast to many Protestant Fundamentalists, who often have either eschewed higher education or have expressed wariness about it, Mormonism has historically placed, and continues to place, a strong emphasis upon not only religious education but also secular education. As a consequence, Mormons have struggled with literal and allegorical interpretations of the Bible as well as their own sacred scriptures.

Mormonism, Critical Biblical Studies, and Science in the Late Nineteenth and Early Twentieth Centuries

Like most Protestant Christians and Roman Catholics, nineteenth-century Mormons subscribed to a literal interpretation of the Bible. In addition to accepting the *Book of Mormon*, Mormons rely upon the King James version of the Bible as well as an "inspired translation" written by Joseph Smith (1805–1844), founder of the Mormon Church. As he did with many theological matters, the Mormon prophet felt free to interpret the Bible according to his own spiritual insights and stated that "there are many things in the Bible which do not, as they now stand, accord with the revelations of the Holy Ghost to me" (Barlow 1991: 57). Sociologist Thomas O'Dea captures the essence of the Mormon approach to the Bible in the following quote:

> [D]espite Joseph Smith's recognition that the Bible need not necessarily be taken literally in all cases, the modern scriptures were certainly to be so understood. Literalism became and has largely remained characteristic of the Mormon approach to the text of modern revelation. The Bible, recopied for generations, translated over the centuries into various languages, may be unclear, may even be seriously corrupted, but the scriptures presented to the world in our own time by a man [namely Joseph Smith] who talked with God, translated by a modern prophet through divine inspiration and miraculous assistance—these scriptures must be literally true, or the very foundations of Mormon faith are threatened. (O'Dea 1957: 226)

Nevertheless, the debates over biological evolution and biblical studies that Protestants and Catholics struggled over in the early decades of the twentieth century also impacted Mormonism. Various Mormon leaders, theologians, and scholars argued that religion and science are mutually compatible endeavors. Such views were expressed by John A. Widtsoe, a member of the Quorum of the Twelve, in his *Joseph Smith As Scientist* (1908), *Science and the Gospel* (1908–1909), and *The Earth and Man* (1930); B. H. Roberts, a member of the First Quorum of the Seventy, in his *Joseph Smith: The Prophet-Teacher* (1908–1912); and Joseph F. Merrill in his *The Truth-Seeker and Mormonism* (1946). Roberts believed that the earth was at least two billion years old and accepted the existence of pre-Adamic humans (Barlow 1991: 114). William H. Chamberlain, who had studied biblical criticism at the University of Chicago, in his *Essay on Nature* (1915) and Fredrick J. Pack in his *Science and Belief in God* (1924), argued that Mormonism is compatible with both Darwinian evolutionary theory and geological studies that ascribe an old age to the earth. Although a number of church leaders accepted the notion of an old earth, most of them, with the possible exception of Roberts, rejected the Darwinian evolutionary theory. Conversely, various other early-twentieth-century church leaders, such as Joseph Field Smith, vehemently rejected both evolutionary and geological theories. According to Paul (1992: 26), many Mormon Church leaders, scientists, and laypersons regarded science as a "quest for knowledge" that would contribute to "eternal betterment." Evolutionary theory and geology have been and continue to be taught at various Mormon universities and colleges, including Brigham Young University in Provo, Utah. Despite the existence of a relatively large proportion of scientists within the church, Mormon anthropologist John L. Sorenson (1997: 75) states that "scientists generally do not know much about Mormonism and rarely care to know more; few Mormons are sufficiently informed about science to see how it might, or might not, relate to their religious life."

Institutional Forces Promoting Fundamentalism among Mormons

Mormon sociologist Armand Mauss delineates five institutional developments that have contributed to a growing pattern of Fundamentalism among Mormons (1994: 159–174). The first of these is a heavy reliance upon a lay clergy, including at the highest echelons, which results in the promotion of a "folk wisdom" with a "quaintly fundamentalist flavor" (Mauss 1994: 160). The second development is the "priesthood correlation movement" within the church since the 1960s that has entailed a concerted effort to create a standardized curriculum in religious study classes. The third is the seniority system for succession to the presidency of the church that has made it possible for assertive church leaders or even church bureaucrats with Fundamentalist leanings to override the opinions of the top leaders who often have been both elderly and ailing individuals. The fourth is the church hierarchy's effort to squelch the views of liberal Mormon intellectuals, some of whom are based at Brigham Young University and the church bureaucracy, but others who are based at secular colleges and universities around the country. The fifth development is the disproportionately high number of converts from the American South that historically has been the bastion of Protestant Fundamentalist thought.

Mauss asserts that whereas Mormonism exhibited a certain openness to secular scholarship, the Social Gospel, evolutionary theory, and biblical criticism during its assimilationist period in the early twentieth century, it has embraced more fundamentalist tendencies during its more recent retrenchment period. Elsewhere, Cummings (1992: 97) asserts that the "marked swing toward political and ideological conservatism which has characterized the Church since the early seventies has created a climate which is almost as favorable to institutional literalism as was the garrison mentality of the Church during much of the latter half of the nineteenth century when political opposition and national unpopularity justified such a mentality." Sociologist O. Kendall White (1987) discusses in detail three trends in the development of what he terms "Mormon neo-orthodoxy" that also depict the growing convergence between mainstream Mormonism and Protestant Fundamentalism. These are (1) a redefinition of God in infinite, ambiguous terms associated with traditional Christianity rather in the more anthropomorphic and finite terms found in early Mormonism; (2) a reformulation of human nature as depraved and sinful rather than the early conception of humans as eternally spiritually progressing entities who will retain their bodies in the afterlife and can advance to the status of Godhood; and (3) a redefinition of salvation more in terms of grace than good works.

Mauss (1994: 177–195) cites four concrete examples of how mainstream Mormonism has come to take on a Fundamentalist tone over the past several decades: (1) its concerted efforts to control intellectuals within its own ranks, (2) the susceptibility of some of its members to perceive the occurrence of Satanic conspiracies in the Intermountain West, (3) a strong millennial survivalist mentality that suggests that the world indeed has entered into the latter days, and (4) socially conservative attitudes, such as sexual Puritanism and disapproval of contraception.

In the past two decades or so, the Mormon hierarchy in particular has targeted its most vehement attacks against intellectuals, feminists, and homosexuals within the church (Anderson 1993). Throughout the 1980s, various Mormon Church leaders criticized professional Mormon scholars who had been involved in the development of the "New Mormon history"—a perspective that attempts to employ secular standards in the examination of Mormonism. Although one of these historians, Leonard Arrington,

FRONT MATTER FROM: *THE BOOK OF MORMON*

THE BOOK OF MORMON
An Account Written by
THE HAND OF MORMON
Upon Plates
Taken from the Plates of Nephi

Wherefore, it is an abridgment of the record of the people of Nephi, and also of the Lamanites—Written to the Lamanites, who are a remnant of the house of Israel; and also to Jew and Gentile—Written by way of commandment, and also by the spirit of prophecy and of revelation—Written and sealed up, and hid up unto the Lord, that they might not be destroyed—To come forth by the gift and power of God unto the interpretation thereof—Sealed by the hand of Moroni, and hid up unto the Lord, to come forth in due time by way of the Gentile—The interpretation thereof by the gift of God.

   An abridgment taken from the Book of Ether also, which is a record of the people of Jared, who were scattered at the time the Lord confounded the language of the people, when they were building a tower to get to heaven—Which is to show unto the remnant of the House of Israel what great things the Lord hath done for their fathers; and that they may know the covenants of the Lord, that they are not cast off forever—And also to the convincing of the Jew and Gentile that JESUS is the CHRIST, the ETERNAL GOD, manifesting himself unto all nations—And now, if there are faults they are the mistakes of men; where-fore, condemn not the things of God, that ye may be found spotless at the judgment-seat of Christ.

TRANSLATED BY JOSEPH SMITH, JUN.

Source: The Church of Jesus Christ of Latter-day Saints. (1981).
Salt Lake City, Utah.

---

a former professor at the University of Utah and the author of the highly touted *Great Basin Kingdom* (1958), had been appointed in 1972 to serve as the church historian, the Mormon hierarchy stripped him of his duties in 1980 and sent him into exile as a faculty member at Brigham Young University. As a result of the withdrawal of research funds and ecclesiastical sanctions, D. Michael Quinn, a renowned professor of Mormon history at Brigham Young University, opted to resign his teaching position in 1988 (Waterman and Kagel 1998: 13). Despite his excommunication from the church in 1993, he asserted that "I remain a Mormon in heritage, culture, and belief" and "I regard Joseph Smith as a prophet in the same way that Moses was" (Quinn 1994: 67–68). In addition to Quinn, the Mormon Church excommunicated at least seven other well-known intellectuals between 1993 and 1995 for heretical views

(Knowlton 1996: 113). In 1993, Brigham Young University dismissed Cecilia Konchar Farr, an assistant professor of English, for her feminist politics, and David Knowlton, a popular assistant professor of anthropology, for his writings and statements about how Mormon missionaries in Latin America had been targeted by terrorists as scapegoats due to the church's pattern of siding with authoritarian governments (Waterman and Kagel 1998) Church authorities have also criticized other Mormon intellectuals for writing articles in independent Mormon periodicals, such as *Dialogue: A Mormon Journal of Thought*, the *Journal of Mormon History*, and *Sunstone*, and presenting papers at the popular annual *Sunstone* conference. *Sunstone* in particular has published articles that have challenged antihomosexual, antifeminist, and pro-Republican proclivities on the part of the General Authorities of the church.

Rather than relying upon the views of new Mormon historians and liberal-minded Mormon religious scholars, the Mormon hierarchy has tended to grant unofficial recognition to the views of selected lay theologians within its own ranks. The most obvious example of this pattern was the late apostle Bruce R. McConkie, the author of *Mormon Doctrine*—a volume that went through several editions (Barlow 1991: 182–194). He adopts a literal interpretation of the Bible and vehemently rejects both biological evolutionary theory and geological dating of the earth. McConkie maintains that humanity is on the brink of embarking upon the seventh millennium at which time "Missouri will be wiped clean of the Gentile descendants of those who so horribly persecuted the States" and the "earth will return to its telestial state in which the world's land masses will be joined together and leveled, while the countryside is filled with trees and sweet grasses, and all thistles, thorns, briars, and weeds are no more" (Coates 1991: 171). Mauss argues that McConkie's view converges strongly with Protestant Fundamentalism,

> given (1) his antimodernist and anti-intellectual understanding of Mormonism; (2) his authoritarian expectation of unquestioning obedience by church members; (3) his readiness to label as "heresies" certain doctrines with which he disagreed, even though they had no settled canonical status in the church; and (4) the admixture of traditional religious folklore and some of his doctrinal teachings, especially where racial issues were concerned. (Mauss 1994: 162)

In reality, Mormon intellectuals exist along a continuum with some of them clearly espousing views essentially in harmony with the church hierarchy and others espousing views that are regarded as heretical. White and White (1998) delineate the following types of Mormon intellectuals: (1) "apologists" who are staunch defenders of the faith; (2) "compartmentalizers" who manage to retain a faith in Mormon tenets while accepting secular scientific, philosophical, and historical perspectives; (3) "integrators" who modify their Mormonism to conform to secular perspectives; (4) "cultural Mormons" who reject many of the Mormon doctrines but who choose to remain in the Mormon community; and (5) "apostates" who have broken their ties both with the church and Mormon culture.

Ties between Mormonism and the Religious Right

Protestant Fundamentalists have often referred to the Mormon Church as a "cult" due to the latter's theological teachings on the Godhead, the Trinity, and the afterlife as well as the use of the *Book of Mormon* and *Doctrine and Covenants* as forms of ongoing revelation. The Baptist-oriented Moody Bible Institute based in Chicago publishes numerous anti-Mormon books, including *Mormonism, Mama, and Me* written by Thelma Greer, a former Mormon, "who devotes particular emphasis to the implications of treating God as a married entity with a wife and offspring" (Coates 1991: 213). Despite such examples of Protestant Fundamentalist antipathy toward Mormonism, various scholars have pointed to the emergence of a coalition between Mormonism and the religious Right or Moral Majority (Shupe and Heinerman 1985). Certain ultraconservative Mormon politicians, such as U.S. senator Orrin Hatch from Utah, have served as a link between the church hierarchy and Protestant Fundamentalists on social issues such as abortion. The Mormon-based Freeman Institute, now the Center for Constitutional Studies, forged an alliance with Phyllis Schlafly's Stop ERA (Equal Rights Amendment) campaign in states such as Nevada, Florida, Virginia, Georgia, Missouri, Illinois, and North Carolina. Despite the unstable nature of a Mormon–new religious Right coalition, as White (1986: 186) so astutely observes, "the present political climate in American society and the Mormon church has presented opportunistic conservatives with the option of using the social structure and moral spirit of Mormonism to advance their political agenda." It is important to point out that this political coalition is very tenuous. Many Fundamentalist Protestants continue to be highly skeptical of mainstream Mormonism because of its drastic differences with the former on theological matters.

Hans A. Baer

Bibliography

Anderson, Lavina Fielding. (1993) "The LDS Intellectual Community and Church Leadership: A Contemporary Chronology." *Dialogue* 26, 1: 7–64.

Barlow, Philip L. (1991) *Mormons and the Bible: The Place of the Latter-day Saints in American Religion*. New York: Oxford University Press.

Coates, James. (1991) *In Mormon Circles: Gentiles, Jack Mormons, and Latter-day Saints.* Reading, MA: Addison-Wesley Publishing.

Cummings, Richard J. (1992) "Quintessential Mormonism: Literal-Mindedness As a Way of Life." *Dialogue* 15, 4: 93–102.

Knowlton, David Clark. (1996) "Authority and Authenticity in the Mormon Church." *Religion and the Social Order* 6: 113–134.

Mauss, Armand. (1994) *The Angel and the Beehive: The Mormon Struggle with Assimilation.* Urbana: University of Illinois Press.

O'Dea, Thomas F. (1957) *The Mormons.* Chicago: University of Chicago Press.

Paul, Erich Robert. (1992) *Science, Religion, and Mormon Cosmology.* Urbana: University of Illinois Press.

Quinn, D. Michael. (1994) "Dilemmas of Feminists and Intellectuals in the Contemporary LDS Church." *Sunstone* (June): 67–73.

Shupe, Anson, and John Heinerman (1985) "Mormonism and the New Christian Right: An Emerging Coalition." *Review of Religious Research* 27: 146–157.

Sorenson, John L. (1997) *Mormon Culture: Four Decades of Essays on Mormon Society and Personality.* Salt Lake City, UT: New Sage Books.

Waterman, Bryan, and Brian Kagel. (1998) *The Lord's University: Freedom and Authority at BYU.* Salt Lake City, UT: Signature Books.

White, Jr., O. Kendall. (1987) *Mormon Neo-orthodoxy: A Crisis Theology.* Salt Lake City, UT: Signature Books.

White, Jr., O. Kendall, and Daryl White. (1998) "Mormon Intellectuals: Living on the Boundary." Paper presented at the Society for the Scientific Study of Religion meeting, 6–8 November 1998, Montreal.

Mount of Olives

Some of the most sacred events in Christianity occurred on the Mount of Olives and it is a significant place in both the Old and New Testaments. It was a favorite retreat for King David as well as Jesus. Many Old Testament prophecies refer to the Mount of Olives (e.g., 2 Samuel 15:30; Zechariah 14:4). The first biblical mention of the Mount of Olives is that of King David's flight from Jerusalem to escape his son, Abshalom, who was chasing him (2 Samuel 15:30). Under Solomon, the Mount of Olives became infamous for the idol worship of some of his wives (2 Kings 23:13–14). Indeed, according to Jewish tradition, the Mount of Olives is the place from which came the branch carried back to Noah's ark.

In the New Testament, the Mount of Olives was Jesus' usual place to rest and pray in Jerusalem and He often spent the night there. During Holy Week, Jesus and His apostles spent the nights on the eastern slope of the eastern hill. He prophesied about the fall of Jerusalem, prayed there after the Last Supper, and was arrested in the Garden of Gethsemane (Mark 14:32–50).

Historical and Geographical Background

The Mount of Olives, or Oliver, is a double hill outside of Jerusalem. It is the highest hill in the area, rising to about 830 meters, 40 meters higher than the mountain range on which are situated Mt. Zion and the "Old City." From that hill, there was a view of the temple. The Garden of Gethsemane is found at the western base of the Mount of Olives. Today it is housed within the walls of the Church of all Nations. The name "Mount of Olives" describes the whole mountain range running from north to south, directly east of the "Old City" of Jerusalem. The names Har HaZaytim (Mount of Olives) and Har HaMoshcha (Mount of Anointing) derive from the olive trees that flourished on the mountain range. Oil was a precious ointment, used to anoint kings and for religious services in the nearby temple. The hill was a favorite spot for visitors both day and night and it was customary for pilgrims to spend the night there in tents.

According to tradition the Mount of Olives will be the site from which the dead will be judged in the last days (*Bereishit Rabah* 33:11; *Bavli Ketubot*). Therefore, Jews have long desired to be buried in Jerusalem and preferably on the Mount of Olives. There are already about 150,000 grave sites there. The Acts of the Apostles (Acts 1:12) gives the impression that the Mount of Olives was the site of Jesus' ascent into heaven. Following the betrayal of Christ, Judas hung himself from the branches of an olive tree. It is, therefore, not surprising that the Mount of Olives is the site of pilgrimages, a prestigious burial ground, and a location for many churches. Moreover, Jews, Christians, and Muslims consider it a sacred place.

Frank A. Salamone

Myth

In the study of religion, the most general use of the term "myth" refers to a sacred narrative. This definition considers sacred that which engages values, ideas, and beliefs that are considered to be unquestionably true within their own culture. When the terms used to address those values, ideas, and beliefs are placed in a narrative framework, the narrative itself becomes sacred. The essential components of a myth, then, are two: (1) that it be a narrative, and (2) that it engage terms that are sacred. For many Fundamentalist believers, their sacred narratives bear with them the most basic principles of their belief. Differing from non-narrative theological writings, however, myths often present the beliefs and values of a culture or group in ways that are less clear than when those beliefs or values are presented in non-narrative doctrinal statements. Though myths are commonly known and referred to by Fundamentalists, much Fundamentalist belief rests not so much in a particular myth or mythic cycle but in particular interpretations of their mythic narratives.

Definitions of Myth

In the study of myth, however, making determinations of what is and is not mythic is seldom this clear. The folklorist Alan Dundes defines myth as, "a sacred narrative explaining how the world and man came to be in their present form" (Dundes 1984: 1). Dundes's definition coincides with Mircea Eliade's much earlier work. Eliade states that "myth narrates a sacred history; it relates an event that took place in primordial Time." Unlike Dundes, however, Eliade seeks to include prophetic myths or stories containing elements expected to occur in the future among the topics of mythic narrative. He describes these prophetic myths as "the myth of the destruction of the World, followed by a new Creation and the establishment of a Golden Age" (Eliade 1963: 5). In further work on prophetic narrative, he presents an expansive account of how Christian thinking evolved out of earlier belief sets concerned with seasonal regeneration (Eliade 1949). For Eliade, the key component of prophetic myth is its relation to creation, or re-creation, in the myth of the Eternal Return. His concept of the Eternal Return is itself based on the effect of daily and seasonal cycles on the minds and cultures of all humans.

From the Greek *mythos*, which simply means "story," myth has, in common parlance, come to be associated with something that is not true. Because myths deal in stories about the sacred, they often approach philosophical topics of the highest order: the origins of the cosmos, of humanity, or the ultimate purposes of being. Living myths operate to define, with the community that holds them to be true, the very nature of reality for the group. However, these same philosophical and culturally bound beliefs often seem strange or even contradictory to fact when viewed by an individual outside the community that takes the myth to be unquestionably true. Thus, even as early as in the writings of the ancient Greek philosopher Plato, myth carried with it the idea that it was untrue. Nevertheless, even Plato often resorted to using the powerful metaphors of myth to approach the topics of the highest order.

The Study of Myth

With the emergence of scientific methods of inquiry in the beginning of the European Renaissance of the 1400s, many of the myths' claims to truth were called into question. And with this new way of viewing the world, the very concept of myth became synonymous with something that is false. By the 1800s, "mythology," the study of myths, was broken into two distinct areas. First, it had become the study of the sacred narratives of cultures long extinct: the ancient Greeks, the Mesopotamian, or the ancient texts of Asia. Here, it was associated with philology and the study of ancient languages. Second, it had become the study of the sacred narratives of others. In the 1800s, and from a European perspective, it was the study of the sacred narratives native to the North and South Americas, Africa, the South Pacific, and other places in which Europeans were encountering new communities with different and seemingly strange understandings of the world.

Later, it would be generally acknowledged that the European sacred narratives, primarily those of Judaism and Christianity, also constituted myths. At the same time, however, the study of myth began to gain a new currency. In his very influential *The Interpretation of Dreams*, first published in 1901, Sigmund Freud argued that some basic themes common in Greek myth seem to be correlated with psychological function. Later, Freud's student, Carl Gustav Jung, pursued this avenue of psychology at great length. In his 1949, *Essays on a Science of Mythology*, Jung explores his concept of "archetypes." For Jung, archetypes are reoccurring psychological structures that seem to bear primary truths to individuals via myths, dreams, meditation, and in other ways. Jung hypothesized that these primary patterns were somehow encoded in the very shapes and genetics of the human brain. His ideas gained widespread popularity in a simplified form in the work of Joseph Campbell. Best known for his 1968 *Hero of a Thousand Faces*, Campbell argued for the existence of a "monomyth," which helps govern our choices as individuals and which is borne through the ages via Jung's archetypes. While Campbell's work is generally considered more optimistic than it is accurate, in many ways he can be credited with helping to restore the admiration for the mythic mode of understanding lost during the rise of the scientific method.

Conclusion

Like many complicated terms with long histories, "myth" is difficult to pin down. What seems to be most constant in its character is that myths are narratives and that they involve the sacred. This includes the stories of the Bible, the Qur'an, the Hindu Vedas, thousands of Native American oral traditions—and these are only a few among many examples. While the myths foreign to us may seem strange or even ridiculous, because they are sacred they carry some access to wisdom that may very well not be expressible in any other form. Thus, myths deserve our continued admiration, reverence, and study.

Robert Glenn Howard

Bibliography

Bascom, William. (1984) "The Forms of Folklore: Prose Narratives." Reprinted in *Sacred Narrative*, edited by Alan Dundes. Berkeley: University of California Press, 5–29.

Campbell, Joseph. (1972) *The Hero with a Thousand Faces*. Princeton, NJ: Princeton University Press.

Dundes, Alan. (1965) "What Is Folklore?" In *The Study of Folklore*. Englewood Cliffs, NJ: Prentice-Hall, Inc., 1–3.

———. (1984) Preface to *Sacred Narrative*. Berkeley: University of California Press.

Eliade, Mircea. (1949) *The Myth of the Eternal Return*, translated by Willard R. Trask. New York: Pantheon Books.

———. (1963) *Myth and Reality*, translated by Willard R. Trask. New York: Harper and Row Publishers.

Freud, Sigmund. (1923) *The Interpretation of Dreams*, authorized translation of 3rd ed., with introduction by A. A. Brill. New York: Macmillan.

Jung, Carl Gustav. (1969) *Essays on a Science of Mythology; the Myth of the Divine Child and the Mysteries of Eleusis*, translated by R. F. C. Hull. Princeton, NJ: Princeton University Press.

Plato. (1905) *The Myths of Plato*, translated, with introductory and other observations, by J. A. Stewart. New York: Macmillan.

Nationalism

Nationalism is a flexible ideology based on supporting, defending, expanding, or creating a geographic area populated by a community of citizens that share some common interest and has established, or desires to establish, territorial sovereignty and a political governing structure. The common interest can be based on a culture, language, ethnicity, race, religion, political philosophy, historical factors, or a combination of these and other factors. Anthony D. Smith suggests that to understand nationalism, it is first necessary to look at the role of the state, territory, language, religion, history, and the use of rites and ceremonies, "in the creation and maintenance of collective identity and solidarity in different cultures and historic periods" (1998: 226–227). Religious Fundamentalists, defined in the broadest sense, have a history of viewing nations as expressions of God's will, and then attempting to enforce piety and obedience. The unfortunate result can prompt visions or versions of authoritarian theocratic or theonomic regimes.

The Origins of Nationalism

Christianity shaped the rise of nationalism. For centuries European emperors and kings had measured their reach by force, and all those under the sword were subjects to be ruled. In 1215 King John was pressured by barons and bishops to sign the Magna Carta, which limited dynastic rule. Political and religious leaders hotly contested who had ultimate authority over which spheres of life in a society.

Politicized theological disputes between royalty and clergy were commonplace. In 1555 the Religious Peace of Augsburg dulled the disputes by establishing as state religion the specific beliefs of the reigning monarchy. Later, the Enlightenment championed the model of separation of church and state. With these and other developments, the groundwork for nationalism was laid.

Benedict Anderson calls nations "imagined political communities" because the sense of belonging to a specific nation is crafted as a collective consciousness over time with narratives that are creatively malleable and often mythical. He argues that the rise of print media with its mass circulation of ideas accelerated the rise of nationalism. Protestantism was central to this process. Martin Luther's Reformation theses in 1517 were translated into German and spread throughout the country within days. The city of Geneva had forty printing presses that could print the news of John Calvin's death in 1564. "The coalition between Protestantism and print-capitalism, exploiting cheap popular editions, quickly created large new reading publics—not least among merchants and women, who typically knew little or no Latin—and simultaneously mobilized them for politico-religious purposes." This not only helped challenge the Catholic Church but also resulted in "Europe's first non-dynastic, non-city states in the Dutch Republic and the Commonwealth of the Puritans" (Anderson 1991: 40).

E. J. Hobsbawm is one of many to reject the widely held idea "that national identification is somehow so natural, primary and permanent as to precede history." Hobsbawm asserts that the "characteristic modern state [received] its systematic shape in the era of the French revolutions, though in many ways [it was] anticipated by the evolving European principalities of the sixteenth–seventeenth centuries" (1992: 80). During this period colonialism helped spawn nationalism by forcing colonists to define themselves—and those colonized to defend themselves. The process of nation building was inextricably linked to the rise of the modern era, leading Hobsbawm to quip that the "basic characteristic of the modern nation and everything connected with it is its modernity" (14–15). He argues that in the public mind, the routine linking into the concept of nationhood the elements of government, territory, and the inhabitants of a province, country, or kingdom did not occur until the late 1800s. Most analysts, however, place the date somewhat earlier.

By the early twentieth century, after an initial period of novelty, the nation had emerged as the primary form of large-scale sociopolitical organization. Many critics of nationalism claim that nationalism leads to wars, rebellions, and political repression, but Tom Nairn argues that since the mid-1700s the building of nations has been a mainstream project, not a temporary eddy on the way toward some peaceful utopian collective internationalism. "Nationalism has always been invention after nature," claims Nairn, since it reflects a natural "political will to exist" that arises in groups responding to antagonisms created by clashing cultures (1997: 56). Nairn and others point out that reports of the demise of nationalism were premature, especially given its resurgence in the 1990s.

Christian Nationalism in the United States

When the Puritans settled in the New World, they saw themselves on a messianic mission of building a chosen nation that was part of prophetic destiny. For many the idea of the "city on a hill" was hardly a democratic concept, but an authoritarian model of the theocratic society constructed by Calvin in the city of Geneva. Frederick Clarkson suggests that "from the persecution of Quakers, Jesuits, and 'witches' in the Massachusetts Bay Colony during the 1600s through the bitter Presidential election campaign of 1800, and the advent of the Christian Right in the 1980s, an animating, underlying theme of the American experience has been the struggle between democratic and theocratic values" (1997: 4–5).

In 1800 when Thomas Jefferson ran for president his support for the disestablishment of religion was a major campaign issue. Protestant nativist movements from the 1830s through the 1920s demonized Catholics and defined the nation in exclusionary terms. When Fundamentalism emerged at the turn of the century, it had a nationalist subtext built on this history, and quickly engaged in the political process. Embarrassed by the negative publicity surrounding the battle over the teaching of Creation versus evolution exemplified by the Scopes "Monkey Trial," Fundamentalist nationalism retreated for decades, surviving as a low-profile subculture.

Political organizing within a resurgent Fundamentalist Protestant base fueled the rise of the new Christian Right in the 1980s. A leading figure in this distinctive form of apocalyptic religious nationalism was the Rev. Jerry Falwell, a highly visible televangelist who founded the Moral Majority. Warren L. Vinz explains that "fundamentalists in general and Falwell in particular have been dismayed" by the increasing secularization of American culture and the way they see Christian morality being deinstitutionalized. They "draw on their perception of a more glorious past as a model," says Vinz who portrays Falwell as "passionately committed to the values purported to have existed in the past, including the traditional family, rugged individualism, self-reliance, honesty, God-fearing scripture-believing reverence, a peace-loving but always ready-for-war patriotism ('don't tread on me'), discipline, faith in the ordinary man, prosperity, and a mission to the world to show the better way." This recipe for Christian nationalism, according to Vinz, celebrates a past that never was, but nonetheless relieves anxiety by "providing comfort amid confusing social change" (1997: 179).

Invigorated by their organizing acumen and electoral clout, some Fundamentalists now openly call for the recognition of the United States as a Christian nation. They represent a trend sometimes called "dominionism." The most militant wing of dominion theology is Christian Reconstructionism, which seeks to not only make the United States a Christian nation but also wants recognition of biblical law as superseding the U.S. Constitution.

The most zealous example of religious nationalism is Christian Identity, a philosophy that sees a looming race war between white Christians and their God-ordained enemies, the Jews (seen as Satanic), blacks, and other people of color (viewed as subhuman). White supremacist and anti-Semitic theories are interlaced with End-Times eschatology and racial nationalism. Christian Identity forms the core religious belief of Aryan Nations and several other neo-Nazi groups in the United States, and has been denounced by all other forms of Christianity.

Conclusion

In contemporary society religious, racial, and ethnic forms of nationalism are seen in many countries. One factor exacerbating nationalist strife in the former Yugoslavia is long-standing religious animosities among Roman Catholics, the Orthodox, and Muslims. In India, the BJP Party promotes an exclusionary Hindu nationalism. Fundamentalist nationalist movements exist in Iran, Afghanistan, and Israel. Historic examples of religious nationalism include Lebanese Christian nationalism and the colonialist Afrikaner Broederbond of South Africa. During World War II, there were Catholic fascist nationalist movements such as the Ustasha in Croatia and the Arrow Cross in Hungary. In the worst cases, zealous ethnoreligious nationalism in the twentieth century has caused the genocide of Christian Armenians by Turks and later of European Jews by the Nazis.

Nairn has called nationalism the "Modern Janus" after the "two-headed Roman deity who couldn't help looking backwards into the past as well as forward into the future" (1997: 67). In the future Nairn sees a constructive form of nationalism emerging that is distanced from the belligerent ethnic nationalism and "anti-imperial strife" of the past century. "In other words a 'civil' social order (with the sense of 'decency', privacy, individual and group or minority rights, freedom of initiative and enterprise, etc.)" that "depends in the long run upon an appropriately civic form of national identity" (1997: 87–89). This civic brand of nationalism, however, conflicts with religious nationalism—especially Fundamentalist demands for national conformity.

Chip Berlet

See also Anti-Semitism; Aryan Nation; Nativism; New Christian Right

Bibliography

Anderson, Benedict. ([1983] 1991) *Imagined Communities: Reflections on the Origin and Spread of Nationalism*, revised and extended. London: Verso.

Barkun, Michael. (1994) *Religion and the Racist Right: The Origins of the Christian Identity Movement*. Chapel Hill: University of North Carolina Press.

Clarkson, Frederick. (1997) *Eternal Hostility: The Struggle Between Theocracy and Democracy*. Monroe, ME: Common Courage.

Gellner, Ernest. (1997) *Nationalism*. New York: New York University Press.

Hobsbawm, E. J. ([1990] 1992) *Nations and Nationalism Since 1780: Programme, Myth, Reality*, 2nd ed. Cambridge: Cambridge University Press.

Hutchinson, John, and Anthony D. Smith, eds. (1994) *Nationalism*. Oxford Readers. Oxford: Oxford University Press.

Kaplan, Jeffrey, and Tore Bjørgo, eds. (1998) *Nation and Race: The Developing Euro-American Racist Subculture*. Boston: Northeastern University Press.

Nairn, Tom. (1997) *Faces of Nationalism: Janus Revisited*. London: Verso.

Smith, Anthony D. (1998) *Nationalism and Modernism: A Critical Survey of Recent Theories of Nations and Nationalism*. London: Routledge.

Vinz, Warren Lang. (1997) *Pulpit Politics: Faces of American Protestant Nationalism in the Twentieth Century*. Albany: SUNY Press.

Nativism

Nativism is an ideology that combines xenophobia with ultrapatriotic nationalism. The xenophobia appears as a fear of or disdain for people or ideas that are seen as foreign, strange, or subversive. This finds expression in a form of nationalism that doubts the suitability for citizenship (or even residency) of those suspected of being unable or unwilling to function as loyal and patriotic Americans. Thus "real" Americans must protect the nation from these "alien" intruders. The nativist litmus test can use race, country of origin, religion, language, loyalty to foreign regimes, or dissident political philosophy.

The term also has often been used to describe a series of similar mass-based political and social movements between 1830 and 1925. Because Protestant Fundamentalism arose during the end of this period, it both incorporated and influenced several nativist themes. Routine claims in Fundamentalist media that society is collapsing at the hands of an evil conspiracy gain context and meaning when viewed with a knowledge of historic nativism with its apocalyptic calls to defend the American way of life. Nativism in the 1800s mobilized a backlash against immigrants who were different from the common idea of an "ideal" citizen: a White Anglo-Saxon Protestant (sometimes dubbed a WASP). Charles Higham, however, argues that nativism is more than mere antipathy toward immigrant "aliens" and their ideas, but an "intense opposition to an internal minority on the ground of its foreign (i.e., 'un-American') connection" (1972: 4). While nativism as a major mass movement collapsed in the late 1920s, it continues to flourish both thematically and in small subcultures. Some analysts argue that the anti-immigrant and "English-Only" groups that gained popularity in the 1990s represent a revival of nativist sentiments. A racial-nationalist form of nativism resides in the contemporary Far Right, including various Ku Klux Klan units and neo-Nazi groups such as Aryan Nations, The World Church of the Creator, and the National Alliance. Christian Identity churches blend nativism and Fundamentalism, with some preaching white supremacy and anti-Semitism.

Three Varieties of Nativism

According to Higham, distinctively American nativism developed in three varieties, each with roots planted prior to the Civil War: anti-Catholicism, anti-radicalism, and Anglo-Saxon racialism (1972: 3–11). Various strains of Protestant Fundamentalism have embraced one or more of these tendencies during their history.

Richard Hofstader called anti-Catholicism "the pornography of the Puritan," and Catholics were a main target of nativism in the 1800s when most practitioners were Protestant (1965: 21). According to Hofstadter, early Protestant settlers saw a "great war going on in the Western world between political reaction and [Catholic orthodoxy] on one side and political and religious liberties on the other." The common view was that "America was a bastion of freedom, and hence an inevitable target for popes and despots" (1965: 19). Many colonies passed laws restricting the rights of Catholics. Ray Allen Billington notes that by the end of the American Revolution, "seven states, Massachusetts, New Hampshire, New Jersey, Connecticut, North Carolina, South Carolina and Georgia insisted on Protestant office holders and

other states inflicted additional liabilities on Catholics in their constitutions" (1974: 39). In the opinion of many Protestant nativists, "Catholic traditions continued to look dangerously un-American partly because they did not harmonize easily with the concept of individual freedom imbedded in the national culture" (Higham 1972: 6). The authoritarian hierarchy of Catholicism also seemed wedded to feudal or monarchical governments of Europe. The influx of Catholic immigration in the 1800s exacerbated this conflict. In the mid-to-late nineteenth century, as the idea of centralized and standardized public education gained favor among progressive reformers, many people who held conservative religious values felt threatened. One response was the expansion of a system of Catholic parochial educational institutions, which themselves generated Protestant suspicion and occasionally prompted physical attacks.

Nativism also drew sustenance from a long-standing fear that subversive radicals were conspiring to undermine the nation. This antiradical nativism had to overcome the positive image of the American Revolution, which was framed as colonial patriots overthrowing the tyrannical rule of a European power. Anti-elitist European radicals, however, could be portrayed as rabble-rousers threatening a stable republican form of government in the United States with revolutionary anarchy and mob violence. Higham explained that a "persistent contrast between a generally hopeful psychology of mobility in America and the more desperate politics born in class-ridden Europe has fostered the belief that violent and sweeping opposition to the status quo is characteristically European and profoundly un-American" (1972: 7–8). The roots of this fear trace back to the 1790s when a series of books and pamphlets (first published in Europe) warned that a conspiracy of Freemasons (controlled by the shadowy Illuminati group) was plotting to overthrow all world governments. This in turn mimics the prophecies in the Book of Revelation concerning an End-Times conspiracy to build a One World Government based on the global false religion of the Antichrist. This view of prophesy continues to influence many Fundamentalists today.

Anglo-Saxon racialism at its peak claimed that people from superior "white" racial stock were responsible for all the major advances of Western culture, and that inferior racial types were diluting superior bloodlines and harming the future of civilization. In the 1800s, unlike today, the Irish, Italians, or Serbians were not considered "white." Racialism moved from diffuse ideas of ethnic pride and a homogenous national character in the late 1700s to a pseudoscientific theory of supremacy that predominated in the late 1800s.

Madison Grant's seminal racialist book, *The Passing of the Great Race*, was first published in 1916 but gained widespread popularity in the 1920s. In this period the idea of scientific racism was not only popular but also was taught in biology and genetics courses at major universities. When parents hoped their children married someone "with the proper breeding" they meant that in the literal, genetic sense. A nativist "eugenics" movement encouraged people with "good" genes to procreate, while those with "bad" genes were targeted for programs discouraging "dysgenic" reproduction. This sometimes included forced sterilization.

Historic Manifestations

The 1790s Irish insurrection was supported by many Irish-Americans, some of whom were themselves refugees from the struggle. The nativist Federalists, especially John Adams, combined anti-Catholicism and antiradicalism (with the encouragement of English diplomats), to argue "that the presence of such Irish enthusiasts was a menace to American institutions and American liberty. In 1798, the year of the actual rebellion in Ireland, Adams secured the passage of the Alien and Sedition acts" (Billington 1974: 45). When the anti-Federalist (and pro-rebellion) Thomas Jefferson became president, these acts fell into disfavor. Yet Billington notes that even Jefferson at one point suggested barring citizenship from any man "who took a title or gift from European powers" (1974: 46).

In addition, during the late 1790s, sermons by Jedidiah Morse fueled a brief hysteria over a feared plot by members of Masonic lodges to launch a revolutionary attack on church, state, and the status quo. Antimasonry again emerged in the 1820s, but this time the status quo was seen as corrupt, with nativists envisioning the government controlled by secret elites who supposedly networked through Masonic lodges.

The core of nativism in the 1800s was an anti-immigrant backlash. Between the 1820s and 1860s, as the total U.S. population was expanding, the location

and birthplace of residents was also changing. For instance, people living in urban areas more than doubled to about 20 percent. New York City alone saw close to a 750 percent increase in residents as more than 3.5 million immigrants arrived at its docks. A large number of these immigrants were Irish Catholics, with a smaller yet substantial number of Germans, many of whom were also Catholic. While some immigrants remained on the East Coast, others moved on to cities such as Chicago, which grew from a prairie outpost to a city of over 100,000 inhabitants. Dale T. Knobel observes, "the foreign-born in Philadelphia increased from 2 percent of the total population in 1830 to 20 percent at midcentury ... [and by] the end of the 1850s, California's population was nearly 40 percent foreign-born, and immigrants constituted 35 percent of the populations of Wisconsin and Minnesota" (1996: 46–47).

In the mid-1830s distrust of immigrant foreigners was so intense that native-born Protestant political activists in New York formed the New York Native Democratic Association. Their primary target was Irish Catholic immigrants. In New England, Samuel F. B. Morse (the son of Jedidiah) warned that the "evil of immigration brings to these shores illiterate Roman Catholics, the tools of reckless and unprincipled politicians, the obedient instruments of their more knowing priestly leaders" (Bennett 1995: 40). The 1834 burning of the Ursuline convent in Charlestown, Massachusetts, was part of a wave of anti-Catholic bigotry propelled by a popular press which generated lurid (and false) claims of rape, abduction, sexual sadism, and murder inside the walls of Catholic institutions.

Another wave of anti-Catholic nativism crested in the mid-1850s with the appearance of the Order of the Star Spangled Banner known popularly as the "Know Nothings" because the secretive group told its members to reply "I know nothing" when asked about the organization. From its base in New York State the group eventually recruited hundreds of thousands of members nationwide. In 1854 candidates backed by the Know Nothings took control of the Massachusetts state legislature, captured all seats for the U.S. House of Representatives, and sat in the governor's chair. The sentiments of the group were revealed in the title of an 1855 book written for members called *Startling Facts for Native Americans Called "Know-Nothings" or a Vivid Presentation of the Dangers to American Liberty, to Be Apprehended from Foreign Influence*. The book expounds on the anti-Catholic fears of the organization: "Shall TRUE AMERICANS govern themselves, or shall foreigners, unacquainted with our laws and brought up under monarchical governments, rule? Shall those who are temporally and spiritually subject to a foreign prince be our legislators, and change our laws as they are directed by the Pope of Rome?" (Berlet and Lyons 2000: 50).

The Know Nothing movement collapsed as quickly as it had merged, and by 1857 was rapidly disappearing from the national political scene. Nativism retreated but did not vanish. After the Civil War, nativist themes were woven into the "middle-class reform movements" of the late 1800s, and "crusaders for temperance and for women's rights assailed the immigrant's subversive, European attitudes on these questions" (Higham 1972: 41).

The passage of the 1882 Chinese Exclusion Act, which suspended immigration and barred Chinese aliens from U.S. citizenship, resulted from nativist organizing primarily by Americans from the Western states. Chinese immigrants were also targets of violence from the West Coast to the Rocky Mountain States and antipathy toward Chinese and Japanese immigrants flourished nationwide well into the first decade of the twentieth century.

After World War I, the threat of Bolshevism and anarchism emerged as a major nativist issue. The Palmer Raids (starting in late 1919), a campaign against suspected radicals and aliens, were justified as being the sole means to combat anti-American plots. This countersubversion hysteria was often racialized, with deportation ships carrying immigrants and their "alien" ideas back to Italy and Russia. The 1924 National Origins Act set quotas favoring immigrants from northern Europe over those from southern Europe, Asia, and Africa. At this same time, a nativist "Americanization" campaign sought to teach the remaining immigrants the proper character traits for true citizenship.

In the 1920s, the popularity of Americanization helped reinvigorate the Ku Klux Klan, which attracted somewhere between two to five million members. KKK supporters captured political control of Indiana, and influenced state politics nationwide. The Klan's "attacks on Catholics and foreigners and the vows to protect imperiled American women" has tied it to earlier nativist movements, according to Bennett (1995: 220).

Continuing Echoes

The one key feature of the "American Right of the Depression era was . . . the strident racism and anti-Semitism of its large, mass-based organizations" (Diamond 1995: 23). Influential movements were led by charismatic demagogues such as Father Charles E. Coughlin, William Dudley Palley, Gerald Winrod, and Gerald L. K. Smith. They peddled a blend of nativism, populism, anticommunism, anti-Semitism, and conspiracy theories. Coughlin promoted his reactionary views through radio broadcasts, and mobilized previously scapegoated Catholics as participants—a reversal Bennett calls "inverted nativism" (1995: 259).

After World War II, the distaste for European fascism and Nazism made it difficult for nativist activists to build a mass base, although the Red Scare of the McCarthy period in the 1950s contained elements of nativist countersubversion. White segregationist groups in the 1960s, such as the White Citizens' Councils and the Ku Klux Klan, revived racist and nativist themes by attacking and terrorizing the civil rights movement activists, sometimes with murderous consequences. Yet these groups' standing diminished when no national nativist movement emerged, civil rights legislation was passed by Congress, and the 1965 Immigration Act ended the discriminatory quota system installed in 1924. However, nativism continues to exert influence: "Nativism has waxed and waned over the course of U.S. history, but it remains an important perspective that many native-born Americans use to construct and interpret hard economic times. Certain essential components of nativism remain more or less constant: the accent on the racial or cultural inferiority of immigrants, the problematizing of assimilation of immigrants, the idea that immigrants are a serious threat to the U.S. economy, and the notion that immigrants are responsible for government crises" (Feagin 1997: 37). It has also been argued that cultural or social stress can trigger nativist fears in addition to real or anticipated economic hardship. The 1990s saw a renewal of the biological determinist claim that genetic racial differences accounted for social and economic inequalities. *The Bell Curve* (1994), by Richard J. Herrnstein and Charles Murray, suggested that blacks and Latinos were genetically inferior, and that therefore most affirmative action programs and government social welfare programs were doomed to failure. Books such as *Measured Lies: The Bell Curve Examined* (1996), refuted these claims, but racist arguments remained the subtext for many policy debates over street crime, welfare, and immigration, as well as political campaigns by former klansman David Duke and conservative journalist Patrick Buchanan.

Anti-immigrant rallies garnered national headlines with the passage of California's Proposition 187 in 1994. Provisions include barring undocumented immigrants from attending public schools or colleges; denying them medical treatment (with a few exceptions) at hospitals or other institutions receiving tax dollars; and forcing teachers, medical staff, and social workers to inform state and federal agencies of suspected illegal status. Voters in Alabama, Arizona, California, Colorado, and Florida passed popular initiatives and referenda promoting English as the only proper language for education, documents, or signage.

Conclusion

Many people tend to dismiss participants in nativist movements as marginal "extremists" or a "lunatic fringe," but recent scholarship contends that this rhetoric is unfair. According to Bennett, "Those who joined the nativist movements did not invent the crises of values they saw developing around them. The disruption of American life was not the product of their overheated imaginations but of objective conditions. Their 'solutions' to these problems may have been irrelevant, inappropriate, and destructive, but their fears were rooted in reality" (1995: 9).

Nativist groups, some of which achieve significant political clout and mobilize mass populist activism, seek to redress grievances, real or imagined. The prejudices they so often highlight are already embedded in the body politic, waiting for a sympathetic moment to surface and fester. This dynamic has not vanished. Vestigial anti-Catholic bigotry in certain Protestant Fundamentalist institutions such as Bob Jones University became a campaign issue in the 2000 presidential election. Starting in the mid-1980s and continuing today within Southern Baptist congregations is a battle over whether or not Freemasons should be expelled from the church. While racist Christian Identity is denounced by most Fundamentalists, it still is a significant viewpoint within the Far Right, where its hyperbolic blend of

nativist Fundamentalism fuels hatred. Whenever Protestant Fundamentalists and Evangelicals call for the defense of a Christian nation under attack, there are echoes of nativism.

Chip Berlet

Bibliography

Bennett, David H. ([1988] 1995) *The Party of Fear: The American Far Right from Nativism to the Militia Movement*, rev. ed. New York: Vintage Books.

Berlet, Chip, and Matthew N. Lyons. (2000) *Right-Wing Populism in America: Too Close for Comfort*. New York: Guilford Press.

Billington, Ray Allen. ([1933] 1974). *The Origins of Nativism in the United States 1800–1844*. New York: Arno Press.

Davis, David Brion, ed. (1971) *The Fear of Conspiracy: Images of Un-American Subversion from the Revolution to the Present*. Ithaca, NY: Cornell University Press.

Diamond, Sara. (1995) *Roads to Dominion: Right-Wing Movements and Political Power in the United States*. New York: Guilford Press.

Feagin, Joe R. (1997) "Old Poison in New Bottles: The Deep Roots of Modern Nativism." In *Immigrants Out! The New Nativism and the Anti-Immigrant Impulse in the United States*, edited by Juan F. Perea. New York: New York University Press, 13–43.

Grant, Madison. ([1916] 1923) *The Passing of the Great Race: The Racial Basis of European History*, 4th rev. ed. New York: C. Scribner's Sons.

Herrnstein, Richard J., and Charles Murray. (1994) *The Bell Curve: Intelligence and Class Structure in American Life*. New York: Free Press.

Higham, John. ([1955] 1975) *Strangers in the Land: Patterns of American Nativism 1860–1925*. New York: Atheneum.

Hofstadter, Richard. (1965) *The Paranoid Style in American Politics and Other Essays*. New York: Alfred A. Knopf.

Hutchinson, E. (1855) *Startling Facts for Native Americans Called "Know-Nothings" or a Vivid Presentation of the Dangers to American Liberty, to Be Apprehended from Foreign Influence*. New York: published by the author.

Kincheloe, Joe L., Shirley R. Steinberg, and Aaron D. Gresson, III, eds. (1996) *Measured Lies: The Bell Curve Examined*. New York: St. Martin's Press.

Knobel, Dale T. (1996) *America for the Americans: The Nativist Movement in the United States*. New York: Twayne Publishers.

Lipset, Seymour Martin, and Earl Raab. ([1970] 1978) *The Politics of Unreason: Right-Wing Extremism in America, 1790–1970*, 2nd ed. New York: Harper and Row.

Perea, Juan F. (1997) *Immigrants Out! The New Nativism and the Anti-Immigrant Impulse in the United States*. New York: New York University Press.

Ribuffo, Leo P. (1983) *The Old Christian Right: The Protestant Far Right from the Great Depression to the Cold War*. Philadelphia: Temple University Press.

New Age

In the 1980s, the religious community in Europe and North America was swept by a new millennial movement unusual for its being based not in conservative biblical Christianity but in Western esotericism. The Western esoteric tradition has continually challenged Christianity for a place in Western culture but was generally persecuted out of existence whenever it became a popular movement (such as with the medieval Bogomils and Cathars sects). In the seventeenth century, it found new life in the Rosicrucian movement and later expanded through speculative Freemasonry, the Neo-Templar movement, and most notably, nineteenth-century Theosophy. The esoteric tradition would nurture two popular nineteenth-century movements—spiritualism and the metaphysical churches (Christian Science/New Thought)—and through the twentieth century, numerous groups basing their perspective on the widely circulated theosophical texts appeared.

Origins

Movements of the esoteric or metaphysical tradition were distinguished by their rejection of biblical authority usually in favor of perspectives derived from mystical and paranormal experiences with a divine reality. God was not seen as a loving Father so much as a distant reality primarily manifest through the invisible structures underlying the universe (natural laws and the life force). Jesus was often seen as an exemplar who understood those hidden (or occult) realities and manifesting the means of attuning with them. Humans were seen as a spark of the divine trapped in the material world and forgetful of their divine nature. Salvation was seen not as occur-

ring through faith but in gaining wisdom (gnosis) of the unseen realm, coming into contact with it, and doing those things necessary for the soul to return to the spiritual realms.

Emergence of the Contemporary Movement

In the 1970s, several people operating within the esoteric community proposed that a New Age was dawning. This New Age would propel humankind from its present state, characterized by poverty, war, and human conflicts, into a Golden Age of abundance, peace, and human understanding and cooperation. Among the first effective voices in spreading this message was David Spangler (b. 1945). Spangler was a student of the writings of theosophist Alice A. Bailey and a resident of the Findhorn Community, an independent theosophical center in Scotland. In his two seminal works, *Revelation, the Birth of a New Age* (1976) and *Towards a Planetary Vision* (1977) he suggested that new arrangements in the heavens were releasing a flood of spiritual energy, which, if taken in and refocused by humans could bring about the New Age.

The idea of a New Age energized the older esoteric community and spread quickly to all parts of the globe. A highly decentralized and diverse movement, it offered the transformation of culture as a whole in the near future and presaged by the offer of immediate transformation of individuals who were invited to participate in a spectrum of spiritual and occult exercises. Hundreds of thousands of people responded to the New Age message and began such diverse practices as astrology, meditation, channeling, and divination. The New Age found an ally in the parallel holistic health movement that offered transformation in the form of healing utilizing a host of traditional medical procedures that had been left behind or rejected by scientific medicine. Holistic medicine championed naturopathy's older program of noninvasive and drugless therapies.

Through the 1980s the New Age became a mass movement and an estimated one to two percent of the population became involved at more than a superficial level. Notable elements of the New Age included channeling and crystals. Channeling, a form of mediumship in which contact was made with what were believed to be enlightened beings from other realms, provided new revelations accepted by many as religiously authoritative. The wearing of crystals and their use in various healing rituals grew from a belief that crystals stored large quantities of energy.

Opposition to the Movement

As the movement gained popularity, it also came under critical attack. Secular critics denounced it as a rebirth of ancient occult superstitions that fostered much occult nonsense on the public. Critics banded together in the Committee for the Scientific Investigation of the Claims of the Paranormal, which expanded its initial criticism of astrology into a broadside against the whole New Age movement. Evangelical Christians, perceiving the appeal of the New Age to many church members, as well as the movement's rejection of orthodox Christian teachings, focused a considerable amount of attention on the New Age beginning in the mid-1980s. It not only denounced the unbiblical soul-destroying nature of popular New Age teachings but warned church members to stay away from New Age events, books, and paraphernalia.

By the end of the 1980s, the New Age movement had largely run its course. The bottom fell out of the crystal market under the severe criticism of pseudoscientific theories of crystal power. More important, however, the leaders of the movement lost faith in the millennial expectations that had seen such an unprecedented growth in interest in the teachings of the esoteric tradition. By the beginning of the 1990s, the loss of energy by the movement was noticeable. By this time, the movement had been responsible for the founding of a chain of New Age bookstores throughout the Western world, the organization of numerous New Age organizations and businesses, and the circulation of thousands of books and periodicals.

New Focus of the Movement

The New Age movement did not simply go away, however; it radically transformed in the 1990s. Dropping its belief that a Golden Age was imminent, some leaders began to emphasize the primacy of the many transformative tools (occult and mystical practices) now available everywhere, and suggested that the many individual transformations were sufficient for continuing the movement. However, by the mid-1990s, new visions of the transformation of the culture were appearing, most notably in *The Celestine Prophecy*, a best-selling novel by James Redfield. Redfield and others argued that the New Age was dawning, but suggested that it might be limited to a minority of people, and simply influence the culture through the next century rather than dominate it. Thus, a postmillennial perspective came to replace the millennial hope upon which the New Age had originally arrived. This next stage of the movement continues to develop.

The New Age movement brought literally millions into the esoteric world although, like most social movements, it eventually died. However, it left in its wake a significantly enlarged community that has now become a permanent part of the religious landscape.

J. Gordon Melton

Bibliography

Hanegraaff, Wouter J. (1996) *New Age Religion and Western Culture*. Leiden, Netherlands: Brill.

Heelas, Paul. (1996) *The New Age Movement*. Oxford: Blackwell.

Lewis, James R., and J. Gordon Melton. (1992) *Perspective on the New Age*. Albany: SUNY Press.

Melton, J. Gordon, Jerome Clark, and Aidan A. Kelly. (1990) *New Age Encyclopedia*. Detroit, MI: Gale.

Spangler, David. (1976) *Revelation: The Birth of the New Age*. San Francisco: Rainbow Bridge.

The New Christian Right

The New Christian Right (NCR) is a social movement that appeared in the late 1970s in the United States, advancing an agenda of political, cultural, and social conservatism. Consisting of a shifting collage of organizations, the Christian Right was based primarily in the Evangelical Protestant community, although it made efforts to attract other religious conservatives such as traditionalist Catholics. From 1980 to 2000, the NCR sought to influence elections, lobby Congress, and engage the judicial process. Although scholars disagree on the efficacy of these efforts, the NCR remains a considerable force on the American political scene.

Origins

The NCR's rise in the late 1970s surprised veteran observers of American politics, who assumed that religion had become largely irrelevant politically. The new movement arose from the convergence of several social, institutional, and political developments. Perhaps the most important was the growth of a new Evangelical Protestant constituency for political activity. The Evangelical community may be broadly defined as those Protestants who rejected the emerging religious modernism of mainline Protestant denominations in the early twentieth century, vigorously reasserting Christian "fundamentals" such as the inerrancy of the Bible, the Virgin Birth of Jesus, the Resurrection, and salvation through Jesus' substitutionary Atonement. Although the broad Evangelical community comprised a number of sometimes hostile movements, such as Fundamentalism, Pentecostalism, and neo-Evangelicalism, its members not only shared some core beliefs, but adhered to conservative social values as well, emphasizing the centrality of the nuclear family, traditional gender roles, and restrictive sexual attitudes.

Historically concentrated in rural and working-class America, by the 1970s Evangelical Protestants were becoming middle class, well educated, and suburban. They were also increasingly well connected by numerous organizational and communications networks, especially the growing television and radio ministries, by the burgeoning Christian school movement, and by informal clergy associations. All these developments created the potential for the mobilization of Evangelical Christians, who were quite apolitical for most of the twentieth century.

This new political constituency was activated by a series of "trigger issues" that disturbed traditionalist Christians and their religious leaders. Although scholars disagree on their relative importance, these included disenchantment with the Supreme Court's school prayer rulings in the 1960s and legalization of abortion in *Roe v. Wade* (1973), the Carter administration's effort to impose federal nondiscrimination policies on Christian schools, and the growing gay rights movement of the 1970s. Local controversies, often involving school curricula or moral issues, prompted conservative Christian activism in almost every region, but especially in the burgeoning suburban areas of the South, Midwest, and West.

The "first wave" of organizing produced Christian Voice, the Religious Roundtable, and Jerry Falwell's

Moral Majority, a group that for a time became virtually synonymous with the movement. Although journalists at first greatly exaggerated their size, these groups were in reality "checkbook" organizations run by prominent Fundamentalist clergy. Although the Moral Majority and Christian Voice managed to elicit a substantial number of small contributions for a time, none of the first-wave groups attracted a large, sustaining membership, and by the late 1980s most had dissolved. Their narrow religious base, extremely conservative ideology, and reluctance to compromise certainly hastened their demise.

The "second wave" NCR mobilization occurred in the late 1980s, inspired by Christian broadcaster Marion G. "Pat" Robertson's drive for the 1988 Republican presidential nomination. Although that campaign failed, Robertson raised enormous sums of money and mobilized an impressive corps of activists, drawn especially from among Pentecostal and charismatic Christians. Robertson soon hired Ralph Reed, an aggressive young Republican operative, to transform the remnants of the campaign into the Christian Coalition, which soon replaced the defunct Moral Majority as the symbol for the entire "Christian Right." Reed sought to reduce the role of clergy in the NCR, promote greater political pragmatism, promulgate a more "mainstream" message, and, especially, attract a broader coalition of "people of faith," including conservative mainline Protestants, traditionalist Catholics, and religious Jews.

Although the media often seem obsessed with the Christian Coalition, several other NCR groups achieved some prominence during the 1990s. Christian psychologist Dr. James Dobson used his vast radio audiences to create Focus on the Family, which promoted "pro-family" causes. For a time Dobson's organization was affiliated with the Washington-based Family Research Council, headed by former Reagan administration official Gary Bauer, who lobbied assiduously for NCR issues on Capitol Hill. Concerned Women for America (CWA), founded by Beverly LaHaye, organized Fundamentalist women for political action. The American Family Association (AFA), led by Rev. Donald Wildmon, addressed issues such as pornography in the media, largely by boycotting offending corporations. A plethora of smaller national, local, and regional groups buttressed—or sometimes competed with— these major organizations.

Despite sporadic efforts to broaden their religious constituency, these groups drew largely from the

NCR's original Evangelical clientele—and often reflected their founders' religious identity. For example, Jerry Falwell's Moral Majority and Beverly LaHaye's CWA consisted primarily of Fundamentalists, with only a smattering of Pentecostals. The Christian Coalition, on the other hand, attracted many Fundamentalists and Evangelicals, but has always had a strong Pentecostal and charismatic flavor, reflecting Pat Robertson's patronage. Traditional tensions among these historic religious movements still complicate the work of NCR organizations, but such divisions seem to be diminishing. On the other hand, no NCR group has any substantial mainline Protestant, Catholic, or Jewish membership, nor do they attract other religious traditionalists such as Missouri Synod Lutherans, Mormons, or, for that matter conservative African-American Protestants. Even the Christian Coalition's effort to create a loosely affiliated "Catholic Alliance" was soon abandoned.

Electoral Activities

Although the NCR has pursued varied political strategies, from the very start its prime concern has been to elect politicians who support its agenda. In presidential contests, NCR groups have invariably endorsed the Republican ticket, but with varying enthusiasm. In both 1980 and 1984, the first-wave groups gave Ronald Reagan massive support. After Robertson's 1988 campaign disintegrated, NCR groups united around George Bush, who some had favored from the start. Although many of President Bush's policies and appointments subsequently disappointed NCR leaders, most aided his unsuccessful 1992 reelection campaign against Bill Clinton.

In 1996 the NCR played a critical role in the Republican presidential primaries. Initially divided in their preferences, NCR groups eventually coalesced around Senator Robert Dole, helping him turn back challenges from publisher Steve Forbes and journalist Patrick Buchanan. Although Dole subsequently distanced himself from the NCR, most groups still mobilized for him during the general election, distributing millions of voter guides in conservative churches, contacting religious voters, and eliciting clergy endorsements.

The NCR was also a crucial factor in the 2000 Republican nominating process. A Christian Right leader, Gary Bauer, actually sought the nomination, but without attracting broad support. All the other

candidates, including Senator Orrin Hatch, former vice-president Dan Quayle, Steve Forbes, Alan Keyes, Elizabeth Dole, Senator John McCain, and Texas governor George W. Bush, made open appeals to Christian conservatives. Indeed, Bush's ultimate victory owed much to his astute wooing of Christian conservatives, who were also angered by Senator John McCain's calculated attack on Jerry Falwell and Pat Robertson. In the end, Christian conservatives not only supplied Bush with some critical primary victories but also constituted over half his vote in the November election.

While NCR activity in presidential campaigns was often the most visible, the movement has also been active in congressional races, especially for the U.S. House of Representatives. First-wave NCR candidates for Congress were often "self-starters," political amateurs such as local clergy and religious activists. Most lost in the Republican primaries and the rare victors were almost invariably trounced by Democratic candidates in the general election. By the late 1980s, however, second-wave NCR strategy shifted toward backing the most conservative Republican aspirant with a real chance to win. Over time, an increasing number of such candidates were Evangelical Protestants. As a result, the movement enjoyed more success, but sometimes at the cost of moderating its demands and tying its objectives to the fortunes of the Republican Party. A similar shift in strategy occurred in contests for state and local office.

By the end of the 1990s, then, the NCR had demonstrated some electoral prowess. Christian conservatives had assisted several GOP presidential nominees, in the process achieving a strong voice in national and state Republican Party organizations. Evangelical Republican legislators held leadership positions in Congress and, most important, conservative Christians provided a large and crucial bloc of loyal Republican voters. Ironically, however, the movement's successful infiltration of the Republican Party made NCR electoral assistance increasingly dispensable, as more and more conservative Christians worked directly through party and candidate organizations.

Legislative Lobbying

Despite considerable electoral success, the NCR has often been frustrated in achieving its policy agenda. During the early 1980s, the first-wave NCR nominally espoused a comprehensive platform encompassing

339

numerous economic, social, and foreign policy goals, but the real agenda focused on limiting abortion, legalizing school prayer, and providing assistance to Christian schools though tuition tax credits. Although Congress was forced to consider such proposals, very few legislative initiatives passed. The absence of consistent support from the Reagan administration, ineffective NCR lobbying, and lack of favorable public opinion made this campaign a futile one.

The second-wave NCR groups sought the same objectives, but added other conservative goals, such as reducing the tax burden on American families. After the Republican electoral victory in 1994, the Christian Coalition and some other NCR groups joined a coalition of conservative groups lobbying for the House GOP's "Contract with America." Some militant NCR leaders, such as James Dobson and Gary Bauer, soon charged that Republican leaders had put abortion and school prayer on the "back burner" once again, and threatened to withdraw their support. The NCR forces eventually did achieve some legislative goals, such as congressional passage of restrictions on late-term abortions, but their limited victories were often frustrated by President Bill Clinton's veto. Not surprisingly, perhaps, the NCR was in the vanguard of the GOP's failed impeachment drive against President Clinton in 1998. Once again, the movement was frustrated by the absence of broad public support for one of its objectives.

Judicial Campaigns

Although landmark court decisions helped spark the rise of the NCR, the first-wave groups did not try to influence judicial decisions, but rather hoped to transform the courts through appointments by a friendly President Reagan. By the early 1990s, however, Christian groups were deeply engaged in legal activities, hoping to benefit from twelve years of conservative Republican nominations, especially to the lower federal courts. When NCR organizations finally took to the judicial field, they tended to specialize in their activities. The American Center for Law and Justice (ACLJ), sponsored by Pat Robertson and led by Jay Sekulow, initiated important test cases to achieve sympathetic judicial interpretation of contested questions. The Alliance Defense Fund (ADF), created by James Dobson, D. James Kennedy, Donald Wildmon, Bill Bright, and other prominent Fundamentalist and Evangelical leaders, did not litigate but rather provided grants to local Christian attorneys

and other NCR organizations fighting worthy causes. The ADF, for instance, financed the successful plaintiffs in the Supreme Court decision in *Rosenberger v. The University of Virginia* (1995), which provided a Christian journal of opinion with equal access to university publication funds on a nondiscriminatory basis.

Other NCR groups have preferred a less costly strategy, filing *amicus curiae* ("friend of the court") briefs presenting their legal arguments in cases already before the federal courts. The Christian Legal Society (CLS) and the National Association of Evangelicals (NAE), both older organizations, took this approach, as did newer groups such as the Family Research Council, CWA, and Focus on the Family. Besides filing *amicus* briefs, the CLS also assisted potential litigants in quiet negotiated resolution of contentious issues, often involving religious rights in education or in other public settings. Finally, John Whitehead's Rutherford Institute engaged in a seemingly eccentric mix of litigation, *amicus* filings, and pretrial negotiation.

The overall result of these legal strategies has been mixed. The NCR has had little luck reversing federal doctrine on abortion, school prayer, or other core issues. But the movement won more often by entering religious claims as First Amendment "free speech" rights, rather than relying on either the "free exercise of religion" or "no establishment of religion" clauses of that amendment. Unfortunately for the NCR, only some of its legal objectives can be incorporated under the free speech rubric. Nevertheless, for the first time in American history, Christian conservatives are now well represented in the judicial process.

Conclusion

After thirty years of activity, the New Christian Right had experienced both success and frustration. The movement produced a shifting kaleidoscope of organizations, most of which have perished. Those that did survive have failed to expand beyond Evangelical Protestants to include other religious conservatives, but have nevertheless managed to influence elections and plant an important faction within the Republican Party. The NCR has put several controversial social issues on the national agenda, but has achieved only modest policy changes on those issues, whether through executive, legislative, or judicial channels. Nevertheless, despite the repeated obituaries for the NCR written by journalists, politicians, and scholars, the movement will remain an important force in American politics.

James L. Guth

See also Abortion; Moral Majority; Televangelism

Bibliography

Bruce, Steve, Peter Kivisto, and William H. Swatos, Jr., eds. (1995) *The Rapture of Politics: The Christian Right As the United States Approaches the Year 2000.* New Brunswick, NJ: Transaction Publishers.

Diamond, Sara. (1998) *Not by Politics Alone: The Enduring Influence of the Christian Right.* New York: The Guilford Press.

Green, John C., James L. Guth, Corwin E. Smidt, and Lyman A. Kellstedt. (1996) *Religion and the Culture Wars: Dispatches from the Front.* Lanham, MD: Rowman and Littlefield Publishers.

Martin, William. (1996) *With God on Our Side: The Rise of the Religious Right in the United States.* New York: Broadway Books.

Moen, Matthew. (1992) *The Transformation of the Christian Right.* Tuscaloosa: University of Alabama Press.

Watson, Justin. (1997) *The Christian Coalition: Dreams of Restoration, Demands for Recognition.* New York: St. Martin's Press.

Wilcox, Clyde. (1996) *Onward Christian Soldiers: The Religious Right in American Politics.* Boulder, CO: Westview Press.

New Testament

The New Testament is the second and later section of the Christian Bible. It, along with the first and earlier section known as the Old Testament, comprise that which has been established by the Christian Church as Holy Scripture, "containing the final, authoritative deposit of divine revelation" (Meye 1979: 601). The title "New Testament" is derived from references in the Bible concerning a "new covenant," the first one (from a chronological point of view) found in 1 Corinthians 11:25, "this cup is the new covenant in my blood" (Tr. Richard I. McNeely; see also Luke 22:20; Hebrews 8:8, 13; 9:15, NIV). Additionally, the New Testament was composed in Greek and the Greek title translated as "the New Covenant"; the Greek word *diatheke* in the title is translated as both "covenant" and "testament."

Fundamentalist scholars have always approached the New Testament from the presuppositional concept that it is inspired, and consequently, authoritative. In the last two decades, Fundamentalist scholars have studied the works of those who approach the New Testament from a purely literary approach, but these scholars have accepted the works only if they are consonant with a view of verbal inspiration.

The Canon of the New Testament

There has been much debate about the establishment of the traditional canon (or list of officially accepted books) of the New Testament. Some modern scholars have questioned the merit of certain books of the canon and argue that the canon is the product of the powerful and influential church leaders of the first three centuries of the church. Others, such as some members of the "Jesus Seminar," have suggested that the apocryphal and Gnostic *Gospel of Thomas* has as much right to be a part of the canon as the so-called received books.

The Random House Dictionary of the English Language defines the word "canon" as "a standard" or a "criterion" by which something is measured. Two criteria, developed over time, were used to test canonicity. Initially, the books had to pass the test of *apostolicity*, that is, they were written by an apostle or by those who were close to apostles. Then the books were tested on the basis of *inspiration*: Did the book show evidence of the direction of the Holy Spirit in its composition and was it in harmony with the other received books?

In the case of the canon of the New Testament, it began with a series of documents that were circulated through the church. Eventually, some were viewed as having more authority than others. The controversy has to do with inspiration. That is, does this particular book demonstrate internally and by its apostolicity that it has come from God? Not every book of the New Testament came from the pen of an apostle, but it can be substantiated that those traditionally believed to be the authors were either apostles or closely involved with the ministry of one or more of the apostles. The only book that might not fit this criterion is the Epistle to the Hebrews, but it found a place in the canon early on because its doctrine is so clearly the doctrine of the apostles. The process by which the canon of the New Testament was arranged probably began with a collection of Paul's letters (epistles). No clear evidence can be produced to determine *when* such a collection was completed, but because of Paul's importance in the church and his obvious authority as an apostle, it would not have taken long before his letters became a part of the teachings of the early Christian Church. It was believed by some that the collection of the Pauline writings was possibly the work of one person such as Onesimus, mentioned in Paul's very personal letter to Philemon.

That there were questions regarding the establishment of the canon is clear. Martin Luther disputed the canonicity of Hebrews, James, Jude, and the Revelation. The keys to canonicity were then inspiration, apostolicity, and finally, Christology. Meye (1979: 606) clearly states the position of historic Christianity: "The Christian can only believe that this history, set in motion by the earthly Lord, has been superintended by the risen Lord, who will not lead His Church into error. We believe that He has built His Church upon this Scripture, and that all future development must spring from the grateful obedience exercised by a Church that may hear its Lord speak in the OT and NT canon."

The Text of the New Testament

The New Testament was written in common Greek, that is, not classical Greek but the language of the common people. Some of the New Testament authors used more refined Greek, but it was the Greek spoken as lingua franca of the Mediterranean world. When Jerome translated the Greek into Latin, he referred to his translation as being in "vulgar," or common Latin, hence the title *The Vulgate Version*.

There is more evidence for the Greek text of the New Testament than for any other ancient document. More than five thousand texts, some complete, others fragments, contribute to the establishment of what the original text would have been. As of yet, no original documents of the New Testament have been discovered; however, through the process of textual criticism, present editions of the Greek text have a probability factor of 99.9% of the original text. Students must make a clear distinction between the manuscripts, which are in Greek, and the translations in various languages called "versions" (such as the Latin, the Ethiopic, and the King James.). Establishment of the meanings of words must refer back to the Greek of the New Testament rather than to a version of it.

The Divisions of the New Testament

The New Testament is a collection of twenty-seven books divided logically into four parts: the Four Gospels, Matthew, Mark, Luke and John; the Book of the Acts of the Apostles, which includes but one book; the Epistles, which is further divided into the Pauline Epistles and the General Epistles; and the apocalyptic Book of the Revelation of Jesus Christ.

The Gospels

The word "gospel" is a translation of the Greek *euaggelion*, meaning "good news." There are four recognized Gospels: Matthew, Mark, Luke, and John. The authorship of these books is not found within the books themselves, but is the early tradition that has been generally accepted until the last 150 years. The first three are designated as the synoptic Gospels because they can be compared side by side, having so much material that is common to them. Only Matthew and Luke have any record of the birth of the Lord. John, on the other hand, begins his Gospel with the declaration of the deity of Christ, who was present "in the beginning," was "with God" and "was God." John shares only two incidents in the life of the Lord with the other Gospels—Jesus feeding the 5,000 and Jesus walking on the water.

The Gospels focus on presenting the person of Jesus Christ. Matthew portrays Jesus as the Messiah of Israel, citing many Old Testament passages as having been fulfilled in him. Mark shows Jesus as the obedient Servant who "did not come to be served, but to serve, and to give his life as a ransom for many" (Mark 10:45, NIV). Luke's Gospel presents Jesus as the one who is identified with humanity, tracing the genealogy of Jesus back to Adam. In his Gospel, John's evangelistic purpose is stated in John 20:30–31, based on seven miracles or signs that Jesus did to evoke faith in Him.

The Acts of the Apostles

The Acts of the Apostles recounts the early history of the Christian Church. It begins with the Ascension of Christ and ends with Paul being held prisoner in Rome though living in a house and having a great deal of freedom. It was written by Luke and is a sequel to the things "that Jesus began to do and to teach until the day he was taken up to heaven" (Acts 1:1–2, NIV). Acts gives little information about the "apostles," thus many have suggested that it be called "The Acts of the Holy Spirit." The book can be viewed in light of the geographical spread of the gospel (See Acts 1:8) or seen as developed personally around the ministries of Peter, Philip, and Paul.

The Epistles

Thirteen epistles are believed to have been written by Paul and can be further assigned as church letters and personal letters. Romans presents the doctrine of salvation. The Corinthian letters deal with church order and Paul's apostolic authority. Galatians presents a charter of Christian freedom in Christ as the Apostle Paul deals with the question of legalism, whereas Ephesians has as its theme the Christian's election and consequent position in Christ. Colossians is an epistle that addresses the deity of Jesus Christ. Philippians is a tender and compassionate letter in which Paul expresses his concern for them as well as giving them news concerning his possible release from incarceration. The First and Second Thessalonian epistles both have to do with the return of Christ. First and Second Timothy and Titus were written to instruct Timothy and Titus in their leadership roles in the churches for which they had responsibilities, and Philemon is a personal letter to Philemon in which Paul makes a plea for a runaway slave by the name of Onesimus.

Some have placed Romans, Galatians, the Corinthian correspondence, and the Thessalonian correspondence in a separate group, then designating Ephesians, Colossians, Philippians, and Philemon as the Prison Epistles, because, in them Paul refers to himself as a prisoner. Books 1 and 2 Timothy and Titus are viewed as the Pastoral Epistles and Philemon as a personal epistle. The New Testament order of Paul's letters is not a chronological one but rather a logical one with the great treatise on Salvation as the first letter. Though the letters to the Thessalonians may have been his first written epistles, they are placed last because they have to do with eschatology. Critics have presented many arguments against the Pauline authorship of such letters as Ephesians and Colossians as well as the Pastorals, but internal evidence for their Pauline authenticity is compelling as evidence for their Pauline origin. The fact that Paul's name appears in both of the epistles does little to persuade those who attribute these letters to someone else, but Guthrie (1970, 507–8) presents a compelling case against those who argue that the name Paul is a pseudonym: "To maintain that the

Paulinist out of his sheer love for Paul and through his own self-effacement composed the letter [Ephesians], attributed it to Paul and found an astonishing and immediate readiness on the part of the Church to recognize it as such is considerably less credible than the simple alternative of regarding it as Paul's own work."

The remaining eight epistles are called General Epistles because they are written to the church as a whole and not to particular churches. The first of these, Hebrews, is by an unknown author but was long attributed to Paul; however, Pauline authorship was disputed very early on. Hebrews compares the Old Testament sacrificial system with the work of Christ on the Cross and emphasizes Christ's position as the Great High Priest. The central passage of the book is its reference to Psalm 110:4 (NIV): "You are a priest forever, in the order of Melchizedek," and chapter five begins the development of that theme.

The Epistle of James, a half-brother of the Lord, was addressed to Jewish people who had become dispersed into a hostile world that offered many temptations to compromise the faith. It teaches the importance of undergoing trials of faith and overcoming temptation.

Peter's two letters are very different in terms of the Greek texts. They were obviously written by different amanuenses. The First Epistle of Peter is a treatise on "the true grace of God" (5:12) as it relates to salvation, to the areas of submission, to suffering in the name of Jesus and Christian service. The Second Epistle has a much more urgent message—Peter warns about the last days and the judgment to come.

John's three letters center around the themes of truth and love. The First Epistle of John is a treatise on truth and explains how love for God and for others comes through truth. One does not become truthful by loving God, but one who lives the truth of the message of Christ demonstrates that he or she loves God. John demonstrates the Christian life by contrasts with light and darkness. He talks about theology, about the social implications of the Christian life, and expressions of love to God and to others. The Second Epistle of John (9) is a warning to avoid those who would "advance" truth; that is, Christians are to "Love in the truth." The Third Epistle centers around three individuals: Gaius is the author's friend and they find mutual fellowship "in the truth." In contrast to Gaius, who is "faithful in what [he] is doing for the brother even though they are strangers to you" (5, NIV), John writes a scathing denunciation of Diotrophes, "who loves to be first, but will have nothing to do with us." The third person mentioned is Demetrius, "who is well spoken of by everyone" (12, NIV). The lesson here is "Hold the truth in love."

The last of the epistles is written by Jude whom it is believed was a half-brother of the Lord. Its content is similar to that of 2 Peter. The key passage in Jude is an exhortation to Christians to "contend for the faith that was once for all entrusted to the saints" (3, NIV). Jude writes about false teachers who surreptitiously have insinuated themselves into the church. He warns believers about them and their false doctrines, and concludes with a series of commands relating to faithfulness and urgency in the proclamation of the gospel.

The Revelation of Jesus Christ

Though the Book of Revelation is neglected by most Christians, it is rarely overlooked by Fundamentalists. In fact, eschatology has always been of the greatest interest to Fundamentalists, and the Book of Revelation is familiar to most. There is some controversy among Fundamentalists about how the Book of Revelation should be interpreted. Consequently, there is no one interpretation that fits all views. The Book of Revelation emphasizes worship—both true and false. It raises the specter of the worship of falsehood whether in the person designated as the Antichrist, the false prophet, or the character of the earthly culture. Chapters 2 and 3 are letters to seven churches and have been used often as biblical bases to encourage Christians to forsake the temptations of correctness without love (Ephesus), of heresy and compromise (Pergamum and Thyatira), or the lukewarmness of Laodicea, but instead to follow the examples of the churches at Smyrna, Sardis, and Philadelphia.

To those who interpret the book from a "futurist" point of view, it is an accurate account of the events that lead up to the return of Christ and His reign as King of kings and Lord of lords. This is particularly true of dispensationalists, most of whom believe that the command, "Come up here, and I will show you what must take place after this" (4:1b, NIV), demonstrates that this is a portrayal of future events. Dispensationalism is coincidental with premillennialism, and the only serious conflict between dispensationalists is whether the "rapture of the church"(1 Thessalonians 4:16–17) will precede, come in the middle of, or at the end of the "great tribulation," which

dispensational interpreters all believe to be yet future. The tribulation is a seven-year period which is the completion or the seventieth week of Daniel's prophecy in Daniel 9:24ff. It is that time prophesied by the Lord Jesus Christ in Matthew 24:15–25 with special note given to Jesus' words, "For then there will be great distress, unequaled from the beginning of the world until now—and never to be equaled again" (24:21). The events of this period are pictured beginning with Revelation 4 and ending with the nineteenth chapter when the return of Christ in glory is pictured. When that occurs, the Antichrist, called the "beast" in Revelation will gather the kings of the earth to battle the returning Lord Jesus Christ. The end of the battle is that the beast and his false prophet are cast into the "fiery lake of burning sulfur" (Revelation 19:20), and the armies of the earth were destroyed by the one whose name is "The Word of God." Chapters 20 and 21 present the 1000–year reign of Christ, which is followed by the final judgment.

Unity and Purpose

Fundamentalists believe that because "All scripture is God-breathed" (2 Timothy 3:16, NIV), there is a unity to be found within the scriptures, Old Testament and New. That unity is found in the prophetic word of the Old Testament concerning the Messiah, and it finds its fulfillment in the New Testament record of the virginal conception and birth, of His preexistence, the miraculous work in conjunction with the Holy Spirit, His sufferings in life, and in death, His Resurrection and the promises of God's coming kingdom. Indeed, the Lord taught that "beginning with Moses and all the Prophets, he explained to them what said in all the Scriptures concerning himself" (Luke 24:27, NIV). Luke records the Lord's appearance to the disciples on the night following the Resurrection when "he opened their minds so that they could understand the Scriptures." He told them, "This is what is written: The Christ will suffer and rise from the dead on the third day, and repentance and forgiveness of sins will be preached in his name to all nations beginning in Jerusalem" (Luke 24:45–47, NIV).

The purpose of all Scripture is to lead people out of the darkness of sin and into the glorious light of God's righteousness. Since Jesus emphasized that the scriptures spoke of Him (Luke 24:45–47; John 5:39), it is clear that the Bible was not written as a document for the improvement of society, or for the answer to every question that perplexes modern life, but it was written that people might find that righteousness by faith (Romans 1:17). More particularly, the New Testament is a reflection of the promise that Jesus made to His apostles in the Upper Room that the Holy Spirit would teach them all things and "remind [them] of everything [He] said to [them]" (paraphrase of John 14:26). Jesus' teachings and the uniform teachings of the New Testament writers presented the path to salvation and the dire consequences for those enslaved by sin.

Richard I. McNeely

See also Bible; Biblical Criticism; Biblical Inerrancy; Old Testament

Bibliography

Aland, Kurt. (1962) *The Problem of the New Testament Canon.* Oxford: Mowbray.

Bruce, Frederick F. (1988) *The Canon of Scripture.* Downers Grove, IL: InterVarsity Press.

Carson, Donald A., Douglas J. Moo, and Leon Morris. (1992) *An Introduction to the New Testament.* Grand Rapids, MI: Zondervan Publishing.

Gromacki, Robert G. (1974) *New Testament Survey.* Grand Rapids, MI: Baker Book House.

Guthrie, Donald. (1970) *New Testament Introduction.* Downers Grove, IL: InterVarsity Press.

Meye, Robert P. (1979) "Canon of the New Testament." In *International Standard Bible Encyclopedia*, vol. I. Grand Rapids, MI: Wm. B. Eerdmans, 601–606.

Tenney, Merrill C. (1961) *New Testament Survey.* Grand Rapids, MI: Wm. B. Eerdmans.

Noahide Covenant

The Noahide Covenant refers to an agreement between God and Noah in the immediate post-flood period. Genesis 9:8–11 (NIV) makes this promise explicit:

> Then God said to Noah and to his sons with him [9]: "I now establish my covenant with you and with your descendants after you [10] and with every living creature that was with you.... [11] Never again will all life be cut off by the waters of a flood; never again will there be a flood to destroy the earth."

In Genesis 9:12, the rainbow is set by God as the seal of His covenant with man through Noah.

The precise requirements set by God in the Noahide Covenant, however, are not so clearly stated. The text makes explicit only two restrictions: a ban on murder [Genesis 9:6] and on eating meat with the blood still in it [Genesis 9:4]. To arrive at the seven commandments comprising the Noahide Covenant therefore, rabbinic exegetes juxtaposed the Adamic Covenant of Genesis 2:16–17 with that of Genesis 9. Thus, according to Maimonides [d. 1204]:

> Six precepts were given to Adam: prohibition of idolatry, of blasphemy, of murder, of adultery, of robbery, and the command to establish courts of justice. Although there is a tradition to this effect— a tradition dating back to Moses, our teacher, and human reason approves of those precepts—it is evident from the general tenor of Scriptures that he (Adam) was bidden to observe these commandments. An additional commandment was given to Noah: prohibition of (eating) a limb from a living animal. (Hershman 1949: 230–231):

The Noahide Covenant would seem unremarkable, but it has been a source of polemical controversy since the Middle Ages stemming from its application to Gentiles. According to talmudic teachings, Gentiles are deemed Noahides (children of Noah) and are enjoined to obey the seven laws of Noah if they are to be apportioned a share in the life hereafter. According to Tract Sanhedrin of the Babylonian Talmud:

> The rabbis taught: Seven commandments were given to the children of Noah, and they are: Concerning judges, blasphemy, idolatry, adultery, bloodshed, robbery, and that they must not eat of the member of the body while the animal is still alive. R. Hananiah b. Gamaliel said: Also the blood of the same. R. Hidka said: Also castration is forbidden to them. R. Simeon said: Also witchcraft. And R. Jose said: All that is forbidden to them in the portion on witchcraft [Deuteronomy 18:10–12] shall be forbidden to a descendant of Noah.

Whether the Noahide code was ever actually enacted into law is questionable, especially in light of the punishment for transgression of the Noahide laws— death at the hands of a Jewish court. According to Sanhedrin 57b

Rabbi Ya'akov bar Aha found in Sefer Aggadeta deVei Rav: "A descendant of Noah may be put to death on [the ruling of] one witness, without formal preliminary warning [that his crime is a capital offense]. The witness must be a male but may be a relative. In the name of Rabbi Ishmael, it is said "[a] descendant of Noah may be put to death for feticide as well."

This dire sanction was obviated in two ways. First, according to the teachings of Maimonides, no Noahide could be put to death if he or she was ignorant of the transgression of Noahide law. Since virtually no Gentile—and not so many more Jews—was aware of the Noahide code, conviction and sentencing would have been unlikely in a Jewish court. More to the point, in conditions of exile, there were no Jewish courts, and Jews were powerless to enforce any sanctions, however theoretical.

The Noahide Laws remained the province of academics specializing in Jewish thought and learned rabbis steeped in Jewish texts until 1992 with the emergence in the United States of an organized Noahide movement led by David Davis, Jack Saunders, and Vendel Jones. The movement, taking the name B'nai Noah (Children of Noah), teaches that Gentiles should, under the guidance of Jewish rabbis, adopt the Noahide code and live according to its precepts.

Jeffrey Kaplan

Bibliography

Hershman, Abraham M., trans. (1949) *The Code of Maimonides: Book Fourteen, The Book of Judges*. New Haven, CT: Yale University Press.

Kaplan, Jeffrey. (1997) *Radical Religion in America: Millenarian Movements from the Far Right to the Children of Noah*. Syracuse, NY: Syracuse University Press.

Lichtenstein, Aaron. (1986) *The Seven Laws of Noah*, 2nd ed. New York: The Rabbi Jacob Joseph School Press.

Rakover, Nahum. (1991) "Jewish Law and the Noahide Obligation to Preserve Social Order." *Cardozo Law Review* 12 (February/March): 1073–1074.

Old Testament

The Old Testament of the Bible consists of the thirty-nine books that Jewish and Christian traditions recognize as canonical. Most modern biblical scholars see the Old Testament as a record of the religious experiences of ancient Israel. While some would acknowledge that there may be a historical core to some of the stories, they would argue that the present text reflects a long process of theological interpretation by the religious community. Most modern scholars assume that what is reported in the Old Testament are events that correspond to natural cause-and-effect explanations, but which have been interpreted as miraculous acts of God by the religious community. Thus, a determination of what actually occurred requires a modern scientific and historical analysis of the report.

The Fundamentalist understanding of the Old Testament is very different. They believe that the Old Testament is the revelation of God, and is, therefore, true in all its assertions. While the exact mechanism of inspiration is debated, there is agreement that the truth of the revelation was not obscured by the human instrument through whom it came. Clear Old Testament affirmations about science, history, authorship of books, miracles, and moral values are taken as truth that is beyond dispute, and this perspective determines the Fundamentalist understanding of worldview, history and science, and biblical criticism. This understanding also encourages the literal biblical interpretation that is characteristic of Fundamentalism. Christian Fundamentalists see the Old Testament as revelation that prepared the way for the fuller revelation of God's purposes in the New Testament.

The Contents of the Old Testament

The first five books of the Old Testament, traditionally attributed to Moses, are known as the Law or Pentateuch. The first book, Genesis, relates the origins of the world, mankind and civilization, and the beginnings of the Israelite nation. It also describes the entrance of sin into the world, God's judgment, and his redemptive response to peoples' sin. Exodus contains the account of Israel's experience as slaves in Egypt and God's deliverance of his people from that bondage. The book also recounts God's Covenant with Israel at Mt. Sinai in which He agreed to be their God and declared them to be His people. Exodus includes regulations detailing how God wanted His people to live. More detailed regulations for the Israelites and their religious life are given in the Book of Leviticus. The wanderings of Israel following the Exodus from Egypt are described in the Book of Numbers. Deuteronomy is a recounting of the Law to Israel delivered by Moses just prior to Israel's entrance into the land of Canaan.

The books of Moses are followed by the books of History, which are accounts of Israel's history. Joshua describes the conquest of Canaan by the Israelite tribes, while Judges describes the chaotic period between the conquest and the establishment of the monarchy. The Book of Ruth relates a story about David's ancestors during the period of the Judges.

One and 2 Samuel deal with the establishment of the monarchy under Saul and David. One Kings 1–11 depicts the reign of Solomon over a united Israel, while the remainder of 1 and 2 Kings relates the history of the kingdoms of Israel and Judah after the political division following Solomon's death. One and 2 Chronicles also report the nation's history through the return from the Babylonian Exile from a slightly different perspective. Ezra, Nehemiah, and Esther relate events from the post-Exilic period.

These historical books are followed by the Writings, books of poetry and prophecy. The Book of Job explores the problem of righteous suffering as it relates the story of a blameless and upright man who suffered greatly. Psalms contains poems (thanksgiving songs, laments, wisdom songs, etc.) that were set to music and served as the hymnbook for temple worship. Proverbs contains collections of proverbs and other wisdom sayings. Ecclesiastes was a sage who examined complexities of life that seemed to be at variance with the general tone of the wisdom tradition, while Song of Songs is a collection of poems celebrating love.

The rest of the Old Testament consists of the books of Prophets and Minor Prophets. These prophetic books date from the eighth century BCE until the post-Exilic period. The major prophets include the Book of Isaiah. Chapters 1 to 39 concern primarily the events of the eighth century BCE in Judah. Chapters 40 to 66 recount the return from Exile in 538 BCE and the prophet's hopes for the Messianic Kingdom. Jeremiah and Ezekiel describe the events immediately preceding and following the Babylonian destruction of Judah and Jerusalem in 587/86 BCE. Jeremiah writes from the perspective of a prophet living in Judah while Ezekiel, who was exiled to Babylon in 597 BCE, presents his material in an Exilic setting. The Book of Daniel is also set in the context of the Exile. Lamentations is a collection of poems mourning the destruction of Jerusalem. The Hebrew Bible includes it among the Writings, but Christian versions place it after the Book of Jeremiah because tradition attributes the material to that prophet.

The twelve minor prophets (also known as The Twelve) include the books of Hosea, Joel, Amos, Obadiah, Jonah, Micah, Nahum, Habakkuk, Zephaniah, Haggai, Zechariah, and Malachi. These works range from the eighth century BCE to the post-Exilic period and concern issues in both the southern kingdom of Judah and the northern kingdom of Israel. The prophets were primarily preachers who addressed issues of relevance to their own society and called the people to repent and obey God's Covenant. Major themes in the prophets include the need for just and moral government, compassion and fair treatment of the poor, and purity and strict obedience to God in their religious life. The prophets exhorted Israel and Judah to avoid idolatry and syncretistic religion and to worship the Lord alone. They proclaimed God's coming judgment and focused on such themes as the Messianic Kingdom and the Day of the Lord.

The Fundamentalist Perspective on the Old Testament and the Worldview

The worldview reflected in Scripture is considered to be normative and prescriptive by Fundamentalists, and the difference in perspective is clearly articulated by C. C. McCown (1956: 18) as he argues for a rigorous naturalistic approach to biblical studies. He says,

> The nature of divine activity, as seen by the ancient world, was arbitrary, deterministic, and miraculous. God, or the gods, stood outside to foreordain and interfere with the course of events. Modern science and philosophy have no place for miracles and special providences. History is the result of the complex interaction of natural and social forces and the actions and reactions of men. There are neither demons nor angels. God only acts through men. Neither the liberal nor the conservative, neither the historian nor the theologian can afford to neglect the total difference of world view.

The Fundamentalist, advocating a literal interpretation of the text, would argue that the worldview reflected in the Old Testament is an accurate description of reality. That reality includes the spiritual realm, demons and angels, and God's intervention in natural and historical processes.

The Fundamentalist View of Science, History, and Morality

While many Fundamentalists would agree that the Old Testament is not a science textbook, they would maintain that when the Bible speaks about matters of science or history, it is true and authoritative. Old Testament accounts of theophanies and miracles are seen as literal accounts of what occurred in history. Since the Old Testament reports that God intervenes

Isaiah 41:21–29

21. Produce your cause, saith the Lord; bring forth your strong reasons, saith the King of Jacob.

22. Let them bring them forth, and shew us what shall happen: let them shew the former things, what they be, that we may consider them, and know the latter end of them; or declare us things for to come.

23. Shew the things that are to come hereafter, that we may know that ye are gods; yea, do good, or do evil, that we may be dismayed, and behold it together.

24. Behold, ye are nothing, and your work of nought: an abomination is he that chooseth you.

25. I have raised up one from the north, and he shall come: from the rising of the sun shall he call upon my name: and he shall come upon princes as upon mortar, and as the potter treadeth clay.

26. Who hath declared from the beginning, that we may know? and beforetime, that we may say, He is righteous? yea, there is none that declareth, yea, there is none that heareth your words.

27. The first shall say to Zion, Behold, behold them: and I will give to Jerusalem one that bringeth good tidings.

28. For I beheld, and there was no man: even among them, and there was no counsellor, that, when I asked of them, could answer a word.

29. Behold, they are all vanity; their works are nothing: their molten images are wind and confusion.

---

in natural processes to produce miracles that are not amenable to naturalistic cause-and-effect explanations, Fundamentalists accept such declarations as authoritative. God created the heavens and the earth (most would argue in six twenty–four hour days, and perhaps as recently as ten thousand years ago). Human beings, created in God's image, are unique and essentially different from the animals. Human beings fell, and sin and evil entered into human experience. Sin has radically impacted human ability to live as God desires, and humankind is now characterized by an intense rebellion against God and His purposes in the world. There was a universal flood that destroyed all mankind except for Noah and his family, who were delivered along with pairs of all the animals. Noah was saved by building an ark according to the instructions that God gave him, and it came to rest on Mt. Ararat after the flood waters had subsided. God delivered his people from Egyptian bondage through a series of plagues against the Egyptians (some of which distinguished between the Israelites and the Egyptians) and by a miraculous escape when the waters of the Red Sea dried up to allow the Israelites to cross over on dry land. God then allowed the Israelites to conquer the land of Canaan through a series of miraculous victories against more numerous and better equipped Canaanite forces. God did this in fulfillment of a promise made to Abraham some four hundred years earlier. The purpose of such marvelous acts of God was to make it clear to both I srael and to the people around them that Yahweh was the true God, and such awareness was to bring people to obey God, to trust and worship him. While there are significant differences of opinion among Fundamentalists about the exact way in which the Old Testament Law is to be viewed under the New Covenant (often a distinction is made between cultic law, civil law, and moral law, with the claim that only the moral law is binding under the New Covenant), all would see the moral precepts of the Old Testament as authoritative and binding. The basis for their authority comes from the fact that they are set in the context of "Thus saith the Lord," and Fundamentalists see in this a transcendent authority for moral truth.

Fundamentalists and Modern Biblical Criticism

This Fundamentalist belief that the Old Testament results from God's self-revelation also accounts for their rejection of many of the conclusions of critical biblical scholarship, including the Documentary Hypothesis of the origin of the Pentateuch, the multiple authorship of Isaiah, and the Maccabean date for the Book of Daniel.

As Gleason Archer (1996) demonstrates, Fundamentalists can cite considerable evidence in support of their argument for the Mosaic authorship of the Pentateuch, but the statements throughout Deuteronomy and the Pentateuch indicating that Moses spoke or wrote these words, in effect, establish the conclusion about authorship for most Fundamentalists. Fundamentalists reject the claim of modern scholarship that Deuteronomy dates to the time of Josiah and was written to promote his religious reforms. Critical theories about the origin of the other books of the Pentateuch are also rejected in favor of Mosaic authorship.

Modern scholars note the pre-Exilic perspective of Isaiah 1 to 39 and the decidedly post-Exilic perspective of Isaiah 40 to 66. In addition, they point to a number of detailed statements about events that occurred long after the time of the eighth-century prophet Isaiah (e.g., the reference to Cyrus in chapter 45 or the numerous references to the return from Exile or to clearly post-Exilic settings in chapters 40 to 66), and conclude that this material could not have originated in the eighth century BCE Thus, they argue that chapters 40 to 66 were written by a different author (or authors) who lived at the time of these events. Fundamentalists argue that predictive prophecy is a possibility because God is revealing details of future events to the prophet. They maintain that passages such as Isaiah 41:21–29 assert that it is the Lord's ability to accurately predict the future that proves that He is God and that often validates a prophet's message. Thus, Fundamentalists see predictive prophecy as having its origins in God's omniscience, and He reveals that knowledge to His true prophet. The prophet's knowledge of events that transpired long after he lived then becomes, for the Fundamentalist, not a certain basis for conclusions about authorship, but rather evidence for the God-breathed nature of Scripture (2 Timothy 3:16).

According to the book, Daniel was taken from Judah to Babylon in 605 BCE and served there under both Babylonian and Persian kings. Daniel relates several visions that came to him there, and while several of the visions describe future kingdoms in general terms that are amenable to various interpretations, his vision in chapter 11 involves a precise and detailed description of events in the second century BCE. Because of the exactness of the descriptions, it is concluded by most modern biblical scholars that this material could not have been written before the events transpired. Fundamentalists argue that this material was written by the Daniel who went to Babylon in 605 BCE, and is but another example of predictive prophecy that is possible because God has revealed the future to His prophet.

Conclusion

The Fundamentalist understanding of the Old Testament flows out of the assumptions with which they approach it. The text is seen as God's authoritative revelation, and thus its assertions are accepted as true. While commitment to literal interpretation does not produce consensus on the meaning of every text (there are wide differences among Fundamentalists about how prophetic texts are to be interpreted), all would agree that the Old Testament is God's revealed Word to His people. Scripture thus stands as the final authority, not only in matters of morals and theology but in all those matters about which it speaks, including its claims about the nature of reality, the facts of history (both past and future), and statements about science.

Edward M. Curtis

See also Bible; Biblical Criticism; Biblical Inerrancy; Biblical Inspiration; Judaism, Fundamental; New Testament; Temple

Bibliography

Archer, Gleason Leonard. (1994) *A Survey of Old Testament Introduction*, rev. ed. Chicago: Moody Press.

Hill, Andrew E., and John H. Walton (1991) *A Survey of the Old Testament*. Grand Rapids, MI: Zondervan Publishing.

McCown, C. C. (1956) "The Current Plight of Biblical Scholarship." *Journal of Biblical Literature* 18: 12–18.

Ramm, Bernard. (1970) *Protestant Biblical Interpretation*, 3rd rev. ed. Grand Rapids, MI: Baker Book House.

Opus Dei

Opus Dei is an official organization of the Roman Catholic Church with a combined membership of clerics and laity who pledge to lead exemplary personal lives and assist the church to propagate the faith. Members are encouraged to neither proclaim nor deny their allegiance to Opus Dei and this gives rise to suspicion that the organization is needlessly secretive and even subversive. In fact, its leadership is routinely listed in publicly circulated church documents. Opus Dei is entirely supportive of papal authority and does not dispute doctrine.

The Spanish priest Fr. José Maria Escrivá Albás founded Opus Dei in the late 1920s during a time of intense anti-Catholicism in Spanish higher education and politics. He intended it as a foil to the materialism of modern life, whether capitalist or Marxist. In the ensuing Spanish Civil War, Republican and Communist forces attacked the organization and persecuted its membership. After the Falangist victory, Opus Dei reasserted itself and steadily gained adherents among political and religious conservatives, especially in the Spanish church hierarchy. In 1947, Opus Dei, now relocated to Rome, was recognized as an official secular institute of the Roman Catholic Church, dedicated to the papacy. It has since spread throughout the world and can be found in most countries with a substantial Catholic population.

There are four classes of members in Opus Dei. Numeraries are celibates with intensive religious training who devote their entire time to the organization. In practice, they are all in Holy Orders. Associates, also celibate, are trained in theology but do not live communally and need not be priests. Supernumeraries can be married and need only devote part of their time to Opus Dei. The fourth class, the Cooperators, share the goals of the organization but need not be Roman Catholic. There is a separate women's branch that is associated with the men's branch solely by its connection to the president-general of Opus Dei. The membership does not wear identifying dress nor perform any exercises of piety distinct from Catholics in general. The lay membership, drawn from all walks of life, are called to live lives of exemplary moral purity and even asceticism. Included are many prominent, and some influential, Catholic professional people who are asked to live in the world while not being of it.

Members of Opus Dei are enjoined against revealing its workings to the world. This casts an aura of secrecy about it, but, in fact, it is a common provision for organizations under the sway of Rome's Sacred Congregation of Religious. The varied membership of Opus Dei, many of whom are active in work-a-day commercial and family life, works against any military-style discipline. Opus Dei is better described as a loosely associated, although deeply dedicated, group of like-minded Catholics who vow to live sanctified lives under the authority of Rome. At the same time, members are undeniably theological, and often political, conservatives. The veiled nature of Opus Dei and the frequent stature of its international adherents cause some to regard the membership as quasi-Fundamentalist Roman Catholic shock troops, secretive at best and possibly conspiratorial. Catholic scholars emphatically deny this.

Robert K. Whalen

See also Catholic Fundamentalists; Catholics United for Faith; Wanderer, The

Bibliography

Estruch, Juan. (1996) *Saints and Schemers: Opus Dei and Its Paradoxes*, translated by Elizabeth Ladd Glick. New York: Oxford University Press.

Rodriguez, Pedro. (1994) *Opus Dei in the Church: An Ecclesiological Study of the Life and Apostolate of Opus Dei*. Princeton, NJ: Scepter Publishers.

Tapia, Maria del Carmen. (1997) *Beyond the Threshold: A Life in Opus Dei*. New York: Continuum.

Original Sin

Original sin refers primarily to the inherited guilt, and tendency to sin, borne by all human beings for the sin of Adam, the biblical first parent of the human race. Fundamentalist Christianity, largely owing to this doctrine, has maintained a very pessimistic evaluation of natural human capabilities, and has insisted on the universal need for a radical conversion.

Early History

Despite the frequent assertion that original sin is a scriptural teaching, the notion of an inherited taint on human nature did not feature prominently in earliest Christian writings. While some idea of universal human sinfulness might be inferred from certain scriptural texts, especially some Pauline writings (Romans 5:12–19; Ephesians 2:3), well-developed notions of original sin took shape only after some centuries, and were by no means uniform in their portrayal of how the human race was affected by the first sin. Original sin does not figure at all prominently in the earliest Christian writings outside the New Testament. References to Christ's redemptive work in texts like 1 Clement (c. 96) and the letters of Ignatius of Antioch (c. 107) only allude to the source of the evil from which humans are redeemed. From the second century onward, there is a general distinction between Greek and Latin Christian accounts of the consequences of Adamic sin. Early Greek writers from Justin Martyr (second century) to John Chrysostom (fourth to fifth century) univocally denied that human beings share in the guilt for Adam's transgression. Humans can be culpable only insofar as they willingly imitate the first parents by sinning; Adam's sin is a model or prototype. By contrast, early Latin writers beginning with Tertullian of Carthage (c. 200) portray a much more direct and deleterious connection between Adam's sin and the subsequent human condition. Tertullian speaks of a propensity to sin sown in each soul through the parent. Another North African, Cyprian of Carthage (c. 250), was the first to argue that infants are baptized because of a "contagion of death" inherited from Adam.

Views like these continued in the West into the fourth century, and received their fullest and most enduring development in the writings of yet another North African, Augustine of Hippo (354–430), who coined the term "original sin" (from the Latin, *peccatum originale*). The Pelagian controversy, which occupied the latter years of Augustine's life, supplied the context for his seminal writings on original sin. Pelagius, a British spiritual teacher, denied that infant baptism imparted forgiveness of sin, because infants could not be guilty for sins they did not commit. Augustine responded by asserting that the guilt of Adam's sin is passed on to his posterity through the sexual desire (Latin: *libido*) involved in procreation. The human liability to death is the most evident penalty for the first sin. Augustine identifies original sin with "concupiscence," the yearning for self-gratification in humans that turns them away from God, such that the human will invariably fail to choose the good. Because all human beings both inherit the guilt and penalty for Adamic sin and experience its presence as concupiscence, the human race as a whole stands condemned—a "condemned lump" (Latin: *massa damnata*). God could have left humanity to its collective condemnation, but through Christ some receive, freely, the transformation needed to reorient them toward the good. Augustine's anti-Pelagian views on original sin were endorsed in the canons of the Sixteenth Council of Carthage in 418, which were in turn approved by Pope Zosimus (d. 418).

Later Development

Through the Middle Ages discussion about original sin in the West repeated many Augustinian themes, but also departed significantly from Augustine's analysis. From Anselm (d. 1109) onward, discussion of original sin focused not on concupiscence but on the lack of "sanctifying grace" (or original justice) that Adam had possessed before the first sin. Thomas Aquinas (d. 1274) spoke of original sin as a weakened, disordered condition, but was not as pessimistic as Augustine about original sin's effects on human nature.

Protestant Views

The Protestant Reformers repeated Augustine's identification of original sin with concupiscence, and a stern doctrine of original sin characterized Reformational theologies—particularly Calvinism—and their later orthodoxies. The Calvinist *Westminster Shorter Catechism*, for example, states that the sinful human condition "consists in the guilt of Adam's first sin, the want of original righteousness, and the corruption of his whole nature, which is commonly called original sin" (*The Shorter Catechism* A. to Q. 18). New England in the late seventeenth and early eighteenth centuries experienced a series of disputes among various schools of thought concerning precise interpretations of original sin. The religious revival known as the Great Awakening certainly proceeded under the conviction that human beings in their natural state were totally depraved as a result of Adam's sin.

As the spirit of the Enlightenment began to penetrate theology, English liberals like Daniel Whitby (1638–1726) and John Taylor (1694–1761) began to criticize the traditional doctrine of original sin. Taylor, for example, argued that sin could arise only from evil choices made without the control of reason. Thus the notion of an "imputed" human sinfulness made no sense. Through the nineteenth century, hesitations about the Augustinian notion of original sin were widespread among Protestants, and even would-be defenders of the notion of original sin, like Nathaniel Taylor (1786–1858), greatly modified the Augustinian and Calvinist understanding. Taylor held that human beings are born morally free, yet will invariably choose to sin without the infusion of divine grace.

The greatest challenge to traditional notions of the Fall and original sin was posed in the nineteenth and twentieth centuries by the spread of the Darwinian theory of evolution. While for some, evolutionary theory cast all religious worldviews into doubt, proponents of the so-called progressive orthodoxy or "new theology" of the nineteenth century labored to maintain Christian language while accepting a progressive philosophy of the history of humankind. In some renderings, such as that of G. A. Gordon (1853–1929), the darker side of human moral life is cast as a struggle between the lower, brutish aspects of the human and the higher dictates of reason.

Liberal optimism foundered on the rocks of World War I, and the later writings of Walter Rauschenbusch (1861–1918) reflect a renewed consciousness of human perversity. In the twentieth century, Reinhold Niebuhr and Paul Tillich attempted to revive notions of original sin in a manner that de-emphasized the historical Fall and, particularly for Tillich, emphasized original sin in its existential aspect.

Fundamentalist Christians, though not always predictably Augustinian in their account of original sin, have insisted on the universality of human sinfulness apart from the saving grace of God in Christ, and on the concomitant darkened powers of human reason apart from scriptural revelation.

Thomas A. Smith

See also Fall of Humankind; Grace; Sin and Sinners

Bibliography

Blocher, Henri. (1999) *Original Sin: Illuminating the Riddle*. Grand Rapids, MI: Wm. B. Eerdmans.

Foster, Durwood, and Paul Mojzes, eds. (1985) *Society and Original Sin. Ecumenical Essays on the Impact of the Fall*. New York: Paragon House.

Gardella, Peter. (1985) *Innocent Ecstasy*. New York: Oxford University Press.

Haag, Herbert. (1969) *Is Original Sin in Scripture?* Translated by Dorothy Thompson. New York: Sheed & Ward.

Smith, H. Shelton. (1955) *Changing Conceptions of Original Sin*. New York: Charles Scribners' Sons.

Orthodoxy

The relationship of orthodoxy to Fundamentalism is an integral and a subtle one that has often been misunderstood. In recent years this misunderstanding has become particularly acute because the line between expressions of orthodoxy within various confessional traditions and the claims of Fundamentalists has been blurred in the public's eye. The origin of this confusion rests in part in the liberal application of the term "Fundamentalism" as a descriptive for several socially conservative and scriptural-based religious movements. More often than not, observers of religious life have suggested little or no distinction between self-confessed Fundamentalists and conservative Evangelical groups. While the social agendas or expressed convictions of these groups may correspond, their religious beliefs or ecclesiastical practices often remain distinct. Similarly, another important source for the current misunderstanding about the relationship of orthodoxy and Fundamentalism may be found in the diversity of meanings associated with the term "orthodoxy." While the term "orthodox" or "orthodoxy" refers to sound or correct opinion espoused within a religious system, it may also designate a specific social group, practice, or system of belief within a particular religious tradition—such as Greek Orthodox, Orthodox Judaism, or neo-orthodox theology. In the United States and elsewhere, these religious expressions tend to stand outside the cultural mainstream and are often seen as "peculiar" or "backward."

Further misunderstanding of this relationship exists due to the popular assumptions about the meaning of orthodoxy. Though orthodoxy does designate that which is understood as correct or sound belief and practice, it does not simply express a singular view of a religious tradition. In his seminal work on the development of doctrine in Christianity, Jaroslav Pelikan suggests that traditional orthodoxy encompassed a plurality of views and was articulated in a manner that accommodated these views while expressing their underlying consensus (1971: 332–357). Negotiating "orthodox consensus" is not the particular domain of Christianity and is the operative found in the oral traditions of both Judaism and Islam. Some scholars have attempted to nuance comparative studies of Fundamentalism among the three great Western traditions by utilizing this notion of orthodox consensus to eschew charges of Fundamentalism within a particular tradition. These writers have suggested that unlike Christianity, whose profession of orthodoxy is intricately tied to a historically developmental theology, the oral traditions of Judaism and Islam have tempered such innovations. What is popularly viewed as "Jewish" or "Islamic" Fundamentalism, it is argued, is simply an expression of social reactionaries or sects to the proliferation of Western values and cultural modernity. Historically speaking, such a division is somewhat artificial and does not take seriously changes within the respective traditions during the twentieth century.

The greatest contributing factor to existing uncertainty is, however, the elusive social organization of Fundamentalism itself. Historians of religion have described the organizational structure of Fundamentalism among various religions as that of a parachurch, contra-acculturationists, second-generation movements, or as reformists' organizations. Unlike other religious movements, Fundamentalism does not adhere to any single confessional statement that identifies the contours of the faith.

The Emergence of Intransigent Orthodoxy

Traditionally, the term "orthodoxy" has referred to a system of religious belief that is understood as "right belief" over and against heresy. Implicit to this system of religious belief are the subjects of history, consensus, and tradition. Stated simply, orthodoxy is an expression of mainstream beliefs among a particular religious tradition that developed over time. Because orthodoxy is formed by consensus over time, its formulation includes a plurality of religious expression and beliefs. Traditional expressions of orthodoxy derive their authority from a complex system of tradition, history, and hermeneutical principles. Fundamentalism, on the other hand, is a recent historical phenomenon whose determination of right belief is rooted in a particularly literal interpretation of Scripture. Its construction of orthodoxy has been premised upon an entirely different set of governing principles.

Fundamentalism, as it emerged during the early twentieth century, was predicated on the defense of Protestantism against perceived and select challenges of modernity. Although, as a religious system, its nascent form of expression was not unique to the American scene, its ultimate fruition as a culturally significant phenomenon was intricately wedded to the social and intellectual fabric of American society at the turn of the last century. While some debate has occurred over the amount of emphasis to be placed upon the distinctive features of the Progressive Era that nurtured Fundamentalism, scholars generally agree that developments such as the inroads made

by the Darwinist theory, German higher criticism, socialism, and spiritualism, all helped to shape the Fundamentalist agenda of the day. According to those self-professed Fundamentalists of the time, they were championing the cause of an unaltered orthodoxy against such heresies. This was a reified expression of orthodoxy, not based on the working principle of consensus derived through time, but rather one that was a reaction and a disavowal of recent social developments. As one scholar aptly put it, "In a word, fundamentalism is orthodoxy in confrontation with modernity"(Silberstein 1993: 28). It is this conceptual framework that has made Fundamentalism a powerful and viable form of expression among most of the world's major religious traditions. Integral to these systems of belief has been a static understanding and homogeneous conception of what is orthodox.

Orthodoxy Giving Expression to Fundamentalism

In examining the broad conceptual framework of Fundamentalism, one key attribute informing this religious perspective has been a philosophical dualism. At the center of the Fundamentalist perspective stands a type of Manichaeanism that understands the world in terms of oppositional forces of lightness and darkness. The modern world, Fundamentalists assert, has divided God's dominion against itself by introducing elements of darkness, thus corrupting God's intended order, including the revelation of truth. This notion of social and religious declension lends further credence to Fundamentalists' presuppositions about the legitimacy of elements used in determining orthodoxy. Institutionalized religion, it is believed, has succumbed to this modernist impulse, thus abdicating its former authentic claims of apostolic succession and orthodoxy. Members of such religious bodies are presumed to be nominal believers who constitute an apostate church because of their acceptance of modern scientific methods in helping to determine truth. Given these presuppositions, Fundamentalism often demonstrates itself in dramatic tension with traditional expressions of faith in modern society.

Further legitimating this conception of orthodoxy is the Fundamentalist's understanding of Scripture as the literal "Word of God." "The inerrancy of Scripture in every detail" is the a priori principle guiding Fundamentalist exegesis. This presupposition dramatically shapes their convictions about absolute truth and orthodoxy. For the Fundamentalist, the sacred text is understood as a collection of true and precise propositions regarding absolute truth. When properly organized and classified through the epistemological principles that govern the scientific method, the sacred Scripture presents no theological ambiguities or contradictions. Through the application of an empirically based rationalism, Fundamentalism argues that the Scriptures alone are perspicacious to the inquirer. This understanding of revealed truth has significant implications for Fundamentalist conceptions of society and orthopraxy.

By their abandonment of the textually literal commandments found in sacred Scripture, modern states have rejected the revealed and eternally valid principles of God's intended social order. From the Fundamentalists' perspective, the only way to repair such a breech is through a return to the prescriptive social laws found in Holy Scripture. Once such laws are obeyed, orthodoxy will prevail, thus restoring society to a mythical "golden age" when orthodoxy and orthopraxy predominated. It is this worldview, one that situates the dialectic between orthodoxy and modernity at the center of its constitution, that nearly all expressions of Fundamentalism share. As such, essential to the Fundamentalist worldview is the so-called reestablishment of an organic unity between religious and political expressions of orthodoxy.

The strict construction of orthodoxy over and against modernity has led Fundamentalists to reject the current social order. As self-assured bearers of "authentic" orthodoxy, Fundamentalist communities articulate a type of social mastery position. This has resulted in two general forms of response on the part of Fundamentalist communities: one may be characterized as a reformist approach while the other may be understood as revolutionary. While the reformist position seeks to establish orthodoxy by working through existing social and political institutions by means of public protests and pressure on political bodies, the revolutionary perspective seeks to disestablish current institutions, understanding them as illegitimate institutions that prohibit a full expression of the divine order. Failure to accomplish the reformation of society can lead to a more revolutionary agenda on the part of a reformist, as well as to a form of quietism that shuns the world as wholly corruptible and unworthy of change.

The Relationship of Orthodoxy to Orthopraxy

Like all religious orientations, Fundamentalism is an orientation that helps to create meaning and value among its adherents. This understanding of systems of religious belief is particularly important when referring to Fundamentalism and its understanding of orthodoxy. Ideas about what was acceptable belief and practice were not simply imposed on Fundamentalists by a modernist agenda. They did not simply "respond" to the perceived challenges of modernity, but attempted to live out their faith by abiding communally determined rules of orthopraxy that were selective. This correspondence between "right" belief and practice dramatically shaped the Fundamentalist agenda of the past and continues to do so today. Generally speaking, the Fundamentalist system for determining orthopraxy is founded on the acceptance of literal inerrancy of Scripture. A rigid adherence to this principle of interpretation not only secures a sense of certain and knowable truth but also creates a belligerency among scholars who, with the assumed truth on their side, define right and wrong in the arena of social practice. Coupled with their understanding of the corrupt modern age, Fundamentalists lament a "golden age" of social morality, when orthopraxy was the standard of civilized society. Through this hermeneutical approach, the sacred text not only defines boundaries of right and wrong, good and evil but also establishes who are the faithful and who are the nonbelievers.

Approximating Orthodoxy among Various Expressions of Fundamentalism

Scholars generally agree that locating any single or formal expression of Fundamentalist orthodoxy among the various religious traditions in which they appear is a difficult challenge. Because Fundamentalism in its variety of forms is not creedal or confessional in character, those beliefs that constitute Fundamentalist orthodoxy can only be approximated. Since the designation of Fundamentalism was first attributed to groups of American Evangelicals in the early twentieth century, Fundamentalist Christian orthodoxy is key to any discussion of orthodoxy.

Perhaps the most readily identifiable statement that shaped a nascent Fundamentalist movement was the publication of *The Fundamentals*. Published first as a series of paperback articles by Lyman

Stewart, a financial backer and chief promoter of the works, the series ran from 1910 to 1915 and included conservative scholars from both America and Britain. It was distributed freely throughout the countries to clergy, theological students, publishing houses, and educational and religious institutions. By the end of its initial run, more than three million volumes were generated and distributed. While its immediate impact was anything less than what was desired, its long-term effect was substantial. As historian George M. Marsden has suggested, the work "became a symbolic point of reference for identifying a 'fundamentalist' movement" (1982: 119). Not only did its title become a social designation for a particular group of conservative Evangelicals, but it also articulated the now-famous "five points" of Christian faith that, Fundamentalists insisted, every Christian must accept in order to be orthodox. These points are: the inerrancy of Scripture, the divinity of Jesus, the Virgin Birth, substitutionary Atonement of Jesus, and the physical Resurrection and bodily return of Christ.

Like their Christian contemporaries, Jewish Fundamentalists, referred to in general terms as ultra-Orthodox or the Haredim, are interested in delimiting the religious discourse of modern Judaism. Discounting much of the tradition and limiting the meaning and use of key terms of the faith, the Haredim seek to establish a religious "reordering" of society. Through this process, Jewish Fundamentalism seeks to homogenize the history, identity, and practices of historic Judaism and establish an "orthodoxy" that is ahistoric. But unlike its Christian manifestation, the identity of Fundamentalists and conceptualization of "orthodoxy" among Jews is not intimately tied to a body of written work outside the Torah. Instead Jewish Fundamentalism may be properly understood, in large part, as an offshoot of religious Zionism that first developed in nineteenth-century Europe. Zionism has been the conduit through which radical alternatives to prevailing or traditional Jewish concepts have flowed. With the establishment of the Jewish state of Israel, debate over the meaning and place of Zionist beliefs among Jewish Fundamentalists has been an intensive and complex process. Some factions of the Haredim endorse Zionism to varying degrees, while other groups of Fundamentalists, like the *yeshiva* community, reject the idea of the Jewish state. Although the methods or process may be debated among ultra-Orthodox Jews, they all will agree that the Jewish community must seek to reconcile a unitary and omniscient God with an imperfect world. While their Christian counterparts share this general understanding of theodicy, Jewish Fundamentalists also share other world views with Fundamentalists that shape their conception of religious truth and orthodox practice. Like Christian Fundamentalists, the Haredim argue organized religion is a "harlot" among the Jewish people. Based on an assumption of the infallibility of Holy Scripture, they also share ideas about Creationism with Christian Fundamentalists and preach of an apocalyptic judgment upon the world, when the Davidic dynasty will one day be restored among the nations.

In recent years observers of religion have discussed "the Islamic resurgence" throughout the world. The resurgence of Islam they contend is the result of three recent developments: namely, the Western tendency to make divisions between what is secular and what is sacred; a historical determinism that sees secularization as the only option in modern life; and the need to make religious belief relevant to the world of politics, education, law, social life, and economics. While some scholars suggest a prototype of Islamic Fundamentalism began to evolve as early as the eighteenth century, it was the dawning of the twentieth century that gave shape to Islamic Fundamentalism as it appears today (Cohen 1990: 60–61). Unlike Christian Fundamentalists, radical expressions of Islam have tended not to completely marginalize themselves in terms of politics. As historian John Esposito notes, for modern professors of Islam the central issue of faith is clear, "the question is not whether religion should inform life, but when and how" (1998: 159). In both its degree and form, Muslim Fundamentalists conceptualize orthodoxy in ways distinct from their co-religious. Several assumptions inform this body of beliefs, particularly a single way to discovering truth. The acceptance of the call (al-da'wa) to abide by a singular interpretation of Islamic law (Shari'a) that will establish a true Islamic society informs the everyday life of Islamic radicals. This presupposition, in turn, shapes how orthodoxy is discussed in terms of both belief and practice. Like their Christian and Jewish counterparts, Muslim Fundamentalists share a crusader mentality. This understanding, however, pits Islam against the West, which has fallen under the power of Zionism. In addition, Muslim Fundamentalists agree that a system of government based on a strict interpretation of Shari'a is the only legitimate form of government. Furthermore, since Christians and Jews are generally

not regarded as "People of the Book," they are subject to persecution. Moreover, because such groups as
the Taliban in Afghanistan are unwilling to allow a
plurality of voices within or outside of the Islamic
community (*ummah*), Christians and Jews, once considered protected (*dhimmis*) for their religious beliefs,
are now subject to persecution like Hindus and
Sikhs. Similar to earlier expressions of Islam witnessed among groups such as the Kharijites, the
Wahhabi, the Madhi, and Sarekat Islam, to name but
a few, today's Fundamentalists demand total commitment and obedience to the one true faith.

Kent A. McConnell

See also Haredim; Islamic Fundamentalism; Jews;
Judaism, Fundamental; Shi'a Islam

Bibliography

Cohen, Norman J., ed. (1990) *The Fundamentalist Phenomenon: A View from Within; A Response from
Without.* Grand Rapids, MI: Wm. B. Eerdmans.

Eliade, Mircea, Ioan P. Couliano, and Hillary S. Wiesner.
(1991) *The Eliade Guide to World Religions.* San
Francisco: HarperSanFrancisco.

Esposito, John L. (1998) *Islam: The Straight Path.* New
York: Oxford University Press.

Marsden, George M. (1980) *Fundamentalism and American Culture: The Shaping of Twentieth-Century Evangelicalism, 1870–1925.* New York: Oxford University
Press.

Marty, Martin E., and Scott Appleby, eds. (1994) *Accounting for Fundamentalisms.* Chicago: University of
Chicago Press.

Pelikan, Jaroslav. (1971) *The Christian Tradition: A History
of the Development of Doctrine,* vol. 1. Chicago: University of Chicago Press.

Ravitzky, Aviezer. (1996) *Messianism, Zionism, and Jewish
Religious Radicalism.* Chicago: University of Chicago
Press.

Silberstein, Laurence J., ed. (1993) *Jewish Fundamentalism
in Comparative Perspective: Religion, Ideology, and the
Crisis of Modernity.* New York: New York University
Press.

Parousia *See* Second Coming

Pastor's Wife

A pastor's wife is a role that intersects the private sphere of the home and the public realm of the church in Christian Fundamentalist traditions. According to Genesis 3:16, because of the original sin, God punishes Eve by multiplying her pain in childbirth and establishes that her desire would be for her husband and he would "rule over" her. In 1 Corinthians 11:3 (RSV), Paul writes, "I want you to understand that the head of every man is Christ, the head of a woman is her husband, and the head of Christ is God." Interpreting these passages literally, Fundamentalist Christians view men as the head of the household. In the home, women assist their husbands and nurture their children's spiritual growth. Within the church, men occupy the highest leadership offices while women participate within certain circumscribed areas such as the women's ministry programs and the Sunday School. Within this paradigm, the pastor's wife, gaining increased status from her husband's position, becomes the most influential role in the church accessible to women. Because there is only one pastor's wife, no other woman assumes such a place of power in the church. A pastor's wife publicly models the ideal characteristics of the true Christian wife for the congregation, assisting her husband in his ministry without neglecting the private domestic religious life of her family. Her role as assistant to the pastor allows her to exercise authority in the congregation, particularly among female congregants, without impinging upon the divinely ordained relationship between men and women.

Julius H. Bailey

See also Antifeminism; Christian Home, Ideal; Male Headship

Bibliography

Brasher, Brenda E. (1998) *Godly Women: Fundamentalism & Female Power*. New Brunswick, NJ: Rutgers University Press.

Gerami, Shahin. (1996) *Women and Fundamentalism: Islam and Christianity*. New York: Garland Press.

Hawley, John Stratton, ed. (1994) *Fundamentalism & Gender*. New York: Oxford University Press.

Pentecostalism

Pentecostalism, a worldwide Protestant movement that originated in America during the early twentieth century, promotes the belief that the Holy Spirit can reveal itself during divine worship, whether private or assembled, in an immediate and dramatic way. Such a revelation can prompt from its followers intense personal reverence, spontaneous physical healing, speaking in tongues (glossolalia), prophesying, and other physical or mental manifestations. Pentecostalism revels in hortatory preaching and vibrant congregational response. In some forms it stresses personal sanctification—a holistic turning away from sin brought about by the Holy Spirit.

There is no single Pentecostal church, but, rather, a mode of worship and belief that spans dozens of denominations, great and small. Many Pentecostals regard the Bible as infallible. They place a high premium on personal rectitude. Nearly always, they enthusiastically embrace premillennial eschatology. Though notably quarrelsome among themselves over finer theological points, Pentecostals encompass a wide social spectrum. They are found in great numbers among both white and African-American populations and, increasingly, among American Hispanics.

Missionaries have carried the faith overseas, especially to Latin America, where it has grown with astonishing rapidity. In the year 2000, a Pentecostal conference claimed a worldwide following of nearly one-half billion—although this number may be a substantial exaggeration. Nevertheless, Pentecostalism grew more rapidly during the past century than any other aspect of Christianity. As the twenty-first century opened, there seemed to be no reason why it could not continue its remarkable spread.

Pentecostal–Fundamentalist Relationship

There is no settled opinion on whether Pentecostals are Fundamentalists. It is likely that a majority of them, at least in the United States, would lay claim to being so. However, because it is not entirely certain what the term Fundamentalism even means in the opening years of the twenty-first century, such an assertion should be examined carefully. During the last quarter of the twentieth century, the contemporary media scrambled for a term with which to describe Protestants active on the political right. In its confusion, it often used the names "Christian Right," "Fundamentalist Christian," "Religious Right," and "Evangelical" interchangeably. High-profile clergy, such as Jerry Falwell, Oral Roberts, Jimmy Swaggart, and Jim Bakker were lumped together as a sort of generic Elmer Gantry, regardless of their disparate theologies.

It is equally misleading to simply dismiss Pentecostalism as "conservative" or "old-time" religion. So-called mainline Christians find nothing "conservative" about Pentecostal faith healing or speaking in tongues. These practices might, rather, appear a "radical" departure from the theological norm. Nor is Pentecostalism a survival from an earlier era, a sort of vestige from less complicated times, since its ori-

gin and history still lie, for the most part, in living memory. One is on safer ground where social issues are concerned, for here the entire Evangelical community tends toward the right. Even so, the diversity of American religious experience makes generalizations difficult and this is true with Pentecostals.

The relationship of Pentecostalism to Fundamentalism is thus murky because of the lack of a universally accepted definition on what constitutes a Fundamentalist. The term came into use around the time of World War I during a period when journalists such as H. L. Mencken had a field day hurling insults at the "rubes," nearly always identified as Fundamentalists. In addition, Pentecostals shared some of the traits usually assigned to these somewhat vaguely conceived Fundamentalists: an inerrant Bible, premillennial eschatology, hortatory preaching, and traditional—even ultratraditional—social values. Much, then, is held in common between the two religious groups. Yet, as in geometry where all squares are rectangles but not all rectangles are squares, it may be asserted that all Pentecostals are Fundamentalists—but not all Fundamentalists are Pentecostals. The reach of Fundamentalism in modern life thus depends on whether one includes Pentecostals. If one does, then Fundamentalism is a vast phenomenon of truly international scope. If the Pentecostals are defined separately, however, Fundamentalism shrinks greatly in both numbers and importance.

The argument for including Pentecostals in the Fundamentalist camp, the similarities just cited, must not blind us to their differences. Perhaps the foremost distinction is their historical backgrounds. This, at least as much as formal theology, differentiates the two traditions.

The Azusa Street Revival

In 1906, an extraordinary religious revival profoundly affected an interracial congregation in California. For several months, as participants recalled, worshippers were swept by an almost irresistible belief that the Holy Spirit had entered into their midst and filled their souls. So striking did this seem that it was compared at once to the original Pentecost, the event shortly after the Resurrection during which the assembled apostles experienced something similar: "And suddenly a sound came from heaven like the rushing of a mighty wind, and it filled all the house where they were sitting.... And they were all filled with the Holy Spirit and began to speak in other tongues" (Acts 2:1–3, RSV). Note here that the Spirit is a physical presence. It is heard ("a sound, etc") and prompts a striking corporeal response ("began to speak in tongues"). The Acts of the Apostles further recounts that Peter at once recalled the Old Testament prophecy that "your sons and daughters shall prophesy," and that the faithful would be shown "wonders in the heaven above and signs on earth below" (Acts 2:17). Spontaneous healings by the apostles immediately followed. What occurred at the Azusa Street Revival, at least for believers, thus evidenced the Spirit's palpable presence: extraordinary corporeal manifestations among the assembled, speaking in tongues, prophesying, and inexplicable healings. And, in fact, the Pentecostal movement, beginning with the Azusa revival, has never strayed far from the opening chapters of the Acts of the Apostles which, indeed, may be taken for its constitution.

Behind this famous revival lay a long tradition in the Anglo-American Protestant community that stressed immediate and transforming access to the Holy Spirit. This was especially true in Methodism. Although Methodism today is a rather staid, "mainline" faith, it was altogether different in the eighteenth and nineteenth centuries. Then, it was a faith of portents, signs, and wonders: of deeply affecting appeals for conversion and overtly emotional worship. Quickly transplanted from its native England to North America during the close of the eighteenth century, it spread throughout the new United States at a remarkable pace. Its popularity was due, in part, to a broad shift away from Calvinist theology within American Protestantism. Americans were increasingly attracted to Arminian faiths; that is, those that held the human will is free to choose salvation and, even more liberating, to work efficiently toward it. Increasingly, Protestants regarded sin as less as an endemic, irremediable condition of the human soul than a moral disease to be expunged through the work of the Holy Spirit in a willing heart. Well before the outbreak of the Civil War, this optimistic theology produced a perfectionist–Holiness strain in American Protestantism—a belief that the whole personality could be turned away from sin and toward godliness.

Recent scholarship suggests that the later Pentecostal movement in America owed much to the perfectionist–Holiness tradition of the mid-nineteenth century. There is, of course, more to it than this. The biblical account of the first Pentecost was, to American Protestants convinced of the sole authority of Scripture, a stirring example that might someday be repeated. Furthermore, the long American tradition of religious revivals both legitimized and prompted a longing for deeply felt spiritual experience. There was, as well, the hope among some American Protestants that they might recover the "primitive Christianity" of the apostolic and immediate subapostolic period, when spontaneous healing and other wonders (again, see Acts of the Apostles) were proclaimed as corporeal evidence that the Holy Spirit was present among believers. Such a "primitive" faith would contrast with the alleged flummery of the Roman Catholic Church or a seminary Protestantism believed overly intellectualized.

The Azusa Street Revival was thus a spark thrown into a powder magazine kept well stocked through more than a century of American religious history. Almost at once, the revival became famous for its manifestations, as was believed, of the Holy Spirit. This early Pentecostalism was all the more remarkable for its inclusiveness, at least in its early stages. Blacks and whites mixed freely and testified to one another, while women were allowed to prophesy and otherwise manifest the presence of the Lord. What began as a remarkable revival in one congregation soon spread to other churches in the Los Angeles area. At the same time, clergy who regarded its adherents as delusional or undignified denounced the new movement and vigorously contested its spread.

Fundamentalism, too, inherited much from the perfectionist–Holiness movement. And, like Pentecostalism, it owed at least as much to the simple, Bible-based faith of Christians as to theologians. In a time of rapid social change, urbanization, and industrialization especially, there was an enthusiastic audience for a theology grounded in the "literal" word of the Bible that, amid the numbing complexities of modern life, stressed personal salvation. However, early twentieth-century Fundamentalism also had an intellectual core and it was centered on premillennial eschatology. That eschatology, in turn, built on Calvinism. The traditional Calvinist emphasis on human moral inability was magnified by eschatology into a general sociology and theory of history that foresaw inevitable moral declension in the affairs of humankind until Christ returns in judgment. Only then will a millennium of true holiness be possible.

Despite real similarities, then, there is thus a meaningful difference between the historic roots of Fundamentalism and Pentecostalism. The first is rooted in Calvinism filtered through eschatology.

361

Acts 2:1–4

1. And when the day of Pentecost was finally come, they were all with one accord in one place.
2. And suddenly there came a sound from heaven as of a rushing mighty wind, and it filled all the house where they were sitting.
3. And there appeared unto them cloven tongues like as of fire, and it sat upon each of them.
4. And they were filled with the Holy Ghost, and began to speak with other tongues, as the Spirit gave them utterance.

Acts 2:17

17. And it shall come to pass in the last days, saith God, I will pour out of my Spirit upon all flesh: and your sons and your daughters shall prophesy, and your young men shall see visions, and your old men shall dream dreams:

Pentecostalism is traceable (at least in part) to the perfectionist–Holiness tradition of the nineteenth century. Not only are these two traditions not compatible, they are diametric opposites. One stressed humanity's indelible sinfulness, while the other taught that individuals could attain to holiness in this life. Little more than half-a-century before the Azusa Street Revival, the besieged Calvinist Protestant community had regarded the Holiness movement as a snare and a delusion.

Fundamentalism and Pentecostalism may be regarded as two massive but separate pillars of American Evangelical Protestantism, over which there is laid a common lintel of biblical inerrancy, hortatory worship, personal rectitude, premillennialism, and social conservatism. Seen from the outside, these components might appear to be a single structure and it is thus understandable that the public regard them as such and dismiss the whole as simply Fundamentalism. Moreover, there is enough shared history and belief to nearly warrant such an approach. In terms of historical tradition, as well as current practice, however, there is significant disparity as well.

The early Pentecostal movement stirred bitter controversy. Some visitors to the Azusa revival departed calling it fanatical or even Satanic. Glossolalia was singled out for particular condemnation. Among those who condemned Pentecostalism were some of the most prominent clergy in the larger Evangelical community. In addition, several churches in the Wesleyan tradition explicitly disassociated themselves from Pentecostalism. The Pentecostals soon fell to quarreling among themselves, an in-

evitable by-product of American religiosity, and splintered into mutually recriminatory factions that argued incessantly over the meaning of such doctrines as "sanctification" and the "second blessing." The interracial nature of early Pentecostalism faded as well and blacks and whites increasingly worshipped apart. However, the exceptional role accorded women in Pentecostalism remained and female preachers were common in twentieth-century Pentecostal congregations.

Despite criticism from without and acrimony within, the nascent Pentecostal churches grew at an astonishing rate throughout the twentieth century. Congregations of like mind inevitably coalesced into new denominations. In a relatively short time, a matter of a few decades, several of these were national in scope and first rivaled and then overtook many mainline denominations in total membership. For example, the Assemblies of God did not exist prior to 1906, but by the closing years of the century it claimed millions of members. Pentecostalism was, throughout the century, unquestionably the fastest growing strain of American Protestantism. Toward the end of the century, its rocketing membership contrasted with the stasis or even decline that affected longer established Protestant churches.

When Pentecostalism attracted the attention of the general public it often involved a bit of sensationalism. During the century just ended, Pentecostalism produced several preachers who became nationally famous, if intensely controversial. The best known of these was probably Aimee Semple McPherson, founder of the International Church of the Foursquare Gospel. She was known throughout America during the interwar years for her theatrical church worship and flamboyant personal life. A charismatic preacher, purported healer, and superb organizer, she was less well known for her consistent charity to those in need, especially during the Great Depression. From time to time, fringe Pentecostal practices such as snake-handling gained predictable press notoriety. Usually, all of this was lumped together in the popular mind as Fundamentalism.

Pentecostalism spread overseas with remarkable success, especially to Latin America, carried by missionaries from the United States. In both Brazil and the Hispanic community, Pentecostals were immensely effective in wooing the religious from their traditional allegiance to Roman Catholicism. The same trend occurred within the Hispanic population of the United States, most particularly among recent immigrants who found the Pentecostal churches welcoming and helpful. By the early twenty-first century, Pentecostalism had clearly emerged as the most vibrant strain within the larger Evangelical community in the United States.

Robert K. Whalen

See also Angelus Temple; Azusa Street Revival; Biblical Inerrancy; Evangelicalism; Perfectionism; Preaching; Premillennialism; Speaking in Tongues

Bibliography

Epstein, Daniel Mark. (1993) *Sister Aimee: The Life of Aimee Semple McPherson*. New York: Harcourt Brace and Co.

Hatch, Nathan O. (1989) *The Democratization of American Christianity*. New Haven, CT: Yale University Press.

Marsden, George M. (1980) *Fundamentalism and American Culture: The Shaping of Twentieth-Century Evangelicalism 1870–1925*. New York: Oxford University Press.

Synan, Vinson. (1997) *The Holiness–Pentecostal Tradition: Charismatic Movements in the Twentieth Century*. Grand Rapids, MI: Wm. B. Eerdmans.

Perfectionism

Perfectionism in Christian theology is the belief that the individual can, through the influence of the Holy Spirit, attain in this lifetime a state of grace in which one is no longer liable to sin. The doctrine has appeared sporadically in Christian history, often to be regarded as unsound or even heretical. The Roman Catholic Church discouraged and even persecuted those who adhered to perfectionism during the Middle Ages, at least insofar as they were seen as part of a larger heretical community. In modern times, perfectionism was widespread throughout the transatlantic Evangelical community of the nineteenth century.

Historians of religion regard perfectionism as a precursor of today's Pentecostal movement—perhaps the fastest growing strain of Christianity. Something similar to perfectionism, however, occurs as well among non-Christian or even totally secular movements, some of which gained notoriety during the last years of the twentieth century. It is, nevertheless, as a Christian belief that perfectionism has most influenced American culture.

The Biblical Concept of Perfection

Perfectionism is often controversial because it seems at odds with traditional Christian anthropology. Judaism, the parent faith of Christianity, while it asserted that man was created in God's image (Genesis 1:26), also stressed the yawning gap it saw between God's holiness and humankind's failings. In the Psalms, Yahweh chides humankind for the belief that its nature is somehow comparable to His holiness: "You thought that I was one like yourself" (Psalms 51:21, RSV). The Old Testament is replete with such warnings.

The early Christian church inherited Judaism's sense of God's transcendent holiness. Jesus did tell His disciples, "You, therefore, must be perfect, as your heavenly Father is perfect" (Matthew 6:48), but such a counsel of perfection—literally—was understood as prophetic exhortation. More typical of early apostolic thought was Paul's lament, "All have sinned and fall short of the glory of God" (Romans 3:23). There are occasional hints in the New Testament that certain early Christian communities engaged in scandalous behavior under the apprehension that grace received through Christ freed them from sin. There is, however, no mistaking the thrust of early Christian anthropology. Humankind has inherited a fallen nature (Original Sin), is at odds with God, and can be redeemed only through the unmerited grace offered by the Atonement.

363

The Church's Interpretation of Perfection

The church fathers expounded on this theme of natural man's fallen nature, none with more influence than St. Augustine (354–430 CE). In his *Confessions*, this towering figure in church history influenced centuries of theology with his assessment of the ineluctable sinfulness of humanity: "For in your sight no man is free from sin, not even a child who has lived one day on earth" (Augustine, *Confessions*, Bk. I, 7, Tr. R. S. Pine-Coffin). Humanity's desperate need for grace has ever since lain near the heart of Christian thought. Paradoxically, however, a small number of Christian thinkers have seized on grace as a means of liberation altogether from sinfulness.

Even in Paul's time there was evidence that a few interpreted God's grace as license to live unbridled lives. Paul was forced to defend himself against the accusation that he urged others to sin, that they might be more fully forgiven and thus God's grace more abound. While the church has consistently portrayed grace received through Jesus Christ as the means for forgiveness of sin, there have been those who interpret it as a means to expunge sin altogether. As a result they hope, and even claim, to lead holy, sinless, lives.

The Cathar heresy of the late Middle Ages was merely one of the more notorious examples of the recurrent belief that grace could not only free an individual from the penalty of sin but move one into a realm of perfect holiness. Those who had attained this holy status were known as *parfaits* and regarded as spiritual masters. A fourteenth-century *parfait* alleged, "We good men can absolve anyone of his sins. Our power of absolution is equal to that of the Apostles Peter and Paul." (Tr. LeRoy Ladurie) Other, furtive, medieval groups, such as the Free Spirit, kept the perfectionist doctrine alive. Of these, Professor Norman Cohn wrote, "The core of the heresy of the Free Spirit lay in the adept's attitude toward himself: he believed that he had attained a perfection so absolute that he was incapable of sin." There were other, similar, creeds, during the Reformation, such as the Ranters of the English Civil War.

Methodism

Historically, perfectionism led a furtive existence in Western life, always in danger from the Catholic Church and its ally, the civil authorities. This fugitive existence ceased after the Reformation when the doctrine was taken up by one of the most prominent religious movements in the history of Christianity—Methodism. This persuasion originated in eighteenth-century England, largely under the leadership of the Wesley brothers, and the *A Plain Account of Christian Perfection As Believed and Taught by the Reverend Mr. John Wesley* stimulated perfectionism. Wesley taught that an individual could receive a "second blessing" (the first being conversion), an infusion of the Holy Spirit that oriented the soul of the recipient away from sin and toward holiness. Humans might still fall short of holiness through errors in judgment or occasional weakening before temptation but, overall, the desire of the soul would now be only for God.

Methodism spread rapidly in North America during the late eighteenth and early nineteenth centuries. It is, in fact, now regarded by some religious scholars to be the decisive vehicle in the transmission of the perfectionist–Holiness movement to the new United States and thus a precursor of today's Pentecostalism. Its steady and spectacular expansion throughout the former colonies was, in part, due to the peculiar religious history of the republic, especially its insatiable appetite for "enthusiasm" in religion

The Great Awakening and the Pentecostal Movement

The American colonies experienced occasional revivals of religion from their earliest settlement, but in the mid-eighteenth century, the Great Awakening, prompted in part by the great Anglican preacher George Whitefield, swept the North American settlements with intense religious fervor. The Great Awakening, however, differed from Wesleyan Methodism in its general adherence to Calvinist doctrine, especially as expounded by the great Massachusett's theologian Jonathan Edwards. But, by stressing the irresistible influence of the Holy Spirit in conversion, thus sanctioning "enthusiasm" in religion, distinct from the rationalism that marked "Old Light" clergy, the Awakening prepared the ground for the intensely emotional revivals of the next century, the wider reception of Wesleyan doctrine, and the rapid spread of perfectionism.

The nineteenth century opened in America with a stunning series of revivals—sometimes styled the Second Great Awakening—which transformed the religious landscape. The best known of these was the

1801 Cane Ridge, Kentucky, revival, labeled "America's Pentecost" by one historian. This intensely emotional style of worship proved highly popular and was, initially, frequently accompanied by extraordinary physical manifestations among worshippers, such as speaking in tongues (glossolalia), the "jerks," and other symptoms regarded as manifestations of the Holy Spirit. Methodism spread like wildfire in this environment and by the Civil War it was America's largest Protestant denomination.

The perceived presence of the Holy Spirit in revivals and the spread of Wesleyan doctrine tended inevitably to popularize perfectionism (also known as the Holiness Movement) in the United States. In Wesleyan terms this meant, once again, a sanctification of the individual will toward holiness, a reorientation of spiritual life wholly toward God, although not an absolute absence of sin. Regardless, Wesley's doctrine of the second blessing spread with Methodism, especially in the emerging urban areas of antebellum America, and was often accompanied by a desire to extend personal holiness to society by reforming vicious personal and social ills, from drunkenness to slavery.

Charles Grandison Finney, a towering figure in nineteenth-century Evangelical life, was perhaps the most influential exponent of perfectionism, which he championed on the revival circuit and then from Oberlin College in Ohio. Phoebe Palmer, a remarkable churchwoman, also propagated the belief. After Appomattox, the reformist impulse of perfectionism was partially transmuted into the Social Gospel in response to the ills attendant on industrialization.

Christian perfectionism was taken up, as well, by small, sectarian movements, some of which scandalized society. Most prominent of these was the Oneida Movement of the latter half of the nineteenth century, led by John Humphery Noyes. A blend of the Holiness Movement and utopian socialism, Noyes's upstate New York settlement enthusiastically practiced free love. The belief that the perfected individual was free from sin (and so could freely indulge one's sexual appetite) was reminiscent of the libertine theologies that accompanied earlier perfectionism movements such as the medieval Cathars.

Neither scandal nor social reforms, however, are what chiefly distinguished the continuation of the perfectionist movement down to our own day. Its chief, and continuing, influence lay in helping to engender the modern Pentecostal movement. By the closing decades of the nineteenth century, as its clergy grew more settled and its worship more sedate, Methodism was increasingly removed from the intensely personal experience of the Holy Spirit that so typified its early decades. Yet, the desire of individuals and congregations, of whatever denomination, for a dramatic outpouring of the Spirit continued unabated, along with the hope that such a visitation might be manifested in personal holiness. In a sense, there was in American religion a considerable fund of spiritual longing on deposit, created over the years by the perfectionist–Holiness tradition, for a direct experience of sanctity and receptiveness to overt manifestations of the Spirit. At the turn of the century, this longing exploded into Pentecostalism—the most rapidly growing religious tradition in the world.

Historians commonly date the modern Pentecostal movement from the 1906 Azusa Street Revival in Los Angeles, California. This date is somewhat arbitrary, as behind it lay a century of the Holiness tradition. Regardless, there was in that year, for those who believed, an outpouring of the Holy Spirit such as had rarely been seen since the days of the Apostles. Perfectionism lived on in Pentecostalism as sanctification, a belief that is spiritual kin to Wesley's second blessing. Although the modern Pentecostal movement is divided on this point, its larger denominations—such as the Church of God in Christ—teach that Christians may hope to be sanctified in such a way that the taint of sin is dampened and the heart prepared for the Holy Spirit. This sanctification is, as was true of earlier Methodist doctrine, in addition to conversion.

Perfectionism is central to modern Fundamentalism to the extent that one regards Pentecostalism as part of a larger Fundamentalist tradition —but this point is debatable. It is likely that most Pentecostals consider themselves Fundamentalists and there is an unmistakable kinship between the two beliefs. Both draw their inspiration from a Bible that is believed to be infallible, revel in exhortatory preaching, and are centered, in part, on millenarian eschatology. In addition, most intellectuals regard Fundamentalism and Pentecostalism as equally alien, as do the so-called mainline Protestant denominations. There are, however, certain differences as well. From at least as early as the 1920s, Fundamentalists have rejected Pentecostal belief in glossolalia and are generally skeptical of miraculous claims involving faith healing. The intense outward manifestations of the Holy Spirit, which Pentecostals believe often attend their worship, are likewise regarded with some suspicion, while certain fringe Pentecostal beliefs—such as serpent-handling—are regarded as little more than lunacy. These objections notwithstanding, it is likely that the public at large conflates the two traditions.

Perfectionism Today

Contemporary perfectionism is not limited to the Pentecostals. It occurs from time to time among the exotic sects that seem to come and go in American religious life. These beliefs occasionally claim a knowledge that enables believers to move beyond the limitations of everyday moral and physical life and ascend to a spiritual realm devoid of sin and error. A notorious recent example was the 1997 mass suicide of the Heaven's Gate faithful. They were convinced that a combination of right belief and suicide would enable them to ascend to "The Level above Human" and dozens were subsequently found dead by their own hands.

There are, as well, other strains of perfectionist thinking in modern religious life. Christian Science insists that study of the teachings of Mrs. Eddy, combined with the resolute casting out of "Error," can free the individual from all manner of moral and physical affliction. In fact, sin itself—so central to historic Christian belief—is seen as one of those "errors" that can be destroyed altogether by the right application of the tenets taught in *Science and Health with Key to the Scriptures*. There are, as well, other perfectionist sects, although most are small and usually short-lived.

Perfectionism continues today, albeit under the rubric of sanctification, as a key component of Pentecostal belief. If, then, one places Pentecostalism within the larger Fundamentalist tradition, it follows that perfectionism is a key component aspect of Fundamentalism as well, both in the United States and worldwide. Since the Pentecostal movement now claims that it holds the allegiance of nearly one-half billion followers, it can be argued that perfectionism, in its latest manifestation, has never been more widely held than at present.

Robert K. Whalen

See also Fall of Humankind; Grace; Great Awakening; Pentecostalism; Sanctification; Sin and Sinners

Bibliography

Cohn, Norman. (1961) *The Pursuit of the Millennium.* New York: Harper Torchbooks.

Klaw, Spencer. (1993) *Without Sin: The Life and Death of the Oneida Community.* New York: Penguin Books.

Ladurie, LeRoy. (1978) *Montaillou: The Promised Land of Error.* New York: George Braziller.

Smith, Timothy L. (1965) *Revivalism and Social Reform.* New York: Harper Torchbooks.

Synan, Vinson. (1997) *The Holiness–Pentecostal Tradition: Charismatic Movements in the Twentieth Century.* Grand Rapids, MI: Wm. B. Eerdmans.

Postmillennialism

Postmillennialism, often called simply millennialism, was a Protestant Christian eschatology that originated during the eighteenth century, flourished during the early nineteenth century, but largely disappeared during its final decades. The millennium, a period of earthly bliss, was extrapolated from the prophecy of Revelation 20:1–3 (RSV) that Satan shall be bound "for a thousand years," and thus "deceive the nations no more." Christ's return in judgment would follow the thousand years and was, thus, *post*millennial.

The Christian Eschatological Tradition

From its earliest days, Christianity cleaved to the doctrine of the Second Advent. Christ will return in glory "to judge the living and the dead" (Apostle's Creed) and wind up history. The Second Advent remained normative belief in nearly all Christian traditions—Catholic, Orthodox, and Protestant—to the present. The doctrine of a millennium enjoys no such historical sanction. Its scriptural basis is limited to the brief and controverted passage in Revelation just mentioned. From the Patristic Period onward, an occasional theologian speculated about a millennium. The Christian church, however, from at least the time of its establishment as an official religion of the Roman Empire, deemphasized eschatology in favor of building Christ's church on earth. Throughout the long medieval era, one or another self-proclaimed prophet announced that the Second Advent was imminent. Occasionally, a millennium was also prophesied. For the most part, however, these episodes centered not on a millennium but Christ's return to doom the world.

There is a corollary between apocalyptic thinking and Christian anthropology in the basic Christian belief that humankind is alienated from God. Humanity cannot hope to ascend, through its sole effort, to the holiness required of it. It follows that human society must always be imperfect, sinful, and, at its best, merely a hedge against the race's worst instincts. Only grace, received through Jesus Christ, can bridges the yawning gap between God and humanity.

The salient thinkers of the Protestant Reformation, John Calvin most especially, stressed anew humanity's innate depravity. Thus it was that, up until the eighteenth century, those (never very numerous) who prophesied a millennium predicted, first, a time of worsening persecution of God's people. Christ's return in judgment would precede the millennium (*pre*millennialism) and the time of bliss would follow for the faithful remnant saved from utter annihilation. More than just eschatology, this apocalyptic scenario is, as well, a philosophy of history. The world is in a state of steady moral decay and history is but the working through of this vast declension.

The European Enlightenment

Although Protestantism might subscribe to such a severe anthropology, European civilization as a whole began to look in other directions. Seventeenth-century Europe was a cockpit for more than just religious conflict. It experienced, as well, the high humanism of the late Renaissance. And, most importantly, it created what we today recognize as the physical sciences. The work of the English mathematician and physicist, Sir Isaac Newton, in particular, was so wide ranging, explanatory, and undergirt with brilliant mathematics that it seemed to de-mystify Creation. New methods of reasoning combined with epochal discoveries in the physical sciences to evoke an almost unprecedented intellectual excitement in the European mind.

These discoveries prompted a reevaluation of history. Since antiquity, Western thought had regarded civilization as in steady decline when compared with the achievements of the classical world. However, by the late Renaissance, and certainly by the seven-teenth century, progress in the arts and sciences called this historiography of social degeneration into question. Europeans began increasingly to believe that the ancients had a lot to learn and that modern civilization had far outstripped them.

This surging European optimism blossomed during the eighteenth-century Enlightenment. The French writer Voltaire exemplified the era, for although he satirized its optimistic pretensions he also popularized Newtonian physics. The great political revolutions that closed that century in Europe and America seemingly announced, despite their bloodshed, limitless possibilities for transforming society. Finally, the nascent Industrial Revolution thrilled observers as it harnessed nature to provide endless power.

Such was the European background from which issued postmillennialism. With the long obeisance to classical thought at an end, undisputed progress in the physical sciences, and political liberation at hand, it was inevitable that some theologians should look anew at sacred history. Was it, as long believed, a tale of sin and degeneracy, leading to the Apocalypse? Enlightenment thinkers such as Turgot and Condorcet articulated theories of linear historical progress and Christian writers soon joined their ranks. It was then but a short step from the revolutionary idea of history as progress to a revised eschatology that incorporated this social optimism.

Among the first to articulate a systematic postmillennialism was Daniel Whitby (b. 1638) whose *Paraphrase and Commentary on the New Testament* (1703) set forth a "new hypothesis" on the millennium. The novelty lay in placing it *before* the Second Advent. At some future, but not too far distant date the world must be Christianized, the Turks and the Pope both overthrown, and the Jews restored to Palestine. But, this would happen in history, not at its end. It was a cheery prospect and, in effect, a sacred counterpart of the still a-borning secular Idea of Progress.

The Apogee of Postmillennialism

Postmillennialism came into its own during the nineteenth century, aided by the gradual abandonment of Calvinist depravity, a burgeoning Methodist movement, and new confidence in the perfectibility of the human soul. On both sides of the Atlantic, Evangelical Christians of the early and mid-Victorian era heralded the imminence of a millennium achieved through history and based largely on technology and political liberation. Christ's return would be merely the crown placed on humanity's brow.

Technology was the key. In 1853, for instance, the *Methodist Quarterly Review* praised the nineteenth century: "It is an age of steam, of electricity, of prodigious movement and significance." The millennium could be expected as early as 1900. That same year, the *Presbyterian Quarterly Review* surveyed the marvels of industrializing America and announced: "We regard the Millennium as a mere extension and perfection of the *present dispensation*." Earlier, another Methodist writer marveled: "Rail-roads are fast girdling the globe. . . . the increase of knowledge is a not insignificant sign of the coming morning."

Political progress, defined largely in terms of the white "race," was as important as technology. In the 1850s, an English author, Hollis Read, proclaimed: " We cannot be mistaken that Anglo-Saxondom is now being used as the right hand of Providence to civilize, enlighten, and Christianize the Pagan World." S. D. Baldwin, author of the 1854 *Armageddon*, pontificated: "The Millennium is a political era of Christian republicanism, confined mainly to the white race."

Postmillennialism prompted a host of social reforms in both England and America. Anti-slavery flourished, since human bondage was incompatible with a millennium. Crusades to reform vicious personal habits burgeoned, since drunkenness, prostitution, Sabbath-breaking, and the like had to perish before the approaching era of blessedness. Today, some of these reforms seem trivial and officious. Others sought—with some success—to meliorate the worst ills of modern life. Anti-slavery benefited especially.

Charles Grandison Finney, the great evangelist, predicted in 1835 that the millennium might come about as early as in three years. Shortly thereafter, he veered toward Methodist perfectionism, the belief that the human soul could be so "sanctified" by the Holy Spirit as to be free from the propensity to sin. There was an obvious affinity between the perfectibility of society and the perfectibility of the individual soul and it is not surprising that the two doctrines were soon intertwined in popular religious opinion.

Millennialism also spilled into nineteenth-century secular life. Robert Owen adopted its language and optimistic anthropology to publicize his utopian scheme to relieve the ills of industrialism. Even Karl Marx, resolutely atheistic, interpreted history as a long march to ever more advanced economic systems, socialism the last and best. Theorists, such as John Humphery Noyes, set up utopian communities, which combined millennialism with scandalous sexual mores. During the High Victorian era, from 1840 to 1870, a belief in progress seemed almost universal. No longer must humanity suffer in dread of a last judgment; knowledge, democracy, and goodwill would achieve the millennium peacefully. And soon, at that.

Postmillennialism was popular but paid the price. Cheerleading for Western civilization was no theology. No religious thinker arose, on a par with Calvin or Luther, to integrate traditional Christian doctrine into the new eschatology. No one, for instance, explained how the ancient belief in Original Sin was reconcilable with human perfectibility. There was optimism in plenty: serious intellectual labor was absent. Postmillennialism was like a vase of cut flowers: lovely to behold but not rooted in soil that could sustain it over time.

The weakened Calvinists, who did possess a rigorous intellectual heritage, struck a cautionary note. This was especially true among premillennial Christians, a loosely associated group that, in many ways, formed the nucleus of modern Fundamentalism. It was they, as much as anyone, who dissented from the broad optimism of the mid-nineteenth century. Reformed doctrine stressed human sinfulness and alienation from God. It was impossible, they insisted, to maintain simultaneously that humankind was innately depraved and yet could somehow create a paradise on earth. These proto-Fundamentalists, if we may call them such, warned that postmillennial optimism discounted, or ignored altogether, the abiding presence of evil in human life.

The proto-Fundamentalists warned, especially, against science and technology. Historians have long noted that certain nineteenth-century thinkers, Thoreau for instance, were wary of industrial life. This, however, was largely a matter of agrarian nostalgia. However, Calvinist critics of postmillennialism went beyond nostalgia to warn that evil, as one of them put it in 1859, "derives as powerful aid for the spread and propagation of its empire, as pure Christianity does, from the improvements of the age." Yet another had warned in 1846 that "Steam Ships & Rail Roads" were "precipitating the stew of human wickedness, whose end is death." Derided or ignored in their time, these warnings gained a certain resonance in the century to follow.

Revelation 20:1–3

1. **And I saw an angel come down from heaven, having the key of the bottomless pit and a great chain in his hand.**
2. **And he laid hold upon the dragon, that old serpent, which is the Devil, and Satan, and bound him a thousand years,**
3. **And cast him into the bottomless pit, and shut him up, and set a seal upon him, that he should deceive the nations no more, till the thousand years should be fulfilled: and after that he must be loosed a little season.**

This same Calvinistic bent caused a few to dissent, as well, from the reflexive nationalism of postmillennialists who anointed the United States as a millennial nation. Entirely typical of this postmillennial gush was S. D. Baldwin who, in 1854, smugly assured readers: "It will be a democracy or it will be no millennium; and the United States is likely to be that incipient democracy." But, a few years later, a leading premillennalist scorned such talk: "The American Republic is no more set up by the God of heaven ... than the English provinces of Canada and Nova Scotia, England itself, Prussia, the Sandwich Islands, or New Zealand. It is a work of man, as absolutely as they are." In 1873, the *Prophetic Times*, already an exponent of such Fundamentalist themes as an inerrant Bible, warned against spread-eagle patriotism as so much "idolatry."

Decline and Irrelevance

The apogee of postmillennialism in American Protestantism was reached during the two or three decades just prior to the Civil War. The expansion of American power over the North American continent, the nation's phenomenal economic growth, and its marvelous facility with technology seemed harbingers of the millennium. This euphoria did not survive the massive bloodletting of 1861 to 1865. Its cheery optimism was replaced by, for instance, the apocalyptic rhetoric of Julia Ward Howe's *Battle Hymn of the Republic*, which featured no millennium in three years but, rather, the "terrible, swift sword." Postmillennial optimism was not lost altogether. America remained an optimistic place. Once civil conflict was over, however, the nation confronted the cold realities of a ruthless age of industrialization. The postmillennialism of an earlier generation seemed hopelessly naive and a younger generation was content to mitigate the evils of the new urban society, a realizable goal, than labor for an age of perfect bliss. In time, this more modest effort was labeled the "Social Gospel" and did much to awaken American conscience and meliorate social ills. It sometimes used millennial language to exhort reform, but it was far distant from the flamboyant optimism that marked so much Evangelical thought during the antebellum period.

Postmillennialism, had it survived the nineteenth century, would have seemed especially ridiculous throughout the bloody catastrophes of 1914 to 1945. Protestant thought, in fact, moved in the other direction during that period and rediscovered sin. Neo-orthodox theologians such as Paul Tillich, Rudolph Bultmann and, especially, Karl Barth, stressed anew humanity's propensity to create, not a millennium, but a hell on earth. The controversial Fundamentalist movement, which gained notoriety in the 1920s, was devoid of such intellectual giants; however, its anthropology and sociology proved more in consonance with what the world experienced under the Third Reich and the Soviet leader Joseph Stalin than did the easy optimism of nineteenth-century postmillennialists.

The carnage of twentieth-century warfare and the looming threat of thermonuclear annihilation, combined with neo-orthodox theology, would seem to relegate postmillennialism to oblivion. And, indeed, as a serious Christian eschatology, it utterly ceased to exist quite early in the century. Its purely secular twin, Marxist utopianism, followed it to the grave at century's end. Yet, the dramatic lessening of international tension, the communications explosion (for example, the Internet), and the rise of a truly global economy have prompted visions of a peaceful, prosperous world which, though devoid of theism, are redolent of earlier postmillennialism. Whether this new optimism fares any better than its nineteenth-century predecessor is yet to be seen.

Robert K. Whalen

See also Premillennialism

Bibliography

Baumer, Franklin L. (1977) *Modern European Thought.* New York: Macmillan Publishing Co.

Block, Ruth. (1985) *Visionary Republic: Millennial Themes in American Thought, 1756–1800.* New York: Cambridge University Press.

Harrison, J. F. C. (1969) *Quest for the New Moral World.* New York: Charles Scribner's Sons.

Tuveson, Ernest L. (1964) *Millennium and Utopia.* New York: Harper Torchbooks.

———. (1968) *Redeemer Nation.* Chicago: University of Chicago Press.

Whalen, Robert K. (1992) "Calvinism and Chiliasm: The Sociology of Nineteenth Century American Millennarianism." *American Presbyterians* 70 (Fall): 163–172.

Post-Tribulationism

Post-Tribulational premillennialists maintain that the Rapture of the church will occur *after* the Great Tribulation. All premillennialists look forward to the Rapture or "catching away"of the church (1 Thessalonians 4:15–17), but they debate when it will occur in relation to the seven years of Tribulation in the Last Days and the Second Coming of Christ.

Post-Tribulationists claim the oldest perspective among premillennialists in the history of Christianity. They believe that the Rapture and the Second Coming will occur at the same time—*after* the Tribulation. Contrary to dispensational premillennialists, post-Tribulationists, who like to call their perspective "historic premillennialism," find no biblical warrant for dividing the Rapture and Second Coming into two phases: Christ's coming *for* His saints before the Tribulation and *with* His saints at the end of the Tribulation. They point out that in his most explicit passage on the Rapture, the apostle Paul does not mention any chronological relationship between the Rapture and the Tribulation (1 Thessalonians 4). However, many of the phenomena of the Rapture that

Paul does mention (e.g., loud command, the trumpet of God, the sending of angels to gather the saints, and Christ's coming on the clouds) are found in other passages that clearly place them *after* the Tribulation (Matthew 24; Mark 13; Luke 21). Because this view places the Rapture at the end of the Tribulation, post-Tribulationists hold that believers will not escape its horrors. Christians will have to steel themselves for the rise of the Antichrist and the False Prophet, the systematic persecution of those who refuse to accept the "mark of the Beast"—which is required for buying or selling in a world controlled by the Antichrist—and the Battle of Armageddon. Unlike dispensationalists who promise "escape" from such horrors in the pre-Tribulational Rapture, post-Tribulationists foresee inevitable suffering, persecution, and even death. Despite such difficulties, during the Tribulation believers will not suffer the wrath of God, which is reserved for those who swear loyalty to the Antichrist and receive his mark on their foreheads (Revelation 7). Thus, "this calls for patient endurance on the part of the saints who obey God's commandments and remain faithful to Jesus" (Revelation 14:12).

During the revival of premillennialism after the Civil War, post-Tribulationists like Nathaniel West, John T. Duffield, and A. J. Gordon were among the leaders of the Niagara Bible Conference and the various prophetic conferences in the 1880s and 1890s. However, their numbers were soon eclipsed by those of the dispensationalists, whose more salutary pre-Tribulational Rapture doctrine attracted the majority of Fundamentalists by World War I. After World War II, the post-Tribulational Rapture doctrine experienced a revival through the exegetical studies of George Ladd, Robert Gundry, and Robert Mounce. Such reconnections to older premillennial views proved to be most popular among American Evangelicals, who desired to abandon dispensationalism without giving up premillennialism altogether.

On the popular level, the post-Tribulational Rapture doctrine remained less insignificant than its pre-Tribulational rival, but it did produce some interesting connections with advocates of survivalism. During the 1970s and 1980s, people like Jim McKeever and evangelist Pat Robertson used post-Tribulationism to promote serious preparation for the tough times ahead. They preached self-sufficiency, such as stockpiling food, developing alternate sources for energy and water, and even becoming armed to the teeth to protect one's supplies from marauding neighbors. Christians may not be able to avoid suffering and persecution in the Great Tribulation, but those believers who take precautions will increase their chances of survival until Jesus arrives to rescue them from the Antichrist. Likewise, other post-Tribulational survivalists counseled people to get out of debt, pay off their mortgages, convert their financial resources to gold or silver, and move to the country where they could live off the land and be independent of city services during the Antichrist's reign of terror. Despite such fervency, post-Tribulationists have not succeeded in creating a large popular movement within American religious life.

Timothy P. Weber

See also Mid-Tribulationism; Premillennialism; Pre-Tribulationism; Rapture; Tribulation

Bibliography

Archer, Gleason L., et. al. (1984) *The Rapture: Pre-, Mid-, or Post-tribulational?* Grand Rapids, MI: Zondervan Publishing.

Gundry, Robert. (1973) *The Church and the Tribulation.* Grand Rapids, MI: Zondervan Publishing.

Ladd, George. (1956) *The Blessed Hope.* Grand Rapids, MI: Wm. B. Eerdmans.

McKeever, Jim. (1978) *Christians Will Go Through the Tribulation.* N.p.: Omega.

Mounce, Robert. (1977) *The Book of Revelation.* Grand Rapids, MI: Wm. B. Eerdmans.

Weber, Timothy P. (1987) *Living in the Shadow of the Second Coming: American Premillennialism, 1875–1982.* Chicago: University of Chicago Press.

Prayer

Prayer is the vehicle for individual and communal communication between God and God's people that affects both personal and institutional spheres. For Protestant Fundamentalists in the United States, prayer has been and continues to be a central practice with impact in virtually every area of life and thought. Prayer is often described in terms of (1) supplication: prayer which asks for the fulfillment of needs; (2) intercession: prayer on behalf of a person or cause; (3) thanksgiving: prayer which responds in gratitude for God's benevolence; (4) adoration: prayer which highlights the attributes of God; and (5) confession: prayer that admits the believer's sinfulness and seeks forgiveness.

Although Fundamentalists draw most of their justification for and information about prayer from the Bible, they also recognize that prayer has been a prominent part of Christian tradition and history. Therefore, retention of this practice and its continuing centrality in Fundamentalist thought rests on arguments of both a biblical and a traditional nature. Fundamentalists perceive themselves as those Christians who preserve the original Christian faith in its purity against the modernizing and secularizing tendencies of the broader culture. The persistence of prayer as a central religious practice modeled on biblical examples reflects their attempt to sustain the true Christian faith. Fundamentalists have consistently maintained, in the face of growing theological and scientific criticism of their positions, that the biblical God is a God who wants His people to pray, who hears their prayers, and who answers those prayers for benevolent and disciplinary reasons.

Fundamentalists did not disappear in the early twentieth century after their defeats in the ecclesiastical arenas. They reorganized and restructured their ministries and their intellectual life in the 1930s and 1940s to create a unique and vibrant subculture throughout the middle decades of the twentieth century. This subculture remains a thriving strand in the religious landscape of the United States. Yet, the long presence and persistence of prayer as a force in Fundamentalist life and thought indicates that Fundamentalism is not merely a phenomenon centered on institutional organization and social and political activity. Instead, it has a strong devotional or pietistic element at its root. Fundamentalism is as much about personal faith and devotion as anything else. Thus, prayer as a theological doctrine and practice provides a window into the Protestant Fundamentalist world. To better understand that world, it is first essential to discern (1) how the Fundamentalist doctrine of prayer motivates other aspects of Fundamentalist practice and (2) what theological elements comprise the doctrine and its practice.

Theological Elements of the Fundamentalist Doctrine of Prayer

For Fundamentalists, the manner in which a Christian prays and the standards that must be met to pray effectively (i.e., the "right" way and to the desired ends) are extremely important. The extensive requirements, methods, and theological beliefs that the Christian Fundamentalist follows in order to practice the act of prayer for benefit and efficacy include positions about God, the Bible, the Holy Spirit, and Jesus Christ.

The Hearing God

At its most basic level, the Fundamentalist doctrine of prayer rests on the belief in the Hearing God. Fundamentalists maintained throughout the twentieth century a belief in a transcendent God. This preservation of a more traditional doctrine of God carried with it the belief that God wanted His people to pray to Him and consequently, He answered their prayers. These answers, furthermore, were not merely masks for naturalistic phenomena. Instead, the biblical God would intervene personally, corporately, and naturalistically into the affairs of the world on behalf of His followers. All that the true believer needed to do was live a faithful, Spirit-filled life and pray correctly in order to benefit from the practice of prayer.

The Bible

Coupled with this belief in the Hearing God is the prominent place of the Bible in the practice of prayer. Bible reading and study often accompany other suggestions for effective prayer. The Fundamentalist must daily and earnestly study the Bible to understand and discover the will of God for his or her life as well as to find biblical examples of effective prayer to model. Biblical study also increases the believer's level of obedience to God's moral and religious instruction that in turn aids the practice of prayer.

The Holy Spirit

The presence and function of the Holy Spirit in the practice of prayer is a primary element for the Christian Fundamentalist. Not only do Fundamentalist interpreters see the integral nature for prayer of the Spirit of God portrayed in the Old and New Testaments, but the Holy Spirit itself functions as a channel through which the individual Christian may address God in the present. The central concern surrounding the role of the Holy Spirit in the Fundamentalist doctrine of prayer, however, is the inadequacy of the believer's self-sufficiency in this devotional practice. The believer is inadequately prepared to participate in this devotional act without the work of God's Spirit in his or her life and on his or her behalf.

In fact, the Holy Spirit actively gives light and guidance to the act of prayer itself by interceding to correct this deficiency. Thus, the individual may be too spiritually weak or immature to pray correctly or effectively to God, so the Holy Spirit makes the prayer on his or her behalf. Yet, some Fundamentalist theologians also understand the function of the Holy Spirit in prayer extending to the advanced Christian who has entered a realm of spiritual maturity with such depth that the Spirit of God is needed to aid the believer in reaching even higher levels of faithfulness and devotion.

There are other influences of the Holy Spirit in the Fundamentalist practice of prayer. Fundamentalists throughout the twentieth century have viewed themselves as revivalists of a stale Christianity. Therefore, the presence of the Holy Spirit encourages earnestness in praying in order to remove the arid formality that often accompanies prayer. The Holy Spirit also disciplines the individual to surrender his or her will to the will of God, thereby spurring the believer to pray according to the divine will and not out of selfish motives. Determination and persistence mark the faithful prayer of a believer who is guided by the Holy Spirit. This indicates a willingness to pray even when results of prayer are not readily forthcoming. These influences and characteristics of the role of the Holy Spirit in the doctrine of prayer point to the theocentric concern of the Fundamentalist. The value of prayer influenced by the Holy Spirit is its ability to turn the believer away from selfish concerns and toward the concerns of God.

In the Name of Christ

A final element for effective prayer in the Fundamentalist doctrine involves the person of Jesus Christ, and particularly the efficacy of praying "in the name of Christ." For Fundamentalists, the name of Christ contributes power and authority to prayers. By praying to God through Christ, the believer can approach God and make requests. The foundation for this is the Fundamentalist belief in the atoning death of Jesus Christ, in which Jesus took upon Himself the sins of humanity to bridge the gap between humanity and God. Fundamentalists affirm that using the name of Christ for more efficacious and powerful prayer is not some magic formula nor is it merely the attachment of a rotely used phrase to a prayer. When invoking the name of Christ, the inadequacy of the believer in prayer is once again assumed. Fundamentalists argue that the believer has no claim on God, so God is not required to answer any prayer offered. Instead, the believer is only able to pray effectively to God because of Christ's intercession on his or her behalf. Christ, in a sense, places the believer in His place before God on the merits of His atoning work. Yet, not every believer has access to this kind of power and authority in the practice of prayer. Prayer is only effective when Christ's name is evoked out of an intimate relationship with Him. The use of the name implies a closeness that must be undergirded by a particular character and by specific acts. For example, Fundamentalists reserve the right to pray "in the name of Christ" for those who believe in Jesus, love Him, and keep His commandments. Believing in Jesus makes the individual worthy to use His name in prayer because it reflects a living or vital faith in Jesus as Savior and Lord. Love of Christ and obedience to His commandments reflect the faithfulness of the believer. If prayer is to be effective in the name of Christ, then love of Christ must be demonstrated by following His teachings. These stipulations ensure that an individual's prayers are consistent with the will of God. With these stipulations in place, it is assumed that individual prayer will not reflect inappropriate requests or demands from God. Without these stipulations, there is no guarantee that there will be a return from God.

Impact and Use of Prayer for the Fundamentalist

Fundamentalists consistently use prayer for an ever-widening sphere of influence beginning with the individual's personal needs, moving on to the needs of the church, and finally working in the wider culture or society.

Prayer for Personal Need

Throughout the twentieth century the personal needs of Fundamentalists most readily addressed by prayer have focused on the spiritual advancement of the individual. Although material needs have not been neglected in the Fundamentalist doctrine of prayer, their fulfillment has been at least dependent on the spiritual status of the individual in relation to God. Prayer is a way to increase spiritual power,

faithfulness, and perseverance in the face of difficulty. Fundamentalists wish to increase and preserve spiritual power in their personal lives. This power comes from God. The search for spiritual power does not come from other sources, but only from a relationship with God. This power is the sustenance that the Fundamentalist needs to live the holy and truly Christian life and to work in the service of God and the church effectively and faithfully. One early analogy used in Fundamentalism to express this connection of the individual believer to the power of God was the image of the battery. This image illustrates the charging energy of God filling the believer with power in order to live with victory over weakness, anxiety, or worry. As the believer's power drains out, God reenergizes him or her through the avenue of prayer.

The power received from God through prayer serves in the struggle to remain faithful to God's will and to the truths of the gospel. Prayer, coupled with Scripture, functions as God's avenue of revelation to the individual. For many Fundamentalists, the greatest need for an individual, or humanity in general, is the presence of a higher standard of faithfulness. Prayers, either as supplication or intercession, provide the constant contact needed for spiritual growth. Christian characteristics like patience, obedience, love for enemies, and personal holiness all derive from the persistent practice of prayer. Prayer enables the believer to see the ways of God more clearly and to better obey the laws of God.

Fundamentalists were constantly aware of the potential for failure, on both the personal and corporate level. Yet, their doctrine of prayer has sustained a sense of perseverance. In fact, they often saw the full efficacy of prayer emerge with complete failure and defeat. Negative experiences, it was believed, produced a defense against hypocrisy, and answered prayer provided the evidence needed to support the truth of Fundamentalist belief and practice.

Prayer As a Vocational Aid

Fundamentalists readily use the practice of prayer for their work in mission and evangelization, both foreign and domestic. Prayer encourages the giving of monetary and physical support for the evangelistic work of the church and individuals. Fundamentalists often recount great acts of prayer from both the Bible and history to demonstrate the necessity of this doctrine and the importance of its earnest practice for contemporary believers. Examples of answered prayer serve as a witness to the efficacy of true prayer. Here, the fulfillment of material needs for the service of God's work, often against overwhelming odds, is an encouragement for further prayer and for material contribution to the work of mission or evangelization.

Prayer for the Wider Culture and Society

Ever-present among Fundamentalists is the sense of apostasy, or the decline in faithfulness to the truths of the Christian faith and the dilution of the remaining truths due to modernistic developments, in the wider church and society. Protestant Fundamentalists speak of revival in church and culture as a way to stem the tide of apostasy, and the key to revival is prayer. Without the church engaging in true prayer, that is, Spirit-filled prayer in the name of Christ practiced by faithful students of the Bible, Fundamentalists see little reason for optimism through revival.

William Carter Booker

See also Bible; Biblical Inerrancy; Holy Spirit; Jesus; Preaching

Bibliography

Biblical Prayers: Messages on Prayer from the World Congress of Fundamentalists. (1976) Greeneville, SC: Bob Jones University Press.

Biederwolf, William Edward. (1910) *How Can God Answer Prayer?* New York: Fleming H. Revell.

Bounds, Edward M. (1912) *Power through Prayer.* Grand Rapids, MI: Zondervan Publishing.

Carpenter, Joel A. (1997) *Revive Us Again: The Reawakening of American Fundamentalism.* New York: Oxford University Press.

Falwell, Jerry, ed. (1981) *The Fundamentalist Phenomenon.* Garden City, NY: Doubleday.

The Fundamentals: A Testimony to the Truth. (1910–1915) Chicago: Testimony Publishing Company, IX: 66–83; XII: 97–107.

God Hath Spoken. (1919) Philadelphia: Bible Conference Committee.

Marsden, George M. (1980) *Fundamentalism and American Culture: The Shaping of Twentieth-Century Evangelicalism, 1870–1925.* New York: Oxford University Press.

Needham, George C. (1886) *Prophetic Studies of the International Prophetic Conference.* Chicago: Fleming H. Revell.

Ostrander, Rick. (2000) *The Life of Prayer in a World of Science.* New York: Oxford University Press.

Rice, John R. (1945) *Prayer.* Wheaton, IL: Sword of the Lord.

Simpson, Albert B. (1925) *The Life of Prayer.* Harrisburg, PA: Christian Publications, Inc.

Torrey, Reuben A. (1924) *The Power of Prayer.* New York: Fleming H. Revell.

Preaching

Preaching based on the scriptural text is at the heart of Fundamentalism. While some stand in the temple–priest–sacrifice worship tradition in which liturgy and ritual dominate, Fundamentalists stand self-consciously in the synagogue–prophet–preaching tradition in which the proclamation of the Word of God dominates. Taking the synagogue as their model, they emphasize Jesus in the synagogue in Nazareth reading the biblical text and then explaining and applying that text (Luke 4:16–22).

The impassioned prophets of the Old Testament in all of their diversity of theme and emphasis are seen as the forebearers of Fundamentalists in delivering the "Thus saith the Lord" to their generation. The fidelity of Jesus to the Old Testament documents and His insistence that "it shall be fulfilled which was spoken" has supplied the pattern for Fundamentalist preaching. The apostolic preaching with its heralding of the death, Resurrection, and Second Coming of Jesus Christ presents the critical paradigm for pulpit proclamation.

Since what we believe about the Bible shapes in large part our view and value of preaching, we can readily see that Fundamentalism's insistence on the total reliability and trustworthiness of Scripture necessarily translates into a high view of preaching. While variously termed "verbal inspiration" or "inerrancy," the bottom line for the Fundamentalist is the axiom that the Bible can always be trusted. The overall rejection of evolutionary higher criticism does not mean that Fundamentalists lack interest in lower or textual criticism in terms of which we virtually possess the original autographs, given the abundance of ancient manuscripts. While a few have preference for the *textus receptus* (the basis of the King James Version), most have used Westcott and Hort's general theory about manuscript families. (The Anglicans, Bishop B. F. Westcott and professor F. J. A.

Hort used what they felt were earlier and more recently discovered manuscripts as the basis for translating the Bible.)

Concern for the text in preaching has tended to involve an emphasis on historical/grammatical exegesis or seeking the original author's intent in the text. Ordinarily this has meant seeking the plain, natural, simple meaning of the text, literal wherever possible. Some Fundamentalists have yielded to extensive allegorization and spiritualization of the text beyond anything Scripture itself would authorize. Explicit types (such as Christ the rock in the wilderness) or implicit types (such as the Cities of Refuge) are one thing, but making the gates of Jerusalem (Nehemiah 2) into the steps to salvation is quite another. Some Fundamentalists have not seen that the case for the absolute reliability of everything the Scripture addresses can be severely undercut by a wrong hermeneutic. The key is seen to be the Apostle Paul's exhortation to Timothy: "Preach the Word" (2 Timothy 4:2). Here is the authorization for the centrality and importance of preaching in worship and the life of the Christian community (note also 2 Timothy 3:15–17).

The Roots and Sources of Preaching in Fundamentalism

A primary influence on Fundamentalist preaching has been the Protestant Reformation, chiefly the return to the centrality and priority of preaching as seen in Martin Luther (1483–1546), John Calvin (1509–1546), Huldrych Zwingli (1484–1531), and Menno Simons (1496–1561). The English Reformers were also strong in their emphasis on preaching as were their immediate predecessors like John Wycliffe (1325–1384) and John Hus of Prague (1369–1415), both of whom were martyred for their ministry. Hus had a strong preaching ministry in the famous Bethlehem Chapel in Prague. He steeped himself in Scripture and drew huge crowds who came to hear the Word of God. The Reformers gave wide berth to the complicated medieval university sermon and doggedly used the ancient homily, a loosely structured exposition of a scriptural text employed by both St. Chrysostom and St. Augustine as well as many others in the early church.

Direct heirs of the Reformers were the Puritans in England and North America and the Continental Pietists, both of whom reveled in the opening of the Bible to eager congregations. While the Pietists in Germany, such as Philipp Spener (1605–1705) and August Franke (1663–1727), tended to retain the homily, the Puritans developed their own sermonic form; that is, a small piece of text is exposed, as when Thomas Shepard, first president of Harvard University, preached for four years in a Sunday morning series on the parable of the ten virgins in Matthew 25:1–13. The average Puritan preacher preached 7,000 sermons in his lifetime, utilizing more than 15,000 hours to do so. The Puritans were strong in their application of the interpreted text (what they called "uses"). Richard Baxter (1615–1691) of Kidderminster in England identified sixty-six uses in one of his sermons and recapitulated all of these "uses" at the conclusion of the sermon. Although the Puritan sermon fell out of favor, Charles Haddon Spurgeon, the great London preacher (1834–1892), effectively used the Puritan sermon form in his long and powerful ministry at the Metropolitan Tabernacle, as did Dr.

Evangelical preacher at Speaker's Corner, Hyde Park, London, January 1999. PHOTO COURTESY OF KAREN CHRISTENSEN.

375

2 Timothy 4:1–5

1. I charge thee therefore before God, and the Lord Jesus Christ, who shall judge the quick and the dead at his appearing and his kingdom;
2. Preach the word; be instant in season, out of season; reprove, rebuke, exhort with all longsuffering and doctrine.
3. For the time will come when they will not endure sound doctrine; but after their own lusts shall they heap to themselves teachers, having itching ears.
4. And they shall turn away their ears from the truth, and shall be turned unto fables.
5. But watch thou in all things, endure afflictions, do the work of an evangelist, make full proof of thy ministry.

2 Timothy 3:15–17

15. And that from a child thou hast known the holy scriptures, which are able to make thee wise unto salvation through faith which is in Christ Jesus.
16. All scripture is given by inspiration of God, and is profitable for doctrine, for reproof, for correction, for instruction in righteousness:
17. That the man of God may be perfect, throughly furnished unto all good works.

David Martyn Lloyd-Jones in the next century at Westminster Chapel. Both of these preachers exerted tremendous influence on Fundamentalist preaching in North America and around the world.

Still a third root for Fundamentalist preaching and as strong if not stronger than either of the aforementioned, was the Great Awakening of the eighteenth century, which deeply stirred the British Isles and North America. The revivalist flavor of so much Fundamentalist preaching traces its origin to the gospel preaching of George Whitefield (1714–1770) and John Wesley (1703–1791). Both were members of the Holy Club at Oxford University, England, and experienced a transforming personal conversion. Although Whitefield was more Reformed (stressing the decrees of God) and Wesley more Arminian (stressing free moral choice), they were colleagues and collaborators in preaching the death and Resurrection of Jesus Christ as the basis for the transforming experience of the New Birth through the power of divine grace. The preaching of Whitefield in New England greatly influenced Jonathan Edwards (1703–1758), whose ministry at Northampton, Massachusetts, shook a continent for God. The Second Evangelical Awakening (1776–1810) featured Edwards' grandson, Timothy Dwight (1752–1817), president of Yale University, Connecticut, and was characterized by repeated outpourings of the Holy Spirit on the student body and faculty at Yale. In this uprush, Francis Asbury (1745–1816), a Methodist bishop and circuit-rider, brought the gospel message 16,500 times, discarding Wesley's liturgical and sacramental style and clerical dress. This was the era of the Cane Ridge Camp Meeting and so many others like it when thousands came forward in profound repentance for sin and prayed to receive Jesus Christ as their own personal Savior. Among Baptists, Methodists, Disciples of Christ (the Campbellite connection), and others there was an amazing networking that surmounted the distinctions peculiar to each and favored a common allegiance to the supernatural gospel of the New Testament. Then followed the Presbyterian-Congregationalist Charles G. Finney (1792–1875), who saw more than 500,000 profess conversion in his meetings, and the eccentric frontier preacher, Peter Cartwright (1785–1872) as well as a host of others in the United States and Britain. Thus, revivalism was the matrix for the rise of Fundamentalism and its preaching of the new life in Christ and biblical holiness to encompass the whole of human life (Hatch, 3ff).

We can attribute the new shape of the sermon in this time frame to the French Protestant pastor, Jean Claude (1619–1687), and his extensive piece entitled

Essay on the Composition of the Sermon. This seminal analysis was translated by the Cambridge preacher, Robert Robinson and it molded the preaching of Charles Simeon (1789–1836), who for fifty-four years was the highly influential rector of Holy Trinity Church in Cambridge, England, and founder of the Evangelical wing of the Church of England. Claude, departing from the rather rambling form of the historic homily, urged the division of the text with corresponding divisions in the sermon, thus making the sermon say what the text says. This was the birth of the modern textual and expository sermon, the favorites of Fundamentalist preachers (Larsen 1998: 208ff, 402ff). John Broadus of the Southern Baptist Seminary and his northern counterpart, Austin Phelps of Andover, were the modern fathers of expository preaching. This sermonic form recommends the use of a natural thought unit of Scripture and letting its progression shape the sermon. Haddon Robinson, Lloyd Perry, and Bryan Chapell are some of the more recent advocates of the teaching sermon.

The expository sermon is a rhetorically influenced revision of the historic homily and not all Fundamentalists have gone with it. H. A. Ironside (1876–1951), who served historic Moody Church in Chicago from 1930 to 1948, used the Plymouth Brethren Bible reading style, which is really a verse-by-verse running commentary on the Scripture. His content was solid as he interpreted and effectively illustrated verse by verse, but an embracing unity in the sermon was often to prove elusive. The notion that one thereby escapes rhetorical influence is dubious since rhetoric is "how" we say it and the Bible reading is another rhetorical method.

Representatives and Examples of Preaching in Fundamentalism

Fundamentalism is an aggressive orthodoxy. As Enlightenment rationalism and evolutionary naturalism began to influence the church in the eighteenth century, there were those who were willing to make substantial accommodations in biblical and theological areas and this altered their preaching. Walter Rauschenbusch (1861–1918), Washington Gladden (1836–1918), and later, Harry Emerson Fosdick (1878–1969) are just some examples in the United States. Fosdick's famous sermon in 1922 at the First Presbyterian Church in New York City entitled "Shall the Fundamentalists Win?" led to his resignation.

Many champions of what the Apostle Paul called "sound doctrine" rose up to defend and expound "the faith that was once for all entrusted to the saints" (Jude 3, NIV).

Evangelists like Dwight Lyman Moody (1837–1899) carried the simple gospel message to the masses on both sides of the Atlantic. Inclined more to the Plymouth Brethren model of preaching, Moody sprinkled his sermons with anecdotes. Billy Sunday (1862–1935), a former baseball player and a Presbyterian, used a somewhat similar rough-and-tumble style. More than 100,000,000 heard his colorful sermons in which he inveighed against evolution and liquor and presented Jesus Christ as the only Savior. Even great universities opened to his ministry. Following in this succession were such flaming preachers as Sam Jones, the southern Methodist, R. A. Torrey, J. Wilbur Chapman, and William E. Biederwolf. The remarkable worldwide ministry of Billy Graham (1918–) must be seen as part of the resistance to the advancing tide of scepticism and unbelief. His simple method of delivery based on his deep and unwavering confidence in the Bible and his dedication to the efficacy of the Cross of Christ for humanity's salvation have led untold thousands to make their commitment to Christ. The ripple effect of his mammoth crusades can be seen in *Christianity Today* and *Decision* magazines, radio, television, films, and worldwide conferences on evangelism.

The preaching of these evangelists indicates that Fundamentalism may be countercultural but not culturally isolated. Billy Graham, like his predecessors, has interacted with the critical issues of the day, such as racism. The influence of revivalism on the slavery issue (as in England where the Evangelical William Wilberforce led the charge) and in the United States (with Lyman Beecher and many others at the forefront) is typical. General William Booth, who with his wife Catherine founded the Salvation Army, are cases in point.

Strong advocates of the fundamentals of the faith—Theodore Cuyler (1822–1909) and T. Dewitt Talmage (1832–1902) in Brooklyn and A. J. Gordon (1836–1895) in Boston—were heard throughout the land, and Bishop Matthew Simpson (1811–1884), a staunch conservative in the Methodist Church preached the funeral sermon for President Abraham Lincoln in Springfield, Illinois. The Civil War had a harmful effect on the churches, although powerful revivals did sweep through both the Union and Confederate armies.

377

Historically, the Southern Baptist Convention has been a bastion of the faith. Leading it early on in this direction was B. H. Carroll (1843–1914), who was converted in a Methodist camp meeting and founder of the Southwestern Baptist Seminary. His masterful *Interpretation of the English Bible* in thirteen volumes underscores the great biblicality of his preaching. Such pulpit giants as George W. Truett of Dallas (1867–1944), Robert G. Lee of Memphis (1886–1978), and W. A. Criswell (1909–) of the First Baptist Church, Dallas, whose volume *Why I Believe That the Bible is Literally True* became a Fundamentalist landmark, preached fearlessly. Criswell's strong preaching through the Bible (*lectio continua*) has made him one of the great expository preachers of modern times.

John Roach Straton of New York City (1875–1929) was one of the Baptists in the north who were particularly articulate during the Fundamentalist–modernist struggle of the 1920s and 1930s over denominational institutions and agencies. He led the Calvary Baptist Church to a great outreach. William Bell Riley (1861–1947), forty-five years pastor of the First Baptist Church in Minneapolis, founder of Northwestern Schools, and president of the World Christian Fundamentals Association, was a prince of the pulpit. His magisterial *The Bible of the Expositor and the Evangelist* struck a fine balance between probing Bible preaching and a clear enunciation of the evangelic for the unconverted. Riley's preaching on the Bible and science presents an excellent case study on this topic and the times. A. C. Dixon (1854–1925) of Baltimore and Chicago was also a commanding figure.

Presbyterians whose biblical preaching enthralled a city must include Mark A. Matthews (1867–1940) of Seattle and Clarence E. Macartney (1879–1957), long-time pastor of First Presbyterian Church in Pittsburgh. Macartney was nominated as the moderator of the Presbyterian General Assembly by William Jennings Bryan in 1924, which led to the departure of Harry Emerson Fosdick. Donald Grey Barnhouse (1895–1960), whose immense gifts as a preacher of the Word moved far beyond his Ten Presbyterian Church of Philadelphia. Americans have always had an inordinate love for British preachers. Considerable support for the conservative cause came from G. Campbell Morgan (1863–1945) and the Baptist, F. B. Meyer, (1847–1929), who traveled widely throughout the United States.

At the bottom line, the African-American Church in all of its branches has stood for the miracles and mysteries of the historic faith, and its pulpits have been filled with many extraordinarily gifted proclaimers such as E. V. Hill and Gardiner Taylor, both examples of authentic biblical preaching and true exegetical conscience.

Among the more separatist preachers of immense power and impact we must recognize the Methodist Bob Jones, Sr. (1883–1968), who had a wondrously winsome style; John R. Rice (1895–1980), whose preaching and whose paper, *The Sword of the Lord*, extended the message of supernatural salvation to an unbelievably wide audience; and Robert T. Ketchum (1889–1978), leader of the General Association of Regular Baptists, who had an unusually effective ministry as a preacher of divine grace.

The growing ranks of the Pentecostal preachers stateside and abroad bear witness to the great vitality of this movement that is faithful to the Scriptures and increasingly interested in depth biblical preaching. Next of kin A. B. Simpson (1842–1919), founder of the dynamic Christian and Missionary Alliance, was himself a careful student and preacher of the scriptural text. The lively preacher at Jarvis Street Baptist Church in Toronto, T. T. Shields (1873–1955), and the missionary-minded Oswald J. Smith (1889–1986) of the great People's Church of Toronto, were Canadian stalwarts in the Fundamentals' cause.

Fundamentalism was not lacking its own eminent scholars in many fields including the brilliant J. Gresham Machen (1881–1937), who taught at Princeton Theological Seminary in New Jersey, and then founded Westminster Seminary in Philadelphia. His classic defense of the Virgin Birth of Jesus [(Machen 1930) was a sterling contribution to the cause, as were his lucid and forceful sermons. Wilbur M. Smith (1894–1977) of Moody Bible Institute and Fuller Theological Seminary was the world's foremost theological bibliographer and a deeply gripping expositor of Scripture. Walter A. Maier (1893–1950), distinguished professor of Hebrew (and author of the classic commentary on the Book of Nahum) and skilled preacher of Christ over the Lutheran Hour, was a member of the Missouri Synod of the Lutheran Church and advocated steadfast adherence to scriptural infallibility.

Thus, with a rich legacy and heritage from the biblical preaching of the ages, Fundamentalism majored in preaching the scriptural text. Drawing upon a striking breadth and range of denominations and personalities, Fundamentalism and conservative Evangelicals gave voice to historic Christianity in a tense time of grave challenge to biblical supernaturalism. This address of Bible preaching to the times continues to thrive.

David L. Larsen

See also Angelus Temple; Azusa Street Revival; Evangelicalism; Great Awakening; Pentecostalism; Radio; Salvation Army; Televangelism

Bibliography

Dorsett, Lyle W. (1991) *Billy Sunday and the Redemption of Urban America.* Grand Rapids, MI: Wm. B. Eerdmans.

Hatch, Nathan O. (1989) *The Democratization of American Christianity.* New Haven, CT: Yale University Press.

Hattersley, Roy. (1999) *Blood and Fire: William and Catherine Booth and Their Salvation Army.* New York: Doubleday.

Larsen, David L. (1998) *The Company of the Preachers: A History of Biblical Preaching from the Old Testament to the Modern Era.* Grand Rapids, MI: Kregel Publications.

Machen, Gresham J. (1923) *Christianity and Liberalism.* New York: Macmillan.

———. (1930) *The Virgin Birth of Christ.* New York: Harper.

Smith, Timothy L. (1957; rev. 1980) *Revivalism and Social Reform: American Protestantism on the Eve of the Civil War.* Nashville, TN: Abingdon.

Stout, Harry S. (1986) *The New England Soul: Preaching and Religious Culture in Colonial New England.* New York: Oxford University Press.

Trollinger, William Vance, Jr. (1990) *God's Empire: William Bell Riley and Midwestern Fundamentalism.* Madison: University of Wisconsin Press.

Predestination

The doctrine of predestination has been a cause of controversy throughout Christian history. While few Christian thinkers have placed the doctrine as the central pillar of their thinking, some reflection on it has been deemed necessary because of the emphasis in both Testaments on the teaching that God alone chose nations, groups, or individual persons for salvation or condemnation. In the New Testament, texts such as John 6, Romans 8–11, Ephesians 1, and 1 Peter 1–2, among others, show that even the earliest Christians grappled with this doctrine.

Predestination should not be confused with the idea of providence, providence being a more general concept that denotes God's sovereign, often mysterious intervention in all that has been made. Instead, predestination is related to salvation, which notes how the Creator God enters into right relations with humans who are sinners and therefore in need of "saving" if they are going to "relate" correctly to their Maker. Predestination serves as part of the answer as to why some choose this salvation and others do not.

In Christianity, mankind receives salvation through the Incarnation, life, death, Resurrection, and Ascension of Jesus Christ, but it is here that the debate ensues. Questions arise such as whether a sinful person has enough strength of free will to make a choice for Christ or whether God must work a merciful newness on those chosen for salvation so that they can now choose Christ while leaving others to freely reject God's gift of Christ. Christian thinkers have tried to make a clear distinction between predestination and fatalism (people have no free will) or chance (God has no sovereignty). The distinction between these views, however, encompasses a wide diversity of opinions.

Predestination and the American Context

Throughout American history, the concept of predestination has varied. One concept that is of some interest because American Fundamentalists still promote it today, is the idea of America as an "elect nation" with a "manifest destiny." From the time of the Puritan John Winthrop's (1588–1649) famous 1630 *Arbella* speech where he called the Puritan experiment "a city set on a hill" to ventures in foreign policy and home social construction, Americans, both believers and nonbelievers, have sought to align the American political, cultural, and social calling as a special nation with that of Israel in the Hebrew Scriptures. A book like Jerry Falwell's (1933–) *Listen America* (1980) fits this genre well.

For American Christians who believe the Bible to be God's infallible word that explains the way to a right relationship with Him through Jesus Christ, the predestination debate, however, has generally taken on a more personal character. The American Puritans in the colonies of New England, of whom Winthrop was an important leader, believed that salvation was a pure gift from God because humans, who were innately sinful, were so bent against God that they would not turn to God through their own freedom of will. But, this did not mean pure fatalism to these Christians seeking a new world wherein to worship and work for God freely. Rather, it meant that when a sinner chose to turn to God and away from sin for a right relationship with God through Jesus Christ, he or she would praise God recognizing that the impulse for that choice came from God. Such beliefs also strongly included teaching that through the regular church exercises of preaching, teaching, administering the sacraments, and the like, God opened the eyes of an "elect" few so they could freely and willfully embrace Christ for salvation while the rest of humanity would remain freely and willfully obstinately opposed to God. Their English Puritan compatriots codified this understanding in *The Westminster Confession of Faith* (1647).

In the next century, the First Great Awakening brought such an enthusiastic response to the "good news" of sovereign gracious salvation in Christ that scores of people claimed conversion (turning from sin and turning to Christ). A number of more status quo–oriented clergy thought the revival was a mere exciting of people's own desires and declared the awakening to be human engineering and not God ordained. Jonathan Edwards (1703–1758), the greatest theologian who favored the Great Awakening, argued vehemently against this view in his *Freedom of the Will*, charging that his opponents knew nothing of God's sovereignty and grace but relied instead on their own free will for a religion that was but a sham religion of man. Edwards, however, in works like *The Religious Affections*, also warned those awakened against frivolous enthusiasm, reminding them that revival was a "surprising work of God" in them and thus part of God's sovereign plan of salvation.

Not all revivalists were so sanguine about God's sovereignty in salvation. John Wesley (1703–1791) of England (which was having its own Great Revival) sent his own emissaries to America in the aftermath of the Awakening. These emissaries sought a greater role for human decision making in the relationship with God for salvation. This is sometimes called Arminianism, a term denoting the followers of Jacob Arminius (1560–1609), an early-seventeenth-century Dutch theologian, who sought to curtail some of the predestinarian language of his own Dutch Reformed Church. The Wesleyans or "Methodists" shared an idea of free will with the Dutch Arminians but their theology differed in several basic ways. The major difference related to predestination centered on the fallen human ability to respond to the gospel message. While both had a place for free will, the Dutch tradition tended to see such ability as still native, although quite harmed after the Fall. Wesleyans followed Calvinistic views of a more radical and pervasive depravity since the Fall, with the proviso that Christ's atonement procured a new "chance" for all humans to exercise their wills rightly. While the Wesleyan movement has had a pronounced effect on traditional Protestant Christianity in America, it did not play as major a role in America's Fundamentalist–modernist controversy as some other conservative Christian groups, except in the way some of these groups appropriated aspects of Wesley's teaching on holy living. (For more on the overall impact of Wesleyan teaching amidst the wider conservative Evangelical ethos, see Synan 1997.)

Nevertheless, one cannot downplay this tension between revivalist views because a "revivalist" impulse has been present in America since at least the First Great Awakening and today's American Fundamentalists are, for the most part, typically revivalist in their views. Indeed, the nineteenth century witnessed several revivals of a traditional Protestant Christianity in America, the most notable figures of these being Charles Finney (1792–1875) and Dwight L. Moody (1837–1899). Although Finney was an ordained Presbyterian clergyman and thus part of a tradition that held the *Westminster Confession* as a doctrinal standard, he railed against predestination teaching of any sort, viewing salvation as virtually in the hands of the human recipient to choose or refuse. Finney found an ally in this through the writings of the Yale theologian Nathaniel William Taylor (1786–1858), who himself had modified the strong predestinarian elements of his forbears like Edwards in favor of an emphasis on human freedom of the will. Finney advanced his position much further than Taylor, to the point that even many revivalist friends accused him of "Pelagianism" (named for the British monk Pelagius who in the fifth century C.E. asserted that the power to live right in the sight of God resided in humans because the Fall of Adam and Eve harmed only themselves; in this, Pelagius was primarily opposed by Augustine [354–430] who had strong predestinarian leanings because of his belief that after the Fall, humans inherited a sin nature from which they could not extricate themselves without God's grace in Christ).

Moody, who came after Finney, never directly challenged Finney's reconstruction of revival from a "surprising work of God" to a regular happening "through the right use of the right constituted means," nor did he directly refute Finney's "pelagianizing" turn. Nevertheless, as part of a revival that lasted from the late nineteenth to the early twentieth century (during which time, American "Fundamentalism" as a movement was born), he and his followers dismissed Finney's emphasis on the power of the human will and instead advanced the graciousness and love of God in Jesus Christ for sinners. In doing so, however, they reverted not to the Edwardsean idea of salvation solely by sovereign grace but rather simply bypassed the predestination debate by speaking both about God's sovereign love and the call to each and every person to "receive Christ" by an act of the will.

Yet, not all those who applauded the revivalists' preaching of a supernatural method of redemption in Christ were satisfied with the rather watered-down approach to the doctrine of predestination. Among these detractors of Finney in particular but also of those like Moody, the theologians and clergy from Princeton Theological Seminary (a Presbyterian school) proved the most prominent and powerful advocates of a traditional Reformed or Calvinistic stance on these issues. Benjamin Warfield (1851–1921) of Princeton delivered a series of lectures published as *The Plan of Salvation* (1914) in which he called all types of "free will" Protestantism an "inconsistent evangelicalism," that is, a classic Protestant expression of the good news of salvation in Jesus Christ. It was at just this time that battle lines were being drawn in what was to become the Fundamentalist–modernist controversy of the 1920s. Thus, although the Princetonians joined ranks with the Fundamentalists and other traditional Christians in the movement against the modernists, even supplying such noteworthy manifestoes as J. Gresham Machen's (1881–1937) *Christianity and Liberalism* (1923) in the very midst of the controversy's flash point, they looked askance at the number of allies who either modified or simply ignored classic Reformed statements of belief or teachings by the likes of Augustine, Calvin, or Edwards on the role of God's sovereign grace in salvation. For a time, they

welcomed these other Christians who like them stressed the supernatural and redemptive character of the Christian message. They shared the fear that "modernism" would corrupt the church with its teaching that Christianity was all about ethical guidelines for the truly good life given by a merely human Jesus who served as moral exemplar. Yet they also found that the Fundamentalist position needed to be rebuked for a human-centeredness that though different from modernism would, like modernism, take the focus off the glory of God in salvation. The problem was not the idea of "revival" but instead, what "revivalism" had become.

After the Fundamentalist–modernist controversy, the name "Fundamentalist" was used primarily by the more recalcitrant and separatistic heirs of the Finney and Moody awakenings and not by those who saw themselves as part of the older Reformed or Calvinistic tradition (although Carl McIntire [1906–], himself of Reformed leanings, did continue to wear the label with a rather militant "America as chosen nation" pride). Also by this time, most self-styled Fundamentalists had added a new weapon in their arsenal against modernism, namely dispensationalism. Originally proposed by John Nelson Darby (1800–1882) and popularized by C. I. Scofield (1843–1921) in the *Scofield Reference Bible* (1909, 1917), the dispensationalist interpretation of Scripture had comforted Christians of the late nineteenth and early twentieth centuries alarmed at an increasingly (in their minds) secular church and continued to do so for those now in the separate "post-controversy" Christian communities.

Darby tied God's absolute sovereignty not only to matters of personal salvation but also to what he deemed to be a clear sovereign schematic of history revealed in the Scriptures. This scheme included seven distinct periods, or dispensations, of human testing, the end of which resulted always in human failure. The world since New Testament times lived in the sixth such dispensation, the "age of grace," which would end with a cataclysmic seven-year "tribulation" period and the establishment of a 1,000 year earthly kingdom in which Jesus physically reigned from Jerusalem. Darby and his immediate heirs thought that the book of Revelation and certain "unfulfilled" Old Testament prophesies plainly told this story, and that a wise believer could if "rightly dividing the word of truth" actually see when the times showed the power of the sovereign

God moving this dispensation to a close. When Darbyism was translated to America, it kept the strong reference to God's sovereign control of the "signs of the times" but mixed with this the American cultural emphasis on freedom of choice that had been such a major factor in American revivalism since the Second Great Awakening of the early nineteenth century.

Indeed, in the second half of the twentieth century, the American Fundamentalist movement has continued to be informed by both its revivalist and dispensationalist inheritances. It has therefore kept something of a paradox concerning predestination. In terms of personal salvation, there is still primarily an appeal to human free will to appropriate God's salvation in Christ (similar to the revival preaching of Moody), but in terms of world history, there is a strongly deterministic bent which sees "signs of times" (like Israel becoming a nation in 1948) as God's sovereign governing of all events to a very detailed and determined end of world history and final judgment (building on its dispensationalism). This history schematic has appeared and reappeared especially at times of social or cultural crisis in America (the secularization process of the late nineteenth century, World War II, the Cold War with the Soviet Union, the Gulf War, etc.). For example, Hal Lindsey's *The Late Great Planet Earth* (1970) appeared in the midst of the upheavals of the 1960s and 1970s and Tim LaHaye's "End-Times" novels are bestsellers in this new millennium. Culture may go by the wayside, it is said, but God has all the times, even the worst, under absolute sovereign control. When this "predestined End-Times/free will personal salvation" paradox is added to the "freely chosen separatistic communities/America as chosen nation" paradox of an avowed Fundamentalist and dispensationalist like Jerry Falwell, one can see the complexities of contemporary American Fundamentalism as an intellectual and cultural phenomenon.

Conclusion

Predestination continues to be a concern both to self-proclaimed "Fundamentalists" and to those who reject the label but nevertheless are heirs of the Fundamentalist–modernist controversy. Part of the complexity of the doctrine is its application, especially when the application being sought is political ("chosen nation"), social and moral ("light of the world"), or eschatological (End-Times mentality chronicled in supermarket tabloids).

Even so, the central issue has more often than not been a reflection on the main thrust of biblical teaching on the subject, namely, the relationship between a sovereign God and responsible albeit sinful humanity. How can Christian preaching best affirm the biblical teaching of God's sovereign grace and human responsibility as it tries to explain the good news of Jesus in contemporary terms? That has been the main question of predestination and continues to be so for Evangelical Christians who hold to a high view of the authority of the Bible. And, in answering it by proclaiming that God has provided a cure for human sinfulness (which is itself the main barrier to right relations with a God who is holy) through the grace found in Jesus Christ and His cross and that humans have the call to respond to this gracious offer in a faith that trusts Christ alone, Christian teachers of a traditional understanding will continue to have to work out how such a scheme becomes neither fatalism (an overemphasis on God's power where God becomes an impersonal force that randomly selects everything to such a degree that all acts by other agents are but a legal fiction) on the one hand or chance (an overemphasis on human ability and power against a sovereign God) on the other.

Paul R. Schaefer, Jr.

See also Dispensationalism; Salvation; Sin and Sinners

Bibliography

Edwards, Jonathan. (1959) *A Treatise Concerning Religious Affections*, edited by John E. Smith. New Haven, CT: Yale University Press.

———. (1996) *The Freedom of the Will.* Ligonier, PA: Soli Deo Gloria Publishers. [Original edition published by Thomas Nelson in London, England, in 1845.]

Falwell, Jerry. (1980) *Listen America.* New York: Doubleday.

Finney, Charles G. (1976) *Finney's Systematic Theology*, abridged ed. Minneapolis, MN: Bethany House. [Originally published in London, England, as *Lectures on Systematic Theology*, 1846–1847.]

Hart, D. G. (1994) *Defending the Faith: J. Gresham Machen and the Crisis of Conservative Protestantism in Modern America.* Baltimore: Johns Hopkins University Press.

Hatch, Nathan. (1989) *The Democratization of American Christianity.* New Haven, CT: Yale University Press.

LaHaye, Tim. (1996) *Left Behind*. Grand Rapids, MI: Zondervan Publishing.

Lindsey, Hal. (1970) *The Late Great Planet Earth*. Grand Rapids, MI: Zondervan Publishing.

Machen, J. Gresham. (1977) *Christianity and Liberalism*, reprint ed. Grand Rapids, MI: Wm. B. Eerdmans.

Marsden, George M. (1980) *Fundamentalism and American Culture: The Shaping of Twentieth-Century Evangelicalism, 1870–1925*. New York: Oxford University Press.

———. (1984) *Reforming Fundamentalism: Fuller Seminary and the New Evangelicalism*. Grand Rapids, MI: Wm. B. Eerdmans.

———. (1991) *Understanding Fundamentalism and Evangelicalism*. Grand Rapids, MI: Wm. B. Eerdmans.

McIntire, Carl. (1946) *Twentieth Century Reformation*. Collingswood, NJ: Christian Beacon Press.

McLoughlin, William. (1978) *Revivals, Awakening, and Reform, 1607–1977*. Chicago: University of Chicago Press.

Noll, Mark. (1983) *The Princeton Theology*. Grand Rapids, MI: Baker Book House.

———. (1992) *A History of Christianity in the United States and Canada*. Grand Rapids, MI: Wm. B. Eerdmans.

Reid, Daniel, et. al. (1990) *Dictionary of Christianity in America*. Downers Grove, IL: InterVarsity Press.

Reid, W. S. (1984) "Predestination." In *Evangelical Dictionary of Theology*, edited by Walter Elwell. Grand Rapids, MI: Baker Book House.

Scofield, C. I. (1896) *Rightly Dividing the Word of Truth*. Neptune, NJ: Loizeaux Brothers.

Synan, Vincent. (1997) *The Holiness-Pentecostal Tradition: Charismatic Movements in the Twentieth Century*. Grand Rapids, MI: Wm. B. Eerdmans.

Warfield, Benjamin B. (1935) *The Plan of Salvation*, new rev. ed. Grand Rapids, MI: Wm. B. Eerdmans.

Premillennialism

Premillennialism is a Christian eschatology that forms part of the core theology of Protestant Fundamentalism in the United States. It is an ancient Christian belief, although never normative within the larger church, that appeared sporadically in Western religious thought, accompanied at times with local social disturbance. It is concerned with how God will close out history and bring the earth and its inhabitants to judgment. Its central tenet is that Jesus Christ will return in glory to institute a thousand-year reign of sinless peace upon the earth—the millennium—and that when this blessed era is over there will be a final confrontation between Satan and God that will end in the final overthrow of evil.

Eschatology was part of Christian belief from the days of Jesus' ministry on earth. In the years prior to the beginning of the Christian era there were sects and teachers within Judaism that proclaimed an imminent day of judgment. Jesus Himself frequently used eschatological language, most especially in the "Little Apocalypse" of Mark 13: "For in those days there will be such tribulation as has not been from the beginning of the creation which God created until now" (Mark 13:19, RSV). After His death and Resurrection, early Christians clearly believed that Jesus would soon return in judgment. This belief is central to the Book of Revelation, the prophecies of which still order modern premillennialism. Revelation 20 is especially important and often used to justify belief in a millennium: "Then I saw an angel coming down from heaven, holding in his hand the key of the bottomless pit and a great chain. And he seized the dragon, that ancient serpent, who is the Devil and Satan, and bound him for a thousand years" (Revelation 20:1–2).

Early Millennialism

The early church was not, however, premillennial and when applied to the early church the word itself is anachronistic. Not until several generations after the Crucifixion did a few of the early fathers speculate about a millennium to come and, even so, there was no systematic premillennial doctrine. As first decades, and then centuries, passed without the Second Coming, Christian theologians deemphasized eschatology and concentrated on the business of building a church and living in the often hostile Roman world. Belief in Christ's Second Coming remained—and is to this day—part of orthodox Christian belief. For example, the Apostles' Creed states of Jesus that "He will come again in glory to judge the living and the dead." From the Patristic Period onward, however, the church discouraged attempts to date the Parousia and few of the church fathers paid much attention to millennialism. (Although a few, such as Ireaneus, considered it.) St. Augustine was especially influential in defusing eschatology as an issue for the church when he stressed that a spiritual community of the elect, the City of God, was the goal of the faith, and not an earthly millennium under Christ's personal rule.

Medieval and Reformation Millennialism

During the long medieval era, groups that claimed knowledge of the End Times occasionally displayed millenarianism (a common synonym for premillennialism) and held up their way of life as a precursor to the millennium. We know relatively little about popular medieval eschatology, but historians have long been intrigued by episodic millenarian outbursts that triggered—or were triggered by—social unrest. In some instances, such as the fifteenth-century Taborites of Bohemia, this social unrest was suppressed by the civil authorities, often at the behest of the church, with terrible bloodshed. The very notoriety of these outbursts may, however, make them somewhat atypical of more widespread popular piety.

The Reformation was a period of intense eschatological speculation and a direct line can be drawn between the millenarianism of that era and today's Fundamentalist premillennialism. Not all the great reformers advocated eschatology. Martin Luther positively discouraged attempts to fix the date of Christ's return and doubted whether the Book of Revelation should even be considered canonical. Local sects, however, interpreted the conflict with Rome through the lens of eschatology and prophecy. Nowhere was this truer than in the English Reformation.

English Reformation

The seventeenth-century English Civil War, prompted in great part by religious as well as political differences (which were often one and the same, in any event) saw the rise of an especially intense interest in biblical prophecy. In addition, the English Reformation prompted a scholarly interest in scriptural translation that resulted in the Authorized Version. The desire to translate led, in turn, to a new interest in the sacred languages, Hebrew among them. And, as they became proficient in Hebrew, English divines had increased access to Jewish prophetic literature. The political and religious turmoil of the seventeenth century thus combined with the wider availability of prophetic literature to create a cockpit of eschatological speculation. The urge to label one's opponent the Antichrist or otherwise validate one's own religious-political stance as fulfillment of prophecy proved irresistible to all sides. Radical political groups, such as the Fifth Monarchy Men, called for a complete revamping of English political life, based on expectation of Christ's imminent return in judgment.

For the most part, this eschatological ferment in the mother country was little felt in the North American colonies. Certain Puritan divines did, from time to time, dabble in prophecy and there is no doubt that millenarian literature crossed the Atlantic. It was, as well, a common practice of Protestant preachers to excoriate the Roman Catholic Church in eschatological terms and identify it with the "whore of Babylon" mentioned in Revelation. But, in the political environment of the seventeenth-century colonies, far removed from England's turmoil, there was little impetus toward millenarianism.

In time, eschatological speculation faded in England. With the travails of the Civil War in the past, prophecy became a sort of low-voltage hobby of the occasional divine or layman. Isaac Newton was the most famous of those who attempted to understand Bible prophecy, but there were others as well, such as Anglican Bishop Thomas Newton. For the most part, however, the subject drew little popular attention. This changed dramatically toward the end of the eighteenth century.

Modern Millenarian Theology

Scholars have, for some decades now, identified the French Revolution as the event that impelled millenarianism in modern times. So startling did that event appear to contemporaries that they opened their Bibles to locate events in France in what they regarded as a sort of prophetic timetable. There was a vast outpouring of millenarian books, tracts, and sermons that lasted well into the nineteenth century. This literature quickly crossed to the United States where it inspired a millenarian movement that soon rivaled, and then overtook, that of the mother country. During the late nineteenth century, as the popularity of premillennialism largely faded in England, it grew and flourished in America, and continues to do so today.

The "millenarian revival," to use the words of one scholar, that flourished in the early nineteenth-century Anglo-American Evangelical community occurred as momentous changes took place in Protestant Christianity. Fundamentalism, in part, is a result of the interplay between premillennial eschatology and the tensions those changes generated. The authority of the Bible, on which Protestantism rests, was challenged by the new biblical criticism, along

Selection from: *SYNOPSIS OF THE BOOK OF THE BIBLE, THE REVELATION* BY JOHN NELSON DARBY

Finally, Christ announced Himself, having taken up the word in Person in verse 12, as Alpha and Omega, the beginning and the end—God before and after all; and filling duration. I suppose we are to take as the true reading: "Blessed are they that wash their robes, that they may have a right to the tree of life, and may enter in through the gates into the city." The redeemed, cleansed ones, can enter there and feed on the tree of life; for I suppose it is the fruit here. Without are the unclean and violent, and those who love Satanic falsehood and idolatry, sin against purity, against their neighbor, against God, and follow Satan.

This closes the summing up. The Lord Jesus now reveals Himself in His own Person, speaking to John and the saints, and declares who He is, in what character He appears to say it to them. "I am the root and offspring of David"—the origin and heir of the temporal promises of Israel; but much more than that—He is the bright and morning Star. It is what He is before He appears, in both respects; only the former regards Israel born of the seed of David according to the flesh. But the Lord has taken another character. He has not yet arisen as the Sun of Righteousness on this benighted globe; but, to faith, the dawn is there, and the assembly sees Him in the now far-spent night as the Morning Star, knows Him, while watching according to His own word, in His bright heavenly character—a character which does not wake a sleeping world, but is the delight and love of those who watch. When the sun arises, he will not be thus known: the earth will never know Him, bright as the day may be. When Christ is in this place, the Spirit dwells in the assembly below, and the assembly has its own relationship. It is the bride of Christ, and her desire is toward Him.

Source: Christian Classics Ethereal Library. ccel.org.

---

with science—geology and zoology (Darwin) most especially. It was, as well, an era during which clergy and laity, grown disillusioned with its determinist theology, slowly abandoned Calvinism. Finally, the antebellum period witnessed increased interest in social amelioration, such as antislavery, from Protestants convinced that both the individual and the world were capable of meaningful reform. Such optimism was, in itself, a challenge to traditional Calvinism.

There was a natural affinity between Calvinist doctrine, whether theology, sociology, or anthropology, and premillennialism that encouraged religious traditionalists to view millenarianism as a sort of lifeboat from the ongoing wreck of sound Protestant belief. Biblical inerrancy was the core issue. Premillennialism can hardly exist without an inerrant Bible, based as it is on the word of prophecy. If, as European scholars insisted, much of the Bible was myth, mere poetry, historically wrong, or just plain nonsense, then the relevance of prophecy—and pre-

millennialism with it—crumbled. There was thus an immediate rapport between premillennialists and other Protestants who insisted on a "literal" reading of the Scripture.

Predestination was a second issue where minds met. To simplify a complex issue, Calvinism had historically stressed the inability of the will to work its own salvation, or even to choose salvation. All depended on God's sovereign will. Premillennialism was the natural ally of Calvinism because it insisted that God determined the course of history and that prophecy revealed an unalterable future of social disintegration in the period leading up to Christ's return. If men could not save themselves corporately, as prophecy revealed, then how could they save themselves as individuals? Thus, premillennialism upheld traditional Calvinist anthropology. Finally, the dark premillennial view of the future corresponded exactly with those religious conservatives who saw society as unreformable and stressed that only individual hearts—brands plucked from the burning—could be redeemed through God's grace.

Premillennialism was, as well, the source of a core tenet of Fundamentalism that today has political as well as religious ramifications; that is, the belief that the Jews must be "restored" to Israel. In 1844, for example, the *American Millenarian and Prophetic Review* stated: "The Jews ... shall be restored to their own land, converted, and become the centre of unity of the visible church of Christ ... during the millennial reign." Protestant Zionism thus joined biblical inerrancy, Augustinian theology, social conservatism, and hostility toward science in the nascent Fundamentalism of the first half of the nineteenth century.

The 1840s and 1850s spawned several premillennial journals, countless tracts and books, as well as local associations. Such journals as the *American Millenarian and Prophetic Review, Waymarks In the Wilderness, The Prophetic Times,* and, especially, the massive *Theological and Literary Review,* popularized the eschatology. A determined coterie of clergy and laity, located in Manhattan, publicized premillennialism with signal success just prior to the Civil War. Then, during the immediate post–Civil War decades, a series of well-attended "prophetic conferences," held largely in New York City and Ontario, provided rallying points for the growing ranks of premillennialists.

Millenarian theology was enriched during the second half of the nineteenth century by two doctrines identified especially with the Irish cleric John Nelson Darby (1800–1882). The first was dispensationalism, which fit premillennialism like a glove. Christianity uniformly regards the Old and New Testaments as distinct periods in God's revelation to humankind. The anticipated millennium constitutes, in effect, a third such period or "dispensation." Darby's contribution was to further divide sacred history into seven discrete periods, during each of which humankind is offered salvation on a slightly different basis.

Darby further extrapolated the doctrine of the Rapture from his reading of Scripture. Prophecy forewarns, he taught, that Christ will bodily remove His elect from out of the world just prior to the Tribulation, the brief period of Satanic triumph that precedes Christ's final return in glory. These two doctrines, dispensationalism and the Rapture, largely completed the formation of a premillennial theology. In time, they too became integral to modern Fundamentalism.

Darby's dispensationalism largely developed the idea of multiple and discreet periods of grace inherent in premillennialism, although the Rapture was a unique contribution. Otherwise, it must be noted that the emergent premillennial–Fundamentalist theology of the nineteenth century continued the oldest traditions of Protestantism. Prophecy, a Bible of unchallenged veracity, fascination with the Jews, and a sociology and anthropology both thoroughly Augustinian, are traceable to the early Reformation, particularly in England. Fundamentalism, then, has good claim to antiquity and cannot be dismissed as merely a "reaction" to modernity. Premillennialism became the vehicle for the continuation of its values in American religious life.

It is important, as the late professor Ernest Sandeen stated, to distinguish between Fundamentalism and the Fundamentalist Controversy. Fundamentalism is a constellation of religious values that stands in contradistinction to much twentieth-century Protestant thought. Its essential elements, grouped around millenarian eschatology, were in place by the 1850s in the United States. The "Controversy," however, dates largely from the 1920s, when the Scopes "Monkey Trial" brought Fundamentalism into the public eye and "progressive" churchmen, such as Harry Emerson Fosdick, all but declared war on it.

As the twentieth century progressed, the Fundamentalist tail came to wag the premillennial dog. With its "literalist" hermeneutics, inerrant Bible, Calvinist anthropology, social conservatism, and Protestant Zionism, premillennialism incubated the core beliefs of what we loosely call Fundamentalism. In time, however, millenarian eschatology was regarded as but one belief common to Fundamentalists. The stupendous growth of Pentecostalism, which largely endorses premillennialism, throughout the twentieth century broadened the spectrum of conservative Christianity so that the rubric "Fundamentalism" now seems outdated. Today, the term *Evangelical* is often used to describe a spectrum of beliefs that includes, among others, historical Fundamentalism, Pentecostalism, some Anabaptists, the Charismatic Movement, and moderate conservative Christians along the lines of Billy Graham. Within this "Evangelical" community, premillennialism is a common, almost expected, substratum of theology. Despite its protean role in the creation of Fundamentalism, premillennialism today is merely the eschatology that members of this broadly defined Evangelical community generally hold in common.

Robert K. Whalen

See also Calvinism; Dispensationalism; Postmillennialism; Predestination

Bibliography

Boyer, Paul. (1992) *When Time Shall Be No More: Prophecy Belief in Modern American Culture.* Cambridge, MA: The Belknap Press of Harvard University Press.

Garrett, Clark. (1975) *Respectable Folly: Millenarians and the French Revolution in France and England.* Baltimore: Johns Hopkins University Press.

Marsden, George M. (1980) *Fundamentalism and American Culture.* New York: Oxford University Press.

Sandeen, Ernest R. (1970) *The Roots of Fundamentalism: British and American Millenarianism, 1800–1930.* Chicago: University of Chicago Press.

Weber, Timothy P. (1992) *Living in the Shadow of the Second Coming: American Premillennialism, 1875–1925.* New York: Oxford University Press.

Pre-Tribulationism

Pre-Tribulationism, the view espoused by dispensational premillennialists, places the Rapture of the church *before* the beginning of the Great Tribulation. All premillennialists expect Christ to return to rapture (from the Latin *rapio*) or "catch up" the church around the time of the Second Coming (1 Thessalonians 4:15–17). There is profound disagreement among them, however, over the exact timing of the Rapture in relation to the Great Tribulation. Specifically, different premillennialists place the Rapture before, during, or after the seven-year period of the Tribulation.

Most American Fundamentalists have expected a pre-Tribulational Rapture of the church, thanks to the prevalence of dispensationalism among them. Brought to the United States after the Civil War, dispensationalism originated in Great Britain in the teachings of John Nelson Darby (1800–1882), a former clergyman in the (Anglican) Church of Ireland who became one of the dominant leaders in the fledgling Plymouth Brethren movement. Unlike other premillennialists of his time, in about 1830 Darby began making a distinction between Christ's return *for* His saints (at the Rapture) and His coming *with* His saints (the Second Coming per se). Before Darby, premillennialists believed that the Rapture would occur at the time of the Second Coming. Between the two phases of Christ's return Darby placed the seven-year Tribulation period. Consequently, for the first time, premillennialists who followed Darby's teaching expected believers to be raptured before the horrors of the Tribulation began.

Darby based this novel position on a number of important assumptions. The most significant was his conviction that God had two completely separate plans operating in history: one for an earthly people (Israel) and one for a heavenly people (the church). Darby also believed that God operated only one plan at a time. Based mainly on his complicated reading of the "Seventy Weeks of Daniel" prophecy (Daniel 9), Darby taught that after the sixty-ninth week (actually sixty-nine weeks of *years*), God unplugged the prophetic clock for God's earthly people (due to the Jews' rejection of Jesus as Messiah) and began forming a new "heavenly" people, the church. Thus the church occupied the "Great Parenthesis" of prophetic time until the "Church Age" and the "times of the Gentiles" were complete. Before the prophetic clock could be restarted, however, God had to remove the church from the earth in the Rapture so that Daniel's seventieth week, the Great Tribulation, could begin and God's plan for the Jews could move ahead to its conclusion.

Pre-Tribulationists point to a number of biblical texts to support their views. There is Paul's teaching that before the Antichrist is revealed, a "restrainer" or "restraining force" must be taken away (2 Thessalonians 2:6–8), which dispensationalists understand as either the Holy Spirit or the church. They also emphasize that the church per se is not explicitly mentioned in Revelation after the third chapter, which would indicate that the church has been raptured and that the attention has thus shifted to God's earthly people, Israel. Also decisive for their teaching is the sense of imminence that pervades biblical warnings about the return of the Lord. Pre-Tribulationists claim that there are no prophesied events between the present and the Rapture of the church. Consequently, it may occur at any time, which is why advocates often refer to their view as the "any-moment Rapture."

One of the most interesting features of this view is the claim that Christ's return will be a secret. Without any warning, Christian believers will suddenly disappear from the earth, pulled away from whatever activity they are engaged in: "in a flash, in the twinkling of an eye" (1 Corinthians 15:51) dead Christians will be resurrected and those still alive will be caught up to meet the Lord in the air. According to standard dispensationalist teaching, the non-Christian population, who will be left behind, will not actually witness the Rapture, only the results: empty beds, suddenly missing conversation partners, vacated church pews. As the popular bumper sticker proclaimed in the 1980s, "In Case of Rapture, This Car Will Be *Driver-less*."

Belief in the secret, any-moment, pre-Tribulational Rapture spread rapidly in the late nineteenth and early twentieth centuries among American Evangelicals through a series of well-attended and reported Bible conferences; the teaching and preaching of prominent pastors, evangelists, and Bible teachers; and a ubiquitous popular literature. Chief among the latter was the *Scofield Reference Bible* (1909), whose study notes presented a dispensational premillennialist interpretation of biblical texts. Also crucial in the spread of the pre-Tribulation Rapture idea were Bible institutes, colleges, and seminaries where such views were championed. Schools like Moody Bible Institute in Chicago and Dallas Seminary turned out enthusiastic and well-taught graduates who believed that the pre-Tribulational Rapture was a non-negotiable part of Christian orthodoxy. Dispensational publishing houses, parachurch agencies, radio preachers and televangelists, and an enormous popular press created a strong and self-sustaining subculture that dominated most of American Fundamentalism from World War I through the rest of the twentieth century.

The acceptance of belief in the pre-Tribulational Rapture had some interesting side-effects in Fundamentalist religion. Evangelistic preachers used the doctrine to great advantage: because the Rapture may occur at any time, sinners should not put off making their decision for Christ now. Would-be deviants from Fundamentalism's many do's and don'ts were restrained when they pondered the question: Would you want to be doing *that* when Jesus comes? In addition, any young person growing up with the doctrine has worried about being "left

behind" by the Rapture. The doctrine has been a powerful shaper of belief and behavior.

By the end of the twentieth century, this view had found its way into the popular culture through the success of such books as Hal Lindsey's *The Late Great Planet Earth* (1970) and those of its leading teachers, John F. Walvoord, Dwight Pentecost, Charles Ryrie, Chuck Smith, and more. By the beginning of the twenty-first century, advocates were spreading their views through Christian cable television, film, and even fiction; for example, the immensely popular series of *Left Behind* novels (1995–) that depicts what will happen *after* the pre-Tribulational Rapture of the church.

Timothy P. Weber

See also Dispensationalism; Mid-Tribulationism; Post-Tribulationism; Premillennialism; Rapture; Tribulation

Bibliography

Boyer, Paul. (1992) *When Time Shall Be No More: Prophecy Belief in Modern American Culture*. Cambridge, MA: The Belknap Press of the Harvard University Press.

Ladd, George. (1956) *The Blessed Hope*. Grand Rapids, MI: Wm. B. Eerdmans.

Lindsey, Hal. (1983) *The Rapture*. New York: Bantam Press.

Sandeen, Ernest R. (1970) *The Roots of Fundamentalism: British and American Millenarianism, 1800–1930*. Chicago: University of Chicago Press.

Walvoord, John F. (1979) *The Rapture Question*. Grand Rapids, MI: Zondervan Publishing.

Weber, Timothy P. (1987) *Living in the Shadow of the Second Coming: American Premillennialism, 1875–1982*. Chicago: University of Chicago Press.

Pride

"Pride goes before destruction, and a haughty spirit before a fall" (Proverbs 16:18, NIV). This verse from the Bible's Book of Proverbs is often misquoted as "Pride goes before a fall," but the sentiment is the same. Pride is ultimately the root of all sin and is seen by the universal church as the foremost of the seven deadly sins, the others being envy, gluttony, lust, anger, covetousness, and sloth. These are juxtaposed against the virtues of faith, hope, charity, justice, fortitude, temperance, and prudence. The list of seven deadly sins was officially formulated as early as the sixth century CE by St. Gregory the Great. Pride was classified as deadly because it gives rise to other sins that together begin to kill the soul. Pride is essentially the elevation of oneself above others and the testimony of reality.

Pride has its followers, but the Bible provides insight into the consequences of this sin. Traditionally, Lucifer has been associated with the sin of pride, if not being its creator. He was cast out of heaven for seeing himself equal to God. In Genesis, Adam and Eve were cast out of Eden for believing their judgment and understanding were superior to God's. Another biblical example of pride is when the prophet Nathan told King David a parable of a wicked man, Uriah, who killed to gain what he desired. When Nathan asked David what should happen to such a man, David decried the man's actions and called for his death. Nathan exposed David's proud actions that brought on the soldier Uriah's death and his subsequent taking of Uriah's wife Bathsheba. For this Nathan foretold of the death of David and Bathsheba's son (2 Samuel 11). As king, David rationalized that he was entitled to Bathsheba despite her being married to Uriah. Because of pride David was able to see the wickedness and failures of others but was blinded to his own.

Dante Alighieri, the fourteenth-century author, saw the seven deadly sins as love misdirected, misapplied, or misused. He understood pride as perverted love, as it is love in the wrong direction. In his *Divine Comedy* ([c. 1314] 1932), he placed each of the seven deadly sins on a level in Purgatory. Pride is placed on the first and lowest level, the furthest from Paradise, because it is the most difficult sin to overcome and it compounds and weighs upon itself until it can go no lower.

Pride is also the excessive belief in personal human endeavors and activities rather than God's character and actions. It impacts one's view of oneself and of others: as Pierre Payne has said, "was not pride the soul confronting itself in the mirror, overjoyed at the recognition?" (1960: 1). The British scholar and novelist, C. S. Lewis, too, shared this imagery. Lewis, writing to Arthur Greeves, describes his battle with pride and his metaphoric "posturing before a mirror" congratulating himself first on his subduing pride and then his emerging pride at his skill at defeating it. Lewis felt that fighting pride was "like fighting the hydra" (Lewis 1986: 339).

In *Murder in the Cathedral*, playwright T. S. Eliot presents a tale of pride through the lives of Thomas Becket and Henry II. Becket is enticed by pride and hungers for power. For this he is exiled to France. Because he has been humbled, he forsakes his former pride. In his humility he is killed by the pride and power he previously so earnestly sought. Pride is destructive and as Thomas Jefferson said, it "costs us more than hunger, thirst, and cold" (Randall 1972: v. 3, 525).

Fundamentalism stresses absolutes. The world is presented in black and white. Right and wrong and truth and error are absolutes that are often unclouded by the gray relativity of life. Truth and rightness are easily known, understood, and put into action. Fundamentalism emphasizes right doctrine coupled with right action and encourages adherents to bring others into line with this doctrine and action. It is in this atmosphere that pride can emerge. Pride comes in knowing something, not in necessarily knowing correctly, but in the belief in that knowing. It is interesting to note that pride does not thrive in doubt, because doubt implies ignorance, which is a humble state. Pride emerges when faith is placed solely in oneself and in the correctness and adherence to one's own truth or revelation. It is the conviction that those who do not believe similarly are not "true" believers.

One theologian has written that pride is a "mole-like blindness which thinks its narrow view to be the perimeter of the universe" (Olsson 1962: 15). Pride expresses itself in many ways, but essentially is a skewed view of oneself and one's place in the world, and its consequences impact more than the prideful. The love that should be directed toward God and others instead is directed toward oneself. In the Gospels, Jesus was asked, "Teacher, which is the greatest commandment in the Law?" Jesus replied, "Love the Lord your God with all your heart and with all your soul and with all your mind. This is the first and greatest commandment. And the second is like it: Love your neighbor as yourself" (Matthew 22:36–39).

David B. Malone

See also Fall of Humankind; Sin and Sinners

Bibliography

Baasten, Matthew. (1986) *Pride According to Gregory the Great: A Study of the Moralia.* Lewiston, NY: Edwin Mellen Press.

Baxter, Richard. (1996) *A Christian Directory*. Morgan, PA: Soli Deo Gloria.

Bloomfield, Morton W. (1967) *The Seven Deadly Sins*. East Lansing: Michigan State University Press.

Capps, Donald. (1987) *Deadly Sins and Saving Virtues*. Philadelphia: Fortress Press.

Dante Alighieri. (1932) *The Divine Comedy*. New York: Modern Library.

Eliot, T. S. (1935) *Murder in the Cathedral*. New York: Harcourt, Brace and Company.

Fairlie, Henry. (1979) *The Seven Deadly Sins Today*. Notre Dame, IN: University of Notre Dame Press.

Lewis, Clive Staples. (1986) *They Stand Together: The Letters of C. S. Lewis to Arthur Greeves (1914–1963)*. New York: Collier Books.

Olsson, Karl A. (1962) *Seven Sins and Seven Virtues*. New York: Harper and Brothers.

Payne, Pierre S. R. (1960) *Hubris, A Study of Pride*. New York: Harper and Brothers.

Randall, Henry Stephens. (1972) *The Life of Thomas Jefferson*, 3 vols. New York: Da Capo Press.

Primitivism

In American Protestantism the ideal to restore or reproduce the beliefs, practices, and behaviors of the primitive (earliest) Christians as found in the New Testament Scriptures is called primitivism. Primitivism is sometimes used interchangeably with the terms "restorationism" (although this is most often a reference to the nineteenth-century Restoration movement of Alexander Campbell and Barton W. Stone) or "restitutionism." The proponents of primitivism advance the concepts of religious democratization and a populist understanding of the Bible through the principles of Scottish Common Sense Realism.

History and Development

The roots of primitivism reach deep into the soil of Christian history. Nearly every reform effort in the history of Christianity has been inspired to some degree by a desire to return the Christian religion to its pristine form. Additional momentum was given to the concept of primitivism by the rise of the Protestant Reformation and the importance the reformers afforded to Scripture. Martin Luther's insistence upon *Sola Scriptora* (Scripture alone) as the source for the Christian belief system and John Calvin's efforts to create a community based on New Testament principles went a long way toward promoting a conviction that the church must divest itself of human traditions and doctrinal inventions. Thus, the English Puritans sought to remove the taint of Roman Catholicism on the Church of England by restoring the church to its New Testament form and practice. When confronted with opposition, many of the Puritans sought a safe haven where they could isolate themselves from their present religious circumstances and work to reestablish the primitive Christian pattern.

Primitivism in America

North America became the site where the Puritans attempted their grand experiment of restoring the early Christian church. The characterization of America as a pure and unspoiled land prompted the New England Puritans to believe that they had settled an area where they could reinstitute an undefiled primeval form of Christianity. Convinced that their efforts would succeed and that the entire world would ultimately accept the success of their mission and become participants in it, the Puritans felt certain that they were taking the first steps that would be necessary to establish Christ's millennial reign on earth. The accomplishment of their plan, it was believed, would be the return of both mankind and the church to their initial untainted appearances.

The religious primitivist thought of the Puritans also found its way into the national ideology of America. Just as the Puritans believed they had the power to inaugurate a new order in humanity, the Founding Fathers of the American nation were convinced that they could institute a new governmental order. By breaking away from the traditions and confines of the Old World, the American revolutionary leaders believed they were establishing a nation that offered the new beginnings and abundant opportunities that were designed as man's "inalienable rights" from the very beginning. As American pioneers settled the western frontier, the primitivist feelings of independence, fresh beginnings, and plentiful opportunities continued to manifest themselves in American thought.

Primitivism had its most significant effect on American religious thought in the period that fol-

Acts 2:44–47

44. And all that believed were together, and had all things common;

45. And sold their possessions and goods, and parted them to all men, as every man had need.

46. And they, continuing daily with one accord in the temple, and breaking bread from house to house, did eat their meat with gladness and singleness of heart,

47. Praising God, and having favour with all the people. And the Lord added to the church daily such as should be saved.

---

lowed the American Revolution. As Baptists, Methodists, and other European denominations came to America, they soon found themselves influenced by their new nation's democracy and religious plurality. The democratizing influence of the American Revolution raised a popular appeal for a new age that stretched far beyond political boundaries. Just as the government had broken the chains of European tradition, Christianity was expected to abandon Old World customs and create a new era of Christianity. Furthermore, the lack of a nationally sanctioned religion, when coupled with the variety of Christian denominations that were present in America, provided for a state of religious confusion. To avoid the confusion produced by this plurality of religions, Americans sought a return to the original, undefiled system of Christianity found in the Bible.

The most outstanding example of American primitivism found expression in the nineteenth-century Restoration movement of Alexander Campbell (1788–1866) and Barton W. Stone (1772–1844). Claiming to "Speak where the Scriptures speak and be silent where the Scriptures are silent," the Stone–Campbell fellowship (which developed into the Disciples of Christ, Christian Churches, and Churches of Christ) sought a "restoration of the Ancient Order of Things" as found in the New Testament. They further hoped to bring about the demise of denominational factions in favor of a single church that would unite around a restoration of the first-century church's pattern for belief and worship.

The primitivist impulse also displayed itself in the Pentecostal movement of the early twentieth century. Declaring the reappearance of such apostolic powers as divine healing and tongue-speaking to be evidence that God had poured His Spirit upon them, Pentecostals claimed to be a restoration of the first-century church and all of its power. Furthermore, they were convinced that their miraculous gifts and the revival of the "full gospel" of Christ were signs of His imminent return.

As part of the countercultural movement of the 1960s, the Jesus People (sometimes referred to as the Jesus Movement or the Jesus Freaks) also promoted a desire to return to the primitive form of Christianity. Disillusioned by their culture and the traditional church, the Jesus People withdrew from their society to form communal groups that would replicate the communal lifestyles of the early church (Acts 2:44–47). Promoting a simple understanding of the gospel and an intense spirituality, the Jesus People were certain that they could restore the genuine, simple faith of the early Christian church.

The primitivist concept of restoring the church to its New Testament pattern for belief and organization has profoundly influenced American Christianity. Many theological positions and denominations within the American church bear the imprint of primitivist idealism. Furthermore, among Fundamentalists and Evangelicals—those who believe that the Bible should be one's guide to life and worship—the desire to return to the early church's form of doctrine and worship is more than a theological speculation, it is a conscious part of their religious lives.

Richard J. Cherok

See also America as a Christian nation; Common Sense Philosophy; Great Awakening

Bibliography

Bozeman, Theodore Dwight. (1988) *To Live Ancient Lives: The Primitivist Dimension of Puritanism.* Chapel Hill: University of North Carolina Press.

Hatch, Nathan O. (1989) *The Democratization of American Christianity.* New Haven, CT, and London: Yale University Press.

Hughes, Richard T., and C. Leonard Allen. (1988) *Illusions of Innocence: Protestant Primitivism in America, 1630–1875.* Chicago and London: University of Chicago Press.

Hughes, Richard T., ed. (1988) *The American Quest for the Primitive Church.* Urbana and Chicago: University of Illinois Press.

Promise Keepers

Promise Keepers (PK) is a parachurch Christian men's ministry founded in 1990 by former University of Colorado football coach Bill McCartney and is concentrated in the continental United States. PK is dedicated to helping men come together and grow spiritually to become promise keepers who live in accord with seven promises. According to the ministry's website (www.promisekeepers.org/faqs/core/faqscore24.htm), the Promise Keeper is committed to: (1) "honoring Jesus Christ through worship, prayer and obedience to God's Word in the power of the Holy Spirit"; (2) "pursuing vital relationships with a few other men, understanding that he needs brothers to help him keep his promises"; (3) "practicing spiritual, moral, ethical, and sexual purity"; (4) "building strong marriages and families through love, protection and biblical values"; (5) "supporting the mission of his church by honoring and praying for his pastor, and by actively giving his time and resources"; (6) "reaching beyond any racial and denominational barriers to demonstrate the power of biblical unity"; and (7) "influencing the world, being obedient to the Great Commandment (see Mark 12:30–31) and the Great Commission (see Matthew 28:19–20)."

PK garnered significant public recognition for its ability to draw huge crowds to the all-male religious conventions held in sports arenas across the United States. As a follow-up to convention attendance, PK encourages men to form small accountability groups of four to ten men in their local communities; the purpose of these groups is to monitor the extent to which men keep their PK promises. The PK organization subsequently established regional offices to oversee these accountability groups, and area task forces that organize followers' interests and actions, especially in the area of race relations.

 Much of PK's unique style of combining popular Christian music, multiethnic preachers, and pithy doctrines in support of a family-centered Christian masculinity (whose adoption was deemed urgent in light of the potentially imminent return of Jesus) is traceable to founder McCartney's personal background and interests. Born Roman Catholic, McCartney affiliated with the neo-Evangelical Vineyard Christian Fellowship as an adult. There he was regularly exposed both to the modern, laid-back worship styles that PK eventually adopted, as well as to the biblically literal millennialism that energized its principal organizers. Elements of McCartney's personal history also informed PK's doctrinal emphasis on racial reconciliation. As a football coach, McCartney regularly forged all-male teams from ever-changing collections of racially diverse young men. When he became the lay leader of one of the most successful parachurch ministries of the twentieth century, McCartney worked to infuse the PK organization with a similar, proactive attitude toward racial differences among men. His efforts were only partly successful, however, as the PK persistently remained a movement constituted mainly of white, middle-class men.

Although the organization is characterized by explicitly evangelistic appeals, PK leaders insist they do not wish PK to compete with local congregations or denominations for men's religious loyalty. The evangelistic goal of PK is not to encourage men to join the PK organization, but commit men to become promise keepers; hence, another of the seven promises PK asks men to make is to support their local pastor.

Arising during an era when women's rights were on the upswing, major controversies surround the PK movement for its stance on the role of women in religion and in the home. The National Organization for Women has been especially critical of the language of submission PK uses to depict a marital ideal. Additionally, PK has been criticized for its invitations to male pastors to attend workshops on men's ministries while ignoring the existence of female ministers and their interest in men's ministries. Even some men within its folds who want to involve their spouses in PK activities question its exclusive targeting of men. In response to this barrage of criticism, PK has altered some of its practices. Most notably, it now invites female ministers to the men's ministry workshops.

The substantial material culture that developed around the PK organization contributes to its appeal. This primarily consists of PK baseball caps, t-shirts, and sweatshirts, but is supplemented by a wide variety of other miscellaneous personal items. As an extension of this, there is a huge array of books and magazines targeted at Christian men that PK encourages men to use in their accountability group studies.

By the mid-1990s, PK was one of the best-known Christian ministries in the United States. Its substantial popular appeal was demonstrated on a national stage when it drew approximately one million men to its first national meeting, Stand in the Gap, held in Washington, D.C., on 4 October 1997. Yet this watershed event was quickly followed by considerable intra-organizational turbulence and decline. A policy change that curtailed the PK practice of charging admission to attend its stadium conferences plunged the organization into financial chaos, and resulted in large staff layoffs. The poor publicity that ensued fueled a trajectory of diminished popularity for the organization and placed its long-range continuance in serious doubt.

Though its laid-back dress code and willingness to embrace men from all Christian denominations can make PK seem like a "Fundamentalism lite" movement, its commitment to biblical inerrancy, biblical literalism, and male headship, combined with its aggressive assault on modern culture, clearly align PK with the second-wave Fundamentalism movement.

Brenda E. Brasher

See also Christian Home, Ideal; Male Headship

Bibliography

Brasher, Brenda E. (1998) "On Politics and Transcendence: The Fleeting Reflections of a [Female] Academic Observer at the 4 October 1997 Promise Keepers Rally in Washington, DC." *Nova Religio* 1, 2 (April): 289–292.

Bright, Bill. (1999) *Seven Promises of a Promise Keeper*, rev. and expanded ed. Nashville, TN: Word Pub. Edition.

Claussen, Dane S. (1999) *Standing on the Promises: The Promise Keepers and the Revival of Manhood*. Cleveland, OH: Pilgrim Press.

Lippy, Charles H. (1997) "Miles to Go: Promise Keepers in Historical and Cultural Context [Comparison with Men and Religion Forward (1911–1912)]." *Soundings* 80 (Summer–Fall): 289–304.

Rhys Williams. (2001) *Promise Keepers and the New Masculinity: Private Lives and Public Morality*. Lanham, MD: Lexington Books.

Prophecy

The Christian faith has always been advanced in terms of three tenses: what Christ has done, what Christ is now doing, and what Christ will do (1 Thessalonians 1:9–10; Hebrews 9:23–28). Christianity's perspective on the future involves a linear view of history in contrast with that of the Greco-Roman cyclical view. In Christian theology, time–space history begins with the creation of all things as described in Genesis 1; then a decisive mid-point in the Christ event, His death, burial, and Resurrection; and finally, the omega point or the climax with the Second Advent of Jesus Christ and related events.

Three terms are indispensable: *eschatology,* or the doctrine of last things; *prophecy,* or that body of supernaturally revealed prediction of future events, primarily related to Israel and the nations, the coming of the Messiah Jesus Christ, and the end of the age; and *apocalyptic,* a specific kind of prophetic literature such as is found in Daniel, Zechariah, the Olivet Discourse of Jesus (Matthew 34–25; Mark 13; Luke 21), and the Book of Revelation. In apocalyptic literature, the curtain is raised on the final scenes of history in a very vivid way and with a sense of the impending.

Both biblical testaments are built on this age and the age-to-come tension. The powers of the age to come have broken into this present evil age (Hebrews 6:5), but the ultimate fulfillment is yet to come. Christ has come but He is coming again. We live in the "now" but there is a "not yet." One verse out of every four in the New Testament deals with the Second Coming of Christ. The early church lived in the vigor of apocalyptic expectation and greeted one another with "Maranatha," Aramaic for "The Lord is coming." Working from quite a literal interpretation of "the kingdom promised to Israel" (Acts 1:6, NIV), the early believers were quite generally millennialists or chiliasts, holding that at Christ's return the promised Kingdom of Heaven would be established on earth when Christ would rule for one thousand years (Daniel 7:1–28; Revelation 20:4–6). Fundamentalists stand in this earliest tradition of understanding Bible prophecy (Peters 1952).

The Fundamentalist System of Understanding Prophecy

While the five points of historic Fundamentalism do not include reference to the Second Advent of Christ,

1 Thessalonians 1:9–10

9. For they themselves shew of us what manner of entering in we had unto you, and how ye turned to God from idols to serve the living and true God;

10. And to wait for his Son from heaven, whom he raised from the dead, even Jesus, which delivered us from the wrath to come.

Hebrews 9:23–28

23. It was therefore necessary that the patterns of things in the heavens should be purified with these; but the heavenly things themselves with better sacrifices than these.

24. For Christ is not entered into the holy places made with hands, which are the figures of the true; but into heaven itself, now to appear in the presence of God for us:

25. Nor yet that he should offer himself often, as the high priest entereth into the holy place every year with blood of others;

26. For then must he often have suffered since the foundation of the world: but now once in the end of the world hath he appeared to put away sin by the sacrifice of himself.

27. And as it is appointed unto men once to die, but after this the judgment:

28. So Christ was once offered to bear the sins of many; and unto them that look for him shall he appear the second time without sin unto salvation.

---

the last half of the nineteenth century did see the development of a millenarian movement that became quite definitive in Fundamentalism. There were pockets of conflicting conviction, such as Charles Hodge and B. B. Warfield of old Princeton (who were postmillennialists), and J. Gresham Machen of Westminster Seminary and T. T. Shields of Canada (who were amillennialists). In England, Bible teachers such as H. Grattan Guinness were historicists (believing that the Crusades and the Napoleonic Wars were prophesied in the Bible) and praeterists like R. C. Sproul in our time (believing that Christ's prophecies find their basic fulfillment in the destruction of Jerusalem in 70 CE).

The vast preponderance of Fundamentalists, as the history of the Niagara and New York Bible conferences shows, were becoming dispensational premillennialists (Sandeen [1970] 1978: xviiiff). Dispensational premillennialism is a system of interpreting Bible prophecy that insists on a plain, simple, natural meaning of the text, literal where possible. While noting that the mountains singing and the trees clapping their hands and the sea of glass are not literal, it is imperative to maintain a consistent historical-grammatical exegesis, taking into account the intent of the original author. Thus, the theocratic kingdom and Messiah's literal reign on earth as

understood and taught by the prophets and the early believers were jettisoned by Augustine who spiritualized the kingdom and equated it with the church (Payne 1973). The argument of premillennialists would be that the seventy-three instances of the word "Israel" in the New Testament all have to do with national Israel and that God has something very special planned for His ancient covenant people (Romans 11). The hermeneutical issue is crucial (Couch 1996: 142ff).

With a moral and ethical free-fall and spiritual apostasy prevailing as history draws toward a close, Fundamentalists were looking for the imminent return of the Savior and the translation of the bridal church to heaven (Larsen 1995: 227ff). Since the New Testament writers all seem to be looking for the return of Christ in their own lifetimes (e.g., 1 Thessalonians 4:13–18) and since Jesus told His disciples to "watch for my coming" (Matthew 25:13, NIV) and warned them not to expect anything before His coming (Luke 12:45), the proper posture of believers is that "Jesus is coming to earth again.... What if it were today?"

The deferred seven years of the great prophecy of Daniel 9:24–27 then ensue with the church "raptured" and the emergence of the Man of Sin or Antichrist (2 Thessalonians 2:1–12). This epoch of unparalleled suffering and judgment is in fact The Day of the Lord as described by the Old Testament prophets. In its depiction of the Four Horsemen and the great woes, the Book of Revelation makes this dreadful time very real. Yet, even the outpouring of judgments does not sidetrack God's plan of saving Israel (now restored to her land) and the many Gentiles who will not take the mark of the beast (cf. Revelation 7:1–17). Only the return of Christ in power and great glory with His saints and angels (Zechariah 14; Revelation 19:11–20) defeats Satan, the Antichrist, and all of his minions. Then Christ will set up the theocratic kingdom and rule for one thousand years after which the eternal future will flow in and on—thus, Fundamentalists believed and preached throughout the world and taught in their schools, expounded in their publications, and cherished in their hearts in increasingly apocalyptic times. "Even so, come quickly Lord Jesus" (Revelation 22:20, KJV).

The Shaping of the Fundamentalists' Understanding of Prophecy

The key figures in shaping this system of interpretation in the United States included C. I. Scofield (1842–1921), a Congregational-Presbyterian and editor of the highly influential *Scofield Reference Bible*; J. A. Seiss (1823–1904), a Lutheran; James H. Brookes (1837–1897), a Presbyterian; A. C. Gaebelein (1861–1945), a German Methodist; James M. Gray (1820–1893), an Episcopalian with a longtime association with Moody Bible Institute; and W. B. Riley (1861–1947), a Baptist pastor, school founder, and prolific writer. The networking in these circles is striking, as when Scofield and Moody worked closely in many ventures. Thus, Moody, as well as Billy Sunday (1862–1935) and Billy Graham (1918–), were all steadfast devotees of dispensational premillennialism. Charles Haddon Spurgeon (1834–1892) called himself a premillennialist and Bishop J. C. Ryle (1816–1900) of Liverpool was staunchly premillennial and saw something very distinctly ahead for the Jews at the end of history, as did many postmillennialists (such as Charles Hodge and many of the Puritans), Pietists (like Spener and Francke), and amillennialists (like D. Martyn Lloyd-Jones).

The case for a premillennial position by Fundamentalists is made primarily on the basis of a literal interpretation of prophecy in the Bible (Campbell and Townsend 1992). Prophecies about many subjects have already been fulfilled and have been fulfilled quite literally, as, for example, Israel's sojourn in Egypt (Genesis 15:13–16), the many prophecies about the Messiah (Micah 5:2; Isaiah 53), the prophecies about the seventy years of captivity in Babylon and Persia (Jeremiah 25:11–14), or about the nations such as Assyria (Nahum 1–3), Tyre and Sidon (Ezekiel 26, 28), and so many others. If the prophecies of judgment have been fulfilled so literally, shall we not expect that the prophecies of blessing will likewise be fulfilled literally? Can we literalize the judgments and spiritualize the blessings? Fulfilled prophecy has always been a strong Fundamentalist apologetic for the faith.

The strong premillennialism of the early church fathers has been a reinforcing strength to the understanding of prophecy in Fundamentalism. Hippolytus (d. circa 236 CE), a bishop of Rome and a student of Irenaeus, clearly placed a gap between the sixty-ninth and seventieth week of Daniel (Couch 1996: 171). The serious challenges to premillennial orthodoxy by Origen and then the domestication of the kingdom by Augustine hit premillennialism hard but did not demolish it and it would rise to flourish in a later day.

A key figure in the premillennial renewal of more modern times was John Nelson Darby (1800–1882). Deeply disturbed by what he saw as the established church in ruins, Darby left the Church of England and joined others in founding the Plymouth Brethren movement and what we call "dispensationalism" today. Darby became convinced of the unique future of the Jews in the plan of God while he was a student of Richard Graves at Trinity College, Dublin (Weremchuk 1992). He was a gifted linguist (translating the Bible into French, German, and English) and his collected works exceed thirty-four volumes. He insisted that the New Covenant must be literally experienced by national Israel and he saw the heavenly and spiritual nature of "the church which is Christ's body" (Ephesians 2:22, NIV). A primary emphasis for Darby is the two-phase Second Advent missed by so many students of Bible prophecy paralleling the two-phase coming of the Messiah missed by so many in the Old Testament—that is, the First Advent in humiliation and the Second Advent in power and glory.

Arguably there were dispensational schemes in Augustine himself (who exhorted, "Distinguish the ages and the Scriptures harmonize") and in that fascinating abbot of medieval times, Joachim of Fiore

(1145–1202), who abandoned Augustinian amillennialism and displayed an "incipient dispensationalism" (Reeves 1969; also Cohn 1957). It is alleged that traces of the pre-Tribulational hope of the church can be found in the fourth-century poet and preacher Ephraem the Syrian; in Morgan Edwards in Wales (1722–1792); and in Thomas Shepard, the first president of Harvard University. Joseph Mede (1586–1638), one of John Milton's teachers at Cambridge University, is called "the father of English premillennialism." He saw the seven churches in Revelation 2–3 as not only a picture of seven existing churches but as a projection of seven periods in church history. Sir Isaac Newton (1642–1727) was an astute student of the books of Daniel and Revelation. He lectured on the evidential value of fulfilled prophecy and saw that Daniel 9:24–27 led to the Crucifixion of Christ and that there would a future siege of Jerusalem at the time of Christ's Second Coming (Whitla 1922).

Thus, the strands and threads of Jewish eschatology, the teaching of Jesus and the apostles, insights from the convictions and controversies of the ages, and a renewal of serious Bible study, all came together in a remarkably resilient and explosive system of prophetic interpretation that, at the bottom line, was critical for Fundamentalism.

The Strong Impact of Prophecy on Fundamentalism

Critics of premillennialism often cite the pessimism of the premillennial system as an obstacle to any meaningful involvement in society and in current affairs. Of course, amillennialists share the truly biblical view that the final scenario in human history will be a spiritual and moral decline (Matthew 24:10–13; Luke 18:8; 1 Timothy 4:1–2; 2 Timothy 3:1–17; 4:3–4; 2 Peter 3:3–5, etc.). Where is the biblical case for the world getting increasingly better? Premillennialists are short-term pessimists but long-term optimists. Christ will reign!

Belief in the any-moment Rapture stimulated dispensational premillennialists to alertness and readiness; to biblical holiness and purity of life (1 John 3:3); to living life on short accounts; and, above all, to service and soul-winning because the door of grace could close at any time. Much missionary impetus was kindled in denominations and in the new independent missionary societies under the premillennial banner. Schools like the Moody Bible Institute, the Bible Institute of Los Angeles (BIOLA), Philadelphia College of the Bible, Northwestern Schools, Dallas Theological Seminary, and many others were born out of this movement. Who worked the rescue missions and carried on innumerable parachurch ministries as prominently as those who stood on the tiptoes of expectancy waiting for the Rapture? Who but premillennialists sponsored societies around the world to reach Jews for Christ?

Activists as different as the Presbyterian Donald Grey Barnhouse (1895–1960), the independent J. Vernon McGee (1904–1988), or the Christian and Missionary Alliance A. W. Tozer (1897–1963) all cherished the hope of the imminent return of the Savior for His church. The movement gave rise to a whole new hymnody about the Second Advent and to fictional works communicating "the blessed hope," such as Sidney Watson's earlier *In the Twinkling of an Eye* (1923) or the "Left Behind" series of recent vintage, written by Tim LaHaye and Jerry B. Jenkins. Apocalyptic has become a significant literary and cinematic genre and no one has used the media to greater creative advantage than premillennialists. Hal Lindsey's *The Late Great Planet Earth* (1970) sold over 10,000,000 copies and, as a consequence, uncounted thousands came to profess Christ (Zamora 1989), even though Lindsey has been a date-setter.

The underside to the prophetic tenets of Fundamentalism was, on the one hand, the tendency of some to become obsessed with the subject and, on the other hand, the temptation to set dates and find contemporary specificity for biblical prophecies that exceeded textual bounds. In our times, Tozer lamented what he called "the decline of apocalyptic expectation" in a culture of great prosperity and affluence (*The Alliance Witness* 1952: 3ff). We tend to think more about heaven and the Second Coming when we are in difficulty or duress. Of Fundamentalism, Webber has well observed: "In the last analysis, premillennialism must be seen as an authentic part of the conservative evangelical movement at the end of the nineteenth century that gained popularity among those conservatives who favored a rather literalistic interpretation of Scripture and who recognize in premillennialism a way to remain Biblical and evangelical under difficult circumstances" (1983: 42). Still, notwithstanding the ups and downs of prophetic interest and insight and the general hostility of a secular society to notions of a return to earth by Jesus Christ, the lamp of prophecy has continued to shine in a dark and squalid time of human history and will "until the day dawns" (2 Peter 1:19, NIV).

David L. Larsen

See also Apocalypse; Dispensationalism; End Times; Eschatology; Premillennialism; Rapture

Bibliography

The Alliance Witness. (1952) 28 November: 3ff.

Campbell, Donald K., and Jeffrey L. Townsend, eds. (1992) *A Case for Premillennialism: A New Consensus,* foreward by Kenneth S. Kantzer. Chicago: Moody Press.

Cohn, Norman. (1957) *The Pursuit of the Millennium.* Oxford: Oxford University Press.

Couch, Mal, ed. (1996) *Dictionary of Premillennial Theology.* Grand Rapids, MI: Kregel Publications.

Larsen, David L. (1995) *Jews, Gentiles and the Church: A New Perspective on History and Prophecy.* Grand Rapids, MI: Discovery House.

Payne, J. Barton. (1973) *Encyclopedia of Biblical Prophecy: The Complete Guide to Scriptural Predictions and Their Fulfillment.* Grand Rapids, MI: Baker Book House.

Peters, George N. H. (reprint 1952) *The Theocratic Kingdom of Our Lord Jesus Christ, As Covenanted in the Old Testament and Presented in the New Testament,* 3 vols. Grand Rapids, MI: Kregel Publications.

Reeves, Marjorie. (1969) *The Influence of Prophecy in the Later Middle Ages.* Oxford: Oxford University Press.

———. (1976) *Joachim of Fiore and the Prophetic Future.* New York: Harper Torch Books.

Sandeen, Ernest R. ([1970] 1978) *The Roots of Fundamentalism: British and American Millennarianism 1800–1930.* Grand Rapids, MI: Baker Book House.

Webber, Timothy P. (1983) *Living in the Shadow of the Second Coming: American Premillennialism, 1875–1982.* Grand Rapids, MI: Zondervan Publishing.

Weremchuk, Max S. (1992) *John Nelson Darby.* Neptune, NJ: Loizeaux Brothers.

Whitla, William. (1922) *Sir Isaac Newton's Daniel and the Apocalypse with an Introductory Study.* London: John Murray.

Zamora, Lois Parkinson. (1989) *Writing the Apocalypse: Historical Vision in Contemporary U.S. and Latin American Fiction.* Cambridge: Cambridge University Press.

Protestantism

In a broad definition the term "Protestant" labels all groups who have separated themselves from the Roman Catholic Church since the sixteenth-century Reformation. Protestants reject the notion that divine authority is channeled through one particular human institution or person such as the Roman Catholic pope. Instead, most believe in the doctrines of the authority of Scripture and the priesthood of all believers. The majority of Protestants date the beginning of their movement to 1517, when the German monk Martin Luther posted for debate a series of affirmations known as the Ninety-five Theses, which challenged Roman Catholic teaching on indulgences.

Protestantism took its name at the second Diet of Speyer in 1529. A group of Evangelical German princes of Lutheran and Zwinglian beliefs issued a formal "protest"(*protestatio*) after the Roman Catholic party rescinded a ruling that allowed individual German states the right to self-determination of their religious position. Of the four hundred states represented at the Diet (assembly), only nineteen opposed the decision of the emperor. The majority of the Diet was working toward the reestablishment of the teachings and practices of the Roman Catholic Church throughout Germany, along with suppressing what they considered "heresy." Matters of conscience, it was felt by the protesters, could not be decided by government action. The verb *protestari*, from which the adjective "protestant" is derived, means "to witness or confess." After the second Diet of Speyer, this individual protest became the confession of thousands in Germany and all over Europe. The protesters and their supporters came to be called "Protestants." Protestantism now includes the Lutheran, Reformed, Anglican, Anabaptist, Congregational, Baptist, and Methodist traditions as well as many smaller denominations.

Fundamental Beliefs

Like the orthodox theology of the early church, most Protestants share faith in the Trinity—God the Father, Son, and Holy Spirit. Most keep alive the ancient creedal witness to the fact that Jesus Christ was and is both divine and human. From the Reformation on, Protestantism has developed certain unique theological directions. They emphasize the Bible over tradition and the authority of Scripture. It is Scripture

SELECTION FROM: THE NINETY-FIVE THESES

DISPUTATION OF DOCTOR MARTIN LUTHER. ON THE POWER AND EFFICACY OF INDULGENCES. OCTOBER 31, 1517.

Out of love for the truth and the desire to bring it to light, the following propositions will be discussed at Wittenberg, under the presidency of the Reverend Father Martin Luther, Master of Arts and of Sacred Theology, and Lecturer in Ordinary on the same at that place. Wherefore he requests that those who are unable to be present and debate orally with us, may do so by letter. In the Name our Lord Jesus Christ. Amen.

1. Our Lord and Master Jesus Christ, when He said "Poenitentiam agite", willed that the whole life of believers should be repentance.

2. This word cannot be understood to mean sacramental penance, i.e., confession and satisfaction, which is administered by the priests.

3. Yet it means not inward repentance only; nay, there is no inward repentance which does not out-wardly work divers mortifications of the flesh.

4. The penalty [of sin], therefore, continues so long as hatred of self continues; for this is the true inward repentance, and continues until our entrance into the kingdom of heaven.

5. The pope does not intend to remit, and cannot remit any penalties other than those which he has imposed either by his own authority or by that of the Canons.

6. The pope cannot remit any guilt, except by declaring that it has been remitted by God and by assenting to God's remission; though, to be sure, he may grant remission in cases reserved to his judgment. If his right to grant remission in such cases were despised, the guilt would remain entirely unforgiven.

7. God remits guilt to no one whom He does not, at the same time, humble in all things and bring into subjection to His vicar, the priest.

8. The penitential canons are imposed only on the living, and, according to them, nothing should be imposed on the dying.

9. Therefore the Holy Spirit in the pope is kind to us, because in his decrees he always makes exception of the article of death and of necessity.

10. Ignorant and wicked are the doings of those priests who, in the case of the dying, reserve canonical penances for purgatory.

11. This changing of the canonical penalty to the penalty of purgatory is quite evidently one of the tares that were sown while the bishops slept.

12. In former times the canonical penalties were imposed not after, but before absolution, as tests of true contrition.

13. The dying are freed by death from all penalties; they are already dead to canonical rules, and have a right to be released from them.

14. The imperfect health [of soul], that is to say, the imperfect love, of the dying brings with it, of necessity, great fear; and the smaller the love, the greater is the fear.

Source: Martin Luther (1915) "Disputation of Doctor Martin Luther on the Power and Efficacy of Indulgences. In *Works of Martin Luther*, translated and edited by Adolph Spaeth, L.D. Reed, Henry Eyster Jacobs, et al.

Philadelphia: A. J. Holman Company, Vol.1, pp. 29–30.

itself and not the exegetical traditions of the church that is the final norm of Christian doctrine. Protestants accept the canon of Scripture containing sixty-six books.

Protestantism announces the Reformation belief in justification by God's grace alone. They assert that in the relationship of God and man, it is God who takes the initiative. However, there are differences of opinion as to the manner in which God accomplishes this goal and the degree of human cooperation necessary.

The priesthood of all believers is an important Protestant doctrine. There is the understanding of the church as the fellowship of saints. The ordained ministry is seen by most Protestants as a functional office and not as a different spiritual status or as a sacrament. Another doctrine of Protestantism is the emphasis on personal faith. Protestants use the term "justification by faith" or its Latin phrase, "sola fide." This faith comes from a complete trust in Jesus Christ as the revelation of God and the answer to the meaning of life (Romans 3:28). According to Protestant belief, man and all human institutions are fallible; therefore the church must be open to an ongoing reformation.

There are differences in the doctrine of the Sacraments within Protestantism, but the majority of Protestants accept two Sacraments or ordinances: baptism and the Lord's Supper (or Holy Communion). Protestants only accept those Sacraments or ordinances for which there is warrant in the New Testament. Because Protestants tend to be independent, many denominations have developed. The Protestant concept of independence has also led to numerous denominational splits and a loss of unity.

Protestant Liberalism

Out of the eighteenth-century Enlightenment arose nineteenth-century liberal Protestantism, which emphasized reason, religious experience, and took the principle of private judgment beyond the understanding of the original reformers. The rise of biblical criticism, Darwinian evolution, and the study of comparative religions led to the designation "New Protestant" to describe a movement within mainline churches that stressed tolerance, a more liberal theology, and the social concerns of the church. This form of Protestantism is still present today, but because of the labors of such thinkers as Søren Kierkegaard and Karl Barth, a "neo-orthodoxy" has arisen that has had such influence that many theologians and pastors would use the label "post-liberal" to define themselves.

Protestantism and Fundamentalism

Within twentieth-century Protestantism there were those of conservative beliefs who held to the doctrine of the verbal inerrancy of Scripture. From Protestantism came Protestant Fundamentalism as a reaction against modernism. (The common definition of "Fundamentalism" as a synonym for religious extremism of any form in whatever setting does not describe all of Protestantism.) Most Protestants did not become Fundamentalists, whereas, on the other extreme, there are some who would define themselves as theological liberals or as "modernists." A large percentage would label themselves as within the "broad church" or the basic confessionalism of the mainline denominations.

Contemporary Protestantism

Although mainline Protestant churches are losing membership, overall church attendance is not declining. This is due to the emergence of new churches that have discarded many of the attributes of established religion. Donald E. Miller has labeled these new churches "new paradigm churches." He sees them as the initial phase of a "Second Reformation" (Miller 1997: 1–2). These churches have appropriated contemporary cultural forms, are using a new genre of worship music, are restructuring the organizational character of institutional religion, and are radicalizing the Protestant principle of the priesthood of all believers. Some of these "new paradigm churches" have remained in older denominations but their worship and organizational style differ decidedly from those of the more institutionalized churches. Miller sees this new form of church as appealing to people who would probably be only marginally involved in institutional religion and believes that their success comes from mediating the sacred by radicalizing the priesthood of all believers.

Leland Edward Wilshire

See also Arminianism; Black Church, The; Calvinism; Free Methodist Church; Holiness, Wesleyan; Megachurches; Salvation Army; World Council of Churches

Bibliography

Brown, Robert McAffe. (1974) *The Spirit of Protestantism.* New York: Oxford University Press.

Dillenberger, John, and Claude Welch. (1954) *Protestant Christianity, Interpreted through Its Development.* New York: Charles Scribner's Sons.

Forell, George W. (1960) *The Protestant Faith.* Englewood Cliffs, NJ: Prentice Hall.

Jacobson, Douglas, and William Vance Trollinger, Jr. (1998) *Re-forming the Center. American Protestantism 1900 to the Present.* Grand Rapids, MI: Wm. B. Eerdmans.

Marty, Martin. (1986) *Protestantism in the United States,* 2nd ed. New York: C. Scribner's Sons.

Miller, Donald E. (1997) *Reinventing American Protestantism. Christianity in the New Millennium.* Los Angeles: University of California Press.

Radio

Protestant Fundamentalism and radio came of age at the same time, so it is not surprising to find them linked in the remarkable story of American culture. Given how common religious radio is today, it is difficult to imagine the airwaves without the strains of old-time hymns, the voice of familiar preachers, the soothing sounds of a Christian deejay, or the driving beat of the new wave of "Christian rock." But this was not always the story. While radio has played an important role in the story of American Fundamentalism, its daily presence on a regional or even national level proved to be a long and difficult fight.

One of those battles was within Fundamentalism itself. In its early days, many conservative Christians feared that radio, seemingly another invention that drew people away from the quiet rhythms of church and family, would prove yet another weapon in modernism's assault on traditional values and ways of life. Accordingly, they pointed out that the Bible referred to Satan as "the prince of the power of the air" (Ephesians 2:2, KJV), and wondered whether that was perhaps a prophecy of radio waves. Moreover, they argued, if everyone began listening to religious services over the radio, why should they bother going to church at all? But these hardliners were opposed by a forceful group of Evangelical preachers in the vanguard of Charles Finney, Dwight L. Moody, and Billy Sunday, who sought to use whatever means were available to spread the gospel. They considered radio a godsend to be used for evangelistic and teaching purposes.

The Early Radio Ministries

It is therefore not surprising that many evangelically minded Fundamentalists, along with other conservative Protestants, were among the first to use radio during the 1920s. Pittsburgh's KDKA broadcast the first religious program in January 1921. Soon thereafter Paul Rader, of the Chicago Gospel Tabernacle, and R. R. Brown, of the Omaha Gospel Tabernacle, joined Los Angeles Pentecostal Aimee Semple McPherson on the airwaves. Rader's ministry was particularly influential, as he sought out every avenue to promote the gospel, a practice that affected a number of young men who would take that message to an international audience. Often seen running from station to station between shows, Rader put together a schedule of Fundamentalist radio for Chicago's most powerful stations, offering live music, children's shows, and late-night inspirational messages to accompany his gospel preaching.

As more Americans bought radios, religious programming increased. The number of religious broadcasting licenses augmented nearly fivefold from 1923 to 1925. The Department of Commerce, which oversaw radio in its early days, reacted to this rush to register stations by confining public service stations (which included religious stations) to a single radio wave. While today it would be impossible to share time with others broadcasting in the same area on a single wavelength, few religious stations during the mid-1920s ran more than a few hours of programming each day. With no recorded sermons or music, most programming consisted of live preaching or music. Though sharing a single wavelength with other stations could have become a problem if the programs overlapped, this rarely occurred.

The Emergence of the Networks

The seemingly endless opportunities of radio that many Fundamentalists foresaw in those early days came to a crashing halt in 1927, when the Federal Radio Commission (FRC)—a new government agency—ironically ended the one-wavelength restriction for religious broadcasting but increased technical standards for radio licenses. About half of those religious stations holding licenses failed in their efforts to renew them. Their only option, then, was to purchase air time from those whose licenses were renewed by the FRC. Thus began a decades-long struggle over the issue of paid-time religious programming. Heeding the call of the powerful Greater New York Federation of Churches, and later the Federal Council of Churches, the giant National Broadcasting Company (NBC) provided free, or "sustaining," time for traditional religious groups drawn from Protestants, Catholics, and Jews. Those who fell outside that "mainstream"—including Protestant Fundamentalists—would not receive this free service, nor could they purchase time on the national network. (Local affiliates of NBC could still sell time to nonmainline groups if they chose to do so, but were encouraged to follow the practice of the network, which delivered the top programming to them.) In 1935 the Columbia Broadcasting System (CBS) followed suit, effectively ending what little conservative Protestant radio there was on a national level.

How could Fundamentalist preachers, who hoped to heed the command to evangelize and make disciples, now make their voices heard over radio? The answer came in three advances that occurred in radio, itself. The first was the development of electronic transcriptions—wax recordings that could be reproduced and sent out to stations around the country on which time could be purchased. The forerunner of present-day syndication, this practice enabled programs to be produced locally and then distributed to contracted NBC and CBS affiliates who were willing to sell local broadcasting time outside the strictures of the national networks. It also made it possible for programs to purchase time on non-network stations around the country, in a sense, creating one's own "grid" of national coverage without going through NBC or CBS.

Great strides were also made in shortwave radio. Though these facilities were expensive to build, their coverage proved far greater than the AM wavelengths used by stations throughout the country. It became especially popular among Fundamentalist missionaries to build shortwave stations internationally in order to reach as many listeners as possible. Equador's HCJB, co-founded by Paul Rader-protégé Clarence W. Jones, is a prime example. Broadcasting in Spanish, it reached the entire continent of South America. A few such stations were operated in the United States, and they were the envy of conservative preachers who could afford to support such an expensive ministry.

Finally, in 1934 the upstart Mutual Broadcasting System (MBS) attempted to break the stranglehold of NBC and CBS. Though MBS never achieved the audience share of either of the other two networks, it did particularly well selling time to Fundamentalist and other conservative Protestant programming. It paid off handsomely for MBS during its first decade. By World War II, fully one-quarter of Mutual's income came from religious programs.

Charles E. Fuller, Radio Preacher

No doubt the prime example of how these developments saved Fundamentalist radio appears in the *Old Fashioned Revival Hour*, hosted by Charles E. Fuller of Los Angeles, California. Using electronic transcriptions, international shortwave radio, and the MBS, Fuller's program took the radio world by storm. First broadcasting from his church in Placentia, California, in 1931, he was quick to learn the value of mass evangelism through radio when he received letters from as far east as Iowa. Having been converted under the ministry of Paul Rader when the Chicago pastor was on an evangelistic tour of the West Coast, Fuller began to pattern his radio work after that early giant in the field. During the early-1930s, he experimented with a variety of formats before settling on two: a nostalgic program recalling the sawdust trail of revivalism and a teaching program patterned after Sunday School lessons. Eventually, both were picked up by Mutual Broadcasting in 1937 as the *Old Fashioned Revival Hour* and the *Pilgrim's Hour*, respectively. Operating on a shoestring budget paid for weekly by unsolicited offerings from the listening audience, Fuller's programs grew along with the fledgling Mutual system. The *Revival Hour* increased from 128 stations with an audience estimated at five million in 1938 to 575 stations with twenty million listeners in 1944. Receiving approximately two thousand letters each day from his worldwide parish, Fundamentalist Charles E. Fuller was by then the most listened-to nonpolitical voice in the United States, with more than one thousand outlets broadcasting his two programs worldwide.

The format of the *Old Fashioned Revival Hour* is important to understand later developments in Fundamentalist radio and even television. Fuller followed the lead of Paul Rader by incorporating enjoyable, upbeat music into a repertoire of gospel songs—a combination that drew audiences from the young and old alike. His message was clearly cut to the essentials of Fundamentalism, but his style was nonconfrontational. Indeed, his genial manner, mixed with Grace Fuller's motherly reading of listeners' letters, created a homey atmosphere that many conservative Protestants felt slipping away. That appeal was particularly important during World War II, when American families, spread around the globe, could still gather together around radio sets and listen to Fuller, via Mutual, or syndication, or international shortwave.

At the height of the program's popularity in 1944, Mutual Broadcasting announced it would no longer accept paid-for religious programs. Fuller and his Fundamentalist broadcasting cohorts were exasperated. Despite garnering one-fourth of its income from religious shows (and one-eighth of its income just from Fuller's two programs), Mutual joined NBC and CBS in following the guidelines laid down by the more liberal Federal (soon to be National) Council of Churches. In response, Fuller and other Fundamentalist leaders created an association to deal with the political and press-related attacks conservatives faced. The National Association of Evangelicals (NAE), thus, was born in the midst of a series of Fuller revival broadcasts around the country used as a platform to announce the NAE's existence. A subcommittee for radio broadcasting concerns was created and immediately began lobbying efforts in Washington, D.C. Within two years this group formed the National Religious Broadcasters, an organization for conservative Protestants with sound financial practices who needed a lobby in state houses.

The Start of Syndication

Despite their efforts, Fundamentalists were now forced to syndicate their programs through individual stations or even remain solely on local radio where possible. While syndication required a great deal of effort, a number of programs achieved national followings, including M. R. DeHaan's *Radio Bible Class*, Theodore Epp's *Back to the Bible*, and Paul Myers's *Haven of Rest*. Other notable programs remained regional in their appeal during the 1930s and 1940s, including the ministries of Robert Schuler in Los Angeles, W. A. Criswell in Dallas, or Howard Cadle in Indianapolis.

Walter Maier's *The Lutheran Hour* proves the major exception to the circumstances governing Fundamentalists' experience with radio. Although he was forced to leave CBS for Mutual in 1935, he was able to do so with two things his colleagues in the business lacked: denominational support through the Walther League (the youth auxiliary of the Missouri Synod Lutheran Church) and underwriting by General Motors. This enabled Maier to put on his half-hour program without the same sort of worries that faced Charles E. Fuller, the only person who surpassed his listenership of fifteen million. But Maier faced his own problems. Many within his conservative denomination appreciated neither the program's secular funding nor the broad appeal Maier sought to fashion, which they thought ignored their Lutheran heritage. When Mutual joined the ban on purchased religious time, his program was allowed to remain since he had denominational backing in a way the independent Fuller did not. But Maier's untimely death in 1950 left Fuller alone at the top of the charts.

The Move to FM Stations and Television

The 1950s and 1960s saw great expansion in Fundamentalist radio. Again, changes within radio, itself, accounted for new opportunities. In 1949, the American Broadcasting Company (ABC)—previously the "Blue Network" of NBC, whose monopoly was broken up by the Federal Communications Commission—announced it would accept paid-for religious programming. Naturally, Fuller's *Old Fashioned Revival Hour* became its lead religious program. But within a year the voice of a young Billy Graham could be heard on the network's *Hour of Decision*. Throughout the decade ABC would reap the rewards of religious radio that once stuffed the coffers of Mutual.

The second major change of the 1950s was the wholesale purchase by Fundamentalists of FM radio stations. Initially developed in the 1930s, both FM and television technology were mothballed during

World War II. And while television soon dominated America's postwar culture, many were cautious about whether the millions of listeners accustomed to AM's greater range would switch to FM, which has better sound but less power. Most industry analysts bet against it. With FM stations losing money, stations equipped with that technology were selling cheaply throughout the 1950s. Here was the opportunity Fundamentalists had waited for: affordable and Federal Communications Commission–approved stations. Hundreds jumped on it. When the FCC decided to push FM by allowing simulcasting on both modulations, the nation suddenly realized the increased sound quality of FM radio. So by the early-1960s, many Fundamentalists held stations and licenses in the most prized treasure in radio, FM.

That development led to the incredible number and power of religious—particularly Fundamentalist—radio today. Many of the familiar voices, and eventually faces, of today arose out of that time. Jerry Falwell, Pat Robertson, and James Kennedy all got their starts in inexpensive FM radio, and then rode its wave of popularity through the 1960s into television. Much of their success was due also to the 1960 compromise between the National Council of Churches and the National Religious Broadcasters stating that stations could count purchased religious programming as their "public service"—something previously reserved for sustaining time programs approved by the NCC. Naturally, radio and television stations longed to profit from the time they had been forced to give away for many years. Now, Fundamentalist ministers were given the opportunity to buy a place at the table of mass communications, and many stations were more than willing to assist.

More important, however, with so many local Christian stations on FM, Fundamentalists and other conservative Protestants could promote their own form of syndication by buying time on stations around the country. There was no longer any need to go through national networks, or even local secular stations. Now, a grid of Christian radio existed for national coverage. The 1970s saw the rise of several programs that dominated Christian airwaves, including James Dobson's *Focus on the Family* and Charles Swindoll's *Insight for Family Living*.

Conclusion

In many ways, the story of Fundamentalism and radio has come full circle. What began with such

promise in the 1920s and then entered a period of long struggle with intolerant mainline denominations and government agencies has arrived again at a point where local stations provide platforms for regional and national star preachers in the Fundamentalist tradition.

Philip Goff

See also Media, Mass; Televangelism

Bibliography

Barfield, Ray. (1996) *Listening to Radio, 1920–1950.* Westport, CT: Praeger.

Erickson, Hal. (1992) *Religious Radio and Television in the United States, 1921–1991: The Programs and Personalities.* Jefferson, NC, and London: McFarland and Company.

Fuller, Daniel. (1972) *Give the Winds a Mighty Voice: The Story of Charles E. Fuller.* Waco, TX: Word Books.

Greenfield, Thomas Allen. (1989) *Radio: A Reference Guide.* Westport, CT: Greenwood Press.

Hilmes, Michele. (1997) *Radio Voices: American Broadcasting, 1922–1952.* Minneapolis: University of Minnesota Press.

Hoover, Stewart. (1988) *Mass Media Religion: The Social Sources of the Electronic Church.* Newbury Park, CA: Sage Publications.

Schultze, Quentin, ed. (1990) *Evangelicals and the Mass Media.* Grand Rapids, MI: Zondervan Publishing.

Stout, Daniel, and Judith M. Buddenhaum, eds. (1996) *Religion and Mass Media: Audiences and Adaptations.* Thousand Oaks, CA: Sage Publications.

Rapture

A cornerstone doctrine in premillennialist Christian eschatology, the Rapture is the much-anticipated and oft-debated "snatching away" of living Christians from earth into the clouds, through the air to meet Jesus Christ (1 Thessalonians 4:13–18). Alternately designated the "Translation of the Saints" or the "Great Hope" (from the phrase "blessed hope" in Titus 2:13, KJV), the Rapture occurs at the parousia (Second Coming) of Christ and follows the resurrection of Christians who have died. Like the resurrected, the raptured miraculously receive spiritual, imperishable bodies that enable them to inherit the kingdom of God and to live forever (1 Corinthians

15:50–55). These basic beliefs about what happens to living Christians at the parousia come directly from Paul's letters and have been part of orthodox Christian eschatology since the first century CE.

Modern proponents of the Rapture, however, introduced an important innovation into the doctrine of the parousia by dividing it into two stages. First, in the "Secret Rapture" Christ will come, invisible to unbelievers, *for the church* alone, resurrect dead believers, and "rapture" those still alive. Those left behind will be stunned by the sudden disappearance of millions of Christians. Seven years of the "Great Tribulation" will follow, during which the prophecies of Daniel 9:27–12:13 and the Revelation 4–22 will be fulfilled. At the end of the Tribulation Christ will return a second time *with the church*, this time visible to the entire world, to gather those who became believers during the Tribulation, to defeat the Antichrist and his forces, and to establish his millennial kingdom on earth. This scenario is premillennial, because Christ returns before the millennium; futurist, because the prophecies of Daniel and Revelation refer exclusively to future events and not to past events in church history; and pre-Tribulational, because the Rapture takes place before the seven-year period of Tribulation. It is by far the most commonly taught scenario among Christian Fundamentalists, and is the most important in the history of modern belief in a two-stage parousia. While postmillennial and amillennial doctrines of the parousia persist, as do historicist interpretations of the prophecies of Daniel and Revelation—which assume that these refer to events from the founding of the church in the first century CE to the present day—and while some groups teach that the Rapture will occur mid- or post-Tribulation, this futurist, premillennial, pre-Tribulational doctrine came first and established the Rapture as a distinct and conventional eschatological subject that modern millennialists of all convictions must address in their treatments of the End Times.

History of the Doctrine

The doctrine of the "Secret Rapture" was one of the key innovations of dispensationalism, a version of futurist premillennialism developed and popularized in Great Britain and the United States by British evangelist John Nelson Darby (1800–1882). Darby's division of the parousia into the Secret Rapture and the establishing of the millennial kingdom resulted from another of his innovations: Darby argued that all biblical prophecy, in both Testaments, pertained to the people of Israel alone. God sent Jesus Christ to Israel as the Messiah who would reclaim the throne of David in fulfillment of the promises of Scripture (2 Samuel 7:4–17), which the prophet Daniel predicted would occur 490 years after Israel returned from the Babylonian exile (Daniel 9:24–27). Darby calculated that Jesus was crucified 483 years after the return and claimed that God originally intended for Jesus to return to earth seven years after his Resurrection to claim the Davidic throne, judge the earth, and establish his millennial kingdom. During the seven years between Christ's Ascension and parousia the events of the Great Tribulation (Daniel 9:27; Revelation 4–20; also Mark 13; Matthew 24) were to have occurred. After the Jews rejected Jesus as Messiah, however, God suspended his dealings with Israel, postponed the fulfillment of the prophecies regarding the final seven years, and turned his attention to the Gentiles. When God has completed his dealings with the Gentiles he will return his attention to Israel and resume fulfilling the prophecies related to the final seven years, after which Christ will return to establish the millennial kingdom. Because the prophecies do not pertain to the Gentile church, however, the church cannot be in the world when they are fulfilled, since the entire world will be affected by relentless succession of devastations (Revelation 8–9), and those who follow Christ will be persecuted (Revelation 13:5–10; Mark 13:9–13; Matthew 24:9–13). Darby argued that the Gentile church would be removed from earth in the Secret Rapture, immediately after which God would resume fulfilling the final seven years of prophecy, and then Christ would return again with the church to establish the millennial kingdom with the remnant of Israel that came to believe in Jesus Christ during the Tribulation.

By the time the Fundamentalist movement was underway in early-twentieth-century American and British circles, a number of prominent participants advocated central tenets of Darbyite dispensationalism, including the doctrine of the Secret Rapture. Although the sixty-four authors who contributed to *The Fundamentals* (1910–1915) (the twelve-volume collection of articles in defense of Christian doctrine for which the Fundamentalist movement was named) included scholars who did not accept dispensationalism or even premillennialism, many of the contributors were dispensationalists, and two articles defended the premillennialist view of the parousia (Sandeen 1970). The moderate treatment of

1 Thessalonians 4:15–18

15. For this we say unto you by the word of the Lord, that we which are alive and remain unto the coming of the Lord shall not prevent them which are asleep.

16. For the Lord himself shall descend from heaven with a shout, with the voice of the archangel, and with the trump of God: and the dead in Christ shall rise first:

17. Then we which are alive and remain shall be caught up together with them in the clouds to meet the Lord in the air: and so shall we ever be with the Lord.

18. Wherefore comfort one another with these words.

1 Corinthians 15:50–55

50. Now this I say, brethren, that flesh and blood cannot inherit the kingdom of God; neither doth corruption inherit incorruption.

51. Behold, I slew you a mystery; We shall not all sleep, but shall all be changed.

52. In a moment, in the twinkling of an eye, at the last trump: for the trumpet shall sound, and the dead shall be raised incorruptible, and we shall be changed.

53. For this corruptible must put on incruption, and this mortal must put on immortality.

54. So when this corruptible shall have put on incorruption, and this mortal shall have put on immortality, then shall be brought to pass the saying that is written, Death is swallowed up in victory.

55. O death, where is they sting? O grave, where is thy victory?

---

eschatology in *The Fundamentals* represents a compromise on the part of millennialists who cooperated with nonmillennialists to defend doctrines such as the inerrancy of Scripture, the deity of Christ, and the necessity of a literal interpretation, against the assault on such tenets that higher criticism and liberal theology represented. When contributors such as A. C. Dixon (1854–1925) and R. A. Torrey (1856–1928), both of whom were general editors of the series, wrote and preached in other settings, the message they spread was that of Darbyite dispensationalism. Torrey wrote a glowing commendation for the front pages of *Jesus Is Coming* (3d edition, 1916), a popular presentation of dispensationalist eschatology by W. E. Blackstone (b. 1841), which was translated into thirty-one languages and distributed worldwide. As influential as such tracts were, no publication did more to promote the Secret Rapture among Fundamentalists than C. I. Scofield's (1843–1921) *Scofield Reference Bible* (1909), a sophisticated, well-produced, and accessible presentation of Scripture. With copious cross references and marginal notes that strongly promote a dispensationalist eschatology, this book continues to be a best-seller to this day.

Popular Depictions of the Rapture

In the hands of evangelists and missionaries the doctrine of the Rapture and the premillennial parousia spread explosively from pulpits in the United States, Europe, and worldwide. Dwight L. Moody (1837–1899), an early convert to premillennialism, confessed that awareness of the imminence of the parousia fueled his efforts to win converts more than any other Christian doctrine. Historian Timothy Weber (1983: 52) notes that, since Moody, nearly every major American revivalist has been a premillennialist. Crowd-gatherers like the evangelist Billy Sunday (1862–1935) warned thousands of the terrors they would face if they missed the Rapture, and local ministers and missionaries spread the word to their respective audiences. At the end of the twentieth century, high-profile Fundamentalist evangelists such as Jimmy Swaggart, a former televangelist associated with the Pentecostal Assemblies of God denomination, and Tim LaHaye, a Baptist minister, continued to make the Rapture a central theme in their preaching and publishing. LaHaye, a prolific apologist for dispensationalism and the founder of the Pre-Trib Research Center, a "think-tank committed to the study, proclaiming, teaching, and defending of the Pretribulational Rapture" (www.millennianet.com/atpro4sel/petri2.html), continues to coauthor the *Left Behind* series of novels (1995–), a fictional account of premillennial dispensationalism, with Jerry B. Jenkins, writer-in-residence at the Moody Bible Institute. The series follows the post-Rapture struggles of the "Tribulation Force," a Christian underground, against the Antichrist as the prophecies of Revelation are sensationally fulfilled. Each installment in the series has made national best-seller lists, and a direct-to-video movie based on the first novel and starring Kirk Cameron was released in 2000. The intention of these popular presentations of the Rapture is the same as that in evangelism: to gain converts to Christianity. The authors boast that thousands of people have become born-again believers after reading the *Left Behind* books.

Opposing Views of the Rapture Doctrine

A glance at the statements of doctrine of some of the most powerful Fundamentalist denominations at the end of the twentieth century reveals that dispensationalist eschatology does not completely dominate. The Assemblies of God, the largest Pentecostal denomination in the world, includes the doctrine of the premillennial, pre-Tribulation Rapture of the saints among its sixteen Statements of Fundamental Truths (http://www.ag.org/top/about/truths.cfm#14). However, the Southern Baptist Convention's official statement on "last things" in the "Baptist Faith and Message" says only that "God, in His own time and in His own way, will bring the world to its appropriate end" (http://www.sbc.net/default.asp?/url=bfam_2000.html). Similarly, the Presbyterian Church of America's synopsis of beliefs contains no reference to the relationship of the parousia to the millennial reign of Christ, nor to the Rapture; indeed, their statement refers only to a single coming of Christ, "at a time when he is not expected, to consummate history and the eternal plan of God" (http://www.pcanet.org/general/beliefs.htm). The Christian and Missionary Alliance extends the premillennial return of Jesus Christ as the hope of believers without any reference to the Rapture (http://www.cmalliance.org/whoweare/doctrine.htm). A survey of the official statement of belief of major denominations does not tell the whole story, however: there are thousands of independent Fundamentalist churches and organizations in America that maintain the Rapture at the center of their preaching and evangelism. Tracts published by Jack T. Chick, for example, which appear in public bathroom stalls, in the hands of evangelists on street corners, and every other conceivable location, make the Rapture the central hope of the Christians in these times (www.chick.com). Likewise, the Rapture is central to the teachings of the Bible Believers Association, another major tract distribution center in Sherman, Texas (http://www.biblebelievers.com/Dispensation_Chart.html). Hundreds, if not thousands, of websites designed by Fundamentalists are devoted to promoting the doctrine of the Rapture. Moreover, the persistent international success of the *Left Behind* series demonstrates that the doctrine continues to capture the religious imagination at the beginning of the twenty-first century—and, therefore, is still very useful for Fundamentalist evangelism.

Yonder Moynihan Gillihan

See also Dispensationalism; Premillennialism; Second Coming; Tribulation

Bibliography

Archer, Gleason L., et al. (1996) *Three Views on the Rapture: Pre-, Mid-, or Post-Tribulation?* Grand Rapids, MI: Zondervan Publishing.

LaHaye, Timothy, and Jerry B. Jenkins. (1995) *Left Behind.* Carol Stream, IL: Tyndale House Publishers.

Sandeen, Ernest R. (1970) *The Roots of Fundamentalism: British and American Millenarianism, 1800–1930.* Chicago: University of Chicago Press.

Weber, Timothy P. (1983) *Living in the Shadow of the Second Coming: American Premillennialism, 1875–1982.* Enlarged edition. Grand Rapids, MI: Zondervan Publishing.

Reconstructionism, Christian

Christian Reconstructionism is a theological and political movement that has had tremendous impact on the early development of the New Christian Right (NCR). Well before the establishment of the Washington-based NCR political organizations designed to harness the growing dissatisfaction among conservative Christians, Reconstructionists were laying an intellectual foundation for what would become the religious Right's critique of the late-twentieth-century American social order, and developing strategies to bring about change.

Writers and Theologians of the Reconstructionist Movement

In 1960, Rousas John Rushdoony, patriarch of the Christian Reconstruction Movement, founded the think tank called the Chalcedon Foundation. By 1977 (one year before most scholars date the beginnings of the NCR), he had already written more than twenty books, including his massive *Institutes of Biblical Law* (1973), which outlined the Reconstructionist vision for a society ordered under Old Testament biblical law. The works of other Reconstructionists were also widely available to Fundamentalist Christians across the nation. Gary North, Rushdoony's son-in-law and once heir apparent, was writing for the Chalcedon Foundation's journal, *The Journal of Christian Reconstruction* (*JCR*) in 1974. North had already written two important Reconstructionist books, one of which was his *Introduction to Christian Economics* (1973). Greg Bahnsen, a young American theologian, was also on staff at the Chalcedon Foundation in 1974, and his *Theonomy and Christian Ethics* went to press that year. By 1976, Bahnsen was teaching at Reformed Theological Seminary in Jackson, Mississippi, and future Reconstructionist pastor and theologian James Jordan was one of his students and also writing for the *JCR*. By 1978 (one of the earliest dates set for the beginnings of the Christian Right), David Chilton (who would later write the definitive works on Reconstructionist postmillennialism) was also on staff at the Chalcedon Foundation and writing for *JCR*. In that same year, Rus Walton founded his Plymouth Rock Foundation to disseminate Reconstructionist ideas in churches and Christian schools and had written *One Nation Under God* (1975), advocating Christian involvement in politics for the purpose of returning America to its "biblical roots."

Although these books and authors were largely unknown outside Fundamentalist circles, they were highly influential within the subculture. Moreover, while there were a few self-identified Christian Reconstructionist churches, more often there were a handful of Reconstructionists in non-Reconstructionist Fundamentalist churches who were working to promote Reconstructionist ideas. They ordered books by mail from the Fairfax Christian bookstore, located outside Washington, D.C., in suburban Virginia, which carried all the important Reconstructionist works. These scattered Reconstructionists then distributed these books in their churches. In addition, before the explosion of "small group meetings" in conservative churches, they held weekly Bible studies in which they led their fellow church members in reading Reconstructionist books. They also encouraged their churches to establish Christian schools, a key component of the Reconstructionist plan to reshape society. These schools, in turn, used Reconstructionist materials in their classrooms. Many of these Reconstructionist theologians taught, at one time or another, in one of the many private Christian schools around the country that were grounded in Reconstructionist ideas.

Christian Reconstructionist Theology

The theological core of Christian Reconstructionism is historic Calvinism, read through the lens of the apologetics of Cornelius van Til, who taught at "Old Princeton" (the Princeton Theological Seminary) and Westminster Theological Seminary. In fact, Reconstructionists trace their own theological heritage to these two institutions as well as the Orthodox Presbyterian Church.

Two variations on traditional Calvinism became theological distinctives of this movement: postmillennialism and presuppositionalism, each of which was translated into popular theology among Fundamentalists. Essentially, Reconstructionists teach that God's law, as it is laid out in the Old Testament, is binding on Christians still today. They believe that when Christians are obedient to God's law (bringing every aspect of their lives "under the Lordship of Christ"), they will see the fruition of the Kingdom of God on earth (or the millennium). In short, Christians are charged with "working out their salvation" in such a way as to "usher in the Kingdom of God" as promised in the Bible.

Reconstructionists teach that the Bible ordains three spheres of government, each of which has specific areas of authority and responsibility, and is subject to biblical law. The first sphere of government is the family, whose primary task is to raise children in the "fear and admonition of the Lord." Thus, Reconstructionists oppose "government schools" and legislation that "intrudes" on family prerogatives. The second sphere of government is the church: the locus of spiritual authority on earth. Reconstructionists take seriously church discipline and excommunication. For example, civil disputes between Christians should be settled in church courts. Third, civil government should have limited powers. ("Legitimate" functions are limited to national security and the punishment of "evildoers.") Reconstructionists believe in an institutional separation of church and state but insist that all three spheres of government derive their authority specifically from God, so there can be no separation of religion and politics. Further, taxes should be limited to a flat rate of ten percent of income (based on the tithe); abortion and homosexuality are "abominations" to be punished by government; and a combination of restitution (for nonviolent offenders and property crimes) and the death penalty (for repeat offenders and for violent crimes against persons) should replace our existing criminal justice system.

Conclusion

Despite the fact that many in the religious Right deny the influence of the movement, Rushdoony and the Reconstructionists had tremendous impact on the leaders of the Washington-based political organizations that were so prominent in the early 1980s. In fact, Reconstructionist books could usually be found in the offices of religious Right organizations, and Reconstructionists worked on staff for numerous members of Congress (e.g., one of Jack Kemp's staffers wrote for the *JCR* as early as 1976). At a 1996 birthday celebration for Rushdoony, Howard Phillips, one of the "political operatives" credited with building the NCR's organizational structure at the end of the 1970s, called Rushdoony the "most influential man of the 21st century" and said that Rushdoony had brought "historic changes in the thinking of countless leaders" (http://ustaxpayers.org/hp-rushdoony-bday.html). While most of these NCR leaders never adopted the Reconstructionist agenda wholesale, they did adapt various aspects of it and they brought those aspects to the center of the American political debate.

Julie J. Ingersoll

See also Dominion Theology; Theonomy

Bibliography

Ammerman, Nancy. (1990) *Baptist Battles*. New Brunswick, NJ: Rutgers University Press.

Bahnsen, Greg. (1974) *Theonomy and Christian Ethics*. Vallecito, CA: Craig Press.

Barron, Bruce. (1992) *Heaven on Earth*? Grand Rapids, MI: Zondervan Publishing.

Berkowitz, Laura, and John C. Green. (1997) "Charting the Coalition." In *Sojourners in the Wilderness*, edited by Corwin E. Smidt and James M. Penning. New York: Rowman and Littlefield, 57–72.

Chilton, David. (1985) *Paradise Restored*. Tyler, TX: Reconstruction Press.

———. (1987) *Days of Vengeance*. Fort Worth, TX: Dominion Press.

Hadden, Jeffrey K., and Anson Shupe. (1988) *Televangelism*. New York: Henry Holt and Company.

Lienesch, Michael. (1993) *Redeeming America: Piety and Politics in the New Christian Right*. Chapel Hill: University of North Carolina Press.

Marsden, George. (1991) "Preachers of Paradox." In *Understanding Fundamentalism and Evangelicalism*. Grand Rapids, MI: Wm. B. Eerdmans, 91–121.

Moen, Matthew C. (1989) *The Christian Right and Congress*. Tuscaloosa: University of Alabama Press.

———. (1992) *The Transformation of the Christian Right*. Tuscaloosa: University of Alabama Press.

North, Gary. (1973) *Introduction to Christian Economics*. Vallecito, CA: Craig Press.

Rushdoony, Rousas John. (1973) *Institutes of Biblical Law*. Vallecito, CA: Presbyterian and Reformed Publishing Company.

———. (1981) *The Philosophy of the Christian Curriculum*. Vallecito, CA: Ross House Books.

Shupe, Anson. (1997) "Christian Reconstruction and the Angry Rhetoric of Neo-Postmillennialism." In *Millennium, Messiah's and Mayhem*, edited by Thomas Robbins and Susan J. Palmer. New York: Routledge, 195–210.

Thoburn, Robert L. (1984) *The Christian and Politics*. Tyler TX: Thoburn Press.

Whitehead, John W. (1977) *The Separation Illusion*. Milford, MI: Mott Media.

Reformed Theology

By tradition, the term "reformed theology" is applied to the beliefs and doctrines of the early Protestant Reformation leaders Ulrich Zwingli (1484–1531) and John Calvin (1509–1564) and to those who have inherited and extended these theological commitments into the present day. As such, it draws

SELECTION FROM: *THE ARTICLES OF THE BELGIC CONFESSION* (1619)

Article 1: The Only God

We all believe in our hearts and confess with our mouths that there is a single and simple spiritual being, whom we call God - eternal, incomprehensible, invisible, unchangeable, infinite, almighty; completely wise, just, and good, and the overflowing source of all good.

Article 2: The Means by Which We Know God

We know him by two means: First, by the creation, preservation, and government of the universe, since that universe is before our eyes like a beautiful book in which all creatures, great and small, are as letters to make us ponder the invisible things of God: his eternal power and his divinity, as the apostle Paul says in Romans 1:20.

All these things are enough to convict men and to leave them without excuse.

Second, he makes himself known to us more openly by his holy and divine Word, as much as we need in this life, for his glory and for the salvation of his own.

Article 3: The Written Word of God

We confess that this Word of God was not sent nor delivered by the will of men, but that holy men of God spoke, being moved by the Holy Spirit, as Peter says. 1

Afterwards our God—because of the special care he has for us and our salvation—commanded his servants, the prophets and apostles, to commit this revealed Word to writing. He himself wrote with his own finger the two tables of the law.

Therefore we call such writings holy and divine Scriptures. 1 2 Pet. 1:21

Article 4: The Canonical Books

We include in the Holy Scripture the two volumes of the Old and New Testaments. They are canonical books with which there can be no quarrel at all.

---

together the different strains of Calvinist thought as they developed in Germany, Switzerland, France, the Netherlands, Great Britain, and the United States, chiefly through the work of such influential scholars and church leaders as John Knox (1513–1572), William Perkins (1558–1602), Richard Baxter (1615–1691), Abraham Kuyper (1837–1920), and Karl Barth (1886–1968). Reformed theology played a large role in the emergence of twentieth-century Fundamentalism in the United States through the agency of Princeton Theological Seminary professors Benjamin Breckinridge Warfield (1851–1921) and John Gresham Machen (1881–1937), whose published writings on the subject of the inerrancy of Scripture influenced a generation of conservative Protestant theologians and clergymen.

The Protestant Reformation

The Protestant Reformation of the sixteenth century began as a protest against certain objectionable religious practices, such as the selling of indulgences. Ulrich Zwingli, the chief minister at Zurich, encouraged the continuation of the Reformation in the Swiss city, and insisted that the Bible become the sole measure of what religious forms should be retained. He successfully campaigned against the use of images and the high Latin mass, while developing his view of the Eucharist as a commemorative act, in contrast to the Roman Catholic view of transubstantiation. These views brought Zwingli to plumb the depths of Scripture to reconstruct Christian theology from its very foundations. He stressed the absolute all-

In the church of God the list is as follows: In the Old Testament, the five books of Moses—Genesis, Exodus, Leviticus, Numbers, Deuteronomy; the books of Joshua, Judges, and Ruth; the two books of Samuel, and two of Kings; the two books of Chronicles, called Paralipomenon; the first book of Ezra; Nehemiah, Esther, Job; the Psalms of David; the three books of Solomon—Proverbs, Ecclesiastes, and the Song; the four major prophets—Isaiah, Jeremiah, Ezekiel, Daniel; and then the other twelve minor prophets—Hosea, Joel, Amos, Obadiah, Jonah, Micah, Nahum, Habakkuk, Zephaniah, Haggai, Zechariah, Malachi.

In the New Testament, the four gospels—Matthew, Mark, Luke, and John; the Acts of the Apostles; the fourteen letters of Paul—to the Romans; the two letters to the Corinthians; to the Galatians, Ephesians, Philippians, and Colossians; the two letters to the Thessalonians; the two letters to Timothy; to Titus, Philemon, and to the Hebrews; the seven letters of the other apostles—one of James; two of Peter; three of John; one of Jude; and the Revelation of the apostle John.

Article 5: The Authority of Scripture

We receive all these books and these only as holy and canonical, for the regulating, founding, and establishing of our faith.

And we believe without a doubt all things contained in them—not so much because the church receives and approves them as such but above all because the Holy Spirit testifies in our hearts that they are from God, and also because they prove themselves to be from God.

For even the blind themselves are able to see that the things predicted in them do happen.

Source: *Historic Church Documents*. www.reformed.org

knowing and all-powerful character of God, who presented His Gospel to the fallen world to instruct the human race and to make known His will. This brought Zwingli to expound upon the Augustinian doctrine of election: that certain individuals are predestined to receive the free gift of God's grace. Some reformed theologians added the notion that if certain individuals are predestined for grace, then others are predestined for damnation, which is commonly referred to as "double predestination." As a second-generation reformer, John Calvin assumed the task of systematizing the Protestant Reformation, publishing his influential *Institutes of the Christian Religion* (1536) as a response to the charges of heterodoxy lodged against the reformers by their Roman Catholic disputants. In the later editions of this work, he developed the "reformed" system of theology with its focus on the unsurpassed majesty of God and humankind's capacity to achieve union with Christ.

Like Zwingli, Calvin made extensive use of Scripture in support of his doctrinal positions on the nature of God, Jesus Christ, the Holy Spirit, and the church, which were the focal points of the four books of his final edition of the *Institutes* (1559).

In the work of Zwingli and Calvin, Protestant theology acquired certain doctrinal commitments that influenced theological reflection in the ensuing decades and centuries. These included the notion of God's all-encompassing sovereignty, the idea of sin as an inherited "nature" rather than a specific act, the belief in the election of those destined for grace, an understanding that the sacraments bring the church into communion with Christ, and perhaps above all, the centrality of the Bible in formulating doctrine. These commitments and others were expressed in several key confessions and catechisms, including the Helvetic Confession (1536, 1566), the Belgic Confession of Faith (1561), and the Heidelberg Catechism

(1563). The reformed tradition is therefore "confessional" in the sense that such documents have been used to clarify theological and doctrinal positions and to create uniformity of worship and church governance in certain states and provinces in Western Europe, Great Britain, and the British American colonies. Through John Knox, a Scottish expatriate in Calvin's Geneva, reformed theology was introduced into the Church of Scotland in the sixteenth century. Likewise, many English clergymen who were exiled to the continent during England's turbulent engagement with the Reformation returned as "Puritans," or Calvinists committed to reformed theology in doctrine, liturgy, and church governance. English Calvinists like William Perkins and William Ames (1576–1633) further developed reformed theology into a system of "covenants," or agreements entered into by God and Adam, God and Christ, and God and the elect, by which God provides for the salvation of His people. Thus, covenant theology became the principal expression of Calvinist and reformed theology for much of the English-speaking world, and gave structure to the most important reformed confession in the English language, the Westminster Confession (1647).

The Americas

Reformed theology was brought to the American colonies by Puritans in Plymouth Colony and Massachusetts Bay, who made extensive use of covenant theology in their writings and sermons and affirmed the Westminster Confession and Longer and Shorter Catechisms. It also entered the colonies through Scottish and Scots-Irish Presbyterians who settled in the middle colonies, particularly Pennsylvania and New Jersey, and were influential in establishing the Princeton Theological Seminary (1812). Princeton Theology, under the leadership of Archibald Alexander (1772–1851) and Charles Hodge (1797–1878), utilized the covenant system of theology and the main reformed confessions of faith in training hundreds of ministers for service in the expanding American West. Princeton Theology dominated conservative Protestant thought in the nineteenth-century United States, and thus became embroiled in the Fundamentalist controversy of the early twentieth century.

In the face of new, "liberal" modes of biblical scholarship emanating from Europe and taking root in American seminaries, Charles Hodge and Benjamin B. Warfield developed a doctrine of scriptural inerrancy that held that the "inspired Word, as it came from God [that is, in the 'original autograph'], is without error" ("Portland Deliverance" [1892], Ahlstrom: 814). The Presbyterian General Assembly made this doctrine the centerpiece of its "Five Points" in 1910, triggering a fierce controversy within the denomination that continued for a quarter-century. Conservative reformed theologians joined with like-minded theologians from other Protestant traditions to advance the Hodge–Warfield doctrine, most notably in a series of tracts published between 1910 and 1915 called *The Fundamentals*, which gave the new conservative movement its name. J. Gresham Machen of Princeton Seminary took up the conservative cause in his book *Christianity and Liberalism* (1923), giving new life to the Hodge–Warfield position on scriptural inerrancy and leading to the establishment of a Fundamentalist seminary in the reformed theological tradition, Westminster Seminary in Philadelphia. Thus, reformed theology played a role in shaping the Fundamentalist–modernist controversy through its emphasis on the Bible as the chief rule for the establishment of doctrine, worship, and church governance.

Jeffrey B. Webb

See also America, as a Christian nation; Bible; Biblical Inerrancy; Fundamentals, The

Bibliography

Ahlstrom, Sidney E. (1972) *A Religious History of the American People*. New Haven, CT: Yale University Press.

Marsden, George M. (1980) *Fundamentalism and American Culture: The Shaping of Twentieth-Century Evangelicalism, 1870–1925*. New York: Oxford University Press.

McKim, Donald K. (1992) *Major Themes in the Reformed Tradition*. Grand Rapids, MI: Wm. B. Eerdmans.

Piepkorn, Arthur Carl. (1977) *Profiles in Belief: The Religious Bodies of the United States and Canada*, vol. II. San Francisco: Harper and Row.

Wells, David F. (1985) *Reformed Theology in America: A History of Its Modern Development*. Grand Rapids, MI: Wm. B. Eerdmans.

Rescue Missions

Rescue missions have been an important outlet for American Fundamentalist social action from the late nineteenth century to the present day. The early-twentieth-century division in American Protestantism between those who emphasized social action, and traditions that focused on the salvation of the individual, left Fundamentalists without a framework for service to the urban poor. Drawing on the revivalist heritage of evangelism and temperance work, rescue missions made it possible for Fundamentalists to meet the physical needs of the poor without embracing the Social Gospel. More a loose confederation of independent ministries than a unified movement, rescue missions developed localized funding sources that joined business and civic leaders with churches and other traditional organizations. The missions were strongly evangelistic in style and emphasis, and provided food, clothing, and shelter to the urban poor and others living in poverty. As the United States became increasingly industrialized, and as more of its population settled in large cities, rescue missions adapted revivalist religion to the new cultural landscape.

Three representative figures illustrate the groups that founded, supported, and gave shape to rescue missions across the United States. Jerry McCauley (1839–1884) is credited with founding the first rescue mission, best known as the Water Street Mission in New York City in 1872. Lyman and Milton Stewart, the owners of Union Oil Company who funded the Bible Institute of Los Angeles (Biola) and the publication of *The Fundamentals*, also provided support for the founding and operation of what would become the Union Rescue Mission in Los Angeles (1891). Mel Trotter (1870–1940) was the best known preacher and leader of the rescue mission effort. Though most closely linked with the mission in Grand Rapids, Michigan, which now bears his name, Trotter led crusades in missions across the country.

Though intentionally traditional in style, rescue missions have often been at the forefront of new methodologies in both evangelism and faith-based addiction recovery. The Pacific Garden Mission in Chicago is one of the most influential facilities in the history of the movement, working with Mel Trotter in the early years of the twentieth century to found several other missions in the Midwest. Pacific Garden boasts many famous converts, including evangelist Billy Sunday (1862–1935) and Trotter himself, and has broadcast a radio program, *Unshackled*, since just after World War II. Union Rescue Mission in Los Angeles is a model for missions around the United States and the world, and has become known for its innovative programs. As early as 1907 Union Rescue provided services for Spanish-speaking homeless men, and now houses state-of-the-art health, dental, counseling, and legal clinics at its main facility.

Rescue missions represent an important facet of the Fundamentalist experience in America. Still fervently evangelistic, today many rescue missions have moved away from their traditional Fundamentalist theological roots, and toward a more dynamic form of urban Pentecostalism. These missions continue to offer conservative Evangelicals an opportunity to join their passion for "soul-winning" with concern for the poor and homeless.

John A. D'Elia

Bibliography

Henry, Helga Bender. (1955) *Mission on Main Street*. Los Angeles, CA: W. A. Wilde Company.

Marsden, George M. (1980) *Fundamentalism and American Culture: The Shaping of Twentieth-Century Evangelicalism, 1870–1925*. New York: Oxford University Press.

Moberg, David O. (1977) *The Great Reversal*. Philadelphia: Holman Publishing.

Zarfas, Fred C. (1950) *Mel Trotter: A Biography*. Grand Rapids, MI: Zondervan Publishing.

Resurrection (Christ)

Belief in the Resurrection of Jesus of Nazareth following His death lies at the foundation of Christianity as a religion. Related to that belief is the idea that all people will be regenerated in order to face a final, eternal judgment. Formulations in the Christian New Testament indicate that the early Christians believed the Resurrection of Jesus to be linked to human salvation and eternal life (I Corinthians 15:3f.; Romans 10:9), God's purposes for Creation (1 Peter 1:3f.), possession of the Holy Spirit (Romans 8:9f.), and ethical behavior (Romans 6:5f., 7:4f.). The New Testament gospel accounts present the Resurrection of Jesus as essential to His role as Messiah (Mark 8:12), the universal Savior (Luke 24:47), and the mediator between God and humanity (John 20:17). Resurrection was not therefore a neutral concept, but one which from the start possessed a richly nuanced theological significance. This idea is largely absent from the Hebrew Bible, which considers the underworldly realm of *Sheol* to be the permanent abode of all the departed. There is, however, mention of resurrection to a heavenly afterlife in the late apocalyptic book of Daniel as well as in the various inter-testamental writings. Historical and literary criticism of the New Testament Gospels have revealed in recent years that the historical reliability of the biblical accounts of the Resurrection is not something that can be taken for granted. In response, several theologians have sought to speculate on what might have actually happened following the death of Jesus, and to reformulate the significance of the idea of resurrection against that new background. Nevertheless, the bodily Resurrection of Jesus remains a fundamental belief among more conservative Christians.

The Meaning of the Resurrection

The word "resurrection" contains the Latin root, *surgere*, which means "to rise"; hence, resurrection means "to rise again." The word is used specifically to refer to the rising again to life of Jesus following His Crucifixion and burial. It is also used in a more general sense to indicate that event in the future—the "resurrection of the dead"—at which time, or so it is believed, all people who have died will be resurrected to life in order to face God's eternal judgment. At issue in both of these uses is a question that many consider to be the most central, if not the most vexing, question raised by the study of resurrection: Is resurrection of the physical body as well as the soul, or is it purely a nonphysical event? It must be noted here that this is very much a modern question. As a recent study by Caroline Walker Bynum illustrates, medieval Christendom consistently attributed both to the Resurrection of Jesus and the general resurrection the resurrection of the flesh as it was before death. Notwithstanding the learned disquisitions of theologians and philosophers about the finer points of distinction between form and substance, spirit and matter, popular Christianity as it came to be ratified in church doctrine held that, although death manages to disintegrate bodies by various means, God shall triumph over death in the end by reintegrat-

ing them to wholeness. The recurring concern in medieval Christianity, writes Walker Bynum, was not whether the body is resurrected, but rather how the body, when it rises again in glory, can be reassembled entire and identical to the earthly body. Believers wanted to know how a body that had undergone normal disintegration in the grave could be the same one reconstituted in heaven. And in the worst case, how could a body that had suffered violence and mutilation be resurrected whole and unblemished? The dominant metaphors used to depict such transformations are of death devouring, dismembering, and consuming bodies and finally regurgitating them. Similarly, paintings from the time show animals at the general resurrection restoring to their owners human limbs they had consumed. This theme of death chewing and swallowing flesh and vomiting it back again seems to have provided for a largely illiterate populace the necessary imaginative material they needed to support the doctrine of bodily resurrection. In more modern times, however, with the problem of the connection between body and mind at the forefront of philosophical discussion, the notion of a bodily resurrection has come into some disrepute. Moreover, recent emphasis by social theorists upon the body as primarily the locus of human sexuality and gender have made it increasingly difficult for supporters of a bodily resurrection, for these traits are considered nontransferable after death. Finally, historical and literary criticism of the resurrection narratives in the New Testament have generated the scholarly consensus that the several references to the body and physicality of Jesus at His Resurrection—namely, references to the empty tomb, His eating, His willingness to be touched, and so on—are later interpolations aimed at a Jewish, or possibly Greek, audience. This forwards the possibility of the historical corruption of the texts upon which the idea of a bodily resurrection is based. Theologically, the Resurrection of Jesus represents His entrance into the condition of "glory," a state free from suffering and guilt and a reward for a life lived in perfect devotion to God. The Resurrection is not considered to be meritorious of human salvation in the same way that the death of Jesus is; rather it is taught in Christianity that the Resurrection of Jesus is a sign that the redemption has already taken place. Moreover, Jesus' rising again is considered by Christians to be the symbol of humanity's spiritual resurrection from a life of sin, and the exemplar and pledge of humanity's future resurrection, which is its greatest hope.

Conclusion

The Resurrection of Jesus is based on the belief that Jesus of Nazareth was raised from the dead on the third day after His Crucifixion and that through His conquering of death all believers will subsequently share in His victory over "sin, sickness, death, and the devil." The celebration of this event, called Easter—or more formally, the Feast of the Resurrection—is the most sacred festival celebrated by the Christian Church. According to the New Testament accounts, certain women disciples went to the tomb of Jesus and found the stone sealing the tomb moved and the tomb empty. Later, various disciples claimed to have seen Jesus in Jerusalem; He was also seen in Galilee (here the accounts differ). Critical discussion of these texts has brought the historical reliability of these accounts into question. Competing scenarios for what actually happened have been offered. Dutch theologian Edward Schillebeeckx has argued that what took place between the death of Jesus and the church's proclamation that He had risen from the dead was a kind of intellectual conversion wherein the early Christians, in reflecting on Jesus' life, concluded that He must have been delivered from death even if they had no empirical evidence to verify that claim. More recently, Bishop John Shelby Spong has speculated that the first disciples, a long while after the Crucifixion, had some kind of spiritual "vision" of Jesus very much alive and with God, and that this vision instigated their missionary activity. Conservative theologians have, for the most part, rejected these theories as contrary to the teaching of Scripture and the apostolic tradition of the church.

Thomas Kinsell Carr

See also Ascension

Bibliography

Ott, Ludwig. (1992) *The Fundamentals of Catholic Dogma.* Rockford, IL: Tan Books and Publishers.

Schillebeeckx, Edward. (1983) *Christ: The Experience of Jesus As Lord.* New York: Crossroad/Herder and Herder.

Spong, John Shelby. (1994) *Resurrection.* San Francisco: HarperSanFrancisco.

Walker Bynum, Carol. (1997) *Resurrection of the Body in Western Christendom.* New York: Columbia University Press.

Resurrection (of the Dead)

The word "resurrection" is derived from the Greek word *anastasis*, meaning "standing up again." The concept implies that in some future time God will reassemble and reanimate the decomposed and scattered corpses of the dead. Early Christians took this doctrine literally, and a literal view is prevalent not only among Fundamentalist Christians but as the official doctrine within many branches of Judaism, Christianity, and Islam.

The Hebrew Bible

A focus on bodily resurrection comes relatively late in Judaism. There are few references to life after death in the Hebrew Bible, and some biblical passages appear to be outright denials of the possibility of bodily resurrection (e.g., Job 14:14). The earliest reference to resurrection is Isaiah 26:19: "The dead shall live; their bodies shall rise" (OEB). This verse is often seen as a later addition to the Book of Isaiah. The most explicit reference to life after death can be found in the apocalyptic Book of Daniel 12:2: "And many of those who sleep in the dust of the earth shall awake, some to everlasting life, and some to shame and everlasting contempt." Despite the lack of textual justification, rabbinic Judaism came to see resurrection as fixed dogma. It was feared that Jews who denied the resurrection of the dead might be excluded from the world to come. While differing considerably as to the nature of resurrection, Jewish theologians and philosophers of the Middle Ages considered resurrection as an important article of faith. Moses Maimonides (1135–1204), for example, included bodily resurrection of the dead as one of his thirteen "binding articles." Today, the doctrine of resurrection is affirmed in Orthodox and Conservative circles, but is openly rejected by liberal and Reform Jews.

The Apocalyptic Literature

Belief in resurrection of the dead became widespread—but it was by no means universal—by the

APHRAAHAT, THE PERSIAN SAGE

Therefore be instructed by this, you fool, that each and every one of the seeds is clothed in its own body. Never do you sow wheat and reap barley, and never did you plant a vine and have it produce figs. But everything grows in accord with its own nature. So also the body which has been laid in the ground is the same which will rise again.

Source: *Treatises* 8:3 (340 CE).

second century CE. Christian and Jewish Scriptures contain many references pertaining to resurrection. Some Jewish interpreters stressed the resurrection of righteous Israelites only, while other interpreters insisted on the resurrection of both righteous and unrighteous Israelites. Some Christians and Jews emphasized resurrection of all who have ever lived, but they differed as to *where* such resurrection would take place. Would it be resurrection to earth, to a transformed earth, or to paradise? They also differed as to *how* resurrection would occur. Would it be a resurrection in a body, in a transformed body, or without a body? Some Jewish theologians posited a resurrection to life for those who had been loyal in the fight against Rome and resurrection followed by immediate condemnation for those who had not. Only much later did Christians combine the idea of bodily resurrection and Greek ideas surrounding the immortality of the soul.

Fundamentalist Christians

For most Christians, belief in the bodily Resurrection of Jesus is a central tenant of their faith. When Christ rose from the dead, He did so in a representative capacity (Romans 6:4, "All are raised with Christ"). According to Acts 13:30, Jesus was raised from the dead to fulfill God's promises to King David. In addition, Fundamentalist Christians stress that the Resurrection of Jesus marks a turning point in Christ's identity as the "last Adam" (1 Corinthians 15:45) and signifies the beginning of a new creation. Christ is said to have died in an age dominated by sin, but He rose to a new era.

Thus, Fundamentalists' views of history are teleological, universal, linear, and disjunctive in as much as "history is punctuated by divine intervention" (cf. Crapanzano 2000: 180). The Resurrection of Jesus

concentrates the whole of salvation into a single event. It becomes the turning point of the ages and the center of all time. George Eldon Ladd (1967: 184) summarizes the Fundamentalist position by arguing that resurrection is "a miracle, not in the sense that it is a violation of the laws of nature and human history, but in the sense that it is an appearance within history of a higher order that transcends the world of nature and history—the realm of eternal life which belongs to the world to come." Fundamentalist sermons highlight the works of Christ after the Resurrection when he gave His Spirit at Pentecost (Acts 2:33), apprehended Saul on the Damascus road (Acts 9:5), and directed Paul to continue His work in Corinth (Acts 18:2).

Belief in Christ's Resurrection is central for all Christians. Fundamentalist Christians maintain that Christ rose not only in the minds of His followers, but in time and space as well. For Fundamentalists, the Resurrection of Jesus underscores Christianity's place as a religion that is firmly based in history. It is seen as an indication of God's attitude toward the material world. It reasserts the Fundamentalist belief that their God is committed to redeem the material world in the body of Christ, in the bodies of believers, and ultimately, in the entire cosmos.

Christian Fundamentalists contend that Jesus conquered death by rising physically from His tomb and that His Resurrection foreshadows what will happen to all humankind at the end of time. This is not a new position nor is it unique to Protestantism. The Fourth Lateran Council of the Catholic Church, for example, proclaimed that at the end of time "the actual particles composing each individual's flesh will be collected together" and "the identical structure which death had destroyed will be restored intact." This belief was later incorporated into the Apostles' Creed and is generally accepted among the Eastern Orthodox, by early Protestant theologians (Calvin and Luther), in Judaism (Maimonides), and in Islam.

Modernist Interpretations

Some contemporary Christian theologians have claimed that the idea of resurrection expresses the hope for eternal life without necessarily implying a physical restoration and/or "raising up" of the dead. They also question the physical resurrection of bodies and the ascension of these bodies into heaven. In part, this is a result of changing ideas about the cosmos. It has become increasingly difficult in an age of space exploration for modernists to sustain a belief in heaven as a place located "in the skies above the earth." To get around this problem, a number of modernists have argued that after death humans will be granted new, "spiritual" bodies better suited to life in heaven. Even within Islam, Fundamentalist theologians contend that while Allah clearly has the power "to create the like of them" (Sura 17:99), the resurrected body may be "like" but not identical to the body of the flesh.

An extreme, modernist reinterpretation of the doctrine of resurrection was formulated by Rudolph Bultmann, who suggested that resurrection implies a new experience of life in the here-and-now. Bultmann attempted to give a wholly existential interpretation to the Resurrection of Jesus. Other, less radical theologians posited that humans may again live, but only in the eternal memory of God. This, too, represents a significant departure from traditional Christian doctrine and has been rejected by Fundamentalist theologians.

Social Consequences

Resurrection has myriad implications for Fundamentalist Christians in their daily lives. Belief in resurrection, for example, makes union with Christ possible. The New Testament states not only that Christians are in Christ, but Christ dwells in all Christians. This has been an impetus for missionizing. Because Christ dwells in all Christians, Christ was able to charge the church to accomplish the difficult task of evangelizing the world. For many Fundamentalists, resurrection also provides assurances that the universe is moral. Christ's Resurrection is seen as the ultimate indication of the triumph of good over evil.

Belief in resurrection has been a dynamic force in human history (e.g., Jews willing to sacrifice their lives in the Maccabean revolt in the second century; Christian martyrs in first-century Rome; and Shiite Muslims facing certain death in the Iran–Iraq war). Moreover, belief in resurrection changes people's values and their willingness to act on them. Individuals may be more willing to take risks when they believe that this life is not all, but that out of death one can "rise to life anew."

Stephen D. Glazier

Bibliography

Badham, Paul. (1976) *Christian Beliefs About Life After Death*. New York: Macmillan.

Bowker, John. (1991) *The Meaning of Death*. New York: Cambridge University Press.

Crapanzano, Vincent. (2000) *Serving the Word: Literalism in America from the Pulpit to the Bench*. New York: The New Press.

Hick, John. (1976) *Death and Eternal Life*. New York: Macmillan.

Ladd, George Eldon. (1967) *The New Testament and Criticism*. Grand Rapids, MI: Wm. B. Eerdmans.

Wong, John D. (2000) *The Resurrected Body: Y2K and Beyond: A New Concept of the Resurrected Body from Biblical, Theological, Philosophical, and Scientific Perspectives*. Lanham, MD: University Press of America.

Revelation

In response to the effort of the priests of Zeus and the people of Lystra to worship Paul and Barnabas as human embodiments of their gods, Zeus and Hermes, Paul acted to turn the attention of the mob "from these vain things to the living God," indicating that God had long since "permitted all the nations to go their own ways," adding that nevertheless, "He did not leave Himself without witness ..." (Acts 14:16–17, NASB). The concept of "revelation" has to do with the "witness" mentioned by Paul. Revelation is that work/operation of God by which He makes known to human beings those things about Himself that they could not know in any other way. He has revealed and is in the process of revealing Himself to mankind made in His image so that they may know Him and fellowship with Him. The self-revelation of God is usually divided into two major categories: general revelation and special revelation.

General Revelation

The means by which God makes Himself known to all people everywhere, through the natural world, the miraculous and providential events of history, and the nature and constitution of man constitutes the general revelation.

The Natural World

While there are a number of biblical passages that speak to the point of divine self-revelation by means of the natural world, there are several "key" passages that need to be specifically mentioned. In Psalm 19:1–6 this reality is clearly expressed as the psalmist points out that the heavens above are constantly pouring forth the message of the glory of God and revealing knowledge of Him as expressed through the work of His hands. The message has gone throughout the whole world as evidenced by the circuit of the sun from whose effects there is no escape. A striking truth regarding the revelation of God in nature is that it is a constant revelation that the unbeliever must face all day every day, for "day to day pours forth speech and night to night reveals knowledge" (Psalms 19:2). The apostle Paul informs the reader in Romans 1:18–28 that since the creation of the world the invisible attributes of God, His eternal power and deity, have been clearly seen, being understood through the created world, and these attributes are clearly seen because God made it evident to them so that it is evident within them.

As noted earlier, Paul called on the people of Lystra, bent on worshipping him and Barnabas as gods, to turn to the "living God, who made heaven and the earth and the sea, and all that is in them" (Acts 14:15–17). That is, to turn to the God Who though He had permitted rebellious peoples to go their own way, had revealed His goodness through the natural order of things over which He exercises control in providing rain and fruitful seasons for them, satisfying their hearts with food and gladness.

Miraculous and Providential Events in History

While the exodus of Israel from Egypt is often mentioned in Scripture as the greatest demonstration in history of the greatness and the power of God, one of God's major purposes was to reveal to His people the truth that He alone is God, and that there is none like Him. Israel had spent more than four hundred years in idolatrous polytheistic Egypt, thus it was essential that the foundational truth of the unity of God be revealed in a striking way. As God informed Moses of His plan for the last judgment on Egypt—the death of the firstborn—He said "against all the gods of Egypt I will execute judgment—I am the Lord" (Exodus 12:12). Later, after reminding the people of Israel of His activities in the exodus, God said, "To you it was shown that you might know that the Lord He is God; there is no other besides Him" (Deuteronomy 4:35), and again, "Know therefore today, and take it to your heart, that the Lord, He is God in heaven above and on the earth below; there is no other" (Deuteronomy 4:39). The same fundamental truth of God's unity was emphasized in the days of Isaiah when God through the prophet named the Persian king Cyrus as His anointed to act in behalf of "Jacob My servant, and Israel My chosen one" (Isaiah 45:4) 150 years or more in advance of his birth and activity. The prophecy, brought to fulfillment by providential rather than miraculous means, was designed in part to remind oft-wandering Israel that, "I am the Lord, and there is no other; besides Me there is no God.... That men may know from the rising to the setting of the sun that there is no one besides Me. I am the Lord, and there is no other" (Isaiah 45:5–6).

The Nature and Constitution of Man

In Paul's approach to the philosophers and leaders of Athens (Acts 17:16–31) on the Areopagus, he began with the observation that the Areopagites were "very religious." In fact, he identified the unknown god they sensed by their speculations as the God he represented, who is the Creator of the world and all things in it, and Who gives life and breath to all things. Further, he affirmed the statement of one of their own Greek poets, arrived at apart from special revelation, "For we are His offspring" (Acts 17:29), arguing that if we are the offspring of God ("God's kind"), then one should be able to learn something about God by observing man. In this case, one should learn that God is not an idol but is the living God. Following the principle that man is "God's kind," there are certain basic characteristics of man that one can postulate of God. For instance, since man is a personal being, and is God's kind, one would expect to find that God is a personal being with a number of the characteristics of personhood that are found in man, such as life, intelligence, purpose, activity, freedom, self-consciousness, and emotional capacity. Moreover, man is a moral being with a sense of right and wrong and a conscience that "accuses or defends" him (Romans 2:15). Paul declares that those who do not have the Law of God have a law written in their hearts that makes them responsible to God. One would expect to find that God, man's Creator, is a moral being on an infinitely greater scale. Post-Reformation Protestants have generally held to the validity of natural revelation, but have regarded it as inadequate to provide a way of salvation. However, from the evidence available in the natural world, from the findings of history, and from man's moral consciousness, man ought to be able to draw the conclusion of the existence of a supreme being called God. General revelation demonstrates God's grace as He reaches out to man, it leads to an affirmation of theism, and it provides an explanation for God's righteous condemnation of the so-called heathen.

Special Revelation

Those acts of God by which He has revealed Himself and His truth to specific people at specific times in the unveiling of essential hidden realities concerning His person, His purposes, and His plans that can be known now only in and through Scripture comprise special revelation. Hebrews 1:1–2a clearly divides God's means of revelation between the Hebrews in the Old Testament era and the church in the New Testament era. We are clearly told that in time past God spoke to the (Hebrew) fathers by the prophets, and He did it in many portions and in many ways.

Many Parts and Many Ways

The phrase "many portions" relates to "progressive revelation," the concept that later revelation builds on earlier revelation in a complementary and supplementary way. The phrase "many ways" has to do with the many creative methods that God used in making His "Word" known to those for whom it was intended, such as the direct voice of God (Exodus 33:11), the hand of God (Exodus 31:18), dreams and their interpretation (Genesis 40–41), visions (Ezekiel 1:1), and the message of the prophets. His use of prophetic utterance was the major Old Testament means of revelation, as Hebrews 1:1 suggests. The prophets were chosen and gifted by God, and hence

were very aware that their message was God's, not their own. The words, "Thus says the Lord" and "The Lord said" appear over two thousand times in the Old Testament. God said to Ezekiel, "When I speak to you, I will open your mouth, and you will say to them, 'thus says the Lord God" (Ezekiel 3:27). Peter explains, "For no prophecy was ever made by an act of human will, but men moved by the Holy Spirit spoke from God" (2 Peter 1:21). Paul adds, "All Scripture is God-breathed" (2 Timothy 3:16), including both Old and New Testaments in the statements. Special revelation clearly includes propositional truth that is contained in the Scriptures and that is an accurate reproduction of that originally given. While general revelation is of great value in influencing the mind with reference to the existence of God, the Scriptures include revelation of broad areas of truth that could never be made known through it (e.g., regarding Christ and salvation). In God's providence, the Scripture includes revelation from all other sources, presents this revelation in original pure form, supplies the correct interpretation of such revelation, and is vastly superior to general revelation in nature, history, and man.

The Lord Jesus Christ

"God ... in the last of these days has spoken to us in His Son" (Hebrews 1:1–2). The final and greatest revelation of God to mankind is seen in the incarnation, in which the Son of God took upon Himself human nature and form in which He as the God-man perfectly revealed God to the world. The eternal Word of God became flesh (John 1:14); He did not come simply to bring a new revelation. He is that revelation. "No man has seen God at any time; the only begotten God. . . . He has explained Him" (John 1:18). Jesus Himself said, "He who has seen me has seen the Father" (John 14:9). The revelation of God in Christ is complete, for Paul says, "In Him all the fulness of Deity dwells in bodily form" (Colossians 2:9). It is perfect, for the writer to the Hebrews tells us that "He is the forthshining of God's glory and the exact representation of His nature" (Hebrews 1:3). It is also final, for Jesus said, "He who has seen me has seen the Father" (John 14:9). What more could God do to reveal Himself than He has already done in coming into human life and allowing mankind to see God in action in the scenes of life that he himself knows by his own experience?

The revelation of God in Christ is not limited to the expression of the whole complex of divine attributes (characteristics that are inseparable from the idea of God) in His person. He is called by divine names (God, Lord, Son of God); divine works are predicated of Him (Creation, preservation, providential guidance of history, forgiveness of sin, answered prayer, Resurrection, final judgment); worship that belongs to God alone is offered to Christ now by the heavenly host and by believers, and ultimately will be offered to Him by all created intelligence; and claims were made by Christ for Himself that could be true only of one who is God. Recorded in the Gospel of John, for example, are the following: "I am the door" (10:9), "I am the bread of life" (6:35), "I am the Light of the world" (8:12, 9:5), " I am the resurrection and the life"(11:25), "I am the true vine" (15:1), "I am the way, and the truth, and the life" (14:6). In addition to all this, He spoke the message of God to the people of His day ("I speak these things as the Father has taught Me," John 8:28); salvation and eternal life are through Jesus Christ alone (John 3:16–18; 6:29); worship is not a matter of place but of inner relationship to God (John 4:21–24); the Holy Spirit will come to indwell believers (John 7:37–39; 14:16–26; 15:26–27; 16:7–15; Acts 1:5); Christ will return for His own (John 14:1–3); and these words embody the message of God for us today. While the revelation of God in Christ is the complete, perfect, and final revelation of God, that revelation is found in the Bible, which presents the only authentic portrait of Christ in His revelation of God.

Conclusion

The revelation of God in the natural world, in history, in the constitutional makeup of man, in the Bible, and in Jesus Christ gives rich meaning to the statement of Paul in Acts 14:16–17, "He did not leave Himself without witness." The witness of God to the world is complete, containing in it sufficient light to illumine the mind and heart of every person. It is the responsibility of human beings to turn to the light, embrace it, and find their whole beings enlightened by Him who said, "I am the Light of the world" (John 8:12, 9:5).

Wayne S. Flory

See also Second Coming

Bibliography

Arndt, William F., and F. Wilbur Gingrich, trans. and ed. (1979) *A Greek-English Lexicon of the New Testament*. Chicago: University of Chicago Press.

Erickson, Millard J. (1997) *Introducing Christian Doctrine*. Grand Rapids, MI: Baker Book House.

Friedrich, Gerhard, ed. (1974) *Theological Dictionary of the New Testament*, vol. III. Grand Rapids, MI: Wm. B. Eerdmans.

Pache, Rene. (1969) *The Inspiration and Authority of Scripture*. Chicago: Moody Press.

Ryrie, Charles Caldwell. (1986) *Basic Theology*. Chicago: Moody Press.

Tenney, Merrill C., ed. (1968). *The Bible the Living Word of Revelation*. Grand Rapids, MI: Zondervan Publishing.

Thiessen, Henry Clarence, and Rev. Vernon D. Doerksen. (1979) *Lectures in Systematic Theology*. Grand Rapids, MI: William B. Eerdmans.

Warfield, Benjamin Breckinridge. (1948) *The Inspiration and Authority of the Bible*. Philadelphia: The Presbyterian and Reformed Publishing Company.

Revival

Revival is a bringing back to life, or a renewal of activity, effectiveness, or vigor. Revival brings improvement to existing customs, traditions, practices, ideas, or methods. Among Evangelicals, the word means a reawakening of believers to be more active and committed in their spiritual responsibilities both to God and man. Revival is also a call to repentance and being born again.

The term "revival" has been applied to facets of human endeavors other than religious ones. There is economic revival, indicating an improvement in the economic situation of a country and betterment in the living conditions. There is also sociocultural revival, which deals with the process by which a people seek to improve on the existing customs and traditions. Closely related to sociocultural revival is political revival, which involves changes in the political system, government, foreign policy, or electoral system. Despite its varied application, the term is used frequently in the religious sphere, connoting a call to awake the faithful from syncretism, permissiveness, and indifference to the tenets of religion. When there is spiritual laxity, there is usually a need for an awakening to spiritual fervency, inciting the faithful to be more sober and more vigilant in their religious obligations and spiritual responsibilities. The synonym "renewal" is also commonly used.

Spiritual Revival in the Bible

The Bible contains several calls for spiritual revival, and evidences the course and results of revivals. These calls were from the prophets to the people to return to God. Two prominent examples of such calls were those of Hosea and Amos. Hosea, a prophet in eighth century BCE, was married to Gomer, a harlot, who continued her waywardness while still married to Hosea. This story was used to illustrate Israel's disloyalty and unfaithfulness to God. Hosea preached of God's judgment, and called for a religious revival. Prophet Amos, a contemporary of Hosea, preached in the northern kingdom of Israel against oppression, moral laxity, and spiritual apostasy, and emphasized the need for a national revival to stem God's judgment. The prophet Samuel promoted a revival early in his ministry (1 Samuel 7:3–6), but a more detailed illustration of the course of revival was that of King Josiah whose religious reform was preceded by a revival (2 Kings 22, 23; 2 Chronicles 34, 35). The Pentecost in Acts 2, which marked the inauguration of the Christian Church, was another major revival. New Testament books such as the Hebrews and Paul's letters to the Corinthians also contain messages calling for repentance and revival.

Religious Revivals in History

The history of Christianity contains numerous instances of revivals, commonly occurring following a period of religious apathy. Some of the revivals gave rise to significant religious and social movements in human history. Monasticism, which began in the Egyptian desert in the third century CE, was one of the earliest movements; however, its seclusion and the withdrawal of hermits from the society limited its impact. The religious Crusades of the eleventh and thirteenth centuries were sustained by calls to uphold the Christian ideal and its noble past. The Protestant Reformation of the sixteenth and early seventeenth centuries brought much revival to an ailing church, and eventually had great impact on the political and social history of Europe. Martin Luther's attack on indulgences and papal abuses

and his call for a reform of the church's structures in the tract *An Appeal to the Ruling Class of German Nationality As to the Amelioration of the State of Christendom* (1520) were projected further by the radical reformers to include a personal moral renewal. Catholic Reformation of the sixteenth century marked the beginning of a revivalist tradition in the Roman Catholic Church. German Pietism of the seventeenth and early eighteenth centuries is yet another example of a religious revival. William Carey's sermon at a meeting of a Baptist association in England in 1791 initiated a revival of Christian missions among Protestant churches. But perhaps the most enduring revival has been the Pentecostal and Charismatic Renewal of the twentieth century, which centered on a new awareness of the Holy Spirit and its various manifestations. Not all revivals have been worldwide, however. The Great Awakening in North America in the eighteenth century, the Welsh Revivals in the mid-nineteenth and early twentieth centuries, the Balokole in East Africa in the 1930s to the 1950s, and the Aladura revivals in Nigeria in the 1930s and 1940s are some examples of national revivals. A common denominator to all these revivals is the expansion of the frontiers of religion, resulting in an increase in converts and territorial acquisition. Moreover, their impact has permeated the social and political spheres of their societies.

Revivals are not a phenomenon limited to the Christian faith; they have been documented in other religions, particularly in Islam. In 1979, the call of Ayatollah Khomeini in Iran to a revival had an important political and social impact. Traditional religions in Africa have witnessed somewhat of a revival in the post-independence era of the 1960s and 1970s. However, it is among Christian Fundamentalists and Evangelicals that revival has had the most impact in the mid-twentieth century.

Sources of Revival

There is no general agreement on the source or initiator of religious revival. Some opined that revival is of divine origin, hence God is the sole initiator, and He is the only one who can revive people from their spiritual inertia. To others, revival is purely of human origin. It occurs as humans perceive their spiritual conditions and see the need for revival. Necessary steps are then taken to bring about this revival. However, humans must be ready for revival because if they are not, God cannot help them attain it. Others have taken the middle course, maintaining that revival is both of divine and human origins. In this view, revival occurs as a result of God's mercy on human's pathetic and deplorable spiritual state. Thus, God can inspire believers to yearn and pray for revival, after which God answers. Even when God decides to send revival, man must still cooperate with God; without man's cooperation, the needed revival will not occur.

Steps to revival may include intense prayer coupled with fasting, evangelistic sermons, and devotion to the word of God. In recent times, religious services or evangelistic meetings called "revival services" are often organized with guest ministers. These services can last from a few days to several weeks. The objective of these services is to seek the face of God so that His people can be revived spiritually.

The revivalistic methods are as varied as the locations of the revival meetings. The English Methodists in the eighteenth century used itinerant preachers, while the American Methodists and Baptists of the late-eighteenth-century Second Great Awakening held camp meetings. Dwight L. Moody, a prominent evangelist of this same period, organized mass evangelistic campaigns. In the latter half of the twentieth century, some revivalists appropriated media technology, particularly the television, to reach a wider audience over a greater distance. Whatever the method, evangelistic preaching has always dominated revivals. Great evangelists such as Charles G. Finney, William B. Sprague, Dwight L. Moody, John Wesley, George Whitefield, Charles Spurgeon, were not only great preachers, but also wrote inspirational lectures on revival.

Phases and Modes of Revival

The revival process seems to follow two alternating phases. The first phase is that of indifference and degeneration. The pathetic situation will then be discussed along with ways in which to improve it. An appropriate solution will then be debated. The second phase is that of renewal or revival. During this time, the situation will have improved, and solutions will have been found. This phase will continue until a new degeneration sets in and the process will start all over again.

Revival can be corporate in that all the people will see their pathetic condition and the need for improvement. The people will then work together to

bring about the desired improvement. In other cases, a single person or several persons will first see the need for an improvement in their religious situation and may instigate the revivals. They will start to enlighten others on how they can corporately seek improvement in the situation. In this type of revival, the process may be prolonged and slow. Revival may also be spontaneous in which nobody planned for it; it just occurred unexpectedly. However, in many cases it is planned for and expected. Some revivals are peaceful and quiet while others may be violent and chaotic. Any revival that is not managed well will eventually result in degeneration, necessitating a call for yet another revival.

The Character and Results of Revivals

Religious revival meetings usually appeal to the emotions of believers, and religious activities such as loud singing, clapping, dancing, rolling, weeping, and in the 1990s, "holy laughter" are common experiences. These experiential elements also go simultaneously with personal commitment. Very often revival meetings are marked by a conversion experience with public confession and testimonies. In fact, pietistic concerns for personal spiritual faith become the overriding concern. Traditional rites and ceremonies are of less importance, and may be derided. Religious formalism is the first casualty in any revival. The laity assume prominence and constant Bible studies become the bulwark sustaining revivals.

Some revivals could assume national dimension when sins are projected beyond the sphere of the individual and made central to the society as a whole. In such cases, the believers would claim to confess the sins of the entire population and seek national repentance. Moreover, revivals engender creativity and allow for consideration of new patterns of worship. Hence, Christian practices, rather than rational knowledge, receive much attention. Revivalists often call believers to be faithful to the Scriptures. However, revivals often breed an antimodernist ideology because liberalism is closely associated with modern tendencies.

Evangelical and Fundamentalist philosophies often converge in revivalism. The centrality of the authority of the Scriptures has always been the basis of the direct evangelistic preaching in revival services, and the acceptance of the universal need of the new birth has enabled both Evangelicals and Fundamentalists to call for repentance and faith in Jesus Christ. Lastly, both accept that evangelization and world missions are imperative to prolonging revivals.

Revivals, apart from producing zealousness in religious matters, have regularly stimulated social actions much as the English Evangelicals did in the late eighteenth and early nineteenth centuries, and the Salvation Army in the late nineteenth century. For Fundamentalists, revivals generally resulted in greater commitment to evangelistic and missionary activities for individual Christians and churches. Some revivals, however, produced results not initially envisaged. For example, the revival promoted by John Wesley eventually produced a separate Methodist Church. The Pentecostal and Charismatic Renewal effectuated a plethora of independent churches and Bible study groups in the twentieth century.

Conclusion

Revivals contribute to and sustain the growth of Evangelicalism and Fundamentalism. Rapid growth of churches following significant revivals was commonplace in Christian history. Significant moral, social, and cultural changes accompanied some past awakenings. Divisions among Christian churches often lessened during revivals; instead, ecumenical cooperation was encouraged. Critics have, however, derided the unbridled emotionalism and extremism, the propensity to separatism, occasional intolerance and a holier-than-thou attitude on the part of revivalists and their followers, as well as the promotion of morality based largely on legalistic codes, anticlericalism, and anti-intellectualism. Nevertheless, revivalism has continued to inspire church leaders to greater heights, mobilized laypersons for Christian ministry, encouraged an intimate relationship with God, and generally advanced the frontiers of Christianity into new epochs and new territories.

Matthews A. Ojo

See also African-American Holiness-Pentecostal Movement; Evangelicalism; Great Awakening; Hinduism, Fundamental; Islamic Fundamentalism; Judaism, Fundamental; Preaching

Bibliography

Ammerman Nancy T. (1991) "North American Protestant Fundamentalism." In *Fundamentalism Observed,* edited by Marty E. Martin and R. Scott Appleby. Chicago: University of Chicago Press.

Chadwick, Owen. (1972) *The Reformation.* Harmondsworth, UK: Penguin Books.

Hoover, Stewart M. (1988) *Mass Media Religion: The Social Sources of the Electronic Church.* Newbury Park, CA: Sage.

Isichei, Elizabeth. (1995) *A History of Christianity in Africa: From Antiquity to the Present.* Grand Rapids, MI: Wm. B. Eerdmans.

Marsden, George M. (1980) *Fundamentalism and American Culture: The Shaping of Twentieth-Century Evangelicalism, 1870–1925.* New York: Oxford University Press.

McLaughlin, W. G. (1959) *Modern Revivalism: Charles Grandison Finney to Billy Graham.* New York: Ronald Press Co.

———. (1978) *Revivals, Awakenings, and Reform.* Chicago: University of Chicago Press.

Pousson, Edward Keith. (1994) "A 'Great Century' of Pentecostal/Charismatic Renewal and Missions." *PNEUMA: The Journal of the Society for Pentecostal Studies* 1 (16): 81–100.

Sprague, William B. (1958) *Lectures on Revivals of Religion.* Edinburgh: The Banner of Truth Trust.

Rock Music

Fundamentalists and Evangelicals have given rock music a mixed reception since its emergence in the 1950s. Some have decried rock and roll as a tool of the devil, while others have embraced it as the best way to evangelize modern youth. The history of this reception has involved the appearance in the 1970s of the contemporary Christian music (CCM) industry, today a $300– to $500–million-dollar enterprise. The drive for market share on the part of CCM executives has profoundly shaped acceptance or rejection of rock music among conservative Protestants.

Evangelicals and Fundamentalists in the 1950s and 1960s shared with many middle-class Americans a racially influenced distaste for rock music. They deemed it both sexually explicit and, because of its beat, savage "jungle music." Some held that rock music's beat could actually lead to demon possession. A story circulated among Fundamentalists (probably apocryphal) in which a missionary to Africa played rock music to native Africans. They quickly begged the missionary to turn off the music because it was calling up demons.

These reactions only intensified in the 1970s as rock musicians increasingly incorporated overt themes of drugs, sex, and the occult into their music. This decade marked the beginnings of a concerted Fundamentalist attack on the forces of rock music. Small Christian publishers released widely circulating books by authors such as Bob Larson and Jeff Godwin, documenting in painstaking detail the alleged evils of rock music. These works gave voice to anxieties about the future of the American youth, and they questioned teen idolization of morally compromised rock stars. The most impassioned, however, held that rock and roll itself was a tool of Satan to destroy moral civilization. They evidenced heavy metal album covers visually representing Satanic forces on the loose and apocalyptic lyrics decrying organized Christianity. Some even found hidden Satanic messages imbedded in the music when played backwards, called *backward masking*. According to Fundamentalists, all of these trends stemmed naturally from rock music's Satanic beat, making it dangerous to susceptible young minds. By the late 1970s church youth groups were sponsoring rock music seminars, such as Dan and Steve Peters's "Truth about Rock" seminar, which purported to expose demonic influences as well as give youth opportunities to set their rock records and cassettes on fire. According to Jeff Godwin, "Rock & Roll and Jesus Christ are completely incompatible" (1985: 277).

This Manichaean stance among Fundamentalists toward culture generally and rock music specifically challenged emerging CCM labels and artists. Except for gospel-style lyrics, CCM was virtually indistinguishable from its "secular" counterpart. While the CCM industry welcomed critiques of secular rock and roll, they endeavored to weaken the appeal of the Fundamentalist argument against rock as a music form. The burgeoning contemporary Christian market thus fed a divided mind among Fundamentalists and Evangelicals. While some condemned rock music outright, increasingly more discriminated between Christian rock's evangelistic orientation and secular rock's humanistic and profiteering goals. William Romanowski (2000) argues that CCM actually helped to create an Evangelical popular culture separated from the life of churches. Christian concerts, like the revival services in the nineteenth century, became places of worship; CCM

compact disks and T-shirts became symbols of religious faith.

The 1980s and 1990s brought respectability to CCM, but not without further controversy. When Amy Grant's *Age to Age* (1982) reached platinum sales, major record companies like A&M began to seek distribution arrangements with CCM labels. The result was that within a decade a handful of songs by Christian artists "crossed over" to secular pop charts. This crossover caused another wave of alarm among Fundamentalists who had awkwardly made their peace with CCM during the 1980s. Now, Christian crossover music contained little that would distinguish it from secular rock. For example, when Grant's lyrics dropped much of their explicitly Christian content in the late 1980s and 1990s, many Christian bookstores and radio stations refused to carry and play her music. Overall, however, the general trend in the past twenty years has been the spread of a relatively more sophisticated theology of art and culture among conservative Protestants (Peacock 1999; Lawhead 1987).

R. Bryan Bademan

See also Antimodernism; Gospel Music; Secularism

Bibliography

Godwin, Jeff. (1985) *The Devil's Disciples: The Truth about Rock*. Chino, CA: Chick Publications.

Howard, Jay R., and John M. Streck. (1999) *Apostles of Rock: The Splintered World of Contemporary Christian Music*. Lexington: University Press of Kentucky.

Joseph, Mark. (1999) *The Rock & Roll Rebellion: Why People of Faith Abandoned Rock Music and Why They're Coming Back*. Nashville, TN: Broadman and Holman Publishers.

Larson, Bob. (1971) *Rock and the Church*. Carol Stream, IL: Creation House.

Lawhead, Steve. (1987) *Rock of This Age: The Real & Imagined Dangers of Rock Music*. Downers Grove, IL: InterVarsity Press.

Peacock, Charlie. (1999) *At the Crossroads: An Insider's Look at the Past, Present, and Future of Contemporary Christian Music*. Nashville, TN: Broadman and Holman Publishers.

Peters, Dan, and Steve Peters, with Cher Merrill. (1984) *Why Knock Rock?* Minneapolis, MN: Bethany House Publishers.

———. (1985) *Rock's Hidden Persuader: The Truth about Backmasking*. Minneapolis, MN: Bethany House Publishers.

Romanowski, William D. (1992) "Roll Over Beethoven, Tell Martin Luther the News: American Evangelicals and Rock Music." *Journal of American Culture* 15 (Fall): 79–88.

———. (1996) *Pop Culture Wars: Religion and the Role of Entertainment in American Life*. Downers Grove, IL: InterVarsity Press.

———. (2000) "Evangelicals and Popular Music: The Contemporary Christian Music Industry." In *Religion and Popular Culture in America*, edited by Bruce David Forbes and Jeffrey H. Mahan. Berkeley: University of California Press.

S

Sacrament

The word "sacrament" is from the Latin *sacraméntum*, meaning sacred, holy, or consecrated. A sacrament, in an ecclesial sense, refers to an ordinance or ceremonial rite that the church performs and participates in. This word is used in Jerome's (c. 347–420) Latin Vulgate (completed in c. 384) for the Greek *mystçrion*, which is most often translated as "mystery" in the New Testament (e.g., Ephesians 1:9; 3:3, 9; 5:32; Colossians 1:27; 1 Timothy 3:16; Revelation 1:20; 17:7), but can also refer to a secret, oath, or a rite in Greek classical literature.

Baptism and the Lord's Supper are the two primary sacramental rites of the early church. Both are rites instituted by Jesus Christ (Matthew 28:19–20; Luke 22:19–20). Significantly, the two sacraments are linked together in several passages in the Old and New Testaments. Not only are baptism and the Lord's Supper found in succession but circumcision and the Passover meal are seen as the counterparts of baptism and the Lord's Supper. The Israelites are commanded in Exodus 12 to observe regulations concerning the Passover meal (43). Circumcision is a prerequisite for Passover participation: "No uncircumcised male may eat of it" (48, NIV). Circumcision as a sign of the covenant represented inauguration into the covenant community. Passover represented the deliverance and liberation of Israel from the Egyptians.

The same succession of the two rites is found in the New Testament. Paul writes about the Exodus event and connects baptism and the Lord's Supper with the baptism in the Red Sea and the eating of the wilderness manna and the water from the Rock (1 Corinthians 10:1–2; cf. Acts 2:37–47; Colossians 2:11–12).

The apologist Justin Martyr (c.100–165) records the first instance of the sacraments of baptism and the Lord's Supper. Although, church fathers Tertullian (c. 196–212) and Augustine (c. 354–430) used the word "sacrament" to refer to many mysterious and spiritual theological topics, they did develop and systemize the rites into doctrines. In particular, Augustine viewed the sacraments as outward visible signs of the invisible graces of God. In medieval scholasticism, two figures expand the list of sacraments from two to seven. Peter Lombard (c. 1100–1159), in his work *Libri Quattuor Sententiarum* (Four Books of Sentences), added five lesser sacraments: confirmation, matrimony, penance, ordination, and extreme unction. These were confirmed by Thomas Aquinas (1225–1274) and adapted by the Catholic Church at the Council of Florence (1439) and reaffirmed at the Council of Trent (1547). Hugo of Victor (c1142) named as many as thirty sacraments in his *De Sacramentis Christianae Fidei*. Today, Greek Orthodoxy, Roman Catholicism, and Anglicanism accept all seven sacraments.

The Reformers viewed the five additional sacraments as not only an exaggeration of the Bible but as the product of institutionalism. They acknowledge only the two primary sacraments, baptism and the Lord's Supper, as instituted by Christ. The doctrine of *ex ópere operáto*, which is the belief that God works through the act of administering the sacrament in its outward form, in favor of the primacy of faith as the

Matthew 28:19–20

19. Go ye therefore, and teach all nations, baptizing them in the name of the Father, and of the Son, and of the Holy Ghost:

20. Teaching them to observe all things whatsoever I have commanded you: and, lo, I am with you always, even unto the end of the world. Amen.

Luke 22:19–20

19. And he took bread, and gave thanks, and brake it, and gave unto them, saying, This is my body which is given for you: this do in remembrance of me.

20. Likewise also the cup after supper, saying, This cup is the new testament in my blood, which is shed for you.

efficacy of the sacrament, was also denied. The Reformers recaptured the conviction that the two sacraments are two movements of the one mystery of Christ. Christ works in and through the sacraments as both the gift and the giver, the offering and the one who offers. The double movement of Christ in the sacraments is a means by which He sustains His body, the Church, between his First and Second Comings (Calvin 1989: 492). Therefore, baptism is the mystery of incorporation into the body of Christ and the Lord's Supper is the renewal of incorporation into the body of Christ. It is neither the act of baptism or partaking of the Lord's Supper, nor the elements of water, bread, and wine, nor the one who administers the sacraments, that evokes the movement of grace as sustenance. Only as the mystery of Christ works through the sacraments by means of His Holy Spirit do the rites have meaning and effectiveness.

Apart from Reformed churches, most Evangelical and Fundamentalist churches use the language of "ordinance," "ceremony," or "rite" when referring to baptism and the Lord's Supper. Sacramentalism is seen as being a carry-over from Catholicism and implies an institutionalization of tradition that is viewed as a supersession of the New Testament teachings on the matter. Unlike Augustine or Calvin, contemporary Evangelicals understand baptism and the Lord's Supper as being simply a visible sign or commemorative event of what Christ *did* and does not refer to what Christ is *doing*. In this manner, the sacraments are to teach and admonish believers the great truths of the New Testament (Hodge 1995: 498) and to represent the separation of believers from the world. They are not a means of sustaining the church. Baptism represents the believer's cleansing from all sin and guilt. The Lord's Supper is understood as a commemorative meal to remind believers of Christ's sacrificial atonement on their behalf. In both of these instances the sacraments are understood as personal reminders of the work of Christ on behalf of the individual. Catholicism, Greek Orthodoxy, and some Reformed churches have a more communal understanding of sacrament; baptism is an inauguration into the body of Christ (the Church) and the Lord's Supper (Eucharist) is a means of continual participation (communion) with Christ and His body.

Robert T. Leach

See also Baptism; Lord's Supper

Bibliography

Beveridge, Henry, tr. (1989) "Calvin, John." In *Institutes of the Christian Religion*, reprint ed. Grand Rapids, MI: Wm. B. Eerdmans, 491–511.

Erikson, Millard. (1985) *Christian Theology*. Grand Rapids, MI: Baker Book House.

Hodge, Charles. (1995) *Systematic Theology*, vol. 3. Grand Rapids, MI: Wm. B. Eerdmans.

Schaff, Philip. (1996) *History of the Christian Church*, vols. 5 and 6. Peabody, MA: Hendrickson.

Torrance, Thomas F. (1976) "The Paschal Mystery of Christ and the Eucharist." *Liturgical Review* 1: 6–12.

Westminster Confession of Faith (1646). Electronic version © 1991 by BibleWorks, L.L.C.

Salvation

The doctrine of salvation is one of the most explored Christian teachings. In the early developments of the doctrine, attempts focused on interpreting the word from the premises of the Scriptures. While salvation is still a primary doctrine of Christianity, different perspectives from which the notion has been approached lately seem to be of interest. For example, attempts have been made to define salvation from cultural perspectives. Hence, it is possible to look at salvation from an African perspective, from an Asian perspective, and so on. Soteriology, the systematic treatment of the doctrine of salvation, is very broad in scope and includes aspects such as the historical development of the doctrine, analysis, comparison and interpretation of all biblical terms applying to salvation, especially as taught by Jesus Christ, and the relationship of His death to atonement, and much more. Hence, only a brief and general discussion of salvation can be attempted here.

The Meaning of Salvation

The simplest definition of salvation is of rescue, deliverance, and liberation. It is deliverance from some real or potential danger. Examples may include deliverance from physical illness, or from visible enemies. In the biblical and theological perspectives, salvation portrays an experience in which a person is made spiritually whole in God through Christ. Salvation is often restricted to deliverance from the consequences of Satanic influence and sin. This conception of salvation emphasizes undeserved mercy when God graciously brings restoration and wholeness to a person. The understanding of salvation as deliverance from sin and its consequence of spiritual death is an important doctrine in Evangelical Christianity.

Salvation in the Bible

In the Old Testament, salvation is depicted concretely and is usually described as deliverance and liberation from adverse situations and negative conditions of life such as physical liberation from visible things, and deliverance from danger or evil. The history of the Israelites furnishes adequate examples of God's acts of salvation to the entire nation. These include salvation from the bondage in Egypt, from dangers of aggression from enemies, from exile in Babylon, and from famine. God always consciously delivered His people. Individuals also experienced salvation, particularly when healed of their diseases.

During the intertestamental period, the idea of a messianic deliverance became a general Jewish religious thought. This salvation to be wrought by the Messiah was expected to include political, national, and religious elements. However, Jews opposed the ministry of Jesus because He did not fulfill the messianic expectation of the people, though He frequently ascribed messianic titles to Himself.

The Old Testament concept was continued in the New Testament, especially in the Gospel narratives. Jesus' miraculous healings of the sick, the blind, the lame, the deaf and dumb, and His miracles, which include bringing relief to those tormented by evil forces, feeding the hungry, are examples of deliverance from dangers. Early in His ministry, Jesus applies a prophecy from Isaiah 61:1–2 to Himself indicating that the salvation He brings is comprehensive enough to take care of most physical and spiritual needs of humans (see Luke 4:17–21). Later in Jesus' ministry, the notion of salvation took on a new dimension that emphasized salvation from sin. In the letters of apostle Paul, salvation was elaborated upon to mean primarily deliverance from sin and the wrath of God. This salvation was available only in the atoning death of Jesus and could be received by faith alone. This spiritual perception was derived from a new understanding of the significance of the death of Jesus on the cross. To Paul and the apostles, the historical Jesus was the Messiah, but not in the manner the Jewish nation was expecting. His vicarious death has a universal application to all people everywhere. The understanding of salvation from this context makes it a present, continuous, and future event.

The Need for Salvation

The need for salvation arises from the desire of humans to be free from troubles, problems, and bondage. The helplessness of humans in the face of grievous situations and predicaments necessitates a solution. In Christian theology, salvation is needed because of the depravity and sinfulness of humans, which has made God to declare them guilty of sin. Sin is any failure to conform to the moral laws of God in act, attitude, or nature. It includes every personal wrongdoing, such as infringement of the laws of a society, and all attitudes contrary to God's moral laws. Salvation is therefore seen as a willing submission to God's provision in Christ as the only source of redemption from the penalty of sin. To Evangelicals and Fundamentalists, the genesis of man's depravity occurred with the Fall of Adam and Eve when they disobeyed God's instruction not to eat from the Tree of Knowledge. Their death, after eating "the forbidden fruit," was a spiritual rather than a physical one. God promptly punished them and drove them out of the Garden of Eden. Christians believe that this event marked the beginning of the strained relationship between God and humankind. The consequences of this sin were passed on to the entire human race; thus, all humans are born with a sinful nature and are under the judgment of God.

The Process of Obtaining Salvation

The process of obtaining salvation varies from one religion to the other. Even within Christianity, there is no general agreement on whether salvation can be obtained by faith alone or by faith and good works, which Catholics have traditionally affirmed. The position of faith alone was popularized about 1512 by Martin Luther from his own experience and his study of the Book of Romans. In the traditional religions, the means of salvation is mainly by propitiation of the gods through sacrifices and rituals that would appease the supreme deity to have mercy on the adherents and forgive them their sins. In the Asian religions, the means of salvation is meditation, which helps to liberate the soul from earthly bondage and forces of evil. In Islam, salvation from future punishment is by obedience and submission to Allah, and particularly the observance of the five pillars of Islam, which are *Shahaddah* (faith), *salawat* (praying five times daily), *zakat* (alms giving), *ºaum* (fasting during the month of Ramadan), and *hajj* (going on pilgrimage to the Holy land at least once in one's life). In Christianity, Christ is the only means of salvation. Salvation begins for the sinner when he or she considers the precarious situation, the impending penalty, and decides to accept God's offer of salvation. Accepting this offer begins first with repentance. By exercising repentance the sinner is forgiven and reconciled to God from whom he or she has previously been estranged. Thereafter, the believer accepts by faith the atoning death of Jesus as applicable to his or her situation. Thus, the sinner is "born again."

Some Christians argue that humans can earn their salvation through their own initiatives and efforts. Hence, people engage in "good work" so that they can please God, get His pardon, and earn salvation. Good works include abstinence from certain food, drink and sex, denial of worldly pleasure, celibacy, fasting, meditation, and ascetic living. However, Evangelicals believe that salvation is not earned by any human effort or merit, but is a gift of God. God, and not the sinner, is the initiator and provider of the means of salvation; the sinner is powerless to save him or herself. Acts of goodwill are only beneficial after the gracious offer of God's salvation in Christ has been accepted and appropriated into a sinner's life by faith and repentance. However, others have taken a middle course, maintaining that offers of salvation, although initiated by God, can either be accepted or rejected by humans.

Conservative Evangelicals believe that salvation is essentially spiritual, and must be in the foreground of any discussion of the issue. Therefore, salvation must not be understood only in terms of deliverance from negative conditions of contemporary life such as famine, wars, disease, poverty, economic and political exploitation, as the liberals affirm. Although these physical issues are biblical and desirable, Evangelicals still insist that sin is at the root of all human problems, hence, salvation must be accomplished by virtue of voluntary faith in Jesus Christ and the subsequent redemption from sin.

Stages of Salvation

To some, salvation is a one-time experience. Salvation is not a physical event but when it occurs, it is life-changing; there is a complete transformation in lifestyle, thinking, disposition, affection, and behavior. Others insist that salvation is not instantaneous but gradual and progressive. As one increases in the knowledge of God, one continues to realize one's shortcomings and make amendments, and continue to grow in salvation.

Can salvation be lost? This is a controversial issue among the Evangelicals and Fundamentalists. To some, salvation is lost when a saved person commits a sin. Others maintain that salvation cannot be lost because a saved person is kept by the power of God. Even when a responsible person sins, he or she will soon realize it and come back to God. Is salvation for all? This is another controversial issue. Calvinists maintain that salvation is only for the elect, that is, those who have been predestined to be saved. Hence, those who have not been predestined for salvation cannot be saved even when they hear the gospel. The Arminians, on the other hand, insist that salvation is for all. All humans can be saved provided they hear the gospel that can transform their lives. Evangelism is therefore the responsibility of all Christians so that everyone can hear the gospel and obtain salvation.

Contemporary and Fundamentalists' Emphases on Salvation

Sociologists have stated that salvation can be understood culturally. For example, African charismatics often interpret salvation beyond the biblical concept to include deliverance from idolatry, ancestral curses, and social bondage, which prevent a fulfilling life for the present generation. In addition, they strive for the removal of all those factors and forces adversely affecting the sociopolitical and economic situation of the countries. In Fundamentalism, salvation is the idea around which all doctrinal emphases and practices are built. Because Fundamentalists see salvation as a life-changing event, it has also become the most important doctrine distinguishing them from the unbelieving world and other Christians. Fundamentalists are proud to claim the assurance of salvation. This salvation centers on the acceptance of Jesus as a personal Savior. In addition, boundaries and limits are set for acceptable and unacceptable behaviors for Fundamentalists. A sanctified life and a life of separation from worldly values are important characteristics of this religious culture.

Having this personal assurance of salvation, every Fundamentalist is expected to evangelize about Jesus to nonbelievers and bring them into the Kingdom of God. Radio and television broadcasts, tract distribution, in addition to the traditional method of personal witnessing, are some of the methods regularly used. Within church services, evangelistic sermons are followed by an invitation to accept the message of salvation.

Conclusion

While salvation is a universal religious belief, it is considered a primary doctrine of Christianity. Although Christians generally agree on the definition of salvation, and that it is a need of all humans regard-less of their spiritual or physical situation, there are countless other views that depend on the religious background of the person. Evangelicals and Fundamentalists, however, center their understanding of salvation on the atoning death of Jesus. Were it not for this insistence, Fundamentalism might have disintegrated or fossilized from the onslaught of modernism.

The doctrine of salvation has been shaped not only by the biblical understanding of the word but also from a variety of cultural, theological, and ideological forces. The paradigm of deliverance has been taken up by many seeking to improve humankind. It is as relevant to liberation theology as it is to those who fought to overthrow colonialism in the twentieth century, and to those still struggling to eradicate poverty in developing countries. However, Fundamentalists insist that the spiritual dimension must always be the primary focus of the term. Only then can sinners be redeemed from the condemnation of sin and thus obtain salvation.

Matthews A. Ojo

See also Fall of Humankind; Sanctification; Sin and Sinners

Bibliography

Ammerman, Nancy T. (1987) *Bible Believers: Fundamentalists in the Modern World.* New Brunswick, NJ: Rutgers University Press.

Brown, D. Lavonn. (1978) *The Doctrine of Salvation.* Nashville, TN: Convention Press.

Dillistone, F. W. (1967) *The Christian Understanding of Atonement.* Welwyn, Herts, UK: James Nisbet and Company.

Green, E. M. B. (1965) *The Meaning of Salvation.* London: Hodder and Stoughton.

Grudem, Wayne. (1994) *Systematic Theology.* Grand Rapids, MI: Zondervan Publishing.

Hogue, C. B. (1978) *The Doctrine of Salvation.* Nashville, TN: Convention Press.

McIntyre, John. (1992) *The Shape of Soteriology.* Edinburgh: T and T Clark.

Salvation Army, The

The Salvation Army is an Evangelical Christian body with one million members in 108 countries and

Statues of William Booth and Catherine Booth in front of the William Booth Memorial Training College of the Salvation Army in Camberwell, London. PHOTO COURTESY OF KAREN CHRISTENSEN.

territories, and 125,000 members in the United States. While it is technically a church, the Army also acts as a social service provider, and offers humanitarian aid during crises and emergencies. In the United States, the Army is best known for its philanthropy and, during the 1990s, became the nation's largest charitable fund-raiser.

A British-based movement, the Salvation Army began in 1865 as the Christian Mission. Thirteen years later, William Booth, the group's founder, changed its name to the Salvation Army, adopting both martial language and a military structure. Members were called soldiers, clergy were officers, and churches became corps. The Army undertook a religious crusade to save the unchurched, using colorful antics, including brass bands, women preachers, and bois-

terous parades to attract the masses. In 1880, Booth sent his first official missionaries to the New World. Disembarking at Castle Garden, the immigrant absorption center in lower Manhattan, the eight-member landing party dropped to the ground and claimed America for God. For the next several days, the group proselytized throughout the city—marching from uptown street corners to downtown missions and from Harry Hill's Concert Saloon on the Lower East Side to the Hudson River Hall in midtown's West Side.

The Army was as controversial in America as it was in Great Britain. Its rigorous faith and commitment to full-time service attracted many young people. Officers worked full-time, and rules of discipline regulated what they wore, where they lived, and

MISSION STATEMENT OF THE SALVATION ARMY USA

The Salvation Army, an international movement, is an evangelical part of the universal Christian Church. Its message is based on the Bible. Its ministry is motivated by the Love of God. Its mission is to preach the gospel of Jesus Christ and to meet human needs in His name without discrimination.

Source: The Salvation Army USA. www.salvationarmyusa.org.

VISION STATEMENT OF THE UK TERRITORY OF THE SALVATION ARMY

We will be a Spirit-filled, radical, growing movement with a burning desire to:
   lead people into a saving knowledge of Jesus Christ
   actively serve the community
   fight for social justice

Source: www.salvationarmy.org.uk

---

how they behaved in all circumstances. Women were particularly drawn to the movement since, treated as men's equals, they had opportunities for adventure and leadership that few others avenues offered. While the Army was, first and foremost, an Evangelical mission, its leaders soon realized the difficulty of reaching people whose desperate physical needs prevented them from hearing a spiritual message. In an 1890 book, *In Darkest England and the Way Out*, William Booth proposed a scheme for "social salvation" to complement religious outreach. American Salvationists, also moving in this direction, were establishing a national network of social services including shelters, cheap hotels, and "rescue homes" for fallen women. Today that network includes homes for families with AIDS, adult rehabilitation centers for substance abusers, and after-school centers for children and youth.

Salvationist theology draws on Wesleyan, Holiness, and Quaker strains. Adherents subscribe to eleven doctrines, including an inerrant Bible, justification by grace through faith, and bodily resurrection, which mark them as conservative Christians. Salvationists also believe in sanctification, a second baptism that cleanses the heart (enabling believers to lead simple, holy lives) and empowers them for service (attending to others' spiritual and material welfare). William Booth's theology, while definitive, was subordinate to his notion of "practical religion." Thus, even though Army theology leads to social and political convictions consonant with conservative Christianity, Salvationists generally refuse to take sides in theological (and political) controversies because they distract from saving souls. Salvationists also part company with many religious conservatives in their understanding of women's roles. William Booth's wife Catherine believed women were men's equals and convinced her husband that they should preach and teach in God's army.

Diane Winston

See also Rescue Missions

Bibliography

McKinley, Edward H. (1995) *Marching to Glory: The History of the Salvation Army in the United States, 1880–1992*. Grand Rapids, MI: Wm. B. Eerdmans.

Murdoch, Norman H. (1994) *Origins of the Salvation Army*. Knoxville, TN: University of Tennessee Press.

Winston, Diane. (1999) *Red Hot and Righteous: The Urban Religion of the Salvation Army*. Cambridge, MA: Harvard University Press.

Sanctification

Derived from the Latin word *sanctus*, meaning "holy," sanctification is the process by which someone or something becomes holy. The emphasis upon the holy life is of special importance to Christianity in general, inspiring theologians and laymen alike. For Protestants, salvation is achieved through a two-tiered process of justification followed by sanctification, wherein the convert is forgiven of sin, then is gradually freed from the power of sin in a lifelong process of growing in grace. The advent of Methodism in the late eighteenth century brought about a different view. John Wesley (1703–1791), Evangelical Anglican and founder of Methodism, argued that sanctification could take place within a relatively short space in one's life. Protestant Fundamentalism places great emphasis on this more sudden, life-changing transformation, and interpretations of sanctification gave rise to new Fundamentalist denominations in the nineteenth and twentieth centuries.

According to the tenets of Calvinism, while the sanctified individual can never be confident of his or her election, such a person does exhibit the unmistakable signs of election in the performance of good works. A saintly demeanor, faithful attendance at church services, the dispensation of charity, and the high esteem of family, friends, and neighbors, are all indications of sanctification, as the individual steadily improves the quality of his or her spirit in strict obedience to God. Whereas a person receives grace through faith alone (*solo fide*), the performance of good works acts as a visible indication that he or she has indeed received grace. Radical Calvinists have variously focused upon sanctification as a process of becoming spiritually perfected, oftentimes scandalized as Donatists and antinomians. Quakers and Shakers are most noted for their beliefs in perfectionism, but such notions have had their influence upon other Protestant denominations, as well as upon Catholicism.

John Wesley was particularly interested in the possibility of achieving spiritual purity. Influenced by German Moravians as a young missionary in Georgia, Wesley began to believe in a "second blessing" that he felt he underwent after a period of "unusually frequent lapses into sin" following his failure in Georgia and return to England. In *A Plain Account of Christian Perfection* (1766), Wesley suggested that at such moments of spiritual crisis the convert can achieve "entire sanctification" leading to "Christian perfection." Justification leaves a "residue of sin within" that the second blessing washes away in a moment of spiritual ecstasy. However, the perfectionism Wesley taught was not sinless perfection, but merely a life of daily victory over sin. His colleague and successor, John Fletcher, took this concept further in *Checks to Antinomianism* (1771), in which he referred to this experience as a "baptism in the Holy Spirit" that cleanses the soul as well as conferring spiritual power upon the recipient. Other effects of this spiritual baptism are episodes of fainting, trembling, shouting, weeping, and other charismata noted by observers of Methodist services in late-eighteenth-century Virginia.

During the Second Great Awakening in the early nineteenth century, issues of sanctification and perfectionism asserted a new primacy in American Protestant theology. Asa Mahan, president of Oberlin College in Ohio, and colleague of Charles G. Finney, argued in *Scripture Doctrine of Christian Perfection* (1839) that spiritual perfection is an attainable goal for those who give themselves completely to Christ. This became especially influential in Methodism after the Civil War, where a wing emerged that propagated the doctrine that sanctification confers absolute, sinless perfection upon the convert. Other denominations were similarly affected, as Holiness and Pentecostal movements emerged that subscribed to more radical interpretations of sanctification. The second blessing of sanctification gradually became connected as much to the experience of the conferral of inner power over sin and Satan as to being merely cleansed of sin. The most notable manifestation of sanctification according to Pentecostals and Holiness church members is the phenomenon of glossolalia, or "speaking in tongues." Though sporadically witnessed at revivals in the eighteenth and somewhat more commonly in the nineteenth centuries, glossolalia was elevated by Charles Fox Parham in 1900 to a higher significance. It achieved even greater importance with the 1906 Azusa Street Revival in Los Angeles, where white Holiness worship forms merged with African-American forms to create the Church of God in Christ denomination. Among other such charismata as uncontrollable trembling, spontaneous singing and shouting, and trance states, glossolalia is taken as direct evidence of sanctification.

The Wesleyan interpretation of entire sanctification dominated the American Holiness and Pentecostal movements in the late nineteenth century, while in England a divergent view arose that shied away from perfectionism. At a Holiness convention in Keswick, England, leaders there saw the second blessing only as a spiritual baptism and not as sanctification, and also denied Wesley's eradicationist language with regard to sin, arguing instead that the second blessing only suppresses the convert's sinful nature. Sticking instead with Wesley's more equivocal term of "Christian perfection," the Keswick view influenced the American Holiness opponents of the excesses of the Azusa Street Revivalists. The ensuing doctrinal schism over sanctification involved those Holiness denominations claiming Methodist roots who maintained the interpretation that the second blessing destroyed "inbred sin," as opposed by those Pentecostal denominations emerging from non-Methodist backgrounds who questioned the necessity of the second blessing and argued instead that conversion and sanctification occur simultaneously. William H. Durham of Chicago instigated the cleavage by preaching in 1910 that sanctification happens at the moment of conversion because Christ eliminated original sin by His sacrifice on Calvary. Durham's "Finished Work" theology negated the need for a "second change," and reverted to the much older conception that sanctification is a lifelong process of growing in grace. At a 1914 Pentecostal convention in Hot Springs, Arkansas, the Assembly of God denomination emerged, which repudiated the Wesleyan conception of sanctification and adopted Durham's doctrine of the "Finished Work."

The Pentecostal and Holiness denominations remain divided over the issue of sanctification. The Pentecostal denominations generally adhere to the "second blessing" interpretation originally devised by Wesley, while the Holiness denominations are more attached to Durham's "Finished Work" theology.

John Howard Smith

See also Azusa Street Revival; Calvinism; Great Awakening; Justification; Keswick Movement; Salvation; Saved, The; Speaking in Tongues

Bibliography

Dieter, Melvin E., ed. (1987) *Five Views on Sanctification.* Grand Rapids, MI: Zondervan Publishing.

Synan, Vinson. (1997) *The Holiness–Pentecostal Tradition: Charismatic Movements in the Twentieth Century.* Grand Rapids, MI: Wm. B. Eerdmans.

Saved, The

In Protestant Fundamentalist usage, to be saved is to be forgiven of one's sins and to receive a new status and identity as a child of God, no longer in rebellion against God, but loving Him and living according to His will. This process is also called "being born again," from the words of Jesus in John 3:3: "Unless a man is born again, he cannot see the kingdom of God" (NIV). The saved, therefore, are those who can demonstrate some evidence of their status as children of God through a verbal testimony of God's inner renewing grace in their lives and through the outward manifestation of a righteous or sanctified life. The conscious experience of salvation is called conversion, when a sinner repents of former sins and chooses to follow Christ and live a life pleasing to God. Fundamentalists have been careful to point out, however, that an experience of conversion is not a guarantee of inner spiritual rebirth, and some converts later fall away from their initial profession of faith. There has been a division of opinion about why this occurs. For Fundamentalists influenced by Arminian traditions, a convert can lose the initial gift of salvation. For others in the Reformed traditions, however, once a Christian is truly "born again," that is, given a new spiritual nature, salvation cannot be lost. This is called the doctrine of perseverance, or "eternal security of the believer." Moral lapses, therefore, represent either the yielding of a professed Christian to the desires and weaknesses of the flesh, or in extreme cases, become the evidence that the person had never actually been born again.

In the Fundamentalist worldview, there are either the saved or the unsaved—there is no middle ground. Although it is often acknowledged that the final destiny of a human's soul is known only to God, Fundamentalists affirm that humans can know whether or not they are saved, thus giving rise to the frequently asked question: "Brother, are you saved?" It is also assumed on this basis that those who are not saved can be recognized with some degree of certainty. Typically, the unsaved include the heathen, who have never heard the gospel, as well as members of non-Christian religions. The unsaved may also include members of Christian communions, such as Roman Catholics or mainline Protestants, who profess to be Christians but have not been born again. Opinion about the Jews, however, has been divided: many believe that all Jews will someday be saved because of biblical promises made to the people of Israel. Others have argued that all these promises have been either fulfilled or abrogated and, therefore, not all Jews will be saved but only those who repent and trust in Christ.

Fundamentalists consider revivalism and personal evangelism as the key means of salvation. Sharing the gospel is believed to be an obligation of every believer. Properly speaking, it is God who saves, but Fundamentalists have emphasized to a greater extent the role of human initiative and methods that can lead to repentance and conversion. Some of these methods, such as the practice of threatening sinners with eternal punishment in hell, have been severely criticized. Fundamentalists also have been particularly adept at using modern communication technology, such as radio and television, for evangelism. Fundamentalists differ somewhat from the broader Christian tradition by their widespread insistence that salvation must be an explicit experience of conversion as opposed to a gradual process of Christian growth and nurture. Indeed, for many, the ability to recite a personal testimony of salvation, and even to identify the precise time and place that one was saved, has been considered an essential aspect of Christian identity. This became particularly important as a response to the tendency of liberals to interpret salvation in ethical terms rather than in terms of sin and forgiveness. However, it was also seen as a corrective to the Roman Catholic tradition, which appeared to subordinate the experience of conversion to a lifelong process of sacramental observance.

Fundamentalists have often been accused of narrowing their concept of the saved to those who hold particular doctrinal views. In their efforts to oppose modernism, they sometimes emphasize the spiritual necessity of believing certain doctrines or following certain practices. Some, for example, have expressed the sentiment that it is not possible to be a Christian without believing in the "fundamentals," such as the Virgin Birth of Jesus or the inerrancy of the Bible, because to deny these must inevitably lead to infidelity and unbelief. The same has been said regarding belief in biological evolution. More extreme sects have either tended to broaden the list of essential doctrines and practices or to focus exclusively on one particular doctrine or practice. Certain sects, for example, have held that the mode and words used during baptism, worship on Saturdays, foot washing as a liturgical act, beliefs about the Second Coming of Christ, and numerous pious practices serve to distinguish the believers from the nonbelievers. For some Pentecostal Fundamentalists, speaking in tongues as a sign of baptism in the Holy Spirit has sometimes served as a way of identifying the saved. In all these instances, Fundamentalists have been characterized by a tendency toward sectarianism that excludes any that do not conform to the behavior and beliefs of the sect. This has usually been an implicit assumption of Fundamentalist sects rather than an overtly expressed theological position.

Although Fundamentalists have not been opposed to providing physical and social assistance to the needy, all such efforts are seen as secondary to the primary task of soul saving. Organizations such as the Salvation Army and urban Union Rescue Missions have specialized in providing relief for the poor and indigent. These efforts, however, are typically accompanied by explicit appeals for spiritual conversion. In a Union Rescue Mission, for example, homeless people seeking food and shelter must first listen to an evangelistic sermon before receiving a meal.

Daniel W. Draney

See also Born Again; Conversion; Grace; Rescue Missions; Revival; Salvation; Sin and Sinners

Bibliography

Marsden, George M. (1991) *Understanding Fundamentalism and Evangelicalism.* Grand Rapids, MI: Wm. B. Eerdsmans.

Smith, Timothy L. (1957) *Revivalism and Social Reform.* New York: Abingdon Press.

Torrey, R. A. (1905) *Real Salvation.* New York: Fleming H. Revell Co.

Scofield Reference Bible

First published by Oxford University Press in 1909, the Scofield Reference Bible is probably the most popular study Bible. Using explanatory notes at the bottom of the pages, Cyrus Ingerson Scofield (1843–1921) put forth a dispensational premillennialist interpretation of Scripture. More notes were added in a 1917 revision and another revised version was published in 1967. The Scofield Bible became the most widely held defense of dispensational premillennialism within the American Fundamentalist movement. Dispensationalism claims to be a method of "rightly dividing the world of truth" using the concept of dispensations. A dispensation as defined by Scofield is "a period of time during which man is tested in respect of obedience to some specific revelation of the will of God." Scofield found seven dispensations in the Bible: (l) the dispensation of innocence (Genesis 1:28–3:13), (2) the dispensation of conscience (Genesis 3:23–7:23), (3) the dispensation of human government (Genesis 8:20–11:9), (4) the dispensation of promise (Genesis 12:1–Exodus 19:8), (5) the dispensation of law (Exodus 19:8–Matthew 27:53), (6) the dispensation of grace (Matthew 27:35; John 1:17), and (7) a final dispensation will include the pre-Tribulation rapture of the church, the Great Tribulation, and Christ's return to set up a millennial kingdom (Ephesians 1:10; Daniel 9:20–27; Revelation 20, 21). The word "millennium" interestingly is not used by Scofield in his notes on chapter twenty in the Book of Revelation, but the word "kingdom" is substituted. In the 1917 edition, the Ussher dating of Creation was added with the year 4004 BCE given for the creation of the world. (James Ussher [1581–1656], Irish scholar and archbishop of Armagh, proposed the age of the earth by adding together the life spans of the patriarchs in the book of Genesis, coming up with the date of 4004 BCE for the world's creation.)

The authors Frank E. Gaebelein (1959) and Charles G. Trumbull (1920) have written appreciative biographies of C. I. Scofield and Joseph M. Canfield (1988) writes of accusations of forgeries in his early life, his divorce from his first wife, his lack of support for the children of his first marriage, his assumption of a doctor of divinity degree with no evidence of it ever being granted to him by an educational institution, and an award from a French university that cannot be substantiated. His supporters stress his conversion experience, his successful pastoral work later in his life in churches in Texas and New York, and his leadership in the early American dispensational premillennialist movement. Scofield's belief that women were unfit for leadership became a prevalent belief among his followers.

Scofield did not elaborate on the theories of Creation, although he proposed a cataclysmic event in Genesis 1:3. He believed that fossils could be accounted for as residuals from this destroyed primitive creation. The Scofield Reference Bible appealed to many conservative Protestant Christians as it offered a unified interpretive pattern to the whole Bible. Quoting Augustine (as Scofield did in the introduction to the 1917 revision of his study Bible), "Distinguish the ages, and the Scriptures harmonize." Scofield used the dispensations as a means to show the progressive ordering of the dealings of God with humanity in one uniting biblical scheme. Its great popularity speaks to the desire of many Christian readers for just such a unifying interpretive model.

Leland Edward Wilshire

See also Dispensationalism; Premillennialism

Bibliography

Canfield, Joseph M. (1988) *The Incredible Scofield and His Book*. Vallecito, CA: Ross House Books.

Gaebelein, Frank Ely. (1959) *The Story of the Scofield Reference Bible, 1909–1959*. New York: Oxford University Press.

Trumbull, Charles Gallaudet. (1920) *The Life Story of C. I. Scofield*. New York: Oxford University Press.

Second Coming

Although many religious traditions describe an anticipated arrival of one or more divine beings on earth, the "Second Coming" specifically refers to the future return of Christ in the religious traditions of Christianity. In Christianity, it is believed that Christ, who first came to earth in the human form of Jesus as the Son of God, would return at the end of time. The Greek term for this event is *parousia*, which literally means "presence," but often refers to an "arriving." In all Christian theological writings (including the New Testament), parousia specifically refers to Christ's return at the end of earthly time.

The Second Coming in The Bible

The New Testament never uses the term Second Coming. It refers instead to the imminent return of Christ—Christ's parousia. One Thessalonians speaks of the parousia of the "Lord Jesus" (2:19). The Gospel of Matthew mentions the parousia of the "Son of Man" (24:27; 37:39). In the Gospel of John, Jesus himself states that He "will come again" (14:3). Hebrews affirms that Christ will come a "second time": "For then must he often have suffered since the foundation of the world: but now once in the end of world hath he appeared to put away sin by the sacrifice of himself. And as it is appointed unto men once to die, but after this the judgment: So Christ was once offered to bear the sins of many; and unto them that look for him shall he appear the second time without sin unto salvation" (9:26–28). This Second Coming is described in powerful, haunting, and enigmatic metaphors in the final book of the Bible: the Apocalypse of John. Most scholars agree that the Apocalypse of John is an example of a whole genre of apocalyptic writing that uses a complex system of metaphors to describe the destruction of the Roman Empire, which oppressed Christians at the time of its writing. However, its very powerful and obscure metaphors have given rise to complex beliefs for many Fundamentalist Christians.

In Christian theology generally, Jesus is thought to have come to the earth at the command of God t he Father so that the sins of all humans could be placed into Him. Then, after His brutal torture and death, the sins that were placed into Him were lifted from humanity. Because death was the result of an original sin of the very first humans created by God, Jesus, as proof of His power over sin and death, arose from the grave three days after being executed. Although this forgiveness of sin or grace is thought to be offered to all humans by Christ, the risen Jesus, the individual must first be judged worthy to gain this grace. Typically, Christian thought has placed most emphasis on the necessity to love ones' neighbors without reservation as the basis for this judgment.

However, various Christian sects and theologies have considered the nature of this judgment and "brotherly love" in different ways. Whatever the case, theologians who focus on the Second Coming generally consider the Apocalypse of John to describe a future return of the risen Christ during which the evil kingdoms of the world will be destroyed, the living and dead will be judged, and Christ will rule a peaceful world for one thousand years. After this time, evil will be finally and forever conquered and those judged well will be joined with God in an eternal "holy city, new Jerusalem, coming down from God out of heaven" (John 21:2, KJV).

From the Christian texts of the Bible, it would seem that the contemporary followers of Christ believed that this Second Coming would occur in their near future. The Gospel of Mark 9:1 recounts Jesus saying: "there be some of them that stand here, which shall not taste of death, till they have seen the kingdom of God come with power."

Similarly, in the Gospel of Luke 9:27, Jesus says: "But I tell you of a truth, there be some standing here, which shall not taste of death, till they see the kingdom of God." Both of these passages seem to indicate that the Second Coming will occur with Jesus' own generation. However, this has not kept individuals from reinterpreting the passages of the New Testament that refer to some sort of Second Coming in ways that make this future event seem, as yet, unfulfilled.

The Second Coming in Theology

With the adoption of Christianity as the official religion of the Roman Empire by Constantine in 325 CE, it is clear that the failure of Christ to return as soon as expected did not diminish the power of the Christian message. About 417 CE, St. Augustine of Hippo wrote the definitive text of institutionalized Roman Christianity *The City of God*. This "city" refers to the kingdom Christ would bring into being with his Second Coming. However, in Augustine's interpretation of the texts, this Second Coming has become a metaphor for the ongoing struggle of good and evil in each individual's life. This interpretation remains the official perspective of the Catholic Church. Nevertheless, with the inclusion of the Apocalypse of John in the canonical texts of the Bible, the idea of an imminent Second Coming has played a powerful role in Christian thought. Although the evidence is scant, throughout the Middle Ages there seems to have been a number of movements in Europe that focused on the Second Coming. Most famous among these seems to have been founded by Joachim of Fiore. Fiore was a Cistercian monk who predicted the Second Coming would occur in 1260, which turned out to be ten years after his death in 1250. With the disintegration of Roman Catholicism into many Protestant sects that arose after the Reformation, spurred on by Martin Luther's public outcry against many Catholic Church practices in 1517, numerous new religious groups began to focus on the Second Coming with a new intensity.

The Puritans were among the early Protestants who expected an imminent Second Coming. Even as they established colonies in North America, early American Puritans seem to have been convinced that the return of Christ was imminent. Furthermore, this sense of the Second Coming being at hand has had an incredible longevity. In the 1840s, John Nelson

Darby (1800–1882) gained a substantial following in Britain, America, Australia, and New Zealand, preaching that this Second Coming, or the "Third Dispensation" as he called it, was near at hand. In 1844, a sect of American Christians following the charismatic leader William Miller (1782–1849), known as the Millerites, left their crops to rot and climbed a hill expecting Christ to arrive after Miller set the date for the Second Coming on October 22, of that year. Similarly, the best-selling nonfiction book of the 1970s, Hal Lindsey's *Late Great Planet Earth*, reinterpreted Darby's ideas based on contemporary current events. Fundamentalist breakaway groups from such mainstream Protestant movements as the Jehovah's Witnesses, The Seventh-Day Adventists, The Church of the Latter-day Saints, and many others occasionally proclaim that they have seen signs of an imminent Second Coming. Probably most fresh in recent memory was the U.S. law enforcement's attack on the Branch Davidians in Waco, Texas, who felt that the Second Coming was at hand. Most recently, Tim Lahaye and Jerry B. Jenkins's best-selling *Left Behind* series of novels (1995–1999) describe contemporary events that would proceed a very near Second Coming.

Conclusion

Despite the long history of the Christian community both expecting and predicting an eminent Second Coming, the texts of the Bible are themselves unclear on whether it is possible for individuals to recognize the signs that will proceed the Second Coming. The Gospel of Mark 13:32–33 specifically states that humans will not be able to predict the time of the Second Coming: "But of that day and *that* hour knoweth no man, no, not the angels which are in heaven, neither the Son, but the Father. Take ye heed, watch and pray: for ye know not when the time." However, 2 Thessalonians 2:1–12 seems to lay out a series of specific signs that will proceed His return. This very ambivalence, coupled with the powerful imagery of the Second Coming in the Apocalypse of John, has given rise to powerful beliefs about the near return of Christ. In particular, these beliefs, and the groups who espouse these beliefs, tend to emphasize a strict adherence to a particular interpretation of the biblical texts. Thus, in general, many Fundamentalist Christian believers are deeply committed to and heavily focused on the Apocalypse

of John and its depiction of the Second Coming of their Christ.

Robert Glenn Howard

See also End Times; Eschatology; Jesus Christ

Bibliography

Augustine. (1950) *The City of God*, translated by Rev. George Wilson and Rev. J. J. Smith. New York: Random House.

Boyer, Paul S. (1992) *When Time Shall Be No More: Prophecy Belief in Modern America*. Cambridge, MA: Harvard University Press.

Cohn, Norman. (1970) *The Pursuit of the Millennium: Revolution and Mystical Anarchists of the Middle Ages*. Bristol: J. W. Arrowsmith Ltd.

Emmerson, Richard K., and Bernard McGinn, eds. (1992) *The Apocalypse in the Middle Ages*. Ithaca, NY: Cornell University Press.

LaHaye, Tim, and Jerry B. Jenkins. (1995) *Left Behind: A Novel of Earth's Last Days*. Wheaton, IL: Tyndale House Publishers.

O'Leary, Stephen D. (1994) *Arguing the Apocalypse: A Theory of Millennial Rhetoric*. New York: Oxford University Press.

Tickle, John. (1983) *The Book of Revelation: A Catholic Interpretation of the Apocalypse*. Liguori, MO: Liguori Publications.

Wojcik, Daniel. (1997) *The End of the World As We Know It: Faith, Fatalism, and Apocalypse in America*. New York: New York University Press.

Secularism

Secularism is a vital concept in how we understand the interaction of religion and society. On the one hand, social scientists use it to understand the relation between modern life and religion. On the other hand, Fundamentalists evoke it as a word of opprobrium toward those who do not meet their standards of piety. To analyze its history is to tap the heart of the issue where Fundamentalism meets modernity and scholars interpret Fundamentalism.

Definitions

Secularism has a colorful definitional history. Early in the Christian era the Latin word *saeculum* referred to an age or era. By the fourth and fifth century it was defined as "the world" or the "spirit of an age." It was used in Latin Christian liturgy meaning "the world to come" or "world without end." In time priests who served parishes in "the world" were called "secular," as opposed to cloistered priests who served God in the monasteries (Swatos and Olson 2000: 3–4). It was not until the early twentieth century that Max Weber, the German sociologist, used the term "secularization" to describe the effects of modernity on the life of culture, religious and otherwise. The Enlightenment's focus on reason was the source of secularism and thus a secularizing process. Reason conquered and domesticated mystery, divine or otherwise. The process of rationalization penetrated every human activity. The supernatural was no longer the source or cause of events. Every aspect of life must be explained by material causes understood by human reason. Weber most often used the term "disenchantment" to describe this movement in history. This meant that one could no longer appeal to divine authority for explanation. Human reason ruled in scholarship and religion.

For intellectuals, secularism or secularization meant three things: 1) a decline in religious institutional participation and religious piety; 2) the differentiation of social institutions, whereby every function in society could and should be performed by specific institutions serving particular needs; and 3) the privatization of religion, meaning that religion and specifically Christianity no longer shaped public life but was demoted to the private chambers of the heart (Casanova 1994: 7).

It was supposed by most Western European scholars of the modern period that religion had and would decline. Moreover, secularism and its emphasis on human reason would lead inevitably to the extinction of religion and its public authority and finally to a loss of its meaning in the lives of individuals. It was argued that individual autonomy was and should be the core of all decision-making in private and public life. This turn to reason led ineluctably to the separation of the church and state. Thus, religion lost its throne not only as the queen of science but as the king of the state. Its consolation prize became the soul, and even that reward would fade according to most experts in the academic study of religion.

Secularism Revisited

Secularism thus ended religion. This, of course, proved not to be true and the predictions by social scientists up until the 1970s about the decline of religion in the world were simply wrong. Religion, across the world and particularly in the United States, has boomed. Secularism—and the secularization process as a predictive theory—is in wide disrepute. Indeed, Peter Berger, the most forceful predictor of religion's decline, recently published an edited volume called *The Desecularization of the World: Resurgent Religion and World Politics* (1999). With the rise of Fundamentalism worldwide, religion has not only gone public, but private belief has blossomed as well. Moreover, for Fundamentalists secularism is the "enemy" and various religious groups use it as a term to pillory the authenticity of other religionists. Fundamentalist groups identify secularism as the source of religious corruption, tantamount to unbelief. Secularism empties the divine dimension from the world, encourages doubt toward the supernatural, and seeks scientific or "worldly" explanations for events. Secularism gives priority to the individual and sacrifices the group's interest, something Fundamentalists find corrosive at best. Fundamentalists, particularly in the Islam and Jewish religions, argue that secularism gave rise to the secular state and the separation of church and state, each of which undercut the authority of religion and undermine the validity and the absolute nature of religious beliefs.

To be sure, Fundamentalists pick and choose what to reject from modernity and its bedfellows. Modernity produced both technical advances and the belief in the authority and rationality of the individual. Fundamentalists tend to protest secularism and its focus on individual rights, particularly when it comes to minority groups like women and homosexuals. Nonetheless, Fundamentalists use the technical advances of the secular age (including the media) to promote their more traditional message. This message includes advocating the interests of the group over the individual; seeking a new inscription of patriarchal norms, that is, the authority of the male in families and in public leadership; and finally, a focus on religious nationalism (Lawrence 1989: xix). Religious nationalism is most potently embodied in the Islamic State of Iran. In American Fundamentalism the flirtation with religious nationalism is less intense. American Fundamentalists, for the most part, do not seek a theocratic state but simply the reestablishment of Protestantism as the American civil religion.

Secularism in American Fundamentalism

The meaning of secularism for American Fundamentalists has changed over time. In the nineteenth century, postmillennialist Christians sought to advance God's kingdom in order to bring on the millennium, which would end with Christ's Second Coming. They saw in each point of American national progress a sign of God's coming kingdom. Optimism flowed from an American sense of Manifest Destiny, that America was God's tool to bring about the coming of Christ's kingdom. By the end of the nineteenth century, liberal Evangelicals had moved away from the supernatural and apocalyptic notions of their more conservative Evangelical fellows. The Social Gospel was a this-worldly effort to ameliorate problems of poverty and race across the nation. It was no longer about a millennialist hope, but transformation for the sake of social justice. Conservative Evangelicals interpreted their northern Evangelical brothers and sisters as having secularized and lost the faith. Moreover, with Darwin and the rise of evolutionary theory, conservatives redoubled their rejection of "secular science" and in particular rejected the use of historical criticism on the Bible that for them undercut its authority and was a secularist slap in the face. Scripture was deemed "inerrant," without error relative to history and science. *The Fundamentals*, a series of booklets finished in 1915, set out the principles from which "Fundamentalists" would not budge. The controversy broke out in nearly every American Christian denomination. For conservatives it was the Fundamentalists who were faithful to God and God's word. It was the Bible against the secularizing liberal Christians corrupted by the world. The modernist–Fundamentalist controversy of the 1920s sealed the divide between the two groups. From 1930 until the 1970s American Fundamentalists developed their own vibrant culture set apart from American mainstream secular culture. Indeed, even Billy Graham, the popular Evangelical preacher, was excluded from Fundamentalist pulpits from 1957 on. Graham was accused of accommodating to secularist

Christianity and thus rejected. The pure minority set itself up as a righteous remnant dedicated for the most part to a premillennialist hope. That is, the thousand-year kingdom of Christ would not come by means of human effort but only begin by a divine intervention of Christ, who would judge the righteous and the sinful and set up His kingdom on earth.

In 1979 the world of Fundamentalism changed. In Iran the Ayatollah Khomeini came to power and an Islamic Republic was founded. It was ruled by Islamic clerics. In that same year, led by the Baptist Jerry Falwell, three organizations of the American Christian religious Right were set in place: the Moral Majority, the Christian Voice, and the Religious Roundtable. In the 1960s Falwell had joined his Fundamentalists' leadership in rejecting any involvement in secular public politics. He agreed that to save the soul before the coming of Christ was the task of the church. Jose Casanova argues that up until the 1970s Fundamentalists, for the most part, could sustain a Christian lifestyle or "lifeworld" that was separate and sealed off from the wider secular culture. Moreover, in general, America maintained a Protestant civil religion, an ethos and public life that supported and nurtured the Protestant ethic. This quasi-Protestant establishment began to deteriorate in the 1960s with the Supreme Court decisions against Scripture-reading and prayer in the public schools. Moreover, the civil rights movement for African Americans and in particular for women began to impact the cultural and religious life of the Christian religious Right. In others words, things had gone too far and it was time, at least in Falwell's mind, to take a stand. The Moral Majority in name and in its rhetoric attempted to persuade Americans that the cultural changes of the 1960s had corrupted the American character and the American way of life. Not all Fundamentalists agreed with Falwell's decision to join the political fray. Nonetheless, his impact, though much debated, did have some influence on the election of Ronald Reagan and conservative social politics of the Republican Party. Falwell made plain that sources of American corruption were from secularist sources, including the women's movement, secular humanism in the schools, and the Supreme Court and its legalization of abortion and the easing of restrictions on divorce. The ideal of the nuclear family as the source of religious and moral education had been undercut by the moral depredation of the 1960s. Falwell's agenda was clear and pointed: prolife, profamily, promoral, and pro-American (Casanova 1994: 152–154).

For many Fundamentalists what is most inconsistent about the American Protestant Fundamentalist movement is its tendency to maintain the distinction between church and state. As noted earlier, this separation is a secularist heresy for Fundamentalist Jews, Muslims, and even some Roman Catholics. How can the truth of faith be maintained when one is under the legal authority of a secular state? Certainly Falwell's Baptist roots nurtured the church–state separation. Baptists were initially a religious minority in the colonies and needed this separation for the sake of their very existence. American Fundamentalism has always lived in the tension of believing that religious liberty is critical for American political polity and yet maintaining a theology that demands a separation from any sources of secularism.

This discomfiture over secular authority is not the only incongruity within American Fundamentalism. It also tends toward individualism in its rhetoric and in its church polity. The salvation of the individual is at the core of its salvific message. De jure and de facto congregationalism undercuts most organizational accountability. Thus, group standards are difficult to enforce and individualism undermines the authority of its leadership. Moreover, American Fundamentalists wholeheartedly support American laissez-faire capitalism and American dominance militarily. Falwell and other American Fundamentalists seem unaware that their economic and political positions may tend to lead to the erosion of the faith that they proclaim with such certainty. Autonomy in one cultural sphere cannot help but bleed into other cultural fields.

To be sure, American Fundamentalists at the beginning of the twenty-first century remain a potent force in the culture, in politics, and in American denominations. By the end of the 1990s the Fundamentalist takeover of the Southern Baptist denomination was complete. Theologically and politically liberal and moderate professors at Southern Baptist seminaries were systematically fired. Fundamentalists took over denominational leadership and as a result, the role of women in church was curtailed and a new hierarchy of male leadership in the family was instituted and prescribed. These oppositional movements are predictable because Fundamentalists seek traditional gender roles, the norms for families of the American 1950s, and a push toward an American civil religion that would proscribe the rights of minority groups and forestall the expression of alternative

forms of morality in the media and in the culture. The power of American Fundamentalism remains a great threat to many in American public life, but social scientists that study the field assert that their power numerically and politically is limited. Nonetheless, with the election of George W. Bush, a candidate strongly supported by many American Fundamentalists, their public agenda is far from dead.

Conclusion

The word "secularism" has enjoyed a motley history. It began as a part of the sacred Catholic liturgy and through time became a favored and then condemned word in the arena of social scientists. Even today, this word continues to be used by Fundamentalists as a negative descriptor—as the source and origin of religious and moral corruption. The negative use of "secularism" tends to lead toward a definitional generality and elusiveness. The word and its use remain intrinsically fluid. Nonetheless, its history is central to how religion, and particularly Fundamentalism, is understood and interpreted in the modern world. How it is used and by whom tells us much more about that group or individual than it does about the word. As in so many cases in the field of religion, context is everything.

James K. Wellman, Jr.

See also Antimodernism; Liberalism

Bibliography

Berger, Peter L. (1967) *The Sacred Canopy: Elements of a Sociological Theory of Religion*. Garden City, NY: Doubleday and Company.

———. (1999) *The Desecularization of the World: Resurgent Religion and World Politics*. Grand Rapids, MI: Wm. B. Eerdmans.

Casanova, Jose. (1994) *Public Religions in the Modern World*. Chicago: University of Chicago Press.

Lawrence, Bruce B. (1989) *Defenders of God: The Fundamentalist Revolt Against the Modern Age*. Columbia: University of South Carolina.

Marsden, George M. (1980) *Fundamentalism and American Culture: The Shaping of Twentieth-Century Evangelicalism, 1870–1925*. Oxford: Oxford University Press.

Stark, Rodney, and Roger Finke. (2000) *Acts of Faith: Explaining the Human Side of Religion*. Berkeley: University of California Press.

Swatos, William H., Jr., and Daniel V. A. Olson. (2000) *The Secularization Debate*. New York: Rowman and Littlefield Publishers.

Sermon on the Mount

Contributors to *The Fundamentals* (published between 1910 and 1915) presented a common front against modernism and gave cohesiveness to the Fundamentalist movement, but this unity sometimes dissolved into squabbles over doctrinal and interpretive issues. Such is the case with their understanding of the Sermon on the Mount (Matthew 5–7). This is most clearly illustrated in the writings of Philip Mauro (1859–1952), as well as the reactions to them in the premillennial dispensationalist community. Mauro, a successful New York patent attorney, was converted at the Gospel Tabernacle under the ministry of Albert Benjamin Simpson (1843–1919) and had initially adopted John Nelson Darby's (1800–1882) dispensationalist system of interpretation and End-Times scenario. An influential contributor to *The Fundamentals*, Mauro rethought dispensationalism and began writing about his newfound understanding of the New Testament teachings on the "kingdom" in 1918, focusing much attention on the Sermon on the Mount.

In the dispensationalist framework, enshrined and popularized in the notes of the *Scofield Reference Bible* (1909) and the elaborate charts of Clarence Larkin (1850–1924), the Sermon is primarily related to a "Messianic kingdom" and only secondarily to believers in this age. "What most concerns us," wrote Mauro, "is that the theory under consideration sets aside the commandments of the Lord Jesus Christ contained in the 'Sermon on the Mount,' as being not for the children of God of this present dispensation, but as being 'principles' of that *earthly* kingdom which, according to this theory, was offered to the Jews, refused by them, withdrawn by the Lord, and postponed to a future age" (Mauro n.d.: 22). Cyrus Ingerson Scofield (1843–1921) and others rightly recognized that Mauro's criticism was not simply a difference of opinion on a passage of Scripture, but an attack on their whole interpretive approach to the Bible. Mauro was thereafter excluded from dispensationalist conferences.

Both Mauro and the dispensationalists, each in their own way, were trying to preserve a literal understanding of the Bible and protect the Bible itself. Mauro took the Sermon's admonition to "turn the other cheek" quite literally and advocated pacifism throughout World War I. He also later championed the superiority of the 1611 King James Version of the Bible against the 1881 Revised Version. Likewise, many dispensationalists (past and present)

Matthew 5:1–12

1. And seeing the multitudes, he went up into a mountain: and when he was set, his disciples came unto him:
2. And he opened his mouth, and taught them, saying,
3. Blessed are the poor in spirit: for theirs is the kingdom of heaven.
4. Blessed are they that mourn: for they shall be comforted.
5. Blessed are the meek: for they shall inherit the earth.
6. Blessed are they which do hunger and thirst after righteousness: for they shall be filled.
7. Blessed are the merciful: for they shall obtain mercy.
8. Blessed are the pure in heart: for they shall see God.
9. Blessed are the peacemakers: for they shall be called the children of God.
10. Blessed are they which are persecuted for righteousness' sake: for theirs is the kingdom of heaven.
11. Blessed are ye, when men shall revile you, and persecute you, and shall say all manner of evil against you falsely, for my sake.
12. Rejoice, and be exceeding glad: for great is your reward in heaven: for so persecuted they the prophets which were before you.

believe "that the full, nonfudging, unadjusted fulfill-ment of the Sermon relates to the kingdom of Messiah" (Ryrie 1965: 108) that will begin after the Rapture of the church. Postmillennial and other inter-pretations deemed to be nonliteral were considered an accommodation to theological liberalism or worse, though many present-day dispensationalists have moderated this position and even acknowledge the possibility that Jesus employed speech in the Sermon that was not meant to be taken literally.

Different approaches to the Sermon on the Mount can also be viewed in the larger context of the rela-tionship between law and gospel. Today Evangelicals and Fundamentalists have conflicting opinions about the words of Jesus contained in the Sermon: "Do not think that I have come to abolish the law or the prophets; I have not come to abolish but to fulfill. For truly I tell you, until heaven and earth pass away, not one letter, not one stroke of a letter, will pass from the law until all is accomplished (Matthew 5:17–18, NRSV). Opinions range from radical continuity among some theonomists (who believe that the Old Testament laws—except for the sacrificial and purity codes—still apply to Christians and society today) to radical discontinuity among some dispensationalists, though these polar extremities are not usually pres-ent in their best educational institutions.

Douglas Milford

See also Dispensationalism; Jesus Christ; Theonomy

Bibliography

Gardiner, Gordon P. (1961) *Champion of the Kingdom: The Story of Philip Mauro.* Brooklyn, NY: Bread of Life.

Larkin, Clarence. (1920) *Dispensational Truth or God's Plan and Purpose for the Ages.* Philadelphia: Rev. Clarence Larkin Estate.

Marsden, George, M. (1980) *Fundamentalism and Ameri-can Culture: The Shaping of Twentieth-Century Evangel-icalism, 1870–1925.* Oxford: Oxford University Press.

Mauro, Philip. (n.d.) *A Kingdom Which Cannot Be Shaken.* Boston: Scripture Truth Depot.

Ryrie, Charles H. (1965) *Dispensationalism Today.* Chi-cago: Moody Press.

Saucy, Robert L. (1993) *The Case for Progressive Dis-pensationalsim.* Grand Rapids, MI: Zondervan Pub-lishing.

Strickland, Wayne G., ed. (1993) *The Law, the Gospel, and the Modern Christian.* Grand Rapids, MI: Zondervan Publishing.

Seventh-Day Adventists

Seventh-Day Adventists trace their roots to the Millerite movement of the early 1840s, which at-tracted upward of fifty thousand followers in the American Northeast. When the prediction of Baptist lay-preacher, William Miller (1782–1849), that Christ would return on 22 October 1844 proved false, his movement shattered. One fragment, whose leaders included a young visionary, Ellen White (1827–1915), reinterpreted the prophecy: the pre-advent judgment had begun in heaven on that day. However, Christ's return was imminent, and Adventists believed that it was their God-given task to warn the world to pre-pare for that event. (The movement eventually incor-porated in 1862.)

Early Adventism was, to use a descriptive socio-logical term that does not imply a value judgment, highly sectarian. That is, it was in high tension in many ways with government, other churches, and society in general. Adventists observed Saturday as the Sabbath at a time when it was considered a regu-lar workday in America, making it difficult for them to secure employment. The Adventists were antago-nistic to the U.S. government because it allowed slav-ery and had enacted laws criminalizing those who aided fugitive slaves. As a challenge to the legitimacy of the government they discussed whether they should refuse to vote. Their expectation of persecu-tion from that government in collaboration with other Christian churches (which seemed confirmed when members were turned in by neighbors and prosecuted under the prevailing state "blue laws" for working on their farms on Sundays) and of the imminent end of the world led to their rejection of the American Dream. Tensions with the govern-ment were exacerbated when they announced that they were conscientious objectors and refused to serve in the military during the Civil War. In addi-tion, their observance of the Sabbath, their embrace of vegetarianism, and their rejection of most forms of popular entertainment and of the then-current women's fashions separated them from others, mak-ing them objects of scorn.

Expansion of the Adventist Community

Adventists sent out their first foreign missionaries in the 1870s, and soon built a network of missions in every continent. As part of their outreach, they estab-lished schools and "sanitariums," which eventually developed into extensive networks of educational and medical institutions. Unlike the mainstream Protestant denominations, Adventist missionary work did not culminate in the spinning off of independent national churches, but instead helped build a highly centralized, and increasingly bureaucratized, multilayered system. Because tithes were not retained at the congregational level, but were passed up the structure, the hierarchy was able to redistribute funds from the wealthier parts of the world church to the newer and poorer segments, and thus to orchestrate expansion. The control of the American-based hierarchy over finances and its voice in the choice of leaders at lower levels also enabled it to exercise considerable control over the operation of the church as a whole, in spite of its representative features.

As Adventism expanded both geographically and in membership, its educational and medical institutions created increasing opportunities for the upward mobility of members. Although most converts were working class and poor, second-generation members often gained professional qualifications. The clergy gradually came to think of themselves as professionals, and administrators as corporate executives. As time passed, Adventists sought positive relationships with governments; for example, they modified their stance on military service in order to embrace patriotism, initiated contacts with other churches in which they presented themselves as fellow Christians, and pursued positive public relations. Their image was also bolstered when many societies adopted a five-day work week, thus making Sabbath observance less of a problem. Medical research endorsed their rejection of smoking and the value of many of their diet and health-related practices. In short, they became much more comfortable with society, thus moving steadily from a sect toward a denomination as they closely followed the trajectory outlined by sociological church-sect theory.

Nevertheless, Adventists have remained sufficiently distinct, and therefore retained enough sectarianism, to stoke the enthusiasm and commitment that fosters outreach and growth. This is especially so in much of the developing world, where members are mostly first-generation converts and the process of upward mobility and accommodation to society is still in its early stages. Of the worldwide community of 1,068,329 members added through baptism in 1999, 95.7% were in the developing world. Consequently, the proportion of the world membership in the United States, where Adventism was born, and indeed in the developed world, has fallen steeply in recent decades: of a total of 11,496,912 members in September 2000, only 7.6% were in the United States and 10.6% in the developed world. Within the Christian community today, where most of the mainline denominations are declining in numbers, Seventh-Day Adventists are one of four American-born religious movements that are expanding rapidly, along with Pentecostals, Jehovah's Witnesses, and Mormons.

Developing an Adventist Hermeneutic

William Miller was a Baptist lay-preacher, and Ellen White had been raised in a Methodist home. Early Adventists were drawn from the milieu and membership of these "upstart sects," which had begun by that time to accommodate to society. They embraced the view of the Scriptures as the inspired Word of God, together with biblical literalism and the methodology of proof-texting that were common at that time among such religious groups. To this they added a special emphasis on the apocalyptic books of the Bible, especially Daniel and Revelation. Since they did not include biblical scholars among their number and had not been trained in biblical languages, they were dependent on the King James Version of the Bible, which was then in common use. For example, Miller's interpretation of Daniel 8:14, which had led him to expect the return of Christ in 1844, and also its reinterpretation by Adventists after the "great disappointment," were peculiarly dependent on the rendering of the verse in that version. Modern translations all render it very differently.

Ellen White came to be viewed as a prophet and counselor to the Adventist Church, or "the messenger of the Lord," as she dubbed herself. She was a prolific writer who published twenty-four books and contributed more than five thousand articles to church magazines during her lifetime. Although she insisted that her writings were subsidiary to the Bible, her standing and their specificity made them highly influential in shaping the thought and behavior of Adventists.

Adventists initially focused on their special insights—their "message": the Sabbath, the unconscious state of man in death awaiting the Resurrection, the heavenly sanctuary and pre-advent judgment, the urgent apocalyptic and expectations regarding last-day events, and the rejection of the belief in eternal torment for the damned. They lived with diversity in other areas for several decades—for example,

Trinitarianism versus Arianism—and were slow to embrace righteousness by faith and to place a personal relationship with Christ at the core of their belief system.

Because of their commitment to observing the Sabbath on Saturday, Adventists placed great weight on the belief in a literal Creation in six days, for the two were inextricably linked in both the Creation story in Genesis and the Fourth Commandment in Exodus 20. They therefore rejected Darwin's theory of evolution, and came to view it as a scheme by Satan to muddy the waters just as they had been called by God to proclaim the forgotten commandment. Darwin's claim that the fossils were evidence that the world was a huge cemetery long before the presence of human beings was also seen as a direct challenge to their belief that all death was a result of human sin, and ultimately also to their apocalyptic. Similarly, Adventists gave short shrift to the rise of liberal biblical scholarship toward the end of the nineteenth century and its product, higher criticism, which seemed intended to undermine their whole doctrinal edifice. At the same time, however, they distanced themselves to some extent from the conservative biblical literalists. White held that the thought of the biblical writers was inspired, but that the Scriptures were not dictated by God, and she inevitably rejected the conservatives' opposition to the emancipation and enfranchisement of women, which they based on a literalistic reading of particular biblical passages, as well as their related attempts to reclaim the church for men and the image of God and Christianity as masculine.

The death of White in 1915 and the rapid growth of Adventism during World War I—as its public expositions of biblical prophecy attracted religious conservatives who had been drawn to apocalyptic issues by the times—helped change its face, for the newcomers were not aware of the earlier hermeneutic nuances. Adventist leaders therefore responded to the rise to prominence of the Fundamentalist movement as the champion of orthodoxy within American Christianity with a sense of relief, embracing it in large part for its affirmation of the inspiration and infallibility of the Bible and especially for its rejection of Darwinism. Indeed, their unexpected decision to replace their long-term president, A. G. Daniells (1858–1935), who had led Adventism from 1901 to 1922, with the more conservative W. A. Spicer (1865–1952) has been interpreted as symbolizing support of Fundamentalism. Francis Wilcox (1865–1951),

editor of *Review and Herald*, the official church paper, declared that "Adventists should count themselves the chief of Fundamentalists today." (Land: 1986: 283). With George McCready Price (1870–1963) as their champion, Adventists set the course of contemporary "scientific creationism." A worldwide flood at the time of Noah became the chief bulwark in their defense of the beliefs that God had created the world through special fiat about six thousand years ago and that all death—and therefore the fossils—was the result of, and therefore occurred after, Adam's sin. Similarly, they applied a literalistic hermeneutic, rooted in a proof-texting methodology, to the writings of White. Her authority was strengthened considerably at this time, with the issuing of a stream of books compiled from such sources as her magazine articles, whose excerpts were used with little concern for the context in which they were originally written.

However, the affinity between Adventism and Fundamentalism was far from complete. Many Fundamentalists felt a deep antagonism toward Adventism because of some of its peculiar doctrines, especially its reliance on the writings of White as an extra-biblical source of authority and its perceived legalism, which led them to conclude that Adventism was a non-Christian "cult." Fundamentalists also resented the Adventists' aggressive evangelism and persistent attempts to win over their members. For its part, the Adventist Church also held back, in order to distinguish itself and the "specialness" of its message. It therefore challenged the Fundamentalist champions of the infallibility of the Bible to obey it fully—including the Sabbath commandment.

Changing Relationships—and Hermeneutics

Coincidentally, the rise of the Fundamentalist movement occurred just as authority in American medicine was clarified and then organized. This obliged the Adventist medical school to seek accreditation, and this in turn forced the Adventist colleges to follow suit if their graduates were to be admitted to the medical school or receive certification as nurses or teachers. Consequently, the colleges had to send their faculty members to study for higher degrees at secular universities, where they were exposed to concepts and interpretations from which they had previously been sheltered. Although the biblical studies departments did not have to seek accreditation, it was inevitable that that faculty would not be left behind once others began to pursue graduate degrees.

The first steps were taken to upgrade the education of clergy with the founding of a seminary in 1937. Initially, only older biblical faculty members were sent to graduate school because their loyalty was certain, and their participation in the programs was limited to intermittent and part-time attendance. Moreover, these students initially restricted their studies to "tool" subjects such as biblical languages, archeology, church history, and speech, and thus, refrained from exposing themselves to the more threatening influences. Nevertheless, the founding of the seminary represented a major turning point in Adventist theology. Thereafter, the formerly dominant "proof-text" approach to the Scriptures became unacceptable among scholars, who replaced it with the "historical-critical" approach, which they began to teach to their students. Thenceforth their approach to the Bible was to use all available tools to discern what was meant when it was written rather than using it merely to bolster views that were already held.

The higher education of the biblical faculty began to make itself felt as early as World War II. A group at one college, disturbed at the tendency of Adventist evangelists and publications to declare that the current headlines were a direct fulfillment of biblical prophecy, formed an "Eschatology Society" to share their research. This rapidly evolved into a "Biblical Research Fellowship" (BRF) embracing scholars at all English-language colleges throughout the world. Although the independence of the BRF made church administrators so nervous that it was brought under the control of a General Conference department in 1952, the ten-volume *Seventh-Day Adventist Bible Commentary*, which was released between 1953 and 1957 and whose authors were inevitably mostly BRF members, showed an openness to the historical-critical method. For the first time, it presented Adventists with alternative interpretations of Scripture, reflecting scholarly debate—even though the editors felt they could not include all the positions they themselves held and acknowledged traditional Adventist interpretations they felt were without biblical basis.

The accreditation of the Adventist colleges in the United States led to greater opportunities for upward mobility among young members. An Adventist education, instead of being merely a route to church employment, now opened the door to the professions. Tensions eased between Adventists and the broader society, as Adventism accommodated to it. The process of assimilation was perhaps best symbolized by colleges replacing their names from those that referred to their mission at the time of their founding with titles better befitting the educational mainstream. The College of Medical Evangelists became Loma Linda University in 1945, Emmanuel Missionary College became Andrews University in 1960, and Washington Missionary College was renamed Columbia Union College in 1961.

Meanwhile, Adventist leaders also sought opportunities to improve their standing with other Christian churches, especially with Evangelicals, with whom Adventists had most in common but with whom tensions were the greatest. In 1955, Walter Martin, the director of cult apologetics for Zondervan Publishing Company, who had earlier classified Seventh-Day Adventism as a "cult" in his book, *The Rise of the Cults*, set out to make a comprehensive evaluation of Adventist theology for a new book that would focus solely on Adventists. Donald Grey Barnhouse, a nationally known Bible scholar and founder and editor of the *Evangelical Eternity* magazine, who had also written critically of Adventist theology, put Martin in contact with an Adventist pastor who had written him. The leadership of the General Conference had no wish to have their church classified as a cult. Not only would it be bad public relations, but inaccurate, for the Adventists now had closer ties to the Protestant mainstream than to groups like the Jehovah's Witnesses, who had already received stern treatment at the hands of Martin. They therefore chose to cooperate with Martin's researchers, appointing three men to work with them. After extensive research and meetings, during which the Adventists answered Martin's written questions, Barnhouse and Martin reversed their opinions, concluding that Adventists were Christian brethren. They announced their favorable conclusions in an article in *Eternity* magazine, even though they predicted that this would cost them circulation. Meanwhile, Adventists published their answers to Martin in a volume entitled *Seventh-Day Adventists Answer Questions on Doctrine* (1957), which disowned several positions embraced in earlier publications: for example, it now affirmed that Ellen White's writings were neither free of error nor equal to the Scriptures. Martin's book, *The Truth about Seventh-Day Adventism*, appeared in 1960.

The number of Adventist students seeking college education increased considerably in the mid-1960s, which greatly augmented the demand for new faculty members in Adventist institutions. Consequently, clusters of bright young full-time graduate students appeared at such schools as Harvard Divinity School and the Graduate Theological Union. These young scholars now felt free to build on what they had learned in the Adventist Seminary by exposing themselves to more "daring" disciplines, such as theology and ethics. They formed both in-formal networks and a formal organization, the Association of Adventist Forums. The association issued a journal, *Spectrum*, which was—and remains—both scholarly and independent of church authorities. When these scholars took up teaching positions at Adventist colleges they continued their interest in reforming church doctrine, and used their networks, journal, and the annual meetings of their professional organization, the Adventist Society for Religious Studies, to keep abreast of and build on the work of one another.

Although the more recent availability of doctoral degrees in various biblical and theological fields at Andrews University (the home of the Adventist Seminary) has allowed increasing numbers of teachers in religion to gain their entire education at Adventist schools, the majority of Adventist biblical scholars in the United States today have adopted a hermeneutic that is far from Fundamentalism, but has been strongly influenced by the historical-critical method. They consider the original context and intention of the writer and draw on the best available scholarship to understand this. Similarly, interviews with the science teachers at Adventist colleges in the United States show that while they continue to believe in a Creator God, the majority now personally hold that both the earth and life on it are very old and that the fossil record predates man (Lawson [forthcoming]). However, because of the antagonism of church leadership to the historical-critical method, and its misunderstanding of it, biblical scholars often avoid the term in their teaching and writing, and many of the scientists are so afraid of landing in hot water that they disguise their personal stances in their teaching.

Internal Tensions

In recent decades, the international Adventist Church has become very diverse culturally, racially, in terms of social class and level of education, and inevitably in beliefs. Internal tensions have caused a fear of disunity, and many church leaders feel as if they have to do a delicate balancing act to keep the church from flying apart. Two controversial issues have been prominent in recent years. At the General Conference Sessions of 1990 and 1995, the issue of ordination of women pastors was debated. Although this proposal was broadly supported within the United States, it was overwhelmingly defeated because of strong opposition from delegates from the developing world. The opposition stance was rooted in a literalist, proof-texting hermeneutic. This difference of opinion in turn ignited a bitter attack by Samuel Koranteng-Pipim, a Ghanaian scholar resident in the United States, on the scholarship of Alden Thompson, known for promoting the more liberal view of biblical inspiration. The second issue involved the writings of Ellen White. The church hierarchy initially ignored the mounting evidence of her gross dependence on the writings of several contemporary scholars, some of the earliest of which was published by *Spectrum*. However, when the evidence of her plagiarism was revealed to the church membership at large in 1980 in a front-page story in the *Los Angeles Times*, with follow-up analyses in the major news magazines, the church was obliged to enter the fray. Unable to refute the evidence, church leaders chose to defend the Adventist prophet by arguing that she had only done what scholars have shown was common among the Bible writers. They thus embraced modern biblical scholarship for pragmatic reasons. However, this shift seems to have had little impact on the theological understanding and use of her writings.

Conclusion

Seventh-Day Adventists, like other sectarian Christian groups in the mid-nineteenth century, held positions on the authority of Scripture and Darwinism that were similar to those later embraced by the Fundamentalist movement. They welcomed that movement when it emerged in the 1920s. However, the tension between Adventism and society diminished over time. Once Adventist colleges sought accreditation so that their faculty members were exposed to higher education at secular universities and the degrees they awarded their students became a means for widespread upward mobility within American Adventism, Adventist biblical scholars and scientists increasingly adopted stances contrary to the earlier Fundamentalist positions. This has exacerbated the conflicts that have resulted from increasing internal diversity. A bitter battle is currently being waged within international Adventism over the issue of whether or not it will be essentially Fundamentalist in its approach.

Ronald Lawson

See also Millerites

Bibliography

Barnhouse, Donald Grey. (1956) "Are Seventh-Day Adventists Christians?" *Eternity* (September): 6–7, 43–45.

Bull, Malcolm, and Keith Lockart. (1989) *Seeking a Sanctuary: Seventh-Day Adventism and the American Dream.* New York: Harper and Row.

Butler, Jonathan. (1974) "Adventism and the American Experience." In *The Rise of Adventism: Religion and Society in Mid-Nineteenth-Century America,* edited by Edwin S. Gaustad. New York: Harper and Row, 173–206.

Dudley, Roger L., and Edwin I. Hernandez. (1992) *Citizens of Two Worlds: Religion and Politics among American Seventh-Day Adventists.* Berrien Springs, MI: Andrews University Press.

Finke, Roger, and Rodney Stark. (1992) *The Churching of America, 1776–1990: Winners and Losers in Our Religious Economy.* New Brunswick, NJ: Rutgers University Press.

General Conference of Seventh-Day Adventists. (1996) *Seventh-Day Adventist Encyclopedia,* 2 vols. Hagerstown, MD: Review and Herald.

Hammil, Richard L. (1992) *Pilgrimage: Memoirs of an Adventist Administrator.* Berrien Springs, MI: Andrews University Press.

Haywood, James L., ed. (2000) *Creation Reconsidered: Scientific, Biblical, and Theological Perspectives.* Roseville, CA: Association of Adventist Forums.

Koranteng-Pipim, Samuel. (1996) *Receiving the Word: How New Approaches to the Bible Impact Our Biblical Faith and Lifestyle.* Berrien Springs, MI: Berean Books.

Land, Gary, ed. (1986) *Adventism in America: A History.* Grand Rapids, MI: Wm. B. Eerdmans.

Lawson, Ronald. (1995) "Seventh-Day Adventist Responses to Branch Davidian Notoriety: Patterns of Diversity within a Sect Reducing Tension with Society." *Journal for the Scientific Study of Religion* 34, 3: 323–341.

———. (1996a) "Church and State at Home and Abroad: The Evolution of Seventh-Day Adventist Relations with Governments." *Journal of the American Academy of Religion* 64, 2: 279–311.

———. (1996b) "Onward Christian Soldiers?: Seventh-Day Adventists and the Issue of Military Service." *Review of Religious Research* 37, 3: 97–122.

———. (1998) "From American Church to Immigrant Church: The Changing Face of Seventh-Day Adventism in Metropolitan New York." *Sociology of Religion* 59, 4: 329–351.

———. (Forthcoming) *Apocalypse Postponed: Global Seventh-Day Adventism Faces Dilemmas of Diversity and Direction.* Walnut Creek, CA: Alta Mira.

Martin, Walter. (1960) *The Truth about Seventh-Day Adventism.* Grand Rapids, MI: Zondervan Publishing.

Morgan, Douglas. (2001) *Adventism and the American Republic: The Public Involvement of a Major Apocalyptic Movement.* Knoxville: University of Tennessee Press.

Numbers, Ronald L. (1992) *The Creationists: The Evolution of Scientific Creationism.* Berkeley: University of California Press.

Schwarz, Richard W. (1979) *Light Bearers to the Remnant.* Mountain View, CA: Pacific Press.

Thompson, Alden. (1991) *Inspiration: Hard Questions, Honest Answers.* Hagerstown, MD: Review and Herald.

White, Ellen G. (1888) *The Great Controversy between Christ and Satan.* Oakland, CA: Pacific Press.

Sheol

The Hebrew word "Sheol" denotes the unseen dwelling place of the dead. The Bible frequently portrays Sheol as being in the midst of the earth (Isaiah 7:11; Ezekiel 31:14–16) and as a place devoid of earthly activity (Ecclesiastes 9:10). It is not the ultimate place of eternal torment, but an intermediary holding place where the souls of the dead await their final judgment and the sentence of eternal punishment in hell (Revelation 20:13). The Greek equivalent to Sheol is "Hades," a term used in both the Septuagint (the Greek Old Testament) and the Greek New Testament.

Initially, Sheol (or Hades) had two compartments: a place of torment for the unrighteous dead, and a place of contentment for the righteous dead. Jesus' parable of Lazarus and the rich man (Luke 16:19–31) pictures the two places as being separated by a gulf. While the rich man suffered torment in Sheol after his death, the righteous man, Lazarus, was comforted in Abraham's bosom (considered by many scholars to be the same place Jesus called "Paradise" in Luke 23:43), After Jesus' death on the cross, He descended into Sheol and delivered Paradise (i.e., the righteous dead) into heaven (Ephesians 4:8–10). Ultimately, those held in Sheol's single remaining compartment, the souls of the unrighteous dead, will be cast into hell (Revelation 20:14).

The etymology of the Hebrew word "Sheol" is unknown. English translators of the Bible have often assigned the terms "hell," "grave," and "pit" as the proper renderings for Sheol's sixty-six occurrences in the Old Testament. More recent translations have opted to use "Sheol" rather than an attempted translation of the word.

Richard J. Cherok

See also Hell, Heaven, and Purgatory

Bibliography

Lutzer, Erwin W. (1997) *One Minute After You Die: A Preview of Your Final Destination*. Chicago: Moody Press.

Sutcliffe, Edmund F. (1946) *The Old Testament and the Future Life*. London: Barns, Oates and Washbourne.

Thompson, Fred P., Jr. (1983) *What the Bible Says about Heaven and Hell*. Joplin, MO: College Press Publishing Company.

Tromp, Nicholas J. (1969) *Primitive Conceptions of Death and the Nether World in the Old Testament*. Rome: Pontifical Biblical Institute.

Wensing, Michael G. (1993) *Death and Destiny in the Bible*. Collegeville, MN: Liturgical Press.

Shi'a Islam

Islam is a major world religion that, though possessing clearly described principles, nevertheless is not monolithic. Islam can be divided into three major sects: Sunni, Sufi, and Shi'a. The Sunnis form the majority and are the most identifiable to non-Muslims. Sufi Islam constitutes a very small minority that is primarily characterized by various forms of mysticism and a strong belief in the existence of the supernatural. However, the Shi'a sect of Islam is most often seen as being in the vanguard of Islamic Fundamentalism and has, in recent years, garnered a great deal of attention in the international news media. With slightly over 900 million adherents to Islam worldwide, approximately eleven percent would identify themselves as Shi'ite.

Origins

The roots of this Fundamentalist sect of Islam can best be understood by a look at the years immedi-ately following the death of the founder of Islam ("submission"), Muhammed ibn Abdallah (570–632 CE). Islamic doctrine is heavily dependent upon the teachings of this one man and on the subsequent interpretation by Islamic scholars of the Prophet's teachings. When Muhammed died at Medina, he left no orders regarding the governance of the *umma*, the Muslim community. Nor did he leave a male heir who might naturally have assumed Muhammed's place of leadership. Consequently, two claimants asserted their rights: Abu Bakr, a close friend and father-in-law of Muhammed, who became the first caliph, and Ali, the husband of Muhammed's daughter Fatima. Ali was an imam, a leader of daily prayers, and considered to have special infallible guidance by Allah. He was also believed to have been the first convert Muhammed made to this new, monotheistic religion. The Prophet himself claimed that Ali had special revelation and lived a sinless life in action and word. On several occasions, Ali is said to have been willing to lay down his life for Muhammed. Ali would also later claim that it was he who finished the compilation of the Qur'an. His followers called themselves *Shi'at Ali* (the party of Ali). Thereafter, the descendants of Ali are believed by Shi'ites to be the true leaders of Islam.

Ali was highly respected as the one who not only vanquished enemies but also had a deeper understanding of the Qur'an. The *Shi'at Ali* held that a ruler should also be a religious authority, free from doctrinal distortion because an Islamic government must carry out the divine law of the Shariah. In the minds of his followers, only an imam of the stature of Ali was qualified for such a position. He was schooled in metaphysics and served to train other religious scholars. Throughout its long tradition, Shi'a Islam has placed an emphasis upon natural and intuitive discovery as well as intellectual inquisitiveness. Most important of all, however, is divine revelation such as that exhibited by Imam Ali. Moreover, as the husband of Fatima, Ali maintained a lofty position in the eyes of his followers because this surviving daughter of the Prophet had long been considered to have been a major influence on her father. Thus, the Shi'ites combined both a sense of spiritual destiny and a political claim to power in their movement.

In the years that followed, not only did the followers of Ali insist that he and subsequent imams were the true inheritors of Muhammed's leadership position, but also refused to recognize the caliphate status of such rulers as Abu Bakr and his successors

Umar and Uthman. Ironically, after four and one-half years in power, Ali was later assassinated by a disgruntled follower who thought Ali had compromised the cause of those who followed him. Following Ali's death, the Umayyad dynasty of Syria attempted to bring about some cohesion within the Islamic body politic but such was not to be. Husain, the son of Ali, mounted a fierce campaign to avenge his father's death and to establish his claim as the rightful heir to the rule of his grandfather Muhammed, The Prophet.

Thus the stage was set for the watershed event that would forever forge Shi'a Islam. The Shi'a Islamic movement took on a more passionate and even romantic quality following the historic Battle of Kerbela in 680 in which Ali's son Husain and a number of members of his family were killed. It appears that Husain was on his way to Kufa to establish his claim to rule when he was ambushed. All the men were killed and the women and children were taken as prisoners to Damascus. The severed head of Husain was placed on display to symbolize the end of the Shi'ite movement. Today, Kerbela, which is located in southern Iraq, is second only to Mecca in sacred importance to a Shi'ite. The death of the Prophet's grandson is still observed and mourned with great intensity and emotion by Shi'ites on the tenth day of the month of Muharram in the Islamic calendar. Husain's death is viewed not only as a martyrdom but also as a form of redemptive analogy through death and suffering and even the hope for an eventual savior at the end of the age. Likewise, after 680, Muhammed's daughter Fatima was imbued with qualities not unlike those of the Virgin Mary, as a suffering mother to be venerated. Since the battle of Kerbela, Shi'a Islam has maintained a sense of tragedy and emphasis upon the role of suffering and martyrdom. Understandably, Shi'a Islam first gained strength in Iraq, the site of Kerbela. There it became a political force in opposition to and defiance of caliphs located in Mecca and eventually elsewhere. Indeed, some historians have concluded that Shi'a Islam is, at its heart, also a Persian versus Arab movement.

Development and Spread

In time, Shi'ites added additional traditions and lore to their unique belief system. Speculation about theology led some to believe that imams would return from the hidden world in an almost messianic form.

Shi'a Islam itself split between the followers of Ismail, the Seventh Imam and are thus referred to as the "Seveners," and the followers of the Twelfth Imam known as the "Twelvers." The Twelvers believe that the last imam, Mahdi, will return as a Muslim messiah.

Today, however, Shi'a Islam is most evident in Iran where it has been the official state religion since 1501. At that time, Shah Ismail, a fourteen year old, established the Safavid dynasty, which was Shi'ite in its doctrinal identification. This placed the Shi'ites in the eastern Ottoman Empire in opposition to the Sunnis of the western Ottoman Empire, a fact that still influences Middle Eastern spiritual and political leanings to this day. The Safavids encouraged Shi'ites from all over the Islamic world to move to Iran, which further served to solidify Shi'ite dominance. A number of Mughal emperors in India also had Shi'ite leanings.

In addition to Iran and Iraq, Shi'ite minorities exert influence in Pakistan, Turkey, Syria, and India as well. But ultimately it was in Iran that the surprising 1979 Iranian Revolution overthrew Shah Mohammed Reza Pahlavi and placed Shi'ites in political power, thus giving impetus to Islamic Fundamentalism (although the term "fundamentalism" is thought of by most Muslims as a "Christian" term). The revolution served to rekindle historic roots and give the revolutionaries a sense of return to the past. Strong emphasis is placed upon the role of the imam as the one who inherits and interprets the divine meaning of Islamic doctrine. The Imam Ayatollah Ruhollah Khomeini was the epitome of the revered Shi'ite figure who is looked upon as the inspired leader and anointed interpreter of the faith. For Shi'ite Muslims of Iran, the leadership of the Ayatollah Khomeini represented a return to the glory days of the past when Ali led his followers in the true steps of the Prophet. His anti-Western stance struck a chord with Muslims concerned about the corrupting influence of Westernization and also by those who harbored animosities from the recent imperialist influence in the Middle East. Khomeini was able to assert a Shi'ite tradition known as *taqiyyah* or "dissimulation." This doctrine suggests that an imam or other spiritual leader may say or do whatever is needed to defend the faith and pursue the true way. Such activities advance the larger interests of Allah and, ultimately of the ummah, and are thus acceptable. Such a belief therefore explained and justified some of the violence of the Iranian Revolution in 1979, such as the taking of American hostages and also the vitriolic words of the Ayatollah Khomeini. The Ayatollah was viewed as the ultimate representative and interpreter of the divine will of Allah and could thus exercise a moral veto, even in matters that would otherwise have been political.

Following in the tradition of the seventh century, Shi'ite heroes are still venerated and their tombs are pilgrimage sites. During Ramadan, Shi'ites set aside a day to mourn the death of Husain. The city of Kerbela, where the great battle ensued, is considered to have special significance as a place where Allah can work through Husain for the salvation of the truly faithful. Kerbela has become a major burial site for thousands of Shi'ites who believe that it is desirable to be buried there. Other sacred cities of Shi'a Islam include Najaf in Iraq where Ali is buried on the site that is believed to be the burial site of Adam and Noah. Likewise, Qum in Iran, where Fatima is believed to be buried, has also become a sacred pilgrimage site. The faithful pilgrims circle the tombs in a counterclockwise pattern as they repeat prayers in the belief that such pilgrimages will relieve them from the torments of the afterlife. The building of monuments to the dead by Shi'ites is a radical departure from the practice of Sunni Muslims who do not believe in placing marked tombstones or mausoleums to the dead. Today, the mausoleum of Ayatollah Khomeini, located outside of Tehran, has also become a pilgrimage site around which something of a cult has developed.

One distinctive ritual of Shi'a Islam is *ta'ziya*, which means "consolation." Ta'ziya is a form of passion play or morality drama that not only depicts the death of Husain at the Battle of Kerbela, but also portrays the principal characters as valiant heroes in a struggle with the larger forces of evil. Often the audience becomes involved in a highly emotional way that may end with a processional formed by young Shi'ite men who flagellate themselves with chains and smear blood on their bodies and faces. The color green is always worn by Husain's followers in the *ta'ziya*, which, along with the red for blood, has taken on special meaning in Shi'ite symbolism. In Iran, the colors red and green played a significant role in the 1979 revolution.

Not only is the Battle of Kerbela reenacted once a year, but the stories of Ali, Husain, and other Shi'ite heroes are recited again and again in small towns and villages in a simplified form. The story may be sung or conveyed in poetic form. While Islam prohibits the making of graven images, Shi'ites use other forms of representational art such as black draping to commemorate the events of Kerbela. In keeping with the motif of suffering, young men may carry portable shrines with pictures of Ali and other imams through the streets and often hold up large photos of recently deceased persons. During the Iran–Iraq War (1980–1988), this practice could be seen in mass demonstrations in both nations.

Thus it is the holy places and the reenactment of historic events that greatly contribute to the sense of unique community among Shi'a Muslims today. While Shi'ites certainly adhere strictly to the Five Pillars, they group the daily prayers into two points of the day: midday and afternoon prayers are prayed together as are the evening and night prayers. Their strongly emotional responses are encouraged by a special historical sense of suffering, of spiritual revelation, and of passion. In recent years, Shi'ites have countered the influence of the West by a renewed sense of destiny that they are the true carriers of the teachings of the Prophet and subsequent imams. Liberalism and materialism are viewed as destructive factors upon the essence of Islam, which can only be countered by a strict adherence to the way of Shi'a Islam.

Mary Ann Lind

See also Imam, the Last; Islamic Fundamentalism; Mahdi

Bibliography

Anderson, Roy, Robert F. Seibert, and John G. Wagner. (1990) *Politics and Change in the Middle East.* Englewood Cliffs, NJ: Prentice Hall.

Denny, Frederick Mathewson. (1985) *An Introduction to Islam.* New York: Macmillan.

Fisher, Sydney Nettleton, and William Ochsenwald. (1990) *The Middle East: A History.* New York: McGraw Hill.

Goldschmidt, Arthur. (1988) *A Concise History of the Middle East.* Boulder, CO: Westview Press.

Kelly, Marjorie, ed. (1984) *Islam: The Religious and Political Life of a World Community.* New York: Praeger.

Schimmel, Annemarie. (1992) *Islam: An Introduction.* Albany: SUNY Press.

Sin and Sinners

In Fundamentalist usage, sin has usually been construed as a failure to live up to the requirements of God's moral will, which can be known through Scripture and through the special leading of the Holy Spirit in one's life. The Christian tradition has universally recognized the pervasive influence of sin in human life in at least three important ways: as individual acts of thought and deed that violate God's will; as a condition or state of existence affecting the human soul; and as a universal power or influence affecting the ordering of creation itself. The central theme of Christian faith is forgiveness of sin, the power to defeat sin in daily life, and finally the inheritance of eternal life in heaven, which finally separates the believer from the power of sin and the dominion of the devil. In all these considerations, Protestant Fundamentalists hold to an essentially catholic and orthodox theology of sin.

The Origin of Sin

Christians have traditionally held that sin entered the world through the disobedience of Adam and Eve in the Garden of Eden, although there is also a tradition that sin entered cosmic history through a rebellion of angels prior to the creation of the world (Jude 6). This cosmic rebellion resulted in a host of fallen angels, or demons, led by the fallen archangel, Lucifer, also identified as the devil or Satan. The disobedience of Adam and Eve, called the Fall, is the cause of sin in human life, of physical death, and of spiritual death, which is the state of the soul without grace. The final consequence of sin will be judgment at the end of history and, for those not saved, the final separation of the soul from God and the community of saints in eternity.

Fundamentalists, in accord with most orthodox Christians, believe in the historical reality of the traditions of Adam and Eve, the Garden of Eden, their disobedience, the existence of Satan and demons, and a final judgment at the end of history. A principal difference between Fundamentalists and the broader Christian tradition does not lie in the affirmation of these beliefs, but in their vigorous and accentuated defense in opposition to modern skepticism. Whereas the Christian tradition had been more or less content to assume the historical reality of the Fall, Fundamentalists emphasized it, and interpreted the Genesis narrative as an objective scientific description of what actually took place about 6,000 years ago. This defense was regarded as a chief counterargument to the post-Enlightenment liberal viewpoint that human history is not a story of Fall and redemption, but of gradual moral progress, from primitive to more advanced ethical understanding, and of the gradual realization of innate human potential for goodness. It is sometimes charged that this Fundamentalist emphasis on historical literalism narrowed and obscured the Christian tradition of interpretation of Genesis and the Fall.

In spite of the universal agreement among Fundamentalists on the origin of sin, they disagree on the effects of the Fall, the nature of sin, and its extent in human life and history. Generally, Fundamentalists in North America have been influenced by three traditions with respect to sin: the Reformed or Calvinist tradition; the Arminian tradition, particularly as mediated through John Wesley and the Methodist movement; and the revivalist theology of evangelist Charles Finney (1792–1875). Some Fundamentalists, particularly Presbyterians, influenced by the Reformed tradition of Princeton Seminary, believe that Adam's sin corrupted human nature, and that this corruption along with Adam's guilt is passed on from generation to generation. In Reformed terminology, the Fall has resulted in the total depravity of the human being. Total depravity does not mean that people are incapable of good deeds; rather, it means that no part of human nature is left untouched by the effects of sin, and therefore, that no human acts are intrinsically and completely holy and free from corruption. Even acts arising from the redeemed nature of a Christian believer are not completely free from the taint of sin, due to the continuing presence of a "sin nature." The most prominent representative of this tradition during the Fundamentalist–modernist conflicts of the 1920s and 1930s was John Gresham Machen, a Princeton Seminary professor who later founded the Orthodox Presbyterian Church.

The Doctrines of Sin

Other Fundamentalists, influenced by the Methodist movement, particularly the Holiness and Pentecostal traditions, deny the Reformed doctrine of total depravity. Although John Wesley himself seems to have held to a Reformed view of human nature, his

Selection from: DEATH TO SIN, BY THE REV. C. G. FINNEY, 1840

Text.—Romans 6:7: "For he that is dead is freed from sin."

I. **Different kinds of death.**
   1. **Natural death.** This is the death of the body.
   2. **Spiritual death.** This is death in sin. It is total depravity or a state of entire alienation from God.
   3. **Eternal death.** This consists in the endless curse of God.
   4. **Death to sin.**

II. **The kind of death mentioned in the text.**

   The death here spoken of is manifestly a death to sin. This is very evident from the context. At the close of the preceding chapter, Paul had been speaking of the super-abounding grace of Christ, and commences the sixth chapter by saying, "What shall we say then? shall we continue in sin, that grace may abound? God forbid. How shall we that are dead to sin live any longer therein?"

   Here Paul is speaking of those who were alive and yet dead to sin. He spoke of their having received a baptism into the death of Christ. By their spiritual baptism they had been solemnly set apart or consecrated to the death of Christ. "Know ye not, that so many of us as were baptized into Jesus Christ were baptized into His death? Therefore we are buried with Him by baptism into death; that like as Christ was raised up from the dead by the glory of the Father, even so we also should walk in newness of life.

   For if we have been planted together in the likeness of His death, we shall be also in the likeness of His resurrection; knowing this, that our old man is crucified with Him, that the body of sin might be destroyed, that henceforth we should not serve sin. For he that is dead is freed from sin. Now, if we be dead with Christ, we believe that we shall also live with Him." He speaks of them as not only dead, but, by their spiritual baptism buried into the death of Christ. And to carry the idea of their being still farther from the life of sin; he speaks of them as being planted into the likeness of His death, and crucified with Him that the body of sin might be destroyed. And then adds in the words of the text, "Now he that is dead is freed from sin." The term here rendered justification may be rendered "is made righteous."

   It is plain from this connection, that Paul is speaking of those who had been so baptized by the Holy Spirit so as to be dead to sin, buried, planted, crucified, as it respects sin.

III. **What it consists in.**

   Summarily, death to sin consists in the annihilation of selfishness, and the reign of perfect love to God and man in the heart and life.

Source: Finney, Charles Gradison (1840) " Lecture XIV. Death to Sin."
The Oberlin Evangelist, July 15. www.whatsaiththescripture.com

followers tended to interpret the Fall as a loss of original righteousness, not as a total corruption of human nature. Having lost the grace that sustained Adam's righteousness, human beings lack the moral willpower to do the right thing. Though not corrupt by nature, without the sustaining grace of original righteousness, they invariably make sinful choices and consequently acquire guilt and corruption—though rarely as to completely eradicate their ability to repent and accept the saving grace of Christ. The influential Methodist theologian, Richard Watson (1781–1833), articulated this viewpoint.

Finally, the "New School" tradition of Charles Finney modified the traditional Reformed emphasis on total depravity. According to Finney, human beings possessed a natural ability to know right from wrong, and the natural ability to act on that knowledge by repentance. Although universal, the power of sin over human life was not conceived as so pervasive that it rendered human beings impotent or incapable of right reason, for if it did, evangelism and exhortations to moral improvement would be superfluous. Sinful acts do not, therefore, inevitably arise from a sin nature, but from natural desires lacking in supernatural grace, and an absence of intellectual awareness of the moral purpose of God. Finney's understanding of sin and sinners became the unexamined assumptions of many Fundamentalists.

Teachings on the Power of Sin

The effects of sin in the Christian life must also be considered. Fundamentalists in the Reformed tradition believe that the Christian, after having been saved by accepting the promise of forgiveness in the gospel, continues to struggle against the sin nature with the assistance of God's grace. This sin nature is never completely eradicated in this life, although through growth in righteousness it is weakened and its power destroyed. This viewpoint has been widely held by Fundamentalists, giving rise to frequent exhortations against "backsliding." A backslider is a Christian who has yielded to the sin nature and by repeated acts of sin fallen into a state of moral weakness and degradation.

Fundamentalists in the Wesleyan-Holiness traditions have a different view of the power of sin in the Christian life. They argue that God did not intend for the believer to struggle with a sin nature, and that the sin nature can be eradicated through a second work of sanctifying grace. The state of freedom from sinful desires and from actual sin is called "entire sanctification." This distinctive view stemming from John Wesley's teaching on perfection often led to a separation between Reformed and Wesleyan Fundamentalists. This could be seen in early Los Angeles, for example, where Fundamentalists at the Bible Institute of Los Angeles appeared to have little contact with Holiness Fundamentalists at the across-town Training School for Christian Workers.

However, a moderate form of Holiness teaching did influence Presbyterian and Baptist Fundamentalists. This teaching was called the "Keswick doctrine of sanctification," and it gained a widespread hearing in the United States through English interpreters like G. Campbell Morgan (1863–1945) and W. H. Griffith Thomas (1861–1924), and through the influence of Dwight L. Moody in his Northfield Bible Conferences. Keswick leaders argued that the sin nature was not eradicated in this life, but the power of sin could be broken by a second application of grace, so that one could live a victorious Christian life without a continuing struggle against sin. This idea provided a halfway point between Reformed views and the practical Holiness views popular in American revivalism.

The Fundamentalist Concept of Sin

Fundamentalists generally focused less on sin as a fallen condition of existence, emphasizing instead the practical common sense view of Charles Finney— that people are not born sinners, but become sinners as they commit individual acts of sin. This viewpoint led both Reformed and Wesleyan Fundamentalists to regard sin as particular acts that could be resisted by living a spiritual life infused with practices of piety and devotion, such as reading the Bible, memorizing and reciting Scripture, praying, and avoiding worldly temptations. Moreover, the role of the devil as a tempter to sin received greater attention in Fundamentalist institutions than it did in the mainline Protestant denominations. Individual acts of sin have often been regarded as the result of the temptations of the devil combined with natural lusts of the flesh; hence, the popular anti-Fundamentalist parody, "the devil made me do it."

The Fundamentalist conception of sin has also been shaped by the biblical precept of "being in the world but not of the world" (see John 15:19, 17:14, 18:36; 2 Corinthians 10:3). For many Fundamentalists, separation from the world is considered the defining feature of Fundamentalism, though it should be noted that religious separatism has characterized many Christian movements. Fundamentalists often focused on specific sins that were considered worldly, such as smoking, drinking alcoholic beverages, dancing, attending movies, wearing jewelry and make-up, and playing cards. Other practices that could lead to entanglement in the world included crude language and humor, immodest dress, preoccupation with fashion, and neglect of the Christian Sabbath. For some pietistic Fundamentalists avoiding the world could also mean shunning political involvement, which might subject the believer to spiritual compromises and the use of worldly means

455

to achieve political objectives. During the 1970s and 1980s, however, many Fundamentalists rejected this form of piety and acquired a new voice in American politics through the conservative coalition known as the Moral Majority. Earlier in the century, revivalist Billy Sunday found a wide hearing for his fast-talking attacks on social sins, which included spitting, playing baseball on Sundays, alcoholism, prostitution, and communism. Support for temperance in the nineteenth century led Fundamentalists to substitute grape juice for wine in the Holy Communion, and sometimes even to claim that the wine that Jesus and His disciples drank was not fermented.

Fundamentalists and their revivalist forbears have often been criticized for their emphasis on moralism, that is, creating lists of forbidden behaviors and preaching with great fervor against them. While it is true that revivalists were concerned about sin and sometimes used the threat of punishment in hell as an inducement for people to repent, it was not the dominant motif of revival preaching. Historians have pointed out that the famous sermon of Jonathan Edwards, "Sinners in the Hands of an Angry God," which compared the sinner to a spider dangling above the flame of a candle, was not necessarily typical of revival preaching. Moreover, although Charles Finney sometimes identified sinners by name in his revivals, this did not become a common practice. Indeed, Moody quite explicitly rejected "hell fire and brimstone preaching," favoring instead a sentimental emphasis on love and forgiveness.

Fundamentalists have not distinguished between mortal and venial sins as in the Roman Catholic tradition. Distrust of subtle distinctions encouraged Fundamentalists to treat all sins as equally bad before the standard of God's righteousness, and as equally forgivable through repentance and faith. An interesting exception to this arises from the problem of the "sin against the Holy Spirit," which Jesus said was the only sin that would not be forgiven (Matthew 12:31). Taking Jesus' words literally, Fundamentalists attempted to explain what this sin is and how to avoid it.

Opposition to nineteenth-century liberal assumptions about sin and human nature also shaped Fundamentalist ideas of sin. In contrast to Unitarians and mainline Protestant liberals, who asserted an innate potential for the moral goodness of human beings, Fundamentalists emphasized the sinfulness of humanity. Fundamentalist opposition to the Social Gospel was also key. In this early-twentieth-century movement, religious leaders regarded sin not merely as personal moral failings, but as a corporate reality caused by class divisions and the unjust distribution of wealth. Ironically, pre-Civil War revivalists like Charles Finney had been considered social progressives, but by the late nineteenth century, revivalism tended to be allied with industrial capitalism and social conservatism. This was most evident in the ministry of Dwight L. Moody, who believed that poverty was the result of laziness and a lack of thrift. For his Fundamentalist successors, society would not be changed by fighting social injustice, but by converting one sinner at a time through the preaching of the gospel.

During the second half of the twentieth century, some Fundamentalists mounted a challenge to this narrowly individualistic conception of sin. Carl F. H. Henry published a critique in 1947 entitled *The Uneasy Conscience of Modern Fundamentalism*, in which he called for a new social consciousness among Fundamentalists. Although not forsaking a traditional revivalist emphasis on soul saving, Billy Graham identified himself with this emerging perspective. As a result of these developments, Fundamentalists have attempted to broaden their conception of sin and take into account the social factors that lead to sin, problems of injustice, and the psychological roots of sin.

Daniel W. Draney

See also Eternal Life; Fall of Humankind; Grace; Original Sin; Perfectionism; Sanctification

Bibliography

Dorsett, Lyle W. (1991) *Billy Sunday and the Redemption of Urban America*. Grand Rapids, MI: Wm. B. Eerdmans.

Draney, Daniel W. (1996) "John Murdoch MacInnis and the Crisis of Authority in American Protestant Fundamentalism, 1925–1929." Unpublished Ph.D. diss., Pasadena, CA: Fuller Theological Seminary.

Findlay, J. F. (1969) *Dwight L Moody: American Evangelist, 1837–1899*. Chicago: University of Chicago Press.

Henry, Carl F. H. (1947) *The Uneasy Conscience of Modern Fundamentalism*. Grand Rapids, MI: Wm. B. Eerdmans.

Ramm, Bernard. (1985) *Offense to Reason: A Theology of Sin*. New York: Harper and Row Publishers.

Weisberger, Bernard. (1958) *They Gathered at the River: The Story of the Great Revivialists and Their Impact Upon Religion in America*. Boston: Little, Brown and Co.

Soul

The notion of the soul is of primary importance in Fundamentalist thinking because it motivates much of Fundamentalist church life, preaching, and even family activities. The Fundamentalists' understanding of the soul comes from a long historical, philosophical, and theological development in Western thought which gave birth to the Fundamentalist tradition. The primary focus of the life and ministry of the Fundamentalist church is the saving of souls. In fact, the Fundamentalist church finds more value in the soul than the body.

Early Western Thought

The study of the soul has its origins in Western thought as far back as pre-Platonic and pre-Socratic philosophy. Plato was the father of this discipline in the golden era of Greek philosophy. Plato (429–347 BCE), a student of the philosopher Socrates (469–399 BCE), raised many of the questions that modern theology and philosophy still ask today. The soul or *psyche* was the primary focus of the pursuit of happiness and all things good and pleasurable. To the Greek philosopher the alleviation of pain and the increase of pleasure were the goals of life. Pleasure was experienced by the soul through the activities of the body. The body was secondary, the soul and its pleasure was primary.

Plato divided the soul or *psyche* into three main parts: (1) The appetites, which includes all human myriad desires for various pleasures, comforts, physical satisfactions, and bodily ease. These appetites are so numerous that Plato does not bother to enumerate them all, and he notes that they are often in conflict with each other. (2) The spirited, or hot-blooded, part, that is, the emotional part of the soul that gets angry, for example, when it perceives an injustice being done. This is the part of the soul that loves to face and overcome great challenges, that can steel itself to adversity, and that loves victory, winning, challenge, and honor. Plato's use of the term "spir-

ited" here is not the same as "spiritual," but instead is used in the same sense as when speaking of a high-spirited horse with lots of energy and power. (3) The mind (*nous*), our conscious awareness, is represented by the charioteer who guides the horses and chariot. This is the part of the soul that thinks, analyzes, looks ahead, rationally weighs options, and tries to gauge what is best and truest overall.

According to Plato, the soul is a complex part of the human creation and the center of human experience. The body is the house in which the soul dwells. The dichotomy between body and soul is a hallmark of early Western philosophical thought. In this dichotomy the soul and body are often at war because of differing priorities. In his Dialogue "Cratylus," Plato contrasts this body-soul dichotomy. The body is a "prison" that the soul inhabits. "Note also that we have nothing to do with men while they are in the body, but only when the soul is liberated from the desires and evils of the body" (see Cratylus in Hamilton and Cairns 1987: 403). Fundamentalists parallel this view in that they see humans as corrupt and in need of cleansing through spiritual renewal (see *The Baptist Confession, 1689*: 17).

Plato claims that the soul has eternal value and worth. He states that "there exists: first, the unchanging form, uncreated and indestructible, admitting no modification and entering no combination, . . . second, that which bears the same name as the form and resembles it . . and third, space which is eternal and indestructible, which provides a position for everything that comes to be" (see Timeus in Hamilton and Cairns 1987: 20). The soul is eternal and indestructible.

Aristotle (384–322 BCE), Plato's student, corrected some of the errors he saw in Plato's thinking. Aristotle believed that the soul was that which animates each individual. In Aristotle's logic the error of the soul/body distinction is avoided. His definition of the soul as a physical organized body potentially possessing life emphasizes the closeness of the union of soul and body. The difficulty in his theory is to determine what degree of distinction or separation from the matter of the body is to be conceded to the human soul. He fully recognizes the spiritual element in thought and describes the "active intellect" (*nous poetikos*) as "separate and impassible," but the precise relation of this active intellect to the individual mind is a hopelessly obscure question in Aristotle's psychology (Shahan 1917: 153).

The Stoics, representing another branch of Greek thought, taught that all existence is material, and described the soul as a breath pervading the body. They also called it Divine, a particle of God, composed of the most refined and ethereal matter. They recognized eight distinct parts of the soul: the ruling reason, the five senses, and the procreative powers (Shahan 1917: 153).

Gnostic Thought

The Gnostics created a distorted variation of Plato's philosophy of the soul in that they held that the body and soul were warring inside each person. The body is material, temporal, and created by evil while the soul is immaterial and essentially good. Thus, the body and soul struggle for domination. Salvation comes to those who can free themselves from the control of the material body to the control of the immaterial soul. This freedom is obtained through divine revelation or knowledge (*gnosis*) received from above. The Gnostics divided man into three classes: spiritual (*pneumatici*), animal (*psychici*), and earthy (*choici*). They believed that the soul-body is the lowly animal urges that each person experiences and most overcome. Divine knowledge is obtained by buffeting the body into submission until the seeker is brought into an ecstatic experience and eternal knowledge is found.

Judeo-Christian Thought

Fundamentalism at its core affirms the literal truth of the Old and New Testaments. The method of interpreting the Scriptures was in normal or plain sense. This high view of Scripture forms Fundamentalist thinking in all areas of life and practice. Issues of creation, sin, death, heaven, hell, rebirth, and resurrection are all interpreted in a literal sense.

Old Testament

From the very early chapters of Scripture the soul is seen as irrevocably united to the body. In Genesis 2:7 at the creation of man "the LORD God formed man *of the dust of the ground*, and breathed into his nostrils the breath of life; and man became a living being" (NKJV). Living being or *nephesh* is the Hebrew word for the soul and in the Hebrew culture it was inseparable from the body. The soul and body were eternally united. After the creation of Adam and Eve, God made a covenant with them that on condition of perfect obedience they would have eternal life. However, if they disobeyed the one command of God, eating of the Tree of the Knowledge of Good and Evil, "on that day they would surely die" (Genesis 2:17). Adam did eat and his soul died immediately and his body soon after. Because of Adam's sinful disobedience (original sin) all of his offspring also receive this same spiritual death—the death of the soul. Soon after Adam's disobedience God made another promise to Adam that He would deliver him from his sin and disobedience. The Scriptures teach that this deliverance is for both body and soul, because both felt the effects of sin and both were to be delivered from those effects.

As the Old Testament unfolds it is the soul that grieves over its sins and is in anguish due to the trials of life. The psalmist writes: "Have mercy on me, O LORD, for I am weak; O LORD, heal me, for my bones are troubled. My soul also is greatly troubled" (Psalm 6:2–3). Both body and soul are united in the struggles of life. The Old Testament develops a unity of body and soul that is expressed in a proto-resurrection doctrine as found in Isaiah 29:19, which foretells of a bodily resurrection of those who are delivered by the Lord God of Scripture: "your dead shall live; together with my dead body they shall arise. Awake and sing, you who dwell in dust; for your dew is like the dew of herbs, And the earth shall cast out the dead."

New Testament

In the New Testament God is described as the creator of things material and immaterial: "For by Him all things were created that are in heaven and that are on earth, visible and invisible. . . . All things were created through Him and for Him" (Colossians 1:16). According to Paul, the soul, an invisible creation, was created by God and for His purposes. The material and immaterial have an ongoing relationship in biblical understanding and are not easily separated.

The early followers of Jesus Christ were aware of the ongoing debate between two factions within the Hebrew community. One group, the Sadducees, followed the Greek thought of Aristotle and believed that there was no reality after death and no resurrection of the dead. They held to a form of annihilation. The Pharisees, a more Platonic group, promoted the resurrection of the dead and looked forward to the uniting of the delivered bodies and souls (Matthew 22:23).

Jesus Christ taught much concerning the soul and its relation to the body, particularly that God alone had authority over the destiny of the soul: "Do not fear those who kill the body but cannot kill the soul. But rather fear Him who is able to destroy both soul and body in hell" (Matthew 10:28). He also taught that the soul had tremendous value, "For what profit is it to a man if he gains the whole world, and loses his own soul? Or what will a man give in exchange for his soul?" (Matthew 16:26).

In the New Testament the notion of soul and spirit are interchangeable. Therefore, the soul must experience a new birth since it is dead from sin. In Scripture, souls are born in a state of death to those who are not followers of Christ: "And you He made alive, who were dead in trespasses and sins" (Ephesians 2:1). Souls then are in need of being reborn. John records Jesus' words in his gospel, "Jesus answered, 'Most assuredly, I say to you, unless one is born of water and the Spirit, he cannot enter the kingdom of God. That which is born of the flesh is flesh, and that which is born of the Spirit is spirit. Do not marvel that I said to you, You must be born again'" (John 3:5–7).

Because of Adam's sin of disobedience in the Garden of Eden the soul of each person is dead. This death continues until it is the recipient of new life by the Holy Spirit of God. Fundamentalists are highly motivated to see the souls of all people receive this new birth when faith is put in Christ and His death on the cross. In the Fundamentalist view, new birth occurs when a "sinner" puts his or her trust in the substitutionary work of Jesus Christ. Christ's death and the sinner's faith in His death are the signs of new birth or being "born again." When a sinner is born again or receives new birth there is a restoration of the soul that will be completed at the uniting of the soul with the body at the resurrection.

The apostle Paul, a convert to Christianity from Hebrew Phariseeism, brought much of the latter's view of the body and soul with him to his new religion. Paul wrote that the new birth that Jesus spoke of was a new birth of the whole person, body, soul, and spirit: "Now may the God of peace Himself sanctify you completely; and may your whole spirit, soul, and body be preserved blameless at the coming of our Lord Jesus Christ" (1 Thessalonians 5:23). Paul, to whom the Resurrection of Christ was a primary doctrine, taught that the followers of Jesus, those who were "born again," would experience the resurrection of body and soul. Paul's teaching was integral to the Fundamentalist tradition.

The Early Church Fathers

The early church fathers, the leaders of the post-apostolic church, took either the views of Plato or Aristotle as they developed the doctrine and theology of the church. The early fathers struggled with the question of the soul and its origin. These theologians advanced three main doctrines for the origin of the soul. The doctrine of preexistence was inspired by Platonism. It held that the soul had a higher existence prior to joining the body. Moreover, the material world was inherently evil and was linked to the transmigration of the soul. Gnostics saw the soul as having a divine substance. This view was promoted by Origen (c. 185–c. 254 CE), but was condemned in the fifth century. Traducianism held that the soul was created at the exact moment as the body at procreation by the parents. The soul is a material creation. Traducianism was promoted by Tertullian (c.160–c. 236 CE), who was influenced by the Greek Stoics. This doctrine is the official teaching of the Lutheran tradition. The doctrine of creationism holds that the soul is a unique creation of God *ex nihilo*, "out of nothing," and that He implants the soul in the person at the moment of conception. This is the most widely held view among Christians today (Berkouwer 1962).

Two divergent views concerning the soul developed later in early church theology. St. Augustine (354–430 CE) followed the teaching of the apostle Paul that all souls are spiritually dead and need new birth to bring them to life. A more popular view was advanced by Pelagius (c. 400 CE), a British monk. He saw the soul as merely weak and which only needed strengthening and help to gain salvation. These two views run through all of church history and caused considerable debate.

Protestantism

Sixteenth-century Protestantism brought to the forefront the doctrines of justification and salvation. The reformers and their progeny—pietism, revivalism, and Fundamentalism—believed that the soul was the primary focus of redemption. The salvation of the soul was eminent. As Protestantism developed, the reformers such as John Calvin (1509–1564), Martin Luther (1483–1546), John Knox (1514–1572), Jonathan Edwards (1703–1758), and George Whitefield (1714–1770) took the Augustian view of the spiritual deadness of the soul. This view was challenged by others such as Phillip Melanchthon (1497–1565), a follower of Martin Luther, John (1703–1791) and Charles

(1707–1788) Wesley, the schools of pietism, revivalism, and much of Fundamentalism, who took either the Pelagian or semi-Pelagian view.

Fundamentalism

Fundamentalism maintains that the soul is lost, sinful, and in need of a spiritual birth of recovery. Fundamentalist Jack Hyles writes, "Every Christian must be soul conscience" (1962: 26). Souls are eternally valuable and need salvation. To the Fundamentalist the human soul can either be saved or lost. The mission of the Fundamentalist church and every individual believer is to lead lost souls/lost sinners to salvation that is based on the work and ministry of Jesus Christ. Salvation is founded on putting faith in the substitutionary work of Christ and his death on the cross. The so-called Great Commission is at the root of Fundamentalist thought concerning the soul: "Go therefore and make disciples of all the nations, baptizing them in the name of the Father and of the Son and of the Holy Spirit, teaching them to observe all things that I have commanded you" (Matthew 28:19–20). These words recorded as spoken by Jesus are a serious command for Fundamentalists.

Church services, revival meetings, and evangelistic crusades all focused on the mission of saving lost souls from punishment in hell because a soul that is not saved/born again will spend eternity in hell. Fundamentalist church services emphasize the salvation of the lost soul. The music, prayer, and preaching are all directed at saving lost souls from the torment of hell.

Conclusion

Fundamentalists are a part of the long tradition of Western theological and philosophical development. Their notion of the soul is consistent with this Western legacy. The Fundamentalist believes that the soul has eternal immeasurable value and is in need of salvation because of its sinful nature. The Fundamentalist church values the soul more than the body. Therefore, the Fundamentalist believes that salvation can only be achieved by faith in the work of Jesus Christ as He died on the cross for human sins.

Patrick W. Malone

See also Holy Spirit; New Testament; Old Testament; Original Sin; Sin and Sinners

Bibliography

The Baptist Confession, 1689. (1981) Sterling, VA: GAM Publications.

Berkouwer, Gerrit C. (1962) *Man: The Image of God.* Grand Rapids, MI: Wm. B. Eerdmans.

Ferguson, Sinclair, ed. (1988) *New Dictionary of Theology.* Downers Grove, IL: InterVarsity Press.

Gonzalez, Justo. (1984) *The Story of Christianity.* New York: Harper and Row.

Hamilton, Edith, and Huntington Cairns, eds. (1987) *Plato, The Collected Dialogues.* Princeton, NJ: Princeton University Press.

Hyles, Jack. (1962) *Let's Go Soul Winning.* Hammond, IN: Hyles-Anderson Press.

Orr, James, ed. (1994) *The International Standard Bible Encyclopedia,* vols. I–IV. Grand Rapids, MI: Wm. B. Eerdmans.

Shahan, Rt. Rev. Thomas J., ed. (1917) *The Catholic Encyclopedia,* vol. XIV. The Encyclopedia Press, Inc.

Walton, Robert. (1986) *Church History.* Grand Rapids, MI: Zondervan Publishing.

Southeast Asia

Protestant Fundamentalism in Southeast Asia is best understood within the political, geographical, religious, and historic context of the region. Comprehension of this subject is also enhanced given the background to the birth of Protestant Fundamentalism and its interest in missions in general, and Southeast Asia in particular. Therefore, this article is divided under four main headings consisting of a brief political-religious overview of Southeast Asian history, the emergence of Protestant Fundamentalism, Protestant Fundamentalism in Southeast Asia, and the future of Fundamentalism in the region.

Political-Religious Overview of Southeast Asia

Southeast Asia is comprised of ten countries: Myanmar (also known as Burma), Thailand, Laos, Cambodia, Vietnam, Malaysia, Singapore, Brunei, Indonesia, and the Philippines. The designate Southeast Asia came about during World War II to clarify, for the

Allies, the geographical boundaries of the war effort. Situated between the two great civilizations of India and China, this area was formerly identified by various names such as "Little China," "Greater India," and "Indo-Pacific." Past scholars of this region wondered whether the Philippines should be included with the rest of the Southeast Asian states because this country's history is quite distinct from the rest of the region. Similarly, Vietnam is considered by many scholars as part of East Asia (China, Japan, the Koreas) more than Southeast Asia because China's influence in Vietnam is much more profound than in any other part of Southeast Asia. Indeed, Vietnam was considered part of East Asia during the first millennium of the common era.

Broken down even further, Southeast Asia is divided into two sections: mainland Southeast Asia (Myanmar, Thailand, Vietnam, Laos, Cambodia) and insular Southeast Asia (Malaysia, Singapore, Brunei, Indonesia, Philippines). Dissecting this region into these two parts assists the casual observer to understand its religious foundations. Indeed, it might be said that Southeast Asia has the greatest diversity of religions found anywhere in the world. Take, for example, mainland Southeast Asia. In the countries of Thailand, Myanmar, Laos, and Cambodia the populations are overwhelmingly Therevada (orthodox) Buddhists. In Vietnam, Mahayana Buddhism prevails as the dominant religion, although Catholicism still claims to have several million adherents among the Vietnamese.

The insular Southeast Asian states have an even more amazing diversity of world religions. Indonesia is the largest Islamic nation on the planet and the peoples of Brunei and Malaysia also are predominantly Islamic. Singapore, the city-state overwhelmingly made up of ethnic Chinese, celebrates its diversity of religion including various Buddhist, Taoist, and Confucian sects from China. Inhabitants of Java, one of the islands of Indonesia, are said to be the only predominantly Hindu community outside of South Asia. Finally, the Philippines, with a population of eighty million, is identified as Asia's only Christian nation.

Southeast Asia's religious diversity is rooted in the region's historical experience. Buddhist, Islamic, and Christian missionaries, as well as early Brahman priests, came to the different states and disseminated their belief systems. The area's religious diversity attests to the varying degrees of success that each of these world religions had on the ten states of Southeast Asia.

The Emergence of Protestant Fundamentalism

In his award-winning book, *Fundamentalism and American Culture*, Marsden (1980) accurately demonstrates that the roots of American Protestant Fundamentalism are found in nineteenth-century religious movements. During this period there was a shift away from the doctrine of total depravity of humanity, to the belief that humanity was not as lost as St. Augustine and the Protestant Reformers claimed. Based on the philosophy of Scottish Common Sense Realism, seminary professors taught that every aspect of the Bible and God could be understood based on intuitive study and reason.

Three major implications of this theological and philosophical shift would eventually affect Southeast Asian peoples. First, the idea that humans had the ability to convince people to become "saved" opened the floodgate of innovations to produce converts. Charles Finney, the trendsetter in this area, began to announce that revivals would take place at various locales. His assumption was that through human innovation—a vibrant song leader, a dynamic preacher whose sermons would climax with sentimental stories, and a public invitation for people to come forward and accept Christ as their personal savior—revivals could be instigated. Success was based on the number of people an evangelist could "get saved" at such meetings.

This first theological divergence from orthodox Christianity led to a second idea, which, like the first, came to affect Southeast Asia. This was the belief that individuals had the ability to choose or reject God. While this was antithetical to the writings of St. Paul, St. Augustine, Martin Luther, and Jonathan Edwards, this idea of free will became the dominant theological position of the growing Fundamentalist movement.

Finally, the third theological shift that affected Southeast Asia was a new eschatological system called "dispensational premillenialism." In short, this system taught that the world was a lost cause, and that it was a Christian's duty to save as many people as quickly as possible because God was about to "rapture" all Christians out of the world, and then a "great tribulation" period would begin on earth. These three changes in the historic orthodox theology of the Christian Church gave rise to the modern missionary movement. It was incumbent on Christians to travel around the world and give everyone an opportunity to choose Christ, and to save as many people as possible before the Rapture.

It is important to remember that the theology of Fundamentalists affected every aspect of their worldview. An emphasis was placed on remaining separate from general culture because the complete focus of the convert had to be on heaven and not on this world, which was the domain of Satan. There was also an anti-intellectual bent among Fundamentalists due to the growth of science and Darwinism in the nineteenth century, and the inability of Fundamentalists to properly respond to this. Concomitantly, Fundamentalists remained ignorant of the basic aspects of Church history. They became skeptical of any Christian Church that was not completely independent of a denominational hierarchy.

Fundamentalism in Southeast Asia

Christianity came to Southeast Asia during the early sixteenth century. Portuguese and Spanish friars moved to the area and established missions. In 1565, the Philippines became part of Spain's empire and for the next three centuries the archipelago was politically dominated by the friars. During the eighteenth and nineteenth centuries, Catholic priests from France brought their religion to Vietnam, and cathedrals were built there. Thus, Roman Catholicism was the early Christian influence in Southeast Asia. During the nineteenth century, Catholic priests were joined by Protestant missionaries. Yet, we must distinguish these early Protestant missionaries from the later Protestant Fundamentalist zealots. The first Protestant missionaries in Southeast Asia were from the mainline denominations, and they did not have the theological bent of the later Fundamentalists. Instead, they were more concerned with improving the indigenous peoples' societies, whether through improved agricultural techniques or the introduction of new medicines.

After World War II, Protestant Fundamentalist missionaries flocked to Southeast Asia for various reasons. Primarily, the Fundamentalists had been in retreat since the 1925 Scopes "Monkey Trial" debacle, wherein they were labeled as ignorant. After the war, however, they believed that they had been vindicated by the horrendous aspects of war, and the creation of weapons of mass destruction. Further, there was an increased distance between mainline denominations and independent (mostly Baptist) organizations.

Southeast Asia soon became very attractive to Fundamentalist missionaries. Nine of the ten countries in the region had been colonized by Western powers, with Thailand being the sole exception. This meant that a modicum of Western imperialism was in place—something that the missionaries could build on. Southeast Asia was also a battleground for the stemming of communism and Vietnam, in particular, was targeted as an area where Christian influence could stem the anti-God Marxist ideology. The Buddhist countries of mainland Southeast Asia were also open to missionaries, while the Islamic countries of Malaysia, Brunei, and Indonesia were more wary of Protestant zealots. If success is measured by results, it was the Philippines that provided the greatest opportunities for Fundamentalist missionaries. Today, on this archipelago, one can spot independent Baptist churches throughout the towns and cities.

Despite the ubiquity of Fundamentalist churches in Southeast Asia, this radical arm of Protestantism has not experienced the same success that Roman Catholicism and other world religions have enjoyed in the region. Several factors make Fundamentalism unpalatable in Southeast Asian communities. First, a major tenet of Fundamentalist theology is the belief that true Christians must not become entangled in popular society and culture. In Southeast Asia this means that Fundamentalists do not participate in animistic-based rituals, non-Christian religious celebrations, or any social gathering that does not have conservative Christian overtones. In Thailand, Burma, Vietnam, Laos, and Cambodia—where Buddhism is the state religion—the implication of Christian Fundamentalist separatism affects every area of social interaction. In the predominantly Islamic countries of Brunei, Malaysia, and Indonesia, conservative Christians are a subculture and considered societal pariahs who gladly accept the persecution that is promised to all who truly follow the teachings of Jesus. Even in the Philippines, a predominantly Christian nation, there is a distinction made between Fundamentalists and mainline Catholic or other Protestant citizens. The separation between these groups is based on the Fundamentalists' claim that anyone who follows religious tradition rather than the Bible is not a Christian. Consequently, Filipino Fundamentalists refuse to participate in corporate celebrations such as a town's annual fiesta celebrating the municipality's patron saint.

Another reason that Fundamentalism has not spread widely in Southeast Asian communities is that a social characteristic of this region is the emphasis placed on kinship loyalty and corporate behavior. In contrast, Fundamentalism stresses the primacy of individual spirituality. Finally, as an anti-intellectual movement, Fundamentalism in this region does not attract the professional elite. Demographically, it is the economic lower class that fills the conservative Christian congregations. A dominant theme in the preaching to these believers, then, is that their poverty and persecution in this life are due to the wickedness of this world and to the devil's rule on this earth. Since the focus of the Fundamentalist message is on the brevity of this life because of the imminent return of Christ, adherents to this doctrine are encouraged to just hold on for awhile and soon their suffering will be turned to joy.

Nevertheless, with the emphasis on abandoning tradition and corporate behavior, it is somewhat surprising that there are thousands of Fundamentalist congregations throughout Southeast Asia. What would possess individuals to take such a radical step and depart from tradition and culture? The answer to this question is multifaceted, but is certainly rooted in several aspects of Fundamentalist doctrine: the explanation for current suffering, the guarantee of a glorious future, and the personal aspect of this conservative community.

Another motivation for conversion is the biblical promise that in the end, the last will be first and the first will be last. Fundamentalists proudly hold to the literal translation of the Bible; therefore, they promise that every believer will receive a mansion and walk on streets of gold when they get to heaven. It only takes a prayer to guarantee that one will be rich for eternity. Pastors and missionaries tell their followers that although every true believer must wear the badge of an antisocial religious fanatic, this brief humiliation will result in eternal rewards.

Finally, in a region where monks, priests, nuns, and imams must minister to millions of people, there often arises a sense of impersonal religious relations. Many Southeast Asians claim that their spiritual needs are not met because of the sheer volume of people that their spiritual leaders must minister to. Fundamentalists, on the other hand, emphasize the duty of pastors to make weekly visitations to all their church members, and to create a community where accountability, emotional and financial support, and a close-knit subculture are nurtured.

The Future of Fundamentalism in Southeast Asia

There are trends that point to a current and future shift among Southeast Asian Fundamentalists. Frustrated by the lack of meaningful worship services, many are returning to either a more historic form of Christianity, either in Roman Catholic or mainline Protestant churches. They are not returning to non-Christian world religions, but, instead, are seeking a more historic understanding of the Christian faith. Results are the basis of success for Fundamentalists, and therefore there is little surprise that many Southeast Asian indigenous pastors and foreign missionaries are studying the techniques of mega-churches and incorporating their methods. One example of this is that the services are noted to be "seeker friendly," that is, attractive and comfortable for visitors who might be seeking the truth. Finally, Fundamentalists in Southeast Asia will continue to maintain their methods and ministries among the rural, relatively poorly educated population because the message to this group is that the harshness of this life will be replaced with a glorious heavenly life. This populace is also unaware of the fact that while Fundamentalist leaders assert that they are preaching the "true gospel," the fact is that most of their theology and methods are rooted in the nineteenth century.

L. Shelton Woods

Bibliography

Anderson, Gerald H., ed. (1969) *Studies in Philippine Church History*. Ithaca, NY: Cornell University Press.

Caplan, Lionel. (1987) *Class and Culture in Urban India: Fundamentalism in a Christian Community*. New York: Clarendon Press.

Chopra, V. D., ed. (1994) *Religious Fundamentalism in Asia*. New Delhi, India: Gyan Publishing House.

Clymer, Kenton J. (1986) *Protestant Missionaries in the Philippines, 1898–1916: An Inquiry into the American Colonial Mentality*. Chicago: University of Illinois Press.

Cooley, Frank L. (1982) *The Growing Seed: The Christian Church in Indonesia*. New York: Division of Overseas Ministries.

Frank, Douglas W. (1986) *Less Than Conquerors: How Evangelicals Entered the Twentieth Century.* Grand Rapids, MI: Wm. B. Eerdmans.

Hutchinson, William R. (1987) *Errand to the World: American Protestant Thought and Foreign Missions.* Chicago: University of Chicago Press.

Marsden, George M. (1980) *Fundamentalism and American Culture: The Shaping of Twentieth-Century Evangelicalism, 1870–1925.* New York: Oxford University Press.

Tarling, Nicholas, ed. (1992) *The Cambridge History of Southeast Asia,* 2 vols. Cambridge: Cambridge University Press.

Speaking in Tongues (Glossolalia)

Having tarried for days during the middle of a snowy Canadian winter in 1908, the teenage Aimee Semple McPherson shivered as she longed to receive the "baptism of the Holy Spirit." Finally, her prayer seemed to be answered when her body began to tremble, she slipped completely to the ground, and out of her lips escaped syllables in "other tongues." McPherson's religious experience exemplifies a phenomenon that occurred in the lives of thousands of North American Christians at the turn of the century.

"Glossolalia" is the term historians and theologians have used to describe people's experiences of speaking in unknown languages. Derived from the Greek New Testament expression translated "speaking in tongues," the word *glossolalia* came into use in the late nineteenth century. The phenomenon itself has a long and controversial history dating back to the origins of the Christian Church. The first men and women to speak in tongues were Christ's disciples who patiently waited together for the promised descent of the Holy Spirit, which occurred on the Day of Pentecost. Suddenly, the biblical author wrote, the disciples were filled with the Spirit and "began to speak in other languages, as the Spirit gave them ability" (Acts 2:4, NRSV). Some observers claimed that the languages being spoken by the disciples were authentic human dialects, which they recognized, although unknown to the speakers. Others have since argued that tongues can also be unknown personal languages. The apostle Paul defined speaking in tongues as one of the "Gifts of the Holy Spirit" (1 Corinthians 12:10).

The phenomenon of glossolalia has occurred infrequently over the course of Christian history. It has, however, consistently appeared in pockets of Christian sects. In the early nineteenth century, the Shakers became the first group known to have practiced glossolalia in the United States. Mormons spoke in tongues later in that century as well. Although many sources indicate that there were other groups in the United States and around the world who practiced glossolalia, it was in 1900 that the modern Evangelical tongues movement was born. In Charles Parham's church in Topeka, Kansas, petitioners who were expecting the "baptism of the Holy Spirit" experienced glossolalia, which they believed evidenced God's restoration of the New Testament Church. One of Parham's disciples was William J. Seymour, an African American who carried his Kansas experience to a small Los Angeles mission on Azusa Street. There, in 1906, more Christians spoke in tongues, capturing the attention of the *Los Angeles Times*, which ran a front-page headline on the new interracial religious movement and subsequently informed the nation of this phenomenon. As the revivals of glossolalia spread, the Pentecostal movement was born.

In the subsequent decades, the practice of glossolalia was hotly contested. Some Pentecostals, such as Aimee Semple McPherson, often sought to minimize its importance rather than offend more conservative Fundamentalists. Her irenic disposition allowed her to regularly work alongside many other Fundamentalists who did not practice glossolalia. Other Pentecostals, like the leaders of the Assemblies of God, insisted that speaking in tongues was *the* evidence of the baptism of the Holy Spirit, which more divisively pitted the different sects of Fundamentalists against each other.

In the 1960s, glossolalia again became a nationally publicized phenomenon. The rector of St. Mark's Episcopal Church in Van Nuys, California, Dennis Bennett, announced to his congregation that he had spoken in tongues. This began the charismatic movement, a new outbreak of glossolalia in traditional Protestant and even some Catholic churches. The controversies of the 1910s and 1920s were reborn, as different segments of the Protestant Church lined up against each other over this controversial practice, which continues to be contested.

Matthew A. Sutton

See also Angelus Temple; Azusa Street Revival; Evangelicalism; Pentecostalism

Bibliography

Anderson, Robert M. (1979) *Vision of the Disinherited: The Making of American Pentecostalism.* New York: Oxford University Press.

Blumhofer, Edith L., Russell P. Spittler, and Grant A. Wacker, eds. (1999) *Pentecostal Currents in American Protestantism.* Urbana: University of Illinois Press.

Dayton, Donald W. (1987) *Theological Roots of Pentecostalism.* Metuchen, NJ: Hendrickson Publishers, Inc.

Submission

Submission is a ruling dynamic in Fundamentalisms worldwide. A central tenet of Fundamentalist religious groups or movements is that individuals must submit to a religious authority outside the self, most typically a sacred text defined as unmediated revelation. In Christian Fundamentalism, the term "submission" primarily refers to relations between spouses; however, it begins with a divine anchor. To Fundamentalists, the family, not the individual, is the basic unit of human community. Within families, men are expected to submit to Christ, women to men, and children to their parents. In Fundamentalist congregations, women are taught that they should not mind submitting to the authority of a man who is submitted to Christ, as he is bound to treat her as Christ treated the church, giving his life for her if necessary. In the 1980s, second-wave Christian Fundamentalist pastors began to claim that spouses must mutually submit to each other; however, this "softer" submission ideal also left major decision-making within the family with men.

The submission interrelationships found in the Christian Fundamentalist family life are further reflected in congregations that circumscribe access to authority dependent on sex, by church roles assigned by sex, and by senior pastor/pastor's wife behavioral modeling. Males lead all men's groups and all mixed-sex groups, yet their authority is not absolute. As in the submission ideal of family order, male church leaders are considered responsible to Christ for the well-being of their followers. Some opportunities are available for Fundamentalist women in all-female networks that tend to flourish in conjunction with Fundamentalist congregational life, but the energies of these groups generally are channeled into nonsubversive activities that support the agendas of male leaders.

Islamic, Jewish, and Hindu Fundamentalist groups are similar in that leaders propound patterns of submission that require the male to submit to the authority of a transcendent, revelatory entity, text, or religious leader, and elevate the male/father figure within the family over the female/mother, and their children. One difference is that it is rarely the case that a family pattern of submission serves as a model for the submission expected within communal religious activities because in these traditions male Fundamentalist leaders have minimal expectations of female involvement in public religious life.

Brenda E. Brasher

See also Christian Family, Ideal; Male Headship; Pastor's Wife

Bibliography

Brasher, Brenda E. (1998) *Godly Women: Fundamentalism and Female Power.* New Brunswick, NJ: Rutgers University Press.

Griffith, R. Marie. (1997) *God's Daughters: Evangelical Women and the Power of Submission.* Berkeley: University of California Press.

Lawrence, Bruce B. (1998) *Shattering the Myth: Islam beyond Violence.* Princeton, NJ: Princeton University Press.

Sunday Schools

The Sunday school has been a primary vehicle for evangelism and Christian education in American Fundamentalist churches from the beginning of the movement. The inception of the Sunday school can be traced to the late-eighteenth-century revivals in Britain where, under the influence of such preachers and reformers as George Whitefield and John Wesley, several new forms of organizations emerged in churches, including missionary, Bible and tract societies, as well as Christian education initiatives. The

The D. L. Moody Memorial Church and Sunday School in Chicago, Illinois. PHOTO COURTESY OF ROBIN O'SULLIVAN.

first Sunday schools were opened in 1769 by Hannah Ball, a Methodist, and then later popularized by Anglican layman Robert Raikes. The Sunday school movement originated in the Church of England and then spread to the United States by missionaries and circuit-riding Methodist preachers establishing outposts of the faith. Formative influences in American Fundamentalism, such as Dwight L. Moody, remolded the various local Sunday school associations into a powerful national vehicle for evangelism, known as the International Sunday School Association. Uniform standards for teachers and curriculum for students not only increased the sense of unity among American Evangelicals, but gave them a common language—similar to how the Latin Mass united Catholics before the Second Vatican Council. By 1911, the Sunday school movement was reaching an estimated 15,000,000 people in 173,000 Sunday schools in the United States and Canada.

The denominations became the primary publishers of Sunday school literature, often staffed by professionals who worked cooperatively with other denominations. In fact, it was the concern over Sunday school curriculums and the influence of theological liberalism in church educational literature that led to the official launching of the Fundamentalist movement. Organizations such as the Religious Education Association in 1903 sought to integrate the insights of progressive education into Christianity and gradually these ideas found their way into Sunday school curricula published by the major denominations. Conservatives in these churches attempted to counteract these influences by publishing *The Fundamentals* (1910–1915), a twelve-volume series of books dedicated to a reaffirmation of conservative Christian theological teachings and serving as the founding documents of American Fundamentalists.

Fundamentalist Sunday Schools Geared for Evangelism

The Sunday school became a very effective vehicle for outreach and church growth for the Southern Baptist Convention and for Fundamentalist associations that had withdrawn from their liberal denominations after the modernist–Fundamentalist battles of the early twentieth century. Church associations such as the General Association of Regular Baptist Churches broke with mainline Christianity because they viewed the Sunday school as far more than a means of educating the children of church members into a particular faith. Sunday schools were widely used by Fundamentalists as a way to reach out to the community. Once children from the surrounding community attended Sunday school, it was not difficult to invite their parents to the main service or to adult-oriented classes where they would also be evangelized.

The evangelistic or "soul-winning" mission of Sunday schools was most pronounced in the independent Fundamentalist Baptist churches that either withdrew from or refused to align themselves with the Southern Baptist Convention, which was accused of being tolerant of liberalism These churches were strongly pastor-led and separatistic in doctrine and lifestyle. They taught that believers should no longer participate in theologically liberal associations or in worldly activities such as dancing and attending Hollywood films.

In the 1960s and 1970s, these congregations became the first generation of what are now known as megachurches, drawing thousands of people to their Sunday schools and church services. Churches such as First Baptist Church in Hammond, Indiana; First Baptist Church in Dallas, Texas; and Highland Park Baptist Church in Chattanooga, Tennessee, gained national fame for their extensive Sunday schools that attracted individuals from a wide range of ages, social classes, and races.

These churches featured extravaganzas with famous athletes and contests, and dispatched fleets of buses to bring children to classes and church services. Elmer Towns, a religious education specialist who championed and publicized these churches in books and magazine articles, noted that they revolutionized Sunday schools by the large size of the classes, aggressively seeking conversions (and often baptisms) of each student, their independence from traditional denominations, informality, and the au-

thoritative and charismatic pastors who ran the Sunday schools. In many cases, Fundamentalist pastors established their Sunday schools before they started church services or built church structures. The large Sunday schools were often the catalysts for establishing other educational arms of these "super churches," such as Christian schools and even colleges.

New Reforms in Sunday Schools

Yet by the beginning of the 1980s, the growth and expansion of Fundamentalist Sunday schools and church in general had waned considerably. Sunday school busing and the hell-fire preaching of First Baptist Church pastor Jack Hyles and other preachers had given way to the more moderate Fundamentalist, Evangelical, and charismatic approaches of Jerry Falwell of Thomas Road Baptist Church, Bill Hybels of the Willow Creek Community Church, and John Wimber of the Vineyard churches. The largest and fastest growing churches were those that emphasized contemporary music over traditional hymns, mainstream acceptance over separation from the world, and teaching rather than revivalistic preaching. The traditional Sunday schools with a single teacher presenting doctrine to rows of silent students was less favored than an approach stressing team teaching and outreach ministries using marketing and interactive, high-tech aids such as videos and computers.

The new approach gained the support of Sunday school powerhouses such as Southern Baptists and some influential independent churches, as well as leaders such as Jerry Falwell and Elmer Towns. Just as the pastors of the large Fundamentalist Baptist churches had held Sunday school clinics and conventions to bring their methods to smaller churches across the United States, the megachurches are now influencing many small and average-sized Fundamentalist and Evangelical churches. The overriding concern of these Sunday school reforms is that the baby boom generation and their children have little grounding in basic Christian teachings and therefore teachers have to reach such students on their own levels and in their own cultural idioms.

Richard P. Cimino

See also Bible Schools

Bibliography

Dowley, Tim. (1977) *Handbook to the History of Christianity*. Grand Rapids, MI: Wm. B. Eerdmans.

Handy, Robert. (1977) *A History of the Churches in the United States and Canada*. New York: Oxford University Press.

Midgett, Linda. (1993) "Emerging Sunday School Avant Garde." *Christianity Today* 37, 1 (11 January): 45.

Towns, Elmer. (1969) *The Ten Largest Sunday Schools*. Grand Rapids, MI: Baker Book House.

———. (1990) *Ten of Today's Most Innovative Churches*. Ventura, CA: Regal Books.

Taliban

Taliban is a political, cultural, and religious movement and organization in Afghanistan. The word "Taliban" (Taleban) is the plural of Talib, which in Arabic/Persian means "student of Islamic law." In the Western world, the Taliban is viewed as the most extreme Islamic Fundamentalist movement and organization of the late twentieth and early twenty-first centuries. The founders of the movement were Afghan students living in exile in Pakistan. The organization gained power in Afghanistan at the end of 1994 under the leadership of Mullah Muhammad Omar (b. 1959). The Taliban and other factions, with military and financial help from the United States, Saudi Arabia, and Pakistan, ousted the Soviet forces in 1989, ending the ten-year (1979–1989) Afghan–Soviet War. Civil war broke out in 1992 as different rival factions battled for control of the nation. The Taliban triumphed in 1995 when their forces captured the capital city of Kabul, which had been severely damaged during the civil war as rival factions bombarded the city. The Taliban went on to defeat rival groups across the nation and established peace and security over ninety-five percent of Afghanistan, with only a small territory in the north remaining free of Taliban control. According to media reports, Saudi Arabia and Pakistan support the Taliban, while the rival Northern Alliance receives money and military hardware from the United States, Russia, Iran, and India, who are opposed to Taliban rule.

Taliban rule is absolute and all-encompassing and is based on a strict and literal interpretation and application of Islamic law (*shari'a*). Under the Taliban, Islamic law was the basis for establishing and remains the basis for maintaining social order and political control. From the viewpoint of the international community, restrictions on the employment and education of women have been especially severe. Schools for girls and young women have been closed, woman may not leave home unless accompanied by a male relative and fully covered by the traditional Afghan veil (*burqa*), and women are prohibited from working outside the home on the grounds that social and political instability make it unsafe for them to be outside the protection of male relatives. The application of Islamic law is not only restricted to women. Men are required to grow beards and strictly observe all Islamic rituals, including the daily five prayers. The Taliban's attempts to eradicate crime and antisocial behavior is reinforced by Islamic law to carry out public punishments, which include stoning to death for adultery, fornication, or any, even consensual, sexual relations outside of wedlock; amputation of hands for theft; and lashing for gambling and intoxication. While these strict applications of Islamic law have been criticized by other Islamic nations and condemned by many Western nations, others note that the Taliban has succeeded in creating and maintaining social order and political stability following fifteen years of turmoil. Because much of Afghanistan is off-limits to outside observers, the true nature of life under Taliban rule is not known.

The Taliban have also been criticized and isolated from much of the world community because of allegations that they support international terrorism and

TALIBAN DESTRUCTION OF PRE-ISLAMIC STATUES CONFIRMED

Taliban soldiers blasted two towering ancient statues of Buddha with anti-aircraft weapons, according to the first eyewitness account from the area today. . . .

Residents of central Bamiyan, where the two ancient statues of Buddha hewn from a cliff face in the third and fifth centuries are located, said Taliban soldiers began attacking the statues at least three days ago.

"I could see the Taliban soldiers firing anti-aircraft weapons at the two statues. That was three days ago," said Safdar Ali, a resident. . . .

Source: *The Tribune of India,* March 4, 2001. www.tribuneindia.com.

drug trafficking. The United States has been a leader in making these accusations and in encouraging isolation, especially because the Taliban are believed to be protecting Osama bin Ladin, a Saudi millionaire, who has been accused of plotting and funding the August 1998 bombing of U.S. embassies in Kenya and Tanzania,, which killed more than two hundred people. In retaliation, the United States launched a missile attack on suspected terrorist facilities in Afghanistan and Somalia. On the urging of the United States, the United Nations has imposed sanctions on the Taliban regime for not handing over Osama bin Ladin for trial in an international court of justice. In March 2001, the Taliban came in for additional condemnation. The international community questioned the Taliban interpretation of Islamic law, which prohibits the depiction of the human form in painting and sculpture, as the rationale for the mass destruction of all pre-Islamic art (mainly Buddhist art and sculpture) in Afghanistan, including sculptures and stone statues of the Buddha that were of significant artistic and archaeological value. Even other Islamic nations and scholars were outraged by the destruction, which points to the reality that belief and practice in Islam are diverse. As there were no Buddhists in Afghanistan, these acts of destruction were seen by some outside observers as a political attack on the Western world, which highly values such works of religious art.

Abdul Karim Khan

Bibliography

Matinuddin, Kamal. (1999) *The Taliban Phenomenon: Afghanistan 1994–1997.* Karachi: Oxford University Press.

Rashid, Ahmed. (2000) *Taliban: Militant Islam, Oil and Fundamentalism in Central Asia.* New Haven, CT: Yale University Press.

Televangelism

In the wake of the televangelism scandals of the late 1980s, many observers, especially in the news media, depicted televangelism within the United States as a crafty business designed to defraud the faithful out of their money. Critics of televangelism often invoke the image of Sinclair Lewis's fictional character Elmer Gantry, a suave, yet unscrupulous Fundamentalist preacher who readily engaged in sexual and financial indiscretions without apparent concern about his duplicity. While the comparison to the fictional Gantry might fit some televangelists, it is not indicative of televangelism as a whole. Yet televangelism is a business, and among Fundamentalist Christians in the United States it is skillfully choreographed and boasts a variety of talented performers.

The Historical Roots of Televangelism

Contemporary televangelism in the United States is rooted in the Evangelical revivals known as the First and Second Great Awakenings. During the First Great Awakening in the eighteenth century, Jonathan Edwards combined his capable intellect with an appreciation of human emotion to stir his listeners up to righteous action. The noted evangelist and orator George Whitefield used his speaking skill and stage presence to appeal to broad audiences. Whitefield's success in attracting large crowds is also partially attributable to his ability to jettison theological discourse in favor of simple, moving exhortation. This approach became especially effective during the Second Great Awakening in the early to mid-nineteenth century as revival spread along the American frontier to a less urbanized and less educated audience. The capacity to reduce the Christian gospel to easy-to-understand phrases during an emotional appeal meshed well with a gradually evolving democratic society that idealized the common man. The Second Great Awakening likewise fostered the growth of numerous sects and denominations within Evangelical Christianity and the constituent rise of countless preachers who became adept at marketing their messages to a mass audience.

The most famed nineteenth-century revivalist, Charles Finney, openly relied on what he termed "excitements" to awaken the populace to the gravity of his message, and his approach is illustrative of the emerging character of American Evangelicalism. Finney declared that the "great political, and other worldly excitements that agitate Christendom, are all unfriendly to Christendom, and divert the mind from the interests of the soul. Now these excitements can only be counteracted by *religious* excitements" (Finney 1993: 194). Finney attacked the widespread belief that revival is a divine miracle and he outlined the means whereby revival could be humanly engineered. His sensationalism drew heavy crowds and influenced a generation of later revivalists, although some such as Dwight Moody practiced a more sublime, yet equally effective method of outreach. Moody's urban evangelistic campaigns attracted a cadre of local pastors who formed missionary schools to train individuals to further the message.

After the turn of the twentieth century, former baseball player turned evangelist Billy Sunday kept alive the revivalist tradition pioneered by individuals such as Whitefield, Finney, and Moody. A master showman, Sunday's crusades regularly featured shouting and comic parody, capturing public attention and making him a popular circuit speaker. After 1920, a number of radio ministries emerged, and

Sunday himself began to use the medium in 1929 until his death in 1935, bringing to radio the same feisty wit that won him fans during his revivals. But Sunday shared the radio with a number of other charismatic personalities who garnered solid followings during the 1920s and 1930s. Chief among them was Aimee Semple McPherson, whose initial ambition to become an actress likely aided her in mastering both stage and radio presentation, and Charles Fuller, whose down-to-earth manner made his *Old Fashion Revival Hour* a hit in Evangelical circles during the 1930s and 1940s.

Following World War II, an economic boom in the United States fostered the development of a consumer culture that pervaded almost every aspect of everyday life. The austere days of the Great Depression and the wartime rationing of the early to mid-1940s seemed like another world. During the 1950s, middle-class Americans enjoyed previously unheard of conveniences, including credit cards, automatic dishwashers, and garbage disposals. And, as increasingly more Americans owned automobiles, fast food restaurants such as McDonald's began to dot the nation's landscape, typifying the relative ease with which life in the consumer society could be conducted. The thriving advertising profession eagerly catered to developing middle-class tastes and reduced much of commercial discourse to a "catchy phrase" or "sound bite" that would appeal to consumers. Yet no innovation appeared to hold more promise for both consumers and advertisers than television, which came into widespread use around 1950. Although there are many uses for television, it became the primary medium for advancing and confirming the middle-class consumer culture on a national scale.

The Beginning of Televangelism

Fundamentalists, and the broader Evangelical coalition in general, quickly realized the value of the new technology, but they encountered early opposition. The National Council of Churches, successor to the Federal Council of Churches, which thwarted most Fundamentalist radio broadcasting on major networks in the 1930s and 1940s, attempted to do the same with television in 1950. Television evangelism was at first limited, but it was not eradicated. In 1950, Fundamentalist Percy Crawford became the first independent broadcaster to air over the major networks. His live *Youth on the March* ran on the

American Broadcasting Company (ABC) until 1953. Crawford expanded his media interests, eventually buying his own television station in Philadelphia in 1960.

As with radio, Fundamentalists were willing to buy time on local television stations, and they were initially more successful in this venue. Broadcast time was less expensive and it proved a better training arena because television was considerably more complex than radio broadcasting. Yet these early efforts produced some of the most enduring television ministries in American religious history. In 1953, Pentecostal minister Rex Humbard bought time on a local station in Akron, Ohio. Talented and articulate, Humbard set the standard for later television evangelism. Like the major revivalists before him, he downplayed doctrinal issues and focused on the simplicity of his message, which enabled him to appeal to a broad television audience. Humbard's program, eventually named *Cathedral of Tomorrow*, regularly featured other Humbard family members and reached most of North America and much of the world by the 1970s.

Other notable entries to religious television quickly emerged. Oral Roberts, who rose from poverty to organize a prominent faith-healing ministry in 1948, began television broadcasting of his studio-produced *Your Faith is Power* in 1954. The following year, Roberts began airing his tent revivals, which soon gained additional outlets nationwide. A skilled tactician, the young Roberts relied on advertising professionals to promote his ventures. Another newcomer, Jerry Falwell, began local television broadcasting in 1956, a program later modified and recast as the *Old Time Gospel Hour*, which obtained international coverage by the 1970s. Not to be outdone, Billy Graham, who rose to fame as a result of tent revivals in Los Angeles in 1949, became the first evangelist to have a revival broadcast nationally on a major network when ABC aired his New York crusade in 1957. The first decade of televangelism aptly demonstrated that the small screen presented an ideal forum for orchestrating the religious excitements that Charles Finney earlier considered necessary to revival.

The Expansion of Televangelism

Religious broadcasts over television began to increase steadily after 1960 when the Federal Communications Commission decreed that federally mandated public service programming could be met with paid broadcasts, which then made religious programs more attractive to commercial television stations. As a result of experience in producing commercial quality programming, Evangelicals benefited immensely from this move. Three years later, the invention of ultrahigh frequency (UHF) television opened local television airwaves to community evangelists at inexpensive cost. In 1961, Pat Robertson began airing programs over his Christian Broadcasting Network (CBN), at that time a local station in Portsmouth, Virginia. Robertson inaugurated his popular *700 Club* program five years later with the then-unknown Jim Bakker as co-host. Robertson's network grew steadily, and his programming, especially the *700 Club*, became more sophisticated and polished, placing it on par with the professionalism of secular newscasts over the major networks. By the early 1970s, Jim Bakker left CBN and, along with his wife Tammy Faye Bakker, began hosting the equally popular *PTL Club*, where he again offered a professionally crafted program that, while high on emotion, appealed to a large audience. In 1973, the musically inclined Jimmy Swaggart launched his well-received *Jimmy Swaggart Telecast*, a revival-style presentation that quickly made the skilled evangelist well known among viewers of religious television. Also in 1973, Paul Crouch founded the Trinity Broadcasting Network, which soon mushroomed into a media empire, inaugurating twenty-four hour broadcasting in 1977. That same year, Robertson's CBN began using satellite to beam its programming around the globe. Other broadcasters soon followed, exporting a staple of American culture abroad. By the early 1990s, Crouch became a pioneer in broadcasting in the former Soviet Union. A host of other broadcasters likewise built impressive television followings during the 1970s and 1980s, some of whom focused almost exclusively on a premillennial interpretation of prophetic events. These included Garner Ted Armstrong, who initially broadcast for the Worldwide Church of God until 1978 when his father Herbert W. Armstrong successfully resumed broadcasting for the denomination, and Jack Van Impe, who along with his wife Rexella built a dedicated cadre of followers for their dispensationalist *Jack Van Impe Presents!*

The Scandal of Televangelism

Aside from the emergence of Jerry Falwell's Moral Majority in 1979, the mainstream media spent relatively little time focusing on televangelism until 1987. That year veteran broadcaster Oral Roberts declared that God would "call him home" if he did not raise eight million dollars, a declaration that solicited media ridicule. Meanwhile, Jim Bakker faced accusations of sexual misconduct with Jessica Hahn, a former PTL secretary. The scandal undermined Bakker's ministry and contributed to investigations of financial abuse within the organization. Despite a vain attempt by Jerry Falwell to save the PTL ministry, it eventually crumbled and Bakker spent time in prison for his financial dealings. In 1988, Jimmy Swaggart was reduced to a well-orchestrated, yet admittedly tearful confession for his sexual misconduct with a prostitute. After being caught with another prostitute in 1991, Swaggart barely retained his once successful ministry. Also in 1991, ABC aired a segment on its *Prime Time Live* that included allegations of financial irregularities by Texas televangelist Robert Tilton. The report led to a criminal investigation into Tilton's ministry, resulting in its collapse two years later. However, not all coverage of the world of televangelism involved scandal. In 1988, Pat Robertson, the son of a former United States senator, conducted an abortive, albeit highly publicized attempt to gain the Republican presidential nomination, provoking a flurry of media attention.

Televangelism As a Reflection of American Society

The scandals of the late 1980s initiated growing public concern over televangelism, heightening awareness of the sophisticated marketing techniques that made American televangelism a multimillion-dollar industry. Many critics attacked the lifestyles and personal conduct of televangelists, often invoking the Gantry comparison. But the personal failings of individual televangelists notwithstanding, the limits of televangelism rest primarily in its inability to effectively critique the excesses of American society that its exemplars regularly condemn. The so-called electronic church, rather than being a benign medium for expressing divine precepts, is a high-profile manifestation of a peculiarly American religion.

Evangelical revivals during the eighteenth and nineteenth centuries gradually distanced themselves from theological discourse, eagerly adopting the common vernacular in an attempt to appeal to mass audiences. This approach, while popular, made Evangelical Christianity in the United States a reflection of American democracy, with its inherent idealization of simplicity and its often overt anti-intellectualism. This revival style worked well on radio, and it also meshed well with the burgeoning consumer culture after World War II. It met its perfect match in television, a medium that, however informative, thrives on entertainment and sensationalism. As televangelism became more developed it too became an outgrowth of the consumer culture, transforming Evangelical Christianity into a product often marketed by celebrity-seeking preachers. This process further diluted the intellectual aspects of the message by focusing on emotion, and by leading the audience into a perceived pseudo-relationship with the televangelist. In those instances when the personal failings or excessive lifestyles of popular broadcasters became known, many of their followers felt as though they had been betrayed by a personal friend or even by the divine.

The Future of Televangelism

While Fundamentalists argue that television is a prime venue to spread the gospel—and most major televangelists identify themselves loosely as Fundamentalists—studies show that the majority of viewers of religious television are already believers and that televangelism simply confirms their faith. Televangelism does, however, raise the profile of conservative Evangelical Christianity, heightening its perceived importance in American life. As increasing numbers of televangelists expand their ministries in the United States and abroad, it is doubtful that the scandals of the past, or unforeseen troubles ahead, will end this thriving business. Nevertheless, if televangelists are to be credible critics of secular culture in the United States, they must honestly recognize its impact on their profession. Failure to realize and react constructively to the limits of televanglism will undoubtedly lead to further charges of hypocrisy in the future as televangelists and the media operations they manage mimic the often superficial marketing techniques characteristic of American consumerism.

Scott Lupo

See also Evangelicalism; Media, Mass; Radio

Bibliography

Bruce, Steve. (1990) *Pray TV: Televangelism in America*. London: Routledge.

Erickson, Hal. (1992) *Religious Radio and Television in the United States, 1921–1991: The Programs and Personalities*. Jefferson, NC: McFarland and Co.

Finney, Charles Grandison. ([1835] 1993) "What a Revival of Religion Is." In *The American Intellectual Tradition*, vol. 1, 2nd ed., edited by David A. Hollinger and Charles Capper. New York: Oxford University Press, 192–201.

Fishwick, Marshall W. (1995) *Great Awakenings: Popular Religion and Popular Culture*. Binghamton, NY: Haworth Press.

Hadden, Jeffrey K., and Charles E. Swann. (1981) *Prime Time Preachers: The Rising Power of Televangelism*. Reading, MA: Addison-Wesley.

Hadden, Jeffrey K., and Anson Shupe. (1988) *Televangelism: Power and Politics on God's Frontier*. New York: Henry Holt.

Hoover, Stewart M. (1988) *Mass Media Religion: The Social Sources of the Electronic Church*. Newbury Park, CA: Sage Publications.

Horsfield, Peter G. (1984) *Religious Television: The American Experience*. New York: Longman.

Jorstad, Erling. (1993) *Popular Religion in America: The Evangelical Voice*. Westport, CT: Greenwood Press.

Kintz, Linda, and Julia Lesage, eds. (1998) *Media, Culture, and the Religious Right*. Minneapolis: University of Minnesota Press.

Melton, J. Gordon, Phillip Charles Lucas, and Jon R. Stone. (1997) *Prime-Time Religion: An Encyclopedia of Religious Broadcasting*. Phoenix, AZ: Oryx Press.

Morris, James. (1973) *The Preachers*. New York: St. Martin's Press.

Noll, Mark A. (1994) *The Scandal of the Evangelical Mind*. Grand Rapids, MI: Wm. B. Eerdmans.

Peck, Janice. (1993) *The Gods of Televangelism: The Crisis of Meaning and the Appeal of Religious Television*. Cresskill, NJ: Hampton Press.

Schultze, Quentin J. (1991) *Televangelism and American Culture: The Business of Popular Religion*. Grand Rapids, MI: Baker Book House.

Temple

The Jerusalem Temple was the seat of the Yahweh cult of ancient Israel and a place of unrivaled sacredness. Although today only a few ruins remain of the Second Temple, some Christian Protestant Fundamentalists believe that a new temple will be raised at the site of the old and that this will coincide with the Second Advent of Jesus Christ. At the same time, a controversial faction within modern Judaism also lobbies for the reconstruction of the biblical temple. However, the Temple Mount (as Christians and Jews know it) is sacred, as well, to Muslims, and they vehemently object to this restoration. There exists, therefore, the possibility for violent confrontation between the three Abrahamic religions over this shared heritage. (Something of this potential was realized in September 2000 when former Israeli defense minister Ariel Sharon visited the Temple Mount and Muslims reacted with sustained violent protest.)

First Kings 5–8 describes the building of King Solomon's Temple during the tenth century BCE. Other locales were sacred to the ancient Hebrews but the temple reinforced the preeminence of Jerusalem as a holy city. "And so I propose to built a house for the name of the Lord" (1 Kings 5:5), are the words credited to the king as he commanded "that the cedars of Lebanon be cut" (1 Kings 5:6) and "great and costly stones" (1 Kings 5:17) be quarried to build the mighty edifice. The temple housed the Ark of the Covenant and its precincts grew into a vast, priestly complex dedicated to Yahweh.

For several centuries, Solomon's Temple was the focus for worship until it, along with most settlements in the ancient Hebrew kingdoms, was destroyed during the sixth century BCE Babylonian invasion. Later in that century, when Cyrus the Great allowed the Hebrew elite to return from exile in Babylon, rebuilding the temple was a first order of business. It was recorded: "And all the people shouted with a great shout, when they praised the Lord, because the foundation of the house of the Lord was laid" (Ezra 3:11). For nearly six centuries, the rebuilt temple was the locus of Jewish worship and a place of unspeakable sacredness. Its importance carried over into Christianity, for the ministry of Jesus carried Him to Jerusalem, where His actions and words provoked great controversy in and about the temple. During the first century CE, Rome destroyed this Second Temple when it crushed the rebellious Jewish state. Only a fragment, known today as the "Wailing Wall," survives.

The centrality of this temple in Jewish thought down to our own day is understandable. While it stood, it was the holiest place in Israel and when destroyed, a reminder of the great days of Jewish faith and glory. It should not be surprising, then, that

1 Kings 6:11–14

11. And the word of the LORD came to Solomon, saying,

12. Concerning this house which thou art in building, if thou wilt walk in my statutes, and execute my judgments, and keep all my commandments to walk in them; then will I perform my word with thee, which I spake unto David thy father:

13. And I will dwell among the children of Israel, and will not forsake my people Israel.

14. So Solomon built the house, and finished it.

a small band of Jewish zealots wishes the temple rebuilt, regardless of what violence this might provoke. More puzzling, perhaps, is how the temple became important to Christian Fundamentalists during the modern era. The key to this puzzle lies in eschatology, the study of the Last Days, which underlies contemporary Protestant Evangelical fascination with the temple. It is a fascination not felt elsewhere in Christianity. Mainline American Protestant denominations, along with Roman Catholic and Orthodox Christians, revere the City of David simply as the scene of the final days of Jesus' ministry. For Fundamentalists, however, the temple is key to the future Kingdom of God.

American Fundamentalists are most often premillennialists. That is, they expect that Jesus Christ will return in glory to initiate a holy kingdom on earth. Christians almost universally agree that Jesus will return. However, premillennialists couple the Second Advent with the onset of the millennium, a period during which Jesus will visibly reign over the earth with His capital in Jerusalem. Some assert, as well, that during the millennium the ancient biblical sacrifices will be reinstituted and it is for this purpose that the temple must be rebuilt. Thus, a significant Fundamentalist Christian constituency supports building a third temple on the site of the Temple Mount. This constitutes, as noted, political dynamite within the cauldron of Middle Eastern religious and ethnic politics—especially when coupled with Jewish Fundamentalists who likewise hope for a third temple.

Protestant fascination with the temple dates only from the late eighteenth and early nineteenth centuries. This was when premillennialism, largely dormant within European Christianity, revived as students of prophecy proclaimed the French Revolution a sign of the Last Days. Originating in England, this revived premillennialism quickly spread to America where it has flourished ever since. It included a conviction that the Jerusalem Temple must be rebuilt. David Nevins Lord, an American, wrote in 1849 ("The Restoration of the Israelites," in *Theological and Literary Journal*): "The descendents of Levi are to be the ministers of the temple, sacrifices are to be offered in it, and all nations are to go to it to worship." Although from the century before last, this sentence encapsulates a belief which, carried into the twenty-first century, has scarcely changed. The temple will once again be the center of worship, only now not just for the Jews but the entire human race. The Jews, though, will regain their priestly preeminence as the "descendents of Levi" and offer sacrifice in the temple during the millennium on behalf of all humankind.

While Fundamentalist Protestants are generally premillennialists, there are many, perhaps a majority, who do not share this vision of the temple's restoration. Those who do, however, are frequently quite dedicated, such as the American rancher who, at the end of the 1990s, bred a strain of spotless red cattle to be used as fitting temple sacrifice. Muslims, for whom the Temple Mount is sacred because of the presence there of the Dome of the Rock, the spot from which Muhammed is believed to have ascended to heaven, are aghast at the idea of a rebuilt temple. They regard the entire scheme as little more than Jewish–Christian profanation of a holy site. As the twenty-first century opened, the possibility existed that religious Fundamentalists, whether Christians or Jews, might attempt to anticipate prophecy by rebuilding the temple. Beyond certain ultra-observant groups, however, there was little sentiment among Israelis to provoke Muslim outrage with such an extraordinary deed.

Robert K. Whalen

See also Prophecy; Second Coming

Bibliography

Boyer, Paul. (1992) *When Time Shall Be No More: Prophecy Belief in Modern American Culture.* Cambridge, MA: Harvard University Press.

Sandeen, Ernest. (1970) *The Roots of Fundamentalism: British and American Millenarianism, 1800–1930.* Chicago: University of Chicago Press.

Weber, Timothy P. (1979) *Living in the Shadow of the Second Coming: American Premillennialism, 1875–1927.* New York: Oxford University Press.

Whalen, Robert K. (1966) "'Christians Love the Jews!' The Development of American Philo-Semitism, 1790–1860." *Religion and American Culture* 6 (Summer): 226–260.

Testimony

A testimony is evidence in support of a cause. To give testimony is to authenticate firsthand or bear witness to a fact or an event. Legally, a testimony is a spoken or written statement made under oath by a witness in a legal proceeding. Within the Christian context, the word "testimony" has three different connotations, but in its contemporary, more popular usage, a testimony is a personal narrative professing to the goodness of, or benefits one has received from, God through one's association or membership in a group or by upholding the ideals of the group. Some believe that the benefits received are rewards for one's faithfulness, or the product of the Supreme Being's munificence, while others regard testimonies as a method of self-portrayal.

In the Old Testament, "testimony" refers to the Ten Commandments or any ordinance of God. The stone tablets, on which these laws were inscribed, constituted concrete evidence or a reminder and a "testimony" of Israel's relationship with, and responsibility to, God. Evidence of this testimony can be found in Exodus 25:16; 31:18; 32:15, and more. In Psalms 19:7, the word is used for the entire law of God given to humankind. In the New Testament, "testimony" is used synonymously with "witness." The witness to be borne is to the truth of the gospel. This is not only about verifiable events, but includes the proclamation that Jesus is the Savior. Hence, the term refers to the witness given by Christians of Christ and His saving power.

A more popular usage of testimony is proclaiming the goodness of God in one's lives. The giving of testimonies dates back to the Old Testament when God delivered the Israelites from Egypt, instructing them to make known His miraculous power by testifying before their children (Exodus 13:14). Moreover, there are many Bible verses that call on Christians to testify to God's goodness. One example is Psalms 96:3 (RSV): "Declare his glory among the nations, his marvelous works among all the peoples!" Consequently, Evangelicals and Fundamentalists maintain that Christians must make known God's goodness by giving testimonies.

The Scope of Testimonies

There are various types of testimonies. Testimonies of conversion experience are basic to Christianity and many other religions. Adherents to a faith give accounts of how they were converted and recruited. Testimonies of healing, deliverance, and life-changing miracles bear witness to the power of God. There are numerous examples of these testimonies, such as healing of diseases, overcoming infertility, and escaping disasters. Most religions encourage their adherents to give public testimony as evidence of the saving grace of the Supreme Being. There are also testimonies of God's provision of material blessings to meet personal and family responsibilities, as well as God's intervention in career development such as a promotion, divine direction in the choice of a career, or in the execution of specific tasks. Biographical testimonies tell of a person's journey through life or of an experience in a religious group. Finally, though less common, there are testimonies of individual spiritual growth within a specific religious group.

The essential qualification of a testimony is that it must be truthful. Testimonies can be oral and spontaneous or planned, or they may be in written form or occasionally recorded electronically. A recorded testimony is filtered and digested to determine its authenticity before public presentation. To prevent the giving of false testimonies, some religious leaders insist that the testifier must first be heard privately and the contents verified before public presentation. Usually, a testimony is given personally, but occasionally it is given on behalf of others. Testimonies have often been exaggerated and at times falsely given for publicity purposes, to protect something or someone, to harm others, or for various other reasons.

Significance of Testimonies

Testimonies are an important part of religious practice for several reasons. A testimony is given to acknowledge and affirm the power and benevolence of the supernatural over human affairs. Thus, there is recognition of the limitations of humans in determining their own affairs. Testimonies are sometimes used to encourage and challenge believers, by demonstrating that if the problems of others can be solved, it should be assumed that one's own problems can be solved. Testimonies can also serve as a means of socialization when new members are introduced to the culture of the groups. Moreover, they serve to release emotions, particularly for members experiencing difficulties in life. They also act as a mechanism for determining the commitment of members to the religious leaders and their groups. The testimonies of members' faith can also serve as the subject for sermons, to prove the efficacy of prayers, and to illustrate why it is important to trust in God. Furthermore, by portraying the benefits available to members, testimonies also serve to recruit potential converts from the outside. Finally, when taken out of their primary religious context, testimonies advertise certain churches or religious groups, and project the image of religious leaders as powerful people of God whose ministries are attested to by miracles.

Though testimonies are a part of Christian history, the Pentecostal, charismatic, and Fundamentalist groups gave them prominence in the twentieth century. Initially, Pentecostals and charismatics encouraged testimonies of baptism of the Holy Spirit and speaking in tongues, but later every kind of testimony was accepted. Testimonies were usually given orally, but the more inspiring ones were later printed for wider circulation. In fact, many of today's religious magazines devote substantial space or whole editions to testimonies of members and readers.

Conclusion

Because testimonies are narratives of personal experience, they are best understood within their cultural context, and within the expectations of the religious group. Not only do testimonies express objective facts, they also portray moral principles. They are a tool of religion, serving to incorporate new members, determine the commitment of existent members, and strengthen the position of religious leaders. Finally, testimonies bear witness to a powerful and benevolent God, and confirm that the human world is under the absolute sovereign control of God.

Matthews A. Ojo

See also Conversion; Witnesses, Two

Bibliography

Ammerman, Nancy T. (1987) *Bible Believers: Fundamentalists in the Modern World.* New Brunswick, NJ: Rutgers University Press.

Bueno, Ronald N. (1999) "Listening to the Margins: Rehistoricizing Pentecostal Experiences and Identities." In *The Globalisation of Pentecostalism: A Religion Made to Travel,* edited by Murray W. Dempster, Byron D. Klaus, and Douglas Petersen. Oxford: Regnum Books International, 268–288.

McGuire, M. B. (1977) "Testimony As a Commitment Mechanism in Catholic Pentecostal Prayer Groups." *Journal for the Scientific Study of Religion* 16: 165–168.

Theology

The term "theology" is an etymological form of the Greek words *theos* (God) and *logos* (word), which together means "a word about God." The word "theology" is not found in Scripture, though the concept of "a word about God" is intrinsic to the study of the Bible. The heart of Fundamentalism was its application of the Scriptures to the building of a theology that was faithful to the biblical text. It is abundantly clear when reading the table of contents in *The Fundamentals,* the twelve-volume set of books published in the second decade of the twentieth century, that the authors were theologians. In the modern studies of theology, however, it was considered important to follow a scientific or inductive method. Hodge noted, "The Bible is no more a system of theology, than nature is a system of chemistry or of mechanics. We find in nature the facts which the chemist or the mechanical philosopher has to examine, and from them to ascertain the laws by which they are determined. So the Bible contains the truths which the theologian has to collect, authenticate, arrange, and exhibit in their internal relation to each other" (1952: I, 1). The study of theology has a number of facets, all of which contribute to the development of what has been termed "systematic theology."

Biblical Theology

Fundamentalism inherited the Reformed concept that theology should be based on the Scriptures, not on a dogmatic approach that amounted to little more than using Scripture and tradition to reinforce the teachings of the church. One of the Reformed phrases was *scriptura sola*, or "Scripture alone." As a result of this approach, there was a renewed emphasis on the study of the biblical languages, Hebrew and Greek, the sense of the historical setting of the texts, and the development of theological principles based on that study. The study of biblical history then formed the matrix out of which theology evolved. Hodge (1952: I, 1–2) noted that the purpose of biblical theology was "to ascertain and state the facts of Scripture." From a Fundamentalist point of view, the question to be asked is "In light of its historic context, what does this passage mean?"

This early emphasis, however, drifted off in two directions. In more conservative circles, there developed a system of "proof texting," and in more liberal circles, influenced by the application of the theories of evolution, the study of the Bible gave way to the development of religion. The drift in the liberal direction led to contemporary biblical studies dominated by the historical-critical method. Unfortunately, in its essence, this approach denigrates the concept of the transcendence of God and of His supernatural self-revelation revealed in the Scriptures. Clear understanding of the doctrines of inspiration and Revelation are integral to the Fundamentalist approach to the study of the Word of God. When Fundamentalist scholars recovered their pursuit of academic studies, they embraced the historical-critical approach in their research, with attention given to scholarship outside a strict Fundamentalist theological view. Indeed, Millard J. Erickson has pointed out that when biblical criticism is "used and based upon assumptions that are consistent with the full authority of the Bible, [it] can be a helpful means of shedding further light on the meaning of Scripture" (1983: I, 104). Although Erickson would probably not consider himself a Fundamentalist, many in the Fundamentalist camp are in agreement with his theological positions.

The Bible is not a book that presents a series of propositional truths to be believed, but rather a historical unfolding of God's revelation to humankind; it records the history of Israel, the life of Jesus the Messiah, and the history of the early church. Because God's revelation occurred in historical events, it is subject to historical study and analysis, which is the basis of biblical theology. Ladd (1979: 506) explains how biblical theology should work: "The events themselves, however, are not self-explanatory; there was always a divinely initiated prophetic or apostolic word of interpretation. That Jesus died is an objective fact that even the Pharisees could affirm. That Jesus died *for our sins* is no less an 'objective' fact: but it is a theological event occurring within the historical fact which could be understood only from the prophetic word of interpretation. Revelation, therefore, occurred in the complex of event—Word" [italics in original].

The studies embodied in biblical theology include such works as *A Theology of the Pentateuch, The Theology of the Book of Job, Isaiah's Portrait of God,* or in the New Testament, *Johannine Theology, The Theology of the Gospel of Matthew,* and *A Study of Pauline Theology.* For the Fundamentalist theologian, this research is not an academic exercise alone, but is a responsibility to obedience to the truth.

Systematic Theology

Hodge (1952: I, 2) states that the practice of systematic theology "is to take the facts, determine their relation to each other and to other cognate truths, as well as to vindicate them and *show their harmony and consistency*" [italics added]. The development of systematic theology properly includes a knowledge of the biblical languages, a clear conception of ancient history and society, and the contributions of biblical theology that led to the development of a theological system. Chafer (1947: I, v) observes that "systematic theology, the greatest of the sciences, has fallen upon evil days. Between the rejection and ridicule of it by the so-called progressives and the neglect and abridgement [sic] of it by the orthodox, it, as a potent influence, is approaching the point of extinction." This same observation is shared by James Daane (1988: 827): "Few modern theologians have great interest in systematic theology, and even fewer attempt to construct one." Chafer certainly is a notable exception, and his work has been followed by theologians such as Millard Erickson, Wayne Grudem, Charles Ryrie, and the late James Boice's popular modern adaptation of Calvin's *Institutes, Foundations of the Christian Faith* (1985). Though theology simply means "a word about God," systematic theology develops the "word about God" into systematic categories that ideally are reflections of the background studies of the biblical languages and biblical theology. Chafer's *Systematic Theology* is representative of the theological divisions in systematic theology. He includes nine major divisions, or branches, of systematic theology. Chafer used theological titles such as Bibliology, Angelology, and Soteriology, but much simpler titles will be used here.

Bible

Since the Scriptures are basic to a study of God, Bibliology, "a consideration of the essential facts concerning the Bible" (Chafer, 1974: I, 15), is a proper starting place for the study of theology. To establish the worth of the Scriptures as the source for theological study, it is important that the Bible's supernatural origin be acknowledged. It is properly "a book of God." Bibliology includes such topics as the structure of the Bible, its division into the Old and New Testaments, the Bible as a Revelation from God, and the biblical concepts of inspiration, canonicity, and authority. Fundamentalist theology proceeds from the presuppositional basis that the Bible is the written Word of God, inerrant and infallible. It is "God-breathed" (2 Timothy 3:16, NIV) in terms of its origin. The words embodied in the original manuscripts are those God directed the human authors to write. The Bible is God's *full* revelation of Himself to man. This is referred to as "verbal-plenary" inspiration. The thirty-nine books in the Old Testament and the twenty-seven in the New Testament comprise the received canon of Scripture. Though the Apocryphal books and the Pseudepigrapha may be of interest to the scholar, they are not recognized as canonical and therefore are not equivalent to Scripture. Further, the Bible is authoritative because it is inspired by God. Paul's words positing the fact of inspiration are followed with a declaration that the Scriptures are "useful for teaching, rebuking, correcting and training in righteousness, so that the man of God may be thoroughly equipped for every good work" (2 Timothy 3:17).

God

Having determined the source from which theology is to flow (i.e., Bibliology), the next topic would be a study of the person and nature of God, and how God may be known. This is the section of theology that theologians have designated as Theology Proper. The first question in Theology Proper has to do with the ways in which God has made Himself known. (God cannot be known unless He makes Himself known.) The Scriptures declare that there are two ways in which God reveals Himself. The first way is through nature: "The heavens declare the glory of God; the skies proclaim the work of his hands" (Psalms 19:1); and in Paul's sermon to the people of Lystra, he declared, "We are bringing you good news, telling you to turn from these worthless things to the living God, who made heaven and earth and sea and everything in them. In the past, He let all nations go their own way. *Yet He has not left himself without testimony: He has shown kindness by giving you crops in their seasons; He provides you with plenty of food and fills your hearts with joy*" (Acts 14:15b–17, italics added). The second and fullest revelation that God has given concerning Himself is found in the Scriptures. Principally, Theology Proper is a thorough study of the Bible to ascertain what God has revealed concerning Himself.

The second question in Theology Proper has to do with the personality of God. The evidence for God's personality is found in His attributes: God is intelligent; God is sensitive; and God can act according to His will. In addition, the Scriptures speak of other attributes, such as God's omnipotence and omnipresence, infinitude and immutability, which are God's alone.

God's sovereignty and the way in which He works are best stated in the Westminster Shorter Catechism. It defines the decree of God as "[God's] eternal purpose, according to the counsel of his will, whereby, for his own glory, he hath foreordained whatsoever comes to pass" (Question 7, Westminster Shorter Catechism; see Ryrie 1986).

God is known also by the names and titles ascribed to Him. These names and titles given to God enhance knowledge of God. In the New Testament, the title "Lord," which is the Old Testament name Yahweh, has been ascribed to Jesus (Isaiah 42:8; cf. Philippians 2:11; Romans 10:9).

The doctrine of the Triunity of God comes under Theology Proper. The Scriptures teach that God is triune in persons but one in essence. It is a doctrine that is too complex to be explained; it is revealed truth about the Infinite One whom cannot be dissected and exegeted.

Angels

Some theologians include a study of angelic beings under Theology Proper. Angels are referred to in Scripture as God's messengers, sent by Him, to declare His will toward man. Angels are spirit beings created as higher than man (Psalms 8:5). Some rebelled and lost their holy estate. They are viewed as the demonic forces that continue to oppose God. Chief among those who oppose God and who leads the demonic forces is the devil, called Satan, and described as a dragon (Isaiah 14:12–15; Revelation 12:9).

Man

The biblical doctrine of mankind begins with the Creation. Man was created in the image and likeness of God. What that entailed is still a matter of discussion among theologians. The simplest explanation is that man was created a personal being having intellect, by which he could come to know God; emotions, by which he could come to love God; and volition, by which he could come to obey God. Others have added to the list, but the most important concept is that of personality. No biblical theologian will make the "image and likeness" to be physical likeness, for God is Spirit. Adam was created first, then Eve, and in time he disobeyed God and became estranged from God. By his disobedience, sin entered the world and death came as a result of that sin. The description of man without God is that such a one is "dead in trespasses and sins" (Ephesians 2:1). Theologians recognize both original sin inherited from Adam and the personal sin that each person has willfully chosen to commit. The Scriptures note that the rebellion of man became so intense that God brought a flood upon the earth and wiped out all but the family of Noah. God never abandoned man to his sin, but in the call of Abraham and the election of the people of Israel, God continued to call people to Himself. The system of sacrifices and priesthood were the means by which God dealt with the sins of mankind in the Old Testament. But in the midst of all this was the progressing revelation that God would finally deal with the problem of sin through the one who He would send—the Messiah, the Son of God. God's Son accomplished this by becoming human, taking upon Himself human flesh. Paul notes that this was a humiliating act (Philippians 2:6–8). God's Son then voluntarily gave up His life as a substitute for men. He took upon Himself human sinfulness (1 Peter 2:24), and imputed to mankind the righteousness of God (2 Corinthians 5:21).

Sin

The biblical teaching about mankind leads naturally to the teaching of the doctrine of sin. The Hebrew word for sin, as well as the principal word in Greek, means "missing the mark." The Westminster Shorter Catechism defines sin as "any want of conformity unto, or transgression of the law of God" (Question 14, Westminster Shorter Catechism; see Ryrie 1986). The origin of the sin of mankind is to be found in the disobedience in the Garden of Eden. There is no man who is without sin except for the Son of God, though He became "sin for us" (2 Corinthians 5:21). This is the "good news" of the gospel. "Christ Jesus came into the world to save sinners"(1 Timothy 1:15).

Salvation

The doctrinal teaching about salvation could just as easily be considered alongside the study of Christ, for this topic is related to the work of Christ. Salvation, however, involves all three members of the Triune Godhead. Fundamentalist theologians have conflicting views about salvation. To be sure, all agree on the need for salvation, but not on how salvation is procured. The viewpoint most often embraced by reformers or Calvinist theologians is that God chooses particular individuals to be saved. Others argue that the choice to accept or reject God's saving grace depends on the individual. Another important part of the study of salvation has to do with the nature of the Atonement. Most Fundamentalists hold the Vicarious Atonement view of Christ's death: that Christ died as a substitute for the sinners to appease the judgment of God against the sinner. He became the Vicar or Substitute to bring salvation.

Another area of disagreement among Fundamentalists has to do with the permanence of salvation. Those who have followed a Calvinistic theological viewpoint believe in what has been called "the perseverance of the saints." In churches that have not used Calvinistic language, the idea is that once a person has been genuinely "born again," that person is saved once and for all. However, there are some within the Fundamentalist camp who believe that a person can lose salvation because of apostasy of flagrant sin. Those who hold this view generally believe that a person can be "resaved" a number of times. Obviously, there is a great difference. Perhaps one of the major questions relating to this is to clearly define what is meant by "salvation." Those of the Calvinist persuasion would question the genuineness of the salvation of someone who left the faith and rejected it.

Salvation is given by divine grace, that is, it cannot be earned by any human action or attitude. It is received by faith—faith in the work of Jesus Christ on the cross as a substitute for the sinner. Even the principle of faith is a "gift of God—not by works, so that no one can boast" (Ephesians 2:8–9). To "believe in Jesus" is more than some fuzzy idea about Jesus, but must be associated with the idea of mankind receiving salvation through His sacrificial death and triumphant Resurrection (Romans 10:9–10).

Church

Fundamentalism included both those who embraced a dispensational theology as well as those who referred to themselves as covenant theologians. Covenant theologians identify the nature of the church as being the present body of believers as one with the Old Testament believers. Dispensationalists, on the other hand, believe that the church is a distinct body of believers who were gathered by God on the Day of Pentecost (Acts 2) and who will be spirited out of the world with the Rapture (1 Thessalonians 4:13).

Future Things

Just as there are differences of views on the church, so there are wide differences of interpretation regarding the future. Dispensational theologians are also premillennial in their beliefs concerning the future. They hold that a literal thousand-year reign by Jesus Christ will take place on the earth following Christ's return. Amillennial theologians, however, believe that the thousand-year period is metaphorical and that it is being fulfilled at the present time. When Jesus returns, there will be the judgment of all, followed by the eternal state. Also included in this division is the doctrine of Resurrection and Final Judgment.

Christ

In Chafer's divisions, the study of Christ has to do with the background of the person of Christ. He includes discussion of the preincarnate Christ, His incarnation, baptism, temptation, ministry of teaching and miracles, sufferings, death, Resurrection, Ascension, and return.

The Holy Spirit

The third member of the Trinity is the least known. He is often referred to as a force or as an extension either of the Father or the Son. But to speak of the Holy Spirit as a "force" is not biblical. In fact, referring to the Spirit as a force would destroy the true idea of the Trinity, which includes that each member of the Trinity is personal, though still being One. So to speak of the Holy Spirit as a force or extension is not biblical. The Holy Spirit is a distinct person, equal in power and glory with the Father and the Son. The Scriptures give less information about the Holy Spirit than about the Father and the Son. However, what little information there is, makes a clear distinction between the Father, the Son, and the Holy Spirit (e.g. John 14–16). An over-simplification speaks of the Father as the Creator, the Son as the Redeemer, and the Spirit as the Sustainer, but this does nothing to show the distinctness of the Spirit.

The Holy Spirit is present in the post-Resurrection time in a different way than in the Old Testament times. Jesus taught, "he lives with you and will be in you" (John 14:17). The fulfillment of that promise took place on the Day of Pentecost (Acts 2), and marked much of the teaching of the New Testament Epistles in that through the indwelling Spirit, the Son and the Father were present with believers (John 14:23).

Conclusion

Though there are many concepts of theology in this postmodern world, those who are directed by the fundamentals of the faith do not easily fall prey to conflicting theologies. Most of their work is centered on the development of a biblical theology that will enhance a systematic theology.

Richard I. McNeely

See also Angels; Bible; Bible Study; Biblical Inerrancy; Christ; Dispensationalism; God and God's Will; Holy Spirit; Premillennialism; Salvation; Sin and Sinners; Trinity

Bibliography

Berkhof, Louis. (1966) *Systematic Theology*. London: The Banner of Truth Trust.

Boice, James. (1985) *Foundations of the Christian Faith*. Downers Grove, IL: InterVarsity Press.

Chafer, Lewis Sperry. (1947) *Systematic Theology*, 8 vols. Dallas TX: Dallas Seminary Press.

Daane, James. (1988) "Theology." In *International Standard Bible Encyclopedia*, 4 vols., edited by Geoffrey W. Bromiley, F. Everett Harrison, William Sanford LaSor, and Edgar W. Smith. Grand Rapids, MI: Wm. B. Eerdmans, IV, 826–827.

Erickson, Millard J. (1983–1985) *Christian Theology*, 3 vols. Grand Rapids, MI: Baker Book House.

Grudem, Wayne. (1996). *Systematic Theology*. Grand Rapids, MI: Zondervan Publishing.

Hodge, Charles. (1952) *Systematic Theology*, 3 vols. Grand Rapids, MI: Wm. B. Eerdmans.

Ladd, George E. (1979) "Biblical Theology, Nature of." In *International Standard Bible Encyclopedia*, 4 vols., edited by Geoffrey W. Bromiley, F. Everett Harrison, William Sanford LaSor, and Edgar W. Smith. Grand Rapids, MI: Wm. B. Eerdmans, I, 505–509.

Lightner, Robert P. (1986) *Evangelical Theology*. Grand Rapids, MI: Baker Book House.

Murray, John. (1984) *Select Lectures in Systematic Theology*. Vol. 2 of *Collected Writings of John Murray*, 4 vols. Edinburgh: The Banner of Truth Trust.

Ryrie, Charles C. (1986) *Basic Theology*. Wheaton, IL: Victor Books.

"The Westminster Shorter Catechism." In *The Constitution of the Presbyterian Church (U.S.A.), Part I, Book of Confessions*. Louisville, KY: The Office of the General Assembly, 181–193.

Theonomy

Theonomy is a central aspect of the theology of Christian Reconstructionism. Translated as "God's Law" and grounded in the presuppositional apologetics of Cornelius van Til, this perspective has been reshaped in popular forms, including the Fundamentalists' critique of secular humanism. Theonomists hold that all knowledge is derived from presuppositions; reasoning always begins with premises that cannot be proven. There is, for example, no proof that God exists; yet, neither can it be proven that God does not exist. Christianity and atheism each requires a "leap of faith," as it were. Inasmuch as presuppositional epistemology asserts that there can be no objective or neutral reasoning, theonomy asserts that there can be no neutral, objective way to determine ethics and law. Humans must live under God's law or substitute some humanistic value system; the only alternatives in this worldview are an objective absolute (the Bible) or abject moral relativism resulting in chaos (which they view as tyranny.) In this regard, theonomists believe that submission to "Biblical Law" is the only path to authentic liberty.

The founder of Christian Reconstructionism, Rousas John Rushdoony, laid out his theonomist perspective and its implications in his *Institutes of Biblical Law* (1973), an 890–page commentary on the Ten Commandments and elaborated this further in the second volume (another 752 pages) entitled *Law and Society: Volume II of the Institutes of Biblical Law* (1982). Other important Reconstructionist works on this topic include Gary North's *The Dominion Covenant* (1981) and Greg Bahnsen's *Theonomy and Christian Ethics* (1974) as well as his *By This Standard: The Authority of God's Law Today* (1985). Theonomists believe that the Bible sets out three spheres of authority, each of which is subject to appropriate biblical law: the family, the church, and the civil society. God's law refers to the principles governing each sphere, not merely the civil sphere in which we might expect to find "legal" concepts.

Rushdoony (1973) uses the Ten Commandments as basic legal principles, which he then elaborates with what he calls "case law" drawn primarily from Exodus, Deuteronomy, and Leviticus. As an example, he argues that property taxes violate biblical law because such taxes are based on the principle that land is owned by the government (rather than owned by God and loaned to humans as stewards). According to Reconstructionists, property taxes violate the First Commandment in that it is idolatrous to make the civil government Lord over the earth. In support of his position, Rushdoony (1973: 283) cites "The earth is the Lord's, and the fullness thereof" (Psalms 24:1, KJV; also Exodus 9:29, Deuteronomy 10:14, 1 Corinthians 10:26). Theonomists believe that the Bible provides all the legal insight necessary to resolve even modern questions. There is, however, among theonomists, some disagreement over the interpretation and appropriate application of biblical law. Some, for example, believe that the "ceremonial laws" (dietary regulations, sacrifice requirements, etc.) are still applicable to Christians, while others do not. In another example, it is often noted that theonomists embrace widespread use of the death penalty (for adulterers, homosexuals, "incorrigible" teenagers, and so on). Theonomists actually disagree over whether the Bible requires those penalties or whether it is setting limits on the most extreme penalties permitted by God.

Reconstructionist theonomy was translated to a popular level and gave shape to the New Christian Right in the form of the critique of "secular humanism" and efforts to make America a "Christian nation." As Rushdoony wrote (on many occasions), if there can be no knowledge without presuppositions, and presuppositions are inherently religious, then there can be no religious neutrality. There can be no religiously neutral legal systems or economic systems (all law is someone's view of what is right imposed on others; the originator of law can be God or "man" but it can never be neutral.) Neither can there be religiously neutral educational systems or curricula. Believers and nonbelievers have no common ground on which to engage. All presuppositions not derived from God (that is, from the Bible) are derived from human beings' desire to be gods unto themselves, determining good and evil for themselves: humanism. Theonomists take great umbrage at the oft-heard expression that Christians are "not under law but under grace." If this is correct, argue the theonomists, then we have no standard for evaluating right from wrong; we have source of authority for our views other than ourselves. Adam and Eve's determining good and evil for themselves or "each being a law unto himself," theonomists remind us, was the original sin in the Garden of Eden.

Sometimes explicitly acknowledged—but often not—the intellectual/theological foundation for the religious Right's critique of secular humanism is presuppositionalism and theonomy as translated through Reconstructionist writings. For example, Rus Walton's *One Nation under God* (1975), lays out the critique of secular humanism, and cites Rushdoony's works throughout. Another Christian Right leader, John Whitehead, in his *The Separation Illusion* (1977), aligns himself with Christian Reconstructionists by "documenting" the shift from America as a "nation founded on God's law," to one founded on "secular humanism." His Rutherford Institute uses the American legal system to further this viewpoint.

Julie J. Ingersoll

See also Reconstructionism, Christian; Secularism

Bibliography

Bahnsen, Greg. (1974) *Theonomy and Christian Ethics.* Vallecito, CA: Craig Press.

———. (1985) *By This Standard: The Authenticity of God's Law Today*, prologue by Gary North. Tyler, TX: Institute for Christian Economics.

Barron, Bruce. (1992) *Heaven on Earth?* Grand Rapids, MI: Zondervan Publishing.

DeMar, Gary. (1989) *God and Government*, 2nd ed. Brentwood, TN: Wolgemuth and Hyatt.

North, Gary. (1973) *Introduction to Christian Economics.* Vallecito, CA: Craig Press.

———. (1981) *The Dominion Covenant.* Tyler, TX: Institute for Christian Economics.

———. (1987) *Biblical Blueprint series*, 10 vols. Fort Worth, TX: Dominion Press.

Rushdoony, Rousas John. (1973) *Institutes of Biblical Law.* Nutley, NJ: The Craig Press.

———. (1974) *By What Standard?* Fairfax, VA: Thoburn Press.

———. (1977) *Law and Liberty.* Fairfax, VA: Thoburn Press.

———. (1982) *Law and Society: Volume II of the Institutes of Biblical Law.* Vallecito, CA: Ross House Books.

Walton, Rus. (1988) *Biblical Solutions to Contemporary Problems: A Handbook.* Brentwood, TN: Wolgemuth and Hyatt.

———. (1975) *One Nation Under God.* Marborough, NH: Plymouth Rock Foundation.

Whitehead, John W. (1977) *The Separation Illusion: A Lawyer Examines the First Amendment*, forward by R. J. Rushdoony. Milford, MI: Mott Media.

Tribe of Dan

Throughout the Old and New Testaments is the tradition that Israel was composed of twelve tribes, each descended from an eponymous ancestor who is a son (or grandson in the case of Ephraim and Manasseh) of Jacob. According to the story of the birth of Jacob's children in Genesis 29:31–30:24, Dan was one of two sons of Jacob by Rachel's handmaid Bilhah (the other being Naphtali). The conquest and settlement traditions claim that Dan's descendants settled territory along the coastal plain in the vicinity of Philistia. Perhaps the best-known stories about the tribe of Dan, the Samson narratives preserved in Judges 13–16, reflect Philistine military pressure on

> **Revelation 7:4–8**
>
> 4. And I heard the number of them which were sealed: and there were sealed an hundred and forty and four thousand of all the tribes of the children of Israel.
>
> 5. Of the tribe of Juda were sealed twelve thousand. Of the tribe of Reuben were sealed twelve thousand. Of the tribe of Gad were sealed twelve thousand.
>
> 6. Of the tribe of Aser were sealed twelve thousand. Of the tribe of Nepthalim were sealed twelve thousand. Of the tribe of Manasses were sealed twelve thousand.
>
> 7. Of the tribe of Simeon were sealed twelve thousand. Of the tribe of Levi were sealed twelve thousand. Of the tribe of Issachar were sealed twelve thousand.
>
> 8. Of the tribe of Zabulon were sealed twelve thousand. Of the tribe of Joseph were sealed twelve thousand. Of the tribe of Benjamin were sealed twelve thousand.

the tribe's territory in the period before the establishment of the monarchy in Israel. Due to external pressures Dan was forced to migrate north, capturing the city of Laish and renaming it Dan, and thus establishing the tribe in the far north of Israel (Judges 18:27–29).

This picture of Dan as a roving tribe that left its mark by renaming geographic locales plays a significant role in the nineteenth-century ideology known as British or Anglo Israelism. Anglo Israelism holds, at base, that the tribes of Israel "lost" in the Assyrian and Babylonian exiles are actually the direct, linear ancestors of people of Anglo-Saxon heritage. While most attention is devoted to the identification of peoples with the tribe of Ephraim, Dan holds a special place as a tribe that, through its roaming, had an impact throughout the Old World. So, for example, in John Gawler's (1880) classic treatment of the subject, the claim is made that Dan's presence can be divined from the names Mace*don*, Cale*don*ia, the *Dan*ube, and of course the ultimate home of Dan, *Den*mark, from where the Danes (that is, Danites) proceeded on to Ireland, Scotland, and England. These views remained strong in some circles throughout the twentieth century, as can be seen in Herbert W. Armstrong's *United States and British Commonwealth in Prophecy* (1967).

In the New Testament, by far the most famous reference to the tribe of Dan is one that is *not* made. Revelation 7:4–8 (NRSV) contains a roster of the 144,000 who are to be sealed "out of every tribe of the people of Israel." The tribe of Dan, however, is not mentioned. This omission, as well as other scriptural notices such as Jeremiah 8:16, has led to the view of some that the Antichrist will come from the tribe of Dan. Indeed, the earliest reference to the idea that the Antichrist would be Jewish comes from Irenaeus, who explicitly identifies him as a Danite. It is unclear precisely how old this tradition is, but it was fueled by the extensive treatment of the subject by Hippolytus, writing shortly after Irenaeus; the association by certain Christians of Dan with Antichrist traditions survives to the present day. Finally, it should be noted that the controversial Mormon group known as the Danites take their name from the biblical Book of Daniel, not from association with the tribe of Dan.

Matthew Neujahr

See also Antichrist; Aryan Nations

Bibliography

Armstrong, Herbert W. (1967) *The United States and British Commonwealth in Prophecy*. Pasadena: Ambassador College.

Gawlor, John C. (1880) *Dan, the Pioneer of Israel*. London: W. H. Grant.

Hill, C. E. (1995) "Antichrist from the Tribe of Dan." *Journal of Theological Studies* 46: 99–117.

Niemann, Hermann Michael. (1985) *Die Daniten*. Göttingen: Vandenhoeck and Ruprecht.

Tribulation

The majority of American Protestant Fundamentalists have held that the Great Tribulation will be a seven-year period of unparalleled political and social oppression that will take place after the Rapture of the church and immediately prior to the millennial, or thousand-year, reign of Jesus Christ. Christians who hold to this notion of the Tribulation are premillennialists, believing that the Second Coming of Christ will *precede* His millennial reign. Dispensational premillennialism, the dominant strand of premillennialism among Fundamentalists, teaches that the Great Tribulation will feature the ascendance of the satanically inspired Antichrist—a religio-political leader who will proclaim himself the Messiah of the Jews and help bring about a revived Roman Empire. Fleeing worldwide persecution, Jews will return to Palestine, reestablish Israel, and sign a peace treaty with the Antichrist. In the second half of the Tribulation, however, the Antichrist will turn on the Jews, causing some to convert to Christianity. The persecution will end only when Christ returns bodily at the end of the Tribulation, defeating Antichrist and the Gentile nations at the Battle of Armageddon.

Views of the Tribulation

Premillennialists have spilled much ink debating the specifics of this coming Tribulation, but views fall into three general camps. All three attempt to account for certain prophetic passages of the Bible. The most popular among Fundamentalists, pre-Tribulationism (discussed above), posits that Christ will appear immediately prior to the Tribulation, calling the church out of the world in the Rapture and giving reign to Antichrist. Christ's pre-Tribulational return will be secret and unexpected, though the attentive soul might discern in the "signs of the times" that it is imminent. For pre-Tribulationists, the Tribulation marks when God will attend once again to the Jews and begin to fulfill all outstanding Old Testament prophecies concerning the nation of Israel. God will at this time unleash the judgments of the seven seals, seven trumpets, and seven bowls recorded in Revelation 6–18. Post-Tribulationists, on the other hand, maintain that Christ will come for His church *after* the Tribulation. Biblically, theirs is a less literal version of premillennialism. For instance, post-Tribulationists usually do not adhere to a literal seven-year Tribulation and typically avoid reference to the Rapture of the church. Similarly, unlike pre-Tribulationists, post-Tribulationists argue that scriptural references to "Israel" often refer to the church, thus eliminating the need for a renewed nation of Israel. In this scheme, the church will endure a more

generic Tribulation, or testing, of their faith prior to the millennial reign of Christ (not necessarily taken as a literal one thousand years). A smaller number of inquirers have discerned a third view of the Tribulation, which features a Rapture midway through the Tribulation. This mid-Tribulational view insists that the church will experience the relatively mild, first three-and-a-half years of Tribulation and be "raptured" before the more perilous second half. Something of a family quarrel over the precise nature of the Tribulation has characterized premillennialism since the 1890s, though pre-Tribulationism became dominant among Fundamentalists from the 1920s. Although these views are highly specific in detail and sometimes rest heavily on literal readings of prophetic books and passages in Scripture (especially Daniel and Revelation), their influence, as Paul Boyer has argued (1992), extends well beyond those who might be considered End-Times "experts." Millions of people worldwide consider the Bible to contain important clues about End-Times events.

Historical Development of Tribulational Views

Since belief in a premillennial Tribulation does not always accompany an Evangelical faithfulness to the Bible, extra-biblical sources are equally important for understanding tribulational views. Adherence to premillennialism rose dramatically in the late nineteenth century as postmillennialism—the view that the present world would progressively realize the kingdom of God—declined among theological conservatives. Premillennialism seemed more attuned to modern times. In the premillennial scheme, the world (and organized religion with it) would steadily increase in corruption until the Second Coming of Christ. Though various forms of millennialism already existed in the United States in diverse figures like William Miller, Alexander Campbell, and Ann Lee, the most influential form of premillennialism for Fundamentalists would come to America through British Plymouth Brethren founder John Nelson Darby (1800–1882). Darby brought premillennialism to a new level of cohesiveness and respectability by supplementing it with hundreds of biblical proof-texts and by refusing to predict dates for the Second Coming. His "dispensationalist" and pre-Tribulational system taught that God's promises to Israel would be literally fulfilled during the Tribulation and millennium. (In fact, twentieth-century Evangelical and Fundamentalist pro-Israel political stances stem in part from the pervasiveness of Darbyite premillennialism.) His views were codified in C. I. Scofield's (1843–1921) best-selling *Scofield's Reference Bible* (1909, revised in 1917 and again in 1967) and taught widely at Bible conferences and Bible schools, most famously the Niagara Conference and the Moody Bible Institute in Chicago.

Twentieth-century history fed the dispensationalist premillennial imagination in remarkable ways. World wars and racial genocide fueled premillennial hopes that the End was near, and candidates for Antichrist abounded from Mussolini to Gorbachev. The British capture of Jerusalem in 1917 and the promise of a Jewish homeland appeared to fulfill the promise of a renewed Jewish state. (Christian and Missionary Alliance founder A. B. Simpson [1843–1919] read the Balfour Declaration to his congregation in tears, believing it to be one of the last "signs" before Christ's return.) For many, the Allied nations in Europe seemed at least to be a forerunner of the ten-nation revived Roman Empire foretold in the Book of Daniel. Likewise, the creation of the state of Israel in 1948, the Cold War, and the European Common Market seemed to confirm dispensationalist premillennial themes. Computer technology revealed how Antichrist might administer his global reign. Thermonuclear weapons finally made possible the cataclysmic destruction predicted in the Book of Revelation. Plus, according to Fundamentalists, civilization seemed to be fast unraveling: morality was in decline, nations rose against themselves, fascism and communism threatened good government, and established religion slowly followed its destined course to apostasy. For many, reading the "signs of the times" became a favorite pastime.

Continuing Legacies

Even with the demise of many of these realities—such as the Cold War and the threat of a nuclear holocaust—dispensational premillennialism remains a compelling ideology. Many Fundamentalists and their institutions continue to relate contemporary events to biblical prophecies. For example, Moody Bible Institute and Dallas Theological Seminary (DTS) professors have continued to propagate dispensational premillennialism in courses on eschatology and the prophetic books. Hal Lindsey's *The Late Great Planet Earth* (1970), which sold twenty-eight million copies by 1990, brought dispensationalist

themes politically up to date, making them compelling to politicians such as President Ronald Reagan. During the Middle East crisis in 1990, interest in Bible prophecy reached a fever pitch, causing John Walvoord's (then president of DTS) publisher to re-release a million additional copies of his *Armageddon, Oil, and the Middle East* (1974). Christian television networks are presently replete with prophecy programs and speakers on prophetic themes. Fundamentalists and others have also learned that Tribulational themes sell well. Since the 1930s, End-Times novels, often with overtly evangelistic themes, have received a wide Christian as well as non-Christian readership. Tim LaHaye and Jerry Jenkins's amazingly successful series *Left Behind* (1996–), with titles such as *The Rise of Antichrist* and *Tribulation Force*, is taking this popular literary genre to new heights. As the series demonstrates, belief in a coming Tribulation (and premillennialism more broadly) is not exclusive to Fundamentalists. Though dispensational premillennialism's generally pessimistic reading of contemporary history fits well with Fundamentalism's militant antimodernism, many non-Fundamentalist Evangelicals share a fascination with dispensationalist themes.

R. Bryan Bademan

See also Dispensationalism; End Times; Premillennialism; Rapture

Bibliography

Boyer, Paul. (1992) *When Time Shall Be No More: Prophecy Belief in Modern American Culture.* Cambridge, MA: The Belknap Press of Harvard University Press.

Carpenter, Joel A. (1997) *Revive Us Again: The Reawakening of American Fundamentalism.* New York: Oxford University Press.

LaHaye, Timothy F., and Jerry B. Jenkins. (1996–) *Left Behind.* Wheaton, IL: Tyndale House Publishers.

Lindsey, Hal, with C. C. Carlson. (1970) *The Late Great Planet Earth.* Grand Rapids, MI: Zondervan Publishing.

Marsden, George M. (1980). *Fundamentalism and American Culture: The Shaping of Twentieth-Century Evangelicalism, 1870–1925.* Oxford: Oxford University Press.

Moorhead, James H. (1999) *World Without End: Mainstream American Protestant Visions of the Last Things, 1880–1925.* Bloomington: Indiana University Press.

Ryrie, Charles C. (1965) *Dispensationalism Today*. Chicago: Moody Press.

Sandeen, Ernest R. (1970) *The Roots of Fundamentalism: British and American Millenarianism, 1800–1930*. Chicago: University of Chicago Press.

Scofield, Cyrus I. (1909) *Scofield's Reference Bible*. Oxford: Oxford University Press.

Walvoord, John F., with John E. Walvoord. (1974) *Armageddon, Oil, and the Middle East Crisis: What the Bible Says about the Future of the Middle East and the End of Western Civilization*. Grand Rapids, MI: Zondervan Publishing.

Weber, Timothy P. (1979) *Living in the Shadow of the Second Coming: American Premillennialism, 1875–1925*. New York: Oxford University Press.

Tridentine Mass

The Tridentine Mass is the name commonly given to the Roman Missal (order of Mass), which was revised according to the decrees of the Council of Trent (1545–1563) and promulgated by Pope Pius V in 1570. The Tridentine Missal remained in effect with minor revisions for four hundred years, until acts of the Second Vatican Council, known as Vatican II (1959–1963), resulted in the publication of a new Roman Missal (*Novus Ordo Missae*) by Pope Paul VI in 1969 to 1970.

The decisions of Vatican II in general, and changes in the order of Mass in particular, galvanized into action Catholics who saw the *Novus Ordo* as a symbol of the invasion of modernity, liberalism, ecumenism, and Protestant heresies into the church. Believing that Pius V had intended to establish the 1570 Missal for all time as the liturgy of the Roman Catholic Church, Catholic traditionalists have established a variety of organizations, both separatist and nonseparatist, that celebrate the Tridentine rite and work for the expulsion of modernism from Catholic liturgy and polity.

How the Tridentine Mass Became a Rallying Point

In 1965, while Vatican II was ongoing, American priest Fr. Gommar De Pauw (1918–) published a "Catholic Traditionalist Manifesto," which attacked modernist Catholicism and its influence on liturgical reform. He also founded a group known as the Catholic Traditionalist Movement (CTM). De Pauw remained "a controversial symbol of traditionalist discontent with Vatican II throughout the later 1960s" (Dinges 1991: 71). However, he was soon eclipsed by a French traditionalist archbishop, Msgr. Marcel Lefebvre (1905–1991). Lefebvre had been a member of the Central Preparatory Commission, which prepared documents for consideration during Vatican II. During the council he sided with conservatives and refused to sign two major conciliar documents on Religious Liberty and the Church in the Modern World. In 1970 he established a traditionalist seminary in Ecône, Switzerland, and a priestly fraternity called the Society of St. Pius X (SSPX). In the early 1970s the first traditionalist American priests ordained by Lefebvre began to establish chapels in America. Many groups inspired by De Pauw had already been meeting underground in houses and rented spaces in order to say and hear the Tridentine liturgy.

During the 1970s relations between Lefebvre and the Vatican grew increasingly strained, and in 1983, he threatened to consecrate some of his priests to the episcopacy. In 1984, in an attempt to conciliate with him, the Vatican issued a papal indult, or circular letter, which granted Catholic priests permission to celebrate the Tridentine rite and Catholic laity to attend it under carefully regulated conditions. These conditions included considering Vatican II's decisions and the *Novus Ordo* to be legitimate. In addition, the Tridentine Mass could only be celebrated on request and with permission of a bishop. However, this did not satisfy Lefebvre, and in 1988 he consecrated four priests as bishops in defiance of the Vatican's orders. Shortly afterward he was excommunicated and the SSPX formally separated from the church.

In response to the secession of the Lefebvreites, Pope John Paul II (1920–) issued a *moto proprio*, or papal act, known as *Ecclesia Dei*, which argued for "a wide and generous application of the directives already issued some time ago by the Apostolic See [i.e., the 1984 indult] for the use of the Roman Missal according to the typical edition of 1962 [the last edition of the Tridentine rite]" (John Paul II 1988: 3). This was followed in 1991 by a pastoral letter to the bishops of the United States, which considerably relaxed the restrictions on celebration of the Tridentine rite as long as the legitimacy of the pope and the validity of the *Novus Ordo* were recognized. In

COMPARISON OF PARTS OF THE EUCHARISTIC LITURGY IN THE TRIDENTINE MISSAL AND THE *NOVUS ORDO MISSAE*

P=Presider, R=Response (congregational)

1) *Liturgy from the middle of the canon or Eucharistic prayer*

The Consecration of the Host

P: Who, the day before He suffered, took bread into His holy and venerable hands, and having lifted up His eyes to heaven, to Thee, God, His almighty Father, giving thanks to Thee, blessed it (+), broke it, and gave it to His disciples, saying:
Take ye and eat ye all of this:

The priest bends over the Host and says: FOR THIS IS MY BODY. *Then the priest adores and elevates the Sacred Host. The bell is rung.*

The Consecration of the Wine

The priest uncovers the Chalice and says:

P: In like manner, after He had supped, taking also into His holy and venerable hands this goodly chalice again giving thanks to Thee, He blessed it (+), and gave it to His disciples, saying:
Take ye, and drink ye all of this:

The priest bends over the Chalice and says:

FOR THIS IS THE CHALICE OF MY BLOOD, OF THE NEW AND EVERLASTING TESTAMENT, THE MYSTERY OF FAITH, WHICH FOR YOU AND FOR MANY [*pro multis*] SHALL BE SHED UNTO THE REMISSION OF SINS.
P: As often as ye shall do these things, ye shall do them in memory of Me.

The priest adores and elevates the Chalice. The bell is rung.

2) *Liturgy for the administration of Communion*

At the Communion

The priest genuflects, rises and says:

P: I will take the bread of heaven, and will call upon the name of the Lord.

Taking the Sacred Host with his left hand, the priest strikes his breast three times, saying (here the bell is rung each of the three times with the priest):

---

some cases the Tridentine Mass could even become the principal Sunday Mass of a parish church, provided permission was obtained from the bishop.

Traditionalist Catholic Criticisms of the 1970 Missal

Catholic traditionalists criticize the *Novus Ordo* on a number of counts. Overall, they feel the liturgy has been overly "Protestantized" and modernized, and that emphasis on the Mass as a sacrifice has been severely reduced. They argue that the new liturgy has decreased respect for the priesthood and the institutions of the church and has led to declines in Mass attendance and the number of young men entering the priesthood. Many also associate the new Mass with other distrusted reforms implemented by Vatican II, such as the move toward ecumenical

P: Lord, I am not worthy that Thou shouldst enter under my roof; but only say the word, and my soul shall be healed. (three times)

Holding the Sacred Host in his right hand, the priest makes the sign of the cross with it and says:

P: May the Body of Our Lord Jesus Christ keep my soul unto life everlasting. Amen.

The priest receives Holy Communion and after a brief meditation continues:

P: What shall I render unto the Lord for all the things that He hath rendered unto me? I will take the chalice of salvation and will call upon the name of the Lord. With high praises will I call upon the Lord, and I shall be saved from all mine enemies.

The priest takes the Chalice in his right hand and makes the sign of the cross, saying:

P: May the Blood of Our Lord Jesus Christ keep my soul unto life everlasting. Amen.

Then, the priest faces the people with the Ciborium and, holding up one of the Sacred Particles before the communicants, he says:

P: Behold the Lamb of God, behold Him who taketh away the sins of the world. P: Lord, I am not worthy that Thou shouldst enter under my roof; but only say the word, and my soul shall be healed. (three times)

Communion of the Faithful

Here Holy Communion is administered to those of the faithful who desire to receive it. The priest gives Holy Communion to each communicant saying:

P: May the Body of Our Lord Jesus Christ keep your soul unto life everlasting. Amen.

When all have received Communion, he returns to the altar and replaces the Ciborium in the tabernacle. He then receives wine in the Chalice and says:

P: Into a pure heart, O Lord, may we receive the heavenly food which has passed our lips; bestowed upon us in time, may it be the healing of our souls for eternity.

The priest goes to the Epistle side [of the altar] *and, while the server pours wine and water over his fingers, he says:*

P: May Thy Body, O Lord, which I have received, and Thy Blood which I have drunk cleave to mine inmost parts: and do Thou grant that no stain of sin remain in me, whom pure and holy mysteries have refreshed: Who livest and reignest world without end. Amen.

New Roman Missal in Latin and English by Rev. F. X. Lasance and Rev. Francis Augustine Walsh, O.S.B., 1945.

1) *Liturgy from the middle of the canon or Eucharistic prayer*

P: Before he was given up to death, a death he freely accepted, he took bread and gave you thanks. He broke the bread, gave it to his disciples, and said:

(cont.)

COMPARISON OF PARTS OF THE EUCHARISTIC LITURGY IN THE TRIDENTINE MISSAL AND THE *NOVUS ORDO MISSAE* (cont.)

Take this, all of you and eat it:

THIS IS MY BODY WHICH WILL BE GIVEN UP FOR YOU.

P: When supper was ended, he took the cup. Again he gave you thanks and praise, gave the cup to his disciples and said:

Take this all of you, and drink from it:

THIS IS THE CUP OF MY BLOOD, THE BLOOD OF THE NEW AND EVERLASTING COVENANT, IT WILL BE SHED FOR YOU AND FOR ALL MEN [*pro multis*] SO THAT SINS MAY BE FORGIVEN.

P: Do this in memory of me.

The bell is rung as the priest elevates the Chalice to be seen by the people. He then genuflects

P: Let us proclaim the mystery of faith.

The people acclaim one of the following formulas:

R: Christ has died, Christ is risen, Christ will come again.

R: Dying you destroyed our death, rising you restored our life, Lord Jesus, come in glory.

R: When we eat this bread and drink this cup, we proclaim your death, Lord Jesus, until you come in glory.

R: Lord, by your cross and resurrection you have set us free. You are the Saviour of the world.

2) *Liturgy for the administration of Communion*

At the Communion

P: This is the Lamb of God who takes away the sins of the world. Happy are those who are called to his supper.

A: Lord I am not worthy to receive you, but only say the word and I shall be healed. (once)

Before consuming the Host, the priest saying silently:

P: May the Body of Christ bring me to everlasting life.

Before drinking the precious Blood, he says silently:

P: May the Blood of Christ bring me to everlasting life.

Communion of the Faithful

Here Holy Communion is administered to those of the faithful who desire to receive it. The priest goes to the communicants and says to each:

P: The Body of Christ.

R: Amen.

P: Lord, may I receive these gifts in purity of heart. May they bring me healing and strength, now and for ever.

New Missal, 1973 English translation, Eucharistic Prayer I.

relationships with Protestant denominations and the end of many traditional Catholic lifestyle practices.

One of the primary promoters of the traditionalist agenda is writer and Catholic convert Michael Davies (1936–), who has written extensively on Archbishop Lefebvre, the errors of modernism and Vatican II, and the value of the Tridentine liturgy. Davies and others are specifically critical of a number of reforms in the *Novus Ordo*, many of which do resemble the Eucharistic liturgy and rubrics of mainline Protestant denominations who have also been participating in liturgical renewal and ecumenical cooperation. Criticized reforms include an almost universal move to saying Mass in the vernacular, the removal of sacrificial language in many prayers, the addition of "excessive" Scripture reading and the move to a three-year lectionary, the use of laity to distribute Communion, the reception of Communion by the laity in their hands and while standing, the reception of Communion in both kinds (i.e., bread and wine), the translation of the term *pro multis* in the liturgy as "for all" rather than "for many" (suggesting universalism), the audible recitation of many parts of the service that were formally recited silently, the use of "secular" and "new" music rather than Gregorian chant, the removal of many images and side altars from sanctuaries, and the use of women as altar girls and readers. Catholic traditionalists compare many of these revisions, particularly the emphasis on Scripture, the removal of sacrificial language, and the liturgy's attempt to give a stronger idea of the priesthood of all believers and the Eucharist as a common meal, to the Reformation-era liturgical revisions of Martin Luther (1483–1546) and Thomas Cranmer (1489–1556). In fact, Pope Pius V's 1570 Missal was originally intended to combat those Reformation reforms. Davies and others blame some changes on Protestant observers, many of them liturgical experts, who were present at Vatican II. Other changes are the result of the encroachment of modernity and liberalism in general. In fact, support for the Tridentine Mass in many cases has become deeply intertwined with support for other Fundamentalist social and political causes.

Conclusion: The Present Situation

The celebration of the Tridentine liturgy is alive and well in the Roman Catholic Church. Many of its promoters are not separatists and pledge allegiance to the current pope and to the church, but are busy working within Catholicism to establish Tridentine-rite chapels and parishes. Davies is now the president of Una Voce Federation, an international organization founded in 1964 to encourage the use of Latin in the Roman rite and currently devoted to "the promotion and support of the traditional Latin mass within the church, in union with Rome" (Una Voce website). Una Voce and other organizations publish directories of the growing number of parishes and other locations where the Tridentine liturgy is being used. The Tridentine Mass remains both a symbolic and actual focus of the Fundamentalist movement within the Roman Catholic Church.

Jennifer Lynn Woodruff

See also Catholic Fundamentalism

Bibliography

Congar, Yves. (1976) *Challenge to the Church: The Case of Archbishop Lefebvre*. Huntingdon, IN: Our Sunday Visitor.

Congregation for Divine Worship. (1984) "Quattuor Abhinc Annos" (papal indult). *L'Osservatore Romano* (English) 43: 9.

Cuneo, Michael. (1997) *The Smoke of Satan: Conservative and Traditionalist Dissent in Contemporary American Catholicism*. New York and Oxford: Oxford University Press.

Davies, Michael. (1976) *Cranmer's Godly Order: The Destruction of Catholicism Through Liturgical Change*. Vol. 1 of *Liturgical Revolution*. New Rochelle, NY: Arlington House.

———. (1977a) *Archbishop Lefebvre: The Truth*. No. 1 of *Augustine Pamphlets*. Chawleigh, Chumleigh, and Devon, UK: Augustine Publishing Co.

———. (1977b) *The New Mass*. No. 3 of *Augustine Pamphlets*. Chawleigh, Chumleigh, and Devon, UK: Augustine Publishing Co.

———. (1977c) *Pope John's Council*. Vol. 2 of *Liturgical Revolution*. New Rochelle, NY: Arlington House.

———. (1977d) *The Tridentine Mass*. No. 2 of *Augustine Pamphlets*. Chawleigh, Chumleigh, and Devon, UK: Augustine Publishing Co.

———. (1980) *Pope Paul's New Mass*. Vol. 3 of *Liturgical Revolution*. Dickinson, TX: Angelus Press.

Dinges, William D. (1983) "Catholic Traditionalist Movement." In *Alternatives to American Mainline Churches*, edited by Joseph H. Ficheter. Barrytown, NY: Unification Theological Seminary, 137–158.

———. (1989) "The Quandary of Dissent on the Catholic Right." In *Sociological Studies in Roman Catholicism: Historical and Contemporary Perspectives*, edited by Roger O'Toole. Lewiston, NY: Edwin Mellen Press, 107–126.

———, and James Hitchcock. (1991) "Roman Catholic Traditionalism and Activist Conservatism in the United States." In *Fundamentalisms Observed*, edited by Martin E. Marty and R. Scott Appleby. Chicago: University of Chicago Press, 66–141. Eccelsia Dei Commission. (1991) "Guidelines on Tridentine Mass." *Origins* 21: 144–145.

Latin Mass Society. http://www.latin-mass-society.org

Lefebvre, Msgr. Marcel. (1986) *Open Letter to Confused Catholics*. Kansas City, MO: Angelus Press.

———. (1997) *Against the Heresies*. Kansas City, MO: Angelus Press.

Leonard, George. (1978) *Light on Archbishop Lefebvre*. London: Incorporated Catholic Truth Society.

Lex Orandi, Lex Credendi. http://sonnet.co.uk/credo/lex.html.

Liberatore, Albert M. (1994) "Beyond Nightmares and Dreams: Trent and Vatican II." *America* 170 (13): 16–17.

Likoudis, James, and Kenneth D. Whitehead. (1981) *The Pope, the Council, and the Mass*. West Hanover, MA: Christopher Publishing House.

Liturgy Training Program. (1980) *The Liturgy Documents: A Parish Resource*. Chicago: Liturgy Training Program.

Lothian, James. (2000) "Novus Ordo Missae: The Record After Thirty Years." *Homiletic and Pastoral Review* 101 (1): 26–31, 48.

Pope John Paul II. (1988) "Eccelsia Dei." http://www.vatican.va/holy_father/john_paul_ii/motu_proprio/documents/hf_jp-ii_motu-proprio_02071988_ecclesia-dei_en.html

Pruter, Karl, and J. Gordon Melton. (1983) *The Old Catholic Sourcebook*. New York and London: Garland Publishing.

Una Voce. http://www.unavoce.org.

Weakland, Msgr. Rembert G. (1997) "Liturgical Renewal: Two Latin Rites?" *America* 176 (20): 12–15.

Weaver, Mary Jo, and R. Scott Appleby, eds. (1995) *Being Right: Conservative Catholics in America*. Bloomington: Indiana University Press.

White, James F. (1995) *Roman Catholic Worship: Trent to Today*. New York and Mahwah, NJ: Paulist Press.

Trinity

The doctrine of the Trinity is a principal concept of historic Christianity. If Jesus Christ is not God, and the Holy Spirit is not God, there would be no Christianity. Though the word "trinity" is not found in Scripture, there exists what some have termed the "building materials" for the construction of the doctrine. Interestingly, although the twelve-volume series of articles known as *The Fundamentals* (1910–1915, republished in 1917) does not have a separate article on the Trinity, there are a number of articles in Volume II of that work that relate to the deity of Christ and the deity of the Holy Spirit.

A Working Definition

What is meant when speaking of the triunity of God? It is certain that if someone declares that the doctrine of the Trinity is easily explained, that person does not know what the doctrine entails. The Athanasian Creed states, "We worship one God in trinity, and trinity in unity." Chafer (1947) explains the triunity by citing Dr. John Dick: "While there is only one divine nature, there are three subsistences, or persons, called the Father, the Son, and the Holy Ghost, who possess, not a similar, but the same numerical essence, and the distinction between them is not merely nominal, but real" (II: 283). In reality, this doctrine is not explicable—it is revealed truth. "The doctrine of the Trinity is truth for the heart," declared A. W. Tozer (1961: 20). He later observed, "The fact that it cannot be satisfactorily explained, instead of being against it, is in its favor. Such a truth had to be revealed; no one could have imagined it" (23).

Misrepresentations

Through the centuries of church history, there have been divergent ideas about this doctrine. In the first and second centuries of the Christian era some advocates of Judaism believed that Christians were teaching tritheism, the belief that there are three separate Gods. Trying to understand Christianity from a rational point of view, they could not accept the idea that there were three distinct personalities who shared an essential Oneness.

The most persistent idea concerning this triunity is called "modalism." This view holds that there is but one personality, God, who sometimes is portrayed as Father, at other times as Son, and at other times, the Holy Spirit. Another modern approach portraying God as Creator, Redeemer, and Sustainer—though it could be interpreted as a Trinitarian statement—nevertheless is still ambiguous enough to be a form of modalism in that there is no clear delineation of the persons of the Godhead.

Certainly one of the most pernicious concepts used in contemporary life is that God is a woman. It must be recognized, however, that the triune God is neither masculine nor feminine, but to speak of God as feminine is contrary to the revelation given in Scripture and has led to convolutions of terms; for example, speaking of the Father as "the divine parent" and of the Son as "the child." Rather than strengthening the biblical information, such concepts weaken and more often distort the truth.

Unitarianism is also a denial of the triunity of God. Historic Unitarianism was a serious attempt to emphasize the unity of God as one being, but Trinitarians also emphasize the Oneness of the Godhead. To some, it seems that Christians are still cutting God into three equal pieces. The emphasis on the unity of God is biblical and logical, but when Trinitarian thought is criticized, it generally stems from a failure to understand what the Trinitarians are saying, and more important, it takes away the importance of the death and Resurrection of Christ and of the present ministry of the Holy Spirit.

Old Testament Concepts

The Old Testament does not present a full-orbed view of the Trinity. Yet, there are some indicators. Though not all agree, the use of the word *elohim* throughout the Old Testament is one such intimation of the Trinity. It is a masculine plural noun, which translates as "God." Trinitarians base their view of the triunity of God on the plural. However, the use of the plural may not be conclusive in that there are other uses of the plural that still embrace the singularity of the object. Yet when *elohim* is combined with the use of plural pronouns, as in "Let us make man in our image, after our likeness" (Genesis 1:26, NIV), and God's observation following the fall, "The man has now become like one of us" (Genesis 3:22), it seems apparent that there is more than a single person. Another line of evidence is proposed from the record of the three strangers who approached Abraham (Genesis 18), one of them being identified as the Lord (Yahweh). If three appeared, why does Abraham only address one of them? Bray (1993: 140)

cites the Jewish philosopher, Philo, as seeing in this incident a clue that Yahweh could be known in more than one person.

Two Old Testament passages speak of God having a Son. In Psalm 2, it is evident that the son spoken of is not the Israelite king, though such kings were called "anointed ones." This king, too, is called "the annointed" (Messiah). This does not mean that this psalm was originally considered a messianic psalm, that is, it could not be adduced from this evidence alone. However, it seems clear that by the New Testament period it was considered to have alluded to the Messiah. In fact, the Epistle of St. Paul to the Hebrews (1:5) begins with this reference. The second passage in the Old Testament is Proverbs 30:2–4, in which Agur, son of Jakeh, admits his ignorance of God. Speaking of God, the "Holy One" he asks a series of questions that relate to God's omnipotent sovereignty, but then concludes by asking, "What is his name, and name of his son? Tell me if you know."

There are also many Old Testament passages that speak of the Holy Spirit as "breath" or "wind" (Hebrew, *ruach*), which is similar to Jesus' teachings to Nicodemus (John 3). Even in the Old Testament, the Spirit is frequently involved in personal activities (Genesis 6:3; Exodus 31:2–3; 2 Samuel 23:2; Nehemiah 9:20; Isaiah 34:16; 63:10).

Some writers have commented on the threefold "Holy, holy, holy" uttered by the seraphs in Isaiah 6 as being indicative of a plurality in the Godhead. Even such passages as Isaiah 8:13, with its threefold statement about the Lord Almighty as "the one you are to regard as holy," "the one you are to fear," and "the one you are to dread," would indicate such a plurality. Even though such passages are interesting, they are hardly conclusive.

Morey (1996) has made an interesting case for the word *achad*, which means "one." It is used in Deuteronomy 6:4, "Hear O Israel, The Lord our God, the Lord is *one* [italics added]." As Moray demonstrates the use of the word, he shows that it is a "compound or unified" oneness. Of the nine Hebrew words for "one," this one opens the door for a Trinitarian interpretation, and as Morey concludes, "the implication is obvious, God is a compound unity, i.e., multi-personal" (90). Other passages that speak of plurality are Ecclesiastes 12:1, "Remember now your Creators," and Isaiah 54:5, which speaks of God as the "Makers" of Israel. Jesus used the first verse of Psalm 110 when He asks His detractors, "What do you think about the Christ? Whose son is he?" They answer, "The son of David." Jesus then asks, "How is it then that David, speaking by the Spirit, calls him 'Lord'?" citing Psalm 110:1.

The New Testament Witness to the Deity of Jesus Christ

In the New Testament, there is clear Trinitarian evidence. Matthew's portrayal of what has been called the "Great Commission" unifies the Father, the Son, and the Holy Spirit together in the singular "name" (Matthew 28:19). The Father, the Son, and the Holy Spirit are not names, so the concept of the name must go back to the Old Testament name for God—Jehovah or Yahweh, translated "Lord" in the Old Testament. Fundamentalists and Evangelicals believe that the majority of passages in which Jesus is called "Lord" are attributing the Divine Name to him (see e.g., 1 Corinthians 9:1). The Holy Spirit is called Lord in 2 Corinthians 3:18, "And we who with unveiled faces all reflect the Lord's glory are being transformed into his likeness with increasing glory, which comes from the *Lord, who is the Spirit*. [italics added]."

If the reading of Mark 1:1, "Jesus, the Son of God," is accepted, a case can be made that Mark's Gospel is clearly presenting Jesus as deity. The same could be noted for the Gospel according to John. The very first verse is a clear statement that "the Word," identified clearly with Jesus, "was God." His preexistence, even eternity, is clearly portrayed, and the fact that nothing was created apart from Him clearly demonstrates that He was not a created being. Though the New Testament writers rarely called him "God," as Plantinga (1998: 915) notes, "Still, Jesus Christ in the NT is 'what God is,' i.e., He is divine."

Many theologians have listed the evidence in Scripture for the divinity (deity) of Jesus Christ. These lists almost always include:

1. Jesus is given the titles belonging to deity. He is called "God" (John 1:1; 20:28; Romans 9:5; Timothy 2:13; Hebrews 1:8). He is called "Lord," which, in many cases, is indisputably a transfer of the Old Testament title "Yahweh" to Him (Romans 10:9; Philippians 2:9–11; Hebrews 1:10; Revelation 19:16). He is also called the "Son of God" (John 5:18f; 1 John 4:15; Revelation 19:16).

2. Passages that have to do with Yahweh are applied to Jesus. In Isaiah 45:23–24, God is speaking, "Before me every knee will bow; by me every tongue will swear. They will say of me, 'In the Lord alone are righteousness and strength'" as compared with the New Testament Philippians (2:10 and 11), "that at the name of Jesus, every knee should bow, in heaven and on earth and under the earth, and every tongue confess that Jesus Christ is Lord, to the glory of God the Father." Other New Testament passages that are based on Old Testament references include Hebrews 1:10 and Romans 10:13. Moreover, as Plantinga (1998: 915) points out, Jesus "expresses Himself in magisterial 'I am' language (e.g., John 8:58)."

3. Jesus does the works of God. He is the Creator (John 1:3; Colossians 1:16; Hebrews 1:10). He can forgive sin (Mark 2:10); He can save (2 Timothy 1:10); and He has been appointed judge by the Father (John 5:27, 30; Revelation 22:12).

4. Jesus is spoken of as being "equal with God" (Philippians 2:6) and as the unique ("only begotten") of the Father (John 1:18; cf. Hebrews 1:3; Colossians 1:19; 2:9).

5. Jesus is the focus in both the baptism and the Lord's Supper (Matthew 28:19; John 6:54; 1 Corinthians 11:23–26). People were baptized in the name of Jesus and the Supper is to be partaken in remembrance of Him.

The New Testament Witness to the Deity of the Holy Spirit

By comparing the references to Jesus Christ with those to the Holy Spirit, there is a sharp contrast in the numbers. This does not mean, however, that the Holy Spirit is unimportant or that there is too little evidence to support the doctrine that the Spirit is a part of the triune Godhead. First, the New Testament reveals that the Holy Spirit is a personal being; that is, the Spirit is not just some kind of force or dynamic. He can be blasphemed (Matthew 12:31–32); He can be grieved (Ephesians 4:30). Both of these are actions that only affect persons, not forces. In Acts (5:3–4) the Spirit is called God. A second and important line of evidence for the Spirit's deity is found in the revelation of the Spirit that Jesus delivers to His apostles in John's report of the Upper Room Discourse (John 14–16). Jesus spoke words of assurance to the eleven who were with Him as He announced, "I will ask the Father, and he will give you *another* [italics added] Counselor to be with you forever—the Spirit of truth." The word that the Lord uses for "another" means "another of the same kind" as He was, not a different kind of being. This is Christ's assurance that He will not leave them "orphans" (14:18). This is a clear narrative that involves Father, Son, and Holy Spirit. Jesus speaks to the Father as an equal and this One who will come to them is "of the same kind." There is no room for modalism or Unitarianism in this bold proclamation.

The New Testament Trinitarian Statements

The more important of the Trinitarian statements is the Baptismal Formula of Matthew 28:19–20. The principal command is "Make disciples" and this includes "baptizing them in the name of the Father and of the Son and of the Holy Spirit." Bray (1993: 142) declares, "For something as central and important as the rite of Christian initiation, the practice of the church at this stage must have rested on very good authority." An incident recorded in Acts 8 supports this formula: the apostles in Jerusalem were forced to respond to such a thing as Samaritan salvation, but noted that many of them had "simply been baptized into the name of the Lord Jesus" (8:16).

The second clear Trinitarian statement is Paul's benediction in 2 Corinthians 13:14: "May the grace of the Lord Jesus Christ, and the love of God and the fellowship of the Holy Spirit be with you all." A question, of course, comes in relation to the reference merely to God, but not to the "Father." Paul uses similar formulas in several other passages as well (Romans 15:16, 30; 2 Corinthians 1:21–22; 3:3; Ephesians 2:8). Peter opens his first epistle with a specific triadic pattern, speaking of the election of God's people "according to the foreknowledge of God the Father, through the sanctifying work of the Spirit, for obedience to Jesus Christ and sprinkling by his blood" (1:2). Jude also presents a clear triadic pattern as he writes, "But you, dear friends, build yourselves up in your most holy faith and pray in the Holy Spirit. Keep yourselves in God's love as you wait for the mercy of our Lord Jesus Christ to bring you to eternal life" (1:20–21). It is significant that in this passage, the Holy Spirit is placed first.

The doctrine of the triunity of the Godhead was not developed at Nicea in 325 CE. It was already the position of the first-century church in the revelation given to the apostles of Jesus Christ and is a basic tenet of the Christian faith.

Richard I. McNeely

See also Christ, The; Holy Spirit; Jesus

Bibliography

Boice, James M. (1978) "God in Three Persons." In *The Sovereign God.* Downers Grove, IL: InterVarsity Press.

Bray, Gerald. (1993) "One God in Trinity." In *The Doctrine of God.* Downers Grove, IL: InterVarsity Press.

Chafer, Lewis Sperry. (1947) *Systematic Theology*, 8 vols. Dallas: Dallas Seminary Press., .

Morey, Robert. (1996) *The Trinity.* Iowa Falls, IA: World Bible Publishers.

Plantinga, Cornelius, Jr. (1988) "Trinity." In *International Bible Encyclopedia,* vol. IV. Grand Rapids, MI: Wm. B. Eerdmans.

Tozer, A. W. (1961) *The Knowledge of the Holy.* San Francisco: HarperCollins.

UFOs

While the popular belief in unidentified flying objects (UFOs) is about a hundred years old, public interest in UFOs, extraterrestrials, and the field of ufology has dramatically increased in recent years. In addition, beliefs in UFOs and extraterrestrials have fused with more traditional religious beliefs to produce new hybrid forms of religions. A tragic example of this fusion involved the March 1997 group suicide of the millennial UFO cult, Heaven's Gate. By taking their own lives, the thirty-eight members thought they would be freeing their extraterrestrial spirits from their human repositories, allowing the group to rendezvous with a UFO following the comet Hale-Bop. Melding contemporary or secular beliefs in extraterrestrials and intergalactic space travel with classic millennial mythology, including the apocalyptic destruction of the planet and the return of the "messiah," Heaven's Gate had created a modern UFO theology. While most UFO religions do not preach suicide as a way to achieve cosmic enlightenment, as did Heaven's Gate, apocalyptic beliefs are commonly found among many new ufology religions.

Ufologists, such as Heaven's Gate and the Greater Community Way, founded by Marshall Vian Summers in 1992, are fearful of the so-called gray aliens, who they believe harbor malicious intentions and a plan to colonize Earth. Yet most UFO religions demonstrate a more optimistic or millennial view of human–alien contact. Millennial ufologists, such as the Ground Crew Project, the Raelians, Summum, Unarius, Outpost Kauai, and the New World Com-

forters, see the extraterrestrials as benevolent, even messianic, returning to Earth to save humanity and the planet and to assist their "cosmic brothers" in their further evolution. From the perspective of some Christian Fundamentalist groups, UFOs and extraterrestrials are manifestations of the fallen angels of Genesis, forces of the great deceiver who is now alive in the world. According to Cutting Edge Ministries, a Christian group that professes belief in UFOs, the main objective of the aliens and the entire New Age subculture, "is to successfully stage the appearance of the Anti-Christ":

> These supernatural or seemingly supernatural miracles will lead men directly to the worship of Anti-Christ. This is precisely the planned result of these UFO's and Aliens. The shocking reality is that Satan has been manipulating world events to achieve his One-World Government, Economy, and Religion through Secret Societies, Communism, Nazism, the New Age, and UFO's. The final merger into the New World Order is almost complete. UFO Aliens and Spaceships are nothing more than demons which the Holy Spirit has allowed in this final age to physically manifest themselves in our realm. (Bay 1997: para. 40–41)

The Watcher Ministries, another Christian group located in Montana, point out that the language of ufology, especially in the literature of alien abductions and channeling (for example,"Ascended Masters," "spirit communication," "Elohim"), hint at the Satanic origins of extraterrestrials. If the extraterrestrials themselves are not "the rebel Ben Elohim of the Bible," argues the writer in a website document entitled "Apocalyptic Signs in the Heaven," then "they are under the jurisdiction of Satan, the Prince of the Powers of the Air" (Bay 1997: para. 30).

Philip Lamy

See also Antichrist

Bibliography

Bay, David. (1997) "Anti-Christ, Aliens, and UFOs," Cutting Edge Ministries. http://www.cuttingedge.org/ce1030.html.

Clark, Jerome. (1998) *The UFO Book: Encyclopedia of the Extraterrestrial*. Detroit: Visible Ink Press.

Lamy, Philip. (2000) "UFOs, Extraterrestrials, and the Apocalypse: The Making of a Subculture." In *Millennial Visions: Essays on Twentieth Century Millenarianism*, edited by Martha F. Lee. Westport, CT: Praeger.

Lewis, James R., ed. (1995) *The Gods Have Landed: New Religions From Other Worlds*. Albany: State University of New York Press.

United Nations

The United Nations is an international organization that was formally established on 24 October 1945 in the aftermath of the devastation of World War II. It was the second major world organization dedicated to international cooperation and the prevention of war, the first being the League of Nations, which existed from 1920 to 1946.

The UN's Mission

The main objectives of the United Nations are to help stabilize international relations and maintain world peace and security. The organization is more than a peace keeper and forum for conflict resolution, however. It also works for child survival and development, environmental protection, human rights, health and medical research, the alleviation of poverty and economic development, agricultural development, family planning, emergency and disaster relief, and the peaceful uses of atomic energy.

The Administration

There are six basic organs of the United Nations. The General Assembly is the deliberative body of the United Nations. All member countries are represented in the General Assembly. The 15–member Security Council has five permanent seats—the United Kingdom, China, France, Russia, and the United States. The Council is responsible for maintaining international peace and security. The International Court of Justice, also known as the World Court, is the "supreme court" of the United Nations. The Economic and Social Council coordinates the work of specialized agencies that attempt to achieve higher standards of living, improve health conditions, and promote respect for human rights and freedoms. The Secretariat carries on the day-to-day work of the United Nations. It is headed by the secretary-general, the chief administrative officer of the United Nations. The Trusteeship Council seeks to protect the interests of people who live in trust territories and to lead them toward self-government.

The Fundamentalist View

Fundamentalists were generally opposed to the United Nations primarily because they saw it as an attack on American sovereignty. The American Council of Christian Churches urged that "restraints must be written into the Constitution to protect us from the schemes and subtleties of those who are working for a One World Church" (Gasper 1963: 52). Some Fundamentalists thought that the United Nations was a communist front and that it wanted the United States to become a communist nation." America's support of the United Nations, 'that tower of Red Babel,' crippled its sovereignty and drained off tax-payers' dollars that should have been spent on more armaments" (Jorstad 1970: 86). Many Fundamentalists repudiate the United Nations and the World Council of Churches. "In the Book of Revelation, the scarlet woman, representing the ecclesiastical world power, rides upon the back of the beast, representing the one-world political power. Here we see the World Council of Churches counselling and seeking to direct the affairs of the governments of the world as they deal with communism, and this pressure is on the side of surrender to communism in the Far East" (Jorstad 1970: 134).

Donald S. Armentrout

ONE WORLD WORSHIP BY MEANS OF THE UNITED NATIONS?

Undergirding the UN's quest for "sustainable development" is a pagan religious world view that is utterly incompatible with biblical faiths. Known as the "Gaia Hypothesis" or the Gaian world view, the "UN's pantheist perspective holds that the earth itself is the deity which we should worship, and that the UN is the [*sic*] through which the earth goddess will dictate our forms of devotion. Gaia Atlas of Future Worlds, Dr. Norman Myers, who has been an adviser to the UN, the World Bank, the Department [*sic*], and the Rockefeller Brothers Fund, sets forth the basic tenets of the Gaian religion, declaring that there is no longer any 'we' and 'they.' For the first time, and for all time, there is only 'us' - all of us humans, together with all our fellow species and other members of the Gaian community." Of course, the "Gaian community" will require a governing ethic – one that teaches, in Myers's words, "a new humanism, a New World view, a new planetary concern." Ultimately this would require a UN ministry of religion. The September/October 1994 issue of *The Futurist* magazine reported, "Religions are now headed toward what may eventually form a United Religions Organization (URO), structured in much the same way as the United Nations and with the same goals." Once created, the URO would be given the task of creating a 'new covenant' for the planet: "The URO will discern the nature of that covenant, and with it the responsibility's, rather than the rights, of planetary citizenship."

Source: Matrix Message Board. www.parascope.com

Bibliography

Gasper, Louis. (1981) *The Fundamentalist Movement, 1930–1956.* Grand Rapids, MI: Baker Book House.

Hovet, Thomas, Jr., and Erica Hovet. (1986) *A Chronology and Fact Book of the United Nations, 1941–1985.* Dobbs Ferry, NY: Oceana Publications, Inc.

Jorstad, Erling. (1970) *The Politics of Doomsday: Fundamentalism of the Far Right.* Nashville and New York: Abingdon Press.

Meisler, Stanley. (1995) *The United Nations: The First Fifty Years.* New York: Atlantic Monthly Press.

V

Virgin Birth

A virgin birth or *parthenogenesis* (Greek, *parthenos*, "virgin"; *genesis*, "birth") is one in which a woman without loss of her virginity miraculously conceives and bears a child to term. Stories of the miraculous births of heroes and gods are found in a wide variety of religious mythologies. Traditionally, Christianity has held that Mary, the mother of Jesus, was a virgin at the point of conception. Roman Catholic theology adds that Mary remained a virgin following Jesus' birth. In recent years, the stories about the Virgin Birth of Jesus in the Gospels of Matthew and Luke have been the subject of intense scrutiny by scholars trained in historical and literary criticisms. Their findings suggest that much about these stories is not historical but mythological in origin. Nevertheless the literal, historical Virgin Birth of Jesus remains a required belief among conservative Christians.

The story of Jesus' miraculous birth to a virgin has a lengthy pedigree of similar stories found in a wide variety of religious and mythological traditions. One possible root source of such stories is the archetypal genre of the sacred marriage between a human woman and a divine being. Ancient Babylon and Egypt both built temples to house selected virgins who were chosen to act as brides to the gods. In ancient Greece there was an annual ceremony established to celebrate the ritual marriage between Dionysus, the god of wine, and a royal virgin. The Peruvian Indians performed an annual ceremony involving the ritual sacrifice of a young virgin before a stone effigy representing the god Huaca to whom she was to be betrothed.

Another possible strand of tradition lying behind the Virgin Birth myth is the genre of miraculous births attributed to contact between a virgin and some sort of supernatural force hidden in nature. The Toltec and Aztec god, Quetzalcoatl, was conceived when his mother, Chimalman, was breathed upon by a god who had taken the form of the "morning wind." Similarly, the fiery desert wind of the sun god, Re, was thought to be responsible for impregnating the virgin mothers of certain Egyptian pharaohs. Stories told about the Buddha's birth involve a chaste woman who in a dreamlike state encountered a "superb white elephant" whose mere touch brought about conception.

These and other similar stories—like the story about Jesus' birth—seem to convey a dual meaning: (1) that human survival necessitates a vital connection between humanity and the ultimate source of the natural world; and (2) that at the center of this connection is the virgin, symbol of purity and creative power, within whom a kind of "sacred creation" can take place. We see this latter emphasis particularly in the Judeo-Christian tradition, where the image of the virgin is related to the primal element active at the first creation—the "face of the waters" on which the "spirit of God moved" in the Genesis creation account—and to other symbols of latent fecundity, like the "plugged spring," the "enclosed garden," and the "sealed fountain" of the Song of Songs. These images found in the Hebrew Bible were applied by early Christian apologists to Mary as a way of demonstrating that the promise of virginal creativity, through which the divine becomes active in the human realm, had now been fulfilled in her.

Sandro Botticelli, *The Cestello Annunciation*

A relatively late Virgin Birth story is that told about the birth of Jesus in the gospels of Matthew and Luke of the Christian New Testament. Despite significant differences between the two accounts, the story of Jesus' birth can be broken down into four essential components: (1) the angelic announcement to the Virgin Mary of her conception of God's son (Matthew, Luke); (2) Mary's humble acceptance of her fate (Luke); (3) the post-conception marriage of Mary to Joseph (Matthew, Luke); and (4) the birth itself, which is witnessed either by figures representing wisdom (Matthew) or humility (Luke). Roman Catholic theology appends three further stipulations. First, that Mary was herself conceived "immaculately"—without the "stain of original sin"—thus enabling her to bear a divine child without risk of impurity. Second, Mary is believed "to have given birth [to Jesus] and nevertheless remained a virgin" (St. Ambrose, Epistle 42.4). This is to say that Mary's birthing of Jesus, by means of another miracle, left her hymen intact—a physical sign that Mary's virginity had been preserved. The third is that, despite her marriage to Joseph, Mary committed herself to a life of continued virginity after Jesus' birth. Protestant theologians reject the doctrines of Mary's "immaculate conception," "virginity in parturition," and her "perpetual virginity."

Conservative Christian traditions, both Catholic and Protestant, generally require belief in the Virgin Birth as a sign of orthodoxy. The publication in 1910

to 1915 of *The Fundamentals* by a group of Protestant Christian theologians included the Virgin Birth of Jesus as one of the five essential tenets of orthodox Christian faith. This was echoed in 1985 when an article in the *The Southern Baptist Journal* included the Virgin Birth as the first of six essential Christian doctrines. Most liberal theologians, Protestant and Catholic, agree that certain mythological elements have been woven into the birth narratives and that the actual circumstances of Jesus' conception and birth can no longer be reconstructed.

Thomas Kinsell Carr

See also Cult of Mary

Bibliography

Brown, Raymond S. J. (1978) *The Virginal Conception and Bodily Resurrection of Jesus*. Boston: Paulist Press.

Ludemann, Gerd. (1998) *Virgin Birth: The Real Story of Mary and Her Son Jesus*. New York: Trinity Press International.

Ott, Ludwig. (1992) *The Fundamentals of Catholic Dogma*. Rockford, IL: Tan Books and Publishers.

Pagels, Elaine. (1989) *Adam, Eve and the Serpent*. New York: Vintage Books.

Virtue

Virtue focuses upon attributes of moral goodness as contrasted by vice. Recently repopularized by William Bennetts's *Book of Virtues* (1993), virtue has traditionally been articulated by the Christian Church as at least seven traits that one is encouraged to obtain: faith, hope, charity (love), justice, fortitude, temperance, and prudence. The apostle Paul, writing to the fledgling church in Colossi, stated, "Therefore, as God's chosen people, holy and dearly loved, clothe yourselves with compassion, kindness, humility, gentleness and patience. Bear with each other and forgive whatever grievances you may have against one another. Forgive as the Lord forgave you. And over all these virtues put on love, which binds them all together in perfect unity" (Colossians 3:12–15, NIV).

Virtue has its roots in ancient Western philosophy. In the *Nicomachean Ethics*, Greek philosopher Aristotle wrote that we acquire virtues "by first having actually practiced them, just as we do the arts" (1934: 73). Aristotle believed that virtue came through action, particularly habit, and that it was beneficial for the community because it made better citizens. Furthermore, virtue moved from a Greek philosophical idea to a Christian theological one as definitions and uses changed. The fourth-century CE African theologian Augustine advanced that virtue was a result of one's conformity to God's character. This introduced concepts relating to the individual, which over the centuries has become increasingly the focus of Western Christian theology.

Virtue comes to an individual through actions as they are based on a particular set of beliefs. The difficulty is in the doing, however. The English philosopher, David Hume, wrote in *Of the Immortality of the Soul* that "heaven and hell suppose two distinct species of men, the good and the bad. But the greatest part of mankind floats between vice and virtue" (1965: 164). Since we rest in the middle of heaven and hell, or Middle-Earth as J. R. R. Tolkien called this life, we must strive for virtue and work against vice. One does not simply strive for virtue by battling vice, but it is the changes in character brought through the practice of the virtues that enables one to battle vice. The struggle for virtue and against vice is often a difficult one. It is strenuous to keep proper perspective and focus. The apostle Peter in his second Epistle wrote, "His divine power has granted to us all things that pertain to life and godliness ... that through these you may escape from the corruption that is in the world because of passion, and become partakers of the divine nature. For this very reason make every effort to supplement your faith with virtue, and virtue with knowledge, and knowledge with self-control, and self-control with steadfastness, and steadfastness with godliness, and godliness with brotherly affection, and brotherly affection with love" (1:4–7, RSV). Peter raises some key aspects relating to the virtues: the practice of virtue can be done with or without divine power and the virtues can be compounded. Just as the results of vices such as pride can be exponential and made more severe, similarly the results of compounded virtue can be multiplied.

For Fundamentalists, the virtues are imperiled by the tendency toward legalism, that is, the attempt to earn God's approval through good works, as exemplified by the Pharisees in Jesus' day. Legalism emphasizes action, as do the virtues, but it can focus too easily on a list of proper and improper activities and beliefs detached from the virtues. The Pharisees were diligent to tithe even a portion of their spices, though it was disconnected from any heartfelt motivation. Lists of proscribed activities can soon replace the practice of charity, hope, and faith. It is simpler to determine and objectify what can and cannot be done, rather than be presented with a never-ending stream of decisions to be charitable, faithful, and hopeful. What ensues is a complex code of do's and don'ts. Challenging this complexity, Augustine provided a simpler code when he said "love God and do as you please." He believed that if the former were done then the latter would take care of itself.

Fundamentalism as a religious movement is often defined by its relationship to modernity and secularism. Purposefully separated from a corrupt world, obedience to doctrinal and lifestyle code is for many the first virtue. The second virtue may be chastising those who do not follow these codes. However, these virtues have their pitfalls. The poet Ralph Waldo Emerson commented that "there is no virtue which is final; all are initial. The virtues of society are vices of the saint. The terror of reform is the discovery that we must cast away our virtues, or what we have always esteemed such, into the same pit that has consumed our grosser vices" (n.d.: v. 1, 225). The philosopher Jean-Jacques Rousseau puts it plainly: "the Romans had been content to practice virtue; all was lost when they began to study it" and "there are a thousand prizes for fine discourses, none for fine action" (1992: 11 and 19). Being virtuous is not as simple as going through the motions. Virtues are best implemented and practiced when they are habits borne out of good intentions.

David B. Malone

See also Antimodernism; Law, Old Testament; Secularism

Bibliography

Aquinas, Thomas. (1961–1984) *Summa Theologiae*: *Latin text and English translation, introductions, notes, appendices, and glossaries*. New York: McGraw Hill. [particularly *Prima Secundae*, questions 55–67]

Aristotle. (1934) *The Nicomachean Ethics*, translated by H. Rackham. Cambridge, MA: Harvard University Press.

Barr, James. (1978) *Fundamentalism*. Philadelphia: Westminster Press.

Emerson, Ralph Waldo. (n.d.) *The Works of Ralph Waldo Emerson*, 6 vols. New York: Nottingham Society.

Geach, Peter Thomas. (1977) *The Virtues*. Cambridge, UK: Cambridge University Press.

Hume, David. (1965) *Of the Standard of Taste, and Other Essays,* edited, with an introduction, by John W. Lenz. Indianapolis: Bobbs-Merrill.

Kreeft, Peter. (1992) *Back to Virtue: Traditional Moral Wisdom for Modern Moral Confusion.* San Francisco: Ignatius.

Lee, Cameron. (1998) *Beyond Family Values: A Call to Christian Virtue.* Downers Grove, IL: Intervarsity Press.

MacIntyre, Alasdair C. (1984) *After Virtue: A Study in Moral Theory.* Notre Dame, IN: University of Notre Dame Press.

Meilaender, Gilbert. (1984) *The Theory and Practice of Virtue.* Notre Dame, IN: University of Notre Dame Press.

Pieper, Josef. (1966) *The Four Cardinal Virtues: Prudence, Justice, Fortitude, Temperance.* Notre Dame, IN: University of Notre Dame Press.

Rousseau, Jean Jacques. (1992) *Discourse on the Sciences and Arts: (First Discourse) and Polemics.* Hanover, NH: University Press of New England.

Sommers, Christina, and Fred Sommers. (1993) *Vice & Virtue in Everyday Life: Introductory Readings in Ethics.* Fort Worth, TX: Harcourt Brace Jovanovich.

Wallace, James D. (1978) *Virtues and Vices.* Ithaca, NY: Cornell University Press.

Vocation

Vocation comes from the Latin word *vocare*, meaning "to call." It has several different connotations in the Christian tradition. On one level, it simply refers to the call to Christian faith, that is, the call of Christ offered to all the baptized. The Christian's calling is to be a witness to the life, death, and Resurrection of Jesus Christ: "I [Jesus] came not to call the righteous, but sinners" (Mark 2:17, RSV). "But you are a chosen race, a royal priesthood, a holy nation, God's own people, that you may declare the wonderful deeds of him who called you out of darkness into his marvelous light" (1 Peter 2:9). On another level, it invokes the particular work, labor, profession, or business that every person is called to. One's calling is one's work or vocation. Vocations are the structured channels through which Christians serve their neighbors in love. The primary way the Christian serves the neighbor in love is through his or her vocation. All God-fearing vocations are of equal importance. The vocation of ordained ministry is no greater than that of milkmaid or custodian. Vocations are a structure of creation through which persons serve one another. Although Martin Luther was not the first person to apply the word "vocation" to the work, trade, or profession of persons, there is no doubt that he popularized this terminology. He extended the term "calling" to include all honest and productive vocations. Not only an ecclesiastical office, but all honest work and every occupation is a calling, a vocation, according to Luther. He believed that the primary way an individual does good works is through his or her vocation. The Lutheran confessions continued this theme: " . . . therefore perfection means to grow in the fear of God, in trust in the mercy promised in Christ, and in dedication to one's calling" (Kolb and Wengert 2000: 282).

Vocation is also used to refer to the work of those who are called to ordained ministry and to the religious life, that is, a call to the ecclesiastical state. In the more Catholic traditions, vocation is frequently limited to those who have an ecclesiastical position. In discussing high priesthood, the writer of Hebrews states, "And one does not take the honor upon himself, but is called by God, just as Aaron was" (5:4). Almost all the Christian traditions stress that one who is ordained for public ministry must have a call. Article XXIII of the Thirty-nine Articles states, "It is not lawful for any man to take upon him the office of public preaching, or ministering the Sacraments in the Congregation, before he be lawfully called, and sent to execute the same. And those we ought to judge lawfully called and sent, which be chosen and called to this work by men who have public authority given unto them in the Congregation, to call and send Ministers into the Lord's vineyard" (Bicknell 1963: 321).

Donald S. Armentrout

See also Calling; Love; Preaching

Bibliography

Bicknell, Edgar John. (1963) *A Theological Introduction to the Thirty-nine Articles of the Church of England,* 3rd ed. rev., edited by H. J. Carpenter. London: Longmans, Green and Co., Ltd.

Kolb, Robert, and Timothy J. Wengert, eds. (2000) *The Book of Concord: The Confessions of the Evangelical Lutheran Church.* Minneapolis, MN: Fortress Press.

W

Wanderer, The

The Wanderer, founded in 1867 as a German-language newspaper, is the staunchest voice of resistance to modern culture in American Catholicism. Its circulation is currently estimated at 35,000.*The Wanderer* has been edited and published by the Matt family of St. Paul, Minnesota, since 1897, first in German, and then, beginning in 1931, in English (though the German edition did not cease publication until 1957). The paper's editorial policy is grounded in Catholic orthodoxy as defined by the popes and "loyal" bishops and priests. As such, it condemns all forms of liberalism. In the Catholic Church, it opposes any changes in church laws governing divorce, abortion, or homosexuality and has been vehemently critical of theological and liturgical "innovations" since the Second Vatican Council (1962–1965). Because *The Wanderer* tends to see the feminist movement as the source of a variety of social evils, it condemns any incursions of the women's movement into Catholicism (nuns who do not wear habits and/or who work in nontraditional places, those who support women's ordination, feminist theologians, and critics). As a staunch and faithful supporter of papal policy, the paper has historically condemned what the Vatican condemns ("Americanism," for example, or modernism) and supported all papal directives (against artificial birth control, or against "erring" theologians like Hans Küng or Charles Curran). Its politically conservative editorial policy has condemned socialism, the New Deal, and the Kennedy administration, while giving strong support to Senator Joseph McCarthy and Franco. *The Wanderer* continues to oppose socialism and communism ("liberation theology") in all forms.

Mary Jo Weaver

See also Abortion; Antifeminism; Antimodernism; Catholic Fundamentalism; Catholics United for the Faith; Liberalism

Westminster Confession

The *Westminster Confession* is a seventeenth-century Calvinist doctrinal statement of faith of English-speaking Presbyterians. It was produced during the initial phase of the English Revolution (1640–1660), when the Long Parliament convened the Assembly of Divines at the Westminster Abbey. The Assembly was charged with the responsibility of reforming the church government and producing an ecumenical theological statement that could unite the English and Scottish churches. This gathering of English Puritan and Scottish Presbyterian ministers and theologians met regularly from 1643 until 1648 and produced several documents, including the *Westminster Confession*. The *Confession* covered the range of conventional Protestant doctrines, such as justification by faith and the inspiration and authority of the Bible, with a precision characteristic of seventeenth-century Protestant scholasticism. The *Confession*'s distinctive characteristics include the doctrine of double predestination, which held that

Selection from:
WESTMINSTER CONFESSION OF FAITH (1646)

CHAPTER I.
Of the holy Scripture.

I. Although the light of nature, and the works of creation and providence, do so far manifest the goodness, wisdom, and power of God, as to leave men inexcusable; yet are they not sufficient to give that knowledge of God, and of his will, which is necessary unto salvation; therefore it pleased the Lord, at sundry times, and in divers manners, to reveal himself, and to declare that his will unto his Church; and afterwards for the better preserving and propagating of the truth, and for the more sure establishment and comfort of the Church against the corruption of the flesh, and

the malice of Satan and of the world, to commit the same wholly unto writing; which maketh the holy Scripture to be most necessary; those former ways of God's revealing his will unto his people being now ceased.

II. Under the name of holy Scripture, or the Word of God written, are now contained all the Books of the Old and New Testament, which are these: . . .

All which are given by inspiration of God, to be the rule of faith and life.

III. The books commonly called Apocrypha, not being of divine inspiration, are no part of the Canon of Scripture; and therefore are of no authority in the Church of God, nor to be any otherwise approved, or made use of, than other human writings.

IV. The authority of the holy Scripture, for which it ought to be believed and obeyed, dependeth not upon the testimony of any man or Church, but wholly upon God (who is truth itself), the Author thereof; and therefore it is to be received, because it is the Word of God.

V. We may be moved and induced by the testimony of the Church to an high and reverent esteem of the holy Scripture; and the heavenliness of the matter, the efficacy of the doctrine, the majesty of the style, the consent of all the parts, the scope of the whole (which is to give all glory to God), the full discovery it makes of the only way of man's salvation, the many other incomparable excellencies, and the entire perfection thereof, are arguments whereby it doth abundantly evidence itself to be the Word of God; yet, notwithstanding, our full persuasion and assurance of the infallible truth and divine authority thereof, is from the inward work of the Holy Spirit, bearing witness by and with the Word in our hearts.

VI. The whole counsel of God, concerning all things necessary for his own glory, man's salvation, faith, and life, is either expressly set down in Scripture, or by good and necessary consequence may be deduced from Scripture: unto which nothing at any time is to be added, whether by new revelations of the Spirit, or traditions of men. Nevertheless we acknowledge the inward illumination of the Spirit of God to be necessary for the saving understanding of such things as are revealed in the Word; and that there are some circumstances concerning the worship of God, and the government of the Church, common to human actions and societies, which are to be ordered by the light of nature and Christian prudence, according to the general rules of the Word, which are always to be observed.

VII. All things in Scripture are not alike plain in themselves, nor alike clear unto all; yet those things which are necessary to be known, believed, and observed, for salvation, are so clearly propounded and opened in some place of Scripture or other, that not only the learned, but the unlearned, in a due use of the ordinary means, may attain unto a sufficient understanding of them.

VIII. The Old Testament in Hebrew (which was the native language of the people of God of old), and the New Testament in Greek (which at the time of the writing of it was most generally known to the nations), being immediately inspired by God, and by his singular care and providence kept pure in all ages, are therefore authentical; so as in all controversies of religion the Church is finally to appeal unto them. But because these original tongues are not known to all the people of God who have right unto, and interest in, the Scriptures, and are commanded, in the fear of God, to read and search them, therefore they are to be translated into the language of every people unto which they come, that the Word of God dwelling plentifully in all, they may worship him in an acceptable manner, and, through patience and comfort of the Scriptures, may have hope.

IX. The infallible rule of interpretation of Scripture, is the Scripture itself; and therefore, when there is a question about the true and full sense of any scripture (which is not manifold, but one), it may be searched and known by other places that speak more clearly.

X. The Supreme Judge, by which all controversies of religion are to be determined, and all decrees of councils, opinions of ancient writers, doctrines of men, and private spirits, are to be examined, and in whose sentence we are to rest, can be no other but the Holy Spirit speaking in the Scripture.

Source: *Historic Church Documents*. www.reformed.org

God preordains the elect to heaven and the lost to hell, as well as sabbatarianism, which proscribed work or recreation on Sundays.

The document was adopted by the Church of Scotland in 1647 and by the English Parliament in 1649. Even so, subsequent political developments prevented Presbyterians from becoming the state religion of England. As Presbyterianism grew as an international movement, however, the *Confession*'s influence spread. With minor revisions of its statement on church–state relations, American Presbyterians adopted the *Confession* as their official theological standard in 1729. During the late nineteenth and especially in the early twentieth centuries, debates between Fundamentalists and modernists over doctrines expressed in the *Confession* divided the Presbyterian Church, USA. Although a more theologically inclusive position eventually prevailed within the so-called mainline Presbyterian church, some members of smaller and more conservative Presbyterian denominations often espouse the *Confession*'s Calvinist theology as the definitive expression of the Bible's

teaching on various doctrines with a sectarian zeal characteristic of Protestant Fundamentalism.

Paul C. Kemeny

See also Calvinism

Bibliography

Balmer, Randall, and John R. Fitzmier. (1994) *The Presbyterians*. Westport, CT: Praeger.
Heron, Alistar I. C., ed. (1982) *The Westminster Confession in the Church Today*. Edinburgh: Saint Andrews Press.
Paul, Robert. (1985) *The Assembly of the Lord*. Edinburgh: T. & T. Clark.

Witnesses, Two

The two witnesses are introduced in chapter 11 of the Revelation to John. The author sees in his vision, beginning in Revelation 8, an angel of God sounding

Revelation 11:3–19

3. And I will give power unto my two witnesses, and they shall prophesy a thousand two hundred and threescore days, clothed in sackcloth.

4. These are the two olive trees, and the two candlesticks standing before the God of the earth.

5. And if any man will hurt them, fire proceedeth out of their mouth, and devoureth their enemies: and if any man will hurt them, he must in this manner be killed.

6. These have power to shut heaven, that it rain not in the days of their prophecy: and have power over waters to turn them to blood, and to smite the earth with all plagues, as often as they will.

7. And when they shall have finished their testimony, the beast that ascendeth out of the bottomless pit shall make war against them, and shall overcome them, and kill them.

8. And their dead bodies shall lie in the street of the great city, which spiritually is called Sodom and Egypt, where also our Lord was crucified.

9. And they of the people and kindreds and tongues and nations shall see their dead bodies three days and an half, and shall not suffer their dead bodies to be put in graves.

10. And they that dwell upon the earth shall rejoice over them, and make merry, and shall send gifts one to another; because these two prophets tormented them that dwelt on the earth.

11. And after three days and an half the Spirit of life from God entered into them, and they stood upon their feet; and great fear fell upon them which saw them.

12. And they heard a great voice from heaven saying unto them, Come up hither. And they ascended up to heaven in a cloud; and their enemies beheld them.

13. And the same hour was there a great earthquake, and the tenth part of the city fell, and in the earthquake were slain of men seven thousand: and the remnant were affrighted, and gave glory to the God of heaven.

14. The second woe is past; and, behold, the third woe cometh quickly.

15. And the seventh angel sounded; and there were great voices in heaven, saying, The kingdoms of this world are become the kingdoms of our Lord, and of his Christ; and he shall reign for ever and ever.

16. And the four and twenty elders, which sat before God on their seats, fell upon their faces, and worshipped God,

17. Saying, We give thee thanks, O Lord God Almighty, which art, and wast, and art to come; because thou hast taken to thee thy great power, and hast reigned.

18. And the nations were angry, and thy wrath is come, and the time of the dead, that they should be judged, and that thou shouldest give reward unto thy servants the prophets, and to the saints, and them that fear thy name, small and great; and shouldest destroy them which destroy the earth.

19. And the temple of God was opened in heaven, and there was seen in his temple the ark of his testament: and there were lightnings, and voices, and thunderings, and an earthquake, and great hail.

seven trumpets of judgment, with each bringing about some particularly destructive event upon the earth. Between the sixth trumpet, which marks the destruction of one-third of humankind, and the seventh trumpet, which marks the end of human rule over the earth, the two witnesses appear in Jerusalem to prophesy for three-and-one-half years. These two witnesses are endowed with divine authority and power, which both aids their prophetic work and defends them against attack from those offended by their preaching. At the end of their testimony, the beast arises from the abyss and kills them, thus making them martyrs. Their deaths become an occasion for celebration because their offensive message is now silenced. Their bodies lie in the street of Jerusalem for three-and-one-half days at the end of which God resurrects them and they ascend into heaven.

For Fundamentalists concerned with deciphering the complex imagery and symbolism of this text, these biblical figures have remained somewhat enigmatic and have not been subject to extensive attempts at interpretation. The most complex question concerning these unnamed witnesses is their identity. In Revelation 11:4 they are identified as the two olive trees and the two candlesticks, which is imagery drawn from the Old Testament, Zechariah 4:2–3. They are also clearly prophets as they are clothed in sackcloth (Revelation 11:3) and they come to Jerusalem to prophesy (11:8). In light of these descriptions from the text, Fundamentalist interpreters often have looked to more traditional identities for the two witnesses. Early interpreters like Louis S. Bauman (1875–1950) and Isaac M. Haldeman (1845–1933) identify the first witness as Elijah, mainly as a fulfillment of Malachi 4:5 (KJV) where Elijah is prophesied to return before "the coming of the great and dreadful day of the Lord." They interpret the second witness as either Moses, who had appeared with Elijah at Jesus' transfiguration, or Enoch, who, like Elijah, did not die an earthly death. A later interpreter, Tim LaHaye (b. 1926), also finds Elijah and Moses as the most compelling identities for the two witnesses. Arno C. Gaebelein (1861–1945) represents another strain in Fundamentalist interpretation as he sees them as representative figures of a larger witness for Jesus Christ. A third approach, as evidenced by John F. Walvoord (b. 1910), takes seriously the anonymity of their identities and interprets them as individuals whose identities will be revealed during their prophetic ministries. In either case, Fundamentalist interpreters read the importance of these two witnesses as both embodiments of the greatest prophetic powers ever to appear on Earth and judgments of God's impending wrath upon the world.

William Carter Booker

See also Prophecy; Revelation

Bibliography

Bauman, Louis. (1940) *Light from Bible Prophecy*. New York: Fleming H. Revell.
Gaebelein, Arno C. (1915) *The Revelation*. New York: Our Hope Publication Office.
Haldeman, I. M. (n.d.) *Synopsis of the Book of Revelation*. Published by author.
LaHaye, Timothy. (1973) *Revelation*. Grand Rapids, MI: Zondervan Publishing.
Walvoord, John F. (1966) *The Revelation of Jesus Christ*. Chicago: Moody Press.

Women *See* Antifeminism; Christian Home, Ideal; Male Headship; Pastor's Wife; Salvation Army, The; and Scofield Reference Bible

World Council of Churches

The World Council of Churches (WCC) is a fellowship of more than 300 member churches that speaks for non-Catholic Christendom around the globe. Founded in 1948, the WCC combined the Social Gospel movement with groups that stressed faith and order. While the latter groups focused on ecclesiastical unity and theological doctrine, the Social Gospel movement concerned itself primarily with social ethics and politics. The missionary movement remained outside of the WCC until the International Missionary Council was integrated into it in 1961.

Involvement in politics is not new for the WCC. The Geneva-based organization relies on programs to promote its interests. Its vast program area is divided into three major units: Faith and Witness, Justice and Service, and Education and Renewal. Every year, the Central Committee draws on the report from the Justice and Service unit to adopt a number of public issues. These public issues are statements on the political situation in a given country or on trends in international affairs. As some of these statements are controversial, the WCC has gained a reputation for being pro-leftist and anti-Western. In fact, the WCC has drawn heavy fire from the right for offering financial support and a public stage to liberal causes. Consequently, its many other activities, such as evangelism and support for religious freedom, draw less attention and are barely noticed by the international media.

In the WCC, Western influence faded as churches and theologians from Africa, Asia, and Latin America increasingly dominated the ecumenical debate starting about 1961. The WCC grew more radical and

THE FUNDAMENTAL EVANGELISTIC ASSOCIATION ON THE WCC

IF ONLY GOD'S PEOPLE WOULD WAKE UP AND SEE HOW THE WORLD COUNCIL OF CHURCHES IS USING THE CHURCHES TO DESTROY THE VERY FOUNDATIONS OF FAITH AND FREEDOM, what a difference it could make! If only God's people would immediately withhold support and withdraw membership from the WCC and then begin attending and supporting only those churches that refuse to compromise with the ecumenical apostasy, what a difference it would make! Further loss of support now could be critical for the WCC. Are you one of those who are supporting the WCC by your finances and membership even while decrying its heretical, radical programs? If so, why not obey God - **COME OUT AND BE SEPARATE** (11 Corinthians 6:14–18) and join hands with those who are willing to stand up and speak out for our God-given liberties which enable us to preach the gospel (good news) of Jesus Christ instead of a socialist revolution.

Source: Reynolds, M. H. "The Truth about the World Council of Churches."
FEA News & Views. http://cnview.com

established its controversial Program to Combat Racism (PCR) in 1969. This program draws attention to the policies of governments or transnational corporations that provide economic support to racism as well as examining how theology is used to promote racism and how it might be used to combat it. The PCR has a fund to financially support organizations of the racially oppressed. The bulk of grants from the PCR have gone to liberation movements, some of them violent, in southern Africa. Other recipients include Australian aboriginals and indigenous people in North America and Latin America. Both the Presbyterian Church of Ireland and the Salvation Army have withdrawn from the WCC because of PCR grants to groups that support terrorism.

Another controversial strategy, liberation theology, has also made deep inroads within the WCC. At its Nairobi Assembly in 1975, the WCC declared that churches should develop activities through which poor people, industrial and rural workers, women, minority groups, and others who suffer from any form of oppression can be made aware of their condition and influence the course of society. Linking racism with sexism, the WCC further argued that the liberation of women from structures of injustice must be taken seriously as seen in the light of the liberation of all oppressed people. By the 1980s, the WCC denounced capitalism and imperialism as lay-ing the foundations of much oppression throughout the world.

In attempting to enlighten its members about injustice and encourage them to act as pressure groups, the WCC has enraged many groups. Nevertheless, it has never wavered in its call for men and women to place their responsibility to God above their loyalty to any earthly community.

Caryn E. Neumann

Bibliography

Lefever, Ernest W. (1979) *Amsterdam to Nairobi: The World Council of Churches and the Third World.* Washington, DC: Ethics and Public Policy Center.

Vermaat, J. A. Emerson. (1989) *The World Council of Churches and Politics.* New York: Freedom House.

World Council of Churches. (1974) *Words to the Churches: Voices of the Sisters,* vol. 10, no. 2.

World Evangelical Fellowship

The World Evangelical Fellowship (WEF) was born following the formation of new institutions to promote international cooperation and unity, both political (United Nations) and religious (World Council of

Churches [WCC]). The occasion was the assembly of ninety-one people representing twenty-one countries at the Woudschoten hostel near Zeist, Holland, in August 1951. The need to begin a world fellowship of Evangelicals was keenly felt by the vast majority present. (Only delegates from Denmark, Norway, Sweden, and France voted against it, some objecting to the word "infallible" to describe the Scriptures in the proposed statement of faith.) The following purposes, derived from the first chapter of Philippians, were approved at this organizing conference: "the furtherance of the Gospel" (1:11), "the defense and confirmation of the Gospel" (1:7), and "fellowship in the Gospel." (1:5) (Howard 1986: 31). The current mission statement continues in line with these purposes: "to establish and help regional and national evangelical alliances empower and mobilize local churches and Christian organizations to disciple the nations for Christ." (Fuller 1996: 194)

While the founding of the WEF followed on the heels of the WCC, it was not merely a reaction to it. There were several precursors, most notably the Evangelical Alliance (formed in 1846), which brought together many churches throughout the world in prayer, in missions mobilization, and in highlighting the plight of Protestant Christians undergoing persecution. WEF remains committed to all of these concerns. Nevertheless, it is undeniable that the direction of the WEF has been influenced by the WCC throughout its history.

J. Elwin Wright (1890–1973), a key figure at the beginning of both the National Association of Evangelicals in the United States and the WEF, illustrates the tightrope many North American Evangelicals walked between separatist Fundamentalism and what they considered to be unacceptable compromise on the part of the ecumenical movement represented by the WCC. With Carl McIntire (1906—), founder of the American Council of Churches and the International Council of Christian Churches, Wright shared disdain for the WCC. However, he also believed that McIntire's form of doctrinal purity and separatism ignored what the Bible itself had to say about Christian unity. His attempts to soften McIntire's views on separation and to woo him into a more open Evangelicalism were to no avail.

Waldron Scott, who headed WEF from 1975 to 1980, encountered opposition when he suggested an end to active hostility toward the WCC. "Rather," he argued, "WEF and its national bodies should culti-vate a position of courteous but perceptive criticism of the World Council of Churches while, at the same time, serving as a rallying point for the estimated 35 million evangelicals within the WCC." (Scott n.d.: 12) Scott lamented the inability of Evangelicals to work together, except on discreet projects, and noted how the individualism and entrepreneurial spirit of Western Evangelicals often worked against Christian cooperation. This was no doubt a factor in the failed attempt to merge with the Lausanne Committee on World Evangelism in the mid-1970s. Evangelical suspicion of ecumenical unity also helps to explain the fund-raising difficulties WEF has always faced.

Despite the strong desire by many of the WEF's highest leaders for stronger leadership from the Third World and an international headquarters outside of North America or Western Europe, it was not until 1987 that the headquarters was moved to Singapore. The election of Augustin Vencer (from the Philippines) to the WEF's highest office in 1992 has helped to dampen the perception that the WEF is primarily a Western agency with Western leaders. The same is true of the increasingly international make-up of its commissions.

The WEF's most visible work is accomplished through its commissions. The founders envisioned commissions on Evangelism, missions, literature, and "Christian Action" that would coordinate and enhance the work already going on among its members. However, it was the Theological Commission, established in 1968, that became a model of action for others by launching new publications, convening consultations, cultivating leadership training, and supporting institutional development for theological education. Increasing attention has been given to social justice issues. In addition to the Theological Commission, there are currently commissions on women's concerns, missions, religious liberty, youth, and the International Council for Evangelical Theological Education.

Douglas Milford

See also World Council of Churches

Bibliography

Fuller, Harold W. (1996) *People of the Mandate: The Story of the World Evangelical Fellowship.* Carlisle, Cumbria and Grand Rapids, MI: WEF with Paternoster Publishing and Baker Book House.

Howard, David. (1986) *The Dream That Would Not Die: The Birth and Growth of the World Evangelical Fellowship 1846–1986*. Exeter: WEF with Paternoster Publishing.

McIntire, Carl. (1943–1952) Records of WEF. Billy Graham Center Archives, Wheaton, IL, Assession #338, Box 10, Folder 18.

Scott, Waldron. (n.d.) "Evangelical Ecumenism." Records of WEF. Billy Graham Center Archives, Wheaton, IL, Assession #338, Box 1, Folder 21.

World Evangelical Fellowship. http://www.worldevangelical.org

World Vision

In the 1940s, Fundamentalists reemerged from the winter of their discontent. Having been relegated to the fringes of American culture by intellectuals, journalists, and novelists after the infamous Scopes "Monkey Trial," thousands of Fundamentalists abandoned their isolationist tendencies and sought once again to improve their world. Only this time, some integrated their conservative theology with a burden for social activism, which had previously been associated with their Social Gospel rivals. Robert Pierce, founder of World Vision International, was chief among the new Evangelicals.

Pierce, an ordained Baptist minister, worked in the mid-1940s with the newly established Youth for Christ (YFC), a national parachurch organization that sought to energize American young people with a broad international vision and a passion for worldwide evangelism. Serving as YFC vice president in 1947, Pierce seized numerous opportunities to lead evangelistic rallies all over the world. However, on one fateful trip to China, he realized that his American style of preaching lacked relevance for many people who needed food and clothing much more than they needed inspirational talks. In 1950, after spending a few years working in war-ravaged Europe and Asia, and encountering "communist atrocities" in Korea, he organized a new ministry, World Vision International. Its purpose was to meet emergency needs in crisis areas by assisting local churches and missionaries, and ultimately, to provide humanitarian relief around the globe.

Over the course of the next couple of decades, World Vision engaged in a flurry of activities. The most successful strategy for financing community development was the Child Sponsorship program, started under Pierce's administration, which continues to be a cornerstone of World Vision. By persuading people to make a monthly donation, this program siphons resources into health care, education, food, and clothing for needy communities worldwide. Among the most innovative tactics Pierce introduced to garner support was the organization's use of visual technology. World Vision produced about a dozen early films, which were distributed to local churches. The films increased awareness about the needs of missionaries and foreign communities, and contained a very strong anti-communist message typical of the 1950s era. As the organization grew in strength in the United States, Pierce opened new offices around the world.

In the late 1960s, Pierce retired and was eventually succeeded by W. Stanley Mooneyham. The new president carefully sought to redirect the organization's work away from implicitly bolstering right-wing U.S. foreign policy programs by refocusing the mission of World Vision. He inculcated the ministry with progressive ideas about health care, poverty, the environment, and the population explosion, to better assist their work with developing nations. Rather than partnering with local ministers to obtain church support, he took his plea for aid directly to parishioners, which created some controversy for the organization. Mooneyham completed what Pierce had begun, thoroughly "internationalizing" the organization by working more directly with other relief agencies around the world.

Robert Seiple, president of World Vision's U.S. branch from 1987 to 1998, continued Mooneyham's progressive initiates. He oversaw World Vision's evolution into the largest privately funded relief and development agency in the world. Since retiring from World Vision, Seiple has been appointed "Ambassador at Large for Religious Freedom" by President Bill Clinton, a testament to the rapid rise into respectability that characterized some segments of Fundamentalism in the second half of the twentieth century. World Vision is currently engaged in 4,500 projects in ninety-four countries, including long-term development endeavors and short-term emergency relief.

Matthew A. Sutton

Bibliography

Carpenter, Joel. (1997) *Revive Us Again: The Reawakening of American Fundamentalism*. New York: Oxford University Press.

Goffin, Alvin M. (1994) *The Rise of Protestant Evangelism in Ecuador, 1895–1990*. Gainesville: University Press of Florida. .

Graham, Franklin, and Jeanette Lockerbie. (1983) *Bob Pierce: This One Thing I Do*. Waco: Word Publishing.

Rohrer, Norman. (1987) *Open Arms*. Wheaton: Tyndale House Publishers, Inc.

Seiple, Robert A. (1990) *Making a World of Difference, One Life at a Time*. Dallas: Word Publishing.

World War I

Millions of Americans rushed to the streets on Armistice Day, 11 November 1918, celebrating the end of the Great War. Unified by a patriotism that had characterized the war years, few Protestant women and men realized the tension that had enveloped their denominations, challenging their seemingly sacrosanct religious communities. While there had been prewar skirmishes between conservative Evangelicals and liberal modernists, the war forced the burgeoning Fundamentalist movement to explicitly define itself.

The Progressive Era (c. 1880–1916) was a period of intense political, social, religious, and cultural renewal. Many Protestants, called modernists, employed the tools of modern science and liberal philosophy to reconfigure their faith for the modern world, assuming that progress was inevitable and that the gospel contained an inherently social dimension. However, other Protestants, who remained skeptical of contemporary trends, outlined and defended their understanding of the "fundamentals" of the Christian faith. By the end of World War I, modernists and Fundamentalists were no longer engaged simply in academic debates, but were permanently divided over the nature of the gospel.

When the United States entered the war, Fundamentalists lacked a consensus on what their individual roles should entail. Some leaders, like Billy Sunday, were extremely nationalistic and willing to fight. Others, such as William Jennings Bryan, leaned toward isolationism and pacifism. But, along with the rest of the American public, most Christians became increasingly patriotic as the war progressed. Modernists captured President Woodrow Wilson's vision of "making the world safe for democracy" and conservatives, who had previously devoted little time to social matters, found themselves drawn to politics. The most energized group of Fundamentalists was premillennialists, who believed that the imbroglio in Europe was the culmination of biblical prophecy. Before the war, premillennialists had a limited following but the apparent vindication of their long-standing predictions of an apocalypse caused their numbers to swell. Modernists were disturbed by such premillennial teachings, arguing that premillennialists lacked patriotism and encouraged apathy, which inherently undermined the "Social Gospel" that modernists had worked so hard to develop. The mounting tension erupted in Chicago where a rhetorical battle unfolded between modernists at the University of Chicago and premillennialists at the Moody Bible Institute. What began as a local debate between rival schools quickly became a national dispute culminating in the "Fundamentalist–modernist" controversies of the 1920s.

Historians have long wrestled with the reasons why Fundamentalism took on a militant form after the war. The most likely explanation is that the Fundamentalists' experience in World War I heightened their sense of calling and mission; they believed that the Second Coming of Christ was truly imminent. They were no longer content to remain on the margins of Protestantism. Had the differences between modernists and Fundamentalists been purely theological in nature, they would never have provoked the reactions they did. However, since a cultural crisis, involving no less than the nature of the Christian faith in the United States, seemed to be at stake, differences were suddenly polarizing. Thus, World War I sparked the exodus of many conservatives from traditional Protestant denominations and foreshadowed the Fundamentalist–modernist schism.

Matthew A. Sutton

See also Antimodernism; Secularism

Bibliography

Boyer, Paul. (1992) *When Time Shall Be No More: Prophecy Belief in Modern American Culture*. Cambridge, MA: Harvard University Press.

Handy, Robert T. (1991) *Undetermined Establishment: Church–State Relations in America, 1880–1920.* Princeton, NJ: Princeton University Press.

Marsden, George M. (1980) *Fundamentalism and American Culture: The Shaping of Twentieth-Century Evangelicalism 1870–1925.* New York: Oxford University Press.

Piper, John F. (1985) *The American Churches in World War I.* Athens: Ohio University Press.

Weber, Timothy P. (1983) *Living in the Shadow of the Second Coming: American Premillennialism 1875–1982.* Grand Rapids, MI: Zondervan Publishing.

World War II

Germany's invasion of Poland on 1 September 1939 was the commencement of World War II. Despite strong isolationist sentiment at home, the United States entered the conflict a little more than two years later. During the course of the next four years, the world witnessed unparalleled losses in human life, massive destruction of physical properties, and severe economic hardships in numerous nations. While the unconditional surrender of Germany and Japan to the Allied forces in 1945 brought an official close to this destructive period of history, the residual effects of these extraordinary years, particularly in America's religious life, were only beginning to be realized. The evils witnessed in the Holocaust and the devastation wrought by atomic weapons brought to the fore profound questions of faith and morality for religious Americans. For Protestants of either a conservative or liberal ilk, with their emphasis on human sin, God's omnipotence, and covenantal theology, these events invited speculation about the very nature and the course of human history. Among Protestant Fundamentalists, the gravity of this turbulent epoch seemed to further substantiate a worldview premised upon the dialectic between good and evil.

The 1930s and 1940s were a gestation period among Evangelicals and Fundamentalists. During these years, Fundamentalism acquired a more limited meaning as a new generation began to distance themselves from the Protestant mainstream and their fundamentalist legacy. Few clear lines of distinction can be drawn between these conservative factions during these years. Yet, the malleable antiliberal unity displayed among Fundamentalists at the time

would, in the years after the war, congeal to threaten the very establishment from which it emerged.

Amid the interwar years, several of America's prominent religious voices espoused support for world peace movements and organized labor. Leaders such as Harry Emerson Fosdick championed these causes while also making overtures toward Fundamentalists asking for tolerance and solidarity among Protestant circles. Fundamentalists generally distanced themselves from such advances, displaying an overall political conservatism. This "neo-Evangelical" agenda espoused by Fundamentalists rejected ecumenism based on the belief that liberals had made too many concessions to modernity concerning higher criticism and a supernatural basis for Christian belief. A variant form of premillennialism that was asserting itself at the time formidably shaped these separatist beliefs. Yet within this conservative circle, held together by a tenuous antiliberal unity, several factions would emerge during the war years in response to political developments.

Events in Europe and during World War II helped to reveal this religious perspective. The dispensational premillennialism espoused by this new generation of Fundamentalists led them to interpret world events in light of sacred history—a foreordained divine plan for Creation and the apostolic church they believed to be revealed in Scripture. Given this outlook, ecclesiastical perspectives carried with them political overtones. Individuals like John R. Rice adopted a moderate stance toward current events, emphasizing neutrality on issues of the state while seeking further separation from the corrupt forces within Protestantism and society at large. But to suggest that Fundamentalists were simply apolitical overlooks one of the intriguing ironies of the dispensationalist perspective. Many Fundamentalists were highly conversant with the day's events, espousing a vigorous patriotism. Others, like Carl McIntire, the founder of the American Council of Christian Churches who gained a wide following of highly motivated political activists, railed against such patriotism, urging, instead, pacifism and peaceful coexistence with communism. Yet, on occasion, such forms of historicism and political activity could be carried to its extreme. Such was the case with Gerald Burton Winrod, a preacher from Wichita, Kansas, whose dispensationalism led him to interpret the Nazi crackdown on Jews in Europe as part of God's plan. He espoused these anti-Semitic views in *The*

Defender Magazine, a Fundamentalist publication of the 1930s. In 1938, Winrod ran as a candidate for the U.S. Senate, but was defeated in the primary.

Kent A. McConnell

See also Anti-Semitism; Communism; United Nations

Bibliography

Bowden, Henry Warner. (1993) *Dictionary of American Religious Bibliography*, 2nd ed. Westport, CT: Greenwood Press.

Brouwer, Steve, Paul Gifford, and Susan D. Rose, eds. (1996) *Exporting the American Gospel: Global Christian Fundamentalism*. New York: Routledge.

Hutchison, William R., ed. (1989) *Between The Times: The Travail of the Protestant Establishment in America, 1900–1960*. New York: Cambridge University Press.

Marsden, George M. (1991) *Understanding Fundamentalism and Evangelicalism*. Grand Rapids, MI: Wm. B. Eerdmans.

Meyer, Donald. (1988) *The Protestant Search for Political Realism, 1919–1941*. Middleton, CT: Wesleyan University Press.

Miller, Robert Moats. (1985) *Harry Emerson Fosdick: Preacher, Pastor, Prophet*. New York: Oxford University Press.

World's Christian Fundamentals Association

The World's Christian Fundamentals Association (WCFA) was an interdenominational association of North American Protestant Fundamentalist churches and societies from the 1920s to 1940s. Under the leadership of its founder and original president, William Bell Riley, the WCFA became the largest and longest-lasting international Fundamentalist association and the principal organization of the premillennial wing of the Fundamentalist movement. Theologically and culturally conservative, the WCFA opposed modernism in North America's largest Protestant denominations and the teaching of evolution in public schools. Like the Fundamentalist movement it represented, the WCFA reached its zenith of cultural influence in the mid-1920s only to fade from national importance after the Scopes "Monkey Trial" in 1925.

The WCFA originated at a prophecy conference held in Philadelphia, Pennsylvania, from 25 May to 1 June 1919. During the previous summer, Riley had met with leaders of the prophecy conference movement at the summer home of Reuben A. Torrey (dean of the Bible Institute of Los Angeles) in Montrose, Pennsylvania, to plan the conference and the founding of the WCFA. More than six thousand people attended the conference, which featured many of the heroes of North American premillennialism who had spoken at prophecy conferences across the country for decades: Riley, Reuben A. Torrey, Charles G. Trumbull (editor of *The Sunday School Times*), James M. Gray, John Campbell, W. H. Griffith Thomas, I. M. Haldeman, J. C. Massee, Peter W. Philpott, Lewis S. Chafer, William L. Pettingill, John Roach Straton, and others. The conference proceedings, published in 1919 as *God Hath Spoken: 25 Addresses*, identified Fundamentalism's enemies, such as modernism, Darwinism, theological liberalism, higher criticism of the Bible, moral laxity, rationalism, and Roman Catholicism. Leaders saved their most vitriolic language for liberal institutions of higher learning, expressing their desire to produce theologically sound graduates. Because education was key to their program, the WCFA advocated increased numbers of Bible conferences and the founding of Bible colleges. During the conference proceedings a doctrinal statement drafted by Charles A. Blanchard (president of Wheaton College in Illinois) was presented which emphasized the verbal inspiration of the Scriptures, the Virgin Birth, the "premillennial and imminent return" of Jesus Christ, substitutionary atonement, and hell as a place of eternal conscious torment.

The founding of the WCFA marked a significant change in North American Fundamentalism. Prior to American entrance into World War I in 1917, Fundamentalist attacks on theological liberalism and modernism had been muted and moderate. Fundamentalists were more interested in evangelizing, praying, and waiting for the premillennial Second Coming of Christ than they were in the state of American civilization. *The Fundamentals*, a twelve-volume series of articles that defined Fundamentalist theological and philosophical beliefs, had been completed by 1915 but had produced little national effect. After World War I, however, the fear of cultural decline and the threat of postwar Bolshevism prodded Fundamentalists to concern themselves with halting degenerate moral trends. Whereas leaders had previously dealt primarily with End-Times prophecy, after 1919 they would emphasize the state of the church and the spreading of false, modernistic doctrines. Conference organizers claimed, "The Great Apostasy is spreading like a plague throughout Christendom" (*God Hath Spoken: 25 Addresses* 1919: 7). Only an all-out cultural offensive would rescue the church and American culture from the dangerous effects of modernism and theological liberalism. The WCFA and its official organ, Riley's *Christian Fundamentals in School and Church*, galvanized Fundamentalist forces on a national scale.

After 1923, the WCFA concerned itself less with modernism in North America's Protestant denominations and more with preventing the teaching of evolution in tax-supported public schools. The WCFA actively influenced numerous state legislatures to pass antievolution laws and was responsible for recruiting William Jennings Bryan, a nationally influential Fundamentalist and antievolutionist, to defend the Tennessee legislature against John Scopes and the American Civil Liberties Union in 1925. The Scopes trial signaled the decline of national Fundamentalism and therefore the demise of the WCFA as a major force in American life. Although the organization lasted until the 1940s under the leadership of Paul W. Rood, it continually waned in its impact. The failure of antievolution forces in general, the growing multiplicity of local Fundamentalist institutions, and the persistence of modernism in North America's largest denominations all contributed to the demise of the WCFA.

Kurt W. Peterson

See also Evolution and Antievolution; Modernism

Bibliography

Cole, Stewart. (1931) *The History of Fundamentalism.* New York: Richard Smith.

Dollar, George W. (1973) *A History of Fundamentalism in America.* Greenville, SC: Bob Jones University Press.

Furniss, Norman F. (1954) *The Fundamentalist Controversy, 1918–1931.* New Haven, CT: Yale University Press.

Marsden, George M. (1980) *Fundamentalism and American Culture. The Shaping of Twentieth-Century Evangelicalism, 1870–1925.* New York: Oxford University Press.

Sandeen, Ernest R. (1970) *The Roots of Fundamentalism: British and American Millennarianism, 1800–1930.* Chicago: University of Chicago Press.

Trollinger, William Vance, Jr. (1990) *God's Empire: William Bell Riley and Midwestern Fundamentalism.* Madison: University of Wisconsin Press.

WWJD (What Would Jesus Do?)

Distilled in these five syllables is a vital spiritual problem: what are the behavioral obligations of belief? This ethical dilemma dates to Christianity's earliest moments. Even Paul was moved to ask, "Lord, what wilt Thou have me to do?" (Acts 9:6, KJV) Generally, only monastic orders have been expected to strictly imitate Christ's ascetic example. However, in the early nineteenth century, this emulative theme gained popularity as part of a wider effort to define the social obligations of Protestant faith in an urbanizing, industrial society. Readers of the *Princeton Review* in 1832, for example, were asked to observe their "Christian obligation with respect to the conversion of the world" by making "the Bible their test of character" (310). In this Evangelical formulation, true inner faith informs everyday mien and radiates purposefully into the realm of economic and political conduct.

The phrase "What Would Jesus Do?" assumed iconic status at the height of the Social Gospel. In 1889 Rev. Charles M. Sheldon, fresh from a London settlement house, arrived in Topeka, Kansas, eager to involve his Congregational parish more fully in the problems of the laboring poor. His Sunday "sermon stories" were compiled and published as a single volume in 1896. *In His Steps* used sentimental clichés to celebrate Christian charity. Over six million volumes have been sold, making it one of the top selling books ever. (Sheldon never saw direct profits, however, due to a copyright defect.)

In the novel's opening scenes, the tragic death of a sickly homeless man forces a complacent middle-class parish to clarify its social responsibilities. Rev. Henry Maxwell challenged his flock to apply a simple test to all things: "What Would Jesus Do?" The pledge spread to Chicago, where it moved beggars and bishops alike to serve the commonweal. Critics cautioned that while the zealous characters of *In His Steps* sang, prayed, and avoided drink, they rarely

"Once I saw that someone put [WWJD] on a necklace that cost $400—$400!—I knew it had gotten out of hand."

Janie Tinklenberg, quoted in Cave (2000)

consulted Scripture. Some feared that this unsystematic approach would produce only the most superficial of behavioral changes. Nevertheless, by avoiding sticky theological issues, the "What Would Jesus Do?" pledge found widespread application as a means of translating moral inquiry into practical answers on issues ranging from the prosaic to the profound (e.g., "Would Jesus support McKinley or Bryan for president?").

The pledge resurfaced in the late twentieth century as a lay youth movement and merchandising phenomenon. In 1989 Janie Tinklenberg presented Sheldon's book to her youth group at the Calvary Reformed Church in Holland, Michigan. The idea caught on. The inscription served as both a public declaration of faith and a coded communication with other Christians. A local manufacturer began making bracelets—then in fashion among adolescents—inscribed with the acronym "WWJD?" By 2000 several companies were plying a multimillion dollar trade in WWJD-themed Bible covers, musical recordings, key chains, t-shirts, ball caps, bumper stickers, and rhinestone pins. A federal ruling that year awarded Tinklenberg limited control over the trademark while defining WWJD as part of the public domain.

Fundamentalists never fully reconciled themselves with WWJD. On one hand, they applauded its inversion of "Just Do It" epicureanism. But ironically, WWJD unleashed an unseemly commercialism. In addition, some ministers detected a pharisaical plot to reduce Jesus to a secular role model. Fueling these fears were reports that youths were giving the acronym secular meanings, such as What Would [Michael] Jordan Do?, or that suburban favorite, Why

Waste Jack Daniels? Most troubling, some liberals used WWJD to challenge the Christian Right's grip on public God talk. Rev. Jerry Falwell's call for Southern Baptists to defeat the 2000 presidential campaign of Democratic candidate Al Gore—a Southern Baptist who had boasted that he often made decisions by asking, "What Jesus would do"—was a potent reminder of Fundamentalism's continuing power to shape culture and politics.

Andrew C. Rieser

Bibliography

Boyer, Paul. (1971) "*In His Steps*: A Reappraisal." *American Quarterly* 23: 60–78.

———. (1978) *Urban Masses and Moral Order in America, 1820–1920*. Cambridge, MA: Harvard University Press.

Cave, Damien. "What Would Jesus Do—About Copyright?" www.salon.com (25 October 2000).

"Christian Obligation with Respect to the Conversion of the World." (1832) *Princeton Review* 4, 3 (July): 309–342.

Miller, Timothy. (1987) *Following in His Steps: A Biography of Charles M. Sheldon*. Knoxville: University of Tennessee Press.

Sheldon, Charles M. (1898) *In His Steps: What Would Jesus Do?* Chicago: Advance Publishing Co.

———. (1914) *"Jesus Is Here!" Continuing the Narrative of In His Steps (What Would Jesus Do?)*. New York: Hodder & Stoughton.

Sheldon, Garrett Ward, and Deborah Morris. (1998) *What Would Jesus Do?* Nashville, TN: Broadman & Holman Publishers.

Year of the Evangelical

A 1976 Gallup poll reported that half of American Protestants claimed to be "born again" or to have made, at some point in their lives, a personal commitment to Jesus Christ as their personal Savior. The poll also revealed that considerable numbers of Americans believed that the Bible was inspired by God and to be interpreted literally—word for word. Furthermore, fifty-eight percent of those surveyed had tried to convert others to Christian faith. Such a proliferation of belief in America prompted Gallup to declare 1976 the "year of the evangelical." *Newsweek* magazine would soon follow, with a cover story entitled "Born Again: The Year of the Evangelicals."

For historians and other scholars of American religion, the rising tide of Evangelical religion was not unusual. America had always been a country driven by a certain affinity for Evangelical religion. What made 1976 unique was the fact that Evangelicalism was emerging as an important factor in presidential politics. Both presidential candidates—Jimmy Carter and Gerald Ford—openly claimed Evangelical faith. Carter, the eventual winner of the election, claimed to be "born again." The Southern Baptist Sunday school teacher, moreover, openly shared his struggle with sin and lust in a controversial interview in *Playboy* magazine.

The religious convictions of the presidential candidates, especially Carter, sent journalists scrambling to understand the contours of Evangelical faith in America. What they found was a thriving subculture of churches, television preachers, mission organizations, and associations that would provide much of the support for the religious-based political movements of the 1980s such as the Moral Majority and the Christian Coalition.

John Fea

Bibliography

Wells, David, and John D. Woodbridge. (1975) *The Evangelicals: What They Believe, Who They Are, Where They Are Changing.* Nashville, TN: Abingdon Press.

Woodward, Kenneth L. (1976) "Born Again: The Year of the Evangelicals." *Newsweek* (25 October):

Young Life

Young Life is an Evangelical youth organization working primarily with predominantly urban junior high and high school age youth in school-based clubs and camping programs. In Gainesville, Texas, in 1938, Jim Rayburn (1909–1970), a student at Dallas Theological Seminary (DTS) started a weekend Bible club on school property, and concentrated on attracting youth from unchurched backgrounds. He soon moved his program to weeknight meetings in area homes. Like the founders of the youth ministries that eventually coalesced around the Youth for Christ (YFC) movement, Rayburn was a critic of stuffy formalism in the churches and was even more skeptical than they of traditional Fundamentalist taboos in recreation and entertainment. Rather than relying primarily on area-wide rallies like YFC, from the beginning, Young Life emphasized individual club meetings with a lively, entertaining format and an emphasis on physical activity and the outdoors. With the help of DTS President Lewis Sperry Chafer (1871–1952), Rayburn recruited a number of fellow seminarians who helped him spread his concept to other cities in Texas. Young Life was officially incorporated in October 1941.

The organization experienced moderate growth during World War II, but through one of his seminary friends Rayburn met influential Chicago businessman Herbert J. Taylor (1893–1978), a backer of many Evangelical religious causes, including Child Evangelism and InterVarsity Christian Fellowship. With Taylor's help, Young Life was able to expand its staff and its ministry throughout most of the United States. Taylor was also instrumental in helping Young Life acquire and equip camp facilities in Colorado, Minnesota, and British Columbia.

Young Life has, with a few rare periods, experienced steady growth since its inception. International expansion began in the late 1950s with work initially established in Brazil, France, and West Germany. By 1977, the organization's 600 full-time workers interacted with 70,000 American youth each week. As of the year 2000, Young Life utilized over 1,000 full-time staff and more than 12,000 volunteers to work weekly with an estimated 100,000 young people in the United States. With a total of nearly 2,900 full-time staff, 22 camp facilities, and chapters in 40 foreign countries, its annual operating budget was reported at over $150 million per year.

Larry Eskridge

Bibliography

Calliet, Emile. (1963) *Young Life*. New York: Harper & Row.

Meredith, Char. 1978) *It's a Sin to Bore a Kid: The Story of Young Life*. Waco, TX: Word Books.

Rayburn, Jim, III. (1984) *Dance, Children, Dance: The Story of Jim Rayburn, Founder of Young Life*. Wheaton, IL: Tyndale House.

Shelley, Bruce L. (1986) "The Rise of Evangelical Youth Movements." *Fides et Historia* 18: 47–63.

Youth

Modern Fundamentalist and Evangelical attempts to evangelize and train adolescents for ministry are rooted in late-nineteenth-century Protestant responses to social, cultural, and economic changes in the United States. Most important in this regard was the Christian Endeavor Society (1881), an interdenominational congregation-based youth organization promoting prayer, Bible study, church attendance, evangelism, and the training of youth for future leadership positions in the church. By the late 1880s it numbered more than 500,000 members, mostly in the northeastern and midwestern states. Christian Endeavor served as the model for a number of new denominational youth organizations that were created during the late nineteenth and early twentieth centuries, a development that ironically led to its subsequent decline.

While models of Protestant youth ministry remained fairly constant into the 1930s, there was by that time growing concern among Fundamentalists about the direction of American culture and the inroads of liberalism in organizations such as Christian Endeavor, the Young Men's Christian Association (YMCA) (1844), and the Student Volunteer Movement (1888). New Fundamentalist efforts to reach the young drew both from the cultural store of traditional revivalism and the energy of contemporary popular culture. In the New York City area, the Association of Christian Youth in America (1933) used rallies, local meetings, banquets, retreats, and occasional radio broadcasts to sustain over forty local chapters. In Philadelphia, Percy Crawford (1902–1960), a young Canadian evangelist, built a successful regional youth ministry around his radio program, the "Young People's Church of the Air" (1932). As independent youth efforts flourished in northern cities, the Southern Baptists sponsored similar programs through interchurch rallies held by the Baptist Young People's Union.

In the early 1940s a "Youth for Christ" (YFC) movement—largely influenced by Crawford and his New York-based protégé Jack Wyrtzen's (1913–1996) Word of Life ministry—appeared in a number of cities, including Indianapolis, Washington, D.C., Detroit, St. Louis, Minneapolis, and Chicago. Tying the groups together was a format combining revivalism with the influence of popular entertainment. Meetings were well-advertised, tightly structured rallies, and the up-tempo music more closely reflected popular music familiar to teenage audiences than it did the typical hymns sung at church on Sunday mornings. Headlining the events were a new breed of young, energetic preachers who wore flashy clothes, could speak teen jargon, and mimicked the delivery styles of famous broadcasters. The newly created Chicago YFC, led by young pastor Torrey Johnson (1909–), was particularly successful, attracting a crowd of more than 70,000 to a spectacular May 1945 Memorial Day rally in Chicago's Soldier Field. On the heels of media publicity a national YFC organization was created at a July meeting held at Winona Lake, Indiana. By 1946 it was estimated that nine hundred city-wide and regional YFC branches were operating rallies with monthly attendance of over a million youth. While there was some criticism of YFC from ultraconservative Protestants for being too "worldly," overall the movement was looked upon with great favor as a positive national force and a bulwark against juvenile delinquency.

By the mid-1950s the rally-model had lost its impetus and YFC shifted its strategy toward school-based Bible clubs. By this time, a number of important new youth-oriented Evangelical organizations had emerged and established their own constituencies among junior high and high school age youth (Young Life in 1941), school-age athletes (Fellowship of Christian Athletes in 1955), and college students (InterVarsity Christian Fellowship in 1941 in the United States, and Campus Crusade for Christ in 1951). All of these groups experienced steady growth into the 1960s, enjoying their greatest success in the sprawling new white, middle-class suburbs. One major exception was David Wilkerson's (1931–) Teen Challenge (1958) organization. Teen Challenge targeted urban gang members, at-risk teenage girls, and drug addicts and was in place in dozens of large cities by the late 1960s, aided greatly by Wilkerson's best-selling book, *The Cross and the Switchblade* (1963). Teen Challenge's success along with the growth of the civil rights movement augured an increased effort by Evangelical youth organizations to minister to urban and minority youth in the 1960s.

The mid-1960s ushered in a major period of growth and change for Evangelical youth ministry. The prosperity of the postwar period, the growing professionalization of youth ministry, and the "pig-in-the-python" effect caused by baby boom demographics all worked to bring about tremendous growth for groups like Campus Crusade, which saw its budgets and staff grow more than fourfold during the decade. On the congregational level, lay volunteers were increasingly relegated to assisting and advisory roles as part- and full-time professional "youth directors," "youth pastors," and "Ministers of Youth" became fixtures in a growing number of Evangelical churches.

Not all of the changes were favorable, however. One major flash point was the growing allure of the larger youth culture. The increasing influence of film, television, teen fashions, and, above all, rock and roll music, coupled with rising levels of leisure time and disposable teen income, were viewed as vehicles for worldliness and immorality. The subsequent rise of the 1960s hippie "counterculture" made this dilemma even more problematic as the youth culture drifted further away from the norms of the Evangelical subculture.

The emergence of the Jesus People movement in the late 1960s eased this dilemma. Originating largely in California and the Pacific Northwest with a few Evangelical pastors and youth workers' efforts to evangelize hippies, the Jesus People were a countercultural, Pentecostal-leaning take on traditional Evangelical religion. While they advocated a strict Evangelical moral code, and a literalistic, apocalyptic-tinged Bible-based faith, the Jesus People retained many of the trappings of the counterculture, such as long hair, casual dress, and the playing of folk and rock-based music in their worship. In 1971 the Jesus People movement received a great deal of publicity in the secular and religious media. Evangelical youth, attracted by the movement's exuberant spirit, Christian rock music, and hip trappings, enthusiastically adapted the Jesus People persona as their own. Many pastors and youth workers, seeing the movement as an effective way to reach youth, backed it over the objections of more conservative laypeople and some leaders who criticized the movement's identification with the hippie counterculture and use of rock music. However, a great many more Evangelical leaders, including Billy Graham (1918–), proclaimed the Jesus People movement as evidence of Christianity's relevance to societal problems and a sign of impending national revival. This movement marked a major milestone in the history of Evangelical and Fundamentalist dealings with youth. A softened, Evangelical version of the trends and styles of the larger youth culture(s) became an accepted strategy among a majority of the nation's conservative Protestant congregations and youth organizations. Buttressed by the Contemporary Christian Music (CCM) industry that emerged out of "Jesus Music," a number of different Evangelical youth culture styles aping secular counterparts—new wave, punk, heavy metal, rap, and even hip-hop dance—

were available for Evangelical teen self-identification during the 1980s and 1990s. Indeed, resistance to this accommodation was one of the clearest indicators of the cultural divide between Evangelicals and Fundamentalists.

Among recent developments in Evangelical youth ministry is an increased emphasis on global responsibility and the plight of the world's poor. Short-term mission trips and summer projects have become an increasingly important dimension of congregational and denominational youth programs and several agencies arose whose main task was to organize such trips. Additionally, cultural and political tension regarding the role of religion within society has given wider impetus to public affirmations of youthful faith including marches and events such as the annual "See You at the Pole" (1990) school rallies every September. For the most part, however, Evangelical youth work at the end of the twentieth century was still structured around the youth programs of the local congregation and the Bible study, Bible club, and camping programs of now long-established Evangelical youth ministries like the YFC, Young Life, or Fellowship of Christian Athletes. By the late 1990s these organizations, and programs for college-age youth like Campus Crusade and InterVarsity, had combined budgets approaching the half-billion mark. It was clear as the twentieth century came to a close that a highly organized, well-funded network of youth programs was an essential factor in the continued health of conservative American Protestantism.

Larry Eskridge

See also Campus Crusade for Christ; Youth for Christ

Bibliography

Benson, Warren S., and Roy B. Zuck. (1978) *Youth Education in the Church.* Chicago: Moody Press.

Carpenter, Joel A. (1997) *Revive Us Again: The Reawakening of American Fundamentalism.* New York: Oxford University Press.

DiSabatino, David. (1999) *The Jesus People Movement: An Annotated Bibliography and General Resource.* Westport, CT: Greenwood Press.

Hefley, James. (1970) *God Goes to High School.* Waco, TX: Word Books.

Larson, Mel. (1947) *Youth For Christ, Twentieth Century Wonder.* Grand Rapids, MI: Zondervan Publishing.

Meredith, Char. (1978) *It's a Sin to Bore a Kid: The Story of Young Life.* Waco, TX: Word Books.

Pahl, Jon. (2000) *Youth Ministry in Modern America: 1930 to the Present.* Peabody, MA: Hendrickson Publishers.

Romanowski, William. (2000) "Evangelicals and Popular Music: The Contemporary Christian Music Industry." In *Religion and Popular Culture in America,* edited by Bruce David Forbes and Jeffrey H. Mahan. Berkeley: University of California Press, 105–124.

Shelley, Bruce L. (1986) "The Rise of Evangelical Youth Movements." *Fides et Historia* 18: 47–63.

Wilkerson, David. (1963) *The Cross and the Switchblade.* Old Tappan, NJ: Fleming H. Revell.

Youth for Christ

Youth for Christ (YFC) is a nondenominational youth organization that played a key role in the emergence of the "New Evangelical" movement in the years following World War II. YFC's origins trace back to the efforts of a number of progressive, youth-oriented Fundamentalist ministries that emerged in the late 1930s and early 1940s. Working mostly through local rallies featuring lively music, humor, audience participation skits, and dynamic young preachers, the new youth ministries were a novel revamping of timeworn revivalist methods. In July 1945, a number of these groups centralized their efforts at an organizing meeting in Winona Lake, Indiana. Torrey Johnson (1909–) of Chicago was elected YFC's first president and Billy Graham (1918–), a young Chicago-area pastor, was named its first field representative.

With a central organization in place, YFC experienced tremendous growth in the next few years. In 1946 it was estimated that nine hundred separate YFC branches were sponsoring monthly rallies attracting nearly one million youth. While the group was criticized as faddish and too entertainment-oriented by theological critics on both the Left and Right, YFC was hailed by many civic leaders who saw it as a bulwark against juvenile delinquency and the threat of communism.

In the early 1950s, YFC shifted its focus to the nation's growing suburbs. Rallies receded in importance and the establishment of local high–school based clubs became the dominant organizational strategy. By 1960, there were nearly 2,700 YFC-sponsored clubs in the United States and Canada. Since the 1960s, the high school Bible club (dubbed "Campus Life" in the early 1960s), sponsored through local and regional YFC chapters, has remained the organization's basic structure and there has been a conscious effort to expand overseas and target urban and minority youth.

YFC peaked during the mid-1970s with the convergence of baby boom demographics and the popularity of the Jesus People Movement. A subsequent decline and attendant financial pressures during the 1980s resulted in a number of cutbacks and the eventual relocation of YFC offices from Wheaton, Illinois, to Denver, Colorado, in 1991. As of 2000, YFC had more than 1,800 full-time staff members and an annual operating budget of over $15,000,000; there were 235 local chapters in the United States sponsoring over two thousand programs in schools, neighborhoods, and juvenile institutions as well as YFC branches in 127 foreign countries.

Larry Eskridge

See also World War II

Bibliography

Carpenter, Joel A. (1997) *Revive Us Again: The Reawakening of American Fundamentalism*. New York: Oxford University Press.

Hefley, James. (1970) *God Goes to High School*. Waco, TX: Word Books.

Larson, Mel. (1945) *Young Man on Fire: The Story of Torrey Johnson and Youth For Christ*. Chicago: Youth Publications.

Shelley, Bruce L. (1986) "The Rise of Evangelical Youth Movements." *Fides et Historia* 18: 47–63.

List of Contributors

Aho, James
Idaho State University
Antimodernism

Akinade, Akintunde E.
High Point University
Incarnation

Altany, Alan
Marshall University
Biblical Criticism
Ecumenical Movement

Ariel, Yaakov S.
University of North Carolina–Chapel Hill
Jews
Jews for Jesus

Armentrout, Donald S.
Sewanee–The University of the South
Ascension
Assumption
United Nations
Vocation

Bademan, R. Bryan
University of Notre Dame
Atonement
Rock Music
Tribulation

Baer, Hans A.
University of Arkansas
African-American Holiness-Pentecostal

Black Church, The
Mormons, Fundamentalist (Polygamous)
Mormons, Mainstream and Protestant

Bailey, Julius H.
University of North Carolina
Pastor's Wife

Balaban, Victor
Emory University
Cult of Mary

Balmer, Randall
Barnard College, Columbia University
Evangelicalism

Berlet, Chip
Political Research Associates
Apocalypse
Devil and Satan, The
Illuminati, The
Nationalism
Nativism

Blee, Kathleen
University of Pittsburgh
Ku Klux Klan

Booker, Carter
University of Iowa
Prayer
Witnesses, Two

Boyer, Paul
University of Wisconsin
Eschatology

Brasher, Brenda E.
Mount Union College
Promise Keepers
Submission

Bromley, David
Virginia Commonwealth University
Covenant

Brugaletta, John J.
California State University–Fullerton
Bible

Burkholder, Jared S.
Waukegan, IL
Heresy

Carr, Thomas Kinsell
Mount Union College
Doubt
Eternal Life
Hell, Heaven, and Purgatory
Resurrection (Christ)
Virgin Birth

Cherok, Richard J.
Cincinnati Bible College and Seminary
Common Sense Philosophy
Primitivism
Sheol

Cimino, Richard P.
Wantagh, NY
Sunday Schools

Clark, Lynn Schofield
University of Colorado–Boulder
Entertainment Industry

Clements, William
Arkansas State University
Azusa Street Revival
Evil Empire

Cook, David
University of Chicago
Imam, The Last

Curtis, Edward M.
Biola University
Old Testament

Daschke, Dereck
Truman State University
False Prophets

D'Elia, John A.
Fuller Theological Seminary and University of Stirling
Rescue Missions

Draney, Daniel W.
Fuller Theological Seminary
Free Will
Kingdom of God
Saved, The
Sin and Sinners

Elliott, Joel
University of North Carolina–Chapel Hil
Jehovah's Witnesses

Eskridge, Larry
Wheaton College
Campus Crusade for Christ
Young Life
Youth
Youth for Christ

Fackre, Gabriel
Andover Newton Theological School
Biblical Inerrancy
Biblical Inspiration

Fea, John
Valparaiso University
Year of the Evangelical

Flory, Richard W.
Biola University
Bible Schools
Fundamentals, The

Flory, Wayne S.
Biola University
Body of Christ, The
Christ, The
Grace
Revelation

Forrest, Beth Marie
Center for Millenial Studies at Boston University
Christian Research Institute

Fuller, Robert C.
Bradley University
Antichrist

Furnish, Timothy R.
Georgia Perimeter College
Islamic Fundamentalism

Gillihan, Yonder Moynihan
University of Chicago
Rapture

Glazier, Jack
Oberlin College
Anti-Semitism

Glazier, Stephen D.
University of Nebraska–Lincoln
Evolution and Antievolution
Resurrection (of the Dead)

Gloege, Timothy E.
Wheaton College
Healing, Faith

Goff, Matthew
University of Chicago
Apocalyptic Literature
Messiah

Goff, Philip
Indiana University–Purdue University, Indianapolis
Radio

Griffin, Roger
Oxford Brookes University
Fascism

Guth, James
Furman University
New Christian Right

Hayward, Douglas
Biola University
Missions

Hewitson, James
University of Toronto
Great Awakening

Holt, Zachary P.
Fullerton, CA
Baptism
Blasphemy

Howard, Robert Glenn
University of Oregon
Final Judgment
Myth
Second Coming

Huff, Peter A.
Centenary College of Louisiana
Haredim

Hutchison, John C.
Biola University
Bible Study
Jesus Christ

Ingersoll, Julie J.
University of North Florida
Dominion Theology
Male headship
Reconstructionism, Christian
Theonomy

Kaplan, Jeffrey
University of Alaska–Anchorage
Aryan Nations
Mahdi
Mark of the Beast
Noahide Covenant

Kemeny, Paul C.
Grove City College
Westminster Confession

Ketchell, Aaron
University of Kansas
Liberalism

Khan, Abdul Karim
University of Hawaii–Leeward
Taliban

Kostlevy, William C.
Asbury Theological Seminary
Holiness, Wesleyan

Lamy, Philip
Castleton State College
Militia
UFOs

Landes, Richard
Center for Millennial Studies at Boston University
Chiliasm

Larsen, David L.
Trinity Evangelical Divinity School
Preaching
Prophecy

Lawson, Ronald
Queens College–City University of New York
Seventh-Day Adventists

Leach, Robert T.
Indiana Wesleyan University
Israel
Lord's Supper
Sacrament

Lind, Mary Ann
Biola University
Angelus Temple
Hinduism, Fundamental
Shi'a Islam

Luft, Shanny
Boston University
Evil

Lupo, Scott
University of Nevada–Reno
Baconian Science
Beast, The
Christian Coalition
Media, Mass
Millerites
Televangelism

Maiba, Hermann
University of Illinois at Chicago
Gush Emunim
Judaism, Fundamental

Malone, David B.
Wheaton College
Gospel Music
Pride
Virtue

Malone, Patrick W.
Ashland Theological Seminary
Soul

McConnell, Kent A.
University of Virginia
Elohim
Gospel
Orthodoxy
World War II

McNeely, Richard I.
Bozeman, MT
Gifts of the Spirit
God and God's Will
Holy Spirit
New Testament
Theology
Trinity

Melton, J. Gordon
Institute for the Study of American Religion
Church of God
Church of the Nazarene
Churches of Christ
Free Methodist Church
New Age

Milford, Douglas
Wheaton University
Calling
Keswick Movement
Sermon on the Mount
World Evangelical Fellowship

Nestingen, James
Luther Seminary
Justification

Neujahr, Matthew
Yale University
Tribe of Dan

Neumann, Caryn E.
Ohio State University
World Council of Churches

Newman, Robert C.
Biblical Theological Seminary
Creation
Creationism

Ojo, Matthews A.
Obafemi Awolowo University
Born Again
Christian Home, Ideal
Last Things
Miracles
Revival
Salvation
Testimony

Peterson, Kurt W.
Judson College
Higher Criticism
World's Christian Fundamentals Association

Rausch, Thomas P., S.J.
Loyola Marymount University–Los Angeles
Immaculate Conception

Reeves, Russ P.
Trinity Christian College
Depravity
Fall of Humankind

Richardson, James T.
University of Nevada–Reno
Conversion

Rieser, Andrew C.
St. Cloud State University
WWJD (What Would Jesus Do?)

Rose, Susan D.
Dickinson College
Antifeminism

Salamone, Frank A.
Iona College
Decalogue
Justice
Love
Mount of Olives

Schaefer, Paul R., Jr.
Grove City College
Predestination

Sidwell, Mark
Bob Jones University
Bible Conferences

Smith, John Howard
State University of New York–Albany
Sanctification

Smith, Thomas A.
Loyola University–New Orleans
Original Sin

Sutton, Matthew A.
University of California–Santa Barbara
America, as a Christian nation
Speaking in Tongues (Glossolalia)
World Vision
World War I

Talley, David Lee
Biola University
Law, Old Testament

Thumma, Scott
Hartford Institute for Religion Research
Megachurches

Weaver, Mary Jo
Indiana University
Catholic Fundamentalism
Catholics United for the Faith
Wanderer, The

Webb, Jeffrey B.
Huntington College
Reformed Theology

Weber, Timothy P.
Northern Baptist Theological Seminary
Armageddon
Mid-Tribulationism
Post-Tribulationism
Pre-Tribulationism

Wellman, James K., Jr.
University of Washington
Secularism

Whalen, Robert K.
State University of New York–Stony Brook
Abortion
Angels
Communism
Dispensationalism
End Times
Literalism
Moral Majority
Opus Dei
Pentecostalism
Perfectionism
Postmillennialism
Premillennialism
Temple

Wilshire, Leland Edward
Biola University
Arminianism

Baptists
Calvinism
Church
Protestantism
Scofield Reference Bible

Winston, Diane
Pew Charitable Trusts
Salvation Army, The

Woodruff, Jennifer Lynn
Duke University
Tridentine Mass

Woods, L. Shelton
Boise State University
Southeast Asia

Index

Boldface page numbers indicate extended treatment of a subject.